D1278284

Football Outsiders Almanac 2016

THE ESSENTIAL GUIDE TO THE 2016 NFL AND COLLEGE FOOTBALL SEASONS

Edited by Aaron Schatz

With Bill Connelly, Cian Fahey, Brian Fremeau, Tom Gower,

Scott Kacsmar, Rivers McCown, Chad Peltier,

Mike Tanier, Vincent Verhei, and Robert Weintraub

Copyright 2016 Football Outsiders, Inc.

ISBN-10: 1536851175

ISBN-13: 978-1536851175

Table of Contents

Introduction

The lesson of 2016 is that the Browns could win the Super Bowl this season.

Over the last few months, the Cleveland Browns have publicly dedicated themselves to the football analytics revolution. That's exciting news for the staff of Football Outsiders. After all, we're the people who launched that revolution, when Football Outsiders went online in July 2003.

However, that's not the reason the Browns could win the Super Bowl. They're probably still going to be terrible this season. The defense doesn't have a lot of talent. The offense is depending on two quarterbacks who have been dismal over the past couple seasons, plus a bunch of rookie receivers and one stellar superstar receiver who can't stay away from his weed.

On the other hand, even the improbable is possible in the world of sports. *That's* the lesson of the last few months.

It's the lesson of Leicester City, the 5,000-to-1 longshot soccer team that won the English Premier League. It's the lesson of Iceland, the smallest nation to ever make the knockout phase of the UEFA European Championship tournament, a nation of 323,000 people whose top soccer players beat the best players from Austria (8.5 million) and England (53 million) in a two-week period.

Cleveland's chances of winning Super Bowl LI—yes, the league is going back to roman numerals, so we will too—are pretty terrible. But it's not impossible. Most bookmakers in Las Vegas list the Browns as a 200-to-1 longshot to win the Super Bowl this season. Those odds are actually better than the Browns' odds according to our 2016 season simulation. Believeland claimed a Lombardi Trophy to go with LeBron's Larry O'Brien Trophy in 772 of our one million runs. That simulation suggests that the odds of the Browns winning the Super Bowl are more like 1,300-to-1. But still, it's possible. Crazy things happen in sports. Like Leicester City, and Iceland.

Watching the improbable happen is a lot of fun. But when you love football, watching the probable happen is a lot of fun too. Watching great players such as Cam Newton and Von Miller be great is a lot of fun, even when you already knew they were great. And the truth is, the probable happens a lot more often than the improbable. More talented players usually outplay less talented players. More talented teams usually outplay less talented teams. That is why you are reading *Football Outsiders Almanac 2016* right now.

The staff of Football Outsiders has watched a lot of football, and we've run a lot of numbers. We have a lot of statistics that tell you more about the players on the field than the standard yardage and touchdown totals. We can't tell you exactly what will happen in the upcoming NFL and college football seasons. But we can tell you what's more likely to happen, and which players are likely to be better or worse than they were a year ago. We want to make you a smarter, more informed football fan, and hopefully a better entertained fan as well.

At its heart, the football analytics revolution is about learning more about the intricacies of the game instead of just accepting the boilerplate storylines produced by insipid pregame shows and crotchety old players from the past. It's about not accepting the idea that some guy "just wins." It's about understanding that the "skill players" aren't the only guys on the team with skills. It's about gaining insight into the complexity behind the modern offense, and that you don't just shove the ball into the line hoping to gain yardage. It's about understanding the dramatic way that strength of schedule affects the way we see a team's performance, especially at the college level. It's about figuring out which player skills translate from college to the pros, and which skills just produce meaningless scoutspeak. And it's about accepting that the pass dominates the run in the National Football League, and that it's been that way for 30 years.

There's more to this analysis than just numbers. Numbers are just one way to look at what happens on the football field. Words are the meat of our analysis; numbers are just the spice. There's a rumor that stat analysts don't watch game tape. In reality, stat analysts watch more tape than most beat writers or national Internet columnists, and *a lot* more tape than the average fan. We take everything we learn off the tape, synthesize it with the statistics, and deliver it to you.

Everybody who writes about football uses both statistics (whether they be basic yardage totals or more advanced stats like ours) and scouting (whether scouting reports by professionals or just their own eyes). The same goes for us, except that the statistics portion of our analysis is far more accurate than what you normally see from football coverage. Those numbers are based on two ideas:

1) Conventional football statistics are heavily dependent on context. If you want to see which teams are good and which are bad, which strategies work and which do not, you first need to filter out that context. Down and distance, field position, the current score, time left on the clock, the quality of the opponent—all of these elements influence the objective of the play and/or its outcome. Yet, the official NFL stats add together all yardage gained by a specific team or player without considering the impact of that particular yardage on wins and losses.

A close football game can turn on a single bounce of the ball. In a season of only 16 games, those effects can have a huge impact on a team's win-loss record, thus obscuring the team's true talent level. If we can filter out these bits of luck and random chance, we can figure out which teams are really more likely to play better for the rest of the season, or even in the following season.

2) On any one play, the majority of the important action is not tracked by the conventional NFL play-by-play. That's why we started the Football Outsiders game charting project in 2005. As of 2015, we now partner with both ESPN Stats & Info and Sports Info Solutions to collect data on every single NFL regular-season and postseason play. We know how many pass rushers teams send on each pass, how often teams go three-wide or use two tight ends, how often teams use a play-fake or a zone blitz, and which defensive backs are in coverage, even when they don't get a tackle in the standard play-by-play.

There's also a third important precept that governs the work we do at Football Outsiders, although it's more about how to interpret numbers and not the numbers themselves. **A player's production in one year does not necessarily equal his production the next year.** This also applies to teams, of course. Even when stats are accurate, they're often extremely variable from year to year and subject to heavy forces of regression to the mean. Field goal percentage, red zone performance, third-down performance on defense, interceptions and fumble recoveries—these are but a few examples. In addition, the age curves for football players are much steeper than in other sports. Old players break down faster, and young players often improve faster. A number of football analysts concentrate on looking at what players did last year. We'll talk about that as well, but we're more interested in what players are going to do *this* year. Which performances from a year ago are flukes, and which ones represent long-term improvement or decline? What will one more year of experience do to this player's production? And how will a player's role change this year, and what does it mean for the team?

As with past books, *Football Outsiders Almanac 2016* starts off with "Pregame Show" (reviewing the most important research we've done in past books) and "Statistical Toolbox" (explaining all our stats). Once again, we preserve the ridiculousness of the football season for posterity with another version of "The Year in Quotes" and we introduce you to some of the more promising (and lesser-known) young bench players with our seventh annual list of Top 25 Prospects chosen in the third round or later.

Each NFL team gets a full chapter covering what happened in 2015 and our projections for the upcoming season. Are there reasons to believe that the team was actually better or worse than its record last year? What did the team do in the offseason, and what does that mean for the team's chances to win in 2016? Each chapter also includes all kinds of advanced statistics covering 2015 performance and strategic tendencies, plus detailed commentary on each of the major units of the team: offensive line, defensive front seven, defensive secondary, special teams, and coaching staff.

"Skill players" (by which we mean "players who get counted in fantasy football") get their own section in the back of the book. We list the major players at each position alphabetically, along with commentary and a 2016 KUBIAK projection that will help you win your fantasy football league. We also have the most accurate projections anywhere for two fantasy football positions that people wrongly consider impossible to predict: kickers and team defense.

Next comes our preview of the college football season. We go in-depth with the top 50 projected teams in the nation. Just like with our NFL coverage, the goal of our college previews is to focus as much as possible on "why" and how," not just "which team is better." We're not just here to rank the Football Bowl Subdivision teams from 1 to 128. We break things down to look at offense and defense, pass and run, and clutch situations compared to all plays.

We hope our book helps you raise your level of football expertise, win arguments with your friends, and win your fantasy football league. Occasionally, there are also jokes. It's a fun job. Thanks for buying this book and helping us continue to make a living out of our love for football.

Aaron Schatz
Framingham, MA
July 31, 2016

P.S. Don't forget to visit FootballOutsiders.com every day for fresh coverage of the NFL and college football, plus the most intelligent football discussion threads on the Internet.

Pregame Show

It has now been 13 years since we launched Football Outsiders. In that time, we've done a lot of primary research on the National Football League, and we reference that research in many of the articles and comments in *Football Outsiders Almanac 2016*. New readers may come across an offhand comment in a team chapter about, for example, the idea that fumble recovery is not a skill, and wonder what in the heck we are talking about. We can't repeat all our research in every new edition of *Football Outsiders Almanac*, so we start each year with a basic look at some of the most important precepts that have emerged from Football Outsiders research. You will see these issues come up again and again throughout the book.

You can also find this introduction online at http://www.footballoutsiders.com/info/FO-basics, along with links to the original research in the cases in which that research appeared online instead of (or as well as) in print.

Our various methods for projecting NFL success for college prospects are not listed below, but are referenced at times during the book. Those methods are detailed in an essay on page 415.

You run when you win, not win when you run.

If we could only share one piece of anti-conventional wisdom with you before you read the rest of our book, this would be it. The first article ever written for Football Outsiders was devoted to debunking the myth of "establishing the run." There is no correlation whatsoever between giving your running backs a lot of carries early in the game and winning the game. Just running the ball is not going to help a team score; it has to run successfully.

There are two reasons why nearly every beat writer and television analyst still repeats the tired old school mantra that "establishing the run" is the secret to winning football games. The first problem is confusing cause and effect. There are exceptions, but for the most part, winning teams have a lot of carries because their running backs are running out the clock at the end of wins, not because they are running wild early in games.

The second problem is history. Most of the current crop of NFL analysts came of age or actually played the game during the 1970s. They believe that the run-heavy game of that decade is how football is meant to be, and today's pass-first game is an aberration. As we addressed in an essay in *Pro Football Prospectus 2006* on the history of NFL stats, it was actually the game of the 1970s that was the aberration. The seventies were far more slanted towards the run than any era since the arrival of Paul Brown, Otto Graham, and the Cleveland Browns in 1946. Optimal strategies from 1974 are not optimal strategies for 2012.

A sister statement to "you have to establish the run" is "team X is 5-1 when running back John Doe runs for at least 100 yards." Unless John Doe is possessed by otherworldly spirits the way Adrian Peterson was a couple years ago, the team isn't winning because of his 100-yard games. He's putting up 100-yard games because his team is winning.

A great defense against the run is nothing without a good pass defense.

This is a corollary to the absurdity of "establish the run." With rare exceptions, teams win or lose with the passing game more than the running game—and by stopping the passing game more than the running game. Ron Jaworski puts it best: "The pass gives you the lead, and the run solidifies it." The reason why teams need a strong run defense in the playoffs is not to shut the run down early; it's to keep the other team from icing the clock if they get a lead. You can't mount a comeback if you can't stop the run.

Note that "good pass defense" may mean "good pass rush" rather than "good defensive backs."

Running on third-and-short is more likely to convert than passing on third-and-short.

On average, passing will always gain more yardage than running, with one very important exception: when a team is just 1 or 2 yards away from a new set of downs or the goal line. On third-and-1, a run will convert for a new set of downs 36 percent more often than a pass. Expand that to all third or fourth downs with 1 or 2 yards to go, and the run is successful 40 percent more often. With these percentages, the possibility of a long gain with a pass is not worth the tradeoff of an incomplete that kills a drive.

This is one reason why teams have to be able to both run and pass. The offense also has to keep some semblance of balance so they can use their play-action fakes, and so the defense doesn't just run their nickel and dime packages all game. Balance also means that teams do need to pass occasionally in short-yardage situations; they just need to do it less than they do now. Teams pass roughly 60 percent of the time on third-and-2 even though runs in that situation convert 20 percent more often than passes. They pass 68 percent of the time on fourth-and-2 even though runs in that situation convert twice as often as passes.

Standard team rankings based on total yardage are inherently flawed.

Check out the schedule page on NFL.com, and you will find that each game is listed with league rankings based on total yardage. That is still how the NFL "officially" ranks teams, but these rankings rarely match up with common sense. That is because total team yardage may be the most context-dependent number in football.

It starts with the basic concept that rate stats are generally more valuable than cumulative stats. Yards per carry says more about a running back's quality than total yardage, completion percentage says more than just a quarterback's total number of completions. The same thing is true for teams; in fact, it is even more important because of the way football strategy influences the number of runs and passes in the game plan. Poor teams will give up fewer passing yards and more rushing yards because opponents will stop passing once they have a late-game lead and will run out the clock instead. For winning teams, the opposite is true. For example, which team had a better pass defense last year: Arizona or Chicago? The answer is obviously Arizona, yet according to the official NFL rankings, Chicago (3,593 net yards allowed on 548 pass attempts, 6.6 net yards per pass) was a better pass defense than Arizona (3,687 net yards allowed on 609 pass attempts, 6.1 net yards per pass).

Total yardage rankings are also skewed because some teams play at a faster pace than other teams. For example, last year Indianapolis (5,142) had roughly the same number of yards as Minnesota (5,139). However, the Vikings were the superior offense and much more efficient; they gained those yards on only 166 drives while the Colts needed 187 drives.

A team will score more when playing a bad defense, and will give up more points when playing a good offense.

This sounds absurdly basic, but when people consider team and player stats without looking at strength of schedule, they are ignoring this. In 2004, Carson Palmer and Byron Leftwich had very similar numbers, but Palmer faced a much tougher schedule than Leftwich did. Palmer was better that year, and better in the long run. A similar comparison can be made between Russell Wilson and Robert Griffin III in their rookie years: Wilson had a higher DVOA rating because he faced a more difficult schedule, even though Griffin had slightly better standard stats.

If their overall yards per carry are equal, a running back who consistently gains yardage on every play is more valuable than a boom-and-bust running back who is frequently stuffed at the line but occasionally breaks a long highlight-worthy run.

Our brethren at Baseball Prospectus believe that the most precious commodity in baseball is outs. Teams only get 27 of them per game, and you can't afford to give one up for very little return. So imagine if there was a new rule in baseball that gave a team a way to earn another three outs in the middle of the inning. That would be pretty useful, right?

That's the way football works. You may start a drive 80 yards away from scoring, but as long as you can earn 10 yards in four chances, you get another four chances. Long gains have plenty of value, but if those long gains are mixed with a lot of short gains, you are going to put the quarterback in a lot of difficult third-and-long situations. That means more punts and more giving the ball back to the other team rather than moving the chains and giving the offense four more plays to work with.

The running back who gains consistent yardage is also going to do a lot more for you late in the game, when the goal of running the ball is not just to gain yardage but to eat clock time. If you are a Chargers fan watching your team with a late lead, you don't want to see three straight Melvin Gordon stuffs at the line followed by a punt. You want to see a game-icing first down.

A common historical misconception is that our preference for consistent running backs means that "Football Outsiders believes that Barry Sanders was overrated." Sanders wasn't just any boom-and-bust running back, though; he was the greatest boom-and-bust runner of all time, with bigger booms and fewer busts. Sanders ranked in the top five in DYAR five times (third in 1989, first in 1990, and second in 1994, 1996, and 1997).

Rushing is more dependent on the offensive line than people realize, but pass protection is more dependent on the quarterback himself than people realize.

Some readers complain that this idea contradicts the previous one. Aren't those consistent running backs just the product of good offensive lines? The truth is somewhere in between. There are certainly good running backs who suffer because their offensive lines cannot create consistent holes, but most boom-and-bust running backs contribute to their own problems by hesitating behind the line whenever the hole is unclear, looking for the home run instead of charging forward for the 4-yard gain that keeps the offense moving.

As for pass protection, some quarterbacks have better instincts for the rush than others, and are thus better at getting out of trouble by moving around in the pocket or throwing the ball away. Others will hesitate, hold onto the ball too long, and lose yardage over and over.

Note that "moving around in the pocket" does not necessarily mean "scrambling." In fact, a scrambling quarterback will often take more sacks than a pocket quarterback, because while he's running around trying to make something happen, a defensive lineman will catch up with him.

Shotgun formations are generally more efficient than formations with the quarterback under center.

Over the past five seasons, offenses have averaged roughly 5.9 yards per play from Shotgun (or Pistol), but just 5.1 yards per play with the quarterback under center. This wide split exists even if you analyze the data to try to weed out biases like teams using Shotgun more often on third-and-long, or against prevent defenses in the fourth quarter. Shotgun offense is more efficient if you only look at the first half, on every down, and even if you only look at running back carries rather than passes and scrambles.

It's hard to think of a Football Outsiders axiom that has been better assimilated by the people running NFL teams since we started doing this a decade ago. In 2001, NFL teams only used Shotgun on 14 percent of plays. Five years later, in 2006, that had increased slightly, to 20 percent of plays. By 2012, Shotgun was used on a 47.5 percent of plays (including the Pistol, but not counting the Wildcat or other direct snaps to non-quarterbacks). Last year, the league as a whole was up to an average of 62.7 percent of plays from Shotgun or Pistol. Remember, before 2007, no team had ever used Shotgun on more than half its offensive plays. Now, the league *averages* over 60 percent. At some point, defenses will adapt and the benefit of the formation will become less pronounced, but it doesn't look like it is happening yet.

A running back with 370 or more carries during the regular season will usually suffer either a major injury or a loss of effectiveness the following year, unless he is named Eric Dickerson.

Terrell Davis, Jamal Anderson, and Edgerrin James all blew out their knees. Larry Johnson broke his foot. Earl Campbell and Eddie George went from legendary powerhouses to plodding, replacement-level players. Shaun Alexander broke his foot *and* became a plodding, replacement-level player. This is what happens when a running back is overworked to the point of having at least 370 carries during the regular season. DeMarco Murray was the latest player to follow up a high workload with a disappointing season.

The "Curse of 370" was expanded in our book *Pro Football Prospectus 2005*, and now includes seasons with 390 or more carries in the regular season and postseason combined. Research also shows that receptions don't cause a problem, only workload on the ground.

Plenty of running backs get injured without hitting 370 carries in a season, but there is a clear difference. On average, running backs with 300 to 369 carries and no postseason appearance will see their total rushing yardage decline by 15 percent the following year and their yards per carry decline by two percent. The average running back with 370 or more regular-season carries, or 390 including the postseason, will see their rushing yardage decline by 35 percent, and their yards per carry decline by eight percent. However, the Curse of 370 is not a hard and fast line where running backs suddenly become injury risks. It is more of a concept where 370 carries is roughly the point at which additional carries start to become more and more of a problem.

Wide receivers must be judged on both complete and incomplete passes.

Last year, for example, Rishard Matthews had 662 receiving yards for Miami while Nate Washington had 658 receiving yards for Tennessee. Neither played with one of the better quarterbacks in the league, and both ran their average route roughly 11.4 yards downfield. But there was a big difference between them: Matthews caught 70 percent of intended passes, while Washington caught 50 percent. That's why the Titans brought in Matthews to replace Washington.

Some work has been done on splitting responsibility for incomplete passes between quarterbacks and receivers, but not enough that we can incorporate this into our advanced stats at this time. We know that wide receiver catch rates are almost as consistent from year to year as quarterback completion percentages, but it is also important to look at catch rate in the context of the types of routes each receiver runs. Five years ago, we expanded on this idea with a new plus-minus metric, which is explained in the introduction to the chapter on wide receivers and tight ends.

The total quality of an NFL team is four parts offense, three parts defense, and one part special teams.

There are three units on a football team, but they are not of equal importance. For a long time, the saying from Football Outsiders was that the total quality of an NFL team is three parts offense, three parts defense, and one part special teams. Further recent research suggests that offense is even more important than we originally believed. Recent recent work by Chase Stuart, Neil Paine, and Brian Burke suggests a split between offense and defense of roughly 58-42, without considering special teams. Our research suggests that special teams contributes about 13 percent to total performance; if you measure the remaining 87 percent with a 58-42 ratio, you get roughly 4:3:1. When we compare the range of offense, defense, and special teams DVOA ratings, we get the same results, with the best and worst offenses roughly 130 percent stronger than the best and worst defenses, and roughly four times stronger than the best and worst special teams.

Offense is more consistent from year to year than defense, and offensive performance is easier to project than defensive performance. Special teams is less consistent than either.

Nobody in the NFL understood this concept better than former Indianapolis Colts general manager Bill Polian. Both the Super Bowl champion Colts and the four-time AFC champion Buffalo Bills of the early 1990s were built around the idea that if you put together an offense that can dominate the league year after year, eventually you will luck into a year where good health and a few smart decisions will give you a defense good enough to win a championship. (As the Colts learned in 2006, you don't even need a year, just four weeks.) Even the New England Patriots, who are led by a defense-first head coach in Bill Belichick, have been more consistent on offense than on defense since they began their run of success in 2001.

Field goal percentage is almost entirely random from season to season, while kickoff distance is one of the most consistent statistics in football.

This theory, which originally appeared in the *New York Times* in October 2006, is one of our most controversial, but it is hard to argue against the evidence. Measuring every kicker from 1999 to 2006 who had at least ten field goal attempts in each of two consecutive years, the year-to-year correlation coefficient for field goal percentage was an insignificant .05. Mike Vanderjagt didn't miss a single field goal in 2003, but his percentage was a below-average 74 percent the year before and 80 percent the year after. Adam Vinatieri has long been considered the best kicker in the game. But even he had never enjoyed two straight seasons with accuracy better than the NFL average of 85 percent until 2010 and 2011.

On the other hand, the year-to-year correlation coefficient for kickoff distance, over the same period as our measurement of field-goal percentage and with the same minimum of ten kicks per year, is .61. The same players consistently lead the league in kickoff distance. In recent years, that group includes Steven Hauschka, Graham Gano, Stephen Gostkowski, Pat McAfee, and Justin Tucker.

Teams with more offensive penalties generally lose more games, but there is no correlation between defensive penalties and losses.

Specific defensive penalties of course lose games; we've all sworn at the television when the cornerback on our favorite team gets flagged for a 50-yard pass interference penalty. Yet overall, there is no correlation between losses and the total of defensive penalties or even the total yardage on defensive penalties. One reason is that defensive penalties often represent *good* play, not bad. Cornerbacks who play tight coverage may be just on the edge of a penalty on most plays, only occasionally earning a flag. Defensive ends who get a good jump on rushing the passer will gladly trade an encroachment penalty or two for ten snaps where they get off the blocks a split-second before the linemen trying to block them.

In addition, offensive penalties have a higher correlation from year to year than defensive penalties. The penalty that correlates highest with losses is the false start, and the penalty that teams will have called most consistently from year to year is also the false start.

Recovery of a fumble, despite being the product of hard work, is almost entirely random.

Stripping the ball is a skill. Holding onto the ball is a skill. Pouncing on the ball as it is bouncing all over the place is not a skill. There is no correlation whatsoever between the percentage of fumbles recovered by a team in one year and the percentage they recover in the next year. The odds of recovery are based solely on the type of play involved, not the teams or any of their players.

Fans like to insist that specific coaches can teach their teams to recover more fumbles by swarming to the ball. Chicago's Lovie Smith, in particular, is supposed to have this ability. However, in Smith's first three seasons as head coach of the Bears, their rate of fumble recovery on defense went from a league-best 76 percent in 2004 to a league-worst 33 percent in 2005, then back to 67 percent in 2006. And the last two years when he was in Tampa Bay, the defense recovered roughly half all fumbles each season.

The Dallas Cowboys over the last three seasons provide another example. The Cowboys recovered 11 of 14 forced fumbles in 2013. Then they recovered only three of 10 fumbles in 2014. And they were back to recovering 10 of 16 fumbles in 2015.

Fumble recovery is equally erratic on offense. In 2014, the San Francisco 49ers fumbled 15 times and only recovered four of them. Last year, the 49ers fumbled 15 times and instead recovered 12 of them.

Fumble recovery is a major reason why the general public overestimates or underestimates certain teams. Fumbles are huge, turning-point plays that dramatically impact wins and losses in the past, while fumble recovery percentage says absolutely nothing about a team's chances of winning games in the future. With this in mind, Football Outsiders stats treat all fumbles as equal, penalizing them based on the likelihood of each type of fumble (run, pass, sack, etc.) being recovered by the defense.

Other plays that qualify as "non-predictive events" include two-point conversions, blocked kicks, and touchdowns during turnover returns. These plays are not "lucky," per se, but they have no value whatsoever for predicting future performance.

Field position is fluid.

As discussed in the Statistical Toolbox, every yard line on the field has a value based on how likely a team is to score from that location on the field as opposed to from a yard further back. The change in value from one yard to the next is the same whether the team has the ball or not. The goal of a defense is not just to prevent scoring, but to hold the opposition so that the offense can get the ball back in the best possible field position. A bad offense will score as many points as a good offense if it starts each drive 5 yards closer to the goal line.

A corollary to this precept: The most underrated aspect of an NFL team's performance is the field position gained or lost on kickoffs and punts. This is part of why players such as Tyler Lockett and Cordarrelle Patterson can have such an impact on the game, even when they aren't taking a kickoff or punt all the way back for a touchdown.

The red zone is the most important place on the field to play well, but performance in the red zone from year to year is much less consistent than overall performance.

Although play in the red zone has a disproportionately high importance to the outcome of games relative to plays on the rest of the field, NFL teams do not exhibit a level of performance in the red zone that is consistently better or worse than their performance elsewhere, year after year. The simplest explanation why is a small(er) sample size and the inherent variance of football, with contributing factors like injuries and changes in personnel.

Defenses which are strong on first and second down, but weak on third down, will tend to improve the following year. Defenses which are weak on first and second down, but strong on third down, will tend to decline the following year.

Teams get fewer opportunities on third down, so third-down performance is more volatile—but it's also is a bigger part of a team's overall performance than first or second down, because the result is usually either very good (four more downs) or very bad (losing the ball to the other team with a punt). Over time, a team will play as well in those situations as it does in other situations, which will bring the overall defense in line with the = defense on first and second down.

This trend is even stronger between seasons. Struggles on third down are a pretty obvious problem, and teams will generally target their off-season moves at improving their third-down performance ... which often leads to an improvement in third-down performance.

However, we have discovered something surprising over the past few years. Originally, we discovered this effect on both offense and defense. But the third-down rebound effect seems to have disappeared on offense, as we explained in the Philadelphia chapter of *Football Outsiders Almanac 2010*. We still plan to do additional research on this to look at whether the third-down effect still exists, and how strong it is on offense and/or defense.

Injuries regress to the mean on the seasonal level, and teams that avoid injuries in a given season tend to win more games.

There are no doubt teams with streaks of good or bad health over multiple years. However, teams who were especially healthy or especially unhealthy, as measured by our adjusted games lost (AGL) metric, almost always head towards league average in the subsequent season. Furthermore, injury—or the absence thereof—has a huge correlation with wins, and a significant impact on a team's success. There's no doubt that a few high-profile teams have resisted this trend in recent years. The Patriots seem to overcome injuries every year, and a number of recent Super Bowl champions such as the 2010 Packers and 2011 Giants have overcome injuries to win the championship. Nonetheless, the overall rule still applies. In 2014, six of the seven teams with the lowest AGL won at least 10 games. Last year wasn't quite as extreme, but the ten teams with the lowest AGL included both Carolina and Denver as well as Cincinnati, Seattle, and Kansas City. Meanwhile, out of the teams with the dozen highest AGL totals, only Washington and New England made the playoffs.

In the past, we have written that teams with a high number of injuries are a good bet to improve the following season. However, work we did on last year's new team projection system suggests this may not actually be the case. AGL totals correlate strongly with how well a team plays in that year, but not necessarily with improvement or decline the following season.

By and large, a team built on depth is better than a team built on stars and scrubs.

Connected to the previous statement, because teams need to go into the season expecting that they will suffer an average number of injuries no matter how healthy they were the previous year. You cannot concentrate your salaries on a handful of star players because there is no such thing as avoiding injuries in the NFL. The game is too fast and the players too strong to build a team based around the idea that "if we can avoid all injuries this year, we'll win."

Running backs usually decline after age 28, tight ends after age 29, wide receivers after age 30, and quarterbacks after age 32.

This research was originally done by Doug Drinen (editor of pro-football-reference.com) in 2000. In recent years, a few players have had huge seasons above these general age limits, but the peak ages Drinen found a few years ago still apply to the majority of players.

As for "non-skill players," research we did in 2007 for *ESPN The Magazine* suggested that defensive ends and defensive backs generally begin to decline after age 29, linebackers and offensive linemen after age 30, and defensive tackles after age 31. However, because we still have so few statistics to use to study linemen and defensive players, this research should not be considered definitive.

The strongest indicator of how a college football team will perform in the upcoming season is their performance in recent seasons.

It may seem strange because graduation enforces constant player turnover, but college football teams are actually much more consistent from year to year than NFL teams. Thanks in large part to consistency in recruiting, teams can be expected to play within a reasonable range of their baseline program expectations each season. Our Program F/+ ratings, which represent a rolling five-year period of play-by-play and drive efficiency data, have an extremely strong (.76) correlation with the next year's F/+ rating.

Championship teams are generally defined by their ability to dominate inferior opponents, not their ability to win close games.

Football games are often decided by just one or two plays: a missed field goal, a bouncing fumble, the subjective spot of an official on fourth-and-1. One missed assignment by a cornerback or one slightly askew pass that bounces off a receiver's hands and into those of a defensive back five yards away and the game could be over. In a blowout, however, one lucky bounce isn't going to change things. Championship teams—in both professional and college football—typically beat their good opponents convincingly and destroy the cupcakes on the schedule.

Aaron Schatz

Statistical Toolbox

After 13 years of Football Outsiders, some of our readers are as comfortable with DVOA and ALY as they are with touchdowns and tackles. Yet to most fans, including our newer readers, it still looks like a lot of alphabet soup. That's what this chapter is for. The next few pages define and explain all of all the unique NFL statistics you'll find in this book: how we calculate them, what the numbers mean, and what they tell us about why teams win or lose football games. We'll go through the information in each of the tables that appear in each team chapter, pointing out whether those stats come from advanced mathematical manipulation of the standard play-by-play or simple counting of what we see on television with the Football Outsiders game charting project. This chapter covers NFL statistics only. College metrics such as Adjusted POE and F/+ are explained in the introduction to the college football section on page 363.

We've done our best to present these numbers in a way that makes them easy to understand. This explanation is long, so feel free to read some of it, flip around the rest of the book, and then come back. It will still be here.

Defense-Adjusted Value Over Average (DVOA)

One running back runs for three yards. Another running back runs for three yards. Which is the better run?

This sounds like a stupid question, but it isn't. In fact, this question is at the heart of nearly all of the analysis in this book.

Several factors can differentiate one three-yard run from another. What is the down and distance? Is it third-and-2, or second-and-15? Where on the field is the ball? Does the player get only three yards because he hits the goal line and scores? Is the player's team up by two touchdowns in the fourth quarter and thus running out the clock, or down by two touchdowns and thus facing a defense that is playing purely against the pass? Is the running back playing against the porous defense of the Saints, or the stalwart defense of the Seahawks?

Conventional NFL statistics value plays based solely on their net yardage. The NFL determines the best players by adding up all their yards no matter what situations they came in or how many plays it took to get them. Now, why would they do that? Football has one objective—to get to the end zone—and two ways to achieve that, by gaining yards and achieving first downs. These two goals need to be balanced to determine a player's value or a team's performance. All the yards in the world won't help a team win if they all come in six-yard chunks on third-and-10.

The popularity of fantasy football only exacerbates the problem. Fans have gotten used to judging players based on how much they help fantasy teams win and lose, not how much they help *real* teams win and lose. Typical fantasy scoring further skews things by counting the yard between the one and the goal line as 61 times more important than all the other yards on the field (each yard worth 0.1 points, a touchdown worth 6.0). Let's say Odell Beckham catches a pass on third-and-15 and goes 50 yards but gets tackled two yards from the goal line, and then Andre Williams takes the ball on first-and-goal from the two-yard line and plunges in for the score. Has Williams done something special? Not really. When an offense gets the ball on first-and-goal at the two-yard line, they are going to score a touchdown five out of six times. Williams is getting credit for the work done by the passing game.

Doing a better job of distributing credit for scoring points and winning games is the goal of **DVOA**, or Defense-adjusted Value Over Average. DVOA breaks down every single play of the NFL season, assigning each play a value based on both total yards and yards towards a first down, based on work done by Pete Palmer, Bob Carroll, and John Thorn in their seminal book, *The Hidden Game of Football*. On first down, a play is considered a success if it gains 45 percent of needed yards; on second down, a play needs to gain 60 percent of needed yards; on third or fourth down, only gaining a new first down is considered success.

We then expand upon that basic idea with a more complicated system of "success points," improved over the past four years with a lot of mathematics and a bit of trial and error. A successful play is worth one point, an unsuccessful play zero points with fractional points in between (for example, eight yards on third-and-10 is worth 0.54 "success points"). Extra points are awarded for big plays, gradually increasing to three points for 10 yards (assuming those yards result in a first down), four points for 20 yards, and five points for 40 yards or more. Losing three or more yards is -1 point. Interceptions average -6 points, with an adjustment for the length of the pass and the location of the interception (since an interception tipped at the line is more likely to produce a long return than an interception on a 40-yard pass). A fumble is worth anywhere from -1.7 to -4.0 points depending on how often a fumble in that situation is lost to the defense—no matter who actually recovers the fumble. Red zone plays get a bonus: 20 percent for team offense, five percent for team defense, and 10 percent for individual players. There is a bonus given for a touchdown that acknowledges that the goal line is significantly more difficult to cross than the previous 99 yards (although this bonus is nowhere near as large as the one used in fantasy football).

(Our system is a bit more complex than the one in *Hidden Game* thanks to our subsequent research, which added larger penalty for turnovers, the fractional points, and a slightly higher baseline for success on first down. The reason why all fumbles are counted, no matter whether they are recovered by the offense or defense, is explained in the essay "Pregame Show.")

Every single play run in the NFL gets a "success value" based on this system, and then that number gets compared to the average success values of plays in similar situations for all players, adjusted for a number of variables. These include down and distance, field location, time remaining in game, and the team's lead or deficit in the game score. Teams are always compared to the overall offensive average, as the team made its own choice whether to pass or rush. When it comes to individual players, however, rushing plays are compared to other rushing plays, passing plays to other passing plays, tight ends to tight ends, wideouts to wideouts, and so on.

Going back to our example of the three-yard rush, if Player A gains three yards under a set of circumstances in which the average NFL running back gains only one yard, then Player A has a certain amount of value above others at his position. Likewise, if Player B gains three yards on a play on which, under similar circumstances, an average NFL back gains four yards, that Player B has negative value relative to others at his position. Once we make all our adjustments, we can evaluate the difference between this player's rate of success and the expected success rate of an average running back in the same situation (or between the opposing defense and the average defense in the same situation, etc.). Add up every play by a certain team or player, divide by the total of the various baselines for success in all those situations, and you get VOA, or Value Over Average.

Of course, the biggest variable in football is the fact that each team plays a different schedule against teams of disparate quality. By adjusting each play based on the opposing defense's average success in stopping that type of play over the course of a season, we get DVOA, or Defense-adjusted Value Over Average. Rushing and passing plays are adjusted based on down and location on the field; passing plays are also adjusted based on how the defense performs against passes to running backs, tight ends, or wide receivers. Defenses are adjusted based on the average success of the *offenses* they are facing. (Yes, technically the defensive stats are actually "offense-adjusted." If it seems weird, think of the "D" in "DVOA" as standing for "opponent-Dependent" or something.)

The biggest advantage of DVOA is the ability to break teams and players down to find strengths and weaknesses in a variety of situations. In the aggregate, DVOA may not be quite as accurate as some of the other, similar "power ratings" formulas based on comparing drives rather than individual plays, but, unlike those other ratings, DVOA can be separated not only by player, but also by down, or by week, or by distance needed for a first down. This can give us a better idea of not just which team is better, but why, and what a team has to do in order to improve itself in the future. You will find DVOA used in this book in a lot of different ways—because it takes every single play into account, it can be used to measure a player or a team's performance in any situation. All Pittsburgh third downs can be compared to how an average team does on third down. Blaine Gabbert and Colin Kaepernick can each be compared to how an average quarterback performs in the red zone, or with a lead, or in the second half of the game.

Since it compares each play only to plays with similar circumstances, it gives a more accurate picture of how much better a team really is compared to the league as a whole. The list of top DVOA offenses on third down, for example, is more accurate than the conventional NFL conversion statistic because it takes into account that converting third-and-long is more difficult than converting third-and-short, and that a turnover is worse than an incomplete pass because it eliminates the opportunity to move the other team back with a punt on fourth down.

One of the hardest parts of understanding a new statistic is interpreting its scale, or what numbers represent good performance or bad performance. We've made that easy with DVOA. For each season, ratings are normalized so that 0% represents league average. A positive DVOA represents a situation that favors the offense, while a negative DVOA represents a situation that favors the defense. This is why the best offenses have positive DVOA ratings (last year, Seattle led the NFL at 18.7%) and the best defenses have negative DVOA ratings (with Denver on top at -25.8%).

The scale of offensive ratings is wider than the scale of defensive ratings. In most years, the best and worst offenses tend to rate around +/- 30%, while the best and worst defenses tend to rate around +/- 20%. (2015 was a unique year where the strongest and weakest defenses were farther from average than the strongest and weakest offenses. Seattle had the lowest offensive DVOA ever for a team ranked No. 1, and Tennessee was the first team to ever finish in last place with an offensive DVOA above -20%.) For starting players, the scale tends to reach roughly +/-40% for passing and receiving, and +/- 30% for rushing. As you might imagine, some players with fewer attempts will surpass both extremes.

Team DVOA totals combine offense and defense by subtracting the latter from the former because the better defenses will have negative DVOA ratings. (Special teams performance is also added, as described later in this essay.) Certain plays are counted in DVOA for offense and not for defense, leading to separate baselines on each side of the ball. In addition, although the league ratings for offense and defense are always 0%, the league averages for passing and rushing separately are *not* 0%. Because passing is more efficient than rushing, the average for team passing is almost always positive and the average for team rushing is almost always negative. However, ratings for individual players only compare passes to other passes and runs to other runs, so the league average for individual passing is 0%, as are the league averages for rushing and the three separate league averages for receiving by wide receivers, tight ends, and running backs.

Some other important notes about DVOA:

• Only four penalties are included in DVOA. Two penalties count as pass plays on both sides of the ball: intentional grounding and defensive pass interference. The other two penalties are included for offense only: false starts and delay of game. Because the inclusion of these penalties means a group of negative plays that don't count as either passes or runs, the league averages for pass offense and run offense are higher than the league averages for pass defense and run defense.

• Aborted snaps and incomplete backwards lateral passes are only penalized on offense, not rewarded on defense.

• Adjustments for playing from behind or with a lead in the fourth quarter are different for offense and defense, as are adjustments for the final two minutes of the first half when the offense is not near field-goal range.

• Offense gets a slight penalty and defense gets a slight bonus for games indoors.

How well does DVOA work? Using correlation coefficients, we can show that only actual points scored are better than DVOA at indicating how many games a team has won (Table 1) and DVOA does a better job of predicting wins in the coming season than either wins or points scored in the previous season (Table 2).

(Correlation coefficient is a statistical tool that measures how two variables are related by using a number between 1 and -1. The closer to -1 or 1, the stronger the relationship, but the closer to 0, the weaker the relationship.)

Table 1. Correlation of Various Stats to Wins, 2002-2014

Stat	Offense	Defense	Total
Points Scored/Allowed	.755	-.676	.920
DVOA	.708	-.490	.859
Yards Gained/Allowed	.546	-.371	.681
Yards Gained/Allowed per Play	.546	-.339	.725

Table 2. Correlation of Various Stats to Wins Following Year, 2002-2014

Stat	Correlation	Stat	Correlation
DVOA	.370	Yards per Play Differential	.316
Point Differential	.353	Wins	.307
Pythagorean Wins	.347	Yardage Differential	.298

Special Teams

The problem with a system based on measuring both yardage and yardage towards a first down is what to do with plays that don't have the possibility of a first down. Special teams are an important part of football and we needed a way to add that performance to the team DVOA rankings. Our special teams metric includes five separate measurements: field goals and extra points, net punting, punt returns, net kickoffs, and kick returns.

The foundation of most of these special teams ratings is the concept that each yard line has a different value based on the likelihood of scoring from that position on the field. In *Hidden Game*, the authors suggested that the each additional yard for the offense had equal value, with a team's own goal line being worth -2 points, the 50-yard line 2 points, and the opposing goal line 6 points. (-2 points is not only the value of a safety, but also reflects the fact that when a team is backed up in its own territory, it is likely that its drive will stall, forcing a punt

that will give the ball to the other team in good field position. Thus, the negative point value reflects the fact that the defense is more likely to score next.) Our studies have updated this concept to reflect the actual likelihood that the offense or defense will have the next score from a given position on the field based on actual results from the past few seasons. The line that represents the value of field position is not straight, but curved, with the value of each yard increasing as teams approach either goal line.

Our special teams ratings compare each kick or punt to league average based on the point value of the position of the kick, catch, and return. We've determined a league average for how far a kick goes based on the line of scrimmage for each kick (almost always the 35-yard line for kickoffs, variable for punts) and a league average for how far a return goes based on both the yard line where the ball is caught and the distance that it traveled in the air.

The kicking or punting team is rated based on net points compared to average, taking into account both the kick and the return if there is one. Because the average return is always positive, punts that are not returnable (touchbacks, out of bounds, fair catches, and punts downed by the coverage unit) will rate higher than punts of the same distance which are returnable. (This is also true of touchbacks on kickoffs.) There are also separate individual ratings for kickers and punters that are based on distance and whether the kick is returnable, assuming an average return in order to judge the kicker separate from the coverage.

For the return team, the rating is based on how many points the return is worth compared to average, based on the location of the catch and the distance the ball traveled in the air. Return teams are not judged on the distance of kicks, nor are they judged on kicks that cannot be returned. As explained below, blocked kicks are so rare as to be statistically insignificant as predictors for future performance and are thus ignored. For the kicking team they simply count as missed field goals, for the defense they are gathered with their opponents' other missed field goals in Hidden value (also explained below).

Field goal kicking is measured differently. Measuring kickers by field goal percentage is a bit absurd, as it assumes that all field goals are of equal difficulty. In our metric, each field goal is compared to the average number of points scored on all field goal attempts from that distance over the past 15 years. The value of a field goal increases as distance from the goal line increases. Kickoffs, punts, and field goals are then adjusted based on weather and altitude. It will surprise no one to learn that it is easier to kick the ball in Denver or a dome than it is to kick the ball in Buffalo in December. Because we do not yet have enough data to tailor our adjustments specifically to each stadium, each one is assigned to one of four categories: Cold, Warm, Dome, and Denver. There is also an additional adjustment dropping the value of field goals in Florida (because the warm temperatures allow the ball to carry better).

The baselines for special teams are adjusted in each year for rule changes such as the introduction of the special teams-only "k-ball" in 1999 as well as the move of the kickoff line from the 35 to the 30 in 1994 and then back to the 35 in 2011.

Baselines have also been adjusted each year to make up for the gradual improvement of kickers over the last two decades, and a new baseline was set last year for the longer distance on extra points.

Once we've totaled how many points above or below average can be attributed to special teams, we translate those points into DVOA so the ratings can be added to offense and defense to get total team DVOA.

There are three aspects of special teams that have an impact on wins and losses, but don't show up in the standard special teams rating because a team has little or no influence on them. The first is the length of kickoffs by the opposing team, with an asterisk. Obviously, there are no defenders standing on the 35-yard line, ready to block a kickoff after the whistle blows. However, over the past few years, some teams have deliberately kicked short in order to avoid certain top return men, such as Devin Hester and Cordarrelle Patterson. The special teams formula now includes adjustments to give teams extra credit for field position on kick returns if kickers are deliberately trying to avoid a return.

The other two items that special teams have little control over are field goals against your team, and punt distance against your team. Research shows no indication that teams can influence the accuracy or strength of field goal kickers and punters, except for blocks. As mentioned above, although blocked field goals and punts are definitely skillful plays, they are so rare that they have no correlation to how well teams have played in the past or will play in the future, thus they are included here as if they were any other missed field goal or botched punt, giving the defense no additional credit for their efforts. The value of these three elements is listed separately as "Hidden" value.

Special teams ratings also do not include two-point conversions or onside kick attempts, both of which, like blocks, are so infrequent as to be statistically insignificant in judging future performance.

Defense-Adjusted Yards Above Replacement (DYAR)

DVOA is a good stat, but of course it is not a perfect one. One problem is that DVOA, by virtue of being a percentage or rate statistic, doesn't take into account the cumulative value of having a player producing at a league-average level over the course of an above-average number of plays. By definition, an average level of performance is better than that provided by half of the league and the ability to maintain that level of performance while carrying a heavy work load is very valuable indeed. In addition, a player who is involved in a high number of plays can draw the defense's attention away from other parts of the offense, and, if that player is a running back, he can take time off the clock with repeated runs.

Let's say you have a running back who carries the ball 300 times in a season. What would happen if you were to remove this player from his team's offense? What would happen to those 300 plays? Those plays don't disappear with the player, though some might be lost to the defense because of the associated loss of first downs. Rather those plays would have to be distributed among the remaining players in the offense, with the bulk of them being given to a replacement running back. This is where we arrive at the concept of replacement level, borrowed from our friends at Baseball Prospectus. When a player is removed from an offense, he is usually not replaced by a player of similar ability. Nearly every starting player in the NFL is a starter because he is better than the alternative. Those 300 plays will typically be given to a significantly worse player, someone who is the backup because he doesn't have as much experience and/or talent. A player's true value can then be measured by the level of performance he provides above that replacement level baseline, totaled over all of his run or pass attempts.

Of course, the *real* replacement player is different for each team in the NFL. Last year, the player who originally was the third-string running back in Seattle (Thomas Rawls) ended up as the starter with a much higher DVOA than either Marshawn Lynch or Fred Jackson. Sometimes a player such as Gary Barnidge or Danny Woodhead will be cut by one team and turn into a star for another. On other teams, the drop from the starter to the backup can be even greater than the general drop to replacement level. (The 2011 Indianapolis Colts will be the hallmark example of this until the end of time.) The choice to start an inferior player or to employ a sub-replacement level backup, however, falls to the team, not the starter being evaluated. Thus we generalize replacement level for the league as a whole as the ultimate goal is to evaluate players independent of the quality of their teammates.

Our estimates of replacement level are computed differently for each position. For quarterbacks, we analyzed situations where two or more quarterbacks had played meaningful snaps for a team in the same season, then compared the overall DVOA of the original starters to the overall DVOA of the replacements. We did not include situations where the backup was actually a top prospect waiting his turn on the bench, since a first-round pick is by no means a "replacement-level" player.

At other positions, there is no easy way to separate players into "starters" and "replacements," since unlike at quarterback, being the starter doesn't make you the only guy who gets in the game. Instead, we used a simpler method, ranking players at each position in each season by attempts. The players who made up the final 10 percent of passes or runs were split out as "replacement players" and then compared to the players making up the other 90 percent of plays at that position. This took care of the fact that not every non-starter is a freely available talent. (Think of Giovani Bernard or Duke Johnson, for example.)

As noted earlier, the challenge of any new stat is to present it on a scale that's meaningful to those attempting to use it. Saying that Andy Dalton's passes were worth 116 success value points over replacement in 2015 has very little value without a context to tell us if 116 is good total or a bad one. Therefore, we translate these success values into a number called "Defense-adjusted Yards Above Replacement, or DYAR. Thus, Dalton was fourth among quarterbacks with 1,135 passing DYAR. It is our estimate that a generic replacement-level quarterback, throwing in the same situations as Dalton, would have been worth 1,135 fewer yards. Note that this doesn't mean the replacement level quarterback would have gained exactly 1,135 fewer yards. First downs, touchdowns, and turnovers all have an estimated yardage value in this system, so what we are saying is that a generic replacement-level quarterback would have fewer yards and touchdowns (and more turnovers) that would total up to be equivalent to the value of 1,135 yards.

Problems with DVOA and DYAR

Football is a game in which nearly every action requires the work of two or more teammates—in fact, usually 11 teammates all working in unison. Unfortunately, when it comes to individual player ratings, we are still far from the point at which we can determine the value of a player independent from the performance of his teammates. That means that when we say, "In 2014, Le'Veon Bell had a DVOA of 8.6%," what we really are saying is, "In 2014, Le'Veon Bell, playing in Todd Haley's offensive system with the Pittsburgh offensive line blocking for him and Ben Roethlisberger selling the fake when necessary, had a DVOA of 8.6%."

DVOA is limited by what's included in the official NFL play-by-play or tracked by our game charting partners (explained below). Because we need to have the entire play-by-play of a season in order to compute DVOA and DYAR, these metrics are not yet ready to compare players of today to players throughout the league's history. As of this writing, we have processed 27 seasons, 1989 through 2015, and we add seasons at a rate of roughly two per year (the most recent season, plus one season back into history.) We're close to finishing up with 1986-1988 and will unveiling those numbers on our website in the next few months. (Yes, we wrote this last year as well, but the regular season got in the way. They're coming soon.)

In addition, because we need to turn around DVOA and DYAR quickly during the season before charting can be completed, we do not yet have charting data such as dropped passes incorporated into these advanced metrics. Eventually we will have two sets of metrics, one incorporating charting data and going back to 2005 or 2006, and another that does not incorporate charting and can be used to compare current players and teams to players and teams all the way back to 1986 or earlier.

Pythagorean Projection

The Pythagorean projection is an approximation of each team's wins based solely on their points scored and allowed. This basic concept was introduced by baseball analyst Bill James, who discovered that the record of a baseball team could be very closely approximated by taking the square of team runs scored and dividing it by the sum of the squares of team runs scored and allowed. Statistician Daryl Morey, now general manager of the Houston Rockets, later extended this theorem to professional football, refining the exponent to 2.37 rather than 2.

The problem with that exponent is the same problem we've had with DVOA in recent years: the changing offensive levels in the NFL. 2.37 worked great based on the league 20 years ago, but in the current NFL it ends up slightly underproject-

ing teams that play high-scoring games. The most accurate method is actually to adjust the exponent based on the scoring environment of each individual team. Saints games have a lot of points. Jaguars games feature fewer points.

This became known as Pythagenport when Clay Davenport of Baseball Prospectus started doing it with baseball teams. In the middle of the 2011 season, we switched our measurement of Pythagorean wins to a Pythagenport-style equation, modified for the NFL.[1] The improvement is slight, but noticeable due to the high-scoring teams that have dominated the last few years.

For a long time, Pythagorean projections did a remarkable job of predicting Super Bowl champions. From 1984 through 2004, 10 of 21 Super Bowls were won by the team that led the NFL in Pythagorean wins. Seven other Super Bowls during that time were won by the team that finished second. Super Bowl champions that led the league in Pythagorean wins but not actual wins include the 2004 Patriots, 2000 Ravens, 1999 Rams, and 1997 Broncos.

Super Bowl champions have been much less predictable over the last few seasons. As of 2005, the 1980 Oakland Raiders held the mark for the fewest Pythagorean wins by a Super Bowl champion, 9.7. Then, between 2006 and 2012, four different teams won the Super Bowl with a lower Pythagorean win total: the 2006 Colts (9.6), the 2012 Ravens (9.4), the 2007 Giants (8.6), and the 2011 Giants (7.9), the first team in the 90-year history of the National Football League to ever be outscored during the regular season and still go on to win the championship. In the past three seasons, we've returned to more standard playoff results: five of the past six Super Bowl teams ranked first or second in Pythagorean wins during the regular season, although Denver ranked tenth last season with 9.7 Pythagorean wins.

Pythagorean wins are also useful as a predictor of year-to-year improvement. Teams that win a minimum of one full game more than their Pythagorean projection tend to regress the following year; teams that win a minimum of one full game less than their Pythagorean projection tend to improve the following year, particularly if they were at or above .500 despite their underachieving. Seattle is the team favored to rebound in 2016 according to this trend; the Seahawks went 10-6 despite 11.7 Pythagorean wins. On the other hand, both Super Bowl teams outperformed their Pythagorean projections: Carolina led the league with 12.1 Pythagorean wins but that's nowhere near 15-1, and Denver went 12-4 with 9.7 Pythagorean wins. The Colts also should see the return of Andrew Luck somewhat countered by a reversion of luck, as they went 8-8 despite only 6.1 Pythagorean wins.

Adjusted Line Yards

One of the most difficult goals of statistical analysis in football is isolating the degree to which each of the 22 men on the field is responsible for the result of a given play. Nowhere is this as significant as the running game, in which one player

---

1   The equation, for those curious, is 1.5 x log ((PF+PA)/G).

runs while up to nine other players—including not just linemen but also wideouts and tight ends—block in different directions. None of the statistics we use for measuring rushing—yards, touchdowns, yards per carry—differentiate between the contribution of the running back and the contribution of the offensive line. Neither do our advanced metrics DVOA and DYAR.

We do, however, have enough play-by-play data amassed that we can try to separate the effect that the running back has on a particular play from the effects of the offensive line (and other offensive blockers) and the opposing defense. A team might have two running backs in its stable: RB A, who averages 3.0 yards per carry, and RB B, who averages 3.5 yards per carry. Who is the better back? Imagine that RB A doesn't just average 3.0 yards per carry, but gets exactly 3 yards on every single carry, while RB B has a highly variable yardage output: sometimes 5 yards, sometimes minus-2 yards, sometimes 20 yards. The difference in variability between the runners can be exploited not only to determine the difference between the runners, but the effect the offensive line has on every running play.

At some point in every long running play, the running back passes all of his offensive line blocks as well as additional blocking backs or receivers. From there on, the rest of the play is dependent on the runner's own speed and elusiveness and the speed and tackling ability of the opposing defense. If David Johnson breaks through the line for 50 yards, avoiding tacklers all the way to the goal line, his offensive line has done a great job—but they aren't responsible for the majority of the yards gained. The trick is figuring out exactly how much they *are* responsible for.

For each running back carry, we calculated the probability that the back involved would run for the specific yardage on that play based on that back's average yardage per carry and the variability of their yardage from play to play. We also calculated the probability that the offense would get the yardage based on the team's rushing average and variability using all backs *other* than the one involved in the given play, and the probability that the defense would give up the specific amount of yardage based on its average rushing yards allowed per carry and variability.

A regression analysis breaks the value for rushing yardage into the following categories: losses, 0-4 yards, 5-10 yards, and 11+ yards. In general, the offensive line is 20 percent more responsible for lost yardage than it is for positive gains up to four yards, but 50 percent less responsible for additional yardage gained between five and ten yards, and not at all responsible for additional yardage past ten yards.

By applying those percentages to every running back carry, we were able to create **Adjusted Line Yards**, a statistic that measured offensive line performance. (We don't include carries by receivers, which are usually based on deception rather than straight blocking, or carries by quarterbacks, although we may need to reconsider that given the recent use of the read option in the NFL.) Those numbers are then adjusted based on down, distance, situation, opponent and whether or not a team is in the shotgun. (Because defenses are generally playing pass when the quarterback is in shotgun, the average running back carry from shotgun last year gained 4.46 yards, compared to just 3.92 yards on other carries.) The adjusted numbers are then normalized so that the league average for adjusted line yards per carry is the same as the league average for RB yards per carry. (Historically, this is roughly 4.25 yards. Last year, it was only 4.09 yards. We will be looking in the next few months to change the way we normalize adjusted line yards to account for the drop in overall league rushing efficiency.)

The NFL distinguishes between runs made to seven different locations on the line: left/right end, left/right tackle, left/right guard, and middle. Further research showed no statistically significant difference between how well a team performed on runs listed as having gone up the middle or past a guard, so we separated runs into just five different directions (left/right end, left/right tackle, and middle). Note that there may not be a statistically significant difference between right tackle and middle/guard either, but pending further research (and for the sake of symmetry) we still list runs behind the right tackle separately. These splits allow us to evaluate subsections of a team's offensive line, but not necessarily individual linesmen, as we can't account for blocking assignments or guards who pull towards the opposite side of the line after the snap.

Success Rate

Success rate is a statistic for running backs that measures how consistently they achieve the yardage necessary for a play to be deemed successful. Some running backs will mix a few long runs with a lot of failed runs of one or two yards, while others with similar yards-per-carry averages will consistently gain five yards on first down, or as many yards as necessary on third down. This statistic helps us differentiate between the two.

Since Success Rate compares rush attempts to other rush attempts, without consideration of passing, the standard for success on first down is slightly lower than those described above for DVOA. In addition, the standard for success changes slightly in the fourth quarter when running backs are used to run out the clock. A team with the lead is satisfied with a shorter run as long as it stays in bounds. Conversely, for a team down by a couple of touchdowns in the fourth quarter, four yards on first down isn't going to be a big help.

The formula for Success Rate is as follows:

• A successful play must gain 40 percent of needed yards on first down, 60 percent of needed yards on second down, and 100 percent of needed yards on third or fourth down.

• If the offense is behind by more than a touchdown in the fourth quarter, the benchmarks switch to 50 percent, 65 percent, and 100 percent.

• If the offense is ahead by any amount in the fourth quarter, the benchmarks switch to 30 percent, 50 percent, and 100 percent.

The league-average Success Rate in 2015 was 45.2 percent. Success Rate is not adjusted based on defenses faced, and is not calculated for quarterbacks and wide receivers who occasionally carry the ball.

Similarity Scores

Similarity scores were first introduced by Bill James to compare baseball players to other baseball players from the past. It was only natural that the idea would spread to other sports as statistical analysis spread to other sports. NBA analyst John Hollinger has created his own version to compare basketball players, and we have created our own version to compare football players.

Similarity scores have a lot of uses, and we aren't the only football analysts who use them. Doug Drinen of the website Footballguys.com has his own system that is specific to comparing fantasy football performances. The major goal of our similarity scores is to compare career progressions to try to determine when players have a higher chance of a breakout, a decline, or—due to age or usage—an injury (much like Baseball Prospectus's PECOTA player projection system). Therefore we not only compare numbers such as attempts, yards, and touchdowns, but also age and experience. We often are looking not for players who had similar seasons, but for players who had similar two- or three-year spans in their careers.

Similarity scores have some important weaknesses. The database for player comparison begins in 1978, the year the 16-game season began and passing rules were liberalized (a reasonable starting point to measure the "modern" NFL), thus the method only compares standard statistics such as yards and attempts, which are of course subject to all kinds of biases from strength of schedule to quality of receiver corps. For our comparisons, we project full-season statistics for the strike years of 1982 and 1987, although we cannot correct for players who crossed the 1987 picket line to play more than 12 games.

In addition to our similarity scores for skill players, we also have a similarity score system for defensive players based on FO's advanced statistics going back to 1997. It measures things like average distance on run tackles or pass tackles, as well as Stops and Defeats. It does not account for game-charting stats like hurries or Success Rate in coverage.

If you are interested in the specific computations behind our similarity scores system, we have listed the standards for each skill position online at http://www.footballoutsiders.com/stats/similarity. (The defensive system is not yet listed.) In addition, as part of our online premium package, all player pages for current players—both offensive and defensive—list the top ten similar players over one-, two-, and three-year spans.

KUBIAK Projection System

Most "skill position" players whom we expect to play a role this season receive a projection of their standard 2016 NFL statistics using the KUBIAK projection system. KUBIAK takes into account a number of different factors including expected role, performance over the past two seasons, age, height, weight, historical comparables, and projected team performance on offense and defense. When we named our system KUBIAK, it was a play on the PECOTA system used by our partners at Baseball Prospectus—if they were going to name their system after a long-time eighties backup, we would name our system after a long-time eighties backup. Little did we know that Gary Kubiak would finally get a head coaching job the very next season. After some debate, we decided to keep the name, although discussing projections for Denver players can be a bit awkward.

To clear up a common misconception among our readers, KUBIAK projects individual player performances only, not teams.

2016 Win Projection System

In this book, each of the 32 NFL teams receives a **2016 Mean Projection** at the beginning of its chapter. These projections stem from three equations that forecast 2016 DVOA for offense, defense, and special teams based on a number of different factors. This offseason, we overhauled and improved the team projection system for the first time in a few years. The new system starts by considering the team's DVOA over the past three seasons and, on offense, a separate projection for the starting quarterback. The new system also does a much better job of measuring the value of offseason personnel changes by incorporating a measure that's based on the net personnel change in DYAR among non-quarterbacks (for offense) and the net change in Pro Football Reference's Approximate Value stat above replacement level (for defense). Other factors include coaching experience, recent draft history, certain players returning from injury, and combined tenure on the offensive line.

These three equations produce precise numbers representing the most likely outcome, but also produce a range of possibilities, used to determine the probability of each possible offensive, defensive, and special teams DVOA for each team. This is particularly important when projecting football teams, because with only 16 games in a season, a team's performance may vary wildly from its actual talent level due to a couple of random bounces of the ball or badly timed injuries. In addition, the economic structure of the NFL allows teams to make sudden jumps or drops in overall ability more often than in other sports.

From 2003-2014, the mean DVOA forecast by the new projection system had a correlation coefficient of .539 with actual wins and a correlation coefficient of .642 with actual DVOA.

The next step in our forecast involves simulating the season one million times. We use the projected range of DVOA possibilities to produce 1,000 different simulated seasons with 32 sets of DVOA ratings. We then plug those season-long DVOA ratings into the same equation we use during the season to determine each team's likely remaining wins for our Playoff Odds Report. The simulation takes each season game-by-game, determining the home or road team's chance of winning each game based on the DVOA ratings of each team as well as home-field advantage. A random number between 0 and 100 determines whether the home or road team has won that game. We ran 1,000 simulations with each of the 1,000 sets of DVOA ratings, creating a million different simulations. The simulation was programmed by Mike Harris.

Last year, we began using a system we call a "dynamic simulation" to better approximate the true distribution of wins in the NFL. When simulating the season, each team had 2.0% DVOA added or subtracted after a win or loss, reflecting the fact that a win or loss tends to tell us whether a team is truly better or worse than whatever their mean projection had been before the season. Using this method, a team projected with 20.0% DVOA which goes 13-3 will have a 40.0% DVOA entering the playoffs, which is much more realistic. This change gave us more projected seasons at the margins, with fewer seasons at 8-8 and more seasons at 14-2 or 2-14. The dynamic simulation also meant a slight increase in projected wins for the best teams, and a slight decrease for the worst teams. However, the conservative nature of our projection system still means the distribution of mean projected wins has a much smaller spread than the actual win-loss records we will see by the end of December. We will continue to experiment with changes to the simulation in order to produce the most accurate possible forecast of the NFL season in future years.

In addition, this year's simulation is programmed to account for the fact that Jimmy Garoppolo will be quarterback of the New England Patriots in Weeks 1-4 before Tom Brady returns in Week 5, and to account for the likelihood of Kansas City edge rusher Justin Houston beginning the year on the PUP list. No other suspensions or injuries were specifically incorporated into this year's simulation.

Football Outsiders Game Charting Data

Each of the formulas listed above relies primarily on the play-by-play data published by the NFL. When we began to analyze the NFL, this was all that we had to work with. Just as a television broadcast has a color commentator who gives more detail to the facts related by the play-by-play announcer, so too do we need some color commentary to provide contextual information that breathes life into these plain lines of numbers and text. We added this color commentary with game charting.

Beginning in 2005, Football Outsiders began using a number of volunteers to chart every single play of every regular-season and postseason NFL game. To put it into perspective, there were over 54,000 lines of play-by-play information in each NFL season and our goal is to add several layers of detail to nearly all of them.

It gradually became clear that attempting to chart so much football with a crew of volunteers was simply not feasible, especially given our financial resources compared to those of our competitors. Over the past few years, we have partnered with larger companies to take on the responsibilities of game charting so that we can devote more time to analysis.

This began in 2012 with an agreement between Football

Outsiders and the ESPN Stats & Info group. ESPN charts games live on Sundays and our agreement allowed us to get access to their data immediately rather than waiting two to three weeks for our game charters to complete each game. In return, we provided suggestions to correct mistakes in the data—the more eyes we have on data like this, the more accurate it will be—and supplied ESPN with some of our older charting data, which allowed them to produce their new Total QBR metric for the 2006 and 2007 seasons.

In 2015, Football Outsiders reached an agreement with Sports Info Solutions, formerly Baseball Info Solutions, to begin a large charting project that would replace our use of volunteers to collect data not yet collected by ESPN Stats & Info. All charting data for the 2015 season is provided by one of these two companies. Our partnership with Baseball Info Solutions has resulted in the Off The Charts podcast, which explores data from game charting in a weekly discussion of the NFL season.[2] We are also working on an expansion of our Football Outsiders Premium section online. which will provide weekly updates of charting data such as pressures and cornerback coverage metrics for an annual subscription fee.

Game charting is significantly easier now that the NFL makes coaches' film available through NFL Game Rewind. This tape, which was not publicly available when we began charting with volunteers in 2005, includes sideline and end zone perspectives for each play, and shows all 22 players at all times, making it easier to see the cause-and-effect of certain actions taken on the field. Nonetheless, all game charting is still imperfect. You often cannot tell which players did their jobs particularly well or made mistakes without knowing the play call and each player's assignment, particularly when it comes to zone coverage or pass rushers who reach the quarterback without being blocked. Therefore, the goal of game charting from both ESPN Stats & Info and Sports Info Solutions is *not* to "grade" players, but rather to attempt to mark specific events: a pass pressure, a blown block, a dropped interception, and so on.

We emphasize that all data from game charting is unofficial. Other sources for football statistics may keep their own measurements of yards after catch or how teams perform against the blitz. Our data will not necessarily match theirs. Even ESPN Stats & Info and Sports Info Solutions had a number of disagreements, marking different events on the same play because it can be difficult to determine the definition of a "pressure" or a "dropped pass." However, any other group that is publicly tracking this data is also working off the same footage, and thus will run into the same issues of difficulty and subjectivity.

There are lots of things we would like to do with all-22 film that we simply haven't been able to do yet, such as charting coverage by cornerbacks when they aren't the target of a given pass, or even when pass pressure prevents the pass from getting into the air. Unfortunately, we are limited by what our partners are able to chart given time constraints.

In the description of data below, we have tried to designate which data from 2015 comes from ESPN Stats & Info group

---

2   Find links to all FO podcasts at http://www.footballoutsiders.com/podcasts

(ESPN S&I), which data comes from Sports Info Solutions (SIS), and where we have combined data from both companies with our own analysis.

Formation/Personnel

For each play, we have the number of running backs, wide receivers, and tight ends on the field courtesy of ESPN S&I. Players were marked based on their designation on the roster, not based on where they lined up on the field. Obviously, this could be difficult with some hybrid players or players changing positions in 2015, but we did our best to keep things as consistent as possible.

SIS also tracked this data and added the names of players who were lined up in unexpected positions. This included marking tight ends or wide receivers in the backfield, and running backs or tight ends who were lined up either wide or in the slot (often referred to as "flexing" a tight end). SIS also marked when a fullback or tight end was actually a sixth (or sometimes even seventh) offensive lineman, and they marked the backfield formation as empty back, single back, I formation, offset I, split backs, full house, or "other." These notations of backfield formation were recorded directly before the snap and do not account for positions before pre-snap motion.

SIS then marked defensive formations by listing the number of linemen, linebackers, and defensive backs. There will be mistakes—a box safety may occasionally be confused for a linebacker, for example—but for the most part the data for defensive backs will be accurate. Figuring out how to mark whether a player is a defensive end or a linebacker is a different story. The rise of hybrid defenses has led to a lot of confusion. Edge rushers in a 4-3 defense may play standing up because they used to play for a 3-4 defense and that's what they are used to. A player who is usually considered an outside linebacker for a 3-4 defense may put his hand on the ground on third down (thus looking like a 4-3 defensive end), but the tackle next to him is still two-gapping (which is generally a 3-4 principle). SIS marked personnel in a simplified fashion by designating any front seven player in a standing position as a linebacker and designating any front seven player in a crouching position as a defensive lineman.

Mark Barron of the Rams and Deone Buccanon of the Cardinals were marked as defensive backs in Weeks 1-4 and then as linebackers from Week 5 onward.

Rushers and Blockers

ESPN Stats & Info provided us with two data points regarding the pass rush: the number of pass rushers on a given play, and the number defensive backs blitzing on a given play. SIS also tracked this data for comparison purposes and then added a count of blockers. Counting blockers is an art as much as a science. Offenses base their blocking schemes on how many rushers they expect. A running back or tight end's assignment may depend on how many pass-rushers cross the line at the snap. Therefore, an offensive player was deemed to be a blocker if he engaged in an actual block, or there was some hesitation before running a route. A running back that immediately heads out into the flat is not a blocker, but one that waits to verify that the blocking scheme is working and then goes out to the flat would, in fact, be considered a blocker.

Pass Play Details

Both companies recorded the following data for all pass plays:

• Did the play begin with a play-action fake, including read-option fakes that developed into pass plays instead of being handed to a running back. Was the quarterback in or out of the pocket.
• Was the quarterback under pressure in making his pass.
• Was this a screen pass.

SIS game charting also marks the name of the defender who caused the pass pressure. Charters were allowed to list two names if necessary, and could also attribute a hurry to "overall pressure." No defender was given a hurry and a sack on the same play, but defenders were given hurries if they helped force a quarterback into a sack that was finished by another player. SIS also identified which defender(s) caused the pass pressure which forced a quarterback to scramble for yardage. If the quarterback wasn't under pressure but ran anyway, the play could be marked either as "coverage scramble" (if the quarterback ran because there were no open receivers) or "hole opens up" (if the quarterback ran because he knew he could gain significant yardage).

Football Outsiders (using our past game charting volunteers) reviewed a number of plays where there was disagreement between the two companies on pass pressure. Therefore, our count of pass pressures represents a combination of the data. Unfortunately, we did not have the time to review all plays with disagreement. All team pressure rate stats in this book are based on ESPN S&I data, adjusting for the plays where Football Outsiders felt that SIS charting was more accurate. All individual pressure counts for defenders are based on SIS data combined with Football Outsiders adjustments, even if ESPN S&I did not mark the play in question as a pass pressure.

Some places in this book, we divide pass yardage into two numbers: distance in the air and yards after catch. This information is tracked by the NFL, but it can be hard to find and the official scorers often make errors, so we corrected the original data based on input from both ESPN S&I and SIS. Distance in the air is based on the distance from the line of scrimmage to the place where the receiver either caught or was supposed to catch the pass. We do not count how far the quarterback was behind the line or horizontal yardage if the quarterback threw across the field. All touchdowns are counted to the goal line, so that distance in the air added to yards after catch always equals the official yardage total kept by the league.

Incomplete Passes

Quarterbacks are evaluated based on their ability to complete passes. However, not all incompletes should have the same weight. Throwing a ball away to avoid a sack is actually a valuable incomplete, and a receiver dropping an otherwise quality pass is hardly a reflection on the quarterback.

This year, our evaluation of incomplete passes began with ESPN Stats & Info, which marked passes as Overthrown, Underthrown, Thrown Away, Batted Down at the Line, Defensed, or Dropped. We then compared this data to similar data from SIS and made some changes. We also changed some plays to reflect a couple of additional categories we have kept in past years for Football Outsiders: Hit in Motion (indicating the quarterback was hit as his arm was coming forward to make a pass), Caught out of Bounds, and Hail Mary.

Our count of passes defensed will be different from the unofficial totals kept by the league for reasons explained below in the section on Defensive Secondary tables.

ESPN S&I and SIS also marked when a defender dropped an interception; Football Outsiders volunteers then analyzed plays where the two companies disagreed to come up with a final total. When a play is close, we tend to err on the side of not marking a dropped interception, as we don't want to blame a defender who, for example, jumps high for a ball and has it tip off his fingers. We also counted a few "defensed" interceptions, when a quarterback threw a pass that would have been picked off if not for the receiver playing defense on the ball. These passes counted as dropped interceptions for quarterbacks but not for the defensive players.

Defenders

The NFL play-by-play lists tackles and, occasionally, tipped balls, but it does not definitively list the defender on the play. SIS charters attempted to determine which defender was primarily responsible for covering either the receiver at the time of the throw or the location to which the pass was thrown, regardless of whether the pass was complete or not.

Every defense in the league plays zone coverage at times, some more than others, which leaves us with the question of how to handle plays without a clear man assigned to that receiver. Charters (SIS employees in 2015, and FO volunteers in past seasons) had three alternatives:

• We asked charters to mark passes that found the holes in zone coverage as Hole in Zone, rather than straining to assign that pass to an individual defender. We asked the charter to also note the player who appeared to be responsible for that zone, and these defenders are assigned half credit for those passes. Some holes were so large that no defender could be listed along with the Hole in Zone designation.

• Charters were free to list two defenders instead of one. This could be used for actual double coverage, or for zone coverage in which the receiver was right between two close defenders rather than sitting in a gaping hole. When two defenders are listed, ratings assign each with half credit.

• Screen passes and dumpoffs are marked as Uncovered unless a defender (normally a linebacker) is obviously shadowing that specific receiver on the other side of the line of scrimmage.

Since we began the charting project in 2005, nothing has changed our analysis more than this information on pass coverage. However, even now with the ability to view all-22 film,

it can be difficult to identify the responsible defender except when there is strict man-to-man coverage. There were particular changes in the frequency of zone coverage marked, due to the change from Football Outsiders volunteers to Sports Info Solutions employees. SIS and FO are working together so that this charting data becomes more and more accurate as we have more experience marking coverage. The change in the frequency of "Hole in Zone" is why we have not given a "Hole in Zone" percentage for each team on this year's Strategic Tendencies tables (explained further below).

Additional Details from ESPN Stats & Info

All draw plays were marked, whether by halfbacks or quarterbacks. Option runs and zone reads were also marked.

ESPN S&I tracked when the formation was pistol as opposed to shotgun; the official play-by-play simply marks these plays all as shotgun.

ESPN S&I also marks the number of defenders in the box for each snap, and tags each play as either "loaded" or "not loaded." A loaded box is when the defense has more players in the box than the offense has available blockers for running plays. Finally, ESPN S&I marks yards after contact for each play.

Additional Details from Sports Info Solutions

SIS charters marked each quarterback sack with one of the following terms: Blown Block, Coverage Sack, QB Fault, Failed Scramble, or Blitz/Overall Pressure. Blown Blocks were listed with the name of a specific offensive player who allowed the defender to come through. (Some blown block sacks are listed with two blockers, who each get a half-sack..) Coverage Sack denotes when the quarterback has plenty of time to throw but cannot find an open receiver. QB Fault represents "self sacks" listed without a defender, such as when the quarterback drops back, only to find the ball slip out of his hands with no pass-rusher touching him. Failed Scramble represents plays where a quarterback began to run without major pass pressure because he thought he could get a positive gain, only to be tackled before he reached the line of scrimmage.

SIS tracked "broken tackles" on all runs or pass plays. We define a "broken tackle" as one of two events: Either the ballcarrier escapes from the grasp of the defender, or the defender is in good position for a tackle but the ballcarrier jukes him out of his shoes. If the ballcarrier sped by a slow defender who dived and missed, that did not count as a broken tackle. If the defender couldn't bring the ballcarrier down because he is being blocked out of the play by another offensive player, this did not count as a broken tackle. It was possible to mark multiple broken tackles on the same play. Broken tackles are not marked for special teams.`

Please note that broken tackle numbers have gone up substantially over the past two years because of a change in methodology in 2014 and a looser definition of broken tackles used by Sports Info Solutions in 2015. Because of these changes, the league-wide total of broken tackles went up roughly 25 percent in 2014 and then another 25 percent in 2015. It is important to account for this when comparing a player's total in one year to his total in another year.

Sports Info Solutions also tracked a couple of new items which Football Outsiders had not tracked in the past. We'll be working in the future to add this data into our analysis, including designating every run by the type of blocking scheme and marking when the intended receiver on each pass began the play wide, tight, in the slot, or in the backfield.

Acknowledgements

Thank you to all the past game charting volunteers who helped us collect data from 2005 through 2014, and who helped us clean data from our partners in 2015.

Thanks as well to our two game charting partners that have helped free us up to do more analysis and less data collection, including ESPN Stats & Info (particularly John McTigue, Allison Loucks, and Henry Gargiulo) and Sports Info Solutions (particularly Greg Thomas, Scott Spratt, and Ben Jedlovic).

How to Read the Team Summary Box

Here is a rundown of all the tables and stats that appear in the 32 team chapters. Each team chapter begins with a box in the upper-right hand corner that gives a summary of our statistics for that team, as follows:

2015 Record gives each team's actual win-loss record. **Pythagorean Wins** gives the approximate number of wins expected last year based on this team's raw totals of points scored and allowed, along with their NFL rank. **Snap-Weighted Age** gives the average age of the team in 2015, weighted based on how many snaps each player was on the field and ranked from oldest (New York Jets, first at 27.6) to youngest (St. Louis/Los Angeles, 32nd at 25.5). **Average Opponent** gives a ranking of last year's schedule strength based on the average DVOA of all 16 opponents faced during the regular season. Teams are ranked from the hardest schedule of 2015 (Cleveland) to the easiest (Carolina).

Total DVOA gives the team's total DVOA rating, with rank. **Offense, Defense**, and **Special Teams** list the team's DVOA rating in each category, along with NFL rank. Remember that good offenses and special teams have positive DVOA numbers, while a negative DVOA means better defense, so the lowest defensive DVOA is ranked No. 1 (last year, Denver).

2016 Mean Projection gives the average number of wins for this team based on the 2016 Win Projection System described earlier in this chapter. Please note that we do not expect any teams to win the exact number of games in their mean projection. First of all, no team can win 0.8 of a game. Second, because these projections represent a whole range of possible values, the averages naturally tend to drift towards 8-8. Obviously, we're not expecting a season where no team goes 4-12 or 12-4. For a better way to look at the projections, we offer **Postseason Odds**, which give each team's chance of making the postseason based on our simulation, and **Super Bowl Appearance** odds, which give each team's chance of

representing its conference in Super Bowl XLIX. The average team will make the playoffs in 37.5 percent of simulations, and the Super Bowl in 6.3 percent of simulations.

Projected Average Opponent gives the team's strength of schedule for 2016; like the listing for last year's schedule strength in the first column of the box, this number is based not on last year's record but on the mean projected DVOA for each opponent. A positive schedule is harder, a negative schedule easier. Teams are ranked from the hardest projected schedule (San Francisco, first) to the easiest (Tennessee, 32nd). This strength of schedule projection does not take into account which games are home or away, or the timing of the bye week. The strength of schedule projections for Arizona, Buffalo, Houston, and Miami are based on facing the Patriots with Jimmy Garoppolo rather than Tom Brady.

The final column of the box gives the team's chances of finishing in four different basic categories of success:

- On the Clock (0-4 wins; NFL average 12%)
- Mediocrity (5-7 wins; NFL average 32%)
- Playoff Contender (8-10 wins; NFL average 36%)
- Super Bowl Contender (11+ wins; NFL average 20%)

The percentage given for each category is dependent not only on how good we project the team to be in 2016, but the level of variation possible in that projection, and the expected performance of the teams on the schedule.

You'll also find a table with the team's 2016 schedule placed within each chapter, along with a graph showing each team's 2015 week-to-week performance by single-game DVOA. The second, dotted line on the graph represents a five-week moving average of each team's performance, in order to show a longer-term view of when they were improving and declining. After the essays come statistical tables and comments related to that team and its specific units.

Weekly Performance

The first table gives a quick look at the team's week-to-week performance in 2015. (Table 1, next page) This includes the playoffs for those teams that made the postseason, with the four weeks of playoffs numbered 18 (wild card) through 21 (Super Bowl). All other tables in the team chapters represent regular-season performance only unless otherwise noted.

Looking at the first week for the Arizona Cardinals in 2015, the first five columns are fairly obvious: the Cardinals opened the season with a 31-19 win at home against New Orleans. **YDF** and **YDA** are net yards on offense and net yards against the defense. These numbers do not include penalty yardage or special teams yardage. **TO** represents the turnover margin. Unlike other parts of the book in which we consider all fumbles as equal, this only represents actual turnovers: fumbles lost and interceptions. So, for example, the Cardinals forced two more turnovers than Baltimore in Week 7, but then com-

Table 1. 2015 Cardinals Stats by Week

Wk	vs.	W-L	PF	PA	YDF	YDA	TO	Total	Off	Def	ST
1	NO	W	31	19	427	408	0	57%	30%	-22%	5%
2	at CHI	W	48	23	300	335	0	100%	56%	-27%	17%
3	SF	W	47	7	446	156	3	57%	-2%	-64%	-5%
4	STL	L	22	24	447	328	-3	-4%	11%	11%	-4%
5	at DET	W	42	17	345	435	6	85%	47%	-33%	4%
6	at PIT	L	13	25	469	310	-3	22%	19%	-11%	-8%
7	BAL	W	26	18	414	276	2	-4%	21%	0%	-26%
8	at CLE	W	34	20	491	254	-2	13%	2%	-7%	4%
9	BYE										
10	at SEA	W	39	32	451	343	-2	25%	12%	-2%	11%
11	CIN	W	34	31	383	377	-1	31%	27%	-7%	-4%
12	at SF	W	19	13	337	368	2	-37%	-22%	17%	2%
13	at STL	W	27	3	524	212	1	74%	54%	-31%	-11%
14	MIN	W	23	20	393	389	3	-3%	15%	15%	-3%
15	at PHI	W	40	17	493	424	4	51%	53%	-7%	-8%
16	GB	W	38	8	381	178	2	79%	12%	-67%	0%
17	SEA	L	6	36	232	354	-3	-84%	-48%	-3%	-38%
18	BYE										
19	GB	W	26	20	368	386	-1	-10%	-18%	-3%	5%
20	at CAR	L	15	49	287	476	-6	-42%	-17%	22%	-3%

Table 2: 2015 Cardinals Trends and Splits

	Offense	Rank	Defense	Rank
Total DVOA	15.8%	4	-15.6%	3
Unadjusted VOA	17.0%	2	-13.9%	5
Weighted Trend	13.0%	4	-10.4%	7
Variance	7.9%	21	6.2%	25
Average Opponent	0.4%	19	0.5%	15
Passing	42.4%	3	-9.4%	4
Rushing	-8.0%	16	-24.4%	2
First Down	12.6%	5	-6.6%	8
Second Down	10.5%	9	-17.5%	3
Third Down	31.6%	3	-29.9%	2
First Half	16.4%	6	-11.8%	9
Second Half	15.1%	4	-19.5%	3
Red Zone	-2.6%	19	10.6%	23
Late and Close	18.0%	1	-26.3%	2

mitted two more turnovers than Cleveland in Week 8.

Finally, you'll see DVOA ratings for this game: Total **DVOA** first, then offense (**Off**), defense (**Def**), and special teams (**ST**). Note that these are DVOA ratings, adjusted for opponent, so a loss to a good team will often be listed with a higher rating than a close win over a bad team. For example, the Cardinals have a positive DVOA for their Week 6 loss to Pittsburgh, but a negative DVOA for their Week 12 win in San Francisco.

Trends and Splits

Next to the week-to-week performance is a table giving DVOA for different portions of a team's performance, on both offense and defense. Each split is listed with the team's rank among the 32 NFL teams. These numbers represent regular season performance only.

Total DVOA gives total offensive, and defensive DVOA in all situations. **Unadjusted VOA** represents the breakdown of play-by-play considering situation but not opponent. A team whose offensive DVOA is higher than its offensive VOA played a harder-than-average schedule of opposing defenses; a team with a lower defensive DVOA than defensive VOA player a harder-than-average schedule of opposing offenses.

Weighted Trend lowers the importance of earlier games to give a better idea of how the team was playing at the end of the regular season. The final four weeks of the season are full strength; moving backwards through the season, each week is given less and less weight until the first three weeks of the season, which are not included at all. **Variance** is the same as noted above, with a higher percentage representing less consistency. This is true for both offense and defense: Oakland, for example, was very consistent on defense (2.7%, third) but

the league's most inconsistent offense (12.3%, 32nd). **Average Opponent** is that the same thing that appears in the box to open each chapter, except split in half: the average DVOA of all opposing defenses (for offense) or the average DVOA of all opposing offenses (for defense).

Passing and **Rushing** are fairly self-explanatory. Note that rushing DVOA includes all rushes, not just those by running backs, including quarterback scrambles that may have begun as pass plays.

The next three lines split out DVOA on **First Down, Second Down**, and **Third Down**. Third Down here includes fourth downs on which a team runs a regular offensive play instead of punting or attempting a field goal. **First Half** and **Second Half** represent the first two quarters and last two quarters (plus overtime), not the first eight and last eight games of the regular season. Next comes DVOA in the **Red Zone**, which is any offensive play starting from the defense's 20-yard line through the goal line. The final split is **Late and Close**, which includes any play in the second half or overtime when the teams are within eight points of each other in either direction. (Eight points, of course, is the biggest deficit that can be made up with a single score, a touchdown and two-point conversion.)

Five-Year Performance

This table gives each team's performance over the past five seasons. (Table X) It includes win-loss record, Pythagorean Wins, **Estimated Wins**, points scored and allowed, and turnover margin. Estimated wins are based on a formula that estimates how many games a team would have been expected to win based on 2015 performance in specific situations, normalized to eliminate luck (fumble recoveries, opponents' missed field goals, etc.) and assuming average schedule strength. The formula emphasizes consistency and overall DVOA as well

Table 3. Minnesota Vikings' Five-Year Performance

Year	W-L	Pyth W	Est W	PF	PA	TO	Total	Rk	Off	Rk	Def	Rk	ST	Rk	Off AGL	Rk	Def AGL	Rk	Off Age	Rk	Def Age	Rk	ST Age	Rk
2011	3-13	5.3	4.6	340	449	-3	-22.2%	29	-10.2%	24	8.0%	23	-4.1%	27	20.5	8	28.3	19	27.7	10	27.3	14	26.4	15
2012	10-6	8.8	8.8	379	348	-1	2.0%	14	0.3%	15	3.1%	21	4.7%	5	10.4	3	18.5	8	25.5	31	27.2	12	25.5	28
2013	5-10-1	6.1	6.5	391	480	-12	-11.4%	26	-4.7%	21	10.5%	27	3.8%	6	21.4	8	32.5	21	26.6	19	27.1	12	25.8	24
2014	7-9	7.5	7.2	325	343	-1	-8.7%	25	-7.4%	22	4.3%	23	3.0%	10	39.0	23	17.1	3	26.7	17	25.9	29	25.6	28
2015	11-5	9.8	9.5	365	302	+5	5.7%	11	0.0%	16	-1.8%	14	3.9%	4	36.5	17	22.5	7	26.4	19	27.5	4	25.7	22

as DVOA in a few specifically important situations. The next columns of this table give total DVOA along with DVOA for offense, defense, and special teams, and the rank for each among that season's 32 NFL teams.

The next four columns give the adjusted games lost (AGL) for starters on both offense and defense, along with rank. (Our total for starters here includes players who take over as starters due to another injury, such as Thomas Rawls or Ryan Fitzpatrick last year, as well as important situational players who may not necessarily start, such as pass-rush specialists and slot receivers.) Adjusted games lost was introduced in *Pro Football Prospectus 2008*; it gives a weighted estimate of the probability that players would miss games based on how they are listed on the injury report. Unlike a count of "starter games missed," this accounts for the fact that a player listed as questionable who does in fact play is not playing at 100 percent capability. Teams are ranked from the fewest injuries (2015: Cincinnati on offense, New York Jets on defense) to the most (2015: Baltimore on offense, Washington on defense).

Individual Offensive Statistics

Each team chapter contains a table giving passing and receiving numbers for any player who either threw five passes or was thrown five passes, along with rushing numbers for any players who carried the ball at least five times. These numbers also appear in the player comments at the end of the book (except for wide receiver rushing attempts). By putting them together in the team chapters we hope we make it easier to compare the performances of different players on the same team.

Players who are no longer on the team are marked with an asterisk. New players who were on a different team in 2015 are in italics. Changes should be accurate as of July 15. Rookies are not included.

All players are listed with DYAR and DVOA. Passing statistics then list total pass plays (**Plays**), net yardage (**NtYds**), and net yards per pass (**Avg**). These numbers include not just passes (and the positive yardage from them) but aborted snaps and sacks (and the negative yardage from them). Then comes

average yards after catch (**YAC**), as determined by the game charting project. This average is based on charted receptions, not total pass attempts. The final three numbers are completion percentage (**C%**), passing touchdowns (**TD**), and interceptions (**Int**).

It is important to note that the tables in the team chapters contain Football Outsiders stats, while the tables in the player comments later in the book contain official NFL totals, at least when it comes to standard numbers like receptions and yardage. This results in a number of differences between the two:

- Team chapter tables list aborted snaps as passes, not runs, although aborted handoffs are still listed as runs. Net yardage for quarterbacks in the team chapter tables includes the lost yardage from aborted snaps, sacks, and intentional grounding penalties. For official NFL stats, all aborted snaps are listed as runs.
- Football Outsiders stats omit kneeldowns from run totals and clock-stopping spikes from pass totals.
- In the Football Outsiders stats, we have changed a number of lateral passes to count as passes rather than runs, under the theory that a pass play is still a pass play, even if the receiver is standing five inches behind the quarterback. This results in some small differences in totals.
- "Skill players" who played for multiple teams in 2015 are only listed in team chapters with stats from that specific team; combined stats are listed in the player comments section.

Table 4. WAS 2015 Passing

Player	DYAR	DVOA	Plays	NtYds	Avg	YAC	C%	TD	Int
K.Cousins	1023	16.9%	570	3979	7.0	5.0	69.8%	29	11
C.McCoy	22	20.9%	12	114	9.5	11.6	63.6%	1	0

Rushing statistics start with DYAR and DVOA, then list rushing plays and net yards along with average yards per carry and rushing touchdowns. The final two columns are fumbles (**Fum**)—both those lost to the defense and those recovered by the offense—and Success Rate (**Suc**), explained earlier in this chapter. Fumbles listed in the rushing table include all quarterback fumbles on sacks and aborted snaps, as well as running back fumbles on receptions, but not wide receiver fumbles.

Table 5. TEN 2015 Rushing

Player	DYAR	DVOA	Plays	Yds	Avg	TD	Fum	Suc
A.Andrews	-6	-9.5%	143	520	3.6	3	1	42%
D.McCluster	-12	-14.9%	55	247	4.5	1	1	31%
D.Cobb	-16	-16.4%	52	146	2.8	1	0	33%
B.Sankey	12	-1.5%	47	193	4.1	1	1	45%
M.Mariota	20	-0.6%	32	253	7.9	2	1	-
T.West*	-31	-51.8%	16	51	3.2	0	2	50%
J.Fowler	11	13.0%	7	13	1.9	1	0	71%
K.Wright	2	-31.1%	5	17	3.4	0	0	-
M.Cassel	-10	-29.3%	14	85	6.1	0	2	-
D.Murray	-29	-12.1%	193	704	3.6	6	2	45%

Receiving statistics start with DYAR and DVOA and then list the number of passes thrown to this receiver (**Plays**), the number of passes caught (**Catch**) and the total receiving yards (**Yds**). Yards per catch (**Y/C**) includes total yardage per reception, based on standard play-by-play, while yards after catch (**YAC**) is based on information from our game charting project. Finally we list total receiving touchdowns, and catch percentage (**C%**), which is the percentage of passes intended for this receiver which were caught. Wide receivers, tight ends, and running backs are separated on the table by horizontal lines.

Table 6. CIN 2015 Receiving

Player	DYAR	DVOA	Plays	Ctch	Yds	Y/C	YAC	TD	C%
A.J.Green	414	26.5%	132	86	1297	15.1	3.9	10	65%
M.Jones*	171	7.6%	104	66	818	12.4	4.6	4	63%
M.Sanu*	16	-8.3%	49	33	394	11.9	6.2	0	67%
B.LaFell	-43	-20.1%	74	37	515	13.9	6.1	0	50%
T.Eifert	247	42.0%	74	52	615	11.8	4.5	13	70%
T.Kroft	27	24.9%	15	11	129	11.7	6.2	1	73%
R.Hewitt	15	11.8%	12	8	99	12.4	7.4	0	67%
G.Bernard	97	14.6%	66	49	472	9.6	9.4	0	74%
J.Hill	0	-13.4%	19	15	79	5.3	5.8	1	79%
R.Burkhead	13	0.9%	15	10	94	9.4	2.5	1	67%

Performance Based on Personnel

These tables provide a look at performance in 2015 based on personnel packages, as defined above in the section on marking formation/personnel as part of the Football Outsiders game charting project. There are four different tables, representing:

- Offense based on personnel
- Offense based on opponent's defensive personnel
- Defense based on personnel
- Defense based on opponent's offensive personnel

Most of these tables feature the top five personnel groupings for each team. Occasionally, we will list the personnel group which ranks sixth if the sixth group is either particularly interesting or nearly as common as the fifth group. Each personnel group is listed with its frequency among 2015 plays, yards per play, and DVOA. Offensive personnel are also listed with how often the team in question called a running play instead of a pass play from given personnel. (Quarterback scrambles are included as pass plays, not runs.)

Offensive personnel are given in the standard two-digit format where the first digit is running backs and the second digit is tight ends. You can figure out wide receivers by subtracting that total from five, with a couple of exceptions. Plays with six or seven offensive linemen will have a three-digit listing such as "611" or "622." Any play with a direct snap to a non-quarterback, or with a specific running quarterback taking the snap instead of the regular quarterback, was counted as "Wildcat." No team ends up with Wildcat listed among its top five offensive personnel groups.

When defensive players come in to play offense, defensive backs are counted as wide receivers and linebackers as tight ends. Defensive linemen who come in as offensive linemen are counted as offensive linemen; if they come in as blocking fullbacks, we count them as running backs.).

This year, we are not giving personnel data based on the number of defensive linemen and linebackers. This is because of the difficulty in separating between the two, especially with our simplified designation of players as defensive linemen or

Table 7. DEN 2015 Performance Based on Most Common Personnel Groups

DEN Offense					DEN Offense vs. Opponents					DEN Defense				DEN Defense vs. Opponents			
Pers	Freq	Yds	DVOA	Run%	Pers	Freq	Yds	DVOA	Run%	Pers	Freq	Yds	DVOA	Pers	Freq	Yds	DVOA
11	57%	5.9	-6.4%	30%	Base	32%	4.7	-21.1%	50%	Base	57%	4.4	-26.2%	11	41%	5.1	-26.9%
12	32%	5.4	-3.7%	47%	Nickel	54%	5.9	0.0%	35%	Nickel	11%	3.8	-70.9%	12	28%	4.9	-26.7%
10	2%	3.8	-17.1%	48%	Dime+	13%	6.1	12.0%	7%	Dime+	29%	5.7	-7.5%	21	12%	3.3	-40.3%
02	2%	4.5	28.8%	11%	Goal Line	1%	-0.4	-28.7%	63%	Big	3%	1.8	-17.3%	13	8%	4.0	-18.7%
13	2%	2.3	-27.2%	72%	Big	0%	1.2	16.4%	100%					22	5%	2.7	-38.6%

linebackers based simply on who has a hand on the ground. There are just too many hybrid defensive schemes in today's game: 4-3 schemes where one or both ends rush the passer from a standing position, or hybrid schemes that one-gap on one side of the nose tackle and two-gap on the other. Therefore, defensive personnel is listed in only five categories:

- Base (four defensive backs)
- Nickel (five defensive backs)
- Dime+ (six or more defensive backs)
- Big (either 4-4-3 or 3-5-3)
- Goal Line (all other personnel groups with fewer than four defensive backs)

11, or three-wide personnel, was by far the most common grouping in the NFL last year, used on 55 percent of plays, followed the standard two-tight end set 12 personnel (21 percent of plays) and the more traditional (and slowly dying) 21 personnel (8 percent). Defenses lined up in Base on 33 percent of plays, Nickel on 51 percent of plays, Dime+ on 14 percent of plays, and either Big or Goal Line on 1.4 percent of plays.

Strategic Tendencies

The Strategic Tendencies table presents a mix of information garnered from both the standard play by play and the Football Outsiders game charting project. It gives you an idea of what kind of plays teams run in what situations and with what personnel. Each category is given a league-wide **Rank** from most often (1) to least often (32) except as noted below. The sample table shown here lists the NFL average in each category for 2015.

The first column of strategic tendencies lists how often teams ran in different situations. These ratios are based on the type of play, not the actual result, so quarterback scrambles count as "passes" while quarterback sneaks, draws and option plays count as "runs."

Runs, first half and **Runs, first down** should be self-evident. **Runs, second-and-long** is the percentage of runs on second down with seven or more yards to go, giving you an idea of how teams follow up a failed first down. **Runs, power situations** is the percentage of runs on third or fourth down with 1-2 yards to go, or at the goal line with 1-2 yards to go. **Runs, behind 2H** tells you how often teams ran when they were behind in the second half, generally a passing situation.

Pass, ahead 2H tells you how often teams passed when they had the lead in the second half, generally a running situation.

In each case, you can determine the percentage of plays that were passes by subtracting the run percentage from 100 (the reverse being true for "Pass, ahead 2H," of course).

The second column gives information about offensive formations and personnel, as tracked by ESPN Stats & Info.

The first two entries detail formation, i.e. where players were lined up on the field. **Form: Single Back** lists how often the team lined up with only one player in the backfield, and **Form: Empty Back** lists how often the team lined up with no players in the backfield.

The next three entries are based on personnel, no matter where players were lined up in the formation. **Pers: 3+ WR** marks how often the team plays with three or more wide receivers. **Pers: 2+ TE/6+ OL** marks how often the team plays with either more than one tight end or more than five offensive linemen. **Pers: 6+ OL** marks just plays with more than five offensive linemen. Finally, we give the percentage of plays where a team used **Shotgun or Pistol** in 2015. This does not count "Wildcat" or direct snap plays involving a non-quarterback.

The third column shows how the defensive **Pass Rush** worked in 2015.

Rush 3/Rush 4/Rush 5/Rush 6+: The percentage of pass plays (including quarterback scrambles) on which ESPN Stats & Info recorded this team rushing the passer with three or fewer defenders, four defenders, five defenders, and six or more defenders. These percentages do not include goal-line plays on the one- or two-yard line.

Sacks by LB/Sacks by DB: The percentage of this team's sacks that came from linebackers and defensive backs. To figure out the percentage of sacks from defensive linemen, simply subtract the sum of these numbers from 100 percent.

The fourth column has more data on the use of defensive backs.

4 DB/5 DB/6+ DB: The percentage of plays where this defense lined up with four, five, and six or more defensive backs, according to Sports Info Solutions.

CB by Sides: One of the most important lessons from game charting is that each team's best cornerback does not necessarily match up against the opponent's best receiver. Most cornerbacks play a particular side of the field and in fact cover a wider range of receivers than we assumed before we saw the charting data. This metric looks at which teams prefer to leave their starting cornerbacks on specific sides of the field.

To figure CB by Sides, we took the top two cornerbacks from each team and looked at the percentage of passes where

Table 8. NFL Average Strategic Tendencies

Run/Pass		Rk	Formation		Rk	Pass Rush		Rk	Secondary		Rk	Strategy		Rk
Runs, first half	38%	--	Form: Single Back	75%	--	Rush 3	7.0%	--	4 DB	33%	--	Play action	19%	--
Runs, first down	48%	--	Form: Empty Back	8%	--	Rush 4	62.8%	--	5 DB	51%	--	Avg Box (Off)	6.24	--
Runs, second-long	30%	--	Pers: 3+ WR	60%	--	Rush 5	23.0%	--	6+ DB	14%	--	Avg Box (Def)	6.24	--
Runs, power sit.	55%	--	Pers: 2+ TE/6+ OL	33%	--	Rush 6+	7.2%	--	CB by Sides	75%	--	Offensive Pace	30.30	--
Runs, behind 2H	25%	--	Pers: 6+ OL	4%	--	Sacks by LB	37.6%	--	S/CB Cover Ratio	23%	--	Defensive Pace	30.25	--
Pass, ahead 2H	48%	--	Shotgun/Pistol	62%	--	Sacks by DB	8.6%	--	DB Blitz	10%	--	Go for it on 4th	1.00	--

that cornerback was in coverage on the left or right side of the field, ignoring passes marked as "middle." For each of the two cornerbacks, we took the higher number, right or left, and then we averaged the two cornerbacks to get the final CB by Sides rating. Teams which preferred to leave their cornerbacks in the same place last season, such as Cincinnati and Philadelphia, will have high ratings. Teams that did more to move their best cornerback around to cover the opponent's top targets, such as Arizona, Carolina, and New England, will have low ratings.

S/CB Cover Ratio: A new metric for this year's book, this is our attempt to track which teams like to use their safeties as hybrid safety/corners and put them in man coverage on wide receivers. This ratio takes all pass targets with a defensive back in coverage, and then gives what percentage of those targets belonged to a player who is rostered as a safety, ranging from Arizona, which used safety Tyrann Mathieu as a nickel-back (41 percent) to Oakland, which often used cornerback T.J. Carrie as a safety (13 percent).

DB Blitz: We have data on how often the defense used at least one defensive back in the pass rush courtesy of ESPN Stats & Info.

Finally, in the final column, we have some elements of game strategy.

Play action: The percentage of pass plays (including quarterback scrambles) which began with a play-action fake to the running back. This percentage does not include fake end-arounds unless there was also a fake handoff. It does include flea flickers.

Average Box: Another item added to our charting courtesy of ESPN Stats & Info Group is the number of defenders in the box before the snap. We list the average box faced by each team's offense and the average box used by this team's defense.

Offensive Pace: Situation-neutral pace represents the seconds of game clock per offensive play, with the following restrictions: no drives are included if they start in the fourth quarter or final five minutes of the first half, and drives are only included if the score is within six points or less. Teams are ranked from quickest pace (Philadelphia, the quickest situation-neutral pace we've ever measured at 22.2 seconds) to slowest pace (St. Louis, 33.1 seconds)

Defensive Pace: Situation-neutral pace based on seconds of game clock per defensive play. This is a representation of how a defense was approached by its opponents, not the strategy of the defense itself. Teams are ranked from quickest pace (Houston, 28.0 seconds) to slowest pace (Seattle, 31.8 seconds).

Go for it on fourth: This is the aggressiveness index (AI) introduced by Jim Armstrong in *Pro Football Prospectus 2006*, which measures how often a team goes for a first down in various fourth down situations compared to the league average. A coach over 1.00 is more aggressive, and one below 1.00 is less aggressive. Coaches are ranked from most aggressive to least aggressive.

Following each strategic tendencies table, you'll find a series of comments highlighting interesting data from that team's charting numbers. This includes DVOA ratings split for things like different formations, draw plays, or play-action passing. Please note that all DVOA ratings given in these comments are standard DVOA with no adjustments for the specific situation being analyzed. The average DVOA for a specific situation will not necessarily be 0%, and it won't necessarily be the same for offense and defense. For example, the average offensive DVOA on play-action passes in 2015 was 25.3%, while the average defensive DVOA was 20.6%. The average offensive DVOA when the quarterback was hurried was -66.9%; even if we remove sacks, scrambles, and intentional grounding and only look at actual passes, the average offensive DVOA was -10.1%. On average last year, there was pressure marked on 25.6 percent of pass plays.

How to Read the Offensive Line Tables

SIS charters mark blown blocks not just on sacks but also on hurries, hits, and runs stuffed at the line. (There are fewer blown blocks marked in 2015 than in previous seasons, because of the transition to new charters from SIS.) However, while we have blown blocks to mark bad plays, we still don't have a metric that consistently marks good plays, so blown blocks should not be taken as the end all and be all of judg-

Table 9. 2015 Houston Texans Offensive Line

Player	Pos	Age	GS	Snaps	Pen	Sk	Pass	Run	Player	Pos	Age	GS	Snaps	Pen	Sk	Pass	Run
Ben Jones*	C	27	16/16	1186	6	2.0	5.0	1.0	Chris Clark	RT	31	11/4	431	2	0.0	5.0	0.0
Derek Newton	RT	29	16/16	1166	5	7.0	11.0	4.0	Oday Aboushi	LG	25	7/5	398	3	0.5	1.5	3.0
Brandon Brooks*	RG	27	14/14	983	6	1.0	5.0	5.0	Kendall Lamm	OT	24	15/4	257	2	0.0	1.0	1.0
Duane Brown	LT	31	14/14	908	7	1.0	6.0	2.0	Jeff Allen	RT	26	12/8	429	2	0.0	2.0	1.0
Xavier Su'a-Filo	LG	25	11/9	628	1	1.0	4.0	2.0	Tony Bergstrom	OT	30	16/3	250	1	0.0	0.0	0.0

Year	Yards	ALY	Rank	Power	Rank	Stuff	Rank	2nd Lev	Rank	Open Field	Rank	Sacks	ASR	Rank	Press	Rank	F-Start	Cont.
2013	4.20	4.10	6	56%	26	20%	17	1.31	3	0.53	26	42	6.6%	11	31.8%	31	19	38
2014	4.07	3.72	23	67%	13	21%	25	1.07	22	0.80	12	26	4.9%	8	24.8%	19	15	39
2015	3.79	3.72	18	65%	16	19%	9	1.02	25	0.47	29	36	6.3%	17	21.3%	8	18	24

| 2015 ALY by direction: | Left End 3.85 (12) | Left Tackle 4.29 (7) | Mid/Guard 3.77 (18) | Right Tackle 3.77 (17) | Right End 2.63 (27) |

ing individual linemen. It's simply one measurement that goes into the conversation.

All offensive linemen who had at least 160 snaps in 2015 (not including special teams) are listed in the offensive line tables along with the position they played most often and their **Age** as of the 2016 season, listed simply as the difference between birth year and 2016. Players born in January and December of the same year will have the same listed age.

Then we list games, games started, snaps, and offensive penalties (**Pen**) for each lineman. Finally, there are three numbers for blown blocks in 2015.

- Blown blocks leading directly to sacks
- All blown blocks on pass plays, not only including those that lead to sacks but also those that lead to hurries, hits, or offensive holding penalties
- All blown blocks on run plays; generally, this means plays where the running back is tackled for a loss or no gain, but it also includes a handful of plays where the running back would have been tackled for a loss if not for a broken tackle, as well as offensive holding penalties on running plays

Players are given half a blown block when two offensive players are listed with blown blocks on the same play.

As with all player tables in the team chapters, players who are no longer on the team have an asterisk and those new to the team in 2016 are in italics.

The second offensive line table lists the last three years of our various line stats.

The first column gives standard yards per carry by each team's running backs (**Yds**). The next two columns give adjusted line yards (**ALY**) followed by rank among the 32 teams.

Power gives the percentage of runs in "power situations" that achieved a first down or touchdown. Those situations include any third or fourth down with one or two yards to go, and any runs in goal-to-go situations from the two-yard line or closer. Unlike the other rushing numbers on the Offensive Line table, Power includes quarterbacks.

Stuff gives the percentage of runs that are stuffed for zero or negative gain. Since being stuffed is bad, teams are ranked from stuffed least often (1) to most often (32).

Second-Level (**2nd Lev**) Yards and **Open-Field** Yards represent yardage where the running back has the most power over the amount of the gain. Second-level yards represent the number of yards per carry that come five to ten yards past the line of scrimmage. Open-field yards represent the number of yards per carry that come 11 or more yards past the line of scrimmage. A team with a low ranking in adjusted line yards but a high ranking in open-field yards is heavily dependent on its running back breaking long runs to make the running game work, and therefore tends to have a less consistent running attack. Second-level yards fall somewhere in between.

The next five columns give information about pass protection. That starts with total sacks, followed by adjusted sack rate (**ASR**) and its rank among the 32 teams. Some teams allow a lot of sacks because they throw a lot of passes; adjusted sack rate accounts for this by dividing sacks and intentional grounding by total pass plays. It is also adjusted for situation (sacks are much more common on third down, particularly third-and-long) and opponent, all of which makes it a better measurement than raw sacks totals. Remember that quarterbacks share responsibility for sacks, and two different quarterbacks behind the same line can have very different adjusted sack rates. This year, we've also listed pressure rate: this is the percentage of pass plays where we have marked pass pressure, based on a combination of ESPN Stats & Info and Sports Info Solutions charting. Sacks or scrambles due to coverage are not counted as passes with pressure.

F-Start gives the number of false starts, which is the offensive penalty which best correlates to both wins and wins the following season. This total includes false starts by players other than offensive linemen, but it does not include false starts on special teams. Oakland led the league with 28, Jacksonville was last with 8, and the NFL average was 16.3. Finally, Continuity score (**Cont.**) tells you how much continuity each offensive line had from game-to-game in that season. It was introduced in the Cleveland chapter of *Pro Football Prospectus 2007*. Continuity score starts with 48 and then subtracts:

- The number of players over five who started at least one game on the offensive line;
- The number of times the team started at least one different lineman compared to the game before; and
- The difference between 16 and that team's longest streak where the same line started consecutive games.

The perfect continuity score is 48, which Minnesota received by starting the same five linemen in all 16 games. Last year's lowest score, and lowest score since we began tracking this stat, was New England at 15.

Finally, underneath the table in italics we give 2015 Adjusted Line Yards in each of the five directions with rank among the 32 teams. As noted earlier, these averages were down from past years. The league average was 3.63 on left end runs (**LE**), 3.81 on left tackle runs (**LT**), 3.87 on runs up the middle (**MID**), 3.71 on right tackle runs (**RT**), and 3.50 on right end runs (**RE**).

How to Read the Defensive Front Seven Tables

Defensive players make plays. Plays aren't just tackles—interceptions and pass deflections change the course of the game, and so does the act of forcing a fumble or beating the offensive players to a fumbled ball. While some plays stop a team on third down and force a punt, others merely stop a receiver after he's caught a 30-yard pass. We still cannot measure each player's opportunities to make a tackle. We can measure opportunities in pass coverage, however, thanks to the Football Outsiders game charting project.

Defensive players are listed in these tables if they made at least 20 plays during the 2015 season, or if they played at least eight games and played 25 percent of defensive snaps in those games. We made a couple of exceptions to list a handful of players who just missed these minimums, including Johnson Bademosi, Ryan Davis, Barkevious Mingo, Rahim Moore, Cameron Wake, and Kyle Williams. Defensive players who were with two teams last year are only listed with the final team they played with.

Defensive Linemen/Edge Rushers

As we've noted earlier in this toolbox: as hybrid defenses become more popular, it becomes more and more difficult to tell the difference between a defensive end and an outside linebacker. What we do know is that there are certain players whose job is to rush the passer, even if they occasionally drop into coverage. We also know that the defensive ends in a two-gapping 3-4 system have a lot more in common with run-stuffing 4-3 tackles than with smaller 4-3 defensive ends.

Therefore, we have separated front seven players into three tables rather than two. All defensive tackles and defensive ends from 3-4 teams are listed as **Defensive Linemen**, and all ranked together. Defensive ends from 4-3 teams and outside linebackers from 3-4 teams are listed as **Edge Rushers**, and all ranked together. All 4-3 linebackers are ranked along with 3-4 inside linebackers, and listed simply as **Linebackers**. For the most part this categorization puts players with similar roles together.

The tables for defensive linemen and edge rushers are the same, although the players are ranked in two separate categories. Players are listed with the following numbers:

Age in 2016, determined by 2016 minus birth year, plus position (**Pos**) and the number of defensive **Snaps** played in 2015.

Plays (**Plays**): The total defensive plays including tackles, pass deflections, interceptions, fumbles forced, and fumble recoveries. This number comes from the official NFL gamebooks and therefore does not include plays on which the player is listed by the Football Outsiders game charting project as in coverage, but does not appear in the standard play-by-play. Special teams tackles are also not included.

Percentage of team plays (**TmPct**): The percentage of total team plays involving this defender. The sum of the percentages of team plays for all defenders on a given team will exceed 100 percent, primarily due to shared tackles. This number is adjusted based on games played, so an injured player may be fifth on his team in plays but third in **TmPct**.

Stops (**Stop**): The total number of plays which prevent a "success" by the offense (45 percent of needed yards on first down, 60 percent on second down, 100 percent on third or fourth down).

Defeats (**Dfts**): The total number of plays which stop the offense from gaining first down yardage on third or fourth down, stop the offense behind the line of scrimmage, or result in a fumble (regardless of which team recovers) or interception.

Broken tackles (**BTkl**): The number of broken tackles recorded by SIS game charters.

The next five columns represent runs only, starting with the number of plays each player made on **Runs**. Stop rate (**St%**) gives the percentage of these run plays which were stops. Average yards (**AvYd**) gives the average number of yards gained by the runner when this player is credited with making the play.

Finally, we have pass rush numbers, starting with standard NFL **Sack** totals.

Hit: To qualify as a quarterback hit, the defender must knock the quarterback to the ground in the act of throwing or after the pass is thrown. We have listed hits on all plays, including those cancelled by penalties. (After all, many of the hardest hits come on plays cancelled because the hit itself draws a roughing the passer penalty.)

Hurries (**Hur**): The number of quarterback hurries recorded by Sports Info Solutions game charters. This includes both hurries on standard plays and hurries that force an offensive holding penalty that cancels the play and costs the offense yardage.

Disruptions (**Dsrpt**): This stat combines two different but similar types of plays. First, plays where a pass-rusher forced an incomplete pass or interception by hitting the quarterback as he was throwing the ball. These plays are generally not counted as passes defended, so we wanted a way to count

Table 10. New England Patriots 2015 Defensive Linemen

Defensive Line	Age	Pos	G	Snaps	Plays	TmPct	Rk	Stop	Dfts	BTkl	Runs	St%	Rk	RuYd	Rk	Sack	Hit	Hur	Dsrpt
						Overall							vs. Run				Pass Rush		
Malcom Brown	22	DT	16	509	48	5.8%	34	38	7	1	44	80%	32	2.3	47	3.0	2	5.0	0
Alan Branch	32	DT	16	434	38	4.6%	--	27	5	0	32	72%	--	2.3	--	1.0	2	2.0	2
Akiem Hicks*	27	DT	16	399	22	2.7%	--	19	7	2	19	84%	--	2.1	--	3.0	4	6.5	0
Dominique Easley*	24	DT	11	275	14	2.5%	--	12	7	0	9	78%	--	1.9	--	2.0	7	12.5	0
Sealver Siliga*	26	DT	13	254	28	4.2%	--	21	2	1	27	74%	--	2.5	--	0.0	0	1.0	0
Terrance Knighton	30	DT	15	369	29	3.9%	--	27	8	4	25	92%	--	1.0	--	1.5	2	2.0	0

Edge Rushers	Age	Pos	G	Snaps	Plays	TmPct	Rk	Stop	Dfts	BTkl	Runs	St%	Rk	RuYd	Rk	Sack	Hit	Hur	Dsrpt
						Overall							vs. Run				Pass Rush		
Rob Ninkovich	32	DE	16	891	59	7.2%	7	42	15	6	31	71%	60	2.8	69	6.5	12	24.5	5
Chandler Jones*	26	DE	15	863	45	5.8%	28	41	19	6	27	85%	11	1.6	22	12.5	7	17.5	0
Jabaal Sheard	27	DE	13	558	38	5.7%	32	34	17	6	26	88%	7	1.0	6	8.0	5	16.5	1
Chris Long	31	DE	12	485	19	2.8%	86	14	4	2	13	77%	34	3.2	82	3.0	1	9.0	0

them. Second, plays where the pass-rusher batted the ball down at the line of scrimmage or tipped it in the air. These plays are usually incomplete, but occasionally they lead to interceptions, and even more rarely they fall into the hands of offensive receivers. As with the "hit in motion" disruptions, some plays counted as tips by Football Outsiders were not counted as passes defensed by the NFL.

Defensive linemen and edge rushers are both ranked by percentage of team plays, run stop rate, and average yards per run tackle. The lowest number of average yards earns the top rank (negative numbers indicate the average play ending behind the line of scrimmage). Defensive linemen and edge rushers are ranked if they played at least 40 percent of defensive snaps in the games they were active. There are 84 defensive linemen ranked, and 97 edge rushers.

Linebackers

Most of the stats for linebackers are the same as those for defensive linemen, except that the sections for pass rush and run tackles are reversed.[3] Linebackers are ranked in percentage of team plays, and also in stop rate and average yards for running plays specifically. Linebackers are ranked in these stats if they played at least 40 percent of defensive snaps in the games they were active, with 89 linebackers ranked.

The final six columns in the linebacker stats come from Sports Info Solutions game charting.

Targets (**Tgts**): The number of pass players on which game charters listed this player in coverage.

Success rate (**Suc%**): The percentage plays of targeting this player on which the offense did not have a successful play. This means not only incomplete passes and interceptions, but also short completions which do not meet our baselines for success (45 percent of needed yards on first down, 60 percent on second down, 100 percent on third or fourth down). Success rate is adjusted for the quality of the receiver covered.

Adjusted yards per pass (**AdjYd**): The average number of yards gained on plays on which this defender was the listed target, adjusted for the quality of the receiver covered.

Passes defensed (**PD**): Football Outsiders' count of passes defensed. Unlike the official NFL count of passes defensed, this does not include passes batted down or tipped at the line.

These stats, including other differences between the NFL's count of passes defensed and our own, are explained in more detail in the section on secondary tables. Plays listed with two

---

3   This is a vestigial remnant of how we built these tables in previous books and we keep forgetting to fix it.

defenders or as "Hole in Zone" with this defender as the closest player count only for half credit in computing both success rate and average yards per pass. Seventy-three linebackers are ranked in the charting stats, based on hitting one of two minimums: 14 charted passes with fewer than eight games started, or 11 charted passes with eight or more games started. As a result of the different thresholds, some linebackers are ranked in standard stats but not charting stats.

Further Details

Just as in the offensive tables, players who are no longer on the team are marked with asterisks, and players who were on other teams last year are in italics. Other than the game charting statistics for linebackers, defensive front seven player statistics are not adjusted for opponent.

Numbers for defensive linemen and linebackers unfortunately do not reflect all of the opportunities a player had to make a play, but they do show us which players were most active on the field. A large number of plays could mean a strong defensive performance, or it could mean that the linebacker in question plays behind a poor part of the line. In general, defensive numbers should be taken as information that tells us what happened on the field in 2015, but not as a strict, unassailable judgment of which players are better than others—particularly when the difference between two players is small (for example, players ranked 20th and 30th) instead of large (players ranked 20th and 70th).

After the individual statistics for linemen and linebackers, the Defensive Front Seven section contains a table that looks exactly like the table in the Offensive Line section. The difference is that the numbers here are for all opposing running backs against this team's defensive front. As we're on the opposite side of the ball, teams are now ranked in the opposite order, so the No. 1 defensive front seven is the one that allows the fewest adjusted line yards, the lowest percentage in Power situations, and has the highest adjusted sack rate. Directions for adjusted line yards are given from the offense's perspective, so runs left end and left tackle are aimed at the right defensive end and (assuming the tight end is on the other side) weakside linebacker.

How to Read the Secondary Tables

The first few columns in the secondary tables are based on standard play-by-play, not game charting, with the exception

Table 11. Carolina Panthers Linebackers, 2015

Linebackers	Age	Pos	G	Snaps	Plays	TmPct	Rk	Stop	Dfts	BTkl	Runs	St%	Rk	RuYd	Rk	Sack	Hit	Hur	Tgts	Suc%	Rk	AdjYd	Rk	PD	Int
						Overall						vs. Run				Pass Rush				vs. Pass				
Thomas Davis	33	OLB	16	1003	111	13.4%	32	68	20	10	53	70%	19	3.9	64	5.5	6	13.5	38	62%	20	4.0	10	6	4
Luke Kuechly	25	MLB	13	767	128	19.0%	1	75	24	9	64	69%	22	3.0	26	1.0	4	10	37	63%	19	5.9	31	9	4
Shaq Thompson	22	OLB	14	365	50	6.9%	--	37	13	5	29	76%	--	2.6	--	1.0	1	3	9	77%	--	2.4	--	2	0
A.J. Klein	25	OLB	15	318	49	6.3%	--	26	13	2	25	64%	--	1.8	--	1.0	0	0	6	48%	--	4.9	--	1	1

of broken tackles. Age, total plays, percentage of team plays, stops, and defeats are computed the same way they are for other defensive players, so that the secondary can be compared to the defensive line and linebackers. That means that total plays here includes passes defensed, sacks, tackles after receptions, tipped passes, and interceptions, but not pass plays on which this player was in coverage but was not given a tackle or passed defense by the NFL's official scorer.

The middle five columns address each defensive back's role in stopping the run. Average yardage and stop rate for running plays is computed in the same manner as for defensive linemen and linebackers.

The third section of statistics represents data from Sports Info Solutions game charting. In all game charting coverage stats, passes where two defenders are listed and those listed as "Hole in Zone" with this player as the closest zone defender count for half credit. We do not count pass plays on which this player was in coverage, but the incomplete was listed as Thrown Away, Batted Down, or Hit in Motion. Hail Mary passes are also not included.

Targets (**Tgts**): The number of pass plays on which our game charters listed this player in coverage.

Target percentage (**Tgt%**): The number of plays on which this player was targeted divided by the total number of charted passes against his defense, not including plays listed as Uncovered. Like percentage of team plays, this metric is adjusted based on number of games played.

Distance (**Dist**): The average distance in the air beyond the line of scrimmage of all passes targeted at this defender. It does not include yards after catch, and is useful for seeing which defenders were covering receivers deeper or shorter.

Adjusted Success rate (**Suc%**): The percentage plays of targeting this player on which the offense did not have a successful play. This means not only incomplete passes and interceptions, but also short completions which do not meet our baselines for success (45 percent of needed yards on first down, 60 percent on second down, 100 percent on third or fourth down). Defensive pass interference is counted as a failure for the defensive player similar to a completion of equal yardage (and a new first down). This number is adjusted based

on the quality of the receiver covered.

Adjusted Yards per Pass (**AdjYd**): The average number of yards gained on plays on which this defender was the listed target, adjusted for the quality of the receiver covered.

Passes Defensed (**PD**): This is our count of passes defensed, and will differ from the total found in NFL gamebooks. Our count includes:

• All passes listed by our charting as Defensed, based on ESPN Stats & Info data checked against Sports Info Solutions data.

• All interceptions, or tipped passes leading to interceptions.

• Any pass on which the defender is given a pass defensed by the official scorer, and our game charting is marked either Miscommunication or Catch Out of Bounds.

Our count of passes defensed does not include passes marked as defensed in the official gamebooks but listed by our charters as Overthrown, Underthrown, or Thrown Away. It also does not include passes tipped in the act of rushing the passer. In addition, we did a lot of work with both the NFL head office and the folks from ESPN Stats & Info and Sports Info Solutions to get the most accurate numbers possible for both drops and passes defensed. Official scorers and game charters will sometimes disagree on a drop vs. a pass defensed, or even an overthrown/underthrown ball vs. a pass defensed, and there are a number of passes where the league marked the official stats in one way and ESPN S&I or SIS marked their stats the other way.

Interceptions (**Int**) represent the standard NFL interception total.

With more and more wide receivers playing, that means more and more cornerbacks are playing, so we've had to increase our minimums so we aren't ranking a zillion cornerbacks. Cornerbacks need 50 charted passes or eight games started to be ranked in the defensive stats, with 75 cornerbacks ranked in total. Safeties require 20 charted passes or eight games started, with 70 safeties ranked in total. (However, we did not rank Johnson Bademosi of Cleveland, who

Table 12. Green Bay Packers Defensive Secondary, 2015

Secondary	Age	Pos	G	Snaps	Plays	TmPct	Rk	Stop	Dfts	BTkl	Runs	St%	Rk	RuYd	Rk	Tgts	Tgt%	Rk	Dist	Suc%	Rk	AdjYd	Rk	PD	Int
						Overall						vs. Run							vs. Pass						
Ha Ha Clinton-Dix	24	FS	16	1048	102	12.6%	14	37	12	11	53	42%	33	8.1	51	25	6.4%	23	13.9	60%	26	7.9	45	2	2
Casey Hayward*	27	CB	16	914	70	8.6%	36	39	15	9	19	68%	7	5.4	18	46	13.6%	3	9.4	57%	19	6.8	15	5	0
Damarious Randall	24	CB	15	755	70	9.2%	29	23	14	6	13	23%	63	11.2	65	74	26.6%	70	14.4	48%	57	8.8	61	13	3
Sam Shields	29	CB	12	697	52	8.5%	40	22	14	7	3	0%	74	15.7	75	45	17.6%	18	14.3	57%	20	6.5	13	13	3
Morgan Burnett	27	SS	11	683	72	12.9%	12	29	7	5	40	53%	15	6.4	31	14	5.4%	15	15.2	67%	10	5.5	13	4	0
Micah Hyde	26	SS/CB	15	652	55	7.2%	63	19	13	7	15	20%	63	13.6	68	40	16.5%	69	9.6	52%	49	6.8	35	6	3
Quinten Rollins	24	CB	14	323	32	4.5%	–	16	11	4	9	56%	–	4.6	–	31	25.8%	--	13.1	57%	–	7.7	–	6	2

Year	Pass D Rank	vs. #1 WR	Rk	vs. #2 WR	Rk	vs. Other WR	Rk	vs. TE	Rk	vs. RB	Rk
2013	28	20.0%	28	16.7%	27	-8.1%	11	15.4%	25	13.3%	27
2014	11	-1.5%	15	-14.2%	7	-11.4%	9	-5.8%	14	1.0%	19
2015	6	7.5%	21	-31.7%	2	6.4%	19	-20.8%	4	-24.7%	4

had 22 charted targets but only 12 "plays.") Strong and free safeties are ranked together. Players listed with two positions, usually safeties who move to slot cornerback in nickel, are ranked at the first position listed.

Just like the front seven, the secondary has a table of team statistics following the individual numbers. This table gives DVOA figured against different types of receivers. Each offense's wide receivers have had one receiver designated as No. 1, and another as No. 2. (Occasionally this is difficult, due to injury or a situation with "co-No. 1 receivers," but it's usually pretty obvious.) The other receivers form a third category, with tight ends and running backs as fourth and fifth categories. The defense is then judged on the performance of each receiver based on the standard DVOA method, with each rating adjusted based on strength of schedule. (Obviously, it's a lot harder to cover the No. 1 receiver of the Pittsburgh Steelers than to cover the No.1 receiver of the Los Angeles Rams.) **Pass D Rank** is the total ranking of the pass defense, as seen before in the Trends and Splits table, and combines all five categories plus sacks and passes with no intended target.

The "defense vs. types of receivers" table should be used to analyze the defense as a whole rather than individual players. The ratings against types of receivers are generally based on defensive schemes, not specific cornerbacks, except for certain defenses that really do move one cornerback around to cover the opponent's top weapon (i.e., Arizona). The ratings against tight ends and running backs are in large part due to the performance of linebackers.

How to Read the Special Teams Tables

The special teams tables list the last three years of kick, punt, and return numbers for each team.

The first two columns list total special teams DVOA and rank among the 32 teams. The next two columns list the value in actual points of field goals and extra points (**FG/XP**) when compared to how a league average kicker would do from the same distances, adjusted for weather and altitude, and rank among the 32 teams. Next, we list the estimated value in actual points of field position over or under the league average based on net kickoffs (**Net Kick**), and rank that value among the 32 teams. That is followed by the estimated point values of field position for kick returns (**Kick Ret**), net punting (**Net Punt**), and punt returns (**Punt Ret**) and their respective ranks.

The final two columns represent the value of "**Hidden**" special teams, plays which throughout the past decade have usu-

ally been based on the performance of opponents without this team being able to control the outcome. We combine the opposing team's value on field goals, kickoff distance, and punt distance, adjusted for weather and altitude, and then switch the sign to represent that good special teams by the opponent will cost the listed team points, and bad special teams will effectively hand them points. We have to give the qualifier of "usually" because, as explained above, certain returners such as Cordarrelle Patterson will affect opposing special teams strategy, and a handful of the missed field goals are blocked. Nonetheless, the "hidden" value is still "hidden" for most teams, and they are ranked from the most hidden value gained (Miami, 18.8 points) to the most value lost (Philadelphia, minus-13.8 points).

We also have methods for measuring the gross value of kickoffs and punts. These measures assume that all kickoffs or punts will have average returns unless they are touchbacks or kicked out of bounds, then judge the kicker or punter on the value with those assumed returns. These metrics may be listed in special teams comments as **KickPts+** and **PuntPts+**. We also count special teams tackles; these include both tackles and assists, but do not include tackles on two-point conversions, tackles after onside kicks, or tackles of the player who recovers a fumble after the punt or kick returner loses the ball. The best and worst individual values for kickers, punters, returners, and kick gunners (i.e. tackle totals) are listed in the statistical appendix at the end of the book.

Administrative Minutia

Receiving statistics include all passes intended for the receiver in question, including those that are incomplete or intercepted. The word passes refers to both complete and incomplete pass attempts. When rating receivers, interceptions are treated as incomplete passes with no penalty.

For the computation of DVOA and DYAR, passing statistics include sacks as well as fumbles on aborted snaps. We do not include kneeldown plays or spikes for the purpose of stopping the clock. Some interceptions which we have determined to be "Hail Mary" plays that end the first half or game are counted as regular incomplete passes, not turnovers.

All statistics generated by ESPN Stats & Info or Sports Info Solutions game charting, or our combination of the two sources, may be different from totals compiled by other sources.

Unless we say otherwise, when we refer to third-down performance in this book we are referring to a combination of third down and the handful of rushing and passing plays that take place on fourth down (primarily fourth-and-1).

Table 13. Kansas City Chiefs Special Teams, 2015

Year	DVOA	Rank	FG/XP	Rank	Net Kick	Rank	Kick Ret	Rank	Net Punt	Rank	Punt Ret	Rank	Hidden	Rank
2013	7.8%	1	-5.6	26	3.0	12	19.8	2	4.6	13	17.2	1	5.2	9
2014	6.7%	3	-1.5	20	-2.7	23	12.4	1	11.6	4	13.7	2	0.1	15
2015	2.0%	9	-2.9	25	0.6	16	-0.8	16	16.2	1	-3.1	20	2.8	12

The Year In Quotes

NOT GOOD UNLESS IT'S COMING FROM A TODDLER

"I don't know how many fingers he has."

—New York Giants co-owner **John Mara**, on the extent of his knowledge of defensive end Jason Pierre-Paul's hand injuries suffered during a Fourth of July fireworks accident. (Eye on Football)

USUALLY I JUST STAND ON THE SHORE AND CAST A LINE

"I'm ready for whatever. I go fishing and the forecast says it isn't going to rain, but it might rain. Guess what: I got me a 100-mile-an-hour Bass Pro Shop dry suit right next to me, right in the drop storage hatch, and I can easily walk to the front of my boat, pull it out and put it on and be ready for the occasion."

—Chicago Bears defensive lineman turned linebacker **Willie Young**, making an interesting fishing analogy while describing his mentality towards his position switch after the Bears moved to a 3-4 scheme. (Chicago Sun-Times)

'OH COME, I'LL SHOW YOU MY FAVORITE FOUNTAIN IN THE CITY!'

"I'd like to drink from the same fountain as Vernon drinks from because he's not a 31-year-old athlete. This guy takes care of his body, he can really run, he's athletic and still very, very explosive. For me, what's neat is I don't have any knowledge of what happened in the past. When I came in here, it was a blank slate."

—San Francisco 49ers tight ends coach **Tony Sparano** in August, heaping praise on the conditioning of 31-year-old tight end Vernon Davis. (San Francisco Chronicle)

DAY-TO-DAY: FLESH WOUND

"It's a leg. I don't know, just one of them. I don't know. I know it's one of the two. And there's a lot of leg there too, so I don't know that it's a knee. It's in the leg, so I don't know. Anyway."

—University of Florida head coach **Jim McElwain**, discussing the extent and severity of offensive tackle Martez Ivey's August leg injury, which was in fact a partially torn meniscus in his left knee. (Twitter)

THIS SEEMS LIKE A SOCIETAL ISSUE

"Quarterbacks get protected more than any other player. I mean, he gets hit in his knees and he's about to cry. 'They hit me in my legs.' Everybody gets hit in their legs. Every play somebody tries to hit me in my legs. So what makes him different? What makes his life better than mine? I've got kids. I've got stuff I like to do on the weekend. But because he gets hit in his legs, he gets a flag. He gets up with a sad face like the world just ended because he got hit. I mean, you got hit in an NFL game. Who cares? Get back up and be like, 'Good job.' ... There's some mediocre quarterbacks in the NFL that make a lot of money. You take a guy like Sam Bradford—he's never played really in the last three years, but he's made more money than most guys in the NFL. Quarterback is the only position in the NFL where you could be mediocre and get paid. At every other position, you can't be mediocre."

—Seattle Seahawks defensive end **Michael Bennett**, speaking his mind once again, this time about average and overpaid quarterbacks. (CSN Philly)

GOD TOLD STEVE NOT TO TAKE JORDY NELSON IN THE FOURTH ROUND OF THE FANTASY DRAFT, SO WHAT DID YOU THINK WOULD HAPPEN?

"I hated Jordy got hurt, but in my beliefs, and the way I believe, it was—God meant for Jordy to get hurt. If he wouldn't have got hurt [on Sunday], if he wouldn't have played in that game, if he wouldn't have practiced anymore, and the next time he walked on the field would have been opening day, I feel like he would have got hurt opening day."

—Detroit Lions safety **Glover Quin**, commenting on Green Bay Packers wide receiver Jordy Nelson tearing his ACL in a preseason game. (MLive.com)

IF THEY STILL HAD OTTO GRAHAM, BEAR BRYANT WOULD STILL BE COACHING THE NAVY

"If we'd had Drew Brees, I might still be in Miami."

—University of Alabama head coach **Nick Saban**, saying that had the Miami Dolphins signed quarterback Drew Brees in 2006 instead of Daunte Culpepper, Saban might still be the coach of the Dolphins. (Pro Football Talk)

ELIAS: FIRST PLAYER NAMED 'TYROD' TO START AT QB IN NFL HISTORY

"It doesn't mean that they couldn't throw another guy in there at some point during the course of that game, but you can kind of hone in on what you want to do, especially from a pass-rush standpoint, if you have a pure pocket passer that is not mobile, can't run around, you're probably going to go after him a certain way. If you've got a guy that's as athletic and mobile as Tyrod is, then you have to plan accordingly."

—Indianapolis Colts head coach **Chuck Pagano**, discussing the challenges of defending Bills quarterback Tyrod Taylor. (NFL Nation Blog)

NEVER LOOK TO THE RIGHT OR THE LEFT—EVER

"He's been great. He's always been classy. I don't feel a distraction in the building. The distraction is if I turn on the TV, answer my phone, get on Twitter. As long as I'm in the building working hard and ignoring the noise even if there is something on the outside being said I don't feel it. We're playing in Washington, D.C., and for the Redskins and in the NFL, there's always going to be something going on there and it's so important to look forward and not look right or left."

—Washington Redskins quarterback **Kirk Cousins**, talking about backup and former franchise quarterback Robert Griffin III. (ESPN)

STEP ONE TO BEING IN THE NFL SUBSTANCE ABUSE PROGRAM

"Red wine is the key. Get it in your veins, baby. Keeps you strong."

—Minnesota Vikings cornerback **Terence Newman**, the oldest cornerback in the league at 37 years old, revealing the secret to his longevity. (Pioneer Press)

YOU CAUGHT JERRY GOING THROUGH HIS OLD AIKMAN DVDS AGAIN

"This quarterback Weeden can drive the ball downfield. He's a thing of beauty on throwing a football. His passing motion and his arm, frankly, you won't see a more gifted passer, power, accuracy, the entire aspect of it. If he can basically prepare, be the starting quarterback, come in and execute and keep his head right, then I feel good about Weeden."

—Dallas Cowboys owner **Jerry Jones,** painting an optimistic picture of his backup quarterback after Tony Romo's injury. (CBS DFW)

"I almost crashed my car. Listen, we played against Brandon Weeden when he was in Cleveland, and man, he threw me an interception—I thought I was playing catch with my kid in the park or in the backyard, man."

—Former NFL linebacker **London Fletcher**, reacting to Jones' compliment. (Gio and Jones)

WHY DOES THIS HAVE TO BE A BLACK AND WHITE THING?

"They get mad because my cleats are too black but they're perfect for my feet. I feel like they're supposed to protect the players. I have a certain shoe that feels the best for my foot. I've had foot problems over the last two years. They fine me because they're too black and they don't make them in white. I've got a kid at home. She's smart, too, so I'm gonna have to pay for Harvard or something."

—Chicago Bears tight end **Martellus Bennett**, saying that he is "pissed off" at the NFL over for a fine for wearing black Jordan brand shoes. (Chicago Sun-Times)

AWESOME

"There's also been a lot of talk about bringing back the helmet stickers. We're not gonna be handing these out for potty training or reciting the alphabet like they do in Columbus. You want a Wolverine sticker on that famous winged helmet; you gotta do one of the following things: hit someone so hard his eyes switch sockets, catch a pass with your junk, tell Mrs. Harbaugh she looks lovely in the regulation sized football earrings I bought her, or make such a spectacular play I start to cry. That's the list."

—University of Michigan head coach **Jim Harbaugh**, outlining his policy on helmet stickers which, quite frankly, we can get behind. (Twitter)

KICKERS ARE LIKE THE APPENDIX OF THE NFL

"I honestly don't think of it that way. That's just me personally. Obviously kicking is very mental and if you do struggle it is a little harder to go out there with confidence, but the good ones, if they miss they can bounce right back and make the next one. There are a lot of reasons why guys can miss—it isn't always just black and white—but you just have to learn to move on from it. That's just the approach I take. I've missed plenty of kicks before. I think the kickers have been so good the past couple years that it just looks different. There are still plenty of guys doing well; it's just easier to point out the guys that miss."

—New England Patriots kicker **Stephen Gostkowski**, when asked whether or not he thinks the craft of kicking is suffering in the NFL after a series of high-profile kicking failures in Week 4. (NFL Nation Blog)

IT'S HARD OUT THERE FOR A COACH

"That's all media bullcrap. I can tell you how they [the Clemson players] feel about it—they don't like it. It's a lack of respect. It's not doing your homework and paying attention to what reality is. Bullcrap. People need to quit talking about that. It's like people are trying to push their own agenda out there, and I can't believe I've gotta come in here with a 5-0 football team that just had a great win and have to be talked about 'Clemsoning.'"

—University of Clemson head coach **Dabo Swinney**, responding to a reporter's question following a win against Georgia Tech about what the team needs to do to avoid "Clemsoning," which is apparently losing games that you should win. (The Post and Courier)

MARK EMMERT WILL ADDRESS THAT AFTER HIS DAILY MONEY BATH

"I just don't understand how this happens when you play 12 straight games, then you play night road games and then we are going to play an 8 p.m. road game at Washington, get back at 5 in the morning and then have to go back on the road again. If the conference is really concerned about student-athlete welfare, I think someone should step in, because when do guys get a chance to get healthy? They are not getting treatments on the plane. They can try to sleep, but they are not getting a whole lot of rest when they are traveling. It is just ridiculous in my opinion."

—Arizona head coach **Rich Rodriguez**, voicing his displeasure with the Pac-12's scheduling of his team. (Sports Illustrated)

LOOKS AROUND I THINK THE PANTHERS ARE GOING TO WIN THIS WEEK

"No offense, but I find all media comical at times, I think in your guys' profession, you can easily take back what you say. There's no danger when somebody says, 'Oh, I'm going to pick this team to win.' If it was a pay cut or if it was an incentive, picking teams each and every week you get a raise, I guarantee people would watch what they say."

—Carolina Panthers quarterback **Cam Newton**, throwing some shade at the media. (Black and Blue Review)

THE NEW YORK MEDIA FINDS THIS ILLOGICAL

"I wouldn't say we made a statement because personally, I ignore everything you guys say anyway."

—New York Giants defensive end **Robert Ayers**, on whether October's Sunday night game against the Cowboys was a statement game for the Giants. (Twitter)

I HOPE HE DOESN'T GO OUT ON SATURDAY NIGHT

"The way we go about our business around here—from [coach John] Harbaugh down—no one is freaking out. We're not walking around in a zombie apocalypse."

—Baltimore Ravens tight end **Crockett Gillmore**, assuring everyone that despite their 1-6 start, the Ravens were not freaking out because it's not like there's a zombie apocalypse going on or something. (NFL Nation Blog)

HOW COULD YOU NOT GET UP FOR A GUY WITH THAT NAME?

"I mean, that's just—I didn't make a conscious decision. I think maybe my parents were really into marketing, so we were trying to sell some T-shirts from an early age."

—Detroit Lions offensive coordinator **Jim Bob Cooter**, explaining how he went from James Robert Cooter to Jim Bob. (Detroit Free-Press)

I HAVE MORE FACETS TO MY GAME THAN ANY OF YOU!

"You see Jimmy [Graham]. Jimmy can't block worth shit. They get a lot of credit and a lot of love. But Julius Thomas doesn't block anybody. Antonio Gates doesn't really block anybody. But they do a great job in the passing game. It all depends on the system that they're in."

—Chicago Bears tight end **Martellus Bennett**, throwing some shade on other tight ends throughout the league for being one-dimensional. (ESPN)

DOESN'T HE KNOW PHILADELPHIA WAS AN ORIGINAL USPS CITY? BOOOOOOOO

"That offer must have gotten lost in the mail."

—Philadelphia Eagles quarterback **Sam Bradford**, on reports that he turned down a four-year contract extension from the Eagles in November. (Eye on Football)

DEREK CARR TO AMARI COOPER COULD BE FUN FOR A WHILE

"He's awesome, man. It was fun watching him out there. They had a great game plan moving him, and a lot of places to give him the ball. Awesome. The sky is the limit for him. A special player, he is. They played well today. Like I said, Amari is a special player. They try to move him around a lot in the offense to try to get him the ball in many ways."

—New York Jets cornerback **Darrelle Revis**, praising rookie Raiders wide receiver Amari Cooper following the Raiders victory over the Jets. (OaklandRaiders.com)

THE YEAR IN RYANS

"It's pretty satisfying, without question. You know what? Now I can talk the truth. This thing's kind of like, well, like being dumped by some girl you had the hots for. That's what it feels like. Hey, you move on and every now and then they call you back. But they can't get you back."

—Buffalo Bills head coach **Rex Ryan**, finally acknowledging that a November 12 win at the offices of his former employer was quite satisfying, thank you very much. (The Buffalo News)

"The quarterback [Tom Brady] never gets worse. What's wrong with him? That quarterback never gets worse. Like what is wrong with him. You know what I mean? When you get older, you're supposed to get worse. This dude's getting better. Like, it's sick. It's not right. I'm waiting for the wheels to fall off."

—Ryan, commenting on Patriots quarterback and oft-Ryan thorn-in-side Tom Brady. (NFL Nation Blog)

"For me, and I'll speak for myself on this, I have an extra hunger... At the end of the day, the last two years in New Orleans were a waste of time for me. I want to give everything I have to a team that I want to be a part of, with a head coach I want to be a part of. Not only is Rex a great head coach, but he is also a great defensive coach. He's going to be the best coach that I can work for, anytime... I was hired to be in a multiple system in New Orleans, and I did a damn good job and got fired for it. I am more hungry now than I have ever been."

—Buffalo Bills "assistant head coach/defense" **Rob Ryan**, after reuniting with his brother Rex as the Bills' new, explaining what led him to Buffalo. Possibly, wings were also a factor.

"I said I was going to build a bully, it wasn't the appropriate word, but I want to be physical. I think we are getting it right. We brought in Richie Incognito."

—Brother Rex, on bringing Rob in. (SI.com)

YOU HEAR THAT PATRICK PETERSON (BUT MOSTLY RASHAD JOHNSON)?

"Not me. I didn't get my ass run over. Hopefully with the guys that got their ass run over, it motivates them."

—Arizona Cardinals head coach **Bruce Arians**, on whether Seahawks running back Marshawn Lynch's "Beastquake 2.0" run and crotch grab against Arizona in 2014 motivated the Cardinals at all in 2015. (Twitter)

DO YOU KNOW HOW MANY CARROTS I HAVE EATEN IN MY LIFE?

"No. I trust my eyes. I trust my eyes, OK? I watch the tape. I watch a lot of tape and I trust what my eyes tell me. So I don't need a freaking piece of paper with a bunch of numbers on there to tell me something my eyes can see. I mean, not to get pissed off, but that whole thing of looking at a piece of paper and telling you how to call a football game is a freaking joke in my opinion. That's why I watch tape. Half the stuff on that paper, you can sort those stats out any way you want to. But I'm sticking by eyes. It's worked OK for me so far."

—Tampa Bay Buccaneers then-offensive coordinator, now-head coach **Dirk Koetter**, when asked if he uses statistical research to prepare the plays he calls. The Buccaneers are one of many teams with an analytics department, not to mention quality control coaches, but Dirk Koetter thinks they are all nerds. (Tampa Bay Times)

OH THAT CLEARS IT UP THEN

"We're going to have plays where it's looks like a catch but it isn't."

—Vice President of Officiating **Dean Blandino**, discussing the new, updated criteria for what is considered a catch in the NFL. (Marc Sessler, NFL.com)

THE YEAR IN SHERMAN

"Like I said before, you don't have a bunch of guys ... let Jerry Rice and Michael Irvin talk about it for about 20, 30 minutes. Maybe Cris Carter. Randy Moss, let those guys have a roundtable discussion about what a catch should be and come up with a rule."

—Seahawks cornerback **Richard Sherman**, talking about the confusion regarding what is and what is not a catch in the NFL at the current moment. (ESPN.com)

"Critics are people with no talent dealing with people who have talent."

—Sherman giving his opinion on detractors and doubters of the Seahawks when they started 4-5 in 2015. (Twitter)

"It sounds like something somebody who's never played the game would say, something that they would suggest, because he doesn't understand. He's just a face. He's just a suit. He's never stepped foot on the field and understood how you can get a personal foul."

—Sherman, showing his disdain for Roger Goodell, as well as the new NFL rules regarding multiple personal fouls. (ESPN.com)

WHAT IF IT WAS A BOBBY BOUCHER-TYPE DEAL?

"We're going to talk every day until he figures it out and we figure it out as a team. He knows full well that he can't do that. He can't put himself and this team in jeopardy. You love the grit, and you love the toughness and all that stuff. But playing the position like a linebacker? You can't."

—Indianapolis Colts head coach **Chuck Pagano**, evaluating the play of quarterback Andrew Luck. (Indianapolis Star)

...HE SAID FACETIOUSLY INTO HIS PERSONAL TAPE RECORDER

"I think our officials do an extraordinary job. I think what we see now through technology is we see things we could never see before. But I think what it does is it validates the quality of our officiating."

—NFL commissioner **Roger Goodell**, addressing the state of NFL officiating which, we don't know if you've noticed lately, has been great! (NFL.com)

THEY SHOULD HAVE REPLACEMENT REFS! THAT WOULD GO OVER REALLY WELL

"The officials were struggling. Mightily. They can't count to three. I got tired of them because they were just running out of [explanations]. It was a FUBAR on their part. They can try to explain it. They're wrong."

—Arizona Cardinals head coach **Bruce Arians**, complaining about the officiating during their November 29 win against the 49ers and then explaining why he complained to officials during the game while using a cool acronym to describe the situation. (Arizona Republic)

BECAUSE PLAYING YOUR DEFENSIVE END AT TAILBACK IS A NORMAL FORMATION

"Anytime plays like that don't work—it wasn't a gadget play. It was a goal-line formation, goal-line play, blocked like a goal-line play and it didn't work. When those plays don't work, that obviously lays at the foot of me and I take that blame. I understand that. I'm not going to get into the schematics of it. It just didn't work."

—Houston Texans Coach **Bill O'Brien** when asked his thoughts regarding J.J. Watt's goal-line run in the wild-card loss to Kansas City. (HoustonTexans.com)

COULDN'T AGREE ANYMORE RON—WHO CARES ABOUT THE SUPER BOWL?

"We're not worried about the Super Bowl. That's irrelevant."

—Carolina Panthers head coach **Ron Rivera**, talking about the possibility of making it to the Super Bowl. (Black and Blue Review)

I'D KILL A MAN FOR A SLICE OF HAWAIIAN

"So if a man has the last piece of pizza in the world, are you going to take that last piece? One of y'all got to live! One of us has to win, and I'm not trying to lose. It's you and that one man. You gonna live or not? I'm trying to win. I don't care who you are."

—Panthers defensive back **Tre Boston**, saying he would have no qualms about sending Peyton Manning home without another Super Bowl ring. (NFL.com)

THIS AIN'T NO DISCO/AND IT AIN'T NO COUNTRY CLUB EITHER/THIS IS L.A.

"I didn't start looking for places yet. They told us to hold on. We still don't know the full scoop in terms of where we'll be in OTAs and stuff. I'll wait a little but—they told us to wait and they'll let us know from there."

—Rams defensive tackle **Aaron Donald**, still living in St. Louis but knowing that he will soon be moving somewhere in the Los Angeles area. (NFL.com)

HE WOULD HAVE BEEN BETTER OFF SAYING HE WAS JUST THERE SO HE WOULDN'T GET FINED

"We'll be back."

—Carolina Panthers quarterback **Cam Newton**, speaking at a postgame press conference, when asked if he had a message to Panthers fans after the team's 24-10 loss to Denver in Super Bowl 50.

"No."

—Newton, when asked if he could take it to heart that Denver had won a Super Bowl two years after losing one.

"Got outplayed."

—Newton, when asked to put a finger on why Carolina didn't play the way it normally played.

"Got outplayed, bro."

—Newton, when asked why the Panthers were outplayed.

"Nothing different."

—Newton, when asked if the Broncos had done anything different in the game than what they had shown on film.

"No."

—Newton, when asked if fans and/or media forgot that defenses could still take apart offenses in this game.

"He told us a lot of things."

—Newton, when asked what Panthers coach Ron Rivera had said to his team after the game.

"Nope."

—Newton, when asked if any of those things were particularly memorable.

[Silent nodding]
—Newton's response when told "Obviously you're disappointed. On the biggest stage it's difficult, I know."

"They just played better than us. I don't know what you want me to say. They made more plays than us, and that's what it comes down to. We had our opportunities. It wasn't nothing special that they did. We dropped balls, we turned the ball over, gave up sacks, threw errant passes. That's it. They scored more points than us."
—Newton, when asked if he had seen anything unexpected from Denver.

"We lost."
—Newton, when asked if he could put his disappointment into words.

"No."
—Newton, when asked if Denver had changed anything defensively to take away his running lanes.

[Shakes head] "I'm done, man." [Stands up, walks away]
—Newton's response when told "I know you're disappointed not just for yourself, but for your teammates. It's got to be real tough." (ABC News)

TWO SIDES OF THE STORY

"You can't do that. A Manning, a Brady, all these guys that has been the prototypical quarterbacks in our league... they would not do that... You're opening yourself up for more criticism. Everybody's going to say, 'You're dabbin' and smilin' and stylin' and profiling when you're winning. So this is how you're gonna act when you lose?'"
—Super Bowl winner **Deion Sanders,** criticizing Newton's behavior.

"I've been on that podium in that very same seat. It's tough. It's hard. When I look back at how I handled it, I promised to never be that person again. And Cam is gonna learn from this. Not just as a person, but definitely as an athlete. For some people, just like me, just like Cam, losing is hard. You can talk to whoever you want to, but until you've lost this game and sat on that stage and you had those feelings in you, you have no idea how it feels to get peppered with questions about how you played, how your team played and what woulda, coulda, shoulda. Talking to Cam does no good right now. When Cam watches this, he's gonna learn from it."
—Super Bowl winner (and loser) **Marshall Faulk** empathizing with Newton. (Charlotte Observer)

MANNING QUOTES ARE LIKE A BOX OF CHOCOLATES

"We all think it's blasphemy, because Peyton, he still has it. You know, he has what it takes. I think it's just a matter of time because it's a new offense. It's the beginning of the season ... just the chemistry with the O-line and the receivers, everybody gotta get in sync. I definitely think it's going to turn around. I have no issues, or no worries about anything."
—Denver Broncos linebacker **Brandon Marshall** in September, saying that it was blasphemous to doubt quarterback Peyton Manning's arm. (NFL.com)

"You guys are getting so desperate here. I had like these big throws and it almost reminds me of The Bad News Bears when Buttermaker was trying to encourage his team when they're really bad. He asked whoever kept the stats—I can't remember if it was Rudi or whatever—he said, 'Come on guys, get me the stats. Look on the bright side. Two of our runners have almost reached first base and we did hit 17 foul balls. That's the spirit.' Well, two good throws in there. I'll take it. Hey, I love it. I'm just going to keep trying to hit foul balls and almost reach first base. Maybe we'll get on base on some point and get going."
—**Peyton Manning,** when asked if a pair of long throws he made against the Lions in September were a result of some of the increased agility work he was doing. (Denver Post)

"I hate football."
—Former NFL quarterback **Archie Manning,** commenting on the results of Week 10 of the 2015 season. Peyton had arguably the worst game of his career against Kansas City while Eli lost to the Patriots at the last second. (Associated Press)

"Hey listen... This might be my last rodeo, so, it sure has been a pleasure."
—Peyton, to Patriots coach Bill Belichick after Denver defeated New England 20-18 to advance to the Super Bowl. (NFL.com)

"I don't know if that's been confirmed... What happened to private conversations on the 50-yard line? They just don't exist anymore. ... There's no confirmation on that whatsoever... We are on to Carolina."
—Peyton, refusing to discuss the possibility of retirement with reporters while also bemoaning the fishbowl life of an NFL quarterback. (NFL.com)

"I'm going to drink a lot of Budweiser tonight."
—Peyton after winning the Super Bowl, with perhaps the best post-game comment of all time. (ESPN.com)

"Like Forrest Gump said, 'that's all I have to say about that.'"
—Now-former NFL quarterback Peyton, during his retirement press conference. (FOX Sports)

"God bless all of you. And God bless football."
—Peyton, during his retirement press conference. (NFL.com)

"Then she asked, 'Daddy, is this the last game ever?' And that's just when I shook my head in amazement because I was thinking, '[ESPN reporters Chris Mortensen] and Adam Schefter had gotten to my 5-year-old daughter to cultivate a new source.'"
—Peyton, also during his retirement press conference. (NFL.com)

"Just like Jim Morrison's grave, even though it's not a grave Peyton, it will be a destination for people to leave cans of Budweiser or notes for you, so we'll collect those and get them to you as years pass."
—Indianapolis Colts owner **Jim Irsay,** revealing his plans for a Peyton Manning statue to be placed by Lucas Oil Stadium. (NFL.com)

BELIEVE ME, CURRENTLY THERE IS PLENTY OF ROOM ON THE BANDWAGON
"I can't wait until everybody jumps on the bandwagon when things are going good. I know some things will take time, but I'm not built that way to where I'm comfortable with ever losing. And I don't think anybody in our organization is."
—New Cleveland Browns head coach **Hue Jackson,** commenting on the Browns' lack of activity in free agency. (NFL.com)

WATCH OUT FOR YOUR TAIL, SAM
"I'm excited to be back on the field today with my teammates and coaches. The business side of football is sometimes a necessary consideration. My attention and efforts are focused on the participation in and preparation for a championship season: I am committed to my teammates and the Eagles organization for nothing less."
—Incumbent Eagles quarterback **Sam Bradford,** upon ending his pointless holdout after the Eagles traded up to select North Dakota State quarterback Carson Wentz in April's draft. (Adam Schefter on Facebook)

FORTUNATELY, MOST PLAYERS AREN'T HUMAN
"Injuries are a part of it. It's a violent game that I personally don't think humans are supposed to play. But we trust in our medical staff and we trust in each individual athlete to do what they have to do to get back on the field."
—Bills GM **Doug Whaley,** apparently unaware of the current issues surrounding the NFL with regards to player safety. (WGR 550 SportsRadio)

"Clearly, I used a poor choice of words in my comment yesterday morning... The point I was trying to make is that football is a physical game and that injuries are a part of it. Playing football is very physically, mentally, and emotionally challenging, and that is all part of what makes the game so compelling to play and watch."
—Whaley again, in a statement via the Bills' official Media Relations channel, clarifying his previous comments. (Twitter)

THEY ACTUALLY SCORE THE MOST POINTS ON THE TEAM
"Not a lot of people will ever admit that a kicker is worth a first-round pick. I'm going to be jumping for joy when a few of the people in your business realize that some are... If we love a player we're going to go get him. Don't worry about it. Go get him. Don't worry about how other teams had him ranked, either. If you read that this guy is a sixth-round pick and you take him in the second, it doesn't matter. Get your guy."
—Bucs GM **Jason Licht,** defending the decision to trade up and select Robert Aguayo in the second round of April's draft . (Pewter Report)

ANYONE KNOW WHO WEARS THE 5 JERSEY?
"A Bills quarterback with a jersey number that is the square root of 25 threw a football that missed its intended target."
—Buffalo Bills reporter Mike Rodak reporting from team OTAs, after the Bills published a strict set of media guidelines preventing media from reporting which players dropped passes or threw interceptions during camp. (Twitter)

"This is my 38th year covering the NFL. I've asked many, many coaches to give me one instance in which media won or lost a game. None could."
—*Houston Chronicle* writer **John McClain,** confirming suspicions that, indeed, there is no competitive advantage to be gained by knowing who threw an incompletion in their shorts in May. (Twitter)

THE SNAKE SPEAKS
"Like Jerry Jones, who says it's 'absurd' that there would be a link between brain trauma, football, and CTE. Shame on him for saying that, that billionaire asshole. It's the worst thing in the world for a guy like that to say."
—Former Cardinals and Broncos quarterback **Jake Plummer,** comparing Dallas Cowboys owner Jerry Jones to everyone's favorite orifice.

"There was, still is, and always has been a pretty high use of whatever drug of choice it is to keep you on the field."
—Plummer on drug culture in the NFL.

"It's basically really nice, really good heroin and we're going to give it to you so you can go out and actually damage your body even more and we'll insure you for a few years afterward, but then you're on your own."

—Plummer on the NFL's liberal policy with narcotics in alleviating players' pain.

"They should be able to say, 'I'm going to have some CBD and puff on this fatty, relax after a football game and take the pain away.' Not get tested for it like Josh Gordon, who now can't play the game that he's been playing since he was a kid because he smokes marijuana. It didn't derail him or cause him to underachieve from what I witnessed. He dominated the league for two straight years, and now he's out of the league because he chose an alternative form of medicine."

—Plummer on the case of Josh Gordon. (BSNDenver.com)

PRESIDENT OF THE MUSHROOM SOCIETY?

"Like mushrooms, offensive linemen are kept in the dark and fed [manure] with the expectation that good things will grow."

—Veteran NFL offensive line coach **Howard Mudd** in his new book <i>The View from the O-line: Football According to NFL Offensive Linemen and an Uncommon Coach.</i>

THE YEAR IN DEFLATEGATE (a.k.a. THE YEAR OF NOTHING BUT DEFLATEGATE)

"I would equate what [Tom Brady] did to driving 66 [mph] in a 65 speed zone, and getting the death penalty."

—Cleveland Browns left tackle **Joe Thomas,** discussing the penalties from Deflategate. (ESPN)

"While I am pleased to be eligible to play, I am sorry our league had to endure this. I don't think it has been good for our sport—to a large degree, we have all lost. I am also sorry to anyone whose feelings I may have hurt as I have tried to work to resolve this situation. I love the NFL. It is a privilege to be a member of the NFL community and I will always try to do my best in representing my team and the league in a way that would make all members of this community proud. I look forward to the competition on the playing field and I hope the attention of NFL fans can return to where it belongs—on the many great players and coaches who work so hard every week, and sacrifice so much, to make this game great. Most importantly, I look forward to representing the New England Patriots on Thursday night in our season opener. I hope to make all of our fans proud this year ... and beyond!"

—New England Patriots quarterback **Tom Brady,** in a statement following the decision to have his four-game suspension overturned. (Pro Football Talk)

"He never left."

—New England Patriots head coach **Bill Belichick,** when asked what his thoughts were on Tom Brady re-joining the team. (Twitter)

"If it was J.J. Watt, I think he would have been cooperative, and it wouldn't be a question. ... I don't think J.J. would destroy his cell phone."

—Houston Texans owner **Bob McNair,** claiming that if defensive end J.J. Watt were involved in Deflategate, Watt would not have destroyed his cell phone. (ESPN)

"It's not healthy for the NFL to be in the kind of litigious position that it's been for last several years. I think that the commissioner is working hard to hold up the respect and integrity of the game, the competitive balance of the game and the shield. Having said that, I think we have to find ways to get to a better place sooner with the NFLPA than the process that we've gone through."

—Atlanta Falcons owner **Arthur Blank,** saying that it might be time to look into commissioner Roger Goodell's power. (Atlanta Journal Constitution)

"Everybody does their things a little differently, but at the end of the day, it's handled between the lines. And if they man up and they beat you straight up, they beat you straight up. You can say they knew your plays or they watched this or they watched that, but a lot of times if you watch film good enough, you find good indicators. You find things. So if you're studying the game the right way, you go out there understanding what plays are coming, and you know when the plays are coming. But can you execute? Can 11 guys stop the other 11 from executing their play? You can say you stole scripts or whatever it is, but they still have to win the game. They still have to intercept the ball. They still have to execute. Eleven guys have to execute at the same time. And that's what they did, so give them credit. If there's hanky-panky going on, they've gotten away with it. Like they say, if you didn't get caught, then it wasn't cheating."

—Seattle Seahawks cornerback **Richard Sherman,** offering his opinion. (Eye on Football)

"They always say, 'If you ain't cheating you ain't trying.' So they're trying hard.

—Hall of Fame quarterback **Joe Montana,** giving us his two cents.

"You know, everybody does everything they can to possibly get a little bit of an edge. I mean, back then it wasn't illegal but it was illegal, like our guys used to spray—and everybody did it at the time—silicone on their jerseys, the linemen, so that the defensive linemen couldn't get a hold of them. And the defensive linemen did it so the offensive linemen couldn't hold them. It's a game. Everybody wants to win, so you do whatever you can to make it happen."

—Montana, on cheating back in the good ol' days. (Pro Football Talk)

"I'm very grateful for the overwhelming support I've received from Mr. Kraft, the Kraft family, coach Belichick, my coaches and teammates, the NFLPA, my agents, my loving family and most of all, our fans. It has been a challenging 18 months and I have made the difficult decision to no longer proceed with the legal process. I'm going to work hard to be the best player I can be for the New England Patriots and I look forward to having the opportunity to return to the field this fall. "

—Brady finally, possibly, just maybe drawing a line under the most ridiculous saga in the history of top-level professional sports.

Full 2016 Projections

The following table lists the mean DVOA projections for all 32 NFL teams. We also list the average number of wins for each team in our one million simulations, along with how often each team made the playoffs, reached the Super Bowl, and won the NFL Championship.

New England projections for both wins and DVOA assume that Tom Brady will serve a four-game suspension to start the season. This is also accounted for in the schedule strength of New England's first four opponents.

Full 2016 Projections

Team	Avg Wins	Postseason Odds			Mean DVOA Projections									Schedule	
		Make Playoffs	Reach Super Bowl	Win Super Bowl	Total DVOA	Rk	Off DVOA	Rk	Def DVOA	Rk	ST DVOA	Rk		Average Opponent	Rk
SEA	10.5	72.2%	23.1%	13.7%	23.6%	1	11.3%	4	-10.1%	2	2.2%	5		1.0%	10
ARI	10.4	69.3%	19.7%	12.2%	20.8%	2	14.4%	3	-8.2%	3	-1.8%	25		-0.3%	17
NE	9.8	65.5%	19.2%	10.4%	17.1%	3	9.3%	5	-3.8%	6	4.0%	2		-0.3%	16
PIT	10.1	66.9%	18.1%	9.4%	16.9%	4	17.0%	1	-0.2%	17	-0.3%	16		-1.7%	25
GB	10.0	64.8%	15.5%	8.4%	14.9%	5	16.5%	2	0.3%	19	-1.2%	21		-2.6%	29
KC	9.6	60.3%	14.1%	7.0%	13.8%	6	8.8%	6	-3.4%	7	1.6%	8		-1.6%	24
BAL	9.1	50.7%	9.0%	4.2%	7.4%	7	-3.6%	22	-5.1%	5	5.9%	1		-2.1%	27
CAR	8.6	47.7%	6.8%	3.3%	5.8%	8	4.6%	9	-3.2%	8	-2.0%	27		0.8%	12
DAL	8.8	50.5%	6.5%	3.0%	3.7%	11	3.3%	10	-0.4%	16	0.0%	15		-3.3%	31
MIN	8.6	41.4%	5.9%	2.8%	4.0%	10	2.0%	12	0.3%	18	2.2%	4		-0.9%	19
CIN	8.5	40.9%	6.1%	2.7%	4.0%	9	1.1%	14	-2.7%	9	0.2%	13		-1.1%	21
BUF	8.2	39.9%	5.7%	2.5%	2.5%	12	2.2%	11	1.6%	22	2.0%	6		0.7%	13
DEN	8.2	37.0%	5.1%	2.2%	2.2%	13	-8.3%	27	-11.3%	1	-0.8%	20		0.5%	14
SD	8.2	37.2%	4.6%	1.9%	-1.2%	16	4.9%	8	6.7%	30	0.6%	10		-3.0%	30
DET	8.1	33.7%	3.6%	1.6%	-1.0%	15	-0.1%	15	-0.4%	15	-1.3%	23		-2.1%	26
IND	7.8	38.9%	4.0%	1.6%	-3.2%	20	-2.4%	19	1.4%	21	0.6%	12		-1.4%	23
LARM	7.7	28.0%	3.2%	1.4%	1.3%	14	-4.6%	25	-6.3%	4	-0.4%	17		3.0%	3
OAK	7.6	29.7%	3.5%	1.4%	-2.5%	17	-1.0%	18	-0.7%	14	-2.2%	28		0.3%	15
NYG	7.8	34.5%	3.1%	1.3%	-3.7%	22	-1.0%	17	0.7%	20	-2.0%	26		-1.1%	22
NO	7.4	29.9%	2.8%	1.2%	-3.2%	19	6.4%	7	7.2%	31	-2.4%	31		2.0%	8
NYJ	7.2	25.7%	2.8%	1.1%	-3.5%	21	-2.8%	20	-1.2%	13	-1.8%	24		3.7%	2
ATL	7.3	28.1%	2.6%	1.1%	-2.8%	18	1.6%	13	6.3%	28	1.9%	7		2.7%	5
HOU	7.4	32.2%	2.7%	1.0%	-7.2%	24	-11.0%	30	-2.4%	10	1.3%	9		-1.0%	20
TB	7.2	26.4%	2.3%	1.0%	-4.7%	23	-4.2%	23	-1.7%	11	-2.3%	30		2.1%	6
TEN	7.2	28.9%	2.1%	0.7%	-10.3%	29	-4.2%	24	6.7%	29	0.6%	11		-3.8%	32
JAC	6.9	26.2%	1.9%	0.7%	-10.2%	28	-10.9%	29	-1.4%	12	-0.7%	18		-0.7%	18
PHI	6.9	23.5%	1.7%	0.7%	-7.9%	25	-5.3%	26	6.0%	27	3.4%	3		0.8%	11
CHI	7.2	21.7%	1.6%	0.6%	-9.8%	26	-0.8%	16	5.9%	26	-3.1%	32		-2.2%	28
WAS	6.8	21.5%	1.4%	0.5%	-10.1%	27	-3.5%	21	5.9%	25	-0.7%	19		1.5%	9
MIA	6.1	13.3%	0.8%	0.3%	-14.8%	30	-9.7%	28	3.9%	24	-1.2%	22		2.9%	4
SF	5.4	6.7%	0.3%	0.1%	-17.4%	31	-13.1%	31	2.1%	23	-2.2%	29		5.3%	1
CLE	5.2	6.8%	0.3%	0.1%	-24.5%	32	-17.0%	32	7.5%	32	0.1%	14		2.1%	7

Arizona Cardinals

2015 record: 13-3	**Total DVOA:** 27.4% (3rd)	**2016 Mean Projection:** 10.4 wins	**On the Clock (0-4):** 2%
Pythagorean Wins: 12.1 (2nd)	**Offense:** 15.7% (4th)	**Postseason Odds:** 69.3%	**Mediocrity (5-7):** 11%
Snap-Weighted Age: 26.9 (11th)	**Defense:** -15.6% (3rd)	**Super Bowl Odds:** 19.7%	**Playoff Contender (8-10):** 37%
Average Opponent: 1.3% (16th)	**Special Teams:** -4.0% (29th)	**Proj. Avg. Opponent:** -0.3% (17th)	**Super Bowl Contender (11+):** 51%

2015: The best team in the league thru Week 16.

2016: If only Carson Palmer and Tyrann Mathieu could play in a protective bubble.

Why has Bruce Arians been a legitimate Coach of the Year candidate for each of the last four seasons? He keeps exceeding expectations, especially from Football Outsiders, with an aggressive style of football. Are we overcompensating this year by making his Cardinals one of our top two favorites to win Super Bowl LI? Not really. For much of 2015, Arizona looked like the best team in the NFL. Carson Palmer was the most consistent quarterback, playing at an MVP level to lead one of the best offenses. The defense was again excellent despite changing defensive coordinators and losing several starters from the previous year. Outside factors were also helping to make it look like Arizona's year. Green Bay was not the same without Jordy Nelson, and it was probably a year too early for Minnesota to emerge as a serious contender. Dallas almost never had Tony Romo and Dez Bryant on the field together. Arizona was a formidable challenger to Carolina and Seattle.

But NFL seasons can turn on a dime, and Week 15 in Philadelphia may have been the beginning of the end for the 2015 Cardinals. Arizona won comfortably, by a 40-17 final score, but two big injuries made it a Pyrrhic victory. First, Palmer jammed his right index finger after hitting a defensive player as he followed through on a pass. The severity of this remains debatable, but Palmer never looked right again the rest of the season. What's not in question is the huge loss Arizona suffered with just 2:33 left in the game and a 23-point lead. At the end of an interception, versatile defensive back Tyrann Mathieu tore his ACL and was lost for the remainder of the season. Mathieu, who also tore his ACL as a rookie in 2013, had been a Defensive Player of the Year candidate and was named to his first All-Pro team. He was as valuable as anyone on Arizona's defense.

Concerns over these injuries briefly subsided when Arizona destroyed Green Bay 38-8 in Week 16. Led by an incredible pass rush that produced nine sacks, the defense posted its best single-game DVOA (-66.9%) of the season. Of course, we had learned by this point that the Packers were not the offensive powerhouse they have usually been. Two fumble return touchdowns by the defense made it an easy day for Palmer and the offense. In Week 17, Arians may not have been going full tilt to win a game against Seattle; Arizona still had a shot at the No. 1 seed, but a Tampa Bay upset in Carolina was unlikely. In reality, the final regular-season game only decided which

team would finish No. 1 in DVOA for the season. Seattle blew the doors off the Cardinals, taking a 30-6 halftime lead before winning 36-6. Palmer had his first poor game of the season and did not play in the second half.

That awful performance was followed by a week of rest, which only extended the time to ponder if the absence of recent playoff success made Arizona vulnerable heading into the NFC divisional-round rematch with Green Bay. Despite the comeback win in overtime, Palmer looked very shaky, as did Arians' aggressive coaching as the two narrowly collected their first playoff win. Then in the NFC Championship Game in Carolina, the biggest game of his career, Palmer vindicated his critics by turning the ball over six times in a 49-15 slaughter. The loss of Mathieu was also significant here as the Arizona safeties had a miserable game, and no one looked athletic enough to keep up with Cam Newton.

Good teams usually find a way to bounce back, even from a 34-point season-ending blowout. The Cardinals have won at least 10 games three years in a row because they have found stability at head coach, quarterback and general manager. They have some of the best defensive talent in the league. These are the ingredients for a consistent winner. If your best players remain healthy at season's end and the ball bounces your way enough, you have all the ingredients for that elusive championship season.

Some have been waiting for the other shoe to drop on Arians. His record in close games has been nothing short of phenomenal over the last four years, including his time as an interim coach with the 2012 Colts. Arians is 19-8 (.704) in games where his offense has a fourth-quarter comeback and/or game-winning drive opportunity. No other active head coach is above .500 (Table 1).

And when Arians gets a late lead of 1 to 8 points, he hangs onto it better than anyone. Since 2012, Arians is 31-1 (.969) when holding a one-score lead in the fourth quarter. The rest of the NFL wins 66.1 percent of the time in that situation, and the rival Seahawks with Pete Carroll are just 23-15 (.605) in that span. Arians' only loss was in his first game as Arizona's coach, blowing a 24-13 lead in St. Louis in 2013.

Naturally, you would expect Arians' record in close games to regress to the mean. There will come a time when John Brown doesn't haul in that long touchdown pass, or Patrick Peterson doesn't make that game-clinching interception. But

2016 Cardinals Schedule

Week	Opp.	Week	Opp.	Week	Opp.
1	NE	7	SEA	13	WAS
2	TB	8	at CAR	14	at MIA
3	at BUF	9	BYE	15	NO
4	LARM	10	SF	16	at SEA (Sat.)
5	at SF (Thu.)	11	at MIN	17	at LARM
6	NYJ (Mon.)	12	at ATL		

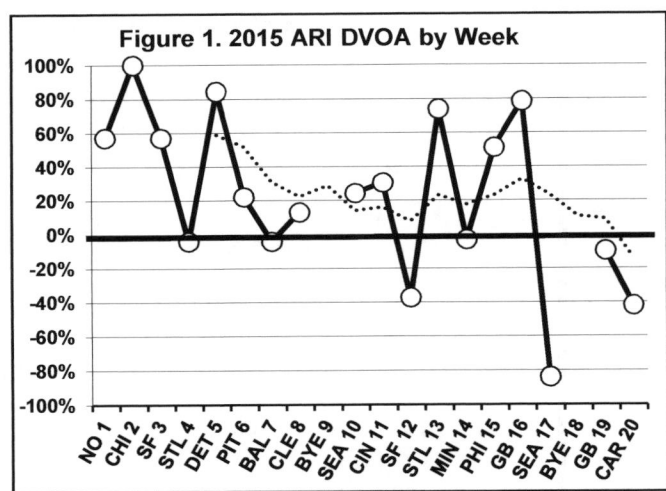

Figure 1. 2015 ARI DVOA by Week

for the last four seasons, Arians has had the magic beans in crunch time. His "no risk it, no biscuit" motto is not just coach speak. He backs it up with pressure in situations where most defenses are comfortable at going to the prevent, and he'll throw the ball down the field when most offenses just want to run clock. The results speak for themselves, but every hot streak comes to an end.

Arians has used "Whip Somebody's Ass," a five-line song written by a pastor, as the team's battle hymn in the past. The sentiment is clear, but no one stomps through a whole season on the way to a title anymore. Close games are inevitable. Nine of the last 10 Super Bowl winners needed a fourth-quarter comeback in the playoffs. The one who didn't, the 2010 Packers, had to thwart drives in the final minute while clinging to leads of less than a touchdown against each of the two Pennsylvania teams. Arians, as an offensive coordinator, was on the losing end of Pittsburgh's 31-25 loss in Super Bowl XLV. Two years earlier, he watched Ben Roethlisberger lead the Steelers down the field to beat the Arizona Cardinals in Super Bowl XLIII. Arians knows as well as anyone how small the margin is between success and failure. For Arizona to play its best football in the most important games, the team has to be less dependent on Palmer and Mathieu, and get more from the supporting cast.

We have enough evidence to conclude that Palmer has not

Table 1. Head Coaches: Active 4QC/GWD Opportunity Records (Includes Playoffs)

Rk	Coach	4QC/GWD Record	Pct.	Rk	Coach	4QC/GWD Record	Pct.
1	Bruce Arians	19-8	.704	15	Jack Del Rio	33-50	.398
2	Chuck Pagano	10-10	.500	16	Andy Reid	45-69-1	.396
2	Mike Zimmer	6-6	.500	17	Marvin Lewis	39-62-2	.388
2	Dan Quinn	5-5	.500	18	Pete Carroll	29-47	.382
5	Bill Belichick	62-77	.446	19	John Harbaugh	24-40	.375
6	Jim Caldwell	18-23	.439	19	Jay Gruden	6-10	.375
7	Jason Garrett	24-31	.436	21	Bill O'Brien	4-7	.364
8	John Fox	45-59	.433	22	Chip Kelly	6-11	.353
9	Todd Bowles	3-4	.429	23	Ron Rivera	12-23-1	.347
10	Sean Payton	28-39	.418	24	Mike McCoy	9-17	.346
11	Mike Tomlin	31-45	.408	25	Jeff Fisher	52-99-1	.345
12	Gary Kubiak	26-39	.400	26	Mike McCarthy	22-45-1	.331
12	Rex Ryan	22-33	.400	27	Gus Bradley	6-14	.300
12	Hue Jackson	2-3	.400	28	Mike Mularkey	4-19	.174

been good in the postseason (-4.1% DVOA) in his career. We *do not* have enough evidence to assume he will be bad in future postseasons. His postseason career began with the Bengals in 2005 against the Steelers, where Palmer tore his ACL after completing a 66-yard pass. He played poorly at home against the 2009 Jets, one of the best pass defenses this century. His stat line (349 yards and three touchdowns) against Green Bay this past January will hide some of his sloppiness, such as the red zone interception he threw, and the one Sam Shields dropped in the same fourth quarter. Palmer's go-ahead touchdown pass to Michael Floyd was a dangerous, deflected ball, and while he had the awareness to find Larry Fitzgerald in overtime, that 75-yard play was mostly YAC. Then we saw Palmer turn into 2008 Jake Delhomme with six giveaways in his first road playoff game, turning it over any time the Cardinals seemed to find a glimmer of hope. It's not a good record, but it's not a horrible one, and there's no reason to believe it holds predictive value. All it takes is one postseason run to change his career narrative.

Let's not forget that the real Carson Palmer is a talented player who has overcome several serious injuries to become the 18th quarterback in NFL history with 40,000 passing yards. At his best, Palmer is a very accurate passer, threading the needle in big prime-time wins over the Bengals and Seahawks last season. He can also go vertical; Palmer averaged 8.7 yards per pass, the fifth-highest average ever in a season with at least 500 attempts. There have been issues over the years with consistency, durability, and decision-making, but Palmer is one of the more gifted quarterbacks in the league.

We always caution to expect regression from a career year. The good news is that Palmer does not have to lead the league in DYAR, DVOA and QBR again for Arizona to be a top Super Bowl contender. After a shaky start in 2013, Palmer has found a comfort level in Arizona. There was a 15-game stretch in 2013-14 where Palmer averaged 7.85 yards per attempt and completed 64.5 percent of his passes for 4,159 yards, 27 touchdowns and 12 interceptions. That's a strong performance, but not the transcendent one Palmer delivered in 2015, and Arizona went 13-2 in those games anyway. Many of them came against soft competition, but that record is a reminder that this team can win at a high rate without MVP-level quarterback play. As the 2015 Broncos reminded us, you don't necessarily need MVP-level quarterback play to get through the playoffs either.

Palmer just has to avoid the big mistakes, which can be difficult in Arians' unique offense, built on the three b's: bubble screens, bombs, and broken plays. Arizona's 46 receiver screens were tied for the fourth most in the league. No offense threw deep more often than Arizona (27 percent of passes went at least 16 yards past the line of scrimmage), and Palmer's average pass traveled a league-high 11.1 yards. The Cardinals used shotgun a league-low 40 percent of the time, but Palmer had higher DVOA (36.1%) from under center than he did in shotgun (33.3%), and the deeper drops just enhanced the downfield passing game. Arians is used to his quarterbacks holding the ball without maximum protection, and while Palmer is no Ben Roethlisberger or Andrew Luck, he moved around well enough last season. Only Jay Cutler had a higher DVOA while pressured than Palmer did in 2015.

It helps that Arizona has the deepest wide receiver corps in the NFL. While many expected 2015 to be the year of John Brown, Larry Fitzgerald was still the No. 1 target, catching 44 more passes than his next closest teammate. Should a 33-year-old Fitzgerald start to fall off this year, Brown is right there to snatch the torch. Floyd is also a very talented big-play weapon with 1,000-yard potential, and J.J. Nelson might be the fastest receiver in the league.

Perhaps the most exciting change to the offense was rookie David Johnson taking over when Chris Johnson was injured. Johnson scored 12 touchdowns on limited touches and showed a knack for big plays as a receiver and returner. While Arians has been upfront about still starting Chris Johnson this year, his history suggests he loves to use a workhorse, and it should be David that sees the majority of touches in 2016. The offensive line is really built more for the running game, led by veteran guards Mike Iupati and Evan Mathis. Left tackle Jared Veldheer ranked third at his position in snaps per blown block in 2015, and D.J. Humphries should take over at right tackle after being the only healthy first-round pick to not play a single game last year. If the new line gels quickly, then we could see Johnson emerge as the star of this offense even more than Palmer this season.

Since Palmer turns 37 in December, his age is the limiting factor in Arizona's Super Bowl window. With the team so close to the top, you would expect to see some bold moves from general manager Steve Keim. He delivered this spring with the controversial first-round selection of defensive tackle Robert Nkemdiche. This is a classic example of a player with freakish athletic talent, major potential, little actual production (only six sacks in three seasons), and considerable character concerns. By now you are probably aware of the incident from last December in which Nkemdiche fell from a hotel room window in Atlanta and was charged with drug possession for seven marijuana cigarettes. A locker room with players who have overcome their own problems, such as Mathieu and Frostee Rucker, may be the perfect spot for enlightening Nkemdiche, as well as learning from a great player like Calais Campbell.

But the biggest move was trading a second-round pick and disappointing guard Jonathan Cooper to New England for Chandler Jones. This may not be a one-year rental à la Deion Sanders (1994 49ers) or Darrelle Revis (2014 Patriots), two corners who were the last pieces to Super Bowl teams. If Jones produces as expected, he'll get a rich contract from the Cardinals next offseason, but his performance in 2016 is crucial. Arizona needed a pass-rusher capable of winning one-on-one battles. This has really been a need ever since injury ended John Abraham's career.

While former defensive coordinator Todd Bowles took his blitzing ways to the Jets, his replacement James Bettcher kept up the pressure on Arians' command. In 2015, the Jets (47.9 percent) and Cardinals (48.1 percent) were the only two defenses to use a four-man rush on less than 50 percent of plays. The Jets (89) and Cardinals (66) led the league in six-man blitzes, and were both in the top four in defensive back blitzes. This aggressive approach led to the third-best pressure rate in the league (29.3 percent), but Arizona really needed to finish plays with sacks to make the pressure pay off. With sacks excluded, Arizona's defense ranked 10th in DVOA when getting pressure—good, but not great.

"Good, but not great" is also a good description of Jones' career so far. Sacks can be overrated, but this is not a trade to make without expecting big production in that department. Jones is a very versatile player, but will likely spend most of his time in Arizona on the right edge, replacing Dwight Freeney. This is a situation where simpler can be better if Jones is just asked to be a 3-4 outside linebacker, capable of rushing the passer and being stout against the run. However, Jones' reputation for inconsistency in New England is justified. In 2013, he recorded 32.5 quarterback hurries, but only has a total of 32.0 hurries in the two seasons since then. Last year, Jones had a career-high 12.5 sacks on 863 snaps, but only 17.5 hurries. A 35-year-old Freeney, playing in a similar role for the Cardinals, picked up 8.0 sacks and 17 hurries on just 255 snaps. In 2014, a young Alex Okafor had 8.0 sacks and 20.5 hurries. Last year, second-round rookie Markus Golden had 14.5 hurries on 518 snaps. Jones turns a high percentage of his pressures into sacks, which is good, but his overall pass-rushing production does not stack up to the likes of J.J. Watt and Von Miller.

Jones is the 26th player since 1982 to change teams after recording at least 35 sacks in his first four seasons (Table 2). Seven of the previous 25 players had at least 10 sacks in their debut season with their new team, but none had more than Jared Allen's 14.5 sacks with Minnesota. Some players only moved on well past their prime; others, such as Shawne Merriman and Aldon Smith, changed teams young due to personal issues. Given that Richard Dent only played in three games for the 1994 49ers, Charles Haley (1992 Cowboys) was really the only player on this list to help his new team immediately win a Super Bowl.

While only a small number of these players had a transformative effect on their new defense, there were some great success stories. Trevor Pryce improved the 2006 Ravens to the No. 1 defense in DVOA with a 13-sack season. The aforementioned Allen had Minnesota one Brett Favre decision away from Super Bowl XLIV. Julius Peppers had an All-Pro season for the Bears, reaching the NFC Championship Game in 2010. Jevon Kearse helped the Eagles to a Super Bowl appearance in 2004. While they may not have sealed the deal in Year 1, Reggie White (1996 Packers), Simeon Rice (2002 Buccaneers), and DeMarcus Ware (2015 Broncos) all eventually helped their new teams to a No. 1 defense and Super Bowl win. It would have to be viewed as a failure for the Cardinals to not at least get back to the NFC Championship Game with this roster after the Jones trade.

When you consider the potential of Nkemdiche and return of Corey Peters from injury, the defensive line should have better depth this season. With Golden expected to improve in his sec-

Table 2. When a Sack Producer Moves On

Player	1st Tm	Sk Yrs 1-4	Age	XP	New Tm	Debut	Sacks	Result
B.Pickel	LARD	42.5	32	9	NYJ	1991	2.0	Lost AFC-WC
T.Harris	GB	48.0	27	6	SF	1991	3.0	No Playoffs
C.Haley	SF	40.5	28	7	DAL	1992	6.0	Won SB
R.White	PHI	70.0	32	9	GB	1993	13.0	Lost NFC-DIV
P.Swilling	NO	38.0	29	8	DET	1993	6.5	Lost NFC-WC
F.J.Nunn	STLC	35.0	32	10	IND	1994	1.0	No Playoffs
G.Townsend	LARD	39.0	33	12	PHI	1994	2.0	No Playoffs
T.Bennett	GB	36.0	27	5	IND	1994	9.0	No Playoffs
R.Dent	CHI	49.0	34	12	SF	1994	2.0	Won SB
J.Jeffcoat	DAL	39.5	34	13	BUF	1995	2.5	Lost AFC-DIV
L.O'Neal	SD	42.5	32	10	STL	1996	7.0	No Playoffs
B.Smith	BUF	44.5	37	16	WAS	2000	10.0	No Playoffs
S.Rice	ARI	44.0	27	6	TB	2001	11.0	Lost NFC-WC
K.Carter	STL	35.0	28	7	TEN	2001	2.0	No Playoffs
J.Kearse	TEN	38.0	28	6	PHI	2004	7.5	Lost SB
T.Pryce	DEN	35.5	31	10	BAL	2006	13.0	Lost AFC-DIV
J.Allen	KC	43.0	26	5	MIN	2008	14.5	Lost NFC-WC
J.Peppers	CAR	40.5	30	9	CHI	2010	8.0	Lost NFC-CG
S.Merriman	SD	39.5	26	6	BUF	2010	0.0	No Playoffs
M.Williams	HOU	39.5	27	7	BUF	2012	10.5	No Playoffs
D.Freeney	IND	51.0	33	12	SD	2013	0.5	Lost AFC-DIV
E.Dumervil	DEN	43.0	29	7	BAL	2013	9.5	No Playoffs
D.Ware	DAL	53.5	32	10	DEN	2014	10.0	Lost AFC-DIV
L.Woodley	PIT	39.0	30	8	OAK	2014	0.0	No Playoffs
A.Smith	SF	44.0	26	5	OAK	2015	3.5	No Playoffs
C.Jones	**NE**	**36.0**	**26**	**5**	**ARI**	**2016**	**--**	**--**

ond season opposite of Jones, Arizona's pass rush is definitely getting a boost with talent and youth. While you cannot expect Arizona to abandon the pressure game—hell, this team rushed seven at Aaron Rodgers on a Hail Mary attempt and was burned for it in the playoffs—less blitzing could be beneficial against the better offenses. This can allow a player like Deone Bucannon, the current prototype for the dollar linebacker, to spy a mobile quarterback such as Cam Newton or Russell Wilson. Mathieu, who had 10 hurries himself last year, can drop back into coverage more and attack the ball.

The defense has more options if Jones can be a consistent source of pressure, but it can be tough to implement a veteran in an established defense. If winning another Super Bowl isn't enough motivation, Jones should also be thinking about the contracts Fletcher Cox and Olivier Vernon received this off-season. He can certainly be that level of player for Arizona, but this isn't quite Reggie White going to Green Bay.

After ending the last two seasons with playoff losses in Carolina, the onus is really on Arizona to earn home-field advantage. The Cardinals are 20-5 at home since 2013, but three of those losses came at the hands of Seattle, which is not going away as a major contender in the same division. Fortunately, the schedule should give a little edge to Arizona. The Cardinals were a hidden beneficiary when Tom Brady finally ended his appeal process; they get to host Jimmy Garoppolo's first NFL start at home in Week 1 while Seattle has to travel to Foxborough in Week 10, after Brady's return. In fact, Arizona's early schedule is very favorable before the huge two-game stretch against Seattle and at Carolina in Weeks 7 and 8. Seattle also has a December game in Green Bay, where the Packers should be much improved, while the Cardinals do not play the Packers in 2016. And while the Seahawks have had good success in Arizona, the Cardinals with Palmer at quarterback are 2-0 in Seattle (where the Seahawks are otherwise 31-3 at home since 2012) despite Palmer's seven combined turnovers in those games. The two meet in Seattle on Christmas Eve in a game likely to decide the NFC West, if not more.

Aggressive blitzes, downfield passing, a big trade acquisition, and a history of ACL tears for its most valuable players: Arizona is definitely playing with fire. If this was any other coach, we would might be pessimistic about this team's chances of putting it all together for a title run. But Arians has done something rare among the mostly conservative figures who revolve around the NFL's coaching carousel: he has earned our trust.

Scott Kacsmar

2015 Cardinals Stats by Week

Wk	vs.	W-L	PF	PA	YDF	YDA	TO	Total	Off	Def	ST
1	NO	W	31	19	427	408	0	57%	30%	-22%	5%
2	at CHI	W	48	23	300	335	0	100%	56%	-27%	17%
3	SF	W	47	7	446	156	3	57%	-2%	-64%	-5%
4	STL	L	22	24	447	328	-3	-4%	11%	11%	-4%
5	at DET	W	42	17	345	435	6	85%	47%	-33%	4%
6	at PIT	L	13	25	469	310	-3	22%	19%	-11%	-8%
7	BAL	W	26	18	414	276	2	-4%	21%	0%	-26%
8	at CLE	W	34	20	491	254	-2	13%	2%	-7%	4%
9	BYE										
10	at SEA	W	39	32	451	343	-2	25%	12%	-2%	11%
11	CIN	W	34	31	383	377	-1	31%	27%	-7%	-4%
12	at SF	W	19	13	337	368	2	-37%	-22%	17%	2%
13	at STL	W	27	3	524	212	1	74%	54%	-31%	-11%
14	MIN	W	23	20	393	389	3	-3%	15%	15%	-3%
15	at PHI	W	40	17	493	424	4	51%	53%	-7%	-8%
16	GB	W	38	8	381	178	2	79%	12%	-67%	0%
17	SEA	L	6	36	232	354	-3	-84%	-48%	-3%	-38%
18	BYE										
19	GB	W	26	20	368	386	-1	-10%	-18%	-3%	5%
20	at CAR	L	15	49	287	476	-6	-42%	-17%	22%	-3%

Trends and Splits

	Offense	Rank	Defense	Rank
Total DVOA	15.8%	4	-15.6%	3
Unadjusted VOA	17.0%	2	-13.9%	5
Weighted Trend	13.0%	4	-10.4%	7
Variance	7.9%	21	6.2%	25
Average Opponent	0.4%	19	0.5%	15
Passing	42.4%	3	-9.4%	4
Rushing	-8.0%	16	-24.4%	2
First Down	12.6%	5	-6.6%	8
Second Down	10.5%	9	-17.5%	3
Third Down	31.6%	3	-29.9%	2
First Half	16.4%	6	-11.8%	9
Second Half	15.1%	4	-19.5%	3
Red Zone	-2.6%	19	10.6%	23
Late and Close	18.0%	1	-26.3%	2

Five-Year Performance

Year	W-L	Pyth W	Est W	PF	PA	TO	Total	Rk	Off	Rk	Def	Rk	ST	Rk	Off AGL	Rk	Def AGL	Rk	Off Age	Rk	Def Age	Rk	ST Age	Rk
2011	8-8	6.9	4.9	312	348	-13	-19.7%	28	-18.4%	28	2.4%	20	1.2%	11	46.3	28	40.5	25	27.0	17	27.5	11	27.0	2
2012	5-11	4.8	4.8	250	357	-1	-16.3%	26	-30.9%	32	-13.5%	6	1.1%	11	50.3	28	22.0	12	26.7	18	27.6	8	27.1	4
2013	10-6	9.5	10.4	379	324	-1	10.0%	10	-2.4%	20	-16.4%	2	-4.1%	27	26.8	11	36.1	22	27.9	4	28.0	2	27.0	3
2014	11-5	8.3	7.4	310	299	+8	-6.4%	22	-9.3%	23	-5.0%	7	-2.2%	21	24.0	8	48.8	24	27.3	10	27.1	9	26.4	5
2015	13-3	12.1	11.6	489	313	+9	27.4%	3	15.7%	4	-15.6%	3	-4.0%	29	21.2	4	41.3	25	28.2	3	26.0	26	25.8	21

2015 Performance Based on Most Common Personnel Groups

ARI Offense					ARI Offense vs. Opponents					ARI Defense					ARI Defense vs. Opponents			
Pers	Freq	Yds	DVOA	Run%	Pers	Freq	Yds	DVOA	Run%	Pers	Freq	Yds	DVOA		Pers	Freq	Yds	DVOA
11	46%	6.8	23.0%	35%	Base	31%	5.6	1.1%	56%	Base	10%	4.1	-12.2%		11	62%	5.6	-21.0%
12	29%	7.0	26.5%	53%	Nickel	50%	7.4	39.3%	39%	Nickel	31%	5.3	-9.8%		12	18%	5.7	4.7%
10	13%	7.0	17.7%	12%	Dime+	17%	7.0	6.4%	16%	Dime+	59%	5.6	-21.2%		21	12%	4.2	-34.2%
13	5%	5.4	15.6%	76%	Goal Line	1%	0.0	-6.8%	70%	Goal Line	1%	0.6	26.1%		22	2%	3.8	14.4%
612	1%	3.9	-35.3%	86%											20	2%	1.3	-57.7%

Strategic Tendencies

Run/Pass		Rk	Formation		Rk	Pass Rush		Rk	Secondary		Rk	Strategy		Rk
Runs, first half	37%	17	Form: Single Back	79%	9	Rush 3	5.6%	20	4 DB	10%	31	Play action	17%	21
Runs, first down	53%	7	Form: Empty Back	14%	2	Rush 4	48.1%	31	5 DB	31%	31	Avg Box (Off)	6.31	11
Runs, second-long	30%	18	Pers: 3+ WR	61%	15	Rush 5	32.9%	4	6+ DB	59%	1	Avg Box (Def)	6.40	4
Runs, power sit.	54%	19	Pers: 2+ TE/6+ OL	39%	10	Rush 6+	13.4%	2	CB by Sides	58%	28	Offensive Pace	31.04	22
Runs, behind 2H	22%	24	Pers: 6+ OL	4%	12	Sacks by LB	57.1%	9	S/CB Cover Ratio	41%	1	Defensive Pace	31.34	29
Pass, ahead 2H	48%	13	Shotgun/Pistol	40%	32	Sacks by DB	11.4%	11	DB Blitz	17%	4	Go for it on 4th	0.84	19

The Cardinals benefited from a league-high 151 opponent penalties and 1,202 opponent penalty yards. The penalties were evenly split (64 by offenses, 64 by defenses, and 23 on special teams). Historically, there is very little year-to-year correlation in opponent penalties, but the Cardinals may be an exception; they've ranked in the top five for opponent penalties for three straight seasons, and also led the league in opponent penalty yards in 2014. (Or, perhaps, the entire 2015 season was an exception: the year-to-year correlation of opponent penalties was 0.10 from 2010-2014 but 0.53 for just 2014-2015.) ☜ Meanwhile, the Cardinals themselves ranked 30th with 110 penalties and dead last with only 758 penalty yards. ☜ For eight straight years, Arizona has ranked either first or second in the league in the percentage of plays with four or more wide receivers. Their 14 percent of plays last year paled in comparison to the Jets going four-wide 38 percent of the time, but no other NFL team was above 10 percent. ☜ The Cardinals ranked second in time of possession (32:04) and saw the second-largest increase in TOP from 2014 (+2:16). Only the Falcons eclipsed them in both categories. ☜ On a per-possession basis, Arizona may have had the league's most consistent offense. The Cardinals ranked first in yards per drive, second in points per drive and first in fewest three-and-outs per drive. However, the Cardinals stalled a bit in the red zone, dropping to 19th in DVOA including 24th in goal-to-go situations. ☜ Carson Palmer ate up blitzes: Arizona went from 7.9 yards per play with a standard pass rush to 9.1 yards per play against a blitz even though Cam Newton was the only quarterback blitzed more often than Palmer (38 percent of passes). ☜ Arizona once again used more dime packages than any other defense—and the count of six defensive backs doesn't include Deone Bucannon once he was officially moved to linebacker in Week 5. ☜ The Cardinals were far and away the best third-and-long defense with -97.6% DVOA, well ahead of second-ranked Houston and its -61.7% DVOA. ☜ Don't go to Arizona games expecting to see draw plays. The Cards only called seven running back draws in 2015, and the defense faced only one. (Congratulations, Isaiah Crowell, you are a special snowflake.) ☜ Arizona also didn't like to use its backs on screens, calling a league-low 10 all year. But screens aren't the only way to throw the ball to your running backs. The Cardinals led all offenses with 11.5 YAC on passes thrown behind the line of scrimmage, and were second with 44.5% DVOA on such passes.

Passing

Player	DYAR	DVOA	Plays	NtYds	Avg	YAC	C%	TD	Int
C.Palmer	1698	34.4%	557	4495	8.1	5.1	64.5%	35	11
D.Stanton	-82	-57.4%	27	96	3.6	2.4	44.0%	0	2

Rushing

Player	DYAR	DVOA	Plays	Yds	Avg	TD	Fum	Suc
C.Johnson	26	-5.4%	196	812	4.1	3	2	47%
D.Johnson	133	15.7%	125	581	4.6	8	2	56%
A.Ellington	64	24.4%	45	289	6.4	3	1	58%
K.Williams	-19	-27.1%	27	142	5.3	1	1	37%
S.Taylor	-9	-21.1%	17	58	3.4	0	0	41%

Receiving

Player	DYAR	DVOA	Plays	Ctch	Yds	Y/C	YAC	TD	C%
L.Fitzgerald	363	18.9%	146	109	1215	11.1	4.2	9	75%
Jo.Brown	352	29.9%	101	65	1003	15.4	4.8	7	64%
M.Floyd	256	24.0%	89	52	849	16.3	4.1	6	58%
J.Nelson	84	25.7%	27	11	299	27.2	5.1	2	41%
Ja.Brown	-7	-16.1%	23	11	144	13.1	2.0	1	48%
J.Gresham	-16	-14.0%	32	18	223	12.4	4.1	1	56%
D.Fells	86	35.8%	28	21	311	14.8	6.7	3	75%
D.Johnson	120	22.1%	57	36	457	12.7	9.6	4	63%
A.Ellington	27	3.7%	24	15	148	9.9	5.3	0	63%
C.Johnson	-23	-47.0%	13	6	58	9.7	10.5	0	46%

Offensive Line

Player	Pos	Age	GS	Snaps	Pen	Sk	Pass	Run	Player	Pos	Age	GS	Snaps	Pen	Sk	Pass	Run
Jared Veldheer	LT	29	16/16	1071	7	2.0	4.0	2.0	Ted Larsen*	G	29	10/10	679	4	1.0	6.0	2.0
Lyle Sendlein*	C	32	15/15	994	1	1.0	2.5	3.0	Jonathan Cooper*	RG	26	14/9	638	4	1.0	2.0	3.0
Bobby Massie*	RT	27	14/14	979	6	2.0	9.0	3.5	Earl Watford	G	26	8/2	199	1	1.0	4.0	1.0
Mike Iupati	LG	29	13/13	814	2	2.0	6.5	2.0	Evan Mathis	LG	35	16/12	809	2	2.0	7.5	3.0

Year	Yards	ALY	Rank	Power	Rank	Stuff	Rank	2nd Lev	Rank	Open Field	Rank	Sacks	ASR	Rank	Press	Rank	F-Start	Cont.
2013	3.89	3.84	17	73%	6	19%	16	1.00	24	0.71	15	41	6.8%	13	26.7%	23	19	42
2014	3.47	3.68	24	59%	24	19%	14	0.92	32	0.42	30	28	4.8%	6	24.5%	17	22	42
2015	4.59	4.18	3	51%	29	20%	16	1.22	6	1.15	4	27	5.0%	5	28.1%	23	16	32
2015 ALY by direction:			Left End 4.45 (7)			Left Tackle 4.25 (9)			Mid/Guard 3.66 (22)			Right Tackle 4.62 (3)			Right End 5.63 (1)			

Jared Veldheer's significant improvement in his second season with the Cardinals was crucial in allowing the team to run such a vertical passing attack. Veldheer's charted blown blocks on pass plays decreased from 17.5 to 4.0, as he finished 2015 with the third-best snaps per blown block average (178.5) among all left tackles. Arizona climbed from 32nd in adjusted line yards on runs off left tackle in 2014 to ninth last season. ☜ Left guard Mike Iupati missed the first three games of the season with an injury, but returned to earn his reputation as a strong run blocker and a Pro Bowl nod. Iupati's bugaboo was pass protection, but after allowing 25 quarterback hits and hurries in his last two years in San Francisco, Iupati allowed just 4.5 with the Cardinals. ✎ Center Lyle Sendlein's probable retirement opens the door for A.Q. Shipley, who has followed Bruce Arians from Pittsburgh to Indianapolis to Arizona. He has started 22 games in his career and will have to compete with rookie fourth-rounder Evan Boehm (Missouri), who has more desirable physical traits. ✎ Evan Mathis is looking to repeat as a Super Bowl champion after spending one season in Denver. He signed a one-year deal worth $6 million in March to play right guard for Arizona. His 2015 started slowly, but this year he'll have more time to prepare for his new offense. It's not like the Cardinals got much out of Jonathan Cooper here. ✎ D.J. Humphries has a lot to prove at right tackle after not playing a down in his rookie season despite his first-round status. Last summer, Humphries earned the nickname of "Knee Deep" as Arians said you have to keep "a knee in his ass every day" to keep him motivated. He can certainly improve on what Bobby Massie gave the team last year, but he has to prove it.

Defensive Front Seven

Defensive Line	Age	Pos	G	Snaps	Plays	Overall TmPct	Rk	Stop	Dfts	BTkl	vs. Run Runs	St%	Rk	RuYd	Rk	Pass Rush Sack	Hit	Hur	Dsrpt
Calais Campbell	30	DE	16	816	62	8.1%	8	49	20	3	48	79%	35	1.7	21	5.0	16	16.5	2
Frostee Rucker	33	DE	13	511	27	4.3%	54	23	7	6	22	91%	5	1.8	28	3.0	12	12.5	0
Rodney Gunter	24	DT	16	414	20	2.6%	--	15	5	4	18	78%	--	2.1	--	1.0	4	6.5	0
Ed Stinson	26	DE	15	377	11	1.5%	--	6	4	1	9	44%	--	2.2	--	1.0	2	5.0	0
Josh Mauro	25	DE	14	249	16	2.4%	--	14	5	2	14	86%	--	1.4	--	1.0	2	5.0	1

Edge Rushers	Age	Pos	G	Snaps	Plays	Overall TmPct	Rk	Stop	Dfts	BTkl	vs. Run Runs	St%	Rk	RuYd	Rk	Pass Rush Sack	Hit	Hur	Dsrpt
Alex Okafor	25	OLB	13	613	31	5.0%	48	20	5	5	19	68%	69	2.5	57	2.0	9	12.5	1
Markus Golden	25	OLB	15	518	29	4.0%	67	18	13	3	14	64%	77	2.0	34	4.0	7	14.5	0
LaMarr Woodley*	32	OLB	10	279	10	2.1%	95	8	4	4	4	75%	40	0.0	1	1.0	1	5.0	0
Dwight Freeney*	36	OLB	11	255	9	1.7%	--	9	8	0	1	100%	--	1.0	--	8.0	3	17.0	0
Chandler Jones	26	DE	15	863	45	5.8%	28	41	19	6	27	85%	11	1.6	22	12.5	7	17.5	0

Linebackers	Age	Pos	G	Snaps	Plays	Overall TmPct	Rk	Stop	Dfts	BTkl	vs. Run Runs	St%	Rk	RuYd	Rk	Pass Rush Sack	Hit	Hur	vs. Pass Tgts	Suc%	Rk	AdjYd	Rk	PD	Int
Deone Bucannon	24	ILB	16	995	111	14.5%	25	54	23	10	53	60%	55	3.2	31	3.0	3	5.5	32	55%	44	5.9	32	3	1
Keith Minter	26	ILB	16	927	95	12.4%	41	68	19	9	59	83%	1	2.0	2	0.5	5	11	20	59%	29	6.5	43	1	0

Year	Yards	ALY	Rank	Power	Rank	Stuff	Rank	2nd Level	Rank	Open Field	Rank	Sacks	ASR	Rank	Press	Rank
2013	3.19	3.09	1	48%	2	28%	1	1.01	8	0.46	7	47	7.2%	12	27.6%	5
2014	4.10	3.50	6	43%	1	26%	2	1.14	16	0.98	28	35	5.3%	28	29.1%	3
2015	3.71	3.05	2	62%	13	27%	2	1.05	8	0.87	21	36	5.7%	27	29.3%	3

2015 ALY by direction: Left End 2.70 (7) | Left Tackle 2.55 (3) | Mid/Guard 3.63 (8) | Right Tackle 2.22 (1) | Right End 1.99 (3)

Calais Campbell has yet to have a double-digit sack season, but he has consistently given Arizona around 20 defeats and 20 hurries for each of the last six seasons. Campbell is a free agent after this season, but don't look at the selection of first-round rookie Robert Nkemdiche as a replacement. He could make a great duo with Campbell as Darnell Dockett once did. ✎ Nkemdiche had just 6.0 sacks and 16 tackles for loss in three seasons at Ole Miss, but NFL.com does note he doubled his pressures to 26 in his final season. Don't expect rookie dominance on a crowded line which also includes Frostee Rucker, returning veteran nose tackle Corey Peters, and last year's fourth-round pick Rodney Gunter. ✎ Instead of trying to drain the remaining pass rush left in LaMarr Woodley and Dwight Freeney, this year's Cardinals are going younger with Markus Golden and Chandler Jones. Even the backups are young in Alex Okafor and Kareem Martin, a 2014 third-rounder who has played limited time in his first two seasons. ✎ Linebacker Daryl Washington actually has the sixth-highest cap hit ($7.5 million) on the team this year, but Arizona would be best to move on from a troubled player who has missed the last two seasons to suspension. ✎ Kevin Minter did well in replacing veteran Larry Foote, and he was as successful as any interior linebacker at stopping the run last year. ✎ Safety Deone Bucannon does not like being called a (dollar) linebacker, but the decision to move him there worked out really well for the defense last season.

Defensive Secondary

Secondary	Age	Pos	G	Snaps	Plays	TmPct	Rk	Stop	Dfts	BTkl	Runs	St%	Rk	RuYd	Rk	Tgts	Tgt%	Rk	Dist	Suc%	Rk	AdjYd	Rk	PD	Int
						Overall						vs. Run					vs. Pass								
Patrick Peterson	26	CB	16	990	41	5.4%	75	19	5	3	7	14%	71	13.6	70	51	13.7%	4	13.5	70%	1	4.4	1	7	2
Tyrann Mathieu	24	FS/CB	14	886	105	15.7%	3	56	31	17	32	47%	22	6.6	32	61	18.4%	70	10.4	62%	23	6.4	25	13	5
Rashad Johnson*	30	FS	14	845	63	9.4%	41	17	10	8	29	21%	62	11.4	65	17	5.4%	16	21.1	68%	9	8.1	47	7	5
Jerraud Powers*	29	CB	13	785	59	9.5%	23	22	5	6	16	44%	35	7.9	44	60	20.6%	48	14.9	51%	46	8.8	58	7	1
Tony Jefferson	24	SS	16	756	79	10.3%	30	25	13	7	30	40%	36	4.6	4	33	11.7%	60	10.2	56%	39	5.4	10	5	2
Justin Bethel	26	CB	16	443	42	5.5%	74	16	10	4	6	17%	69	9.0	56	54	32.8%	75	13.5	52%	42	7.2	22	9	2
D.J. Swearinger	25	SS	11	265	19	3.2%	--	9	5	7	13	46%	--	5.8	--	4	4.6%	--	6.6	62%	--	7.3	--	1	0
Tyvon Branch	30	SS	16	428	45	5.5%	69	18	8	4	14	43%	30	5.1	16	28	15.1%	68	10.4	67%	11	6.4	26	6	1

Year	Pass D Rank	vs. #1 WR	Rk	vs. #2 WR	Rk	vs. Other WR	Rk	vs. TE	Rk	vs. RB	Rk
2013	5	-27.3%	1	-10.5%	9	-9.3%	10	6.4%	20	-11.3%	8
2014	14	-4.0%	12	2.7%	19	-40.0%	1	16.9%	27	-26.2%	3
2015	4	-12.4%	6	-24.8%	3	-20.5%	5	-13.1%	7	9.7%	23

Patrick Peterson pulled off the rare feat of leading all cornerbacks in adjusted success rate and adjusted yards per pass allowed in his All-Pro season. Arizona opponents threw a league-low 19.5 percent of passes to No. 1 receivers. ☞ Tyrann Mathieu can make his case as the second-best corner on the team, and the versatile defender was actually the most targeted member of this unit in 2015. There were 46 players with at least three disruptions in 2015—passes batted down or disrupted through contact while the quarterback was throwing—and Mathieu was the only one that plays defensive back. If there was a knock on his game, it was the 17 missed tackles after having only seven combined in 2013-14. But he is a magnet for the ball and allows Arizona to use Bucannon as a linebacker. ☞ While known more for his work on special teams, Justin Bethel is more than capable of replacing Jerraud Powers as the No. 2 cornerback. ☞ Safety Rashad Johnson had a miserable performance in the NFC Championship Game loss and signed with Tennessee in the offseason. He could be replaced by veteran Tyvon Branch (ex-Chiefs), who finally played a full season as a backup after missing 27 games in 2013-14.

Special Teams

Year	DVOA	Rank	FG/XP	Rank	Net Kick	Rank	Kick Ret	Rank	Net Punt	Rank	Punt Ret	Rank	Hidden	Rank
2013	-4.1%	27	-4.9	25	-1.0	18	-6.5	30	3.9	14	-11.8	31	3.4	10
2014	-2.2%	21	0.0	16	2.0	13	-6.2	30	-9.6	30	3.0	11	-0.3	18
2015	-4.0%	29	-1.8	24	0.4	17	0.5	11	-12.7	30	-6.3	29	-11.4	31

Kicker Chandler Catanzaro has been nothing special through his first two seasons. He only produces a touchback 50.3 percent of the time. He has only made two field goals longer than 50 yards, and they were both 51 yards. He also missed five extra points last season, in the inaugural year of the 33-yard extra point. For a team that loves to pull out close games, a shaky kicker is likely to bite you eventually. ☞ Drew Butler was one of the NFL's least effective punters in 2014, and nothing changed in 2015. Arizona's punt coverage hasn't been very good, but Butler is the real problem: even assuming average returns, his punts were worth minus-9.4 points of estimated field position value in 2015 and minus-11.9 points in 2014. ☞ David Johnson wowed fans with a 108-yard kick return touchdown in Week 2, but he lost the return job after becoming the workhorse back. Kerwynn Williams' negative value as his replacement essentially cancelled out Johnson's positive value. ☞ Remember when Patrick Peterson had four punt return touchdowns as a rookie? He's taken none of his last 116 returns to the house, and has been one of the least effective return men in the league since 2012.

Atlanta Falcons

2015 record: 8-8	**Total DVOA:** -16.3% (26th)	**2016 Mean Projection:** 7.3 wins	**On the Clock (0-4):** 14%
Pythagorean Wins: 7.8 (15th)	**Offense:** -7.3% (23rd)	**Postseason Odds:** 28.1%	**Mediocrity (5-7):** 40%
Snap-Weighted Age: 27.1 (6th)	**Defense:** 6.9% (22nd)	**Super Bowl Odds:** 2.6%	**Playoff Contender (8-10):** 35%
Average Opponent: -7.6% (30th)	**Special Teams:** -2.1% (22nd)	**Proj. Avg. Opponent:** 2.7% (5th)	**Super Bowl Contender (11+):** 11%

2015: For the next few years, destined to be the easy comparison for any fast-starting team that inspires skepticism.

2016: So, hey, about that quick defensive rebuild…

Five weeks into the 2015 season, after a 25-19 overtime victory over Washington, the Atlanta Falcons stood at 5-0. They weren't doing it in dominant fashion, but they'd authored four tight wins against NFC East opponents and a thorough butt-kicking of the Texans. Still, DVOA only ranked them 13th after Week 5, and we weren't the only people suggesting the Falcons were not suddenly a major Super Bowl contender. Even the mainstream football media has become more skeptical of fast starts in recent seasons. Combine that with the general lack of national media coverage for the Falcons, and it meant there weren't an avalanche of people rushing to pat Atlanta on the back. This was more of a "sneak Matt Ryan on to the bottom of your MVP ballot" start.

And that's fine. Every year we have teams that ride easy schedules and hot starts to the playoffs before fading. That schedule was one of the main reasons *Football Outsiders Almanac 2015* gave Atlanta the best odds to win the NFC South. Atlanta was headed towards one of those seasons that earns "What a great story and great job by [INSERT HEAD COACH WHO COACHES TEAM I DON'T WATCH]" two-sentence blurbs and a first-round exit.

Except, rather than fulfil that destiny, the Falcons lost eight of their last 11 games. They lost to Tampa Bay twice. They lost to Matt Hasselbeck. They lost to Blaine Gabbert. They narrowly avoided losing to Zach Mettenberger. It wasn't

that the schedule got harder. It was that the offense suddenly couldn't score points.

After starting the season with four consecutive weeks with a single-game passing DVOA above 33.0%, the Falcons managed to pull that off again just once over the last 12 games (Figure 1). They didn't even have another game above 10.0% until Week 15. Julio Jones played through injury, but the real issue was that he was the only target the Falcons had who could make anything happen. Roddy White proved he was, as the kids say, *washed.* 2015 third-round pick Justin Hardy wasn't ready to get on the field, and Leonard Hankerson was hurt and then waived before he could recover. Jacob Tamme is a fine fourth or fifth receiving option, and Devonta Freeman is a capable receiving back. But they were pressed into bigger roles than the talent merited because Atlanta didn't have anything else.

Quarterback Matt Ryan also had some uncharacteristic struggles in new offensive coordinator Kyle Shanahan's system. White's lack of speed hurt—Shanahan's money routes like the play-action post and cross weren't able to create the separation they needed. But Ryan also mixed them with some bone-headed mental errors, including interceptions that went right to defenders.

It's hard for us to sit here with all-22 tape and say we know exactly what a quarterback is thinking when he fires one right to an underneath linebacker (besides expletives). Ryan lacks prototype arm strength, but has every other trait you'd want in a quarterback. Perhaps he was pressing to do more to make up for the players around him. Perhaps they were the sort of mishaps that happen when you try to teach an old veteran quarterback new tricks. (See: Manning, Eli, 2014.) Or perhaps it was the start of an early decline. We're more inclined to be skeptical that Ryan's skill went down a level, but non-elite quarterbacks don't tend to have pretty ends.

Atlanta didn't make much in the way of moves on offense this offseason. Mohamed Sanu comes in from Cincinnati to replace White, and center Alex Mack was finally allowed to leave Cleveland. Sanu never shined in Cincinnati, but as long as he can be a reliable target, he slides everyone else on this offense into positions for which they are better suited. Both moves profile as upgrades, and the Falcons shouldn't have a problem improving their offense so long as Ryan is still up to being a top-10 quarterback. All outward appearances show they believe Ryan will be just fine.

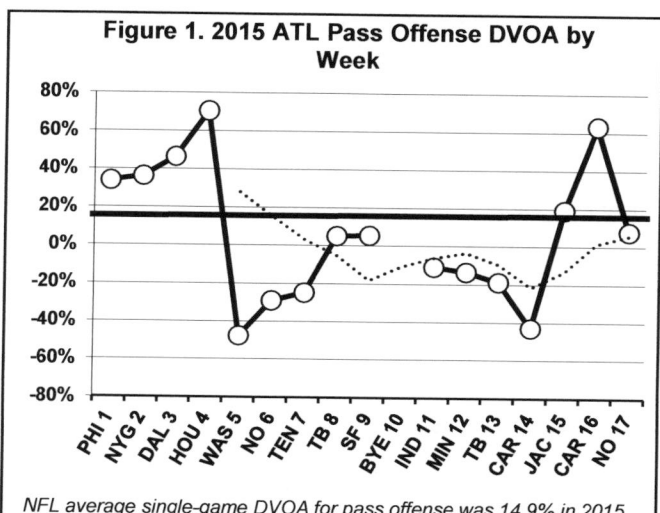

Figure 1. 2015 ATL Pass Offense DVOA by Week

NFL average single-game DVOA for pass offense was 14.9% in 2015

9

2016 Falcons Schedule

Week	Opp.	Week	Opp.	Week	Opp.
1	TB	7	SD	13	KC
2	at OAK	8	GB	14	at LARM
3	at NO (Mon.)	9	at TB (Thu.)	15	SF
4	CAR	10	at PHI	16	at CAR (Sat.)
5	at DEN	11	BYE	17	NO
6	at SEA	12	ARI		

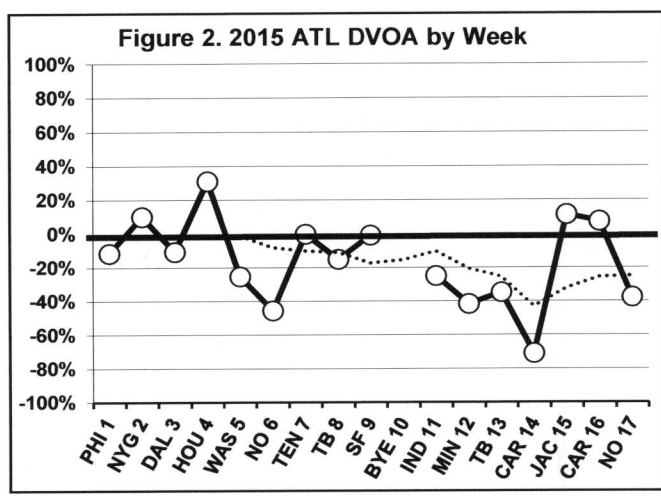

Figure 2. 2015 ATL DVOA by Week

Dan Quinn's defense, though, is an area where skepticism is warranted. The Falcons improved from 32nd in defensive DVOA in 2014 to 22nd in 2015. But the issues that we talked about in *Football Outsiders Almanac 2015*—poor depth and bad drafts—continued to haunt. The Atlanta defense is the sort of long-running conundrum that reminds us of the Rams offensive line. The free agents they can throw at it aren't impactful enough to change much before they grow old. The draft picks they made in the last two offseasons have been reaches or system projections rather than the best talents. It creates this perfect circle of underachievement where neither input actually fixes anything.

The Falcons drafted a keeper when they got Clemson's Vic Beasley last year, but instead of letting him rush off the edge, they moved him to strong-side linebacker. Creating a hybrid role for a good pass rusher is an interesting idea when you've got Cliff Avril and Michael Bennett up front. When only one other Falcon had as many as three sacks in 2015, a better descriptor might be "overly cute."

Now, to their credit, the Falcons did go out and sign Derrick Shelby away from the Dolphins. Shelby notched 3.5 sacks and 20.5 hurries last season even though he wasn't a starter until Week 9, and he has always been stellar as a run defender. He's clearly the kind of gamble a team like Atlanta should be taking. But the odds that Shelby is the next Avril and the rest of the league blew its evaluation of him seem to be pretty low. Even if he is, that still seems a weird reason to shunt your most promising pass-rusher into a hybrid role.

The Seattle defensive blueprint demands up-the-middle players who can cover and tackle. Atlanta spent its first two draft picks on a pair of players to try to fit that mold. Florida safety Keanu Neal was a surprise first-round pick to fill the void the Falcons had at the position last season. If you want to imagine Neal's college play, picture Kam Chancellor—and then imagine if Chancellor missed tackles left and right and wasn't much of a pass defender. There you go, that's the college Neal experience. All the physical dimensions, little of the production.

Atlanta's second-round selection was linebacker Deion Jones of LSU, who doesn't have to clear much of a hurdle to be better than incumbent whipping boy Paul Worrilow. He is fast (4.38 40-yard dash at LSU's pro day) and was productive in 2015. He also is seen as severely undersized, missed a lot of tackles, and didn't exactly have great coverage numbers in college. Jones didn't even start until his senior season.

Now, to leave the snark behind for a brief interlude, drafting on projection isn't inherently a bad thing. There are plenty of players who were misused, hurt, or changed positions in college and wound up as productive NFL stars. But when you go as far in on projection as the Falcons have, and your first two draft picks happen to be players who should start at two of your weakest positions, it's hard to not get the scent of reach. It's hard to look at what the Falcons have done with Beasley and its other recent draft picks (including Jalen Collins, a 6-foot-1 cornerback drafted out of LSU in last year's second round) and not see the attempt to build their own Seahawks defense. But, as Gus Bradley has also discovered in Jacksonville, building a Seahawks defense cover band does not guarantee you Seahawks results. If you want those, you need to find your own Richard Sherman and Bobby Wagner. And, most importantly, you need to find your own Earl Thomas. That's easier said than done.

Looking at the lack of improvement in the secondary and the significant number of snaps likely to go to rookie defenders, it's little surprise our projection system expects another consolidation year. You may think this isn't a big deal. Between a public relations desire to spin a positive message of continuous development and the influences of college football and corporate America, the NFL media has gotten hooked on the idea of "building a culture." Think a little bit about how ridiculous this would sound outside of the context of football. Imagine telling your significant other that the dishes aren't done because you're trying to establish a culture of dish-washing.

Wade Phillips comes in and immediately turns around any defense he sets his hands on. Nobody's campaigning for him to be a head coach again—put your hand down, Rob Johnson—and he spent a year unemployed before Gary Kubiak brought him back to Denver. He turned a pass rush that underachieved in 2014 into one that single-handedly won the Super Bowl. Building a culture is nice, and an organization should want everyone to be on the same page. But everything in this life you can get paid for boils down to a simple truth: you're only as valued as the value you produce for somebody else. And if this culture doesn't create actual, tangible on-field value, what is it worth?

It's a shame, because Ryan should bounce back. The Atlanta offense should be better, and that should give them a fighting chance to make the playoffs. But unlike last season, we project the Falcons to have the fifth-toughest schedule in the league. Swapping the AFC South and NFC East for the NFC West and AFC West is a stark contrast. Because of this, six different teams have a higher mean win projection than the Falcons despite having a lower mean DVOA projection.

There's a lot at stake for the Falcons this year. They're one year from opening a ridiculously expensive new stadium to replace the Georgia Dome. General manager Thomas Dimitroff and his Justice League of Ex-GMs (Scott Pioli, Phil Emery, Ruston Webster) need to prove that they can protect

Quinn. ("Of course, I'm on the hot seat," Dimitroff told the *Atlanta Journal-Constitution* this offseason, "this is a very urgent league right now.") Ryan needs to hold up his end of the bargain and show he can execute Shanahan's scheme without mental errors.

But, most of all, Quinn's defense needs to show Falcons fans signs of life. Real, actual results. Dimitroff has survived the axe a few years in a row with media lining up to bury him, but Quinn is one 5-11 season from being the lame-duck coach inherited by a totally new football operations department. We're told that's bad for culture.

Rivers McCown

2015 Falcons Stats by Week

Wk	vs.	W-L	PF	PA	YDF	YDA	TO	Total	Off	Def	ST
1	PHI	W	26	24	395	399	0	-12%	-7%	8%	4%
2	at NYG	W	24	20	402	388	1	10%	22%	2%	-10%
3	at DAL	W	39	28	438	347	1	-11%	36%	49%	2%
4	HOU	W	48	21	378	428	4	31%	32%	3%	2%
5	WAS	W	25	19	418	270	-1	-25%	-24%	-18%	-19%
6	at NO	L	21	31	413	385	-3	-46%	-19%	8%	-18%
7	at TEN	W	10	7	378	256	0	0%	-13%	-15%	-2%
8	TB	L	20	23	496	290	-4	-15%	-10%	7%	2%
9	at SF	L	16	17	302	318	2	-1%	-15%	3%	17%
10	BYE										
11	IND	L	21	24	375	276	-1	-25%	-24%	-13%	-13%
12	MIN	L	10	20	329	365	-2	-42%	-26%	20%	4%
13	at TB	L	19	23	319	388	1	-35%	-16%	16%	-3%
14	at CAR	L	0	38	230	424	-4	-71%	-46%	28%	2%
15	at JAC	W	23	17	328	370	0	11%	-5%	-6%	10%
16	CAR	W	20	13	373	268	0	7%	12%	-1%	-5%
17	NO	L	17	20	414	390	-1	-38%	-16%	15%	-7%

Trends and Splits

	Offense	Rank	Defense	Rank
Total DVOA	-7.3%	23	6.7%	22
Unadjusted VOA	-3.3%	20	5.3%	21
Weighted Trend	-15.4%	28	6.2%	22
Variance	5.0%	10	2.8%	4
Average Opponent	3.7%	30	-2.9%	27
Passing	2.8%	23	15.3%	21
Rushing	-15.4%	25	-3.9%	25
First Down	-3.7%	18	10.1%	25
Second Down	-15.9%	26	2.1%	17
Third Down	-1.9%	16	6.9%	19
First Half	-4.7%	20	11.2%	29
Second Half	-10.2%	27	2.1%	15
Red Zone	-23.9%	29	13.0%	26
Late and Close	-14.5%	26	-13.8%	10

Five-Year Performance

Year	W-L	Pyth W	Est W	PF	PA	TO	Total	Rk	Off	Rk	Def	Rk	ST	Rk	Off AGL	Rk	Def AGL	Rk	Off Age	Rk	Def Age	Rk	ST Age	Rk
2011	10-6	9.4	10.2	402	350	+8	13.9%	8	6.1%	11	-9.1%	8	-1.3%	22	22.2	11	26.4	16	28.0	4	26.7	20	26.4	12
2012	13-3	11.2	9.1	419	299	+13	9.1%	10	6.1%	12	-2.9%	12	0.1%	16	17.3	7	35.6	21	28.6	1	28.0	3	26.5	9
2013	4-12	5.9	6.5	353	443	-7	-10.4%	25	3.2%	14	13.5%	29	-0.1%	17	53.9	27	36.1	23	27.6	7	26.7	15	25.9	21
2014	6-10	7.1	7.2	381	417	+5	-5.4%	20	7.2%	10	15.7%	32	3.0%	9	60.6	30	33.2	12	26.8	16	26.6	21	26.4	7
2015	8-8	7.8	5.8	339	345	-7	-16.3%	26	-7.3%	23	6.9%	22	-2.1%	22	10.9	2	17.8	5	27.5	8	26.9	14	26.7	5

2015 Performance Based on Most Common Personnel Groups

ATL Offense					ATL Offense vs. Opponents					ATL Defense					ATL Defense vs. Opponents			
Pers	Freq	Yds	DVOA	Run%	Pers	Freq	Yds	DVOA	Run%	Pers	Freq	Yds	DVOA		Pers	Freq	Yds	DVOA
11	54%	6.0	-1.8%	22%	Base	47%	5.1	-12.5%	51%	Base	46%	5.3	-1.8%		11	57%	6.6	15.9%
21	25%	6.1	7.9%	55%	Nickel	46%	6.2	3.5%	25%	Nickel	49%	6.3	13.9%		12	19%	5.2	-11.5%
12	14%	4.2	-35.1%	47%	Dime+	6%	6.8	16.8%	3%	Dime+	4%	6.9	-9.5%		21	7%	5.1	-22.8%
13	3%	5.8	1.1%	62%	Goal Line	1%	0.5	-47.3%	75%	Goal Line	1%	1.1	100.4%		13	7%	5.4	21.3%
22	2%	2.9	-35.5%	71%											22	5%	4.3	-22.2%

Strategic Tendencies

Run/Pass		Rk	Formation		Rk	Pass Rush		Rk	Secondary		Rk	Strategy		Rk
Runs, first half	35%	27	Form: Single Back	64%	29	Rush 3	5.6%	21	4 DB	46%	5	Play action	22%	7
Runs, first down	47%	15	Form: Empty Back	7%	17	Rush 4	71.3%	4	5 DB	49%	22	Avg Box (Off)	6.39	4
Runs, second-long	28%	21	Pers: 3+ WR	55%	20	Rush 5	20.4%	19	6+ DB	4%	24	Avg Box (Def)	6.26	16
Runs, power sit.	50%	25	Pers: 2+ TE/6+ OL	20%	28	Rush 6+	2.7%	30	CB by Sides	86%	8	Offensive Pace	30.38	17
Runs, behind 2H	29%	9	Pers: 6+ OL	0%	30	Sacks by LB	21.1%	23	S/CB Cover Ratio	29%	5	Defensive Pace	30.31	15
Pass, ahead 2H	47%	17	Shotgun/Pistol	49%	27	Sacks by DB	10.5%	12	DB Blitz	5%	28	Go for it on 4th	1.59	2

The Falcons threw a league-high 29 percent of passes in the middle of the field even though they ranked 31st in DVOA on passes up the middle, ahead of only the Rams. ☞ Falcons receivers had the most drops (32) and the highest drop rate (5.5 percent) in the NFL. ☞ Fat lot of good it did them, but Atlanta led the league in time of possession (32:12) and increased its TOP from 2014 more than any team in the league (+2:50). ☞ Part of the problem: although Atlanta ranked first in plays per drive, it also ranked 31st in turnovers per drive. ☞ Atlanta's run offense was 15th in DVOA in Weeks 1-9, but dead last in Weeks 10-17. ☞ Atlanta opponents stacked the box after the Falcons ranked just 30th in average box faced in 2014. But that's not the reason for the running game's midseason decline—Devonta Freeman faced the same average number of defenders in the box for the whole season. ☞ Opponents clearly think the weakness of the Atlanta defense is short and inside. The Falcons faced both more passes to tight ends than any other team (26.5 percent of passes) and more passes to running backs than any other team (24.9 percent of passes). ☞ The Falcons did not do well sending extra pass-rushers, going from 6.5 yards per pass with a standard pass rush to 9.2 yards per pass with a blitz.

Passing

Player	DYAR	DVOA	Plays	NtYds	Avg	YAC	C%	TD	Int
M.Ryan	389	-1.9%	647	4372	6.8	4.5	66.4%	21	15
S.Renfree	-40	-97.2%	9	-6	-0.7	7.0	42.9%	0	1
M.Schaub	-146	-38.4%	83	513	6.2	4.1	65.0%	3	4

Rushing

Player	DYAR	DVOA	Plays	Yds	Avg	TD	Fum	Suc
D.Freeman	90	-0.5%	264	1062	4.0	11	2	46%
T.Coleman	-12	-11.9%	87	393	4.5	1	3	49%
T.Ward	-4	-12.3%	29	95	3.3	1	0	38%
M.Ryan	3	-9.6%	17	73	4.3	0	1	-
M.Sanu	62	77.2%	10	71	7.1	2	0	-

Receiving

Player	DYAR	DVOA	Plays	Ctch	Yds	Y/C	YAC	TD	C%
J.Jones	343	8.5%	203	136	1871	13.8	4.7	8	67%
R.White*	23	-8.5%	70	43	506	11.8	2.4	1	61%
L.Hankerson*	51	1.1%	46	26	327	12.6	4.6	3	57%
J.Hardy	-32	-24.8%	36	21	194	9.2	3.1	0	58%
N.Williams	27	0.8%	25	17	159	9.4	5.7	2	68%
M.Sanu	16	-8.3%	49	33	394	11.9	6.2	0	67%
J.Tamme	68	5.7%	81	59	657	11.1	3.3	1	73%
L.Toilolo	-26	-40.7%	12	7	44	6.3	2.9	0	58%
D.Freeman	68	-1.2%	97	73	578	7.9	6.0	3	75%
P.DiMarco	55	31.2%	17	13	110	8.5	3.7	2	76%
T.Ward	-11	-33.4%	13	9	73	8.1	6.6	0	69%
T.Coleman	-46	-99.5%	11	2	14	7.0	5.5	0	18%

Offensive Line

Player	Pos	Age	GS	Snaps	Pen	Sk	Pass	Run	Player	Pos	Age	GS	Snaps	Pen	Sk	Pass	Run
Chris Chester	RG	33	16/16	1140	3	4.0	9.0	3.5	Mike Person	C	28	14/14	952	3	0.0	2.0	4.0
Ryan Schraeder	RT	28	16/16	1130	5	1.0	3.5	3.5	Alex Mack	C	31	16/16	1106	4	1.5	2.5	3.0
Jake Matthews	LT	24	16/16	1127	4	2.0	6.0	2.0	Tom Compton	RT	27	13/1	210	1	0.0	1.0	0.0
Andy Levitre	LG	30	16/16	1127	11	1.5	2.5	5.0									

Year	Yards	ALY	Rank	Power	Rank	Stuff	Rank	2nd Lev	Rank	Open Field	Rank	Sacks	ASR	Rank	Press	Rank	F-Start	Cont.
2013	3.91	3.74	24	63%	18	21%	25	0.98	25	0.76	14	44	5.9%	7	28.4%	27	18	23
2014	3.93	3.96	14	67%	13	21%	20	1.02	24	0.68	17	31	5.1%	11	26.4%	22	16	27
2015	4.07	3.82	15	61%	21	22%	22	1.33	1	0.67	19	32	5.4%	9	24.3%	13	12	36

2015 ALY by direction:	Left End 3.46 (19)	Left Tackle 3.93 (15)	Mid/Guard 4.41 (1)	Right Tackle 3.64 (20)	Right End 3.38 (18)

In a challenging year for the Falcons offense, it was unsettling how well their offensive line played. You expect first-round talents like Jake Matthews to put it together, but Atlanta also got stellar years from the 30-something guard pairing of Chris Chester and Andy Levitre. Right tackle Ryan Schraeder had by far the best season of his career. It's rare you see a zone-blocking scheme take hold right away, so remember this team when you see the next nugget about how the decrease in padded practices hurts. ☞ Alex Mack opted out of his contract with the Browns this offseason, trusting that the broken leg which cost him most of 2014 would not affect his market in 2016. His return last season was not as dominant as we were used to seeing, to put it bluntly. He was dipped over more in pass protection than you'd like to see from the center you just gave $28.5 million in guaranteed money to. But this was by far his worst season. His established level of play is a top-three center in this league. And nobody will miss Mike Person or his tendency to botch snaps if Mack plays like Mack can.

Defensive Front Seven

Defensive Line	Age	Pos	G	Snaps	Plays	TmPct	Rk	Stop	Dfts	BTkl	Runs	St%	Rk	RuYd	Rk	Sack	Hit	Hur	Dsrpt
						Overall						**vs. Run**				**Pass Rush**			
Ra'Shede Hageman	26	DT	16	419	28	3.5%	--	20	5	5	24	71%	--	2.8	--	1.0	5	9.0	1
Paul Soliai*	33	DT	14	357	22	3.2%	--	19	3	1	20	90%	--	0.9	--	0.0	5	7.0	0
Grady Jarrett	23	DT	15	267	23	3.1%	--	20	5	0	22	86%	--	1.6	--	1.0	1	2.0	0

Edge Rushers	Age	Pos	G	Snaps	Plays	TmPct	Rk	Stop	Dfts	BTkl	Runs	St%	Rk	RuYd	Rk	Sack	Hit	Hur	Dsrpt
						Overall						**vs. Run**				**Pass Rush**			
Jonathan Babineaux	35	DE	16	549	31	3.9%	70	25	17	5	18	78%	30	0.2	2	1.5	7	15.0	1
Vic Beasley	24	DE	16	539	29	3.6%	76	23	10	2	13	85%	12	1.6	23	4.0	3	12.5	2
Adrian Clayborn	28	DE	16	523	15	1.9%	96	8	6	3	8	63%	83	1.8	25	3.0	14	14.5	0
Kroy Biermann*	31	DE	16	516	51	6.4%	22	37	9	3	42	76%	36	2.5	58	2.5	3	8.0	0
Tyson Jackson	30	DE	16	463	31	3.9%	70	22	4	0	29	72%	55	2.0	37	0.0	1	5.0	0
Derrick Shelby	27	DE	16	836	41	4.7%	50	34	13	6	31	81%	22	1.1	9	3.5	7	20.5	4
Courtney Upshaw	27	OLB	16	799	53	6.6%	18	37	12	7	40	73%	54	2.8	70	2.0	7	14.5	1

Linebackers	Age	Pos	G	Snaps	Plays	TmPct	Rk	Stop	Dfts	BTkl	Runs	St%	Rk	RuYd	Rk	Sack	Hit	Hur	Tgts	Suc%	Rk	AdjYd	Rk	PD	Int
						Overall						**vs. Run**				**Pass Rush**				**vs. Pass**					
Paul Worrilow	26	MLB	15	873	99	13.3%	33	55	20	20	52	67%	31	3.0	27	0.0	4	6.5	24	60%	26	5.0	17	4	2
Justin Durant*	31	OLB	13	657	83	12.8%	38	46	13	12	31	74%	8	2.7	14	0.0	0	3	24	53%	47	6.9	50	1	0
O'Brien Schofield*	29	OLB	16	500	28	3.5%	88	16	8	1	22	59%	56	3.6	48	2.0	14	15	6	37%	--	6.4	--	0	0
Brooks Reed	29	OLB	13	345	17	2.6%	89	12	4	2	12	75%	6	1.1	1	0.0	2	5.5	4	58%	--	1.8	--	0	0
Nate Stupar*	28	OLB	16	257	33	4.2%	--	15	4	4	16	44%	--	3.9	--	1.0	1	1.5	8	61%	--	4.9	--	2	0
Philip Wheeler	32	OLB	9	144	29	6.5%	--	19	5	1	23	65%	--	3.3	--	1.0	2	1	3	8%	--	10.2	--	0	0

Year	Yards	ALY	Rank	Power	Rank	Stuff	Rank	2nd Level	Rank	Open Field	Rank	Sacks	ASR	Rank	Press	Rank
2013	4.85	4.30	27	68%	20	16%	25	1.17	23	1.26	31	32	5.3%	32	21.5%	29
2014	4.09	4.16	24	80%	30	15%	30	1.11	12	0.54	6	22	4.5%	30	22.2%	26
2015	4.06	3.80	19	73%	27	18%	22	1.15	20	0.80	17	19	3.7%	32	21.5%	31

2015 ALY by direction: Left End 4.74 (27) Left Tackle 2.92 (4) Mid/Guard 4.11 (23) Right Tackle 3.88 (21) Right End 2.77 (8)

Fifth-round pick Grady Jarrett was one of the Chosen Draftnik Media Values in the 2015 draft, and he'll be asked to make due on that this season. With Paul Soliai's release, he's expected to take over the starting job at nose tackle. Jarrett had a low snap count in his rookie season, but played the run well. ☞ How do you feel about 6-foot-4 linebackers who run a 4.58 40-yard dash? DeVondre Campbell showed well in coverage for Minnesota last year, and though he's only a fourth-round pick, this is not a depth chart overflowing in those types of athletes. Don't be surprised if he's a factor sooner rather than later as Atlanta tries to get more athletic. ☞ Jonathan Babineaux is good against the run, but he's not *that* good. His average run tackle distance of 0.2 yards is a bit of a fluke caused by a couple extra tackles on plays that lost 4 or 5 yards instead of just 1 or 2, plus a 12-yard loss by DeMarco Murray in Week 1. In other years, Babineaux usually ranks around 30th in both run stats.

Defensive Secondary

Secondary	Age	Pos	G	Snaps	Plays	TmPct	Rk	Stop	Dfts	BTkl	Runs	St%	Rk	RuYd	Rk	Tgts	Tgt%	Rk	Dist	Suc%	Rk	AdjYd	Rk	PD	Int
Desmond Trufant	26	CB	16	968	53	6.7%	67	21	7	6	12	17%	69	11.6	67	52	14.5%	6	12.7	53%	35	7.3	30	11	1
Robert Alford	28	CB	15	908	65	8.7%	34	26	10	3	15	20%	66	8.7	54	60	17.8%	20	15.6	65%	2	7.2	24	10	2
Ricardo Allen	25	FS	15	840	73	9.8%	35	17	9	11	31	19%	65	10.9	64	17	5.3%	14	13.3	52%	50	8.4	50	5	3
William Moore*	31	SS	11	504	55	10.1%	32	21	6	4	24	46%	26	6.1	26	16	8.5%	48	9.5	64%	20	4.7	6	3	2
Phillip Adams*	28	CB	13	429	40	6.2%	--	12	6	4	9	22%	--	7.6	--	28	17.6%	--	13.8	36%	--	12.3	--	3	1
Kemal Ishmael	25	SS	16	375	45	5.7%	--	20	3	4	18	61%	--	3.4	--	11	7.9%	--	8.0	65%	--	3.4	--	4	1
Jalen Collins	23	CB	16	300	13	1.6%	--	1	1	3	2	50%	--	6.5	--	25	22.4%	--	15.1	40%	--	10.5	--	0	0
Robenson Therezie	25	SS	13	289	33	5.1%	--	7	3	6	8	25%	--	11.8	--	12	11.2%	--	15.1	39%	--	9.2	--	2	1
Charles Godfrey	31	SS	8	145	14	3.5%	--	6	2	3	3	67%	--	1.7	--	8	14.9%	--	8.0	64%	--	5.7	--	1	0

Year	Pass D Rank	vs. #1 WR	Rk	vs. #2 WR	Rk	vs. Other WR	Rk	vs. TE	Rk	vs. RB	Rk
2013	32	24.1%	30	18.6%	30	22.5%	30	9.1%	23	-8.8%	12
2014	31	-12.9%	8	28.9%	28	15.7%	27	-8.9%	12	27.4%	30
2015	22	-11.1%	7	8.0%	20	-11.7%	7	-14.0%	6	31.9%	32

In *Football Outsiders Almanac 2015*, we talked about how the scheme hid Desmond Trufant's ascension. This year, he did some pretty nice ascension on the stat sheet. He tied with Vontae Davis in allowing the fewest charted YAC of any cornerback in the NFL. He was also targeted an obscenely small amount of the time because opposing offenses have tape of both Trufant and Atlanta's other cornerbacks. ☞ Robert Alford's phenomenal success rate seems like a massive fluke, a huge example of the year-to-year inconsistency we've seen in these cornerback charting metrics. Alford had a 42 percent success rate in 2014 and was at 45 percent in 2013. Yes, Alford improved last year, but not as much as the charting stats suggest, and opponents are certainly happier to throw at him than at Trufant. ☞ With Joplo Bartu gone and Paul Worrilow likely to come off the bench, it's up to Ricardo Allen to carry on Atlanta's tradition of *Look At This Undrafted Free Agent We're Starting Because We Have No One Better*. Allen's rookie season was really nice if you consider his humble roots and the fact that it was his first season at safety after playing cornerback at Purdue.

Special Teams

Year	DVOA	Rank	FG/XP	Rank	Net Kick	Rank	Kick Ret	Rank	Net Punt	Rank	Punt Ret	Rank	Hidden	Rank
2013	-0.1%	17	0.0	18	-0.4	16	1.2	10	4.8	12	-6.2	25	-6.2	25
2014	3.0%	9	8.8	2	-6.2	26	-0.3	16	5.2	8	7.7	6	-1.2	20
2015	-2.1%	22	-4.3	28	-3.9	26	0.2	13	-4.6	21	2.1	12	7.8	5

Atlanta finished second in Adjusted Games Lost, but AGL doesn't include special teams, and they did lose both return man Devin Hester and kicker Matt Bryant for part of the season. A quad injury last year and Bryant's age has the team considering undrafted rookie Nick Rose (Texas) in camp. We're rooting for Bryant: with Matt Hasselbeck gone, there are only so many NFL players left who could pass for Moby. ☞ With Devin Hester cut loose before the season, Atlanta's returns will shift to the capable Eric Weems. Weems has been quite good over the years, but expecting anybody to come in and replace what a healthy Hester could do may be a stretch.

Baltimore Ravens

2015 record: 5-11	Total DVOA: -3.0% (17th)	2016 Mean Projection: 9.1 wins	On the Clock (0-4): 4%
Pythagorean Wins: 6.0 (25th)	Offense: -5.2% (20th)	Postseason Odds: 50.7%	Mediocrity (5-7): 22%
Snap-Weighted Age: 26.6 (16th)	Defense: 5.1% (20th)	Super Bowl Odds: 9.0%	Playoff Contender (8-10): 44%
Average Opponent: 5.1% (6th)	Special Teams: 7.3% (1st)	Proj. Avg. Opponent: -2.1% (27th)	Super Bowl Contender (11+): 30%

2015: The foxholes got emptier as the close battles took their toll.

2016: You can't keep a good (general) man(ager) down for long.

What's more likely to go stale first: our annual Ozzie Newsome quips in the header box, or the way the Baltimore Ravens play football?

We didn't mention Newsome by name in the box above, but the expectations that he and coach John Harbaugh will get the Ravens back on track in 2016 are still there. After all, 5-11 is out of character for a franchise which has not gone consecutive years without a winning record since 1999. Some regression on the injury front and in close games alone should get the Ravens back to .500.

For a 5-11 team, Baltimore sure kept things exciting last season. The Ravens played a league-high 14 games with a fourth-quarter comeback or game-winning drive opportunity. The only games that were not close were predictable: two blowout losses to Seattle and Kansas City with the J.V. Ravens starting Jimmy Clausen at quarterback. Otherwise, the Ravens became the first team in NFL history to have its first 12 games of a season decided by one score, and tied the 1994 Giants for the most games in a season (14) decided by 1 to 8 points. Unfortunately, Baltimore went 5-9 in those games, with some heart-breaking outcomes. What looked like a potential game-winning touchdown pass in Denver turned into a game-ending interception in the end zone in Week 1. Baltimore dropped a game-ending interception against Blake Bortles, then picked up a facemask flag after Bortles fell down

on the last play of the game. The rare untimed down sunk the Ravens on a 53-yard field goal in a 22-20 loss. Justin Tucker was clutch again with three game-winning field goals, but missed on a 55-yard kick in Miami that would have taken a late lead. The Ravens actually became the second team in history to win on a blocked field goal return touchdown, doing so in epic fashion on *Monday Night Football* in Cleveland in Week 12.

This competitive level of play is how the 2015 Ravens became the 11th team since 1989 to win no more than five games yet still finish 18th or better in DVOA. Among the 10 previous teams, nine of them won more games the next season, with an average increase of 3.7 wins (Table 1). Five teams finished at least .500 and three made the playoffs (the 1991 Broncos, 1992 Chargers, and 2005 Buccaneers).

Generally, a 5-11 team that usually kept it close is going to perform better in the future than one that was often blown out. Baltimore blew four fourth-quarter leads last year, a whole quarter of the season. Since 2001, 56 teams have blown at least four fourth-quarter leads in the regular season, and they averaged 2.0 more wins the following year. Baltimore and Dallas join a group of 13 other teams that had at least nine failed fourth-quarter comeback attempts in a season since 2001. Those teams averaged 4.2 more wins the following season, which would put the Ravens just over nine wins in 2016—right in line with our mean projection (Table 2).

Table 1. 5-11 or 4-12 Teams Ranked in DVOA Top 18, 1989-2015

Team	Year	DVOA	Rk	W-L	DVOA Y+1	Rk	W-L Y+1
PHX	1990	-7.3%	16	5-11	-20.4%	24	4-12
DEN	1990	-7.5%	17	5-11	-1.8%	18	12-4
SD	1991	1.6%	14	4-12	8.7%	9	11-5
PHX	1992	-4.0%	15	4-12	4.1%	11	7-9
CHI	1992	-6.6%	16	5-11	-14.7%	26	7-9
BAL	1996	5.1%	13	4-12	1.8%	15	6-9-1
SD	2001	6.9%	13	5-11	1.8%	15	8-8
JAC	2003	0.5%	17	5-11	-3.5%	18	9-7
TB	2004	-3.6%	16	5-11	-5.1%	17	11-5
DET	2012	0.1%	16	4-12	-1.9%	19	7-9
BAL	**2015**	**-3.0%**	**17**	**5-11**	-	-	-

Table 2. Losing Close Is Good for Your Future

Failed 4QC	Teams (2001-2014)	Avg Change in Wins Following Year
1	29	-2.7
2	54	-1.9
3	76	-1.1
4	88	-0.3
5	74	1.0
6	55	1.3
7	36	1.9
8	16	2.9
9	11	4.1
10	2	4.5

2016 Ravens Schedule

Week	Opp.	Week	Opp.	Week	Opp.
1	BUF	7	at NYJ	13	MIA
2	at CLE	8	BYE	14	at NE (Mon.)
3	at JAC	9	PIT	15	PHI
4	OAK	10	CLE (Thu.)	16	at PIT (Xmas)
5	WAS	11	at DAL	17	at CIN
6	at NYG	12	CIN		

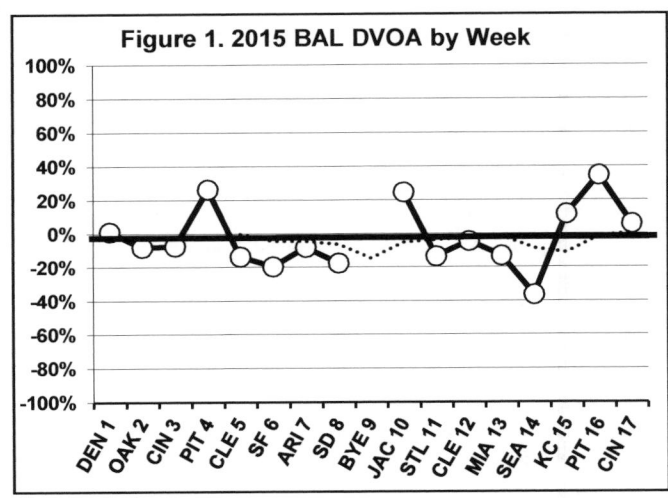

Figure 1. 2015 BAL DVOA by Week

But is this the same old reliable Baltimore team that won at least one playoff game from 2008 through 2012? One look at a team photo offers a resounding "no." Just five of Baltimore's projected 2016 starters were even on the 2012 roster. Such turnover is becoming more common in today's NFL, but the Ravens seemed better equipped to handle that with stability at general manager, head coach, and quarterback. And yet, since winning Super Bowl XLVII, the Ravens are just 23-25 in the regular season and 1-1 in their lone playoff appearance.

That title triumph came at a hefty cost in the form of Joe Flacco's historic contract: a six-year deal signed in 2013 worth a total of $120.6 million. Even though his cap hit has not topped $15 million in the last three years, the burden of fulfilling that contract has no doubt limited Newsome's ability to extend players or bring in significant free agents. Players such as wide receiver Torrey Smith and guard Kelechi Osemele sure would have made a lot of sense to sign to a second contract to keep talent around Flacco. The nightmare scenario with this deal was always paying a premium for non-premium quarterback play. Three years later, and the Ravens are still following that formula of "play great defense/special teams, and hope the offense doesn't screw things up." However, the supporting cast is looking weaker while the B-list quarterback is making superstar money. In fact, the Ravens doubled down on Flacco's salary this past offseason, making him (briefly) the league's highest-paid quarterback for a second time with a contract extension this past March.

You may not have noticed, but a sequel to the 1996 film *Independence Day* came out this summer. It was a flop both critically and commercially, grossing just $41 million domestically in its opening weekend. Many pointed to Will Smith's absence as the cause of the flop, but who really viewed him as the reason the original was such a success? At that time, Smith had just finished his run as TV's *Fresh Prince of Bel-Air* and was not a summer blockbuster machine. We remember that movie's ensemble cast just as much for Bill Pullman's speech, Vivica A. Fox's thong, and the heroics of Jeff Goldblum and Randy Quaid. Smith was the central character, but did not have to carry the film. So when Smith demanded $50 million as his salary for two sequels, Fox was absolutely right in writing him out of the franchise. The Ravens were in a similar position after Super Bowl XLVII. While Flacco played the crucial position of quarterback, Baltimore was not a quarterback-driven team. We also remember the championship run for Anquan Boldin's effort on 50/50 balls, Ray Lewis' emotional return, and the heroics of Jacoby Jones. It was a great team effort, but keeping that team together proved to be impossible.

Unfortunately, the Ravens somewhat had their financial hand forced on them. Flacco bet on himself before the 2012 season, reportedly turning down an extension offer of $16 million per year. He was set to become a free agent after the best four-game stretch of his career. Baltimore may have let Trent Dilfer go after winning Super Bowl XXXV, but how could it happen this time with a 28-year-old Super Bowl MVP just hitting his prime? Flacco and his agent had all the leverage, and the team faced a PR nightmare if this deal did not get done. The result was, at the time, the richest contract for a quarterback in NFL history, and its significance across the league cannot be overstated.

Since Flacco's record deal, the *minimum* price of a veteran field general has essentially climbed to $1 million per game—the type of deal Flacco shot down in 2012. Flacco, at $22.1 million, trails only Andrew Luck in a group of 22 quarterbacks who currently have contracts that average at least $16 million per season. Nick Foles ($12.3 million), who may not even be second-string anymore with the Rams, is the only quarterback between $7.5 million and $16 million per year. The middle tier was obliterated like the White House in *ID4*. You either get paid like a rookie or a stud, but there are few studs in this league. Baltimore was cornered into a bad deal, but *no team* would have had the courage to tell Flacco in 2013 to go move with his auntie and uncle in Bel-Air (or Arizona or Buffalo).

Obviously, the Ravens expected more from Flacco, who is 22-22 as a starter since 2013. Last season's ACL tear in Week 11 did not destroy the Ravens' season; they were already 3-7 with Flacco healthy. Statistically, Flacco was always more stable than stellar. From 2008-2012, you could count on him to throw for about 3,600 yards, complete 60 percent of his passes, throw in the low 20s for touchdowns, and somehow only get picked off 10 or 12 times despite a love for the deep ball. Advanced stats (DVOA and QBR) usually painted a picture of Flacco as a mediocre passer, peaking in 2014 with the year's eighth-highest DVOA (15.5%). Drop-adjusted passing plus-minus only ranks Flacco (+31.9) 25th among quarterbacks since 2006, right between Matt Cassel (+34.1) and Jake Delhomme (+27.7). Since 2013, Flacco's plus-minus on passes thrown deeper than 10 yards (-21.0) is the second lowest in the NFL. While he is throwing for about 34 more yards per game since 2013, Flacco has seen his touchdowns decline, suffered the two worst interception seasons of his career, and declined in yards per attempt from 7.1 to 6.8.

Essentially, Flacco sits at the same lunch table as Matthew Stafford, Matt Ryan, and Jay Cutler, but they have to bring him iced tea because of the power of the ring. That level of play is not worth the salary Baltimore is paying. The Ravens expected more of the postseason version of Flacco, but you won't even get to many postseasons with this type of play in the regular season. The other difference between Flacco and those other quarterbacks was that Baltimore had a better defense to help accumulate those postseason berths. That too was always going to be hard to sustain when legends such as Ray Lewis, Ed Reed, and Haloti Ngata moved on.

Obviously, the major problems on offense in two of the last three seasons have not all been on Flacco. When the unit was healthy and coached well by coordinator Gary Kubiak in 2014, it ranked ninth in DVOA and Flacco had quite arguably his best season. But the pity party is a quiet one, because Baltimore made the type of financial investment you would make into a quarterback capable of overcoming deficiencies around him. If Peyton Manning and Tom Brady had wholesale changes on the offensive line and got new tight ends and running backs, we would still expect them to run a great offense and make the playoffs. Flacco never needed to be Manning or Brady in the past for Baltimore to succeed, but that was when the Ravens had a better team. How does one build a strong team when so much money is invested into a needy quarterback?

It's not like we expect Flacco to play at an MVP level, but we at least have some higher expectations for the (twice) former highest-paid player in the league. For instance, since he was drafted in 2008, Flacco has never thrown for 4,000 yards, never had more than 27 touchdown passes in a season, and never had a passer rating above 95.0. Since 2008, 24 quarterbacks have had a 4,000-yard season, 23 have thrown more than 27 touchdowns in a season, and 28 have had a passer rating above 95.0 (minimum 200 passes). Maybe the most damning fact is that Flacco has never averaged 7.5 yards per attempt, while 35 quarterbacks have done that at least once since 2008. These are rudimentary milestones that other quarterbacks hit with ease, but not in Baltimore, and certainly not since the big contract (Table 3). As passing stats around the league have improved, Flacco's have only gotten worse.

Pro Bowl invitations are as common as McDonald's coupons in the Sunday paper, but Flacco has never been to one. Tyrod Taylor, Flacco's backup from 2011-14, already made the Pro Bowl as an alternate in Buffalo last year. In his first crack as a starter, Taylor had a higher touchdown percentage (5.3 percent), yards per attempt (8.0), passer rating (99.4) and QBR (67.8) than Flacco has had in any of his eight seasons. Taylor is also a dynamic runner and Buffalo went 8-6 in his games last year. It would have been incredible foresight by Newsome and Harbaugh to let Flacco go and turn to Taylor in 2013, but the more Taylor succeeds in Buffalo, the more that decision will sting if things do not improve in Baltimore.

The current dynamics of the AFC North demand more from Flacco. Ben Roethlisberger has always been a superior quarterback, and he is still in his prime with a strong Pittsburgh offense. The real surprise was Andy Dalton's career season in Cincinnati last year, quieting some of his critics with a level of efficiency previously unseen in his first four seasons. That type of jump has never happened for Flacco over a sustained period of time, and it's hard to expect that this late into his career. When you are no better than the third-best quarterback in your division, that makes any playoff success extremely difficult. Flacco is 5-8 in games against Pittsburgh when Roethlisberger has started. Dalton has also improved his play against the Ravens, and has led four game-winning drives in his last four starts in the rivalry. If Hue Jackson cooks up some magic with Robert Griffin III in Cleveland, Flacco could be in the strangest juxtaposition: the worst starting quarterback in his division, but the second-highest paid in the NFL.

In *Football Outsiders Almanac 2014*, we compared Baltimore's Super Bowl journey to the *Lord of the Rings* franchise. As an addendum, we want to note the power of the ring: it shields you from criticism. In 2013, offensive coordinator Jim Caldwell fell on the sword for Baltimore's poor showing, and the struggles of the offensive line and Ray Rice were given plenty of attention. While his 2014 performance lived up to the deal, it should be noted that Flacco essentially forced a game-ending interception in the end zone in the AFC divisional round loss in New England. If someone like Tony Romo threw that pass, we would still see highlights of it today.

Last season, Baltimore's offense had the most adjusted games lost to injury (70.1). Flacco's consecutive starts streak of 137 games, the second longest by a quarterback in NFL history to begin a career (Peyton Manning, 227), was snapped by a torn ACL. By season's end, Baltimore's quarterback, top two running backs (Justin Forsett and Lorenzo Taliaferro), top two wide receivers (Steve Smith and Breshad Perriman), top two tight ends (Dennis Pitta and Crockett Gillmore), left tackle (Eugene Monroe), and center (Jeremy Zuttah) were all on injured reserve. Most of those players lasted at least half the year and the offense was never consistent from Week

Table 3. Elite? We're Going to Need a Bigger Tier

Statistic	Joe Flacco, 2008-2012	Rk	Joe Flacco, 2013-2015	Rk
Passing yards	17,633	11	10,689	13
Touchdown passes	102	12	60	20
Interceptions (most)	56	12	46	3
Completion percentage	60.6%	20	61.5%	21
Yards per attempt	7.08	19	6.76	31
Touchdown percentage	4.10%	25	3.80%	30
Interception percentage (lowest)	2.25%	6	2.91%	29
Passer rating	86.3	16	82.0	31
Wins as a starter	54	2	21	17
Pass DYAR	2,366	11	708	21
Pass DVOA	2.8%	18	-4.6%	23

Note: Minimum 500 passes for ranking in rate stats

1, but that is still a massive injury list. If anyone deserves a pass here, it was offensive coordinator Marc Trestman, who reverted to some of his pass-happy ways despite all the injuries and low caliber of passers. The 2015 Ravens are the third team in NFL history to have four quarterbacks pass for at least 500 yards in a season, along with the 2007 Panthers and 2015 Cowboys, and it's an undesirable achievement.

As long as James Hurst remains on the bench, the offensive line should be one of the best units in the league, so it really comes down to the skill players staying healthy. Newsome has overstocked the shelves with options, but not all of them are sweet and savory. Steve Smith is 37, coming off a torn Achilles, and has the goal of reaching 1,000 career receptions. His days as a big-time No. 1 target are about over. Breshad Perriman was supposed to replace Torrey Smith last year, but missed his entire rookie season due to a PCL tear. He almost lost this season with another knee injury, but early reports of a partially torn ACL proved to be false. Still, Perriman received a stem-cell injection in his knee and is very much an unknown in the NFL. Kamar Aiken took advantage of the injuries with a surprising 75-catch, 944-yard season, and he should see significant targets again.

Or will he? Newsome made the curious decision of signing Mike Wallace to a two-year deal worth $11.5 million, not chump change for someone to sit on the bench. Wallace, still a legend in his own mind, believes he's a better receiver now than he was in Pittsburgh, even though he has been on a decline for four years after failed stints with Miami and Minnesota. Wallace will still likely serve as a deep threat, but that could hamper the progression of the young Perriman. With Smith and Aiken in the fold, Wallace looks like an unnecessary signing.

Likewise, Newsome inked tight end Benjamin Watson after a year of career-best receiving numbers in New Orleans, but he'll be 36 in December. Crockett Gillmore looked pretty good before getting hurt last season, and Maxx Williams was a second-round pick in 2015. Again, this looks like veteran overkill from Newsome on positions he seemingly already filled.

If Newsome has flown over the cuckoo's nest, consider the Ravens deliberated and still signed Trent Richardson, Twitter's favorite laughingstock. He probably won't make the team with five better running backs ahead of him, but just let it sink in that Newsome actually thought it was worth the time to sign T-Rich after using a fourth-round pick on a running back three years in a row. Granted, Trestman offenses also love throwing to the backs, 127 receptions by running backs last season.

So many options for skill players, but not many blue-chip talents. We would be remiss to not question Newsome's recent draft performance. Some of the problems have clearly been out of his control, such as Sergio Kindle falling down the steps and fracturing his skull in his rookie year, and the lower-body injuries to Pitta and Perriman. Three members of the 2014 draft class finished last season on injured reserve (Gillmore, Taliaferro, and Michael Campanaro). 2015 fourth-round corner Tray Walker tragically died in March after a dirt bike accident, and fifth-round tight end Nick Boyle is suspended for

the first 10 games of the season for what is already his second violation of the league's performance-enhancing drug policy.

But there are legitimate knocks on Newsome as well. For a long time, his track record in the first round was magnificent outside of Kyle Boller. However, Matt Elam never worked out as the heir apparent to Ed Reed, forcing of the team to move Lardarius Webb to safety this year. Meanwhile, Newsome drafted six players in the second round from 2009 to 2012, and none of those players are still with the team, including disappointments such as Courtney Upshaw and Terrence Cody. 2013's second-round pick, Arthur Brown, has yet to start a game and is well on his way to "bust" status with 17 career tackles.

Late-round gems have also been hard to come by. ESPN had a graphic this offseason that showed the Ravens have drafted the most Pro Bowlers (six) in Rounds 4 through 7 since Newsome was officially promoted to general manager in 2002. That sounds good until you realize it includes Derek Anderson (who made the Pro Bowl with the Browns), fullback Ovie Mughelli (Falcons), Cedric Peerman (Bengals; never played for Baltimore), and the aforementioned Tyrod Taylor (Bills). That leaves fullback Le'Ron McClain and punter Sam Koch as Newsome's late-round honorees. Baltimore drafted five players in the fourth round this season, and ESPN's Todd McShay called it the best fourth-round class he's ever seen from one team. Let's wait and see.

Since 2009, the only player Newsome drafted in any round that actually made the Pro Bowl as a Raven was linebacker C.J. Mosley in 2014. Using the Pro Bowl as an indicator of quality is not an exact science by any means, but it's a bit shocking that Jacksonville is the only other team in the league to draft just one Pro Bowl player in that time. Twenty-one teams drafted at least four Pro Bowlers (Table 4). Newsome built his early reputation by consistently selecting talent at that level: Ray Lewis, Jonathan Ogden, Jamal Lewis, Peter Boulware, Todd Heap, Chris McAlister, Terrell Suggs, Ed Reed, Haloti Ngata. But in recent years, the parade of incoming talent has slowed down significantly.

Table 4. Pro Bowlers Drafted Since 2009

Team	No. PB	Team	No. PB	Team	No. PB	Team	No. PB
MIN	9	ARI	4	NO	4	MIA	3
SEA	8	ATL	4	OAK	4	SD	3
CIN	7	BUF	4	PHI	4	STL	3
CAR	6	CHI	4	SF	4	TEN	3
DAL	6	CLE	4	TB	4	NYG	2
KC	6	DEN	4	DET	3	NYJ	2
PIT	5	GB	4	HOU	3	**BAL**	**1**
WAS	5	NE	4	IND	3	JAC	1

If any player in the 2016 draft was considered a future perennial Pro Bowler, it was Mississippi tackle Laremy Tunsil, whom many experts felt was worth the No. 1 overall pick prior to the quarterback-hungry trades at the top. NFL analyst Lance Zierlein, for example, said "[Tunsil] to me is going to be the best left tackle in the league, or one of the top two, within three years." Baltimore was clearly in the tackle market with the No.6 pick, but just minutes before the draft began, a video surfaced on Tunsil's hacked Twitter account that showed him smoking from a bong while wearing a gas mask. ESPN's Adam Schefter has reported from a team source that the Ravens were set to select Tunsil, but a team official saw the video and showed it to Newsome and owner Steve Bisciotti. The Ravens ended up selecting Notre Dame tackle Ronnie Stanley while Tunsil fell to Miami at No. 13. Naturally, Baltimore talked up Stanley as the pick all along, with one source claiming he was a top-four player on the team's board while Tunsil was only top 15. Harbaugh declined to answer if Tunsil was ever the planned pick, which tells us plenty in addition to the "No. No. I mean there's a lot of speculation" answer from Newsome. Given that the team did its homework on the kid, it is hard to believe this (old) video and the fact that Tunsil smokes weed were even news to them, or that it would make them change their minds and choose a backup plan at the last second. Only time will tell if this was the right move, but given Newsome's recent track record, he does not get the usual benefit of the doubt.

Stanley will start immediately at left tackle after the Ravens cut Eugene Monroe, but pundits don't expect much instant impact from the rest of Baltimore's 2016 draft class—especially on the defensive side of the ball, where an aging unit could really use a shot of youth. Baltimore's defense fell to 20th in DVOA in 2015, its lowest ranking since being 29th in 1996. There was a serious early blow when edge-rusher and

vocal leader Terrell Suggs tore his Achilles in Denver in Week 1, but otherwise this unit stayed relatively healthy. Free agent Eric Weddle should be an upgrade over fellow veteran Kendrick Lewis, but at age 31 he's not helping the defense get any younger. Last year, the Ravens set franchise-worst marks for touchdown passes allowed (30) and interceptions collected (six). The 14 takeaways were also easily the worst in team history; the Ravens had only 6.6 percent of drives end with a takeaway, one of the 10 lowest figures for any team in the last two decades. The good news is that extreme turnover totals tend to heavily regress towards the mean, making this a very strong indicator of Baltimore improvement in 2016. (A full table of similar teams is found in the Dallas chapter.)

Finally, the schedule is another valid reason to like a Ravens' resurgence this year. The first seven games of the season feature just one playoff team (middling Washington) from last year. Then the bye week comes before a big home showdown with Pittsburgh in Week 9. To win the division, Baltimore will likely need to steal a road game in Pittsburgh on Christmas or in Cincinnati on New Year's Day.

Over the last three years, Harbaugh, one of the league's best coaches, has done fairly well with the hands he has been dealt. If Newsome has only built the third-best roster with the third-best quarterback in the AFC North, then it is hard to see Baltimore doing more than chasing a wild card. But that's still better than last year, and there are plenty of fans who wish their teams were chasing a wild card as often as the Ravens.

Scott Kacsmar

2015 Ravens Stats by Week

Wk	vs.	W-L	PF	PA	YDF	YDA	TO	Total	Off	Def	ST
1	at DEN	L	13	19	173	219	-1	1%	-31%	-27%	5%
2	at OAK	L	33	37	493	448	-1	-8%	30%	40%	2%
3	CIN	L	24	28	398	458	1	-7%	2%	3%	-7%
4	at PIT	W	23	20	356	263	-2	26%	-12%	-30%	9%
5	CLE	L	30	33	377	505	0	-14%	8%	32%	10%
6	at SF	L	20	25	420	391	-2	-20%	-9%	19%	8%
7	at ARI	L	18	26	276	414	-2	-8%	2%	11%	0%
8	SD	W	29	26	365	371	0	-18%	-2%	33%	17%
9	BYE										
10	JAC	L	20	22	397	258	-3	25%	3%	-19%	3%
11	STL	W	16	13	388	213	2	-14%	-16%	-5%	-3%
12	at CLE	W	33	27	336	338	-2	-5%	-22%	10%	27%
13	at MIA	L	13	15	375	219	-1	-13%	-28%	-19%	-4%
14	SEA	L	6	35	302	424	-1	-37%	-21%	25%	10%
15	KC	L	14	34	366	277	-3	12%	-1%	1%	13%
16	PIT	W	20	17	386	308	3	35%	15%	-10%	10%
17	at CIN	L	16	24	341	292	-2	6%	-14%	-4%	16%

Trends and Splits

	Offense	Rank	Defense	Rank
Total DVOA	-5.3%	20	5.1%	20
Unadjusted VOA	-6.1%	23	6.7%	26
Weighted Trend	-8.3%	22	3.3%	18
Variance	2.7%	1	4.8%	20
Average Opponent	-2.6%	8	2.5%	5
Passing	4.1%	21	19.9%	25
Rushing	-9.2%	18	-14.4%	12
First Down	-11.5%	28	1.1%	17
Second Down	3.9%	15	3.9%	21
Third Down	-7.2%	20	14.8%	26
First Half	-2.9%	19	6.7%	22
Second Half	-7.3%	24	3.3%	16
Red Zone	-7.3%	20	-0.7%	14
Late and Close	-18.8%	29	-1.1%	20

Five-Year Performance

Year	W-L	Pyth W	Est W	PF	PA	TO	Total	Rk	Off	Rk	Def	Rk	ST	Rk	Off AGL	Rk	Def AGL	Rk	Off Age	Rk	Def Age	Rk	ST Age	Rk
2011	12-4	11.2	10.6	378	266	+2	14.5%	7	2.9%	13	-17.1%	1	-5.6%	30	8.0	1	10.9	4	27.8	9	28.2	3	26.6	6
2012	10-6	9.4	9.2	398	344	+9	9.8%	8	3.0%	13	2.2%	19	9.0%	1	8.1	2	46.4	25	27.3	10	27.7	7	26.9	7
2013	8-8	7.1	6.8	320	352	-5	-6.7%	23	-21.7%	30	-8.7%	7	6.3%	3	34.0	16	13.4	5	26.6	18	27.5	6	25.9	22
2014	10-6	10.9	11.5	409	302	+2	21.9%	5	9.4%	9	-4.6%	8	8.0%	2	25.0	10	27.6	8	27.4	8	26.8	15	25.4	31
2015	5-11	6.0	7.5	328	401	-14	-3.0%	17	-5.2%	20	5.1%	20	7.3%	1	70.1	32	26.0	12	26.5	18	27.1	10	25.6	27

2015 Performance Based on Most Common Personnel Groups

BAL Offense					BAL Offense vs. Opponents						BAL Defense					BAL Defense vs. Opponents			
Pers	Freq	Yds	DVOA	Run%	Pers	Freq	Yds	DVOA	Run%		Pers	Freq	Yds	DVOA		Pers	Freq	Yds	DVOA
11	51%	5.0	-9.8%	30%	Base	35%	5.4	7.2%	46%		Base	43%	5.4	3.0%		11	55%	5.9	11.7%
21	21%	5.0	-0.3%	44%	Nickel	47%	5.4	-5.5%	30%		Nickel	53%	5.8	6.5%		12	21%	4.9	-12.2%
12	15%	6.4	15.9%	36%	Dime+	15%	4.9	-9.2%	17%		Dime+	3%	5.2	18.2%		21	8%	5.4	0.3%
10	4%	7.5	20.6%	14%	Goal Line	1%	0.9	0.0%	78%		Goal Line	1%	0.7	36.3%		13	4%	3.4	-29.9%
22	2%	3.4	-19.8%	32%	Big	1%	7.9	14.7%	25%		Big	1%	8.7	-29.6%		22	3%	6.9	18.6%
13	2%	8.0	49.0%	57%												10	2%	7.3	29.4%

Strategic Tendencies

Run/Pass		Rk	Formation		Rk	Pass Rush		Rk	Secondary		Rk	Strategy		Rk
Runs, first half	35%	28	Form: Single Back	76%	14	Rush 3	7.5%	13	4 DB	43%	6	Play action	24%	5
Runs, first down	41%	30	Form: Empty Back	5%	25	Rush 4	63.9%	17	5 DB	53%	17	Avg Box (Off)	6.32	9
Runs, second-long	23%	28	Pers: 3+ WR	57%	17	Rush 5	23.3%	13	6+ DB	3%	28	Avg Box (Def)	6.32	11
Runs, power sit.	55%	17	Pers: 2+ TE/6+ OL	22%	27	Rush 6+	5.4%	19	CB by Sides	81%	12	Offensive Pace	29.37	7
Runs, behind 2H	29%	8	Pers: 6+ OL	3%	14	Sacks by LB	60.8%	3	S/CB Cover Ratio	21%	21	Defensive Pace	30.36	16
Pass, ahead 2H	56%	4	Shotgun/Pistol	47%	28	Sacks by DB	5.4%	21	DB Blitz	11%	10	Go for it on 4th	1.56	5

Marc Trestman keeps telling the press he wants Baltimore to be a run-first offense, but actions speak louder than words. In run/pass ratio, the Ravens went from ranking among the top 10 teams in 2014 to the bottom five teams in 2015, both in the first half and on first downs. And it wasn't just an issue of losing games. In 2014, the Ravens passed only 37 percent of the time when ahead in the second half (32nd). Last year, that went up to 56 percent (fourth). Baltimore used play-action on 42 percent of first-down passes, but then fell to NFL average levels (21 percent, 3 percent) on second and third downs. Despite all the injuries to their fantasy players, the Ravens did manage to drop only 2.7 percent of passes, the lowest rate in the NFL. The Ravens used an extra offensive lineman on 33 plays last year and passed on 52 percent of those plays. No other team passed more than 41 percent of the time when they used six or more O-linemen. Deep passes (16 or more yards past the line of scrimmage) are still a huge issue for the Baltimore defense. The Ravens finished 31st in defensive DVOA against deep passes for the second straight season. For the second straight year, the Ravens got killed by big plays when they blitzed a defensive back, allowing a league-high 10.1 yards per pass. The Ravens defense ranked fifth in DVOA against the run on first downs but 25th against the pass. No defense allowed fewer yards per running back screen than the Ravens, who conceded just 2.5 yards per pass on 17 such plays with -48.0% DVOA (third). You may not be surprised to learn that the Ravens weren't great at closing. Baltimore's offense ranked 29th in late-and-close DVOA (second half or overtime, game within one score), while its defense ranked 20th.

Passing

Player	DYAR	DVOA	Plays	NtYds	Avg	YAC	C%	TD	Int
J.Flacco	17	-10.5%	428	2637	6.2	5.6	65.2%	14	12
R.Mallett	87	3.1%	97	537	5.5	4.2	61.7%	2	2
J.Clausen*	69	1.1%	88	547	6.2	3.9	57.6%	2	3
M.Schaub*	-146	-38.4%	83	513	6.2	4.1	65.0%	3	4

Rushing

Player	DYAR	DVOA	Plays	Yds	Avg	TD	Fum	Suc
J.Forsett	117	9.1%	151	641	4.2	2	0	46%
J.Allen	31	-3.2%	137	518	3.8	1	2	47%
T.West	9	-3.9%	46	180	3.9	0	0	39%
L.Taliaferro	22	31.4%	13	47	3.6	1	0	54%
J.Clausen*	3	1.4%	5	30	6.0	0	0	-
T.West	-31	-51.8%	16	51	3.2	0	2	50%

Receiving

Player	DYAR	DVOA	Plays	Ctch	Yds	Y/C	YAC	TD	C%
K.Aiken	101	-2.7%	127	75	944	12.6	2.8	5	59%
S.Smith	125	9.4%	73	46	670	14.6	5.6	3	63%
C.Givens*	-69	-29.5%	53	19	346	18.2	2.6	1	36%
J.Butler	38	-1.4%	44	31	363	11.7	4.8	0	70%
M.Brown*	-91	-52.1%	30	14	112	8.0	3.3	0	47%
C.Matthews	3	-10.2%	16	9	97	10.8	3.1	1	56%
J.Ross*	-3	-14.9%	14	9	88	9.8	8.0	0	64%
D.Brown	4	-7.4%	11	6	64	10.7	3.8	0	55%
M.Campanaro	1	-10.9%	6	5	35	7.0	5.4	0	83%
D.Waller	-27	-77.0%	6	2	18	9.0	6.5	0	33%
M.Wallace	36	-6.4%	72	39	473	12.1	4.3	2	54%
M.Williams	-23	-14.6%	48	32	268	8.4	4.6	1	67%
C.Gillmore	95	22.7%	47	33	412	12.5	7.4	4	70%
N.Boyle	6	-3.6%	23	18	153	8.5	5.6	0	78%
B.Watson	87	4.9%	110	74	825	11.1	3.3	6	67%
J.Allen	27	-6.2%	62	45	343	7.6	6.7	2	73%
K.Juszczyk	72	7.0%	56	41	321	7.8	6.6	4	73%
J.Forsett	-64	-42.6%	41	31	153	4.9	4.5	0	76%

Offensive Line

Player	Pos	Age	GS	Snaps	Pen	Sk	Pass	Run	Player	Pos	Age	GS	Snaps	Pen	Sk	Pass	Run
Marshal Yanda	RG	32	16/16	1133	4	0.0	2.0	2.5	John Urschel	C/G	25	16/7	547	5	1.0	1.0	1.5
Ricky Wagner	RT	27	16/16	1129	5	0.0	5.0	3.0	Ryan Jensen	C	25	11/6	419	5	1.0	1.0	1.0
Kelechi Osemele*	LG	27	14/14	976	8	0.0	0.0	5.0	Eugene Monroe*	LT	29	6/6	317	2	2.0	3.0	2.0
Jeremy Zuttah	C	30	9/9	613	3	1.0	1.0	1.0	Vladimir Ducasse	G	29	16/11	752	9	2.0	5.0	5.0
James Hurst	LT	25	16/8	572	3	1.5	9.0	0.0									

Year	Yards	ALY	Rank	Power	Rank	Stuff	Rank	2nd Lev	Rank	Open Field	Rank	Sacks	ASR	Rank	Press	Rank	F-Start	Cont.
2013	2.95	3.01	32	49%	31	26%	32	0.76	32	0.30	32	48	7.3%	16	25.0%	16	25	37
2014	4.83	4.25	3	55%	28	21%	23	1.36	3	1.30	1	19	4.5%	4	23.0%	13	16	34
2015	3.97	3.87	14	54%	28	23%	25	1.21	11	0.62	21	24	3.8%	2	23.5%	12	18	25

2015 ALY by direction: Left End 3.3 (20) Left Tackle 3.43 (21) Mid/Guard 4.01 (11) Right Tackle 3.82 (16) Right End 4.59 (3)

Exactly why were the Ravens in the left tackle market when Eugene Monroe had a base salary of $6.5 million? On one side, you can argue the draft presented great young options and Monroe had not offered stellar play or consistent presence (with 15 games missed over the last two seasons). On the other hand, this was an easy way to move on from a player who was outspoken about the use of medical marijuana. Either way, Monroe is gone and the Ravens have a new left tackle. ☞ While Laremy Tunsil was the draft's grand prize in the eyes of most, Ronnie Stanley has the potential to be this team's best tackle since Jonathan Ogden. ☞ By any means necessary, Baltimore needs to keep backup James Hurst on the bench. Hurst was the only starter on the Ravens last year to rank outside of the top 12 in snaps per blown block at his position. He was 24th with 63.6 snaps per blown block, which at least was better than the horrible 23.0 snaps per blown block he had as a rookie in 2014. ☞ While Kelechi Osemele was at his best last season, it's hard to argue with Baltimore's decision to let Oakland make him the highest-paid guard in the NFL. Marshal Yanda is one of the game's best guards, and John Urschel fared well at center last year when Jeremy Zuttah was injured. Urschel should be able to handle the left guard spot this year without a noticeable drop.

Defensive Front Seven

Defensive Line	Age	Pos	G	Snaps	Plays	TmPct	Rk	Stop	Dfts	BTkl	Runs	St%	Rk	RuYd	Rk	Sack	Hit	Hur	Dsrpt
							Overall					vs. Run				Pass Rush			
Brandon Williams	27	DT	16	727	55	6.9%	22	46	14	6	50	84%	17	2.0	36	2.0	2	5.0	2
Timmy Jernigan	24	DE	15	531	37	4.9%	42	30	11	3	30	80%	26	2.9	64	4.0	9	12.0	0
Lawrence Guy	26	DE	16	485	47	5.9%	33	38	12	3	38	79%	37	2.7	61	4.5	7	5.0	0
Chris Canty*	34	DE	9	286	20	4.4%	53	15	5	1	17	76%	42	1.6	20	1.0	3	6.5	1
Carl Davis	24	DT	13	239	13	2.0%	--	9	1	0	10	70%	--	3.6	--	0.0	0	2.5	2

Edge Rushers	Age	Pos	G	Snaps	Plays	TmPct	Rk	Stop	Dfts	BTkl	Runs	St%	Rk	RuYd	Rk	Sack	Hit	Hur	Dsrpt
							Overall					vs. Run				Pass Rush			
Courtney Upshaw*	27	OLB	16	799	53	6.6%	18	37	12	7	40	73%	54	2.8	70	2.0	7	14.5	1
Elvis Dumervil	32	OLB	16	792	49	6.1%	25	41	17	3	33	88%	8	2.7	64	6.0	16	28.5	1
Za'Darius Smith	24	OLB	15	405	31	4.1%	65	21	9	1	17	65%	75	2.6	62	5.5	3	7.0	1

Linebackers	Age	Pos	G	Snaps	Plays	TmPct	Rk	Stop	Dfts	BTkl	Runs	St%	Rk	RuYd	Rk	Sack	Hit	Hur	Tgts	Suc%	Rk	AdjYd	Rk	PD	Int
							Overall					vs. Run				Pass Rush				vs. Pass				
C.J. Mosley	24	ILB	16	1053	123	15.3%	13	72	27	11	63	67%	32	4.0	68	4.0	5	9.5	40	54%	45	6.2	38	2	0
Daryl Smith*	34	ILB	16	981	124	15.5%	11	68	18	14	83	58%	61	3.7	54	3.0	1	2	23	44%	61	6.8	46	3	1

Year	Yards	ALY	Rank	Power	Rank	Stuff	Rank	2nd Level	Rank	Open Field	Rank	Sacks	ASR	Rank	Press	Rank
2013	3.92	3.95	19	59%	8	18%	16	1.08	14	0.48	9	40	7.3%	10	24.8%	15
2014	3.53	3.55	7	55%	4	18%	19	0.86	2	0.46	2	49	8.0%	5	25.1%	15
2015	3.96	3.90	20	68%	21	18%	24	0.94	2	0.67	12	37	6.1%	19	23.9%	26

2015 ALY by direction:	Left End 4.29 (24)	Left Tackle 4.27 (25)	Mid/Guard 3.93 (16)	Right Tackle 3.77 (19)	Right End 2.95 (10)

Life without Haloti Ngata did not suck as Baltimore still finished 12th in rush defense DVOA, led by nose tackle Brandon Williams, arguably the most underrated player on the team. ☞ Timmy Jernigan and Lawrence Guy were also helpful against the run and helped the pass rush. ☞ While Chris Canty's departure leaves a hole in veteran depth, the Ravens do have two recent mid-round picks ready to contribute after early injury issues: nose tackle Carl Davis, a 2015 third-rounder from Iowa, and Brent Urban, a 2014 fourth-rounder from Virginia. Urban is the player who blocked the game-winning field goal that led to Baltimore's shocking Week 12 win over Cleveland, in his first game back from a torn bicep. ☞ C.J. Mosley flashed a bit more in his rookie season, but he also had more help around him then. ☞ Daryl Smith's release leaves an open job at inside linebacker, which could be filled by second-round rookie Kamalei Correa. He was known more as an edge rusher at Boise State, but has been versatile enough to play inside, which could be the easiest way to get him on the field right away. If not, this could be Arthur Brown's last chance to not go down as a bust. The third option would be third-year backup Zach Orr, who played a bit in the second half of the season and had horrible stats against the pass in a small sample size. Only one of Orr's eight tackles after a pass reception stopped the ballcarrier short of a successful play. ☞ Last year's torn Achilles could be damaging to Terrell Suggs' Hall of Fame case. His 106.5 sacks rank 24th since 1982, but this is a hard injury to return from at age 34. Only 15 players have had a double-digit sack season at age 34 or older. ☞ Elvis Dumervil, now 32, had his lowest sack total (6.0) since 2008, but at least the hurries were still there. He may be getting a step too slow to finish, or perhaps it was easier for quarterbacks to get the ball away under pressure without Suggs coming from the other side. ☞ Dumervil, who fell in the 2006 draft due to size despite his massive collegiate production, could be a good mentor for fifth-round rookie Matt Judon, who had 20 sacks for Division II Grand Valley State last year.

Defensive Secondary

Secondary	Age	Pos	G	Snaps	Plays	TmPct	Rk	Stop	Dfts	BTkl	Runs	St%	Rk	RuYd	Rk	Tgts	Tgt%	Rk	Dist	Suc%	Rk	AdjYd	Rk	PD	Int
							Overall					vs. Run					vs. Pass							
Jimmy Smith	28	CB	16	1001	64	8.0%	48	22	9	8	10	40%	39	5.1	15	64	18.2%	26	15.3	49%	53	8.6	55	7	3
Will Hill*	26	SS	16	955	70	8.7%	50	27	17	6	25	36%	45	10.2	61	25	7.4%	35	13.0	63%	22	9.1	54	5	1
Kendrick Lewis	28	FS	15	930	63	8.4%	52	27	8	5	33	39%	40	5.9	22	21	6.3%	20	14.9	59%	32	10.7	66	4	0
Lardarius Webb	31	CB	15	889	65	8.6%	35	30	8	7	16	38%	44	5.5	19	58	18.5%	29	12.3	61%	6	7.4	33	10	1
Shareece Wright	29	CB	11	485	45	8.2%	--	17	6	2	8	25%	--	8.0	--	44	25.8%	--	12.4	58%	--	6.3	--	5	0
Kyle Arrington	30	CB	15	339	31	4.1%	--	9	1	0	1	0%	--	11.0	--	28	23.5%	--	11.3	36%	--	9.2	--	2	0
Eric Weddle	31	FS	13	751	81	13.1%	10	36	15	9	45	40%	36	6.8	35	19	6.9%	29	9.5	64%	19	6.5	29	5	0

Year	Pass D Rank	vs. #1 WR	Rk	vs. #2 WR	Rk	vs. Other WR	Rk	vs. TE	Rk	vs. RB	Rk
2013	9	-27.2%	2	-1.8%	13	5.9%	22	2.1%	16	-10.6%	9
2014	15	3.4%	18	8.6%	23	11.7%	24	4.8%	21	-13.5%	9
2015	25	-5.4%	10	18.3%	26	21.5%	29	10.7%	23	-0.4%	16

Cornerback Jimmy Smith looked like a rising star following his 2013 season, but he missed half of 2014 and had his most disappointing charting metrics yet in 2015. Still, Smith grabbed three of Baltimore's paltry six interceptions and remains the No. 1 corner on the team. ☞ A 31-year-old Eric Weddle is not going to improve your defense's takeaways, but he gives the Ravens more run-stopping ability than Kendrick Lewis did. Lewis stays as the first safety off the bench at a position where Baltimore needed bodies following the disappointment of Matt Elam (who missed all of 2015 with a torn biceps) and the 10-game suspension that led to Will Hill's release. ☞ Lardarius Webb once looked poised to ascend to the elite tier of corners, but has not been the same since an ACL tear in 2012. He is making a full conversion to safety after tinkering with it late last year. This is not uncommon for an older player, and it was very successful in prolonging the careers of Rod Woodson and Charles Woodson. Webb still displayed good coverage skills last season, but this should help keep him active in the middle of the field and covering mostly slot receivers. ☞ The only problem with Webb's move are the holes left behind Smith at cornerback. Kyle Arrington was roasted in limited action last season after coming over from New England. Shareece Wright has been up and down in his career; he signed with San Francisco last spring and only ended up in Baltimore because the 49ers cut him before he ever played a down for them. Will Davis, a 2013 third-round pick, has yet to start a game in his three-year career. ☞ The draft provides some hope, as Tavon Young (Temple) could ascend to a nickelback role, but his lack of size dropped him to the fourth round.

Special Teams

Year	DVOA	Rank	FG/XP	Rank	Net Kick	Rank	Kick Ret	Rank	Net Punt	Rank	Punt Ret	Rank	Hidden	Rank
2013	6.3%	3	11.4	2	-1.4	21	9.2	3	-2.9	24	15.5	2	-1.1	17
2014	8.0%	2	5.3	7	8.3	4	10.2	3	17.9	1	-1.9	14	-3.2	24
2015	7.3%	1	4.5	7	4.5	6	4.7	6	16.0	2	7.0	6	-0.6	17

While Flacco and the revamped defensive core have both been inconsistent, John Harbaugh's experience with special teams continues to shine through after another No. 1 finish in DVOA in 2015. It was Baltimore's fourth-straight top-three finish on special teams, a feat that has only been equaled by the 1990-93 Falcons since 1989. ☞ Another team that came close to this accomplishment was the 2001-04 Eagles, but the 2002 team finished fifth. Who was the special teams coordinator for that team? Oh, yes… it was John Harbaugh. ☞ It helps when kicker Justin Tucker and punter Sam Koch are among the best in the league. Tucker led all kickers in gross kickoff value for the second year in a row and has been more consistent than most kickers on field goals. ESPN's Kevin Seifert wrote an article last December about how Koch has quietly changed the punting game[1] with unpredictable directional kicks. We tend to gloss over the punting unit, but it is an advantage for the Ravens. ☞ On the return front, Kaelin Clay did a respectable job down the stretch, but his roster spot could be challenged by an intriguing sixth-round prospect. Navy quarterback Keenan Reynolds has made the conversion to wide receiver and returner, and he scored an FBS-record 88 career touchdowns in the triple-option offense. He has permission from the Navy to play for Baltimore this year and could be an exciting player to watch, as well as a good story.

---

1 http://espn.go.com/blog/nflnation/post/_/id/191948/sam-koch-has-changed-the-punting-game-and-almost-no-one-noticed

Buffalo Bills

2015 record: 8-8	Total DVOA: 2.7% (12th)	2016 Mean Projection: 8.2 wins	On the Clock (0-4): 8%
Pythagorean Wins: 8.5 (13th)	Offense: 9.8% (9th)	Postseason Odds: 39.9%	Mediocrity (5-7): 31%
Snap-Weighted Age: 26.3 (23rd)	Defense: 8.6% (24th)	Super Bowl Odds: 5.7%	Playoff Contender (8-10): 42%
Average Opponent: -0.7% (18th)	Special Teams: 1.5% (12th)	Proj. Avg. Opponent: 0.7% (13th)	Super Bowl Contender (11+): 19%

2015: Rex Ryan's team is explosive and dynamic on offense but cannot generate a pass rush. Wait … what!?

2016: You'll lose your mind when Ryan Twins are two of a kind.

The 2015 Buffalo Bills made absolutely no sense.

They weren't nonsensical in the ways Rex Ryan teams are usually nonsensical. Not exclusively, anyway. Oh, there were goofy press conferences. There was some excessive bragging and beefing. There were too many sloppy penalties, too much attention on picking controversial weekly captains. There was the usual roller coaster of great efforts against heated rivals (A sweep of the Jets! A Monday night scare of the Patriots!) mixed with flat performances when no personal Ryan grudges were at stake (losses to the Jaguars and most of the NFC East).

That's the kind of nonsense that longtime Ryan observers can make sense of.

The 2015 Bills made no sense because they finished ninth in the NFL in offensive DVOA and 24th in the NFL in defensive DVOA.

Ryan is a defense-oriented coach, of course. Tyrod Taylor was a novice quarterback; he missed a pair of starts and the only times he looked at his second-read receiver was when Taylor wanted him to block while he scrambled. LeSean McCoy also missed four starts; the Bills relied on their third and fourth running backs to get them through several games. Percy Harvin had the most Percy Harvinest season ever, playing five games and catching 19 passes while earning $6 million. The offensive line, whose biggest name was a guy who spent a year out of the NFL for having the social graces of a cornered warthog, finished 23rd in the NFL in adjusted line yards and 27th in adjusted sack rate.

The Bills offense had every reason to be below average, if not terrible. Yet the Bills led the NFL in rushing yards and yards per carry. They finished eighth in the NFL in yards per offensive play, ninth in yards per pass play, seventh in interception rate, and 12th in points scored.

The defense, meanwhile, was coming off two straight seasons ranked in the DVOA top five, thanks to one of the most talented lines in the NFL: Mario Williams, Kyle Williams, Marcell Dareus, and Jerry Hughes. That quartet combined for 40 sacks in 2014, with the Bills totaling a league-leading 54 sacks. The combination of the devastating incumbent pass rushers and Ryan's desire to unleash anarchy looked like the formula for a 60-sack season, with a talented secondary (Leodis McKelvin, Stephon Gilmore, Corey Graham, rookie Ronald Darby) relegated to mop-up duty.

Inexplicably, almost impossibly, the Bills finished next-to-last in the NFL in both adjusted sack rate and total sacks (with 21). Only the Falcons fielded a more hapless pass rush. The Bills finished 29th in adjusted line yards, despite the fact that Dareus and Kyle Williams are well-regarded run defenders and Corbin Bryant played well when Kyle Williams got injured. The secondary played well, and Darby performed at a Rookie of the Year level, yet the Bills ranked 19th in the NFL in passing yards allowed per game and 23rd in defensive DVOA on third down: if you cannot rush the opposing quarterback at all, even the Legion of Boom won't do you much good.

None of this adds up. At all. Even if you wrap your brain around the good offense-bad defense-zero pass rush paradigm, you are faced with the internal inconsistencies. If the Bills offensive line looks so mediocre in the metrics, how did Mike Gillislee and Karlos Williams combine to average 5.7 yards per rush? Even if Mario Williams was unhappy playing in Ryan's scheme, what happened to the rest of the pass rush? How does a team that never sacks a quarterback somehow rack up 12 unnecessary roughness penalties?

Even the official storylines don't hold water. Take Subpar Mario, who was released after a season of disgruntled gold-bricking. Mario (there are so many Williamses on the Bills that calling the most famous one by his first name will make life easier for all of us) was unhappy with his role in the defense, leading to a tall tale that Ryan was dropping him into coverage a dozen times per game instead of letting him rush the edge. Extensive tape grinding reveals, however, that Mario only dropped into flat zones once or twice per game for most of the season, no more than any marquee pass-rusher is used as a zone-blitz decoy.

Mario was often shifted inside so Manny Lawson could blitz the edge, which may be closer to both the crux of his complaint and the problem with the Bills defense. Lawson was terrible in most phases of the game, as was fellow linebacker Preston Brown, but in particular both were shockingly slow and ineffective pass-rushers who combined for just one sack on well over 100 blitzes. Mario wasn't just mad about dropping into coverage ten times per month. He was mad about crashing into the tackle and guard as a sacrificial pawn while Lawson huffed and puffed around the edge.

Limiting a great pass-rusher to feature an awful one was a

2016 Bills Schedule

Week	Opp.	Week	Opp.	Week	Opp.
1	at BAL	7	at MIA	13	at OAK
2	NYJ (Thu.)	8	NE	14	PIT
3	ARI	9	at SEA (Mon.)	15	CLE
4	at NE	10	BYE	16	MIA (Sat.)
5	at LA	11	at CIN	17	at NYJ
6	SF	12	JAC		

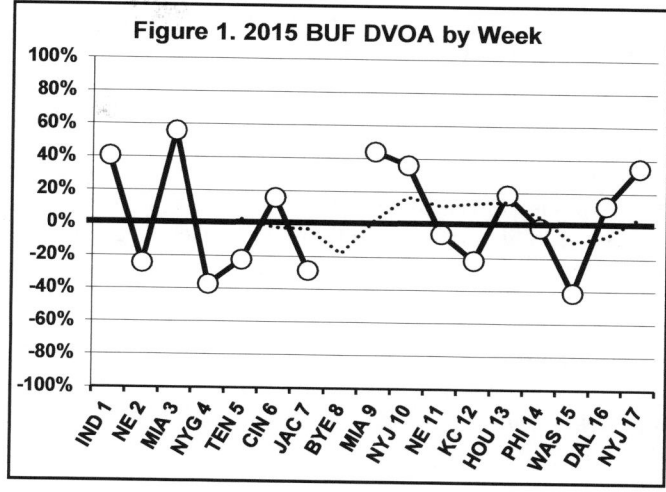

Figure 1. 2015 BUF DVOA by Week

dumb strategy, but it doesn't excuse the fact that Mario was clearly chicken-fighting his blockers late in the year: see the Week 15 Redskins game, where right tackle Morgan Moses defeated him all afternoon with no difficulty, as Exhibit A against the Dolphins having acquired a bargain.

While Stupor Mario shadowboxed, Jerry Hughes overcompensated by trying to jump offside and decapitate the nearest offensive player. Hughes committed 14 penalties for 109 yards. He was always foul-prone (13 for 84 in 2014) and Ryan's philosophy and rhetoric aren't calculated to make the fellas rein themselves in.

The Bills led the NFL with 169 penalties (including declined and offsetting) and 1,249 penalty yards. Everybody got in on the action, as the Bills were second in offensive penalties, second in special teams penalties, and eighth in defensive penalties. Bills penalties on both sides of the ball came in mini sprees, sometimes with Hughes putting the cherry of an unsportsmanlike conduct foul atop a penalty sundae that gave the offense 30 yards of free field position.

The secrets of the inscrutable 2015 Bills defense are starting to reveal themselves: star players behaved counterproductively, bad players were given high-profile roles, and penalties bundled together to give opponents "free trip to the red zone" coupons.

A close look at the offense reveals similar mysteries, starting with an offensive line that committed 38 holding penalties (third highest in the NFL) and a healthy sprinkling of chop blocks, face-mask penalties and other acts of villainy/sloppiness. Offensive penalties cost the Bills a few games (the Eagles game, primarily) while working in the background to negate the offense's greatest strength: the ability to mix runs and passes while keeping down-and-distance "on schedule" to create big-play opportunities.

Offensive coordinator Greg Roman arrived from San Francisco and installed the Colin Kaepernick Starter Kit for Tyrod Taylor, who quickly established himself as the starting quarterback in training camp. Roman's take on the mobile quarterback deluxe option package is dynamic and multi-faceted. Roman likes intricate pull-trap blocking patterns, complex formations with lots of versatile H-back types, occasional flea flickers and other gadgets, and well-timed play-action deep passes.

The general philosophy was perfect for the Bills. It suited Taylor's athleticism and inexperience. It satisfied Rex Ryan's desire for both turnover-free offensive conservatism and unpredictability. The Bills were short on playmakers besides

Sammy Watkins but had roles for fullback/H-back types Jerome Felton and Charles Clay. Richie Incognito, Cordy Glenn, and other Bills linemen took pride in disemboweling defenders after a running start. McCoy and the other backs were deadly in the open field. The Bills became explosive, if inefficient. They finished second in the NFL in both second-level and open-field yards. Taylor and Watkins connected for ten passes of 30-plus yards. The Bills were a nasty team to defend when they could coat simple sweeps and rollout bombs with read-option and pulling-guard gingerbread.

Unfortunately, the Bills were not nearly as effective when forced to move systematically down the field. They led the league in three-and-out drives, with a whopping 27.8 percent. (The league average was 22.6 percent.) The Bills were a run-oriented team with a bad habit of putting itself in pass-oriented down-and-distance situations because of penalties and their boom-or-bust running style. Once forced to throw, their lack of secondary targets and Taylor's tendency to run from a clean pocket if he didn't like his first read hamstrung their ability to sustain drives or play catch-up. When the slobberknocker tactics and option trappings failed, the Bills offense was doomed, and the defense wasn't good enough to pick up the slack.

We've spent a long time dissecting the 2015 Bills here because:

a) Not much has changed;
b) Most of the changes were not positive; and
c) No matter how analytic-minded you try to be, projecting the future of a Rex Ryan team often descends into psychoanalysis of Rex Ryan.

Distressing health news dominated the Bills' spring. Edgerusher Shaq Lawson, the team's first-round pick out of Clemson, needed offseason shoulder surgery. Watkins had surgery to repair a broken bone in his foot. Two critical players would miss weeks of offseason activities. Watkins is optimistically slated for a Week 1 return. Lawson's status is less certain.

Lawson appeared to be an excellent replacement for Mario Williams: similarly talented but cheaper and much less entitled. With training camp in doubt, it's hard to imagine Lawson having anything close to a Mario-level impact as a rookie.

Watkins isn't just the Bills' top receiving threat, but practically their only receiving threat. The team lost Chris Hogan from a thin receiving corps and added only sixth-round speedster Kolby Listenbee (TCU). Marquise Goodwin (another one-dimensional burner) spent the summer participating in the Olympics, Harvin is off the grid, and the depth chart is clogged with hangers-on like Greg Salas and Greg Little. If Watkins suffers any setback, Robert Woods will be the Bills' go-to receiver, and defenses will load up against the run like they are facing a Big 8 team from the 1970s.

Other draft picks brought linebacker Reggie Ragland, defensive tackle Adolphus Washington, and quarterback Cardale Jones. Ragland, an old-school between-the-tackles middle linebacker, should upgrade the gap integrity against the run; the Lawson-Brown gang was often slow to react and easy to root out of the hole. Washington adds beef to the interior line and that special Ryan touch: he was arrested for soliciting a prostitute from a print want-ad who turned out to be an undercover cop.

As for Jones, he's the worst kind of hedged-bet quarterback prospect. He's famous enough to excite the fan base, talented and streaky enough to cause training camp man-crushes, but unreliable enough to get benched in his final season at Ohio State, squandering a chance to lead one of the most talented teams in college football history. Jones has many of Taylor's strengths but more of his weaknesses; given Ryan's mercurial nature and Roman's past history of quarterback swapping, it's easy to imagine the Bills deciding to "go with the hot hand" if Jones makes a big play or two, but hard to imagine that decision resulting in more wins.

There's one other high-profile arrival who demands attention. Rob Ryan, fired at midseason by a Saints team that finished with the worst defensive DVOA in history, was hired by his twin brother in February and eventually handed the title of Assistant Head Coach/Defense. Rob explained to Jenny Vrentas at MMQB.com in May that he actually "did a damn good job and got fired for it" in New Orleans, claiming that he was hamstrung by Jairus Byrd's unavailability and the Saints' insistence that he run a Seahawks-style defense.

Sean Payton shot back hours later, stating that the Saints defense had basic, fundamental problems like getting the proper number of players on the field and communicating assignments. Anyone who watched Saints film or spent any time at their practices (I spent a few days at Saints camp last summer) knows that Payton is right: few teams had more trouble getting 11 players onto the field and ready for the snap than the Rob Ryan Saints. The Rob Ryan Cowboys, Browns, and Raiders were rarely much better. Rob Ryan is just a fundamentally bad coach.

Rex's decision to rescue and reward his twin brother, then allow him to cut loose with stereophonic Ryan lunacy that falls apart against even the slightest scrutiny, reminds us that self-awareness is a fundamental problem for any Ryan-coached team. Rex underlined the point by declaring that the Bills "won the offseason" at the end of June minicamps, an odd assertion for a coach who lost his top draft pick and top receiver to injuries. Our projection system doesn't play by the Ryan Rules, so it's hard to tell if obvious problems will be addressed, worsened or just spackled over with tough-guy speeches and one-liners.

Normally, we point out that penalties fluctuate heavily from year to year and point out that the Bills are unlikely to commit another 169 of them this year. But Hughes and Incognito remain notorious penalty machines, the Ryan Twins can't help but stress rootin'-tootin' outlaw tactics which inevitably cause an extra personal foul or two, and Rob Ryan could even cause an uptick in 12-men-on-the-field penalties and encroachment fouls.

Normally, we would expect the Bills defense to improve by sheer regression to the mean, plus the addition of three high draft picks and the presence of a defense-oriented staff. But Lawson's injury and Rob Ryan's presence throw that prediction into doubt.

Normally, a 26-year-old quarterback finishing seventh in the NFL in DVOA despite a depleted offensive skill-position corps would be an encouraging sign of offensive growth potential. But the Bills did nothing to support Taylor in the offseason and everything to undermine him, from drafting Jones to letting Hogan walk without a replacement to making their pursuit of other quarterbacks a poorly kept spring secret.

Nothing is really certain, or even all that predictable, about the 2016 Bills, except that they will be a Rex Ryan team. Any hope that Rex would be less Rexy in Buffalo than he was in New York was abandoned when he signed IK Enemkpali after the Geno Smith punching incident last summer. Ryan has spent years claiming to have "learned his lesson" but has a blind spot about making real, substantive changes to the way he runs a team. The carnival atmosphere is the only thing you can always depend upon when Rex is calling the shots. As long as it prevails, you can count upon not counting upon anything else.

Mike Tanier

2015 Bills Stats by Week

Wk	vs.	W-L	PF	PA	YDF	YDA	TO	Total	Off	Def	ST
1	IND	W	27	14	342	304	3	41%	41%	19%	19%
2	NE	L	32	40	349	507	-1	-24%	-2%	13%	-9%
3	at MIA	W	41	14	428	391	3	56%	43%	-20%	-8%
4	NYG	L	10	24	313	303	-1	-37%	-41%	-10%	-6%
5	at TEN	W	14	13	209	276	0	-22%	-20%	0%	-2%
6	CIN	L	21	34	368	355	-1	16%	45%	22%	-7%
7	vs. JAC (UK)	L	31	34	375	295	-3	-28%	-38%	6%	16%
8	BYE										
9	MIA	W	33	17	420	397	1	44%	69%	34%	8%
10	at NYJ	W	22	17	280	318	4	36%	7%	-21%	9%
11	at NE	L	13	20	319	356	0	-6%	0%	-5%	-11%
12	at KC	L	22	30	415	413	-2	-22%	16%	36%	-2%
13	HOU	W	30	21	390	401	1	19%	50%	37%	6%
14	at PHI	L	20	23	412	348	-1	-1%	-3%	3%	4%
15	at WAS	L	25	35	452	431	1	-41%	17%	58%	1%
16	DAL	W	16	6	408	307	0	12%	10%	-1%	1%
17	NYJ	W	22	17	295	300	2	35%	-3%	-32%	7%

Trends and Splits

	Offense	Rank	Defense	Rank
Total DVOA	9.8%	9	8.6%	24
Unadjusted VOA	12.0%	7	6.5%	18
Weighted Trend	10.8%	8	11.5%	29
Variance	9.9%	28	6.0%	24
Average Opponent	-0.4%	15	-1.3%	21
Passing	20.5%	12	13.1%	18
Rushing	8.8%	2	2.0%	30
First Down	10.3%	8	5.8%	22
Second Down	19.7%	4	11.0%	29
Third Down	-6.4%	19	10.2%	23
First Half	3.6%	12	14.0%	30
Second Half	17.1%	2	3.8%	17
Red Zone	1.6%	16	11.2%	24
Late and Close	-3.3%	19	-10.4%	13

Five-Year Performance

Year	W-L	Pyth W	Est W	PF	PA	TO	Total	Rk	Off	Rk	Def	Rk	ST	Rk	Off AGL	Rk	Def AGL	Rk	Off Age	Rk	Def Age	Rk	ST Age	Rk
2011	6-10	6.4	7.1	372	434	+1	-9.7%	23	0.3%	16	8.3%	24	-1.7%	24	33.8	20	37.1	21	26.3	27	27.4	12	26.7	5
2012	6-10	5.7	6.5	344	435	-13	-12.1%	23	-4.2%	20	10.6%	27	2.7%	9	51.5	29	28.2	16	26.2	25	26.7	18	26.5	10
2013	6-10	6.7	7.1	339	388	+3	-3.3%	18	-11.5%	25	-13.8%	4	-5.6%	30	17.9	6	26.4	12	26.4	24	26.0	26	26.1	12
2014	9-7	9.6	9.0	343	289	+7	10.5%	9	-11.2%	26	-15.5%	2	6.2%	4	27.2	14	31.9	11	26.6	21	26.1	26	26.1	15
2015	8-8	8.5	8.8	379	359	+6	2.7%	12	9.8%	9	8.6%	24	1.5%	12	37.2	19	43.3	28	26.2	21	26.4	21	26.5	9

2015 Performance Based on Most Common Personnel Groups

BUF Offense					BUF Offense vs. Opponents					BUF Defense					BUF Defense vs. Opponents			
Pers	Freq	Yds	DVOA	Run%	Pers	Freq	Yds	DVOA	Run%	Pers	Freq	Yds	DVOA		Pers	Freq	Yds	DVOA
11	45%	6.2	21.1%	32%	Base	48%	5.5	7.1%	59%	Base	33%	5.6	4.9%		11	51%	6.1	17.9%
12	21%	5.7	17.5%	41%	Nickel	36%	6.6	29.6%	35%	Nickel	52%	5.6	5.8%		12	25%	5.9	13.8%
21	15%	6.4	5.3%	55%	Dime+	15%	5.5	-4.8%	10%	Dime+	12%	8.0	54.6%		21	5%	5.5	-1.3%
22	6%	5.1	9.8%	76%	Goal Line	0%	0.8	16.1%	100%	Goal Line	1%	1.0	-24.1%		10	5%	5.8	-43.3%
620	2%	6.5	42.3%	95%	Big	1%	5.2	31.3%	58%	Big	2%	1.5	-43.4%		13	4%	5.0	-18.3%
621	2%	7.1	76.0%	60%											611	2%	4.1	-26.7%
															612	2%	3.7	-18.3%

Strategic Tendencies

Run/Pass		Rk	Formation		Rk	Pass Rush		Rk	Secondary		Rk	Strategy		Rk
Runs, first half	45%	2	Form: Single Back	67%	26	Rush 3	13.6%	2	4 DB	33%	16	Play action	17%	24
Runs, first down	55%	3	Form: Empty Back	5%	23	Rush 4	55.3%	24	5 DB	52%	18	Avg Box (Off)	6.37	6
Runs, second-long	35%	9	Pers: 3+ WR	48%	28	Rush 5	18.2%	25	6+ DB	12%	15	Avg Box (Def)	6.21	20
Runs, power sit.	67%	4	Pers: 2+ TE/6+ OL	37%	13	Rush 6+	12.9%	3	CB by Sides	87%	6	Offensive Pace	31.39	23
Runs, behind 2H	29%	6	Pers: 6+ OL	8%	5	Sacks by LB	11.9%	29	S/CB Cover Ratio	21%	23	Defensive Pace	28.58	1
Pass, ahead 2H	39%	31	Shotgun/Pistol	78%	3	Sacks by DB	19.0%	1	DB Blitz	15%	5	Go for it on 4th	1.33	8

Regression warning: Buffalo had strong luck on fumble recoveries in 2015, recovering 14 of 21 fumbles on offense and five of eight fumbles on defense. ☜ When it came to passes with and without play-action fakes, only the Rams had a bigger DVOA gap than the Bills. Buffalo gained 9.9 yards per play with a league-high 72.3% DVOA when using play-action, but just 6.2 yards per play and 13.6% DVOA without play-action. ☜ The Bills defense had the opposite trend. They had a league-high gap in DVOA the other way, allowing 6.0 yards per play and -9.6% DVOA with play-action but 6.7 yards per play and 20.4% DVOA without. ☜ Buffalo had a 24.4% rushing DVOA when running with three or more receivers on the field, the best in the league (5.59 yards per carry, fourth). However, the Bills defense allowed a 11.7% rushing DVOA with three or more receivers, the worst in the league (5.15 yards per carry, 29th). ☜ Buffalo's offense threw only 14 percent of passes to the middle of the field; only Chicago threw less to the middle. ☜ On third and fourth downs, the Bills offense ranked second in rushing DVOA but 29th in passing DVOA. ☜ Bills opponents threw a league-high 28.9 percent of passes to their No. 1 receivers. ☜ Also, Bills opponents only threw 13.1 percent of passes to running backs. Every other defense in the NFL was above 17 percent.

Passing

Player	DYAR	DVOA	Plays	NtYds	Avg	YAC	C%	TD	Int
T.Taylor	536	9.8%	417	2810	6.7	4.7	63.7%	20	6
EJ.Manuel	-26	-16.0%	89	509	5.7	3.2	63.4%	3	3

Rushing

Player	DYAR	DVOA	Plays	Yds	Avg	TD	Fum	Suc
L.McCoy	139	8.8%	202	895	4.4	3	1	47%
K.Williams	159	30.4%	93	517	5.6	7	1	56%
T.Taylor	133	19.8%	87	586	6.7	4	2	–
M.Gillislee	54	20.9%	47	267	5.7	3	1	36%
A.Dixon*	-18	-26.9%	21	44	2.1	1	0	29%
EJ.Manuel	34	20.8%	16	66	4.1	1	0	–
D.Herron*	-23	-60.4%	11	37	3.4	0	1	55%
P.Harvin*	27	47.8%	5	31	6.2	0	0	–

Receiving

Player	DYAR	DVOA	Plays	Ctch	Yds	Y/C	YAC	TD	C%
S.Watkins	312	28.9%	96	60	1047	17.5	3.0	9	63%
R.Woods	-12	-14.6%	80	47	552	11.7	3.3	3	59%
C.Hogan*	1	-12.4%	59	36	450	12.5	3.0	2	61%
P.Harvin*	14	-6.5%	30	19	218	11.5	4.4	1	63%
L.Hankerson	51	1.1%	46	26	327	12.6	4.6	3	57%
C.Clay	6	-6.0%	77	51	528	10.4	4.6	3	66%
C.Gragg	0	-7.6%	20	12	150	12.5	4.2	0	60%
J.Dray	-41	-43.7%	16	6	61	10.2	5.7	0	38%
L.McCoy	30	-2.0%	50	32	295	9.2	9.0	2	64%
K.Williams	11	-2.0%	14	11	96	8.7	4.0	2	79%
A.Dixon*	6	3.5%	7	6	44	7.3	4.0	0	86%
M.Gillislee	4	-4.0%	7	6	29	4.8	5.2	0	86%

Offensive Line

Player	Pos	Age	GS	Snaps	Pen	Sk	Pass	Run	Player	Pos	Age	GS	Snaps	Pen	Sk	Pass	Run
Richie Incognito	LG	33	16/16	1075	7	2.0	7.0	5.0	Seantrel Henderson	RT	24	10/10	593	7	1.0	7.0	2.0
Eric Wood	C	30	16/16	1075	3	2.0	2.0	5.5	Kraig Urbik*	LG	31	16/4	432	4	1.0	3.0	1.5
Cordy Glenn	LT	27	16/16	1059	7	4.0	9.0	5.0	Jordan Mills	RT	26	10/5	354	6	1.0	5.0	2.0
John Miller	RG	23	12/12	647	5	3.0	14.0	2.0	Cyrus Kouandjio	OL	23	12/2	227	5	1.0	1.0	0.0

Year	Yards	ALY	Rank	Power	Rank	Stuff	Rank	2nd Lev	Rank	Open Field	Rank	Sacks	ASR	Rank	Press	Rank	F-Start	Cont.
2013	4.38	3.85	16	65%	14	18%	11	1.14	14	0.96	6	48	8.5%	29	21.4%	6	12	41
2014	3.83	3.62	26	63%	16	17%	7	0.94	30	0.64	20	39	6.9%	20	21.7%	8	19	37
2015	4.68	3.59	23	71%	10	21%	17	1.28	2	1.18	2	42	8.4%	27	26.8%	19	15	26
2015 ALY by direction:			Left End 3.53 (18)			Left Tackle 4.28 (8)			Mid/Guard 3.55 (29)			Right Tackle 3.63 (22)			Right End 3.23 (21)			

The Bills' penalty issues on the line were a byproduct of everyone chipping in rather than one egregious offender. No Buffalo lineman finished among the top 40 linemen in penalties, but the Bills were one of just two teams not to have a single qualifying offensive lineman (at least 160 snaps) commit fewer than three penalties. (The other was Minnesota, which had a good excuse: the same five linemen started all 16 games.) ☜ Early word suggests that Jordan Mills, who joined the Bills midseason off of Detroit's practice squad, has the upper hand over 2014 draftees Seantrel Henderson and Cyrus Kouandjio for the starting right tackle job. Mills was subpar as Chicago's starter in 2014, ranking 50th out of 71 offensive tackles in snaps per blown block (37.0). Of course, this probably says more about Buffalo's opinion of Henderson and Kouandjio than it does about Mills. Henderson could still win the job back if he can rebound from a bout with Crohn's Disease that cost him the last six games of last season and a lot of weight. ☜ Cordy Glenn got paid like a franchise left tackle this offseason, as his $12 million average annual salary now ranks fourth at the position. However, during his four-year career, Glenn has never ranked among the top 10 left tackles in snaps per blown block, finishing 18th in 2015.

Defensive Front Seven

Defensive Line	Age	Pos	G	Snaps	Plays	TmPct	Rk	Stop	Dfts	BTkl	Runs	St%	Rk	RuYd	Rk	Sack	Hit	Hur	Dsrpt
Marcell Dareus	27	DT	15	754	51	7.0%	18	37	6	3	47	72%	53	2.6	58	2.0	3	13.0	0
Corbin Bryant	28	DT	16	634	45	5.8%	35	31	3	5	42	69%	58	3.1	73	0.5	6	8.0	0
Kyle Williams	33	DT	6	346	14	4.8%	--	8	5	3	12	50%	--	4.3	--	1.0	5	3.0	0
Stefan Charles*	28	DT	13	228	13	2.1%	–	7	2	3	12	50%	--	2.8	--	1.0	3	1.0	0
Leger Douzable	*30*	*DE*	*16*	*291*	*13*	*1.7%*	*--*	*8*	*1*	*1*	*11*	*73%*	*--*	*2.9*	*--*	*0.0*	*3*	*6.0*	*0*

Edge Rushers	Age	Pos	G	Snaps	Plays	TmPct	Rk	Stop	Dfts	BTkl	Runs	St%	Rk	RuYd	Rk	Sack	Hit	Hur	Dsrpt
Jerry Hughes	28	DE	16	1007	55	7.1%	9	40	13	5	36	78%	30	2.8	71	5.0	9	32.5	3
Mario Williams*	31	DE	15	885	19	2.6%	91	15	7	3	11	82%	17	1.0	5	5.0	6	14.5	0

Linebackers	Age	Pos	G	Snaps	Plays	TmPct	Rk	Stop	Dfts	BTkl	Runs	St%	Rk	RuYd	Rk	Sack	Hit	Hur	Tgts	Suc%	Rk	AdjYd	Rk	PD	Int
Preston Brown	24	MLB	16	1069	120	15.4%	12	62	13	13	89	54%	74	3.6	47	0.0	6	7.5	17	56%	37	5.3	22	2	2
Nigel Bradham*	27	OLB	11	729	60	11.2%	51	33	11	8	31	65%	42	4.2	70	0.5	2	3	21	56%	36	7.2	54	2	0
Manny Lawson	32	OLB	16	701	50	6.4%	80	35	12	7	30	73%	10	2.8	17	1.0	4	4	9	51%	–	3.8	–	2	1
Zach Brown	27	ILB	16	493	80	10.2%	59	42	16	6	47	55%	71	5.6	88	0.5	1	2	17	66%	16	7.5	57	3	2

Year	Yards	ALY	Rank	Power	Rank	Stuff	Rank	2nd Level	Rank	Open Field	Rank	Sacks	ASR	Rank	Press	Rank
2013	4.54	3.99	20	65%	15	17%	24	1.13	20	1.07	28	57	8.7%	3	27.2%	6
2014	3.99	3.34	4	64%	16	26%	1	1.14	17	0.83	23	54	8.8%	1	26.4%	7
2015	4.52	4.32	29	72%	25	16%	31	1.24	26	0.77	16	21	3.8%	31	21.8%	29
2015 ALY by direction:			*Left End 4.48 (26)*			*Left Tackle 3.76 (16)*			*Mid/Guard 4.39 (32)*			*Right Tackle 3.72 (17)*			*Right End 5.17 (31)*	

The front office wasn't exactly subtle with its draft strategy, spending its first three picks on the front seven. The headliner is Shaq Lawson, whose career is already off to an inauspicious start. A shoulder injury which raised red flags before the draft has already flared up and forced Lawson to undergo surgery, which could sideline him as long as November. Even without the injury, SackSEER wasn't high on the Clemson product because of his nonexistent sack production until last season. As for the other two picks, Buffalo seems set to plug Ohio State 3-technique Adolphus Washington and thumping Alabama linebacker Reggie Ragland into its Week 1 starting lineup. ☻ Lost in the rest of the defensive fiasco was Marcell Dareus severely underperforming after his $96 million extension. Dareus regressed noticeably from 2013-14 against both the pass and the run, posting his worst run stop percentage and sack total in that time. Dareus' five-year extension actually just kicked in starting this offseason, so Buffalo sure hopes that 2015 was a one-year aberration.

Defensive Secondary

Secondary	Age	Pos	G	Snaps	Plays	TmPct	Rk	Stop	Dfts	BTkl	Runs	St%	Rk	RuYd	Rk	Tgts	Tgt%	Rk	Dist	Suc%	Rk	AdjYd	Rk	PD	Int
Corey Graham	31	FS	16	979	126	16.2%	2	45	20	3	66	41%	34	7.6	45	36	8.6%	49	13.2	44%	64	11.6	68	4	2
Ronald Darby	22	CB	15	914	89	12.2%	2	33	13	5	15	27%	61	6.7	36	91	23.2%	62	14.5	56%	22	5.3	6	18	2
Stephon Gilmore	26	CB	12	793	54	9.3%	26	23	8	6	6	33%	50	6.3	28	85	25.1%	68	13.2	50%	47	7.2	25	18	3
Bacarri Rambo*	26	SS	15	685	64	8.8%	48	19	12	6	23	30%	53	9.3	55	22	7.4%	33	13.1	56%	42	6.6	31	6	1
Nickell Robey	24	CB	16	673	50	6.4%	--	21	9	2	6	50%	--	5.8	--	48	16.7%	--	12.0	50%	--	8.7	--	2	0
Leodis McKelvin*	31	CB	9	388	41	9.4%	--	19	11	4	6	33%	--	13.2	--	45	27.2%	--	13.5	59%	--	7.1	--	9	2
Duke Williams	26	FS	16	283	24	3.1%	--	9	3	6	12	42%	--	5.5	--	9	7.0%	--	5.1	78%	--	3.3	--	1	0
Sterling Moore	*26*	*CB*	*16*	*706*	*51*	*5.8%*	*71*	*22*	*13*	*8*	*7*	*86%*	*2*	*2.6*	*1*	*47*	*18.8%*	*35*	*10.1*	*46%*	*66*	*8.0*	*42*	*6*	*1*
Robert Blanton	*27*	*SS*	*16*	*231*	*30*	*3.6%*	*--*	*8*	*2*	*2*	*12*	*33%*	*--*	*8.3*	*--*	*8*	*9.4%*	*--*	*17.9*	*48%*	*--*	*8.1*	*--*	*2*	*0*

Year	Pass D Rank	vs. #1 WR	Rk	vs. #2 WR	Rk	vs. Other WR	Rk	vs. TE	Rk	vs. RB	Rk
2013	2	1.9%	20	-45.2%	1	5.2%	20	-27.4%	4	-29.7%	2
2014	1	-22.6%	3	6.6%	22	-5.8%	12	-26.2%	2	-20.0%	5
2015	18	-13.3%	5	-12.9%	8	6.0%	18	-9.0%	13	16.5%	29

Ronald Darby and Defensive Rookie of the Year Marcus Peters of Kansas City faced a similar high volume of targets. The two were neck-and-neck in adjusted success rate, but Darby far outperformed Peters in adjusted yards per target (5.3 versus 7.9). Too bad surface stats like interceptions will always rule the day when it comes to awards voting. ☜ Corey Graham may have led all qualifying cornerbacks in adjusted success rate two seasons ago, but that didn't stop the Bills from moving him to safety last year. In fairness, the move effectively became one of necessity once Aaron Williams suffered a scary neck injury in Week 2, limiting him to three games on the season. Graham's charting stats were considerably worse at his new position, but he was a tackling machine when ballcarriers got past the underperforming front seven. ☜ Stephon Gilmore's charting stats have never quite matched his reputation as a No. 1 corner. Last year was no different, as he has never ranked inside the top 20 in lowest target percentage or highest success rate. In fact, he ranked outside the top 40 two of the past three seasons, including 2015. ☜ With Leodis McKelvin off to Philly, Nickell Robey and newcomer Sterling Moore will most likely compete for the vacant nickel corner job. Robey is a long way removed from his stunning 68 percent adjusted success rate as an undrafted rookie in 2013, which ranked second among corners, while Moore is even further removed from his AFC Championship Game heroics in New England, by far the most notable moment of his journeyman career. If neither seizes the job, don't rule out Graham playing a Malcolm Jenkins-type role, sliding down to the slot in sub packages and letting the likes of Aaron and Duke Williams, Baccari Rambo, and Robert Blanton figure it out on the back end.

Special Teams

Year	DVOA	Rank	FG/XP	Rank	Net Kick	Rank	Kick Ret	Rank	Net Punt	Rank	Punt Ret	Rank	Hidden	Rank
2013	-5.6%	30	5.7	7	-1.5	23	-4.4	25	-15.7	29	-12.1	32	-9.8	29
2014	6.2%	4	8.5	3	7.9	5	5.3	6	2.2	13	7.1	7	1.4	14
2015	1.5%	12	-1.7	23	18.2	1	-6.1	30	4.0	10	-6.9	31	-5.2	22

If the kickoff coverage unit can come close to 2015's performance, the Bills have good reason to kick short of the end zone and circumvent the new kickoff rule. Buffalo's kickoff coverage was worth 15.5 points in isolated field-position value, more than double any other team. The Bills have been a top-five kickoff coverage team since signing kickoff specialist Jordan Gay in 2014. ☜ However, the return game regressed severely after finishing as a top-10 unit on both kickoffs and punts in 2014. The sad trio of Percy Harvin, Denarius Moore, and Marcus Thigpen combined to provide minus-4.9 points below expected on kick returns, while Leodis McKelvin regressed on punt returns after a strong 2014. The departure of those players leaves journeyman Walter Powell or wide receiver Robert Woods as the most likely return men. ☜ Only Jason Myers missed more extra points than Dan Carpenter, who shanked six of them. Carpenter will face camp competition from undrafted rookie Marshall Morgan out of Georgia. But Morgan isn't exactly Roberto Aguayo, converting just 74 percent of his field goals the last two seasons.

Carolina Panthers

2015 record: 15-1	**Total DVOA:** 26% (4th)	**2016 Mean Projection:** 8.6 wins	**On the Clock (0-4):** 6%
Pythagorean Wins: 12.4 (1st)	**Offense:** 10.1% (8th)	**Postseason Odds:** 47.7%	**Mediocrity (5-7):** 27%
Snap-Weighted Age: 27.4 (3rd)	**Defense:** -18.4% (2nd)	**Super Bowl Odds:** 6.8%	**Playoff Contender (8-10):** 43%
Average Opponent: -8.6% (32nd)	**Special Teams:** -2.4% (23rd)	**Proj. Avg. Opponent:** 0.8% (12th)	**Super Bowl Contender (11+):** 24%

2015: Two strokes from perfection, numbers be damned.

2016: In Gettleman We Trust, Part II?

Since 1989, the first year in the DVOA database, the only players to be named NFL Most Valuable Player have been quarterbacks and running backs. None of them ever had a worse DVOA rating than Cam Newton did in 2015. In fact, none of them are even close (Table 1).

Table 1. Lowest DVOA Ratings by AP MVP Winners, 1989-2015

Player	Position	Year	Pass/Rush DVOA	Positional Rank
Shaun Alexander	RB	2005	19.5%	3
Brett Favre*	QB	1997	19.4%	6
Brett Favre	QB	1996	18.0%	4
Thurman Thomas	RB	1991	17.0%	3
Cam Newton	**QB**	**2015**	**7.6%**	**12**

*Co-MVP with Barry Sanders

No, the MVP doesn't always lead the league in DVOA, but remember that DVOA is a rate stat, and you can finish high in the rankings even while missing a quarter-season or more. And sometimes the DVOA leaders play for non-playoff teams and have no shot at the MVP award. Still, Newton is a major outlier here, not finishing among the top ten quarterbacks in either DVOA or DYAR, where he finished 11th. To be fair, those are passing numbers only, and Newton did lead all quarterbacks in rushing DYAR last year. However, even adding his passing and rushing numbers together gives us a total of 772 DYAR, making Newton the first quarterback to make the All-Pro first team with less than 1,100 combined DYAR. Good quarterbacks always get more DYAR than good running backs, so we can't directly compare the two positions in that metric, but the positional rankings make it clear that Newton had some underwhelming statistics for an MVP. How did the man who was theoretically the league's best player come out so shockingly unspectacular on the stat sheet? The answer is all in the context.

As we detailed in the Carolina chapter of *Football Outsiders Almanac 2015*, the Panthers have an unconventional allocation of resources. Their blueprint features some very specific areas of strength, such as linebacker. There are other positions where the Panthers are more willing than other teams

to accept weakness, including offensive tackle. The Panthers went into last season with journeyman/cautionary tale about the truths of book premises Michael Oher as their starting left tackle. The undrafted Mike Remmers, who played for six different teams between 2012 and 2014, manned the right side in his first starting role ever.

And while general manager Dave Gettleman has focused on creating a good receiving corps for Newton, 2015 was not a year that showcased it. 2014 first-round pick Kelvin Benjamin was lost for the season with a torn ACL in mid-August. 2015 second-round pick Devin Funchess was raw and unready for the expanded role that opened up with Benjamin's injury. Tight end Greg Olsen, as always, offered Newton a reliably great target over the middle. Other than that, Newton was throwing at Ted Ginn, a deep threat with no hands, and Corey "Don't Call Me Philly" Brown, an undrafted second-year receiver who had caught 21 passes in his rookie season.

DVOA doesn't give Newton extra credit for making big plays in the clutch. (He had 37.1% DVOA when the Panthers were losing or tied in the fourth quarter, although that only measures 49 plays in five games.) It also doesn't—and isn't meant to—properly account for the pieces around Newton. The game plan Newton was asked to engineer was tailored to the few strengths the rest of his offense had. That meant the Panthers were chucking it deep often, usually with extra blockers to give the tackles help, and asking Newton to perform the impossible. Carolina finished in the top 10 in six-lineman sets, Once the ball was thrown, Newton was relying on a receiving group that made a habit of leaving big plays on the field. Per Sports Info Solutions, Newton's receivers cost him 362 yards on passes that were dropped or dropped/defensed. That was by far the most in the league—Jameis Winston was second with 297 lost yards, and only seven other quarterbacks crossed the 200-lost yard threshold. And that's only counting air yards, and not what receivers might have done with the ball in their hands after gaining possession. Ginn alone dropped four different passes over 30 yards downfield.

Going beyond drops, Cian Fahey counts "failed receptions" in his *Pre-Snap Reads Quarterback Catalogue*, tallying any accurate pass that fell incomplete due to a receiver's mistake, including failure to fight off a defender or poorly tracking a pass in the air. By Fahey's count, Panthers receivers led the NFL in both failed receptions and lost yards on those recep-

2016 Panthers Schedule

Week	Opp.	Week	Opp.	Week	Opp.
1	at DEN (Thu.)	7	BYE	13	at SEA
2	SF	8	ARI	14	SD
3	MIN	9	at LA	15	at WAS (Mon.)
4	at ATL	10	KC	16	ATL (Sat.)
5	TB (Mon.)	11	NO (Thu.)	17	at TB
6	at NO	12	at OAK		

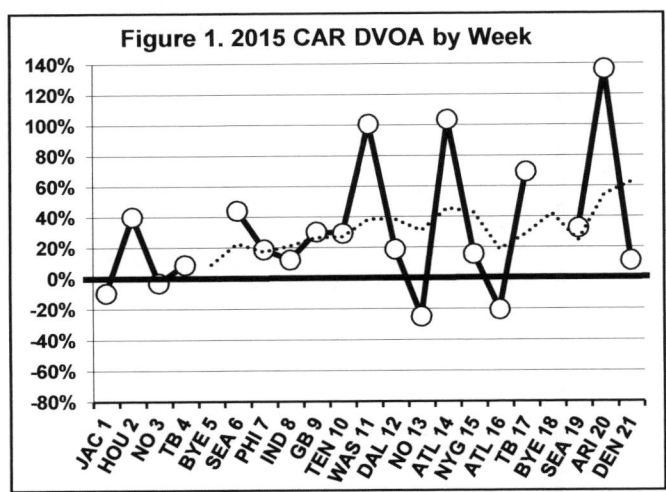

Figure 1. 2015 CAR DVOA by Week

tions. That's two totally different but experienced sets of observers, both saying that Newton and the Panthers lost more yardage due to receiver mistakes than anyone else. And it's not as if Carolina was putting up so many passes that some were bound to be dropped—Newton was just 16th in pass attempts.

In short, Newton's season was about overcoming. He was Jon Snow awaiting that giant Bolton cavalry charge and somehow surviving. (The Panthers' receivers were the equivalent of a bunch of untrained, outnumbered wildlings, and without Benjamin, they didn't even have a giant to help even the odds.) That's how you win an MVP award despite being asked to buck the odds on every passing down.

Normally when a team has a 15-1 season led by the league MVP, the groundwork is laid for a quiet offseason. Of course, most teams that go 15-1 with the league MVP have a deeper talent base than these Panthers. But we were still on track for that quiet, retain-everyone offseason until Gettleman shocked the NFL landscape by revoking star cornerback Josh Norman's franchise tag a week before the draft.

Norman's 2015 season was incredible. He finished third in adjusted success rate among all cornerbacks, fifth in yards per pass allowed, and third in YAC allowed. He was quickly picked up by Washington after the tag was revoked, and given a huge contract with $50 million in guarantees. It is clear that other teams around the league put a value higher on Norman

than the Carolina franchise tag was worth.

In listening to Gettleman talk about it, you get the sense that he felt he was making the easy decision and not necessarily the right one in franchising Norman. He described a one-year deal as unattractive for the Panthers, and apparently didn't think a middle ground could be reached. Gettleman can now shift that money towards extensions for other good players such as defensive tackle Kawaan Short, who has one year left on his rookie contract.

But the bigger factor in this decision was a bit simpler: Dave Gettleman doesn't particularly care for big-money cornerbacks. This is something that we delved into with a big table in *FOA 2015*: not one of Carolina's top seven defensive backs over the past two seasons was drafted higher than the fourth round. They used stopgaps liberally at those positions, especially at safety. The 2015 Panthers had more stability in the secondary than usual, when Norman, Bene Benwikere, and Roman Harper all returned from the previous season. But there were still the usual hallmarks of a Gettleman-built secondary: seemingly washed-up veteran cornerbacks like Pea-

Table 2. Effect of 3+ Rookie DBs from Rounds 1-5 on Pass Defense DVOA, 2007-2016

Team	Draft Year	Players selected	DVOA Y-1	DVOA	DVOA Y+1	DVOA Y+2
IND	2007	Dante Hughes (3), Brannon Condren (4), Michael Coe (5)	0.1% (13)	-15.7% (2)	-1.3% (12)	0.1% (11)
KC	2008	Brandon Flowers (2), DaJuan Morgan (3), Brandon Carr (5)	-5.9% (9)	20.6% (28)	10.1% (20)	4.0% (16)
MIA	2009	Vontae Davis (1), Sean Smith (2), Chris Clemons (5)	2.9% (15)	1.7% (13)	8.6% (22)	0.4% (13)
ATL	2009	William Moore (2), Chris Owens (3), William Middleton (5)	9.1% (17)	22.5% (27)	0.8% (11)	-1.8% (11)
DEN	2009	Alphonso Smith (2), Darcel McBath (2), David Bruton (4)	32.2% (31)	-15.8% (6)	32.6% (31)	10.2% (22)
KC	2010	Eric Berry (1), Javier Arenas (2), Kendrick Lewis (5)	10.1% (20)	4.0% (16)	-0.3% (12)	23.3% (31)
CLE	2010	Joe Haden (1), T.J. Ward (2), Larry Asante (5)	27.1% (28)	4.6% (18)	4.7% (17)	11.8% (20)
SEA	2010	Earl Thomas (1), Walter Thurmond (4), Kam Chancellor (5)	30.9% (30)	23.8% (29)	-5.8% (9)	-18.8% (3)
HOU	2011	Brandon Harris (2), Roc Carmichael (4), Shiloh Keo (5)	17.5% (31)	-6.6% (7)	-12.4% (4)	15.1% (24)
MIN	2012	Harrison Smith (1), Josh Robinson (3), Robert Blanton (5)	22.9% (32)	15.1% (24)	22.1% (30)	8.8% (19)
CIN	2012	Dre Kirkpatrick (1), Shaun Prater (5), George Iloka (5)	6.7% (18)	-5.6% (9)	-14.5% (4)	-5.0% (7)
SF	2014	Jimmie Ward (1), Dontae Johnson (4), Keith Reaser (5)	-2.1% (10)	-7.6% (4)	25.0% (30)	--
CAR	**2016**	**James Bradberry (2), Daryl Worley (3), Zach Sanchez (5)**	**-18.2% (2)**	--	--	--
AVERAGE (2007-2015)				10.2%	3.4%	5.8%	4.3%

nut Tillman and Cortland Finnegan, and the token journeyman safety in Kurt Coleman.

In 2016, the Panthers will again see plenty of turnover in the secondary. Gone are Harper, Finnegan, and Tillman. Coleman and Tre Boston should see snaps at safety, but except for Benwikere, the cornerback crew looks like it will be all new (at least until the typical August reinforcements come in). And, in a surprising twist, Carolina stocked up in cornerbacks in the draft. The Panthers spent second-, third-, and fifth-round picks at the position—by far the most interest they've ever shown in a draft under Gettleman. The Panthers GM insisted he did not "shop hungry," as he called it. "If he's a fifth-rounder and we drafted in the third, well then, shame on us. We really worked hard at not inflating the grades on the corners," he said at a post-draft presser. Gettleman had second-round grades on new corners James Bradberry (Samford) and Daryl Worley (West Virginia), who were absent from most draftnik conversations about this year's top cornerback talent.

Since the beginning of the DVOA era in 1989, roughly one team per year has invested this much draft capital at defensive back in a single draft. There have been 13 such teams in the past decade which selected three defensive backs in the first five rounds. As you'd expect, this is a group that tended to have bad pass defenses the year before. And looking at the development of these pass defenses over the next couple years, we generally just see the natural effect of regression take over these numbers (Table 2).

It's hard to find a single narrative thread that ties most of these 13 teams together. Earl Thomas and Kam Chancellor jump-started the Seahawks on their way to an NFC dynasty, but not until their second season. Harrison Smith would eventually lead the Vikings defense, but not until they hired Mike Zimmer to coach. Two of the strongest defenses on the list, the 2007 Colts and 2009 Broncos, improved with almost no contribution from their three rookie defensive backs. The Texans drafted three disappointing defensive backs in 2011, but also drafted J.J. Watt the same year.

Nonetheless, it is interesting to note that there are not many teams in the recent past that drafted three defensive backs as a pure luxury situation. Perhaps the 2014 49ers qualify, but a) they had a ton of extra draft picks and b) the "after" numbers are skewed by the whole "firing Jim Harbaugh" thing. Carolina's draft is fascinating not only because they were the best pass defense on the list but because they drafted three defensive backs despite having only five total picks.

The Panthers have vacillated from good-to-very good at pass defense with a ton of turnover. It should shock nobody if they continue to play to that level. Projections, of course, don't see it that way. Our defensive projections factor in loss of defensive talent based on Pro Football Reference's Approximate Value stat. Only six teams lost as much "Approximate Value over Replacement" than the 2016 Panthers. Norman is the obvious leader in the clubhouse, but productive veterans Tillman, Harper, and Jared Allen are off the squad as well. Carolina's history offers evidence that this shouldn't concern us as much as it would with other franchises, but as a whole, teams with this much lost talent are at a disadvantage (Table 3). The 13 teams with the most net lost value on defense since 2003 fell an average of seven spots in the defensive DVOA rankings.

Our projections see a lot to be optimistic about beyond that, so Panthers fans shouldn't get too concerned about the low mean wins forecast. This is just what happens when a great year meets a statistical projection system. We anticipate turnover regression for the defense, which forced an offensive

Table 3. Biggest Net Loss in AV Over Replacement on Defense, 2003-2016

Team	Year	Net AV Change	DVOA Y-1	Rk	DVOA	Rk	Change	Players Added	Players Lost
TB	2009	-32	-10.7%	6	8.0%	25	18.6%	NONE	D.Brooks (8), G.Adams (6), P.Buchanon (5), K.Carter (5), J.Haye (4), C.June (4)
NYJ	2013	-24	-4.2%	9	-5.6%	12	-1.3%	D.Landry (3)	B.Scott (7), L.Landry (5), Y.Bell (4), S.Pouha (4), B.Thomas (4), M.Devito (3)
CAR	2010	-23	-12.8%	6	-1.1%	16	11.7%	NONE	J.Peppers (12), D.Lewis (5), C.Harris (4), N.Diggs (2)
PHI	2003	-20	-11.2%	4	3.0%	17	14.2%	M.Coleman (4), N.Wayne (6)	H.Douglas (14), S.Barber (8), L.Kirkland (6), B.Bishop (2)
SF	2015	-20	-10.1%	5	9.9%	27	20.0%	S.Wright (2)	J.Smith (5), P.Cox (4), C.Culliver (4), R.McDonald (4), C.Borland (3), D.Skuta (2)
CAR	2006	-18	-14.2%	2	-10.9%	4	3.3%	K.Lucas (6), M.Kemoeatu (5), R.Howard (1)	W.Witherspoon (7), B.Buckner (6), K.Lucas (6), M.McCree (5), B.Short (5), R.Manning (1)
CAR	**2016**	**-17**	**-18.4%**	**2**	**--**	**--**	**--**	**P.Soliai (2)**	**J.Norman (12), J.Allen (3), R.Harper (3), C.Tillman (1)**
SD	2013	-17	2.0%	18	17.5%	32	15.5%	D.Freeney (3), D.Cox (2)	Q.Jammer (5), S.Phillips (5), T.Spikes (4), A.Cason (3), V.Martin (2), A.Bigby (1), A.Franklin (1), D.Williams (1)
CLE	2011	-17	1.7%	18	4.2%	22	2.6%	D.Patterson (1)	K.Coleman (5), A.Elam (4), M.Roth (4), E.Barton (3), D.Bowens (1), E.Wright (1)
CLE	2003	-17	-5.1%	10	-1.9%	14	3.2%	NONE	E.Holmes (5), D.Hambrick (4), D.Rudd (4), D.Bush (2), C.Fuller (2)
HOU	2013	-16	-14.2%	4	2.5%	18	16.7%	NONE	B.James (5), C.Barwin (5), G.Quin (4), S.Cody (2)
SEA	2011	-16	12.0%	29	-7.1%	10	-19.1%	NONE	L.Tatupu (4), A.Curry (3), L.Milloy (3), K.Balmer (2), C.Cole (2), K.Jennings (2)
NE	2009	-16	3.6%	17	-1.1%	14	-4.7%	L.Bodden (2), D.Burgess (1), S.Springs (1)	E.Hobbs (6), R.Seymour (5), M.Vrabel (4), T.Bruschi (3), D.O'Neal (2)
NYJ	2005	-16	-3.7%	14	1.0%	18	4.7%	L.Legree (1)	D.Abraham (7), J.Ferguson (5), R.Tongue (5)
AVERAGE (2003-2015)			-5.2%	10.9	1.4%	17.6	6.6%		

miscue on a league-leading 19.6 percent of their drives last year. Carolina is no longer playing the easiest schedule in the NFL, as they did last year. And as they had the biggest 2015 gap between actual wins and Pythagorean wins, we wouldn't expect as many wins even if they played at exactly the same level as last year. Yet even with all the expected regression,

the Panthers are easy favorites to win the NFC South for a fourth straight year.

Plus, these projections are just new numbers for Cam Newton to make a fool of. He's gotten pretty good at that.

Rivers McCown

2015 Panthers Stats by Week

Wk	vs.	W-L	PF	PA	YDF	YDA	TO	Total	Off	Def	ST
1	at JAC	W	20	9	263	265	2	-9%	-28%	-30%	-11%
2	HOU	W	24	17	350	300	0	40%	19%	-30%	-10%
3	NO	W	27	22	431	380	2	-3%	24%	9%	-18%
4	at TB	W	37	23	244	411	4	9%	-12%	-29%	-7%
5	BYE										
6	at SEA	W	27	23	383	334	-2	44%	20%	-20%	4%
7	PHI	W	27	16	394	349	-2	19%	0%	-15%	3%
8	IND	W	29	26	379	359	1	12%	-10%	-23%	-1%
9	GB	W	37	29	427	402	1	30%	33%	-3%	-6%
10	at TEN	W	27	10	303	242	2	29%	17%	6%	18%
11	WAS	W	44	16	368	186	5	101%	19%	-100%	-18%
12	at DAL	W	33	14	294	210	3	19%	-16%	-38%	-3%
13	at NO	W	41	38	497	334	-2	-25%	-11%	11%	-2%
14	ATL	W	38	0	424	230	4	104%	43%	-59%	1%
15	at NYG	W	38	35	480	406	1	16%	24%	7%	-1%
16	at ATL	L	13	20	268	373	0	-20%	-1%	22%	3%
17	TB	W	38	10	366	386	1	70%	39%	-21%	10%
18	BYE										
19	SEA	W	31	24	295	403	2	33%	30%	-7%	-4%
20	ARI	W	49	15	476	287	6	137%	55%	-69%	13%
21	DEN	L	10	24	315	194	-2	12%	-30%	-58%	-17%

Trends and Splits

	Offense	Rank	Defense	Rank
Total DVOA	9.9%	8	-18.4%	2
Unadjusted VOA	12.3%	6	-20.3%	2
Weighted Trend	12.5%	6	-17.7%	5
Variance	4.6%	8	9.2%	30
Average Opponent	4.9%	32	-2.9%	26
Passing	23.8%	9	-18.2%	2
Rushing	3.8%	6	-18.7%	6
First Down	1.7%	14	-37.8%	1
Second Down	8.7%	10	-6.4%	9
Third Down	31.4%	4	0.3%	17
First Half	13.6%	8	-24.8%	1
Second Half	5.8%	12	-11.9%	5
Red Zone	32.3%	3	3.4%	18
Late and Close	-0.5%	15	-19.4%	3

Five-Year Performance

Year	W-L	Pyth W	Est W	PF	PA	TO	Total	Rk	Off	Rk	Def	Rk	ST	Rk	Off AGL	Rk	Def AGL	Rk	Off Age	Rk	Def Age	Rk	ST Age	Rk
2011	6-10	7.4	6.9	406	429	+1	-4.1%	20	18.2%	4	15.8%	32	-6.5%	32	47.6	29	61.5	32	27.2	15	25.3	32	26.0	25
2012	7-9	7.8	8.8	357	363	+1	5.5%	13	7.2%	10	-3.1%	11	-4.8%	29	23.1	10	53.0	27	27.1	15	25.7	28	26.0	19
2013	12-4	11.7	11.0	366	241	+11	24.6%	3	7.9%	10	-15.7%	3	1.0%	13	42.4	21	28.4	17	28.2	2	26.6	16	26.6	7
2014	7-8-1	7.0	7.4	339	374	+3	-8.5%	24	-4.7%	20	-1.7%	15	-5.5%	30	39.7	25	11.7	1	26.4	26	27.2	8	26.4	6
2015	15-1	12.4	11.1	500	308	+20	26.0%	4	10.1%	8	-18.4%	2	-2.4%	23	28.2	14	22.7	8	27.0	14	28.1	3	26.8	3

2015 Performance Based on Most Common Personnel Groups

CAR Offense					CAR Offense vs. Opponents					CAR Defense					CAR Defense vs. Opponents			
Pers	Freq	Yds	DVOA	Run%	Pers	Freq	Yds	DVOA	Run%	Pers	Freq	Yds	DVOA	Pers	Freq	Yds	DVOA
11	42%	6.5	25.7%	38%	Base	47%	5.1	2.3%	56%	Base	26%	4.1	-40.5%	11	66%	5.3	-17.1%
12	36%	6.0	14.5%	40%	Nickel	46%	6.6	33.9%	37%	Nickel	72%	5.2	-10.9%	12	16%	4.2	-20.0%
22	9%	4.6	-1.7%	78%	Dime+	5%	5.0	-68.2%	16%	Dime+	1%	5.4	33.4%	21	8%	5.2	-11.3%
21	6%	2.7	-19.3%	49%	Goal Line	1%	-0.4	-19.3%	87%	Goal Line	0%	1.0	93.3%	13	2%	2.5	-33.0%
612	3%	3.1	-29.8%	93%	Big	0%	9.0	71.9%	80%					22	2%	1.6	-63.3%
622	2%	3.6	14.4%	83%										611	2%	10.3	61.6%

Strategic Tendencies

Run/Pass		Rk	Formation		Rk	Pass Rush		Rk	Secondary		Rk	Strategy		Rk
Runs, first half	42%	7	Form: Single Back	63%	30	Rush 3	2.4%	30	4 DB	26%	28	Play action	27%	2
Runs, first down	55%	4	Form: Empty Back	5%	26	Rush 4	69.5%	8	5 DB	72%	1	Avg Box (Off)	6.52	1
Runs, second-long	36%	4	Pers: 3+ WR	43%	30	Rush 5	22.0%	16	6+ DB	1%	29	Avg Box (Def)	6.13	24
Runs, power sit.	67%	6	Pers: 2+ TE/6+ OL	51%	3	Rush 6+	6.0%	16	CB by Sides	54%	30	Offensive Pace	29.74	12
Runs, behind 2H	32%	2	Pers: 6+ OL	5%	9	Sacks by LB	19.3%	25	S/CB Cover Ratio	24%	11	Defensive Pace	29.25	5
Pass, ahead 2H	45%	20	Shotgun/Pistol	72%	7	Sacks by DB	4.5%	25	DB Blitz	10%	17	Go for it on 4th	0.72	25

Carolina held the lead for an average of 39:47 every game, tops in the league. As a result of these frequent leads, the Panthers often sat on the ball after halftime. Carolina ranked ninth in first-half pace (26.91 seconds between plays) but 29th in second-half pace (29.36 seconds between plays). Opposing defenses sped up to try to catch up, and their situation-neutral pace of 29.25 seconds zoomed up to one play every 25.27 seconds when we count all plays against the Panthers. ☞ Cam Newton was blitzed on a league-high 39 percent of passes, even though the Panthers gained 7.5 yards per play against the blitz compared to an average 6.8 yards on other pass plays. ☞ The Panthers ran the ball 38 percent of the time with three or more receivers on the field, by far the highest percentage in the league. And Carolina running backs were much better running from single-back formations, with 4.9 yards per carry and 1.3% DVOA compared to 3.1 yards per carry and 22.3% DVOA with two backs. However, the Panthers' numbers were opposite in 2014, so this may have been fluke variation rather than a real issue with blocking. ☞ Somewhat connected: for a run-first offense, the Panthers were shockingly impotent when the quarterback lined up under center, ranking 31st in DVOA at -19.8%. Carolina had the sixth-best shotgun (or pistol) DVOA at 24.3%, so only San Diego had a larger gap between shotgun/pistol and traditional formations. ☞ Carolina ran a play-action fake on 12 percent of third-down passes, the highest rate in the NFL. ☞ The Panthers offense only recovered three of 12 fumbles. ☞ We only tracked Carolina with 15 wide receiver or tight end screens in 2015, 30th in the NFL. However, the Panthers had 55.9% DVOA and 7.5 yards per play on these passes. ☞ On the flip side, the Carolina defense was the league's best at defending wide receiver and tight end screens, compiling a -75.8% DVOA.

Passing

Player	DYAR	DVOA	Plays	NtYds	Avg	YAC	C%	TD	Int
C.Newton	630	7.6%	526	3558	6.8	5.0	60.0%	35	10
D.Anderson	0	-11.9%	6	36	6.0	5.3	66.7%	0	0

Rushing

Player	DYAR	DVOA	Plays	Yds	Avg	TD	Fum	Suc
J.Stewart	23	-6.2%	242	988	4.1	6	3	43%
C.Newton	142	8.1%	119	645	5.4	10	4	-
M.Tolbert	54	9.8%	62	256	4.1	1	0	56%
C.Artis-Payne	-1	-9.2%	45	183	4.1	1	0	38%
F.Whittaker	11	2.0%	25	108	4.3	1	0	44%
C.Brown	31	58.3%	6	38	6.3	0	0	-

Receiving

Player	DYAR	DVOA	Plays	Ctch	Yds	Y/C	YAC	TD	C%
T.Ginn	77	-2.5%	96	44	739	16.8	5.5	10	46%
D.Funchess	9	-10.7%	63	31	474	15.3	3.6	5	49%
J.Cotchery*	112	14.8%	54	39	485	12.4	5.0	3	72%
C.Brown	89	8.8%	54	31	447	14.4	2.6	4	57%
B.Bersin	-2	-15.0%	11	9	119	13.2	3.7	0	82%
G.Olsen	132	8.9%	124	77	1105	14.4	4.5	7	62%
E.Dickson	-35	-26.3%	26	17	121	7.1	3.1	2	65%
M.Tolbert	56	25.3%	23	18	154	8.6	7.7	3	78%
J.Stewart	10	-5.4%	21	16	99	6.2	7.3	1	76%
F.Whittaker	-21	-42.5%	15	12	64	5.3	9.3	0	80%

Offensive Line

Player	Pos	Age	GS	Snaps	Pen	Sk	Pass	Run	Player	Pos	Age	GS	Snaps	Pen	Sk	Pass	Run
Mike Remmers	RT	27	16/16	1102	13	3.0	9.0	2.0	Ryan Kalil	C	31	15/15	1000	4	0.5	2.5	0.0
Michael Oher	LT	30	16/16	1084	4	6.0	10.0	3.0	Andrew Norwell	LG	25	13/13	818	0	2.0	6.0	1.0
Trai Turner	RG	23	16/16	1074	6	1.5	1.5	1.0	Amini Silatolu*	LG	28	9/3	238	0	1.0	2.0	0.0

Year	Yards	ALY	Rank	Power	Rank	Stuff	Rank	2nd Lev	Rank	Open Field	Rank	Sacks	ASR	Rank	Press	Rank	F-Start	Cont.
2013	3.87	3.91	14	72%	8	19%	14	1.04	22	0.54	25	43	8.2%	25	24.2%	13	9	25
2014	3.93	3.60	27	68%	10	20%	17	1.14	18	0.59	25	42	7.9%	22	21.5%	7	17	26
2015	4.10	3.89	12	76%	2	18%	8	1.23	5	0.61	22	33	6.9%	21	25.7%	17	12	34

2015 ALY by direction: Left End 4.3 (9)   Left Tackle 3.69 (17)   Mid/Guard 3.8 (17)   Right Tackle 4.72 (2)   Right End 3.63 (14)

So the tackles were pretty bad, yes, but the Panthers win from the inside out. It was Ryan Kalil, Trai Turner, and Andrew Norwell that were blunting interior rushers and helping the Panthers win in the trenches. Kalil and Turner each ranked third at their position in snaps per blown block. Kalil is getting a little bit up there in years, and was hurt at the end of last season. The Panthers should be in wait-and-see mode with him, but until his play slips, this is going to be an offensive line that can pound the rock on anyone. ☞ Waiting for Oher and Remmers to slip is tackle Daryl Williams, whom the Panthers traded up to select in 2015's fourth round. Williams has been decried as not being mobile enough to be an NFL left tackle, but he sure played at Oklahoma like a player who could thrive there.

Defensive Front Seven

Defensive Line	Age	Pos	G	Snaps	Plays	TmPct	Rk	Stop	Dfts	BTkl	Runs	St%	Rk	RuYd	Rk	Sack	Hit	Hur	Dsrpt
						Overall						vs. Run				Pass Rush			
Kawann Short	27	DT	16	759	56	6.8%	23	48	24	3	40	83%	21	1.6	17	11.0	9	14.5	4
Star Lotulelei	27	DT	14	533	23	3.2%	72	20	6	1	19	84%	15	1.2	3	1.0	2	5.0	2
Dwan Edwards*	35	DT	12	375	13	2.1%	84	12	2	0	10	90%	6	1.9	31	1.0	2	2.5	0
Kyle Love	30	DT	15	328	17	2.2%	--	12	4	2	13	69%	--	1.9	--	3.0	1	2.5	0
Paul Soliai	33	DT	14	357	22	3.2%	--	19	3	1	20	90%	--	0.9	--	0.0	5	7.0	0

Edge Rushers	Age	Pos	G	Snaps	Plays	TmPct	Rk	Stop	Dfts	BTkl	Runs	St%	Rk	RuYd	Rk	Sack	Hit	Hur	Dsrpt
						Overall						vs. Run				Pass Rush			
Jared Allen*	34	DE	15	654	33	4.3%	63	26	7	7	20	80%	23	1.8	25	2.0	14	18.0	2
Kony Ealy	25	DE	16	648	34	4.1%	66	26	7	8	25	72%	57	3.2	81	5.0	9	21.0	2
Mario Addison	29	DE	14	392	19	2.6%	89	15	9	0	8	75%	40	2.4	48	6.0	10	15.0	0
Charles Johnson	30	DE	9	388	13	2.8%	87	10	4	0	11	73%	53	1.1	8	1.0	5	4.5	0
Ryan Delaire	24	DE	9	225	8	1.7%	--	7	3	0	5	80%	--	2.2	--	2.5	2	7.5	0
Wes Horton	26	DE	8	155	6	1.5%	--	3	1	0	4	50%	--	2.5	--	1.0	3	5.0	0

Linebackers	Age	Pos	G	Snaps	Plays	TmPct	Rk	Stop	Dfts	BTkl	Runs	St%	Rk	RuYd	Rk	Sack	Hit	Hur	Tgts	Suc%	Rk	AdjYd	Rk	PD	Int
						Overall						vs. Run				Pass Rush				vs. Pass				
Thomas Davis	33	OLB	16	1003	111	13.4%	32	68	20	10	53	70%	19	3.9	64	5.5	6	13.5	38	62%	20	4.0	10	6	4
Luke Kuechly	25	MLB	13	767	128	19.0%	1	75	24	9	64	69%	22	3.0	26	1.0	4	10	37	63%	19	5.9	31	9	4
Shaq Thompson	22	OLB	14	365	50	6.9%	--	37	13	5	29	76%	--	2.6	--	1.0	1	3	9	77%	--	2.4	--	2	0
A.J. Klein	25	OLB	15	318	49	6.3%	--	26	13	2	25	64%	--	1.8	--	1.0	0	0	6	48%	--	4.9	--	1	1

Year	Yards	ALY	Rank	Power	Rank	Stuff	Rank	2nd Level	Rank	Open Field	Rank	Sacks	ASR	Rank	Press	Rank
2013	4.07	3.65	9	74%	27	22%	8	1.19	27	0.83	23	60	9.2%	2	27.8%	3
2014	4.51	3.65	10	79%	29	21%	8	1.07	10	1.27	32	40	7.5%	7	25.0%	17
2015	3.78	3.21	4	87%	32	24%	6	1.02	6	0.76	15	44	7.1%	11	26.3%	12
2015 ALY by direction:		Left End 2.27 (1)			Left Tackle 3.04 (7)			Mid/Guard 3.45 (6)			Right Tackle 3.10 (6)			Right End 3.04 (13)		

Part of the reason the Panthers are able to plug in random old cornerbacks in as starters is the presence of Thomas Davis and Luke Kuechly in front of them. Kuechly has become the hands-down best linebacker in the NFL, developing his cover skills to the point where it's surprising when a Carolina opponent completes a crossing pattern. Davis is an athletic freak, even at age 33, and excelled in both pass-rushing and pass coverage last season. Shaq Thompson, a first-round pick out of Washington last year, is on site to learn from and eventually replace Davis. ☞ The Panthers stumbled into Star Lotulelei and Kawaan Short with the first two picks of Gettleman's tenure. Short is on the short list of great 3-techs in the NFL right now, along with Geno Atkins and Aaron Donald. Lotulelei is the rare Planetoid lineman who can even generate some spare pass-rush. ☞ Vernon Butler (Louisiana Tech) fell into Carolina's lap at the end of the first round. He's in the Short mold of having some pass-rush ability and some problems with his college tape. If Butler can smooth out his run defense, he could play either tackle spot effectively. For now, he's a rotational lineman. ☞ The Panthers were able to get Charles Johnson to come back after his surprising release, which should help them patch things over at defensive end, a relatively weak spot. Super Bowl star Kony Ealy is still developing, but his hurry numbers indicate a breakout could be in the cards.

Defensive Secondary

Secondary	Age	Pos	G	Snaps	Plays	Overall TmPct	Rk	Stop	Dfts	BTkl	vs. Run Runs	St%	Rk	RuYd	Rk	vs. Pass Tgts	Tgt%	Rk	Dist	Suc%	Rk	AdjYd	Rk	PD	Int
Josh Norman*	29	CB	16	1061	75	9.1%	30	39	15	9	12	50%	20	5.6	21	80	18.7%	32	14.2	63%	3	4.9	4	18	4
Kurt Coleman	28	FS	15	1018	97	12.5%	16	39	18	8	40	40%	36	6.7	33	27	6.5%	24	16.1	69%	8	9.3	57	9	7
Roman Harper*	34	SS	16	951	78	9.4%	40	34	6	6	41	54%	13	5.1	13	22	5.8%	18	10.8	63%	21	5.4	12	7	0
Bene' Benwikere	25	CB	13	788	67	10.0%	19	31	12	10	18	61%	9	5.5	19	50	15.8%	11	7.9	53%	34	7.3	27	8	0
Charles Tillman*	35	CB	12	711	62	10.0%	18	23	8	4	17	59%	11	4.5	11	45	15.8%	10	14.1	59%	11	8.0	44	7	2
Tre Boston	24	FS	16	222	21	2.5%	--	6	4	2	7	29%	--	14.0	--	4	4.5%	--	5.0	50%	--	6.2	--	0	0
Trenton Robinson	26	SS	9	439	53	11.9%	--	17	5	7	33	39%	--	7.1	--	6	3.5%	--	13.3	61%	--	6.6	--	1	1

Year	Pass D Rank	vs. #1 WR	Rk	vs. #2 WR	Rk	vs. Other WR	Rk	vs. TE	Rk	vs. RB	Rk
2013	3	-2.3%	15	-20.0%	4	-28.1%	2	-4.0%	12	4.8%	18
2014	9	15.1%	27	-0.6%	16	7.9%	23	-11.6%	7	-29.5%	2
2015	2	-24.7%	3	-9.5%	12	-30.4%	3	-40.4%	1	-10.5%	8

Earlier in this chapter, we talked about James Bradberry and Daryl Worley in abstract terms. How are they as players? Bradberry is a bit of a projection after playing in the FCS Southern Conference, and he didn't stand out at the Senior Bowl at all. However, he's got two of the longest arms among combine corners (33 3/8th inches) and carries a lot of weight (211 pounds). Plenty of teams have jumped on the long arms trend as press coverage becomes more important. Worley has a similar profile (another 33 3/8-inch arm length guy), but ran a slow 4.64 40-yard dash at the combine. He wasn't bad at West Virginia, but he did have a tendency to give up big plays—search YouTube for what Corey Coleman did to him. ☞ Should these guys not be ready immediately, journeyman Robert McClain is the likely stand-in. McClain is one of the patron saints of that Football Outsiders precept, "One Year of Awesome Slot Corner Stats Does Not Mean You Are Good," alongside Brice McCain.

Special Teams

Year	DVOA	Rank	FG/XP	Rank	Net Kick	Rank	Kick Ret	Rank	Net Punt	Rank	Punt Ret	Rank	Hidden	Rank
2013	1.0%	13	2.4	14	5.0	8	-3.1	20	1.6	16	-1.0	17	-3.8	21
2014	-5.5%	30	-0.2	18	-2.2	20	2.3	9	-23.1	32	-4.1	22	0.0	17
2015	-2.4%	23	-1.5	21	-5.1	28	-1.8	19	-6.3	24	2.8	11	5.5	10

This was a sensitive spot last year, as coordinator Bruce DeHaven fought cancer and was given multiple leaves of absence. The Panthers have struggled on special teams the past two seasons despite a nominally good punt returner in Ted Ginn. Fozzy Whittaker and Joe Webb both returned kicks poorly, and Whittaker will be first in line for the job if he makes the roster. ☞ Mike Scifres replaces Brad Nortman as the punter; he's coming off some abysmal recent years in San Diego, but can still produce hang time. ☞ Graham Gano is essentially a journeyman kicker without the journey, since he's now been in Carolina for four seasons. ☞ Teddy Williams had 10 special teams tackles and a rather unsustainable 100 percent stop rate on them.

Chicago Bears

2015 record: 6-10	Total DVOA: -5.7% (19th)	2016 Mean Projection: 7.2 wins	On the Clock (0-4): 15%
Pythagorean Wins: 6.3 (22nd)	Offense: 6.9% (10th)	Postseason Odds: 21.7%	Mediocrity (5-7): 41%
Snap-Weighted Age: 26.6 (17th)	Defense: 11.3% (31st)	Super Bowl Odds: 1.6%	Playoff Contender (8-10): 34%
Average Opponent: 5.5% (4th)	Special Teams: -1.2% (21st)	Proj. Avg. Opponent: -2.2% (28th)	Super Bowl Contender (11+): 11%

2015: Looking at my own reflection, when suddenly it changes, violently it changes.

2016: I'm listening with one foot out the door, and something has to die to be reborn.

Some chapters in *Football Outsiders Almanac* are simple to write: just drop a couple thousand words on the biggest change the team made in the offseason. The Rams drafted a new quarterback? Let's discuss Jared Goff and the success or failure he'll have throwing to Kenny Britt and Tavon Austin. Doug Pederson is now the coach of the Eagles? Why don't we look at the system he's likely to use, and how it will work with the scorched earth Chip Kelly left in Philadelphia. Other chapters are more of a puzzle, usually because the team stood pat and there's not much change to discuss.

And then there's a team like Chicago, which made so many changes it's hard to know where to begin. Ever since general manager Ryan Pace and head coach John Fox were hired in January of 2015, the Bears have undergone a rebuilding phase the likes of which we have rarely seen. Partly by chance but mostly by design, the Bears we see this fall will bear little resemblance to those we saw in 2015, and even less to those from the year before. Collectively, Chicago's 24 projected starters for 2016 (including slot receiver Eddie Royal and nickelback Bryce Callahan) played fewer than half the snaps available on offense and defense in 2015. Those same players were on the field for barely a quarter of Chicago's offensive snaps before Fox and Pace arrived in 2014, and just 11 percent of snaps on defense that season. Here's another way to look at it: the projected offensive starters for the Bears in 2016 started only 85 games in Chicago last year, while the defense is getting back 81 starts. For comparison, the Cowboys are getting back 75 starts from their offensive line alone.

If there's one unit that needed an overhaul, it was the defense. Fox and Pace took over a team that had finished 28th in total defensive DVOA in 2014: 29th against the pass and 21st against the rush. And thus, The Great Rebuilding began. First, they opened their wallets, signing defensive end Mitch Unrein, linebacker Pernell McPhee, cornerbacks Tracy Porter and Alan Ball, and safeties Antrel Rolle and Chris Prosinski. Then they turned to the draft, taking nose tackle Eddie Goldman and safety Adrian Amos. Their pool of undrafted free agents produced aforementioned cornerback Bryce Callahan. They added more talent after the season had started, claiming undrafted free-agent strong safety Harold Jones-Quartey after Arizona waived him.

So what was the net result of all those moves? The defense got *worse*, falling from 10.6% DVOA in 2014 to 11.3% in 2015. For those keeping score at home, that's worse than everyone save for the Saints, the worst defensive team we have ever measured. The pass defense did improve (from a 22.6% DVOA to 17.3%), but the run defense fell apart (from -5.0% to 4.2%, the worst in the league in 2015).

So it was time for *Rebuilding Part Deux: The Rebuildening.* The Bears went back to the free-agent well to add a pair of inside linebackers, Denver's Danny Trevathan and Indianapolis' Jerrell Freeman. They supplemented these additions by signing veteran lineman Akiem Hicks, a longtime member of the Saints who had joined the Patriots in 2015 via midseason trade.

That leaves us with the following lineup for the Bears. It starts up front with Goldman at nose tackle and Unrein and Hicks at end. As is typical for 3-4 linemen, none of them were huge playmakers last season, and Goldman and Unrein were part of the problem in Chicago last year. Hicks brings a modicum of pass-rush ability, with 13.5 total sacks, hits, hurries, and disruptions in 399 snaps last year. On a per-snap basis, that almost exactly matches the 21.5 pass rush events that Jarvin Jenkins had in 636 snaps for Chicago last season. With Jenkins now a New York Jet, Hicks becomes a Bears starter, but that looks like a lateral move for Chicago. Will Sutton returns to add depth, along with Jonathan Bullard, a third-round rookie out of Florida.

McPhee will man one outside linebacker spot, with Lamarr Houston taking over the other side. That duo played 30 total games last season even though both were hampered by knee injuries. McPhee underwent arthroscopic surgery after the season, but is expected to be ready for training camp. Houston is a more interesting case. Signed as a free agent from Oakland in 2014, Houston's first season in Chicago ended after just eight games when he tore his ACL while celebrating his only sack of the season. Though he recovered to play all 16 games in 2015, the Bears still brought him along slowly. He played 83 snaps in the first four games, followed by 63 in the second four, 125 in the third, and 160 in the fourth, with his only starts of the year coming in Weeks 16 and 17. He had two sacks in a season-ending loss to Detroit, giving him eight on the year: good enough to lead the team even though he was on the field barely 40 percent of the time. Both McPhee and Houston should be even more productive in 2016 with better health. The Bears have depth here too. After years as an undersized defensive end who didn't accomplish much in Detroit's

2016 Bears Schedule

Week	Opp.	Week	Opp.	Week	Opp.
1	at HOU	7	at GB (Thu.)	13	SF
2	PHI (Mon.)	8	MIN (Mon.)	14	at DET
3	at DAL	9	BYE	15	GB
4	DET	10	at TB	16	WAS (Sat.)
5	at IND	11	at NYG	17	at MIN
6	JAC	12	TEN		

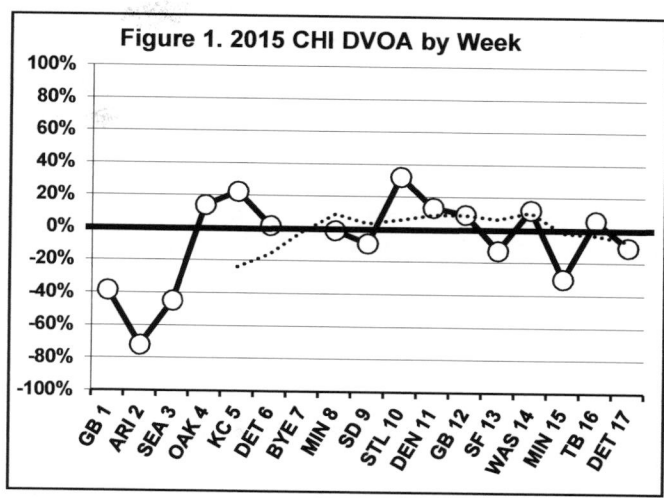

Figure 1. 2015 CHI DVOA by Week

4-3, Willie Young has flourished in Chicago's 3-4, with ten sacks in 2014 and 6.5 last year despite a total of only 1,188 snaps—basically one full season's worth of playing time. The Bears also used their first-round draft pick this year on linebacker Leonard Floyd out of Georgia, though he looks like a long-term project. He weighed 244 pounds at the combine and just doesn't have the mass to set the edge at the NFL level. However, his SackSEER projection of 26.9 sacks in his first five NFL seasons was the best in this year's draft class, and there are worse ideas than bringing in an explosive speed-rusher to bring outside pressure on third-and-long.

At inside linebacker, the newly formed duo of Trevathan and Freeman should be a huge improvement over last year's tandem of Christian Jones and Shea McClellin, whose main assignment in 2015 seemed to be watching running backs go by them for big gains. In almost exactly the same amount of playing time last season (1,490 snaps for Trevathan and Freeman compared to 1,420 for Jones and McClellin), the newcomers made significantly more total plays than the old guard (228 to 169), with nearly double the stops (149 to 75) and triple the defeats (30 to 11), all while missing *fewer* tackles (17 to 19). With McClellin off to New England, Jones remains the top backup here.

For all the upheaval in the front seven, the secondary remains mostly stable. Kyle Fuller, the 14th overall pick in 2014, posted terrible charting numbers as a rookie, but improved to average in his second season. Alan Ball opened 2015 as the starter on the other side, but was ineffective and quickly benched for Tracy Porter. That switch was permanent: after the season, Porter was re-signed, but Ball was not. Bryce Callahan started the year on the practice squad and ended it hurt, but in between played surprisingly well at nickelback.

The only question mark in the secondary is at strong safety, where the Bears tried a trio of players last year. The plan going into the year was for Antrel Rolle, the 11-year veteran, to man the position, but he was limited to just seven games due to knee and ankle injuries. Chris Prosinski and Harold Jones-Quartey each got their turns at the position as well. Rolle was released after just one season in Chicago for cap-related reasons. That leaves Prosinski and Jones-Quartey to battle a pair of rookies—fourth-rounder Deon Bush (Miami) and sixth-rounder DeAndre Houston-Carson (William & Mary)—for the starting role. It's a wide-open race, but early reports out of training camp had Jones-Quartey as a slight favorite. (It's also theoretically possible the Bears could field a tandem of Jones-Quartey and Houston-Carson, which would be a nightmare for announcers everywhere.)

While the Bears' new faces on defense came from free agency and the draft, their new faces at wide receiver are coming from the disabled list. Technically, Chicago didn't add any wideouts to the roster, but they suffered so many injuries last season that having everyone healthy is like having a whole new crew. The woes started when Kevin White, the seventh overall pick of the 2015 draft out of West Virginia, underwent surgery shortly before the season began to repair a stress fracture in his shin. There was initial hope he would only be sidelined a couple of months, but White ended up missing all of his rookie season. Then Alshon Jeffery suffered a calf injury in the preseason, followed by injuries to his (deep inhale) hamstring, groin, shoulder, calf (again), and hamstring (again). He finished with only nine games played and 506 snaps, less than half the Bears' total. Finally, Eddie Royal was limited to 477 snaps over nine games by ankle and knee injuries and an undisclosed illness. If you're keeping track, that's 983 total snaps from Chicago's top three wide receivers. There were ten individual wideouts in the NFL last season who played more than that. Chicago finished with 35.3 adjusted games lost at wide receiver, the most any team has suffered since at least 2002.

Injuries also hit the Bears at center, where Will Montgomery lasted only four games before a broken leg ended his season. This caused shuffling all over the offensive line. Hroniss Grasu, a third-round rookie out of Oregon, moved in and out of the lineup and finished with eight starts. Given his part-time status last year, it's hard to say whether he should count as a returning starter or not. After the season, the Bears drafted and signed a bevy of linemen, and also shifted Kyle Long from right tackle back to right guard. With all that in mind, left tackle Charles Leno is the only starter on last year's line certain to start at the same position this year.

It says something about the volume of Chicago's transactions this year that we're nearly 2,000 words into this essay and only now getting to Matt Forte. Since the Bears drafted Forte in the second round in 2008, the Tulane product is fourth in the NFL with 8,602 rushing yards, and he leads all running backs with 4,116 receiving yards and 12,718 yards from scrimmage. Despite all the shuffling on the line in front of him, he was still effective last year, finishing second among running backs in rushing DYAR and seventh in receiving DYAR even though he missed three games. He turned 30 in December, though, and with his contract up, the Bears opted to let him join the Jets in free agency. That leaves Jeremy Langford the lead back in the Windy City. The fourth-round rookie out of Michigan State actually had a higher rushing DVOA than Forte last year, and produced some big gains in the passing game as well.

Forte wasn't the only key weapon to say goodbye to Chicago this offseason. The Bears also traded Martellus Bennett to New England just one year after the tight end made the Pro Bowl. That move was made possible in part by the resurgence of Zach Miller, who set career highs in catches, yards, and touchdowns as a 31-year-old last season. New offensive coordinator Dowell Loggains likes to use a lot of two-tight end sets, which means Bears fans will also see a lot of Khari Lee, who joined Houston as an undrafted free agent last year only to get traded to Chicago right before the season started.

(Oh, did we forget to mention that the Bears have a new offensive coordinator too? Loggains, the quarterbacks coach last season, takes over for Adam Gase, now the head coach in Miami. Loggains doesn't plan to change much, though. "The shell of the offense will stay the same," he told reporters in May. "It's been the same since coach Fox has been a head coach. The language and everything will be the same, but it will evolve like it would have if Adam would have been here." Fox expressed similar sentiments in March, saying consistency was one of the reasons he liked to promote from within. So we can expect the Bears offense to look much like it did in 2015: a lot of shotgun, a lot of runs, and plenty of short perimeter passes.)

Perhaps the departures of Forte and Bennett should have been somewhat expected. Fox and Pace have a track record of saying goodbye to productive offensive players to make room for cheaper, younger alternatives. Don't forget that one of their first personnel moves after taking over the team was to trade Brandon Marshall to the Jets, when it was clear Marshall still had a lot to offer in the NFL. All of which brings us to Jay Cutler, the lone constant in Chicago amidst all the moving pieces. Aside from kicker Robbie Gould, Cutler is the only player on the Bears left from just five years ago, but it's fair to wonder just how much longer he'll be around. He is coming off one of his best seasons, which is impressive when you consider that for a good chunk of the year he was playing with Josh Bellamy and Marc Mariani as his top receivers. He is also 33 years old, and while the Peyton Mannings and Tom Bradys of the world have changed what we can expect of older quar-

terbacks, Cutler has never been at their level, and likely won't be able to hold off Father Time for as long as they have. Cutler is also something of an odd fit on this team. The Bears have put together a very young roster, especially on defense, and it will probably take two or three years for that roster to develop before they are ready to contend for a championship. When that time comes, will Cutler still be around to lead them? Or will he join Marshall, Forte, and Bennett on the list of players who have been shown the door by Fox and Pace?

In fact, Cutler likely would have been gone already were it not for his contract. In January of 2014, then-Bears GM Phil Emery inked Cutler to a seven-year extension worth up to $126 million, with $54 million in guarantees. Almost immediately, the move looked like a huge mistake—ESPN's Mike Sando has called it the worst contract in the league—but Fox and Pace couldn't cut the quarterback without taking a cap hit of tens of millions of dollars. So instead they tried to find a trading partner. Just before the 2015 draft, Jason Cole at Bleacher Report reported that Fox and Pace were trying to trade Cutler and a package of picks to Tennessee to move up in the first round and take Marcus Mariota. Obviously, that deal never happened, but that doesn't mean Cutler will be in Chicago forever. Come 2017, the cap hit for releasing Cutler will be just $2 million.

The Bears could also be facing a big change at receiver. Alshon Jeffery will play 2016 under the franchise tag, and is hoping to sign a long-term deal after the season. If he does, it likely won't be in Chicago. If the Bears wanted to make a long-term investment in Jeffery, they could have gotten it done this year. Now consider this: Jeffery needs only 1,332 yards this year to break Johnny Morris' Chicago record of 5,059 receiving yards (which is amazing, considering Jeffery has only played 51 career games). Suppose he gains 1,400 or more yards this season—and we know he can, he had 1,421 in 2013—and then another team outbids the Bears for his services. And then, whether through trade or release, Cutler's time in Chicago finally comes to an end. If all that happens, then the Bears could be looking at a third straight year of upheaval, trying to replace their all-time leading passer *and* their all-time leading receiver at the same time.

This is why the 2016 season is so important for Chicago. They are a long shot to make the playoffs this year, but they must show signs of growth, indications that all these changes on the roster are actually leading to better things down the line. If not, it could be time for the Bears to say goodbye to Cutler and farewell to Jeffery, and hello to *Rebuilding 3: Rebuildageddon*.

Vincent Verhei

2015 Bears Stats by Week

Wk	vs.	W-L	PF	PA	YDF	YDA	TO	Total	Off	Def	ST
1	GB	L	23	31	402	322	-1	-39%	9%	50%	3%
2	ARI	L	23	48	335	300	0	-72%	-22%	35%	-15%
3	at SEA	L	0	26	146	371	0	-45%	-21%	-5%	-29%
4	OAK	W	22	20	371	243	-1	14%	3%	-17%	-5%
5	at KC	W	18	17	328	287	-1	22%	13%	-4%	5%
6	at DET	L	34	37	444	546	2	2%	0%	8%	10%
7	BYE										
8	MIN	L	20	23	305	327	1	-1%	25%	3%	-22%
9	at SD	W	22	19	446	339	-1	-9%	11%	8%	-12%
10	at STL	W	37	13	397	285	0	32%	21%	-21%	-10%
11	DEN	L	15	17	347	389	-2	13%	30%	26%	9%
12	at GB	W	17	13	290	365	2	9%	-1%	-10%	0%
13	SF	L	20	26	364	291	-1	-13%	-15%	7%	10%
14	WAS	L	21	24	377	374	0	12%	30%	19%	1%
15	at MIN	L	17	38	293	350	-2	-30%	6%	50%	13%
16	at TB	W	26	21	327	389	3	6%	21%	16%	2%
17	DET	L	20	24	345	349	-3	-10%	-3%	28%	21%

Trends and Splits

	Offense	Rank	Defense	Rank
Total DVOA	6.8%	10	11.3%	31
Unadjusted VOA	3.1%	12	11.5%	24
Weighted Trend	10.5%	9	11.5%	28
Variance	2.8%	2	4.7%	19
Average Opponent	-4.1%	2	1.1%	13
Passing	19.1%	13	17.3%	23
Rushing	4.2%	5	4.2%	31
First Down	-2.9%	17	1.4%	18
Second Down	1.9%	17	12.6%	30
Third Down	33.1%	2	29.2%	31
First Half	5.4%	11	10.4%	28
Second Half	8.3%	7	12.2%	25
Red Zone	-1.8%	17	35.9%	31
Late and Close	6.4%	8	10.1%	26

Five-Year Performance

Year	W-L	Pyth W	Est W	PF	PA	TO	Total	Rk	Off	Rk	Def	Rk	ST	Rk	Off AGL	Rk	Def AGL	Rk	Off Age	Rk	Def Age	Rk	ST Age	Rk
2011	8-8	8.3	7.3	353	341	+2	1.3%	15	-21.4%	30	-14.2%	4	8.5%	1	42.2	24	12.4	6	26.9	18	28.0	4	26.5	9
2012	10-6	10.8	11.0	375	277	+20	20.5%	6	-10.9%	26	-26.7%	1	4.7%	6	17.6	8	13.6	4	27.2	12	27.9	4	26.9	6
2013	8-8	7.3	9.2	445	478	+5	6.6%	11	13.3%	6	8.7%	25	2.0%	11	6.9	1	55.6	30	27.5	8	27.3	10	27.5	1
2014	5-11	4.9	6.4	319	442	-5	-13.8%	26	-0.1%	14	10.6%	28	-3.1%	25	41.0	27	60.6	26	27.9	3	27.0	12	26.3	9
2015	6-10	6.3	6.8	335	397	-4	-5.7%	19	6.9%	10	11.3%	31	-1.2%	21	64.7	30	28.2	16	27.4	10	25.8	31	26.2	13

2015 Performance Based on Most Common Personnel Groups

CHI Offense					CHI Offense vs. Opponents					CHI Defense				CHI Defense vs. Opponents			
Pers	Freq	Yds	DVOA	Run%	Pers	Freq	Yds	DVOA	Run%	Pers	Freq	Yds	DVOA	Pers	Freq	Yds	DVOA
11	64%	5.8	14.8%	32%	Base	26%	4.6	-9.4%	64%	Base	30%	5.4	3.0%	11	60%	6.0	18.0%
12	23%	5.7	1.4%	55%	Nickel	56%	5.9	12.1%	39%	Nickel	60%	6.1	13.4%	12	14%	6.1	12.1%
611	4%	4.3	-4.8%	81%	Dime+	16%	6.4	40.3%	19%	Dime+	8%	6.3	29.3%	21	9%	5.9	-2.8%
13	3%	4.7	-14.8%	69%	Goal Line	1%	1.0	92.4%	80%	Goal Line	1%	2.4	74.7%	22	4%	4.2	-17.8%
612	2%	4.5	11.5%	89%						Big	1%	3.4	-41.9%	13	4%	3.7	-11.0%

Strategic Tendencies

Run/Pass		Rk	Formation		Rk	Pass Rush		Rk	Secondary		Rk	Strategy		Rk
Runs, first half	47%	1	Form: Single Back	82%	7	Rush 3	9.8%	5	4 DB	30%	21	Play action	17%	22
Runs, first down	54%	5	Form: Empty Back	10%	11	Rush 4	69.6%	7	5 DB	60%	8	Avg Box (Off)	6.16	23
Runs, second-long	36%	5	Pers: 3+ WR	65%	11	Rush 5	17.6%	27	6+ DB	8%	20	Avg Box (Def)	6.04	29
Runs, power sit.	53%	23	Pers: 2+ TE/6+ OL	34%	15	Rush 6+	3.0%	29	CB by Sides	75%	17	Offensive Pace	31.74	27
Runs, behind 2H	32%	1	Pers: 6+ OL	6%	6	Sacks by LB	58.6%	8	S/CB Cover Ratio	18%	30	Defensive Pace	30.96	27
Pass, ahead 2H	43%	28	Shotgun/Pistol	74%	5	Sacks by DB	8.6%	14	DB Blitz	5%	29	Go for it on 4th	0.74	23

In case you were wondering if Marc Trestman and John Fox had different coaching philosophies, the Bears went from dead last in first-half run/pass ratio in 2014 (30 percent) to first in 2015. ⬤ The Bears were again among the teams that most frequently used six linemen (6.1 percent of plays, sixth) but passed on ⬤ plays a lot less often than they did the year before.

No offense called more wide receiver screens than Chicago with 58. However, the Bears only had a -12.7% DVOA on these plays, which ranked 21st. Chicago threw only 12 percent of its passes to the middle of the field, the lowest figure in the league. They threw a league-high 47 percent of passes to the right side. The Bears defense was surprisingly good at ending possessions quickly, ranking seventh in three-and-outs forced per drive. However, they were bad at ending possessions suddenly, ranking 29th in turnovers forced per drive. Chicago had the worst tackling defense in the league, with a broken tackle recorded on 11.3 percent of plays. The perils of a Man-2 coverage scheme: Chicago gave up 300 rushing yards on scrambles last year, the most in the league. They only gave up 6 yards on designed quarterback runs, the fewest in the league. The defense was usually at its worst when the stakes were highest. When leading by one score, the Bears had the worst defensive DVOA in the league at 26.0%. And in late-and-close situations, Chicago ranked 26th with a 10.1% DVOA. On the other hand, the offense ranked eighth in late-and-close DVOA.

Passing

Player	DYAR	DVOA	Plays	NtYds	Avg	YAC	C%	TD	Int
J.Cutler	659	8.6%	512	3499	6.8	5.6	64.5%	21	11
J.Clausen*	-63	-41.0%	44	154	3.5	4.4	57.5%	0	1
B.Hoyer	201	-3.0%	394	2400	6.1	4.2	61.0%	19	5

Rushing

Player	DYAR	DVOA	Plays	Yds	Avg	TD	Fum	Suc
M.Forte*	192	12.0%	218	898	4.1	4	1	48%
J.Langford	123	12.7%	148	537	3.6	6	0	47%
K.Carey	56	21.2%	43	161	3.7	2	1	58%
J.Cutler	84	43.7%	28	208	7.4	1	1	-
J.Rodgers	7	2.1%	14	41	2.9	0	0	36%

Receiving

Player	DYAR	DVOA	Plays	Ctch	Yds	Y/C	YAC	TD	C%
A.Jeffery	126	4.1%	94	54	807	14.9	3.3	4	57%
M.Wilson	127	17.0%	51	28	464	16.6	6.6	1	55%
E.Royal	-81	-34.0%	50	37	238	6.4	4.8	1	74%
J.Bellamy	-11	-16.8%	34	19	224	11.8	3.6	2	56%
M.Mariani	82	18.8%	33	22	300	13.6	5.9	0	67%
C.Meredith	7	-6.3%	16	11	120	10.9	3.4	0	69%
M.Bennett*	-18	-10.7%	80	53	443	8.4	4.3	3	66%
Z.Miller	104	25.6%	46	34	439	12.9	6.5	5	74%
M.Forte*	112	23.5%	58	44	389	8.8	8.0	3	76%
J.Langford	16	-6.6%	42	22	279	12.7	10.4	1	52%

Offensive Line

Player	Pos	Age	GS	Snaps	Pen	Sk	Pass	Run	Player	Pos	Age	GS	Snaps	Pen	Sk	Pass	Run
Matt Slauson*	LG/C	30	16/16	1083	5	0.5	5.5	6.0	Hroniss Grasu	C	25	8/8	550	4	0.0	2.0	4.0
Kyle Long	RT	28	16/16	1082	9	6.5	11.5	2.0	Jermon Bushrod*	LT	32	12/4	235	4	0.5	2.5	2.0
Charles Leno	LT	25	16/13	914	8	3.5	8.5	4.0	Will Montgomery*	C	33	4/4	199	1	0.0	1.0	0.0
Vladimir Ducasse*	G	29	16/11	752	9	2.0	5.0	5.0	Bobby Massie	RT	27	14/14	979	6	2.0	9.0	3.5
Patrick Omameh*	RG	27	14/9	665	3	2.0	4.0	1.0	Ted Larsen	G	29	10/10	679	4	1.0	6.0	2.0

Year	Yards	ALY	Rank	Power	Rank	Stuff	Rank	2nd Lev	Rank	Open Field	Rank	Sacks	ASR	Rank	Press	Rank	F-Start	Cont.
2013	4.37	3.80	20	50%	30	21%	26	1.23	11	1.03	3	30	5.5%	5	26.0%	20	8	48
2014	3.97	3.94	15	68%	10	18%	10	1.21	12	0.38	32	41	6.3%	18	22.1%	11	24	23
2015	3.89	4.09	7	74%	4	16%	2	1.05	23	0.30	32	34	5.6%	12	30.1%	27	19	26

2015 ALY by direction: Left End 3.27 (23)   Left Tackle 4.41 (6)   Mid/Guard 4.24 (5)   Right Tackle 3.63 (21)   Right End 4.15 (7)

Between center Will Montgomery, guards Matt Slauson, Vladimir Ducasse, and Patrick Omameh, and Jermon Bushrod (the aging left tackle who lost his job to Charles Leno early in the year), the Bears literally lost an entire offensive line in free agency. Leno remains at left tackle, while Chicago signed Bobby Massie away from Arizona to play on the right side. That will move Kyle Long inside to right guard. Center and left guard remain something of a mystery. Cody Whitehair, a second-round rookie out of Kansas State, is penciled in at right guard, with Hroniss Grasu getting another chance at center. Whitehair also has experience at center and could wind up there. The Bears complicated things by adding two more veteran free-agent interior linemen in Ted Larsen and Manny Ramirez, though Ramirez clarified things somewhat when he surprisingly retired in June. The Bears finished dead last in open-field yards for the second year in a row. This is shocking to see from a franchise with perhaps the NFL's most glorious legacy at running back, from Bronko Nagurski to Gale Sayers to Walter Payton to Neal Anderson to Matt Forte. It explains in part why the Bears were willing to let Forte leave, though Jeremy Langford hardly looks like the kind of speedster to turn this trend around.

Defensive Front Seven

Defensive Line	Age	Pos	G	Snaps	Plays	TmPct	Overall Rk	Stop	Dfts	BTkl	Runs	vs. Run St%	Rk	RuYd	Rk	Pass Rush Sack	Hit	Hur	Dsrpt
Jarvis Jenkins*	28	DE	15	636	33	4.6%	48	25	8	6	25	68%	66	3.4	81	4.0	7	9.5	1
Eddie Goldman	22	DT	15	515	22	3.1%	76	19	6	2	16	88%	11	2.2	44	4.5	1	5.0	0
Will Sutton	25	DE	13	419	26	4.2%	58	18	2	4	20	65%	74	3.0	67	0.0	2	5.0	4
Mitch Unrein	29	DE	16	381	19	2.5%	--	11	1	3	15	60%	--	3.4	--	1.0	2	7.5	0
Bruce Gaston*	25	DE	9	179	12	2.8%	--	10	1	1	11	82%	--	3.3	--	1.0	4	4.5	0
Akiem Hicks	27	DT	16	399	22	2.7%	--	19	7	2	19	84%	--	2.1	--	3.0	4	6.5	0

Edge Rushers	Age	Pos	G	Snaps	Plays	TmPct	Overall Rk	Stop	Dfts	BTkl	Runs	vs. Run St%	Rk	RuYd	Rk	Pass Rush Sack	Hit	Hur	Dsrpt
Pernell McPhee	27	OLB	14	594	56	8.4%	3	40	16	6	41	71%	63	2.4	47	6.0	14	21.5	2
Willie Young	31	OLB	15	524	32	4.5%	56	22	14	0	22	59%	89	2.5	54	6.5	9	15.5	1
Sam Acho	28	OLB	15	447	33	4.6%	52	16	5	7	22	55%	92	3.6	89	0.0	2	4.0	0
Lamarr Houston	29	OLB	16	417	40	5.2%	43	29	11	1	25	76%	38	3.0	76	8.0	6	11.5	0

Linebackers	Age	Pos	G	Snaps	Plays	TmPct	Overall Rk	Stop	Dfts	BTkl	Runs	vs. Run St%	Rk	RuYd	Rk	Pass Rush Sack	Hit	Hur	vs. Pass Tgts	Suc%	Rk	AdjYd	Rk	PD	Int
Christian Jones	25	ILB	15	745	87	12.2%	42	40	5	5	62	53%	77	4.5	79	0.0	3	5.5	18	74%	6	4.0	9	3	0
Shea McClellin*	27	ILB	12	675	82	14.3%	28	35	6	14	49	47%	86	4.6	80	0.0	2	4.5	25	37%	66	9.6	67	1	0
Jonathan Anderson	25	ILB	11	312	36	6.9%	76	17	8	3	12	42%	88	4.8	84	0.0	2	2.5	24	60%	27	8.4	63	2	1
John Timu	24	ILB	7	159	23	6.9%	--	10	1	5	16	63%	--	3.0	--	0.0	0	0	3	66%	--	4.7	--	0	0
Jerrell Freeman	30	ILB	13	753	114	16.7%	9	79	17	4	83	72%	14	3.7	49	3.0	4	5.5	21	78%	4	2.6	1	2	1
Danny Trevathan	26	ILB	15	737	114	14.8%	21	70	13	13	76	68%	23	3.3	32	0.0	3	4	26	67%	15	6.2	37	4	2

Year	Yards	ALY	Rank	Power	Rank	Stuff	Rank	2nd Level	Rank	Open Field	Rank	Sacks	ASR	Rank	Press	Rank
2013	5.34	4.45	32	77%	31	20%	14	1.57	32	1.40	32	31	6.3%	23	21.4%	30
2014	4.45	4.38	30	53%	2	15%	31	1.12	13	0.84	24	39	6.4%	22	24.4%	18
2015	4.33	4.59	32	68%	21	15%	32	1.27	27	0.44	5	35	6.2%	18	24.7%	20

2015 ALY by direction: Left End 3.90 (22)   Left Tackle 4.42 (28)   Mid/Guard 4.38 (31)   Right Tackle 5.12 (32)   Right End 6.08 (32)

Though technically a 3-4 team, the Bears spent most of last season in a nickel defense with two linemen, two outside line-backers, and two inside linebackers in the box. This formation (or the similar 4-2-5) is basically the standard for most NFL defenses these days. ☞ We already mentioned that Danny Trevathan and Jerrell Freeman should be a big upgrade over Shea McClellin and Christian Jones in the run game. As these numbers show, they should also be a big upgrade in pass coverage, especially over McClellin. That's important for a defense such as Chicago that plays a lot of man coverage. It's especially important given the Bears' struggles against opposing tight ends in recent seasons (27th or worse each of the last three years). ☞ It is astounding how the Bears have finished in the bottom three in adjusted line yards three years in a row, after finishing in the top six eight times in the prior nine seasons. It's probably meaningful that the collapse coincides with the retirement of Brian Urlacher. Only after he's gone is it clear what an impact he made on those great Bears defenses early this century. Between Urlacher, Lance Briggs, Mike Singletary, and Dick Butkus, the Bears have historically been as great at linebacker as they have at running back.

Defensive Secondary

Secondary	Age	Pos	G	Snaps	Plays	Overall TmPct	Rk	Stop	Dfts	BTkl	vs. Run Runs	St%	Rk	RuYd	Rk	vs. Pass Tgts	Tgt%	Rk	Dist	Suc%	Rk	AdjYd	Rk	PD	Int
Adrian Amos	23	FS	16	1029	69	9.1%	44	23	9	13	27	44%	28	5.9	21	14	3.9%	6	10.3	34%	70	12.5	70	1	0
Kyle Fuller	24	CB	16	1022	63	8.3%	45	22	9	16	20	30%	54	7.5	40	60	17.3%	15	13.3	51%	45	7.3	31	10	2
Tracy Porter	30	CB	14	843	47	7.0%	64	19	7	7	4	50%	20	5.3	16	66	22.8%	58	14.5	55%	24	7.3	29	12	1
Antrel Rolle	34	SS	7	388	36	10.8%	--	14	1	4	17	35%	--	8.2	--	8	6.1%	--	15.9	44%	--	9.9	--	1	0
Chris Prosinski	29	SS	13	337	23	3.7%	--	8	4	9	11	36%	--	8.8	--	3	2.2%	--	6.8	60%	--	6.0	--	0	0
Bryce Callahan	25	CB	9	321	25	5.8%	--	16	8	2	5	40%	--	2.8	--	20	17.9%	--	8.8	68%	--	5.7	--	2	0
Sherrick McManis	29	CB	16	298	16	2.1%	--	7	4	5	6	50%	--	6.5	--	20	19.7%	--	12.6	35%	--	13.2	--	0	0
Harold Jones-Quartey	23	SS	13	273	23	3.7%	--	5	2	2	7	14%	--	8.1	--	15	15.6%	--	13.0	38%	--	9.8	--	1	1
Alan Ball*	31	CB	15	248	21	2.9%	--	9	4	2	10	40%	--	7.9	--	16	18.4%	--	10.8	51%	--	7.6	--	3	0

Year	Pass D Rank	vs. #1 WR	Rk	vs. #2 WR	Rk	vs. Other WR	Rk	vs. TE	Rk	vs. RB	Rk
2013	17	-10.0%	10	6.6%	18	4.0%	19	18.8%	27	-14.3%	6
2014	29	11.2%	25	10.1%	25	-0.3%	17	30.6%	32	3.0%	21
2015	23	20.7%	31	-12.7%	9	0.8%	15	26.5%	30	-1.8%	14

You can see in the target numbers how frequently the Bears used two deep safeties in coverage last year. Chicago's safeties had only 40 pass targets combined between them, tied with Oakland for the fewest in the league. This is also why opponents threw so few deep passes against Chicago: 17 percent of all passes, third-lowest behind the Rams and Buccaneers. ☞ On the other hand, with safeties playing deep and linebackers turning to chase receivers in man coverage, the Bears were vulnerable to draw plays. Opponents ran draws 29 times against Chicago, the most in the league, though the Bears were in the middle of the pack in average yards allowed (4.7) and DVOA (1.3%) against those draws. ☞ The Bears bolstered their secondary with three draft picks. Safety Deon Bush (fourth round, Miami) is a big hitter with raw coverage technique. Deiondre' Hall (fourth round, Northern Iowa) is one of those hybrid types that coaches love so much right now; he played all over the field in college, including the front seven. But he's a little undersized as a safety and a bit stiff as a man-coverage cornerback. DeAndre Houston-Carson (sixth round, William & Mary) is another very physical player, a three-year cornerback who switched to free safety as a senior. Both NFL Draft Scout and NFL.com projected him to go two rounds earlier. He also blocked four punts in 2014 and should be a core special-teamer.

Special Teams

Year	DVOA	Rank	FG/XP	Rank	Net Kick	Rank	Kick Ret	Rank	Net Punt	Rank	Punt Ret	Rank	Hidden	Rank
2013	2.0%	11	4.0	9	-4.1	26	-1.6	18	5.3	11	6.5	7	-5.6	23
2014	-3.1%	25	-5.9	29	0.2	16	1.6	10	-6.9	25	-4.3	23	-1.4	21
2015	-1.2%	21	3.5	9	-15.0	32	3.3	9	3.0	15	-0.9	18	-8.2	27

Neither Robbie Gould's kickoffs nor Pat O'Donnell's punts were very good by our gross value metrics, but the real issues for Chicago were coverage teams that allowed two touchdowns on kickoff returns and another on a punt. ☞ This is not to say there were no bright spots on the Chicago coverage teams. Sherrick McManis had 11 stops on kick returns—ending a play short of the average return length—and Chris Prosinski had eight. Only four other teams had two gunners so effective (the Patriots had three). ☞ The Bears tried two kickoff returners last year, but Deonte Thompson (29.2-yard average on 14 returns, including a 74-yarder) was clearly superior to Marc Mariani and should be the primary man on kickoffs going forward. ☞ Mariani also had negative value on punt returns, but he is expected to be Chicago's top man there again this season.

Cincinnati Bengals

2015 record: 12-4	Total DVOA: 27.9% (2nd)	2016 Mean Projection: 8.5 wins	On the Clock (0-4): 7%
Pythagorean Wins: 11.7 (4th)	Offense: 18.6% (2nd)	Postseason Odds: 40.9%	Mediocrity (5-7): 28%
Snap-Weighted Age: 27 (8th)	Defense: -7.1% (10th)	Super Bowl Odds: 6.1%	Playoff Contender (8-10): 43%
Average Opponent: 3.3% (12th)	Special Teams: 2.2% (8th)	Proj. Avg. Opponent: -1.1% (21st)	Super Bowl Contender (11+): 22%

2015: Cruel and unusual heartbreak.

2016: Nostalgia for an age that may never come.

Clearly, some things are just not meant to happen.

Once again, the NFL's Charlie Brown (right down to the striped shirt) built up a head of steam, only to have Lucy jerk the ball away before it got kicked to the moon. After four straight one-and-done playoff runs (and six overall under head coach Marvin Lewis) that combined inferior play, superior opposition, and bad luck, Cincinnati took all three ingredients and mixed in a heaping spoonful of self-immolation, conjuring a loss to the hated Steelers out of thin air.

You may not recall all the particulars, which twisted and turned and consumed plot like a full season of *Game of Thrones*. There were the three quarters of offensive futility from backup quarterback AJ McCarron, leading to a 15-0 deficit, including a Pittsburgh touchdown pass that the NFL later admitted was incomplete; the game-changing sack/smash of Ben Roethlisberger; the comeback capped by a late touchdown pass to A.J. Green; the seemingly game-sealing interception and subsequent wind sprint to the tunnel by Vontaze Burfict; the mind-blowing fumble by Jeremy Hill; the Return of Roethlisberger to convert a fourth-down pass despite his damaged shoulder; and of course the end-game meltdown, the personal fouls and subsequent mayhem that gifted Pittsburgh 30 crucial yards and abetted their theft of a seemingly lost game.

Cue the football public: "Only the Bengals."

Obviously, that game won't ever be forgotten in Cincinnati, a city where crimes and misdemeanors at the hands of the hated rivals from Pittsburgh are catalogued with the meticulousness of the Library of Congress. But even while fans were still trying to comprehend why Pittsburgh assistant coach Joey Porter—who once led a gang that jumped former Bengals lineman Levi Jones on the floor of a Vegas casino—was allowed on the field to taunt Cincinnati players and consequently draw critical penalty flags, their team lost its own ultra-valuable assistant coach.

Hue Jackson's contributions to victory were more conventional than Porter's, to be sure. His firm hand on the tiller of the offense led to the league's top passing game (post-season stat fixes slipped them just barely behind Seattle in overall offensive DVOA), as well as quarterback Andy Dalton's finest year as a pro. The defense was sturdy as ever, but it was the explosive attack, featuring Jackson's trademark creativity, that spurred the Bengals to new heights. Twelve wins were the most in Cincinnati since the AFC champions of 1988, even though the team played the final quarter of the season and the playoff game with McCarron behind center. But a dozen victories weren't enough to capture a bye, leaving Cincy at the mercy of their wild-card demon.

Now Jackson is gone, left to coach the rival Cleveland Browns, a spit in the eye on top of a gut punch. But that wasn't the lone loss the elite passing game suffered in the offseason. Wide receivers Marvin Jones and Mohamed Sanu both left for far greener (emphasis on *green*) pastures in free agency. The Bengals replaced them with second- (maybe third-) tier free agent Brandon LaFell and second-round draft pick Tyler Boyd of Pitt, a good prospect but a consolation prize after the consensus top four wideouts in the draft were snagged before Cincinnati could select any of them.

Then in late May came more troubling news. Tight end Tyler Eifert, the ultra-talented and ultra-brittle touchdown machine who scored 13 times in a breakout 2015, underwent ankle surgery after sustaining an injury in the *Pro Bowl*, fergawdsakes. Eifert postponed surgery hoping the ankle would heal without going under the knife, but opted for an operation when pain persisted. He will miss all of the summer, and his status for the first weeks of the season is in doubt.

So in the span of a handful of months, the offense morphed from exclamation point to question mark. Even with the uncertainty, we're forecasting that Cincinnati will once again be one of the NFL's better teams, ranked in the top ten for both mean DVOA and mean win projection. But the Bengals aren't likely to be at the very top of the league again the way they were in 2015. Just in case Cincinnati fans aren't frustrated enough yet, two of the teams likely to outpace the Bengals are division rivals Pittsburgh and Baltimore, which would leave the Stripes you-know-where come the postseason. And even a ten-win season with yet another game on wild-card weekend feels a bit optimistic in light of the hits the offense has taken.

Much will depend on whether Dalton truly broke through in 2015, or if he was a product of Jackson's scheming and the overall brilliance around him. Certainly, Dalton played remarkably well through 12 games, until breaking his thumb against Pittsburgh (naturally) and being lost for the remainder of the season. The injury was particularly cruel, as Dalton sustained it while tackling the interceptor of a rare (in 2015) ill-advised pass. Trying to bring down Stephon Tuitt, the-

2016 Bengals Schedule

Week	Opp.	Week	Opp.	Week	Opp.
1	at NYJ	7	CLE	13	PHI
2	at PIT	8	WAS (U.K.)	14	at CLE
3	DEN	9	BYE	15	PIT
4	MIA (Thu.)	10	at NYG (Mon.)	16	at HOU (Sat.)
5	at DAL	11	BUF	17	BAL
6	at NE	12	at BAL		

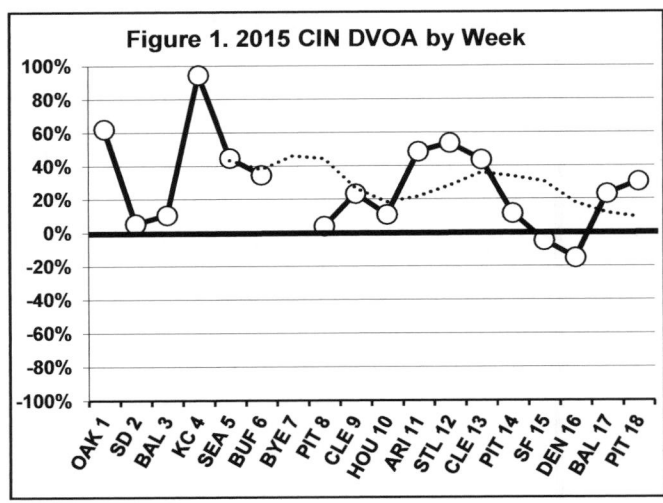

Figure 1. 2015 CIN DVOA by Week

behemoth who picked off the goal-line shovel attempt, was Dalton's second poor decision in as many seconds, and in a flash the play effectively ended Cincinnati's Super Bowl aspirations, despite McCarron's occasional moments of quality in Dalton's stead.

Dalton is healthy, but can he flourish minus his *sensei* and a large chunk of his targets? The Bengals were able to keep defenses on their heels in 2015 thanks to their depth of pass catchers and multiple formations that virtually guaranteed a mismatch somewhere. Dalton's improvement was based around his improved ability to find the right player to target and decisively get the ball to him.

Without Jones, Sanu, and perhaps Eifert, the equation will be flipped on its head—now the onus will be on Dalton to move the team without the luxury of a bevy of open receivers. Aaron Rodgers himself struggled to do just that last season; it's hard to imagine Dalton is suddenly *that* much better than his previous form. Sustaining drives will be difficult unless LaFell regains his 2014 efficiency, *and* Boyd is superb from the very start, *and* backup tight end Tyler Kroft can build upon a promising rookie season, *and* Hill can rebound from a depressing sophomore campaign, etc. There was already a neon sign flashing "regression" in huge letters before the personnel and coaching losses this offseason; after all, the Bengals had ranked either 17th or 18th in offensive DVOA for five straight seasons before last year's dramatic improvement. Even with a healthy Eifert and Green operating with his usual excellence, getting anywhere close to last year's offensive output seems unlikely.

Ironically, Jackson took over two seasons ago vowing to emphasize the running game after his predecessor, Jay Gruden, threw it 587 times in 2013 (Cincy had 505 pass attempts last season and 503 in 2014). Quarterbacks coach Ken Zampese, son of legendary offensive guru Ernie Zampese, was promoted to replace Jackson, and Zampese probably wants to let it fly like his mentor Mike Martz. But with personnel limitations forcing his hand, the Bengals may end up even more run-oriented this season.

Hill's strong 2014 came mostly in the back half of the season, after the Bengals receiver corps was shredded by injury. The Bengals put H-back and ace blocker Ryan Hewitt on the field to lead Hill in power sets, and the Bengals rode him to the playoffs. Hill was out of place in the more wide-open offense of 2015, and wasn't missed; the Bengals were the best shotgun attack in the league. But Hill and fellow back Gio Bernard will likely be counted upon to shoulder a heavier load

with the passing game in transition. The duo will have to come through early, as the schedule is front-heavy, including trips to New York (Jets), Pittsburgh, Dallas, and New England in the first six weeks.

Fortunately, the Bengals can rely on one of the league's best offensive lines to pave the way. The unit led the NFL in adjusted line yards while fronted by sensational left tackle Andrew Whitworth, who gave up just a single sack all season. Yet there is transition here, too. Last year's top draft choice, Cedric Ogbuehi, is ready to take over at right tackle for the departed Andre Smith after what was essentially a redshirt season. Ogbuehi's athleticism is off the charts, and fellow second-year lineman Jake Fisher isn't far behind. Fisher was a backup tackle who was frequently eligible and occasionally targeted for passes. (Heck, he may be asked to play some tight end this season.) The offensive line has been Exhibit A in Lewis' mantra that brute force in the trenches wins in the AFC North. That's true to a point, but the line could use the welcome injection of mobility in space. Cincy was 14th in second-level yards and 15th in adjusted sack rate, average rankings that speak to the need for some quicker feet among the big uglies.

If there is good news for the offense, it's that they don't have far to look for an example of a unit surviving the loss of a hugely respected and effective coordinator. The Bengals defense has marched steadily along despite Mike Zimmer taking the head coaching gig in Minnesota after 2013 (and, like Gruden with Washington, putting his team in the playoffs in Year 2—Lewis may not have much to boast about when it comes to postseason success, but his coaching tree is top-notch). In 2015, the unit was tenth overall defensively in DVOA, and first in variance—there were really no stinkeroos.

Paul Guenther has emerged from Zimmer's shadow as a high-quality coach on his own, though Lewis' defensive acumen surely helps here as well. In Zimmer's last two seasons in Cincinnati, 2012 and 2013, the team ranked ninth and fourth in DVOA against the pass. In Guenther's initial two seasons, the pass defense ranked seventh and tenth. The numbers have remained strong despite wide variance in help from the pass rush. In those four years, Cincy's adjusted sack rate has been as high as second and low as 31st.

High-quality secondary play has thus been a Bengals hallmark in the Lewis era, which figures to continue. The Bengals lost two impact free agents, slot corner Leon Hall and safety Reggie Nelson (whose eight picks tied for the league lead), yet are well positioned in the defensive backfield thanks to the priority the team places on the back four, especially cornerback. Another first-round defensive back (the third in five years) gets added to the mix this season in William Jackson of Houston, whose athleticism and ball skills are reminiscent of former Bengal Johnathan Joseph.

The depth allowed Guenther to employ very basic schemes. Cincinnati stayed in far more 2-high safety zone looks last year than ever before, relying on talent to win in the secondary and along the rush line, where blitzing was rare. The Bengals used just four pass rushers on 504 of their 644 passing snaps, by the far the most in the NFL in number and percentage. Of the Bengals' 42 sacks, a mere 4.5 came from the back seven (that's a league-low 11 percent). The excellence in overall team coverage is borne out by Cincy's 88 percent success rate when rushing just three, also tops in the league.

That output was keyed by the return to greatness of defensive tackle Geno Atkins. Guenther performed some Zimmeresque psy-ops on Geno before the season, calling him "just a guy" after recovery from torn-ACL surgery left him good but hardly great in 2014. Guenther actually hinted that Geno could be replaced. Instead, Atkins returned to his All-Pro quality of yore, destroying the interior of offensive lines and moving with his old lightning-bolt quickness. Only Aaron Donald had more defeats among defensive tackles. His massive inside presence allowed Carlos Dunlap to emerge with 13.5 sacks, most of which he credited to knowing that quarterbacks would be unable to step up in the pocket. Whether Guenther's mind games helped flip Atkins' switch is of course unquantifiable, but it was an important moment for a young coordinator.

Guenther's next challenge will be breaking in virtually an entire new staff beneath him. The Bengals lost coaches on this side of the ball, too. Secondary coach Vance Joseph's move to take over the Miami defense didn't receive a fraction of the attention Jackson's departure did, but Joseph did a sensational job and will be missed. (Joseph was essentially traded for Kevin Coyle, who was fired by the Dolphins, then hired by Cincinnati to replace Joseph.) Defensive line coach Jay Hayes and linebackers coach Matt Burke also left for jobs in the Sunshine State (Burke to the Dolphins, Hayes to the Bucs), to be replaced by Jacob Burney and Jim Haslett, respectively.

The talent on the roster remains formidable, yet the feeling of an opportunity missed permeates the organization. Jackson, Joseph, and other coaches stayed in Cincinnati last offseason specifically for the 2015 run, and the exceptionally deep roster was laden with free agents-to-be who knew they all wouldn't return to the Queen City. The team remained healthy—freakishly so, by Bengals standards, finishing at the top of the league in adjusted games lost with 28.2 (a stat that is doubly crushing when one of the lone key injuries, Dalton's busted thumb, wound up being so costly). The AFC North wasn't its usual snarling self, as Baltimore suffered through an awful season, Ben Roethlisberger was carted off the field on multiple occasions, and Cleveland was Cleveland. In the Week 16 game that essentially determined a first-round bye, Cincinnati led Denver 14-0 and had the ball inside the Broncos' 30 again with four minutes left in the first half. The Bengals lost in overtime, then watched as Denver went on to win a Lombardi Trophy that, with a few breaks, might have been theirs.

It's not unheard of for an NFL team to make a surprise run at glory after blowing what looked like its last, best chance. In fact, the Bengals have seen both archrivals do it. The Steelers botched a 15-1 record in Ben Roethlisberger's rookie season, then won the Super Bowl as a sixth seed the year after. The 12-4 Ravens of 2011 went home when Billy Cundiff couldn't hit a 32-yard field goal in Foxborough, but hoisted the Lombardi Trophy a year later. Yet given recent history and the offseason departures, it makes sense that pessimism outpaces optimism in Bengals Nation. The 2016 season is fraught with uncertainty, and the looming sense that the team is farther from that elusive playoff win, not closer to it.

Robert Weintraub

2015 Bengals Stats by Week

Wk	vs.	W-L	PF	PA	YDF	YDA	TO	Total	Off	Def	ST
1	at OAK	W	33	13	396	246	2	62%	44%	-25%	-6%
2	SD	W	24	19	389	354	1	5%	9%	0%	-3%
3	at BAL	W	28	24	458	398	-1	11%	9%	-1%	1%
4	KC	W	36	21	445	461	1	95%	97%	0%	-2%
5	SEA	W	27	24	419	397	-1	45%	31%	-3%	10%
6	at BUF	W	34	21	355	368	1	35%	34%	15%	16%
7	BYE										
8	at PIT	W	16	10	296	356	1	4%	-28%	-21%	10%
9	CLE	W	31	10	371	213	0	23%	26%	-2%	-5%
10	HOU	L	6	10	256	256	-1	11%	-8%	-18%	1%
11	at ARI	L	31	34	377	383	1	49%	37%	-6%	6%
12	STL	W	31	7	376	345	2	54%	38%	-13%	3%
13	at CLE	W	37	3	377	273	2	44%	14%	-21%	9%
14	PIT	L	20	33	385	354	-2	11%	2%	-7%	3%
15	at SF	W	24	14	242	318	3	-5%	-26%	-26%	-5%
16	at DEN	L	17	20	294	390	0	-15%	23%	30%	-9%
17	BAL	W	24	16	292	341	2	23%	2%	-15%	7%
18	PIT	L	16	18	279	369	-2	31%	-23%	-39%	15%

Trends and Splits

	Offense	Rank	Defense	Rank
Total DVOA	18.6%	1	-7.0%	10
Unadjusted VOA	15.5%	5	-7.2%	9
Weighted Trend	12.4%	7	-7.7%	9
Variance	9.0%	27	2.2%	1
Average Opponent	-2.3%	10	0.4%	17
Passing	48.5%	1	-0.9%	10
Rushing	0.4%	7	-17.2%	8
First Down	12.6%	4	-9.8%	5
Second Down	24.9%	1	-7.5%	7
Third Down	20.0%	7	-1.1%	15
First Half	29.6%	1	-12.1%	8
Second Half	7.7%	8	-2.0%	12
Red Zone	26.9%	6	7.9%	20
Late and Close	3.4%	13	-16.1%	7

Five-Year Performance

Year	W-L	Pyth W	Est W	PF	PA	TO	Total	Rk	Off	Rk	Def	Rk	ST	Rk	Off AGL	Rk	Def AGL	Rk	Off Age	Rk	Def Age	Rk	ST Age	Rk
2011	9-7	8.6	8.5	344	323	0	0.1%	17	-1.4%	17	0.8%	17	2.3%	7	25.2	14	26.5	17	26.5	24	27.4	13	26.4	13
2012	10-6	9.9	8.7	391	320	+4	6.10%	12	-1.8%	17	-3.78%	10	4.1%	7	37.0	21	22.2	13	25.1	32	27.3	11	26.0	17
2013	11-5	11.1	10.1	430	305	+1	14.2%	9	0.4%	17	-12.6%	5	1.2%	12	11.2	2	30.5	19	26.0	29	27.4	8	26.3	9
2014	10-5-1	8.6	9.0	365	344	0	5.0%	12	-1.4%	18	-2.3%	14	4.2%	6	48.5	28	23.2	5	25.9	29	28.1	2	26.1	14
2015	12-4	11.7	12.3	419	279	+11	27.9%	2	18.6%	2	-7.1%	10	2.2%	8	10.0	1	18.2	6	26.2	23	28.1	2	26.5	10

2015 Performance Based on Most Common Personnel Groups

CIN Offense					CIN Offense vs. Opponents					CIN Defense					CIN Defense vs. Opponents			
Pers	Freq	Yds	DVOA	Run%	Pers	Freq	Yds	DVOA	Run%	Pers	Freq	Yds	DVOA		Pers	Freq	Yds	DVOA
11	51%	6.5	36.4%	25%	Base	37%	5.0	12.7%	57%	Base	28%	4.9	-13.1%		11	62%	5.2	-8.6%
12	25%	5.6	13.0%	55%	Nickel	48%	6.8	28.5%	33%	Nickel	68%	5.4	-5.6%		12	17%	5.7	9.5%
13	7%	4.8	-7.2%	63%	Dime+	12%	5.8	56.1%	20%	Dime+	3%	8.0	63.9%		21	10%	4.1	-33.7%
21	5%	5.7	17.5%	44%	Goal Line	2%	1.0	26.5%	56%	Goal Line	1%	1.2	29.2%		22	3%	3.6	-20.4%
611	4%	6.3	24.6%	56%	Big	1%	3.6	-13.7%	82%						10	2%	7.7	-12.3%
612	3%	4.2	0.6%	57%														

Strategic Tendencies

Run/Pass		Rk	Formation		Rk	Pass Rush		Rk	Secondary		Rk	Strategy		Rk
Runs, first half	40%	10	Form: Single Back	72%	21	Rush 3	2.5%	29	4 DB	28%	23	Play-action	20%	11
Runs, first down	48%	14	Form: Empty Back	6%	21	Rush 4	78.3%	1	5 DB	68%	2	Avg Box (Off)	6.38	5
Runs, second-long	29%	20	Pers: 3+ WR	53%	26	Rush 5	13.8%	32	6+ DB	3%	27	Avg Box (Def)	6.00	30
Runs, power sit.	67%	7	Pers: 2+ TE/6+ OL	44%	6	Rush 6+	5.4%	18	CB by Sides	97%	1	Offensive Pace	30.52	18
Runs, behind 2H	21%	25	Pers: 6+ OL	11%	3	Sacks by LB	8.3%	31	S/CB Cover Ratio	21%	22	Defensive Pace	30.55	20
Pass, ahead 2H	45%	21	Shotgun/Pistol	63%	16	Sacks by DB	2.4%	30	DB Blitz	10%	14	Go for it on 4th	1.56	4

The Bengals used at least six offensive linemen on 9.5 percent of plays, fourth in the NFL. They averaged 5.0 yards on these plays with 23.8% DVOA. ☜ The Bengals ranked 17th in the league on defensive DVOA against short passes, but had the best DVOA against deep passes (16 or more yards past the line of scrimmage). ☜ Bengals opponents threw a league-high 30 percent of their passes in the middle of the field, even though the Bengals ranked seventh in defensive DVOA against such passes. ☜ The Bengals had a league-leading -35.4% DVOA against the run on third downs, but ranked only 21st with 6.6% DVOA against the pass. ☜ A league-leading 8.8 percent of running back carries against Cincinnati were draws, and the Bengals have struggled with draws for two seasons: 6.7 yards per carry and 29.3% DVOA in 2015, and 7.4 yards per carry and 58.9% DVOA in 2014.

Passing

Player	DYAR	DVOA	Plays	NtYds	Avg	YAC	C%	TD	Int
A.Dalton	1135	31.7%	409	3103	7.6	5.9	66.1%	26	7
AJ McCarron	151	6.9%	132	781	5.9	4.0	66.4%	6	2

Rushing

Player	DYAR	DVOA	Plays	Yds	Avg	TD	Fum	Suc
J.Hill	85	0.1%	223	792	3.6	11	3	49%
G.Bernard	131	11.8%	154	730	4.7	2	0	49%
A.Dalton	9	-8.1%	42	150	3.6	3	1	-
M.Sanu*	62	77.2%	10	71	7.1	2	0	-
R.Burkhead	-30	-222.9%	4	3	0.8	0	1	0%

Receiving

Player	DYAR	DVOA	Plays	Ctch	Yds	Y/C	YAC	TD	C%
A.J.Green	414	26.5%	132	86	1297	15.1	3.9	10	65%
M.Jones*	171	7.6%	104	66	818	12.4	4.6	4	63%
M.Sanu*	16	-8.3%	49	33	394	11.9	6.2	0	67%
B.LaFell	-43	-20.1%	74	37	515	13.9	6.1	0	50%
T.Eifert	247	42.0%	74	52	615	11.8	4.5	13	70%
T.Kroft	27	24.9%	15	11	129	11.7	6.2	1	73%
R.Hewitt	15	11.8%	12	8	99	12.4	7.4	0	67%
G.Bernard	97	14.6%	66	49	472	9.6	9.4	0	74%
J.Hill	0	-13.4%	19	15	79	5.3	5.8	1	79%
R.Burkhead	13	0.9%	15	10	94	9.4	2.5	1	67%

Offensive Line

Player	Pos	Age	GS	Snaps	Pen	Sk	Pass	Run	Player	Pos	Age	GS	Snaps	Pen	Sk	Pass	Run
Russell Bodine	C	24	16/16	1056	7	1.0	5.0	3.0	Andrew Whitworth	LT	35	16/16	1024	8	1.0	2.5	2.0
Clint Boling	LG	27	16/16	1051	4	2.0	3.5	0.0	Andre Smith*	RT	29	14/14	884	11	1.0	5.0	1.0
Kevin Zeitler	RG	26	16/16	1041	4	0.0	1.0	3.5	Eric Winston	RT	33	13/2	172	1	1.0	1.0	0.5

Year	Yards	ALY	Rank	Power	Rank	Stuff	Rank	2nd Lev	Rank	Open Field	Rank	Sacks	ASR	Rank	Press	Rank	F-Start	Cont.
2013	3.70	4.03	11	63%	19	18%	9	0.96	26	0.37	30	29	5.2%	3	16.5%	2	17	32
2014	4.53	4.03	11	68%	9	15%	3	1.16	16	1.04	3	23	4.6%	5	19.1%	3	18	24
2015	4.00	4.21	1	68%	13	17%	3	1.20	14	0.42	31	32	5.9%	15	21.2%	6	18	36
2015 ALY by direction:		Left End 4.98 (2)			Left Tackle 4.06 (11)			Mid/Guard 4.31 (3)			Right Tackle 3.95 (9)			Right End 3.73 (13)				

The strength here is on the left side, where Andrew Whitworth ranked second among left tackles in snaps per blown block while Clint Boling ranked first among left guards. ☜ The weak link continues to be center Russell Bodine, but offensive line coach Paul Alexander angrily berated reporters at OTAs who repeatedly questioned whether fifth-rounder Christian Westerman (Arizona State) could take over in the middle. Barring injury, Bodine isn't going anywhere. ☜ It's worth noting that we didn't chart a blown block for either Cedric Ogbuehi or Jake Fisher in their combined 191 offensive snaps.

Defensive Front Seven

Defensive Line	Age	Pos	G	Snaps	Plays	Overall TmPct	Rk	Stop	Dfts	BTkl	Runs	vs. Run St%	Rk	RuYd	Rk	Sack	Pass Rush Hit	Hur	Dsrpt
Geno Atkins	28	DT	16	788	42	5.0%	41	39	25	6	29	93%	2	1.1	2	11.0	9	29.5	0
Domata Peko	32	DT	16	544	36	4.3%	57	25	9	3	27	63%	79	2.1	40	5.0	1	4.0	1
Brandon Thompson	27	DT	9	183	8	1.7%	--	7	3	3	6	83%	--	1.0	--	0.5	1	1.0	0
Pat Sims	31	DT	8	180	16	3.8%	--	10	2	1	13	62%	--	3.5	--	0.0	3	3.0	0

Edge Rushers	Age	Pos	G	Snaps	Plays	TmPct	Rk	Stop	Dfts	BTkl	Runs	St%	Rk	RuYd	Rk	Sack	Hit	Hur	Dsrpt
						Overall						vs. Run					Pass Rush		
Carlos Dunlap	27	DE	16	882	56	6.6%	17	45	23	2	35	74%	47	2.5	55	13.5	20	37.5	2
Michael Johnson	29	DE	16	848	43	5.1%	47	27	10	3	29	55%	91	3.3	85	5.0	12	15.5	2
Wallace Gilberry*	32	DE	16	632	23	2.7%	88	19	5	2	14	93%	3	1.1	12	2.0	13	15.0	1

Linebackers	Age	Pos	G	Snaps	Plays	TmPct	Rk	Stop	Dfts	BTkl	Runs	St%	Rk	RuYd	Rk	Sack	Hit	Hur	Tgts	Suc%	Rk	AdjYd	Rk	PD	Int
						Overall						vs. Run				Pass Rush					vs. Pass				
Vincent Rey	29	OLB	16	728	100	11.8%	47	43	14	14	32	53%	78	5.0	85	1.0	1	5	37	35%	67	7.4	56	3	1
Rey Maualuga	29	MLB	15	622	78	9.8%	63	42	7	11	45	62%	49	3.1	29	0.0	1	5	17	58%	31	5.8	30	3	1
Vontaze Burfict	26	OLB	10	467	79	14.9%	19	45	13	6	45	67%	32	2.8	18	1.0	3	3	17	69%	9	3.2	4	4	2
Emmanuel Lamur*	27	OLB	16	340	35	4.1%	–	15	8	3	6	67%	–	5.8	–	0.5	0	2.5	12	39%	–	7.1	–	3	0
A.J. Hawk*	32	MLB	16	286	23	2.7%	–	10	2	2	16	50%	–	3.8	–	1.0	0	2	6	84%	–	0.2	–	1	0
Karlos Dansby	35	ILB	16	1032	113	14.3%	29	64	24	6	72	61%	52	3.8	56	0.0	6	3	20	85%	2	3.3	5	5	3

Year	Yards	ALY	Rank	Power	Rank	Stuff	Rank	2nd Level	Rank	Open Field	Rank	Sacks	ASR	Rank	Press	Rank
2013	3.78	3.82	15	60%	10	15%	29	0.99	5	0.43	3	43	7.0%	14	21.6%	28
2014	4.31	4.24	27	69%	23	17%	24	1.27	27	0.60	12	20	4.5%	31	19.3%	32
2015	4.20	3.64	14	60%	10	22%	11	1.11	16	0.94	26	42	7.0%	12	26.6%	9
2015 ALY by direction:		Left End 3.40 (15)			Left Tackle 4.58 (30)			Mid/Guard 3.70 (10)			Right Tackle 3.16 (9)			Right End 2.42 (5)		

When the Cleveland Browns cut Karlos Dansby after the season, he reacted by predicting the Bengals would sign him. Now NostraDansby indeed is in the fold, replacing A.J. Hawk. Dansby should provide some veteran leadership—as he put it, "I can bring wisdom to these cats"—but also on-field impact. Dansby has ranked among our top three in success rate on pass coverage for two straight years, and was also above average in 2013. ☞ The Bengals added two players to their front seven in this year's draft. Third-rounder Nick Vigil (Utah State) is an instinctive and aggressive linebacker, but somewhat undersized (in terms of weight and strength). Even more intriguing is fourth-round defensive tackle Andrew Billings (Baylor), the presumptive 2017 replacement for free agent-to-be Domata Peko. Though Billings' pass-rush technique is very raw, he boasts an impressive strength-and-speed combo and former FO writer Doug Farrar projected him as a first-round talent. And hey, it's not like the Bengals have a track record of developing undersized defensive tackles or anything.

Defensive Secondary

Secondary	Age	Pos	G	Snaps	Plays	TmPct	Rk	Stop	Dfts	BTkl	Runs	St%	Rk	RuYd	Rk	Tgts	Tgt%	Rk	Dist	Suc%	Rk	AdjYd	Rk	PD	Int
						Overall						vs. Run						vs. Pass						
Reggie Nelson*	33	FS	16	1056	86	10.2%	31	36	17	9	37	46%	25	7.4	41	30	7.1%	31	16.8	54%	47	6.5	30	15	8
Dre Kirkpatrick	27	CB	16	1050	86	10.2%	16	36	14	16	11	27%	60	14.0	71	93	22.2%	54	13.1	54%	32	7.0	18	13	0
Adam Jones	33	CB	14	855	74	10.0%	17	35	16	7	16	50%	20	4.0	5	55	16.0%	12	11.9	62%	5	4.5	2	11	3
Leon Hall*	32	CB	14	666	64	8.6%	–	29	14	4	10	50%	–	4.8	–	39	14.7%	–	8.3	51%	–	6.4	–	8	2
George Iloka	26	SS	12	645	51	8.0%	59	15	7	2	18	39%	41	6.2	27	14	5.2%	12	16.7	65%	17	5.6	17	4	1
Shawn Williams	25	FS	16	474	33	3.9%	–	13	8	4	6	17%	–	11.3	–	13	6.6%	–	19.2	85%	–	1.8	–	5	2
Darqueze Dennard	25	CB	10	189	19	3.6%	–	8	6	1	3	67%	–	2.0	–	17	22.5%	–	12.2	43%	–	11.8	–	3	1

Year	Pass D Rank	vs. #1 WR	Rk	vs. #2 WR	Rk	vs. Other WR	Rk	vs. TE	Rk	vs. RB	Rk
2013	4	-21.9%	3	-27.6%	3	-19.6%	6	-11.7%	9	8.2%	23
2014	7	-28.9%	1	-32.8%	3	-24.4%	2	-20.4%	4	26.6%	29
2015	10	-4.5%	13	2.7%	17	-11.4%	8	-9.5%	12	10.0%	24

The Bengals put a high priority on re-signing safety George Iloka and corner Adam "Pacman" Jones, and both are back in the fold. Now the spotlight turns to Reggie Nelson's replacement at safety, Shawn Williams. The fourth-year man from Cincy's farm team in Athens, Georgia, has impressed in limited action. His diving pick of Roethlisberger to set up the winning score in the first meeting with Pittsburgh was among the plays of the year. The Bengals extended his contract in the offseason, betting on his development. ☞ The Bengals hope Williams is more consistent as a starter than Dre Kirkpatrick, who took on full-time duty in 2015 after years as an understudy and had real problems tackling. (His 16 broken tackles tied for fifth among NFL defensive backs.) However, Kirkpatrick was decent enough in actual coverage, especially given the volume of times he was targeted (93—only Kansas City's Marcus Peters saw more balls thrown his way), but receivers turned his poor angles and instincts into plenty of YAC (an average of 3.7 yards per reception, 48th among 75 cornerbacks, compared to just 2.0 YAC per reception for Jones). Kirkpatrick is a free agent after 2016, and with Jones, Darqueze Dennard, top pick William Jackson, and promising second-year man Josh Shaw pressing for snaps, Kirkpatrick needs to improve if he expects to be re-signed, or find big money elsewhere.

Special Teams

Year	DVOA	Rank	FG/XP	Rank	Net Kick	Rank	Kick Ret	Rank	Net Punt	Rank	Punt Ret	Rank	Hidden	Rank
2013	1.2%	12	-1.5	21	-1.2	19	4.0	6	3.4	15	1.5	12	-1.1	18
2014	4.2%	6	-2.6	23	0.3	15	4.2	7	12.1	3	6.8	8	5.5	7
2015	2.2%	8	1.5	13	7.2	3	-2.0	20	3.4	13	1.1	15	0.9	15

Coverage units were an unheralded part of Cincinnati's overall success, led by running backs Cedric Peerman and Rex Burkhead, who combined for 27 tackles on returns. Brandon Tate turned in another mediocre season on kick and punt returns, but with such an explosive offense, the coaches prized reliable hands more than upfield thrust. With the passing game in flux, that could change this season, with rookie Tyler Boyd and 2015 seventh-rounder Mario Alford getting shots at the gig.

Cleveland Browns

2015 record: 3-13	**Total DVOA:** -23.0% (30th)	**2016 Mean Projection:** 5.2 wins	**On the Clock (0-4):** 41%
Pythagorean Wins: 4.0 (31st)	**Offense:** -13.2% (27th)	**Postseason Odds:** 6.8%	**Mediocrity (5-7):** 43%
Snap-Weighted Age: 27.0 (9th)	**Defense:** 10.5% (29th)	**Super Bowl Odds:** 0.3%	**Playoff Contender (8-10):** 14%
Average Opponent: 8.9% (1st)	**Special Teams:** 0.7% (15th)	**Proj. Avg. Opponent:** 2.1% (7th)	**Super Bowl Contender (11+):** 2%

2015: Working double shifts in the Factory of Sadness.

2016: If they improve, credit Hue. If they don't, blame "analytics."

"From Johnny Football to Moneyball."

That's the shorthand for this, the latest in a series of seemingly endless teardown projects in Cleveland. Johnny Manziel, the party-hearty TMZ magnet, is gone after two depressing seasons of off-field nonsense and on-field deficiency, along with head coach Mike Pettine, general manager Ray Farmer, and anyone else who could grab a life preserver and leap over the deck of the NFL's *Lusitania.*

Into their stead come Bill James, Billy Beane, half of the Ivy League, and the entire staff of Football Outsiders. We made it, guys!

Such was the overblown reaction to the hiring of Paul DePodesta—the real-life basis for Jonah Hill's nerd who did Brad Pitt's dirty work in the movie *Moneyball*—to a front office position with the Browns. Never mind that many if not most teams these days factor data analysis (the kind like your pals here at FO have been doing for years) into franchise decision-making. Never mind that the term "analytics" has been so over-processed and taffy-pulled to fit various arguments, pro and con, that it is devoid of any specific meaning. Never mind that DePodesta is a former college football player (at Harvard, natch) whose first job was in the CFL. Nope, DePodesta was hired for his pocket protector and protractor, and whatever happens on the field in 2016 (especially if the Browns suck again, and they are last in our projections by a fair margin), it is because of spreadsheets and dehumanizing quants and geeks who never had their hands in the dirt.

In other words, the entire Sloan-friendly community has been set up to fail in Cleveland. Any misstep, whether due to injury or bad luck or just plain talent mismatch, will be laid at the feet of the nerds in charge. Should the Browns actually play some decent football—which is hardly implausible, even for a franchise this inept—the gruff ex-jock with the whistle will get all the credit.

That would be new head coach Hue Jackson, fresh off an outstanding run as offensive coordinator in Cincinnati. The Bengals led the league in passing DVOA and were second in overall offense, while Andy Dalton was actually an MVP candidate before breaking his thumb at the three-quarter pole. That alone was enough to demonstrate Jackson's qualifications for a second try as head coach, after his lone season in Oakland in 2011, where he went 8-8.

Jackson unleashed his full frontal lobe on the NFL last season, tossing off unexpected plays, schemes, and formations with abandon. He would not hesitate to motion multiple linemen out wide, use read-option with Dalton (an underrated runner), or bunch three wide receivers to a side in order to isolate his gifted tight end, Tyler Eifert, on an outmatched defender. Defenses were constantly kept guessing by the sheer volume of possibility in the Bengals attack. (Mike Tomlin once called Hue's play calling "thoughtfully non-rhythmic.") Even when Dalton went down, the multiplicity of the offense allowed the Bengals to function adequately with backup AJ McCarron at the helm.

Like many great intellects, Jackson has a tendency to overthink at times. A fine example was his final play call as a Bengal, the 2-point conversion after a late score in the wildcard game against Pittsburgh. Faced with a reeling defense and a slim 1-point margin, Jackson called an unnecessarily complex screen pass behind those split-out linemen, and the slow-developing play went nowhere. A simple handoff might well have done the trick. Jackson often seems to prefer to best opponents by screwing with their heads, rather than simply blasting them with superior talent and execution. Of course in Cleveland that may be his only option, at least at first.

Perhaps Jackson's most important qualities, at least inside in the locker room, are leadership and people skills, traits sure to be mentioned in any anti-analytics jeremiad. He relentlessly makes high demands of his players, calls them out for poor performance, and is able to elicit top effort from oft-jaded professionals. He does it without being branded a martinet, or inflexible, or any of the other media substitutes for "asshole."

True, there is a certain amount of apple-polishing going on here. Hue has made it a point to maintain excellent relations with many members of the national media, which has allowed him to skate on various episodes that might sink others, such as the deer antler spray PED debacle (Jackson introduced the Ravens and Raiders to the supplement, if not other teams), or the nefarious trade for a rusty Carson Palmer midway through 2011 (which ultimately got Hue fired in Oakland), or the halftime fisticuffs with Chad Johnson during the 2005 wild-card game against Pittsburgh (OK, Hue was probably justified there). Voluble and forthright, Jackson offers a tasty cocktail of old-school, no-BS crustiness mixed with an up-to-date approach on the field and with the public.

As such, much like his mentor, Marvin Lewis, when he

2016 Browns Schedule

Week	Opp.	Week	Opp.	Week	Opp.
1	at PHI	7	at CIN	13	BYE
2	BAL	8	NYJ	14	CIN
3	at MIA	9	DAL	15	at BUF
4	at WAS	10	at BAL (Thu.)	16	SD (Sat.)
5	NE	11	PIT	17	at PIT
6	at TEN	12	NYG		

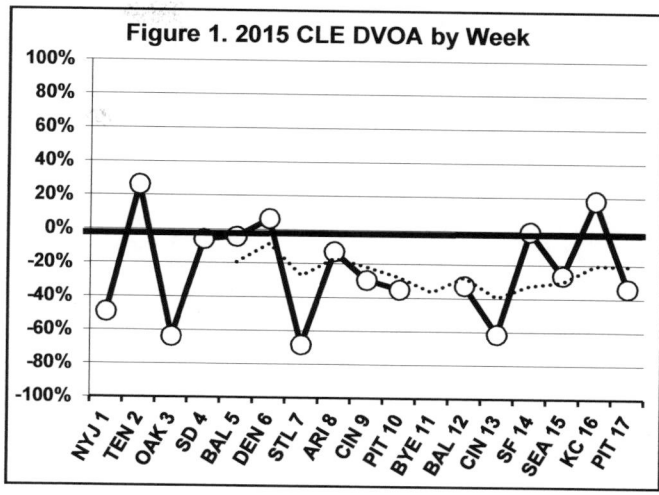

Figure 1. 2015 CLE DVOA by Week

first came to Cincinnati, Jackson is in a near-perfect position as head coach of the Browns. He will get full credit if the Browns turn their leaking ship of state around, whenever that happens. And given the built-in suspicion, ignorance, or flat-out antipathy that remains in the media toward the brainiacs in the front office, Jackson will doubtless be the recipient of some extra Hue-perbole. The coach will be celebrated for the way he brought "old-fashioned football sense" to town and cut the balls off the geeks who thought there might be another path to victory.

All of which will be nonsense, naturally.

Compared to his weapons in Cincinnati, Jackson will have relative popguns at his disposal, starting at quarterback. It will take wizardry indeed to coach Robert Griffin III back into some semblance of an effective quarterback. RG3 was last seen on the field in 2014, when he posted an egregious -34.2% DVOA. He then watched last season as the man picked three rounds behind him in the 2012 draft, Kirk Cousins, had an excellent season and led Washington to the playoffs. The speed and athleticism that made Griffin so special as a rookie has been sapped by numerous leg injuries, and he has never developed as a pocket passer or reader of defenses. Jackson will have his work cut out for him, and hedged his bets by grabbing Cody Kessler of USC in the third round. Oft-injured veteran Josh McCown is still around, at least for now, in case neither of the other guys can hack it.

The new brain trust got off to a rocky start in free agency, when most of the quality players still remaining on the Browns roster left town amid accusations of duplicitous dealings and mixed messages (and plenty of alliteration!). Two talented offensive linemen, center Alex Mack and tackle Mitchell Schwartz, fled, as did fleet wideout Travis Benjamin and safety Tashaun Gipson. Many other veterans (Karlos Dansby and Donte Whitner most prominently) were cut, save a pair of not-so-ordinary Joes: hobbling veteran cornerback Joe Haden, who may miss part of the 2016 season after ankle surgery, and the franchise's bedrock, left tackle Joe Thomas.

In place of all these departed veterans will be a ton of youth. It shouldn't be a bold theory of analytics by now that when it comes to the draft, quantity far outweighs quality, especially for a rebuilding team. Yet Cleveland still managed to deal down for a metric ton of picks, taking advantage of teams

more desperate than them. The Browns selected no fewer than 14 players, headlined by four—count 'em, four—wide receivers, including top pick Corey Coleman of Baylor. The wheeling and dealing left the franchise with enormous draft capital for 2017 as well.

That's where the new administration truly will make its mark, not with any advanced statistical coefficients or by outsmarting mopes in other front offices, but in personnel evaluation. It's not exactly sexy Silicon Valley stuff, but it is an under-appreciated area of the "analytics" rubric. DePodesta is considered a tremendous judge of talent, although we'll have to see if that translates from baseball to football. He has already begun to revamp the scouting department to match his vision.

The new regime can't do worse than the "experienced football hands" who put together recent rosters. The team's drafting has been abysmal. Remember the Trent Richardson/Brandon Weeden debacle at the top of the 2012 draft? Or the Justin Gilbert/Manziel craptacular of 2014? Last year brought defensive tackle Danny Shelton, who was supposed to be a bulwark against the run but underwhelmed. Still, at least he was on the field; Shelton was the lone Browns first-rounder of the last five years to be a regular starter in 2015. Their second pick a year ago was Cam Erving, who was disastrous at guard (he's now the first-string center, replacing the excellent Mack). Third-rounder Xavier Cooper, another defensive lineman, was pushed around as well.

Meanwhile, several Browns the team let slip away, like T.J. Ward to Denver and Jabaal Sheard to New England, have thrived away from the lake. Conversely, Cleveland's splashes in free agency, from Paul Kruger to Dwayne Bowe, have made Louganis-like ripples, not cannonballs. If the new gang can merely halt years of bad drafts and free agency reversals, a turnaround won't be so far away.

And everyone will celebrate Hue Jackson's genius.

Robert Weintraub

2015 Browns Stats by Week

Wk	vs.	W-L	PF	PA	YDF	YDA	TO	Total	Off	Def	ST
1	at NYJ	L	10	31	321	333	-4	-49%	-25%	24%	0%
2	TEN	W	28	14	274	385	3	26%	-1%	1%	28%
3	OAK	L	20	27	355	469	-1	-64%	-25%	39%	1%
4	at SD	L	27	30	432	438	-1	-6%	1%	23%	15%
5	at BAL	W	33	30	505	377	0	-4%	14%	14%	-3%
6	DEN	L	23	26	298	442	0	6%	-12%	-15%	4%
7	at STL	L	6	24	364	308	-3	-68%	-33%	30%	-5%
8	ARI	L	20	34	254	491	2	-13%	-12%	-1%	-2%
9	at CIN	L	10	31	213	371	0	-29%	-11%	14%	-5%
10	at PIT	L	9	30	342	459	-1	-35%	-19%	22%	6%
11	BYE										
12	BAL	L	27	33	338	336	2	-32%	-7%	-1%	-26%
13	CIN	L	3	37	273	377	-2	-61%	-31%	23%	-8%
14	SF	W	24	10	481	221	-2	0%	-2%	-14%	-13%
15	at SEA	L	13	30	230	423	-1	-26%	-7%	31%	12%
16	at KC	L	13	17	368	258	0	18%	19%	-1%	-1%
17	PIT	L	12	28	263	379	-1	-34%	-59%	-17%	8%

Trends and Splits

	Offense	Rank	Defense	Rank
Total DVOA	-13.2%	27	10.5%	29
Unadjusted VOA	-18.3%	32	11.9%	30
Weighted Trend	-15.0%	27	7.0%	23
Variance	3.6%	3	3.1%	5
Average Opponent	-4.9%	1	3.4%	3
Passing	-4.0%	27	22.6%	27
Rushing	-10.3%	20	-2.9%	26
First Down	-17.1%	32	11.5%	27
Second Down	-24.5%	30	8.0%	27
Third Down	12.1%	10	12.2%	24
First Half	-14.0%	26	2.1%	20
Second Half	-12.3%	29	18.7%	31
Red Zone	-50.8%	32	21.5%	27
Late and Close	-18.5%	28	5.1%	25

Five-Year Performance

Year	W-L	Pyth W	Est W	PF	PA	TO	Total	Rk	Off	Rk	Def	Rk	ST	Rk	Off AGL	Rk	Def AGL	Rk	Off Age	Rk	Def Age	Rk	ST Age	Rk
2011	4-12	5.0	5.5	218	307	+1	-14.2%	25	-11.2%	25	4.2%	22	1.3%	10	45.5	27	26.3	15	26.1	29	26.6	24	26.1	23
2012	5-11	6.1	6.2	302	368	+3	-13.5%	24	-15.2%	27	4.5%	22	6.1%	2	26.4	13	57.0	29	25.7	30	26.1	26	25.2	30
2013	4-12	5.5	4.4	308	406	-8	-21.8%	28	-14.4%	26	8.2%	24	0.9%	14	24.8	9	16.3	8	26.6	21	25.4	30	24.9	31
2014	7-9	6.9	7.2	299	337	+6	-6.7%	23	-10.2%	24	-3.0%	11	0.4%	14	30.5	16	36.6	14	26.6	18	26.4	22	25.8	23
2015	3-13	4.0	4.5	278	432	-9	-23.0%	30	-13.2%	27	10.5%	29	0.7%	15	37.1	18	33.7	21	27.4	9	27.1	8	25.6	25

2015 Performance Based on Most Common Personnel Groups

CLE Offense					CLE Offense vs. Opponents					CLE Defense					CLE Defense vs. Opponents			
Pers	Freq	Yds	DVOA	Run%	Pers	Freq	Yds	DVOA	Run%	Pers	Freq	Yds	DVOA		Pers	Freq	Yds	DVOA
11	55%	5.6	1.4%	21%	Base	43%	4.5	-12.2%	44%	Base	36%	5.0	-8.6%		11	50%	6.9	12.9%
12	27%	4.2	-24.5%	42%	Nickel	46%	5.7	2.7%	26%	Nickel	54%	7.2	18.0%		12	22%	6.3	9.4%
21	11%	4.8	-12.8%	47%	Dime+	11%	5.3	-20.4%	6%	Dime+	7%	8.5	81.7%		21	9%	4.9	4.2%
22	3%	5.0	3.3%	70%	Goal Line	1%	0.3	-37.8%	67%	Goal Line	2%	0.7	7.3%		10	5%	7.1	63.6%
13	2%	5.8	19.1%	24%						Big	1%	2.5	-37.3%		13	4%	3.5	-41.5%
															22	3%	4.1	-27.1%

Strategic Tendencies

Run/Pass		Rk	Formation		Rk	Pass Rush		Rk	Secondary		Rk	Strategy		Rk
Runs, first half	36%	20	Form: Single Back	78%	12	Rush 3	8.3%	11	4 DB	36%	12	Play action	15%	28
Runs, first down	45%	20	Form: Empty Back	8%	15	Rush 4	66.9%	15	5 DB	54%	16	Avg Box (Off)	6.25	15
Runs, second-long	22%	30	Pers: 3+ WR	57%	18	Rush 5	19.7%	21	6+ DB	7%	21	Avg Box (Def)	6.34	10
Runs, power sit.	35%	31	Pers: 2+ TE/6+ OL	32%	18	Rush 6+	5.1%	20	CB by Sides	55%	29	Offensive Pace	31.03	21
Runs, behind 2H	23%	19	Pers: 6+ OL	1%	23	Sacks by LB	50.0%	15	S/CB Cover Ratio	19%	28	Defensive Pace	29.62	10
Pass, ahead 2H	47%	17	Shotgun/Pistol	67%	12	Sacks by DB	12.1%	9	DB Blitz	12%	9	Go for it on 4th	1.75	1

Cleveland had the worst offensive DVOA in the league on first down (-17.1%) and third-worst on second down (-24.5%). However, they ranked 10th on third downs (12.2%), in part because they were one of the best third-and-short offenses (35.2%, third overall). ☞ The strength of Cleveland's offense dramatically switched around midseason. Cleveland ranked 16th in passing offense in Weeks 1-9, then ranked dead last in Weeks 10-17. The moment things turned around for the running game was a bit later, but the change was even more dramatic. For the first 12 games, Cleveland had -24.7% DVOA running the ball with just 3.4 yards per carry. In the last four games, Cleveland had 24.5% DVOA with 5.8 yards per carry. ☞ The Browns' rushing defense also improved from awful to average at midseason, ranking 31st in DVOA in Weeks 1-9 but 16th in Weeks 10-17. ☞ The average NFL defense allows 1.5 more yards per play against play-action passes, but Cleveland actually allowed 1.0 yards per play *less* in 2015. The DVOA gap was smaller (-4.5%), but the Browns were one of only nine defenses with a better DVOA when opponents did not use play-action. ☞ No defense was worse at defending running back screens, as Cleveland's 94.7% DVOA against 22 such plays edged out New Orleans for last place. ☞ The Browns benefited from drops less than any other defense, with opponents dropping just 10 passes by our count for a drop rate of just 2.1 percent. ☞ What changes can Cleveland fans expect from the new coaching staff? On offense: more running, especially in power situations (Cincinnati ranked seventh); more play-action (Cincinnati ranked 11th); more extra offensive linemen, some of whom will be lined up in unexpected places (Cincinnati ranked third). On defense, there will be more blitzes, as Ray Horton's Tennessee defense led the league in sending five pass-rushers and ranked sixth in big blitzes of six or more.

Passing

Player	DYAR	DVOA	Plays	NtYds	Avg	YAC	C%	TD	Int
J.McCown	110	-5.8%	315	1963	6.2	5.5	63.7%	12	4
J.Manziel*	-105	-18.4%	241	1350	5.6	5.7	58.4%	7	5
A.Davis	-269	-52.9%	105	425	4.0	3.8	60.9%	1	3

Rushing

Player	DYAR	DVOA	Plays	Yds	Avg	TD	Fum	Suc
I.Crowell	36	-4.0%	185	706	3.8	4	0	41%
D.Johnson	30	-1.4%	104	379	3.6	0	0	45%
J.Manziel*	68	32.6%	32	235	7.3	0	0	-
J.McCown	12	0.7%	19	95	5.0	1	3	-
R.Turbin*	17	13.6%	18	60	3.3	0	0	44%

Receiving

Player	DYAR	DVOA	Plays	Ctch	Yds	Y/C	YAC	TD	C%
T.Benjamin*	38	-8.7%	125	68	973	14.3	4.8	5	54%
B.Hartline*	21	-9.2%	77	46	523	11.4	3.6	2	60%
T.Gabriel	-74	-31.8%	48	28	238	8.5	4.0	0	58%
A.Hawkins	-42	-26.0%	43	27	276	10.2	4.7	0	63%
D.Jennings	-40	-36.8%	21	14	118	8.4	2.7	0	67%
D.Bowe*	-22	-35.2%	13	5	53	10.6	2.8	0	38%
M.Moore	30	26.7%	10	7	81	11.6	4.6	1	70%
T.Pryor	-34	-67.7%	8	1	42	42.0	5.0	0	13%
G.Barnidge	218	19.7%	125	79	1043	13.2	4.6	9	63%
J.Dray*	-41	-43.7%	16	6	61	10.2	5.7	0	38%
D.Johnson	68	2.3%	74	61	534	8.8	8.0	2	82%
I.Crowell	37	17.9%	22	19	182	9.6	11.9	1	86%
M.Johnson	-10	-45.1%	6	4	15	3.8	5.0	0	67%

Offensive Line

Player	Pos	Age	GS	Snaps	Pen	Sk	Pass	Run	Player	Pos	Age	GS	Snaps	Pen	Sk	Pass	Run
Mitchell Schwartz*	RT	27	16/16	1106	5	4.0	6.0	3.0	Joel Bitonio	LG	25	10/10	618	7	1.0	2.0	2.0
Joe Thomas	LT	32	16/16	1106	6	1.0	2.0	0.0	Cameron Erving	C	24	16/4	425	5	4.5	7.0	3.0
Alex Mack*	C	31	16/16	1106	4	1.5	2.5	3.0	Austin Pasztor	RT	26	16/4	295	2	0.0	0.0	0.0
John Greco	RG	31	14/14	892	3	1.0	5.0	1.0	Alvin Bailey	OT	25	14/3	271	3	1.0	4.5	1.0

Year	Yards	ALY	Rank	Power	Rank	Stuff	Rank	2nd Lev	Rank	Open Field	Rank	Sacks	ASR	Rank	Press	Rank	F-Start	Cont.
2013	3.53	3.83	18	70%	9	20%	18	0.95	28	0.36	31	49	7.5%	17	25.7%	18	23	35
2014	3.79	3.63	25	61%	19	22%	31	1.13	19	0.60	22	31	6.0%	15	27.0%	25	19	31
2015	3.75	3.32	29	65%	17	26%	31	0.98	30	0.78	14	53	8.1%	26	33.7%	31	23	35

2015 ALY by direction:	Left End 2.7 (31)	Left Tackle 2.2 (32)	Mid/Guard 3.51 (30)	Right Tackle 3.32 (24)	Right End 3.39 (17)

Once again, the Browns run counter to our "Build an offense from the line out" mantra. The Browns have certainly tried to "build from the line out," but despite all the talent, the offensive line seems to be less than the sum of its parts. The Browns have not ranked in the top ten in either adjusted line yards or adjusted sack rate since 2008, Joe Thomas' second season. Thomas may do his job at left tackle well, but he certainly has never lifted his unit to higher deeds. ☞ Only four players with at least 400 snaps had more blown blocks per snap than Cam Erving, who takes over as center after playing mostly guard as a rookie. At Florida State, Erving made a move to the middle from left tackle, of all positions, with great success. But he is awfully tall (6-foot-5) for an NFL pivot, with long arms that hinder close-in battle. He doesn't sustain blocks particularly well, either. Still, he'll probably be better at center than he was at guard, where he had little feel for the position. ☞ Tackle Shon Coleman, a third-round pick from Auburn, is in the "pull hard for him" category. Coleman discovered at age 18 that he had a form of leukemia, and slogged through thirty months of treatment to make it back to football and, now, the NFL. He will battle journeyman Austin Pasztor for the right tackle slot that Mitchell Schwartz vacated in order to rake in more *shekels* in Kansas City. ☞ Another rookie, fifth-round guard Spencer Drango from Baylor, has the name of an Old West outlaw and what one scout called a "SpongeBob body," i.e., all chest, no ass. For that reason alone, it's hard to imagine him paving many pathways at the pro level.

Defensive Front Seven

Defensive Line	Age	Pos	G	Snaps	Plays	TmPct	Overall Rk	Stop	Dfts	BTkl	Runs	St%	vs. Run Rk	RuYd	Rk	Sack	Hit	Pass Rush Hur	Dsrpt
Desmond Bryant	31	DE	14	528	32	4.6%	47	30	12	2	23	91%	3	2.2	43	6.0	9	11.0	0
Danny Shelton	23	DT	16	506	36	4.6%	50	24	4	1	36	67%	68	2.3	46	0.0	0	0.5	0
Randy Starks*	33	DT	15	467	28	3.8%	61	23	8	5	25	84%	17	1.8	27	1.0	5	9.0	1
John Hughes	28	DE	16	430	24	3.0%	77	16	4	1	22	64%	77	2.6	59	1.5	1	9.0	0
Jamie Meder	25	DE	16	389	33	4.2%	--	23	5	1	31	71%	--	2.5	--	1.0	4	4.0	0
Xavier Cooper	25	DE	14	363	19	2.7%	80	13	4	2	16	69%	60	3.0	67	1.5	0	2.0	0

Edge Rushers	Age	Pos	G	Snaps	Plays	TmPct	Overall Rk	Stop	Dfts	BTkl	Runs	St%	vs. Run Rk	RuYd	Rk	Sack	Hit	Pass Rush Hur	Dsrpt
Paul Kruger	30	OLB	16	681	26	3.3%	79	23	8	5	19	84%	13	1.9	32	2.5	7	26.5	0
Armonty Bryant	26	OLB	14	481	40	5.8%	30	32	16	5	28	82%	15	2.0	38	5.5	6	9.5	0
Nate Orchard	23	OLB	15	473	39	5.3%	42	25	9	3	25	64%	78	2.4	53	3.0	1	2.0	3
Barkevious Mingo	26	OLB	16	256	22	2.8%	--	15	6	4	9	78%	--	3.4	--	0.0	1	6.5	0

Linebackers	Age	Pos	G	Snaps	Plays	TmPct	Overall Rk	Stop	Dfts	BTkl	Runs	St%	vs. Run Rk	RuYd	Rk	Sack	Hit	Pass Rush Hur	Tgts	Suc%	vs. Pass Rk	AdjYd	Rk	PD	Int
Karlos Dansby*	35	ILB	16	1032	113	14.3%	29	64	24	6	72	61%	52	3.8	56	0.0	6	3	20	85%	2	3.3	5	5	3
Christian Kirksey	24	ILB	16	568	54	6.8%	78	29	15	8	26	46%	87	4.8	83	3.5	2	4	15	55%	41	6.8	49	1	0
Craig Robertson*	28	ILB	12	382	55	9.3%	64	37	5	5	40	75%	6	3.5	40	0.0	2	1	10	61%	--	3.7	--	3	1
Demario Davis	27	ILB	16	851	91	11.9%	45	54	15	15	45	80%	2	3.2	30	2.0	7	9	29	52%	49	6.6	44	1	0

Year	Yards	ALY	Rank	Power	Rank	Stuff	Rank	2nd Level	Rank	Open Field	Rank	Sacks	ASR	Rank	Press	Rank
2013	3.94	3.83	16	79%	32	18%	15	0.97	2	0.65	18	40	6.5%	21	23.9%	20
2014	4.45	4.36	29	58%	8	15%	29	1.32	28	0.67	14	31	6.1%	25	20.5%	30
2015	4.57	4.34	30	70%	24	17%	28	1.27	28	0.86	20	29	5.8%	25	23.6%	27

2015 ALY by direction:	Left End 5.97 (32)	Left Tackle 3.79 (17)	Mid/Guard 4.32 (30)	Right Tackle 4.26 (26)	Right End 4.88 (30)

Desmond Bryant was the one bright spot on an otherwise unimpressive defensive line, very quietly leading the team in sacks while finishing third in the NFL in run stop rate. So of course, he tore a pectoral while working out in the offseason and is probably out until 2017. Because Browns. ☞ Bryant's injury does open up more playing time for rookie Carl Nassib from Penn State, the first pick of the third round. Nassib never played a high school game and walked on in Happy Valley, where he worked his way up to leading the Big Ten with a school-record 15.5 sacks in 2015. Tall and relatively slender at 6-foot-7, 277 pounds, he doesn't have the strength to set the edge, so look for him as a pass rush specialist for the time being. John Hughes will play on early downs, with Xavier Cooper on the other side. ☞ New defensive coordinator Ray Horton would be happy to play multiple fronts, but the key to that is nose tackle Danny Shelton. Shelton ballooned to a reported 370 pounds last year during an awful debut campaign. The Browns want to keep him in the 330-pound range so he might show some of the pass-rush skills he displayed at Washington, which were notably absent as a rookie (as were his run-stopping skills). ☞ The linebacking crew lost leader and pass defense savant Karlos Dansby, who was cut in the team's youth movement. Christian Kirksey, who sported a 55 percent success rate against the pass compared to Dansby's 85 percent, takes over. He'll play alongside free-agent arrival Demario Davis, who was seemingly signed from the Jets because he tagged Josh McCown with the shot that removed the scrambling quarterback from the opening game. His pass success rate was even lower (52 percent), though he at least can thump in the run game. And yes, linebacker coverage stats are based on small sample sizes, but Kirksey and Davis were each under 55 percent in 2014 as well. ☞ Kiki Mingo is perilously close to officially being a bust, and will have to work to keep his job from another long, raw rush linebacker, second-round pick Emmanuel Ogbah (Oklahoma State). SackSEER absolutely loved Ogbah's consistent college production, giving him the highest rating in this class. Online draftniks deride him as a hugely inconsistent physical specimen whose effort doesn't match his build. ☞ Paul Kruger was around the quarterback a lot (33.5 combined hits/hurries) without actually taking him down much (2.5 sacks). Cleveland fans can take solace in that players with high pressure numbers but low sack figures often take the passer down more the following season. To wit: Kruger in 2013 had 32.5 hits/hurries but only 4.5 sacks. In 2014, Kruger rebounded with 11 sacks.

Defensive Secondary

Secondary	Age	Pos	G	Snaps	Plays	Overall TmPct	Rk	Stop	Dfts	BTkl	vs. Run Runs	St%	Rk	RuYd	Rk	vs. Pass Tgts	Tgt%	Rk	Dist	Suc%	Rk	AdjYd	Rk	PD	Int
Tramon Williams	33	CB	15	964	79	10.7%	8	24	9	8	17	35%	49	8.8	55	83	23.0%	61	15.4	51%	44	9.3	67	9	1
Donte Whitner*	31	SS	14	850	84	12.1%	18	30	9	5	42	40%	35	8.0	47	19	6.0%	19	11.3	73%	7	4.1	5	4	0
Tashaun Gipson*	26	FS	13	799	62	9.6%	37	20	5	7	41	37%	44	7.4	42	13	4.4%	10	14.8	44%	63	8.3	48	2	2
K'Waun Williams	25	CB	13	516	40	6.2%	--	23	10	5	11	73%	--	4.1	--	33	16.9%	--	10.7	53%	--	7.3	--	1	0
Jordan Poyer	25	CB	14	425	41	5.9%	--	17	10	12	20	45%	--	7.8	--	14	8.9%	--	12.4	70%	--	4.6	--	4	2
Pierre Desir	26	CB	14	388	41	5.9%	--	10	4	4	10	10%	--	8.8	--	46	31.5%	--	14.4	39%	--	11.4	--	6	0
Joe Haden	27	CB	5	286	24	9.7%	--	5	1	2	7	43%	--	12.9	--	27	25.4%	--	14.8	23%	--	13.3	--	2	0
Johnson Bademosi*	26	FS	16	169	12	1.5%	--	5	2	4	5	40%	--	4.8	--	22	34.2%	--	14.1	50%	--	9.9	--	2	0
Jamar Taylor	26	CB	12	712	53	8.1%	--	18	4	1	21	43%	--	5.2	--	48	19.5%	--	13.1	39%	--	10.3	--	2	0
Rahim Moore	26	FS	7	444	18	5.2%	--	5	3	6	11	18%	--	10.9	--	4	2.4%	--	18.0	89%	--	2.3	--	2	1

Year	Pass D Rank	vs. #1 WR	Rk	vs. #2 WR	Rk	vs. Other WR	Rk	vs. TE	Rk	vs. RB	Rk
2013	23	-17.8%	5	8.7%	20	2.9%	17	25.3%	31	20.7%	31
2014	2	-17.6%	6	-5.9%	13	-17.6%	5	-5.7%	15	-41.1%	1
2015	27	4.2%	19	8.7%	21	28.9%	31	-1.7%	17	16.1%	28

The leader of the secondary, corner Joe Haden, was limited to five games by a series of injuries, worst of them a nasty, lingering concussion suffered in Week 5. Then he spent much of the offseason in a walking boot after ankle surgery. He says he'll be ready for the season, but doubts remain. Haden has always been a bit overrated—certainly never in the "shutdown corner" class he is paid to belong to—but the Browns certainly missed him in 2015. ☞ Justin Gilbert, the eighth overall pick in 2014, is at a career crossroads. He's been bustoleum thus far, with little on-field production and immaturity off it. Corners often don't develop until their third or even fourth season, but counting on either Gilbert or fellow third-year corner Pierre Desir, who had a decent rookie season before faltering last year, is folly. A pair of Williamses, Tramon and K'Waun, will likely see the field ahead of either. ☞ Both safeties, Donte Whitner and Tashaun Gipson, are gone. One new starter figures to be promising second-year man Ibraheim Campbell, who showed good instincts and tackling ability as a rookie in spot duty. He looks to be a classic in-the-box safety, lacking the range to be a factor against the pass. Free safety is a major question mark. Rahim Moore, best known for giving up a late-game bomb against Baltimore in a 2013 playoff game while with Denver, was terrible as a free-agent signee in Houston and was cut by the Texans. He has the inside track in Cleveland, though, unless fourth-round pick Derrick Kindred from TCU develops rapidly. Kindred is definitely tough—he made All-Conference while playing all season with a broken collarbone. But he is stiff and not very good at deciphering routes, which is problematic for a deep-field safety. In the short term, he's more likely to make an impact on special teams than in the defensive backfield.

Special Teams

Year	DVOA	Rank	FG/XP	Rank	Net Kick	Rank	Kick Ret	Rank	Net Punt	Rank	Punt Ret	Rank	Hidden	Rank
2013	0.9%	14	-0.5	19	3.5	10	0.0	13	-2.4	23	4.1	10	-9.4	28
2014	0.4%	14	-6.2	30	10.4	1	-5.5	28	9.9	7	-6.6	30	-10.9	29
2015	0.7%	15	-0.3	16	1.4	11	-4.0	25	-2.4	20	8.7	3	-2.6	18

The unit was mostly mediocre overall, but Travis Benjamin was very good on punt returns. Alas, Benjamin is now sunning himself in San Diego. The job for now belongs to either Tramon Williams or Taylor Gabriel, if he can make the team. ☞ Another top special-teamer to bail on Cleveland was ace gunner Johnson Bademosi, who led the team in return tackles four straight seasons, and tied for second in the league in 2015. He signed as a free agent with Detroit, so that's another area of the third phase that will need shoring up under coach Chris Tabor. ☞ In his first NFL season, Travis Coons was middle-of-the-pack on field goals, but his kickoffs were brutal. Only Josh Brown of the Giants finished lower in our gross kickoff value metric. ☞ Punter Andy Lee bounced back in his first year with the Browns, worth 6.4 points of gross punting value, but poor coverage gave away those gains.

Dallas Cowboys

2015 record: 4-12	**Total DVOA:** -18.0% (27th)	**2016 Mean Projection:** 8.8 wins	**On the Clock (0-4):** 5%
Pythagorean Wins: 5.2 (29th)	**Offense:** -15.6% (31st)	**Postseason Odds:** 50.5%	**Mediocrity (5-7):** 25%
Snap-Weighted Age: 26.3 (26th)	**Defense:** 4.1% (19th)	**Super Bowl Odds:** 6.5%	**Playoff Contender (8-10):** 44%
Average Opponent: 0.7% (17th)	**Special Teams:** 1.8% (11th)	**Proj. Avg. Opponent:** -3.3% (31st)	**Super Bowl Contender (11+):** 26%

2015: Even Brandon Weeden made fun of them.

2016: Hit Ctrl + Alt + Del on last year and reboot to 2014.

Next man up is a nice philosophy to preach until you actually need to practice it. When Tony Romo went down, the Cowboys found out that their backup quarterbacks were less Matt Saracen and more a bunch of Uncle Ricos. Consequently, a year after breaking through the .500 glass ceiling, Dallas saw the largest win drop of any team from 2014 to 2015. Poetically, their record since Jason Garrett became the full-time head coach is now 40-40.

When thinking ahead to this season, it's tempting to totally write off the Cowboys' disastrous 2015 campaign. Watching Kellen Moore target Brice Butler nine times in the midst of a December Buffalo snowstorm was surely more horrific than anything Jerry Jones could have imagined in August, but that type of disaster was also an unlikely outcome. Consequently, the Cowboys chose not to overhaul large chunks of their roster this offseason, instead hoping that better health for their two best players will prevent that type of moral hazard from recurring. Romo and Dez Bryant managed to start and finish only one game together the entire season, a Week 11 24-14 win over the Miami Dolphins. The former never completed more than two consecutive games, while the latter was a shadow of himself while playing through foot and ankle injuries which required offseason surgeries.

With that in mind, perhaps it is unsurprising to see the Cowboys largely attempt to maintain the status quo. It is extremely rare for a team to lose the top two cornerstones of its passing offense for most or all of a season. Dating back to 1990, only

nine teams have seen both their starting quarterback and leading receiver from the previous season return, only to start 10 or fewer games in the subsequent season because of injuries (Table 1). Oddly, it didn't happen at all from 2000 to 2010, then happened five times in five seasons and twice last year, to Dallas and Baltimore. Obviously, seven teams are not enough of a sample size to really read into how the Ravens and Cowboys will do this year. However, the overall trend shows that the team's record and offensive DVOA typically rebounds to right around the baseline that was established before the "bad injury luck" season.

There's a wide range of teams here, and not all of them fit the same profile as the Cowboys. The pre-Parcells era Patriots remained a mess regardless of who was healthy, and the Eagles of the mid-'90s were memorably reliant on their great defenses. Among the recent examples, the 2013-14 Packers are the prototype Dallas would like to follow here. Green Bay never bottomed out as badly as the Cowboys did, in part because Aaron Rodgers still played nearly half the season in 2014—and the broken collarbone which nearly torpedoed that season is a mere speed bump in Rodgers' Canton-bound career. The odds of Romo returning as strong from the same injury are slimmer, given his age and more extensive medical history. Still, Romo was a top-five quarterback by both DVOA and DYAR in 2014; he doesn't have to rebound all the way to his pre-injury form for the Cowboys' passing game to be much improved in 2016.

Table 1. Teams with Starting QB and No. 1 WR Playing Less Than 10 Games, 1990-2015

Team	QB-WR	Prev Year		Listed Year		Next Year	
		Record	Off DVOA	Record	Off DVOA	Record	Off DVOA
2015 Cowboys	**Tony Romo / Dez Bryant**	**12-4**	**16.8%**	**4-12**	**-15.6%**	--	--
2015 Ravens	Joe Flacco / Steve Smith	10-6	9.4%	5-11	-5.2%	--	--
2013 Packers	Aaron Rodgers / Randall Cobb	11-5	19.5%	8-7-1	8.6%	12-4	24.7%
2011 Texans	Matt Schaub / Andre Johnson	6-10	21.7%	10-6	8.4%	12-4	0.1%
2011 Rams	Sam Bradford / Danny Amendola	7-9	-18.1%	2-14	-27.2%	7-8-1	-4.2%
1999 Buccaneers	Trent Dilfer / Reidel Anthony	8-8	-7.5%	11-5	-10.2%	10-6	4.7%
1994 Bengals	David Klingler / Jeff Query	3-13	-13.7%	3-13	-16.2%	7-9	2.5%
1993 Eagles	Randall Cunningham / Fred Barnett	11-5	10.5%	8-8	6.3%	7-9	-1.6%
1990 Patriots	Steve Grogan / Hart Lee Dykes	5-11	-4.3%	1-15	-23.4%	6-10	-23.7%
Average (1990-2014)		7.3-8.7	1.2%	6.2-9.8	-7.7%	8.8-7.2	-1.6%

2016 Cowboys Schedule

Week	Opp.	Week	Opp.	Week	Opp.
1	NYG	7	BYE	13	at MIN (Thu.)
2	at WAS	8	PHI	14	at NYG
3	CHI	9	at CLE	15	TB
4	at SF	10	at PIT	16	DET (Mon.)
5	CIN	11	BAL	17	at PHI
6	at GB	12	WAS (Thu.)		

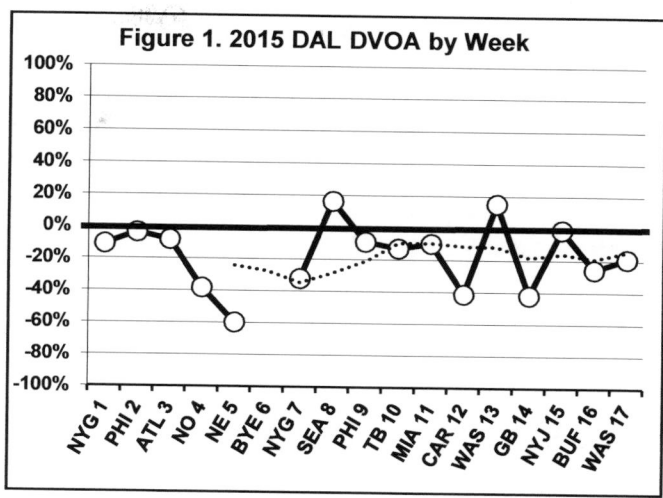

Figure 1. 2015 DAL DVOA by Week

But therein lies the paradox for this Cowboys offense: despite getting the lifeblood of its passing game back healthy, Dallas has deliberately chosen to build around the ground game instead. Taking Ohio State running back Ezekiel Elliott fourth overall was one of the draft's most polarizing decisions, in part because of how dominant the Cowboys' offensive line has been in run-blocking the past two seasons. After finishing first in adjusted line yards while blocking for DeMarco Murray two years ago, the O-line remained sixth in the category last year despite a rotation of mediocrity in the backfield. Most impressively, Dallas managed to spackle together a top-10 rushing offense even though defenses *knew* the ground game was the Cowboys' only real threat. Picking Elliott burned the organization's most valuable draft resource, but it also gave the best unit in the league more wiggle room. A year after the line resuscitated the flagging career of Darren McFadden, perhaps it was wise not to ask the same for Alfred Morris.

With all five starters back under contract, it's hard to imagine how anything besides injuries would prevent the Cowboys from again having the best offensive line in the game. Drafting Elliott also gives the offense its best chance at maximizing its return with this historic line while it remains intact. Every starter apart from Tyron Smith will enter the final year of his deal in 2017, likely forcing some tough decisions over the next couple of offseasons. However, tackling that problem will be less painful if the Cowboys can again become one of the league's most well-rounded offenses.

So as outdated as the whole "3 yards and a cloud of rubber pellets" philosophy may seem, Dallas is as well-equipped as any team in the league to pull it off consistently. Arguably the only strength of the offense last season was its ability to hold onto the ball. Often utilizing multi-tight end sets and a snail-like pace, the Cowboys managed to average 3:00 per offensive drive, the third-best mark in the league. That was almost exactly the same figure they posted in 2014, when their 3:02 TOP per drive ranked second. The problem last year was that these meandering odysseys down the field rarely ended well—despite finishing a respectable 13th in yards per drive and 11th in plays per drive, Dallas was just 27th in points per drive.

That poor bottom line seems incompatible with the other indicators, and indeed, there is lots of evidence screaming that the Cowboys offense should have better luck in 2016. Turnovers tend to regress towards the mean from year to year, and much of Dallas' issues with finishing drives stemmed from giving the ball away before they could actually score. The Cowboys were dead last in turnovers per drive, with just under 19 percent of

their possessions ending in a giveaway. Romo has always had a reputation as a reckless gunslinger, but that perception is an outdated one stemming from his younger days. Across his last two full seasons, Romo posted an interception percentage of 1.96 percent. Only five quarterbacks with at least 20 starts in that span—Alex Smith, Aaron Rodgers, Tom Brady, Russell Wilson, and Ben Roethlisberger—were better at protecting the ball. If Romo stays healthy, these long drives should bear much more fruitful results this season.

The Cowboys are certainly banking on that reality playing out, as the front office has promised repeatedly that winning time of possession will aid a precariously built defense. At this point, the Dallas defense resembles a car nearing the 200,000-mile mark. The "check engine" light keeps blinking, the upholstery is wearing thin, and you're vaguely aware that the timing belt probably needs changing. In the Cowboys' case, the suspension has also been suspended for PED usage.

The Cowboys have finished 16th or worse in defensive DVOA every season since 2010, yet made no major alterations to their defensive personnel this offseason. Other than run-stuffing defensive tackle Cedric Thornton, no free agent signed a deal in excess of $2 million a year in annual average salary. And their top defensive draft pick, Notre Dame linebacker Jaylon Smith, will likely miss his entire rookie season recovering from his gruesome Fiesta Bowl knee injury. Thus, Dallas will continue holding its breath on the highway while procrastinating the invariably expensive trip to the mechanic.

At the same time, not every aging car has to break down immediately, and the Cowboys defense just might be able to get from Point A to Point B reasonably well in 2016. As unlucky as the offense was in the turnover department, their defensive counterparts were even more ill-fated. The 2014 defense skated by with turnovers, leading the league in takeaways per drive, which helped mask a mediocre unit that ranked 22nd in DVOA. Last year, the Cowboys actually improved their defensive DVOA ranking to 19th. Despite better per-play efficiency, though, the Cowboys' rank in total yardage and points allowed actually regressed. As you can guess, the primary culprit was awful turnover luck, as the house of cards which sustained the foundation in 2014 came crumbling down harder than anyone could have expected.

Last year, the Cowboys went from first to last in turnovers forced per drive, finishing with the fourth-worst takeaway per drive rate since 1997. Between Week 3 and Week 9, they did not force a single turnover, and ended up losing four one-possession games in that stretch. Dallas became the first team to finish last in turnovers per drive on both sides of the ball, an unfathomable feat that should reverse itself and be worth a couple wins on its own. Excluding the four defenses from last year, nine of the other 16 most turnover-starved defenses in our database ended up in the top half of the league in turnovers per drive the next season (Table 2).

Table 2. 20 Worst Defensive TO/Drive Rates, 1997-2015

Year	Team	TO/Dr	TO/Dr Y+1	Rk Y+1	Year	Team	TO/Dr	TO/Dr Y+1	Rk Y+1
2014	NYJ	0.056	0.150	6	2005	HOU	0.078	0.133	23
2006	WAS	0.058	0.128	23	2004	STL	0.079	0.133	20
2013	HOU	0.059	0.166	3	2004	GB	0.080	0.111	26
2015	**DAL**	**0.060**	**--**	**--**	2013	NYJ	0.080	0.056	32
2012	KC	0.064	0.159	3	2008	DEN	0.080	0.162	7
2015	BAL	0.066	--	--	2011	DEN	0.081	0.124	16
2012	PHI	0.068	0.158	4	2009	OAK	0.081	0.094	31
2015	SF	0.068	--	--	1998	PHI	0.082	0.208	1
2014	OAK	0.070	0.117	20	2015	CHI	0.082	--	--
2014	KC	0.071	0.156	3	2012	DAL	0.083	0.141	11

Note: turnover rates have steadily declined throughout NFL history, which is why most of these teams are from recent seasons.

Although the Cowboys were not a good team, it is still hard to overstate how profoundly unfortunate they were during this no-good-very-bad season. Along with Miami and Tennessee, Dallas was one of three teams to post bottom-10 offensive and defensive DVOA figures in the fourth quarter. Moreover, the Cowboys were also a bottom-10 offense and defense in "late and close" situations, a level to which the Lions and Browns also sunk. Quite literally, Dallas was the least clutch team in the league last season. This is where the obligatory Romo jokes would come in, but the Cowboys couldn't even get their #hottaek storylines in order. A Romo-led squad in 2016 will perform better in high-leverage situations, even while the football-watching nation collectively decides to continue ignoring this small detail.

Still, while Dallas almost has to experience significantly better luck, they'll be trotting out much of the same unspectacular unit from the past two years. Seven of the 11 starters from the final 2014 playoff game against Green Bay return as projected starters for this season. That doesn't include Sean Lee, who missed that year with a torn ACL, or Jeremy Mincey, a 32-year-old unsigned free agent who may yet return to Valley Ranch.

Most defenses could afford to move on from the Mincey types, unspectacular vets in the twilight of their careers, but the scary news for Dallas is that Mincey might be the best defensive end in their Week 1 lineup. While the Cowboys did

the moral thing by letting the execrable Greg Hardy walk, the troubled edge rusher did lead the defense in combined hits, knockdowns, pressures, and hurries despite missing four games via suspension. Dallas will eventually be able to start a pair of recent second-round picks in Randy Gregory and Demarcus Lawrence (who led the team with 8.0 sacks in 2015), but continuing an unhappy pattern, both edge rushers are suspended the first four games to start the season. Even the harmless specter of OTAs brought more unhappiness: rookie third-rounder Maliek Collins (Nebraska), who appeared poised to contribute as an interior pass-rusher right away, broke his foot and will miss most if not all of training camp, likely making his season a wash. For the opening month, the Cowboys are either looking at playing 3-techniques Tyrone Crawford and/or Jack Crawford out of position or throwing an inexperienced option such as David Irving, Ryan Russell, or rookie fourth-rounder Charles Tapper (Oklahoma) into the fire.

Clearly, none of these solutions are particularly optimal. Though the Cowboys finished a respectable 16th in adjusted sack rate last season, they were 22nd in pressure rate at 24.6 percent. In the first four weeks, without Hardy in the lineup, their pressure rate was a dismal 17.6 percent. No one says you *have* to have a great pass rush to win—in fact, Dallas fielded an even worse pass rush in 2014, finishing 29th in adjusted sack rate and 27th in pressure rate. Maybe Lawrence and Gregory wreak havoc in their return to the lineup, though banking on the latter seems like wishful thinking after Gregory finished without a sack over 12 games during his rookie season. The point is, apart from Swiss Army knife/defensive back Byron Jones, the Cowboys have done little to add dynamic cost-controlled talent to their defense. Along with excellent coaching from defensive coordinator Rod Marinelli, a handful of useful players should keep this unit afloat, and regression to the mean could very well make this defense a league-average unit. But the ceiling likely isn't much higher than that, as it would be surprising to see a fundamentally different defense from what Dallas has rolled out the past five years.

So now the question is whether or not the Cowboys' biggest strength—a clock-killing offense which should be uber-efficient on paper—provides this team enough of a margin for error. Elliott is exactly the type of talented big personality Dallas tends to fall in love with; the chances of Jerry Jones and Chris Christie attending a game together in crop tops are frighteningly real. At the same time, Elliott may have benefited from Todd Gurley's success as a top-10 pick, thereby restoring some luster to the running back position in the draft. While Elliott is unlikely to bust as badly as the last top-five back, Trent Richardson, neither of our running back projection metrics—Speed Score or the newly developed Back-CAST—ranked the Ohio State product as the best prospect in this class. To be clear, Elliott still did well by either method, finishing third in Speed Score and second in BackCAST. Indeed, Elliott profiles as an extremely well-rounded running back, combining above-average measurables with balanced and prolific collegiate production. Gurley and Adrian Peterson were both top-10 running backs by DVOA and DYAR their rookie seasons, so there is certainly precedent for highly touted backs immediately fulfilling the hype.

While it sounds almost too simple, having actual talent at the offensive skill positions, all working around the best offensive line in recent memory, is likely enough of a base to make the Cowboys real contenders in a top-heavy NFC. The skeleton of a top-five offense is in place; no other NFC East team can claim a unit with that type of realistic upside. Unlike last pre-season, though, no one is really imagining Dallas as a Super Bowl-contending powerhouse. Our projections may bestow them with the title of NFC East favorites, but that's like saying the butterfly shrimp at Popeye's is better fast food seafood than the Filet-O-Fish. Apart from the Texans in the moribund AFC South, the Cowboys are the only projected division winner sitting outside of the top 10 in projected mean DVOA. With every other division rival in the bottom third of our forecast, Dallas is the beneficiary of the easiest projected schedule in the NFC. A return to the playoffs might result more from the rampant incompetence along the Northeast Corridor than anything else.

If Dallas is to revive the championship expectations it harbored at this time last year, though, almost everything needs to click into place. The Cowboys actually finished fifth in adjusted games lost despite the high-profile injuries to Romo and Bryant, and will need to stay healthy again to mask the shaky depth across the board. Elliott needs to excel right away

behind the glorious run-blocking he'll surely receive. It would also be helpful if youngsters like Jones, Lawrence, and La'el Collins continued to ascend, strengthening the top of a roster which lacks a sturdy middle class.

That laundry list is a lot to ask for, though the Cowboys should really prepare to embrace tons of close calls given the lot they've chosen. Football Outsiders has laid its foundation on the notion that the passing game is substantially more important than the running game. Though it's certainly not impossible to win big with a heavier-than-average focus on the ground, as Seattle and Carolina will happily attest, those teams also tend to win the aerial battles as well. Romo and the Dallas front office have both insisted this summer that the 36-year-old quarterback has four to five years remaining. The team's roster construction seems to suggest otherwise, as the Cowboys have ostensibly begun the process of shielding Romo from carrying the offense and transitioning him towards the hackneyed "game manager" label. Ultimately, though, Dallas won't be able to win big by masking its quarterback. For better or worse, Romo remains the driver to whom the Cowboys have hitched their ride.

Sterling Xie

2015 Cowboys Stats by Week

Wk	vs.	W-L	PF	PA	YDF	YDA	TO	Total	Off	Def	ST
1	NYG	W	27	26	436	289	-3	-11%	-3%	5%	-3%
2	at PHI	W	20	10	359	226	1	-4%	-30%	-26%	1%
3	ATL	L	28	39	347	438	-1	-8%	33%	44%	3%
4	at NO	L	20	26	335	438	0	-38%	-17%	11%	-11%
5	NE	L	6	30	264	356	-2	-60%	-46%	10%	-4%
6	BYE										
7	at NYG	L	20	27	460	289	-4	-32%	-1%	8%	-23%
8	SEA	L	12	13	220	323	1	16%	-10%	-24%	2%
9	PHI	L	27	33	411	459	-1	-9%	3%	29%	17%
10	at TB	L	6	10	216	327	1	-13%	-32%	-16%	3%
11	at MIA	W	24	14	386	210	-1	-10%	-28%	-12%	6%
12	CAR	L	14	33	210	294	-3	-41%	-54%	-8%	4%
13	at WAS	W	19	16	318	266	-2	15%	-19%	-18%	16%
14	at GB	L	7	28	270	435	-1	-42%	-25%	19%	2%
15	NYJ	L	16	19	309	372	-3	-1%	-14%	1%	15%
16	at BUF	L	6	16	307	408	0	-26%	-25%	0%	-1%
17	WAS	L	23	34	512	437	-4	-19%	4%	25%	2%

Trends and Splits

	Offense	Rank	Defense	Rank
Total DVOA	-15.6%	31	4.5%	19
Unadjusted VOA	-14.5%	28	6.8%	20
Weighted Trend	-18.4%	30	2.0%	17
Variance	4.4%	5	4.0%	10
Average Opponent	2.1%	25	2.1%	6
Passing	-13.9%	32	8.9%	17
Rushing	-4.6%	9	-0.2%	29
First Down	2.2%	13	16.7%	31
Second Down	-36.4%	32	-4.7%	11
Third Down	-19.9%	28	-4.7%	13
First Half	-18.9%	30	-6.2%	11
Second Half	-12.1%	28	14.8%	29
Red Zone	-35.4%	30	-12.7%	7
Late and Close	-18.2%	27	12.6%	27

Five-Year Performance

Year	W-L	Pyth W	Est W	PF	PA	TO	Total	Rk	Off	Rk	Def	Rk	ST	Rk	Off AGL	Rk	Def AGL	Rk	Off Age	Rk	Def Age	Rk	ST Age	Rk
2011	8-8	8.6	8.4	369	347	+4	3.5%	14	5.9%	12	0.4%	16	-2.1%	25	43.5	25	19.0	11	26.6	22	28.2	2	26.0	27
2012	8-8	7.4	7.9	376	400	-13	-0.4%	17	6.1%	11	6.7%	23	0.2%	15	29.0	17	57.5	30	27.2	11	26.7	19	25.6	26
2013	8-8	8.2	8.2	439	432	+8	-2.8%	17	7.5%	11	13.8%	30	3.4%	8	16.4	5	50.2	29	26.5	22	26.1	24	25.3	28
2014	12-4	10.8	10.3	467	352	+6	13.7%	6	16.8%	4	4.0%	22	0.9%	13	9.3	2	66.8	28	26.4	25	26.1	25	25.6	29
2015	4-12	5.2	4.4	275	374	-22	-18.0%	27	-15.6%	31	4.1%	19	1.8%	11	24.1	11	27.6	15	26.9	15	25.9	29	25.7	23

2015 Performance Based on Most Common Personnel Groups

DAL Offense					DAL Offense vs. Opponents					DAL Defense					DAL Defense vs. Opponents			
Pers	Freq	Yds	DVOA	Run%	Pers	Freq	Yds	DVOA	Run%	Pers	Freq	Yds	DVOA		Pers	Freq	Yds	DVOA
11	52%	5.7	-11.9%	25%	Base	36%	5.7	-1.0%	67%	Base	30%	5.2	-8.4%		11	56%	5.9	3.9%
12	23%	6.1	-11.0%	45%	Nickel	49%	5.7	-12.6%	28%	Nickel	52%	5.6	5.2%		12	12%	6.5	-6.2%
21	8%	6.0	0.0%	72%	Dime+	13%	5.6	-26.3%	2%	Dime+	17%	7.4	21.6%		21	11%	5.1	-2.0%
13	7%	6.1	18.5%	75%	Goal Line	1%	0.9	-12.2%	67%	Goal Line	0%	1.0	103.3%		20	4%	5.4	22.1%
22	3%	2.6	-32.4%	87%	Big	1%	3.6	-31.3%	63%						10	4%	8.5	40.0%
02	3%	4.4	-56.7%	7%											22	3%	1.7	-48.6%
															612	3%	5.2	23.3%

Strategic Tendencies

Run/Pass		Rk	Formation		Rk	Pass Rush		Rk	Secondary		Rk	Strategy		Rk
Runs, first half	42%	8	Form: Single Back	77%	13	Rush 3	9.5%	8	4 DB	30%	20	Play action	15%	30
Runs, first down	51%	9	Form: Empty Back	11%	7	Rush 4	69.1%	9	5 DB	52%	19	Avg Box (Off)	6.14	25
Runs, second-long	28%	22	Pers: 3+ WR	56%	19	Rush 5	17.4%	28	6+ DB	17%	10	Avg Box (Def)	6.23	18
Runs, power sit.	61%	9	Pers: 2+ TE/6+ OL	39%	9	Rush 6+	4.0%	28	CB by Sides	82%	11	Offensive Pace	32.95	31
Runs, behind 2H	29%	5	Pers: 6+ OL	2%	19	Sacks by LB	21.0%	24	S/CB Cover Ratio	16%	31	Defensive Pace	30.39	17
Pass, ahead 2H	45%	22	Shotgun/Pistol	54%	25	Sacks by DB	4.8%	24	DB Blitz	7%	23	Go for it on 4th	1.02	12

One reason for the Cowboys' horrible turnover numbers was poor luck on fumble recoveries. Dallas recovered only six of 15 fumbles on offense and only three of 10 fumbles on defense. ☛ Dallas was tied with its opponent for an average of 16:06 each game, by far the largest figure in the league. The difference between the Cowboys and the second-ranked Giants (14:19) was roughly equivalent to the difference between the Giants and 13th-ranked Dolphins. ☛ The Cowboys had an above-average defense on second and third downs, ranking 10th and 13th, respectively. However, they were worse than any defense other than New Orleans on first downs, posting a 16.7% DVOA. ☛ The running back screen was not the Cowboys' friend in 2015. The offense ran only 12 of these plays (30th in the NFL) but gained a dismal 1.5 yards per play with -118.2% DVOA. Meanwhile, the defense had a 26.1% DVOA against running back screens, which ranked 29th. ☛ The Cowboys' defense ranked sixth in DVOA against short passes but 30th against deep passes. ☛ Dallas dropped from third to 19th in frequency of nickel on defense, using both four and six defensive backs around twice as often as in 2014. ☛ With the departure of DeMarco Murray, Dallas opponents weren't as concerned with stacking the box anymore, as the average box faced by the Dallas offense dropped from 10th to 25th.

Passing

Player	DYAR	DVOA	Plays	NtYds	Avg	YAC	C%	TD	Int
M.Cassel*	-172	-23.7%	216	1190	5.5	4.8	58.9%	5	6
T.Romo	-93	-22.4%	127	847	6.7	5.1	68.6%	5	7
K.Moore	10	-9.7%	110	752	6.8	5.8	58.7%	4	5
B.Weeden*	7	-10.1%	106	677	6.4	5.9	72.4%	2	2

Rushing

Player	DYAR	DVOA	Plays	Yds	Avg	TD	Fum	Suc
D.McFadden	83	-0.4%	239	1089	4.6	3	3	50%
J.Randle*	16	-3.5%	76	315	4.1	4	1	45%
R.Turbin*	28	13.4%	32	139	4.3	1	0	50%
C.Michael*	6	0.0%	15	51	3.4	0	0	40%
M.Cassel*	-10	-29.3%	14	85	6.1	0	2	-
L.Whitehead	73	87.2%	10	107	10.7	0	0	-
L.Dunbar	13	107.9%	5	67	13.4	0	0	40%
A.Morris	-52	-15.0%	202	751	3.7	2	0	39%

Receiving

Player	DYAR	DVOA	Plays	Ctch	Yds	Y/C	YAC	TD	C%
T.Williams	140	7.4%	93	52	840	16.2	5.3	3	56%
C.Beasley	64	-1.9%	75	52	536	10.3	6.2	5	69%
D.Bryant	-86	-26.8%	72	31	401	12.9	4.2	3	43%
B.Butler	28	0.3%	26	12	258	21.5	8.0	0	46%
D.Street	2	-10.1%	13	7	114	16.3	1.9	1	54%
L.Whitehead	-35	-65.7%	8	6	16	2.7	3.3	0	75%
J.Witten	36	-1.9%	104	77	713	9.3	3.0	3	74%
J.Hanna	-25	-41.6%	14	9	79	8.8	8.6	0	64%
G.Escobar	-35	-42.8%	13	8	65	8.1	3.5	1	62%
D.McFadden	56	6.9%	53	40	328	8.2	7.9	0	75%
L.Dunbar	45	23.1%	23	21	215	10.2	7.2	0	91%
J.Randle*	36	41.0%	10	10	86	8.6	7.8	0	100%
R.Turbin*	-26	-126.4%	7	5	15	3.0	3.8	0	71%
A.Morris	-10	-27.6%	13	10	55	5.5	3.8	0	77%

Offensive Line

Player	Pos	Age	GS	Snaps	Pen	Sk	Pass	Run	Player	Pos	Age	GS	Snaps	Pen	Sk	Pass	Run
Doug Free	RT	32	16/16	1027	9	3.0	8.0	3.0	La'el Collins	LG	23	12/11	712	6	0.0	3.0	3.5
Zack Martin	RG	24	16/16	1027	11	0.0	0.0	2.0	Ronald Leary	LG	27	4/4	219	2	2.0	3.0	0.0
Travis Frederick	C	25	16/16	1027	2	1.0	3.0	3.0	Joe Looney	C/LG	26	8/6	425	2	3.0	3.5	2.0
Tyron Smith	LT	26	16/16	1027	10	5.0	8.0	1.0									

Year	Yards	ALY	Rank	Power	Rank	Stuff	Rank	2nd Lev	Rank	Open Field	Rank	Sacks	ASR	Rank	Press	Rank	F-Start	Cont.
2013	4.66	4.23	4	68%	11	15%	2	1.29	6	1.02	4	35	6.2%	10	21.8%	7	16	37
2014	4.86	4.40	1	76%	4	18%	11	1.38	2	1.10	2	30	6.1%	16	22.0%	10	13	32
2015	4.53	4.11	6	66%	15	17%	4	1.21	12	1.01	8	33	6.6%	19	20.9%	5	26	34

2015 ALY by direction: Left End 4.46 (6) Left Tackle 4.19 (10) Mid/Guard 4.09 (10) Right Tackle 3.3 (25) Right End 4.32 (5)

Zack Martin's sophomore encore was a strong follow-up to his sterling rookie debut. Martin finished second among right guards in snaps per blown block behind Manny Ramirez, who played less than half as many snaps. However, Martin did commit 11 penalties, a huge jump after drawing just two flags in his rookie campaign. ☞ Doug Free went the whole year without committing a single holding penalty, the only player on the Cowboys' offensive line to pull off that feat. Unfortunately, Free offset that with a league-high nine false starts. The 32-year-old remains a solid starter at right tackle, but Dallas could save $5 million against the cap by cutting Free in 2017 and handing the job to Chaz Green, a 2015 third-round pick out of Florida. ☞ La'el Collins didn't take long to supplant Ronald Leary at left guard, and with a healthy 2016 seems likely to earn a new contract to replace the three-year pact he signed as an undrafted free agent. Like most young players, Collins remains a little raw with his technique, but his flashes of mauling dominance were frequent enough to evoke the image of someone like Kelechi Osemele (who, by the way, is now the highest paid guard in the league).

Defensive Front Seven

Defensive Line	Age	Pos	G	Snaps	Plays	TmPct	Rk	Stop	Dfts	BTkl	Runs	St%	Rk	RuYd	Rk	Sack	Hit	Hur	Dsrpt
								Overall					vs. Run				Pass Rush		
Nick Hayden*	30	DT	16	581	49	6.1%	31	30	8	2	45	60%	81	3.0	70	0.0	0	1.5	2
David Irving	23	DT	12	199	14	2.3%	--	9	4	0	11	64%	--	2.1	--	0.5	2	7.0	0
Cedric Thornton	28	DE	13	493	33	4.5%	51	22	4	1	30	67%	68	3.3	78	1.0	2	9.0	0

Edge Rushers	Age	Pos	G	Snaps	Plays	TmPct	Rk	Stop	Dfts	BTkl	Runs	St%	Rk	RuYd	Rk	Sack	Hit	Hur	Dsrpt
								Overall					vs. Run				Pass Rush		
Tyrone Crawford	27	DE	16	705	35	4.4%	61	24	10	3	25	72%	57	2.9	72	5.0	4	14.5	0
Demarcus Lawrence	24	DE	16	700	55	6.9%	12	41	23	7	39	77%	34	2.4	51	7.5	7	16.5	0
Greg Hardy*	28	DE	12	595	36	6.0%	27	27	14	6	26	69%	66	1.7	24	6.0	15	18.5	0
Jack Crawford	28	DE	16	488	21	2.6%	90	17	10	3	15	80%	23	1.3	17	4.0	0	2.0	0
Jeremy Mincey*	33	DE	14	379	20	2.9%	85	16	5	2	18	78%	30	2.0	34	0.0	4	5.5	0
Randy Gregory	24	DE	12	245	10	1.7%	--	6	2	0	7	71%	--	3.3	--	0.0	8	11.5	0

Linebackers	Age	Pos	G	Snaps	Plays	TmPct	Rk	Stop	Dfts	BTkl	Runs	St%	Rk	RuYd	Rk	Sack	Hit	Hur	Tgts	Suc%	Rk	AdjYd	Rk	PD	Int
								Overall					vs. Run			Pass Rush					vs. Pass				
Sean Lee	29	OLB	14	814	132	18.8%	3	77	23	10	81	54%	73	3.9	66	2.5	1	4	15	45%	58	6.8	47	3	1
Rolando McClain	27	MLB	11	638	83	15.1%	18	43	15	4	60	53%	76	3.9	65	2.0	4	5	16	61%	22	4.1	11	3	1
Anthony Hitchens	24	OLB	16	538	67	8.4%	71	33	9	8	42	57%	64	4.5	78	2.0	3	5	12	34%	68	12.1	72	1	0

Year	Yards	ALY	Rank	Power	Rank	Stuff	Rank	2nd Level	Rank	Open Field	Rank	Sacks	ASR	Rank	Press	Rank
2013	4.84	4.34	29	76%	29	18%	17	1.48	31	0.98	26	34	6.1%	26	21.8%	27
2014	4.46	3.85	17	67%	20	18%	20	1.16	19	1.02	30	28	4.6%	29	22.1%	27
2015	4.31	3.91	21	76%	30	21%	17	1.35	29	0.74	14	31	6.5%	16	24.6%	22

2015 ALY by direction: Left End 3.11 (12) Left Tackle 3.18 (10) Mid/Guard 4.22 (28) Right Tackle 4.56 (29) Right End 3.93 (25)

Having Sean Lee mostly healthy in 2015 was a welcome change for a defense bereft of playmakers. Lee accounted for 16 percent of all the Cowboys' defensive stops in 2015, a rate eclipsed by only D'Qwell Jackson, Lavonte David, and NaVorro Bowman among linebackers. ☞ If he can make it back from his debilitating knee injury, Jaylon Smith is a strong bet to force Rolando McClain out of Dallas next year. McClain may have finally worn out his welcome, earning a 10-game suspension for another substance abuse policy violation after reports suggested that Jason Garrett had become fed up with the linebacker's annual insistence on skipping OTAs. Smith's drool-worthy collegiate tape and ideal measurables make it easy to justify a change. ☞ Tyrone Crawford is probably the most promising pass-rusher on the Cowboys' roster with Lawrence suspended, so Dallas surely hopes the second season of his five-year extension goes better than the first. Crawford certainly wasn't bad, but despite playing roughly 80 more snaps than the year before, the 3-technique saw declines in counting stats like sacks, hurries, defeats, and stops. Dallas should let Crawford figure things out on the interior and quash any notion of moving him to defensive end, a rumor which has persisted throughout the summer.

Defensive Secondary

Secondary	Age	Pos	G	Snaps	Plays	Overall TmPct	Rk	Stop	Dfts	BTkl	Runs	vs. Run St%	Rk	RuYd	Rk	Tgts	vs. Pass Tgt%	Rk	Dist	Suc%	Rk	AdjYd	Rk	PD	Int
Brandon Carr	30	CB	16	1053	82	10.2%	13	21	8	8	21	33%	50	7.0	38	62	18.0%	23	13.2	48%	56	9.0	65	8	0
Byron Jones	24	CB	16	870	74	9.2%	27	29	14	6	27	37%	46	8.2	46	52	18.2%	27	11.0	59%	12	7.4	32	9	0
Barry Church	28	SS	15	862	113	15.0%	4	55	17	18	63	57%	7	4.9	8	23	8.0%	41	7.7	31%	71	9.4	59	0	0
J.J. Wilcox	25	FS	16	821	51	6.4%	65	11	2	13	28	11%	69	7.5	44	10	3.7%	5	8.7	100%	1	0.4	1	3	1
Morris Claiborne	26	CB	11	662	44	8.0%	46	12	2	4	8	25%	62	8.0	45	52	24.2%	66	11.1	47%	63	8.7	57	7	0
Tyler Patmon*	25	CB	13	308	19	2.9%	--	12	6	2	4	75%	--	3.5	--	26	25.5%	--	9.5	66%	--	6.1	--	5	0
Jeff Heath	25	FS	16	205	20	2.5%	--	7	4	2	8	13%	--	9.5	--	9	13.5%	--	15.8	59%	--	7.1	--	2	2

Year	Pass D Rank	vs. #1 WR	Rk	vs. #2 WR	Rk	vs. Other WR	Rk	vs. TE	Rk	vs. RB	Rk
2013	27	12.4%	25	17.6%	28	-11.4%	8	26.8%	32	9.6%	24
2014	22	-2.2%	14	29.5%	29	-24.3%	3	-9.0%	11	-6.3%	12
2015	17	19.6%	30	-11.5%	10	9.0%	21	-25.0%	3	8.2%	20

Athleticism doesn't always transfer onto the field, but combine star Byron Jones proved adept enough to become the Cowboys' most versatile defensive back as a rookie. Jones lined up at every position in the secondary apart from box safety, and early word is that he'll play free safety in 2016. No rookie posted a higher adjusted success rate in coverage than Jones, which is even more impressive considering the variety of receivers he covered on a weekly basis. ☞ Orlando Scandrick will be a most welcome return to Dallas' cornerback corps given the struggles of Brandon Carr and Morris Claiborne last season. Scandrick had the second-lowest estimated target rate of any starting corner in 2014, and ranked in the top 25 in both success rate and yards per pass in both 2013 and 2014. His ability to play outside and in the slot (where he is at his best) affords the Cowboys more flexibility on the back end. ☞ Barry Church was a boom-or-bust thumper in 2015. You can see his shiny run defense stats and the high percentage of plays he was involved in, a reflection of his nose for playing downhill and finding the football. At the same time, Church allowed 18 broken tackles, the most of any safety and second most of all defensive backs behind Antwon Blake. Church has been a durable three-year starter, but as he enters the final year of his current contract, Dallas has to decide whether his cleanups outweigh his messes. ☞ We charted Dallas' safeties in coverage on just 16 percent of passes last season, the second-lowest rate in the league. Typically, opposing quarterbacks were all too happy to isolate Carr or Claiborne on the perimeter and wait for a catch or penalty flag.

Special Teams

Year	DVOA	Rank	FG/XP	Rank	Net Kick	Rank	Kick Ret	Rank	Net Punt	Rank	Punt Ret	Rank	Hidden	Rank
2013	3.4%	8	7.0	5	1.2	14	3.2	7	-1.5	21	7.3	5	0.9	14
2014	0.9%	13	5.3	6	5.0	8	-3.0	23	-0.6	19	-2.5	16	3.1	11
2015	1.8%	11	8.6	3	-6.2	29	-0.1	14	13.3	4	-6.7	30	5.8	8

The Cowboys lost the field-position battle handily in 2015, as the offense ranked 30th in average starting line of scrimmage. Part of that was the continued decline of the punt return game. Cole Beasley has never been an above-average returner, and rookie Lucky Whitehead was better on kick returns (worth 1.9 points on 16 returns) than punt returns (worth minus-4.0 points on 19 returns). ☞ Similarly, Dallas' usually strong kickoff coverage units floundered in 2015. While Dan Bailey has been roughly average on kickoffs, the coverage units gave up net positive value to the opposing kickoff team for the first time in the past three years. ☞ It was a much happier story on punts, where both Chris Jones and the coverage unit were near the top of the league.

Denver Broncos

2015 record: 12-4	**Total DVOA:** 17.7% (8th)	**2016 Mean Projection:** 8.2 wins	**On the Clock (0-4):** 8%
Pythagorean Wins: 9.7 (10th)	**Offense:** -8.7% (25th)	**Postseason Odds:** 37.0%	**Mediocrity (5-7):** 31%
Snap-Weighted Age: 27.1 (7th)	**Defense:** -25.8% (1st)	**Super Bowl Odds:** 5.1%	**Playoff Contender (8-10):** 41%
Average Opponent: 4.1% (10th)	**Special Teams:** 0.7% (14th)	**Proj. Avg. Opponent:** 0.5% (14th)	**Super Bowl Contender (11+):** 19%

2015: Finally, Peyton Manning's teammates do all the work for him, as the Broncos ride one of the ten best defenses in DVOA history to a Super Bowl title.

2016: Great defenses are just not as consistent as great offenses, and this great defense is unlikely to be an exception.

When legendary quarterbacks ride off into the sunset holding the Lombardi Trophy, the horse they ride is a (Denver) bronco. Only John Elway in 1998 and Peyton Manning in 2015 led a team to a Super Bowl victory in their final NFL games. Once again, Denver will try to follow up a title without its leading man, and it could hardly go worse than it did 17 years ago.

In 1999, Denver's title defense foundered from the start. The Broncos led off the season with a 38-21 loss to Miami on Monday Night Football. They lost at home the next two weeks. Then in Week 4, the NFL's reigning MVP, running back Terrell Davis, suffered torn knee ligaments that effectively ended his career. That week's 21-13 loss to the Jets left the Broncos at 0-4. They finished 6-10, the worst winning percentage for any defending champion in the Super Bowl era other than the 1982 49ers (who finished that strike-shortened season 3-6). The defense actually improved in 1999, climbing from No. 20 to No. 10 in DVOA. But without Elway, and mostly without Davis (or Shannon Sharpe, who played only five games), the Broncos' offense slipped from the league's No. 1 spot to No. 14.

This season, our projections see the Broncos again sliding into post-Super Bowl mediocrity, albeit in a very different way. This time, the Broncos were driven not by a great offense but a great defense, ranked No. 8 all-time since our DVOA ratings begin in 1989. That defense is not suddenly going to become mediocre in 2016. Our forecasts consider a range of possibilities, but the average projection for Denver's defense is still the best in the NFL. Nonetheless, even a very good Denver defense will fall far short of last year's dominance. Combine that almost inevitable drop-off with an offense that looks even more impotent than last year, and the Broncos are built around a formula that usually misses the playoffs.

The Broncos optimist would likely challenge the idea that the odds are stacked against the defense repeating its 2015 performance. For years, Football Outsiders has pointed out that defense is less consistent from year to year than offense. Still, maybe it's possible that the gravity of regression tugs the truly great defenses down a little less. The early 1990s Eagles, the early 2000s Ravens, and the recent Seahawks have shown that defenses can dominate year after year, right?

Unfortunately for the Broncos believers—and the fan blogo-

sphere seems to be calling for 12 wins on the low end, so there is a healthy group of them—even those defenses slid substantially after their peak seasons. And the other great defenses of recent history fell further, sometimes much further. Three of the all-time top 10 defenses by DVOA fell all the way to No. 25 the following year. Greatness one year hasn't even been a promise of average defense the following year (Table 1).

Table 1. Best Defensive DVOA Since 1989... and the Year After

Year	Team	Def DVOA	Def DVOA Y+1	Rank Y+1	AV over Replacement Change
1991	PHI	-42.4%	-18.1%	2	-13
2002	TB	-31.8%	-17.6%	3	-4
2008	PIT	-29.0%	-4.6%	9	-7
2004	BUF	-28.5%	8.6%	25	-7
2008	BAL	-27.8%	-14.2%	4	-11
2012	CHI	-26.7%	8.7%	25	-14
2013	SEA	-25.9%	-16.8%	1	-8
2015	**DEN**	**-25.8%**	**--**	**--**	**-12**
2009	NYJ	-25.5%	-10.9%	5	-5
2000	TEN	-25.0%	10.3%	25	-11

Altogether, the other nine teams among the ten best defenses since 1989 averaged a DVOA of -6.1% the following season. Our projection for the Broncos' DVOA in 2015 is more optimistic than that, but the list of comparable teams shows how wide the potential range of outcomes is. It's easy to think of the 1991-1992 Eagles as a potential analogy for the 2015-16 Broncos, but the 2012-13 Bears make just as much sense. The year before their defensive peak, the Bears posted a DVOA of -14.2% in 2011, compared to a DVOA of -13.2% for the Broncos in 2014 (both ranked fourth). More broadly, 22 different defenses from 1989 through 2014 had a DVOA below -20%, but only one of those teams managed to post a defensive DVOA below -20% again the following year: the 1999-2000 Ravens.

But again, maybe the Broncos are different because they return the league's best secondary and best pass-rushing duo. Losing defensive end Malik Jackson and linebacker Danny

2016 Broncos Schedule

Week	Opp.	Week	Opp.	Week	Opp.
1	CAR (Thu.)	7	HOU (Mon.)	13	at JAC
2	IND	8	SD	14	at TEN
3	at CIN	9	at OAK	15	NE
4	at TB	10	at NO	16	at KC (Xmas)
5	ATL	11	BYE	17	at OAK
6	at SD (Thu.)	12	KC		

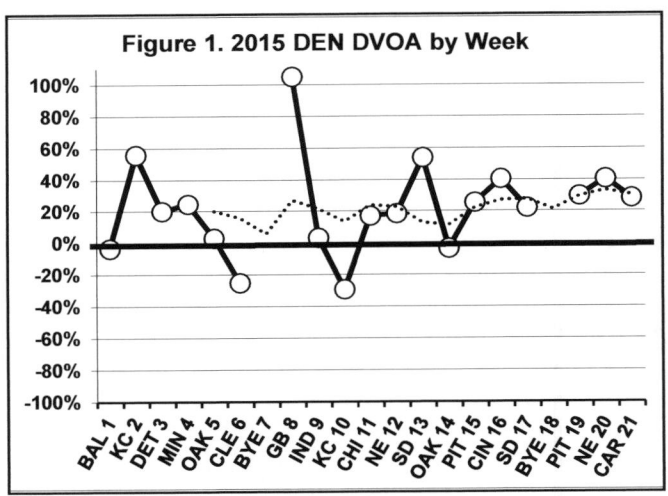

Figure 1. 2015 DEN DVOA by Week

Trevathan in free agency might be less difficult than the changes faced by either the 1992 Eagles (who saw All-Pro defensive tackle Jerome Brown die tragically in the summer of 1992) or the 2013 Bears (who had an aging core and lost Brian Urlacher to retirement).

The lost value in Jackson and Trevathan, however, tends towards the upper end for the best defenses since 1989. The last column in the table lists the Approximate Value (AV) above replacement that the teams lost in net terms through retirement, trades, and free agency. (We're using Pro Football Reference's AV formula and defining replacement level as 3 AV; insert caveat here about all the limitations about AV, which is called "approximate" for a reason.) The Broncos rank just behind the 1992 Eagles and 2013 Bears with 12 points of AV above replacement lost. Though the losses are not totally devastating, they are slightly worse than what previous great defenses have had to overcome. Jackson and Trevathan ranked fourth and fifth in AV last year for Broncos defensive players, trailing only edge rusher Von Miller and cornerbacks Chris Harris and Aqib Talib.

More important, Jackson and Trevathan were two of the three youngest starters on the defense (with defensive end Derek Wolfe being the other 25-year-old). So the Broncos not only lost two key contributors, but two who may still improve. Even with the loss of two young stars, though, the age situation looks considerably more promising for the 2016 Broncos than it did for the 2013 Bears, a group where most of the best players resided on the north side of 30. The Denver defense ranked only 19th in snap-weighted age in 2015. Only edge rusher DeMarcus Ware (34) and Talib (30) will have crossed the 30-year-old barrier by opening day.

To limit Ware's snaps, the Broncos will look for 2015 first-round draft pick Shane Ray to take a big step forward in 2016. As a rookie, Ray posted four sacks while playing 34 percent of the defensive snaps. The degree of pass-rushing difficulty for Ray increases in 2016 with the loss of Jackson's interior pressure. But Ray will still be aided by Wolfe's interior pressure and, more importantly, by all the attention that Miller commands on the opposite side. So the conditions are still favorable for Ray to put up solid numbers in the increased action he is likely to get this season. Unfortunately, our Sack-SEER projections for pass rusher prospects viewed Vernon Gholston as the clearest comparison for Ray, suggesting that his increased role could portend real problems for the pass rush. At Missouri, Ray was a one-year wonder, picking up 14.5 of his 19 sacks in his junior year.

On the other hand, nobody knows how to get the most out of his pass-rushers like Denver defensive coordinator Wade Phillips. The improvement that the Broncos made in Phillips' first year on the job mirrored similar jumps that every one of his previous defenses have made (Table 2). In his previous four stops, Phillips turned four poor defenses into good-to-excellent units. Last year, he took an excellent unit and made it historically great with almost identical personnel. Overall, Phillips has taken over five defenses that averaged a DVOA of 5.1% (average ranking: 20.7) and turned them into units averaging -11.2% (average ranking: 8.5).

Table 2. Wade Phillips in His First Two Years as Defensive Coordinator Since 1995

Year	Team	Pre-Wade DVOA	Pre-Wade Rank	Y1 DVOA	Y1 Rank	Y2 DVOA	Y2 Rank
1995-96	BUF	3.8%	19	-6.5%	10	-9.7%	7
2002-03	ATL	11.8%	26	-4.1%	12	10.6%	27
2004-05	SD	12.0%	30	-4.2%	13	-1.1%	15
2007-08	DAL (HC)	-1.5%	14	-6.8%	9	-4.2%	9
2011-12	HOU	17.5%	31	-9.5%	6	-14.2%	4
2015-16	**DEN**	**-13.2%**	**4**	**-36.0%**	**1**	**--**	**--**

But even with Phillips, the sequel has not been quite as good as the opening act. In his second year as defensive coordinator, two of his defenses (the 1996 Bills and 2012 Texans) got even better, while the other two (the 2003 Falcons and 2005 Chargers) regressed. That regression is no indictment of Phillips. We're talking small samples here. The very large improvements that Phillips achieved likely combine both luck and real coaching contributions. We can come up with a narrative to account for the big first-year improvement followed by the drop-off—such as Phillips being a players' coach—but randomness is both simpler and plausible.

No matter the personnel, Phillips defenses have consistently generated an effective pass rush. We have adjusted sack rate numbers since 1996 and Phillips has been a defensive coordinator for 11 years during that time. Phillips' defenses have ranked in the top six according to adjusted sack rate in eight of those 11 years, with last year marking the first time Philips finished first. The influence of Phillips is the most important factor in countering the regression gods.

Denver's secondary also enters 2016 ready to continue its high level of performance, as all key contributors return. The best player, Harris, is entering his prime at 27; Talib is the oldest starter at the age of 30. Perhaps surprisingly, Harris and Talib both charted as only average in coverage last season by adjusted success rate, although both were better at adjusted yards per pass. Harris' 52 percent success rate ranked 39th (of 83 qualifying cornerbacks) and Talib's 50 percent success rate ranked 48th. Our cornerback charting stats oscillate like Merton Hanks' neck from year to year, so they should be viewed as very noisy. Our numbers for 2014 ranked Harris third among No. 1 corners and Talib ninth among all non-No. 1 corners. (In Denver, that distinction is less clear than on other teams.) Any way you slice the data, Harris and Talib have charted well in the recent past and are likely somewhat underappreciated by their 2015 charting stats. Still, declines in the charting stats for 30-something cornerbacks have foretold further declines in the past. Brent Grimes is one recent example. Particularly with his off-field problems, Talib is a candidate for some slippage in 2016.

If the Broncos do get less from Talib, they will have an even greater need to get more from 2014 first-round pick Bradley Roby. They just may get it. In 2015, Roby had a 54 percent success rate (ranked 30th), facing a similar number of targets as Harris and Talib. He also may have made the single most important play of Denver's playoff run, forcing the fumble that set the Broncos up to complete the divisional-round comeback against the Steelers. Even if Talib stays healthy, Roby may clearly emerge as Denver's second-best cornerback by season's end. The magnitude of his continuing improvement will play an important role in determining the ceiling for the Denver defense in 2016.

The debate on the Broncos defense centers on where it will fall on the spectrum from good to great, but now the chapter turns dark. The situation on offense is the Bizarro version of the situation on defense. The most likely outcomes range from bad to atrocious, with a floor that is as low as the ceiling for the defense is high.

Before last season, the wide receivers looked like the clear strength on offense. Demaryius Thomas has the highest cap number on the team, but saw his effectiveness drop in 2015 for reasons beyond terrible quarterbacking. That our charting credited Thomas with just nine dropped passes (tied for fifth in the NFL) seems a likely case for subjectivity in scorekeeping. His DVOA ranked 70th among wide receivers, falling from 29th the year before. The plummeting stats can be blamed primarily on one of the biggest year-to-year declines in quarterback play that any receiver has experienced, but the tape also shows Thomas having his own issues. Emmanuel Sanders, on the other hand, may comfortably blame his low efficiency numbers entirely on the quarterback calamity. For most of 2015, Sanders looked both like the more reliable target and the more intimidating threat. With the quarterbacking likely to be more of the iffy variety from 2015 rather than the precise variety from 2014, Sanders could again be the receiver most likely to bail his quarterback out rather than his more highly-compensated counterpart.

The Broncos hope to add a receiving threat at tight end with 2015 third-round pick Jeff Heuerman, who missed the entire 2015 season with a knee injury. Denver is betting on Heuerman's physical attributes (6-foot-5, 255 pounds, a 34½-inch vertical jump) outweighing his minimal college production. Limited by a foot injury in his senior season, Heuerman had just 17 catches for 207 yards. He was better as a junior, with 26 catches for 466 yards and four touchdowns.

Heuerman is part of a larger pattern of Denver drafting players coming off injuries in their last college seasons. This year, that included second-round defensive end Adam Gotsis (Georgia Tech) and fourth-round running back Devontae Booker (Utah). Both players were lost to season-ending knee injuries in November. Booker had to undergo a second surgery to repair his torn meniscus, but is reportedly on track to be ready for training camp despite missing OTAs. Leaving his injury issues aside, Booker is a high-variance prospect. On the plus side, Booker's college production projects very well, and he trailed only Ezekiel Elliott and Derrick Henry in our new BackCAST projections for rookie running backs.

The decision to draft Booker makes Elway's offseason negotiations with running back C.J. Anderson all the more confusing. With the option to either pay Anderson $2.6 million, to let him walk, or to try to pay him $1.7 million only to end up matching his deal that comes with a $6 million cap hit this season, Elway ended up picking Door C. Anderson struggled for much of 2015, and letting him walk was the obvious decision. Instead, one of the roster's most replaceable players, someone who was replaced often last season by Ronnie Hillman, will carry the team's eighth-highest cap charge. A better decision would have been to turn the lead back role over to Booker or some other player from the seemingly endless supply of available running backs.

Counteracting the wasted resources at running back, Elway saved money by getting free-agent left tackle Russell Okung at a bargain price ($5.2 million in 2016). Even if Okung is only adequate, he still helps fix an offensive line that struggled last season. Two crucial injuries at left tackle were a big part of the problem: Denver lost Ryan Clady before the season and then his replacement, 2015 second-round pick Ty Sambrailo, in Week 3. This season, the Broncos return just one lineman from the unit that started the Super Bowl: center Matt Paradis, a sixth-round pick in 2014. In addition to Paradis, Okung, and Sambrailo at left guard, the starters on the right side project to be guard Max Garcia, who showed promise as a rookie in 2015, and tackle Dwight Stephenson, a free-agent signee from Kansas City. With so much turnover, the line situation can only be called uncertain.

The situation at quarterback, on the other hand, is more well-defined; for example, the Merriam-Webster dictionary defines the word "horrendous" as "very bad or unpleasant." Probable starter Mark Sanchez has never had a positive

DVOA in seven NFL seasons (he missed one of those with injury). Last season, he had the worst DVOA rating of his career, though with a small sample size of just 100 passes. It seems impossible that Sanchez has been in the league long enough to already be defined as one of those Ryan Fitzpatrick-like veterans who are just good enough to continue to see NFL action, but we're there and the comparison is not entirely fair to Fitzpatrick. Unlike the bearded one, Sanchez has sprinkled in terrible seasons with his recent merely poor ones, giving little reason to think he will suddenly hit the above-average territory that Fitzpatrick has found the last two years. Even for those who argue his situation with the Jets was unusually unfavorable, Sanchez's performance in Philadelphia fell short of Nick Foles' standard. In 2014, Foles (1.8% DVOA) and Sanchez (-1.4% DVOA) each threw nearly the same number of passes. While Foles' peak came in his very fortunate 2013, that 2014 half-season marks Sanchez's high-water mark. The Broncos' situation looks less auspicious.

While Sanchez represents a low-ceiling, low-floor option, rookie first-round pick Paxton Lynch shares only that low floor. Whatever his potential, Lynch seems a strange fit for the Broncos' current situation. Head coach Gary Kubiak, prefers to go to the shotgun less than most offenses—the Broncos even drafted a fullback this year—and Lynch has almost no experience operating under center or taking a deeper drop. Our QBASE projection system gives Lynch a low grade for a first-round pick, assigning him a 67 percent chance of being an NFL bust. Lynch faced some of the softest college competition of any recent early-round prospect; Memphis' slate of opposing defenses last season ranked No. 86 in FBS by our estimates. He did not do as well against that easy schedule as previous prospects, such as Ben Roethlisberger and Chad Pennington, who also feasted on poor defenses but eventually succeeded in the NFL.

Projecting quarterbacks is inherently noisy, perhaps even noisier than projecting other positions. Even if our process is right, there is still a 33 percent chance that Lynch will have some degree of success in the NFL. But his scouting report resembles those of flops such as Jake Locker and Kyle Boller. Scouts rate Lynch highly on athletic skills, "arm talent," and size, but lower on his on-the-move accuracy and his ability to get through progressions. (The latter is admittedly more about the Memphis offense giving us very little on tape to see one way or the other, rather than there being clear evidence of Lynch's limitations.) Lynch seems like much more of a project rather than an immediate contributor, a poor match for a team with a defense ready to win now. That some Bronco-watchers are hoping for 2015 seventh-round pick Trevor Siemian (5.6 yards per attempt as a senior at Northwestern) to challenge for the starting job speaks to the quality of Denver's quarterback options in 2016, not to mention the endless capacity for all of us to instinctively overestimate the probability of unlikely events.

In today's social media-drenched world, NFL players will use anything they can find as evidence of disrespect. That's certainly how the Broncos defense feels about Football Outsiders right now; when we ran our early version of the 2016 projections at ESPN Insider, Chris Harris went on Twitter to thank us for the motivation. But there are three phases of the game, and great players such as Harris can't do anything about what happens when they're off the field. Offensive impotence and defensive excellence add up to a formula that rarely succeeds in today's NFL. Last year, the defense defied that pattern, dragging an albatross of an offense to a championship. This year, the dead weight may be even heavier. As in 1999, a title defense marked by an offense in transition looks unlikely to launch.

Aaron Schatz

2015 Broncos Stats by Week

Wk	vs.	W-L	PF	PA	YDF	YDA	TO	Total	Off	Def	ST
1	BAL	W	19	13	219	173	1	-4%	-59%	-50%	5%
2	at KC	W	31	24	299	314	4	56%	-2%	-47%	11%
3	at DET	W	24	12	354	290	1	20%	-9%	-27%	3%
4	MIN	W	23	20	344	325	-1	25%	-6%	-27%	4%
5	at OAK	W	16	10	297	288	1	3%	-26%	-30%	-1%
6	at CLE	W	26	23	442	298	0	-25%	-36%	-24%	-13%
7	BYE										
8	GB	W	29	10	500	140	-1	105%	53%	-51%	1%
9	at IND	L	24	27	309	365	-2	3%	-1%	18%	22%
10	KC	L	13	29	221	303	-5	-29%	-53%	-20%	3%
11	at CHI	W	17	15	389	347	2	17%	8%	-6%	3%
12	NE	W	30	24	433	301	0	19%	11%	-20%	-12%
13	at SD	W	17	3	293	272	2	54%	-8%	-66%	-4%
14	OAK	L	12	15	310	126	-2	-4%	-38%	-49%	-14%
15	at PIT	L	27	34	385	377	0	26%	16%	-8%	2%
16	CIN	W	20	17	390	294	0	40%	31%	-17%	-8%
17	SD	W	27	20	503	317	-4	22%	-10%	-22%	10%
18	BYE										
19	PIT	W	23	16	324	396	1	30%	3%	-6%	20%
20	NE	W	20	18	244	336	1	41%	-20%	-53%	7%
21	CAR	W	24	10	194	315	2	28%	-50%	-58%	21%

Trends and Splits

	Offense	Rank	Defense	Rank
Total DVOA	-8.8%	25	-25.8%	1
Unadjusted VOA	-7.5%	25	-22.7%	1
Weighted Trend	-4.6%	18	-22.1%	1
Variance	8.8%	24	4.4%	14
Average Opponent	-0.1%	17	3.2%	4
Passing	-3.3%	25	-28.0%	1
Rushing	-10.3%	19	-22.8%	4
First Down	0.4%	15	-22.8%	2
Second Down	-20.6%	28	-33.9%	1
Third Down	-8.2%	21	-18.2%	7
First Half	-10.8%	22	-20.3%	2
Second Half	-6.9%	22	-31.1%	1
Red Zone	-14.7%	26	-2.1%	13
Late and Close	-11.1%	22	-35.5%	1

Five-Year Performance

Year	W-L	Pyth W	Est W	PF	PA	TO	Total	Rk	Off	Rk	Def	Rk	ST	Rk	Off AGL	Rk	Def AGL	Rk	Off Age	Rk	Def Age	Rk	ST Age	Rk
2011	8-8	5.8	7.0	309	390	+1	-11.8%	24	-9.9%	23	1.6%	18	-0.2%	18	15.0	4	40.4	24	25.6	32	27.5	10	25.9	28
2012	13-3	12.5	14.7	481	289	-1	36.5%	2	22.1%	2	-13.8%	5	0.6%	13	27.8	15	21.4	11	28.3	5	27.0	15	25.9	21
2013	13-3	11.7	14.1	606	399	0	32.7%	2	33.5%	1	-0.2%	15	-1.0%	21	37.8	19	45.8	26	27.9	3	26.3	18	26.8	5
2014	12-4	11.0	13.3	482	354	+5	29.5%	2	20.0%	3	-13.2%	4	-3.7%	27	11.7	4	25.2	6	28.6	2	25.7	31	25.6	27
2015	12-4	9.7	10.7	355	296	-4	17.7%	8	-8.7%	25	-25.8%	1	0.7%	14	42.9	22	13.8	2	28.3	2	26.5	19	25.6	26

2015 Performance Based on Most Common Personnel Groups

DEN Offense					DEN Offense vs. Opponents					DEN Defense				DEN Defense vs. Opponents			
Pers	Freq	Yds	DVOA	Run%	Pers	Freq	Yds	DVOA	Run%	Pers	Freq	Yds	DVOA	Pers	Freq	Yds	DVOA
11	57%	5.9	-6.4%	30%	Base	32%	4.7	-21.1%	50%	Base	57%	4.4	-26.2%	11	41%	5.1	-26.9%
12	32%	5.4	-3.7%	47%	Nickel	54%	5.9	0.0%	35%	Nickel	11%	3.8	-70.9%	12	28%	4.9	-26.7%
10	2%	3.8	-17.1%	48%	Dime+	13%	6.1	12.0%	7%	Dime+	29%	5.7	-7.5%	21	12%	3.3	-40.3%
02	2%	4.5	28.8%	11%	Goal Line	1%	-0.4	-28.7%	63%	Big	3%	1.8	-17.3%	13	8%	4.0	-18.7%
13	2%	2.3	-27.2%	72%	Big	0%	1.2	16.4%	100%					22	5%	2.7	-38.6%

Strategic Tendencies

Run/Pass		Rk	Formation		Rk	Pass Rush		Rk	Secondary		Rk	Strategy		Rk
Runs, first half	36%	23	Form: Single Back	87%	3	Rush 3	2.0%	31	4 DB	57%	1	Play action	19%	13
Runs, first down	47%	17	Form: Empty Back	9%	12	Rush 4	55.4%	23	5 DB	11%	32	Avg Box (Off)	6.25	16
Runs, second-long	31%	15	Pers: 3+ WR	63%	13	Rush 5	30.2%	5	6+ DB	29%	5	Avg Box (Def)	6.49	1
Runs, power sit.	51%	24	Pers: 2+ TE/6+ OL	38%	11	Rush 6+	12.4%	4	CB by Sides	68%	24	Offensive Pace	28.92	6
Runs, behind 2H	23%	22	Pers: 6+ OL	2%	18	Sacks by LB	59.6%	5	S/CB Cover Ratio	28%	6	Defensive Pace	30.60	23
Pass, ahead 2H	48%	10	Shotgun/Pistol	65%	14	Sacks by DB	5.8%	19	DB Blitz	7%	22	Go for it on 4th	0.72	26

Only 5.8 percent of carries by Denver running backs came from two-back sets. This number had never been below 47 percent for any previous Gary Kubiak offense—and surprisingly, the rate actually went *down* after Brock Osweiler replaced Peyton Manning at quarterback. Maybe Manning kidnapped Kubiak's brain. ☞ Wade Phillips likes to bring extra pressure, but he does it with linebackers. The Broncos blitzed almost twice as often as they did in 2014 (from 21.9 percent to 42.6 percent), but defensive back blitzes were about the same and Broncos defensive backs had fewer sacks than they did the year before. ☞ Aren't play-action fakes supposed to slow down a great pass rush? The Broncos only faced play-action on 13 percent of opposing pass plays, the lowest figure in the NFL last year. ☞ Denver's defense was historically great without even benefiting from many dropped passes. They had only 14 drops from opponents, 30th in the NFL. ☞ Another reason the Denver defense was even better than it looked: it was often defending short fields. Denver ranked 29th in average starting field position conceded. ☞ Did Denver have any defensive weaknesses? Based on DVOA splits, there were a couple, starting with third-and-short. The Broncos ranked 20th with 8.8% DVOA in those situations, but ranked no worse than eighth in any other down-and-distance combination. Denver also ranked 30th in DVOA against runs in the red zone, though they were ninth against passes in the red zone. ☞ Denver's "CB by Sides" number of 68 percent is a bit confusing because Chris Harris so often moved to the slot in nickel sets. If we measured Aqib Talib and Bradley Roby instead of Talib and Harris, Denver would be around league average at 75 percent.

Passing

Player	DYAR	DVOA	Plays	NtYds	Avg	YAC	C%	TD	Int
P.Manning*	-326	-25.8%	346	2156	6.2	4.9	60.2%	9	17
B.Osweiler*	153	-3.2%	299	1813	6.1	5.2	61.8%	10	6
M.Sanchez	-227	-46.9%	100	562	5.6	5.4	64.8%	4	4

Receiving

Player	DYAR	DVOA	Plays	Ctch	Yds	Y/C	YAC	TD	C%
D.Thomas	56	-8.7%	177	105	1316	12.5	4.7	6	59%
E.Sanders	90	-4.1%	137	76	1135	14.9	4.8	6	55%
J.Norwood	-6	-14.9%	32	22	207	9.4	3.1	0	69%
B.Fowler	20	-3.4%	25	16	203	12.7	6.1	0	64%
A.Caldwell*	-47	-39.8%	22	10	72	7.2	1.6	2	45%
C.Latimer	18	7.5%	11	6	59	9.8	5.3	1	55%
O.Daniels*	26	-2.1%	77	46	517	11.2	5.8	3	60%
V.Davis*	19	3.2%	28	20	201	10.1	3.5	0	71%
V.Green	66	51.3%	15	12	173	14.4	10.1	1	80%
G.Graham	-70	-66.4%	19	4	30	7.5	2.3	1	21%
C.Anderson	-23	-27.8%	36	25	183	7.3	6.0	0	69%
R.Hillman	-89	-59.0%	35	24	111	4.6	5.1	0	69%
J.Thompson	-8	-32.5%	9	6	51	8.5	11.5	0	67%

Rushing

Player	DYAR	DVOA	Plays	Yds	Avg	TD	Fum	Suc
R.Hillman	21	-6.2%	207	863	4.2	7	2	45%
C.Anderson	34	-3.2%	152	720	4.7	5	2	41%
J.Thompson	-24	-40.5%	18	48	2.7	0	0	28%
B.Osweiler*	6	-6.1%	17	65	3.8	1	0	-

Offensive Line

Player	Pos	Age	GS	Snaps	Pen	Sk	Pass	Run	Player	Pos	Age	GS	Snaps	Pen	Sk	Pass	Run
Matt Paradis	C	27	16/16	1109	1	1.0	3.0	5.5	Max Garcia	C	25	16/5	543	6	0.0	5.0	2.0
Ryan Harris*	LT	31	16/16	1006	4	2.0	10.5	4.0	Ty Sambrailo	LT	24	3/3	214	2	1.0	6.0	0.0
Louis Vasquez*	RG	29	16/15	878	3	1.0	7.0	6.0	Russell Okung	LT	29	13/13	851	6	3.0	7.0	7.0
Michael Schofield	RT	26	13/13	872	5	7.0	15.0	4.0	Donald Stephenson	RT	28	16/7	555	6	1.0	8.5	1.0
Evan Mathis*	LG	35	16/12	809	2	2.0	7.5	3.0									

Year	Yards	ALY	Rank	Power	Rank	Stuff	Rank	2nd Lev	Rank	Open Field	Rank	Sacks	ASR	Rank	Press	Rank	F-Start	Cont.
2013	4.38	4.07	8	64%	17	16%	3	1.30	4	0.63	20	20	3.6%	1	15.4%	1	14	36
2014	4.39	3.98	12	75%	5	18%	9	1.24	10	0.83	7	17	3.7%	1	13.4%	1	18	36
2015	4.33	3.73	17	61%	23	23%	23	1.24	3	0.93	9	39	5.8%	13	27.5%	22	11	32

2015 ALY by direction:	Left End 2.92 (27)	Left Tackle 4.46 (5)	Mid/Guard 3.75 (20)	Right Tackle 3.94 (10)	Right End 2.64 (26)

Russell Okung's free-agent deal ($5.2 million in 2016, with just $800,000 guaranteed after that) appears disastrous at first glance. But from the player's perspective, it is similar to the deal Darrelle Revis signed with New England, giving Okung (who turns 29 in October) a one-year audition for a much larger payday in 2017. ☞ 2015 second-rounder Ty Sambrailo projected at left tackle before getting injured last year, but Okung's arrival pushes him inside to left guard. ☞ Fifth-round guard Conor McGovern projects to be the first man off the bench. He's a weight-room stud who played tackle at Missouri; both NFL.com and NFL Draft Scout projected him to go two rounds earlier. ☞ Free-agent signee Donald Stephenson projects to start at right tackle, with Michael Schofield pushed to the bench. Last season in Kansas City, the Chiefs ranked 28th in the league on runs to the outside on Stephenson's side of the field, getting just 2.40 adjusted line yards per carry.

Defensive Front Seven

Defensive Line	Age	Pos	G	Snaps	Plays	TmPct	Rk	Stop	Dfts	BTkl	Runs	St%	Rk	RuYd	Rk	Sack	Hit	Hur	Dsrpt
						Overall						vs. Run				Pass Rush			
Malik Jackson*	26	DE	16	825	50	6.1%	32	36	15	5	31	65%	76	3.1	72	5.0	10	22.0	6
Derek Wolfe	26	DE	12	648	50	8.1%	7	42	14	2	41	83%	20	1.5	12	5.5	9	16.0	1
Sylvester Williams	28	DT	15	535	24	3.1%	75	21	6	1	20	90%	6	1.8	25	3.0	1	3.5	0
Vance Walker	29	DE	15	382	33	4.3%	--	28	5	2	31	84%	--	2.1	--	2.0	1	2.5	0
Antonio Smith*	35	DE	16	364	11	1.3%	--	11	6	1	6	100%	--	-0.2	--	2.5	5	8.5	1
Jared Crick	27	DE	16	783	49	6.3%	27	33	8	4	44	66%	72	3.1	74	2.0	8	4.5	2

Edge Rushers	Age	Pos	G	Snaps	Plays	Overall TmPct	Rk	Stop	Dfts	BTkl	Runs	vs. Run St%	Rk	RuYd	Rk	Pass Rush Sack	Hit	Hur	Dsrpt
Von Miller	27	OLB	16	835	36	4.4%	60	29	15	4	21	76%	36	1.8	28	11.0	23	37.0	1
Shaquil Barrett	24	OLB	16	496	45	5.5%	38	32	14	6	26	69%	66	2.6	61	5.5	6	16.0	1
DeMarcus Ware	34	OLB	11	399	25	4.4%	58	17	12	4	13	54%	93	4.5	94	7.5	8	19.0	0
Shane Ray	23	OLB	14	341	20	2.8%	--	17	6	0	12	83%	--	2.8	--	4.0	3	5.5	0
Benson Mayowa	25	DE	12	377	15	2.3%	93	9	4	0	10	60%	87	3.1	78	1.0	3	7.0	0

Linebackers	Age	Pos	G	Snaps	Plays	Overall TmPct	Rk	Stop	Dfts	BTkl	Runs	vs. Run St%	Rk	RuYd	Rk	Pass Rush Sack	Hit	Hur	vs. Pass Tgts	Suc%	Rk	AdjYd	Rk	PD	Int
Brandon Marshall	27	ILB	16	914	103	12.6%	40	64	19	6	59	71%	16	2.7	11	1.5	1	4	29	61%	23	5.7	28	3	1
Danny Trevathan*	26	ILB	15	737	114	14.8%	21	70	13	13	76	68%	23	3.3	32	0.0	3	4	26	67%	15	6.2	37	4	2

Year	Yards	ALY	Rank	Power	Rank	Stuff	Rank	2nd Level	Rank	Open Field	Rank	Sacks	ASR	Rank	Press	Rank
2013	3.61	3.23	3	64%	13	22%	9	1.03	9	0.63	16	41	6.5%	22	25.9%	11
2014	3.55	3.20	2	55%	7	22%	7	0.97	5	0.60	11	41	6.3%	23	26.8%	5
2015	3.07	3.08	3	83%	31	24%	5	0.73	1	0.37	2	52	8.1%	1	32.7%	1
2015 ALY by direction:		Left End 2.91 (10)			Left Tackle 3.09 (8)			Mid/Guard 3.30 (5)			Right Tackle 2.24 (3)			Right End 1.45 (1)		

2013 first-round defensive tackle Sylvester Williams came off the field on passing downs in 2015, helping make the decision to decline his fifth-year option easier. Williams hopes a new diet will help him generate more speed and with it more of the pass rush he showed in college at North Carolina. ☞ Von Miller finished the 2015 season with two playoff games that rival any other pair of performances for a defensive player in NFL history. He posted five sacks against the Patriots and Panthers, had the game-turning interception against the Patriots, forced the fumble that led to the first touchdown in the Super Bowl, and recovered the fumble that sealed that game. Of course, he can partly thank the matador blocking he faced from the Patriots' Marcus Cannon and Carolina's Mike Remmers. ☞ Miller's sack numbers also understate the overall level of pressure he generated all season long. He trailed Khalil Mack by four sacks, but had 12 more hits and 7.5 more pressures. ☞ The battle to replace Danny Trevathan may come down to two young undrafted players. First shot will go to third-year linebacker Todd Davis, whose 12 run tackles in last year's limited action came at an average depth of just 1.6 yards. Behind Davis is second-year linebacker Zaire Anderson, who didn't play a snap as a rookie but had 13 tackles for loss in his last college season at Nebraska.

Defensive Secondary

Secondary	Age	Pos	G	Snaps	Plays	Overall TmPct	Rk	Stop	Dfts	BTkl	Runs	vs. Run St%	Rk	RuYd	Rk	Tgts	vs. Pass Tgt%	Rk	Dist	Suc%	Rk	AdjYd	Rk	PD	Int
Chris Harris	27	CB	16	1063	64	7.8%	50	31	18	6	10	60%	10	3.6	4	70	17.9%	22	11.3	52%	39	7.2	21	5	2
Aqib Talib	30	CB	15	977	58	7.5%	55	24	9	8	7	43%	36	6.4	30	62	17.4%	16	11.6	50%	48	7.1	19	10	3
Darian Stewart	28	FS	15	848	69	9.0%	46	28	9	8	31	45%	27	6.4	30	22	7.1%	30	12.6	57%	37	7.0	38	8	1
T.J. Ward	30	SS	12	703	67	10.9%	25	32	13	9	26	46%	24	5.0	12	26	9.9%	56	11.9	66%	13	6.1	21	6	0
Bradley Roby	24	CB	16	622	49	6.0%	70	26	14	10	2	50%	20	6.5	31	61	26.9%	72	13.3	54%	30	7.3	26	8	1
David Bruton*	29	SS	13	481	50	7.5%	60	25	12	3	13	62%	3	6.4	29	25	14.2%	65	9.3	60%	27	5.5	14	4	2
Josh Bush*	27	FS	8	232	14	3.4%	--	6	2	2	4	50%	--	4.8	--	3	3.0%	--	20.0	65%	--	4.1	--	1	1

Year	Pass D Rank	vs. #1 WR	Rk	vs. #2 WR	Rk	vs. Other WR	Rk	vs. TE	Rk	vs. RB	Rk
2013	21	-1.1%	17	-4.5%	11	13.7%	27	3.8%	17	-8.7%	13
2014	5	-18.6%	5	-36.0%	2	5.3%	22	-7.0%	13	-1.4%	17
2015	1	-20.7%	4	-22.1%	4	-28.0%	4	-12.0%	8	-33.4%	2

As of this writing, the league is investigating Aqib Talib's incident where he was shot in a Dallas night club. Talib has had issues with guns before. In 2011, Talib was arrested and accused of firing a gun at his sister's boyfriend before the charges were dropped. ☞ Talib was fined but not suspended for his vicious facemask tackle of Corey "Philly" Brown in the Super Bowl. ☞ The secondary charted particularly well by adjusted yards allowed per pass, with all three corners (Talib, Chris Harris, and Bradley Roby) ranking in the top 30. ☞ Safety T.J. Ward will turn 30 in December, but still plays well in coverage. This was the third straight year he ranked in the top 30 safeties for adjusted success rate. ☞ Third-round draft pick Justin Simmons projects as a free safety and could challenge Darian Stewart for playing time. Simmons was second in the ACC with five picks last year, including interceptions of Deshaun Watson and third-round pick Jacoby Brissett.

Special Teams

Year	DVOA	Rank	FG/XP	Rank	Net Kick	Rank	Kick Ret	Rank	Net Punt	Rank	Punt Ret	Rank	Hidden	Rank
2013	-1.0%	21	10.7	3	-11.7	29	5.4	5	-1.9	22	-7.6	28	20.8	1
2014	-3.7%	27	-4.4	27	-6.3	27	6.3	4	-7.7	26	-6.3	29	7.8	4
2015	0.7%	14	-0.6	17	0.1	18	-2.2	22	4.9	7	1.3	14	-2.8	19

Punter Britton Colquitt played an important role in last season's Super Bowl run. He had six punts inside the 20 in the wins over the Patriots and Panthers without a touchback. Against Carolina, Colquitt had eight punts for a net of 45.6 yards, with a total of two return yards. However, Colquitt struggled in the regular season, ranking 26th in gross punt value. (Denver's net punting value was above average because of good punt coverage.) This season, Colquitt is an underdog to make the roster. The Broncos drafted punter Riley Dixon (Syracuse) in the seventh round, and cutting Colquitt would save Denver almost $3 million on the salary cap. ☞ Kicker Brandon McManus made all ten of his playoff field goals, including two from beyond 50 yards. ☞ Emmanuel Sanders was unimpressive on punt returns last season (worth minus-3.9 points of field position). Most of Denver's positive punt-return value came on five returns by Omar Bolden, including a Week 9 touchdown, but he departed for Chicago this offseason.

Detroit Lions

2015 record: 7-9	**Total DVOA:** 1.2% (13th)	**2016 Mean Projection:** 8.1 wins	**On the Clock (0-4):** 9%
Pythagorean Wins: 6.9 (18th)	**Offense:** 1.8% (13th)	**Postseason Odds:** 33.7%	**Mediocrity (5-7):** 32%
Snap-Weighted Age: 26.6 (14th)	**Defense:** 1.6% (16th)	**Super Bowl Odds:** 3.6%	**Playoff Contender (8-10):** 41%
Average Opponent: 3.4% (11th)	**Special Teams:** 1.0% (13th)	**Proj. Avg. Opponent:** -2.1% (26th)	**Super Bowl Contender (11+):** 18%

2015: As *Dukes of Hazzard* fans know, Cooter makes everything better.

2016: Average offense, average defense, and easy schedule should keep them on the edge of the playoffs all season.

Six losses in seven games were enough for Detroit. After watching their offense bumble away a series of winnable contests in September and October last year, the Lions fired offensive coordinator Joe Lombardi and replaced him with quarterbacks coach Jim Bob Cooter. This change jump-started Detroit's offense and kicked off a late-season win streak, and though it was too little, too late to save the 2015 season, it was enough to inspire optimism heading into the 2016 campaign. Can we expect those improvements to carry over into this new year? And even if they do, will they be enough to overcome the loss of an all-time great offensive weapon in Calvin Johnson?

Lombardi's tenure in Detroit was not a long one. He joined the Lions in 2014 along with newly hired head coach Jim Caldwell. It was his first coordinator job at any level after several years kicking around the NFL in various offensive and defensive assistant roles. Immediate results were mediocre—Detroit's offense was 19th in DVOA that season, exactly where they had ranked in the year before Lombardi's arrival—but nobody was paying attention to the offensive mediocrity. With Ndamukong Suh leading the Lions to a third-place finish in the defensive DVOA rankings, the Lions went 11-5 and made the playoffs, losing a heartbreaker to Dallas.

Things started sour for Detroit's offense in 2015. Under Lombardi, the Lions were able to move the ball at times (at the time of his firing, Detroit ranked 21st in yards per play), but couldn't score (25th in points) and really couldn't hang onto the ball (a league-high 18 turnovers). Those numbers were skewed somewhat by a difficult schedule that included games against Denver, Seattle, and Arizona, but at the end of Week 7 the Lions were 21st in offensive DVOA, and dead last in rushing DVOA.

The last straw was a 28-19 loss to Minnesota in which the Lions failed to score on their final seven drives of the game while giving up seven sacks. Detroit responded by sacking Lombardi, along with offensive line coach Jeremiah Washburn and assistant line coach Terry Heffernan. While Cooter took over for Lombardi, tight ends coach Ron Prince was named assistant head coach and put in charge of the offensive line. It was a somewhat surprising move, because Cooter had little experience going into the job. He was just 31 at the time of the promotion, younger than a handful of his own players. His coaching resume consisted mostly of offensive assistant roles with the Tennessee Volunteers and around the NFL, in-

cluding with Caldwell in Indianapolis. Before the promotion, Cooter was best known for two things: being a grown man who went by the name "Jim Bob" in the 21st century, and a shady off-field record. Cooter has been arrested twice in Tennessee, where his playing career ended as a backup quarterback for the Vols. In 2006 he was arrested on suspicion of driving under the influence, with The Tennessean reporting that he blew a 0.19 on a breathalyzer test, well over twice the state limit of 0.08. Then in 2009, he was arrested and charged with aggravated burglary after allegedly climbing into a woman's apartment window, stripping to his underwear, and getting into bed with her. However, when Robert Allen of the Detroit Free Press investigated those arrests, he found that nearly all records had mysteriously vanished from Knox County court documents. Only a booking photo remained. "My guess is that it's been expunged," a sheriff's office spokeswoman told Allen via e-mail.

Cooter's promotion was strange on the surface, and even stranger considering the timing of the move. Detroit had only one game remaining until their bye week, but couldn't even wait that long to pull the plug on Lombardi, promoting Cooter before a Week 8 game against Kansas City. Even stranger, that game against the Chiefs wasn't played in Michigan, or Missouri, or in any of these United States. Instead it was played in London, England. Installing a new offense midweek would be almost impossible even without losing a full day to travel and jet lag. With Cooter hitting the ground running and making things up on the fly, the Lions gave up six more sacks in a 45-10 loss. This resulted in further bloodletting, as Martin Mayhew was fired during the bye week in the midst of his eighth season as general manager.

Following that bye week, though, Cooter changed everything, from player usage to pass patterns to blocking schemes. His first order of business was turning around that league-worst rushing attack, and he did so in a big way. Detroit's offensive line wasn't working well as a unit, so Cooter diversified things, using less zone blocking and more pulling guards to give his linemen better matchups and angles. Our partners at Sports Info Solutions charted Detroit's run-blocking schemes from the 2015 season. Under Lombardi, Detroit ran behind zone blocking 75 percent of the time, and they used a pulling guard only eight times in seven games. Cooter used zone blocking less than half the time, and instead used pulling

2016 Lions Schedule

Week	Opp.	Week	Opp.	Week	Opp.
1	at IND	7	WAS	13	at NO
2	TEN	8	at HOU	14	CHI
3	at GB	9	at MIN	15	at NYG
4	at CHI	10	BYE	16	at DAL (Mon.)
5	PHI	11	JAC	17	GB
6	LARM	12	MIN (Thu.)		

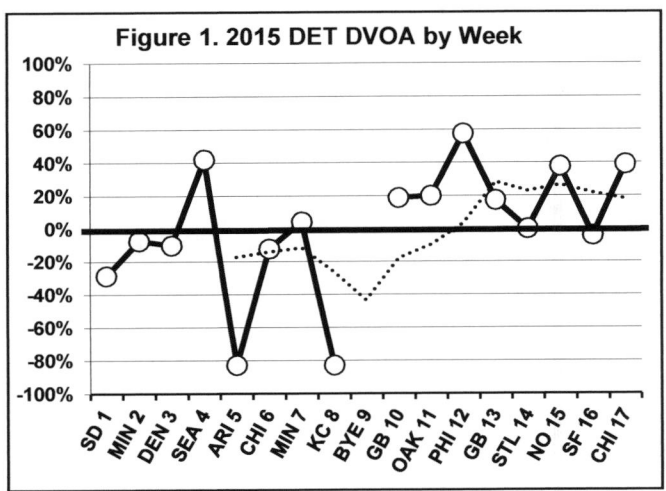

Figure 1. 2015 DET DVOA by Week

guards on nearly a third of his runs. Cooter also stopped trying to run around defenses and ran right at them instead. Only 27 percent of Lombardi's runs were called up the middle, but Cooter's Lions went up the gut 34 percent of the time.

Blocking doesn't mean anything if the ball is on the ground; whether it was a real change or small sample size, fumbles dwindled after Cooter took over. Detroit's running backs fumbled four times in seven games under Lombardi, but only twice in nine games under Cooter despite a heavier workload. This was not exclusive to the running backs: Lions receivers had three fumbles under Lombardi, none under Cooter.

These changes benefited all of Detroit's running backs—the Lions' rushing DVOA after Week 7 was -7.1%, 12th-best in the league—but none more than Joique Bell. The biggest of Detroit's backs at 5-foot-11 and 220 pounds, Bell could barely function in Lombardi's scheme, with a success rate of only 30 percent and a stuff rate of 39 percent. In other words, he was much more likely to get stuffed for no gain or a loss than he was to gain any meaningful yardage on a given play. This is partly due to small sample size; Bell only carried the ball 23 times in four games under Lombardi in 2015. However, Bell had also struggled in Lombardi's offense in 2014, averaging 3.86 yards per carry and finishing among the bottom six running backs in both DYAR and DVOA. Under Cooter, Bell suddenly became a perfectly serviceable power back, and even showed enough explosiveness to produce nine runs of 10 yards or more. That's one fewer than Ameer Abdullah, the 5-foot-8, 198-pounder, had in the same stretch. So it's no surprise that Cooter turned what had been a one-man show into a committee approach (Table 1).

Table 1. Detroit RBs, Before & After

Under Lombardi	Runs/G	Avg	DVOA	Suc Rate	Stuff Rate
A.Abdullah	8.9	3.58	-21.1%	48%	24%
J.Bell	5.8	1.87	-43.5%	30%	39%
Z.Zenner*	2.8	3.53	-0.4%	53%	24%
T.Riddick	1.7	3.83	-40.0%	58%	17%
All Detroit RBs	17.0	3.39	-24.5%	46%	28%
Under Cooter	**Runs/G**	**Avg**	**DVOA**	**Suc Rate**	**Stuff Rate**
A.Abdullah	9.0	4.63	1.2%	53%	16%
J.Bell	7.4	4.00	-1.3%	51%	28%
T.Riddick	3.4	2.81	-18.4%	35%	16%
All Detroit RBs	20.4	3.99	-5.9%	48%	21%

* Zach Zenner didn't play after Week 6 due to broken ribs and a collapsed lung.

Lombardi's god-awful rushing attack was paired with a passing game that was mediocre overall (15th in DVOA at 9.8%) and particularly sloppy and error-prone. Cooter didn't need to re-invent the wheel here, he just needed to cut down on interceptions. And that meant a heavy reliance on shorter pass routes. Stafford threw 11 interceptions before the bye week, and few of those balls were overthrown. Most came due to underthrows, miscommunication, or defensive backs in underneath coverage jumping routes. So Cooter started taking risky patterns like curls and out routes out of the playbook. Those two patterns accounted for 23 percent of all Detroit completions under Lombardi, but only 16 percent under Cooter. Instead, Cooter called more screens, for 13 percent of Detroit's completions, up from just six percent prior to the Chiefs game.

And Cooter would throw screens to just about everyone. Golden Tate caught 11 screens under Lombardi, but 20 under Cooter. For Theo Riddick the number jumped from two to 14; for Bell, from four to eight; for Abdullah, from four to five. Even Calvin Johnson, who was never a consistent threat after the catch (he never ranked higher than 19th in YAC per reception, but five times ranked 40th or worse and three times ranked 70th or worse), was the target of a Jim Bob Cooter screen, even if it was in a meaningless Week 17 game against Chicago. (The play gained 2 yards on first-and-10.)

Something else changed in Lions games after Cooter's promotion, but it wasn't in Detroit's game plan—it was in their opponents'. Defenses rarely blitzed Lombardi's Lions, sending five or more pass rushers barely a quarter of the time. Once Cooter took over, though, the blitz rate soared to nearly 40 percent. There are pros and cons to blitzes, of course, and though Matthew Stafford's sack rate rose slightly in the second half of the year, the Lions' average yards per pass play went up a hair, and their success rate went up from 44.7 percent to 50.0 percent. Most importantly, Stafford threw only two interceptions after that Kansas City game, and as a result the Detroit passing game had a DVOA of 23.8% after Week 7, 10th in the league.

Detroit's overall offensive DVOA under Cooter: 8.8%, ninth in the NFL during that span. The Lions stood at 1-7 after that London game, but then won six of their final eight games. Their only losses were a 27-23 defeat to Green Bay on a Rodgers-to-Rodgers Hail Mary and a 21-14 loss to the Rams that came down to the final possession. Midseason coaching changes don't often accomplish much, but this one was an unqualified success.

The question now is whether that success can carry over into another season. Half-season trends like this are usually somewhat fluky and the result of small sample sizes. And it's doubtful that the Lions will fumble as rarely over a full 16-game season as they did under Cooter. Still, the strategic and schematic changes he implemented do seem a better fit for the Lions' roster than Lombardi's game plan, and now he will have a full offseason to fine-tune his approach while also acquiring and developing players to better fit his power-running, screen-passing scheme.

The most notable of those acquisitions is Taylor Decker, the 16th overall pick in this year's draft. The Ohio State product took every snap at left tackle for the Lions at OTAs and looks to be the final piece in the offensive line puzzle that Detroit has been putting together for several years now. The Lions will also have a new primary power back. Bell was released after the season in a salary-cap move; his carries will now go to either Stevan Ridley or Zach Zenner. Ridley tore his ACL with New England in 2014 and then was quite terrible in limited action with the Jets last year, with a DVOA of -45.5% on his 36 carries, only eight of which gained more than 3 yards. Zenner, a 222-pound undrafted free agent out of South Dakota last year, averaged 5.2 yards on 35 preseason runs and showed promise in the regular season before going on injured reserve with broken ribs. And finally, Matthew Stafford will have a new target in the passing game, as wide receiver Marvin Jones shoots up I-75 from Cincinnati to Detroit.

None of those players, though, will be Calvin Johnson, and the loss of Detroit's all-time leading receiver could more than offset those new faces as well as Cooter's Xs and Os. Johnson's retirement left a gaping hole in the Lions' offense, and it's hard to measure exactly how that will affect Detroit going forward. The massive wideout wasn't just productive but also reliable, missing only nine games in his nine-year career. We should not put too much emphasis on such a small number of games, especially since they came under multiple regimes and quarterbacks, and two of them came in Week 17 when Detroit was resting Johnson for the playoffs. Still, the results are appalling. Yes, Detroit went 5-4 in those games, but they had a negative offensive DVOA in all of them, at an average of -24.0%. And they had a negative pass offense DVOA seven times, at an average of -22.3%. In other words, Detroit without Calvin Johnson has played significantly worse than either the worst offense in the league last year (Tennessee, -15.7% DVOA) or the worst passing offense (Dallas, -14.0%). Again, we shouldn't take this small number of games as a definitive indicator of doom in 2016, but it's certainly not a good sign.

With Johnson enjoying retirement (and enjoying it very much, based on the global travels shared on his Instagram account), Golden Tate will obviously play a larger part in the offense, and he should be up to the task. Like most players

in Detroit, 2015 wasn't his best year, but in the three seasons before that he finished 19th, 24th, and 22nd among wide receivers in DYAR. Don't forget that Tate was once the leading receiver on a Super Bowl champion Seahawks team. Just two years ago, in his first season in Detroit, Tate averaged more targets, catches, and yards per game than Johnson.

Still, in Cooter's offense, Tate should specialize in shorter, YAC-heavy routes, and the Lions will need to find a replacement down the field. The most likely candidate is Jones, who finished among the top 25 wideouts in DYAR in both 2013 and 2015. (In between, he missed all of 2014 with ankle and foot injuries.) He did all that as a second or third receiver behind A.J. Green though, with only two 100-yard games in his career: an 8-of-8, 122-yard, four-touchdown game against the Jets in 2013, and a 130-yard game in a postseason loss to San Diego that same year. The Lions gave Jones a five-year deal worth up to $40 million in hopes he can blossom into a No. 1 receiver in his fifth season. Even if he's a No. 2, though, several teams would swap their top two wideouts for Tate and Jones in a heartbeat.

The bad news is that the depth chart drops off sharply after that. Corey Fuller and T.J. Jones have only 28 combined career catches since the Lions drafted them in the sixth rounds of the 2013 and 2014 drafts, respectively. And veteran additions Jeremy Kerley and Andre Caldwell combined for just 26 catches in 30 games with the Jets and Broncos last year.

While all that is going on, it's easy to forget that Detroit's defense also took several steps backwards in 2015. Detroit's overall defensive DVOA went from -13.9% (third) in 2014 to 1.8% (16th) in 2015. The pass defense slipped from eighth to 19th, while the run defense dropped from first to 14th. Of course, this kind of thing happens to most defenses that lose their top two stars. The Lions watched Suh accept a mammoth Miami contract in free agency, and then lost linebacker DeAndre Levy to a host of injuries that knocked him out for most of the season.

Levy was not alone on the injury report, though. Only Washington and the Giants suffered more adjusted games lost on defense than Detroit last year, and the Giants and Lions were the only teams to make the bottom eight at defensive line, linebacker, and defensive back. Between Levy, defensive tackle Tyrunn Walker, and cornerback Rashean Mathis, the Lions got only 12 starts from three front-line players, one at each level of the defense. You would expect better health for the Lions' defense in 2016, but there appears be a black cloud hanging over their training room—they have now finished 20th or worse in defensive AGL for four years in a row, including two finishes in the bottom three.

Mathis' concussions (and his 36th birthday, which will occur shortly before the season starts) proved to be career-ending, but both Levy and Walker are expected to be fully back this fall. Other new starters on defense include Devin Taylor, who was second on the team in sacks last year despite not starting a game. Longtime backup Tahir Whitehead will compete with a pair of disappointing second-round draft picks (2013's Jon Bostic and 2014's Kyle Van Noy) to fill the spot vacant spot at linebacker left when the team released 10-

year veteran Stephen Tulloch in July. There will also be a new strong safety, though it's very unclear who that will be, or if he will be any better than the middling performance the Lions got out of James Ihedigbo and Isa Abdul-Quddus last season.

In all likelihood, the Lions will be better on defense than they were in 2015, but not nearly as good as they were in 2014. That means the offense may have to carry the team to a handful of shootout victories. They have shown they can operate Caldwell's low-risk, small-ball offense efficiently, and that should keep Detroit in games all season long. On paper, the Lions lack a single dominant unit, but they don't have many glaring weaknesses either, and a weak schedule should have them in the thick of the playoff race come December. But without a Megatron-caliber downfield threat, it's likely a lot of drives will stall before reaching the end zone, leaving Lions fans frustrated once again.

Vincent Verhei

2015 Lions Stats by Week

Wk	vs.	W-L	PF	PA	YDF	YDA	TO	Total	Off	Def	ST
1	at SD	L	28	33	302	483	1	-29%	-20%	14%	5%
2	at MIN	L	16	26	323	350	-2	-7%	3%	3%	-8%
3	DEN	L	12	24	290	354	-1	-10%	-5%	10%	5%
4	at SEA	L	10	13	256	345	2	42%	17%	-31%	-6%
5	ARI	L	17	42	435	345	-6	-83%	-29%	52%	-2%
6	CHI	W	37	34	546	444	-2	-12%	-3%	-3%	-12%
7	MIN	L	19	28	274	425	1	4%	-1%	0%	5%
8	vs. KC (UK)	L	10	45	276	340	-2	-83%	-43%	28%	-11%
9	BYE										
10	at GB	W	18	16	287	372	-1	19%	-10%	0%	28%
11	OAK	W	18	13	375	216	0	20%	3%	-17%	1%
12	PHI	W	45	14	430	227	1	58%	37%	-18%	3%
13	GB	L	23	27	306	313	0	17%	-10%	-17%	10%
14	at STL	L	14	21	331	317	1	0%	15%	12%	-3%
15	at NO	W	35	27	396	399	-1	38%	41%	1%	-2%
16	SF	W	32	17	371	322	1	-4%	9%	21%	8%
17	at CHI	W	24	20	349	345	3	39%	30%	-15%	-6%

Trends and Splits

	Offense	Rank	Defense	Rank
Total DVOA	1.8%	13	1.8%	16
Unadjusted VOA	-1.6%	18	5.2%	22
Weighted Trend	7.7%	11	-0.9%	16
Variance	5.2%	11	4.3%	12
Average Opponent	-1.6%	12	1.7%	7
Passing	17.4%	15	14.1%	20
Rushing	-16.7%	27	-12.8%	14
First Down	11.1%	6	-3.4%	14
Second Down	2.6%	16	4.3%	22
Third Down	-19.2%	27	8.6%	21
First Half	9.1%	10	-6.1%	12
Second Half	-5.3%	21	10.5%	24
Red Zone	50.0%	1	-9.7%	10
Late and Close	-11.2%	23	16.3%	31

Five-Year Performance

Year	W-L	Pyth W	Est W	PF	PA	TO	Total	Rk	Off	Rk	Def	Rk	ST	Rk	Off AGL	Rk	Def AGL	Rk	Off Age	Rk	Def Age	Rk	ST Age	Rk
2011	10-6	10.1	9.4	474	387	+11	10.1%	11	7.1%	10	-8.1%	9	-5.1%	29	29.2	15	14.8	8	27.9	7	26.0	28	27.5	1
2012	4-12	6.4	7.6	372	437	-16	0.1%	16	12.3%	8	7.1%	24	-5.1%	30	23.2	11	58.3	31	28.3	4	26.7	17	27.8	1
2013	7-9	8.5	7.7	395	376	-12	-1.5%	16	-1.9%	19	-0.8%	14	-0.4%	20	31.9	14	30.7	20	27.0	14	27.0	13	26.8	6
2014	11-5	9.2	8.7	321	282	+7	4.4%	14	-3.8%	19	-13.9%	3	-5.7%	31	26.4	13	41.1	21	27.0	15	27.5	6	25.9	20
2015	7-9	6.9	7.4	358	400	-6	1.2%	13	1.8%	13	1.6%	16	1.0%	13	21.7	5	55.0	30	26.2	24	27.3	6	26.2	15

2015 Performance Based on Most Common Personnel Groups

DET Offense					DET Offense vs. Opponents					DET Defense				DET Defense vs. Opponents			
Pers	Freq	Yds	DVOA	Run%	Pers	Freq	Yds	DVOA	Run%	Pers	Freq	Yds	DVOA	Pers	Freq	Yds	DVOA
11	67%	5.6	8.7%	20%	Base	21%	5.3	-6.7%	57%	Base	26%	6.2	13.0%	11	62%	5.8	0.8%
21	15%	4.3	-27.7%	52%	Nickel	52%	5.7	12.8%	29%	Nickel	68%	5.6	-2.8%	12	16%	6.0	10.2%
12	5%	6.4	13.5%	25%	Dime+	26%	5.4	-2.9%	9%	Dime+	4%	8.5	29.0%	21	9%	6.2	2.8%
22	4%	3.7	5.3%	80%	Goal Line	1%	1.8	17.4%	67%	Goal Line	1%	0.3	12.7%	20	3%	4.6	-53.5%
20	3%	5.9	28.1%	24%	Big	1%	0.5	-15.8%	100%	Big	1%	1.2	-222.7%	01	2%	7.7	48.1%
610	2%	8.4	29.5%	68%										10	2%	5.5	3.4%

Strategic Tendencies

Run/Pass		Rk	Formation		Rk	Pass Rush		Rk	Secondary		Rk	Strategy		Rk
Runs, first half	32%	32	Form: Single Back	71%	23	Rush 3	3.1%	27	4 DB	26%	25	Play action	18%	19
Runs, first down	42%	27	Form: Empty Back	7%	16	Rush 4	63.9%	16	5 DB	68%	3	Avg Box (Off)	6.11	26
Runs, second-long	19%	32	Pers: 3+ WR	72%	5	Rush 5	26.5%	10	6+ DB	4%	23	Avg Box (Def)	6.12	26
Runs, power sit.	33%	32	Pers: 2+ TE/6+ OL	15%	29	Rush 6+	6.5%	15	CB by Sides	73%	20	Offensive Pace	32.73	30
Runs, behind 2H	19%	30	Pers: 6+ OL	6%	8	Sacks by LB	14.3%	26	S/CB Cover Ratio	21%	20	Defensive Pace	29.05	3
Pass, ahead 2H	58%	3	Shotgun/Pistol	68%	10	Sacks by DB	6.0%	18	DB Blitz	12%	8	Go for it on 4th	1.31	9

Yes, the Jim Bob Cooter effect was real. From Weeks 1-9 to Weeks 10-17, Detroit's offensive DVOA improved 24.5%, the biggest improvement of any offense outside of Seattle. And it wasn't just Matthew Stafford who benefited from the Cooter offense: Detroit's rushing DVOA also jumped 21.1%. ☞ The Lions also finished with the league's best red zone offense, posting a 50.0% DVOA. ☞ Detroit's offense got worse as the down marker progressed, ranking sixth in offensive DVOA on first downs, 16th on second downs and 27th on third downs. ☞ Detroit ran the ball only 28 percent of the time on second down, the only NFL team below 30 percent last season. ☞ Detroit had the NFL's second-worst defense in late-and-close situations, posting a 16.4% DVOA. Only New Orleans was worse. ☞ The defense was above-average against shotgun formations but one of the worst against formations with the quarterback under center, ranking 30th in DVOA and 31st in yards per play. Fortunately, the Lions faced shotgun on 72 percent of their snaps, more than any defense apart from Kansas City. ☞ Opponents ran the ball 31 percent of the time when lining up with three or more receivers against the Lions defense, tied for the fourth-highest rate in the league. This was a poor choice, as Detroit's -27.9% DVOA on these runs ranked second in the NFL. They also allowed just 3.5 yards per attempt, best of any defense. ☞ Detroit benefited from a league-low 107 opponent penalties.

Passing

Player	DYAR	DVOA	Plays	NtYds	Avg	YAC	C%	TD	Int
M.Stafford	804	8.0%	637	3979	6.2	6.1	67.6%	32	13
D.Orlovsky	31	0.4%	40	201	5.0	3.7	55.0%	1	1

Rushing

Player	DYAR	DVOA	Plays	Yds	Avg	TD	Fum	Suc
A.Abdullah	-2	-8.9%	143	597	4.2	2	4	51%
J.Bell*	-15	-12.5%	90	311	3.5	4	1	46%
T.Riddick	-29	-24.5%	43	133	3.1	0	1	42%
M.Stafford	35	11.4%	29	179	6.2	1	0	-
Z.Zenner	6	-0.4%	17	60	3.5	0	0	53%
G.Tate	33	51.1%	6	41	6.8	0	0	-
M.Burton	-17	-62.4%	4	2	0.5	0	0	25%
G.Winn	-22	-122.9%	4	1	0.3	0	0	0%
S.Ridley	-51	-45.5%	36	90	2.5	0	0	28%

Receiving

Player	DYAR	DVOA	Plays	Ctch	Yds	Y/C	YAC	TD	C%
C.Johnson*	319	14.0%	149	88	1214	13.8	3.4	9	59%
G.Tate	113	-1.7%	128	90	813	9.0	5.9	6	70%
L.Moore*	79	10.1%	43	29	340	11.7	2.1	4	67%
T.J.Jones	7	-7.8%	18	10	132	13.2	4.1	1	56%
C.Fuller	5	-5.7%	9	4	76	19.0	2.3	0	44%
M.Jones	171	7.6%	104	66	818	12.4	4.6	4	63%
J.Kerley	14	-5.3%	26	16	152	9.5	5.9	2	62%
A.Caldwell	-47	-39.8%	22	10	72	7.2	1.6	2	45%
A.Roberts	-26	-28.6%	21	11	135	12.3	3.5	0	52%
E.Ebron	64	6.5%	70	47	537	11.4	6.2	5	67%
T.Wright	-9	-15.2%	16	9	77	8.6	2.8	2	56%
B.Pettigrew	-11	-18.8%	15	7	67	9.6	5.4	1	47%
T.Riddick	201	24.6%	99	80	697	8.7	8.2	3	81%
A.Abdullah	6	-11.3%	38	25	183	7.3	8.1	1	66%
J.Bell*	97	49.3%	27	22	286	13.0	13.9	0	81%
M.Burton	29	48.9%	6	6	39	6.5	4.8	1	100%

Offensive Line

Player	Pos	Age	GS	Snaps	Pen	Sk	Pass	Run	Player	Pos	Age	GS	Snaps	Pen	Sk	Pass	Run
Riley Reiff	LT	28	16/16	1075	6	4.0	8.5	3.0	Manny Ramirez	G/C	33	16/7	490	1	0.0	0.5	0.0
Laken Tomlinson	LG	24	16/14	986	6	2.0	4.0	8.0	Michael Ola	RT	28	10/7	450	2	1.0	1.0	3.0
Travis Swanson	C	25	14/14	949	3	0.0	4.0	0.0	Cornelius Lucas	RT	25	15/3	325	4	1.0	2.0	2.0
Larry Warford	RG	25	13/13	814	5	2.0	3.0	3.0									

Year	Yards	ALY	Rank	Power	Rank	Stuff	Rank	2nd Lev	Rank	Open Field	Rank	Sacks	ASR	Rank	Press	Rank	F-Start	Cont.
2013	4.23	3.94	13	76%	3	19%	12	1.26	9	0.68	17	23	4.5%	2	19.4%	3	11	33
2014	3.75	3.79	21	65%	15	22%	30	0.99	26	0.59	26	45	6.9%	21	20.8%	5	12	23
2015	3.76	3.61	22	69%	12	24%	29	1.11	20	0.59	24	44	6.9%	22	21.6%	9	12	26
2015 ALY by direction:			Left End 3.28 (22)			Left Tackle 3.51 (20)			Mid/Guard 3.64 (23)			Right Tackle 3.87 (14)				Right End 3.52 (16)		

Riley Reiff doesn't turn 28 until December, but he's actually the elder statesman of a unit that has quietly amassed a bevy of young talent. Save for an underrated 2014 campaign, he has never lived up to his status as a first-round pick in the 2012 draft, but the Lions are hopeful a switch to the right side will help him out. The right tackle spot was a disaster last year, with Cornelius Lucas benched and LaAdrian Waddle waived to make room for mid-October waiver-wire pickup Michael Ola. Between Ola and Waddle (who is listed in the New England offensive line table), the Lions got 13 starts at right tackle from players who were waived at some point during the season. ☞ Taking over at left tackle will be Ohio State's Taylor Decker, the 16th pick in this year's draft. His selection, which allowed Reiff to move to the other side, should theoretically make Detroit better at two positions. Scouts noted some inconsistency against edge rushers and worry about his short arms (which are longer than Joe Thomas' arms, so whatever). Otherwise Decker has pretty much everything you want in a tackle, in both measurables and intangibles. ☞ Laken Tomlinson, yet another first-round pick, made a lot of mistakes in his rookie year, but rookies often make mistakes and typically improve in their second season. ☞ That leaves two third-rounders on the inside, 2013's Larry Warford at left guard and 2014's Travis Swanson at center. Warford has been a starter his entire career. Swanson started five games as a rookie and 14 games last year, when he ranked sixth among centers in blown-block rate. ☞ The Lions also filled in their depth with more youth in this year's draft, selecting Michigan center Graham Glasgow in the third round and Washington State guard Joe Dahl in the fifth.

Defensive Front Seven

Defensive Line	Age	Pos	G	Snaps	Plays	TmPct	Rk	Stop	Dfts	BTkl	Runs	St%	Rk	RuYd	Rk	Sack	Hit	Hur	Dsrpt
						Overall							**vs. Run**				**Pass Rush**		
Haloti Ngata	32	DT	14	596	27	3.8%	62	21	9	4	20	75%	45	1.9	31	2.5	7	10.5	3
Caraun Reid	26	DT	14	535	29	4.1%	59	21	8	3	23	74%	50	1.7	22	2.0	4	8.0	0
Stefan Charles	28	DT	13	228	13	2.1%	--	7	2	3	12	50%	--	2.8	--	1.0	3	1.0	0

Edge Rushers	Age	Pos	G	Snaps	Plays	TmPct	Rk	Stop	Dfts	BTkl	Runs	St%	Rk	RuYd	Rk	Sack	Hit	Hur	Dsrpt
						Overall							**vs. Run**				**Pass Rush**		
Ezekiel Ansah	27	DE	16	656	47	5.7%	31	35	22	9	25	64%	78	6.2	96	14.0	23	27.0	0
Devin Taylor	27	DE	15	550	36	4.7%	49	27	18	6	19	63%	82	4.0	92	7.5	4	14.0	1
Jason Jones*	30	DE	15	540	32	4.2%	64	26	13	4	24	79%	28	2.0	34	4.5	6	18.0	1
Darryl Tapp*	32	DE	16	410	26	3.2%	--	17	6	1	20	70%	--	2.7	--	2.0	6	2.0	0
C.J. Wilson*	29	DE	12	224	11	1.8%	--	9	3	1	9	89%	--	1.6	--	1.0	0	1.0	0
Wallace Gilberry	32	DE	16	632	23	2.7%	88	19	5	2	14	93%	3	1.1	12	2.0	13	15.0	1

Linebackers	Age	Pos	G	Snaps	Plays	TmPct	Rk	Stop	Dfts	BTkl	Runs	St%	Rk	RuYd	Rk	Sack	Hit	Hur	Tgts	Suc%	Rk	AdjYd	Rk	PD	Int
						Overall							**vs. Run**			**Pass Rush**					**vs. Pass**				
Josh Bynes	27	OLB	16	816	84	10.3%	58	50	15	9	50	68%	27	3.9	63	0.5	3	6.5	21	64%	18	4.6	14	4	0
Stephen Tulloch*	31	MLB	16	723	107	13.1%	35	59	13	9	64	70%	18	2.7	12	1.0	4	4.5	31	40%	65	6.7	45	2	0
Tahir Whitehead	26	OLB	16	585	52	6.4%	82	24	14	9	17	47%	85	5.5	87	2.0	2	4	27	56%	38	5.3	23	5	1

Year	Yards	ALY	Rank	Power	Rank	Stuff	Rank	2nd Level	Rank	Open Field	Rank	Sacks	ASR	Rank	Press	Rank
2013	4.08	3.13	2	50%	3	26%	4	1.13	19	1.07	29	33	5.8%	31	24.4%	18
2014	3.17	2.82	1	63%	15	25%	3	0.86	1	0.50	5	42	6.6%	18	25.9%	10
2015	4.08	3.30	5	56%	7	24%	4	1.06	11	1.02	28	43	7.3%	8	24.9%	18
2015 ALY by direction:			Left End 3.08 (11)			Left Tackle 4.22 (22)			Mid/Guard 3.07 (3)			Right Tackle 3.73 (18)				Right End 1.69 (2)	

The Lions get back two key contributors who were injured in 2015. The bigger of those names is DeAndre Levy, who ranked third among all players in defeats in 2014, and 14th in 2013. Levy missed the first four games of 2015 with a hip injury, started in Week 5 against Arizona, and then re-injured his hip before halftime and was shelved for the rest of the year. He is expected to be 100 percent for training camp. ☞ Defensive tackle Tyrunn Walker isn't the big star that Levy is, but Detroit did sign him to start after three years on the bench in New Orleans. Unfortunately, he only got in four starts before suffering a broken leg and dislocated ankle against Seattle. He should be ready to start by the fall, but wasn't healthy by OTAs. That gave second-round pick A'Shawn Robinson a chance to take first-team reps next to Haloti Ngata, and Robinson impressed coaches enough that they suggested Walker might get Wally Pipped. Robinson said that after playing in a two-gap scheme at Alabama, he was enjoying the transition to Detroit's aggressive one-gap system. Starter or not, he figures to see plenty of action this fall. ☞ Speaking of Ngata, he was a fine replacement for Ndamukong Suh, as the Lions' front remained its usual stout self even without Suh and Levy. The Lions' overall run defense was mediocre, but that is entirely due to problems giving up long runs. Detroit was still far better than most teams at stopping runners behind the line of scrimmage. ☞ Detroit's other superstar up front is Ezekiel Ansah. The fifth overall pick in 2013 had modest production his first two years, with 8.0 sacks as a rookie and 7.5 as a sophomore. Last year he really shined, finishing third in the NFL in sacks and fourth in hits.

Defensive Secondary

Secondary	Age	Pos	G	Snaps	Plays	Overall TmPct	Rk	Stop	Dfts	BTkl	vs. Run Runs	St%	Rk	RuYd	Rk	vs. Pass Tgts	Tgt%	Rk	Dist	Suc%	Rk	AdjYd	Rk	PD	Int
Darius Slay	25	CB	16	994	70	8.6%	39	25	8	4	10	30%	54	9.7	60	63	17.6%	17	14.1	52%	40	8.4	52	12	2
Glover Quin	30	SS	16	953	72	8.8%	47	8	6	9	27	4%	70	15.9	70	13	3.7%	4	15.1	57%	36	6.7	33	5	4
James Ihedigbo*	33	FS	15	593	64	8.3%	54	29	11	9	33	61%	4	3.9	3	16	7.5%	38	10.1	45%	62	7.7	43	2	1
Isa Abdul-Quddus*	27	FS	16	569	61	7.5%	61	23	10	6	27	33%	46	5.8	20	23	11.3%	58	13.5	46%	58	9.8	62	5	0
Nevin Lawson	25	CB	15	561	48	6.3%	69	17	3	7	7	14%	71	7.0	37	58	28.9%	74	11.3	49%	52	5.6	7	7	0
Quandre Diggs	23	CB	16	471	40	4.9%	--	27	10	9	9	89%	--	1.1	--	38	22.2%	--	13.2	56%	--	8.5	--	7	0
Rashean Mathis*	36	CB	7	435	34	9.5%	--	16	7	1	6	33%	--	5.0	--	28	17.7%	--	10.7	46%	--	10.5	--	6	1
Josh Wilson*	31	CB	8	275	31	7.6%	--	10	2	2	12	50%	--	7.0	--	16	16.3%	--	9.4	27%	--	12.3	--	1	0
Johnson Bademosi	26	FS	16	169	12	1.5%	--	5	2	4	5	40%	--	4.8	--	22	34.2%	--	14.1	50%	--	9.9	--	2	0

Year	Pass D Rank	vs. #1 WR	Rk	vs. #2 WR	Rk	vs. Other WR	Rk	vs. TE	Rk	vs. RB	Rk
2013	20	11.2%	24	-8.7%	10	12.5%	23	-20.6%	5	2.9%	16
2014	8	-26.4%	2	-11.9%	9	2.4%	20	-10.0%	8	14.8%	23
2015	19	9.5%	24	5.5%	18	-5.0%	14	26.0%	29	-10.7%	7

Glover Quin made his average tackle 17.5 yards downfield (not counting passes defensed), while James Ihedigbo made his average tackle just 7.2 yards downfield. That was the largest gap in the league between two starting safeties. Here's a look at the largest and smallest gaps:

Largest and Smallest Gaps Between Average Tackle Distance for Top Two Safeties, 2015

Rk	Team	Gap	Safety 1	Yds	Safety 2	Yds	Rk	Team	Gap	Safety 1	Yds	Safety 2	Yds
1	DET	10.3	G.Quin	17.5	J.Ihedigbo	7.2	32	WAS	0.2	D.Goldson	7.8	K.Jarrett	7.6
2	NO	8.8	J.Byrd	15.8	K.Vaccaro	7.0	31	SF	0.3	E.Reid	11.5	J.Tartt	11.1
3	STL	7.8	R.McLeod	14.5	T.McDonald	6.7	30	CIN	0.4	G.Iloka	10.6	R.Nelson	10.3
4	PIT	7.2	M.Mitchell	14.7	W.Allen	7.5	29	CHI	0.4	A.Amos	10.8	A.Rolle	10.4
5	ARI	6.7	R.Johnson	15.4	T.Mathieu	8.7	28	CLE	0.6	T.Gipson	10.7	D.Whitner	10.1
6	SEA	6.2	E.Thomas	13.8	K.Chancellor	7.6	27	TB	0.9	C.Conte	11.2	B.McDougald	10.3
7	NE	5.9	D.McCourty	12.2	P.Chung	6.3	26	HOU	1.1	A.Hal	11.1	Q.Demps	10.0
8	BAL	4.2	W.Hill	12.2	K.Lewis	8.0	25	CAR	1.7	K.Coleman	10.0	R.Harper	8.3

Not surprisingly, the defenses on the right side of that table tend to play a lot of two-deep schemes, while those on the left typically play with one single-high safety and the other spending more time near the line of scrimmage. In Detroit's case, it was usually Glover Quin patrolling the deep middle while the combination of James Ihedigbo and Isa Abdul-Quddus filled the box. Mind you, given the long runs the Lions gave up, they weren't filling the box particularly well, and their coverage stats show they struggled in that department too. So both are gone now, and it's not clear who will take their place. The Lions signed three safeties in free agency, but Tavon Wilson, Rafael Bush, and Johnson Bademosi have a combined 18 NFL starts between them, never more than seven in a season. The Lions also used a fourth-round pick on Southern Utah's Miles Killebrew; general manager Bob Quinn specifically noted Killebrew's ability to cover tight ends, a real problem for Detroit last year. ☞ Darius Slay is entering the last year of his contract and is openly seeking an extension before the season. He has said he wants to be paid like a top-seven cornerback, naming Darrelle Revis, Richard Sherman, Patrick Peterson, Chris Harris, Aqib Talib, and Joe Haden as the peer group he wishes to join. Neither Slay's individual charting stats nor Detroit's DVOA against No. 1 wide receivers back that up. However, the Lions were eighth in lowest percentage of targets allowed to opposing No. 1s. The seven teams ahead of them include Peterson's Cardinals and Sherman's Seahawks, plus Johnathan Joseph and the Texans, Desmond Trufant and the Falcons, Josh Norman and the Panthers, Dre Kirkpatrick and the Bengals, and Trumaine Johnson and the Rams.

Special Teams

Year	DVOA	Rank	FG/XP	Rank	Net Kick	Rank	Kick Ret	Rank	Net Punt	Rank	Punt Ret	Rank	Hidden	Rank
2013	-0.4%	20	-11.1	30	-1.6	24	5.7	4	-0.7	20	5.8	8	-11.2	31
2014	-5.7%	31	-19.6	32	-4.0	24	-1.7	21	-0.6	17	-2.5	17	-6.6	26
2015	1.0%	13	6.0	5	-2.6	21	3.3	8	3.2	14	-4.7	24	-4.4	20

Sam Martin has been above-average on both punts and kickoffs in each of the last three seasons. That hasn't stopped the Lions from experimenting with David Akers and then Matt Prater on kickoffs, but those results haven't gone as well. ☞ Matt Prater went 22-of-24 on field goals last year, the second-best mark of his career, but he's unlikely to repeat that performance. He was usually a below-average kicker in the better part of seven years with Denver, particularly after adjusting for altitude. ☞ Golden Tate was just adequate as a part-time punt returner. In his last full season in that role, in 2013 with Seattle, he was among the top five punt returners even without scoring a touchdown. ☞ Speaking of not scoring touchdowns, Ameer Abdullah managed to gain 104 yards on a kickoff return against Green Bay and still get tackled at the 1-yard line. Still, he was tenth in the NFL in kickoff return value last year, and could be the long-term star the Lions have sought at that position for years. ☞ Free-agent signing Johnson Bademosi was tied for second in the league with 16 special teams tackles for the Browns last season. Now he'll team with Don Carey, who was tied for fifth with 15 special teams tackles.

Green Bay Packers

2015 record: 10-6	Total DVOA: 9.9% (10th)	2016 Mean Projection: 10.0 wins	On the Clock (0-4): 2%
Pythagorean Wins: 9.3 (11th)	Offense: 2.2% (11th)	Postseason Odds: 64.8%	Mediocrity (5-7): 14%
Snap-Weighted Age: 26.3 (24th)	Defense: -7.3% (9th)	Super Bowl Odds: 15.5%	Playoff Contender (8-10): 40%
Average Opponent: 4.7% (9th)	Special Teams: 0.4% (17th)	Proj. Avg. Opponent: -2.6% (29th)	Super Bowl Contender (11+): 44%

2015: Only in his absence do we learn the value of a top-flight wide receiver.

2016: The NFL's emerald archer has the most dangerous arrow back in his quiver.

Year in and year out, the Green Bay Packers are one of the easiest teams to project, and also one of the most difficult. So long as Aaron Rodgers is throwing passes to a healthy group of receivers, we know that Green Bay's offense will range somewhere between above-average and outright dominant. The Green Bay defense, however, has been much more erratic. Though Dom Capers' scheme has generally been effective, it's also a high-variance approach that has seen its share of flameouts. This makes it difficult to say just how well the Packers will play on defense this year, but with Rodgers and the offense almost certain to get the team into the playoffs, it will be the performance of that defense that determines whether or not the Packers can win another Lombardi Trophy.

Capers was the last cog to join what has been a very stable leadership machine in Green Bay. In 2005, Ted Thompson was named general manager. That same year, Thompson drafted Rodgers, and a year later he hired offensive-minded Mike McCarthy as head coach. Rodgers took over the starting role in 2008, and Capers was signed on as defensive coordinator in 2009. The Thompson-McCarthy-Capers-Rodgers quartet has been together for seven years now, and with tremendous success—only the Patriots have won more games than the Packers since 2009.

Obviously, Rodgers and the offense have spurred most of that success, with an average annual DVOA of 17.0% (again, second only to New England). This is a perennial top-five unit, and even last year, when everything seemed to go wrong, they finished 11th. But Capers' defense has also generally been effective; its average annual DVOA of -3.4% ranks tenth in that same timeframe. Unlike the offense, though, the defensive performance has been all over the map. Capers' defense finished second in DVOA in each of his first two seasons in Green Bay, but then fell to 25th the next year, and has finished eighth, 31st, 16th, and ninth since then. Under Capers, the standard deviation of Green Bay's defensive DVOA has been 11.6 percent. That's not unusual by itself—six other defenses have seen more variance in that same timeframe (Table 1)— but it is unusual considering the stability in the Green Bay coaching staff. Each of the six defenses that have been more erratic than Green Bay's has changed defensive coordinators at least once in that time (Buffalo alone has made five changes), and together they have employed 24 different coordinators, all while Capers has had an uninterrupted run as Green Bay's defensive leader. (Table 1)

Table 1. Highest Year-to-Year Standard Deviation in Defensive DVOA, 2009-2015

Tm	StDev	Defensive Coordinators
CHI	14.8%	B.Babich, R.Marinelli, M.Tucker, V.Fangio
SEA	14.7%	G.Bradley, D.Quinn, K.Richard
DEN	13.7%	M.Nolan, D.Martindale, D.Allen, J.Del Rio, W.Phillips
CAR	11.7%	R.Meeks, S.McDermott
NO	11.6%	G.Williams, S.Spagnuolo, R.Ryan, D.Allen
BUF	11.6%	P.Fewell, G.Edwards, D.Wannstedt, M.Pettine, J.Schwartz, D.Thurman
GB	11.6%	D.Capers
HOU	10.8%	F.Bush, W.Phillips, R.Crennel
DET	10.3%	G.Cunningham, T.Austin
PIT	10.1%	D.LeBeau, K.Butler

Note that wild DVOA swings and coaching changes aren't always bad things. In Seattle's case, this table shows how awful the Seahawks defense was before Pete Carroll arrived, and how its defensive coordinators have left for head coaching opportunities elsewhere after particularly big years. Regardless, it is very unusual for a team to stick with its defensive coach through ups and downs the way the Packers have stuck with Capers.

Longtime readers of our site know that defense is more inconsistent than offense from year to year, but it's hard to find a reason why the Packers' inconsistency is stronger than usual.

Roster turnover isn't the issue; the Packers haven't used any more starters than their division rivals in Chicago, Detroit, or Minnesota. Injuries don't seem to be the cause either. Make no mistake, the Packers defense has seen more than its share of injuries, four times finishing in the bottom ten in defensive adjusted games lost (AGL). However, there's virtually no correlation between Green Bay's injuries and its defensive performance. In 2012, for example, the Packers led the NFL in defensive AGL but still finished eighth in DVOA.

Instead, the Packers' defensive volatility seems due at least in part to Capers' scheme. The Packers theoretically operate out of a 3-4 base, but like most NFL defenses these days they actually use "sub" packages more often than "standard" packages. Green Bay's most frequent personnel package includes two interior linemen, two edge rushers, two coverage linebackers, and five defensive backs (the "2-4-5" nickel). Capers relies heavily on blitzes, while his cornerbacks play aggres-

2016 Packers Schedule

Week	Opp.	Week	Opp.	Week	Opp.
1	at JAC	7	CHI (Thu.)	13	HOU
2	at MIN	8	at ATL	14	SEA
3	DET	9	IND	15	at CHI
4	BYE	10	at TEN	16	MIN (Sat.)
5	NYG	11	at WAS	17	at DET
6	DAL	12	at PHI (Mon.)		

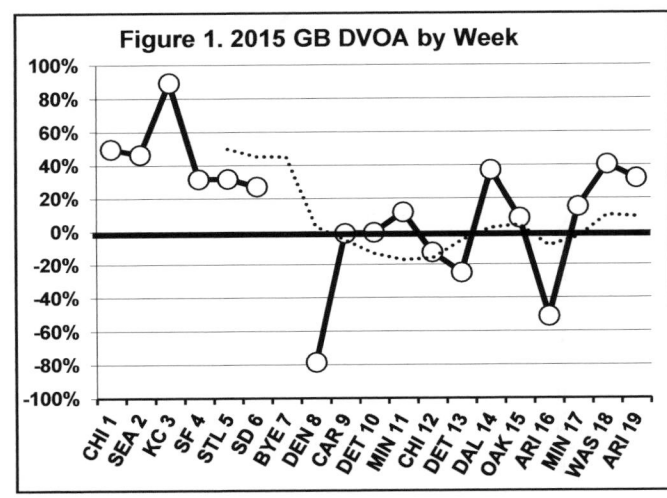

Figure 1. 2015 GB DVOA by Week

sive press coverage on the outside. And on the whole, it has been effective—again, this has been a top-ten defense over the whole of Capers' tenure. But the scheme has notable strengths and weaknesses, and when those vulnerabilities are exposed, things can go south quickly.

Capers' scheme is specifically designed to force mistakes in the passing game, and at that it has certainly been successful. Since he arrived in Green Bay, the Packers lead the NFL with 148 interceptions, 16 more than any other team, and they're fourth with 288 sacks. And all that pressure and tight coverage has also limited opponents to a 58 percent completion rate, third-lowest in the league. On the downside, it has also left them vulnerable to big chunks of yardage, and they have surrendered 371 completions of 20 yards or more (10th since 2009) and 11.3 yards per completion (sixth). Still, Green Bay's average pass defense DVOA under Capers has been -2.9%, one of the five best figures in the league.

Things haven't gone so well against the run, though. With all that speed on the field, the Packers have done a good job limiting big plays and open-field yards, but their other run defense stats have mostly been pretty poor (Table 2).

Table 2. Green Bay Run Defense, 2009-2015

Category	Stat	Rank
DVOA	-4.0%	24
Adjusted line yards	4.09	25
Short-yardage conversions (a.k.a. "power runs")	62.6%	14
Stuff rate	19.0%	19
Second-level yards	1.20	26
Open-field yards	0.66	8

Those numbers aren't very good, but if anything they undersell the sorry history of Green Bay's run defense, because only DVOA and short-yardage conversion rate account for quarterback runs. With abundant pass-rushers madly attacking the line and corners turning to chase receivers in coverage, there's often nobody left in the middle of the field to defend against scrambling quarterbacks. The Packers have also had consistent issues with defenders getting out of position on read-option plays, leading to huge gains.

Overall, Green Bay has allowed 1,522 rushing yards to quarterbacks since 2009. Only the Giants have allowed quarterbacks to gain more yards on the ground in that time, and

they have had the misfortune of playing in the same division as scramblers such as Michael Vick in Philadelphia and Robert Griffin in Washington. The Packers, meanwhile, have struggled to contain players such as Christian Ponder and Jay Cutler. This weakness against running quarterbacks has twice been enough to knock Green Bay out of the playoffs, as they surrendered 279 total rushing yards to Colin Kaepernick in a pair of postseason losses to San Francisco. And it's likely to come up again, considering they will likely need to beat Russell Wilson or Cam Newton (or both) in the playoffs this year.

Green Bay has also been unusually vulnerable to reverses and end-arounds, giving up 436 rushing yards to wideouts, third-most in the league since 2009. Granted, that works out to less than 4 yards per game over seven seasons, but opponents know this weakness and they can exploit it when needed. Green Bay's divisional rivals were sure to test the Packers here, as the Lions and Vikings both called for an end-around in each game against the Packers. (The Bears never did, likely because all their wide receivers were injured.) On a critical third-quarter drive in a must-win game in Green Bay in Week 17, the Vikings called an end-around for Adam Thielen, who has all of 24 touches in 32 NFL games. Thielen gained 26 yards to set up an Adrian Peterson touchdown. (Thielen also gained 41 yards on a fake punt to set up a first-quarter field goal, but it's hard to pin that on Capers or his scheme.)

Between running backs, quarterbacks, and receivers, 36 percent of runs against Capers' teams in Green Bay have gained 5 yards or more, the worst rate of any defense in the league since 2009.

When you take all of this in, you see that a lot can go right for Capers' defenses, but a whole lot can go wrong as well. This might explain why their fortunes can change so radically from one season to the next. You might expect those pros and cons to even out more over the course of 16 games, but perhaps that isn't always the case.

Thus, we know that projecting Green Bay's defense is difficult under the best of circumstances, and now we have to figure out what they're going to do without three starters from last season. Between B.J. Raji, Nate Palmer, and Casey Hayward, the Packers lost one player from each level of their defense, and their ability to replace those men will go a long way in determining their ultimate fate this season. It doesn't help that the Packers signed only one veteran free agent this offseason—and that was a tight end, Jared Cook. Remarkably, Cook, Julius Peppers, and Letroy Guion are the only players on the roster who were drafted by anyone other than the Packers. Thompson's roster strategy is to build from within, and while you can't question his results, it does leave few options on hand to replace a talent drain like this.

The easiest of those starters to replace will be Palmer, and to be fair, this may prove to be a case of addition by subtraction. A sixth-round draft pick in 2013, Palmer entered 2015 as a starter for the first time, but that didn't last long; he was benched after a Week 11 loss to Chicago and played almost exclusively on special teams after that. Green Bay released him after the season, and he signed with Tennessee. Jake Ryan, a fourth-round rookie last year, replaced Palmer in the lineup last season and figures to start again this year alongside Sam Barrington. Barrington missed most of 2015 with a foot injury and has started only eight games since the Packers drafted him in the seventh round in 2013. Other options on hand include Carl Bradford, a 2014 fourth-rounder who has yet to make it into a regular season game, and fourth-round rookie Blake Martinez out of Stanford.

Palmer's release may be more symptom than disease, but with or without him, it's easy to understand why Green Bay is struggling to find starters here. We mentioned five linebackers in that last paragraph: three fourth-round draft picks, a sixth-rounder, and a seventh-rounder. By design or circumstance, the Packers have neglected to grab an inside linebacker in the early rounds of the draft for years now. The last linebacker they took in the first three rounds of the draft was Clay Matthews in the first round of 2009, and he's primarily a perimeter defender. The last pure inside linebacker taken by Green Bay at the top of the draft was A.J. Hawk in the first round of 2006. Matthews spent most of the past two years lining up inside on running downs and outside on passing downs. McCarthy has said that Matthews will spend "a majority" of his time outside this year, but given the scarcity of alternatives, he might line up inside a lot too.

While the Packers themselves made the decision to part ways with Palmer, the team was caught off-guard by Raji's decision to take a year off from football. Raji was entering free agency and Green Bay had a contract ready for him, but the veteran lineman opted for a "hiatus" from football instead. It's hard to quantify just how big this loss is for Green Bay. A two-down defender, Raji played fewer than 60 percent of the Packers' defensive snaps in 2012 and 2013. Then he missed all of 2014 with a torn bicep, and played on 42 percent of the team's snaps last year. Given Green Bay's struggles against the run, perhaps they'd be better off making a change here anyway. Veteran Letroy Guion started 44 games between 2012 and 2014 for the Vikings and Packers, but started only four of 13 games last season (he was suspended three games for an offseason arrest). He weighs 35 pounds less than Raji, but he has started full seasons at nose tackle in both Green Bay and Minnesota. He'll line up next to Kenny Clark, the Packers' first-round draft pick out

of UCLA who should start from Day 1. Datone Jones, a former first-round draft pick himself, never nailed down a spot in Green Bay's starting lineup, and this year will move to outside linebacker to rotate with Matthews and Julius Peppers.

Hayward will likely be the biggest loss for Green Bay. He had the best coverage metrics among Packers cornerbacks last year, and also led the unit in snaps played. He left for San Diego in free agency, once again leaving the Packers with Sam Shields as the top corner on the roster. Shields will partner with Green Bay's top two draft picks from 2015: first-rounder Damarious Randall and second-rounder Quinten Rollins. That's a good little starting trio, and Micah Hyde frequently moves from safety to slot corner, but there is very little depth after that. Demetri Goodson, a 2014 sixth-rounder, has no starts in his first two seasons and will miss the first four games of 2016 due to suspension. And after that, the Packers are left with a bevy of undrafted corners with a combined total of eight defensive snaps in the NFL.

Though the offense is clearly in better shape than the defense, there are questions on that side of the ball, too. Jordy Nelson's return from a torn ACL that knocked him out for all of 2015 should theoretically make the entire receiving corps better, but the way Davante Adams and Randall Cobb struggled without him has to be concerning to Packers fans. They struggled to get open downfield; when they did get open, they had problems catching the ball; and when they did catch the ball, they didn't do a lot to gain yardage after the catch. That last issue may have been their biggest weakness. Rodgers had the second-lowest rate of *expected* failed completions last season based on pass length and down and distance, but he was 23rd in rate of *actual* failed completions. In plain English, this means he was routinely getting the ball to guys who should have been able to make plays with the ball in their hands, but those receivers often failed to gain yards after the catch. Adams, Cobb, and tight end Richard Rodgers were all among the top ten receivers in the difference between expected and actual failed completions last season. Cook, the newly signed tight end, was also in the top ten, which means the Packers could see a lot more completions short of the sticks if this group can't improve their performance.

Green Bay's passing attack was so dysfunctional last year that opponents actually ignored Aaron Rodgers to concentrate on shutting down the run. James Starks faced a loaded box on 35 percent of his carries last year, the highest rate in the league; Eddie Lacy was third at 28 percent. Worse, the Packers were completely unable to make opponents pay for this strategy, because they had by far the league's worst performance on play-action passes. The Packers had a league-low 5.2 yards per play and were the only offense with a negative DVOA (-10.8%) on such plays. That includes an impossibly bad 3-of-18 performance on deep passes after play fakes. The Packers gained only 50 yards on deep play-action completions all season. There were 34 individual *plays* that gained at least 50 yards on play-action deep passes last year; Torrey Smith had three of them by himself.

James Jones, who saved the team by returning in 2015, won't return in 2016. This leaves the Packers with Nelson,

Cobb, and Adams at wide receiver, plus Ty Montgomery (a versatile 2015 third-round pick whose rookie year was ruined by an ankle injury), and playoff heroes Jeff Janis (a pure speedster) and Jared Abbrederis (a possession receiver). As we saw in the postseason, if you give Aaron Rodgers enough chances, he will make plays throwing to bottom-of-the-roster refuse, but it would have been nice to see Green Bay get their quarterback another weapon this offseason.

There have been no immediate changes along the offensive line or in the backfield, where this is Aaron Rodgers' show with Eddie Lacy and James Starks as the primary runners. And all the special-teamers are back, from punter Tim Masthay and kicker Mason Crosby to returners Janis and Micah Hyde. On paper, this is still the best team in the division, and the offense looks like one of the best in the league. It's not clear, though, whether or not they are ready to challenge for a Super Bowl. That's really up to Dom Capers and the defense, and how they'll fare this year is very difficult to say.

Vincent Verhei

2015 Packers Stats by Week

Wk	vs.	W-L	PF	PA	YDF	YDA	TO	Total	Off	Def	ST
1	at CHI	W	31	23	322	402	1	50%	43%	-2%	5%
2	SEA	W	27	17	361	324	1	47%	32%	-10%	5%
3	KC	W	38	28	448	326	1	89%	61%	-29%	0%
4	at SF	W	17	3	362	196	1	32%	6%	-33%	-8%
5	STL	W	24	10	322	334	1	32%	-17%	-50%	-1%
6	SD	W	27	20	370	548	1	27%	22%	3%	9%
7	BYE										
8	at DEN	L	10	29	140	500	1	-78%	-30%	50%	1%
9	at CAR	L	29	37	402	427	-1	-1%	15%	8%	-8%
10	DET	L	16	18	372	287	1	-1%	7%	-15%	-22%
11	at MIN	W	30	13	320	342	1	12%	10%	9%	10%
12	CHI	L	13	17	365	290	-2	-13%	-24%	-8%	3%
13	at DET	W	27	23	313	306	0	-25%	-23%	-5%	-6%
14	DAL	W	28	7	435	270	1	37%	18%	-17%	2%
15	at OAK	W	30	20	293	372	0	8%	-10%	-13%	6%
16	at ARI	L	8	38	178	381	-2	-51%	-56%	3%	8%
17	MIN	L	13	20	350	242	0	15%	-13%	-26%	2%
18	at WAS	W	35	18	346	354	0	59%	28%	-19%	13%
19	at ARI	L	20	26	386	368	1	39%	7%	-37%	-4%

Trends and Splits

	Offense	Rank	Defense	Rank
Total DVOA	2.5%	11	-7.3%	9
Unadjusted VOA	1.2%	14	-4.9%	8
Weighted Trend	-7.8%	21	-3.6%	14
Variance	8.9%	26	5.0%	21
Average Opponent	-3.2%	5	1.2%	10
Passing	14.4%	16	-6.8%	6
Rushing	-5.7%	10	-7.9%	19
First Down	-7.5%	24	-8.2%	6
Second Down	22.5%	3	-2.8%	14
Third Down	-11.9%	23	-12.3%	10
First Half	-0.7%	16	-3.5%	14
Second Half	6.0%	11	-11.4%	6
Red Zone	-12.3%	24	-14.0%	6
Late and Close	17.1%	2	-8.9%	14

Five-Year Performance

Year	W-L	Pyth W	Est W	PF	PA	TO	Total	Rk	Off	Rk	Def	Rk	ST	Rk	Off AGL	Rk	Def AGL	Rk	Off Age	Rk	Def Age	Rk	ST Age	Rk
2011	15-1	12.2	13.3	560	359	+24	27.0%	1	33.8%	1	8.6%	25	1.8%	8	21.3	9	37.5	22	26.3	26	26.7	23	25.1	32
2012	11-5	10.5	11.8	433	336	+7	26.3%	5	19.5%	3	-7.0%	8	-0.2%	18	38.7	23	62.8	32	26.9	16	25.8	27	24.9	32
2013	8-7-1	7.8	7.3	417	428	-3	-6.0%	20	8.6%	9	14.4%	31	-0.3%	19	59.1	29	43.9	24	26.0	30	26.3	19	25.2	29
2014	12-4	11.2	10.8	486	348	+14	23.3%	3	24.7%	1	-1.0%	16	-2.3%	22	11.0	3	31.0	9	25.7	30	26.7	18	25.9	19
2015	10-6	9.3	9.9	368	323	+5	9.9%	10	2.2%	11	-7.3%	9	0.4%	17	29.7	15	26.5	14	26.7	16	26.3	23	25.5	28

2015 Performance Based on Most Common Personnel Groups

GB Offense					GB Offense vs. Opponents					GB Defense					GB Defense vs. Opponents			
Pers	Freq	Yds	DVOA	Run%	Pers	Freq	Yds	DVOA	Run%	Pers	Freq	Yds	DVOA	Pers	Freq	Yds	DVOA
11	66%	5.9	15.3%	29%	Base	13%	4.3	-12.2%	57%	Base	18%	4.6	-21.9%	11	59%	5.7	-3.8%
20	13%	3.4	-43.7%	57%	Nickel	71%	5.6	13.4%	34%	Nickel	57%	5.6	-0.8%	12	20%	6.2	-0.4%
01	4%	7.5	47.0%	12%	Dime+	15%	5.6	-11.1%	22%	Dime+	23%	6.2	-16.6%	22	7%	3.7	-34.4%
10	4%	6.2	37.3%	19%	Goal Line	1%	1.6	7.6%	75%	Goal Line	1%	2.6	8.4%	21	6%	3.9	-22.4%
22	3%	3.2	-50.2%	74%	Big	1%	0.5	-276.5%	83%	Big	1%	2.3	-29.6%	13	3%	8.7	25.7%
21	3%	6.4	0.7%	57%													

Strategic Tendencies

Run/Pass		Rk	Formation		Rk	Pass Rush		Rk	Secondary		Rk	Strategy		Rk
Runs, first half	35%	25	Form: Single Back	65%	28	Rush 3	5.2%	22	4 DB	18%	29	Play action	16%	26
Runs, first down	44%	25	Form: Empty Back	4%	27	Rush 4	54.3%	27	5 DB	57%	12	Avg Box (Off)	6.11	27
Runs, second-long	32%	13	Pers: 3+ WR	89%	1	Rush 5	33.0%	3	6+ DB	23%	7	Avg Box (Def)	6.13	25
Runs, power sit.	57%	13	Pers: 2+ TE/6+ OL	9%	31	Rush 6+	7.5%	13	CB by Sides	79%	14	Offensive Pace	29.40	8
Runs, behind 2H	23%	20	Pers: 6+ OL	2%	20	Sacks by LB	68.6%	1	S/CB Cover Ratio	30%	4	Defensive Pace	30.82	26
Pass, ahead 2H	48%	12	Shotgun/Pistol	73%	6	Sacks by DB	11.6%	10	DB Blitz	14%	6	Go for it on 4th	1.59	3

Even with Jordy Nelson out for the year, the Packers led the league in frequency of using three or more receivers for the third straight season. No team has used three or more wideouts more frequently in 11 years of game charting. (The old record was 82 percent by the 2011 Buffalo Bills.) ☞ 51 percent of runs by Packers running backs came with two backs in the backfield; the Rams were the only other team over 50 percent last year. However, the difference in both DVOA and yards per carry between one-back and two-back runs was negligible. ☞ As you might imagine when you look at the previous two stats together, the Packers led the league by using 20 personnel (two backs, no tight ends) on 13.4 percent of plays. No other offense was above 4.8 percent. ☞ When Aaron Rodgers took a sack, it was almost always on third down. The Packers were fifth in the league with an adjusted sack rate of just 4.7 percent on first and second downs. But they were dead last with an adjusted sack rate of 14.4 percent on third and fourth downs. ☞ The offense had a ghastly -35.4% DVOA on third-and-short, 31st in the NFL. ☞ Green Bay ranked fourth in passing DVOA in Weeks 1-9 but plummeted to 27th in Weeks 10-17. ☞ As much as the offense struggled at times, it often performed its best in high leverage situations. The Packers posted a 17.2% DVOA in late-and-close situations, second-best in the league. ☞ The Packers may have had the league's most effective screen game. Green Bay threw 24 percent of its passes behind the line of scrimmage, the third-highest rate in the league, and compiled a 32.4% DVOA on those passes, the third-best mark in the league. They were especially excellent on running back screens, compiling a league-leading 126.2% DVOA on 48 screens. Only two teams threw more screen passes to running backs. The defense was as good as the offense, compiling a -117.3% DVOA against 22 running back screens, which ranked second overall. ☞ Green Bay finished sixth in red zone defensive DVOA thanks to its pass defense. The Packers ranked third against the pass in the red zone, posting a -34.2% DVOA, but just 27th against the run, posting a 12.4% DVOA. ☞ Green Bay only recovered five of 15 fumbles on defense. ☞ Green Bay's defense has a tackling problem, ranking 30th and 31st the last two seasons in the percentage of plays with broken tackles.

Passing

Player	DYAR	DVOA	Plays	NtYds	Avg	YAC	C%	TD	Int
A.Rodgers	406	-1.0%	617	3489	5.7	5.6	60.9%	31	8

Rushing

Player	DYAR	DVOA	Plays	Yds	Avg	TD	Fum	Suc
E.Lacy	3	-8.3%	187	758	4.1	3	3	49%
J.Starks	-46	-15.8%	148	601	4.1	2	4	43%
A.Rodgers	107	37.1%	45	356	7.9	1	0	-
R.Cobb	22	-9.3%	13	50	3.8	0	0	-
J.Kuhn*	24	40.4%	9	28	3.1	2	0	67%
J.Crockett	1	-4.7%	9	21	2.3	0	0	44%
A.Harris*	5	25.1%	4	19	4.8	0	0	25%

Receiving

Player	DYAR	DVOA	Plays	Ctch	Yds	Y/C	YAC	TD	C%
R.Cobb	77	-5.1%	129	79	829	10.5	5.5	6	61%
J.Jones*	206	13.6%	99	50	890	17.8	4.4	8	51%
D.Adams	-109	-27.8%	94	50	495	9.9	3.0	1	53%
T.Montgomery	74	32.3%	19	15	136	9.1	6.1	2	79%
J.Abbrederis	-29	-36.2%	16	9	111	12.3	1.7	0	56%
J.Janis	-4	-17.0%	12	2	79	39.5	14.5	0	17%
R.Rodgers	21	-3.7%	85	58	526	9.1	4.0	8	68%
J.Perillo	27	22.3%	13	11	102	9.3	1.9	1	85%
J.Cook	-76	-23.5%	75	39	481	12.3	5.1	0	52%
J.Starks	97	17.3%	53	43	392	9.1	11.4	3	81%
E.Lacy	20	-0.6%	28	20	188	9.4	10.7	2	71%
J.Kuhn*	-9	-27.1%	10	6	56	9.3	9.8	0	60%

Offensive Line

Player	Pos	Age	GS	Snaps	Pen	Sk	Pass	Run	Player	Pos	Age	GS	Snaps	Pen	Sk	Pass	Run
Josh Sitton	LG	30	16/16	1140	8	1.0	2.0	4.0	Corey Linsley	C	25	13/13	802	4	2.0	3.0	3.0
T.J. Lang	RG	29	15/15	1033	5	1.0	1.0	2.0	Don Barclay	RT	27	16/5	423	5	8.0	10.0	3.0
David Bakhtiari	LT	25	14/14	957	12	2.0	5.0	3.0	J.C. Tretter	OL	25	16/3	373	1	0.0	1.0	2.0
Bryan Bulaga	RT	27	12/12	808	7	2.0	6.0	4.0									

Year	Yards	ALY	Rank	Power	Rank	Stuff	Rank	2nd Lev	Rank	Open Field	Rank	Sacks	ASR	Rank	Press	Rank	F-Start	Cont.
2013	4.52	4.11	5	83%	1	16%	5	1.24	10	0.95	8	45	8.3%	26	21.0%	5	13	38
2014	4.39	4.08	8	59%	25	21%	24	1.29	5	0.83	8	30	5.5%	13	20.6%	4	11	43
2015	4.00	3.56	25	61%	21	23%	27	1.11	19	0.73	16	47	7.4%	23	30.2%	29	10	28

2015 ALY by direction:	Left End 2.8 (29)	Left Tackle 4.02 (12)	Mid/Guard 3.8 (16)	Right Tackle 3.95 (8)	Right End 2.71 (25)

The Green Bay offensive line will feature some very familiar faces. This will be the third straight season as a starter in Green Bay for center Cory Linsley, the fourth for left tackle David Bakhtiari, the sixth for both right guard T.J. Lang and right tackle Bryan Bulaga, and the eighth for left guard Josh Sitton. That's a continuity that is unheard of in this day and age. ☞ There are signs that this unit could use some new blood, though. Between sacks, runs, and completed passes, the Packers ran 105 plays that lost yardage last year. Only four teams went backwards more often: the Browns, Vikings, Titans, and 49ers. This is not the kind of offensive company you want to keep. ☞ This line could get a radical makeover very soon. Bakhtiari, Sitton, and Lang will all be unrestricted free agents after the upcoming season. It's expected that second-round rookie Jason Spriggs (Indiana) will start sooner or later. J.C. Tretter, a 2013 fourth-rounder who played well in three 2015 starts at center and another at tackle in the playoffs, is also likely to step into a starting role in 2017.

Defensive Front Seven

Defensive Line	Age	Pos	G	Snaps	Plays	TmPct	Rk	Stop	Dfts	BTkl	Runs	St%	Rk	RuYd	Rk	Sack	Hit	Hur	Dsrpt
						Overall						vs. Run				Pass Rush			
Mike Daniels	27	DE	16	706	50	6.2%	29	41	16	6	41	80%	25	1.6	19	4.0	4	12.0	1
B.J. Raji*	30	DT	15	444	24	3.2%	73	20	5	4	20	80%	26	1.6	17	0.5	0	2.0	2
Datone Jones	26	DE	15	364	23	3.0%	--	19	12	2	16	81%	--	1.9	--	3.0	9	15.5	3
Letroy Guion	29	DT	13	330	20	3.0%	--	16	4	1	20	80%	--	1.5	--	0.0	1	1.0	0
Mike Pennel	25	DE	16	287	25	3.1%	--	19	4	2	24	75%	--	2.1	--	1.0	3	5.0	0

Edge Rushers	Age	Pos	G	Snaps	Plays	TmPct	Rk	Stop	Dfts	BTkl	Runs	St%	Rk	RuYd	Rk	Sack	Hit	Hur	Dsrpt
						Overall						vs. Run				Pass Rush			
Mike Neal*	29	OLB	16	734	36	4.4%	57	29	16	5	27	81%	19	1.5	20	4.0	5	14.5	0
Julius Peppers	36	OLB	16	700	37	4.6%	53	27	16	7	23	61%	85	3.3	84	10.5	6	13.5	0
Nick Perry	26	OLB	14	351	30	4.2%	--	22	10	3	23	70%	--	1.7	--	3.5	0	6.5	1

Linebackers	Age	Pos	G	Snaps	Plays	TmPct	Rk	Stop	Dfts	BTkl	Runs	St%	Rk	RuYd	Rk	Sack	Hit	Hur	Tgts	Suc%	Rk	AdjYd	Rk	PD	Int
						Overall						vs. Run				Pass Rush				vs. Pass					
Clay Matthews	30	ILB	16	1020	68	8.4%	70	45	21	12	36	78%	4	2.8	15	6.5	12	25.5	11	81%	3	5.5	--	2	1
Nate Palmer*	26	ILB	16	539	66	8.1%	72	33	3	9	42	55%	72	3.5	44	1.0	1	1	17	55%	42	4.9	16	0	0
Jake Ryan	24	ILB	14	260	46	6.5%	--	28	6	8	38	68%	--	3.4	--	0.0	0	0	10	40%	--	7.5	--	0	0
Joe Thomas	25	ILB	14	250	19	2.7%	--	11	9	5	6	67%	--	6.2	--	1.0	2	1.5	8	66%	--	1.7	--	2	0

Year	Yards	ALY	Rank	Power	Rank	Stuff	Rank	2nd Level	Rank	Open Field	Rank	Sacks	ASR	Rank	Press	Rank
2013	4.67	4.26	26	77%	30	17%	22	1.38	29	0.88	24	44	8.1%	5	21.3%	31
2014	4.09	4.21	26	63%	14	17%	25	1.19	21	0.42	1	41	6.9%	14	25.2%	14
2015	4.15	3.55	11	67%	17	25%	3	1.21	24	0.92	25	43	6.7%	15	26.5%	10

2015 ALY by direction:	Left End 2.68 (6)	Left Tackle 3.39 (11)	Mid/Guard 3.73 (12)	Right Tackle 4.80 (30)	Right End 2.85 (9)

Dom Capers loves the five-man blitz. In the past five years, the Packers have ranked first, first, fifth, third, and third in in frequency of using exactly five pass rushers. Capers hasn't called big blitzes of six or more pass rushers nearly as much, but he has been using them more in recent years. From 2011 to 2013, the Packers ranked 25th, 26th, and 23rd in use of big blitzes, then eighth in 2014 and 13th last year. ☞ Clay Matthews split time between edge rusher and inside linebacker last year, and as a result ended up with some very unusual splits. Matthews and San Diego's Melvin Ingram were the only players in the league in 2015 to get at least 15 quarterback knockdowns and make 15 tackles on completed passes. ☞ Julius Peppers' age has to be concerning. Only eight players age 36 or older have ever had ten sacks in a season, and the last to do it was Bruce Smith in 2000. In the past five years, Jason Taylor (7.0 sacks at age 37 in 2011) and James Harrison (5.5 at 36 in 2014, then 5.0 at 37 last year) are the only pass rushers of any significance at that age.

Defensive Secondary

Secondary	Age	Pos	G	Snaps	Plays	Overall TmPct	Rk	Stop	Dfts	BTkl	vs. Run Runs	St%	Rk	RuYd	Rk	vs. Pass Tgts	Tgt%	Rk	Dist	Suc%	Rk	AdjYd	Rk	PD	Int
Ha Ha Clinton-Dix	24	FS	16	1048	102	12.6%	14	37	12	11	53	42%	33	8.1	51	25	6.4%	23	13.9	60%	26	7.9	45	2	2
Casey Hayward*	27	CB	16	914	70	8.6%	36	39	15	9	19	68%	7	5.4	18	46	13.6%	3	9.4	57%	19	6.8	15	5	0
Damarious Randall	24	CB	15	755	70	9.2%	29	23	14	6	13	23%	63	11.2	65	74	26.6%	70	14.4	48%	57	8.8	61	13	3
Sam Shields	29	CB	12	697	52	8.5%	40	22	14	7	3	0%	74	15.7	75	45	17.6%	18	14.3	57%	20	6.5	13	13	3
Morgan Burnett	27	SS	11	683	72	12.9%	12	29	7	5	40	53%	15	6.4	31	14	5.4%	15	15.2	67%	10	5.5	13	4	0
Micah Hyde	26	SS/CB	15	652	55	7.2%	63	19	13	7	15	20%	63	13.6	68	40	16.5%	69	9.6	52%	49	6.8	35	6	3
Quinten Rollins	24	CB	14	323	32	4.5%	--	16	11	4	9	56%	--	4.6	--	31	25.8%	--	13.1	57%	--	7.7	--	6	2

Year	Pass D Rank	vs. #1 WR	Rk	vs. #2 WR	Rk	vs. Other WR	Rk	vs. TE	Rk	vs. RB	Rk
2013	28	20.0%	28	16.7%	27	-8.1%	11	15.4%	25	13.3%	27
2014	11	-1.5%	15	-14.2%	7	-11.4%	9	-5.8%	14	1.0%	19
2015	6	7.5%	21	-31.7%	2	6.4%	19	-20.8%	4	-24.7%	4

Capers likes to blitz, and he likes to send defensive backs after the quarterback, ranking fourth, second, 11th, and sixth in defensive back blitzes in the past four seasons. In that time, Ha Ha Clinton-Dix has 4.0 sacks, Morgan Burnett has 3.5, and Micah Hyde has 3.0. Ex-Packers Tramon Williams and Davon House had 2.5 and 2.0 sacks respectively in Green Bay. Clinton-Dix is one of ten defensive backs with at least four sacks in the last two seasons, a list that includes safety-linebacker hybrids like Deone Bucannon and Mark Barron. ☞ Clinton-Dix and Morgan Burnett were both among the top 20 safeties in run tackles. That's partly an indictment of Green Bay's front seven, but also a sign of an active secondary—both were in the top 15 in successful run tackles as well, so they weren't just bringing runners down after long gains. ☞ Sam Shields was one of six players (all corners, of course) to play at least 500 snaps and make five or fewer run tackles. Shields, Pittsburgh's Ross Cockrell, and New England's Duron Harmon were the only men to see that much playing time without logging a single run stop.

Special Teams

Year	DVOA	Rank	FG/XP	Rank	Net Kick	Rank	Kick Ret	Rank	Net Punt	Rank	Punt Ret	Rank	Hidden	Rank
2013	-0.3%	19	4.0	10	-12.3	30	-4.2	23	5.4	9	5.6	9	7.5	6
2014	-2.3%	22	-2.9	24	-7.0	28	-2.9	22	-9.4	29	10.5	4	0.1	16
2015	0.4%	17	5.0	6	-7.8	31	5.4	5	4.7	9	-5.6	25	-4.9	21

The Packers should be at the forefront of the movement to eliminate kickoffs, because they damn sure can't cover them. Mason Crosby has been average in kickoff value the last three seasons, but his coverage teams were next-to-last in the league last year after finishing sixth from the bottom in 2014 and third-worst in 2013. The Packers gave up 26.7 yards per kickoff return last year, fourth-highest in the league. And though they gave up no touchdowns, they were the only team with three saves (tackles that stopped long kickoff returns short of the goal line). ☞ Punter Tim Masthay struggled last year, finishing fourth from the bottom in gross punt value after finishing third from the bottom in 2014. In particular, Masthay failed to pin opponents deep. He had only 18 punts downed inside the 20 with six touchbacks, a ratio of 3.0-to-1 that was tied for second-worst in the NFL. (Shane Lechler of Houston was last at 2.4-to-1.) ☞ Green Bay's punt coverage has usually been as poor as the kickoff coverage, but last year it was the third best in the league. Only Philadelphia and Baltimore forced more negative value on punt returns. Jeff Janis is best known for his playoff heroics as a receiver, but he also led the NFL in punt stops (tackles that stop the returner short of an average return). ☞ Speaking of Janis, his 29.0-yard average on 14 kickoff returns was the best of any Packer since Najeh Davenport in 2003. And Ty Montgomery was even better in limited action, averaging 31.1 yards on seven returns. However, Micah Hyde took a big step back in punt returns, near the bottom of the league with minus-3.4 points worth of estimated field position after ranking in the top ten in value in both 2013 and 2014. ☞ Hey, remember that year when Crosby couldn't hit the broad side of a barn and missed 12 of 33 field goal tries? It turns out Crosby has been automatic from short range lately. In the past three seasons, he is 51-of-52 on field goals from inside 40 yards. The Packers were also one of five teams not to miss an extra point last year.

Houston Texans

2015 record: 9-7	**Total DVOA:** -4.8% (18th)	**2016 Mean Projection:** 7.4 wins	**On the Clock (0-4):** 13%
Pythagorean Wins: 8.8 (12th)	**Offense:** -8.5% (24th)	**Postseason Odds:** 32.2%	**Mediocrity (5-7):** 40%
Snap-Weighted Age: 26.3 (25th)	**Defense:** -9.3% (8th)	**Super Bowl Odds:** 2.7%	**Playoff Contender (8-10):** 35%
Average Opponent: -3.6% (22nd)	**Special Teams:** -5.7% (32nd)	**Proj. Avg. Opponent:** -1.0% (20th)	**Super Bowl Contender (11+):** 12%

2015: In the kingdom of the blind, the weak-armed quarterback is king.

2016: 1) Brock Osweiler and Speed, 2) ???, 3) Profit?

Was 2015 a successful season for the Houston Texans? That may sound like a stupid question. After all, the Texans went 9-7, completing the fifth winning season in franchise history. They won an unexpected AFC South title and with it one of the dozen coveted entries into the NFL's postseason tournament.

Or it may not be such a stupid question after all. The 2015 Texans shared many of the underlying qualities of the 2014 Texans. The record of 9-7 was identical. DVOA was actually down a hair, from -4.5% to -4.8%. Even the breakdown by unit was basically the same: a lousy offense that ranked in the low 20s, a defense in the bottom half of the top ten, and dismal special teams.

The postseason appearance ended as soon as it began. The Texans allowed the Chiefs to run the opening kickoff back for a touchdown, and Brian Hoyer's homage to Jake Delhomme made sure Houston would never seriously threaten to score. The home loss to Kansas City was the fourth game of the season where the Texans posted a DVOA of -50.0% or worse, not quite the hallmark of a top team. From this perspective, the Texans won the AFC South because, well, somebody had to. Jacksonville and Tennessee ended up picking in the top five for a second consecutive season, and Indianapolis played the majority of their season sans Andrew Luck. The Texans were default AFC South winners.

Head coach Bill O'Brien and general manager Rick Smith, through their offseason moves, clearly suggested that they would not be content with another repeat of the basic pattern. The offense, too often reduced to "DeAndre Hopkins does something amazing while everybody else does nothing," was unsurprisingly the focal point of the makeover.

After dealing with Ryan Fitzpatrick (plus cameo appearances by Case Keenum, Ryan Mallett, and Tom Savage) in 2014 and Hoyer (plus cameos by Mallett, Brandon Weeden, and T.J. Yates) the past two seasons, Smith and O'Brien went searching for what they hoped would be a long-term solution at quarterback. Looking over the options in the draft and free agency, they chose Brock Osweiler, outbidding John Elway and the Broncos for his services at a cost of $72 million over four years.

The move was a fascinating and bold one. A price tag that more or less just reflects the cost of doing business at the game's most important position was oft-criticized because of Osweiler's inexperience. What teams normally look for and get when adding a player in free agency is a certain level of stability. Osweiler offers approximately none of that.

Four years removed from his selection by Denver in the second round of the 2012 draft, Osweiler has started seven games in the NFL and attempted just 305 passes. All the work in his first three seasons came in garbage time. He was benched late last season and replaced by a washed-up Peyton Manning for Denver's postseason run. Smith and O'Brien made a bold bet that is worth examining in more detail.

The case in favor of Osweiler:

1. He has room to grow as an NFL quarterback. Fitzpatrick turned 32 as a starter, Hoyer 30. Both had had multiple chances with different teams and have shown they are serviceable at best. Osweiler is just 25, approaching the prime of his career. With just 305 NFL passing attempts, a number of his flaws could come from inexperience. Unlike Fitzpatrick and Hoyer, it is reasonable to expect him to grow to become more than he has shown so far.

2. Even if Osweiler is never more than what he was last year, he showed he can be functional. A passing DVOA of -3.2% is not great, but it was significantly better than Manning's was on the same team.

3. He spent the past four seasons being around Peyton Manning, learning what being a committed professional quarterback is all about. He has seen first-hand the work it takes to excel at the highest level.

4. The vast majority of what we have seen out of him (275 of his 305 attempts, and all the non-garbage time) came in Gary Kubiak's highly structured offense, which was not the offense he learned his first three seasons. Bill O'Brien the past two seasons has shown he will adapt to the strength of his quarterback, and runs an offense closer to what Osweiler learned from Adam Gase.

5. What alternatives did the Texans have? Another season starting Hoyer felt untenable, Savage missed the entire 2015 season due to injury, their draft slot was late enough they could not count on getting a quality 2016 or even perhaps 2017 starter, and the defense will not be great forever. The Texans are not a bad team, and Osweiler was the best option for being the best team they could be in (at least) 2016 and 2017.

2016 Texans Schedule

Week	Opp.	Week	Opp.	Week	Opp.
1	CHI	7	at DEN (Mon.)	13	at GB
2	KC	8	DET	14	at IND
3	at NE (Thu.)	9	BYE	15	JAC
4	TEN	10	at JAC	16	CIN (Sat.)
5	at MIN	11	at OAK (Mon./Mex.)	17	at TEN
6	IND	12	SD		

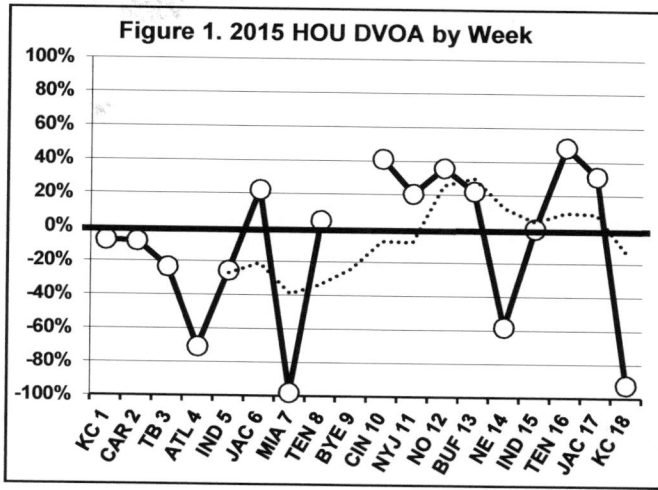

Figure 1. 2015 HOU DVOA by Week

The case against Osweiler:

1. Osweiler will be working closely with O'Brien, whom he did not even meet until his introductory press conference in Houston. This indicates, at least, the rushed nature of the forced marriage.

2. QBASE, our statistical projection system for quarterback prospects, rated Osweiler as the worst highly-drafted prospect of the last two decades when he came out of Arizona State, by a significant margin. His predicted DYAR in Years 3-5 was minus-860, compared to minus-525 for the second-worst prospect. Relying on college stats to say something meaningful about a player heading into his fifth season may feel dubious, but Osweiler threw more than twice as many passes in college as he has in the NFL. QBASE looks down upon Osweiler in part because he only started one year at Arizona State, and in part because of a humdrum completion percentage. The latter critique has been backed up by his inconsistent ball placement in the NFL.

3. Being the backup quarterback to even a top-level passer is no guarantee of future success. Just ask Mallett, whose three years in Foxborough did not instill "do your job" firmly enough for him to consistently make it to team meetings or the team flight to Miami.

4. Osweiler is incredibly tall for a quarterback, listed by the Texans at 6-foot-8. There have been no successful quarterbacks that tall in NFL history (though to be fair, most of the men who might have been ended up as NBA players). The only other 6-foot-8 quarterback with 100 passes in a season is noted first-round bust Dan McGwire. The only other quarterback taller than 6-foot-6 with at least 100 attempts is Mike Glennon, last seen languishing on the bench with Tampa Bay.

5. Why on earth should we think the failed history of tall quarterbacks is anything more than small sample size nonsense? Logically, one of the problems of an awkwardly tall height might be navigating the pocket. Osweiler posted an individual sack rate of 7.2 percent, compared to Manning's 4.5 percent. Sack rate will vary between team and offensive scheme, but the quarterback himself plays an important role in his own pass protection.

6. The team that knew Osweiler intimately was Denver. They benched him for the playoff run and did not do whatever they needed to keep him, at a position where teams do that even for average talents.

The question is a legitimately tricky one. The view from these quarters suggests skepticism. O'Brien made Fitzpatrick and Hoyer about as functional as they had been at other stops, and both came with much lower price tags. Smith and O'Brien bet big on an uncertain proposition, when our logic suggests more and smaller bets—like the Seahawks did from 2010 to 2012 in taking chances on reasonably-priced young former backups Charlie Whitehurst, Tarvaris Jackson, and Matt Flynn and spending a third-round pick on Russell Wilson—might have been a better option than going all-in on a single player. The structure of the contract means Osweiler has little chance of going anywhere before 2018 at the earliest, so we should know in two seasons which side had the better argument.

Sticking with Hoyer or his non-union equivalent might not have been nearly as bad as the Kansas City game suggests, because the Texans also upgraded the supporting cast around their quarterback. The biggest veteran addition was running back Lamar Miller, late of the Dolphins. Miller has been a puzzle for outside observers. He had a phenomenal 2014, leading all backs in DVOA and success rate. He was outstanding at times in 2015, with weeks finishing first, second, and third in rushing DYAR. Yet he finished just 18th in DVOA, 19th in DYAR, and 34th in success rate. O'Brien has spent much of his first two seasons feeding grinders as many carries as he can, yet Miller has reached as many as 20 carries in a game only twice in four years. One thing he does bring is more explosiveness. Arian Foster averaged just 2.6 yards per carry before a torn Achilles in Week 7 ended his season, and ultimately his tenure in Houston. Replacement lead back Alfred Blue finished 43rd (out of 45 qualifying backs) in open-field yards last year; Miller was eighth in 2015 after ranking fifth the year before.

The addition of speed and explosiveness to the ball-handling positions was a theme of the Texans' draft as well. They traded up in the first round to ensure they got Will Fuller, the second receiver off the board. Fuller was a favorite of our Playmaker Score metric, which rated him highly because much of Notre Dame's passing offense ran through him. Receivers with a high yards per catch average, like Fuller's 20.3 yards per catch in 2015, tend to perform better in the NFL. More scouting-oriented analyses were generally less high on Fuller, seeing a drop-prone receiver who ran and was successful on a limited route tree and might only be successful in the NFL as a deep threat.

Technical limitations but athletic explosiveness was also the order of the day when the Texans doubled down on wide receiver by selecting Braxton Miller from Ohio State in the third round. The former Big Ten Offensive Player of the Year has no Playmaker Score projection of his own because of a position switch from quarterback before his final season. He likely projects as a slot receiver and gadget player. Also available for athletic gadgetry is fourth-round running back Tyler Ervin, who averaged 6.0 highlight yards per opportunity and caught 45 passes in his final season at San Jose State.

Even if Fuller and Miller are in some sense limited contributors both in 2016 and going forward, that is not as big a deal as it might be for other teams because of the presence of DeAndre Hopkins. Hopkins is a curious figure—not the fastest receiver, not the quickest, not the most precise route-runner, not the biggest. He ranked just 13th in DYAR and was just a bit average on a per-play basis by DVOA. The instability and inefficiency at quarterback, plus the lack of other quality options resulting him in being force-fed the ball at times, go a long way toward helping explain the mediocre ranking by advanced and per-play efficiency statistics. Hopkins is incredible in how he adjusts to and attacks the football. That helped erase some of the accuracy problems of Fitzpatrick and Hoyer, especially on deep balls, and should help a lot with Osweiler. He also did what he did last season, finishing third in the league in both receptions and receiving yards, despite coverage tilted his direction. Remaining veteran Cecil Shorts will see his job pushed not just by Fuller and Miller, but also by 2015 third-round pick Jaelen Strong, who played better late in the season and significantly reshaped his body in the offseason.

On paper, Osweiler might also be enjoying a significantly better line than Denver's troubled unit last season. But the 2016 Texans line will not be the 2015 Texans line, which allowed pressure on just 22 percent of pass plays last year, fourth-best in the league. Longtime mainstay left tackle Duane Brown's play has slipped, and a torn quad suffered in Week 17 contributed to the postseason offensive ineptitude. He started training camp on the physically unable to perform list, but is expected to be fine for the start of the regular season. The Texans are also remaking their interior line after losing center Ben Jones and right guard Brandon Brooks in free agency. Replacements for both are on hand, in free-agent guard Jeff Allen (late of Kansas City) and second-round pick Nick Martin (brother of Dallas' Zack and South Bend teammate of first-rounder Fuller), but both are likely to cause instability initially. Only right tackle Derek Newton, whom O'Brien praised

for taking on more of a leadership role in Brown and Jones' absence, looks solid.

The big question is whether the defense, a top-ten unit by DVOA four of the past five seasons, will win enough low-scoring games to give the offense the time it needs to stabilize and improve. Befitting the history of success, our numbers are moderately optimistic. J.J. Watt is still an incredible player and the most dominant defensive lineman in the NFL. Kareem Jackson, Kevin Johnson, and Johnathan Joseph form one of the best cornerback trios this side of Denver. Whitney Mercilus blossomed with as many sacks (12.0) as he had in his first two seasons as a starter to provide a complementary pass rush. Jadeveon Clowney, recovering from microfracture surgery, shows flashes of the form that made him the first overall pick. Rookie Bernardrick McKinney solved the weakness at inside linebacker next to Brian Cushing.

However, the situation was not quite as rosy as that picture makes it seem, even before news broke of J.J. Watt's back surgery a week before training camp. The draft's focus on offense meant the defense was neglected, and the Texans were already extremely thin on the defensive line. Jared Crick left in free agency, and the Texans have no obvious replacement for his 783 snaps. Vince Wilfork should be replaced sooner rather than later, and fifth-round pick D.J. Reader (Clemson) will have that job, not replacing Crick. Early reports suggested Watt might miss several games at the start of the regular season. It is not clear how the Texans could manage to deploy a quality defensive front if that happens, likely forcing the offense to come together quicker than they would prefer.

The potential problem areas do not stop up front. Mercilus did a better job of getting to the quarterback, but notching just 20 hurries with those sacks suggests regression is coming this year. The safeties are more workmanlike than positive. The early-season struggles could repeat themselves if last year's schemes do not work as well and Crennel is again slow to adapt.

On balance, our numbers again predict the Texans to be a slightly below-average team. In what is likely to again be the worst division in football, that could be enough to get them to the playoffs. The Colts are our favorites to win the division, but that projection assumes that Andrew Luck returns to his pre-2015 form. If he does not, is the Texans are well-positioned to seize another division crown. Whether they can get beyond that level depends in large part on the right arm of Brock Osweiler. And hey, it could happen.

Tom Gower

2015 x Stats by Week

Wk	vs.	W-L	PF	PA	YDF	YDA	TO	Total	Off	Def	ST
1	KC	L	20	27	396	330	-2	-8%	10%	0%	-18%
2	at CAR	L	17	24	300	350	0	-8%	-10%	-6%	-5%
3	TB	W	19	9	413	318	0	-23%	-16%	-13%	-20%
4	at ATL	L	21	48	428	378	-4	-71%	-22%	37%	-11%
5	IND	L	20	27	444	323	-2	-25%	11%	31%	-6%
6	at JAC	W	31	20	382	394	3	22%	13%	-12%	-2%
7	at MIA	L	26	44	322	503	0	-98%	-51%	49%	2%
8	TEN	W	20	6	270	211	3	4%	-26%	-29%	1%
9	BYE										
10	at CIN	W	10	6	256	256	1	41%	-5%	-40%	6%
11	NYJ	W	24	17	364	267	1	20%	12%	-22%	-14%
12	NO	W	24	6	362	268	0	36%	-5%	-49%	-8%
13	at BUF	L	21	30	401	390	-1	22%	39%	18%	1%
14	NE	L	6	27	189	313	0	-58%	-57%	2%	0%
15	at IND	W	16	10	305	190	0	0%	-11%	-27%	-16%
16	at TEN	W	34	6	330	257	3	49%	10%	-28%	11%
17	JAC	W	30	6	402	215	3	31%	-26%	-70%	-13%
18	KC	L	0	30	226	314	-4	-92%	-77%	-8%	-23%

Trends and Splits

	Offense	Rank	Defense	Rank
Total DVOA	-8.7%	24	-9.3%	8
Unadjusted VOA	-6.5%	24	-11.8%	3
Weighted Trend	-8.9%	24	-17.9%	4
Variance	6.1%	13	10.4%	32
Average Opponent	1.8%	24	-0.7%	19
Passing	3.5%	22	-6.5%	7
Rushing	-16.2%	26	-13.5%	13
First Down	-1.3%	16	3.5%	19
Second Down	-22.2%	29	-12.9%	4
Third Down	-2.3%	17	-28.8%	3
First Half	-22.5%	32	2.1%	19
Second Half	6.4%	10	-21.3%	2
Red Zone	24.1%	7	-18.0%	5
Late and Close	11.3%	5	-17.8%	5

Five-Year Performance

Year	W-L	Pyth W	Est W	PF	PA	TO	Total	Rk	Off	Rk	Def	Rk	ST	Rk	Off AGL	Rk	Def AGL	Rk	Off Age	Rk	Def Age	Rk	ST Age	Rk
2011	10-6	10.9	10.0	381	278	+7	18.6%	5	8.4%	9	-9.5%	6	0.7%	13	31.3	17	18.9	10	28.1	2	25.7	29	26.1	24
2012	12-4	10.2	8.3	416	331	+12	6.7%	11	0.1%	16	-14.2%	4	-7.7%	32	6.7	1	30.6	19	28.1	6	26.5	22	26.4	11
2013	2-14	4.2	3.9	276	428	-20	-26.5%	30	-18.9%	29	2.5%	18	-5.1%	29	35.1	18	28.6	18	27.5	9	26.2	22	25.7	26
2014	9-7	9.8	6.7	372	307	+12	-4.5%	19	-6.8%	21	-6.2%	6	-3.9%	28	18.8	6	41.1	20	27.2	12	26.0	28	26.1	17
2015	9-7	8.8	7.8	339	313	+5	-4.8%	18	-8.5%	24	-9.3%	8	-5.7%	32	49.8	26	15.0	3	26.5	17	26.2	24	25.8	20

2015 Performance Based on Most Common Personnel Groups

HOU Offense

Pers	Freq	Yds	DVOA	Run%
11	55%	5.5	2.8%	31%
12	14%	5.2	-14.5%	37%
10	7%	4.3	-18.6%	24%
21	6%	5.0	-5.3%	60%
611	3%	4.6	-2.6%	57%
22	3%	5.2	-4.4%	87%
621	3%	4.8	-10.4%	86%

HOU Offense vs. Opponents

Pers	Freq	Yds	DVOA	Run%
Base	34%	5.2	-0.1%	57%
Nickel	53%	5.0	-11.9%	34%
Dime+	13%	5.4	18.0%	13%
Goal Line	0%	4.5	3.7%	75%
Big	0%	1.2	-45.5%	100%

HOU Defense

Pers	Freq	Yds	DVOA
Base	37%	5.4	2.7%
Nickel	32%	5.7	-4.0%
Dime+	30%	4.3	-33.5%
Goal Line	0%	-1.7	-44.2%
Big	1%	5.8	24.5%

HOU Defense vs. Opponents

Pers	Freq	Yds	DVOA
11	42%	5.3	-15.9%
12	33%	5.5	3.2%
21	9%	4.3	-16.4%
10	4%	4.1	-34.7%
13	4%	3.3	-16.7%
22	2%	6.6	21.9%
20	2%	5.1	10.8%

Strategic Tendencies

Run/Pass		Rk	Formation		Rk	Pass Rush		Rk	Secondary		Rk	Strategy		Rk
Runs, first half	39%	11	Form: Single Back	76%	17	Rush 3	11.2%	3	4 DB	37%	11	Play action	22%	7
Runs, first down	49%	11	Form: Empty Back	10%	10	Rush 4	55.0%	26	5 DB	32%	30	Avg Box (Off)	6.19	20
Runs, second-long	36%	7	Pers: 3+ WR	68%	7	Rush 5	25.7%	11	6+ DB	30%	4	Avg Box (Def)	6.24	17
Runs, power sit.	54%	20	Pers: 2+ TE/6+ OL	28%	22	Rush 6+	8.1%	10	CB by Sides	73%	19	Offensive Pace	28.28	3
Runs, behind 2H	28%	10	Pers: 6+ OL	10%	4	Sacks by LB	51.1%	14	S/CB Cover Ratio	24%	10	Defensive Pace	30.52	19
Pass, ahead 2H	44%	24	Shotgun/Pistol	54%	23	Sacks by DB	2.2%	31	DB Blitz	6%	24	Go for it on 4th	1.30	10

Houston's defense ranked 20th with 6.0% DVOA through Week 9, but was the best in the league from Week 10 onward (-25.5%). ☞ The Texans had a colossal gap in defense between play-action and non-play action passes. Without play-action, the Texans allowed a league-low 5.0 yards per pass and ranked second behind Denver with -19.2% DVOA. With play-action, the Texans allowed 9.0 yards per pass and 54.9% DVOA, 30th ahead of only Tennessee and New Orleans. Although these numbers tend to fluctuate year-to-year, the Texans have been much weaker against play-action passes for three straight seasons. ☞ The Texans sent a big blitz of six or more pass-rushers half as often as they did in 2014, but these plays were hugely successful, allowing just 2.8 yards per pass. ☞ The defense was at its best when given a lead, ranking seventh in DVOA when leading by one score and first when leading by two or more scores. ☞ Houston's offense was at the bottom of the league with just 68 broken tackles, although this may not cost them the division because the entire AFC South was horrible at breaking tackles last year. Houston, Jacksonville, and Indianapolis were the bottom three teams in percentage of offensive plays with a broken tackle, and Tennessee was 24th. ☞ Houston quarterbacks threw just nine percent of their passes behind the line of scrimmage, the lowest rate in the league. ☞ Houston's offense inexplicably turned it on near the goal line, going from 29th in DVOA on the rest of the field to seventh in DVOA inside the 20. ☞ Houston ran the ball 36 percent of the time on second-and-long despite having a league-worst -71.6% DVOA on these plays. ☞ The offense posted a -22.6% DVOA before halftime, worst in the league. However, they significantly picked it up in the second half with a 6.9% DVOA (ninth). The defense also got stronger as the game went on, posting successively better DVOA figures in each quarter.

Passing

Player	DYAR	DVOA	Plays	NtYds	Avg	YAC	C%	TD	Int
B.Hoyer*	201	-3.0%	394	2400	6.1	4.2	61.0%	19	5
R.Mallett*	-120	-23.5%	151	745	4.9	2.9	53.4%	3	4
T.J.Yates	17	-7.0%	62	337	5.4	4.2	49.1%	3	1
B.Weeden	124	32.2%	43	290	6.7	2.5	63.4%	3	0
B.Osweiler	153	-3.2%	299	1813	6.1	5.2	61.8%	10	6

Rushing

Player	DYAR	DVOA	Plays	Yds	Avg	TD	Fum	Suc
A.Blue	61	-0.2%	183	698	3.8	2	2	45%
C.Polk*	-31	-17.0%	99	334	3.4	1	0	33%
A.Foster*	-51	-29.7%	63	165	2.6	1	2	40%
J.Grimes	54	20.0%	56	282	5.0	1	0	38%
A.Hunt	29	33.7%	17	96	5.6	0	0	47%
C.Shorts	8	-27.2%	10	47	4.7	0	1	-
J.Prosch	12	27.6%	6	33	5.5	0	0	50%
B.Osweiler	6	-6.1%	17	65	3.8	1	0	-
L.Miller	81	1.7%	194	872	4.5	8	1	43%

Receiving

Player	DYAR	DVOA	Plays	Ctch	Yds	Y/C	YAC	TD	C%
D.Hopkins	268	4.8%	192	111	1521	13.7	2.0	11	58%
N.Washington*	-4	-13.2%	94	47	658	14.0	3.4	4	50%
C.Shorts	4	-11.9%	75	42	484	11.5	5.0	2	56%
K.Mumphery	-93	-50.0%	32	14	129	9.2	1.4	0	44%
J.Strong	35	7.1%	24	14	161	11.5	4.5	3	58%
R.Griffin	42	11.5%	34	20	251	12.6	5.0	2	59%
C.Fiedorowicz	-19	-19.6%	24	17	167	9.8	4.5	1	71%
G.Graham*	-70	-66.4%	19	4	30	7.5	2.3	1	21%
J.Grimes	1	-13.3%	31	26	173	6.7	5.0	1	84%
A.Foster*	80	35.0%	28	22	227	10.3	7.3	2	79%
C.Polk*	-26	-30.1%	28	16	109	6.8	3.6	1	57%
A.Blue	31	26.1%	16	15	109	7.3	4.5	1	94%
A.Hunt	-27	-60.1%	10	6	39	6.5	8.2	0	60%
L.Miller	32	-3.6%	57	47	397	8.4	9.0	2	82%

Offensive Line

Player	Pos	Age	GS	Snaps	Pen	Sk	Pass	Run	Player	Pos	Age	GS	Snaps	Pen	Sk	Pass	Run
Ben Jones*	C	27	16/16	1186	6	2.0	5.0	1.0	Chris Clark	RT	31	11/4	431	2	0.0	5.0	0.0
Derek Newton	RT	29	16/16	1166	5	7.0	11.0	4.0	Oday Aboushi	LG	25	7/5	398	3	0.5	1.5	3.0
Brandon Brooks*	RG	27	14/14	983	6	1.0	5.0	5.0	Kendall Lamm	OT	24	15/4	257	2	0.0	1.0	1.0
Duane Brown	LT	31	14/14	908	7	1.0	6.0	2.0	Jeff Allen	RT	26	12/8	429	2	0.0	2.0	1.0
Xavier Su'a-Filo	LG	25	11/9	628	1	1.0	4.0	2.0	Tony Bergstrom	OT	30	16/3	250	1	0.0	0.0	0.0

Year	Yards	ALY	Rank	Power	Rank	Stuff	Rank	2nd Lev	Rank	Open Field	Rank	Sacks	ASR	Rank	Press	Rank	F-Start	Cont.
2013	4.20	4.10	6	56%	26	20%	17	1.31	3	0.53	26	42	6.6%	11	31.8%	31	19	38
2014	4.07	3.72	23	67%	13	21%	25	1.07	22	0.80	12	26	4.9%	8	24.8%	19	15	39
2015	3.79	3.72	18	65%	16	19%	9	1.02	25	0.47	29	36	6.3%	17	21.3%	8	18	24

2015 ALY by direction: Left End 3.85 (12)   Left Tackle 4.29 (7)   Mid/Guard 3.77 (18)   Right Tackle 3.77 (17)   Right End 2.63 (27)

With Duane Brown on the physically unable to perform list to start training camp, veteran Chris Clark's experience makes him the favorite to fill in at left tackle. ☞ The Texans had the NFL's least effective "Jumbo" packages last season. The offense used an extra offensive lineman on 10.2 percent of its plays, the third-highest rate in the league. Unfortunately, Houston's DVOA on these plays was -13.0%, the lowest among the ten teams that used six linemen on a minimum of 40 plays. Undrafted rookie Kendall Lamm was the favored choice as the sixth offensive lineman. ☞ Xavier Su'a-Filo's hold on the left guard spot was not established until after the Week 9 bye. He's vulnerable to competition from the loser of the center camp battle between second-round pick Nick Martin (Notre Dame) and free-agent pickup Tony Bergstrom (ex-Raiders).

Defensive Front Seven

Defensive Line	Age	Pos	G	Snaps	Plays	Overall TmPct	Rk	Stop	Dfts	BTkl	vs. Run Runs	St%	Rk	RuYd	Rk	Pass Rush Sack	Hit	Hur	Dsrpt
J.J. Watt	27	DE	16	1005	84	10.7%	1	79	42	5	56	91%	4	0.7	1	17.0	33	51.0	8
Jared Crick*	27	DE	16	783	49	6.3%	27	33	8	4	44	66%	72	3.1	74	2.0	8	4.5	2
Vince Wilfork	35	DT	16	562	22	2.8%	79	18	5	1	21	81%	24	1.5	14	0.0	0	6.0	0

Edge Rushers	Age	Pos	G	Snaps	Plays	Overall TmPct	Rk	Stop	Dfts	BTkl	vs. Run Runs	St%	Rk	RuYd	Rk	Pass Rush Sack	Hit	Hur	Dsrpt
Whitney Mercilus	26	OLB	16	741	52	6.6%	16	37	23	5	29	76%	39	1.5	21	12.0	4	20.0	1
John Simon	26	OLB	16	639	49	6.3%	24	26	14	10	25	52%	95	3.9	91	5.5	6	9.0	0
Jadeveon Clowney	23	OLB	13	562	46	7.2%	5	36	16	7	30	80%	23	3.1	78	4.5	5	18.5	6

Linebackers	Age	Pos	G	Snaps	Plays	Overall TmPct	Rk	Stop	Dfts	BTkl	vs. Run Runs	St%	Rk	RuYd	Rk	Pass Rush Sack	Hit	Hur	vs. Pass Tgts	Suc%	Rk	AdjYd	Rk	PD	Int
Brian Cushing	29	ILB	16	986	113	14.4%	27	69	15	13	73	73%	13	2.9	19	0.0	3	9	17	60%	25	7.0	51	0	0
Benardrick McKinney	24	ILB	14	411	58	8.5%	67	35	10	3	40	58%	62	3.5	45	1.0	1	1	7	43%	--	6.7	--	0	0

Year	Yards	ALY	Rank	Power	Rank	Stuff	Rank	2nd Level	Rank	Open Field	Rank	Sacks	ASR	Rank	Press	Rank
2013	4.27	3.68	12	53%	6	22%	10	1.10	16	1.04	27	32	6.7%	18	28.0%	2
2014	4.13	3.83	14	64%	17	19%	18	1.25	24	0.59	10	38	6.2%	24	27.2%	4
2015	4.17	3.51	9	59%	8	21%	13	1.14	19	0.88	23	45	7.5%	6	27.0%	8
2015 ALY by direction:			Left End 3.87 (21)			Left Tackle 2.35 (1)			Mid/Guard 3.68 (9)			Right Tackle 2.94 (5)			Right End 3.90 (24)	

The back injury that will probably keep J.J. Watt out for a couple games at the start of the regular season creates a second job opportunity for the collection of unheralded players and cast-offs that were formerly competing for the starting spot opposite him. ☞ Former Bengals second-round pick Devon Still may have been the favorite to win the one job, but Christian Covington (167 snaps last season), Brandon Dunn (102 snaps), Jeoffrey Pagan (44 snaps), and virtually any other defensive lineman could help fill the void. Covington, a 2015 sixth-rounder from Rice, probably has the highest upside of the group. ☞ Any missed games by Watt are especially important because he was the only defensive lineman in the league to play more than 92.5 percent of his team's snaps, though his total snap count was two short of Jerry Hughes' position-leading total. ☞ What Watt did playing so often was more remarkable because of his injuries—not just a broken hand, but several torn adductor muscles that required offseason surgery. ☞ One characteristic of Houston's second-half defensive resurgence was having Watt align in more different places. In his early years, he spent almost all his time as a three- or five-technique. Now he could be anywhere. ☞ Upon Jadeveon Clowney's return from injury, we saw a player who clearly had the burst to get where he wanted to go, but perhaps not the developed package of moves you'd want from an edge rusher. He set the edge well on run plays, and the Texans spent an awful lot of time dropping him into coverage. ☞ Brian Cushing is not the same player he was when he was younger, but he has still made a great recovery from the knee injuries that threatened his career.

Defensive Secondary

Secondary	Age	Pos	G	Snaps	Plays	Overall TmPct	Rk	Stop	Dfts	BTkl	vs. Run Runs	St%	Rk	RuYd	Rk	vs. Pass Tgts	Tgt%	Rk	Dist	Suc%	Rk	AdjYd	Rk	PD	Int
Johnathan Joseph	32	CB	16	876	80	10.2%	15	39	18	10	10	40%	39	10.6	62	77	23.6%	63	13.4	54%	31	5.8	8	21	1
Kevin Johnson	24	CB	16	801	61	7.8%	51	29	14	8	12	42%	38	10.7	63	63	20.9%	49	11.0	56%	23	7.3	28	10	1
Quintin Demps	31	SS	14	764	67	9.8%	36	22	9	7	29	24%	60	7.2	39	21	7.4%	34	17.0	59%	30	6.5	28	6	1
Andre Hal	24	FS	16	725	44	5.6%	68	17	9	9	15	47%	23	6.1	24	23	8.5%	45	13.1	65%	15	5.5	16	9	4
Kareem Jackson	28	CB	12	629	64	10.9%	6	27	10	6	20	50%	20	8.3	48	52	22.2%	53	10.9	40%	74	8.4	50	5	2
Rahim Moore*	26	FS	7	444	18	5.2%	--	5	3	6	11	18%	--	10.9	--	4	2.4%	--	18.0	89%	--	2.3	--	2	1
Eddie Pleasant	28	SS	16	382	34	4.3%	70	18	13	8	8	63%	2	3.5	1	21	14.7%	67	12.5	85%	2	3.2	2	6	2
A.J. Bouye	25	CB	15	185	20	2.7%	--	9	4	1	3	33%	--	7.0	--	20	28.2%	--	13.6	66%	--	5.3	--	4	2
Charles James	26	CB	9	153	15	3.4%	--	5	1	1	3	100%	--	0.0	--	5	8.8%	--	16.8	38%	--	10.3	--	1	0

Year	Pass D Rank	vs. #1 WR	Rk	vs. #2 WR	Rk	vs. Other WR	Rk	vs. TE	Rk	vs. RB	Rk
2013	24	-1.0%	18	5.4%	17	-10.5%	9	24.9%	30	17.6%	30
2014	6	1.0%	16	-39.4%	1	4.5%	21	-24.1%	3	-8.6%	11
2015	7	-7.6%	8	10.7%	23	-39.3%	1	-11.6%	9	2.2%	18

Kevin Johnson is recovering from a pair of offseason surgeries, on his broken wrist and on his foot, but is expected to be ready for the start of the season with no issues. ☞ Heading into his fourth season, A.J. Bouye took the most advantage of Johnson's absence from OTAs. Given the quality of the three cornerbacks ahead of him, however, he is likely limited to depth or injury replacement. ☞ One positional change that mattered a lot: benching Rahim Moore for Andre Hal at safety. The former Broncos goat was too passive in coverage and not physical enough as a tackler in run support or after the catch, contributing to his low number of both plays and targets. Hal's tendency to create big plays shined against the Jaguars, as he picked off Blake Bortles three times in two games. ☞ Eddie Pleasant played mostly as a dime linebacker, thus the high stop rate. The problem is not the plays he makes, but those he does not, thus the high broken-tackle rate. Newcomer Antonio Allen (ex-Jets) may push him or even starter Quintin Demps.

Special Teams

Year	DVOA	Rank	FG/XP	Rank	Net Kick	Rank	Kick Ret	Rank	Net Punt	Rank	Punt Ret	Rank	Hidden	Rank
2013	-5.1%	29	-12.2	31	-1.4	20	-5.0	27	-7.8	27	0.6	13	1.3	13
2014	-3.9%	28	0.5	15	-2.0	19	-5.2	27	-6.5	24	-6.1	27	2.3	13
2015	-5.7%	32	-3.7	27	1.0	12	-2.6	24	-15.1	31	-8.1	32	5.6	9

Larry Izzo is the new special teams coach, just in case you thought there weren't enough ex-Patriots around. He has his work cut out for him. ☞ Kick coverage, until exposed so disastrously when the postseason began, was the relative strength of the Texans special teams unit. In the regular season, Houston limited opponents to kick returns worth minus-3.2 points of estimated field-position value. The bigger problem was Nick Novak, who ranked third-worst with minus-3.6 points of gross kickoff value despite not joining the team until Week 4. Novak replaced Randy Bullock, who missed two extra points and a field goal in the Week 3 win against Tampa Bay. He will be competing in camp with 2015 Lou Groza Award winner Ka'imi Fairbairn (UCLA). The change in kickoffs that emphasizes short returns over touchbacks should help Novak, whose leg strength has declined. ☞ Split the blame for punting between Shane Lechler and punt coverage, both below average. ☞ Ball security was an issue at times for rookie Keith Mumphery. He coughed the ball up on one of 14 kick returns and two of 36 punt returns. Sproles Squad rookie Tyler Ervin (San Jose State) may get a shot at the return jobs.

Indianapolis Colts

On June 29, owner Jim Irsay announced the Colts had signed Andrew Luck to the mega-extension we were all waiting for. Funny money of NFL contracts aside, the flip phone-carrying quarterback earned $47 million fully guaranteed, and the deal brought with it pronouncements that June 29 would be remembered as the day Indianapolis locked up their long-term future. June 29 also marked the official end of another era: the era in which general manager Ryan Grigson and head coach Chuck Pagano enjoyed the services of the most heralded quarterback prospect to enter the NFL this millennium for a relative pittance.

2016 was always going to be the year Grigson and Pagano's gravy train ended. Even before the extension, Luck was due to make nearly $17 million, moving him from the ranks of the lowly-paid rookies to a place that was at least above the bar required to keep even a below-average starter from testing the waters of free agency.

The real meaning of this is significant. For the past four seasons, Irsay permitting, Grigson could—and did—annually engage in short-term gambles such as signing older players and paying role players like starters. He worked frantically to maximize the Colts' chances of hoisting the Lombardi Trophy before the second Luck era began. So why the heck is this chapter about a team that could not even top .500 in the worst division in football?

For one thing, they did not have Luck's services for the entire 2015 season. He started just seven games. First he suffered an injury to his throwing shoulder, then he tore rib cartilage (a possible effect of returning too quickly), and eventually he suffered a lacerated kidney and torn abdominal muscles that ended his season after the Colts upset the previously undefeated Broncos.

For another, Luck was generally not a good quarterback in 2015 even when he was on the field. His passing DVOA of -17.5% ranked 32nd among 37 qualifying quarterbacks, sandwiching him between passing legends Blaine Gabbert and Johnny Manziel. He posted an above-average DVOA in just two of those seven starts, against the Broncos and against the Patriots in a game where his offense went nearly 29 minutes from the second to fourth quarters without crossing midfield.

Luck's numbers were down in 2015 across the board. His interception rate, which had been impressively average for a quarterback who spent so much time throwing deep, skyrocketed. His completion percentage was lousy. The deep throws that drove so much of the Colts' offensive success in his first three seasons were repeatedly off-target.

FO writer Cian Fahey charted Luck's 2014 and 2015 seasons for his Film Room column, and the results[1] showed a marked drop-off in Luck's accuracy throwing more than 10 yards downfield, especially to the right side of the field. Overall 72 percent of Luck's downfield throws to the right were on target in 2014, compared to just 54 percent in 2015. The numbers were especially clear on those deep downfield sideline throws where Luck found T.Y. Hilton (mostly) so productively in 2014. Luck was on target on throws more than 20 yards downfield outside the numbers on the right 75 percent of the time (on a whopping 40 attempts) in 2014, compared to just 47 percent in 2015 (on 17 attempts, so he missed more throws despite less than half as many attempts).

Luck's DVOA splits reinforce the idea of a decline in his play. Using our customary designations of Short (5 yards or less), Mid (6 to 15 yards), Deep (16 to 25 yards), and Bomb (26 yards or more), the decline in his performance is clear (Table 1).

Table 1. Luck DVOA Performance by Pass Distance, 2014-2015

2014	Range	2015
13.4%	Short (up to 5)	2.0%
12.3%	Mid (6-15)	-1.2%
53.4%	Deep (16-25)	-54.6%
121.8%	Bomb (26+)	62.3%

The question for all Colts observers—from Irsay, Grigson, and Pagano to the Colts fan standing on Capitol Avenue outside Lucas Oil Stadium to the author tasked with writing a chapter on the team for an NFL preview annual—is how much weight to put on Luck's 2015 season in evaluating his future performance.

---

1 See the full column at http://www.footballoutsiders.com/film-room/2016/film-room-andrew-luck.

2016 Colts Schedule

Week	Opp.	Week	Opp.	Week	Opp.
1	DET	7	at TEN	13	at NYJ (Mon.)
2	at DEN	8	KC	14	HOU
3	SD	9	at GB	15	at MIN
4	at JAC (U.K.)	10	BYE	16	at OAK (Sat.)
5	CHI	11	TEN	17	JAC
6	at HOU	12	PIT (Thu.)		

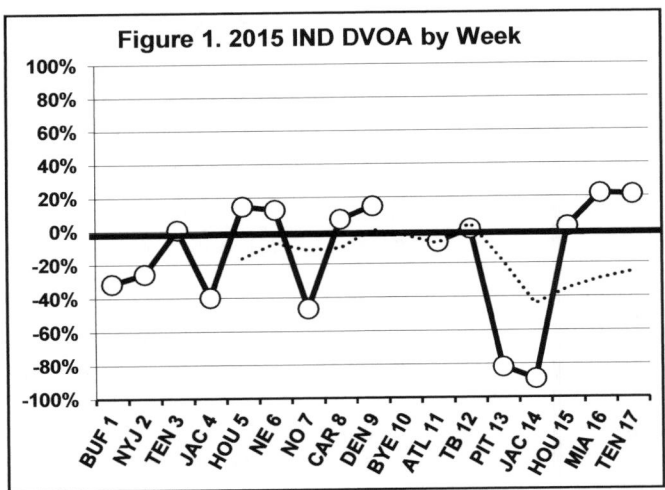

Figure 1. 2015 IND DVOA by Week

After the extension was announced, the answer we got from the troika in charge of the Colts was "very little." Irsay, Grigson, and Pagano seemingly concurred with the outside observers who declared it was easy to see Luck did not look like the Luck we had been used to seeing from the season opener in Buffalo, and those mostly dismal 2015 numbers tell us very little about what Luck will be in 2016 and beyond.

Luck has often been compared to Peyton Manning, for obvious reasons: pedigree (son of an NFL quarterback), draft status (incredibly heralded from early on in his playing career, would likely have been first overall pick if he had come out a year before), and NFL destination (Indianapolis). Especially after last season, though, we should take a step back and reassess that comparison.

Peyton Manning was an incredible quarterback, especially in the regular season, and this was apparent even very early on in his career. Manning was just slightly above average in his rookie year, ranking 18th among quarterbacks with 7.7% passing DVOA, but that was a very strong performance compared to other rookie quarterbacks in the '90s. By his second season, he ranked second in the league in DVOA and DYAR, coming in narrowly behind Kurt Warner of the Greatest Show on Turf Rams. In his third year, he led the league in both categories. Even in his *annus horriblis* when Edgerrin James was injured and the team slumped to 6-10, he still finished in the top eight in both categories. It took until 2015 for him to rank any lower than eighth. Luck has … not been quite the same player (Table 2).

Table 2. Rank by Passing DVOA and DYAR

Manning DVOA	Manning DYAR	Year of Career	Luck DVOA	Luck DYAR
18	12	Year 1	19	19
2	2	Year 2	16	14
1	1	Year 3	11	10
7	6	Year 4	32	33
8	4	Year 5	--	--

That Luck is not (yet?) Manning was not that relevant to the fact of the extension; he was going to get paid, and he was going to get paid *well*, even if his eventual NFL fate is to resemble Eli Manning more than Peyton. The problem Grigson and Pagano have to solve is how to build a team around him.

Thus far, the plan seems to have been for Pagano to talk about running the ball and stopping the run, while Grigson spends draft capital to give Luck weapons in the passing game and more offensive linemen. Since selecting Luck first overall, Grigson has used 15 picks in the top three rounds, 13 in the draft and two in trades for players. Of those 15 picks, ten have been used on offensive players, while just five have been used to buttress the defense.

From at least one perspective, this sort of focus made sense. Our research has shown that offense is much more consistent from season to season than defense, so adding key offensive players tends to create a more consistently good team. Bill Polian built Super Bowl teams and annual contenders in Buffalo and, yes, Manning-era Indianapolis with much the same strategy. Besides, Grigson allocated plenty of those surplus cap dollars to buttress the defense with veteran signings such as D'Qwell Jackson, Trent Cole, Erik Walden, and Mike Adams.

The result of this style of franchise management has been unsurprising: a defense capable of performing competently (the past three seasons, the Colts have ranked 16th, 13th, and 13th again by DVOA) while also leading our age rankings (fourth-oldest in 2013 and the oldest both in 2014 and last season). Eventually those veterans, also including Robert Mathis, will have to be replaced, and the crash when it comes could be harsh. Just ask the Steelers, the former perennially oldest defense in the league, about what happened in 2014.

What ultimately cost the Colts a division title was Luck's lousy 2015 play, plus their inability to win enough games with now-departed backups Matt Hasselbeck and Charlie Whitehurst. The most ignominious defeat was a blown lead at home to the Houston Texans and their fourth-string quarterback. These results raised the obvious question about whether Grigson and/or Pagano should be part of the second Luck era. For most of the season, this seemed very much like an either or neither situation, thanks to a recurring series of organized leaks designed to make one man look good at the expense of the other.

Alternately (sometimes simultaneously) fascinating and incredibly tiresome, the public media war seemed to mostly favor Pagano. The results-oriented business of the NFL meant both men had their jobs on the line, and Pagano in particular seemed headed out the door until a dramatic meeting with Irsay followed by a unity press conference where the top three decision-makers sang kumbaya together. Those who actually lost their jobs included both coordinators, with offensive coordinator and reported Grigson man Pep Hamilton going during the season to be replaced by Pagano man Rob Chudzinski and defensive coordinator Greg Manusky sacked after the season in favor of Pagano's old Baltimore linebackers coach Ted Monachino.

Monachino is largely an unknown, but Pagano remains the dominant defensive voice and any changes to that side of the ball are likely to be tinkering rather than a major overhaul. As for the offense, Chudzinski's best work may have been with the 2007 Cleveland Browns, when Derek Anderson made the Pro Bowl and led the team to a 10-6 mark. That sort of deep pass-oriented scheme fits with what Luck has done best, but it also may play into one of this team's greatest weaknesses.

Quarterback knockdowns often say a lot more about the quarterback and the offensive scheme than they do about the offensive line. Many subjective evaluations say the Colts have had a lousy offensive line for virtually all of Luck's tenure. It is unquestioned that Luck has been sacked and hit a lot over his first four seasons, even after missing over half of 2015.

Improving the offensive line has long been a high priority for Grigson: Hugh Thornton in the third round, Jack Mewhort in the second, and big free-agent contracts to Gosder Cherilus, Donald Thomas, and Todd Herremans (all three of whom are now playing elsewhere). But while everything involving his arm went to pot in 2015, Luck did not go down that much. His adjusted sack rate was 5.4 percent—up a bit from 2014, but below what it was in 2013. Part of the explanation is that his throwing shoulder did not affect his ability to move. Part of it is Luck's size and strength. Part of it may be that Hamilton (fired before Luck's final game, against the Broncos) did at least one of the jobs he was tasked to do. Part of it may be the natural tendency of a young, improvising quarterback like Luck (or Aaron Rodgers or Ben Roethlisberger, to name two successful examples of the type) to take more sacks and hits than a quarterback who gets the ball out more quickly and is exceptional at protecting himself (like Peyton Manning).

Grigson's answer to this problem was the same as it has always been, to throw more resources at the problem. Thus, the Colts selected center Ryan Kelly with their first-round pick in this year's draft, and tackle Le'Raven Clark in the third round. The long-armed Clark is more of a developmental project coming from Texas Tech's unsophisticated passing spread offense, but Kelly is expected to make an immediate impact as a plug-and-play center coming out of Alabama's pro-style system. Nonetheless, as long as Chudzinski's offensive scheme asks Luck to frequently throw the ball downfield, and as long as Luck continues to try to extend plays in search of big gains, he likely will continue to be knocked down as much as or more than any other quarterback in the league regardless of how good Kelly and Clark may be.

If these draft selections did not move the excitement meter for you, well, it was that kind of offseason for the Colts. Their biggest actual decision may have been choosing which tight end to pay. They sensibly opted for Dwayne Allen, the more well-rounded player with an injury history, over Coby Fleener, the receiving threat who was never really that threatening.

But there is no Herremans, no Trent Cole, no Andre Johnson to attract fans and draw attention this presesaon. Instead, the 2016 Colts will look a lot like the 2015 Colts, minus some flotsam and jetsam (Herremans and Johnson the players, rather than the names). The best reasons for optimism are the most obvious. First, they play in the AFC South. Houston, Jacksonville, and Tennessee may be improving, but we still project this to be the worst division in the league. Second, Luck should be healthy. Even if Luck is not Peyton Manning, as he has not been to date, he is the oldest (really!) and most experienced starting quarterback in the AFC South, and we believe he will return to being the best as well.

Being the tallest dwarf may not seem like a great honor. The people of Jacksonville and Nashville, however, might remind you that for some fans it would be enough to reach the NFL's postseason tournament, and that is a much better place to be than picking in the top five of the NFL draft year after year. Sanity has reigned the past couple years, but we do not have to go back too far to see deeply limited and flawed teams making a postseason run to the Super Bowl. Alas, these Colts are probably even more flawed than all of those teams were. Check back next offseason to see if Grigson and Pagano have made any more progress on building a winner while not enjoying a cheap quarterback.

Tom Gower

2015 Colts Stats by Week

Wk	vs.	W-L	PF	PA	YDF	YDA	TO	Total	Off	Def	ST
1	at BUF	L	14	27	304	342	-3	-31%	3%	16%	-18%
2	NYJ	L	7	20	343	344	-4	-26%	-29%	-8%	-5%
3	at TEN	W	35	33	378	433	0	1%	2%	9%	7%
4	JAC	W	16	13	326	431	-2	-40%	-39%	10%	10%
5	at HOU	W	27	20	323	444	2	15%	24%	19%	10%
6	NE	L	27	34	409	417	1	13%	22%	6%	-3%
7	NO	L	21	27	376	449	-2	-47%	-49%	-15%	-12%
8	at CAR	L	26	29	359	379	-1	7%	-19%	-19%	7%
9	DEN	W	27	24	365	309	2	15%	28%	1%	-12%
10	BYE										
11	at ATL	W	24	21	276	375	1	-7%	-36%	-19%	9%
12	TB	W	25	12	336	344	1	1%	-13%	-10%	4%
13	at PIT	L	10	45	240	522	-1	-82%	-67%	17%	2%
14	at JAC	L	16	51	322	380	0	-89%	-49%	24%	-16%
15	HOU	L	10	16	190	305	0	2%	-27%	-14%	15%
16	at MIA	W	18	12	268	361	1	22%	0%	-19%	3%
17	TEN	W	30	24	327	231	0	21%	-13%	-26%	8%

Trends and Splits

	Offense	Rank	Defense	Rank
Total DVOA	-15.6%	30	-2.1%	13
Unadjusted VOA	-16.4%	30	-1.5%	15
Weighted Trend	-19.9%	32	-6.2%	10
Variance	8.0%	22	2.7%	2
Average Opponent	0.2%	18	-1.2%	20
Passing	-6.4%	28	5.4%	12
Rushing	-20.9%	30	-11.8%	16
First Down	-13.6%	29	-5.7%	10
Second Down	-16.7%	27	-3.6%	13
Third Down	-17.3%	26	7.0%	20
First Half	-18.0%	29	-8.5%	10
Second Half	-13.3%	30	4.7%	20
Red Zone	-21.6%	28	-0.6%	15
Late and Close	-22.3%	30	2.4%	22

Five-Year Performance

Year	W-L	Pyth W	Est W	PF	PA	TO	Total	Rk	Off	Rk	Def	Rk	ST	Rk	Off AGL	Rk	Def AGL	Rk	Off Age	Rk	Def Age	Rk	ST Age	Rk
2011	2-14	3.2	3.0	243	430	-12	-32.8%	31	-17.2%	27	9.3%	26	-6.2%	31	37.5	22	47.2	28	27.9	8	26.0	27	25.4	30
2012	11-5	7.2	6.2	357	387	-12	-16.0%	25	-2.9%	18	14.0%	31	0.9%	12	44.4	24	43.1	24	25.9	28	26.6	20	25.2	31
2013	11-5	9.4	9.5	391	336	+13	3.2%	13	4.3%	13	0.9%	16	-0.1%	18	75.5	30	25.2	11	25.8	31	27.7	4	26.0	20
2014	11-5	10.2	8.8	458	369	-5	4.5%	13	-1.1%	17	-2.3%	13	3.3%	8	56.6	29	48.2	23	26.2	28	28.3	1	26.1	12
2015	8-8	6.0	5.5	333	408	-5	-12.9%	23	-15.6%	30	-2.2%	13	0.5%	16	22.0	6	43.1	26	27.1	13	28.6	1	26.3	11

2015 Performance Based on Most Common Personnel Groups

IND Offense					IND Offense vs. Opponents					IND Defense				IND Defense vs. Opponents			
Pers	Freq	Yds	DVOA	Run%	Pers	Freq	Yds	DVOA	Run%	Pers	Freq	Yds	DVOA	Pers	Freq	Yds	DVOA
11	61%	5.3	-5.8%	28%	Base	33%	4.7	-15.6%	46%	Base	55%	5.7	-1.8%	11	39%	6.2	-0.6%
12	24%	5.0	-8.5%	36%	Nickel	55%	5.3	-12.9%	28%	Nickel	33%	5.8	-12.6%	12	35%	5.9	1.4%
13	6%	2.6	-43.2%	68%	Dime+	10%	5.6	19.7%	8%	Dime+	9%	7.6	29.4%	21	9%	5.4	-12.0%
02	2%	4.5	-57.7%	5%	Goal Line	1%	0.4	-107.4%	86%	Goal Line	2%	0.7	18.0%	10	3%	5.5	-4.4%
612	2%	6.8	-0.4%	71%	Big	1%	1.2	-13.8%	78%	Big	1%	2.0	-29.8%	13	3%	5.2	-18.1%
01	2%	5.1	3.3%	0%										22	3%	4.4	-58.2%

Strategic Tendencies

Run/Pass		Rk	Formation		Rk	Pass Rush		Rk	Secondary		Rk	Strategy		Rk
Runs, first half	37%	19	Form: Single Back	76%	16	Rush 3	8.4%	10	4 DB	55%	2	Play action	16%	25
Runs, first down	43%	26	Form: Empty Back	11%	6	Rush 4	53.1%	28	5 DB	33%	28	Avg Box (Off)	6.25	14
Runs, second-long	24%	26	Pers: 3+ WR	66%	10	Rush 5	28.6%	7	6+ DB	9%	18	Avg Box (Def)	6.37	5
Runs, power sit.	47%	27	Pers: 2+ TE/6+ OL	36%	14	Rush 6+	9.9%	8	CB by Sides	85%	9	Offensive Pace	29.63	11
Runs, behind 2H	20%	28	Pers: 6+ OL	4%	13	Sacks by LB	60.0%	4	S/CB Cover Ratio	25%	9	Defensive Pace	28.67	2
Pass, ahead 2H	52%	8	Shotgun/Pistol	60%	20	Sacks by DB	5.7%	20	DB Blitz	9%	19	Go for it on 4th	0.63	30

Though the Indianapolis quarterbacks had less impressive arms than in recent years, the receivers had better hands. The Colts ranked 30th dropping 5.5 percent of passes in 2014 but improved to dropping just 3.0 percent of passes (fourth) in 2015. ☞ The Colts' offense was at its worst when the game was tight. Indy finished dead last in offensive DVOA when tied or trailing by one score, and 30th in late-and-close situations. ☞ The offense compiled a -20.1% DVOA out of empty formations last year, worst in the league. ☞ Although the Indy defense was no better with five pass-rushers than it was with four, it allowed a league-low 2.6 yards per pass when sending a big blitz of six or more. ☞ Despite the strong season from Vontae Davis, Colts opponents threw 27.8 percent of passes to their No. 1 receivers, second only behind Buffalo. Colts opponents only threw 12.5 percent of passes to players we designated as "other wide receivers," which ranked last in the league. ☞ The Colts ended up with the best defensive DVOA in the league against "short middle" passes, although they were below-average against passes on both the left and right sides. ☞ No defense saw fewer shotgun formations than the Colts, who faced it on only 53 percent of their snaps last season. ☞ The Colts benefited from 150 opponent penalties and 1,168 opponent penalty yards, both second in the league behind Arizona.

Passing

Player	DYAR	DVOA	Plays	NtYds	Avg	YAC	C%	TD	Int
A.Luck	-126	-17.5%	306	1783	5.8	4.3	55.9%	15	12
M.Hasselbeck*	-41	-13.4%	273	1588	5.8	5.0	61.3%	9	5
C.Whitehurst*	-99	-58.4%	37	122	3.3	5.8	50.0%	0	1
J.Freeman*	-70	-48.0%	29	142	4.9	4.5	53.6%	1	1
R.Lindley*	28	27.4%	10	58	5.8	1.8	60.0%	1	0

Rushing

Player	DYAR	DVOA	Plays	Yds	Avg	TD	Fum	Suc
F.Gore	0	-8.6%	260	968	3.7	6	4	40%
A.Bradshaw*	-38	-36.0%	31	85	2.7	0	0	32%
A.Luck	59	31.2%	26	202	7.8	0	1	-
J.Robinson*	-34	-56.1%	17	39	2.3	0	1	24%
D.Herron*	5	-1.0%	14	42	3.0	0	0	50%
Z.Tipton*	-7	-41.0%	5	20	4.0	0	0	20%
R.Turbin	45	13.5%	50	199	4.0	1	0	48%
J.Todman	6	34.9%	4	22	5.5	0	0	75%

Receiving

Player	DYAR	DVOA	Plays	Ctch	Yds	Y/C	YAC	TD	C%
T.Y.Hilton	52	-7.7%	134	69	1124	16.3	5.5	5	51%
D.Moncrief	110	1.1%	105	64	733	11.5	4.2	6	61%
A.Johnson*	27	-8.2%	77	41	503	12.3	3.6	4	53%
P.Dorsett	-59	-32.4%	39	18	225	12.5	3.3	1	46%
G.Whalen*	54	14.1%	26	19	205	10.8	2.7	1	73%
R.Turbin	-26	-126.4%	7	5	15	3.0	3.8	0	71%
C.Fleener*	-49	-15.9%	84	54	491	9.1	3.3	3	64%
D.Allen	-48	-31.4%	29	16	109	6.8	3.1	1	55%
J.Doyle	-1	-7.9%	14	12	72	6.0	4.7	1	86%
F.Gore	-60	-32.1%	58	34	267	7.9	8.0	1	59%
A.Bradshaw*	43	34.4%	14	10	64	6.4	5.4	3	71%
Z.Tipton*	-6	-27.5%	8	5	57	11.4	10.0	0	63%
D.Herron*	1	-10.5%	7	6	27	4.5	4.2	0	86%
J.Robinson*	12	16.1%	6	6	33	5.5	6.2	0	100%
R.Turbin	-31	-89.2%	10	7	23	3.3	3.7	0	70%

Offensive Line

Player	Pos	Age	GS	Snaps	Pen	Sk	Pass	Run	Player	Pos	Age	GS	Snaps	Pen	Sk	Pass	Run
Jack Mewhort	LG	25	16/16	1104	6	1.0	5.0	4.0	Jonotthan Harrison	C	25	16/9	671	2	0.0	1.0	0.0
Joe Reitz	RT	31	16/14	950	9	3.0	5.0	2.0	Khaled Holmes*	C	26	9/7	489	3	0.5	3.5	1.0
Anthony Castonzo	LT	28	13/13	897	9	2.5	5.5	1.0	Denzelle Good	OT	25	6/4	274	3	2.0	2.0	0.0
Hugh Thornton	RG	25	13/12	804	6	1.0	3.0	3.0	Lance Louis*	LG	31	11/3	238	1	0.0	3.0	0.0

Year	Yards	ALY	Rank	Power	Rank	Stuff	Rank	2nd Lev	Rank	Open Field	Rank	Sacks	ASR	Rank	Press	Rank	F-Start	Cont.
2013	3.96	3.89	15	65%	15	18%	10	1.09	19	0.63	21	32	5.6%	6	27.0%	24	8	29
2014	3.91	3.94	16	52%	31	19%	15	1.20	13	0.46	29	29	4.8%	7	22.6%	12	20	19
2015	3.52	3.47	27	60%	24	23%	24	0.99	29	0.48	28	37	6.1%	16	25.8%	18	12	26

2015 ALY by direction: Left End 2.44 (32) Left Tackle 3.11 (26) Mid/Guard 3.59 (27) Right Tackle 4.2 (5) Right End 3.28 (19)

The left side is stable with Anthony Castonzo at tackle and Jack Mewhort at guard. First-round rookie Ryan Kelly will start at center immediately. Right guard and right tackle are TBD, and new offensive line coach Joe Philbin has his work cut out for him. ☞ The first-team guard and tackle in the offseason were Jonotthan Harrison, who was much better at center in his second season, and veteran Joe Reitz. Missing in the offseason were Hugh Thornton, definitely the favorite at right guard, and Denzelle Good, who they would probably prefer to start at right tackle. ☞ Third-round pick Le'Raven Clark (Texas Tech) could figure into the tackle mix, but probably not until later in the season, while fifth-round pick Joe Haeg (North Dakota State) provides more depth. ☞ The Colts' offensive line stats were better with Andrew Luck in the lineup. The team had a 5.5 percent adjusted sack rate and 3.69 adjusted line yards per carry with Luck starting, and 6.7 percent adjusted sack rate and 3.33 adjusted line yards per carry otherwise.

Defensive Front Seven

Defensive Line	Age	Pos	G	Snaps	Plays	TmPct	Rk	Stop	Dfts	BTkl	Runs	St%	Rk	RuYd	Rk	Sack	Hit	Hur	Dsrpt
						Overall						vs. Run				Pass Rush			
Kendall Langford	30	DE	16	851	41	4.9%	43	37	15	4	30	90%	6	1.9	31	7.0	10	17.5	3
David Parry	24	DT	16	657	31	3.7%	63	24	6	4	29	79%	33	2.1	41	1.0	2	2.0	0
Henry Anderson	25	DE	9	450	33	7.0%	17	28	9	0	29	86%	12	1.2	4	1.0	3	10.0	2
Billy Winn*	27	DE	12	331	14	2.2%	--	9	2	3	12	67%	--	2.8	--	0.0	1	5.0	0
Zach Kerr	26	DT	12	320	30	4.8%	--	21	4	1	28	68%	--	2.6	--	0.0	3	3.5	2
T.Y. McGill	24	DT	12	222	12	1.9%	--	9	4	0	8	63%	--	2.8	--	3.0	3	3.0	1

Edge Rushers	Age	Pos	G	Snaps	Plays	TmPct	Rk	Stop	Dfts	BTkl	Runs	St%	Rk	RuYd	Rk	Sack	Hit	Hur	Dsrpt
						Overall						vs. Run				Pass Rush			
Erik Walden	31	OLB	15	787	42	5.3%	39	29	19	6	26	73%	51	2.4	52	3.0	10	17.0	0
Robert Mathis	34	OLB	15	543	19	2.4%	92	17	11	2	10	100%	1	1.3	16	7.0	9	12.0	0
Trent Cole	34	OLB	14	529	34	4.6%	51	29	13	5	23	91%	4	1.1	11	3.0	6	14.0	2
Jonathan Newsome*	25	OLB	14	346	20	2.7%	--	14	4	7	16	69%	--	5.5	--	1.0	1	1.5	0

Linebackers	Age	Pos	G	Snaps	Plays	TmPct	Rk	Stop	Dfts	BTkl	Runs	St%	Rk	RuYd	Rk	Sack	Hit	Hur	Tgts	Suc%	Rk	AdjYd	Rk	PD	Int
						Overall						vs. Run				Pass Rush			vs. Pass						
D'Qwell Jackson	33	ILB	16	1090	159	19.0%	2	92	22	17	109	66%	37	2.9	21	3.0	0	9	44	57%	33	5.2	20	8	1
Jerrell Freeman*	30	ILB	13	753	114	16.7%	9	79	17	4	83	72%	14	3.7	49	3.0	4	5.5	21	78%	4	2.6	1	2	1

Year	Yards	ALY	Rank	Power	Rank	Stuff	Rank	2nd Level	Rank	Open Field	Rank	Sacks	ASR	Rank	Press	Rank
2013	4.25	4.30	28	53%	5	16%	26	1.18	24	0.58	14	42	7.6%	8	27.6%	4
2014	4.20	4.05	22	67%	20	20%	15	1.23	23	0.68	15	41	7.3%	9	22.7%	24
2015	4.16	3.75	17	59%	9	20%	18	1.05	9	1.00	27	35	5.7%	28	26.5%	11
2015 ALY by direction:		Left End 3.54 (17)		Left Tackle 4.26 (24)			Mid/Guard 3.97 (19)			Right Tackle 3.68 (16)			Right End 2.76 (7)			

A pair of rookies from Stanford helped create a much better defensive line, at least until one of them went down injured. Third-round pick Henry Anderson ranked seventh in the league in run defeats per snap, but missed the offseason recovering from a Week 9 knee injury. Fifth-round pick David Parry put up 3-4 nose tackle-type numbers. ☞ The Colts are still waiting for big 2014 free-agent acquisition Arthur Jones, who played for Pagano in Baltimore, to play more than a couple games without suffering an ankle injury. Kendall Langford cannot do it all himself, and should not be asked to. (Late note: the NFL announced in late July that Jones will be suspended four games for PED violations. So hey, Kendall, you just go ahead and keep doing it all yourself.) ☞ Jonathan Newsome made our Top 25 Prospects list last year, but did little on the field and was released after a February arrest. Oops. ☞ 2013 first-round pick Bjoern Werner was released after totaling just 6.5 sacks in three seasons. ☞ Trent Cole, Robert Mathis, and Erik Walden are more names than forces at this point, and there is no obvious up-and-coming young talent to support them. Indy only drafted one pass-rusher in April, seventh-round longshot Trevor Bates out of Maine. ☞ The candidates to replace Jerrell Freeman include rookie Antonio Morrison (a fifth-round pick from Florida who is more likely D'Qwell Jackson's eventual replacement) and a trio of 2015 backups: Nate Irving, Josh McNary, and Sio Moore.

Defensive Secondary

Secondary	Age	Pos	G	Snaps	Plays	TmPct	Rk	Stop	Dfts	BTkl	Runs	St%	Rk	RuYd	Rk	Tgts	Tgt%	Rk	Dist	Suc%	Rk	AdjYd	Rk	PD	Int
						Overall						vs. Run				vs. Pass									
Dwight Lowery*	30	FS	16	1088	84	10.0%	33	36	15	10	30	40%	36	8.1	50	39	8.6%	50	12.1	59%	31	7.9	46	9	4
Vontae Davis	28	CB	16	1048	64	7.6%	54	33	14	3	11	36%	47	9.5	59	81	18.8%	34	14.7	60%	9	5.2	5	15	4
Mike Adams	35	SS	13	830	80	11.7%	20	24	13	10	36	33%	46	9.8	57	30	8.8%	53	14.8	45%	60	10.5	64	6	5
Greg Toler*	31	CB	10	684	60	11.5%	4	19	9	3	7	14%	71	15.3	74	76	27.2%	73	14.3	52%	37	9.5	70	9	0
Darius Butler	30	CB	14	576	54	7.4%	59	20	12	7	10	30%	54	14.8	73	53	22.5%	56	13.0	43%	70	10.4	73	4	1
Jalil Brown	29	CB	8	311	25	6.0%	--	13	4	5	8	50%	--	7.5	--	30	23.6%	--	12.2	47%	--	9.7	--	3	0
Clayton Geathers	24	SS	15	271	29	3.7%	--	12	8	1	9	67%	--	6.9	--	14	12.6%	--	13.5	55%	--	8.1	--	0	0
Patrick Robinson	29	CB	16	692	57	7.5%	57	20	8	6	18	28%	59	6.6	33	47	18.8%	37	9.2	58%	13	4.9	3	5	1

Year	Pass D Rank	vs. #1 WR	Rk	vs. #2 WR	Rk	vs. Other WR	Rk	vs. TE	Rk	vs. RB	Rk
2013	13	-6.5%	14	7.6%	19	13.4%	26	17.7%	26	-0.9%	15
2014	10	-11.8%	9	-7.4%	11	-2.6%	14	16.1%	26	29.0%	31
2015	12	-4.8%	11	-10.5%	11	23.4%	30	6.5%	20	-7.9%	11

Vontae Davis is the only corner to rank in the top ten in adjusted success rate in each of the past three seasons. ☞ Patrick Robinson is the best bet to start opposite him, even though the former first-round pick of the Saints saw his career resurgence mostly come out of the slot in San Diego. ☞ Like Robinson, Darius Butler is best suited for the slot. Unlike Robinson, the Colts seem to want him to play there. ☞ 2015 third-round pick D'Joun Smith could challenge at least Butler, if not Robinson, for a role if not for his membership in the offseason injury brigade. He's still recovering from a knee injury that limited him to four short appearances as a rookie. ☞ The resurgence of Mike Adams from journeyman to Pro Bowler continued, as he made his second straight trip to the NFL's increasingly meaningless postseason exhibition game. ☞ Clayton Geathers seemed like Adams' eventual replacement as a strong safety, but will instead start next to him in place of the departed Dwight Lowery. Geathers was dynamic both filling in for Adams and as a dime linebacker as a rookie, and may be asked to fill the dime linebacker role again given how inside linebacker shakes out. ☞ Second-round pick T.J. Green (Clemson) should eventually be the free safety. He brings great speed (4.34 40), limited experience (he was a receiver his first two seasons at Clemson, and played almost exclusively deep safety), and questionable tackling (17 missed tackles in 2015, per NFL.com).

Special Teams

Year	DVOA	Rank	FG/XP	Rank	Net Kick	Rank	Kick Ret	Rank	Net Punt	Rank	Punt Ret	Rank	Hidden	Rank
2013	-0.1%	18	2.9	12	4.4	9	-3.3	21	-3.9	26	-0.6	16	6.2	7
2014	3.3%	8	8.4	4	4.9	9	0.4	14	11.2	6	-8.5	31	2.4	12
2015	0.5%	16	4.5	8	4.8	5	-1.2	18	-0.1	19	-5.6	26	6.9	6

Fifteen of Adam Vinatieri's 27 made field goals from 50-plus have come in the past four seasons, and he connected on 4-of-5 last year. ☞ Only seven of Pat McAfee's 74 non-onside kickoffs were returned. He ranked second in the league in gross kickoff value (4.6 estimated points of field position) and third in gross punt value (11.5 points). However, Indianapolis had one of the league's worst punt coverage units, cancelling out McAfee's ability to boom punts when the offense was pinned back. McAfee averaged a league-high 53.4 gross yards per punt when punting from behind the 20 (NFL average: 49.0 yards). ☞ Quan Bray eventually stabilized both return jobs and was above-average but not spectacular at both of them.

Jacksonville Jaguars

2015 record: 5-11	Total DVOA: -16.0% (25th)	2016 Mean Projection: 6.9 wins	On the Clock (0-4): 18%
Pythagorean Wins: 6.2 (23rd)	Offense: -5.4% (21st)	Postseason Odds: 26.2%	Mediocrity (5-7): 42%
Snap-Weighted Age: 25.9 (31st)	Defense: 9.7% (26th)	Super Bowl Odds: 1.9%	Playoff Contender (8-10): 31%
Average Opponent: -6.6% (28th)	Special Teams: -0.9% (20th)	Proj. Avg. Opponent: -0.7% (18th)	Super Bowl Contender (11+): 9%

2015: The offense put up big fantasy numbers chasing after the huge leads the defense kept handing opponents.

2016: So much more reason for promise, but still plenty of weaknesses to overcome.

NFL owners tend to treat head coaches and general managers like clay pigeons. They release them into the world and give them a moment to get into the air before abruptly shooting them out of the sky. Then they line up the next option and treat them with the same short leash. It's why only six teams have not replaced their head coach since 2010. In that same time, 12 teams have hired one new head coach, seven teams have hired two, and six teams have hired three. The Cleveland Browns have replaced their head coach *four* separate times.

But Jacksonville owner Shad Khan is proving to be an exception. Khan has been an NFL owner since 2011, and even though he has already made two head-coaching changes over that time, he is showing the kind of patience that is scarce in today's NFL.

Khan wouldn't have been criticized by anyone had he fired head coach Gus Bradley and general manager Dave Caldwell after the 2015 season. Bradley and Caldwell had guided the team to its third consecutive third-place finish in the lowly AFC South, finishing 5-11 in 2015, 3-13 in 2014, and 4-12 in 2013. Although there were flashes of potential on offense last season, the only real justification to keep Bradley was continuity on the defensive side of the ball. Bradley came over from the Seattle Seahawks, where he had been the defensive coordinator for three seasons. While the Seahawks have continued to be a dominant defensive unit under Pete Carroll, Bradley's presence in Jacksonville has impacted the Jaguars about as much as his loss has hurt Seattle.

Bradley inherited a bad defense when he took over in 2013. The unit had just finished 28th by DVOA while relying on too many declining veterans. Bradley essentially had a clean slate to work from. He could build a defense from scratch the way his former boss, Carroll, had done in Seattle. While Bradley attempted to use the same schematic principles as Carroll, the acquisition and development skills of the staff in Jacksonville haven't been anywhere close to those in Seattle. The Jaguars defense hasn't ranked higher than 20th in DVOA since Bradley took over, and actually declined to 26th in the league last season.

The Jaguars' main issue on defense has always been that they are a reactive unit. In Seattle, Pete Carroll can rely so heavily on Cover-3 as his base because of the level of execution he gets from his talented personnel. Playing Cover-3 as often as Seattle does should expose your defense because the offense knows what spots on the field to attack and when to attack them. Seattle's defense is so aggressive and so precisely executed that the unit becomes proactive. Carroll is going to run the same coverage over and over, yet in spite of that, his defense is still going to dictate what you do because of how well they execute. From their front four all the way back to Earl Thomas, everyone on the Seahawks defense is tightening windows and rushing the opposition into mistakes. In Jacksonville, the Jaguars have tried to emulate the Seahawks approach with inadequate players.

Teams that have been as bad as the Jaguars have been don't just have one or two issues that need to be corrected. However, the two main issues that have confronted the Jaguars have been at free safety and middle linebacker.

Jonathan Cyprien has yet to live up to his potential as the 33rd overall selection in the 2013 draft. He misses too many tackles to be valuable no matter where he lines up on the field (16 last season, 17 the year before). Cyprien is at his most detrimental when playing free safety, especially as the single-high option in Cover-3 or Cover-1 looks. The Jaguars signed Tashaun Gipson in free agency so they no longer have to rely on Cyprien as their last line of defense. Despite suffering a torn ACL two years ago, Gipson has been a very impressive defender for the Browns over the past three seasons. His 21 pass deflections and 13 interceptions stand out, but those statistics are just a product of the consistently intelligent way he plays the game. Gipson understands positioning and how to diagnose plays as they develop in front of him, while also boasting the ball skills and range to take advantage of those traits. He is the type of defensive back who will intimidate quarterbacks with his presence while upholding the integrity of the defense's design by staying true to his assignment.

Gipson is not the only reason the Jaguars secondary should be dramatically improved in 2016. Davon House was very impressive after Jacksonville signed him away from the Green Bay Packers last year. House was lit up by a few receivers, but the yards he gave up weren't always indicative of the coverage he played. The veteran will start in 2016 across from rookie Jalen Ramsey. Ramsey was very popular with online draftniks, who were surprised to see him fall to the Jaguars with the No. 5 selection. Ramsey's athletic testing was phenomenal and his tape suggested he could be a top

2016 Jaguars Schedule

Week	Opp.	Week	Opp.	Week	Opp.
1	GB	7	OAK	13	DEN
2	at SD	8	at TEN (Thu.)	14	MIN
3	BAL	9	at KC	15	at HOU
4	IND (U.K.)	10	HOU	16	TEN (Sat.)
5	BYE	11	at DET	17	at IND
6	at CHI	12	at BUF		

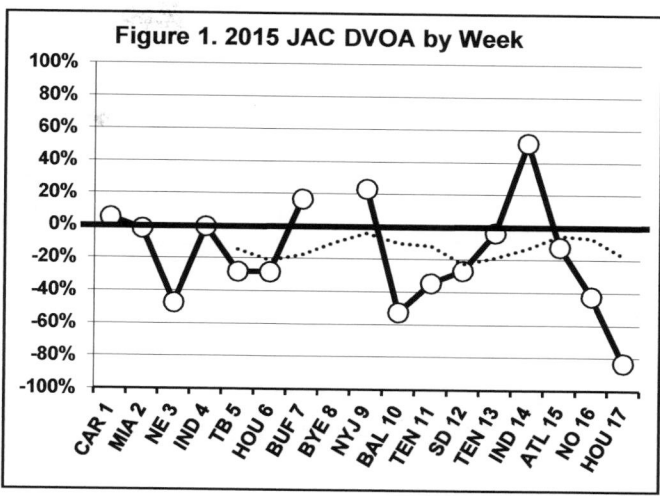

Figure 1. 2015 JAC DVOA by Week

prospect at cornerback or safety. The former Florida State defender suffered a meniscus tear almost immediately after being drafted, but he is expected to return in time for Week 1. Ramsey and House are long, impressive athletes who can disrupt receivers at the line of scrimmage and at the catch point. They should make for an effective pair in a Cover-3 heavy scheme. That said, Prince Amukamara can argue that he is the best cornerback on the roster. In fact, Amukamara can argue he is the best cornerback in the division. Amukamara only finds himself as the nickelback in Jacksonville, on a one-year, $5 million prove-it deal, because his career has been hindered by injuries. He started only 18 games over his last two seasons with the Giants and is looking for the opportunity to prove his worth.

Like the secondary, the linebacker position also has some promising young talent—but there's also much more reason for concern. Paul Posluszny has been the Jaguars' starting middle linebacker for the past five seasons. He has always received plaudits for his ability to consistently rack up tackles, and even made the Pro Bowl in 2013. However, Posluszny's reputation has always been more notable than his actual impact on the field. Posluszny epitomizes what is wrong with the Jaguars defense. He is a reactive player who racks up his production after the offense has already gained what it wants to gain. In 2015, Posluszny played relatively well against the run. His average play against a run gave up 2.6 yards, which ranked seventh among linebackers, while his stop rate was 68 percent, ranking 25th in the league. However, Posluszny was a major liability against the pass. He ranked fourth in the league with 62 tackles after a pass completion, but only 27 percent of those plays counted as stops, giving him the worst figure for a linebacker who had at least 40 tackles after a completion. And Posluszny's 2015 season was actually a bit of a departure from previous years: he has regularly rated worse against the run while remaining just as ineffective against the pass.

You can't afford to rely on a clean-up linebacker like Posluszny in a Cover-3 defense. He will be asked to play in too much space over the middle of the field where opponents can easily attack him in the passing game. Last year, the Jaguars ranked dead last in defensive DVOA on passes listed in the "short middle" of the field. Posluszny's inability to be effective in this role led many to identify Myles Jack as the ideal pick for the Jaguars in the first round of the 2016 draft. In an ideal turn of events, the Jaguars were able to draft both Ramsey and Jack when the latter fell into the second round because of a meniscus injury.

Jack's meniscus problem is more disturbing than Ramsey's. Reports before the draft suggested that Jack's knee will steadily deteriorate and eventually require microfracture surgery to essentially rebuild the cartilage. Those long-term health concerns were severe enough to drop him out of the first round, but his talent was worthy of a top-five pick. And the short-term concerns were clearly overstated, as Jack did not require postseason surgery and was on the field as a full participant at OTAs.

Jack is the antithesis of Posluszny. He excels in space, showing off great athleticism and an understanding of coverages to play with anticipation. He is a proactive defender who won't be repeatedly manipulated by opposing quarterbacks or exposed by tight ends and receivers over the middle of the field. In college, Jack could even line up in press-man against slot receivers, turning to run with them through their routes downfield. Jack is the natural heir to Posluszny, someone who could immediately replace him if the coaching staff shows enough trust in a rookie over a favored veteran.

Even if Posluszny holds onto his middle linebacker spot in the Jaguars base defense—something he is expected to do—Jack and Telvin Smith could take away a huge percentage of his snaps by playing ahead of him in nickel packages. Smith is entering his third year and emerging into one of the better coverage linebackers in the league. He, Jack, and Amukamara, with Gipson behind them, would offer the Jaguars the kind of proactive, intimidating spine that their defense hasn't seen for a very long time.

The Jaguars invested heavily in every level of their defense this offseason. They project to have at least five new starters, with more new additions filling significant roles off the bench. But on the other side of the ball, the Jaguars only added pieces to the periphery of their foundation this offseason: offensive lineman Kelvin Beachum and running back Chris Ivory. And while the offense was better than the defense last year, it still needs to take significant steps forward for the Jaguars to make their first postseason appearance since 2007.

Beachum was signed to compete with Luke Joeckel for the starting left tackle spot, and he was an effective starter in Pittsburgh before tearing his ACL midway through last season. Ivory should act as the goal-line back, a role the Jaguars were reluctant to use T.J. Yeldon in last season. Yeldon only scored two touchdowns last year, partly because he was limited to only 24 carries in the red zone. Of those carries, 10 were within 10 yards of the end zone and only six were within 5 yards of the end zone. As a contrast, Ivory carried the ball for the Jets 39 times in the red zone, scoring five touchdowns on 18 carries within 5 yards of the end zone alone.

Twenty teams had more red zone runs than the Jaguars last year, but only seven teams had more red zone plays. Blake Bortles was the big benefactor, throwing 27 of his 35 touchdowns on red zone plays last year.

Bortles improved in his second NFL season, but needs to take another step forward in 2016. He has proven that he can make big plays and create outside the pocket once the play breaks down, but he hasn't shown any consistency in his accuracy or decision-making. The Jaguars offense led the league in explosive plays: they had 80 plays that gained 20 or more yards, tying the New Orleans Saints for the most passing plays of that kind. Unfortunately, those big plays were offset by too much inefficiency, mostly stemming from the quarterback position. For the second season of his career, Bortles failed to complete more than 59 percent of his passes. Completing fewer than 59 percent of your passes isn't a major issue if you can keep your average yards per attempt high enough to offset it. Yet despite all of the big plays, Bortles still only averaged 7.3 yards per attempt, 15th among quarterbacks with at least 300 attempts. He was also sacked a league-leading 51 times while throwing a league-leading 18 interceptions. If Bortles can correct these problems, he can help the offense make huge strides forward because a large percentage of the sacks were his fault—we charted only 15 of these sacks as blown blocks, or 29 percent compared to the NFL average of 43 percent— and a large number of his interceptions were a result of bad decisions.

If Bortles can refine his craft to the point that his flaws are only hindrances and not fatal, the Jaguars passing game has the potential to be one of the best in the league. Allen Robinson and Allen Hurns established themselves as one of, if not the best, starting receiving tandems in the NFL last year. The duo showed off the ability to dominate defensive backs at the catch point or take advantage of space they were given for big plays while running precise, strong routes against physical or soft coverage. Hurns and Robinson are both complete-package receivers who don't require great service to be productive. Pairing the two together makes it very difficult for opposing defenses to come to the line of scrimmage without offering up an immediate matchup advantage. Robinson and Hurns were supposed to be complemented by the team's marquee free-agent addition from the 2015 offseason, Julius Thomas. Alas, Thomas was injured before he ever played a game for the Jaguars and never looked healthy at any point in the season. Thomas was supposed to be a vertical receiving threat who could be moved around the field, and instead his stomach bloated to the point that he looked more suited to act as an in-line blocker. Lastly, and not to be overlooked, Rashad Greene and Marqise Lee are two very talented slot receivers who could really contribute if they can develop consistency catching the ball.

Three consecutive years picking in the top five of the draft has allowed the Jaguars to build a stacked roster. Now Bradley has to put that talent in position to flourish. He has to structure his rebuilt defense so that it can be successful immediately, while keeping Blake Bortles' development moving in the right direction. Our statistical forecast expects regression from Bortles, a big reason why the Jaguars have the lowest mean win projection in a tightly-packed AFC South. Good coaching can prevent that from happening.

It's hard to know if stability comes from success or if success comes from stability. No team has ever found success by changing regimes every other season, but that doesn't mean that Khan's patience will pay off. Khan risks falling into the same trap that the Rams organization has fallen into with Jeff Fisher, sticking too long with a coach who has never repaid that faith. 2016 should be the decisive year for Bradley and Caldwell. Anything less than a winning season should put their regime under massive scrutiny.

Cian Fahey

2015 Jaguars Stats by Week

Wk	vs.	W-L	PF	PA	YDF	YDA	TO	Total	Off	Def	ST
1	CAR	L	9	20	265	263	-2	5%	-10%	-31%	-16%
2	MIA	W	23	20	396	386	0	-2%	6%	11%	3%
3	at NE	L	17	51	293	471	-1	-47%	-4%	44%	1%
4	at IND	L	13	16	431	326	2	-1%	5%	-10%	-16%
5	at TB	L	31	38	325	369	-2	-28%	9%	26%	-11%
6	HOU	L	20	31	394	382	-3	-28%	-1%	21%	-6%
7	vs. BUF (UK)	W	34	31	295	375	3	17%	-10%	-32%	-6%
8	BYE										
9	at NYJ	L	23	28	436	290	-4	23%	10%	-14%	0%
10	at BAL	W	22	20	258	397	3	-53%	-34%	13%	-6%
11	TEN	W	19	13	308	316	-1	-35%	-32%	20%	18%
12	SD	L	25	31	420	369	-1	-27%	-2%	21%	-4%
13	at TEN	L	39	42	383	467	1	-4%	31%	33%	-2%
14	IND	W	51	16	380	322	0	52%	16%	-14%	22%
15	ATL	L	17	23	370	328	0	-12%	-6%	6%	0%
16	at NO	L	27	38	412	537	-2	-42%	3%	49%	4%
17	at HOU	L	6	30	215	402	-3	-83%	-83%	5%	4%

Trends and Splits

	Offense	Rank	Defense	Rank
Total DVOA	-5.4%	21	9.7%	26
Unadjusted VOA	-3.9%	21	6.8%	27
Weighted Trend	-8.6%	23	11.2%	27
Variance	6.8%	18	5.9%	23
Average Opponent	1.5%	22	-3.3%	31
Passing	5.6%	20	26.8%	31
Rushing	-17.4%	28	-11.7%	17
First Down	-11.2%	27	-8.1%	7
Second Down	7.0%	13	11.0%	28
Third Down	-14.1%	25	43.7%	32
First Half	-13.8%	25	14.7%	31
Second Half	3.4%	15	4.4%	19
Red Zone	-9.4%	22	28.9%	30
Late and Close	-12.4%	24	-1.3%	19

Five-Year Performance

Year	W-L	Pyth W	Est W	PF	PA	TO	Total	Rk	Off	Rk	Def	Rk	ST	Rk	Off AGL	Rk	Def AGL	Rk	Off Age	Rk	Def Age	Rk	ST Age	Rk
2011	5-11	5.3	5.5	243	329	+5	-17.4%	27	-26.5%	31	-11.3%	5	-2.2%	26	23.5	12	52.8	29	26.2	28	26.9	18	26.5	8
2012	2-14	3.3	2.7	255	444	-3	-33.0%	31	-18.4%	28	11.7%	28	-3.0%	25	63.7	30	36.2	22	26.5	20	27.0	14	25.8	23
2013	4-12	3.1	3.2	247	449	-6	-38.2%	32	-29.8%	32	10.9%	28	2.5%	9	47.3	24	26.8	14	26.6	20	26.2	23	24.7	32
2014	3-13	3.6	3.3	249	412	-6	-29.5%	32	-24.3%	31	1.5%	20	-3.6%	26	33.5	19	44.3	22	24.7	32	26.1	27	25.5	30
2015	5-11	6.2	5.8	376	448	-10	-16.0%	25	-5.4%	21	9.7%	26	-0.9%	20	25.7	12	43.2	27	25.6	30	26.4	22	25.4	29

2015 Performance Based on Most Common Personnel Groups

JAC Offense

Pers	Freq	Yds	DVOA	Run%
11	54%	5.8	2.2%	19%
12	37%	5.8	-0.3%	43%
13	6%	4.1	-31.7%	59%
23	1%	-0.2	-72.0%	85%
02	1%	11.8	102.6%	0%
22	1%	2.9	-67.7%	75%

JAC Offense vs. Opponents

Pers	Freq	Yds	DVOA	Run%
Base	34%	5.4	-8.7%	50%
Nickel	50%	6.0	9.3%	25%
Dime+	14%	5.6	-10.8%	1%
Goal Line	1%	-0.3	-77.6%	86%
Big	1%	1.2	-62.7%	67%

JAC Defense

Pers	Freq	Yds	DVOA
Base	39%	5.1	-8.5%
Nickel	55%	6.2	19.1%
Dime+	4%	6.6	79.4%
Goal Line	1%	0.7	33.4%

JAC Defense vs. Opponents

Pers	Freq	Yds	DVOA
11	47%	6.4	28.8%
12	23%	5.7	-7.5%
21	8%	4.3	-26.5%
13	4%	7.3	39.2%
612	3%	4.5	3.0%
621	3%	4.1	-28.6%

Strategic Tendencies

Run/Pass		Rk	Formation		Rk	Pass Rush		Rk	Secondary		Rk	Strategy		Rk
Runs, first half	34%	31	Form: Single Back	88%	2	Rush 3	2.8%	28	4 DB	39%	8	Play action	15%	29
Runs, first down	36%	32	Form: Empty Back	6%	20	Rush 4	68.9%	10	5 DB	55%	15	Avg Box (Off)	6.26	13
Runs, second-long	36%	6	Pers: 3+ WR	55%	21	Rush 5	23.2%	14	6+ DB	4%	25	Avg Box (Def)	6.36	7
Runs, power sit.	54%	21	Pers: 2+ TE/6+ OL	45%	4	Rush 6+	5.1%	21	CB by Sides	70%	23	Offensive Pace	29.50	10
Runs, behind 2H	20%	27	Pers: 6+ OL	0%	31	Sacks by LB	13.9%	27	S/CB Cover Ratio	22%	18	Defensive Pace	29.11	4
Pass, ahead 2H	47%	14	Shotgun/Pistol	61%	19	Sacks by DB	16.7%	4	DB Blitz	10%	16	Go for it on 4th	1.00	14

Jacksonville had a reputation for big plays, but was essentially a boom-and-bust offense. The Jaguars finished in the bottom 10 in yards, turnovers, three-and-outs, plays, and time of possession per drive. ☞ The offense was generally better through the air than on the ground, but not on first downs. Jacksonville had the league's worst first-down passing DVOA (-12.5%). ☞ Jacksonville opponents brought a big blitz of six or more on a league-leading 12.0 percent of passes, and Blake Bortles gained only 4.2 yards per play (compared to 7.0 yards per play otherwise). ☞ The defense was surprisingly competent on first down, posting a -8.1% DVOA (seventh). But it was downhill from there, as the Jags ranked 28th on second downs and dead last on third downs. Jacksonville's 43.6% DVOA on third downs was the league's worst by a wide margin, as 31st-ranked Chicago still managed to post a 29.2% DVOA on the down. ☞ The rushing defense got significantly worse around midseason, dropping from -25.8% DVOA (third) in Weeks 1-9 to 3.0% DVOA (28th) in Weeks 10-17. ☞ The Jaguars ranked 13th with 5.6 percent adjusted sack rate on first and second downs, but 31st with a 13.8 percent adjusted sack rate on third and fourth downs. ☞ Jacksonville discovered the blitz last year, sending five or more pass rushers almost twice as often as they had in 2014 (when they were dead last at 13.0 percent). It seemed to work, as the Jaguars allowed 7.5 yards per pass with four pass rushers but 6.1 yards with five or more. In particular, blitzing a defensive back was successful; Jacksonville allowed only 3.1 yards per pass on these plays.

Passing

Player	DYAR	DVOA	Plays	NtYds	Avg	YAC	C%	TD	Int
B.Bortles	54	-9.9%	657	4089	6.2	5.2	58.9%	35	18

Rushing

Player	DYAR	DVOA	Plays	Yds	Avg	TD	Fum	Suc
T.J.Yeldon	39	-3.2%	182	740	4.1	2	0	42%
D.Robinson	-43	-24.4%	67	265	4.0	1	3	36%
B.Bortles	86	24.5%	42	320	7.6	2	2	-
T.Gerhart	-47	-50.8%	20	44	2.2	0	0	35%
J.Gray	-2	-11.2%	14	54	3.9	0	0	36%
B.Pierce*	-15	-66.6%	6	11	1.8	0	0	17%
C.Grant	-25	-114.1%	6	10	1.7	0	1	33%
M.Lee	19	24.5%	5	38	7.6	0	0	-
C.Ivory	-31	-11.5%	247	1073	4.3	7	3	43%

Receiving

Player	DYAR	DVOA	Plays	Ctch	Yds	Y/C	YAC	TD	C%
A.Robinson	318	14.0%	151	80	1400	17.5	4.5	14	53%
A.Hurns	236	16.1%	105	64	1031	16.1	5.4	10	61%
B.Walters	87	11.4%	45	32	368	11.5	3.8	1	71%
R.Greene	-61	-33.8%	35	19	93	4.9	2.8	2	54%
M.Lee	-2	-13.4%	32	15	191	12.7	6.1	1	47%
J.Thomas	-57	-17.7%	80	46	455	9.9	3.2	5	58%
M.Lewis	-76	-37.0%	37	16	226	14.1	10.1	0	43%
C.Harbor*	17	4.9%	20	14	149	10.6	4.0	1	70%
T.J.Yeldon	52	5.7%	46	36	279	7.8	8.3	1	78%
D.Robinson	9	-8.6%	30	21	164	7.8	7.5	0	70%
C.Ivory	21	-4.3%	37	30	217	7.2	9.2	1	81%

Offensive Line

Player	Pos	Age	GS	Snaps	Pen	Sk	Pass	Run	Player	Pos	Age	GS	Snaps	Pen	Sk	Pass	Run
Stefen Wisniewski*	C	27	16/16	1058	2	2.0	4.0	1.0	A.J. Cann	RG	25	14/13	861	6	0.0	2.0	1.0
Zane Beadles*	LG	30	16/16	1058	4	3.0	8.0	6.0	Sam Young*	RT	29	16/3	233	3	2.0	4.0	2.0
Jermey Parnell	RT	30	15/15	982	8	2.5	9.5	1.0	Brandon Linder	RG	24	3/3	197	3	0.0	0.0	0.0
Luke Joeckel	LT	25	14/14	900	8	3.0	13.0	0.0	Kelvin Beachum	LT	27	6/6	326	5	3.0	5.0	2.0

Year	Yards	ALY	Rank	Power	Rank	Stuff	Rank	2nd Lev	Rank	Open Field	Rank	Sacks	ASR	Rank	Press	Rank	F-Start	Cont.
2013	3.43	3.13	31	58%	24	25%	30	0.93	30	0.59	24	50	7.9%	24	24.8%	15	16	30
2014	3.98	3.52	30	58%	26	21%	22	0.96	27	0.81	10	71	11.3%	32	26.6%	23	8	29
2015	3.80	3.77	16	39%	31	22%	21	1.01	28	0.63	20	51	7.9%	25	27.4%	21	8	41

| 2015 ALY by direction: | Left End 4.04 (11) | Left Tackle 2.31 (31) | Mid/Guard 3.83 (14) | Right Tackle 4.15 (7) | Right End 3.75 (12) |

Brandon Linder is being asked to do a lot this offseason. Not only is Linder returning to the field after missing most of his second season due to a torn labrum, he is also switching positions from guard to center. Linder will be Blake Bortles' third center in as many seasons, replacing the departed Stefen Wisniewski. ☞ There also may be a change at left tackle, as free-agent addition Kelvin Beachum attempts to surpass Luke Joeckel outside. Beachum couldn't be further from Joeckel in terms of pedigree. He was a seventh-round pick in 2012 for the Pittsburgh Steelers. The Steelers hoped to groom him into an interior lineman over the early stages of his career, but instead he was forced to become a starter on Ben Roethlisberger's blind side. Despite his physical limitations and lowly status as a late-round pick, Beachum played disciplined, consistent football to earn the starting role full-time. He could have cashed in if it wasn't for a torn ACL that hit him just before he hit free agency. That injury allowed the Jaguars to sign him to what is essentially a prove-it deal. ☞ Joeckel ranked 23rd among left tackles and 52nd among all tackles in snaps per blown block last season. He and Zane Beadles were the Jaguars' two worst linemen. Beadles was released in the offseason, raising the possibility for Joeckel to move inside. Joeckel doesn't necessarily have that skill set, though. He's a prototype tackle: tall, long, but not very strong by the standards of interior linemen. Defensive tackles would likely overwhelm him with strength and leverage advantages. Not all tackles can move inside and be expected to be effective. It's more likely that A.J. Cann and veteran Mackenzy Bernadeau (ex-Cowboys) start at the guard positions. With Jermey Parnell established at right tackle, Joeckel could be headed for the bench.

Defensive Front Seven

Defensive Line	Age	Pos	G	Snaps	Plays	TmPct	Rk	Stop	Dfts	BTkl	Runs	St%	Rk	RuYd	Rk	Sack	Hit	Hur	Dsrpt
						Overall					vs. Run					Pass Rush			
Jared Odrick	29	DT	16	878	32	3.7%	64	27	14	0	21	76%	43	1.5	9	5.5	2	11.0	3
Roy Miller	29	DT	16	558	40	4.6%	49	31	12	4	33	76%	44	1.5	8	4.0	2	3.0	0
Abry Jones	25	DT	15	366	19	2.3%	--	15	4	2	12	83%	--	1.2	--	2.0	1	2.5	1
Michael Bennett	23	DT	13	297	10	1.4%	--	8	2	3	9	78%	--	2.4	--	0.5	1	1.5	0
Malik Jackson	26	DE	16	825	50	6.1%	32	36	15	5	31	65%	76	3.1	72	5.0	10	22.0	6

Edge Rushers	Age	Pos	G	Snaps	Plays	TmPct	Rk	Stop	Dfts	BTkl	Runs	St%	Rk	RuYd	Rk	Sack	Hit	Hur	Dsrpt
						Overall					vs. Run					Pass Rush			
Tyson Alualu	29	DE	16	689	27	3.1%	83	21	6	2	23	74%	48	2.1	41	2.0	9	15.0	2
Chris Clemons*	35	DE	16	662	14	1.6%	97	13	7	6	8	100%	1	0.5	3	3.0	7	18.5	1
Andre Branch*	27	DE	13	597	26	3.7%	74	21	11	3	15	73%	50	2.9	74	4.0	6	15.5	4
Ryan Davis	27	DE	14	245	7	0.9%	--	7	7	0	1	100%	--	3.0	--	3.5	4	6.5	0

Linebackers	Age	Pos	G	Snaps	Plays	TmPct	Rk	Stop	Dfts	BTkl	Runs	St%	Rk	RuYd	Rk	Sack	Hit	Hur	Tgts	Suc%	Rk	AdjYd	Rk	PD	Int
						Overall					vs. Run					Pass Rush			vs. Pass						
Telvin Smith	25	OLB	14	998	134	17.6%	8	78	30	14	66	68%	25	3.3	34	2.5	1	3	38	45%	59	8.3	61	4	1
Paul Posluszny	32	MLB	14	980	138	18.2%	5	71	24	13	69	68%	26	2.6	7	1.0	7	9.5	24	62%	21	5.9	34	6	3
Dan Skuta	30	OLB	13	417	38	5.4%	86	23	7	4	30	67%	32	2.7	9	1.5	2	2	3	70%	--	5.6	--	0	0
Hayes Pullard	24	MLB	8	150	19	4.4%	--	10	2	2	13	69%	--	3.5	--	0.0	1	1.5	6	35%	--	10.9	--	0	0

Year	Yards	ALY	Rank	Power	Rank	Stuff	Rank	2nd Level	Rank	Open Field	Rank	Sacks	ASR	Rank	Press	Rank
2013	4.12	4.01	21	74%	28	18%	19	1.09	15	0.75	19	31	6.0%	30	22.7%	24
2014	4.06	3.61	9	70%	24	21%	9	1.05	9	0.88	27	45	8.5%	2	20.1%	31
2015	3.68	3.51	8	68%	19	23%	9	1.11	15	0.58	9	36	5.8%	24	21.7%	30
2015 ALY by direction:		Left End 2.59 (5)			Left Tackle 4.50 (29)			Mid/Guard 3.59 (7)			Right Tackle 3.51 (11)			Right End 3.75 (21)		

Myles Jack's arrival in Jacksonville will overshadow the return of Dante Fowler. The third overall selection from the 2015 draft tore his ACL in his first practice with the Jaguars last year, missing out on his whole rookie season. Even when Fowler was coming out, we doubted whether he was truly a difference-making pass-rusher. SackSEER projected him to have 21.7 sacks through five years and gave him a rating of 43.3 percent. Fowler's forecast was boosted by his high projected draft position, as his athletic testing and production in college were underwhelming. He is a versatile player who will offer value against the run and could move around the formation some, but expectations should be muted coming off a significant knee injury. ☞ It was also a significant knee injury that derailed the burgeoning career of defensive tackle Sen'Derrick Marks. Marks was a star before he tore his ACL two years ago. He didn't return to 100 percent effectiveness last year and there are question marks concerning what role he will play this year after the addition of free agent Malik Jackson. Jackson, Marks, Mike Bennett, and Sheldon Day all project to be penetrating interior linemen, giving the Jaguars some versatility that should help to compensate for their limited athleticism coming off the edge.

Defensive Secondary

Secondary	Age	Pos	G	Snaps	Plays	TmPct	Rk	Stop	Dfts	BTkl	Runs	St%	Rk	RuYd	Rk	Tgts	Tgt%	Rk	Dist	Suc%	Rk	AdjYd	Rk	PD	Int
						Overall						**vs. Run**						**vs. Pass**							
Aaron Colvin	25	CB	16	1071	80	9.2%	28	46	15	7	26	77%	4	4.1	6	48	12.4%	2	11.2	53%	36	8.4	51	6	0
Davon House	27	CB	16	1036	83	9.6%	22	37	22	13	13	38%	43	6.7	35	91	24.6%	67	14.2	50%	50	8.0	41	21	4
Johnathan Cyprien	26	SS	14	1015	108	14.2%	7	52	11	16	61	54%	11	6.1	25	30	8.3%	43	11.2	55%	44	6.5	27	2	1
Josh Evans	25	FS	16	621	54	6.2%	66	17	7	8	28	32%	50	7.4	43	10	4.3%	9	11.3	48%	56	9.3	56	1	0
Sergio Brown*	28	FS	15	555	38	4.7%	--	9	4	7	17	29%	--	8.6	--	13	6.6%	--	18.8	40%	--	13.6	--	2	0
Dwayne Gratz	26	CB	12	457	28	4.3%	--	8	1	3	8	63%	--	4.4	--	29	17.8%	--	8.9	50%	--	4.8	--	1	0
Demetrius McCray	25	CB	14	225	22	2.9%	--	7	2	3	2	50%	--	2.5	--	20	24.3%	--	12.1	27%	--	11.9	--	1	0
Tashaun Gipson	26	FS	13	799	62	9.6%	37	20	5	7	41	37%	44	7.4	42	13	4.4%	10	14.8	44%	63	8.3	48	2	2
Prince Amukamara	27	CB	11	765	73	11.9%	3	28	10	3	15	40%	39	8.3	49	55	19.3%	38	12.5	52%	38	7.5	35	6	1

Year	Pass D Rank	vs. #1 WR	Rk	vs. #2 WR	Rk	vs. Other WR	Rk	vs. TE	Rk	vs. RB	Rk
2013	26	13.3%	26	8.9%	21	16.1%	28	19.9%	28	-9.0%	11
2014	17	37.0%	32	-9.8%	10	22.3%	28	5.9%	22	-5.8%	13
2015	31	9.9%	25	13.4%	24	17.7%	26	23.8%	28	14.2%	27

The Jaguars don't really know what they have in second-year safety James Sample. A fourth-round pick out of Louisville last year, Sample played sparingly as a rookie, appearing in just four games because of a forearm injury. When the Jaguars drafted Sample they intended to pair him with Jonathan Cyprien in the hopes of creating an interchangeable safety duo. However, Sample's skill set suggests that he is better suited to stay in the box, so after the signing of Tashaun Gipson, Sample should be expected to compete with Cyprien to be the Jaguars starting strong safety. Cyprien's inconsistency has been such that the Jaguars are desperate for someone to beat him out. He is too reckless of a defender in pursuit while showing off a limited skill set in coverage. The relatively young defender has 33 broken tackles over the past two seasons, and his high tackle totals and strong run stop rate are more a testament to how Jacksonville uses him than to his own performance. Sample only needs to be consistent and disciplined to offer greater value.

Special Teams

Year	DVOA	Rank	FG/XP	Rank	Net Kick	Rank	Kick Ret	Rank	Net Punt	Rank	Punt Ret	Rank	Hidden	Rank
2013	2.5%	9	1.9	15	7.2	5	2.9	8	7.3	8	-6.6	26	9.2	5
2014	-3.6%	26	-1.8	21	2.6	12	0.5	12	-13.2	31	-6.2	28	-3.0	23
2015	-0.9%	20	-4.6	29	2.4	10	-0.9	17	-9.3	27	7.8	5	6.0	7

Now that the Bryan Anger era has come to an end in Jacksonville, we can finally figure out if the punter was the better option than Russell Wilson in the 2012 draft. Wilson may have won a Super Bowl, but Anger averaged 46.3 yards per punt in 2015, with 26 of his 80 punts landing inside the opponent's 20-yard line. He ranked 13th among punters in gross punting last season, worth 1.9 points above average. That was his highest finish in his career. So the verdict is "no." ☜ Unfortunately for Jacksonville, Anger has been better than the man who is set to replace him, Brad Nortman. Nortman ranked 21st in 2015, with a gross punting value worth minus-2.7 points for Carolina. Ryan Quigley (ex-Jets) will also compete for the job in camp. ☜ Field goals weren't an issue for rookie kicker Jason Myers, but extra points were. Myers missed an incredible seven extra points and actually had a higher rate on field goals (86.7 percent) than extra points (82.1 percent). Hopefully he can fix his yips on those point-after tries, because the Jaguars would have a tough time finding someone as strong on kickoffs. ☜ Return duties are likely to be split between slot receiver Rashad Greene and former Auburn quarterback-turned-Jacksonville depth cornerback Nick Marshall. Greene was particularly good in 2015, worth an estimated 11.1 points above average on punt returns. Only Darren Sproles was worth more.

Kansas City Chiefs

2015 record: 11-5	**Total DVOA:** 25.2% (5th)	**2016 Mean Projection:** 9.6 wins	**On the Clock (0-4):** 3%
Pythagorean Wins: 11.2 (6th)	**Offense:** 11.7% (6th)	**Postseason Odds:** 60.3%	**Mediocrity (5-7):** 17%
Snap-Weighted Age: 26.5 (19th)	**Defense:** -11.6% (6th)	**Super Bowl Odds:** 14.1%	**Playoff Contender (8-10):** 42%
Average Opponent: 2.4% (14th)	**Special Teams:** 2.0% (9th)	**Proj. Avg. Opponent:** -1.6% (24th)	**Super Bowl Contender (11+):** 38%

2015: Chiefs roll off 10 straight regular-season wins and a dominant playoff shutout before running out of gas in Foxborough.

2016: Andy Reid's last, best chance to finally win a Super Bowl.

Turn one tie into a loss and Andy Reid would enter the 2016 season with the exact same career record as his mustachioed doppelganger Mike Holmgren. Reid has won his 161 games without the benefit of an all-time great quarterback—and with an 11-11 record in the postseason, he's far from Schottenheimer territory. Last season, he rolled off 11 straight wins without his best offensive player and with Captain Checkdown under center. It's hard to see any coach doing much better with his rosters over the last 17 NFL seasons.

And yet Reid's successes receive less attention than his failures. We think of all those NFC Championship losses with the Eagles, the slow drive to nowhere in Super Bowl XXXIX against the Patriots, and now another clock bungling in the divisional round loss to New England last year. Never mind that Reid managed to piece together the league's best rushing attack by DVOA, and No. 6 offense overall, with one of NFL's most dubious offensive lines, with a quarterback who has never stretched defenses, and without Jamaal Charles. Against the Patriots, his stars on both sides of the ball either did not play or were limited by injuries. His admittedly head-scratching clock management deserved criticism, but there's little justice in that drowning out all that preceded it.

Maybe Reid is forever doomed because his separated-at-birth resemblance to Wilford Brimley evokes New York Knights manager Pop Fisher, respected but more avuncular than commanding. Or maybe his entire narrative comes down to the randomness of whether the bounces of the playoffs go his way enough in a given year to swing a Lombardi Trophy into his ample lap. For all of his strategic shortcomings, Reid's career needed just a little more luck for his flaws to take a back seat to his strengths.

Of course, Reid's flaws are real and played a role in increasing the degree of difficulty needed in last year's playoff run. FO's Andrew Healy wrote a piece on coaching decisions late last year that had just a small group of coaches listed with four or more unambiguous significant errors in 2015: Mike Pettine, Rex Ryan, John Harbaugh, Jim Tomsula, Chuck Pagano, Tom Coughlin, and Reid. While two of Reid's mistakes were on challenges, the other two came in clock management. In Week 2 against the Broncos, Reid chose to run from his own 20-yard line with 37 seconds left in a tie game and one timeout left. While coaches rarely get punished so dramatically for that kind of decision as Reid did with Jamaal Charles' de-

cisive fumble, either passing or playing for overtime would have made more sense. Against the Bears in Week 5, Reid inexplicably let the clock run as the Bears faced a second-and-4 from the Chiefs' 7-yard line with just under a minute left and the Chiefs leading 17-12. Rather than getting the ball back with an extra 25 or 30 seconds to work with following Chicago's eventual touchdown, the Chiefs had to settle for a 66-yard field goal attempt and an 18-17 loss. Those mistakes put the Chiefs in the position of needing to play on wild-card weekend, where receiver Jeremy Maclin suffered a knee injury that limited him the following week, where the Chiefs lost on the road when a division title would have had them playing at home.

This season, Reid is making some changes to try to finally address his weaknesses. The Chiefs are simplifying their two-minute offense in what seems like a direct response to the achingly slow drive against the Patriots. The Chiefs actually were better than average in the last two minutes of either half in 2015 overall (24.6% DVOA, ranked 10th) and close to average in those spots in one-score games (3.0% DVOA, ranked 18th). But the best offenses have been simplifying for a while. Making the calls quicker puts the Chiefs closer to the cutting edge. Now if Reid could only figure out those pesky timeouts.

Reid has already figured out how to get the most out of an offensive roster facing serious limitations. At wide receiver, the Chiefs last year had Jeremy Maclin and a cast of replacement-level talent. On the offensive line, their six offensive linemen who saw the most snaps all ranked 26th or worse at their positions in snaps per blown block. Their quarterback is so limited when throwing downfield that we named a new stat after him last year, an honor in the same way that the Mendoza Line is a tribute to former Pirates shortstop Mario Mendoza. Alex Smith inspired ALEX, or Air Less EXpected, measuring the yards short of the first down that a quarterback's throws travel. For his play on third downs, Smith has been making a strong play to get promoted to Colonel Checkdown. In 2015, Smith set the standard for throwing short of the sticks. His average throw on third down was 3.5 yards short of a conversion, the biggest number in we have recorded so far (back to 2006).

Smith's overly conservative tendencies predate his arrival in Kansas City. Over the last seven years, four of which came with the 49ers, Smith has averaged throwing at least 0.5

2016 Chiefs Schedule

Week	Opp.	Week	Opp.	Week	Opp.
1	SD	7	NO	13	at ATL
2	at HOU	8	at IND	14	OAK (Thu.)
3	NYJ	9	JAC	15	TEN
4	at PIT	10	at CAR	16	DEN (Xmas)
5	BYE	11	TB	17	at SD
6	at OAK	12	at DEN		

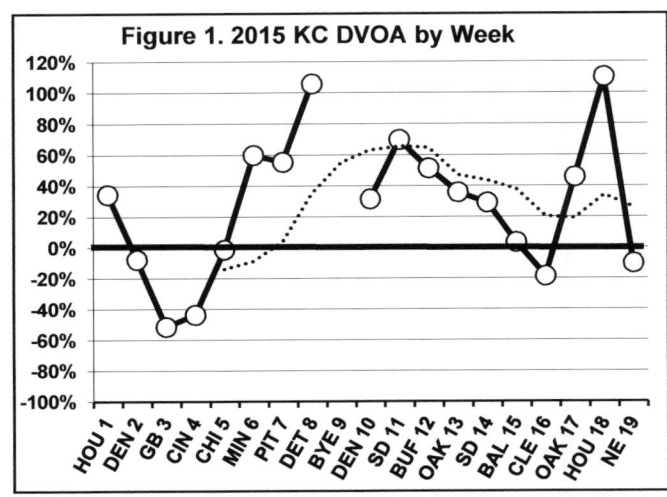

Figure 1. 2015 KC DVOA by Week

yards short of the sticks on third down every year. But some combination of the lack of receiver help and perhaps Reid's play-calling have pushed Smith to another level in Kansas City (Table 1). Given that Reid's offenses in the past usually threw further past the sticks on third down than the rest of the league—average ALEX on third down is generally about 1.5 yards beyond the sticks—Smith's recent tendencies are likely a product of both Smith's own abilities and Kansas City's weakness at receiver.

Table 1. ALEX for Alex Smith and Andy Reid, 2009-2015

Year	Alex Smith	Andy Reid Offenses
2009	-1.0	+3.3
2010	-0.5	+3.3
2011	-1.0	+2.4
2012	-0.9	+0.9
2013	-2.2	
2014	-2.0	
2015	-3.5	

Smith evokes Don Johnson's character in *Tin Cup*: imprudently prudent, cautious to an extreme degree. Despite that weakness, Smith has been consistently around league average in his three years with Reid according to DVOA. Last season, on first and second down—when throwing to the sticks matters less—Smith's DVOA was 6.8%. On third down, Smith's excessive caution helped result in a DVOA of -12.5%. More generally, the Chiefs may need to work in more downfield throws. Last year, they threw more than 15 yards downfield just 64 times, 20 fewer than any other team in the league. It's not as if Smith does unusually poorly on those rare occasions he does go downfield. His DVOA split between deep and short throws (64.2% vs. 20.1%) resembled the split for the rest of the league (52.0% vs. 12.2%). As Reid likely has some low-hanging fruit that could help him improve as a coach, Smith has a clear path to making a big improvement in his 12th NFL season: greater boldness, particularly on third down.

While Smith's long history of checking down makes that improvement unlikely, the Chiefs should improve in at least two areas, making Reid's task easier on offense. First, Charles returns. Charles has rushed for at least 5 yards per carry in each season since entering the league in 2008, although three of those seasons had fewer than 100 carries. After missing

most of 2011 with an ACL tear, Charles returned in 2012 to have his biggest year by rushes (285) and total yards (1,509). It's tempting to think Charles is irrelevant given the Chiefs' success last year without him, but he was a top-ten back in his first two years with Reid and was on an even better pace last year. Spencer Ware put up big numbers on his 72 carries last season, but the sample size is not big enough to suggest he could continue to match what a healthy Charles has consistently produced. Charcandrick West, who started the majority of games, was merely average.

In addition, the offensive line blocking for Charles should be clearly stronger than the leaky unit from 2015. Last year, the primary weakness in run blocking was on the right side of the line. The Chiefs averaged 2.64 adjusted line yards (ALY) on runs charted over right tackle (ranked 30th) and 2.40 ALY on runs around right end (28th). Those numbers contrast sharply with runs to the other side, where Kansas City got 5.08 ALY over left tackle (first) and 4.47 ALY around left end (fifth). To help fix the issues on the right side, the Chiefs signed free-agent tackle Mitchell Schwartz from the Browns. Unlike the Chiefs' incumbent linemen, Schwartz ranked towards the top of his position last year with 122.9 snaps per blown block (ninth among right tackles). 2013 first overall pick Eric Fisher improved last year and has left tackle locked up. 2015 second-round pick Mitch Morse likewise is entrenched at center. The two guard spots are up for grabs with a bunch of contenders, none of them proven. But with Morse a candidate to improve and the addition of Schwartz, the arrow is pointed up on the line.

The line may matter more in Kansas City than elsewhere, too, given Alex Smith's propensity for hanging on to the ball. The Chiefs' high adjusted sack rate of 8.7 percent (ranked 28th) falls largely on Smith's shoulders, but it also underscores that limited quarterbacks receive more help from better line play than quarterbacks at the Brady-Rodgers level. The Chiefs have not had an All-Pro quarterback since Len Dawson claimed the AFL honor in 1966. The last first-round quarterback the Chiefs picked was Todd Blackledge in 1983. Only the Saints have gone longer since their last first-round quarterback. With the exception of some underappreciated years with Trent Green, the Chiefs have been patching the position together ever since, starting other teams' draft choices and 2006 third-rounder Brodie Croyle. Smith is another stopgap, the equivalent of Elvis Grbac from those well-rounded Chiefs' teams of the 1990s that could never quite get over the hump. As with those teams, these Chiefs have a margin of error made smaller by their quarterback's skill set, but improved line play may make a particularly big difference given those limitations.

The offense features improved personnel, but the defense is still depending on an aging cast that hopes it has one more year in the tank. The defense is not aging everywhere, but it is relying on major contributions from inside linebacker Derrick Johnson (34 years old in November) and edge rusher Tamba Hali (33 in November). Largely due to Johnson and Hali, the 2015 Chiefs featured the league's fifth-oldest defense by snap-weighted age.

The biggest question on defense centers on Justin Houston. The edge rusher who led the NFL with 22 sacks in 2014 is just entering his prime at 27, but is trying to recover from surgery to repair an ACL in February. He appears likely to return at some point during the season, but whether he comes back early or late in the year is unclear. Until Von Miller signed his extension this summer, Houston was the highest-paid linebacker in the NFL by a healthy margin. His contract also shows the Chiefs' unsettling habit of taking from the future to stay afloat in the present. Last offseason, Houston signed a six-year $101 million contract which had a 2015 cap hit of just $5.1 million. This year, his cap hit jumps to $19.1 million, and it stays at least that high through 2019. Moreover, his contract almost guarantees the Chiefs will not cut him before 2018. Even then, cutting him would result in $8.2 million in dead money. Houston is obviously really good and someone who every team would love to have, just not at this price. Houston cashed in after his big sack season, but his other pressure numbers that season (seven hits, 33 hurries) fell far short of other players such as Miller or J.J. Watt. Houston's contract looks like an overpay driven by his anomalous sack total in 2014, a contract with almost no upside for the Chiefs.

The Chiefs' salary cap could become a major problem in the next few years, and the first sign is the fact that Sean Smith wears an Oakland Raiders uniform. The Chiefs' top corner last year, Smith signed a reasonable deal (four years, $40 million, but basically a two-year, $20.5 million deal with team options) that the Chiefs ideally would have matched. Smith ranked 16th in adjusted yards per target among all corners last year and would have formed an intimidating tandem with second-year corner Marcus Peters. Last year's Defensive Rookie of the Year, Peters was an all-or-nothing proposition in 2015. He tied for the league lead with eight interceptions and finished an impressive 15th in adjusted success rate. At the same time, his propensity to give up some big plays led him to finish middle of the pack with 7.9 adjusted yards per pass (ranked 39th).

With Smith gone, Peters becomes a promising top corner this year. A host of unproven young players are vying for the other spots. Philip Gaines, a 2014 third-round pick out of Rice, is the presumed heir apparent to Smith; he's coming off an ACL tear but played well in limited opportunities over his two seasons. However, buzz out of OTAs had 2015 third-round pick Steven Nelson (Oregon State), who played just 53 snaps as a rookie, impressing enough that he could supplant Gaines. The Chiefs also drafted three corners this year, with third-round pick KeiVarae Russell (Notre Dame) the most likely player to see action. The Chiefs have youth, depth, and upside at corner.

The task of merging the young cornerback talent in with the veterans elsewhere falls to one of the league's more innovative defensive coordinators, Bob Sutton. Even when injuries limited his best pass-rushing options last season, Sutton managed to scrape together consistent pressure for most of the season. The Chiefs finished fourth in adjusted sack rate, despite getting no more than 7.5 sacks from any single player. This is one example of how Andy Reid's strengths as a head coach extend to hiring coordinators who maximize the opportunities for player talent to shine. The strong job Doug Pederson did overcoming the Chiefs' offensive weaknesses got him the head job in Philadelphia; Brad Childress and Matt Nagy are now co-coordinators, with Reid back to calling the offensive plays. The Chiefs also employ the special teams coordinator who has more than any other defied the usual randomness that rules on special teams. Over his last ten years as a special teams coach (2006-2012 with the Bears and 2013-2015 with the Chiefs), Dave Toub's units have ranked first in DVOA five times and no lower than the No. 7 finish from last year. After Toub left the Bears, their special teams quickly fell off. Before he arrived in Kansas City, the unit ranked No. 22. The blocking on Knile Davis' kickoff return for a touchdown in the wild-card win over the Texans speaks to organization in action and to Toub's indispensability.

The Chiefs' coaching strengths are one more reason to favor Reid's chances to get another ticket to the playoff lottery this year, maybe even his first bye since that 2004 Super Bowl run. The schedule could hardly be more favorable. The AFC West gets to face the shameful Souths as its two divisional opponents. The Broncos, Chargers, and Raiders all have significant flaws, making Kansas City the clear favorite to take the division title. This season looks like the best and maybe last shot for both the Chiefs and their underappreciated head coach. Even if the defense gets through this season, the aging of key players will soon force significant change.

The Chiefs will also be losing more free agents than they keep in upcoming years. Houston's monster deal wasn't the only recent contract extensions to borrow cap relief today in exchange for ballooning payments tomorrow. Both Johnson and Hali signed three-year, $21 million contract extensions this offseason that have cap numbers below $4 million in 2016. Next year, those numbers blow up to $7.75 million for Johnson and $8.58 million for Hali. As reasonable as their contracts look this season, they may be dead weight as soon as next season given those players' ages. According to overthe-cap.com, with more than $161 million in 2017 salaries already committed, the Chiefs have less cap room for 2017 than every team except the Eagles and Cowboys. Only the Eagles have more money allocated in 2018, according to overthecap.com.

And for this season, as of this writing, no team has less cap space to play with than the Chiefs. Despite little wiggle room to make any roster additions, there is still one possible hire that could potentially change the season in a key moment as much as any player could. There is no salary cap on coaches, nothing to stop the Chiefs from hiring that clock-management and challenge-flag specialist who would help fix their head coach's defining flaws. Imagine watching Andy Reid's team without that nagging feeling about some inevitable strategic misstep. Nothing in his control could do more to help Reid finally get his hands on the ultimate prize.

Aaron Schatz

2015 Chiefs Stats by Week

Wk	vs.	W-L	PF	PA	YDF	YDA	TO	Total	Off	Def	ST
1	at HOU	W	27	20	330	396	2	35%	33%	-1%	1%
2	DEN	L	24	31	314	299	-4	-8%	-22%	-10%	5%
3	at GB	L	28	38	326	448	-1	-51%	-10%	42%	1%
4	at CIN	L	21	36	461	445	-1	-44%	15%	65%	7%
5	CHI	L	17	18	287	328	1	-1%	0%	-4%	-5%
6	at MIN	L	10	16	328	321	1	60%	11%	-43%	6%
7	PIT	W	23	13	377	339	3	56%	31%	-20%	4%
8	vs. DET (UK)	W	45	10	340	276	2	106%	46%	-43%	17%
9	BYE										
10	at DEN	W	29	13	303	221	5	31%	2%	-37%	-7%
11	at SD	W	33	3	385	201	2	70%	22%	-41%	7%
12	BUF	W	30	22	413	415	2	52%	49%	0%	2%
13	at OAK	W	34	20	232	361	1	36%	1%	-29%	5%
14	SD	W	10	3	329	280	-1	29%	0%	-34%	-4%
15	at BAL	W	34	14	277	366	3	3%	2%	-2%	-1%
16	CLE	W	17	13	258	368	0	-18%	-8%	12%	1%
17	OAK	W	23	17	339	205	-1	46%	7%	-39%	-1%
18	at HOU	W	30	0	378	340	4	110%	4%	-70%	36%
19	at NE	L	20	27	314	226	-1	-10%	5%	24%	10%

Trends and Splits

	Offense	Rank	Defense	Rank
Total DVOA	11.7%	6	-11.4%	6
Unadjusted VOA	11.1%	8	-11.3%	4
Weighted Trend	13.9%	3	-21.5%	2
Variance	4.1%	4	9.8%	31
Average Opponent	-1.6%	13	0.7%	14
Passing	18.1%	14	-8.6%	5
Rushing	14.0%	1	-15.5%	11
First Down	15.5%	3	-12.6%	4
Second Down	13.4%	7	-7.4%	8
Third Down	0.8%	14	-15.2%	9
First Half	16.4%	5	-19.1%	4
Second Half	6.7%	9	-3.7%	10
Red Zone	41.2%	2	1.6%	17
Late and Close	2.8%	14	-18.3%	4

Five-Year Performance

Year	W-L	Pyth W	Est W	PF	PA	TO	Total	Rk	Off	Rk	Def	Rk	ST	Rk	Off AGL	Rk	Def AGL	Rk	Off Age	Rk	Def Age	Rk	ST Age	Rk
2011	7-9	4.2	6.3	212	338	-2	-16.9%	26	-19.3%	29	-3.2%	13	-0.9%	19	43.8	26	21.7	13	28.0	5	26.3	25	26.1	22
2012	2-14	2.5	2.4	211	425	-24	-40.1%	32	-25.1%	31	13.0%	30	-2.0%	22	50.0	27	29.3	17	26.3	24	26.1	25	26.0	14
2013	11-5	11.1	10.0	430	305	+18	17.5%	6	3.0%	15	-6.7%	9	7.8%	1	29.4	13	10.6	3	26.1	27	26.4	17	25.8	23
2014	9-7	10.1	9.4	353	281	-3	10.4%	10	5.0%	12	1.3%	19	6.7%	3	36.0	20	62.8	27	26.6	19	26.6	20	25.7	26
2015	11-5	11.2	11.4	405	287	+14	25.2%	5	11.7%	6	-11.6%	6	2.0%	9	26.3	13	28.6	18	25.8	28	27.4	5	25.8	19

2015 Performance Based on Most Common Personnel Groups

KC Offense					KC Offense vs. Opponents					KC Defense				KC Defense vs. Opponents			
Pers	Freq	Yds	DVOA	Run%	Pers	Freq	Yds	DVOA	Run%	Pers	Freq	Yds	DVOA	Pers	Freq	Yds	DVOA
11	50%	6.2	21.7%	32%	Base	39%	5.7	21.9%	52%	Base	28%	4.6	-18.4%	11	61%	5.6	-5.5%
12	22%	5.8	21.8%	33%	Nickel	47%	5.8	8.5%	33%	Nickel	39%	6.0	3.9%	12	24%	4.2	-32.8%
21	10%	5.5	15.5%	58%	Dime+	13%	6.1	24.2%	13%	Dime+	32%	4.9	-26.6%	21	5%	5.8	-7.9%
13	9%	4.8	-6.8%	49%	Goal Line	1%	1.1	15.3%	89%	Goal Line	0%	0.7	61.1%	22	3%	5.4	-25.5%
22	5%	3.3	-4.3%	93%	Big	1%	5.5	27.0%	90%	Big	1%	3.2	-43.6%	13	2%	3.8	-22.5%

Strategic Tendencies

Run/Pass		Rk	Formation		Rk	Pass Rush		Rk	Secondary		Rk	Strategy		Rk
Runs, first half	36%	21	Form: Single Back	81%	8	Rush 3	4.1%	24	4 DB	28%	24	Play action	20%	12
Runs, first down	48%	12	Form: Empty Back	3%	30	Rush 4	70.6%	5	5 DB	39%	26	Avg Box (Off)	6.36	7
Runs, second-long	35%	8	Pers: 3+ WR	53%	25	Rush 5	20.8%	17	6+ DB	32%	3	Avg Box (Def)	6.35	8
Runs, power sit.	63%	8	Pers: 2+ TE/6+ OL	37%	12	Rush 6+	4.5%	24	CB by Sides	97%	2	Offensive Pace	33.71	32
Runs, behind 2H	18%	31	Pers: 6+ OL	1%	26	Sacks by LB	55.3%	11	S/CB Cover Ratio	38%	2	Defensive Pace	30.15	13
Pass, ahead 2H	47%	15	Shotgun/Pistol	65%	13	Sacks by DB	14.9%	5	DB Blitz	8%	21	Go for it on 4th	0.57	32

For the third straight season, the Kansas City offense was better in the red zone than it was overall. In 2015, this came almost entirely on the strength of the running game; the Chiefs had the No. 2 DVOA in the red zone, ranking first on runs but just 18th on passes. The same trend existed for the defense in 2013-2014, but that did not continue in 2015, as the Chiefs dropped to 17th in defensive DVOA in the red zone. ◔ Kansas City's offense was handed the best average starting line of scrimmage in the NFL, just past its own 31-yard line. ◔ The Chiefs threw 26 percent of their passes behind the line of scrimmage, the highest rate in the league. It's almost as if Alex Smith likes to throw short or something. ◔ The offense made very effective use of running back draws. Kansas City called draws on eight percent of its runs, tied for the fourth-highest rate in the league, and compiled a 31.7% DVOA, which ranked fifth among offenses. ◔ Kansas City receivers dropped just 3.8 percent of passes (ninth) after dropping a league-worst 6.8 percent of passes in 2014. ◔ When Kansas City was down one score, the defense ranked just 30th in DVOA. But when the Chiefs were up by one score, the defense ranked second overall. ◔ No defense allowed fewer yards per play on wide receiver and tight end screens than the Chiefs at 2.8, and their -28.4% DVOA on these plays ranked fifth.

Passing

Player	DYAR	DVOA	Plays	NtYds	Avg	YAC	C%	TD	Int
A.Smith	468	3.0%	516	3243	6.3	6.3	65.5%	20	7

Rushing

Player	DYAR	DVOA	Plays	Yds	Avg	TD	Fum	Suc
C.West	77	2.8%	160	634	4.0	4	1	45%
S.Ware	106	25.8%	72	403	5.6	6	0	58%
A.Smith	86	11.5%	72	509	7.1	2	2	-
J.Charles	96	24.8%	71	364	5.1	4	2	48%
K.Davis	-19	-25.7%	28	72	2.6	1	0	39%
D.Thomas	32	39.9%	8	41	5.1	1	0	-
A.Wilson	17	30.3%	5	26	5.2	0	0	-

Receiving

Player	DYAR	DVOA	Plays	Ctch	Yds	Y/C	YAC	TD	C%
J.Maclin	234	11.3%	124	87	1095	12.6	3.8	8	70%
A.Wilson	61	1.5%	57	35	451	12.9	6.3	2	61%
C.Conley	39	2.7%	31	17	199	11.7	4.1	1	55%
D.Thomas	-26	-26.4%	25	18	133	7.4	8.3	1	72%
J.Avant*	-6	-15.7%	24	15	119	7.9	3.3	0	63%
T.Kelce	110	9.3%	103	72	875	12.2	7.3	5	70%
D.Harris	-1	-8.6%	11	7	74	10.6	3.1	1	64%
J.O'Shaughnessy	16	21.3%	9	6	87	14.5	9.5	0	67%
C.West	-13	-20.4%	34	20	214	10.7	11.9	1	59%
J.Charles	3	-12.1%	30	21	180	8.6	9.8	1	70%
S.Ware	-42	-167.8%	6	6	5	0.8	2.0	0	100%

Offensive Line

Player	Pos	Age	GS	Snaps	Pen	Sk	Pass	Run	Player	Pos	Age	GS	Snaps	Pen	Sk	Pass	Run
Mitch Morse	C	24	15/15	920	1	3.0	6.5	3.0	Ben Grubbs	LG	32	7/7	463	3	4.0	5.0	0.0
Eric Fisher	LT	25	16/14	826	6	3.0	11.5	3.0	Jeff Allen	RT	26	12/8	429	2	0.0	2.0	1.0
Laurent Duvernay-Tardif	RG	25	16/13	807	7	5.0	7.0	2.0	Zach Fulton	RG	25	16/6	406	2	1.0	3.0	1.0
Jah Reid	RT	27	10/10	608	6	2.0	11.5	3.0	Mitchell Schwartz	RT	27	16/16	1106	5	4.0	6.0	3.0
Donald Stephenson*	OT	28	16/7	555	6	1.0	8.5	1.0	Jordan Devey	RG	28	15/9	390	2	3.5	6.5	2.0

Year	Yards	ALY	Rank	Power	Rank	Stuff	Rank	2nd Lev	Rank	Open Field	Rank	Sacks	ASR	Rank	Press	Rank	F-Start	Cont.
2013	4.58	4.33	2	65%	16	16%	7	1.27	8	0.91	9	41	7.7%	20	22.1%	9	19	28
2014	4.47	4.08	7	60%	21	17%	5	1.15	17	0.97	4	49	9.4%	28	27.0%	26	16	40
2015	4.43	4.15	5	70%	11	18%	6	1.22	8	0.84	11	46	8.7%	28	25.0%	15	15	22

2015 ALY by direction:	Left End 4.47 (5)	Left Tackle 5.08 (1)	Mid/Guard 4.38 (2)	Right Tackle 2.64 (30)	Right End 2.4 (28)

After struggling mightily in his first two seasons, Eric Fisher showed enough in his third year that that the Chiefs picked up his fifth-year option in May; the former first overall pick will make $11.9 million in 2017. ☞ Last year, the Chiefs hoped that free-agent signee Ben Grubbs would fill their hole at left guard. The two-time Pro Bowler will only impact the 2016 Chiefs through the $5.2 million in dead money that he costs against this year's salary cap. After playing in seven games last year, the Chiefs cut Grubbs in the offseason. The 32-year-old now appears likely to retire with a neck injury. ☞ At least five players are in the running for the starting spots at guard, including Laurent Duvernay-Tardif, Jah Reid, Zach Fulton, Jordan Devey, and 2016 fourth-round pick Parker Ehinger (Louisville). 2014 sixth-round pick Duvernay-Tardif saw the most action last year and ranked 32nd (out of 39) right guards with 89.7 snaps per blown block. ☞ Baltimore's John Urschel isn't the only interior lineman pursuing an advanced degree. Duvernay-Tardif attends medical school at McGill for a couple of months each offseason.

Defensive Front Seven

Defensive Line	Age	Pos		Overall							vs. Run					Pass Rush			
			G	Snaps	Plays	TmPct	Rk	Stop	Dfts	BTkl	Runs	St%	Rk	RuYd	Rk	Sack	Hit	Hur	Dsrpt
Dontari Poe	26	DT	15	759	39	5.1%	40	27	4	1	35	74%	48	3.0	66	1.0	2	12.0	0
Jaye Howard	28	DT	16	752	56	6.9%	21	44	16	3	45	82%	22	1.7	23	5.5	6	12.0	0
Allen Bailey	27	DE	12	582	38	6.2%	28	26	11	3	30	63%	78	3.3	77	4.5	3	12.5	0
Mike DeVito*	32	DE	13	293	19	2.9%	--	18	6	3	16	94%	--	0.8	--	3.0	0	9.0	0

Edge Rushers	Age	Pos		Overall							vs. Run					Pass Rush			
			G	Snaps	Plays	TmPct	Rk	Stop	Dfts	BTkl	Runs	St%	Rk	RuYd	Rk	Sack	Hit	Hur	Dsrpt
Tamba Hali	33	OLB	15	838	48	6.3%	23	33	15	1	31	71%	60	1.1	9	6.5	12	24.5	1
Justin Houston	27	OLB	11	621	36	6.4%	20	33	19	2	19	84%	13	1.8	30	7.5	5	23.0	4
Dee Ford	25	OLB	14	480	25	3.5%	78	19	8	4	16	81%	20	2.3	44	4.0	6	13.5	1

Linebackers	Age	Pos		Overall							vs. Run					Pass Rush			vs. Pass					
			G	Snaps	Plays	TmPct	Rk	Stop	Dfts	BTkl	Runs	St%	Rk	RuYd	Rk	Sack	Hit	Hur	Tgts	Suc%	Rk	AdjYd	Rk	PD	Int
Derrick Johnson	34	ILB	16	1062	123	15.1%	17	73	22	16	70	61%	51	3.7	51	4.0	2	11.5	36	67%	12	4.5	13	7	2
Josh Mauga	29	ILB	14	462	60	8.4%	68	28	7	9	37	51%	83	4.2	72	1.0	0	4	12	58%	30	5.4	25	2	2
Ramik Wilson	24	ILB	10	128	20	3.9%	--	10	1	0	16	56%	--	4.9	--	0.0	0	1	2	55%	--	11.1	--	0	0

Year	Yards	ALY	Rank	Power	Rank	Stuff	Rank	2nd Level	Rank	Open Field	Rank	Sacks	ASR	Rank	Press	Rank
2013	4.27	3.67	11	56%	7	18%	18	1.03	10	0.94	25	47	7.9%	6	25.9%	10
2014	4.96	4.57	32	55%	4	18%	23	1.57	32	0.84	25	46	8.3%	3	23.3%	22
2015	3.83	3.50	7	50%	2	22%	10	1.06	10	0.58	8	47	7.7%	4	28.1%	5

2015 ALY by direction:	Left End 3.35 (14)	Left Tackle 3.10 (9)	Mid/Guard 3.72 (11)	Right Tackle 3.51 (12)	Right End 2.27 (4)

Defensive tackle Dontari Poe's contract expires after the season. The Chiefs have expressed the desire to resign the 2012 first-round pick, who may command in the neighborhood of $13 million to $15 million per year. But their salary-cap situation may make it impossible to resign him. Poe's stats generally suffer because he spends most of every game soaking up a double-team. ☜ Much cheaper than Poe is Jaye Howard, a one-time waiver pickup who signed a two-year, $10 million extension in March. ☜ Perhaps preparing for the possibility that Poe will leave next season, the Chiefs spent their first pick of the draft (37th overall) on defensive tackle Chris Jones of Alabama. The 6-foot-6, 308-pound Jones played basketball in high school and apparently "was one heck of a basketball player, too," according to one Chris Jones. ☜ With Hali aging and Houston out, 2014 first-round edge rusher Dee Ford will see more snaps. In his first two years, Ford put up 5.5 sacks altogether. SackSEER viewed Ford as a potential bust before the 2014 draft due to mediocre production before his senior season at Auburn. He had just two passes defensed in his entire collegiate career.

Defensive Secondary

Secondary	Age	Pos	G	Snaps	Plays	TmPct	Rk	Stop	Dfts	BTkl	Runs	St%	Rk	RuYd	Rk	Tgts	Tgt%	Rk	Dist	Suc%	Rk	AdjYd	Rk	PD	Int
						Overall							**vs. Run**						**vs. Pass**						
Ron Parker	29	SS/CB	16	1057	89	10.9%	24	38	20	15	19	26%	55	9.8	58	57	12.4%	62	10.6	49%	54	7.9	44	10	3
Marcus Peters	23	CB	16	1037	86	10.6%	10	44	20	11	9	56%	16	7.8	43	116	25.8%	69	15.4	57%	15	7.9	39	22	8
Eric Berry	28	FS	16	1033	71	8.7%	49	22	8	15	25	32%	51	8.0	48	31	6.8%	28	9.3	59%	29	5.2	9	10	2
Sean Smith*	29	CB	13	834	57	8.6%	37	25	12	2	10	50%	20	12.8	69	66	18.1%	25	14.6	55%	26	6.8	16	11	2
Husain Abdullah*	31	FS	11	434	28	5.0%	--	14	4	3	13	62%	--	4.8	--	17	8.8%	--	7.0	73%	--	5.6	--	2	0
Tyvon Branch*	30	SS	16	428	45	5.5%	69	18	8	4	14	43%	30	5.1	16	28	15.1%	68	10.4	67%	11	6.4	26	6	1

Year	Pass D Rank	vs. #1 WR	Rk	vs. #2 WR	Rk	vs. Other WR	Rk	vs. TE	Rk	vs. RB	Rk
2013	7	-11.7%	8	-4.4%	12	2.8%	16	-36.9%	2	-7.1%	14
2014	13	5.9%	22	-3.9%	14	1.6%	19	7.3%	23	-2.4%	15
2015	5	7.6%	22	-15.7%	7	9.0%	20	-36.4%	2	-28.9%	3

The arrival of Marcus Peters dramatically changed the way Kansas City used its secondary; the Chiefs had ranked 24th in "CB by Sides" in 2014 but ranked second last season. Peters was just the second rookie cornerback since 1983 to record at least eight interceptions. The fact that Anthony Henry (10 picks with the 2001 Browns) is the other player on that list speaks to the randomness of interception totals, but Henry likely needed luck even more than Peters. Peters' combination of aggressiveness and ball-hawking skills resembles New England's third-year corner Malcolm Butler. The pair also shares a proclivity for taking chances, as shown in both players ranking better by success rate than yards per target. ☜ In addition to third-round corner KeiVarae Russell (Notre Dame), the Chiefs drafted fourth-round corner Eric Murray (Minnesota) and sixth-round corner D.J. White (Georgia Tech). White was projected to go in the third round by NFL.com and the fourth by NFL Draft Scout. ☜ All-Pro safety Eric Berry skipped all offseason workouts after not signing the Chiefs' franchise tender ($10.8 million). Last offseason, Justin Houston pursued the same strategy and ended up with a giant payday. The Chiefs' cap situation makes it less likely that Berry sees his own payday in Kansas City.

Special Teams

Year	DVOA	Rank	FG/XP	Rank	Net Kick	Rank	Kick Ret	Rank	Net Punt	Rank	Punt Ret	Rank	Hidden	Rank
2013	7.8%	1	-5.6	26	3.0	12	19.8	2	4.6	13	17.2	1	5.2	9
2014	6.7%	3	-1.5	20	-2.7	23	12.4	1	11.6	4	13.7	2	0.1	15
2015	2.0%	9	-2.9	25	0.6	16	-0.8	16	16.2	1	-3.1	20	2.8	12

Dave Toub's magic touch hits all areas of special teams. In the first eight years of punter Dustin Colquitt's career, the Chiefs' net punting numbers were slightly better than average. In 2015, the Chiefs led the NFL with 16.2 estimated points of added field position on punts. ☜ Toub has compared fifth-round pick Tyreek Hill (West Alabama) to Devin Hester, whom Toub coached with the Bears. Hill, who ran a 4.24-second 40 at his pro day, may be the Chiefs' fastest player and appears to be the leading candidate to return punts and kickoffs. Hill was dismissed from the Oklahoma State football team after he was arrested for punching and choking his pregnant girlfriend in December 2014. He pled guilty last August and was sentenced to three years of probation. While Hill would have been drafted much earlier without the charge, it's hard to avoid the conclusion that he has served a pretty weak penalty for a pretty terrible offense. ☜ While retired tight end Damian Vaughn appears to be the first player who grew up in Brazil to make it to the NFL, he was actually born in Anchorage, Alaska. So Chiefs kicker Cairo Santos is actually the first Brazilian-*born* player to play in the league. Last October against the Bengals, Santos became the seventh kicker in NFL history to make seven field goals in a game.

Los Angeles Rams

2015 record: 7-9	Total DVOA: -2.2% (16th)	2016 Mean Projection: 7.7 wins	On the Clock (0-4): 10%
Pythagorean Wins: 6.5 (20th)	Offense: -15.0% (29th)	Postseason Odds: 28.0%	Mediocrity (5-7): 37%
Snap-Weighted Age: 25.5 (32nd)	Defense: -10.5% (7th)	Super Bowl Odds: 3.2%	Playoff Contender (8-10): 38%
Average Opponent: 6.3% (3rd)	Special Teams: 2.4% (7th)	Proj. Avg. Opponent: 3.0% (3rd)	Super Bowl Contender (11+): 14%

2015: East St. Louis Toodle-Oo.

2016: Los Angeles fans who enjoy watching Mike Trout ply his transcendent talents for an otherwise mediocre team will really love watching Todd Gurley and Aaron Donald ply their transcendent talents for an otherwise mediocre team.

Had Robert Griffin III's NFL career continued on its original trajectory, the framing of Jeff Fisher's decision would be very different. Since trading away the chance to draft Griffin in 2012, Fisher has rapidly propelled his way through a variety of ineffective quarterbacks. Sam Bradford was supposed to be his long-term starter, but Bradford couldn't stay healthy and started only 24 games. Bradford was ultimately traded for Nick Foles after a subsequent contract dispute, but the Rams clearly overestimated what Foles could do for them; he was benched after 11 games started. To make matters worse, Bradford and Foles are the *best* quarterbacks who have started for Fisher over the past four years; the others are Kellen Clemens (nine starts), Austin Davis (eight starts), Shaun Hill (eight starts), and Case Keenum (five starts).

If Griffin had continued to thrive in Washington after his strong rookie year, the desperation at the Rams' quarterback position would have received an exclamation point. Instead, it's more an ellipsis of four successive losing seasons.

Fisher has a 27-36-1 record since taking over as the Rams head coach and de facto general manager (Les Snead holds that title, but Fisher has final say on the roster). That is the seventh-worst record of any team over that span. Most coaches don't last long enough with that record to reach their fourth season, but Fisher has held onto his job for two reasons. First, the Rams have long been anticipating their relocation from St. Louis to Los Angeles, and owner Stan Kroenke wanted stability with a veteran head coach. Second, the Rams had endured the worst five-year stretch in modern NFL history before Fisher took over. From 2007 to 2011, Steve Spagnuolo, Jim Haslett, and Scott Linehan combined to guide the Rams to a 15-65 record, the worst five-year record by any team since the adoption of 16-game schedule. The Rams were so bad during that stretch that they went 3-13 or worse in four of those five seasons.

Now that Fisher is back in his hometown, he should start feeling a bit more pressure to finally rise from mediocrity. And building a winning NFL team always starts at the quarterback position. For as much as they protested publicly, the Rams knew that they couldn't move forward with Case Keenum even though they outrageously applied a first-round tender to

him and named him their prospective starter after the 2015 season. Keenum is a career backup with a limited skill set. Fisher and Les Snead knew they needed to find a new quarterback but weren't in position to draft one.

Because of their situation, it was likely irrelevant whether the Rams believed Jared Goff was a great prospect or not. What was relevant was that Goff was the best quarterback available in the draft, and he wouldn't be available when the Rams were scheduled to select 15th in the first round. Ironically, four years after trading down instead of selecting Griffin, the Rams were on the other side of a blockbuster quarterback trade.

Goff cost the Rams two first-round picks, two second-round picks, and two third-round picks. They also received two lower-round picks that somewhat cancel out next year's third-rounder, but otherwise Chase Stuart's updated NFL draft chart estimates that the Rams gave Tennessee 131 cents on the dollar plus next year's first-round pick. If the Rams match our mean projection for 2016, trading for Goff will essentially cost them 179 cents on the dollar. He better be worth it.

QBASE, Football Outsiders' model that looks at the resumes of the top quarterback prospects, loves Goff. QBASE gives the former Cal prospect only a 28.3 percent chance of busting against a 34.1 percent chance of being an adequate starter, a 23.5 percent chance of being upper tier, and a 14.2 percent chance of being elite.[1] In comparison, Carson Wentz, the quarterback who went second overall behind Goff, received a 61.9 percent chance of busting and just a 3.8 percent chance of being elite. QBASE was so impressed with Goff that he became the ninth-ranked prospect of the past 21 years, the same spot Marcus Mariota assumed last offseason.

However, there is one major reason to be skeptical about how QBASE is interpreting Goff's college production: California's Air Raid offensive scheme. In an article before this year's draft, Jason Kirk of SB Nation described the Air Raid offense as an "efficient, up-tempo, pass-heavy spread offense made famous by Mike Leach and further developed by... Sonny Dykes, Kevin Sumlin, Kliff Kingsbury, and Dana Holgorsen." Kirk went through the history of quarterback prospects who have played for these coaches in this type of scheme and

---

1 These tiers are explained in the Rookie Projections on page 415.

2016 Rams Schedule

Week	Opp.	Week	Opp.	Week	Opp.
1	at SF (Mon.)	7	NYG (U.K.)	13	at NE
2	SEA	8	BYE	14	ATL
3	at TB	9	CAR	15	at SEA (Thu.)
4	at ARI	10	at NYJ	16	SF (Sat.)
5	BUF	11	MIA	17	ARI
6	at DET	12	at NO		

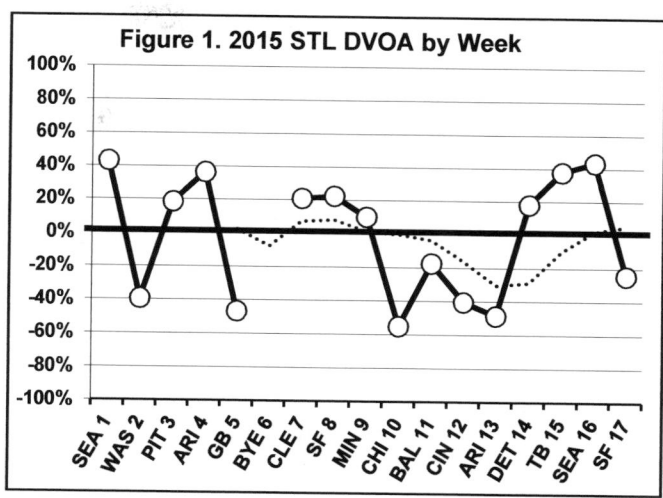

Figure 1. 2015 STL DVOA by Week

it's not pretty. Air Raid quarterbacks chosen in the top 100 picks include some of QBASE's biggest misses, such as John Beck, Geno Smith, and Kevin Kolb (Table 1). The only other Air Raid quarterbacks to start a game in the NFL are Max Hall and, ironically, Case Keenum. Yes, there are other reasons QBASE missed on these players (John Beck and Brandon Weeden's age, Johnny Manziel's mental age of "toddler.") But it is clear that the Air Raid system helps college quarterbacks to put up big numbers against college opponents regardless of the individual quality of the player throwing the ball.

Table 1. Air Raid Quarterbacks, QBASE vs. Actual Performance

Player	College	Team(s)	Round	Pick	Predicted DYAR	Actual DYAR (Yr 3-5)
J.Goff	California	LARM	1	1	1179	--
J.Beck	BYU	MIA/WAS	2	40	1173	-143
G.Smith	West Virginia	NYJ	2	39	1030	72 (Yr 3)
K.Kolb	Houston	PHI/ARI	2	36	875	9
N.Foles	Arizona	PHI/STL	3	88	481	-89 (Yr 3-4)
T.Couch	Kentucky	CLE	1	1	474	-366
J.Manziel	Texas A&M	CLE	1	22	456	--
B.Weeden	Oklahoma St.	CLE/HOU/DAL	1	22	179	152 (Yr 3-4)

The Rams won't employ an Air Raid offense for Goff in 2016. This is Todd Gurley's offense, and the rookie quarterback will just be a complementary piece. Gurley's presence will take pressure off of Goff and allow the Rams to pick and choose how they use him. Less than 12 months removed from the ACL tear that ended his college career, Gurley averaged 20.3 touches in 12 games started, rushing for more than 1,100 yards with 10 touchdowns. Fisher has shown previously that he is willing to run backs into the ground, so expecting the second-year back to carry the ball 400 times isn't unrealistic. Gurley will be tasked with wearing the defense down, primarily running behind left guard Rodger Saffold as his lead blocker.

While Fisher's history tells us that he will build the foundation of his offense on the 21-year-old running back, he has also given voice to his hopes for involving Tavon Austin more. Fisher hopes to give Austin 100 or more catches in 2016, the majority of which will come on YAC plays where Goff can get rid of the ball quickly or throw safely to his diminutive

receiver in space. The combination of Gurley carrying the ball and Austin turning short throws into good gains will help the rookie quarterback sustain drives without making difficult coverage reads or adjustments against pressure.

Putting Goff into favorable situations will be very important. In 2015, the Rams offensive line was a medley of injuries, inexperience, and youth, leading to inconsistent individual and collective performances. It will be especially important to scheme Goff away from pressure. The Rams ranked first in adjusted sack rate last year, giving up just 18 sacks for a 3.5 percent rate, but how they ran their offense played a huge role in creating those results. Despite their low sack rate, the Rams ranked 20th in pressure rate allowed—more in line with the offensive line's performance in recent seasons—and Foles led the league in knockdown rate (both sacks and hits) at 23.0 percent, when no other quarterback had a rate higher than 21.2 percent. The low sack rate despite pressure is partly a product of the quick-throw designs to Austin shot plays off of play-action. Play-action will continue to be a huge part of the Rams' offense; they ranked fourth in the league last year, using play-action on 24 percent of their snaps. Even though the Rams offensive line is young and largely unproven, they do boast the athleticism to be utilized effectively and diversely in both the running and passing games. The Rams have multiple players who can pull outside or across the center in the running game, or act as lead blockers on screens for receivers or running backs.

Gurley and Goff's work won't matter if the Rams defense isn't one of the better units in the league next year. Injuries had a significant impact on the Rams defense in 2015. E.J. Gaines never even made it to the regular season before landing on injured reserve. Chris Long only started five games, playing through pain in a few more. Starting strong safety T.J. McDonald only played in 11 games. Alec Ogletree broke his leg after four games and Robert Quinn started just seven games. Quinn, McDonald, Ogletree, and Long were definite starters, while Gaines was an ascending cornerback who would have played a huge percentage of snaps regardless of whether he was the second or third option. Despite all those absences, the Rams still finished seventh in DVOA. Notably, the Rams finished in the top 10 against the run and against the pass.

Getting players back healthy is one reason the Rams defense will look different in 2016, but an even bigger reason is free-agency departures. Veterans Long and James Laurinaitis were released after serving as foundation pieces of the Rams defense over most of the last decade. Both players were past their primes at this stage and Laurinaitis never really lived up to expectations as an impact middle linebacker. Ogletree will move from outside linebacker to middle linebacker to replace Laurinaitis. Ogletree is a much better athlete who should be an improvement in coverage and with his range from sideline to sideline. The issue that has plagued the young linebacker throughout his career is his ability to get off blocks. Despite his athleticism, Ogletree lacks violent hands and balance to shed offensive linemen. Playing behind Michael Brockers and Aaron Donald will help to hide some of those deficiencies, but Ogletree will need to improve to become a valuable part of the Rams run defense. With Ogletree moving inside, Mark Barron is expected to make his move from safety to linebacker official. Barron essentially played linebacker last year as the third safety behind McDonald and Rodney McLeod. Even with McLeod signing with Philadelphia in free agency, it makes sense to move Barron closer to the line of scrimmage rather than back into a deep role where he lacks the discipline and athleticism to function in space. Finding someone with that discipline and athleticism to play behind McDonald, Ogletree, and Barron will be the Rams' main priority through training camp, as the free safety position looks like a complete mystery at this point.

Cornerback Janoris Jenkins has also moved on, but that departure shouldn't hurt this secondary. Jenkins has really impressive ball skills and could thrive in New York if the Giants pass rush lives up to expectations, but he is also an undisciplined player who tries to intercept every pass that is thrown in his direction. This attitude makes him susceptible to double-moves and creates holes in zone coverages that are easy for the offense to recognize. Jenkins gave up 8.8 adjusted yards per pass last year, ranked 54th in the league, and had a success rate of 47 percent, ranked 61st in the league. With Jenkins gone, Gaines and Trumaine Johnson will start for the Rams outside. Johnson gave up 6.6 yards per pass last year

(12th) and had a success rate of 54 percent (31st). Gaines was a rookie when he last played in 2014, yet he put up phenomenal charting metrics: 6.1 adjusted yards per pass (eighth) with a success rate of 58 percent (11th). Lamarcus Joyner will be the Rams' third cornerback option if he doesn't move to free safety to try and fill the void left by McLeod, who left in free agency.

When it is all put together, it might not matter who plays free safety. Opposing quarterbacks won't have time to throw the ball downfield if Robert Quinn stays healthy all season. Quinn's health issues last year coincided with Aaron Donald's emergence as one of the best players in the league. Even without Quinn's speed coming off the edge pulling the offensive line wider than it wanted to be, Donald was unblockable. He repeatedly destroyed the design of running plays whether he was left unblocked on the backside or targeted with a double-team at the point of attack. As a pass-rusher, Donald had 11 sacks, 27 hits, and 31 hurries. His explosiveness off the line combined with his strong, violent hands and relatively low center of gravity makes him impossible to contain. Putting Donald next to Quinn will stress the very best of offensive lines in ways that they've never been stressed before. If Dominique Easley can stay healthy, he will give the Rams a third pass-rusher with the explosiveness to beat the ball off the ground. Easley is a phenomenal talent whose career has been marred by health issues and personality conflicts that ultimately led to his premature release from the New England Patriots. The Rams will be able to manage his snaps, using him as a situational interior pass-rusher behind Michael Brockers.

With Gurley, the defensive line, the cornerbacks, and an expected improvement at quarterback, the Rams should be a better team in 2016 despite their key losses in free agency. That doesn't guarantee an improvement in the standings, of course, but Fisher should be able to do enough to keep his job for the first two years of Goff's career. Even though Ken Whisenhunt and Lovie Smith drafted quarterbacks before getting fired last season, the Rams would need to suffer a disastrous year for ownership to even consider disrupting the development of a rookie they invested six picks in.

Cian Fahey

2015 Rams Stats by Week

Wk	vs.	W-L	PF	PA	YDF	YDA	TO	Total	Off	Def	ST
1	SEA	W	34	31	352	343	-2	43%	18%	-30%	-5%
2	at WAS	L	10	24	213	373	1	-39%	-35%	10%	6%
3	PIT	L	6	12	258	259	0	19%	-14%	-27%	6%
4	at ARI	W	24	22	328	447	3	37%	14%	-16%	7%
5	at GB	L	10	24	334	322	-1	-47%	-63%	-29%	-12%
6	BYE										
7	CLE	W	24	6	308	364	3	21%	3%	-19%	-1%
8	SF	W	27	6	388	189	-1	23%	-5%	-33%	-6%
9	at MIN	L	18	21	320	293	1	10%	-9%	-13%	6%
10	CHI	L	13	37	285	397	0	-55%	-57%	10%	11%
11	at BAL	L	13	16	213	388	-2	-17%	-32%	-28%	-13%
12	at CIN	L	7	31	345	376	-2	-40%	-34%	4%	-1%
13	ARI	L	3	27	212	524	-1	-49%	-36%	29%	16%
14	DET	W	21	14	317	331	-1	18%	10%	-6%	2%
15	TB	W	31	23	319	509	2	38%	23%	13%	28%
16	at SEA	W	23	17	205	312	3	43%	1%	-45%	-3%
17	at SF	L	16	19	364	458	1	-24%	-15%	7%	-2%

Trends and Splits

	Offense	Rank	Defense	Rank
Total DVOA	-15.0%	29	-10.5%	7
Unadjusted VOA	-15.5%	29	-4.9%	13
Weighted Trend	-15.6%	29	-6.1%	11
Variance	6.8%	19	4.4%	16
Average Opponent	-1.5%	14	4.4%	1
Passing	-13.5%	31	-4.3%	8
Rushing	-6.4%	14	-18.5%	7
First Down	-6.8%	23	-18.5%	3
Second Down	-11.9%	25	6.1%	25
Third Down	-36.3%	31	-21.1%	4
First Half	-16.6%	28	-15.9%	5
Second Half	-13.6%	31	-4.9%	9
Red Zone	-2.4%	18	-29.8%	3
Late and Close	4.8%	10	-8.6%	15

Five-Year Performance

Year	W-L	Pyth W	Est W	PF	PA	TO	Total	Rk	Off	Rk	Def	Rk	ST	Rk	Off AGL	Rk	Def AGL	Rk	Off Age	Rk	Def Age	Rk	ST Age	Rk
2011	2-14	2.3	2.2	193	407	-5	-35.4%	32	-27.2%	32	3.4%	21	-4.8%	28	66.5	32	43.5	27	27.1	16	27.6	7	26.4	11
2012	7-8-1	6.6	8.2	299	348	-1	1.5%	15	-4.2%	21	-9.1%	7	-3.4%	26	28.0	16	8.3	3	26.3	23	26.3	24	25.5	29
2013	7-9	7.6	7.8	348	364	+8	2.4%	14	-9.5%	22	-5.7%	11	6.3%	4	26.1	10	21.4	10	26.1	28	25.0	31	25.0	30
2014	6-10	7.1	6.1	324	354	-2	-3.8%	18	-11.1%	25	-3.8%	9	3.5%	7	37.6	21	26.5	7	26.5	23	25.0	32	25.2	32
2015	7-9	6.5	7.9	280	330	+5	-2.2%	16	-15.0%	29	-10.5%	7	2.4%	7	32.3	16	48.0	29	25.2	32	26.1	25	24.9	32

2015 Performance Based on Most Common Personnel Groups

LARM Offense					LARM Offense vs. Opponents					LARM Defense				LARM Defense vs. Opponents			
Pers	Freq	Yds	DVOA	Run%	Pers	Freq	Yds	DVOA	Run%	Pers	Freq	Yds	DVOA	Pers	Freq	Yds	DVOA
11	50%	5.5	-13.7%	30%	Base	40%	5.2	-3.2%	64%	Base	6%	5.0	-9.8%	11	50%	5.3	-16.0%
12	18%	6.9	12.6%	41%	Nickel	47%	5.8	-12.2%	35%	Nickel	48%	5.8	-8.9%	12	25%	6.2	-0.7%
21	17%	4.7	-9.4%	70%	Dime+	12%	5.0	-38.9%	15%	Dime+	46%	5.4	-11.7%	21	8%	5.4	-11.9%
22	11%	3.1	-44.1%	74%	Goal Line	1%	0.4	78.7%	60%	Goal Line	0%	0.3	-46.8%	22	5%	4.3	-32.1%
01	2%	5.2	2.2%	56%										13	4%	5.5	23.4%
02	1%	5.5	-23.8%	50%										10	2%	6.0	-12.4%

Strategic Tendencies

Run/Pass		Rk	Formation		Rk	Pass Rush		Rk	Secondary		Rk	Strategy		Rk
Runs, first half	45%	3	Form: Single Back	61%	32	Rush 3	7.2%	15	4 DB	6%	32	Play action	24%	4
Runs, first down	61%	2	Form: Empty Back	2%	31	Rush 4	52.1%	30	5 DB	48%	23	Avg Box (Off)	6.32	10
Runs, second-long	32%	14	Pers: 3+ WR	53%	24	Rush 5	28.9%	6	6+ DB	46%	2	Avg Box (Def)	6.30	14
Runs, power sit.	73%	1	Pers: 2+ TE/6+ OL	30%	20	Rush 6+	11.8%	5	CB by Sides	88%	5	Offensive Pace	31.93	28
Runs, behind 2H	31%	3	Pers: 6+ OL	0%	28	Sacks by LB	11.0%	30	S/CB Cover Ratio	19%	26	Defensive Pace	31.62	30
Pass, ahead 2H	40%	30	Shotgun/Pistol	42%	31	Sacks by DB	12.2%	8	DB Blitz	21%	1	Go for it on 4th	0.72	24

Last year was the eighth season in the last nine where the Rams ranked 24th or worse in offensive DVOA on third downs. They were particularly horrendous on third-and-long, where their appalling -120.0% DVOA was more than twice as bad as the No. 31 Titans (-61.6%). That gap was roughly equivalent to the gap between the Titans and the league average. ☞ The Rams' DVOA splits were massively influenced by Todd Gurley. For example, the Rams had the worst passing DVOA in the red zone (-61.9%), but the second-best rushing DVOA in the red zone (59.6%). And the Rams were one of only two offenses to have a positive DVOA running in second-and-long situations (Pittsburgh was the other). ☞ Another aspect of Gurley's influence: the 2014 Rams had the league's lowest run/pass ratio in short-yardage situations, while last year's Rams had the highest. ☞ The Rams also led the NFL with broken tackles on 13.2 percent of plays. Gurley ranked sixth with 46 and Tavon Austin led wide receivers with 34. ☞ The Rams had the league's biggest gap in offensive DVOA using play-action vs. other pass plays. They had 9.0 yards per play and 33.8% DVOA with play-action, but 5.0 yards per play and -28.4% DVOA (both the lowest figure in the league) without play-action. ☞ 62 percent of runs by Rams running backs came with two backs in the formation, far ahead of any other NFL offense. (Green Bay was the only other team above 47 percent.) The Rams actually gained 1.5 yards per carry less on runs from two-back formations, although their DVOA was no different. This was an issue of consistency: it just so happened that only two of the Rams' eight runs over 30 yards came from two-back sets. ☞ After we removed deliberate throwaways and passes batted down at the line, the Rams were the only team in the league that still had a negative offensive DVOA on short passes (up to 15 yards past the line of scrimmage). ☞ Opponents tried to slow down the Rams' defensive line with screens. Many, many screens. The Rams faced the most wide receiver screens (49) and the most running back screens (37). They were good against both plays: -22.2% DVOA against wide receiver screens (eighth) and -20.3% DVOA against running back screens (10th). ☞ The Rams had a top-ten defense against passes on both the left and right sides, but ranked 22nd in DVOA on passes in the middle of the field. ☞ The defense strangely had its issues on second down, posting a 6.1% DVOA which ranked 25th. However, they were a top-four defense on both first down (-18.5%) and third down (-21.1%). ☞ The Rams led the league in special teams penalties (35) and penalty yards (249). This is a consistent problem, as the Rams were tied for second and tied for third, respectively, in 2014.

Passing

Player	DYAR	DVOA	Plays	NtYds	Avg	YAC	C%	TD	Int
N.Foles	-353	-27.9%	350	1944	5.6	6.1	56.9%	7	10
C.Keenum	83	-1.1%	131	795	6.1	5.3	61.1%	4	1
S.Mannion	7	4.3%	7	31	4.4	1.8	85.7%	0	0

Rushing

Player	DYAR	DVOA	Plays	Yds	Avg	TD	Fum	Suc
T.Gurley	170	10.0%	229	1102	4.8	10	3	43%
T.Mason	-99	-41.7%	75	209	2.8	1	3	39%
T.Austin	253	41.5%	51	427	8.4	4	0	-
B.Cunningham	-10	-14.9%	37	140	3.8	0	1	38%
M.Brown	0	-5.9%	4	17	4.3	0	0	50%

Receiving

Player	DYAR	DVOA	Plays	Ctch	Yds	Y/C	YAC	TD	C%
T.Austin	-122	-30.6%	88	53	484	9.1	6.8	5	60%
K.Britt	139	11.0%	72	36	681	18.9	3.3	3	50%
B.Quick	-110	-56.7%	32	10	102	10.2	3.9	0	31%
S.Bailey	-12	-19.4%	25	12	182	15.2	5.9	1	48%
W.Welker*	-36	-34.6%	22	13	102	7.8	3.8	0	59%
B.Marquez	-61	-51.4%	22	13	88	6.8	1.8	0	59%
J.Cook*	-76	-23.5%	75	39	481	12.3	5.1	0	52%
L.Kendricks	-17	-13.6%	40	25	245	9.8	5.2	2	63%
B.Cunningham	67	28.3%	36	26	250	9.6	9.2	0	72%
T.Gurley	25	2.1%	26	21	188	9.0	9.6	0	81%
T.Mason	-18	-31.5%	21	18	88	4.9	6.6	0	86%
C.Harkey	-1	-15.9%	6	5	26	5.2	4.4	0	83%

Offensive Line

Player	Pos	Age	GS	Snaps	Pen	Sk	Pass	Run	Player	Pos	Age	GS	Snaps	Pen	Sk	Pass	Run
Greg Robinson	LT	24	16/16	960	16	3.5	9.5	3.0	Jamon Brown	G	23	9/9	533	3	2.0	3.0	5.0
Tim Barnes	C	28	16/16	956	2	0.5	4.5	6.0	Cody Wichmann	RG	24	12/7	424	0	0.5	0.5	3.0
Garrett Reynolds	G/T	29	16/11	730	5	1.0	2.0	1.0	Rodger Saffold	LG	28	5/5	234	2	0.0	1.0	2.0
Rob Havenstein	RT	24	13/13	728	0	0.0	2.0	0.0									

Year	Yards	ALY	Rank	Power	Rank	Stuff	Rank	2nd Lev	Rank	Open Field	Rank	Sacks	ASR	Rank	Press	Rank	F-Start	Cont.
2013	3.95	3.95	12	58%	25	19%	13	1.05	20	0.68	16	36	6.8%	14	26.6%	22	13	29
2014	4.08	3.90	18	53%	30	21%	29	1.18	14	0.71	16	47	8.6%	23	31.5%	30	20	38
2015	4.24	3.56	24	64%	20	23%	28	1.03	24	1.17	3	18	3.5%	1	27.0%	20	16	25

2015 ALY by direction: Left End 2.95 (26)   Left Tackle 3.98 (13)   Mid/Guard 3.75 (21)   Right Tackle 3.9 (12)   Right End 2.06 (30)

Offensive line coach Paul Boudreau will return all five of his starters for the first time since taking over the role in 2012. Boudreau has never had an opportunity to create an understanding or consistency between his starters because he has never had continuity with his personnel. ☜ Two high picks from last year's draft have finally stabilized this line on the right side. Jamon Brown missed half of his rookie season after an ugly leg fracture, but did enough in the first two months to solidify his spot as the team's starting right guard for the foreseeable future. At right tackle, Rob Havenstein stayed healthy all season and outperformed his fellow rookie. Havenstein showed more precision and control in his play than Greg Robinson has over his two years in the league, and was the only tackle with at least 160 snaps not to commit a penalty all season. ☜ When the Rams selected him second overall in 2014, Robinson was immediately discussed as a generational talent who could solidify the position for a decade or more. He is a great athlete and that athleticism has been put on show regularly when he has worked in space as a run or screen blocker, but Robinson is as raw in pass protection today as he was when he was drafted. Robinson has no technique with his hand placement or balance in his feet, making him a liability in pass protection. The former Auburn player is entering a critical season.

Defensive Front Seven

Defensive Line	Age	Pos	G	Snaps	Plays	TmPct	Rk	Stop	Dfts	BTkl	Runs	St%	Rk	RuYd	Rk	Sack	Hit	Hur	Dsrpt
							Overall					**vs. Run**				**Pass Rush**			
Aaron Donald	25	DT	16	915	70	7.7%	10	57	31	3	54	80%	31	1.3	5	11.0	27	31.0	1
Michael Brockers	26	DT	16	690	43	4.8%	45	34	12	4	37	78%	39	1.5	11	3.0	3	6.0	0
Nick Fairley*	28	DT	15	422	30	3.5%	--	22	3	2	24	79%	--	2.8	--	0.5	7	8.0	1
Dominique Easley	*24*	*DT*	*11*	*275*	*14*	*2.5%*	--	*12*	*7*	*0*	*9*	*78%*	--	*1.9*	--	*2.0*	*7*	*12.5*	*0*

Edge Rushers	Age	Pos	G	Snaps	Plays	TmPct	Rk	Stop	Dfts	BTkl	Runs	St%	Rk	RuYd	Rk	Sack	Hit	Hur	Dsrpt
							Overall					**vs. Run**				**Pass Rush**			
Eugene Sims	30	DE	13	582	24	3.3%	80	14	8	3	13	62%	84	5.4	95	1.5	4	13.5	2
William Hayes	31	DE	16	581	51	5.6%	33	39	19	3	37	78%	29	1.4	18	5.5	8	24.0	0
Chris Long*	31	DE	12	485	19	2.8%	86	14	4	2	13	77%	34	3.2	82	3.0	1	9.0	0
Robert Quinn	26	DE	8	339	24	5.3%	41	19	11	1	15	67%	71	3.5	88	5.0	5	7.5	3
Ethan Westbrooks	26	DE	13	276	19	2.6%	--	14	5	2	16	69%	--	2.3	--	2.0	2	6.5	0

Linebackers	Age	Pos	G	Snaps	Plays	TmPct	Rk	Stop	Dfts	BTkl	Runs	St%	Rk	RuYd	Rk	Sack	Hit	Hur	Tgts	Suc%	Rk	AdjYd	Rk	PD	Int
							Overall					**vs. Run**				**Pass Rush**				**vs. Pass**					
James Laurinaitis*	30	MLB	16	1156	110	12.2%	43	58	19	6	62	65%	42	4.0	67	1.0	9	8	14	55%	43	7.8	59	1	1
Mark Barron	27	OLB	16	920	116	12.8%	39	63	35	10	59	68%	30	3.5	41	1.0	5	9	14	65%	17	2.7	2	3	0
Akeem Ayers	27	OLB	16	527	52	5.7%	84	32	7	12	28	79%	3	2.5	4	0.5	2	5.5	13	60%	24	9.7	68	3	0
Alec Ogletree	25	OLB	4	265	42	18.6%	4	18	7	5	22	64%	46	4.3	75	2.0	1	1	6	40%	--	13.4	--	0	0

Year	Yards	ALY	Rank	Power	Rank	Stuff	Rank	2nd Level	Rank	Open Field	Rank	Sacks	ASR	Rank	Press	Rank
2013	3.80	3.50	5	51%	4	27%	2	1.13	18	0.77	20	53	9.5%	1	25.8%	12
2014	3.88	3.31	3	55%	4	24%	5	1.12	14	0.82	22	40	6.7%	15	26.2%	8
2015	3.97	3.39	6	63%	14	24%	7	1.13	17	0.90	24	41	6.3%	17	28.3%	4
2015 ALY by direction:		*Left End 3.71 (19)*			*Left Tackle 3.69 (13)*			*Mid/Guard 3.28 (4)*			*Right Tackle 3.35 (10)*			*Right End 3.21 (15)*		

The Rams don't know exactly what they are going to get from their defensive line but they can be confident that the unit will be dominant with Aaron Donald and Robert Quinn healthy. Where they will have questions is at middle linebacker. Alec Ogletree barely played in 2015, starting just four games due to a broken leg. He had started all 32 games during his first two seasons before that point, repeatedly showing off the athleticism that made him a first-round pick coming out of Georgia. Athleticism in a linebacker is typically enough to label him a good defender in coverage. Ogletree has 22 career pass deflections and three interceptions, but he hasn't been good in coverage. When he last played a full season, in 2014, Ogletree had a success rate in coverage of 51 percent, making him the 36th-ranked linebacker in the league. The adjusted yards per pass and YAC allowed with Ogletree in coverage were also poor. While he has the physical talent to bully receivers and he can cover ground with ease from sideline to sideline, Ogletree lacks the awareness and subtlety in his feet to be a great coverage linebacker. That will be an issue as he moves from outside linebacker to the inside. To offer value to the Rams, Ogletree needs to excel in coverage, because he has had major issues as a run defender over his first three years in the league.

Defensive Secondary

Secondary	Age	Pos	G	Snaps	Plays	TmPct	Overall Rk	Stop	Dfts	BTkl	vs. Run Runs	St%	Rk	RuYd	Rk	vs. Pass Tgts	Tgt%	Rk	Dist	Suc%	Rk	AdjYd	Rk	PD	Int
Rodney McLeod*	26	FS	16	1154	85	9.4%	42	25	11	9	48	25%	57	12.9	67	13	3.6%	3	16.2	59%	33	8.3	49	2	1
Janoris Jenkins*	28	CB	15	1039	80	9.4%	24	41	15	10	10	70%	6	7.6	42	68	20.5%	46	12.7	49%	51	7.7	37	14	3
Trumaine Johnson	26	CB	14	906	88	11.1%	5	38	17	13	10	50%	20	5.8	22	69	24.1%	65	11.7	55%	28	5.9	10	14	7
T.J. McDonald	25	SS	11	772	62	10.0%	34	27	13	12	34	50%	16	5.5	18	21	8.4%	44	9.0	45%	61	6.2	22	1	0
Lamarcus Joyner	26	CB	16	730	78	8.6%	–	34	19	10	23	39%	–	7.9	–	43	18.4%	–	8.3	59%	–	5.9	–	4	0
Maurice Alexander	25	SS	14	419	35	4.4%	–	15	5	2	9	56%	–	5.8	–	15	10.9%	–	12.4	47%	–	8.7	–	1	0
Marcus Roberson	24	CB	16	328	33	3.6%	–	13	7	3	1	0%	–	15.0	–	27	25.5%	–	10.6	41%	–	8.9	–	5	0
Coty Sensabaugh	28	CB	16	1005	66	8.5%	42	26	11	9	17	47%	31	6.5	32	70	20.0%	41	13.9	47%	59	8.5	53	8	2

Year	Pass D Rank	vs. #1 WR	Rk	vs. #2 WR	Rk	vs. Other WR	Rk	vs. TE	Rk	vs. RB	Rk
2013	15	41.6%	32	-16.1%	5	0.6%	15	-41.6%	1	25.6%	32
2014	20	3.5%	19	33.8%	31	-1.0%	15	-12.2%	6	-9.9%	10
2015	8	-26.4%	2	-19.1%	6	4.1%	16	-4.0%	16	-3.0%	13

T.J. McDonald had a disappointing season in 2015. The Rams' strong safety had thrived in 2014 and looked set to establish himself as one of the best safeties in the league, but his controlled aggression appeared to be less controlled and less aggressive last year. McDonald only played in 11 games because of a shoulder injury and ranked 62nd in adjusted success rate in coverage. That was a real drop from 2014, when he ranked 14th among safeties with an adjusted success rate of 62 percent. McDonald fit perfectly as a complement to Rodney McLeod, but his role could change now that the Rams have less certainty/quality at free safety—and not in a way that emphasizes his strengths. With safety/linebacker hybrid Mark Barron and nickelback Lamarcus Joyner capable of playing underneath zones, McDonald could find himself with more deep zone assignments in 2016. ⊜ The candidates for the other starting safety spot are fairly unknown. Mo Alexander was originally an outside linebacker at Utah State, and much like McDonald, he has been more of a box safety in his two years with the Rams. Cody Davis (undrafted in 2013) and Christian Bryant (seventh round in 2014) have primarily played on special teams. The 5-foot-9 Bryant would be particularly small for a safety; Atlanta's Ricardo Allen and Arizona's Tyrann Mathieu were the only starting safeties at 5-foot-9 last season, and Bryant is probably not the next Honey Badger.

Special Teams

Year	DVOA	Rank	FG/XP	Rank	Net Kick	Rank	Kick Ret	Rank	Net Punt	Rank	Punt Ret	Rank	Hidden	Rank
2013	6.3%	4	1.4	16	12.6	1	-1.4	17	22.4	1	-3.5	19	11.1	4
2014	3.5%	7	-4.7	28	0.1	17	-1.2	19	11.3	5	12.1	3	4.4	10
2015	2.4%	7	-6.7	30	2.5	9	4.0	7	10.4	5	1.6	13	1.0	14

Special teams have been a point of pride for Jeff Fisher's Rams. The franchise has ranked in the top 10 of special teams DVOA in each of the past three seasons, primarily relying on their proficiency punting the ball. Johnny Hekker was the best punter in the league according to our gross punting metric; his punts were worth an estimated 13.0 points worth of field position compared to average. When Hekker hasn't been dropping balls inside the opposition's 20-yard line from 45-plus yards away, he has been completing passes for first downs on fakes. He had his worst year as a passer in 2015, completing just one of four attempts for 20 yards, but the Rams won't mind so long as he continues to excel punting the ball. ⊜ Kicker Greg "The Leg" Zuerlein has been surprisingly subpar for a couple of seasons, but he's not as bad as his raw field goal percentage would indicate. Zuerlein hit only 20 of 30 attempts last season (66.7 percent), but he did hit a 61-yard field goal while six of his 10 misses were 50-plus-yard attempts, two of them 63-yarders. Two of his remaining four misses came from 48 yards away. Zuerlein faces a camp battle with undrafted rookie Taylor Bertolet, but it's hard to see him getting beat out by a guy who only connected on 37 of 56 field goals (66.1 percent) at Texas A&M. ⊜ Tavon Austin returns punts and Benny Cunningham returns kickoffs, and neither is likely to change in 2016.

Miami Dolphins

2015 record: 6-10	Total DVOA: -19.0% (29th)	2016 Mean Projection: 6.1 wins	On the Clock (0-4): 27%
Pythagorean Wins: 5.8 (28th)	Offense: -7.3% (22nd)	Postseason Odds: 13.3%	Mediocrity (5-7): 46%
Snap-Weighted Age: 26.0 (29th)	Defense: 9.0% (25th)	Super Bowl Odds: 0.8%	Playoff Contender (8-10): 23%
Average Opponent: -2.4% (20th)	Special Teams: -2.7% (24th)	Proj. Avg. Opponent: 2.9% (4th)	Super Bowl Contender (11+): 4%

2015: Four months of inscrutable strategy and inconsistent performance.

2016: We have met the enemy and he is us.

Dolphins executive vice president Mike Tannenbaum told a Florida television station in March that the 2016 Dolphins "would beat the crap out of the 2015 Dolphins."

Finally, after nearly a decade, we have evidence of why the Dolphins are so persistently mediocre. They aren't building to beat the Patriots or any of the NFL's other elite teams. They are building to beat themselves.

We should have figured this out years ago. Richie Incognito and Jonathan Martin? A team built to beat the crap out of itself. Dan Campbell ordering midseason Okie drills? A team built to beat the crap out of itself. Endless power struggles among the coaching staff and front office, like the one that elevated Tannenbaum over Dennis Hickey or Campbell over the overmatched Joe Philbin? An organization built to beat the crap out of itself. Ryan Tannehill allegedly getting into beefs with practice squad defenders? You get the idea.

The Dolphins' roster-management strategy has always been based on the most hardheaded approach to self-improvement: massive trades, signings, expenditures and overhauls designed to catapult the team from 7-9 to the giddy heights of 8-8, with no regard for the short-term growing pains or long-term cap ramifications caused by annual upheavals. The Dolphins are the NFL's yo-yo dieters, willing to purchase juicers and treadmills but incapable of walking an extra half-mile, eating a little more broccoli, or making other simple changes that lead to real results.

This offseason's Big Sweeping Changes began with the promotion of Tannenbaum and the arrival of Adam Gase to fumigate away Campbell and his hive of interim decision-makers before they turned team headquarters into a junior high tree fort.

Gase has been on the head-coaching short list since he jerry-rigged a semi-functional offense for Tim Tebow in Denver five years ago. Gase then offered helpful suggestions to Peyton Manning for two years before following John Fox to Chicago, where he performed the dual miracle of: a) making Jay Cutler look efficient when throwing to the likes of Josh Bellamy and Marc Mariani, and b) making Jay Cutler seem content, professional, and pleasant under any circumstances whatsoever.

Gase's ability to adapt to his quarterbacks is great news for Ryan Tannehill, whose growth was stunted by too many sacks and inscrutable Philbin game plans and who clearly wasn't fit to travel on Mad Campbell's Fury Road. The thru line of Gase's chameleon offenses—option concepts (Tebow), high-percentage short passing (Manning, Cutler), a willingness to work with available talent (Tebow, Cutler's injured receivers) and ego-personality-expectation management (all of them)—bodes well for Tannehill, whose career has been defined by peripheral clashes, not his own capabilities.

Gase's arrival was an encouraging sign. Tannenbaum's promotion is a more troubling one. Tannenbaum was the architect of the Mark Sanchez and Santonio Holmes contracts for the Jets, the ones that greased the skids on that organization's downward spiral from contender to comedy. Tannenbaum is an over-spender, and his fingerprints could be seen on the Ndamukong Suh contract (nearly $60 million guaranteed, $5 million more than any human in the NFL, quarterbacks included) and Mike Pouncey's 2015 extension (five years and $44.75 million reported, with rolling guarantees, for a very-good-not-great center) even before he wrested full roster control from Hickey.

With Tannenbaum holding the purse strings—Chris Greer is officially the general manager, but as of May the team website didn't even include a link to his bio, planting the seed for some future revolution—the Dolphins entered the 2016 offseason poised to once again follow the Twin Pillars of Dolphins Sideways Rebuilding:

• Paying a premium to acquire big-name players only slightly better than the players released to clear the necessary cap space to sign them, and
• Leaving one gaping hole somewhere on the roster, despite massive expenditures elsewhere.

Pillar One was erected before free agency even started, when Tannenbaum acquired expensive Chip Kelly extravagancies Byron Maxwell and Kiko Alonso in exchange for a first-round trade-down. The first-round swap worked out well for the Dolphins in the end (more on that in a moment), but Brent Grimes was released days after the Maxwell trade to clear cap space (and, according to some, to rid the Dolphins of Grimes' opinionated wife, which would be a heck of a reason to release a veteran starting cornerback).

Charting shows that replacing Grimes with Maxwell is essentially a wash. The aging Grimes is no longer the Pro Bowl-

2016 Dolphins Schedule

Week	Opp.	Week	Opp.	Week	Opp.
1	at SEA	7	BUF	13	at BAL
2	at NE	8	BYE	14	ARI
3	CLE	9	NYJ	15	at NYJ (Sat.)
4	at CIN (Thu.)	10	at SD	16	at BUF (Sat.)
5	TEN	11	at LARM	17	NE
6	PIT	12	SF		

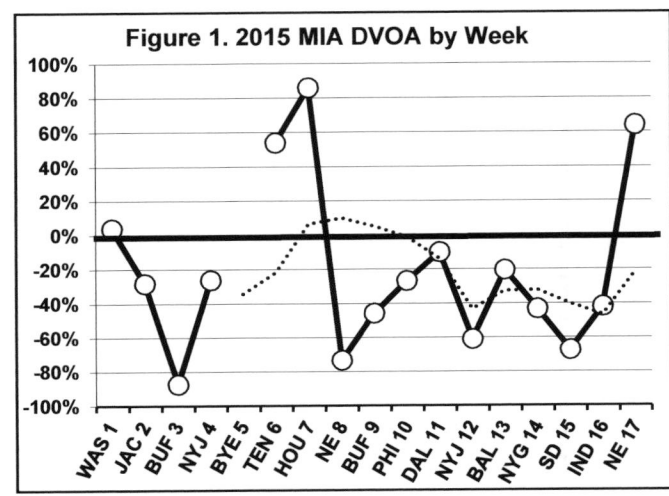

Figure 1. 2015 MIA DVOA by Week

caliber corner of a couple years ago; our game charting last year ranked him 71st out of 75 cornerbacks in adjusted success rate, and 72nd in adjusted yards per pass. But Maxwell was essentially the same, ranked 64th and 71st in the same metrics. Maxwell is five years younger, but he's also in the second year of an outrageous $63 million contract that the Dolphins did not bother to renegotiate. Alonso is a theoretical upgrade at linebacker if you focus on the rookie star of 2013 instead of the injury-prone, limited-use role player he became after the Eagles traded LeSean McCoy to grab him last year.

The Maxwell-Grimes swap at least represented an age and (possibly) attitude upgrade, so the Dolphins quickly undid that by letting 25-year-old Olivier Vernon depart via free agency after signing 31-year-old Bills malcontent Mario Williams. Williams comes with a relatively modest two-year contract; $8.5 million in full guarantees isn't a bad bargain for a four-time Pro Bowler, even a pass-rusher who somehow managed to try Rex Ryan's patience.

Vernon, meanwhile, caught the Giants in a rare generous mood and received $40 million in full guarantees. Perhaps the price tag was a little steep, but successful organizations place a premium on retaining players like Vernon, a pass-rusher on the rise with perennial Pro Bowl potential. Tannenbaum instead spent his money on Williams and a contract extension for Cameron Wake, a 34-year-old coming off an Achilles injury.

When you fit the Maxwell-Grimes-Vernon-Williams-Wake jigsaw pieces together you see the ultimate Dolphins offseason puzzle. The Dolphins made their defense older, younger, cheaper, more expensive, and both more and less likely to turn sour at the first sign of trouble. They acquired Alonso in the shuffle, but they placed themselves in bad position to re-sign running back Lamar Miller at market value, leading to Pillar Two of Dolphins Sideways Rebuilding: the Dolphins left the busy March transaction period without a running back.

Miller is 25 years old, has always had a responsible workload, and is a dynamic rusher-receiver who usually produces positive DVOA results despite offensive philosophies that changed monthly and blockers who sometimes wanted to punch each other. Miller only cost the Texans $14 million in guaranteed money in a four-year contract; retaining a versatile young back at a price like that is a frugal solution. The Dolphins turned it into a complicated problem.

The Dolphins first pursued restricted free agent C.J. Anderson; the Broncos decided to match their offer. The Dolphins then made an unsuccessful run at Chris Johnson. Twice jilted, they grabbed Isaiah Pead from the bottom of the 99 cent bin,

skipped the first two rounds of a running back-heavy draft, selected Alabama change-up back Kenyon Drake in the third round, then skipped the last four rounds of the same running back-heavy draft.

Arian Foster signed with the Dolphins in mid-July. Foster is just two years removed from a 1,200-yard season. He also turns 30 before the start of the season and missed 23 games in the last three seasons with injuries. If Foster has as little left in the tank as it appears—remember, he was available as a street free agent on July 18th—the Dolphins will fold him into a rotation consisting of Drake (whose minicamp injury probably sent the Dolphins to market to fetch Foster), Jay Ajayi, Daniel Thomas (a fumble-prone 28-year-old the team parted ways with last offseason but brought back in December) and Pead, who played three snaps last year but still managed to fumble once. It's a uniquely Dolphins patchwork of creaky veterans, semi-prospects, and guys like Thomas and Pead with no real role or purpose.

At least the draft worked out for the Dolphins, if only by accident. Laremy Tunsil is the best left tackle prospect to enter the NFL in years: a Trent Williams/Tyron Smith-level prospect, if not another Orlando Pace or Walter Jones. Tunsil was expected to be the first or second non-quarterback off the draft board. But a video of Tunsil smoking pot through a surgical mask bong appeared on the Internet just hours before the draft, and NFL front offices reacted like grandmas who saw the bachelor party photos minutes before the wedding. Tunsil slipped to 13th, right where the Dolphins landed after the Maxwell swap meet.

Tunsil joins low-cost, low-risk free agent Jermon Bushrod (yes, the Dolphins sometimes make low-cost/risk moves, too) to improve an offensive line that should remain south of 45 sacks allowed for the first time since Tannehill's rookie year and will open some holes for the Dolphins' hypothetical running backs. Tunsil is likely to start his NFL career at left guard, but will eventually replace left tackle Brandon Albert, the pricey, disappointing solution to the Incognito-Martin mess two years ago. And so the spend-and-purge circle of life continues for the Dolphins, though Tunsil should be a keystone player if the Dolphins ever figure out how to stop paddling their canoe around in a circle.

Could this team kick the crap out of the 2015 Dolphins? Possibly. The 2015 Dolphins won six games. After Philbin (and later coordinator Bill Lazor) were fired, Campbell ran the team as if it was being coached by an Internet message board. They switched from all-run to all-pass philosophies weekly, became weird and evasive about injuries (DeVante Parker, for example, tore scar tissue in his foot sometime last season but was declared "fine" by Campbell), sent mixed messages to Tannehill, and played most of the last two months like they wore themselves out with midseason Okie drills—which is precisely what they did. Gase will at least stabilize the Dolphins. They may not be better immediately, but they can at least regain the professionalism needed to start moving forward.

But can this team actually play competitive football on a week-to-week basis, beating the average teams on its schedule and defeating quality opponents who don't have a Week 17 hand tied behind their backs? Aye, there's the rub.

If pressed to guess how the 2016 Dolphins actually win games, you would probably say that they were a defense-first team built around their front four, with an offense designed for efficient passing and a little option seasoning. The Super Mario-Suh-Earl Mitchell-Wake line represents a heavy investment of money and energy. Even the bench is pricey: Andre Branch will back up Mario and Wake for $2.7 million in 2016, with Jason Jones joining the mix in late May for a reported $1.5 million.

Based on name recognition and sticker price, the Dolphins have a 50-sack line that should give Tom Brady fits. But the Dolphins recorded just 31 sacks last year and finished 22nd in adjusted sack rate, and the Vernon-Williams swap could easily subtract from the sack total instead of adding to it.

Assuming Williams comes to play, Wake stays healthy, and Suh doesn't go to that planet he orbits when things aren't going his way, the Dolphins will generate a consistent pass rush. That's good news, because their projected starting cornerbacks are Maxwell, second-round pick Xavien Howard, and a pair of fifth-round picks from last year named Bobby McCain and Tony Lippett.

Howard was a big cornerback with a slow 40 time who had a bad habit of grabbing receivers at Baylor; he projects as more of a matchup nickelback than The Next Richard Sherman™. McCain and Lippett were passable in limited roles

last year. Safety Reshad Jones can play camp counselor to the youngsters in the secondary, but the Dolphins have second, a third and a pair of fourth cornerbacks vying for the starting and nickel positions. It will take a 1980s Bears-level pass rush to turn them into a playoff-caliber unit.

Jones also skipped OTAs in a contract dispute. Suh and Super Mario skipped because they are important superstar veterans who don't have to attend OTAs. Three of the most important players and best-compensated players on the Dolphins defense are not 100 percent with the program, which is exactly the kind of thing that happens when your "program" consists of overspending and changing management every two years. If the Dolphins were capable of constructing a Seahawks-style defense-and-options contender using their typical tactics, they would have done so by now.

It's shocking that Tannehill, after four healthy seasons as a starter, hasn't even lucked into the kind of playoff season Teddy Bridgewater and Kirk Cousins enjoyed last year or Alex Smith has annually, the one where the quarterback holds down the fort and a few fine seasons at other positions catapult the team to ten or 11 wins. Yes, the Patriots make seasons like that difficult, but the Chiefs share a division with the Broncos yet manage to climb over .500 annually.

The Dolphins can't reach the playoffs with a defense-first philosophy because they don't really have a defense-first philosophy, a build-around-Tannehill philosophy or any other philosophy. They sign players until cap space runs low, and that's the team. Coaching and management regimes fly by so quickly that two general managers have come and gone (Hickey and Jeff Ireland) during the Tannehill era alone. They have been without a coherent blueprint since Jimmy Johnson left town—even Bill Parcells saw the Dolphins as a glorified pension plan—and no longer even recognize the wisdom of having one.

The Dolphins will only get off this hamster wheel if Gase can transform Tannehill into Aaron Rodgers or someone in the front office finally combines organizational vision with the clout to transcend the franchise's endless politics. Gase is good, but the former is a tall order, and the latter won't happen with Tannenbaum at the helm. So the Dolphins will keep running in place and declaring it progress, this year's team locked in ceaseless battle with its mortal enemy: last year's team.

Mike Tanier

2015 Dolphins Stats by Week

Wk	vs.	W-L	PF	PA	YDF	YDA	TO	Total	Off	Def	ST
1	at WAS	W	17	10	256	349	1	4%	-8%	-1%	10%
2	at JAC	L	20	23	386	396	0	-28%	-7%	10%	-11%
3	BUF	L	14	41	391	428	-3	-87%	-56%	31%	0%
4	vs. NYJ (UK)	L	14	27	226	425	-1	-26%	0%	33%	7%
5	BYE										
6	at TEN	W	38	10	434	299	2	54%	31%	-26%	-3%
7	HOU	W	44	26	503	322	0	86%	71%	-23%	-8%
8	at NE	L	7	36	270	437	-2	-73%	-42%	24%	-7%
9	at BUF	L	17	33	397	420	-1	-46%	25%	63%	-7%
10	at PHI	W	20	19	289	436	1	-27%	-22%	-4%	-8%
11	DAL	L	14	24	210	386	1	-10%	-14%	-5%	-1%
12	at NYJ	L	20	38	333	411	-2	-61%	-23%	26%	-12%
13	BAL	W	15	13	219	375	1	-20%	-29%	-15%	-6%
14	NYG	L	24	31	363	429	0	-43%	-4%	45%	7%
15	at SD	L	14	30	231	442	1	-67%	-41%	25%	-2%
16	IND	L	12	18	361	268	-1	-42%	-21%	22%	1%
17	NE	W	20	10	438	196	0	64%	24%	-42%	-2%

Trends and Splits

	Offense	Rank	Defense	Rank
Total DVOA	-7.3%	22	9.0%	25
Unadjusted VOA	-5.4%	22	7.5%	29
Weighted Trend	-4.8%	19	7.1%	24
Variance	10.4%	29	8.1%	28
Average Opponent	1.7%	23	-1.3%	22
Passing	1.0%	24	24.7%	29
Rushing	-6.3%	13	-7.2%	20
First Down	-5.0%	21	15.5%	30
Second Down	7.0%	12	-7.6%	6
Third Down	-36.3%	30	22.3%	29
First Half	-11.0%	23	9.6%	26
Second Half	-3.7%	18	8.2%	23
Red Zone	-8.2%	21	8.2%	21
Late and Close	-13.6%	25	-11.3%	11

Five-Year Performance

Year	W-L	Pyth W	Est W	PF	PA	TO	Total	Rk	Off	Rk	Def	Rk	ST	Rk	Off AGL	Rk	Def AGL	Rk	Off Age	Rk	Def Age	Rk	ST Age	Rk
2011	6-10	8.5	7.7	329	313	-6	-1.3%	18	-7.5%	20	-3.7%	12	2.5%	6	22.1	10	9.6	3	26.6	21	27.7	6	26.3	16
2012	7-9	7.1	7.6	288	317	-10	-7.2%	21	-8.4%	22	-0.8%	14	0.4%	14	19.7	9	18.0	7	25.7	29	26.8	16	25.7	25
2013	8-8	7.5	6.8	317	335	-2	-6.5%	22	-1.8%	18	2.4%	17	-2.4%	23	41.3	20	18.6	9	26.5	23	27.3	11	26.0	18
2014	8-8	8.4	8.8	388	373	+2	3.5%	15	10.1%	8	0.5%	17	-6.1%	32	40.3	26	39.1	18	26.2	27	27.3	7	25.7	25
2015	6-10	5.8	5.8	310	389	-3	-19.0%	29	-7.3%	22	9.0%	25	-2.7%	24	23.0	7	40.5	24	25.5	31	26.6	16	25.3	30

2015 Performance Based on Most Common Personnel Groups

MIA Offense					MIA Offense vs. Opponents					MIA Defense					MIA Defense vs. Opponents			
Pers	Freq	Yds	DVOA	Run%	Pers	Freq	Yds	DVOA	Run%	Pers	Freq	Yds	DVOA		Pers	Freq	Yds	DVOA
11	70%	5.9	-2.3%	24%	Base	28%	5.3	2.0%	56%	Base	38%	5.6	3.0%		11	48%	6.2	20.1%
12	25%	5.2	3.6%	57%	Nickel	59%	5.8	-0.4%	28%	Nickel	58%	5.9	12.1%		12	24%	5.6	0.0%
13	1%	3.2	-17.2%	62%	Dime+	13%	5.7	-21.3%	9%	Dime+	4%	6.8	57.7%		21	14%	6.3	16.5%
21	1%	6.3	24.5%	50%	Goal Line	0%	0.0	-112.3%	100%	Goal Line	0%	-0.5	-55.9%		10	4%	6.7	52.3%
10	1%	3.0	-41.6%	38%											22	3%	1.5	-55.3%
611	1%	-0.8	-104.9%	83%											13	3%	3.5	-36.7%

Strategic Tendencies

Run/Pass		Rk	Formation		Rk	Pass Rush		Rk	Secondary		Rk	Strategy		Rk
Runs, first half	36%	22	Form: Single Back	83%	6	Rush 3	4.9%	23	4 DB	38%	10	Play action	19%	14
Runs, first down	41%	29	Form: Empty Back	10%	9	Rush 4	72.2%	2	5 DB	58%	10	Avg Box (Off)	6.08	29
Runs, second-long	35%	10	Pers: 3+ WR	72%	4	Rush 5	18.4%	24	6+ DB	4%	26	Avg Box (Def)	6.31	13
Runs, power sit.	55%	15	Pers: 2+ TE/6+ OL	28%	23	Rush 6+	4.5%	26	CB by Sides	78%	15	Offensive Pace	30.13	16
Runs, behind 2H	22%	23	Pers: 6+ OL	1%	24	Sacks by LB	3.2%	32	S/CB Cover Ratio	21%	24	Defensive Pace	31.90	32
Pass, ahead 2H	42%	29	Shotgun/Pistol	77%	4	Sacks by DB	9.7%	13	DB Blitz	6%	26	Go for it on 4th	0.59	31

Miami's offense used the middle of the field less than the average NFL team: 19 percent of passes compared to a league average of 23 percent. This could be an even stronger split in 2016, as Adam Gase offenses tend to avoid passes up the middle.

The Bears threw a league-low 12 percent of passes in the middle last year, and the 2014 Broncos ranked 30th at 17 percent. ☞ Ryan Tannehill has struggled against big blitzes for his entire career, and had his worst numbers in 2015. Tannehill gained 6.3 yards per pass against a standard pass rush and 7.4 yards per pass against a five-man blitz, but a league-low 3.4 yards per pass against six or more. The Dolphins also dropped to just 3.1 yards per pass against any blitz that included at least one defensive back. ☞ The Miami defense dramatically changed its pass-rush tendencies in 2015, blitzing far less frequently. The Dolphins went from sending four 50 percent of the time in 2014 (28th) to 72 percent of the time in 2015 (second). ☞ Miami only recovered 3 of 11 fumbles on defense.

Passing

Player	DYAR	DVOA	Plays	NtYds	Avg	YAC	C%	TD	Int
R.Tannehill	20	-10.6%	632	3817	6.0	5.1	62.2%	24	12

Rushing

Player	DYAR	DVOA	Plays	Yds	Avg	TD	Fum	Suc
L.Miller*	81	1.7%	194	872	4.5	8	1	43%
J.Ajayi	-17	-17.7%	49	187	3.8	1	0	39%
J.Gray*	7	-3.4%	31	122	3.9	0	0	45%
R.Tannehill	49	36.5%	23	149	6.5	1	0	-
J.Landry	86	62.6%	17	111	6.5	1	0	-
D.Williams	-28	-49.1%	16	59	3.7	0	1	31%
A.Foster	-51	-29.7%	63	165	2.6	1	2	40%

Receiving

Player	DYAR	DVOA	Plays	Ctch	Yds	Y/C	YAC	TD	C%
J.Landry	72	-7.1%	167	111	1159	10.4	4.9	4	66%
K.Stills	-22	-17.2%	63	27	440	16.3	3.8	3	43%
R.Matthews*	235	36.4%	61	43	662	15.4	5.5	4	70%
D.Parker	93	11.4%	50	26	494	19.0	3.8	3	52%
G.Jennings*	-51	-31.1%	36	19	208	10.9	3.5	1	53%
G.Whalen	54	14.1%	26	19	205	10.8	2.7	1	73%
J.Cameron	-50	-17.9%	70	35	386	11.0	2.3	3	50%
D.Sims	-35	-27.7%	25	18	136	7.6	4.9	1	72%
L.Miller*	32	-3.6%	57	47	397	8.4	9.0	2	82%
D.Williams	10	-7.4%	28	21	142	6.8	4.2	1	75%
J.Ajayi	28	38.1%	11	7	90	12.9	11.1	0	64%
J.Gray	32	115.4%	7	6	72	12.0	9.7	0	86%
A.Foster	80	35.0%	28	22	227	10.3	7.3	2	79%

Offensive Line

Player	Pos	Age	GS	Snaps	Pen	Sk	Pass	Run	Player	Pos	Age	GS	Snaps	Pen	Sk	Pass	Run
Dallas Thomas	LG	27	16/16	1032	8	5.0	14.0	1.0	Jamil Douglas	G	24	16/6	520	2	1.0	4.0	2.0
Jason Fox*	RT	28	15/11	829	10	6.5	10.5	4.0	Ja'Wuan James	RT	24	7/7	393	6	1.0	2.5	0.0
Mike Pouncey	C	27	14/14	788	2	0.5	1.0	0.0	Kraig Urbik	LG	31	16/4	432	4	1.0	3.0	1.5
Branden Albert	LT	32	14/14	787	2	1.5	2.5	2.0	Jermon Bushrod	LT	32	12/4	235	4	0.5	2.5	2.0
Billy Turner	RG	25	13/12	764	5	3.0	5.0	3.0	Sam Young	RT	29	16/3	233	3	2.0	4.0	2.0

Year	Yards	ALY	Rank	Power	Rank	Stuff	Rank	2nd Lev	Rank	Open Field	Rank	Sacks	ASR	Rank	Press	Rank	F-Start	Cont.
2013	3.83	3.62	28	56%	27	21%	27	1.00	23	0.64	19	58	8.6%	30	22.4%	11	9	29
2014	4.63	4.06	9	63%	17	18%	12	1.42	1	0.82	9	46	6.9%	19	26.1%	21	20	26
2015	4.28	3.45	28	58%	27	24%	30	1.22	7	1.01	7	45	7.6%	24	28.2%	25	19	33
2015 ALY by direction:			Left End 3.8 (14)			Left Tackle 3.97 (14)			Mid/Guard 3.6 (26)				Right Tackle 2.91 (27)			Right End 2.91 (23)		

The only bigger shock than Laremy Tunsil's draft night tumble will be if Tunsil can't seize a starting guard spot from the thoroughly mediocre trio of Jamil Douglas, Dallas Thomas, and Billy Turner. Douglas and Thomas were both among the 10 worst players at their position in snaps per blown block, and Turner wasn't far behind. Hopefully all the summer whispers about Tunsil being unable to crack the starting lineup are just posturing about a rookie needing to earn his keep. ☞ Most of this unit has been a mess, but Branden Albert and Mike Pouncey make for a rock-solid foundation. Albert returned from a gruesome knee injury in 2014 to post a career year, ranking fourth among left tackles in snaps per blown block. Meanwhile, after an ill-conceived decision to move Pouncey out to right guard backfired, the three-time Pro Bowler was back at home at his familiar center position. By the same metric of snaps per blown block, Pouncey was the best center in the league. ☞ A toe injury limited right tackle Ja'Wuan James to just seven games, and veteran Jason Fox was less than steady in his place. Only six right tackles committed more penalties than Fox's 10 last season, part of the reason the Dolphins signed Jermon Bushrod to be the new swing tackle.

Defensive Front Seven

Defensive Line	Age	Pos	G	Snaps	Plays	TmPct (Overall)	Rk	Stop	Dfts	BTkl	Runs (vs. Run)	St%	Rk	RuYd	Rk	Sack (Pass Rush)	Hit	Hur	Dsrpt
Ndamukong Suh	29	DT	16	985	66	7.5%	11	51	23	6	48	77%	40	1.5	10	6.0	13	21.5	5
Earl Mitchell	29	DT	12	504	22	3.3%	70	15	6	3	21	67%	68	3.9	83	0.0	3	3.0	0
Jordan Phillips	24	DT	15	430	23	2.8%	--	13	7	3	17	41%	--	3.5	--	2.0	4	4.0	4
C.J. Mosley*	33	DT	11	215	6	1.0%	--	4	2	1	6	67%	--	2.0	--	0.0	3	1.5	0

Edge Rushers	Age	Pos	G	Snaps	Plays	TmPct (Overall)	Rk	Stop	Dfts	BTkl	Runs (vs. Run)	St%	Rk	RuYd	Rk	Sack (Pass Rush)	Hit	Hur	Dsrpt
Olivier Vernon*	26	DE	16	943	59	6.7%	14	52	25	4	43	86%	9	1.4	19	7.5	30	35.5	0
Derrick Shelby*	27	DE	16	836	41	4.7%	50	34	13	6	31	81%	22	1.1	9	3.5	7	20.5	4
Cameron Wake	34	DE	7	249	10	2.6%	--	9	8	0	2	50%	--	2.5	--	7.0	3	8.0	1
Mario Williams	31	DE	15	885	19	2.6%	91	15	7	3	11	82%	17	1.0	5	5.0	6	14.5	0
Andre Branch	27	DE	13	597	26	3.7%	74	21	11	3	15	73%	50	2.9	74	4.0	6	15.5	4
Jason Jones	30	DE	15	540	32	4.2%	64	26	13	4	24	79%	28	2.0	34	4.5	6	18.0	1

Linebackers	Age	Pos	G	Snaps	Plays	TmPct (Overall)	Rk	Stop	Dfts	BTkl	Runs (vs. Run)	St%	Rk	RuYd	Rk	Sack (Pass Rush)	Hit	Hur	Tgts (vs. Pass)	Suc%	Rk	AdjYd	Rk	PD	Int
Koa Misi	29	MLB	13	730	79	11.1%	52	36	15	4	45	49%	84	4.0	69	0.0	1	4	15	28%	72	11.4	70	1	0
Kelvin Sheppard*	28	MLB	16	709	104	11.9%	46	59	21	8	70	59%	59	3.0	25	0.0	0	2	19	46%	56	8.5	64	1	0
Jelani Jenkins	24	OLB	13	700	74	10.4%	56	43	14	10	49	71%	15	2.6	6	0.0	0	1	19	54%	46	6.2	36	3	0
Neville Hewitt	23	OLB	16	341	34	3.9%	--	21	8	9	20	55%	--	4.0	--	0.0	1	2	11	76%	--	2.9	--	3	1
Kiko Alonso	26	ILB	11	472	44	7.1%	75	19	6	3	23	57%	69	4.3	74	0.0	0	2	20	41%	64	7.1	53	2	1

Year	Yards	ALY	Rank	Power	Rank	Stuff	Rank	2nd Level	Rank	Open Field	Rank	Sacks	ASR	Rank	Press	Rank
2013	4.25	4.24	25	64%	14	15%	28	1.20	28	0.58	13	42	6.8%	16	24.9%	14
2014	4.12	3.85	15	65%	19	21%	10	1.08	11	0.80	20	39	7.5%	8	24.1%	20
2015	4.08	3.53	10	66%	16	24%	8	1.21	23	0.84	19	31	5.9%	22	25.3%	15

| 2015 ALY by direction: | Left End 2.50 (3) | Left Tackle 4.25 (23) | Mid/Guard 3.86 (14) | Right Tackle 2.93 (4) | Right End 3.02 (11) |

Don't call Ndamukong Suh a free-agent bust: and not just because he might cause you physical harm if he hears about it. Suh's pass-rushing numbers improved from his final year in Detroit, as his combined hits and hurries increased from 27.0 to 34.5. Additionally, his 23 defeats ranked fourth among defensive tackles, trailing only Aaron Donald, Geno Atkins, and Kawann Short. ☜ Everyone knows about Olivier Vernon's defection, but Derrick Shelby is an underrated loss as well. Shelby almost doubled his hurry total from 2014 and charted quite well against the run as a full-time starter following Cameron Wake's season-ending injury. At age 27, Shelby could have provided strong depth as a rotational rusher entering his prime. Instead, he'll be starting for Atlanta while the Dolphins pray that former third overall pick Dion Jordan can finally keep his head on straight. ☜ Miami linebackers were a mess in coverage last season, so the Dolphins certainly hope Kiko Alonso doesn't resemble the player who looked slowed by knee injuries during his only season in Philadelphia. The thing is, Alonso's coverage abilities were slightly overstated because of his box-score productivity (four interceptions) as a rookie. In reality, Alonso ranked 34th in success rate and 52nd in adjusted yards per target back in 2013, which isn't far off from where he ranked last season.

Defensive Secondary

Secondary	Age	Pos	G	Snaps	Plays	TmPct	Rk	Stop	Dfts	BTkl	Runs	St%	Rk	RuYd	Rk	Tgts	Tgt%	Rk	Dist	Suc%	Rk	AdjYd	Rk	PD	Int
								Overall					**vs. Run**						**vs. Pass**						
Reshad Jones	28	SS	16	1120	145	16.5%	1	65	21	14	79	56%	8	5.0	10	33	8.5%	46	10.6	48%	55	9.8	61	8	5
Brent Grimes*	33	CB	15	960	62	7.5%	56	23	11	10	14	29%	57	10.4	61	75	22.6%	57	14.5	42%	71	9.8	72	13	4
Brice McCain*	30	CB	14	790	49	6.4%	68	22	9	6	15	47%	32	4.5	9	49	17.7%	19	14.9	49%	54	8.5	54	10	1
Jamar Taylor*	26	CB	12	712	53	8.1%	--	18	4	1	21	43%	--	5.2	--	48	19.5%	--	13.1	39%	--	10.3	--	2	0
Michael Thomas	27	FS	16	696	73	8.3%	55	24	6	10	36	47%	20	6.9	36	21	8.7%	51	8.4	40%	68	7.2	39	1	0
Walt Aikens	25	CB	16	447	20	2.3%	--	5	2	4	7	43%	--	9.0	--	10	6.1%	--	11.3	44%	--	8.6	--	1	0
Bobby McCain	23	CB	16	308	26	3.0%	--	7	4	4	5	40%	--	7.8	--	23	21.1%	--	15.0	38%	--	10.6	--	3	0
Byron Maxwell	28	CB	14	908	74	9.4%	25	28	10	3	12	58%	13	8.3	47	72	20.3%	43	13.4	46%	64	9.5	71	10	2
Isa Abdul-Quddus	27	FS	16	569	61	7.5%	61	23	10	6	27	33%	46	5.8	20	23	11.3%	58	13.5	46%	58	9.8	62	5	0
Tyler Patmon	25	CB	13	308	19	2.9%	--	12	6	2	4	75%	--	3.5	--	26	25.5%	--	9.5	66%	--	6.1	--	5	0

Year	Pass D Rank	vs. #1 WR	Rk	vs. #2 WR	Rk	vs. Other WR	Rk	vs. TE	Rk	vs. RB	Rk
2013	12	-12.6%	7	11.9%	25	-39.3%	1	24.5%	29	4.6%	17
2014	16	5.9%	21	-13.4%	8	29.1%	30	-16.5%	5	15.5%	25
2015	29	29.4%	32	21.5%	27	9.2%	22	-10.5%	11	6.3%	19

The Dolphins can exhale now that Reshad Jones isn't following through on his hollow statement to hold out through the season. Jones was by far Miami's most active defender in the back seven. While his coverage numbers took a step back after a strong 2014, he did improve noticeably against the run. Miami has Jones at a decent bargain rate for two more years, at which point he'll turn 30. ☞ For better or worse, Byron Maxwell is locked in as Miami's top corner. Early word has second-round rookie Xavien Howard as the likeliest candidate to emerge as the No. 2 behind Maxwell. The Baylor product was a divisive prospect after surprisingly leaving school a year early. NFL Draft Scout had him pegged for anywhere between Round 2 and 4, so Miami selecting him 38th overall was certainly at the high end of that range. Howard looks the part of a press-man corner with ideal measurables (six feet tall, 200 pounds with 31¼-inch arms), but significant technique issues could make him a penalty machine if he needs to play early. Then again, the alternatives are equally inexperienced (Tony Lippett, Bobby McCain) or uninspiring (Tyler Patmon, Chimdi Chekwa). ☞ The Isa Abdul-Quddus contract raised eyebrows from some, as the longtime Lions and Saints special-teamer is being paid like a definitive starter. Abdul-Quddus fared well in coverage while playing just under 300 snaps two years ago, but regressed when that workload doubled in 2015. Among 70 safeties with at least 20 charted passes or eight starts, Abdul-Quddus ranked in the bottom 12 in both adjusted success rate and adjusted yards per target.

Special Teams

Year	DVOA	Rank	FG/XP	Rank	Net Kick	Rank	Kick Ret	Rank	Net Punt	Rank	Punt Ret	Rank	Hidden	Rank
2013	-2.4%	23	-10.9	28	0.5	15	-6.1	28	9.4	5	-4.6	24	11.9	3
2014	-6.1%	32	-8.8	31	-12.6	32	0.1	15	-4.3	22	-4.8	26	15.3	2
2015	-2.7%	24	-1.7	22	0.8	14	-9.1	31	-11.2	28	7.9	4	18.8	1

The Dolphins didn't have the worst special teams in the league anymore, but they didn't improve too much. The one area where Miami did surge was on punt returns. Jarvis Landry ranked sixth with 6.1 net return points after faring quite poorly (minus-4.8 net points) in his rookie season. ☞ Landry wasn't bad on kickoff returns either, but Miami's rating there is dragged down by Damien Williams, who finished last in the NFL with minus-7.1 net return points on 21 returns. ☞ Andrew Franks attempted only 16 field goals, the lowest total for a kicker who spent all 16 games with a single team. Shayne Graham and Kyle Brindza combined to kick in nine games last year, yet each attempted more 50-plus-yard field goals than Franks (two).

Minnesota Vikings

2015 record: 11-5	Total DVOA: 5.7% (11th)	2016 Mean Projection: 8.6 wins	On the Clock (0-4): 7%
Pythagorean Wins: 9.8 (9th)	Offense: 0.0% (16th)	Postseason Odds: 41.4%	Mediocrity (5-7): 27%
Snap-Weighted Age: 26.7 (13th)	Defense: -1.8% (14th)	Super Bowl Odds: 5.9%	Playoff Contender (8-10): 42%
Average Opponent: 3.2% (13th)	Special Teams: 3.9% (4th)	Proj. Avg. Opponent: -0.9% (19th)	Super Bowl Contender (11+): 24%

2015: How could Blair Walsh leave me standing, alone in a world that's so cold?

2016: Everybody can't be on top. But life, it ain't real funky unless it's got that pop.

This is the story of a team on the rise, a team that overcame catastrophic offensive line injuries and a second-year quarterback to win its division for the first time in more than half a decade. Though a post-Thanksgiving slump threatened to torpedo their season, they rallied to win their final three games of the year, including a winner-take-all victory to take the division crown away from their archrivals in Week 17. Seven days later, they had a two-time Super Bowl team on the ropes and likely would have beaten them if not for a missed field goal from point-blank range. With another year of experience at quarterback, a new target in the passing game added via the draft, and reinforcements aplenty coming in to save the line, there are many reasons for optimism in 2016.

This is also the story of a team in stagnation, a team that only posted two wins against playoff clubs all season, both of which came down to the final drive. It featured an offense with no viable downfield passing threat, and a defense that often looked very ordinary against the pass and outright lousy against the run. A shortage of new talent means a very old defense is likely to get older, and with question marks all over the field, there are plenty of pitfalls on the road back to the postseason in 2016.

As you have probably guessed, these two stories are about the same team, the 2015 Minnesota Vikings. And your outlook on the 2016 Vikings depends mostly on which of these stories you believe to be more true.

Our numbers at Football Outsiders lean towards the latter viewpoint. We see the Vikings as a slightly above-average team that won just enough nail-biters (going 4-2 in games decided by eight points or less) to win the NFC North in a down year. Yes, they nearly upset Seattle, DVOA's favorite team, but that was partly due to an early start and near-record cold temperatures. If the Vikings play at a similar level in 2016, they are likely to return to the playoffs. But they are not the favorites to win the division, and they are certainly not among the stronger candidates to win the Super Bowl.

Obviously, there is a lot to like about this team, but a lot to dislike as well. The question is, can they correct those weaknesses while maintaining those strengths? That's what it will take for the Vikings to fulfill their potential as this year's popular "sleeper" Super Bowl contender.

Let's begin with what Minnesota did best last year, which is what they have usually done best for most of the past de-cade: run the ball. Adrian Peterson, the premiere runner of this generation, returned from a year in exile to win his third rushing title while also leading the league in touchdowns on the ground. Getting little help from an offensive line that was decimated by injury, he did most of the work on his own, finishing third in broken tackles on running plays, and leading the NFL with 43 runs of 10 yards or more—10 more than any other runner. That said, he still had a boom-and-bust running style that limited his advanced stats. He was just 25th out of 44 qualifying runners in success rate and 17th in DVOA, though he finished sixth in DYAR. By that last metric, he was even more valuable than he had been in his last full season in 2013, and once again a top-ten player as he was every year between 2009 and 2012. Peterson is now 31 years old, and at some point he will start to slow down. However, a physical marvel like this could last much longer than his peers.

Minnesota wasn't nearly effective enough when throwing the ball, limiting the upside of the offense. Teddy Bridgewater's sophomore statistics were remarkably similar to his rookie numbers. The only notable changes came in turnovers, where he cut his interceptions (from 12 to nine), but upped his fumbles (from three to eight). The Vikings traded second- and fourth-round picks to take Bridgewater with the last pick of the first round in 2014. Statistically, he has fallen somewhat short of justifying that deal, but this is likely a case where statistics come up short of painting a fully accurate picture. Few quarterbacks were playing with a wide receiver corps as weak as Bridgewater's in 2015, and the Vikings also fielded what might have been the NFL's worst offensive line, due to the yearlong absence of two prospective starters.

Center John Sullivan and tackle Phil Loadholt both entered Minnesota's starting lineup in 2009, and between the two of them they missed only ten starts over six seasons. Neither played a down in 2015, though—Sullivan missed the entire year after a pair of back surgeries, while Loadholt was sidelined with a torn Achilles. The Vikings replaced Sullivan with Joe Berger, who started 16 games for the first time in his ten-year NFL career, while fourth-round rookie T.J. Clemmings stepped in for Loadholt. Berger showed why he's been a career backup, and Clemmings played like a rookie. Between stuffed runs, sacks, and short completions, the Vikings lost yards 113 times in 2015, second-most behind lowly Cleveland. This made things extremely difficult for Bridgewater,

2016 Vikings Schedule

Week	Opp.	Week	Opp.	Week	Opp.
1	at TEN	7	at PHI	13	DAL (Thu.)
2	GB	8	at CHI (Mon.)	14	at JAC
3	at CAR	9	DET	15	IND
4	NYG (Mon.)	10	at WAS	16	at GB (Sat.)
5	HOU	11	ARI	17	CHI
6	BYE	12	at DET (Thu.)		

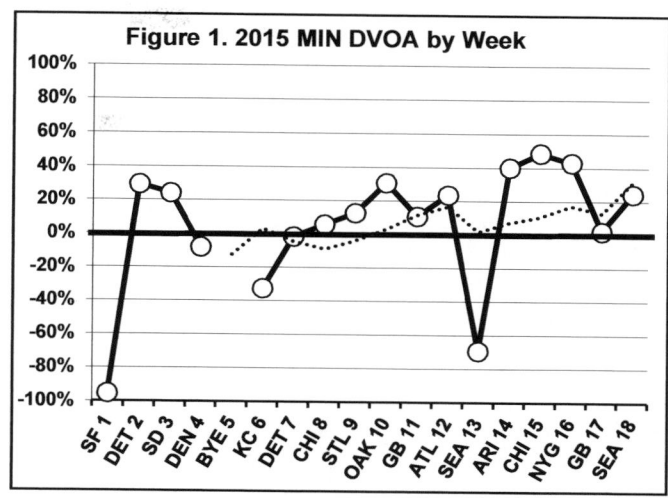

Figure 1. 2015 MIN DVOA by Week

who was pressured on a league-high 36 percent of his drop-backs, and the Vikings finished 29th in adjusted sack rate.

Peterson's skill set is best suited for taking handoffs from deep in the backfield and running downhill. Combine that with Minnesota's problems on the line, and the Vikings' offense fell apart in shotgun formations. Minnesota's offensive DVOA fell from 5.0% under center (fifth in the NFL) to -7.2% in shotgun (20th). Only the Rams had a larger decline when going to shotgun. Bridgewater's personal passing DVOA went from 12.5% under center to -12.8% in shotgun. That's a complete reversal from his rookie year, when he was much better from the shotgun (-2.1%) than under center (-68.7%).

To bolster the line, general manager Rick Spielman doled out free-agent dollars to a pair of veterans, San Francisco's Alex Boone and Cincinnati's Andre Smith. Smith was expected to challenge Loadholt for the right tackle spot, but Loadholt made things much simpler for everyone when he opted to retire shortly before training camp. Boone will move in at left guard, which will let Brandon Fusco move back to the right side. Sullivan will compete with Berger at center.

If all goes well, this offensive line should give Bridgewater much more time to pass in 2016, and the Vikings could add an element that was missing from their playbook almost entirely last season: the deep ball. With pass-rushers constantly in Bridgewater's face, receivers didn't have time to get open downfield, and Bridgewater certainly didn't have time to try to find them. The Vikings only threw 86 deep balls all season, 30th in the league. They were also 30th with 921 yards gained on deep throws. Even considering the ragged state of the offensive line, that's kind of shocking for an offense so run-heavy. With defenses frequently loading the box to stop Peterson, there should have been some opportunities for receivers to beat single coverage for big plays. Instead, Minnesota's targets didn't do much of anything positive. Kyle Rudolph was not among the top 30 tight ends in either DYAR or DVOA, and in limited action MyCole Pruitt and Rhett Ellison were no better. No Vikings made the top 40 wide receivers in DYAR or DVOA either.

Eager to find someone who could make a substantial impact in the passing game, the Vikings grabbed Mississippi receiver Laquon Treadwell with the 23rd pick in the draft, the fourth wideout off the board. Treadwell led the SEC with 1,153 receiving yards and 11 touchdowns in 2015 as a junior, then skipped his senior season to enter the NFL. Football Outsiders' Playmaker Score, however, is not impressed with Treadwell's potential—his total receiving numbers fell short

of other highly-drafted receivers in recent years, and his low average of 11.8 yards per catch in Oxford is a particularly bad omen for his NFL career. In the past ten NFL seasons, 95 different players have produced at least one season with 1,000 or more receiving yards. Only nine of them failed to average at least 12.0 yards per catch in college. Four of those were tight ends (including Antonio Gates, who did not play college football). Two (Randall Cobb and Julian Edelman) were primarily quarterbacks in college. The other three were Steve Breaston, Antonio Brown, and Wes Welker, all of whom are on the small side for NFL receivers. At 6-foot-2 and 221 pounds, Treadwell is much bigger than any of those three, but in this case it's unclear whether or not that's a good thing. Those small, shifty guys were YAC machines who were running plenty of short routes and being asked to break tackles, and that sometimes led to shorter gains when the defense did its job. There's little indication that Treadwell has that kind of athleticism. His lone kick return in college gained only 3 yards, while his six rushes produced a total of minus-10 yards. Treadwell will make for a decent target on short possession routes and in the red zone, but he doesn't look like the home-run threat this offense so badly missed last year.

The Vikings' pass defense was much better than their pass offense last year, and that was almost entirely due to the pass rush. Led by the 10.5 sacks of Everson Griffen, Minnesota was eighth in sacks last year, 10th in adjusted sack rate, and one of four defenses to pressure opposing quarterbacks on at least 30 percent of all dropbacks. (The others: Denver, Seattle, and Arizona. Obviously, harassing opposing quarterbacks goes a long way to getting a team into the playoffs.) When quarterbacks were able to get passes away, however, the results were as bland as tater tot hotdish. Minnesota was essentially average in all standard passing rate metrics, ranking 15th, 16th, or 17th in completion percentage, yards per pass, touchdown rate, and interception rate. That's better than a lot of teams, but mediocre defenses don't typically win championships.

Equally mediocre was the run defense, where Minnesota ranked 18th in DVOA. Minnesota was very good against short-yardage runs, where they ranked third, and they were tenth in open-field yards, which means they didn't give up many long runs. However, they were 23rd or worse in adjusted line yards, stuff rate, and second-level yards. In short, they didn't hit opposing runners in the backfield very often, and once those runners got past the line of scrimmage, Minnesota too often let them turn 4- and 5-yard runs into 9- and 10-yard gains.

All this criticism of Minnesota's defense might be surprising to anyone who saw the Vikings finish fifth in scoring defense and then mostly shut down the vaunted Seattle offense in the playoffs, but their ability to keep teams off the scoreboard had as much to do with circumstance as it did with anything special the Vikings were doing. First of all, Minnesota's defense didn't have to stop opponents very often. The Vikings faced only 170 drives last season, one of the lowest figures in the league (Seattle and Atlanta were below them, tied at 166.) By comparison, the Broncos were fourth in scoring defense, just one spot higher than Minnesota, but they faced 195 drives, the most in the league. When you measure points allowed per drive instead of raw totals, the Broncos move from fourth to first, while the Vikings fall from fifth to 12th. Furthermore, the drives the Vikings defense did face started far away from the end zone—thanks in part to strong special teams, Minnesota opponents started their average drive at the 25.1-yard line, fifth-worst (or best, from the Vikings' perspective) in the league.

In reality, the Vikings were nothing special when it came to stopping opponents from moving the ball. They were 13th in total yards allowed, 14th in yards allowed per play, and 20th in yards allowed per drive. It's true that the Vikings were excellent in the red zone, fourth in the league in DVOA, but that's the kind of split that tends to swing wildly from year to year, so there's no guarantee they can enjoy similar bend-but-don't-break success in 2016.

And speaking of stats that are unlikely to repeat themselves, Minnesota's fumble defense recovered eight of 11 opponent fumbles in 2015. Those balls aren't likely to bounce their way again this year.

There's reason to believe this defense may get worse before it gets better. The Vikings were seventh in adjusted games lost on defense last season, and we can expect them to have more injuries in 2016. And despite the attention paid to young linebackers Eric Kendricks and Anthony Barr, this is actually a very old unit, the fourth-oldest defense in the NFL in 2015 by snap-weighted age. It's possible the defense will return all 11 starters, which obviously means they are going to be another year older in 2016. Some of the more prominent geezers in Minnesota include Greenway as well as linemen Brian Robison and Tom Johnson, all of whom will be 32 or older this fall.

Oldest of all will be Terence Newman, who turns 38 just a week before the Vikings' season starts. Only seven defensive backs in league history have started 10 or more games at age 38 or older, including Hall of Famers Darrell Green, Jimmy Johnson, and Rod Woodson, and future enshrinees Charles Woodson and Brian Dawkins. Only Green and Charles Woodson lasted until 39, so in all likelihood this will be Newman's swan song.

With that in mind, it's worth noting that the Vikings have done their best to replace Newman, who was never intended to be more than a stopgap while younger players developed. With the selections of Xavier Rhodes in 2013, Trae Waynes in 2015, and Clemson's Mackensie Alexander this year, the Vikings have now used a top-60 pick on a cornerback three times in the last four drafts. (This appears to be a philosophy that Mike Zimmer learned from Marvin Lewis; Lewis and the Bengals have taken cornerbacks in the first round three times in the past five years.) So far, though, only Rhodes has developed into a quality starter. Waynes was a huge disappointment as a rookie, barely seeing the field behind Rhodes, Newman, and veteran nickelback Captain Munnerlyn. Going into training camp, the plan is still for Rhodes and Newman to start, with Alexander and Munnerlyn battling to be the third corner and Waynes just trying to fit in.

If there is a glimmer of optimism in Minnesota's 2015 stats, it's that their season-long production was dragged down by two notably bad games, each of which was played under unusual circumstances. In Week 1, they lost 20-3 to what we later learned was a horrible San Francisco team, but that game was the second half of a Monday night double-header on the West Coast, and the ball was not kicked off until 9:20 p.m. Minnesota time. Then in Week 13, the Vikings lost 38-7 to Seattle when Linval Joseph, Harrison Smith, and Anthony Barr missed all or most of the game due to injury. They also had a shockingly low DVOA in a weird 16-10 win over Kansas City, mostly because 12 of Peterson's 26 carries resulted in no gain or a loss, and another was fumbled. These three outliers are dragging Minnesota's full-season numbers down below the level at which they usually played. If we ranked the Vikings by their median game performance rather than their full season numbers, their overall DVOA would improve from 5.7% to 11.8%, their offense from 0.0% to 3.2%, and their defense from -1.8% to -5.3%. The pass offense, however, would actually plummet from 6.7% to -4.7%. In some respects, this may be a more accurate reflection of the way the Vikings typically played last year: an overall very strong team held back by a dreadful passing offense.

In that light, it's easier to see Minnesota making a strong playoff run this fall, especially with what should be a vastly superior offensive line. We have always found, though, that removing outliers makes DVOA's predictions less accurate, not more. Those 49ers and Seahawks losses did happen, and they are an indicator of the Vikings' full range of outcomes. It is games like those that have us questioning Minnesota as a serious Super Bowl contender.

Vincent Verhei

2015 Vikings Stats by Week

Wk	vs.	W-L	PF	PA	YDF	YDA	TO	Total	Off	Def	ST
1	at SF	L	3	20	248	395	0	-95%	-41%	48%	-7%
2	DET	W	26	16	350	323	2	29%	12%	-14%	4%
3	SD	W	31	14	284	369	1	24%	8%	-9%	7%
4	at DEN	L	20	23	325	344	1	-8%	2%	0%	-10%
5	BYE										
6	KC	W	16	10	321	328	-1	-33%	-41%	-6%	3%
7	at DET	W	28	19	425	274	-1	-1%	-6%	-5%	0%
8	at CHI	W	23	20	327	305	-1	6%	-13%	7%	26%
9	STL	W	21	18	293	320	-1	13%	4%	-7%	1%
10	at OAK	W	30	14	385	371	2	31%	20%	-2%	9%
11	GB	L	13	30	342	320	-1	11%	20%	6%	-3%
12	at ATL	W	20	10	365	329	2	24%	18%	-19%	-13%
13	SEA	L	7	38	125	433	0	-69%	-53%	29%	13%
14	at ARI	L	20	23	389	393	-3	40%	30%	-2%	8%
15	CHI	W	38	17	350	293	2	49%	33%	-13%	3%
16	NYG	W	49	17	368	363	3	43%	1%	-25%	17%
17	at GB	W	20	13	242	350	0	2%	-21%	-19%	4%
18	SEA	L	9	10	183	226	0	24%	-12%	-42%	-5%

Trends and Splits

	Offense	Rank	Defense	Rank
Total DVOA	0.0%	16	-1.8%	14
Unadjusted VOA	0.2%	15	-2.1%	11
Weighted Trend	3.0%	15	-4.7%	13
Variance	6.8%	17	3.3%	7
Average Opponent	-1.9%	11	1.3%	9
Passing	6.7%	19	3.2%	11
Rushing	0.1%	8	-8.1%	18
First Down	-9.8%	26	0.8%	16
Second Down	0.4%	19	6.0%	24
Third Down	20.8%	6	-18.7%	6
First Half	-2.8%	18	-2.2%	15
Second Half	3.6%	14	-1.5%	13
Red Zone	-19.0%	27	-21.7%	4
Late and Close	9.9%	6	-10.9%	12

Five-Year Performance

Year	W-L	Pyth W	Est W	PF	PA	TO	Total	Rk	Off	Rk	Def	Rk	ST	Rk	Off AGL	Rk	Def AGL	Rk	Off Age	Rk	Def Age	Rk	ST Age	Rk
2011	3-13	5.3	4.6	340	449	-3	-22.2%	29	-10.2%	24	8.0%	23	-4.1%	27	20.5	8	28.3	19	27.7	10	27.3	14	26.4	15
2012	10-6	8.8	8.8	379	348	-1	2.0%	14	0.3%	15	3.1%	21	4.7%	5	10.4	3	18.5	8	25.5	31	27.2	12	25.5	28
2013	5-10-1	6.1	6.5	391	480	-12	-11.4%	26	-4.7%	21	10.5%	27	3.8%	6	21.4	8	32.5	21	26.6	19	27.1	12	25.8	24
2014	7-9	7.5	7.2	325	343	-1	-8.7%	25	-7.4%	22	4.3%	23	3.0%	10	39.0	23	17.1	3	26.7	17	25.9	29	25.6	28
2015	11-5	9.8	9.5	365	302	+5	5.7%	11	0.0%	16	-1.8%	14	3.9%	4	36.5	17	22.5	7	26.4	19	27.5	4	25.7	22

2015 Performance Based on Most Common Personnel Groups

MIN Offense

Pers	Freq	Yds	DVOA	Run%
11	48%	5.4	0.7%	26%
12	24%	5.4	-4.8%	46%
21	10%	6.4	21.2%	69%
22	9%	3.8	-35.2%	85%
13	7%	7.3	47.0%	81%
622	1%	0.9	51.1%	77%

MIN Offense vs. Opponents

Pers	Freq	Yds	DVOA	Run%
Base	40%	5.6	0.8%	65%
Nickel	41%	5.3	-0.3%	35%
Dime+	17%	5.9	20.0%	16%
Goal Line	1%	0.6	23.3%	71%
Big	1%	3.2	-77.0%	100%

MIN Defense

Pers	Freq	Yds	DVOA
Base	32%	5.5	3.0%
Nickel	67%	5.6	-4.1%
Dime+	1%	10.9	52.5%
Goal Line	1%	0.9	-29.1%

MIN Defense vs. Opponents

Pers	Freq	Yds	DVOA
11	57%	5.7	-0.2%
12	18%	5.0	-10.0%
21	7%	5.9	-3.4%
13	4%	6.0	34.8%
22	4%	4.1	0.3%
20	4%	3.5	-43.1%

Strategic Tendencies

Run/Pass		Rk	Formation		Rk	Pass Rush		Rk	Secondary		Rk	Strategy		Rk
Runs, first half	43%	5	Form: Single Back	73%	20	Rush 3	4.0%	25	4 DB	32%	18	Play action	27%	1
Runs, first down	65%	1	Form: Empty Back	4%	29	Rush 4	68.5%	11	5 DB	67%	4	Avg Box (Off)	6.47	2
Runs, second-long	27%	25	Pers: 3+ WR	48%	27	Rush 5	20.8%	18	6+ DB	1%	31	Avg Box (Def)	6.20	22
Runs, power sit.	58%	12	Pers: 2+ TE/6+ OL	41%	8	Rush 6+	6.7%	14	CB by Sides	84%	10	Offensive Pace	31.57	24
Runs, behind 2H	24%	16	Pers: 6+ OL	1%	22	Sacks by LB	23.3%	20	S/CB Cover Ratio	19%	27	Defensive Pace	31.10	28
Pass, ahead 2H	38%	32	Shotgun/Pistol	45%	29	Sacks by DB	7.0%	16	DB Blitz	8%	20	Go for it on 4th	0.65	28

"Why We Pay Adrian Peterson" Department: The Vikings had the best third-and-short offensive DVOA in the league, posting a 52.8% figure in such situations. ☞ The Vikings led the NFL with 139 broken tackles, though the Minnesota offense was second behind the Rams in the percent of plays that had broken tackles. ☞ If the running game is supposed to stop opponents from blitzing, nobody told the Vikings' opponents. They blitzed Teddy Bridgewater 38.1 percent of the time, third in the NFL behind Cam Newton and Carson Palmer. It didn't work, as the Vikings gained just 5.3 yards per pass with a standard pass rush but 7.2 yards per pass with a blitz. What did work was sending a defensive back at Bridgewater. The Vikings faced a defensive back blitzing on 13.8 percent of passes, second only to Cleveland, and averaged only 3.8 yards on these 68 plays. ☞ Minnesota's run defense ranked 30th in DVOA on first downs but fifth on third downs. ☞ Minnesota's defense was very successful when it brought a blitz. Not only did opponents go from 7.0 yards per pass against a standard pass rush to just 5.2 yards against a Minnesota blitz, but a league-leading 49 percent of Minnesota blitzes were marked as bringing pass pressure. ☞ The Vikings committed only 105 penalties (including declined and offsetting), the lowest total in the league. The defense was near league average but the Vikings were last in penalties on both offense (37) and special teams (13).

Passing

Player	DYAR	DVOA	Plays	NtYds	Avg	YAC	C%	TD	Int
T.Bridgewater	187	-5.1%	491	2923	6.0	6.2	65.3%	14	9
S.Hill	-35	-77.4%	8	4	0.5	4.5	28.6%	0	0

Rushing

Player	DYAR	DVOA	Plays	Yds	Avg	TD	Fum	Suc
A.Peterson	143	2.2%	327	1490	4.6	11	6	45%
J.McKinnon	50	15.3%	52	271	5.2	2	0	50%
T.Bridgewater	32	5.3%	35	203	5.8	3	3	-
M.Asiata	-3	-11.8%	29	112	3.9	0	0	38%
Z.Line	11	19.8%	6	10	1.7	2	0	50%

Receiving

Player	DYAR	DVOA	Plays	Ctch	Yds	Y/C	YAC	TD	C%
S.Diggs	108	3.8%	84	52	720	13.8	5.6	4	62%
M.Wallace*	36	-6.4%	72	39	473	12.1	4.3	2	54%
J.Wright	78	7.6%	50	34	442	13.0	5.1	0	68%
A.Thielen	6	-8.4%	18	12	144	12.0	3.9	0	67%
C.Johnson	37	19.5%	13	9	127	14.1	3.1	0	69%
K.Rudolph	5	-6.3%	73	49	495	10.1	4.1	5	67%
R.Ellison	-2	-8.6%	19	11	124	11.3	11.5	1	58%
M.Pruitt	-17	-23.8%	16	10	89	8.9	4.6	0	63%
A.Peterson	-5	-16.3%	36	30	222	7.4	8.6	0	83%
J.McKinnon	27	2.4%	29	21	173	8.2	8.4	1	72%
M.Asiata	-6	-19.5%	22	19	132	6.9	10.5	0	86%
Z.Line	39	62.1%	9	6	95	15.8	13.7	1	67%

Offensive Line

Player	Pos	Age	GS	Snaps	Pen	Sk	Pass	Run	Player	Pos	Age	GS	Snaps	Pen	Sk	Pass	Run
Michael Harris	RG	28	16/16	1022	4	2.0	3.0	0.0	Matt Kalil	LT	27	16/16	1014	10	6.0	11.5	6.5
Joe Berger	C	34	16/16	1022	3	4.0	8.0	6.0	Andre Smith	RT	29	14/14	884	11	1.0	5.0	1.0
Brandon Fusco	LG	27	16/16	1021	5	1.0	10.0	6.5	Alex Boone	LG	29	13/13	768	4	1.0	3.0	3.0
T.J. Clemmings	RT	25	16/16	1016	2	4.5	12.0	5.0									

Year	Yards	ALY	Rank	Power	Rank	Stuff	Rank	2nd Lev	Rank	Open Field	Rank	Sacks	ASR	Rank	Press	Rank	F-Start	Cont.
2013	4.78	4.04	10	79%	2	20%	20	1.29	7	1.26	1	44	7.8%	23	25.4%	17	11	34
2014	4.11	3.97	13	68%	10	15%	2	1.07	21	0.61	21	51	9.1%	27	29.8%	27	16	28
2015	4.55	3.96	10	76%	2	20%	12	1.24	4	1.12	5	45	8.8%	29	36.0%	32	13	48

2015 ALY by direction: Left End 3.81 (13)   Left Tackle 2.68 (30)   Mid/Guard 4.3 (4)   Right Tackle 3.51 (23)   Right End 3.98 (9)

Blown blocks are not a perfect metric for linemen, but they do show how frequently Minnesota's linemen were clearly beaten last year. Michael Harris had a decent season, ranking fifth out of 39 qualifying right guards. However, Matt Kalil was 30th among left tackles; Brandon Fusco was 35th among left guards; Joe Berger was 37th among centers; and T.J. Clemmings was 31st among right tackles. ☞ The Vikings' pressure numbers give more indication that Teddy Bridgewater was overcoming the failures of his linemen last season. Against blitzes, Minnesota allowed pass pressure 41 percent of the time (24th in the league) but the offense gained 7.2 yards per play (eighth). Against three- and four-man rushes, he Vikings had the NFL's worst offense in terms of pressure rate (37 percent) and yards per play (5.3). ☞ The Vikings gave up a 2016 sixth-rounder in September of 2015 to acquire Jeremiah Sirles from San Diego. He didn't play a snap last year, but took first-team snaps from Kalil in OTAs. This was probably your typical offseason non-news story, but Kalil is entering his contract year, and the Vikings won't be in a big hurry to re-sign him. So they might as well start searching for replacements now.

Defensive Front Seven

Defensive Line	Age	Pos	G	Snaps	Plays	TmPct	Rk	Stop	Dfts	BTkl	Runs	St%	Rk	RuYd	Rk	Sack	Hit	Hur	Dsrpt
						Overall						**vs. Run**				**Pass Rush**			
Tom Johnson	32	DT	16	751	37	4.5%	52	31	12	3	30	80%	26	2.4	49	5.5	15	12.5	0
Sharrif Floyd	25	DT	13	548	35	5.2%	38	24	8	2	28	68%	67	2.4	48	2.5	4	6.0	1
Linval Joseph	28	DT	12	532	56	9.1%	5	38	11	2	51	69%	62	2.5	52	0.5	6	8.0	1
Bruce Gaston	*25*	*DE*	*9*	*179*	*12*	*2.8%*	*--*	*10*	*1*	*1*	*11*	*82%*	*--*	*3.3*	*--*	*1.0*	*4*	*4.5*	*0*

Edge Rushers	Age	Pos	G	Snaps	Plays	TmPct	Rk	Stop	Dfts	BTkl	Runs	St%	Rk	RuYd	Rk	Sack	Hit	Hur	Dsrpt
						Overall						**vs. Run**				**Pass Rush**			
Brian Robison	33	DE	16	897	37	4.5%	54	28	17	6	27	70%	65	1.1	7	5.0	7	25.0	2
Everson Griffen	29	DE	15	865	47	6.1%	26	36	20	5	30	63%	81	3.1	80	10.5	20	29.0	1
Danielle Hunter	22	DE	14	393	29	4.0%	68	21	15	3	20	65%	73	2.9	73	6.0	2	7.0	0

Linebackers	Age	Pos	G	Snaps	Plays	TmPct	Rk	Stop	Dfts	BTkl	Runs	St%	Rk	RuYd	Rk	Sack	Hit	Hur	Tgts	Suc%	Rk	AdjYd	Rk	PD	Int
						Overall						**vs. Run**				**Pass Rush**				**vs. Pass**					
Anthony Barr	24	OLB	14	829	75	10.4%	55	54	23	10	37	73%	11	4.6	81	3.5	6	11	20	67%	13	6.4	42	4	1
Eric Kendricks	24	MLB	14	763	93	12.9%	37	43	14	14	51	57%	66	3.7	55	4.0	4	6	23	32%	70	9.2	65	1	0
Chad Greenway	33	OLB	16	632	69	8.4%	69	39	13	6	37	57%	68	4.7	82	2.5	2	4.5	13	67%	14	3.0	3	1	1
Emmanuel Lamur	*27*	*OLB*	*16*	*340*	*35*	*4.1%*	*--*	*15*	*8*	*3*	*6*	*67%*	*--*	*5.8*	*--*	*0.5*	*0*	*2.5*	*12*	*39%*	*--*	*7.1*	*--*	*3*	*0*

Year	Yards	ALY	Rank	Power	Rank	Stuff	Rank	2nd Level	Rank	Open Field	Rank	Sacks	ASR	Rank	Press	Rank
2013	3.89	3.67	10	60%	9	23%	7	1.19	26	0.64	17	41	6.8%	17	24.6%	17
2014	4.49	4.56	31	73%	26	14%	32	1.25	25	0.64	13	41	7.0%	12	22.9%	23
2015	4.23	4.01	25	53%	3	18%	23	1.22	25	0.63	10	43	7.1%	10	28.0%	7
2015 ALY by direction:		Left End 4.46 (25)			Left Tackle 3.54 (12)			Mid/Guard 3.95 (17)			Right Tackle 4.46 (28)			Right End 3.76 (22)		

Everson Griffen will handle one defensive end spot, but the other is up in the air. Brian Robison is slotted to start with Danielle Hunter coming off the bench, but Robison's age and cap number ($5.1 million) make him a possible camp cut. J.J. Watt, the NFL's sack leader last year, averaged about one sack per 59 snaps played. Hunter nearly matched that with one sack every 65 snaps. ☞ Defensive tackles Sharrif Floyd and Linval Joseph struggled with injuries in 2015. Joseph was bothered by turf toe for the final two months of the season, but should be 100 percent following surgery. Floyd, though, was still being held out of OTAs with knee and ankle issues. This did not stop the Vikings from exercising his fifth-year option, guaranteeing his spot on the team through at least 2017. ☞ Greenway has declared that 2016 will be his final season. Last season he came off the field in Minnesota's nickel package, and this year he could lose his job to free-agent signee Emmanuel Lamur (ex-Bengals). ☞ Eric Kendricks will play in the middle this year, but the Vikings have talked about moving him outside when Greenway retires.

Defensive Secondary

Secondary	Age	Pos	G	Snaps	Plays	TmPct	Rk	Stop	Dfts	BTkl	Runs	St%	Rk	RuYd	Rk	Tgts	Tgt%	Rk	Dist	Suc%	Rk	AdjYd	Rk	PD	Int
						Overall						**vs. Run**							**vs. Pass**					
Xavier Rhodes	26	CB	16	1017	69	8.4%	43	27	8	6	14	43%	36	9.3	58	76	20.1%	42	14.2	47%	60	6.7	14	10	1
Terence Newman	38	CB	16	966	74	9.0%	31	31	11	6	20	50%	20	4.4	8	72	20.0%	40	12.4	52%	41	8.8	60	14	3
Harrison Smith	27	FS	13	795	69	10.3%	28	26	8	7	35	43%	30	4.7	6	16	5.3%	13	9.3	75%	5	3.4	4	3	2
Andrew Sendejo	29	SS	13	777	76	11.4%	22	19	5	11	33	30%	54	6.9	37	21	7.1%	32	15.0	41%	66	13.4	71	3	1
Captain Munnerlyn	28	CB	16	713	59	7.2%	62	32	15	3	8	75%	5	5.9	24	50	18.8%	33	11.4	58%	14	8.0	43	5	2
Robert Blanton*	27	SS	16	231	30	3.6%	--	8	2	2	12	33%	--	8.3	--	8	9.4%	--	17.9	48%	--	8.1	--	2	0
Trae Waynes	24	CB	15	195	26	3.4%	--	11	6	2	3	67%	--	8.0	--	23	31.2%	--	11.2	63%	--	4.9	--	3	0
Michael Griffin	*31*	*FS*	*15*	*940*	*101*	*13.8%*	*8*	*44*	*10*	*10*	*50*	*64%*	*1*	*5.0*	*11*	*25*	*7.5%*	*36*	*12.3*	*38%*	*69*	*12.2*	*69*	*4*	*1*

Year	Pass D Rank	vs. #1 WR	Rk	vs. #2 WR	Rk	vs. Other WR	Rk	vs. TE	Rk	vs. RB	Rk
2013	30	5.1%	22	8.9%	22	44.8%	32	0.1%	15	15.2%	29
2014	19	11.7%	26	-22.3%	5	-15.2%	6	-2.0%	17	15.8%	26
2015	11	-6.1%	9	17.0%	25	-30.4%	2	16.1%	25	8.7%	22

The Vikings have made a concerted effort to acquire more cornerbacks in recent years, through both the draft and free agency, and you can see the effect of their improved depth in their success against "other" wide receivers in the last three years. ☞ Xavier Rhodes will give up some short gains, but he takes away big plays—he has ranked in the top 15 in adjusted yards allowed per target in each of the past three seasons. The Vikings have activated his fifth-year option, and will pay Rhodes more than $8 million in 2017. ☞ The Vikings spent some serious loot on safeties this offseason. In March they re-signed Andrew Sendejo to a four-year deal worth up to $16 million, though only $2.5 million was guaranteed. Four days later they signed Michael Griffin, who had been released by the Titans, for one year and $3 million. The big deal was signing Harrison Smith to a five-year deal worth more than $50 million, with more than $15 million in guarantees. Smith was briefly the top-paid safety in the game, though Eric Berry will pass him if (or when) he signs his franchise tender in Kansas City. Smith had a quiet year in 2015, but he led all safeties with 23 defeats in 2014. ☞ Whether it's from Smith or somebody else, the Vikings need more big plays from their secondary. Vikings defensive backs combined for only 60 defeats (tied for 24th). ☞ Nickelback Captain Munnerlyn led all NFL cornerbacks with 21 stops on tackles after completed passes. He will battle rookie Mackensie Alexander (Clemson) for that job this year.

Special Teams

Year	DVOA	Rank	FG/XP	Rank	Net Kick	Rank	Kick Ret	Rank	Net Punt	Rank	Punt Ret	Rank	Hidden	Rank
2013	3.8%	6	-0.6	20	-15.4	32	22.4	1	0.6	17	11.8	3	-4.6	22
2014	3.0%	10	-3.6	25	6.0	7	5.5	5	3.4	9	3.7	10	7.2	5
2015	3.9%	4	2.0	11	-3.7	25	16.1	1	1.1	16	4.0	7	-8.7	28

Cordarrelle Patterson is a perfect example of the volatile nature of special teams. He led the NFL in kickoff return value in both 2013 and 2015, but in between he had negative value in 2014. Marcus Sherels, on the other hand, has ranked second, 11th, and eighth on punt returns in the past three seasons. ☞ The Vikings favor high, short punts that limit big returns, and as a result Jeff Locke was dead last in our gross punting value metric last year after ranking 27th in 2014 and 22nd in 2013. However, they have done much better in punt coverage, ranking fifth last year, second in 2014, and 19th in 2013. ☞ Blair Walsh has ranked in the middle of the pack on kickoffs for three seasons in a row, but the Vikings have struggled in kickoff coverage, ranking last in 2013 and 28th last year. As for Walsh himself, he's most famous for his missed 27-yarder against Seattle in the playoffs, but that was a fluke. In his career, including the playoffs, he is 33-of-35 from inside 30 yards. He did miss four of 37 extra-point tries in 2015; with the new rules, those are essentially 32-yard field goal tries. ☞ The Vikings ranked very low in "hidden" special teams value, mainly because opposing kickers rarely missed. Vikings opponents went 28-of-31 on field goals. One of those misses was blocked; the others were from 48 and 51 yards. All told, opposing kickers went 6-of-7 from 50-plus yards, including a 61-yarder by the Rams' Greg Zuerlein. They also went 28-of-28 on extra points.

New England Patriots

2015 record: 12-4	**Total DVOA:** 22.6% (6th)	**2016 Mean Projection:** 9.8 wins	**On the Clock (0-4):** 2%
Pythagorean Wins: 11.7 (5th)	**Offense:** 15.4% (5th)	**Postseason Odds:** 65.5%	**Mediocrity (5-7):** 15%
Snap-Weighted Age: 26.5 (20th)	**Defense:** -3.3% (12th)	**Super Bowl Odds:** 19.2%	**Playoff Contender (8-10):** 42%
Average Opponent: -4.1% (23rd)	**Special Teams:** 3.9% (5th)	**Proj. Avg. Opponent:** -0.3% (16th)	**Super Bowl Contender (11+):** 40%

2015: Insanity is doing the same thing over and over and considering it failure to come within a two-point conversion of another Super Bowl.

2016: No matter how many times you repeat $PV=nRT$, it can't make 10 into 12.

For as long as Football Outsiders has existed, for as long as the world has known Twitter, Pro Football Talk, Bleacher Report, smartphones smart enough to set your fantasy lineup, high-definition televisions, midday hot-take talk shows featuring a white sportswriter and a black sportswriter screaming imaginary controversies at each other and all the other things we take for granted as modern football fans, there have only been three types of Patriots teams: Historically Epic Patriots Teams, Excellent Patriots teams, and Really, Really Good Patriots Teams.

The Historically Epic Patriots won Super Bowls XXXVIII and XXXIX. They lost Super Bowls XLII and XLVI.

The Excellent Patriots won Super Bowls XXXVI and XLIX. They lost in the AFC Championship Game last year and in 2006, 2012, and 2013. They lost in the divisional round to the Jets after a 14-2 season in 2010. Strictly using DVOA, the 2010 Patriots might classify as Historically Epic (they led the NFL at 44.6%) and the 2011 team merely Excellent (they finished third at 22.8%), but playoff performance must count for something when you are measuring altitudes on Olympus.

The Really, Really Good Patriots went 9-7 after winning the Super Bowl in 2002, 10-6 in 2005, 11-5 with Matt Cassel at quarterback in 2008, and lost in the wild-card round after a 10-6 season in 2009. These are the worst Patriots teams your typical millennial can even remember, teams that suffered calamities like a season-ending Tom Brady injury and still posted records that would bring parades to Cleveland or Jacksonville.

You have to push back to 2000 and Bill Belichick's first season to find a Patriots team with a losing record. But even back in the late 1990s, the Patriots were toggling in and out of the playoff picture with a legitimate franchise quarterback at the helm (his name was Drew Bledsoe, young'uns) and a head coach who either had won a Super Bowl (Bill Parcells) or would someday (Pete Carroll). The Truly Bad Patriots are buried in early 1990s antiquity. You may not have even had Internet in your home the last time the Patriots had back-to-back losing seasons (in 1992 and 1993). Heck, you may not have been born yet.

All of this is relevant because it frames the parameters of how we think (and write) about the New England Patriots. It's hard to even conceive of how a Patriots team with Belichick and Brady on the payroll would ever produce, say, a 6.8-win projection. There has never been any drama in a *Football Outsiders Almanac* Patriots chapter, not in 12 years we have published under various titles. At least, not "drama" the way an Eagles, Colts or even a Packers fan might experience it: *Are we picked to win the division? Does DVOA like the team's direction? Was last year a fluke, for better or worse?* Patriots chapters exist on a narrow peninsula between explaining a mean forecast of 10 or 11 wins and crowning another likely sovereign, plus varying degrees of kvetching about the latest scandal depending on who from our staff wrote the essay.

With that in mind:

• There is essentially zero chance that we will see the first Truly Bad Patriots Team of the millennium this season.
• The chance that we will see a Historically Epic Patriots team is also pretty small. A 14-win season is an unusual thing to project analytically. A prediction like that would have to include some things this Patriots team clearly lacks. Like a first-round pick. Or a quarterback who isn't facing a four-game suspension, justified or not.

So we are left trying to determine whether this is an Excellent Patriots Team or a Really, Really Good Patriots team. That's a heck of a hair to split in a projection, but it's the only one worth splitting. Can the Patriots win another Super Bowl, given typical performances by their stars, some occasion-rising by others and a break or two? Or are they just another playoff-caliber AFC team?

We regret to inform Patriots fans that it's close. Because of the naturally conservative nature of our season simulation, the mean win projections for the top teams are always lower than most fans expect. Still, this is only the second time in 12 books that we have listed the Patriots with a mean win projection under 10.0. They fall below the Steelers and several of the top NFC contenders. There is a really good chance that this Patriots team is merely Really, Really Good.

As we list the reasons, remember that the Patriots grading curve applies throughout this essay. If the Browns were projected to finish with 9.8 wins, the Alleluia Allegro from Handel's *Messiah* would start playing the moment you opened to this page. But an 11-5 record and (let's speculate) a divisional round loss in the playoffs would represent the Patriots' worst season since 2009. That forces us to nitpick every possible weakness.

2016 Patriots Schedule

Week	Opp.	Week	Opp.	Week	Opp.
1	at ARI	7	at PIT	13	LA
2	MIA	8	at BUF	14	BAL (Mon.)
3	HOU (Thu.)	9	BYE	15	at DEN
4	BUF	10	SEA	16	NYJ (Sat.)
5	at CLE	11	at SF	17	at MIA
6	CIN	12	at NYJ		

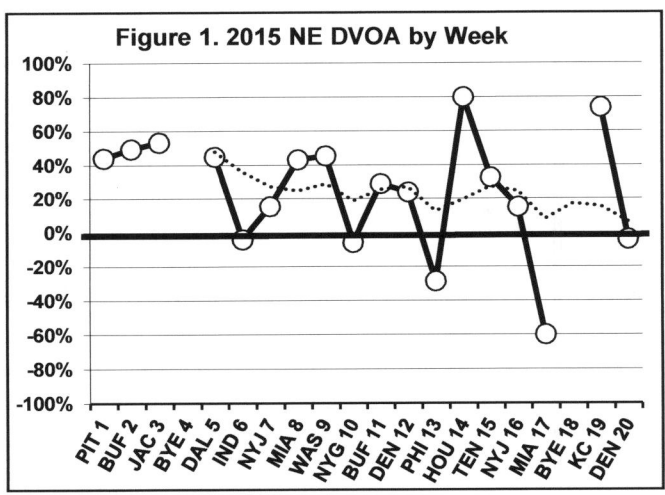

Figure 1. 2015 NE DVOA by Week

The Brady Suspension: There is no sense in vamping or pretending we have some deep knowledge of Jimmy Garoppolo based on three-year-old college scouting reports, some training camp visits, and magical thinking. Garoppolo will probably be OK. He will not be as good as Brady. He will face the Cardinals, Dolphins, Texans, and Bills: one of the NFL's best teams, two divisional opponents, and a conference foe with an outstanding pass rush. Brady's absence will have some impact on the Patriots' record and could affect eventual playoff tiebreakers.

The Offensive Line: Two years of injuries and compulsive juggling have made a mess of this unit. The Patriots finished 18th in adjusted sack rate last year, a figure that would be far worse if Brady wasn't one of the best quarterbacks in NFL history at anticipating and counteracting the pass rush. Brady encountered pressure on a whopping 174 dropbacks last year, 25.7 percent of his pass attempts. That pressure rate has crept up every year since 2012.

A healthier line in 2016 should improve Brady's protection. Nate Solder's return from a bicep injury will move Sebastian Vollmer back to right tackle; Vollmer struggled on the left side last year, while replacements at right tackle like Marcus Cannon and Cameron Fleming were awful. Jonathan Cooper arrives via trade to upgrade the interior blocking, and there are many (maybe too many) prospects vying for roles at center and guard. There are good reasons to expect some improvement along the Patriots line.

On the other hand, injuries aren't the only reason why the Patriots had the lowest offensive continuity score of any team in the 16 seasons we have tracked. The Patriots started 10 different players on the offensive line and never started the same five guys for more than two games in a row. The Patriots have been mixing and matching interior line prospects (Bryan Stork, Tre' Jackson, Shaq Mason, Josh Kline, David Andrews, the departed Jordan Devey, and now third-round pick Joe Thuney) for two years and are still searching for a combination they like. And Cooper, considered one of the best guard prospects of the last decade when he left North Carolina, has been an injury-plagued disappointment for three seasons in Arizona. Brady may not be harassed on one-fourth of his attempts this year, but the days when Logan Mankins and Dan Koppen anchored the middle of the line appear to be long gone.

The Running Game: Patriots fans and stat analysts are conditioned to harrumph at worries about the running game. No, the Patriots' scheme isn't designed to produce 1,500-yard rushers. But the Patriots need some production from their running game.

The Patriots rushed for just 215 yards in their final four regular and postseason games, three of them losses. The Patriots needed more than 49 yards on 18 carries from Steven Jackson, Branden Bolden, and James White when the Jets threw all they could muster at them in Week 16. They needed more than 66 rushing yards on 23 carries from Jackson and Boldin when they went into *Smother Brady with His Own Protection* mode in Week 17 against the Dolphins. They needed something, anything, when Wade Phillips unleashed the Visigoth hordes in the AFC Championship Game.

Yes, Bolden and Jackson were late-season injury replacements, and starters LeGarrette Blount and Dion Lewis are back this year. If this was an essay about any other NFL team, would you expect hosannas about the returns of Blount and Lewis? They are a pair of one-dimensional reclamation projects: Blount a tackle-breaker with personality issues, Lewis a jitterbug prone to fumbles and injuries.

Once upon a time, the Patriots invested in Fred Taylor- and Corey Dillon-types, veterans with 1,000-yard pedigrees, to meet their unique rushing needs. The Patriots even used high draft picks on running backs not too long ago: Stevan Ridley and Shane Vereen were a pair of Day 2 picks in the same draft class, and even "bust" Laurence Maroney averaged 4.5 yards per carry for the team that went 16-0. When BenJarvus Green-Ellis or Danny Woodhead bubbled up the depth chart to semi-stardom, they had to bubble past talented players like Maroney or the aging Taylor.

The current Patriots seem content with letting their system make short-term stars out of Lewis or (two years ago) Jonas Grey. The Patriots ignored the running back position in the draft and free agency, adding only faded Chargers and Colts committee back Donald Brown. So they enter camp expecting to lean upon Blount, Lewis and James White, who posted some excellent receiving numbers when Lewis was hurt but also carried the ball only 22 times for a piddling 56 yards. Receiving backs like White and Lewis can live off the fat of the land as long as Brady is quarterback and the Patriots system creates mismatches for them, just as Blount can munch the clock between the tackles at the end of a 36-7 win. The Patriots offense can make a running back better. What the Patriots lack—what they had in their Excellent and Epic seasons—is a running back who makes the offense better.

The First-Round Famine: The Patriots were without a first-round pick this year because of Deflategate business, of course. Chandler Jones, the team's first-round pick in 2012 and sack leader last year, was traded to the Cardinals to land Cooper and a second-round pick (which became Thumey and some later picks after trades). Dominque Easley, the 2014 first-round pick, was released in the offseason after two seasons of injuries and reported not-with-the-program behavior. The Patriots traded out of the first round in 2013.

That leaves the Patriots with two first-round picks of their own since 2012 on the roster: linebacker Dont'a Hightower, who has been great, and defensive tackle Malcom Brown, who had a promising rookie season.

With little first-round talent in the pipeline, it's difficult to predict vast short- or long-term improvement for the Patriots at positions like cornerback, edge rusher and offensive tackle, where early draft picks are typically part of the champion-building or -maintaining equation. Just as significantly, 12.5 sacks were wiped off the books with the loss of Jones. The Patriots blitzed less than any other team last year yet still notched 49 sacks thanks to Jones (and with underrated contributions from Easley, who was exceptional in situational flashes as a pass rusher). The Patriots will either have to blitz more or get less mileage from their pass rush this year.

The Patriots compensate for the loss of young first-round picks by acquiring other teams' failed or faded first-rounders. They traded for Cooper and signed Shea McClellin from the Bears as an edge defender. Chris Long, an older blue-chip talent, arrives from the Rams as a veteran pass-rush specialist, though Long has recorded just four sacks in two injury-ruined seasons.

Some of the Patriots' offseason moves have obvious merits. Tight end Martellus Bennett provides both Gronk injury insurance and the opportunity to cause the types of two-tight end mismatches the team deployed from 2010 through 2012. Long is finished as a starter but probably has 30 disruptive snaps per game left in him.

But when evaluating Cooper, McClellin, receivers Chris Hogan and Nate Washington and others, we must be careful to resist the logical fallacy of Special Patriots Pleading. *Sure, Cooper was a bust in Arizona, but he will be good because the Patriots know what they are doing. McClellin never found a position in Chicago, but Bill Belichick will create a special role that turns him into a Rob Ninkovich-level contributor, because the Patriots know what they are doing. Hogan and Washington will have the kind of short-term success Brandon LaFell and Brandon Lloyd had in the past, because the Patriots know what they are doing.*

The Patriots do, indeed, know what they are doing. They have spent this entire millennium inventing and reinventing themselves in surprising ways. Fans and experts are both conditioned to assume that even apparent Patriots reaches or miscalculations are part of some fiendish plan too brilliant or intricate for mortal minds to fathom. Those who resist the conditioning overcompensate and start penning Patriots Are Doomed (or Patriots Are Cheaters) columns after every loss or free-agent defection.

Some Patriots decisions are neither signs of transcendent brilliance nor the coming Patsocalypse. They are just maintenance efforts designed to make the best of a situation that works against them even when they aren't forced to surrender draft picks. With first-round talent hard to come by, they surrendered one blue chip (Jones) for a possible blue chip at a position of greater need (Cooper) and an extra pick. Drafting Alabama cornerback Cyrus Jones in the second round solved a talent-and-depth problem in the secondary, but addressing that need pushed other needs to later rounds, forcing the Patriots to the mid-tier free-agent market for McClellin, Hogan, and Washington. Some needs didn't get optimally addressed because the Patriots simply lacked the resources. No Randy Moss or Darrelle Revis is coming to provide a turbo boost this year. The Patriots were too busy spackling the little fissures that inevitably open when a team has been successful since *Friends* was on the air.

By this time next year, those fissures may grow large enough to require more than just a little duct tape and elbow grease to cover up. Jones was only traded in an effort to slough some water off the boat before the Great Free Agent Flood of 2017 arrives. New England has 10 of its projected starters hitting free agency next year, and that doesn't even include one-year rentals Martellus Bennett and Chris Long or important cogs such as Matthew Slater. Seven of them are on a defense that the Pats have slowly rebuilt from a laughingstock into a borderline top-10 unit. Our total does include Malcolm Butler, who's only a restricted free agent, but even Warren Buffett would start sweating at the price of cornerbacks nowadays. If the Pats don't extend Butler after this season, they'll risk having one of their best defenders hit the unrestricted market and demand huge bucks when he's 28. On a related note, Chandler Jones is due to become a 27-year-old unrestricted free agent next summer.

That's a problem for 2017, but it does underline the trepidation we've been hinting at regarding New England's ability to sustain its status as the Death Star of American professional sports. The Patriots have been hovering at 12-4 for three years, with overall DVOA ratings holding remarkably firm between 18 and 24 percent. It's tempting to think they can do this forever, or to just trim them down to 11-5 because of Deflategate but assume they will be breathing vengeful fire come the playoffs.

The AFC East has once again accommodated the Patriots by behaving like a bunch of anxiety-riddled success-phobes. The Jets built a dangerous, veteran-heavy roster, then decapitated themselves at quarterback. The Dolphins continue to equate spending and managerial in-fighting with progress. The Bills are reliving the glory of the 2011-2014 Jets.

Elsewhere in the AFC, the Broncos celebrated their Super Bowl victory by replacing Peyton Manning and Brock Osweiler with Mark Sanchez and Paxton Lynch. The AFC South still looks like Conference USA despite some gains; the division always appears to be one year away from spitting out a serious challenger for the Patriots, and this year is no exception. The road to the playoffs looks as smooth as ever.

Then again, the Patriots face the NFC West and AFC North, two difficult divisions. They will face the Broncos defense and whoever their quarterback is at Denver in December. The Bengals game is a 1:00 kickoff early in the year, so the Bengals won't have a case of stage fright. Maybe that's cutting things way too fine, but we are looking for the 12th win that clinches home-field advantage throughout the playoffs or the sixth loss that forces the Patriots into the wild-card round. The latter is a little easier to find than the former, especially with Brady's absence making a 2-2 start very likely.

As the tone of this essay illustrates, the Patriots have the NFL's version of First World Problems. The Patriots can take many things for granted, even when deprived of Brady for a month. There's Gronk, the coaching, the organization, perennial stalwarts like Devin McCourty, Julian Edelman, Solder and Vollmer, Stephen Gostkowski and others. There are all the hidden benefits of being one of the best-run organizations in professional sports. The special teams are projected to remain top-notch, give or take the blunders that all bunched up in the Eagles loss last year. Because the Patriots can promise both

Super Bowl rings and organizational professionalism, veterans like Long eagerly sign on for comeback opportunities and guys like Blount operate at what passes for their best behavior.

There's just not enough in the cupboard this year to predict absolute conquest. Other teams, even other AFC teams, look a little stronger. Recent Patriots teams look a little stronger. This team is playoff caliber but not overpowering. Maybe that's because they really are facing the beginning of the end, particularly if Brady keeps taking hits and the little injuries like those that quickly swallowed Peyton start mustering for a charge. Maybe it's just another season like 2005 or 2009, the precursor for another reimagining and renaissance.

Los Angelenos wear heavy jackets on 60-degree afternoons. Inuit children eat hunks of seal blubber like they were chocolate brownies. We are all conditioned to be comfortable in our everyday surroundings and uncomfortable with the unfamiliar, including Patriots fans who don't remember what the fans of bad teams endure and classify anything less than an annual Super Bowl prediction to be a sign of disrespect.

Have faith, Patriots fans. This is a Really, Really Good Patriots team. That may not be good enough for you, but after 15 years atop the NFL, it's still rather remarkable.

Mike Tanier

2015 Patriots Stats by Week

Wk	vs.	W-L	PF	PA	YDF	YDA	TO	Total	Off	Def	ST
1	PIT	W	28	21	361	464	1	44%	50%	10%	4%
2	at BUF	W	40	32	507	349	1	49%	21%	-21%	8%
3	JAC	W	51	17	471	293	1	53%	45%	-2%	7%
4	BYE										
5	at DAL	W	30	6	356	264	2	45%	10%	-22%	13%
6	at IND	W	34	27	417	409	-1	-4%	22%	28%	2%
7	NYJ	W	30	23	353	372	1	16%	16%	10%	10%
8	MIA	W	36	7	437	270	2	43%	14%	-18%	12%
9	WAS	W	27	10	460	250	0	45%	10%	-36%	-1%
10	at NYG	W	27	26	406	422	-1	-6%	-14%	8%	16%
11	BUF	W	20	13	356	319	0	29%	0%	-20%	9%
12	at DEN	L	24	30	301	433	0	24%	35%	9%	-1%
13	PHI	L	28	35	427	248	-1	-28%	10%	-7%	-46%
14	at HOU	W	27	6	313	189	0	80%	24%	-50%	6%
15	TEN	W	33	16	346	282	2	33%	14%	-5%	14%
16	at NYJ	L	20	26	284	428	0	15%	12%	11%	14%
17	at MIA	L	10	20	196	438	0	-60%	-39%	17%	-5%
18	BYE										
19	KC	W	27	20	340	378	1	74%	60%	-10%	3%
20	at DEN	L	18	20	336	244	-1	-4%	-15%	-7%	4%

Trends and Splits

	Offense	Rank	Defense	Rank
Total DVOA	15.4%	5	-3.4%	12
Unadjusted VOA	17.2%	1	-4.0%	10
Weighted Trend	8.4%	10	-2.4%	15
Variance	4.5%	7	4.4%	15
Average Opponent	0.4%	20	-3.4%	32
Passing	35.8%	4	5.7%	13
Rushing	-6.1%	12	-16.2%	10
First Down	10.9%	7	-4.4%	13
Second Down	22.9%	2	-4.5%	12
Third Down	12.5%	9	0.3%	16
First Half	19.7%	2	-12.8%	7
Second Half	11.0%	5	6.0%	22
Red Zone	13.3%	11	9.0%	22
Late and Close	4.3%	11	4.1%	23

Five-Year Performance

Year	W-L	Pyth W	Est W	PF	PA	TO	Total	Rk	Off	Rk	Def	Rk	ST	Rk	Off AGL	Rk	Def AGL	Rk	Off Age	Rk	Def Age	Rk	ST Age	Rk
2011	13-3	11.9	12.2	513	342	+17	22.8%	3	31.9%	3	13.2%	30	4.1%	5	40.0	23	57.5	31	28.5	1	26.7	22	26.1	21
2012	12-4	12.7	13.4	557	331	+25	34.9%	3	30.8%	1	1.4%	15	5.5%	4	46.7	25	28.0	15	27.9	7	25.6	29	26.2	12
2013	12-4	10.5	11.0	444	338	+9	18.9%	5	16.4%	4	4.2%	20	6.7%	2	47.8	25	49.8	28	27.6	6	25.8	29	25.6	27
2014	12-4	11.8	10.8	468	313	+12	22.1%	4	13.5%	6	-3.0%	12	5.7%	5	24.4	9	37.6	16	27.7	5	26.6	19	26.1	16
2015	12-4	11.7	10.9	465	315	+7	22.6%	6	15.4%	5	-3.3%	12	3.9%	5	60.6	29	32.7	19	27.2	12	25.9	27	25.9	18

2015 Performance Based on Most Common Personnel Groups

NE Offense					NE Offense vs. Opponents					NE Defense				NE Defense vs. Opponents			
Pers	Freq	Yds	DVOA	Run%	Pers	Freq	Yds	DVOA	Run%	Pers	Freq	Yds	DVOA	Pers	Freq	Yds	DVOA
12	43%	6.1	15.8%	39%	Base	34%	6.3	22.0%	42%	Base	17%	4.8	-12.2%	11	58%	5.6	-3.4%
11	42%	6.6	30.8%	24%	Nickel	43%	5.8	9.2%	33%	Nickel	57%	5.1	-8.6%	12	21%	4.9	-9.2%
13	5%	5.4	-14.5%	46%	Dime+	21%	6.4	40.6%	23%	Dime+	25%	6.4	27.2%	10	6%	7.4	41.3%
613	2%	1.2	-13.2%	90%	Goal Line	1%	0.9	24.1%	64%	Goal Line	1%	0.2	-67.6%	21	6%	4.6	-9.4%
611	2%	7.1	60.0%	68%	Big	1%	1.6	-57.2%	63%					20	2%	4.9	3.8%
612	2%	2.6	-26.7%	82%										13	2%	4.7	3.4%

Strategic Tendencies

Run/Pass		Rk	Formation		Rk	Pass Rush		Rk	Secondary		Rk	Strategy		Rk
Runs, first half	35%	29	Form: Single Back	79%	10	Rush 3	22.0%	1	4 DB	17%	30	Play action	18%	17
Runs, first down	41%	28	Form: Empty Back	15%	1	Rush 4	58.9%	21	5 DB	57%	13	Avg Box (Off)	6.14	24
Runs, second-long	20%	31	Pers: 3+ WR	44%	29	Rush 5	16.9%	29	6+ DB	25%	6	Avg Box (Def)	5.89	32
Runs, power sit.	58%	10	Pers: 2+ TE/6+ OL	55%	2	Rush 6+	2.2%	31	CB by Sides	53%	32	Offensive Pace	28.24	2
Runs, behind 2H	20%	29	Pers: 6+ OL	6%	7	Sacks by LB	22.4%	21	S/CB Cover Ratio	30%	3	Defensive Pace	30.10	12
Pass, ahead 2H	60%	2	Shotgun/Pistol	58%	22	Sacks by DB	2.0%	32	DB Blitz	4%	32	Go for it on 4th	0.84	18

The Patriots offense has been strongly oriented towards the left side for years, but that trend has become even stronger the last two seasons. Last year 44 percent of Patriots passes were on the left side, after a league-leading 45 percent in 2014. The Patriots threw deep passes equally to both sides last year, but their passes that went 15 yards through the air or less were split 46/24/30 between left, middle, and right. Surprisingly, the difference between left and right isn't about Julian Edelman or Danny Amendola, whose passes are more balanced across the field. The issue here is the "X" receiver position. Last year, Brandon LaFell, Keshawn Martin, and Aaron Dobson combined for 84 targets on the left side of the field and only 25 targets on the right side. ☞ For years, one of Tom Brady's only weaknesses was the defensive back blitz; for example, he averaged just 4.2 yards on these passes in 2014. But in 2015, he averaged a league-leading 9.4 yards per pass. The Patriots didn't face many defensive back blitzes—5.8 percent of passes, only the Giants faced fewer—so the improvement could just be case of small sample size. ☞ New England was one of only three teams that didn't have 11 personnel as its most common personnel package. (The Jets and Titans were the others.) ☞ The average NFL team used play-action on 30 percent of first-down passes but just 4 percent of third-down passes. The Patriots, on the other hand, used play-action on 22 percent of first-down passes but 11 percent of third-down passes. Only Carolina was more likely to play-fake on third down. ☞ The Patriots defense ranked seventh in DVOA before halftime but 22nd after halftime. That included a 4.2% DVOA in late-and-close situations, 24th in the league. ☞ Patriots opponents threw deep on a league-leading 26 percent of passes, although this wasn't a particular weakness; the Patriots ranked 13th in the NFL in defensive DVOA against deep passes. ☞ On the flip side, Patriots opponents threw just 12 percent of their passes behind the line of scrimmage, the lowest rate in the league. That may have been a missed opportunity, as the Pats ranked just 23rd in DVOA against those passes. We charted Patriots opponents with only 17 running back screens and only 13 wide receiver screens; both figures were the lowest in the NFL. ☞ Just how big was the gap between the Patriots and the rest of the league when it came to dropping eight defenders into coverage? We recorded the Patriots sending just three pass rushers on 141 plays. The teams ranked second and third, Buffalo and Houston, sent three pass rushers on 141 plays *combined*. ☞ Although the Patriots blitzed less than any other team, they were very successful when they did, allowing 4.8 yards per pass. Only the Broncos allowed fewer average yards when they blitzed. ☞ Without Brandon Browner around, the Patriots finished dead last in the NFL with just 29 penalties on defense.

Passing

Player	DYAR	DVOA	Plays	NtYds	Avg	YAC	C%	TD	Int
T.Brady	1312	19.5%	660	4536	6.9	6.0	64.6%	36	7

Rushing

Player	DYAR	DVOA	Plays	Yds	Avg	TD	Fum	Suc
L.Blount	64	0.2%	165	703	4.3	6	1	52%
B.Bolden	-40	-24.3%	63	207	3.3	0	0	33%
D.Lewis	77	28.1%	49	234	4.8	2	0	55%
J.White	-12	-22.1%	22	56	2.5	2	0	32%
S.Jackson*	11	2.8%	21	50	2.4	1	0	43%
T.Brady	25	6.5%	20	69	3.5	3	1	-
J.Iosefa	-8	-20.7%	15	51	3.4	0	0	60%
D.Brown	21	0.3%	59	229	3.9	1	0	36%

Receiving

Player	DYAR	DVOA	Plays	Ctch	Yds	Y/C	YAC	TD	C%
J.Edelman	144	8.1%	88	61	692	11.3	5.1	7	69%
D.Amendola	139	8.6%	87	65	648	10.0	4.1	3	75%
B.LaFell*	-43	-20.1%	74	37	515	13.9	6.1	0	50%
K.Martin	84	14.9%	37	24	269	11.2	3.2	2	65%
A.Dobson	49	15.1%	21	13	141	10.8	2.2	0	62%
N.Washington	-4	-13.2%	94	47	658	14.0	3.4	4	50%
C.Hogan	1	-12.4%	59	36	450	12.5	3.0	2	61%
R.Gronkowski	235	21.0%	120	72	1176	16.3	7.7	11	60%
S.Chandler*	39	5.8%	42	23	259	11.3	3.1	4	55%
M.Williams	-10	-33.7%	6	3	26	8.7	4.3	0	50%
M.Bennett	-18	-10.7%	80	53	443	8.4	4.3	3	66%
C.Harbor	17	4.9%	20	14	149	10.6	4.0	1	70%
J.White	140	33.3%	54	40	410	10.3	8.7	4	74%
D.Lewis	78	14.7%	50	36	388	10.8	9.4	2	72%
B.Bolden	26	2.2%	30	19	180	9.5	6.8	2	63%
L.Blount	21	39.5%	7	6	43	7.2	5.2	1	86%
D.Brown	-7	-24.8%	13	8	88	11.0	13.8	0	62%

Offensive Line

Player	Pos	Age	GS	Snaps	Pen	Sk	Pass	Run	Player	Pos	Age	GS	Snaps	Pen	Sk	Pass	Run
Josh Kline	G	27	14/13	865	5	1.0	2.0	2.0	Bryan Stork	C	26	8/6	491	4	3.0	7.0	1.0
Sebastian Vollmer	OT	32	14/13	816	6	4.0	8.0	3.0	Cameron Fleming	OT	24	12/7	469	3	2.0	3.0	0.5
David Andrews	C	24	14/11	765	5	1.0	4.0	1.0	LaAdrian Waddle	RT	25	9/6	409	4	2.0	7.0	0.0
Shaq Mason	LG	23	14/10	737	2	2.0	12.0	3.0	Nate Solder	LT	28	4/4	229	2	3.0	3.0	2.0
Marcus Cannon	OT	28	12/8	624	5	1.0	7.0	2.0	Jonathan Cooper	RG	26	14/9	638	4	1.0	2.0	3.0
Tre' Jackson	RG	24	13/9	607	3	1.0	4.0	2.0									

Year	Yards	ALY	Rank	Power	Rank	Stuff	Rank	2nd Lev	Rank	Open Field	Rank	Sacks	ASR	Rank	Press	Rank	F-Start	Cont.
2013	4.69	4.63	1	59%	23	16%	4	1.39	2	0.80	12	40	6.1%	9	20.3%	4	11	32
2014	4.11	4.22	5	59%	23	21%	27	1.22	11	0.59	23	26	4.4%	2	23.3%	14	19	28
2015	3.88	4.19	2	64%	19	16%	1	1.17	16	0.42	30	38	6.5%	18	25.5%	16	13	15
2015 ALY by direction:		Left End 4.31 (8)			Left Tackle 3.64 (18)			Mid/Guard 4.18 (7)				Right Tackle 5 (1)			Right End 2.77 (24)			

As noted earlier in the chapter, the Patriots had the lowest offensive line continuity score in the 16 seasons we have tracked. The only other teams below 20 were the 2007 Rams (17) and 2014 Colts (19). ☞ Newcomer Jonathan Cooper wasn't bad in his first extended stint as a starter, with 127.6 snaps per blown block over nine starts in Arizona. However, a left leg injury sidelined Cooper for two weeks, and Ted Larsen never relinquished the right guard job for the Cardinals when Cooper was healthy again. The former seventh overall pick has been the first-string right guard in offseason practices. Depending on Cooper to stay healthy is a dicey proposition, but so long as he's upright, the Pats will likely give him every chance to earn a starting job. ☞ Completing this spring's new look on the interior line was third-round rookie Joe Thuney lining up as the first-team left guard. The North Carolina State alum checks off all the boxes of a typical New England offensive lineman: a little athletically limited, but a relentless worker with the football IQ to play all over the line. He can't be much worse than Shaq Mason, who ranked last among left guards with 49.1 snaps per blown block.

Defensive Front Seven

Defensive Line	Age	Pos	G	Snaps	Plays	Overall TmPct	Rk	Stop	Dfts	BTkl	Runs	vs. Run St%	Rk	RuYd	Rk	Pass Rush Sack	Hit	Hur	Dsrpt
Malcom Brown	22	DT	16	509	48	5.8%	34	38	7	1	44	80%	32	2.3	47	3.0	2	5.0	0
Alan Branch	32	DT	16	434	38	4.6%	--	27	5	0	32	72%	--	2.3	--	1.0	2	2.0	2
Akiem Hicks*	27	DT	16	399	22	2.7%	--	19	7	2	19	84%	--	2.1	--	3.0	4	6.5	0
Dominique Easley*	24	DT	11	275	14	2.5%	--	12	7	0	9	78%	--	1.9	--	2.0	7	12.5	0
Sealver Siliga*	26	DT	13	254	28	4.2%	--	21	2	1	27	74%	--	2.5	--	0.0	0	1.0	0
Terrance Knighton	30	DT	15	369	29	3.9%	--	27	8	4	25	92%	--	1.0	--	1.5	2	2.0	0

Edge Rushers	Age	Pos	G	Snaps	Plays	Overall TmPct	Rk	Stop	Dfts	BTkl	Runs	vs. Run St%	Rk	RuYd	Rk	Pass Rush Sack	Hit	Hur	Dsrpt
Rob Ninkovich	32	DE	16	891	59	7.2%	7	42	15	6	31	71%	60	2.8	69	6.5	12	24.5	5
Chandler Jones*	26	DE	15	863	45	5.8%	28	41	19	6	27	85%	11	1.6	22	12.5	7	17.5	0
Jabaal Sheard	27	DE	13	558	38	5.7%	32	34	17	6	26	88%	7	1.0	6	8.0	5	16.5	1
Chris Long	31	DE	12	485	19	2.8%	86	14	4	2	13	77%	34	3.2	82	3.0	1	9.0	0

Linebackers	Age	Pos	G	Snaps	Plays	Overall TmPct	Rk	Stop	Dfts	BTkl	Runs	vs. Run St%	Rk	RuYd	Rk	Pass Rush Sack	Hit	Hur	Tgts	vs. Pass Suc%	Rk	AdjYd	Rk	PD	Int
Jamie Collins	26	OLB	12	778	94	15.2%	16	58	25	12	54	65%	40	3.4	35	5.5	2	5	25	69%	10	4.6	15	6	1
Dont'a Hightower	26	MLB	12	594	63	10.2%	60	32	7	4	40	53%	80	4.3	76	3.5	3	9	11	50%	51	6.0	35	1	0
Jerod Mayo*	30	OLB	16	395	45	5.5%	--	28	6	4	29	76%	--	2.3	--	1.0	2	2	6	66%	--	3.9	--	1	0
Jonathan Freeny	27	MLB	13	390	48	7.2%	74	24	3	4	26	65%	38	4.2	73	1.0	0	2	14	47%	54	5.7	29	0	0
Shea McClellin	27	ILB	12	675	82	14.3%	28	35	6	14	49	47%	86	4.6	80	0.0	2	4.5	25	37%	66	9.6	67	1	0
Ramon Humber	29	OLB	14	273	42	5.9%	--	17	4	2	25	52%	--	5.4	--	1.0	1	1	6	65%	--	8.3	--	1	0

Year	Yards	ALY	Rank	Power	Rank	Stuff	Rank	2nd Level	Rank	Open Field	Rank	Sacks	ASR	Rank	Press	Rank
2013	4.24	4.37	30	60%	11	13%	32	1.12	17	0.43	4	48	7.5%	9	23.2%	22
2014	4.08	3.95	18	81%	32	16%	28	1.16	20	0.47	3	40	6.5%	20	22.5%	25
2015	3.92	3.62	13	60%	10	19%	21	1.02	7	0.66	11	49	7.8%	2	24.7%	21

2015 ALY by direction: Left End 3.29 (13)   Left Tackle 3.81 (18)   Mid/Guard 3.89 (15)   Right Tackle 3.58 (13)   Right End 2.49 (6)

The Patriots will miss Chandler Jones. However, Jones' absence won't be too damaging if Jabaal Sheard can sustain anything close to his per-snap production from 2015. Despite playing 305 fewer defensive snaps than Jones, Sheard nearly matched him in quarterback hits (7 to 5), hurries (17.5 to 16.5) and total defeats (19 to 17). There shouldn't be a big drop-off in run defense either. ☞ Jamie Collins was one of eight defenders last season with at least 25 defeats and five sacks. But most of those players were pass rushers like J.J. Watt or Khalil Mack; Collins was also adept at dropping into coverage, ranking 10th among linebackers in adjusted success rate. ☞ The Pats turned over much of their interior defensive line this offseason, but Malcom Brown looks like a rock they can build around. The 2015 first-round pick led New England's defensive tackles in stops with 38, a figure which ranked first among rookie defensive tackles and fourth among all rookie defensive linemen. ☞ Rob Ninkovich drops into coverage more than any other defensive end on a nominally 4-3 team. He led all edge rushers in pass targets in 2013 and 2014 and was second in 2015 (8 targets, trailing only Houston's John Simon).

Defensive Secondary

Secondary	Age	Pos	G	Snaps	Plays	TmPct	Rk	Stop	Dfts	BTkl	Runs	St%	Rk	RuYd	Rk	Tgts	Tgt%	Rk	Dist	Suc%	Rk	AdjYd	Rk	PD	Int
Malcolm Butler	26	CB	16	1082	82	10.0%	20	38	14	5	15	47%	32	4.9	14	93	20.5%	47	16.1	57%	17	8.7	56	17	2
Logan Ryan	25	CB	16	978	87	10.6%	11	36	12	4	21	57%	14	4.2	7	80	19.4%	39	13.2	55%	25	7.8	38	14	4
Devin McCourty	29	FS	14	928	68	9.4%	39	23	12	5	28	25%	57	10.8	63	32	8.2%	42	15.1	54%	46	9.4	58	5	1
Patrick Chung	29	SS	15	887	91	11.8%	19	44	17	6	44	55%	10	3.5	1	50	13.3%	64	11.7	58%	35	5.9	19	11	0
Duron Harmon	25	FS	16	603	24	2.9%	--	5	4	4	9	0%	--	13.9	--	11	4.2%	--	23.3	56%	--	7.4	--	5	3
Justin Coleman	23	CB	10	299	26	5.1%	--	9	3	4	0	0%	--	0.0	--	35	27.6%	--	14.4	45%	--	8.5	--	5	0
Jordan Richards	23	SS	14	239	20	2.8%	--	9	2	2	6	67%	--	4.5	--	12	11.5%	--	11.1	51%	--	4.5	--	2	0
E.J. Biggers	29	CB	16	563	46	5.1%	--	15	6	6	8	25%	--	10.5	--	46	21.0%	--	9.6	53%	--	6.8	--	7	0

Year	Pass D Rank	vs. #1 WR	Rk	vs. #2 WR	Rk	vs. Other WR	Rk	vs. TE	Rk	vs. RB	Rk
2013	14	-1.9%	16	17.9%	29	5.5%	21	-1.1%	13	5.1%	19
2014	12	-14.4%	7	1.8%	17	-13.8%	7	22.0%	30	-4.6%	14
2015	15	-1.2%	17	1.1%	15	21.4%	28	-8.3%	15	1.7%	17

Strong tackling technique is one of the reasons the Patriots defense has been successful the last few years. The Pats were second in the league with just 81 broken tackles last season, after ranking first in 2014 and second in 2013. The defensive backs have played a large role in this success, and the quartet of Malcolm Butler, Devin McCourty, Patrick Chung, and Logan Ryan each had broken tackle rates of under 10 percent. No other defense had four defensive backs with at least 30 tackles and a broken tackle rate in the single digits. ✎ By the Football Outsiders version of passes defended, only eight cornerbacks had more passes defensed than Malcolm Butler's 17. That's partially a byproduct of Butler's heavy volume of targets, but he did finish 17th in both normal and adjusted success rate. However, leaving him on an island did result in a some big plays, which is why he ranks so much lower in adjusted yards per target. ✎ Here's a statement no Patriots fan would have believed two years ago: Patrick Chung is one of the league's best box safeties. Among defensive backs, Chung had the best average depth of tackle (3.5 yards) on rushing plays. In addition, he ranked 19th in adjusted yards per target and either led or finished second among safeties in passes defensed (11), depending on how you consider Tyrann Mathieu. ✎ The biggest weakness in New England's secondary last year was the slot cornerback role, which ended up a revolving door between Justin Coleman, Leonard Johnson and others. Cyrus Jones, the team's top draft selection in 2016, should thus get an immediate chance to play. Jones plays bigger than his listed 5-foot-10, 197-pound size, having thrived in both coverage and run support as a press corner under Nick Saban at LSU. Jones should immediately slot in behind Butler and Ryan on a fairly thin cornerback depth chart, although the Patriots also use plenty of three-safety sub packages.

Special Teams

Year	DVOA	Rank	FG/XP	Rank	Net Kick	Rank	Kick Ret	Rank	Net Punt	Rank	Punt Ret	Rank	Hidden	Rank
2013	6.7%	2	11.4	1	10.5	2	2.0	9	9.0	6	0.5	14	-9.9	30
2014	5.7%	5	10.8	1	8.4	3	0.5	13	0.2	16	8.4	5	8.9	3
2015	3.9%	5	14.1	1	8.2	2	0.7	10	-6.7	25	3.1	10	0.1	16

The Patriots had the worst single-game performance of any special teams unit all year in their shocking Week 13 loss to Philadelphia, but still finished the season in the top five for the fifth straight season. This also marked the 20th straight season the Patriots put up special teams DVOA above 0%. They last time the Patriots had below-average special teams was 1995, the year before they signed undrafted free agent Adam Vinatieri. ✎ Stephen Gostkowski has led the NFL in placekicking value for three straight seasons, and he's strong on kickoffs as well. But the coverage team led by Matthew Slater makes him look even better: we've estimated the Patriots with the most value on kickoff coverage for four straight seasons. ✎ However, last year's punting unit was the worst of the Bill Belichick era, accruing minus-6.7 net points worth of field position less than expected.

New Orleans Saints

A large portion of the NFL media deeply cares about punishments and social norms. These are the old personnel folk who find themselves in the media talking about "building a team the right way." The websites that keep "Days Without an Arrest" countdowns and use the NFL as a broader spectrum to talk about how fair or unfair it is that a minimum salary nobody loses his job for getting arrested while Greg Hardy gets paid like a franchise star. No matter where you look, there's a moral bend to this news, trying to get our attention to tell us how we should feel about things.

A very small subset of this commentary focuses on the NFL salary cap. Writers mock the Cowboys, to give one example, for restructuring deals and tying up a lot of guaranteed money in older players, and they lament how poor the strategy is. You'll see alarming words, set to create concern. "This team could collapse at any minute." "What happens when Romo is anchored to the budget?"

The Saints have been a part of that salary-cap roller-coaster ride the last few seasons. The salary capperatti figured that the Saints didn't have much money under the cap to spend in the 2014 offseason, so they decided that New Orleans "mortgaged their future" by giving safety Jairus Byrd a $56 million contract with $28 million in guarantees. Of course, two years later with perspective—what have the Saints really lost?

New Orleans was forced to trade away Jimmy Graham, which seemed like a huge deal at the time. It's hard to say how he would've fared in New Orleans versus Seattle, which spent half the season not knowing he was supposed to be involved in the offense. One torn patellar tendon later and we're wondering if Graham is even going to be able to get back on the field at 100 percent—and he'll turn 30 in November. The Saints got a first-round pick and an All-Pro center for him. While it's fair to say that quarterback Drew Brees has missed Graham, as the team has struggled to replace him in the pecking order, it's also fair to question if in-his-prime Graham was the one they had under contract—especially given how often he struggled through injury in 2013 and 2014.

The other players New Orleans were "forced" to move on from over the past two years are a litter of once-good, now-old links to their 2009 championship team: wideout Marques Colston, running back Pierre Thomas, guard Jahri Evans, cornerback Jabari Greer. They did let some legitimately good players leave. (Malcolm Jenkins comes to mind.) But the point is: nothing about the salary cap forced New Orleans' hand. The rising salary cap combined with some shrewd management means that the consequences of going all-in can be relatively miniscule. They were able to re-sign Mark Ingram. Drew Brees is still here no matter how big his cap hit gets.

The problem with New Orleans' free-agency spending hasn't been the strategy. It's been the players they've been spending on (Table 1).

New Orleans' splurges just haven't been very good. Some of these failures have been truly unexpected; nobody anticipated that Byrd would collapse in New Orleans the way he has the last two seasons. Still, general manager Mickey Loomis has made a lot of curious judgment calls over the past few offseasons. Brandon Browner was a penalty machine in 2014 on a good New England team, playing in a less-demanding role

Table 1. 2014-2016 Offseason Acquisitions in New Orleans

Year	Player	Pos	Contract	Comments
2014	Jarius Byrd	FS	5 years/$56 million, $28 million guaranteed	Continually injured and ineffective in New Orleans.
2014	Champ Bailey	CB	2 years/$7 million	Retired in training camp.
2015	Brandon Browner	CB	3 years/$15 million	Released after one year; Is holding you as you read this.
2015	Dannell Ellerbe	ILB	Acquired in trade; restructured	Has played seven games in two years, was poor in 2014.
2015	C.J. Spiller	RB	4 years/$16 million	Had no burst last season; also continually hurt.
2015	Max Unger	C	Acquired in trade; restructured	Unger played well last season
2016	James Laurinaitis	ILB	3 years/$8.25 million	Weak link in St. Louis last season.
2016	Coby Fleener	TE	6 years/$36 million, $18 million guaranteed	Drop-prone at his best, nothing special as a receiver.
2016	Nick Fairley	DT	1 year/$3 million	Always seems to play well, but why is he always available in free agency?

2016 Saints Schedule

Week	Opp.	Week	Opp.	Week	Opp.
1	OAK	7	at KC	13	DET
2	at NYG	8	SEA	14	at TB
3	ATL (Mon.)	9	at SF	15	at ARI
4	at SD	10	DEN	16	TB (Sat.)
5	BYE	11	at CAR (Thu.)	17	at ATL
6	CAR	12	LA		

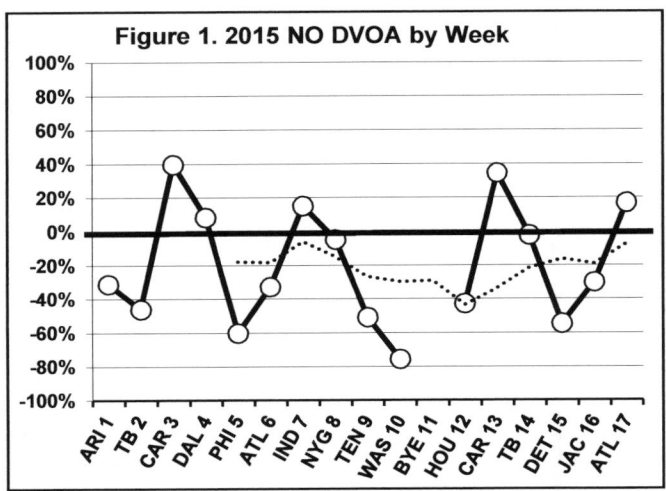

Figure 1. 2015 NO DVOA by Week

with safety help. Why would it be a good idea to run him out as a starter in 2015 without Darrelle Revis shifting extra bodies towards Browner's sideline? If Miami was so desperate to get rid of Dannell Ellerbe that he was a throw-in on a draft pick trade for Kenny Stills, shouldn't that have tipped the Saints off? Why would a cash-strapped team spend money on a running back who's never healthy when the Saints always seem to have a deep stall of cheap, effective running backs?

This year's additions aren't any more promising. James Laurinaitis has never been able to cover, and at this point is nothing more than a thumper-for-hire in the trenches. Coby Fleener was such an enigma for the Colts that they let him walk despite oodles of cap space. Indy even re-signed lower-drafted tight end Dwayne Allen over Fleener. Nick Fairley has played excellent football for a few years now, but always seems to clash with coaching staffs. It's true that an NFL team generally isn't going to build a champion with free agents alone. But you would prefer to see a bit more in the way of quality given the money the Saints have spent.

So, let's not beat around Rafael Bush any longer. The Saints had the worst defensive DVOA we've measured, going all the back to 1989. This makes it hard to win football games. The good news is that a) regression towards the mean is a real concept and b) history shows us that defenses this bad usually take huge strides forward... eventually (Table 2).

Defenses as bad as New Orleans tended to stay pretty bad the year after. The only team in the set that rebounded to a negative DVOA (which means better defense) is the 2009

Table 2. Worst Defensive DVOA, 1989-2015

Year	Team	DVOA	Rank	DVOA Y+1	Rank	DVOA Y+2	Rank
2015	NO	26.1%	32	--	--	--	--
2000	MIN	26.0%	31	18.1%	30	14.5%	30
2008	DET	24.3%	32	17.9%	32	2.9%	22
1999	CLE	22.2%	31	9.8%	25	-13.1%	3
1996	ATL	21.6%	30	4.0%	22	-9.2%	5
2004	MIN	21.6%	32	3.8%	23	-9.3%	6
1992	ATL	21.3%	28	11.9%	25	7.8%	24
2008	DEN	20.7%	31	-9.8%	7	16.6%	30
1999	SF	20.4%	30	16.0%	28	0.1%	15
2005	HOU	20.1%	32	13.7%	31	12.0%	29
AVERAGE		22.0%	31	9.5%	25	2.5%	18

Broncos. You may remember that team best for Josh McDaniels' rookie season as a head coach, with him fist-pumping the Patriots off his field in Week 5. The Broncos turned things around quickly by turning over three-fourths of the starting secondary and getting the fourth (Champ Bailey) back from injury—and the improvement lasted only one year. You may not be surprised to learn that most teams on this list cleaned house on defense. The 2005 Texans, 2008 Broncos, and 2008 Lions fired their head coaches.

Having said that, it was rather puzzling that this team retained Dennis Allen as defensive coordinator. Allen replaced Rob Ryan following a 49-17 shellacking against Kirk Cousins and Washington. New Orleans' DVOA at the time was 25.4%. After Allen took over and used the bye week to his advantage, New Orleans' defense over the last six weeks managed an average DVOA of ... 27.5%. Allen was previously the head coach in Oakland, and the Raiders finished 26th or lower in defensive DVOA in each of his three seasons there. If you don't want to impute Allen's defensive statistics as head coach of the Raiders purely to him, but say he was set up to fail with that roster, that's fine. At the job that got him the Raiders gig—defensive coordinator for the 2011 Broncos—his unit posted a 1.6% DVOA in one Tebow-driven miracle season. There's little statistical evidence that suggests he's going to key a turnaround. This isn't to say that it's unlikely. But when you've finished in the bottom last or next-to-last in defensive DVOA in three of the last four seasons, maybe it's time to look outside the building. And look at who is in the building. And also maybe burn the building to the ground and salt the earth.

When you look back at the teams of Table 2 that retained staff and weren't part of an expansion, you find some exceptionally dysfunctional long-term results. Denny Green's 2000 Vikings were poor on defense all year, but most people didn't notice until they imploded in the NFC Championship Game. They didn't do anything to improve things in the offseason, and that led to Green's dismissal in 2001. New head coach Mike Tice changed defensive coordinators literally every year from 2002 through 2004. The Vikings immediately improved their defense once Brad Childress brought in some young kid named Mike Tomlin as coordinator in 2006, but it was a long woeful stretch.

It was the same story with the early 1990s Falcons, who had two separate regimes of failure under Jerry Glanville and June Jones. Defensive coordinator Doug Shivley survived for one more year after the awful 1992 season, until Jones brought in Jim Bates in 1994. Then in 1996, Jones hired assistant head coach/defense Rod Rust, and both of them went down the tubes in a Jeff George tantrum. Eventually, Dan Reeves took over and spurred a quick turnaround.

The best-case scenario is the 1999 49ers, who kept Steve Mariucci and defensive coordinator Jim Mora on staff until Mora left to become Atlanta's head coach. They took a year to reorient their defense around a new core of Julian Peterson, Lance Schulters, and Andre Carter. However, the 1999 49ers still had some pieces around from the top-rated defense of 1997, which made the turnaround a bit easier. (Think: Bryant Young.)

New Orleans fits more into the Minnesota and Atlanta molds, because finishing 31st or worse in defensive DVOA in three of the last four seasons isn't an accident. It's a trend.

The offseason has also not been kind to New Orleans. Already, 2015 second-round pick Hau'oli Kikaha has torn his ACL and will miss the season. He was penciled in to move down to defensive end with the Saints playing a more standard 4-3 scheme, and that spot is now wide-open on the depth chart. Cornerback Keenan Lewis (leg injury, hip surgery, sports hernia surgery, some other surgeries in all likelihood) hasn't practiced yet, and Kyle Wilson has already been placed on injured reserve with a torn labrum. Byrd is still recovering from back surgery and likely won't play in training camp. Combine that with subpar replacements at middle linebacker and a lack of star power from everyone who isn't Cameron Jordan, and it's hard to see many talent advantages for New Orleans without some very unexpected player development.

To their credit, the Saints have changed some things. There won't be any more two-gapping from the defensive line. 2015 first-rounder Stephone Anthony feels like he'll be able to be more instinctive with Laurinaitis calling the signals. 2016 second-round pick Vonn Bell (Ohio State) is an undersized safety with cornerback experience, and should eventually displace Byrd and his contract. First-round pick Sheldon Rankins (Louisville) made legitimate NFL interior line prospects look like they'd never seen a spin move before at the Senior Bowl.

But despite a depth chart filled with young, high-round picks, we still have New Orleans with the worst mean defensive projection of all 32 teams. The Saints end up with the worst defensive DVOA in the league in 20 percent of our simulations for 2016. They end up with one of the five worst defensive DVOAs in 62 percent of our simulations. They'll rebound a bit, because regression exists, but expecting a huge turnaround is not something we're prepared to forecast.

OK, but the offense is still powerful, right? Somewhat. With so many pieces gone, the New Orleans offense is no longer one of the best five units in the league, but they have more than enough talent to win. Ingram can spearhead a good rushing offense when he's healthy, and Brees is still an objectively good quarterback, even if he is throwing to Fleener and some relatively unknown youngsters. The offense still works just fine. It's just that this team has become the Steve Nash Phoenix Suns of the late 2000s, starring Brees as Nash. The pieces around Brees are no longer boosting his statistical output to 5,000-yard levels, and defense is regarded as almost a chore.

With no massive sea change in place, it's hard to see the defense doing much more than just a dead-cat bounce. That will leave Saints fans with a familiar picture: one more year of Drew Brees wasted.

Rivers McCown

2015 Saints Stats by Week

Wk	vs.	W-L	PF	PA	YDF	YDA	TO	Total	Off	Def	ST
1	at ARI	L	19	31	408	427	0	-31%	6%	33%	-4%
2	TB	L	19	26	323	333	-1	-46%	-25%	-1%	-22%
3	at CAR	L	22	27	380	431	-2	40%	45%	24%	19%
4	DAL	W	26	20	438	335	0	8%	19%	14%	4%
5	at PHI	L	17	39	388	519	-2	-60%	-20%	35%	-5%
6	ATL	W	31	21	385	413	3	-33%	12%	26%	-19%
7	at IND	W	27	21	449	376	2	15%	9%	0%	6%
8	NYG	W	52	49	608	416	-1	-5%	31%	28%	-8%
9	TEN	L	28	34	416	483	-1	-51%	2%	42%	-10%
10	at WAS	L	14	47	350	510	-2	-75%	-27%	52%	4%
11	BYE										
12	at HOU	L	6	24	268	362	0	-43%	-27%	23%	8%
13	CAR	L	38	41	334	497	2	35%	48%	7%	-6%
14	at TB	W	24	17	388	291	0	-2%	12%	12%	-2%
15	DET	L	27	35	399	396	1	-55%	5%	53%	-7%
16	JAC	W	38	27	537	412	2	-30%	43%	55%	-18%
17	at ATL	W	20	17	390	414	1	17%	24%	16%	10%

Trends and Splits

	Offense	Rank	Defense	Rank
Total DVOA	10.5%	7	26.1%	32
Unadjusted VOA	9.6%	9	22.6%	32
Weighted Trend	12.6%	5	28.1%	32
Variance	6.3%	15	3.3%	6
Average Opponent	-0.1%	16	-3.1%	29
Passing	30.1%	7	48.1%	32
Rushing	-7.1%	15	-2.4%	27
First Down	-4.9%	20	20.3%	32
Second Down	18.0%	5	37.3%	32
Third Down	31.1%	5	20.9%	28
First Half	16.8%	4	19.6%	32
Second Half	5.0%	13	33.3%	32
Red Zone	18.8%	9	41.3%	32
Late and Close	4.1%	12	31.9%	32

Five-Year Performance

Year	W-L	Pyth W	Est W	PF	PA	TO	Total	Rk	Off	Rk	Def	Rk	ST	Rk	Off AGL	Rk	Def AGL	Rk	Off Age	Rk	Def Age	Rk	ST Age	Rk
2011	13-3	12.4	12.0	547	339	-3	23.8%	2	33.0%	2	10.2%	28	1.0%	12	17.4	6	7.2	1	27.7	11	26.9	19	26.2	18
2012	7-9	8.2	6.4	461	454	+2	-5.2%	19	11.9%	9	14.8%	32	-2.3%	24	11.5	4	23.6	14	28.3	3	26.6	21	25.9	22
2013	11-5	10.8	10.0	414	304	0	19.3%	4	16.0%	5	-5.8%	10	-2.5%	24	12.3	3	59.0	31	28.4	1	26.0	25	26.2	10
2014	7-9	7.4	7.6	401	424	-13	-0.9%	17	10.6%	7	13.1%	31	1.6%	11	26.4	12	31.6	10	29.0	1	26.2	24	25.9	22
2015	7-9	6.4	5.2	408	476	+2	-18.7%	28	10.5%	7	26.1%	32	-3.2%	26	19.7	3	36.3	23	28.2	4	26.5	20	26.7	4

2015 Performance Based on Most Common Personnel Groups

NO Offense					NO Offense vs. Opponents						NO Defense				NO Defense vs. Opponents			
Pers	Freq	Yds	DVOA	Run%	Pers	Freq	Yds	DVOA	Run%		Pers	Freq	Yds	DVOA	Pers	Freq	Yds	DVOA
11	50%	6.5	18.2%	23%	Base	38%	5.4	4.0%	53%		Base	34%	6.6	21.1%	11	54%	6.4	23.7%
12	25%	5.3	5.2%	45%	Nickel	45%	6.2	20.0%	27%		Nickel	51%	7.3	34.0%	12	23%	8.7	46.4%
13	9%	5.1	-3.6%	63%	Dime+	15%	7.4	26.4%	10%		Dime+	15%	5.8	15.0%	21	9%	5.9	-0.4%
21	4%	4.4	-1.1%	43%	Goal Line	1%	0.7	35.7%	75%		Goal Line	1%	2.3	13.3%	13	3%	6.5	46.7%
612	3%	5.7	35.5%	78%											22	2%	4.4	-11.9%
22	2%	4.0	-19.4%	54%											612	2%	5.2	-3.7%
01	2%	12.2	115.8%	0%											10	2%	6.1	-20.4%

Strategic Tendencies

Run/Pass		Rk	Formation		Rk	Pass Rush		Rk	Secondary		Rk	Strategy		Rk
Runs, first half	35%	26	Form: Single Back	75%	18	Rush 3	9.9%	4	4 DB	34%	14	Play action	18%	20
Runs, first down	47%	18	Form: Empty Back	11%	8	Rush 4	63.4%	18	5 DB	51%	21	Avg Box (Off)	6.18	21
Runs, second-long	22%	29	Pers: 3+ WR	55%	22	Rush 5	18.9%	23	6+ DB	15%	12	Avg Box (Def)	6.32	12
Runs, power sit.	69%	3	Pers: 2+ TE/6+ OL	43%	7	Rush 6+	7.9%	12	CB by Sides	73%	18	Offensive Pace	29.46	9
Runs, behind 2H	28%	11	Pers: 6+ OL	5%	10	Sacks by LB	36.7%	17	S/CB Cover Ratio	18%	29	Defensive Pace	30.57	21
Pass, ahead 2H	54%	6	Shotgun/Pistol	54%	24	Sacks by DB	13.3%	7	DB Blitz	10%	15	Go for it on 4th	1.55	6

The Saints faced the highest rate of play-action in the NFL: 23.9 percent of pass plays, just ahead of San Francisco. Of course they did, because they allowed an absurd 11.1 yards per play on these passes with a league-worst 62.0% DVOA. No other defense allowed more than 10.0 yards per play against play-action. The Saints also had the worst DVOA in the league against non-play action (42.6%) but were 29th in yards allowed per play (7.0). The Saints actually had a good red zone run defense, ranking seventh with a -12.6% DVOA. Unfortunately, their 91.6% red zone pass defense DVOA was the worst in the league by more than 20 percentage points, leading New Orleans to finish last in overall red zone DVOA. The Saints defense ranked 30th in adjusted sack rate on first and second downs but had the highest adjusted sack rate in the league (10.5 percent) on third and fourth downs. New Orleans often found itself needing to speed up down the stretch. The Saints ranked 22nd in first-half pace (28.56 seconds between plays) but fifth in second-half pace (25.49 seconds). The offense averaged 10.0 yards per play with an empty backfield, best in the league, and ranked third with 63.6% DVOA.

Passing

Player	DYAR	DVOA	Plays	NtYds	Avg	YAC	C%	TD	Int
D.Brees	1111	15.8%	657	4625	7.0	5.6	68.6%	32	11
L.McCown	220	77.1%	40	335	8.4	4.8	82.1%	0	1

Rushing

Player	DYAR	DVOA	Plays	Yds	Avg	TD	Fum	Suc
M.Ingram	108	6.6%	166	769	4.6	6	1	45%
T.Hightower	110	16.5%	96	375	3.9	4	0	56%
K.Robinson*	29	3.0%	56	180	3.2	4	0	43%
C.J.Spiller	-29	-28.5%	36	112	3.1	0	1	36%
B.Cooks	-4	-47.8%	7	18	2.6	0	0	-
A.Johnson	17	51.1%	4	9	2.3	1	0	100%
T.Cadet	-15	-87.3%	4	12	3.0	0	1	75%

Receiving

Player	DYAR	DVOA	Plays	Ctch	Yds	Y/C	YAC	TD	C%
B.Cooks	192	7.1%	130	85	1138	13.4	4.6	9	65%
W.Snead	175	10.1%	101	69	984	14.3	5.0	3	68%
M.Colston*	103	7.1%	67	45	520	11.6	4.3	4	67%
B.Coleman	113	17.9%	49	30	454	15.1	4.0	2	61%
B.Watson*	87	4.9%	110	74	825	11.1	3.3	6	67%
J.Hill	-44	-27.9%	30	16	120	7.5	4.8	2	53%
M.Hoomanawanui	-28	-31.2%	16	11	80	7.3	2.6	3	69%
C.Fleener	-49	-15.9%	84	54	491	9.1	3.3	3	64%
M.Ingram	59	4.0%	60	50	408	8.2	9.2	0	83%
C.Spiller	2	-12.9%	44	34	239	7.0	7.5	2	77%
K.Robinson	-1	-14.7%	20	17	115	6.8	9.1	0	85%
T.Hightower	51	56.5%	13	12	129	10.8	11.2	0	92%
T.Cadet	72	91.7%	11	9	146	16.2	9.8	1	82%
A.Johnson	-12	-36.5%	8	5	30	6.0	4.6	0	63%

Offensive Line

Player	Pos	Age	GS	Snaps	Pen	Sk	Pass	Run	Player	Pos	Age	GS	Snaps	Pen	Sk	Pass	Run
Max Unger	C	30	16/16	1158	2	1.0	3.0	4.0	Jahri Evans*	RG	33	11/11	802	5	2.5	4.5	4.0
Zach Strief	RT	33	15/15	1075	10	6.0	8.0	2.5	Andrus Peat	LG/LT	23	12/8	426	2	3.0	4.0	1.5
Tim Lelito	LG	27	15/13	951	2	1.0	6.0	2.0	Senio Kelemete	G	26	16/5	424	2	2.0	4.0	0.0
Terron Armstead	LT	25	13/13	929	5	3.5	5.5	2.0									

Year	Yards	ALY	Rank	Power	Rank	Stuff	Rank	2nd Lev	Rank	Open Field	Rank	Sacks	ASR	Rank	Press	Rank	F-Start	Cont.
2013	4.11	4.08	7	67%	13	21%	23	1.22	12	0.65	18	37	5.3%	4	22.4%	12	13	26
2014	4.36	4.38	2	59%	22	18%	13	1.25	8	0.73	15	30	5.3%	12	21.0%	6	10	33
2015	4.00	3.88	13	74%	5	20%	14	1.17	17	0.68	18	32	5.1%	7	21.3%	7	19	25

2015 ALY by direction: Left End 3.69 (15) Left Tackle 4.5 (4) Mid/Guard 3.89 (13) Right Tackle 3.21 (26) Right End 4.22 (6)

Terron Armstead's breakout year was a long time coming, but boy did it hit hard last year. The supposedly cash-strapped Saints rewarded him with an enormous extension. ☺ Max Unger solidified the middle of this line, but it still had some issues in pass protection. Thus, Andrus Peat, the 13th overall pick of the 2015 draft, will be asked to step in and replace aging icon Jahri Evans at right guard. Evans hadn't received much of a sniff elsewhere as we went to press. Peat makes for one huge guard at 6-foot-7, but the Saints do value pass protection on the interior to help the shorter Drew Brees step up and see the middle of the field. ☺ "Hey Taylor Swift, you wanna wrestle?" is undoubtedly the best Bad Lip Reading line in any of their NFL videos and we'll hear no arguments against it. Thank goodness for you, goofy-looking Zach Strief.

Defensive Front Seven

Defensive Line	Age	Pos	G	Snaps	Plays	TmPct	Rk	Stop	Dfts	BTkl	Runs	St%	Rk	RuYd	Rk	Sack	Hit	Hur	Dsrpt
Kevin Williams*	36	DT	16	555	35	4.3%	55	26	7	5	29	79%	33	1.7	24	0.0	2	5.5	2
John Jenkins	27	DT	14	532	49	6.9%	20	34	6	2	44	73%	51	3.2	75	0.5	1	1.5	1
Tyeler Davison	24	DT	16	528	18	2.2%	83	13	6	0	15	67%	68	1.5	16	1.5	3	7.0	0
Nick Fairley	28	DT	15	422	30	3.5%	--	22	3	2	24	79%	--	2.8	--	0.5	7	8.0	1

Edge Rushers	Age	Pos	G	Snaps	Plays	TmPct	Rk	Stop	Dfts	BTkl	Runs	St%	Rk	RuYd	Rk	Sack	Hit	Hur	Dsrpt
Cameron Jordan	27	DE	16	981	47	5.8%	29	36	17	6	29	72%	55	1.8	27	10.0	11	32.5	5
Bobby Richardson	24	DE	15	583	39	5.1%	45	27	7	4	34	71%	64	2.7	65	0.5	1	7.0	0
Darryl Tapp	32	DE	16	410	26	3.2%	--	17	6	1	20	70%	--	2.7	--	2.0	6	2.0	0

Linebackers	Age	Pos	G	Snaps	Plays	TmPct	Rk	Stop	Dfts	BTkl	Runs	St%	Rk	RuYd	Rk	Sack	Hit	Hur	Tgts	Suc%	Rk	AdjYd	Rk	PD	Int
													vs. Run			Pass Rush						vs. Pass			
Stephone Anthony	24	MLB	16	990	117	14.5%	26	69	21	11	78	63%	47	3.8	62	1.0	3	3	24	42%	63	11.5	71	4	1
Hau'oli Kikaha	24	OLB	15	621	51	6.7%	79	32	12	4	34	74%	9	3.0	23	4.0	4	12	8	32%	--	6.5	--	0	0
Kasim Edebali	27	OLB	16	361	20	2.5%	--	11	8	0	11	36%	--	7.5	--	5.0	1	7	0	0%	--	0.0	--	0	0
Ramon Humber*	29	OLB	14	273	42	5.9%	--	17	4	2	25	52%	--	5.4	--	1.0	1	1	6	65%	--	8.3	--	1	0
Dannell Ellerbe	31	OLB	6	250	40	13.2%	34	20	2	3	18	67%	32	5.9	89	0.0	1	2	16	70%	8	5.5	27	1	0
David Hawthorne*	31	OLB	11	222	31	5.6%	--	15	3	7	19	74%	--	3.1	--	0.0	1	1	6	54%	--	5.5	--	0	0
Michael Mauti	26	OLB	16	175	27	3.3%	--	13	3	1	17	53%	--	5.3	--	0.0	1	2	6	83%	--	2.6	--	0	0
James Laurinaitis	30	MLB	16	1156	110	12.2%	43	58	19	6	62	65%	42	4.0	67	1.0	9	8	14	55%	43	7.8	59	1	1
Craig Robertson	28	ILB	12	382	55	9.3%	64	37	5	5	40	75%	6	3.5	40	0.0	2	1	10	61%	--	3.7	--	3	1
Nate Stupar	28	OLB	16	257	33	4.2%	--	15	4	4	16	44%	--	3.9	--	1.0	1	1.5	8	61%	--	4.9	--	2	0

Year	Yards	ALY	Rank	Power	Rank	Stuff	Rank	2nd Level	Rank	Open Field	Rank	Sacks	ASR	Rank	Press	Rank
2013	4.40	3.75	14	69%	23	21%	12	1.06	12	1.13	30	49	8.6%	4	26.7%	7
2014	4.78	3.99	19	74%	28	18%	22	1.32	29	1.17	31	34	6.0%	26	25.1%	16
2015	5.06	4.35	31	68%	20	16%	30	1.46	32	1.20	31	31	6.0%	20	21.3%	32
2015 ALY by direction:		Left End 4.27 (23)			Left Tackle 4.91 (31)			Mid/Guard 4.01 (21)			Right Tackle 5.01 (31)			Right End 4.49 (28)		

Kikaha's torn ACL puts the Saints on the spot to come up with a real solution at defensive end. In OTAs, Obum Gwachum ran with the first team. Gwachum, a waiver claim who originally signed with the Seahawks as a 2015 UDFA, played wide receiver for most of his career at Oregon State and never started in college. Yes, this is the kind of paragraph you find when discussing the worst DVOA defense of all time. Don't be surprised if New Orleans brings in someone like Dwight Freeney after this book is released. ☞ The Saints traded up to select another potential starter for this unit in the fourth round, David Onyemata of the University of Manitoba. Yet another player in New Orleans' Canadian pipeline, Onyemata impressed scouts at the East-West Shrine game with his explosion off the snap. A 7.25-second three-cone drill at his pro day points to a player who could wreak havoc on the interior. ☞ While James Laurinaitis is getting the offseason hype, fellow free-agent refugee Craig Robertson (ex-Browns) might be a better pure linebacker at this point. Robertson is certainly better in coverage, and Laurinaitis didn't exactly wow anyone with his tackling last year. ☞ By all accounts, Stephone Anthony had a tough year in coverage in his first season. He also put athletic plays on tape that only four or five linebackers in the NFL could make today. If there's one thing that could swing this unit up a notch, it's an Anthony who plays like he knows the scheme.

Defensive Secondary

Secondary	Age	Pos	G	Snaps	Plays	TmPct	Rk	Stop	Dfts	BTkl	Runs	St%	Rk	RuYd	Rk	Tgts	Tgt%	Rk	Dist	Suc%	Rk	AdjYd	Rk	PD	Int
													vs. Run						vs. Pass					
Kenny Vaccaro	25	SS	16	1062	109	13.5%	9	54	15	13	56	55%	9	4.7	5	25	6.3%	22	8.4	47%	57	9.1	53	5	0
Brandon Browner*	32	CB	16	1024	86	10.6%	9	30	6	9	24	54%	17	8.4	51	69	17.9%	21	13.6	44%	67	11.0	75	11	1
Delvin Breaux	27	CB	16	944	64	7.9%	49	36	15	6	16	56%	15	8.4	52	67	18.8%	36	15.1	57%	16	7.4	34	18	3
Jairus Byrd	30	FS	13	811	55	8.4%	53	13	9	6	22	18%	66	14.9	69	14	4.6%	11	14.1	61%	25	7.4	41	3	1
Kyle Wilson	29	CB	15	499	30	4.0%	--	11	5	8	2	0%	--	13.0	--	28	14.7%	--	9.1	43%	--	9.4	--	3	1
Damian Swann	24	CB	7	230	26	7.3%	--	10	4	4	5	60%	--	1.8	--	18	20.9%	--	13.1	50%	--	6.0	--	3	0
Roman Harper	34	SS	16	951	78	9.4%	40	34	6	6	41	54%	13	5.1	13	22	5.8%	18	10.8	63%	21	5.4	12	7	0

Year	Pass D Rank	vs. #1 WR	Rk	vs. #2 WR	Rk	vs. Other WR	Rk	vs. TE	Rk	vs. RB	Rk
2013	6	-9.2%	12	10.7%	24	-5.0%	12	-15.6%	7	-10.4%	10
2014	27	25.1%	30	8.6%	24	-5.2%	13	-26.7%	1	40.7%	32
2015	32	14.9%	29	23.0%	29	18.9%	27	46.0%	32	28.7%	31

Not many teams would entrust a starting cornerback job to someone straight out of the CFL. But these Saints have invested heavily in the CFL, and they also had no other cornerbacks. It was an interesting journey for former LSU Tiger Delvin Breaux. He had a high success rate by our metrics, but he gave up a lot of touchdowns (eight, tied for the league league with Coty Sensabaugh of the Titans) and was called for plenty of penalties (11 flags for 73 yards). Breaux was sort of the football equivalent of baseball's Three True Outcomes hitter. Something was going to be happen, and it was going to be big. ☞ With the return of Roman Harper, the Saints hope to have more three-safety looks this season. Harper was a useful cog with the Panthers, a team that could put Luke Kuechly and Thomas Davis in front of him. Here, working with Not Those Players, his best role is as a dime box linebacker. ☙ Only Detroit had a more clearly differentiated split between strong safety and free safety based on the average tackle distance of the top two safeties. Jarius Byrd made his average tackle after 15.8 yards, Kenny Vaccaro after only 7.0 yards. (For further data, see Detroit secondary comments, page 79.) ☙ Kyle Wilson's injury is hardly a death blow, but with 2015 third-rounder P.J. Williams already being groomed to take over for Brandon Browner, further health issues for Keenan Lewis will force low-rounders and UDFAs into extensive playing time.

Special Teams

Year	DVOA	Rank	FG/XP	Rank	Net Kick	Rank	Kick Ret	Rank	Net Punt	Rank	Punt Ret	Rank	Hidden	Rank
2013	-2.5%	24	-13.8	32	-2.1	25	-0.5	14	11.1	2	-7.3	27	-8.0	27
2014	1.6%	11	-4.1	26	-2.5	21	4.0	8	13.4	2	-2.6	18	-23.1	32
2015	-3.2%	26	-15.4	31	-2.4	20	-2.1	21	3.8	11	0.2	16	14.0	3

Is there a more moving phrase than "kicker camp battle between Connor Barth and Kai Forbath?" Twitter voting now extends to things like All-Star Games and Pro Bowls—why not for this? America needs to know what kind of media campaigns the Forbath family can come up with. ☙ The Saints were fairly average on returns last year behind mighty mite Marcus Murphy, and Thomas Morstead was above average on punts and average on kickoffs. (That's an off-year for him; he's normally above average.) Field goals and extra points were what weighed this unit down so much in our rankings last year. #BarthMakesKickingAnArt #ForBathingYouFrom40

New York Giants

Everything came together for the New York Giants during a pair of charmed Super Bowl runs in 2007 and 2011. One can only imagine the Faustian deeds the Giants committed to earn those Lombardi Trophies, as the ensuing four seasons have largely delivered misfortune and underachievement. This offseason brought more change than the ultra-conservative organization has seen in a long time, but entering 2016, New York seems stuck between a new vision under Ben McAdoo and the old principles of the Tom Coughlin era.

Although Coughlin took the fall for the Giants' 1-6 slump to finish the 2015 season, some of the problems were seemingly out of his control. Start with injuries, which over the long haul will regress to the mean 99 percent of the time. The remaining one percent consists of the Giants, who finished dead last in adjusted games lost for the *third* straight season. AGL is not a straight measure of games lost, but when factoring in adjustments for player role and injury designation, the Giants have lost somewhere between 137 and 141 games worth of production each of the past three seasons. Since 2001, when Football Outsiders began tracking AGL, no other team has lost as many games in any single season. In fact, the Giants have never ranked better than 22nd during the past six seasons of tracking. As you might imagine, injury luck does hold a moderate but meaningful relationship with winning percentage. From 2002-15, the correlation between AGL and winning percentage is -0.21. During the past three years, when the Giants have particularly suffered, the average correlation is -0.19. Of course, as those numbers insinuate, New York can't simply blame injury luck as the overriding factor in their recent disappointments. There are teams like the Patriots, who have won despite ranking 19th or worse in AGL five out of six seasons, and those like the Titans, who haven't won despite ranking seventh or better in half of the past six seasons.

Despite all those injuries, the Giants had the point differential of a roughly .500 team, but underperformed their Pythagorean win expectancy by 1.5 wins. Only three teams undershot their expected win total by a greater margin. New York fared extremely poorly in one-score games, finishing 3-8 in such contests. Again, only four teams had a worse winning percentage in one-score contests. The two are certainly related, and truthfully, the Giants and Coughlin deserve to shoulder the blame for their seemingly weekly shenanigans late in games. New York lost four games in which it was leading after three

quarters, the most of any team in the league. Astoundingly, the Giants lost five games in which they held a lead in the final two minutes of regulation, and lost three games after the opposing team took the lead on a field goal with one or zero seconds remaining.

Unfortunately for the Giants, the answer isn't as simple as retreating to the Hamptons for the summer and waiting for good ol' regression towards the mean to work its magic. After all, the Giants have to improve *past* the mean to make it back to the playoffs. While general manager Jerry Reese narrowly avoided the same fate as Coughlin, he is primarily responsible for the deterioration of the Giants' roster over the past few seasons. The Giants have hit on fewer picks than just about any other team during the past five drafts (2011-2015), a fact that becomes clear when comparing all 32 teams with Pro Football Reference's Approximate Value metric (Table 1).

Table 1. Best and Worst Drafting Teams, 2011-2015

Top 10 in AV from Draft Picks				Bottom 10 in AV from Draft Picks			
Team	Career AV	Pro Bowls	Games Started	Team	Career AV	Pro Bowls	Games Started
1. SEA	449	9	637	23. SD	254	1	514
2. HOU	338	5	598	24. PIT	253	2	417
3. CIN	333	8	520	25. NYJ	252	2	435
4. MIN	325	7	569	26. ATL	242	5	388
5. STL	325	5	595	27. IND	242	5	419
6. BUF	319	2	629	28. SF	235	2	398
7. WAS	313	4	535	29. CHI	233	4	460
8. CAR	299	9	405	30. DET	215	1	393
9. MIA	294	4	546	31. NO	195	3	362
10. ARI	293	9	482	**32. NYG**	**195**	**2**	**337**

Apart from the incandescent Odell Beckham Jr. (who accounts for both of New York's Pro Bowl selections in the table), the Giants have almost completely busted with their draft picks. Out of the 22 selections Reese made from 2011 to 2013, only Justin Pugh and Johnathan Hankins still remain on the roster. On a per-pick basis, the Giants' selections have garnered an average of 5.6 career AV per player, the lowest mark in the league.

2016 Giants Schedule

Week	Opp.	Week	Opp.	Week	Opp.
1	at DAL	7	at LARM (U.K.)	13	at PIT
2	NO	8	BYE	14	DAL
3	WAS	9	PHI	15	DET
4	at MIN (Mon.)	10	CIN (Mon.)	16	at PHI (Thu.)
5	at GB	11	CHI	17	at WAS
6	BAL	12	at CLE		

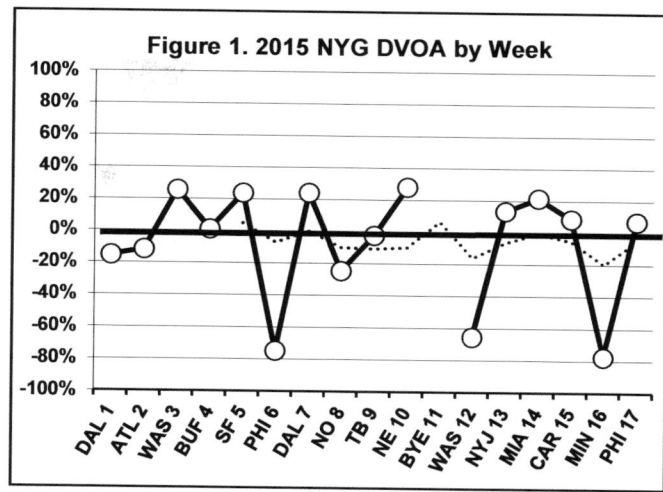

Figure 1. 2015 NYG DVOA by Week

Reese's problems haven't come in the first round. While running back David Wilson saw his career end prematurely due to a neck injury, Reese's four other first-round selections delivered one of game's best receivers (Beckham), two starting offensive linemen (Pugh and Ereck Flowers), and a cornerback who was oft-injured, but a relatively useful starter when healthy (Prince Amukamura). Though he has hardly been a wizard, Reese has been a slightly above-average drafter in the first round. After Round 1, however, Reese has basically morphed into the homeless Cleveland man who purportedly told Browns owner Jimmy Haslam to pick Johnny Manziel. Going back to Approximate Value, Chase Stuart's draft value table comes with an expected marginal AV for each draft slot over the first five years of a player's career (in other words, the amount of value a player produces above a low replacement-level threshold). Obviously not every Reese pick from 2011-15 has played five seasons; to adjust for this, we can divide the expected five-year marginal AV by the number of seasons each draft pick has actually played. Adding up the expected marginal AV for each of New York's Round 1-7 picks from the same timeframe, we can clearly see Reese's failings in the middle and late rounds (Table 2).

Table 2. Expected vs. Actual Value of Giants Draft Picks, 2011-2015

Round	Total Marginal AV	Expected Marginal AV*	Difference
1	46	44.4	+1.6
2	24	29.1	-5.1
3	-14	19.7	-33.7
4	-24	15.6	-39.6
5	-5	3.5	-8.5
6	-24	4.7	-28.7
7	-24	0.4	-24.4

*Five-year expected value adjusted for number of seasons played

The miss rate for later-round picks obviously increases, and this methodology isn't perfect. It's probably not entirely fair to divide Stuart's expected AV the way we did—in theory, a player should steadily improve over his first five seasons and produce increasing AV, not the same AV over each of the five seasons. And almost every team will produce negative value in the later rounds, because how many Round 6 or 7 players even last five seasons in the league?

All that is nice, but it sure doesn't buy Reese a free pass out of this mess. By this method, Weston Richburg, Reuben

Randle, and Devon Kennard (if you're feeling charitable) are the only post-Round 1 players who have contributed anything meaningful above replacement value. Randle now plays for a division rival, while the oft-injured linebacker Kennard has flashed—see Week 4 versus Buffalo last season—but is not a lock to remain in the starting lineup this season. Most mid- to late-round picks will bust and thus produce little value, but it really only takes a couple useful players to break even, or at least come close. This is the idea behind the "quantity over quality" approach when it comes to draft strategy. Perhaps unsurprisingly, Reese has blatantly ignored this widely accepted axiom, failing to trade down even once (!) during the 10 drafts he has overseen in New York.

This approach, coupled with miserable mid-round results, has created a highly stratified stars-and-scrubs roster. The Giants as currently assembled resemble the guy at your fantasy auction who spends all his money on Antonio Brown and Adrian Peterson before checking out for the next few hours. So although any team would struggle to withstand the type of horrid injury luck New York has suffered through, it's the Giants' own fault that the drop-off to their backups is so cavernous. This is how last season's Giants ended up starting a predictably overmatched undrafted first-year middle linebacker on opening day in Uani 'Unga, or asking fullback Nikita Whitlock to double as a modern-day Rudy Reuttiger and play a handful of 3-technique snaps, a role he hadn't occupied since his Wake Forest days.

The logical solution would be to overhaul the draft evaluation system and begin the multi-year process of rebuilding the roster's foundation. For a patient organization with a new head coach, this holds especially true. Naturally, Reese did the exact opposite this offseason, unleashing a small country's GDP on the open market under a brazen win-now operative. The Giants dished out just under $110 million in guarantees to free agents from other teams, by far the most in the league this offseason. By doubling down on the stars-and-scrubs strategy, the Giants probably improved their short-term outlook. Given that Eli Manning turned 35 in January, perhaps New York felt the need to maximize its ceiling for the next two to three seasons, especially considering the dilapidated state of the NFC East.

Of course, for a team with as many holes on its depth chart as the Giants, that large of a spending spree forced Reese to choose which part of the roster to fix and which parts to leave unattended. Consequently, the Giants almost completely ignored their offense (fullback Will Johnson got the biggest new contract with a grand total of $900,000 guaranteed over two seasons) and chose to invest their dollars in fixing a broken pass defense. To Reese's credit, this was probably the correct choice. New York finished 28th in pass defense DVOA in 2015, its worst ranking in the history of the metric (dating back to 1989). And with Amukamura and Robert Ayers leaving in free agency, the Giants desperately needed defensive talent to avoid sliding even further in 2016.

Returning defensive coordinator Steve Spagnuolo hasn't overseen an above-average defense since Taylor Swift was considered the bright new future of country music, which was also back when he could generate pressure with standard four-man rushes. So fittingly, a team whose championship identity was built on a fearsome pass rush reeled in the best pass-rusher on the market. Olivier Vernon isn't the best edge defender in the league, despite what his record-breaking average annual salary might suggest. But he is a significant upgrade on what the Giants rolled out last year, especially when Jason Pierre-Paul was sidelined while recovering from his catastrophic fireworks accident. Although Vernon accrued just 7.5 sacks last season, and has broken double-digit sack totals just once in his four-year career, he became one of the most consistent down-to-down pass-rushers in the league last season. Vernon posted 35.5 quarterback hurries last year, which ranked third among all defenders behind J.J. Watt and Carlos Dunlap. He accumulated an additional 30 quarterback hits, a total only Watt (33 hits) exceeded. In fact, Vernon's QB hit total nearly matched the combined production of New York's five qualifying edge defenders from 2015, as that quintet only managed 33 combined quarterback hits on their own.

Elite pass-rushing territory is new for Vernon, who nearly quadrupled his combined hits and hurries tally (20) from 2014. If he can sustain something close to what he did in 2015, though, Vernon's arrival should give the Giants two of the game's best pass-rushing bookends. The other half of that duo, Pierre-Paul, is coming off one of the more tumultuous seasons any player has endured in recent memory. Quietly, though, JPP reemerged as an elite pass-rusher in the eight games he did play in 2015. As with Vernon, sacks don't tell the full story with Pierre-Paul. Though he had just one sack, Pierre-Paul ended up with a whopping 32 hurries in his half-season, which ranked seventh in the league. That feat would be wildly impressive on its own given the number of games JPP played, but it's even more remarkable considering the life-changing physical adjustments Pierre-Paul had to make midstream. For reference, when JPP played 16 games and had all his digits in 2014, he only accumulated 24 hurries.

Given a whole offseason to adjust his game around his four-fingered reality (not to mention a custom glove which will replace the cumbersome club he played with in 2015), it won't be surprising if the impending free agent produces a season which allows him to blow away Vernon's contract. For now,

the Giants should enjoy a significant rebound in pass pressure. Last season's squad finished 30th in adjusted sack rate, bottoming out with the franchise's second-lowest sack total (23) since the 1970 merger. Vernon's signing might preclude New York from keeping JPP after 2016, but that's a problem for another day.

Unfortunately, Reese's other big-money deals may have only triggered more problems in the present day. Damon Harrison is a safe bet to help out New York's run defense, which has ranked 21st and 27th in DVOA the past two seasons. But even a premier run-clogger like "Big Snacks" isn't likely to fix the run defense on his own. The Giants surrendered plenty of big runs in part because their motley crew of linebackers had trouble sifting through traffic and shedding blocks. Whether you want to measure run defense by how often a defense penetrates the backfield to disrupt a carry or by how well a defense is able to limit big gains, the Giants were a bottom-half unit by all standards in 2015. Maybe Harrison creates more disruptive plays in the backfield and helps out in short-yardage situations, but the Giants could have built up a full rotation of run-stuffers (Terrance Knighton? Steve Mc-Clendon? Ian Williams?) with Harrison's $9.25 million average annual salary.

At least Harrison should supply positive value. It's less clear how the Janoris Jenkins contract might turn out. Jenkins has appeared on plenty of highlight tapes for his five career touchdowns, but his ballhawking borders on reckless and ultimately makes him a net negative over the long haul. By adjusted success rate, Jenkins ranked 51st out of 75 cornerbacks who received at least 50 charted targets or eight starts in 2015. Disturbingly, that was an upgrade from his prior campaign, when he ranked 66th out of 77 qualifiers. As a long-armed corner who piles up lots of pass deflections, Jenkins is effectively a younger, inferior version of the Giants' top corner, Dominique Rodgers-Cromartie, as well as an older, better-tackling version of their first-round pick, Ohio State cornerback Eli Apple.

The capper to all this? The Giants didn't even address the fundamental weakness to their pass coverage by signing Jenkins. While New York was a roughly league-average defense on passes to the perimeter, it floundered in the middle. The Giants ranked 25th in DVOA on passes to that section of the field, hardly a surprise when recalling their woes at linebacker and safety. This isn't a new personnel problem, as New York ranked 32nd in passes up the middle in 2014 and 19th in 2013. While New York did draft safety Darian Thompson (Boise State) and linebacker B.J. Goodson (Clemson), mid-round rookies usually aren't immediate saviors. Both have legitimate chances of starting this fall, a fact that says as much about the current personnel as it does about either prospect. A more measured offseason approach might have seen the Giants draft Apple and let him ripen behind DRC for a season or two, supplementing the pass coverage in the meantime with cheaper upgrades in the slot (Casey Hayward? Patrick Robinson?) and in the box (Tyvon Branch? Daryl Smith?). Instead, by tossing around money in a Leeroy Jenkins-style surge of excitement, Reese has purchased a few expensive ingredients for a recipe still missing several key components.

In the end, the Giants will likely be dependent on their stars in the passing game on both sides of the ball. It feels weird that we've gone this long into the chapter without really discussing Eli Manning and the offense, but routine stability isn't nearly as exciting as total overhaul. Indeed, in promoting McAdoo, New York's primary motivation was to retain the coach who had reigned in the previously erratic Manning. While no offense with Beckham in its lineup is boring, McAdoo's system is inherently meant to limit variance. Manning has cut down on his turnovers, posting identical 2.3 percent interception rates the past two years, well below his 3.4 percent career rate before McAdoo's arrival. However, his passes have also become significantly shorter as more three-step concepts have worked their way into the playbook. Manning set a new career-high for attempts charted as short passes in 2014 at 47 percent, only to surpass that total in 2015 with 50 percent of his passes charted as short. Last season, 40 percent of his deep-ball passes went to Beckham; when Eli isn't targeting his All-Pro superstar, he's most likely checking down to a running back or throwing a short slant or stick route to the numbers.

There's nothing wrong with this approach, but it hasn't been good enough to produce anything beyond a roughly league-average offense. That's a far cry from Eli's 2008-12 heyday, when the Giants finished with a top-10 offense in four out of five seasons. Realistically, even with the money spent on defense, New York probably isn't snapping its four-year playoff drought unless it returns to that level. But given how similar the offense looks to its past two renditions, where can the Giants turn for that leap?

We can most likely rule out any meaningful help from the running game. A rushing attack which has finished 23rd, 23rd, and 30th in DVOA the past three years will probably end up near the cellar again. Lots of draftniks considered Paul Perkins an intriguing sleeper, but for now, the UCLA product is a fifth-round rookie whose skill set is redundant with Shane Vereen. Otherwise, the running game will return the same cast of characters, with several overmatched players receiving far too large a role in both the backfield and on the offensive line. At this point, the likes of Andre Williams, John Jerry, and Marshall Newhouse resemble mediocre *Survivor* contestants who last far too long because everyone else forgets they're still on the island.

Even without any huge improvements, the offense might get a slight boost by simply not being terrible in the red zone. The Giants had the 31st-ranked offensive red zone DVOA, a byproduct of eight turnovers and several late-game gaffes. Remember the earlier bit about New York's league-leading four blown fourth-quarter leads? In each of those instances, a turnover (vs. Atlanta and the Jets) or clock mismanagement (vs. Dallas and New England) helped trigger the eventual comeback. It's too facile to say that New York's late-game woes will disappear with better red zone offense (or that the offense was to blame for those losses in 2015), but when the Giants were merely below average in the red zone in 2014, they were 12th in overall offensive DVOA. Merely regressing back to the top of the bell curve should help out the offense's bottom line.

Still, for the offense to really beat expectations, the passing game might need unexpected contributions from a pair of sources. For different reasons, it's shaky to bet on a huge 2015 season for either Victor Cruz or Sterling Shepard, the two most popular picks to emerge as the No. 2 wide receiver behind Beckham. Cruz will have missed nearly two full years when Week 1 rolls around, and was in the midst of a three-year decline in both DVOA and DYAR at the time of his injury. Meanwhile, Shepard received a lukewarm projection from Playmaker Score, which penalized him for his age and mediocre yards per catch figures at Oklahoma. Moreover, both are slot receivers with minimal experience playing on the perimeter, which may keep one of them glued to the bench even when New York shifts into three-receiver personnel. The opportunity should be there for at least one them; for an offense with a transcendent receiver, the Giants don't force-feed Beckham as much as one might expect. Just under 27 percent of New York's passes went to its No. 1 receiver, which ranked 11th in the league. If either Cruz or Shepard is capable of making plays beyond what the offensive structure calls for, he'll surely have the chance to shine.

Either way, the Giants likely need a couple pleasant surprises to move beyond their recent seven-win ceiling. New York's lineup on paper looks like an upgrade on what the Giants have fielded the past few seasons, especially if they catch some long overdue injury luck. However, this is far from a complete roster, and they no longer have the financial means to significantly alter their current hand or the security of knowing that this core works well together. Long-term, the Giants resemble a homeowner who has fixed up the living room and built a beautiful yard, but still has leaky plumbing, shoddy electricity, and an unfinished basement. That might not affect 2016's short-term results, and a playoff berth would surely appease a fan base which soured on the status quo by the end of 2015. But even as the roster's star power allows the Giants to dream about their ceiling, the floor will once again loom perilously low.

Sterling Xie

2015 Giants Stats by Week

Wk	vs.	W-L	PF	PA	YDF	YDA	TO	Total	Off	Def	ST
1	at DAL	L	26	27	289	436	3	-15%	-6%	18%	9%
2	ATL	L	20	24	388	402	-1	-12%	-2%	24%	14%
3	WAS	W	32	21	363	393	3	26%	24%	-20%	-19%
4	at BUF	W	24	10	303	313	1	1%	-37%	-34%	5%
5	SF	W	30	27	525	380	-1	24%	32%	12%	4%
6	at PHI	L	7	27	247	428	1	-75%	-58%	14%	-3%
7	DAL	W	27	20	289	460	4	24%	14%	13%	23%
8	at NO	L	49	52	416	608	1	-25%	4%	41%	12%
9	at TB	W	32	18	327	383	1	-3%	-17%	-1%	13%
10	NE	L	26	27	422	406	1	28%	13%	-19%	-5%
11	BYE										
12	at WAS	L	14	20	332	407	-3	-66%	-43%	22%	-1%
13	NYJ	L	20	23	355	463	0	13%	-3%	12%	28%
14	at MIA	W	31	24	429	363	0	21%	41%	12%	-8%
15	CAR	L	35	38	406	480	-1	8%	31%	22%	0%
16	at MIN	L	17	49	363	368	-3	-78%	-66%	11%	0%
17	PHI	L	30	35	502	435	1	7%	24%	31%	15%

Trends and Splits

	Offense	Rank	Defense	Rank
Total DVOA	-1.4%	19	10.5%	30
Unadjusted VOA	1.6%	13	10.2%	28
Weighted Trend	-1.8%	16	13.5%	31
Variance	10.8%	30	3.9%	9
Average Opponent	3.2%	27	-1.9%	23
Passing	12.1%	18	23.5%	28
Rushing	-12.2%	23	-6.7%	21
First Down	-8.0%	25	8.5%	24
Second Down	11.2%	8	0.5%	16
Third Down	-9.9%	22	29.2%	30
First Half	-1.0%	17	5.2%	21
Second Half	-1.8%	17	15.5%	30
Red Zone	-39.3%	31	-9.8%	9
Late and Close	14.2%	4	12.6%	28

Five-Year Performance

Year	W-L	Pyth W	Est W	PF	PA	TO	Total	Rk	Off	Rk	Def	Rk	ST	Rk	Off AGL	Rk	Def AGL	Rk	Off Age	Rk	Def Age	Rk	ST Age	Rk
2011	9-7	7.8	9.1	394	400	+7	8.5%	12	10.5%	7	2.4%	19	0.3%	15	25.2	13	53.1	30	27.4	13	27.6	8	26.1	20
2012	9-7	10.2	9.5	429	344	+14	13.4%	7	12.8%	7	1.5%	16	2.0%	10	26.1	12	56.6	28	27.8	8	27.2	13	26.2	13
2013	7-9	5.6	5.5	294	383	-15	-15.7%	27	-22.0%	31	-11.4%	6	-5.1%	28	80.9	32	60.3	32	27.4	12	27.4	7	26.1	15
2014	6-10	7.5	7.0	380	400	-2	-5.8%	21	-0.3%	15	4.9%	24	-0.6%	15	65.9	31	71.3	30	26.6	20	27.6	5	26.7	3
2015	6-10	7.5	7.4	420	442	+7	-7.1%	20	-1.8%	19	10.7%	30	5.4%	2	66.9	31	71.8	31	26.2	22	27.0	13	26.5	8

2015 Performance Based on Most Common Personnel Groups

NYG Offense					NYG Offense vs. Opponents					NYG Defense					NYG Defense vs. Opponents			
Pers	Freq	Yds	DVOA	Run%	Pers	Freq	Yds	DVOA	Run%	Pers	Freq	Yds	DVOA	Pers	Freq	Yds	DVOA
11	81%	6.0	6.1%	30%	Base	19%	4.9	-19.2%	58%	Base	34%	6.4	8.4%	11	53%	6.2	9.1%
21	8%	3.8	-25.8%	74%	Nickel	66%	6.1	10.3%	35%	Nickel	51%	6.4	13.6%	12	23%	6.7	12.6%
12	6%	7.1	20.6%	51%	Dime+	14%	6.0	2.6%	9%	Dime+	12%	6.1	7.5%	21	8%	5.3	-9.4%
22	2%	2.2	-45.5%	94%	Goal Line	1%	-0.3	-80.6%	86%	Goal Line	2%	-0.1	-1.7%	13	4%	9.0	48.6%
01	1%	8.2	58.5%	0%						Big	1%	4.8	23.1%	10	4%	5.8	23.4%

Strategic Tendencies

Run/Pass		Rk	Formation		Rk	Pass Rush		Rk	Secondary		Rk	Strategy		Rk
Runs, first half	37%	18	Form: Single Back	76%	15	Rush 3	6.4%	19	4 DB	34%	13	Play action	17%	23
Runs, first down	50%	10	Form: Empty Back	6%	19	Rush 4	67.6%	14	5 DB	51%	20	Avg Box (Off)	6.10	28
Runs, second-long	28%	23	Pers: 3+ WR	83%	2	Rush 5	15.6%	31	6+ DB	12%	16	Avg Box (Def)	6.21	21
Runs, power sit.	47%	28	Pers: 2+ TE/6+ OL	10%	30	Rush 6+	10.4%	7	CB by Sides	71%	22	Offensive Pace	28.50	4
Runs, behind 2H	24%	17	Pers: 6+ OL	1%	21	Sacks by LB	13.0%	28	S/CB Cover Ratio	27%	8	Defensive Pace	29.52	7
Pass, ahead 2H	53%	7	Shotgun/Pistol	69%	8	Sacks by DB	4.3%	26	DB Blitz	10%	13	Go for it on 4th	0.84	20

Although most teams use 11 personnel as their primary package in today's NFL, nobody has done it quite like the Giants. At 81 percent, they are the first team to use a single personnel package more than 75 percent of the time since we started tracking specific personnel packages six years ago. (That's based on positions, not having the exact same men on the field.) ☞ The

Giants threw 27 percent of their passes in the middle of the field, and the numbers show that was a good strategy. The Giants had only 1.2% DVOA on passes to the left side (31st) and 23.9% DVOA on passes to the right side (22nd) but 101.6% DVOA on passes up the middle (seventh). (Remember that DVOA on passes by side is generally high because sacks, deliberate throwaways, and passes batted down at the line are removed.) ☞ The offense ran just eight wide receiver or tight end screens, the lowest total in the league. ☞ Opponents blitzed Eli Manning on just 16 percent of pass attempts, the lowest figure of any offense we've tracked since we began game charting. Blitzes against the Giants rarely brought pressure (a league-low 24 percent of blitzes were marked with pressure) because Manning excelled at hitting the hot read for a short gain—the Giants dropped from 7.2 yards per play against a standard pass rush to 5.8 against five rushers and 4.5 against six or more. This was a big change from previous seasons, when Manning usually saw his yards per pass go up against big blitzes. ☞ The Giants ranked among the top three teams for running back draws for the fifth straight season. They averaged 4.8 yards with -5.1% DVOA, a slight improvement from 2014. ☞ New York ranked sixth in offensive DVOA when playing at home but just 25th in road contests, the largest home-road split in the league last season. (There's no real consistency in this from year to year; it's just a fun fact.) ☞ The Giants edged out the Saints for the worst third-and-short defense, posting a 40.4% DVOA in such situations.

Passing

Player	DYAR	DVOA	Plays	NtYds	Avg	YAC	C%	TD	Int
E.Manning	404	-1.9%	646	4225	6.5	5.4	62.9%	35	14

Rushing

Player	DYAR	DVOA	Plays	Yds	Avg	TD	Fum	Suc
R.Jennings	117	5.6%	195	863	4.4	3	1	56%
A.Williams	-83	-30.9%	88	257	2.9	1	0	34%
S.Vereen	9	-4.8%	61	260	4.3	0	0	41%
O.Darkwa	27	7.7%	37	153	4.1	1	0	46%
B.Rainey	-16	-118.2%	5	18	3.6	0	1	40%
W.Johnson	-7	-31.2%	4	7	1.8	1	0	25%

Receiving

Player	DYAR	DVOA	Plays	Ctch	Yds	Y/C	YAC	TD	C%
O.Beckham	304	10.3%	158	96	1454	15.1	6.2	13	61%
R.Randle*	167	10.0%	90	57	801	14.1	3.6	8	63%
D.Harris	45	-2.7%	57	36	396	11.0	3.8	4	63%
M.White	-46	-40.2%	20	7	88	12.6	1.0	1	35%
H.Nicks*	-36	-44.5%	14	7	54	7.7	3.1	0	50%
P.Parker*	-32	-47.4%	12	5	40	8.0	5.8	0	42%
W.Tye	51	5.1%	62	42	464	11.0	4.6	3	68%
L.Donnell	-15	-12.6%	41	29	223	7.7	3.0	2	71%
J.Cunningham*	-36	-39.3%	16	8	59	7.4	3.3	0	50%
D.Fells*	12	18.5%	7	6	60	10.0	6.2	0	86%
S.Vereen	103	8.4%	81	59	498	8.4	7.2	4	73%
R.Jennings	29	-0.9%	40	29	296	10.2	10.7	1	73%

Offensive Line

Player	Pos	Age	GS	Snaps	Pen	Sk	Pass	Run	Player	Pos	Age	GS	Snaps	Pen	Sk	Pass	Run
Weston Richburg	C	25	15/15	1016	4	0.0	1.0	4.0	Geoff Schwartz*	RG	30	11/11	673	3	4.0	6.5	1.0
Justin Pugh	LG	26	14/14	967	5	2.0	3.0	2.0	John Jerry	RG	30	16/8	644	3	0.0	2.0	3.0
Ereck Flowers	LT	22	15/15	963	10	3.0	21.0	1.0	Dallas Reynolds*	C	32	16/2	222	1	0.0	1.0	1.0
Marshall Newhouse	RT	28	14/14	937	8	4.0	7.5	2.0									

Year	Yards	ALY	Rank	Power	Rank	Stuff	Rank	2nd Lev	Rank	Open Field	Rank	Sacks	ASR	Rank	Press	Rank	F-Start	Cont.
2013	3.48	3.27	30	70%	10	25%	31	1.10	18	0.45	28	40	7.6%	18	27.4%	25	6	23
2014	3.62	3.76	22	61%	20	20%	18	0.94	29	0.47	28	30	5.0%	10	23.5%	15	18	37
2015	4.02	3.96	11	47%	30	19%	11	1.10	21	0.59	23	27	5.1%	6	23.3%	11	13	28

2015 ALY by direction: Left End 2.71 (30) Left Tackle 3.55 (19) Mid/Guard 4.2 (6) Right Tackle 3.9 (11) Right End 3.25 (20)

It's no exaggeration to suggest that the Giants may have fielded the NFL's worst tackle tandem. Rookie Ereck Flowers assumed blindside duties much earlier than anyone expected, and proceeded to post the second-worst blown blocks per snap rate of any left tackle in the league. Newhouse was also below average by that metric, and drew a team-high five holding penalties. New York will stomach its growing pains with Flowers, who might fare better if he doesn't once again play through a high ankle sprain for much of the season. Newhouse, on the other hand, is someone the Giants seem eager to upgrade from, showing interest in Eugene Monroe earlier this offseason. ☞ The Giants were the only team in the league not to draft or sign an undrafted offensive lineman this offseason. None of New York's backup linemen were drafted higher than the sixth round, though, so the back end of the depth chart isn't exactly filled with promising developmental prospects. The only reserve currently on the roster with more than one career start is Byron Stingily, who served as a fill-in swing tackle on Tennessee's woeful line from 2011-14.

Defensive Front Seven

Defensive Line	Age	Pos	G	Snaps	Plays	TmPct	Rk	Stop	Dfts	BTkl	Runs	St%	Rk	RuYd	Rk	Sack	Hit	Hur	Dsrpt
					Overall						vs. Run					Pass Rush			
Cullen Jenkins*	35	DT	16	733	28	3.1%	74	19	6	3	17	71%	56	1.8	26	3.0	8	15.5	1
Jay Bromley	24	DT	16	479	36	4.0%	60	26	2	1	35	74%	48	2.7	60	0.0	6	2.0	0
Johnathan Hankins	24	DT	9	410	31	6.2%	30	22	2	0	29	69%	59	2.4	51	0.0	2	5.5	1
Markus Kuhn	30	DT	10	313	20	3.6%	66	19	1	0	16	94%	1	1.5	13	0.5	2	3.0	0
Damon Harrison	28	DT	16	568	71	9.3%	3	63	12	1	69	90%	9	1.4	7	0.5	3	4.0	0

Edge Rushers	Age	Pos	G	Snaps	Plays	TmPct	Rk	Stop	Dfts	BTkl	Runs	St%	Rk	RuYd	Rk	Sack	Hit	Hur	Dsrpt
					Overall						vs. Run					Pass Rush			
Kerry Wynn	25	DE	15	579	54	6.4%	21	33	9	2	50	60%	87	3.0	75	0.0	2	4.5	2
Robert Ayers*	31	DE	12	569	45	6.7%	15	38	19	4	28	82%	15	2.0	38	9.5	13	23.0	3
Jason Pierre-Paul	27	DE	8	502	31	6.9%	11	25	8	3	20	80%	23	1.8	29	1.0	6	32.0	6
George Selvie*	29	DE	12	370	25	3.7%	73	21	3	3	20	80%	23	2.8	66	1.0	4	8.5	0
Damontre Moore*	24	DE	14	279	21	2.7%	--	15	8	1	9	56%	--	6.6	--	4.0	8	7.0	1
Olivier Vernon	26	DE	16	943	59	6.7%	14	52	25	4	43	86%	9	1.4	19	7.5	30	35.5	0

Linebackers	Age	Pos	G	Snaps	Plays	TmPct	Rk	Stop	Dfts	BTkl	Runs	St%	Rk	RuYd	Rk	Sack	Hit	Hur	Tgts	Suc%	Rk	AdjYd	Rk	PD	Int
					Overall						vs. Run					Pass Rush			vs. Pass						
Jonathan Casillas	29	OLB	15	673	85	10.1%	61	42	18	5	34	53%	79	4.2	71	2.0	0	4	22	58%	32	5.5	26	3	1
Devon Kennard	25	OLB	9	487	59	11.7%	48	28	7	3	40	53%	80	3.8	57	0.0	5	9	10	56%	--	6.6	--	2	1
Uani' Unga*	29	MLB	13	433	63	8.7%	66	21	10	5	27	41%	89	3.7	50	0.0	1	1	15	27%	73	9.6	66	4	2
Jasper Brinkley	31	MLB	15	420	66	7.9%	--	34	11	6	44	64%	--	2.8	--	1.0	0	0	6	63%	--	7.1	--	0	0
J.T. Thomas	28	OLB	12	400	43	6.4%	81	22	1	5	26	62%	50	3.4	38	0.0	0	4	6	50%	--	8.7	--	1	0
Kelvin Sheppard	28	MLB	16	709	104	11.9%	46	59	21	8	70	59%	59	3.0	25	0.0	0	2	19	46%	56	8.5	64	1	0
Keenan Robinson	27	ILB	12	546	65	10.9%	53	33	10	11	31	58%	60	5.4	86	0.0	0	0	14	57%	34	7.1	52	3	1

Year	Yards	ALY	Rank	Power	Rank	Stuff	Rank	2nd Level	Rank	Open Field	Rank	Sacks	ASR	Rank	Press	Rank
2013	3.56	3.62	8	66%	19	21%	13	1.00	7	0.44	5	34	6.1%	28	22.7%	23
2014	4.81	4.31	28	62%	13	16%	27	1.37	31	1.00	29	47	7.8%	6	29.4%	2
2015	4.35	3.97	22	67%	17	20%	19	1.18	21	0.88	22	23	4.1%	30	25.9%	13

| 2015 ALY by direction: | Left End 5.37 (30) | Left Tackle 3.96 (19) | Mid/Guard 4.04 (22) | Right Tackle 3.11 (7) | Right End 3.51 (19) |

After a strong sophomore season, Johnathan Hankins regressed against both the pass and the run before a torn pectoral prematurely ended his third season. With Damon Harrison's arrival, the Ringo of New York's defensive line should get more pass-rushing opportunities from the 3-technique spot after largely playing the 1-tech in 2015. ☜ There really wasn't a Giants linebacker who was above average at any single skill last season. Devon Kennard showed some extremely promising flashes in coverage as a rookie in 2014, but struggled and couldn't stay healthy under a greater burden in 2015. Keenan Robinson was also excellent in coverage two years ago (for Washington) and could win the starting MIKE role over Jasper Brinkley and Jonathan Casillas. Like Kennard, though, Robinson regressed in coverage last year, and has always been a liability against the run. ☜ B.J. Goodson was the first linebacker Jerry Reese selected before Round 5 since 2010. He went in the fourth round instead. (Tune in next year to see if Reese will ever draft a linebacker before Saturday.) At 6-foot-1 and 245 pounds, Goodson is more of a downhill thumper who can help in run support and as an occasional blitzer (5.5 sacks his senior year). And while he wasn't particularly adept in coverage at Clemson, his strong agility testing at the combine suggests he has the physical tools to help out there eventually.

Defensive Secondary

Secondary	Age	Pos	G	Snaps	Plays	TmPct	Rk	Stop	Dfts	BTkl	Runs	St%	Rk	RuYd	Rk	Tgts	Tgt%	Rk	Dist	Suc%	Rk	AdjYd	Rk	PD	Int
						Overall						vs. Run						vs. Pass							
Landon Collins	22	SS	16	1093	117	13.1%	11	47	16	8	50	58%	6	5.1	15	36	8.8%	52	10.7	44%	65	7.6	42	8	1
D.Rodgers-Cromartie	30	CB	15	889	71	8.5%	41	29	12	7	15	40%	39	6.4	29	68	20.5%	44	13.8	54%	29	6.9	17	14	3
Brandon Meriweather*	32	FS	13	834	66	9.1%	43	21	8	13	33	33%	46	6.7	34	20	6.3%	21	17.4	61%	24	9.7	60	6	2
Prince Amukamara*	27	CB	11	765	73	11.9%	3	28	10	3	15	40%	39	8.3	49	55	19.3%	38	12.5	52%	38	7.5	35	6	1
Trevin Wade	27	CB	16	529	54	6.0%	--	22	13	6	12	50%	--	10.5	--	33	16.7%	--	10.8	46%	--	8.4	--	4	0
Jayron Hosley*	26	CB	14	528	35	4.5%	--	12	2	6	9	22%	--	8.2	--	28	14.0%	--	12.8	49%	--	10.2	--	5	1
Craig Dahl*	31	SS	15	429	48	5.7%	67	14	7	6	16	38%	42	8.8	54	21	12.8%	63	18.0	41%	67	10.5	65	3	0
Trumaine McBride*	31	CB	15	342	30	3.6%	--	11	6	8	4	50%	--	2.8	--	27	21.2%	--	8.3	50%	--	7.5	--	4	3
Janoris Jenkins	28	CB	15	1039	80	9.4%	24	41	15	10	10	70%	6	7.6	42	68	20.5%	46	12.7	49%	51	7.7	37	14	3

Year	Pass D Rank	vs. #1 WR	Rk	vs. #2 WR	Rk	vs. Other WR	Rk	vs. TE	Rk	vs. RB	Rk
2013	8	-11.6%	9	-33.7%	2	-22.0%	5	-18.7%	6	14.9%	28
2014	21	7.8%	23	-3.1%	15	1.1%	18	13.9%	25	2.1%	20
2015	28	-1.7%	15	1.1%	16	-6.0%	12	20.5%	27	8.5%	21

By adjusted yards per target, Dominique Rodgers-Cromartie has improved each of the past three seasons. The degree of difficulty was probably higher in 2015, as DRC toughed out numerous lower-body and back issues to play 15 games, though he had to leave early in three different contests. The 30-year-old is probably more of a health risk now than he has been throughout his durable career, but with a cap hit that stays between $8 million and $8.5 million the next three seasons, DRC's contract looks reasonable amid a booming cornerback market. ☞ Predictably, rookie safety Landon Collins was much more comfortable and productive playing closer to the line. Collins was a positive contributor in the running game, but posted some porous coverage charting numbers. The Giants often had to drop Collins deep because of Brandon Meriweather's even more limited skill set, but that might change with the third-round selection of Darian Thompson. The Boise State product arrives with pro-ready instincts as a deep centerfielder, and is likely the best free safety on the roster. The young safety duo will experience its share of growing pains, but it won't be more painful than watching Meriweather and Craig Dahl play significant snaps again. ☞ Eli Apple isn't likely to play much his rookie year given his redundancy with Rodgers-Cromartie and Janoris Jenkins, and that's fine. Apple was one of the least experienced corners in the draft, and needs to grow out of his tendency to grab receivers and draw penalties. Unfortunately, that leaves some uninspiring options for the slot cornerback job, with Trevin Wade the current favorite.

Special Teams

Year	DVOA	Rank	FG/XP	Rank	Net Kick	Rank	Kick Ret	Rank	Net Punt	Rank	Punt Ret	Rank	Hidden	Rank
2013	-5.1%	28	0.7	17	3.3	11	-4.2	24	-20.5	31	-4.6	23	-12.8	32
2014	-0.6%	15	3.7	8	7.0	6	-5.9	29	-5.2	23	-2.8	19	-13.3	30
2015	5.4%	2	9.5	2	-3.1	24	9.1	2	7.4	6	4.0	8	-6.4	24

Apart from serving as a surprisingly solid fill-in receiver, Dwayne Harris was also back to being one of the game's best returners after a down 2014 in Dallas. Combining kick and punt returns, Harris provided 11.3 points of net value over average. On kickoffs, only Cordarrelle Patterson exceeded Harris' value. ☞ Josh Brown's field goal percentage was above 90 percent for the second consecutive season, but his short kickoffs cancelled out roughly half of that value. Brown was the league's most actively harmful kicker in the latter department, subtracting minus-5.7 points of gross value on his kickoffs. Consequently, the Giants finished 30th in touchback percentage. Of course, with the rule change devaluing touchbacks by moving them to the 25, Brown's weakness may no longer be a disadvantage, significantly upping his value if he can remain accurate on field goals.

New York Jets

2015 record: 10-6	Total DVOA: 12.4% (9th)	2016 Mean Projection: 7.2 wins	On the Clock (0-4): 15%
Pythagorean Wins: 10.0 (8th)	Offense: 1.6% (14th)	Postseason Odds: 25.7%	Mediocrity (5-7): 41%
Snap-Weighted Age: 27.6 (1st)	Defense: -13.8% (5th)	Super Bowl Odds: 2.8%	Playoff Contender (8-10): 34%
Average Opponent: -6.7% (29th)	Special Teams: -2.9% (25th)	Proj. Avg. Opponent: 3.7% (2nd)	Super Bowl Contender (11+): 11%

2015: The best team to miss the playoffs, combining the expected rebound on defense with a surprisingly adequate offense.

2016: Quarterback isn't a really important position, right?

Christian Hackenberg, Bryce Petty, and Geno Smith. It's like a supergroup of John Oates, Art Garfunkel, and Andrew Ridgeley. It's like the brainwash activation code that turns Mike Mayock into the Winter Soldier. It's like an old Johnny Carson "Carnac the Magnificent" skit: "Name three reasons to overpay Ryan Fitzpatrick."

There's no sense in burying the lead here. The Jets have either outsmarted the planet at quarterback or once again outsmarted themselves. General manager Mike Maccagnan is either a genius or an executive who interpreted last year's 10-6 record and league-wide accolades as proof that he's a genius, not a guy who spent a bunch of money on a near-miss wildcard season against a cupcake schedule.

Before we dive into the rest of the Jets organization, let's breakdown the Jets quarterbacks, in descending order of how likely they are to be ridiculed on the back page of the *New York Daily News* in autumn:

Christian Hackenberg was the most perplexing quarterback prospect in a draft class full of perplexing quarterback prospects. Hackenberg had a handful of excellent games in 2013, when Bill O'Brien was his coach, Allen Robinson was his top receiver, and America was just starting to feel OK about Penn State football again.

Hackenberg's entire game downshifted hard into reverse the moment James Franklin replaced O'Brien. By last season, anything longer than a screen pass was a misadventure for Hackenberg, who completed just 53.6 percent of his passes, with 16 touchdowns, six interceptions and a whopping 38 sacks in 359 pass attempts. Don't let the low interception total fool you: Hackenberg ran a stripped-down offense for much of the year, and his downfield passes were sometimes so wild that even defenders had no hope of catching them.

NFL scouting reports can be surprisingly sticky, particularly for quarterbacks. If a quarterback did something successfully two, three, or five years ago, some coaches and scouts will believe he can still do it, despite several seasons of evidence to the contrary. (See Sam Bradford's entire life for an example.) Hackenberg's good tape hasn't quite reached the expiration date where it begins to curdle, so Jets coaches and scouts still saw a prospect who could be "fixed." Hackenberg can also be

thought of as a junior varsity Brian Hoyer-Ryan Mallett-Matt Cassel: if O'Brien (a Bill Belichick proxy) signed off on him, he must be good.

For now, it takes a leap of faith to see the second-round pick the Jets saw. No matter how many draftniks squinted and stared at Hackenberg's 2014-15 tape like a Magic Eye puzzle in search of a franchise quarterback, the best anyone could come away with was "he has a good arm and beat Wisconsin three years ago." Our QBASE projection system hated Hackenberg's horrible college statistics, ranking him one of the five worst quarterback prospects among top-100 picks of the last two decades.

Ryan Fitzpatrick was still a free agent at press time but likely to return to the Jets the moment either side blinks[1]. Fitzpatrick is an object lesson for the triumph of analytics, or at least common sense, over narrative. Fitzpatrick's 3,905-yard, 31-touchdown season was a mirage in a dozen different ways, and the open market suddenly proved immune to FitzMagical thinking when Fitzpatrick tried to cash in with a multi-year deal. The Jets themselves saw through the Fitzpatrick illusion and low-balled him; a tight cap situation no doubt contributed to their lukewarm interest in a 33-year-old journeyman.

The Jets learned the right lesson at the wrong time, because the team could really use a veteran caretaker in 2016. Fitzpatrick can be ready to play with limited practice reps: a valuable skill for a team that wants to devote practice time to developing youngsters. He can be a meeting-room mentor and provide reassurance to some of the veterans (Brandon Marshall, most notably) who openly pined for him in the offseason. His Harvard Hipster Hero routine could shield Hackenberg and the others from the worst of the New York spotlight. These are not intangibles worth a $40 million investment, but they are nothing to brush aside, either. At this writing, the Jets have no safety net quarterback who can provide baseline professionalism and a twinkle-eyed quote to diffuse a drama if and when things go wrong.

Bryce Petty spent half of his career at Baylor enjoying comparisons to Robert Griffin and half his career at Baylor distancing himself from comparisons to Robert Griffin. Petty

---

1 We did 50 percent of our season projections with Smith as the Jets quarterback, and 50 percent of projections expecting the Jets to bring back Fitzpatrick.

2016 Jets Schedule

Week	Opp.	Week	Opp.	Week	Opp.
1	CIN	7	BAL	13	IND (Mon.)
2	at BUF (Thu.)	8	at CLE	14	at SF
3	at KC	9	at MIA	15	MIA (Sat.)
4	DEA	10	LARM	16	at NE (Sat.)
5	at PIT	11	BYE	17	BUF
6	at ARI (Mon.)	12	NE		

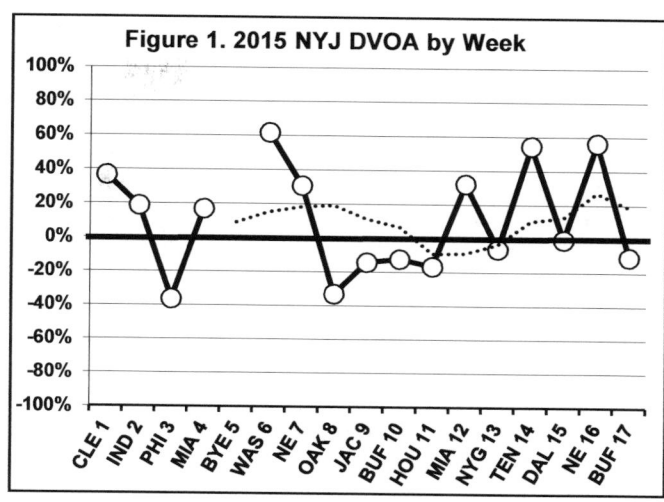

Figure 1. 2015 NYJ DVOA by Week

famously never called a play in the huddle in high school or college, making him raw as a rookie, even by the standard of raw rookies from no-huddle offenses. Petty told NJ.com in May that he now can recognize defensive fronts when calling plays in Madden, meaning he now has the defense-reading chops of an attentive seventh grader.

Geno Smith is the Forgotten Man, and that may be the high point of his NFL career. Whatever you think about Smith's maturity, character, treatment at the hands of some members of the draft community—look, let's just say it, Nolan Freakin' Nawrocki—treatment at the hands of the New York media, accuracy, on-field decision making, off-field decision making, credit rating, or punchability, you have to admit that it's hard to imagine the scenario that results in Geno Smith triumphantly leading the Jets to the playoffs.

The Jets have the quarterback situation of a 4-12 team at the start of a massive rebuilding project. But they are a 10-6 team with their scalps scraping the ceiling of the salary cap. The Jets' roster is loaded with expensive older players. Even when they had opportunities to get younger this offseason, they turned them down.

D'Brickashaw Ferguson retired suddenly in March. The move surprised fans but should not have surprised the Jets, who were trying to renegotiate the 32-year-old's contract. Ferguson's retirement created a massive void at left tackle and exposed a lack of depth across the offensive line. Ferguson had never missed a meaningful snap in ten seasons, and the Jets have only spent two picks in the first three rounds of the draft on the offensive line since they drafted Ferguson and Nick Mangold in the first round in 2006.

Ryan Clady, who will turn 30 before the season opener and spent two of the last three seasons on injured reserve, was imported from Denver to replace Ferguson. As stopgaps go, the Jets could have done far worse. But the Jets then waited until the fifth round of a strong tackle class to select Brandon Shell, a mammoth South Carolina lineman who projects as a right tackle at best. No successor for Mangold arrived in the draft. The closest thing to Clady insurance at left tackle is Ben Ijalana, a former failed Colts prospect.

At running back, the Jets moved on from Chris Ivory after a 1,000-yard season. Again: not a bad move. Ivory, like Fitzpatrick, is an older player (28 is old by running back standards) coming off a career year built on big games against the Browns and Dolphins defenses. But the Jets replaced

Ivory with 30-year-old Matt Forte. Forte is still productive but demonstrated all the warning signs of running back aging last season. He missed three games with an MCL injury and also appeared on injury reports with a back problem. His receptions-per-game rate dropped from 6.4 to 3.4, a sign of a former all-purpose threat starting to tail off. Forte was a committee back in the final weeks of 2015, but the Jets didn't draft a running back, so Forte's backups will be the ubiquitous Bilal Powell and veteran hangers-on Khiry Robinson and Zac Stacy.

You could argue that a veteran-heavy offense featuring Clady, Mangold, Forte, Brandon Marshall, and Eric Decker is perfect for developing Hackenberg or one of the other youngsters at quarterback. The problem is that there is an absolute lack of young talent in the pipeline at most positions.

The Jets defensive line is fully stocked, of course, but there are depth and youth problems everywhere else. Calvin Pryor is a very good safety. Brian Winters is a capable guard. Marcus Williams gets the job done as a nickel or dime defender. The draft brought Derron Lee (first round, Ohio State) and Jordan Jenkins (third round, Georgia), who are expected to make immediate contributions at linebacker.

That's about it. Cornerback Dee Milliner, a first-round pick in 2013, has been vaporware for three years. Jace Amaro is lightly penciled in at tight end after 38 rookie catches (and six drops) in 2014 and a season lost to shoulder surgery. If Amaro doesn't seize the job, the Jets may just forgo the tight end position completely; they barely used one in 2015. Deep threat Devin Smith lost his rookie season to injuries and mistakes. Even if he takes a big leap forward this year, he's trapped behind Marshall and Decker. Last year's success was built almost exclusively on veterans; even supporting roles went to the likes of Jeremy Kerley, Kellen Davis, Calvin Pace, and Erin Henderson, holdovers from the last regime. Player development was just not a priority last year.

The lack of young talent across the roster will become a major problem as the veterans age and contracts expire or come to term. The Jets already had $166 million in liabilities against the salary cap at press time before we consider the big extension Wilkerson signed right as we were finishing this year's book. Marshall, Decker, and Mangold will eat up $25 million combined in 2017, and the Jets will not be in position to replace them (again: no clear successors in the wings) or extend them (they will be old).

Let's not forget the Jets' Once-and-Future Contract Boondoggle. Darrelle Revis is now 30 and coming off another All-Pro season. His most recent contract was front-heavy with incentives; he actually becomes *more* affordable in future years. Of course, Revis is not the kind of guy who settles for less than his absolute market value just because he signed a front-loaded contract. One of two things is likely to happen this year: 1) Revis could start to tail off, turning the Jets' biggest impact player into another expensive veteran on the decline, or 2) Revis has another All-Pro season and turns back into the Money Monster.

The Jets are trapped in a double bind. Their depth chart and financial ledger are built to win now. Their quarterback situation is designed to reap dividends in 2018, but it's impossible to guess who else will form the nucleus of that future roster even if the Jets prove to be right about Hackenberg. It's a scattered organizational model, one that could blow up in the face of Maccagnan, who ended last season as the toast of the Big Apple.

Maccagnan was named NFL Executive of the Year by the Pro Football Writers Association, a jury of our peers that must have missed Dave Gettleman slow-cooking the Panthers into a Super Bowl team, Steve Keim stocking the Cardinals with both young talent and deep-discount veterans, John Elway building the Broncos into a force powerful enough to drag Peyton Manning across the finish line, and so on. Maccagnan traded for Marshall, dropped a cartoon safe full of money on Revis, rented Fitzpatrick and Antonio Cromartie, and rode that expensive veteran turbo boost to the almost-playoffs.

The Jets probably needed the attitude adjustment that the veterans provided; the team had become a perennial laughingstock and suffered a string of mediocre draft classes. Todd Bowles deserved a talent upgrade to get his program off on the right foot. So the expenditures and short-term leases were not a ridiculous idea. But like Fitzpatrick's superlative season, Maccagnan's evaporates when you begin to examine it closely; no wonder Maccagnan and Fitzpatrick were at odds about their relative values to each other in the offseason.

The Jets went 6-2 against the AFC South and NFC East, the two weakest divisions in the NFL. They beat the Browns in the season opener and caught the Dolphins twice when they were playing without the adrenaline rush of a recent coach firing. The Week 16 Patriots win was impressive, a hard-fought effort against the most important opponent on the schedule, but it was the Jets' only win against a truly good opponent; even the Redskins were shorthanded (no DeSean Jackson, Jordan Reed, or several others) when they lost to the Jets.

Everything that has happened since that Patriots victory, from Fitzpatrick's contract demands to Ferguson's retirement to Wilkerson's disenchantment with the franchise tag, appears to have caught Maccagnan and his staff by surprise, even though none of it should have. It's as if he thought his work was done when he built a team good enough to barely upset the Patriots. The Jets spent the offseason flailing and reacting. They are weaker now than they were at several critical positions: quarterback, left tackle, second cornerback. (Cromartie was The Human Torch for most of last year, but he drew a lot of island defense, and replacement Buster Skrine was as bad or worse). Yet long-range problems persist, and Maccagnan almost went out of his way to avoid the simplest solutions to them: Paxton Lynch or a left tackle in the first round instead of Lee, for example.

Maccagnan may turn out to be the wrong man for the job, but the coaching staff on the field inspires a lot more confidence. Bowles had an impressive debut as the anti-Rex Ryan. He defused the Geno Smith punching drama in training camp. The Jets defense played to its reputation for most of the season, and the offense didn't play like it was an afterthought. The Jets finished fifth in the league in fewest penalty yards, with decreases in look-how-macho-we-are penalties like unsportsmanlike conduct (five in 2014, two last year) and roughing the passer (which dropped from five to one). Bowles' Jets were a smart, professional team that won the games they were supposed to win: a huge step up Ryan's bluster-and-blunder teams of the previous four years.

Offensive coordinator Chan Gailey, meanwhile, is the ideal coach for cobbling together an offense around a quarterback who completed less than 53 percent of his passes against Buffalo and Army last year, or one with a 27-to-35 NFL touchdown/interception ratio, or one whose play-calling skills still don't extend to all the buttons on the PS4 controller. Gailey builds his game plans around what he has, not what he wishes he had. Gailey bravely ordered Fitzpatrick to keep forcing footballs downfield from spread formations in the general vicinity of Marshall and Decker last season. The receivers made enough plays to compensate for all of the incompletions, and loosened-up defenses (many of which, remember, were not very good) were more vulnerable to runs and screens underneath.

Gailey will probably use multi-receiver packages to disguise simple concepts this year and let Smith or Hackenberg uncork deep passes to his top targets while everyone learns how to call plays without help from the "Ask Madden" feature. If there really is an NFL quarterback on the roster, Gailey will make him look as good as possible without the aid of a tight end or real weapons at third and fourth receiver.

Jets fans deserved a fresh start last year. For the most part, they got one. They now deserve an encouraging next step, and there's the rub. The 2016 Jets will field a strong defense which will be expected to compensate for mediocre-to-awful quarterbacking. There are cap issues to contend with. There will be some disgruntled veterans if the quarterbacks falter early. It all looks very familiar, right down to Revis Island.

Familiar is bad for the Jets. So is trying to outsmart the planet at quarterback. That tactic hasn't worked for them in 50 years, and there's no reason to believe it will suddenly start working now.

Mike Tanier

2015 Jets Stats by Week

Wk	vs.	W-L	PF	PA	YDF	YDA	TO	Total	Off	Def	ST
1	CLE	W	31	10	333	321	4	37%	13%	-26%	-2%
2	at IND	W	20	7	344	343	4	19%	-9%	-29%	-1%
3	PHI	L	17	24	323	231	-3	-36%	-43%	-16%	-9%
4	vs. MIA (UK)	W	27	14	425	226	1	17%	23%	-13%	-19%
5	BYE										
6	WAS	W	34	20	474	225	-1	62%	33%	-42%	-13%
7	at NE	L	23	30	372	353	-1	31%	17%	-15%	-1%
8	at OAK	L	20	34	366	451	-1	-33%	13%	49%	3%
9	JAC	W	28	23	290	436	4	-14%	-31%	-2%	15%
10	BUF	L	17	22	318	280	-4	-12%	-30%	-26%	-9%
11	at HOU	L	17	24	267	364	-1	-17%	-19%	5%	8%
12	MIA	W	38	20	411	333	2	32%	16%	-6%	10%
13	at NYG	W	23	20	463	355	0	-6%	4%	-14%	-25%
14	TEN	W	30	8	439	292	1	55%	31%	-15%	8%
15	at DAL	W	19	16	372	309	3	-1%	-2%	-15%	-14%
16	NE	W	26	20	428	284	0	57%	26%	-21%	10%
17	at BUF	L	17	22	300	295	-2	-11%	-33%	-29%	-7%

Trends and Splits

	Offense	Rank	Defense	Rank
Total DVOA	1.5%	14	-13.8%	5
Unadjusted VOA	6.5%	11	-17.8%	7
Weighted Trend	3.3%	14	-12.2%	6
Variance	6.2%	14	4.0%	11
Average Opponent	4.1%	31	-3.1%	28
Passing	21.2%	10	-1.2%	9
Rushing	-10.9%	22	-33.3%	1
First Down	-4.7%	19	-5.7%	11
Second Down	6.3%	14	-22.0%	2
Third Down	6.6%	12	-16.1%	8
First Half	-6.7%	21	-19.3%	3
Second Half	9.6%	6	-8.4%	7
Red Zone	32.2%	4	-41.1%	1
Late and Close	5.6%	9	-15.0%	8

Five-Year Performance

Year	W-L	Pyth W	Est W	PF	PA	TO	Total	Rk	Off	Rk	Def	Rk	ST	Rk	Off AGL	Rk	Def AGL	Rk	Off Age	Rk	Def Age	Rk	ST Age	Rk
2011	8-8	8.4	8.4	377	363	-3	13.5%	10	-8.3%	21	-16.1%	2	5.6%	4	9.2	2	21.2	12	27.6	12	27.5	9	26.2	17
2012	6-10	5.3	5.6	281	375	-14	-18.0%	27	-20.7%	30	-4.2%	9	-1.5%	21	37.7	22	41.0	23	26.6	19	28.1	2	26.0	16
2013	8-8	5.4	7.5	290	387	-14	-7.7%	24	-15.3%	27	-5.6%	12	2.1%	10	33.9	15	9.1	1	26.2	26	26.7	14	26.1	13
2014	4-12	4.8	5.9	283	401	-11	-15.5%	27	-11.2%	27	3.5%	21	-0.8%	16	18.7	5	22.8	4	27.3	9	27.0	11	26.1	13
2015	10-6	10.0	9.7	387	314	+6	12.4%	9	1.6%	14	-13.8%	5	-2.9%	25	48.7	25	13.2	1	28.5	1	27.1	9	26.6	6

2015 Performance Based on Most Common Personnel Groups

NYJ Offense					NYJ Offense vs. Opponents					NYJ Defense				NYJ Defense vs. Opponents			
Pers	Freq	Yds	DVOA	Run%	Pers	Freq	Yds	DVOA	Run%	Pers	Freq	Yds	DVOA	Pers	Freq	Yds	DVOA
10	38%	6.7	26.3%	16%	Base	26%	4.9	-15.1%	62%	Base	32%	5.1	-12.3%	11	56%	5.4	-9.8%
11	35%	5.4	9.1%	39%	Nickel	51%	5.7	10.2%	35%	Nickel	57%	5.5	-11.1%	12	24%	4.9	-19.0%
21	15%	5.4	-9.8%	65%	Dime+	22%	6.7	31.4%	11%	Dime+	9%	4.6	-18.0%	21	5%	5.7	-8.5%
20	5%	4.6	0.5%	55%	Goal Line	1%	0.4	0.6%	90%	Goal Line	1%	0.8	-78.7%	01	2%	8.5	33.5%
22	2%	1.8	-54.6%	88%						Big	1%	2.8	-41.9%	611	2%	3.8	-23.6%
12	2%	2.6	-73.3%	64%										10	1%	5.3	35.6%

Strategic Tendencies

Run/Pass		Rk	Formation		Rk	Pass Rush		Rk	Secondary		Rk	Strategy		Rk
Runs, first half	38%	16	Form: Single Back	62%	31	Rush 3	6.4%	18	4 DB	32%	19	Play action	16%	27
Runs, first down	47%	16	Form: Empty Back	13%	3	Rush 4	47.9%	32	5 DB	57%	11	Avg Box (Off)	6.05	32
Runs, second-long	29%	19	Pers: 3+ WR	78%	3	Rush 5	24.4%	12	6+ DB	9%	19	Avg Box (Def)	6.27	15
Runs, power sit.	55%	18	Pers: 2+ TE/6+ OL	7%	32	Rush 6+	21.2%	1	CB by Sides	54%	31	Offensive Pace	30.11	15
Runs, behind 2H	23%	21	Pers: 6+ OL	2%	17	Sacks by LB	38.2%	16	S/CB Cover Ratio	23%	12	Defensive Pace	29.53	8
Pass, ahead 2H	44%	23	Shotgun/Pistol	63%	17	Sacks by DB	5.3%	22	DB Blitz	18%	3	Go for it on 4th	1.18	11

With Jace Amaro out for the year, the Jets almost entirely abandoned the tight end position like no team we've seen in a decade of game charting. 43 percent of the Jets' offensive plays did not have a tight end on the field. The next-highest offense was

Green Bay at 18 percent. In fact, no team had been higher than 20 percent since Buffalo and Chicago in 2011. Only 4.1 percent of Jets passes were thrown to tight ends. ☞ When the Jets did have a tight end in the game, he was often in the backfield to help block. But the Jets' running game was awful with the extra blocker: 3.3 yards per carry and -39.4% DVOA, compared to 4.7 yards per carry and -1.6% DVOA otherwise. Most teams see these numbers (rushing with one back vs. two backs) oscillate wildly from year to year, but not Gang Green. Jets running backs have gained more yards per carry with a higher DVOA from single-back sets (when compared to two-back sets) for four straight seasons. ☞ The Jets have also had better run defense against two-back sets compared to single-back sets for two straight seasons. Last year, they allowed 3.6 yards per carry against single-back sets, but just 2.1 yards per carry when opponents used two backs. ☞ The Jets' red zone defense was strong and balanced: No. 1 in the NFL against the pass and No. 2 against the run behind only the Rams. ☞ The Jets' defense benefited from a league-high 35 dropped passes. ☞ Department of Bowles Being Bowles: The Jets sent a big blitz on 21 percent of pass plays; no other defense was over 13 percent. The Jets allowed only 5.3 yards per pass with a big blitz, but they actually allowed more yards sending five pass-rushers (7.3) than when they sent just three or four (5.9). ☞ Talk about your halftime adjustments: the Jets inexplicably had the league's best offensive DVOA in the third quarter but ranked 20th or lower in the three other quarters.

Passing

Player	DYAR	DVOA	Plays	NtYds	Avg	YAC	C%	TD	Int
R.Fitzpatrick*	542	3.5%	583	3779	6.5	5.4	59.6%	31	15
G.Smith	72	11.0%	45	246	5.5	3.3	64.3%	2	1

Rushing

Player	DYAR	DVOA	Plays	Yds	Avg	TD	Fum	Suc
C.Ivory*	-31	-11.5%	247	1073	4.3	7	3	43%
B.Powell	25	1.0%	70	313	4.5	1	1	46%
R.Fitzpatrick*	73	18.0%	45	281	6.2	2	1	-
S.Ridley*	-51	-45.5%	36	90	2.5	0	0	28%
Z.Stacy	-17	-24.0%	31	89	2.9	1	0	35%
M.Forte	192	12.0%	218	898	4.1	4	1	48%
K.Robinson	29	3.0%	56	180	3.2	4	0	43%

Receiving

Player	DYAR	DVOA	Plays	Ctch	Yds	Y/C	YAC	TD	C%
B.Marshall	303	9.3%	173	109	1502	13.8	4.0	14	63%
E.Decker	278	13.6%	132	80	1027	12.8	2.7	12	61%
Q.Enunwa	-48	-27.0%	46	22	315	14.3	6.7	0	48%
K.Thompkins	-68	-38.8%	33	17	165	9.7	4.0	0	52%
D.Smith	-71	-46.1%	28	9	115	12.8	2.0	1	32%
J.Kerley*	14	-5.3%	26	16	152	9.5	5.9	2	62%
C.Owusu*	-28	-41.1%	13	6	80	13.3	3.7	0	46%
J.Ross	-3	-14.9%	14	9	88	9.8	8.0	0	64%
J.Cumberland*	-35	-45.1%	14	5	77	15.4	10.0	0	36%
K.Davis	-39	-56.7%	11	3	18	6.0	3.3	1	27%
J.Cunningham	-36	-39.3%	16	8	59	7.4	3.3	0	50%
B.Powell	36	-3.3%	63	47	388	8.3	8.9	2	75%
C.Ivory*	21	-4.3%	37	30	217	7.2	9.2	1	81%
Z.Stacy	-3	-18.6%	12	9	65	7.2	8.9	0	75%
T.Bohanon	12	14.9%	8	4	56	14.0	9.5	0	50%
M.Forte	112	23.5%	58	44	389	8.8	8.0	3	76%

Offensive Line

Player	Pos	Age	GS	Snaps	Pen	Sk	Pass	Run	Player	Pos	Age	GS	Snaps	Pen	Sk	Pass	Run
D'Brickashaw Ferguson*	LT	33	16/16	1111	7	4.0	12.0	0.5	Brian Winters	LG	25	16/10	765	7	1.0	4.0	0.0
Breno Giacomini	RT	31	16/16	1107	8	1.0	6.0	1.0	Willie Colon	RG	33	6/6	345	1	0.0	2.0	2.0
James Carpenter	LG	27	16/16	1107	2	2.0	6.0	3.0	Wesley Johnson	OT	25	10/1	170	1	0.0	1.0	1.0
Nick Mangold	C	32	15/15	937	2	1.0	3.0	1.0									

Year	Yards	ALY	Rank	Power	Rank	Stuff	Rank	2nd Lev	Rank	Open Field	Rank	Sacks	ASR	Rank	Press	Rank	F-Start	Cont.
2013	4.27	3.79	21	68%	12	17%	8	0.95	27	0.80	11	47	8.4%	27	28.8%	28	14	42
2014	4.20	3.84	20	75%	5	18%	8	1.12	20	0.65	19	47	8.8%	25	30.2%	28	17	37
2015	4.06	3.55	26	59%	26	23%	26	1.14	18	0.90	10	22	4.1%	3	22.4%	10	21	35
2015 ALY by direction:		Left End 3.28 (21)			Left Tackle 3.38 (23)			Mid/Guard 3.62 (25)			Right Tackle 2.68 (29)			Right End 5.04 (2)				

D'Brickashaw Ferguson was certainly no slouch in his final season, but once he entered his thirties, he became more of a league-average left tackle. Last year, he ranked 14th out of 33 left tackles in snaps per blown block. Ferguson's successor Ryan Clady ranked eighth at the position during his last healthy season in 2014. ☞ Brian Winters became a whipping boy on the line after a poor rookie season in 2013 and an injury-shortened campaign the following year. The Jets signed James Carpenter to push Winters out of the starting lineup, but when Willie Colon went down, the third-year pro turned in a better performance than many might have expected. Over 10 starts, Winters committed just four blown blocks, good for the fifth-best per-snap rating among all right guards. With Colon possibly retiring, Winters might get one more shot to nail down a starting job in the final year of his rookie deal. ☙ At 6-foot-5 and 324 pounds, fifth-round pick Brandon Shell (South Carolina) is a mammoth human being. Starting tackles Clady and Breno Giacomini will both be over 30 when the regular season starts, and with a lack of other young talent on the roster, Shell could be the successor at either position. The great nephew of Art Shell, this Shell will need to build up his technique, particularly with his footwork, as relying on his size will no longer be sufficient.

Defensive Front Seven

Defensive Line	Age	Pos	G	Snaps	Plays	Overall TmPct	Rk	Stop	Dfts	BTkl	Runs	St%	vs. Run Rk	RuYd	Rk	Sack	Pass Rush Hit	Hur	Dsrpt
Muhammad Wilkerson	27	DE	16	940	71	9.3%	3	60	23	10	45	84%	14	2.0	37	12.0	17	30.5	2
Leonard Williams	22	DT	16	809	63	8.2%	6	54	17	4	56	86%	13	1.8	29	3.0	17	19.0	0
Sheldon Richardson	26	DE	11	618	37	7.0%	16	25	14	4	23	61%	80	3.9	84	5.0	9	25.5	2
Damon Harrison*	28	DT	16	568	71	9.3%	3	63	12	1	69	90%	9	1.4	7	0.5	3	4.0	0
Leger Douzable*	30	DE	16	291	13	1.7%	--	8	1	1	11	73%	--	2.9	--	0.0	3	6.0	0
Jarvis Jenkins	28	DE	15	636	33	4.6%	48	25	8	6	25	68%	66	3.4	81	4.0	7	9.5	1
Steve McLendon	30	DT	16	379	14	1.7%	--	10	5	1	12	67%	--	1.8	--	1.0	1	2.0	1

Edge Rushers	Age	Pos	G	Snaps	Plays	Overall TmPct	Rk	Stop	Dfts	BTkl	Runs	St%	vs. Run Rk	RuYd	Rk	Sack	Pass Rush Hit	Hur	Dsrpt
Calvin Pace*	36	OLB	16	523	22	2.9%	84	14	5	4	11	82%	17	2.1	42	3.0	3	11.0	1
Quinton Coples*	26	OLB	15	291	8	1.1%	--	6	1	0	7	86%	--	1.3	--	0.0	4	9.5	0
Lorenzo Mauldin	24	OLB	15	253	10	1.4%	--	8	7	1	5	60%	--	5.2	--	4.0	8	14.5	0

Linebackers	Age	Pos	G	Snaps	Plays	Overall TmPct	Rk	Stop	Dfts	BTkl	Runs	St%	vs. Run Rk	RuYd	Rk	Sack	Pass Rush Hit	Hur	Tgts	vs. Pass Suc%	Rk	AdjYd	Rk	PD	Int
David Harris	32	ILB	16	973	114	14.9%	20	66	23	8	64	64%	44	3.5	42	4.5	3	6	26	71%	7	3.8	8	4	0
Demario Davis*	27	ILB	16	851	91	11.9%	45	54	15	15	45	80%	2	3.2	30	2.0	7	9	29	52%	49	6.6	44	1	0
Erin Henderson	30	ILB	16	226	32	4.2%	--	21	3	2	22	82%	--	2.1	--	0.0	0	3	3	30%	--	8.5	--	1	0

Year	Yards	ALY	Rank	Power	Rank	Stuff	Rank	2nd Level	Rank	Open Field	Rank	Sacks	ASR	Rank	Press	Rank
2013	3.21	3.23	4	39%	1	26%	3	0.80	1	0.48	8	41	6.2%	24	20.6%	32
2014	3.81	3.80	13	64%	18	19%	16	0.89	3	0.69	17	45	8.2%	4	26.7%	6
2015	3.35	2.93	1	62%	12	28%	1	0.96	4	0.55	6	39	6.0%	21	28.0%	6
2015 ALY by direction:		Left End 2.49 (2)			Left Tackle 2.40 (2)			Mid/Guard 2.99 (1)			Right Tackle 3.13 (8)			Right End 3.42 (17)	

The Jets are happy to have Muhammad Wilkerson signed to a long-term extension, but Leonard Williams would have made a fine replacement. That's not a case of hyperbole or projection—as a rookie, Williams posted similar per-snap pass-rushing numbers to Wilkerson, and slightly better run defense numbers. No rookie had more defeats than Williams' 17, and only eight players (rookie or otherwise) had more quarterback hits. ☙ Sheldon Richardson experienced lots of off-field problems in 2015, from a four-game suspension for substance abuse to harrowing tales of his reckless endangerment charges (which led to a one-game suspension for 2016). Still, he largely produced as an interior rusher, increasing his hurry total from 16.5 to 25.5 to offset a slight dip in hits and sacks. With two years left on his rookie deal, Richardson needs to keep his head screwed on if the Jets are to invest in him as a defensive cornerstone next to Williams and Wilkerson. ☙ After spending early picks on Darron Lee and Jordan Jenkins, New York's linebacking corps has gotten much younger and faster. Demario Davis is gone in free agency, Calvin Pace is contemplating retirement, and Quinton Coples finally wore out his welcome. Jenkins in particular will likely need to start right away, taking Pace's old strongside linebacker spot opposite rising edge-rusher Lorenzo Mauldin. First-rounder Lee represents a much more interesting gamble. The Ohio State product has all the athleticism you'd want in a three-down versatile inside linebacker, but he's arguably too small to play right now, and his instincts are still quite raw. With vets Erin Henderson and Bruce Carter still lingering, the Jets might take their time developing Lee physically and mentally.

Defensive Secondary

Secondary	Age	Pos	G	Snaps	Plays	Overall TmPct	Rk	Stop	Dfts	BTkl	vs. Run Runs	St%	Rk	RuYd	Rk	vs. Pass Tgts	Tgt%	Rk	Dist	Suc%	Rk	AdjYd	Rk	PD	Int
Marcus Gilchrist	28	SS	16	1048	89	11.6%	21	25	13	5	36	25%	57	10.4	62	42	9.2%	54	12.3	55%	43	7.0	37	5	3
Antonio Cromartie*	32	CB	15	898	41	5.7%	73	20	10	6	6	50%	20	5.8	23	73	18.6%	31	13.4	55%	27	8.9	64	11	0
Darrelle Revis	31	CB	14	888	48	7.2%	61	20	8	4	8	38%	44	4.8	12	71	18.3%	28	13.6	61%	7	6.2	12	8	5
Buster Skrine	27	CB	16	721	61	8.0%	47	24	16	7	6	67%	8	5.3	17	67	21.3%	50	10.4	47%	62	8.1	46	7	1
Calvin Pryor	24	FS	13	714	76	12.2%	17	37	13	11	32	53%	14	5.5	17	27	8.5%	47	13.3	65%	16	6.0	20	5	2
Marcus Williams	25	CB	13	285	30	4.8%	--	14	10	8	5	40%	--	8.2	--	31	24.6%	--	11.4	54%	--	8.1	--	10	6
Dion Bailey	24	SS	7	154	24	7.2%	--	12	3	1	8	63%	--	5.3	--	10	16.4%	--	10.9	38%	--	9.3	--	2	0

Year	Pass D Rank	vs. #1 WR	Rk	vs. #2 WR	Rk	vs. Other WR	Rk	vs. TE	Rk	vs. RB	Rk
2013	18	-0.6%	19	13.5%	26	-1.3%	13	5.5%	19	-22.3%	3
2014	24	2.7%	17	19.0%	27	34.0%	31	30.5%	31	-23.0%	4
2015	9	-2.1%	14	-51.8%	1	10.6%	24	-8.8%	14	-3.0%	12

The big change with Darrelle Revis last season was that offenses no longer quaked at the notion of targeting him. Revis ranked third in estimated target percentage during his lone Patriots season, checking in at 17.0 percent. However, that figure rose to 18.3 percent in 2015, dropping him to 28th. Revis Island is still dangerous territory, given his solid charting numbers from 2015. But it's no longer an unassailable fortress where passes go to die. ☞ With Antonio Cromartie gone, Buster Skrine should return to playing heavy snaps on the perimeter. The Jets made him a slot corner after signing him away from Cleveland, but Skrine struggled for much of 2015. By adjusted success rate, only 13 out of 85 qualifying cornerbacks (50 charted passes or eight starts) fared worse than Skrine. There's at least a precedent of success, though, as Skrine excelled as the Browns' No. 2 cornerback in 2014. Playing opposite Joe Haden, Skrine ranked third in adjusted yards per target. ☞ Calvin Pryor progressed well in his second season, playing free safety in addition to his customary spot in the box and improving against both the run and the pass. Pryor ranked seventh among safeties in total stops and saw his coverage success rate leap from 43 percent as a rookie to 65 percent in 2015. While most of this team's young talent plays on the defensive line, Pryor stands out as an exception to that rule. ☞ Fourth-round rookie Juston Burris might be a sleeper to play in sub-packages right away. Burris' main competition will come from Dee Milliner and Dexter McDougle, two injury-prone draftees from the John Idzik regime. The long-armed North Carolina State product profiles as a press man coverage corner—gee, think the Jets have a type?—but with Skrine's ability to play the slot, the door is open for Burris to play in the nickel if he earns the job.

Special Teams

Year	DVOA	Rank	FG/XP	Rank	Net Kick	Rank	Kick Ret	Rank	Net Punt	Rank	Punt Ret	Rank	Hidden	Rank
2013	2.1%	10	8.4	4	1.6	13	0.8	12	-0.4	19	-0.1	15	-3.7	20
2014	-0.8%	16	0.5	14	4.8	10	-0.8	18	0.8	15	-9.0	32	-2.6	22
2015	-2.9%	25	0.8	14	4.4	7	-5.6	29	-17.9	32	3.6	9	-7.9	26

The Jets were by far the worst punting team in the league. Ryan Quigley wasn't a star by any means, but most of the blame belongs to the coverage units, which conceded an estimated 13.5 points worth of field position to opposing returners. Regardless, Quigley took the fall for the unit's struggles, as seventh-round rookie Lachlan Edwards (an Australian who attended Sam Houston State) will likely take over the punting job. ☞ Jeremy Kerley saw his offensive role shrink last year, but he was still a good punt returner, contributing 3.4 net points on 45 returns. At the moment, it's a mystery who will succeed Kerley, given that he took 45 out of New York's 46 returns in 2015. Zac Stacy has experience on kick returns; undrafted rookie Jalin Marshall (Ohio State) is also a possibility if he can crack the final roster.

Oakland Raiders

2015 record: 7-9	**Total DVOA:** 0.1% (14th)	**2016 Mean Projection:** 7.6 wins	**On the Clock (0-4):** 12%
Pythagorean Wins: 6.9 (17th)	**Offense:** -1.3% (18th)	**Postseason Odds:** 29.7%	**Mediocrity (5-7):** 36%
Snap-Weighted Age: 26.5 (18th)	**Defense:** -1.5% (15th)	**Super Bowl Odds:** 3.5%	**Playoff Contender (8-10):** 37%
Average Opponent: 4.8% (8th)	**Special Teams:** -0.1% (19th)	**Proj. Avg. Opponent:** 0.3% (15th)	**Super Bowl Contender (11+):** 14%

2015: A surprise playoff contender that ran out of gas a few weeks shy of the goal.

2016: Welcome to the wet blanket that is regression.

ootball Outsiders comment thread legend Raiderjoe got a 2015 season that was straight out of his dreams.

For those of you who don't know Raiderjoe, he drops about 80 words of garbled almost-English at a time. Seventy percent of those words are wildly optimistic, fanboy-esque thoughts about the Raiders, and the other 30 percent are stone-cold coherent takes in that same wacky prose style.

"K. Maiava good lienbCker. Will be nice player for Raiders. Teamon upswing AAnd going to keep swinging upwards with free agency and draft. Going to be like late 1970s and 1985 and1993 and ssome other years. Raiders vs Brobcos for AFC Wets supremacy."

Raiderjoe's warnings of Oakland dominance seemed cute and innocent for a long time. But, after last year's bust out, this may very well be the year we see Oakland battle the Brobcos for AFC Wets supremacy.

A year ago, the Raiders were slotted right next to the Browns in the NFL's cupcake pool. The commonly cited Vegas over/under was 5.5 wins, and they gave you -125 on the under. *Football Outsiders Almanac 2015* gave them a mean projection of 6.3 wins. But eight weeks into the season, Oakland

was in playoff contention at 4-3 despite a tough schedule. The Raiders slowed down in the second half and finished with a losing record, but that doesn't diminish the impressive progress this franchise made in 2015. From 1990 through 2015, only 14 different teams improved their overall DVOA by 20.0% or more after two straight years with a DVOA rating of -20.0% or lower (Table 1). The Raiders and Washington both joined that list in 2015.

Although the Raiders improved their DVOA in all three phases of the game, the driving force behind Oakland's rise was the work that the new coaching staff did with second-year quarterback Derek Carr. Unlike Washington, Oakland also fits into a historical group of teams that dramatically improved upon years of horrible offense (Table 2).

Head coach Jack Del Rio handed responsibility for Carr over to former Minnesota offensive coordinator Bill Musgrave, who had some history of spackling decent seasons out of quarterbacks like Christian Ponder. Musgrave created a spread-offense, collegiate-style scheme for Carr. The quarterback often lined up in shotgun or pistol sets (69 percent of plays, ninth in the NFL). The Raiders finished fourth in

Table 1. Over 20% Improvement in Total DVOA after Two Seasons at -20% or Worse, 1990-2015

Years	Team	Year 1 DVOA	Year 1 W-L	Year 2 DVOA	Year 2 W-L	Year 3 DVOA	Year 3 W-L	Year 4 DVOA	Year 4 W-L
2013-2016	OAK	-34.1%	4-12	-27.4%	3-13	0.1%	7-9	--	--
2013-2016	WAS	-26.2%	3-13	-27.0%	4-12	-0.3%	9-7	--	--
2009-2012	SEA	-30.8%	5-11	-22.9%	7-9	-1.5%	7-9	38.7%	11-5
2008-2011	STL	-47.1%	2-14	-45.1%	1-15	-19.4%	7-9	-35.4%	2-14
2008-2011	OAK	-23.2%	5-11	-34.0%	5-11	-4.1%	8-8	-8.0%	8-8
2008-2011	KC	-29.4%	2-14	-29.2%	4-12	0.3%	10-6	-16.9%	7-9
2008-2011	DET	-48.4%	0-16	-51.6%	2-14	-1.1%	6-10	10.1%	10-6
2004-2007	SF	-41.8%	2-14	-55.5%	4-12	-19.4%	7-9	-33.4%	5-11
1999-2002	CLE	-39.7%	2-14	-40.2%	3-13	-7.3%	7-9	1.6%	9-7
1999-2002	ARI	-28.1%	6-10	-38.7%	3-13	-13.6%	7-9	-36.5%	5-11
1995-1998	NYJ	-23.9%	3-13	-30.9%	1-15	2.6%	9-7	28.3%	12-4
1992-1995	NE	-40.1%	2-14	-23.9%	5-11	5.6%	10-6	-21.2%	6-10
1992-1995	IND	-27.2%	9-7	-37.2%	4-12	-8.1%	8-8	-9.8%	9-7
1990-1993	IND	-24.0%	7-9	-47.7%	1-15	-27.2%	9-7	-37.2%	4-12
AVERAGE (except OAK/WAS)		**-33.7%**	**3.8**	**-38.1%**	**3.3**	**-7.8%**	**7.9**	**-10.0%**	**7.3**

2016 Raiders Schedule

Week	Opp.	Week	Opp.	Week	Opp.
1	at NO	7	at JAC	13	BUF
2	ATL	8	at TB	14	at KC (Thu.)
3	at TEN	9	DEN	15	at SD
4	at BAL	10	BYE	16	IND (Sat.)
5	SD	11	HOU (Mon./Mex.)	17	at DEN
6	KC	12	CAR		

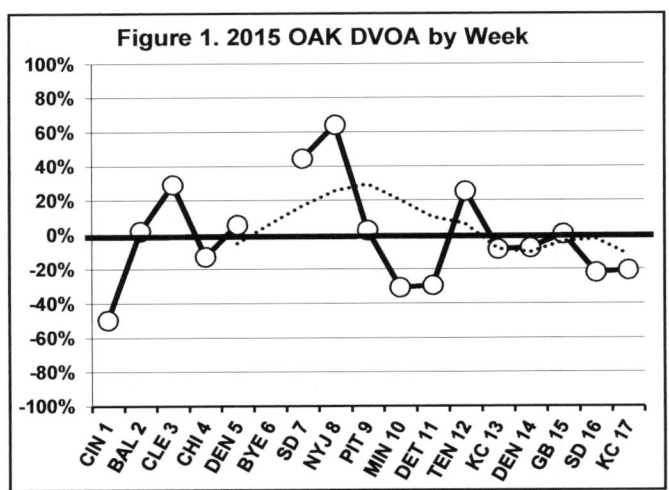

Figure 1. 2015 OAK DVOA by Week

the league in empty-back sets, at 13 percent. They got a ton of mileage out of matching up fullback Marcel Reece against linebackers in space, and used three receivers on one side to get easy short passes. The schematic changes, combined with an offensive line bolstered by ex-Chiefs center Rodney Hudson and the breakout of second-year left guard Gabe Jackson, mitigated Carr's weaknesses. Scouts were confident about Carr's great arm when he came out of Fresno State; it was the issue of how he could handle pressure that worried NFL teams and dropped his selection into the second round. In his rookie season, Carr was shoehorned into a traditional pro-style offense by former offensive coordinator Greg Olsen, and spent all season throwing checkdowns to nowhere on third-and-13. Musgrave changed the dynamic.

By putting Carr in situations where he often didn't need to deal with pressure, Musgrave masked the weaknesses of his young quarterback. The percentage of plays where Carr was charted under pressure dropped from 24.1 percent to 20.5 percent—only three starting quarterbacks were under pressure less often—while Carr's performance under pressure went from 1.8 yards per play in 2014 to 3.4 in 2015. The improve-

ment of the Raiders' offense was particularly interesting given that, outside of Amari Cooper, the offense had exactly zero skill position players of acclaim. Michael Crabtree was on a last-chance contract. Latavius Murray had been buried on the depth chart for two years. Unheralded Andre Holmes and Seth Roberts split third-receiver duties. As a team, Oakland receivers dropped the second-most passes in the NFL.

Things were going well until November hit. Oakland's offense had a 14.3% DVOA through Week 9. In Weeks 10-17, they carried a -18.5% offensive DVOA. And while Carr was prone to suffer through games against defenses where front fours could tee off on him (hello, Broncos), the primary culprit was the running game. The Raiders had just four games all season with a positive rushing offense DVOA, and none of them came after Week 8.

Table 2. Over 15% Improvement in Offensive DVOA after Two Seasons at -15% or Worse, 1990-2015

Years	Team	Year 1 DVOA	Year 1 Rank	Year 2 DVOA	Year 2 Rank	Year 3 DVOA	Year 3 Rank	Year 4 DVOA	Year 4 Rank
2013-2016	OAK	-16.7%	28	-19.4%	30	-1.3%	18	--	--
2011-2014	KC	-19.3%	29	-25.1%	31	3.0%	15	5.0%	12
2011-2014	ARI	-18.4%	28	-30.9%	32	-2.4%	20	-9.3%	23
2010-2013	STL	-18.1%	30	-27.2%	32	-4.2%	21	-9.5%	22
2008-2011	OAK	-26.1%	31	-25.8%	30	-8.3%	23	2.6%	14
2008-2011	DET	-25.3%	30	-28.4%	31	-0.8%	19	7.1%	10
2004-2007	SF	-21.2%	29	-40.4%	32	-8.2%	23	-32.2%	32
2003-2006	CHI	-16.8%	30	-36.5%	32	-17.1%	28	-5.0%	20
2001-2004	DAL	-15.2%	29	-24.5%	29	-6.8%	21	-4.6%	20
2001-2004	CAR	-26.7%	31	-25.2%	31	-5.0%	18	0.0%	13
1999-2002	SD	-18.5%	28	-26.2%	29	0.0%	17	1.8%	15
1999-2002	ARI	-22.9%	30	-19.6%	27	5.2%	9	-12.3%	27
1998-2001	PHI	-23.1%	27	-22.9%	29	0.9%	15	2.9%	12
1998-2001	NO	-23.3%	28	-24.3%	31	-1.3%	19	-6.8%	23
1994-1997	ARI	-16.3%	27	-22.9%	28	-4.2%	20	-13.8%	26
1991-1994	NE	-23.7%	25	-27.6%	27	-12.2%	23	-0.8%	13
1990-1993	TB	-19.9%	25	-28.4%	27	-6.1%	21	-20.8%	28
1989-1992	DAL	-23.3%	28	-23.6%	28	17.6%	4	23.6%	2
AVERAGE (except OAK)		**-21.1%**	**28.5**	**-27.0%**	**29.8**	**-2.9%**	**18.6**	**-4.2%**	**18.4**

Some of Oakland's slowdown could also be attributed to the lingering foot issue Cooper played through in December. Three of the rookie's last four games saw him held under 20 yards. Crabtree is a good technical receiver, but not a burner, and with Cooper playing through an injury so serious that GM Reggie McKenzie opined he was thinking of "shutting him down," there wasn't much to threaten defenses vertically.

Now imagine this from a computer algorithm's perspective. Statistical projection systems are built to look at the macro (large trends) rather than the micro (specific player injuries). They are built to analyze stats, not unquantifiable descriptions of schematic changes. The computer sees a dreadful offensive football team for two years in a row. It sees performance over the full season, not just the good first half when fans outside of Oakland were paying more attention. It sees skill position players that haven't proven much, and no major talent additions in that area. This is where DVOAbot is starting from, and despite a lot of splashy offseason moves by the Raiders, it's one of the reasons we're holding off on projecting them to be easy AFC West contenders.

It's hard to disagree with anything the Raiders did on paper. By signing Baltimore offensive lineman Kelechi Osemele, one of the best guards in the game, Oakland continued to build space for Carr and got a mauler who can help improve the run game. The weakest area on last year's team was the pass defense, so McKenzie went out and brought in Seattle hybrid linebacker Bruce Irvin, cornerback Sean Smith, and safety Reggie Nelson. Irvin isn't a star edge rusher, but can complement Khalil Mack as he grows from star to superstar. Smith has finished in the top 30 in adjusted success rate for two seasons in a row, and was clearly one of the best corners on the market. Nelson lingered on the market a bit because of his age, but he should be an upgrade on the pure castoffs and low-round picks Oakland has been relying on at free safety for a while. Of course, Oakland's best defensive back, strong safety Charles Woodson, retired after the season, but the Raiders invested their first-round pick to replace him with West Virginia's Karl Joseph. Other than Woodson the Raiders retain most of their best players on defense, and they're mostly youngsters.

Unlike the offense, Oakland's defense was clearly improving late in the season, with negative DVOA ratings for the last six games in a row. So it's hard to blame Raiders fans for their optimism. Take the early-season Carr/Cooper combo, the late-season defense, then add a dash of free agency to cover up the warts. Add some "our young players will get better because young players always grow" and, in the words of a wise ex-Raiders linebacker, baby you've got a stew goin'.

We too want to believe, but we have our reservations. Look at the quick risers on Tables 1 and 2, and you'll find that a lot of teams that burst on to the scene needed some time to set themselves—if they ever got there. For every beginning of the Legion of Boom NFC Dynasty, there's a corresponding Stuck in Mediocrity with Matthew Stafford. And for every consolidation year on the way to a Bill Parcells-Drew Bledsoe Super Bowl, there's a tailspin of sadness such as the Sam Bradford-Chris Long Rams.

Ultimately, it's hard to accept the idea that Carr is going to grow into a transcendent quarterback. Statistical growth is nice, but the circumstances that created it are undeniable. That's not necessarily a bad thing. It's wonderfully refreshing to see an NFL team that knows how to get the best out of a player. It also doesn't mean that Carr is going to hold the Raiders back in the future. If Carr is Andy Dalton with a better deep ball, well, the Bengals have been to the playoffs five straight seasons with that formula and good receivers.

It's just that, as meat-and-potatoes as the Oakland draft was, there hasn't really been much of a talent change at the skill positions. Unless you are the world's biggest Maxwell McCaffrey fan, nobody in the receiving corps other than Cooper projects as a good bet to open up the field. Dalton had A.J. Green, but he also had Marvin Jones, Giovani Bernard, Jeremy Hill, Andrew Hawkins, Tyler Eifert, and so on. The Raiders are still trying to find the pieces that fit around Carr, Crabtree, and Cooper to be able to maintain the level of offense the Bengals had last year.

Oakland's rebuild is in the midst of paying off, and what McKenzie has done here is to be commended. It's quite possible the Raiders will be able to parlay an improved defense and Carr small-ball into a playoff berth. That's a sentence that would have been confined to SB Nation comments and Twitter fanboys in 2014.

But we're more of the mind that this team is going to need that consolidation year. The foundation is definitely in place, but even with a friendly schedule that features the two South divisions, a lot has to go right for this team to be a dominant force in 2016.

Plus, if we really did think the Raiders were going to win the Super Bowl, we'd be undermining one of our most loyal customers by depriving him of the opportunity to say he told us so. That's just bad for business.

Rivers McCown

2015 Raiders Stats by Week

Wk	vs.	W-L	PF	PA	YDF	YDA	TO	Total	Off	Def	ST
1	CIN	L	13	33	246	396	-2	-50%	-34%	16%	1%
2	BAL	W	37	33	448	493	1	2%	32%	37%	7%
3	at CLE	W	27	20	469	355	1	29%	22%	-6%	1%
4	at CHI	L	20	22	243	371	1	-13%	-33%	-8%	12%
5	DEN	L	10	16	288	297	-1	6%	-3%	-18%	-9%
6	BYE										
7	at SD	W	37	29	412	417	2	45%	37%	-3%	5%
8	NYJ	W	34	20	451	366	1	64%	77%	8%	-5%
9	at PIT	L	35	38	440	597	-2	3%	16%	13%	-1%
10	MIN	L	14	30	371	385	-2	-31%	7%	13%	-25%
11	at DET	L	13	18	216	375	0	-29%	-25%	6%	2%
12	at TEN	W	24	21	407	249	0	25%	17%	-10%	-2%
13	KC	L	20	34	361	232	-1	-8%	-8%	-10%	-9%
14	at DEN	W	15	12	126	310	2	-7%	-40%	-30%	2%
15	GB	L	20	30	372	293	0	1%	-9%	-14%	-5%
16	SD	W	23	20	281	343	0	-22%	-59%	-12%	25%
17	at KC	L	17	23	205	339	1	-21%	-32%	-12%	-1%

Trends and Splits

	Offense	Rank	Defense	Rank
Total DVOA	-1.3%	17	-1.5%	15
Unadjusted VOA	-1.1%	16	-1.5%	14
Weighted Trend	-5.6%	20	-6.0%	12
Variance	12.3%	32	2.7%	3
Average Opponent	-3.2%	4	1.4%	8
Passing	20.8%	11	6.0%	16
Rushing	-15.0%	24	-12.2%	15
First Down	4.0%	11	4.3%	20
Second Down	-5.8%	21	-1.4%	15
Third Down	-5.1%	18	-12.2%	11
First Half	2.7%	13	0.1%	16
Second Half	-5.2%	20	-3.1%	11
Red Zone	14.6%	10	-7.3%	12
Late and Close	-26.3%	32	-14.4%	9

Five-Year Performance

Year	W-L	Pyth W	Est W	PF	PA	TO	Total	Rk	Off	Rk	Def	Rk	ST	Rk	Off AGL	Rk	Def AGL	Rk	Off Age	Rk	Def Age	Rk	ST Age	Rk
2011	8-8	6.1	7.3	359	433	-4	-8.0%	22	2.6%	14	9.6%	27	-1.0%	20	36.7	21	41.4	26	26.8	19	27.1	16	26.8	4
2012	4-12	4.1	3.7	290	443	-7	-27.8%	29	-9.5%	23	12.5%	29	-5.8%	31	31.8	19	35.0	20	27.1	13	27.5	9	26.6	8
2013	4-12	4.9	2.1	322	453	-9	-34.1%	31	-16.7%	28	10.3%	26	-7.1%	31	49.7	26	27.2	15	26.7	17	27.6	5	26.1	16
2014	3-13	3.1	4.8	253	452	-15	-27.4%	29	-19.4%	30	6.3%	26	-1.7%	18	26.1	11	77.5	32	26.5	22	27.7	4	26.2	11
2015	7-9	6.9	7.4	359	399	+1	0.1%	14	-1.3%	18	-1.5%	15	-0.1%	19	23.7	8	33.9	22	26.2	20	26.6	17	27.2	1

2015 Performance Based on Most Common Personnel Groups

OAK Offense					OAK Offense vs. Opponents					OAK Defense					OAK Defense vs. Opponents			
Pers	Freq	Yds	DVOA	Run%	Pers	Freq	Yds	DVOA	Run%	Pers	Freq	Yds	DVOA		Pers	Freq	Yds	DVOA
11	58%	5.8	9.7%	24%	Base	34%	5.1	-2.4%	51%	Base	50%	5.4	-4.1%		11	46%	5.9	0.8%
12	14%	4.5	-8.9%	41%	Nickel	49%	5.8	10.8%	27%	Nickel	35%	5.8	8.2%		12	24%	4.9	-10.6%
21	10%	6.6	27.6%	31%	Dime+	15%	5.8	11.6%	10%	Dime+	12%	5.7	-2.1%		21	8%	5.6	12.7%
13	5%	4.0	-19.1%	67%	Goal Line	1%	0.9	57.5%	89%	Goal Line	2%	0.9	-34.3%		10	6%	6.3	35.2%
22	5%	5.0	-41.0%	75%	Big	1%	3.0	-29.6%	100%	Big	1%	7.7	-22.1%		13	5%	6.2	-0.6%
10	3%	3.6	-9.0%	21%											22	5%	5.0	-18.0%

Strategic Tendencies

Run/Pass		Rk	Formation		Rk	Pass Rush		Rk	Secondary		Rk	Strategy		Rk
Runs, first half	38%	14	Form: Single Back	67%	27	Rush 3	8.9%	9	4 DB	50%	4	Play action	18%	18
Runs, first down	38%	31	Form: Empty Back	13%	4	Rush 4	55.2%	25	5 DB	35%	27	Avg Box (Off)	6.18	22
Runs, second-long	42%	1	Pers: 3+ WR	62%	14	Rush 5	28.0%	9	6+ DB	12%	17	Avg Box (Def)	6.36	6
Runs, power sit.	58%	11	Pers: 2+ TE/6+ OL	29%	21	Rush 6+	7.9%	11	CB by Sides	62%	26	Offensive Pace	30.61	20
Runs, behind 2H	21%	26	Pers: 6+ OL	4%	11	Sacks by LB	34.2%	18	S/CB Cover Ratio	13%	32	Defensive Pace	30.04	11
Pass, ahead 2H	47%	16	Shotgun/Pistol	69%	9	Sacks by DB	2.6%	29	DB Blitz	6%	27	Go for it on 4th	0.70	27

Oakland receivers dropped 5.4 percent of passes, 31st in the NFL. This has been a problem for years, as the Raiders have ranked 25th or worse in drop rate four straight seasons. Oakland ranked third in the league in DVOA on deep passes but

23rd on short passes (up to 15 yards through the air). ✏ Derek Carr gained 9.3 yards per pass against defensive back blitzes, second only to Tom Brady. ✏ The Raiders recovered 15 of 21 fumbles on offense. ✏ Oakland only called 19 running back screens all season (compared to an NFL average of 25) but had a league-leading 137.4% DVOA on these plays. ✏ When facing second-and-long, the offense called a running play 42 percent of the time, the highest rate in the league. The Raiders were around average on these plays, gaining 4.5 yards per carry with -32.6% DVOA. ✏ The offense was great when Oakland was pulling away, ranking first in DVOA when leading by at least two scores. However, it ranked dead last in DVOA in late-and-close situations. Insert sizzling hot take here. ✏ The defense was at its best when the Raiders were behind, ranking third in DVOA when trailing by at least two scores and fourth when trailing by one score. However, the Raiders ranked just 25th in defensive DVOA when leading by one score and 22nd when leading by two or more scores.

Passing

Player	DYAR	DVOA	Plays	NtYds	Avg	YAC	C%	TD	Int
D.Carr	582	4.1%	603	3763	6.2	5.1	61.3%	32	13
M.McGloin	-26	-21.5%	34	123	3.6	2.8	71.9%	2	1

Rushing

Player	DYAR	DVOA	Plays	Yds	Avg	TD	Fum	Suc
L.Murray	32	-5.6%	266	1066	4.0	6	3	39%
J.Olawale	44	33.5%	24	110	4.6	1	0	58%
D.Carr	-13	-25.3%	21	141	6.7	0	3	-
R.Helu	-16	-30.1%	17	39	2.3	0	0	41%
T.Jones	1	-6.4%	16	74	4.6	0	1	44%
M.Reece	9	13.0%	10	36	3.6	0	0	40%

Receiving

Player	DYAR	DVOA	Plays	Ctch	Yds	Y/C	YAC	TD	C%
M.Crabtree	-4	-13.0%	146	85	922	10.8	3.1	9	58%
A.Cooper	122	-1.0%	130	72	1082	15.0	5.2	6	55%
S.Roberts	114	13.3%	55	32	480	15.0	4.2	5	58%
A.Holmes	-8	-15.9%	33	14	201	14.4	3.1	4	42%
C.Walford	10	-4.1%	50	28	329	11.8	4.4	3	56%
M.Rivera	-51	-25.7%	46	32	280	8.8	3.9	1	70%
L.Smith	-2	-9.5%	13	12	70	5.8	4.8	1	92%
L.Murray	-47	-30.6%	53	41	238	5.8	6.0	0	77%
M.Reece	127	42.3%	37	30	269	9.0	7.2	3	81%
R.Helu	30	18.2%	16	9	75	8.3	9.9	1	56%
J.Olawale	28	28.5%	11	9	84	9.3	7.4	0	82%
T.Jones	38	56.4%	9	7	106	15.1	16.3	1	78%

Offensive Line

Player	Pos	Age	GS	Snaps	Pen	Sk	Pass	Run	Player	Pos	Age	GS	Snaps	Pen	Sk	Pass	Run
Gabe Jackson	LG	25	16/16	1056	3	1.0	4.0	3.5	Rodney Hudson	C	27	13/13	807	5	1.0	2.0	1.5
J'Marcus Webb*	RG	28	16/16	1056	6	2.0	10.0	5.0	Tony Bergstrom*	OT	30	16/3	250	1	0.0	0.0	0.0
Donald Penn	LT	33	16/16	1039	8	4.5	13.5	0.0	Jon Feliciano	G	24	6/3	187	4	1.0	2.0	0.0
Austin Howard	RT	29	13/13	815	9	3.0	6.0	1.5	Kelechi Osemele	LG	27	14/14	976	8	0.0	0.0	5.0

Year	Yards	ALY	Rank	Power	Rank	Stuff	Rank	2nd Lev	Rank	Open Field	Rank	Sacks	ASR	Rank	Press	Rank	F-Start	Cont.
2013	4.09	3.71	26	61%	20	16%	6	0.88	31	0.83	10	44	8.5%	28	29.8%	29	23	22
2014	3.80	3.56	28	55%	29	21%	21	0.94	31	0.65	18	28	4.4%	3	24.6%	18	17	32
2015	3.98	3.69	19	72%	7	18%	6	1.02	26	0.74	15	33	4.6%	4	20.7%	3	28	33

2015 ALY by direction:	Left End 3.06 (24)	Left Tackle 2.93 (28)	Mid/Guard 3.81 (15)	Right Tackle 3.67 (19)	Right End 4.44 (4)

After signing Kelechi Osemele, the Raiders were quickly pitted against the Cowboys in an offseason ranking contest for best offensive line. The winner, as always, were the clicks. Dallas has better stars, but less depth than the Raiders. ✏ The player Osemele is replacing, J'Marcus Webb, was the only Raiders starter who didn't rank in the top half of his position in snaps per blown block. ✏ Donald Penn was a reclamation project gone horribly right for the Raiders, but found a cold market this offseason due to his less-than-ideal physique. He returned to the Raiders for two years and $14 million. Penn's a better pass protector than a mover in the run game at this point. He makes up for his so-so agility with his technique. ✏ Austin Howard, the bookend for Penn, was miscast as a guard in 2014. Moved back to his natural right tackle position, he was having a nice year up until a knee injury took him out. Menelik Watson, a former second-round pick from Florida State, will try to push Howard out of the starting lineup. Watson missed all of last season with a torn Achilles, and hadn't lived up to his draft stock before that.

Defensive Front Seven

Defensive Line	Age	Pos	G	Snaps	Plays	Overall TmPct	Rk	Stop	Dfts	BTkl	vs. Run Runs	St%	Rk	RuYd	Rk	Pass Rush Sack	Hit	Hur	Dsrpt
Dan Williams	29	DT	16	568	49	5.6%	37	40	8	0	45	82%	22	2.0	34	1.0	3	7.5	1
Stacy McGee	26	DT	16	408	22	2.5%	--	17	2	0	20	85%	--	2.0	--	0.0	1	5.0	0
Justin Ellis	26	DT	12	361	23	3.5%	67	17	2	1	22	73%	51	2.4	50	0.0	1	5.0	1

Edge Rushers	Age	Pos	G	Snaps	Plays	Overall TmPct	Rk	Stop	Dfts	BTkl	vs. Run Runs	St%	Rk	RuYd	Rk	Pass Rush Sack	Hit	Hur	Dsrpt
Khalil Mack	25	DE	16	1002	79	9.0%	2	63	32	1	51	75%	46	2.5	56	15.0	11	29.5	2
Denico Autry	26	DE	14	684	24	3.1%	82	18	6	5	16	75%	40	2.3	46	3.0	4	20.0	3
Mario Edwards	22	DE	14	597	43	5.6%	34	33	10	1	31	71%	60	2.3	45	2.0	4	9.5	2
Benson Mayowa*	25	DE	12	377	15	2.3%	93	9	4	0	10	60%	87	3.1	78	1.0	3	7.0	0
Damontre Moore	24	DE	14	279	21	2.7%	--	15	8	1	9	56%	--	6.6	--	4.0	8	7.0	1

Linebackers	Age	Pos	G	Snaps	Plays	Overall TmPct	Rk	Stop	Dfts	BTkl	vs. Run Runs	St%	Rk	RuYd	Rk	Pass Rush Sack	Hit	Hur	vs. Pass Tgts	Suc%	Rk	AdjYd	Rk	PD	Int
Malcolm Smith	27	OLB	16	1141	128	14.6%	24	66	25	18	49	69%	20	2.0	3	4.0	5	8	43	44%	60	7.7	58	6	1
Curtis Lofton*	30	MLB	16	577	64	7.3%	73	26	7	7	31	52%	82	3.7	52	1.0	1	4	10	54%	--	5.3	--	0	0
Aldon Smith	27	OLB	9	517	31	6.3%	83	21	10	2	19	68%	23	2.9	20	3.5	7	26	0	0%	--	0.0	--	0	0
Ben Heeney	24	MLB	15	307	34	4.1%	--	18	9	2	12	67%	--	3.7	--	2.5	0	0	4	81%	--	2.9	--	1	0
Bruce Irvin	29	OLB	15	710	40	5.6%	85	32	14	3	22	77%	5	2.6	8	5.5	11	16.5	6	100%	--	0.3	--	1	0
Bruce Carter	28	MLB	14	307	41	5.4%	--	23	6	2	28	61%	--	3.3	--	2.0	2	4	7	88%	--	1.5	--	2	0

Year	Yards	ALY	Rank	Power	Rank	Stuff	Rank	2nd Level	Rank	Open Field	Rank	Sacks	ASR	Rank	Press	Rank
2013	3.96	3.95	18	73%	25	17%	21	1.16	21	0.45	6	38	7.3%	11	24.7%	16
2014	4.08	3.85	16	62%	12	20%	12	1.13	15	0.72	18	22	4.1%	32	24.4%	19
2015	3.93	3.75	18	53%	4	22%	12	1.07	12	0.72	13	38	5.9%	23	24.1%	25

2015 ALY by direction:	Left End 4.76 (28)	Left Tackle 3.00 (6)	Mid/Guard 4.22 (27)	Right Tackle 2.23 (2)	Right End 3.04 (12)

The big problem area for this team is at inside linebacker, where Curtis Lofton figuratively died on the field last year. Malcolm Smith, in his first real crack as a full-time starter, was below-average in pass coverage. Ben Heeney, last year's fifth-round pick out of Kansas, is likely to get the first crack at filling Lofton's shoes this year. So long as the shoes aren't made of cement, Heeney should be faster than Lofton was. Is he a real solution? The rookie year tape leaned more towards JAG, but that doesn't have to be the final word. ☞ Khalil Mack followed in Mario Williams' footsteps as "high first-round edge rusher who starts slapping people around in Year 2." The only edge rusher with more defeats than Mack last year was J.J. Watt. ☞ The interior of this line is rather unheralded, so let's give them some shine. Dan Williams got a lot of money in free agency when the Raiders had to overpay to get people in the door, but he's been a stellar nose for some time. Mario Edwards struggled a bit when the Raiders tried to use him as an edge rusher after Aldon Smith's suspension, but he was solid as a 3-4 end. Denico Autry, a true McKenzie lifer as a former Packers UDFA, has been a find opposite Edwards and even stumbles into some pressure from time-to-time. ☞ The Raiders reinvigorated their pass-rushing depth with an influx of youth in this draft class. NFL teams were higher on second-round pick Jihad Ward (Illinois) than draftniks. His combine was downright ugly. But between his prototypical end size and his ability to play multiple positions, the Raiders saw enough to pounce on him early. Third-round pick Shilique Calhoun (Michigan State) is rated by SackSEER as an almost perfectly average prospect in terms of both explosion index and college performance. And Oakland wasn't finished after draft day, bringing in James Cowser of Southern Utah as a UDFA. Cowser was SackSEER's favorite sleeper with an 84.2 percent rating. He holds the all-time FCS records for sacks (43) and tackles for loss (80) and had the fastest 3-cone time of any edge rusher at the combine. However, he's overaged (26) because of a two-year LDS mission.

Defensive Secondary

Secondary	Age	Pos	G	Snaps	Plays	TmPct	Overall Rk	Stop	Dfts	BTkl	Runs	vs. Run St%	Rk	RuYd	Rk	Tgts	vs. Pass Tgt%	Rk	Dist	Suc%	Rk	AdjYd	Rk	PD	Int
Charles Woodson*	40	SS	16	1112	83	9.5%	38	21	12	13	35	11%	68	11.6	66	15	3.5%	2	17.1	80%	3	3.3	3	6	5
T.J. Carrie	26	CB/FS	15	931	61	7.4%	58	21	10	12	9	33%	50	9.0	56	54	15.1%	7	12.7	48%	55	8.3	48	7	1
D.J. Hayden	26	CB	16	901	77	8.8%	33	20	7	8	16	19%	68	11.1	64	75	21.6%	51	13.3	38%	75	7.9	40	6	1
David Amerson	25	CB	16	879	85	9.7%	21	38	15	13	11	45%	34	6.6	34	91	26.8%	71	11.8	53%	33	6.0	11	25	4
Neiko Thorpe	26	CB	14	456	42	5.5%	--	15	8	4	4	25%	--	7.8	--	46	26.0%	--	15.7	46%	--	8.7	--	8	1
Larry Asante*	28	SS	16	366	28	3.2%	--	8	3	5	12	42%	--	5.5	--	5	3.6%	--	14.8	81%	--	1.4	--	3	0
Taylor Mays*	28	FS	14	316	28	3.6%	--	14	6	3	9	44%	--	6.8	--	13	10.7%	--	10.1	65%	--	4.0	--	4	0
Reggie Nelson	33	FS	16	1056	86	10.2%	31	36	17	9	37	46%	25	7.4	41	30	7.1%	31	16.8	54%	47	6.5	30	15	8
Sean Smith	29	CB	13	834	57	8.6%	37	25	12	2	10	50%	20	12.8	69	66	18.1%	25	14.6	55%	26	6.8	16	11	2

Year	Pass D Rank	vs. #1 WR	Rk	vs. #2 WR	Rk	vs. Other WR	Rk	vs. TE	Rk	vs. RB	Rk
2013	29	10.8%	23	20.2%	31	28.4%	31	3.9%	18	10.8%	25
2014	28	16.7%	28	2.5%	18	12.1%	25	-9.1%	10	15.4%	24
2015	16	-4.6%	12	-1.1%	14	4.8%	17	-11.0%	10	17.0%	30

How right were things running for the Raiders last year? Their random waiver claim of Washington corner David Amerson hit the jackpot. He suddenly figured it all out, and by midseason had erased first-round bust D.J. Hayden from the starting lineup. Cast as the second corner now that Sean Smith is in town, Amerson has always had the physical tools. Is this a new level of performance we can expect him to sustain, or a blip? ➾ Oakland's "CB by Sides" number from the Strategic Tendencies table is confusing because the Raiders changed the way they used their defensive backs multiple times during the season. Players moved in and out of the lineup, while T.J. Carrie moved back and forth between safety and corner. By the end of the season, Oakland had settled into split-side setup when in nickel or dime, with Amerson at left cornerback, Neiko Thorpe at right cornerback, and Hayden and/or Carrie in the slot. It remains to be seen if they'll keep Smith and Amerson on specific sides or will use Smith to trail the opposition's top receiver. ➾ First-rounder Karl Joseph (West Virginia) is tasked with replacing the future Hall of Famer Charles Woodson. Joseph's 2015 season ended early as he tore his ACL four games into the Mountaineers' season. He had five picks in those four games, though, and looked to be in the midst of a breakout season. His 2014 play was spottier, but he reads well and showed the willingness to tackle that should help him play in the box in the league. The only real concern at the moment is his size: 5-foot-10 and 205 pounds aren't the numbers that get scouts drooling.

Special Teams

Year	DVOA	Rank	FG/XP	Rank	Net Kick	Rank	Kick Ret	Rank	Net Punt	Rank	Punt Ret	Rank	Hidden	Rank
2013	-7.1%	31	-11.1	29	6.0	6	-10.4	32	-16.1	30	-4.1	22	13.5	2
2014	-1.7%	18	8.2	5	-5.4	25	-9.3	32	2.7	12	-4.7	24	6.3	6
2015	-0.1%	19	-1.4	20	-6.2	30	-2.3	23	14.0	3	-4.6	23	16.4	2

Punter Marquette King got a deserved fat contract extension. ➾ Kicker Sebastian Janikowski is 37, closing in on a spot in the oldest active players list next to Adam Vinatieri, Matt Bryant, Phil Dawson, Shane Lechler, and Tom Brady. (One of those names is not like the others.) For as much as we praise his leg strength, Janikowski has only made five attempts of 50 or more yards in each of the last two seasons after eight straight seasons with at least seven of those tries. ➾ The Raiders openly auditioned punt returners all year, finding nobody to their liking. T.J. Carrie is probably the favorite to do it again this year, though he didn't offer much last year. Main kick returner Taiwan Jones is an Al Davis legacy pick who doesn't have much beyond his 40 time; the Raiders can and should do better here.

Philadelphia Eagles

2015 record: 7-9	Total DVOA: -11.2% (22nd)	2016 Mean Projection: 6.9 wins	On the Clock (0-4): 17%
Pythagorean Wins: 6.7 (19th)	Offense: -10.1% (26th)	Postseason Odds: 23.5%	Mediocrity (5-7): 43%
Snap-Weighted Age: 26.9 (10th)	Defense: 3.0% (17th)	Super Bowl Odds: 1.7%	Playoff Contender (8-10): 31%
Average Opponent: -1.3% (19th)	Special Teams: 1.9% (10th)	Proj. Avg. Opponent: 0.8% (11th)	Super Bowl Contender (11+): 9%

2015: Toto, I don't think we're in Oregon anymore.

2016: My kingdom for a quarterback!

Although we often associate words like innovation and flexibility with brilliant football minds, the NFL in general is as conservative as the grandparents from Alabama you see once a year at Thanksgiving. So when Chip Kelly's bold reimagining of the Eagles roster crumbled like the final acts of a Shakespearean tragedy, it was hardly surprising to see Jeffrey Lurie depose Kelly in favor of familiarity by promoting Howie Roseman back to his old general manager post. Kelly may be back on the opposite side of the country, but his maverick philosophies have still shaped how the next decade of Philadelphia football will play out.

One of *Seinfeld's* many memorable moments comes in "The Opposite," when the much beleaguered George Costanza resolves to revolt against all his ingrained behaviors and do the opposite of everything he normally would. This mantra effectively encapsulates the Eagles offseason, with Roseman returning to power after losing a personnel power struggle to Kelly last year. Given how thoroughly Roseman has undone many of Kelly's biggest moves from last year, you can almost picture him locked away in a dungeon underneath the NovaCare Complex in 2015, pacing back and forth and plotting his revenge. The whole episode is practically Napoleonic; Roseman can only hope he lasts longer in his rebirth than the French emperor (or Costanza, who was back to imitating cartoon aliens by episode's end).

Like Roseman, new head coach Doug Pederson holds deep ties to Andy Reid, making him an extremely logical successor to Kelly. Moreover, considering Kelly's reputation as an iconoclastic offensive trailblazer, Pederson's West Coast-derived system should be a welcome sight to the organization. And in tapping Jim Schwartz to run the defense, Roseman chose an aggressive one-gapping 4-3 identity far different from Billy Davis' traditional 3-4 scheme. In the early stages of the offseason, Roseman made quick work in shedding three of Kelly's signature acquisitions from 2015, trading DeMarco Murray for peanuts and packaging Byron Maxwell and Kiko Alonso just to move up five spots in the first round. Other Kelly favorites such as Riley Cooper and Mark Sanchez were also sent packing. The Maxwell-Alonso trade would set up the Eagles' signature move of the offseason, but on paper, these simply appeared to be cap-saving decisions meant to allow Roseman to financial flexibility to chase his own players.

As it turns out, Roseman really wanted to chase quarterbacks.

The Birds spent the spring acting like an obnoxious *Settlers of Catan* player who monopolizes one resource and ignores everything else, making the game harder for everyone without materially improving their own chances of winning. In this instance, Sam Bradford seems akin to Philadelphia's sheep, a mildly useful transitional resource which nevertheless needs help from a diverse collection of resources (or players) to achieve anything meaningful. In length and terms, Bradford's two-year, $35 million deal might be the closest thing in the league to a middle-class quarterback contract. It certainly reflects the uncertainty the Eagles operated with in re-signing their 2015 starter, perhaps preferring to grab the first seat available rather than having no seat at all when the music stopped. At the same time, Bradford's Philly debut was slightly worse than his last two years in St. Louis, based on his passing DVOA and DYAR. In fact, among quarterbacks to re-up with their current teams over the past three seasons, Bradford performed worse in the season leading up to the extension than almost anyone else (Table 1).

Table 1. Passing DVOA and DYAR in Year Before Contract Extension, 2013-2015

Player	Team	Year	DVOA	Rank	DYAR	Rank
Sam Bradford	PHI	2015	-8.2%	24	107	24
Tom Brady	NE	2015	19.5%	5	1,312	2
Kirk Cousins	WAS	2015	16.9%	6	1,023	7
Joe Flacco	BAL	2015	-10.5%	26	17	27
Cam Newton	CAR	2014	-14.5%	33	-105	36
Russell Wilson	SEA	2014	5.5%	14	503	13
Ben Roethlisberger	PIT	2014	26.8%	4	1,572	1
Eli Manning	NYG	2014	4.6%	16	642	11
Philip Rivers	SD	2014	12.6%	10	918	9
Ryan Tannehill	MIA	2014	4.1%	18	630	12
Carson Palmer	ARI	2013	2.7%	17	547	15
Jay Cutler	CHI	2013	5.5%	13	392	18
Colin Kaepernick	SF	2013	16.6%	7	791	8
Andy Dalton	CIN	2013	2.3%	18	541	16
Alex Smith	KC	2013	-3.7%	21	262	20

These quarterbacks didn't always maintain their same prior level of performance after receiving their extensions, as Cam Newton and Colin Kaepernick can attest. But whereas New-

2016 Eagles Schedule

Week	Opp.	Week	Opp.	Week	Opp.
1	CLE	7	MIN	13	at CIN
2	at CHI (Mon.)	8	at DAL	14	WAS
3	PIT	9	at NYG	15	at BAL
4	BYE	10	ATL	16	NYG (Thu.)
5	at DET	11	at SEA	17	DAL
6	at WAS	12	GB (Mon.)		

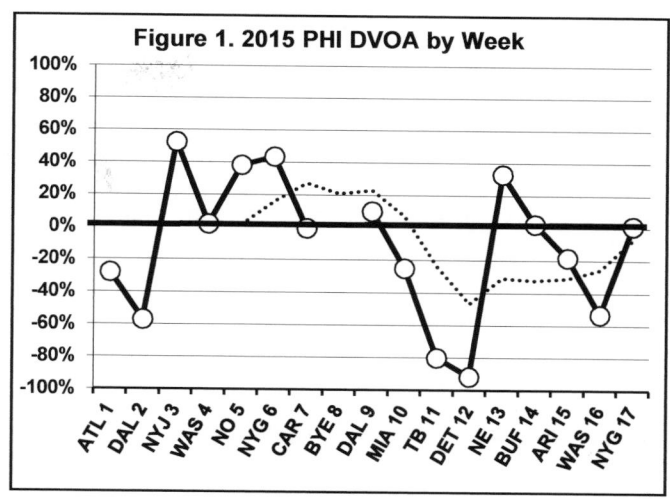

Figure 1. 2015 PHI DVOA by Week

ton, Kaepernick, and several other quarterbacks on this list were still malleable players whose development was in progress, Bradford feels like a finished product. He won't turn the ball over much, with a solid 2.3 percent career interception rate, and showed good short accuracy in completing a career-high 65 percent of his passes last season. Unfortunately, the aforementioned analogy extends beyond *Catan*, as Bradford's limitations have led him to adopt a rather sheepish playing style. Out of 37 qualified quarterbacks, Bradford ranked 29th in failed completion percentage and 34th in Air Less EXpected (ALEX), illustrating his tendency to stick to his conservative comfort zone even when the offense is in need of a bigger downfield play. Essentially, Bradford is a less mobile version of Pederson's last quarterback, Alex Smith. There's really nothing wrong with that fate; the Chiefs have made the postseason two of the past three seasons by surrounding Smith with a strong supporting cast and capable coaching staff.

But Roseman may only get one more chance to construct a roster, and decided he would rather go down by raging against the dying of the light. By trading up for North Dakota State's Carson Wentz, the Eagles have willingly put themselves behind the eight ball in terms of roster construction. Jimmy Johnson's traditional draft trade value chart pegs the difference between what the Eagles acquired and what they gave up as roughly equivalent to the 44th overall pick. Effectively losing a mid-second round pick is far from insignificant, but it seems like a reasonable cost of doing business when trading up for quarterbacks is involved. However, Chase Stuart's empirically derived draft-value chart places more weight in mid-round and future picks, and by that standard, Wentz has a very large gap to bridge. Stuart's chart suggests the net value the Eagles lost in the trade is nearly equivalent to the fourth overall pick, though in reality, Philadelphia's toll will be much more of a slow bleed. The Eagles will not have a first-rounder next year or a second-rounder in 2018. Philly does not have much cost-controlled young talent on its roster, meaning that Wentz will probably need to compensate for a thin supporting cast early in his career.

Still, if you accept the narrative that the Eagles wanted to set fire to the Kelly era, it would make sense that Roseman's chosen quarterback profiles as a fairly different player. Unlike Bradford, who came into the NFL from a spread system at Oklahoma, Wentz played in a traditionally structured pro-style scheme at North Dakota State. In theory, that should ease his transition into Pederson's offense, which will ask Wentz to juggle a potpourri of responsibilities similar to what he expe-

rienced in college. Additionally, Wentz (6-foot-5, 237 pounds) is sturdier than Bradford (6-foot-4, 224 pounds), who has since fulfilled the durability concerns many expressed when he was drafted. None of this ensures that Wentz will become a better or even a different quarterback—ironically, Bradford's deep ball was seen as a strength when he was a prospect—but the Eagles are surely happy to begin with a foundation that appears different from their current status quo.

Of course, cycling through progressions and setting protections while reading coverages against Weber State is not quite the same as doing so against the Seahawks (who Wentz will face if he wins the job by season's end). Overwrought as it may be, the questions about Wentz's level of competition at an FCS school do make it difficult to statistically project him the same way we would an FBS quarterback. QBASE, which just added career projections for top FCS quarterbacks this year, was down on Wentz in its forecast, especially in comparison to Jared Goff. And yet, Wentz projected in the same neighborhood as the likes of Joe Flacco, Andy Dalton, and Blake Bortles, other small-school prospects who defied similarly pessimistic QBASE projections. The point of projections is to show a range of the likeliest outcomes, not to tell everyone exactly what will happen (otherwise, you could just read this book instead of spending Sundays in the fall ignoring your significant others). For Wentz, that range of outcomes is probably wider than it already would be for the typical highly drafted quarterback.

Even if Wentz develops into a long-term starter, though, Philadelphia still needs to bolster the 52-man cast of supporting actors. The short-term future matters too, especially given the weakness of the NFC East. It especially matters while Wentz is on his rookie deal, which for the vast majority of quarterbacks, is the only time they'll ever provide significant surplus value on their contracts. Philly won't enjoy the same edge most teams with young quarterbacks possess; between Wentz, Bradford, and pricey third wheel Chase Daniel, the Eagles rank seventh in cap dollars invested at the position in 2016. Ideally, there would already be a cheap young core in place to accelerate their contention phase while Wentz is cheap, much like Seattle, Baltimore, and San Francisco had in recent seasons. Unfortunately, most of Philly's best home-grown talent has already signed more lucrative second contracts (Fletcher Cox, Brandon Graham, Lane Johnson, Vinny Curry, etc.). Assuming Wentz seizes the starting job at some point, the Eagles roster could resemble the Falcons' roster during Matt Ryan's early years, which were talented but top-heavy and more dependent than most on injury luck.

With limited dollars and draft capital on the horizon, we can tell a lot about the type of team the Eagles hope to build by seeing where they allocate their precious resources. This year, Philly chose the offensive line, which stands out as a strength amid subpar skill position talent. In particular, the Eagles revamped the interior of their line with free-agent signings Brandon Brooks and Stefan Wisniewski, as well as third-round pick Isaac Seumalo (Oregon State), their first post-Wentz selection this year. Despite his reputation as a running game guru, the line was never a priority for Kelly, who preferred to rely on tempo and confusion to help his linemen execute repetitive blocking assignments. Consequently, the Eagles finished 25th or worse in adjusted line yards in all three of Kelly's seasons.

Now, instead of scheming around the unit as Kelly did, Pederson seems likely to accentuate the unit. During his three seasons as Kansas City's offensive coordinator, Pederson's offense never finished worse than seventh in adjusted line yards in spite of consistently unspectacular offensive line personnel. Additionally, the Chiefs always resided in the top half of the league in run/pass ratio during Pederson's tenure. So despite the fact that we just spent the first half of this essay discussing Philly's quarterbacks, the Eagles' best bet at fielding a top-15 or better offense this season probably boils down to how effective the running game can be.

This reality is actually no different from last season, and neither Wentz nor Daniel figures to provide an immediate playmaking upgrade from Bradford. In 2015, Philadelphia posted a positive rushing DVOA seven times. The Eagles went 4-3 in those games with a plus-25 point differential, which doesn't seem so spectacular until you realize what happened when Bradford or Sanchez had to carry the offensive burden. In the nine games where the Eagles had a negative rushing DVOA, the Birds went 3-6 with a minus-78 point differential. You didn't need to watch much beyond the first-down run to see if a drive would pan out, as the Eagles were 22nd in offensive DVOA on second-and-long and 27th on third-and-long.

We know Philly will probably build around the run to protect its quarterback in 2016, but the efficacy of that strategy leaves the Eagles with little margin for error. Unless you're the Cowboys, with the league's best offensive line and a potential All-Pro running back in Ezekiel Elliott, a ground-bound strategy is more likely to leave you sitting next to Jeff Fisher in 7-9 purgatory. Ryan Mathews was excellent as a second fiddle last year, blowing away his previous career-best in rushing DVOA and proving far more effective than the more ballyhooed Murray. Unfortunately, the former first-rounder also has a brittle history and a track record of diminishing returns with higher workloads. But Pederson doesn't necessarily need a star to forge a strong running game, as we saw after Jamaal Charles

went down last season. While the offense doesn't have much upside unless Wentz exceeds rookie expectations, Pederson has proven capable of cobbling together league-average or better offenses with less.

It's less clear whether Pederson's offense will get the defensive support it needs to return the Birds to the playoffs. Philly was a roughly league-average defense over the duration of the Kelly era, but our projections forecast a unit which will most likely be below average in 2016. If you watched the Eagles disintegrate down the stretch, perhaps this news arrives as less of a surprise. With all the heat on Kelly and his offense last season, Philly's defense was quietly as schizophrenic as any unit in the league last season. From the start of the season through their Week 9 win over Dallas, the Eagles had a defensive DVOA similar to what the fifth-ranked Jets ended up posting over the course of the entire season. After that Cowboys win, however, the defense somehow morphed into a group of matadors worse than any unit outside of New Orleans (Table 2).

Table 2. 2015 Philadelphia Defense, Weeks 1-9 vs. Weeks 10-17

	Pass DVOA	Rk	Run DVOA	Rk	TO/ Game	Rk	ALY	Rk	ASR	Rk
Weeks 1-9	-14.9%	4	-11.1%	15	2.50	1	3.72	13	7.8%	5
Weeks 10-17	26.0%	28	9.6%	32	0.75	31	4.24	28	5.9%	24

This alone does not mean the defense is doomed to catastrophe in 2016. There's actually no evidence that playing better or worse in the second half of a season translates to a similar performance the next season. Given the significant personnel turnover most teams experience year to year, that finding shouldn't be too surprising.

At the same time, there's no letting the defense off the hook for that kind of head-scratching incompetence. It's too facile to blame the regression on Kelly's turbo-paced offense, which forced the Eagles defense to face the most plays in the league and finish last in time of possession in 2015. Philly was similarly taxed in both 2013 and 2014, yet their defense regressed only slightly at midseason in 2014 (ninth to 16th) and actually improved significantly in 2013 (30th to 13th). Furthermore, if you buy the fatigue theory, the defense should have played worse in the second halves of games, but that reality never played out. In every season of the Kelly era, the Eagles' defensive DVOA in the second half of games was better than their first-half DVOA.

Much of the Eagles' defensive core was at the heart of that decline, leaving Philadelphia hoping for numerous rebound campaigns in 2016. Start with the front seven, which looks like Philadelphia's greatest strength on paper. The decline coincided with a season-ending injury to impressive rookie linebacker Jordan Hicks, who was an important loss given his range in coverage and ability to stack-and-shed against the run. But Hicks isn't the protagonist in a sports movie—he's a second-year pro recovering from a major injury who played 450 defensive snaps last year (albeit very impressive ones).

His return won't magically cure all that ails the defense. Despite a fair amount of talent in the front seven, the Eagles front had its worst adjusted line yards ranking since 2003 (23rd) and finished 13th in adjusted sack rate after ranking in the top 10 of that category seven of the previous nine years.

If the Eagles are going to defy our defensive projections, it will be because their players translate better and more quickly into Schwartz's scheme than anyone might anticipate. The hallmark of Schwartz's defense is the "wide-9" technique, which refers to alignment of the defensive ends far outside the tackles. Intended to create better pass-rushing angles and provide rushers more space with which to work, the wide-9 should be a godsend for Graham and Curry, both of whom thrived in four-man fronts on passing downs. In addition, Cox and Bennie Logan should see their production increase as one-gapping defensive tackles. Last season, the interior duo often masked the weakness of Philly's run defense by shooting into the backfield and blowing up plays on their own. Indeed, Schwartz has always prioritized disruptiveness in the trenches above all. As defensive coordinator of the 2014 Bills, Buffalo ranked first in both adjusted sack rate and stuffed run percentage and in the process coaxed career years out of 3-4 misfits Jerry Hughes and Mario Williams. And during his tenure as Detroit's head coach, the Lions spent three of their seven first-round picks on defensive linemen (Ndamukong Suh, Nick Fairley, and Ezekiel Ansah) tailor-made for his scheme.

But Schwartz's scheme is far from infallible, and problematically, its biggest weakness stems from its signature strength. The nature of the wide-9 lends itself to yawning gaps in the running game, a problem Schwartz's past teams have always struggled to fix. Even his Bills defense only ranked 12th in run defense DVOA, and his Lions defenses ranked in the bottom half of the league in four of his five seasons at the helm. The defensive ends will not be aligned in the wide-9 on every snap, but when they are, there is extra pressure on the linebackers to hit the interior gaps and shed down-blocking offensive linemen. If you watched Philadelphia's Week 11 debacle against Doug Martin and the Buccaneers last season, you can imagine how poorly this might turn out for the Birds in 2016.

Schwartz brought over a couple players from Buffalo in Leodis McKelvin and Nigel Bradham, both of whom should compete for niche roles as a nickel corner and base package linebacker, respectively. However, his fridge is largely stocked with the groceries from the previous regime, and given the emphasis the front office will likely place on supporting Wentz, he might have to make do for years with Kelly's ingredients. As promising as the pass rush looks on paper, there is a learning curve for the entire defense, as well as legitimate questions surrounding the run defense and coverage.

Making do might ultimately be a theme for the next season or two in Philadelphia. The Eagles' path to contention is dependent on both Wentz developing quickly and Roseman shopping wisely on a budget. It's certainly far from impossible to imagine Philly pushing for a postseason spot this year. After all, their lone playoff berth under Kelly came on the strength of Nick Foles' impossibly efficient season. Most likely, though, 2016 will be a wait-and-see type of year, with the focus on continuing to reconstruct the roster and managing expectations surrounding Wentz for a fan base which can grow just a tad restless at times. The day of reckoning will eventually arrive for this era of Eagles football, but it won't come this season.

Sterling Xie

2015 Eagles Stats by Week

Wk	vs.	W-L	PF	PA	YDF	YDA	TO	Total	Off	Def	ST
1	at ATL	L	24	26	399	395	0	-28%	-9%	10%	-10%
2	DAL	L	10	20	226	359	-1	-57%	-43%	2%	-12%
3	at NYJ	W	24	17	231	323	3	53%	-3%	-44%	11%
4	at WAS	L	20	23	320	417	-1	2%	4%	1%	-1%
5	NO	W	39	17	519	388	2	38%	3%	-29%	7%
6	NYG	W	27	7	428	247	-1	44%	-14%	-56%	2%
7	at CAR	L	16	27	349	394	2	-1%	-4%	-5%	-2%
8	BYE										
9	at DAL	W	33	27	459	411	1	10%	20%	9%	-1%
10	MIA	L	19	20	436	289	-1	-25%	-25%	-14%	-14%
11	TB	L	17	45	383	521	-3	-80%	-45%	35%	0%
12	at DET	L	14	45	227	430	-1	-92%	-45%	42%	-5%
13	at NE	W	35	28	248	427	1	33%	-3%	-11%	26%
14	BUF	W	23	20	348	412	1	3%	-6%	2%	10%
15	ARI	L	17	40	424	493	-4	-18%	0%	30%	12%
16	WAS	L	24	38	398	418	-2	-53%	-19%	38%	4%
17	at NYG	W	35	30	435	502	-1	1%	25%	25%	1%

Trends and Splits

	Offense	Rank	Defense	Rank
Total DVOA	-10.1%	26	3.0%	17
Unadjusted VOA	-8.1%	26	5.6%	16
Weighted Trend	-10.9%	25	11.0%	26
Variance	4.4%	6	8.2%	29
Average Opponent	2.8%	26	1.2%	12
Passing	-3.6%	26	5.7%	14
Rushing	-8.1%	17	-0.4%	28
First Down	-13.8%	30	-5.2%	12
Second Down	-11.1%	24	4.9%	23
Third Down	-0.9%	15	16.7%	27
First Half	-11.3%	24	6.9%	23
Second Half	-8.9%	26	-1.3%	14
Red Zone	-9.4%	23	12.1%	25
Late and Close	-7.8%	21	-2.4%	16

Five-Year Performance

Year	W-L	Pyth W	Est W	PF	PA	TO	Total	Rk	Off	Rk	Def	Rk	ST	Rk	Off AGL	Rk	Def AGL	Rk	Off Age	Rk	Def Age	Rk	ST Age	Rk
2011	8-8	9.8	9.0	396	328	-14	13.5%	9	9.8%	8	-3.7%	11	0.0%	17	10.5	3	11.4	5	26.7	20	26.9	17	25.7	29
2012	4-12	3.9	4.5	280	444	-24	-22.4%	28	-10.8%	25	9.4%	26	-2.2%	23	65.2	32	8.1	2	26.8	17	26.5	23	25.6	27
2013	10-6	9.4	10.2	442	382	+12	15.2%	8	22.9%	3	4.9%	23	-2.8%	25	21.2	7	11.0	4	27.5	11	26.2	21	26.0	19
2014	10-6	9.7	9.7	474	400	-8	12.8%	7	1.1%	13	-3.3%	10	8.3%	1	32.2	18	16.4	2	27.2	11	26.9	13	26.9	1
2015	7-9	6.7	6.8	377	430	-5	-11.2%	22	-10.1%	26	3.0%	17	1.9%	10	23.7	10	28.3	17	27.2	11	26.7	15	26.9	2

2015 Performance Based on Most Common Personnel Groups

PHI Offense					PHI Offense vs. Opponents						PHI Defense					PHI Defense vs. Opponents			
Pers	Freq	Yds	DVOA	Run%	Pers	Freq	Yds	DVOA	Run%		Pers	Freq	Yds	DVOA		Pers	Freq	Yds	DVOA
11	70%	5.5	-7.1%	30%	Base	11%	4.8	-12.0%	59%		Base	33%	6.5	17.8%		11	58%	5.6	0.8%
12	25%	5.7	9.0%	60%	Nickel	74%	5.4	-7.3%	39%		Nickel	48%	5.5	-4.7%		12	18%	6.6	18.8%
21	3%	3.1	-62.9%	37%	Dime+	14%	6.1	11.8%	17%		Dime+	19%	5.4	-6.4%		21	6%	8.3	21.4%
10	1%	1.5	-116.4%	63%							Goal Line	1%	1.0	12.4%		13	4%	3.8	-20.1%
																10	3%	5.4	-57.5%
																22	3%	3.2	-11.4%

Strategic Tendencies

Run/Pass		Rk	Formation		Rk	Pass Rush		Rk	Secondary		Rk	Strategy		Rk
Runs, first half	38%	15	Form: Single Back	93%	1	Rush 3	7.3%	14	4 DB	33%	17	Play action	21%	9
Runs, first down	44%	24	Form: Empty Back	6%	22	Rush 4	67.9%	13	5 DB	48%	24	Avg Box (Off)	6.07	30
Runs, second-long	40%	2	Pers: 3+ WR	71%	6	Rush 5	19.9%	20	6+ DB	19%	8	Avg Box (Def)	6.10	27
Runs, power sit.	71%	2	Pers: 2+ TE/6+ OL	26%	26	Rush 6+	4.9%	22	CB by Sides	91%	4	Offensive Pace	23.94	1
Runs, behind 2H	27%	13	Pers: 6+ OL	0%	32	Sacks by LB	52.6%	13	S/CB Cover Ratio	28%	7	Defensive Pace	30.61	24
Pass, ahead 2H	43%	26	Shotgun/Pistol	94%	1	Sacks by DB	5.3%	22	DB Blitz	5%	31	Go for it on 4th	1.34	7

The Eagles set a new all-time record for using shotgun (or pistol) formations, breaking the previous record of 86 percent—set by themselves in 2013 and 2014. However, they didn't set an all-time record for pace again. In both situation-neutral pace and total pace, they were a little bit slower than they had been the year before. ☞ The Eagles had the 30th-ranked passing attack in the red zone (-52.9% DVOA), but the fourth-ranked rushing attack (29.6%). Alas, that didn't really balance out, as Philly's offense finished 23rd overall in red zone DVOA. ☞ Have you missed the draw play, Eagles fans? Don't worry, it's coming back. The Eagles were the only team that didn't use a single running back draw in 2015, but Doug Pederson's Chiefs ranked fourth in the league using such runs. ☞ For the second straight year, Philly was the only team not to use an extra offensive lineman on any play. That one is less likely to change, as Kansas City rarely used six linemen either. ☞ We only recorded opponents blitzing the Eagles on 17 percent of pass plays. Only the Giants faced fewer blitzes. However, blitzes definitely worked, as the Eagles gained 6.9 yards per play with a standard pass rush but 4.6 yards per play with five or more pass-rushers. ☞ The Eagles compiled a -36.2% DVOA on passes thrown behind the line of scrimmage, by far the worst in the league. No team called more running back screens than Philadelphia's 49, but the Eagles' DVOA on those plays was -46.8%, which ranked 24th. ☞ On the other hand, the Eagles were excellent at defending screens, compiling a -45.3% DVOA against running back screens and a -45.8% DVOA against wide receiver and tight end screens. Overall, Philly's -27.1% DVOA on passes behind the line of scrimmage ranked third in the league. ☞ Only 16.7 percent of passes against the Eagles went to tight ends, the lowest figure in the league. ☞ The Eagles had a top-10 pass defense on first and second downs, but ranked just 27th defending the pass on third down.

Passing

Player	DYAR	DVOA	Plays	NtYds	Avg	YAC	C%	TD	Int
S.Bradford	107	-8.2%	560	3512	6.3	5.6	65.3%	19	14
M.Sanchez*	-227	-46.9%	100	562	5.6	5.4	64.8%	4	4

Rushing

Player	DYAR	DVOA	Plays	Yds	Avg	TD	Fum	Suc
D.Murray*	-29	-12.1%	193	704	3.6	6	2	45%
R.Mathews	133	20.4%	108	539	5.0	6	3	53%
D.Sproles	80	14.8%	83	317	3.8	3	0	49%
K.Barner	30	18.3%	28	124	4.4	0	1	54%
S.Bradford	-43	-76.7%	13	40	3.1	0	3	-

Receiving

Player	DYAR	DVOA	Plays	Ctch	Yds	Y/C	YAC	TD	C%
J.Matthews	112	-1.8%	128	85	1002	11.8	4.9	8	66%
N.Agholor	-31	-21.3%	44	23	279	12.1	4.0	1	52%
R.Cooper*	20	-6.2%	41	21	327	15.6	3.0	2	51%
J.Huff	89	13.5%	40	27	312	11.6	6.7	3	68%
M.Austin*	-10	-16.8%	31	13	224	17.2	4.7	1	42%
R.Randle	167	10.0%	90	57	801	14.1	3.6	8	63%
Z.Ertz	56	0.2%	112	75	853	11.4	4.0	2	67%
B.Celek	107	36.8%	35	27	398	14.7	6.3	3	77%
D.Sproles	-50	-24.9%	83	55	388	7.1	6.5	1	66%
D.Murray*	13	-9.3%	55	44	322	7.3	8.7	1	80%
R.Mathews	-11	-22.2%	28	20	146	7.3	7.6	1	71%
K.Barner	-36	-65.6%	12	9	22	2.4	4.8	0	75%

Offensive Line

Player	Pos	Age	GS	Snaps	Pen	Sk	Pass	Run	Player	Pos	Age	GS	Snaps	Pen	Sk	Pass	Run
Allen Barbre	LG	32	16/16	1156	6	0.5	3.5	4.0	Dennis Kelly	G	26	14/2	393	3	1.5	3.5	1.5
Lane Johnson	RT	26	16/16	1156	13	5.0	7.0	5.0	Andrew Gardner	RG	30	3/3	176	1	0.0	3.0	1.0
Jason Kelce	C	29	16/16	1156	9	0.0	2.0	9.5	Stefen Wisniewski	C	27	16/16	1058	2	2.0	4.0	1.0
Matt Tobin	RG	26	16/13	982	3	4.5	12.5	3.0	Brandon Brooks	RG	27	14/14	983	6	1.0	5.0	5.0
Jason Peters	LT	34	14/14	761	11	4.5	9.5	4.0									

Year	Yards	ALY	Rank	Power	Rank	Stuff	Rank	2nd Lev	Rank	Open Field	Rank	Sacks	ASR	Rank	Press	Rank	F-Start	Cont.
2013	5.02	3.71	25	72%	7	20%	21	1.57	1	1.24	2	46	9.4%	31	28.2%	26	14	48
2014	4.36	3.52	29	81%	1	21%	26	1.24	9	0.93	6	32	4.9%	9	26.7%	24	17	27
2015	4.09	3.25	30	84%	1	21%	18	1.21	10	0.81	13	37	6.6%	20	20.8%	4	20	34
2015 ALY by direction:			Left End 2.89 (28)			Left Tackle 2.87 (29)			Mid/Guard 3.77 (19)			Right Tackle 2.53 (31)			Right End 3.12 (22)			

Between Lane Johnson, Jason Kelce, and Jason Peters, the Eagles started three of the 30 most penalty-prone offensive linemen in the league. That's not great. ☞ Allen Barbre was the Eagles' offensive lineman in 2015 with the best rate of snaps per blown block, missing a block just once every 154.3 snaps. However, Barbre is not a lock to keep his starting spot, with veteran Stefan Wisniewski (formerly of Jacksonville and Oakland) or rookie third-rounder Isaac Seumalo (Oregon State) competing to supplant him at left guard. ☞ It's clear Doug Pederson values athleticism and light feet in his interior linemen. Wisniewski, Seumalo, and Brandon Brooks all possess these qualities, with both veterans having played in zone schemes. Pederson's run game will likely provide a mix of zone- and gap-blocking runs, based on what we saw in Kansas City. ☞ It's incredible that Jason Peters only missed two games last year. Peters exited portions of nine different games due to injury, usually the result of a persistent back ailment. Peters' toughness and history of production is unquestionable, but the 34-year-old is likely nearing the finish line.

Defensive Front Seven

Defensive Line	Age	Pos	G	Snaps	Plays	TmPct	Rk	Stop	Dfts	BTkl	Runs	St%	Rk	RuYd	Rk	Sack	Hit	Hur	Dsrpt
Fletcher Cox	26	DE	16	982	72	8.0%	9	54	20	5	57	70%	57	3.4	79	9.5	11	34.0	2
Bennie Logan	27	DT	14	584	55	7.0%	19	48	12	6	51	88%	10	2.0	35	1.0	1	3.5	0
Cedric Thornton*	28	DE	13	493	33	4.5%	51	22	4	1	30	67%	68	3.3	78	1.0	2	9.0	0
Vinny Curry	28	DE	16	427	12	1.3%	--	11	6	0	7	86%	--	2.4	--	3.5	12	15.0	0
Beau Allen	25	DT	16	341	29	3.2%	--	21	3	0	26	73%	--	2.7	--	0.0	0	0.0	1
Taylor Hart	25	DE	14	327	27	3.4%	--	12	1	1	25	44%	--	3.8	--	0.0	1	1.0	0

Edge Rushers	Age	Pos	G	Snaps	Plays	TmPct	Rk	Stop	Dfts	BTkl	Runs	St%	Rk	RuYd	Rk	Sack	Hit	Hur	Dsrpt
					Overall						vs. Run					Pass Rush			
Connor Barwin	30	OLB	16	1051	61	6.8%	13	36	15	4	35	49%	96	6.3	97	7.0	10	21.0	5
Brandon Graham	28	OLB	16	856	50	5.6%	36	30	17	8	32	53%	94	2.4	48	6.5	5	17.0	1

Linebackers	Age	Pos	G	Snaps	Plays	TmPct	Rk	Stop	Dfts	BTkl	Runs	St%	Rk	RuYd	Rk	Sack	Hit	Hur	Tgts	Suc%	Rk	AdjYd	Rk	PD	Int
					Overall						vs. Run					Pass Rush			vs. Pass						
Mychal Kendricks	26	ILB	13	628	85	11.6%	49	44	17	15	56	59%	57	3.5	43	3.0	4	7	20	53%	48	6.4	39	2	0
DeMeco Ryans*	32	ILB	14	604	54	6.9%	77	30	3	7	33	61%	54	4.4	77	0.0	1	1.5	15	60%	28	5.9	33	5	1
Kiko Alonso*	26	ILB	11	472	44	7.1%	75	19	6	3	23	57%	69	4.3	74	0.0	0	2	20	41%	64	7.1	53	2	1
Jordan Hicks	24	ILB	8	450	52	11.6%	50	23	7	7	23	65%	39	3.4	36	1.0	0	5	18	49%	53	6.8	48	2	2
Nigel Bradham	27	OLB	11	729	60	11.2%	51	33	11	8	31	65%	42	4.2	70	0.5	2	3	21	56%	36	7.2	54	2	0

Year	Yards	ALY	Rank	Power	Rank	Stuff	Rank	2nd Level	Rank	Open Field	Rank	Sacks	ASR	Rank	Press	Rank
2013	3.61	3.89	17	68%	21	18%	20	0.98	3	0.33	1	37	6.7%	19	23.8%	21
2014	3.64	3.72	11	80%	30	21%	11	1.02	7	0.48	4	49	7.1%	10	29.6%	1
2015	4.57	4.00	23	74%	29	17%	27	1.18	22	1.04	29	37	6.8%	13	24.9%	19
2015 ALY by direction:		Left End 3.65 (18)			Left Tackle 4.33 (27)			Mid/Guard 4.16 (25)			Right Tackle 4.37 (27)				Right End 3.63 (20)	

Fletcher Cox isn't the best defender in the NFL, despite what the guaranteed money on his monstrous nine-figure extension might suggest. Nevertheless, he more than doubled his hurry total from 2014, finishing sixth in the category among all front seven players. The hope is that moving Cox to a true 3-technique position will maximize his disruptive potential even further, placing him alongside the likes of Aaron Donald and Gerald McCoy in the league hierarchy. ☞ Even if he's not a natural fit for Jim Schwartz's 4-3, the Eagles need to find a place for Connor Barwin. The Macklemore doppleganger accrued more than 20 hurries for the third straight season, finished tied for fourth in disruptions (combining batted passes with incompletions caused by hitting the quarterback while throwing) and had a broken-tackle rate of under 10 percent for the third straight year. He was also versatile enough to play both end positions and even rush from the interior on occasion. Philly will not be a better front seven without Barwin on the field. ☞ After a big step forward in pass coverage two years ago, Mychal Kendricks gave back many of his gains in 2015. Kendricks remains a strong blitzer from the second level, but the Eagles could really use a healthy season from him to form a dynamic linebacker pairing with Jordan Hicks.

Defensive Secondary

Secondary	Age	Pos	G	Snaps	Plays	TmPct	Rk	Stop	Dfts	BTkl	Runs	St%	Rk	RuYd	Rk	Tgts	Tgt%	Rk	Dist	Suc%	Rk	AdjYd	Rk	PD	Int
					Overall						vs. Run					vs. Pass									
Malcolm Jenkins	29	FS/CB	16	1211	113	12.6%	15	56	29	14	38	61%	5	4.8	7	55	11.6%	59	10.8	64%	18	6.3	23	10	2
Walter Thurmond*	29	SS	16	1197	78	8.7%	51	32	15	12	36	47%	20	8.5	53	31	6.6%	26	14.5	46%	59	10.8	67	8	3
Byron Maxwell*	28	CB	14	908	74	9.4%	25	28	10	3	12	58%	13	8.3	47	72	20.3%	43	13.4	46%	64	9.5	71	10	2
Nolan Carroll	29	CB	11	754	66	10.7%	7	24	8	4	14	21%	65	14.7	72	53	18.0%	24	13.0	47%	58	8.3	49	9	2
E.J. Biggers*	29	CB	16	563	46	5.1%	--	15	6	6	8	25%	--	10.5	--	46	21.0%	--	9.6	53%	--	6.8	--	7	0
Eric Rowe	24	CB	16	503	35	3.9%	--	9	3	4	5	20%	--	12.6	--	49	25.0%	--	15.0	58%	--	5.9	--	6	1
Ed Reynolds	25	FS	6	310	22	6.5%	--	3	2	6	6	33%	--	4.8	--	5	3.7%	--	26.0	46%	--	14.8	--	1	1
Chris Maragos	29	FS	15	304	9	1.1%	--	2	1	2	6	17%	--	12.8	--	1	0.4%	--	3.0	100%	--	-0.6	--	0	0
Rodney McLeod	26	FS	16	1154	85	9.4%	42	25	11	9	48	25%	57	12.9	67	13	3.6%	3	16.2	59%	33	8.3	49	2	1
Leodis McKelvin	31	CB	9	388	41	9.4%	--	19	11	4	6	33%	--	13.2	--	45	27.2%	--	13.5	59%	--	7.1	--	9	2

Year	Pass D Rank	vs. #1 WR	Rk	vs. #2 WR	Rk	vs. Other WR	Rk	vs. TE	Rk	vs. RB	Rk
2013	25	2.6%	21	2.3%	16	12.8%	24	10.0%	24	5.8%	21
2014	18	10.2%	24	4.4%	20	-6.1%	11	0.2%	19	19.7%	28
2015	14	7.8%	23	-5.1%	13	-12.4%	6	4.7%	19	-0.8%	15

Malcolm Jenkins was the stalwart in an otherwise wobbly secondary last season, playing multiple roles as a box safety, a free safety, and a slot corner. However, Jenkins' greatest impact was near the line of scrimmage, as he frequently knifed through gaps on rush attempts to create negative plays in the backfield. Perhaps Philly had this in mind when they signed Rodney McLeod away from the Rams, as McLeod's ranginess should afford Jenkins the freedom to play more near the line of scrimmage. ☞ Eric Rowe was one target short of qualifying to be ranked in our cornerback coverage stats. However, Rowe's adjusted success rate would have ranked 15th among those qualifying corners, one spot ahead of Defensive Rookie of the Year Marcus Peters. ⮌ Rowe may be penciled in to one cornerback spot, but the other two spots in the nickel package are up for grabs. Nolan Carroll had issues preventing big downfield plays and was only slightly better than the much-beleaguered (now departed) Byron Maxwell. Leodis McKelvin had a career year under Jim Schwartz in 2014, finishing 12th in adjusted yards per target, but injuries and regression to the mean intervened last season. Maybe JaCorey Shepherd can re-emerge on the scene: the 2015 sixth-round pick from Kansas surprisingly held the inside track for the slot corner role before tearing his ACL in training camp last August. ⮌ Seventh-round picks don't usually register on the radar, but watch for cornerback Jalen Mills. The LSU product would have gone higher had it not been for injury and character red flags. If he can hold himself together physically and mentally, Mills possesses the versatility and coverage instincts to earn a role, particularly if injuries arise.

Special Teams

Year	DVOA	Rank	FG/XP	Rank	Net Kick	Rank	Kick Ret	Rank	Net Punt	Rank	Punt Ret	Rank	Hidden	Rank
2013	-2.8%	25	-2.8	24	-12.5	31	-0.9	15	5.4	10	-3.4	18	3.3	11
2014	8.3%	1	3.5	9	9.8	2	12.3	2	1.7	14	14.2	1	23.5	1
2015	1.9%	10	-2.9	26	0.7	15	-0.2	15	1.0	18	11.1	2	-13.8	32

The Eagles had as large a split as you'll see between the punt unit and the punt return unit. Darren Sproles was once again indispensable, taking two returns to the house and leading the league in net value. The unit also returned a blocked punt for a touchdown against New England, one of the craziest special teams fueled upsets in recent memory. However, Donnie Jones was a disaster, getting two of his punts blocked and seeing both the net value and the gross value of his punts decline for the third straight year. ⮌ Cody Parkey should win back the kicking job over Caleb Sturgis. Parkey fared significantly better on field goals in 2014 than Sturgis did in 2015; so long as the former recovers from a groin injury which sidelined him after three weeks last season, it's his job to lose. ⮌ The Eagles weren't a particularly unlucky team overall, but yeesh, those hidden special teams points. Eagles opponents did not miss a single field goal attempt all season.

Pittsburgh Steelers

2015 record: 10-6	**Total DVOA:** 21.3% (7th)	**2016 Mean Projection:** 10.1 wins	**On the Clock (0-4):** 2%
Pythagorean Wins: 10.7 (7th)	**Offense:** 17.3% (3rd)	**Postseason Odds:** 66.9%	**Mediocrity (5-7):** 13%
Snap-Weighted Age: 27.4 (4th)	**Defense:** -3.8% (11th)	**Super Bowl Odds:** 18.1%	**Playoff Contender (8-10):** 39%
Average Opponent: 4.9% (7th)	**Special Teams:** 0.1% (18th)	**Proj. Avg. Opponent:** -1.7% (25th)	**Super Bowl Contender (11+):** 45%

2015: Never send to know for whom the Bell tolls, it tolls for too many in Denver loss.

2016: Steelers petition the league to only suspend Tom Brady for Week 7.

Few franchises in sports are as stable as the Pittsburgh Steelers. Since 1992, Pittsburgh has only had two head coaches, two general managers and three losing seasons. Ever since drafting Ben Roethlisberger in 2004, the Steelers have finished at least .500 and outscored their opponents in 12 consecutive seasons. Only seven other teams have done this since 1940, including the 1972-1984 Steelers. Bringing home half as many championships will keep this era behind the "Steel Curtain" days, but what the Steelers have done in the salary-cap era is remarkable. Only New England, also on that list with a 15-year streak, has accomplished more—but we'll get to the Patriots limiting Pittsburgh's success later.

A year ago, no team came closer to preventing Denver from winning its third Super Bowl title than the Steelers. New England and Carolina trailed the Broncos wire-to-wire in their postseason matchups. But Pittsburgh went into Denver with an injured Roethlisberger, without Antonio Brown or its top two running backs, led for 43 minutes and 22 seconds, and still gained more yards (396) than any other offense did against the Broncos all year. The Steelers were driving in Denver territory in the fourth quarter when a fumble by backup running back Fitzgerald Toussaint changed everything.

This season, our numbers favor Pittsburgh for the No. 1 seed in the AFC. Conventional wisdom says that if the Steelers can just keep their top players healthy for a playoff run, they are as well-positioned as anyone to go all the way. However, coach Mike Tomlin has not had much luck in this department. His teams were relatively healthy at the end of 2008 and 2010, and the Steelers reached the Super Bowl in both seasons. In his other four playoff appearances, Tomlin has gone one-and-done three times, and flirted with a fourth had it not been for a total meltdown by Vontaze Burfict and Adam Jones (partially aided by Steelers assistant coach Joey Porter) in Cincinnati this past January.

Consider the impact and lack of time to adjust to these injuries:

- **2007:** Running back Willie Parker was leading the NFL in rushing yards when he fractured his fibula in Week 16. In the wild-card loss to Jacksonville, Roethlisberger handed the ball off 22 times for 31 yards.
- **2011:** Leading rusher Rashard Mendenhall tore his ACL in Week 17. Center Maurkice Pouncey and safety Ryan Clark were also unable to play in the "Tebow 316" wild-card loss in Denver, but the biggest problem was Roethlisberger's high-ankle sprain. He was ineffective in his final three starts after the injury.
- **2014:** All-Pro running back Le'Veon Bell suffered a hyperextended knee in Week 17. Ben Tate was signed just days before the wild-card loss against Baltimore. In the fourth quarter, Tate flubbed a pass that turned into an interception, which the Ravens turned into a 30-15 lead.
- **2015:** Bell was lost with a torn MCL at the season's midway point; DeAngelo Williams was fantastic as his replacement but injured his ankle in Week 16 and never returned to action. The wild-card win in Cincinnati was costly as Roethlisberger sprained his AC joint and Brown's dominant season was ended by a concussion. Brown was unable to play against Denver, a defense he had torched for 16 catches, 189 yards and two touchdowns a month earlier.

Unfortunately, plans for the offense to be at full strength in 2016 went up in smoke with the year-long suspension of wide receiver Martavis Bryant for violating the league's substance-abuse policy. Pittsburgh has built an offense with a passer (Roethlisberger), runner (Bell) and receiver (Brown) each capable of leading their position in yardage. The addition of Bryant in 2014 looked to give the Steelers a dominant, balanced setup arguably not seen since the "Greatest Show on Turf" Rams at the turn of the millennium. But this series of injuries and suspensions means that the four skill players will have only played together in 11 of their first 51 games as teammates (including this season). Even in their lone appearance together last season, Bell tore his MCL in the second quarter against Cincinnati.

Throw in the retirement of Heath Miller, who was such a rock at tight end for 11 seasons, and it might seem odd to project the Steelers as a top-tier offense again. However, this offense has gotten used to change, and there may not be a better set of "triplets" in the NFL than Roethlisberger, Bell, and Brown. We used to spend these Pittsburgh chapters writing about how bad the offensive line was, but Mike Munchak has done wonders in coaching the line the last two years. How many offenses could lose their All-Pro center for the season and their left tackle for 10 games and still finish eighth in adjusted line yards while their primary quarterback had the second-lowest pressure rate in the league?

2016 Steelers Schedule

Week	Opp.	Week	Opp.	Week	Opp.
1	at WAS (Mon.)	7	NE	13	NYG
2	CIN	8	BYE	14	at BUF
3	at PHI	9	at BAL	15	at CIN
4	KC	10	DAL	16	BAL (Xmas)
5	NYJ	11	at CLE	17	CLE
6	at MIA	12	at IND (Thu.)		

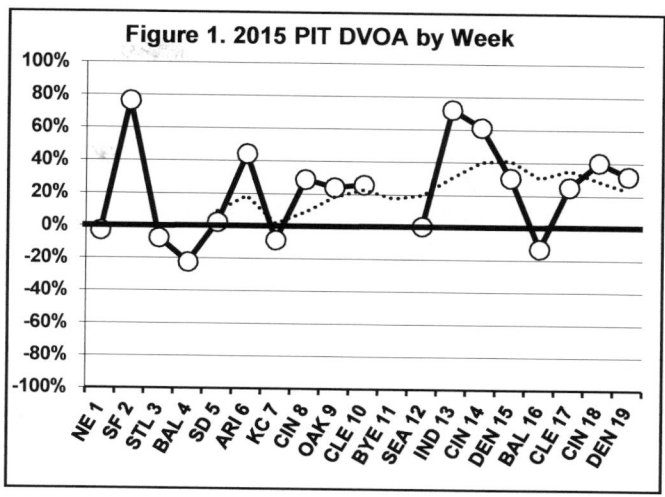

Figure 1. 2015 PIT DVOA by Week

Make no mistake about it: Bryant will be missed and the offense is more dangerous with him, but the 2016 highlight reel is more likely to take a hit than the offensive production will. Bryant's athletic ability made for some sick plays, like the run after the catch on his 88-yard touchdown against Arizona or the postseason front-flip touchdown in Cincinnati. But those drives can be replaced with a "boring" Bell run for six points, or a bomb to Darrius Heyward-Bey where he makes the catch look tougher than it had to be. While Miller was an excellent security blanket for Roethlisberger, the Steelers made a smart pickup in San Diego's Ladarius Green, who was tired of waiting for Antonio Gates to retire. The Steelers may lose a little in the blocking department, but Green improves the position's athleticism and can do some damage down the seam that Miller was getting a bit too slow for.

As long as Roethlisberger is upright, you can trust the offense to be potent and challenge defenses downfield. In 2005, Roethlisberger led the most vertical passing offense in the NFL with a receiving corps of Hines Ward, Antwaan Randle El, and Cedrick Wilson. As much as he has clamored for a tall receiver, he has had plenty of success with the shorter guys and can manufacture big plays in a variety of ways. In the first two games of 2015 when Bryant and Bell were suspended, Roethlisberger was on point, completing 9-of-13 passes thrown at least 25 yards beyond the line of scrimmage. Despite missing a quarter of the season, Roethlisberger finished 2015 with 23 such completions, the most in the NFL. On third downs, Roethlisberger's ALEX (plus-6.8) was the second highest in a season since 2006.

The loss of Bryant would also be more significant if Brown was not on one of the most dominant receiving runs in NFL history. In the 12 games Roethlisberger and Brown played together last season, Brown averaged 9.9 catches for 133 yards. Projected to a 16-game season, that would be 159 catches for 2,132 yards, smashing the NFL's single-season records. If these two can stay healthy all season, those records are in danger. Do not be fooled by "Bryant drawing the coverage." Brown finished 2013 with 110 catches for 1,499 yards while Bryant was in college and Emmanuel Sanders, not yet at his Denver form, was the No. 2 receiver. This is the dominant connection in the NFL right now.

Offensive coordinator Todd Haley's goal of averaging 30 points per game may be optimistic, but this offense showed some aggressive tendencies last season. Pittsburgh was 8-of-11 on 2-point conversions (all passes), the most attempts in the league and a new record for conversions in a season. Some

of the decision-making on when to go for it was puzzling, but Roethlisberger's suggestion this offseason has been to go for two after every touchdown. That would make things easier on Tomlin, but it really is an advantage the Steelers should explore more in this new era of the 33-yard extra point.

There may be some extra motivation for this offense to get things done this season while they are still together. Performing your best in a contract year is an excellent way to cash in. Just ask Von Miller, Malik Jackson, and Josh Norman after Super Bowl 50, or the all-time example of Joe Flacco. After this season, Bell, wide receiver Markus Wheaton and guard David DeCastro are all unrestricted free agents. Pittsburgh has just over $51 million available in 2017 cap space according to overthecap.com, but that may fill up quickly as those players get paid.

Bell has already dropped a hint for his next contract with a lyric in one of his rap songs: "I'm at the top and if not I'm the closest, I'ma need $15 a year and they know this." It is hard to see Pittsburgh shelling out $15 million per year for a running back, but if Bell has another All-Pro season, some team probably will. This could be a franchise-tag situation. Given that Oakland just made Kelechi Osemele (zero Pro Bowls) the highest-paid guard in NFL history, DeCastro will likely aim for at least $12 million per season to top it. Wheaton won't make that kind of money, but Bryant's off-field troubles keep giving him more opportunity to prove himself. With all of this money going around, Brown's 2012 deal (five years, $42 million) looks like a steal, as he is just 19th in average salary at his position. Hines Ward once held out successfully for a raise. Business may be booming now, but Brown must be a saint if he never threatens a holdout on this deal.

Usually, you have to spend some serious money to sustain greatness on one side of the ball. But the defense went down in price after so many stalwarts of the Dick LeBeau era retired. Keith Butler's long-awaited debut as defensive coordinator saw the defense climb from 30th to 11th in DVOA, the biggest improvement in 2015. Oh, the start was disastrous when the Steelers could not even line up properly on opening night in New England, but that was the Patriots and there were communication problems with the headsets. Things got better as the run defense returned to form, and while many big pass plays were given up, the turnovers finally came back as the Steelers intercepted 17 passes and recovered 13 fumbles.

Just as Tomlin let LeBeau have free reign with the 3-4 defense, Butler called the shots last year, and rarely strayed from the system. The Steelers blitzed 35.2 percent of the time under Butler after 35.9 percent in LeBeau's final season. Butler did nearly double the defensive back blitzes—only the Rams had more—to highlight one of William Gay's strengths. Butler also simplified the calls to help younger players contribute. This has some fans channeling the Bobs from *Office Space*, just wanting to ask Tomlin, "what would you say... you do here?" Tomlin came from a Tampa-2 background with expertise in coaching defensive backs. Since joining the Steelers, he has stuck faithfully with LeBeau's 3-4 system, and the Steelers have seen deteriorating defensive back play after neglecting the position for years, both in the draft and free agency.

In April, the Steelers finally addressed that weakness, drafting a defensive back in the first round for the first time since Troy Polamalu in 2003. One thing you can say about general manager Kevin Colbert is that he never forced the cornerback pick out of need in the past. In 2007, Tomlin's first year with the team, local product Darrelle Revis was snatched just one pick ahead of the Steelers by the Jets. That was a tough one to swallow, but outside of 2013 when the Steelers chose Jarvis Jones (17th) over Desmond Trufant (22nd) and Xavier Rhodes (25th), the right value for a corner was just never there.

Given some of the scouting reports on Miami's Artie Burns, Colbert may have forced the pick this time. The athletic traits are there for this track star, but some scouts saw average tape and had a third-round grade on the raw Burns. Pittsburgh has not been a hot spot for developing corners, but this is where Tomlin really needs to make an impact to get this secondary back on track. With Maryland safety Sean Davis chosen in the second round and last year's second-round pick, Ole Miss cornerback Senquez Golson, returning from a shoulder injury that cost him his entire rookie year, the Steelers have three first-time players to develop this season. An immediate impact seems unlikely, but this should be a big part of the future core of the secondary. Letting rookies get over some growing pains cannot be any worse than watching someone like Antwon Blake repeatedly give up completions and miss the most tackles (21) in the league.

Given the roster, it was almost guaranteed that Colbert would draft a cornerback in the first round. The offense is so complete, Cameron Heyward and Stephon Tuitt are leading the defensive line, and Colbert just spent three straight first-round picks on linebackers. What else was left, kicker Roberto Aguayo in the first round? Pittsburgh went through four kickers last year, but save that waste of a pick for Tampa Bay.

Of course, even though the Steelers may start four first-round linebackers this season, that position is the area of real concern. In this system, the outside linebackers need to flourish as pass rushers, yet Tuitt, Heyward, and Lawrence Timmons (who shared some of his pass coverage responsibilities with Ryan Shazier) led the team in sacks. The sack total (47) was nice, but Pittsburgh only ranked 24th in pressure rate (24.2 percent) and 14th in DVOA with pressure (-69.8%). That is not a Super Bowl-caliber defense, and a 37-year-old James Harrison led the team in hurries. Harrison is likely to retire after this season, but who is ready to take his place? Jarvis Jones did not have his fifth-year option picked up for good reason, and he will be a free agent after this season. Arthur Moats was more effective than rookie Bud Dupree, though you expect to see growth in Dupree's second year. Timmons will also be a free agent heading into his age-31 season, so that is another upcoming decision for the Steelers to make. He has been a very good player, but not one to break the bank for when you have to pay so many offensive players big-time money.

Pittsburgh lacks the talent of recent Super Bowl defenses, but the unit was playing well enough down the stretch. If the offense does its share while the defense makes even minor improvements in Butler's second year, there is enough here for a championship run in 2016. Remember, just one timely edge pressure or takeaway can swing a game entirely.

Even after running through the roster, you may still may not be convinced why Pittsburgh is our favorite to win the most games in the AFC. After all, this team needed Ryan Fitzpatrick to implode in Week 17 just to make the playoffs. Well, just check the rest of the conference. Denver is more likely to fall to 8-8 than return to the Super Bowl. Kansas City finished a game ahead of Pittsburgh last year, but a lot of that had to do with Roethlisberger missing that matchup. Baltimore has won five of the last six meetings with the Steelers, but the Ravens are more likely to be buried in the wild-card race with "been a long time since we were contenders" such as Buffalo, Oakland, and Jacksonville.

The Colts are usually contenders, and Andrew Luck is one of the few formidable foes to match scores with Roethlisberger, but Indianapolis has allowed 96 points to the Steelers in the last two matchups. Roethlisberger passed for 886 yards and 10 touchdowns with zero interceptions or sacks in those games, and the Colts have done little to strengthen that defense. Cincinnati is a more talented team, but rarely rises to the occasion to beat the Steelers in a meaningful game. In fact, one of the strangest splits in the NFL is Marvin Lewis having a better road record (6-7) against Pittsburgh than his embarrassing home record (2-13), which includes two playoff losses by his best teams.

Pittsburgh would probably welcome another January trip to Cincinnati, but the goal should be to get a first-round bye with home-field advantage. The biggest rival we have not mentioned, New England, has had a bye for the last six postseasons. Even with Tom Brady suspended for the first four games, the Patriots are favorites for another bye. But between that suspension and the Steelers getting New England at home in Week 7, Pittsburgh should have the inside track to the No. 1 seed.[1]

---

1 This is slightly complicated by the announcement as we finished this year's book that Le'Veon Bell will likely be suspended four games for missing a drug test. The season simulation referenced in this chapter does not account for that suspension.

For the Steelers to turn a good season with 10 or 11 wins into a great season with 12 or 13 wins, they have to stop coming up small in the "small games." Under Tomlin, the Steelers have built up a deserving reputation as a team that plays up or down to the competition, underperforming in games against lesser teams they were expected to beat. Since 2007, the Steelers lead the NFL with 15 losses in games pitting a winning team against a non-winning team (based on final record). Their overall record is 50-15 (.769) in those games, which is a little below the NFL average (.804). Point-spread data from Pro Football Reference shows that in games against non-winning teams, Tomlin's Steelers have been one of the most disappointing bets in the league (Table 1). The results have been especially disappointing on the road despite a fan base that travels as well as any.

As a double-digit favorite on the road, the Steelers are just 4-3 straight up and 1-6 against the spread. None of those games exemplify this better than the last one, Week 16 in Baltimore last season. Pittsburgh could not have been riding any higher. The Steelers had just scored at least 30 points in six consecutive games for the first time in franchise history. They came back from 17 points down to beat Denver in Week 15. Surely they could take care of the rival Ravens with the playoffs on the line, right? Injury-ravaged Baltimore was starting Ryan Mallett and several other players that were just signed in the last month. Yet, Pittsburgh had its worst DVOA (-12.7%) out of the 12 regular-season games with Roethlisberger at quarterback, and the 20-17 loss meant the Steelers needed help from the Bills in Week 17 just to make the playoffs. Pittsburgh was that close to missing the playoffs for the third time in four seasons, because it gave away another "gimme game."

Fans often complain that "we beat ourselves more than the opponent did," but Steelers fans have the best statistical evidence for this claim. Since 2004, the Steelers are the only team to actually outgain their opponents in yardage (plus-748) in games lost. But they've shot themselves in the foot with the worst turnover differential per game (minus-1.6) in losses since 2004. Pittsburgh's margin of defeat (8.5 points per game) is the second smallest, and a league-high 76.4 percent of the Steelers' losses since 2004 still saw the offense have an opportunity for a game-winning drive in the fourth quarter or overtime. The rest of the NFL's average is 57.0 percent.

Year after year, the Steelers are a tough out, unless the opponent is New England. Against that duo of Bill Belichick and Tom Brady, the Steelers are just 2-8 going back to 2001. Most of the games were not close either. In Pittsburgh's six losses with Roethlisberger at quarterback, the Steelers only had one fourth-quarter comeback opportunity (back in 2005).

Somehow these two teams have not met in the playoffs since the 2004 AFC Championship Game. Pittsburgh avoided New England in all three of its Super Bowl seasons, but that seems unlikely in this current AFC. The long-awaited rematch has been one game away from happening five times, and Denver was responsible for breaking up three of those opportunities. All five games would have been in New England, including three AFC Championship Games (2005, 2010, and 2015). Some of those matchups may have turned into bloodbaths for Pittsburgh, but we'll never know. It is worth noting that all nine of Belichick's playoff losses with New England have come in rematches from those regular seasons. Teams have used the experience of the first matchup to their advantage in the playoffs, but arguably Pittsburgh's biggest problem against the Patriots is the refusal to change the script.

LeBeau's scheme worked well against most of the league because it stopped the run and exposed bad quarterback play. Quarterbacks unable to diagnose things quickly would hold onto the ball, allowing the blitz to get home. Quarterbacks unskilled at pre-snap reads would get confused on identifying the pass-rushers and would throw into danger. The best quarterbacks tend to excel against the blitz and could pick this scheme apart with quick, short passes as the defensive backs usually gave up a lot of cushion. Throw in some tempo and no-huddle to disrupt the defense's attempt at creating confusion, and the top passers routinely shredded Pittsburgh's defense with few mistakes.

No team has taken advantage of this scheme more than the Patriots, and it goes back to the 2002 season opener when Brady dropped back to pass on 26 consecutive plays at one point. New England lacks an emotional attachment to establishing the run, which goes against conventional NFL coaching. In Tomlin's first crack against the Patriots, the undefeated 2007 juggernaut version, he watched Brady pass 47 times for 404 yards while the running game only had eight carries for 18 yards. The Patriots won 34-13, and most of the matchups since have looked similar with the Steelers always suffering mental lapses and getting caught in mismatches on defense while the pass rush is nonexistent.

If you look at advanced stats for the last five meetings since 2007, there are not any noticeable trends in how the Patriots' passing game attacks Pittsburgh. The closest one is

Table 1. Steelers Play Small in Small Games (2007-2015)

| Favored by | Split | Straight Up | | | | | Vs. Spread | | | |
		PIT	Pct.	Rk	NFL	Pct.	PIT	Pct.	NFL	Pct.
10-plus	All	16-4	.800	24 of 31	227-31-1	.878	8-12	.400	115-138-6	.456
10-plus	Road	4-3	.571	16 of 18	41-5	.891	1-6	.143	18-28	.391
7-plus	All	29-8	.784	24 of 32	505-102	.830	18-19	.486	295-303-12	.493
7-plus	Road	8-5	.615	23 of 28	117-39	.748	3-10	.231	72-83-2	.465
3-plus	All	49-19	.721	18 of 32	1027-335	.753	31-37	.456	687-635-44	.519
3-plus	Road	19-13	.594	25 of 32	350-126	.735	11-21	.344	253-209-15	.546

that in four of the five games, Brady's average pass traveled between 7.4 and 8.5 yards, which takes advantage of those cushions offered on the outside. In Pittsburgh's 25-17 win in 2011, Tomlin and LeBeau had one of their finest games. From the first two drives of the game, a new plan was apparent: let Roethlisberger control the clock with a Brady-like attack of short passes, and play more press coverage and get physical with the receivers. It was hardly a defensive clinic—Patriots' passing game finished at 39.3% DVOA—but it slowed Brady down while the Steelers played from ahead and controlled the ball for over 39 minutes. Pittsburgh needed a similar approach in last year's season opener, but got caught doing bizarre things like running on third-and-goal from the 5-yard line and putting young linebackers on islands with Rob Gronkowski (if he was covered at all). While some AFC coaches such as John Harbaugh and Gary Kubiak (even going back to his Denver days under Mike Shanahan) have had consistent success in matching wits with Belichick, Tomlin and his assistants have been repeatedly (and obviously) outclassed.

In looking at the 2016 schedule, Pittsburgh should face some good non-New England challenges along the way, but the overall slate is less daunting. The Steelers had one of last year's ten hardest schedules, and are projected with one of the ten easiest for this year. There are no trips to the Patriots or Seahawks this season. According to an article at CBSSports.com, the Steelers will travel just 5,138 miles all season, the lowest total in the league by more than 1,000 miles. The benefits of playing the mediocre NFC East extend beyond opponent strength, with quick trips to D.C. and Philadelphia. Pittsburgh also appreciates getting the Bengals in Week 2 with Vontaze Burfict serving his three-game suspension. Burfict was the tackler on the plays that injured Bell, Roethlisberger, and Brown last season.

But no game is bigger than hosting the Patriots in the national late-afternoon slot for Week 7. A Pittsburgh win could go a long way in securing home-field advantage, as well as removing a mental roadblock. But even the benefits of a win against New England could be thrown away with unexpected losses to losing teams. It may be asking a lot for the Steelers to stay healthy, be logically aggressive, and approach each game with the proper level of importance, but that really is what stands between this team and another trip to the Super Bowl.

Scott Kacsmar

2015 Steelers Stats by Week

Wk	vs.	W-L	PF	PA	YDF	YDA	TO	Total	Off	Def	ST
1	at NE	L	21	28	464	361	-1	-3%	35%	23%	-14%
2	SF	W	43	18	453	409	1	76%	80%	5%	1%
3	at STL	W	12	6	259	258	0	-7%	-2%	1%	-4%
4	BAL	L	20	23	263	356	2	-22%	-23%	-8%	-8%
5	at SD	W	24	20	349	406	1	3%	3%	6%	6%
6	ARI	W	25	13	310	469	3	44%	26%	-8%	11%
7	at KC	L	13	23	339	377	-3	-8%	4%	11%	-1%
8	CIN	L	10	16	356	296	-1	29%	4%	-34%	-9%
9	OAK	W	38	35	597	440	2	24%	32%	3%	-4%
10	CLE	W	30	9	459	342	1	26%	17%	-12%	-3%
11	BYE										
12	at SEA	L	30	39	538	436	-4	1%	24%	24%	1%
13	IND	W	45	10	522	240	1	72%	34%	-34%	5%
14	at CIN	W	33	20	354	385	2	61%	17%	-28%	16%
15	DEN	W	34	27	377	385	0	31%	41%	14%	4%
16	at BAL	L	17	20	308	386	-3	-13%	-2%	15%	4%
17	at CLE	W	28	12	379	263	1	25%	-21%	-46%	0%
18	at CIN	W	18	16	369	279	2	40%	-14%	-48%	7%
19	at DEN	L	16	23	396	324	-1	32%	41%	-1%	-10%

Trends and Splits

	Offense	Rank	Defense	Rank
Total DVOA	17.3%	3	-3.8%	11
Unadjusted VOA	16.2%	3	-4.5%	12
Weighted Trend	16.3%	2	-8.3%	8
Variance	6.5%	16	4.6%	18
Average Opponent	-3.0%	7	0.5%	16
Passing	31.9%	5	5.8%	15
Rushing	7.5%	3	-18.8%	5
First Down	21.7%	2	5.6%	21
Second Down	14.3%	6	-4.8%	10
Third Down	13.5%	8	-19.4%	5
First Half	17.6%	3	1.1%	17
Second Half	17.0%	3	-7.8%	8
Red Zone	27.2%	5	-37.1%	2
Late and Close	-3.0%	18	-16.3%	6

Five-Year Performance

Year	W-L	Pyth W	Est W	PF	PA	TO	Total	Rk	Off	Rk	Def	Rk	ST	Rk	Off AGL	Rk	Def AGL	Rk	Off Age	Rk	Def Age	Rk	ST Age	Rk
2011	12-4	11.1	11.3	325	227	-13	22.6%	4	11.4%	6	-9.4%	7	1.7%	9	33.2	19	27.3	18	26.4	25	29.1	1	26.2	19
2012	8-8	8.7	7.4	336	314	-10	-1.2%	18	-4.0%	19	-2.9%	13	-0.1%	17	64.3	31	19.1	9	26.5	21	29.2	1	25.9	20
2013	8-8	8.2	8.3	379	370	-4	0.9%	15	4.4%	12	4.0%	19	0.5%	16	55.3	28	27.5	16	26.4	25	28.4	1	25.7	25
2014	11-5	9.7	9.4	436	368	0	12.1%	8	22.5%	2	11.3%	30	0.9%	12	4.1	1	38.7	17	26.5	24	27.8	3	26.2	10
2015	10-6	10.7	10.8	423	319	+2	21.3%	7	17.3%	3	-3.8%	11	0.1%	18	43.2	23	23.9	9	28.2	5	27.0	11	26.2	14

2015 Performance Based on Most Common Personnel Groups

PIT Offense					PIT Offense vs. Opponents					PIT Defense				PIT Defense vs. Opponents			
Pers	Freq	Yds	DVOA	Run%	Pers	Freq	Yds	DVOA	Run%	Pers	Freq	Yds	DVOA	Pers	Freq	Yds	DVOA
11	66%	7.1	30.7%	24%	Base	28%	6.2	13.3%	54%	Base	26%	5.2	-5.2%	11	63%	5.8	-3.5%
12	12%	6.1	27.3%	44%	Nickel	52%	6.9	19.5%	30%	Nickel	65%	6.0	-2.2%	12	19%	6.3	14.3%
22	11%	5.9	-3.5%	64%	Dime+	18%	7.2	63.2%	16%	Dime+	7%	4.9	12.5%	21	5%	5.8	-12.1%
21	5%	5.6	1.1%	74%	Goal Line	1%	0.5	21.7%	82%	Goal Line	1%	-0.1	-42.9%	13	3%	3.5	-27.4%
621	1%	9.7	32.6%	67%	Big	1%	1.1	-138.4%	78%					10	2%	6.2	28.1%
														22	2%	3.7	-27.8%

Strategic Tendencies

Run/Pass		Rk	Formation		Rk	Pass Rush		Rk	Secondary		Rk	Strategy		Rk
Runs, first half	35%	30	Form: Single Back	78%	11	Rush 3	7.1%	16	4 DB	26%	25	Play action	14%	31
Runs, first down	44%	23	Form: Empty Back	8%	14	Rush 4	57.6%	22	5 DB	65%	5	Avg Box (Off)	6.24	17
Runs, second-long	31%	17	Pers: 3+ WR	68%	9	Rush 5	33.2%	2	6+ DB	7%	22	Avg Box (Def)	6.16	23
Runs, power sit.	50%	25	Pers: 2+ TE/6+ OL	27%	24	Rush 6+	2.1%	32	CB by Sides	66%	25	Offensive Pace	30.55	19
Runs, behind 2H	24%	18	Pers: 6+ OL	3%	15	Sacks by LB	53.2%	12	S/CB Cover Ratio	19%	25	Defensive Pace	30.21	14
Pass, ahead 2H	56%	5	Shotgun/Pistol	67%	11	Sacks by DB	14.9%	5	DB Blitz	19%	2	Go for it on 4th	0.94	16

The Steelers running game was much better in 2015 when there were two players lined up in the backfield, with 5.9 yards per carry and 16.5% DVOA compared to 4.0 yards per carry and -2.0% DVOA from single-back sets. However, the Steelers' numbers were opposite in 2014, so this may have been fluke variation rather than an argument for putting David Johnson in the Pro Bowl. ☞ Pittsburgh receivers dropped just 16 passes by our count, and were second in dropped-pass rate at 2.8 percent of passes. ☞ The Steelers were one of two offenses to have a positive DVOA when running the ball in second-and-long situations. Pittsburgh's 2.2% DVOA edged out the Rams for the best in the league. ☞ The Steelers dramatically improved their pass defense on short passes compared to the year before, but deep passes were still a problem. The Steelers ranked ninth in defensive DVOA against short passes, but 26th against deep passes. (In 2014, these ranks were 27th and 28th, respectively.) ☞ Pittsburgh allowed 7.3 yards per pass with a standard pass rush but only 5.5 yards per pass when blitzing. (That average includes 10.3 yards per pass with six pass-rushers, but the Steelers only sent six pass-rushers 13 times all season.)

Passing

Player	DYAR	DVOA	Plays	NtYds	Avg	YAC	C%	TD	Int
B.Roethlisberger	1114	22.1%	489	3809	7.8	4.6	68.2%	21	16
M.Vick*	-207	-57.4%	75	321	4.3	4.8	61.5%	2	0
L.Jones	37	-1.5%	57	496	8.7	8.8	58.2%	3	4

Rushing

Player	DYAR	DVOA	Plays	Yds	Avg	TD	Fum	Suc
D.Williams	184	12.1%	200	907	4.5	11	3	50%
L.Bell	162	28.1%	113	556	4.9	3	0	50%
F.Toussaint	-31	-52.3%	18	42	2.3	0	0	39%
M.Vick*	15	12.1%	14	105	7.5	0	1	-
M.Bryant*	37	103.6%	5	37	7.4	1	0	-
J.Todman*	6	34.9%	4	22	5.5	0	0	75%
W.Johnson*	-7	-31.2%	4	7	1.8	1	0	25%

Receiving

Player	DYAR	DVOA	Plays	Ctch	Yds	Y/C	YAC	TD	C%
A.Brown	517	19.7%	193	136	1841	13.5	4.4	10	70%
M.Bryant	75	-2.4%	92	50	765	15.3	7.0	6	54%
M.Wheaton	159	12.4%	79	44	749	17.0	3.6	5	56%
D.Heyward-Bey	25	-4.6%	39	21	314	15.0	3.5	2	54%
H.Miller*	48	1.2%	82	61	537	8.8	3.6	2	74%
J.James	-5	-13.3%	11	8	56	7.0	2.5	1	73%
L.Green	78	11.8%	63	37	429	11.6	6.0	4	59%
D.Williams	109	30.5%	47	40	367	9.2	9.2	0	85%
L.Bell	-10	-21.3%	26	24	136	5.7	5.8	0	92%

Offensive Line

Player	Pos	Age	GS	Snaps	Pen	Sk	Pass	Run	Player	Pos	Age	GS	Snaps	Pen	Sk	Pass	Run
David DeCastro	RG	26	16/16	1075	3	0.0	0.0	3.5	Alejandro Villanueva	LT	28	16/10	753	2	6.0	11.0	3.0
Ramon Foster	LG	30	16/16	1075	4	4.0	4.0	3.0	Kelvin Beachum*	LT	27	6/6	326	5	3.0	5.0	2.0
Cody Wallace	C	32	16/16	1073	13	3.0	8.0	4.5	Ryan Harris	LT	31	16/16	1006	4	2.0	10.5	4.0
Marcus Gilbert	RT	28	16/16	1070	6	1.0	6.0	3.5									

Year	Yards	ALY	Rank	Power	Rank	Stuff	Rank	2nd Lev	Rank	Open Field	Rank	Sacks	ASR	Rank	Press	Rank	F-Start	Cont.
2013	3.57	3.79	22	60%	21	21%	24	0.94	29	0.39	29	43	7.3%	15	22.2%	10	11	27
2014	4.50	4.10	6	69%	8	15%	1	1.18	15	0.96	5	33	5.8%	14	17.5%	2	15	27
2015	4.53	4.08	8	60%	24	19%	10	1.22	9	1.01	6	33	5.4%	8	19.2%	1	17	39
2015 ALY by direction:			Left End 4.78 (4)			Left Tackle 5.02 (2)			Mid/Guard 3.9 (12)			Right Tackle 4.49 (4)			Right End 1.58 (32)			

Left tackle was the only position where Pittsburgh did not have a 16-game starter last season due to Kelvin Beachum's torn ACL. While some teams would be happy to re-sign a 27-year-old tackle with 39 career starts, the Steelers were wise to let Beachum test a tepid market that saw him ink a one-year deal in Jacksonville. In his four seasons, Beachum never averaged at least 50 snaps per blown block, something achieved by 31 left tackles (min. 400 snaps) in 2015 alone. Alejandro Villanueva filled in admirably enough given that he was a tight end at Army and never played in the NFL before 2015. In case Villanueva falters as Beachum's permanent replacement, backup Ryan Harris (70 career starts) was signed from Denver. Center Cody Wallace was never expected to start 16 games, but Maurkice Pouncey was lost in the preseason and went through seven surgical procedures on his left leg. Pouncey is the superior player, but he has been surprisingly replaceable throughout his career—in 2013, the drop from Pouncey to replacement Fernando Velasco wasn't very large either—so at least the Steelers have some insurance in Wallace now. Guards Ramon Foster and David DeCastro each ranked in the top 10 at their position in snaps per blown block for the second year in a row. We haven't charted DeCastro with a sack allowed since the 2013 season. Right tackle Marcus Gilbert was undressed by Von Miller on the crucial fourth-and-5 in Denver, but who didn't Miller embarrass in the postseason?

Defensive Front Seven

Defensive Line	Age	Pos	G	Snaps	Plays	TmPct	Rk	Stop	Dfts	BTkl	Runs	St%	Rk	RuYd	Rk	Sack	Hit	Hur	Dsrpt
					Overall							vs. Run				Pass Rush			
Cameron Heyward	27	DE	16	976	55	6.5%	25	42	18	2	36	75%	45	2.0	38	7.0	8	16.5	1
Stephon Tuitt	23	DE	14	872	55	7.5%	13	45	18	4	40	80%	26	2.2	45	6.5	5	19.5	0
Steve McLendon*	30	DT	16	379	14	1.7%	--	10	5	1	12	67%	--	1.8	--	1.0	1	2.0	1
Ricardo Mathews	29	DE	16	511	22	2.9%	78	15	3	3	20	65%	74	3.7	82	1.0	0	3.5	0

Edge Rushers	Age	Pos	G	Snaps	Plays	TmPct	Rk	Stop	Dfts	BTkl	Runs	St%	Rk	RuYd	Rk	Sack	Hit	Hur	Dsrpt
					Overall							vs. Run				Pass Rush			
James Harrison	38	OLB	15	611	41	5.2%	44	30	12	5	25	72%	57	2.1	40	5.0	10	24.0	2
Bud Dupree	23	OLB	16	563	27	3.2%	81	18	8	0	13	69%	66	3.4	86	4.0	2	8.5	1
Arthur Moats	28	OLB	16	554	37	4.4%	59	24	9	4	23	65%	72	2.6	63	4.0	6	14.5	2
Jarvis Jones	27	OLB	15	454	29	3.7%	75	21	7	6	18	78%	30	2.6	60	2.0	2	5.0	2

Linebackers	Age	Pos	G	Snaps	Plays	TmPct	Rk	Stop	Dfts	BTkl	Runs	St%	Rk	RuYd	Rk	Sack	Hit	Hur	Tgts	Suc%	Rk	AdjYd	Rk	PD	Int
					Overall							vs. Run				Pass Rush				vs. Pass					
Lawrence Timmons	30	ILB	16	1057	124	14.7%	22	63	27	18	58	57%	65	3.8	61	5.0	4	8	31	51%	50	6.4	40	4	1
Ryan Shazier	24	ILB	12	667	90	14.3%	30	49	20	10	44	70%	17	3.0	24	3.5	4	3.5	26	43%	62	5.4	24	4	1
Sean Spence*	26	ILB	15	270	34	4.3%	--	18	6	2	19	58%	--	3.4	--	1.0	0	0	7	45%	--	6.4	--	0	0
Vince Williams	27	ILB	16	192	35	4.2%	--	17	6	1	20	70%	--	2.7	--	0.5	1	0	8	29%	--	5.4	--	1	0

Year	Yards	ALY	Rank	Power	Rank	Stuff	Rank	2nd Level	Rank	Open Field	Rank	Sacks	ASR	Rank	Press	Rank
2013	4.07	4.16	24	65%	16	15%	30	0.98	4	0.60	15	34	6.1%	27	22.3%	25
2014	4.36	4.04	21	53%	3	18%	21	1.32	30	0.75	19	33	6.4%	21	24.0%	21
2015	3.80	3.73	16	55%	5	21%	14	1.13	18	0.56	7	48	7.4%	7	24.2%	24
2015 ALY by direction:			Left End 2.78 (8)			Left Tackle 2.94 (5)			Mid/Guard 3.78 (13)			Right Tackle 4.24 (25)			Right End 3.42 (18)

If Cameron Heyward is the best overall player on Pittsburgh's defense, then Stephon Tuitt is the most improved. The duo combined for 36 hurries and 13.5 sacks in a scheme that is designed to feature the outside linebackers. ☞ Daniel McCullers will have to hold off third-round pick Javon Hargrave (South Carolina State) for the starting nose tackle spot, a position that Steve McClendon filled to the tune of fewer than 400 snaps per season following the retirement of Casey Hampton. This duo has nicknames bigger than their actual roles in the defense: McCullers is "Shade Tree" because he weighed nearly 400 pounds in junior college, while Hargrave is "The Gravedigger." ☞ Ryan Shazier showed his high potential in the wild-card win in Cincinnati with 13 total tackles, two passes defensed and two huge fumbles forced. Now, if he could only stay healthy for an entire season… ☞ Lawrence Timmons' 18 missed tackles were as many as he had in the previous two seasons combined. ☞ While some linebackers take a while to find the field, others such as Jarvis Jones continue to disappoint while on it. In three seasons, Jones has 17 hurries and five sacks in 36 games. A 37-year-old James Harrison, in a limited pass-rusher role, had 24 hurries and five sacks last season. 2016 should be Jones' final chance to prove his worth to the team.

Defensive Secondary

Secondary	Age	Pos	G	Snaps	Plays	Overall TmPct	Rk	Stop	Dfts	BTkl	vs. Run Runs	St%	Rk	RuYd	Rk	vs. Pass Tgts	Tgt%	Rk	Dist	Suc%	Rk	AdjYd	Rk	PD	Int
William Gay	31	CB	16	1065	65	7.7%	53	31	17	6	14	79%	3	2.7	2	49	11.2%	1	11.0	62%	4	5.9	9	7	2
Mike Mitchell	29	SS	16	1048	89	10.6%	27	18	10	10	35	20%	63	10.1	60	11	2.5%	1	16.4	77%	4	9.0	52	7	3
Antwon Blake*	26	CB	16	921	86	10.2%	14	33	14	21	17	53%	18	6.2	26	90	24.0%	64	12.3	40%	73	8.9	63	13	2
Will Allen*	34	FS	13	814	86	12.6%	13	46	20	13	37	54%	12	5.9	23	25	7.5%	37	10.3	56%	41	8.6	51	4	1
Ross Cockrell	25	CB	15	684	54	6.8%	65	22	10	10	3	0%	74	8.3	49	64	23.0%	59	12.6	46%	65	8.9	62	13	2
Robert Golden	26	FS	16	390	40	4.8%	--	18	5	4	17	59%	--	6.6	--	17	10.7%	--	11.5	51%	--	5.1	--	3	1
Brandon Boykin*	26	CB	16	274	26	3.1%	--	10	5	1	5	40%	--	6.6	--	17	14.8%	--	8.7	43%	--	7.7	--	6	1

Year	Pass D Rank	vs. #1 WR	Rk	vs. #2 WR	Rk	vs. Other WR	Rk	vs. TE	Rk	vs. RB	Rk
2013	19	23.9%	29	0.6%	15	-24.2%	4	-0.5%	14	-15.2%	5
2014	30	4.4%	20	-6.8%	12	39.3%	32	17.4%	28	13.3%	22
2015	13	12.2%	26	10.2%	22	-9.2%	11	-16.1%	5	-8.6%	9

William Gay had excellent coverage metrics, but that's partly because quarterbacks sure enjoyed attacking Antwon Blake and Ross Cockrell. ☞ The art of tackling was lost on this secondary: Pittsburgh and St. Louis were the only two teams with four defensive backs having at least 10 broken tackles, and Blake (21) led the NFL. ☞ Tonight on *The Twilight Zone*: When does one of the best slot corners in the league fail to see the field for a secondary that needed him? Last August, Pittsburgh traded a conditional fifth-round pick to the Eagles for Brandon Boykin. Despite playing in all 16 games, Boykin logged just 22 defensive snaps in Weeks 1-12 before moving up to 252 snaps in Weeks 13-17. Some conspiracy theorists believed the Steelers were petty enough to limit his playing time so the traded draft pick would only be a fifth-round pick instead of a fourth. After Boykin was allowed to leave, the new theory came from defensive back coach Carnell Lake: Boykin has a degenerative hip condition. Boykin denies this, but he remains out of work in one of the NFL's more peculiar career tales. ☞ The Steelers are finally trying to develop some young defensive backs, with safety Sean Davis (versatile, heavy hitter) and cornerbacks Artie Burns (athletic freak) and Senquez Golson (short, but good ball skills). Davis has the best shot of making an immediate impact given the departure of veteran Will Allen and the lacking resumé of Shamarko Thomas.

Special Teams

Year	DVOA	Rank	FG/XP	Rank	Net Kick	Rank	Kick Ret	Rank	Net Punt	Rank	Punt Ret	Rank	Hidden	Rank
2013	0.5%	16	2.4	13	-1.5	22	1.0	11	-11.1	28	11.8	4	-6.0	24
2014	0.9%	12	2.5	10	-2.6	22	-4.6	26	3.2	10	5.8	9	-13.5	31
2015	0.1%	18	-1.0	18	3.7	8	-4.8	27	3.4	12	-0.6	17	-11.1	30

The kicker position was looking to doom Pittsburgh's season after some costly early-season misses by Josh Scobee, but Chris Boswell, the team's fourth kicker of 2015, finally solved the problem Although his kickoffs could be better, Boswell made 36 of his 39 field goals, including the game-winning playoff kick in Cincinnati. ☞ Punter Jordan Berry followed an average regular season with a rough playoff game in Denver. ☞ Antonio Brown still handles punt returns, and he finally had a touchdown return against someone (Indianapolis) other than Cincinnati. ☞ Pittsburgh needs a new plan at kick returner after pulling the plug on the Dri Archer experiment. Markus Wheaton and Fitzgerald Toussaint are possibilities.

San Diego Chargers

2015 record: 4-12	**Total DVOA:** -14.8% (24th)	**2016 Mean Projection:** 8.2 wins	**On the Clock (0-4):** 8%
Pythagorean Wins: 5.9 (27th)	**Offense:** 0.9% (15th)	**Postseason Odds:** 37.2%	**Mediocrity (5-7):** 31%
Snap-Weighted Age: 26.8 (12th)	**Defense:** 10.4% (28th)	**Super Bowl Odds:** 4.6%	**Playoff Contender (8-10):** 42%
Average Opponent: 5.3% (5th)	**Special Teams:** -5.3% (31st)	**Proj. Avg. Opponent:** -3.0% (30th)	**Super Bowl Contender (11+):** 20%

2015: Which Offensive Lineman Will Get Hurt This Week Part II: Electric Boogaloo

2016: For all the focus on the run, this team sure can pass well.

Not since LaDainian Tomlinson was on the field has Philip Rivers played with a running game that was more efficient than his passing game. Tomlinson assured himself of a spot in the Hall of Fame during the 2006 season, when he rushed for a career-high 1,815 yards and 28 touchdowns. The Chargers, obviously, ranked first in rushing DVOA that year, while the Rivers-led passing game finished third during his first season as a full-time starter. That was the last time the Chargers finished in the top 10 in rushing DVOA. The following year, the Chargers ranked 11th rushing and 13th passing, and that was the last time their ground game ranked higher than their passing game in DVOA.

During the eight seasons that have passed since 2007, the San Diego pass offense has ranked in the top 10 of DVOA seven times. Even when the passing game finished 16th in 2012, it still ranked more than 10 spots ahead of its running complement. In four of those seven seasons the Chargers ranked either first or second in passing DVOA. Only twice during that time did the running game even rank in the top half of the league, finishing in the bottom five more times than it finished in the top 16.

You can't say that Rivers has never had a running game to rely on, but it has been a long time—and the problem reached a new low in 2015.

The Chargers' running game bottomed out last year, finishing 31st in DVOA. San Diego had also finished No. 31 in 2009, but last year's -21.8% DVOA was 7.5% worse than the rushing DVOA put up by that 2009 squad. There are a couple of reasons for this. Some of it is just the way the league has been trending, as running games on the whole have become less efficient relative to passing over the past decade. All plays together average to 0.0% DVOA in each individual year, but last year had the highest average passing DVOA (13.5%) and the lowest average rushing DVOA (-7.5%) since 1989. The worst rushing DVOA in 2009 would have ranked 24th in 2015.

A bigger issue for the Chargers has been the abnormal amount of injuries they have endured on their offensive line over the past two years. From the first week of last year the Chargers offensive line resembled something that you would find in the aftermath of a *Game of Thrones* battle. San Diego finished last in offensive AGL in 2014, and 26th last year, based mainly on offensive linemen falling left and right. The Chargers got a total of 48 starts from the line they entered the

regular season with. 48 out of a possible 80. Joe Barksdale was the only player to start all 16 games. D.J. Fluker made it to the third quarter of Week 1 before he was sidelined for a week. Fluker started the second-most games of the starters with 12. Orlando Franklin managed to make it to double digits, while King Dunlap and Chris Watt *combined* to reach 10 starts. Backups Trevor Robinson, Chris Hairston and Kenny Wiggins were all forced to play extensive snaps. That lack of stability made it tough for the offense to find its footing.

But offensive line issues and the general direction of the league can't protect Melvin Gordon from taking the brunt of the blame. Gordon was supposed to balance the Chargers offense. He wasn't drafted to be Tomlinson, but he was drafted to do what Tomlinson previously did for Rivers: force opposing defenses to be honest. The former Wisconsin running back became the 17th overall pick of the 2015 draft after the Chargers gave up a first-, a fourth- and a fifth-round pick to select him. Gordon had run for 4,915 yards and 45 touchdowns at Wisconsin. During his final season he rushed for 2,587 yards and 29 touchdowns while averaging 7.5 yards per attempt. Gordon's appeal was built around his speed. He could break off big runs with ease and accelerate to top speed to outrun the angles of college defenders trying to catch him. There were also enough flashes of Gordon running through defenders to suggest that he could consistently break tackles, even though he didn't do it in college. It was easy to understand why the Chargers fell in love with Gordon, but his detractors were proved right during his rookie season. Gordon carried the ball 184 times for 641 yards, 3.5 yards per carry, and didn't score a touchdown.

After the season, Gordon condemned himself, "I was terrible. I have something to prove. I have a year in my back pocket now, so if anything I'm more confident. Pretty much everything went wrong last year that could." Actually, what specifically went wrong is exactly what the draftnik posse predicted could be a downfall for Gordon. Gordon has always had very heavy feet. He got away with it in college because the Wisconsin offensive line gave him a lot of space to work in, but in the NFL that space isn't afforded to running backs. It doesn't matter how fast or how strong you are if you can't adjust behind the line of scrimmage to find or create space to run to. Gordon could be an effective back behind a good offensive line, but he had no chance of elevating the Chargers' depleted line in 2015. He just doesn't possess that level of talent.

2016 Chargers Schedule

Week	Opp.	Week	Opp.	Week	Opp.
1	at KC	7	at ATL	13	TB
2	JAC	8	at DEN	14	at CAR
3	at IND	9	TEN	15	OAK
4	NO	10	MIA	16	at CLE (Sat.)
5	at OAK	11	BYE	17	KC
6	DEN (Thu.)	12	at HOU		

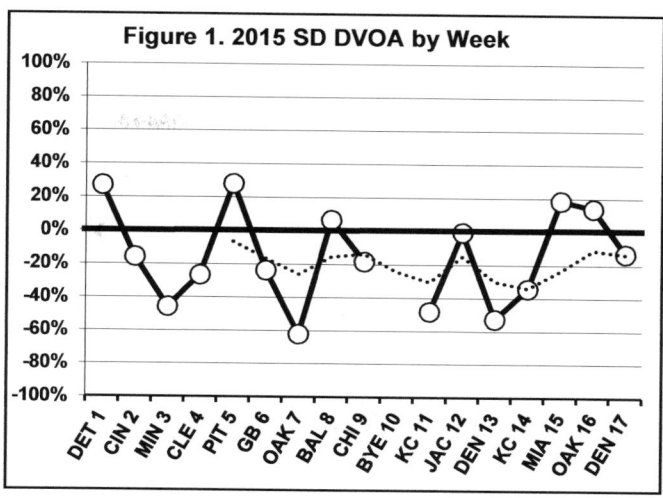

Figure 1. 2015 SD DVOA by Week

The running back's rookie season was ended by a knee injury that ultimately led to microfracture surgery in the offseason. While he's expected to be ready for training camp, microfracture is one of the scarier injury buzzwords any football player can hear. Without a star back, the Chargers can expect to rank low in rushing DVOA again next year. It's a crippling issue, but it's an issue that Rivers has repeatedly proven he can overcome. Rivers is under-appreciated as one of the great quarterbacks in this era because of what he has achieved in extremely difficult circumstances. Despite having no running game or pass protection last year—without even acknowledging the injury and suspension issues with his receivers—Rivers still ranked eighth in DYAR and 11th in DVOA. Rivers was pressured on 24.5 percent of his pass attempts last season. Twenty-one quarterbacks were pressured more often, but Rivers' presence was the only thing keeping that percentage below 30. Rivers reads defenses before and after the snap as well as any quarterback in the league. He throws with touch and anticipation, allowing him to release the ball extremely early no matter where he is throwing. The combination of that acumen and passing ability allows Rivers to regularly get rid of the ball before pass-rushers even have an opportunity to beat the blockers assigned to them.

Rivers doesn't require much coaching. Offensive coordinator Ken Whisenhunt and company need to avoid putting restrictions on him. The easiest way to do this is to leave him in shotgun with multiple receiving options so he can run the offense like an orchestra conductor. Better health and offseason moves may help him write a comeback symphony for the Chargers this year.

Keenan Allen was enjoying the best season of his career last year before he landed on injured reserve. Allen caught 67 passes for 725 yards and four touchdowns in just eight games. He played in 14 games during the previous season … and caught 77 passes for 783 yards and four touchdowns. (Granted, he played hurt in 2014 as well. And he was hurt coming out of college, which is why he was around in the third round in the first place. We swear, he's going to be healthy one of these years.) While Allen's breakout season was ended prematurely, Travis Benjamin's lasted for all 16 games. Benjamin only caught 68 passes for 966 yards and five touchdowns, but he did so with an unsettled, often abhorrent, quarterback situation in Cleveland. Benjamin is a great deep threat with the speed and precision through his routes to easily get open downfield. He will replace retired over-the-top threat Malcom Floyd in the offense. Benjamin is less of a ball winner than

Floyd though, so Rivers' downfield precision will be stressed more. That is somewhat of a concern because there were signs of physical decline from Rivers over the second half of last season. At the very least, Benjamin will perfectly complement Allen and Stevie Johnson's ability to work the short and intermediate routes with Antonio Gates. Gates is undoubtedly in decline as he enters his 7,000th season as the Chargers starting tight end. He is still a reliable weapon for Rivers and he won't need to be relied upon as often with the emergence of Allen and the addition of second-round tight end Hunter Henry (Arkansas). Henry is a receiving tight end who should fit perfectly as another possession-type receiver in the Chargers' passing game.

Henry's addition to the offense was almost an afterthought because of his projected role. Joey Bosa's addition to the defense couldn't have been any bigger. Bosa was the third-overall pick of the 2016 draft, the first non-quarterback selected. He was a bit of a surprise selection for a team that was regularly linked to DeForest Buckner, Laremy Tunsil, and Jalen Ramsey. Bosa wasn't viewed as a fit in the Chargers scheme, as he's not explosive or flexible enough to bend the edge as an outside linebacker, and not big enough to hold up against the run as a defensive end. While Bosa's production at Ohio State was huge, his subpar combine testing numbers—a very slow 4.86-second 40-yard dash in particular—opened some eyes about his athleticism. Combine those times with an average number of passes defensed, and SackSEER isn't particularly wild about Bosa's future. Bosa's Explosion Index, which measures a prospect's scores in the 40, vertical jump, and broad jump, came out at just 0.01. That is one of the worst rankings for a top-10 edge-rusher since 1998. Fellow top-10 picks Greg Ellis (0.12), Dante Fowler (0.14), and Chris Long (0.54) are better comparisons for Bosa than Von Miller (1.87) or Khalil Mack (1.70). The system expects Bosa to have a strong career but called him "below average" for a pass-rusher chosen in the top five.

The Chargers don't see that as an issue. After drafting Bosa, general manager Tom Telesco praised his run-stuffing ability before saying, "We're in a four-man front two-thirds of the time. Joey plays big. The weight doesn't bother us at all. He's an outstanding pass rusher, both on the edge or [as an inside rusher]. He's very balanced." The Chargers view Bosa as a moveable piece along their defensive line. He should play significant snaps alongside Jeremiah Attaochu and Melvin Ingram instead of playing in place of either. Bosa and free-agent addition Brandon Mebane could completely alter the Chargers defensive front. Mebane has proven himself has a high-quality nose tackle, making him the ideal complement to Bosa when he lines up as three-technique inside. The Chargers are being aggressive with both of these moves. They needed to be: their defense ranked 28th in DVOA last year for a reason.

Mebane's arrival will be huge for the defense because the Chargers ranked 31st against the run. Bosa will need to prove that he can hold up inside to be trusted in that role as a starter, or at least as someone who plays close to starter snaps. So will second-year linebacker Denzel Perryman. The Chargers released Donald Butler, a former starter who had previously been given a seven-year, $51.8 million contract extension. Perryman will assume Butler's vacated spot while fourth-round pick Joshua Perry (Ohio State) will compete with the disappointing Manti Te'o for a starting spot. Te'o had an awful 32 percent success rate in coverage last year to rank 69th among linebackers. He lacks the athleticism to be effective in space against NFL offenses.

The Chargers have the makings of a very good pass defense with the potential to be a capable run defense. They can mitigate the impact of their run defense if the offense plays to its potential and forces opponents into shootouts. Rivers deserves better from the Chargers. Since Rivers became the Chargers' starter in 2006, only Drew Brees (his predecessor in San Diego, of all people) has thrown for more yards, and that's mainly because Brees gets more attempts. San Diego's signal-caller averages slightly more yards per attempt than the man he replaced. His 5.3 percent touchdown rate ranks seventh amongst quarterbacks with at least 500 attempts over that time, and his completion percentage ranks ninth.

Rivers' window is closing, so the Chargers were right to be aggressive in their actions over the past two offseasons—even if at least some of those actions were misguided. Quality at quarterback plays a strong role in our season forecast, which is a big reason why our projection system believes the Chargers can bounce back from last year's 4-12 disaster. The Chargers came out with 8.6 mean wins, which puts them among the top dozen teams for 2016. Even if they aren't a powerhouse in the AFC, the Chargers have the kind of roster that could make a surprise playoff run—if they stay healthy and Philip Rivers plays close to his potential.

Cian Fahey

2015 Chargers Stats by Week

Wk	vs.	W-L	PF	PA	YDF	YDA	TO	Total	Off	Def	ST
1	DET	W	33	28	483	302	-1	27%	21%	-18%	-11%
2	at CIN	L	19	24	354	389	-1	-16%	9%	13%	-12%
3	at MIN	L	14	31	369	284	-1	-45%	-25%	15%	-6%
4	CLE	W	30	27	438	432	1	-26%	10%	25%	-11%
5	PIT (Mon)	L	20	24	406	349	-1	28%	22%	-7%	-1%
6	at GB	L	20	27	548	370	-1	-24%	16%	32%	-8%
7	OAK	L	29	37	417	412	-2	-62%	-6%	46%	-10%
8	at BAL	L	26	29	371	365	0	7%	25%	21%	3%
9	CHI	L	19	22	339	446	1	-18%	2%	15%	-5%
10	BYE										
11	KC	L	3	33	201	385	-2	-48%	-33%	18%	3%
12	at JAC	W	31	25	369	420	1	-1%	18%	12%	-7%
13	DEN	L	3	17	272	293	-2	-53%	-44%	7%	-1%
14	at KC	L	3	10	280	329	1	-34%	-23%	10%	-2%
15	MIA	W	30	14	442	231	-1	18%	18%	-12%	-11%
16	at OAK	L	20	23	343	281	0	14%	-9%	-30%	-7%
17	at DEN	L	20	27	317	503	4	-13%	-6%	9%	2%

Trends and Splits

	Offense	Rank	Defense	Rank
Total DVOA	0.9%	15	10.4%	28
Unadjusted VOA	-1.1%	17	9.0%	19
Weighted Trend	-2.5%	17	9.6%	25
Variance	4.6%	9	3.6%	8
Average Opponent	-3.1%	6	1.2%	11
Passing	24.9%	8	15.6%	22
Rushing	-21.7%	31	4.2%	32
First Down	-6.4%	22	14.3%	29
Second Down	7.4%	11	3.4%	19
Third Down	4.2%	13	13.5%	25
First Half	1.0%	15	8.6%	25
Second Half	0.9%	16	12.5%	27
Red Zone	23.5%	8	7.4%	19
Late and Close	9.6%	7	4.1%	24

Five-Year Performance

Year	W-L	Pyth W	Est W	PF	PA	TO	Total	Rk	Off	Rk	Def	Rk	ST	Rk	Off AGL	Rk	Def AGL	Rk	Off Age	Rk	Def Age	Rk	ST Age	Rk
2011	8-8	8.7	7.4	406	377	-7	0.7%	16	13.0%	5	10.8%	29	-1.6%	23	32.6	18	40.0	23	28.0	6	28.0	5	26.4	10
2012	7-9	8.0	6.6	350	350	+2	-9.05%	22	-10.0%	24	2.0%	18	3.0%	8	30.2	18	19.3	10	28.4	2	27.8	6	27.1	2
2013	9-7	9.2	8.8	396	348	-4	6.4%	12	23.1%	2	17.5%	32	0.8%	15	46.3	23	44.8	25	27.5	10	25.8	28	26.0	17
2014	9-7	8.0	8.0	348	348	-5	-0.6%	16	7.0%	11	4.9%	25	-2.7%	23	82.1	32	37.0	15	27.9	4	26.7	17	26.6	4
2015	4-12	5.9	6.0	320	398	-4	-14.8%	24	0.9%	15	10.4%	28	-5.3%	31	55.7	27	25.7	10	27.6	7	25.9	30	26.5	7

2015 Performance Based on Most Common Personnel Groups

SD Offense					SD Offense vs. Opponents					SD Defense				SD Defense vs. Opponents			
Pers	Freq	Yds	DVOA	Run%	Pers	Freq	Yds	DVOA	Run%	Pers	Freq	Yds	DVOA	Pers	Freq	Yds	DVOA
11	65%	5.7	12.6%	30%	Base	21%	4.3	-28.1%	51%	Base	33%	5.5	-4.1%	11	58%	6.7	13.6%
12	25%	5.8	2.0%	35%	Nickel	64%	5.9	15.4%	32%	Nickel	47%	6.3	9.8%	12	20%	4.7	-3.6%
13	6%	3.0	-40.9%	71%	Dime+	14%	5.3	27.2%	13%	Dime+	18%	7.6	38.3%	21	9%	6.9	21.0%
21	3%	5.0	-4.2%	33%	Goal Line	0%	1.0	29.2%	75%	Goal Line	1%	0.9	40.1%	13	5%	6.5	22.9%
02	0%	3.4	34.2%	0%										22	4%	6.8	6.9%

Strategic Tendencies

Run/Pass		Rk	Formation		Rk	Pass Rush		Rk	Secondary		Rk	Strategy		Rk
Runs, first half	36%	24	Form: Single Back	84%	4	Rush 3	7.9%	12	4 DB	33%	15	Play action	10%	32
Runs, first down	46%	19	Form: Empty Back	8%	13	Rush 4	59.4%	20	5 DB	47%	25	Avg Box (Off)	6.05	31
Runs, second-long	23%	27	Pers: 3+ WR	65%	12	Rush 5	28.5%	8	6+ DB	18%	9	Avg Box (Def)	6.34	9
Runs, power sit.	55%	16	Pers: 2+ TE/6+ OL	32%	17	Rush 6+	4.2%	27	CB by Sides	60%	27	Offensive Pace	29.74	13
Runs, behind 2H	30%	4	Pers: 6+ OL	0%	29	Sacks by LB	64.1%	2	S/CB Cover Ratio	23%	13	Defensive Pace	30.57	22
Pass, ahead 2H	63%	1	Shotgun/Pistol	88%	2	Sacks by DB	17.2%	3	DB Blitz	13%	7	Go for it on 4th	0.95	15

The field was dramatically tilted against San Diego last season. The Chargers offense had the worst average starting field position (just inside their own 23-yard line) and the Chargers defense faced the worst average starting field position for their opponents (just past the 31-yard line). Regression to the mean on special teams should help here. ☞ This was the first time in six years that the Chargers did not rank among the bottom ten teams in situation-neutral pace. ☞ Philip Rivers gained 7.2 yards per pass against blitzes compared to just 6.2 yards per pass otherwise. Sometimes these stats fluctuate from year to year, but Rivers has gained more yards against blitzes in four of the last five years. (In the other year, 2013, he had the exact same average against blitzes that he had against a standard pass rush.) ☞ San Diego had a league-worst -37.0% DVOA when Rivers lined up under center, so it's a good thing they used shotgun more than any team other than Philadelphia. ☞ Seventeen percent of San Diego's rushing attempts were draws, easily the highest rate in the league. However, the Chargers' -17.9% DVOA on these plays was well below the league average. ☞ San Diego led the league in passing DVOA in the red zone but ranked only 29th on runs in the red zone. ☞ The Chargers finished dead last in use of play-action fakes for the third straight season. ☞ San Diego ranked 30th in the league on defensive DVOA against short passes, but 14th against deep passes (16 or more yards past the line of scrimmage).

Passing

Player	DYAR	DVOA	Plays	NtYds	Avg	YAC	C%	TD	Int
P.Rivers	847	7.8%	704	4503	6.4	6.0	66.5%	29	13
K.Clemens	67	157.4%	6	63	10.5	0.8	83.3%	1	0
Z.Mettenberger	-408	-46.4%	179	812	4.5	4.1	61.6%	4	7

Rushing

Player	DYAR	DVOA	Plays	Yds	Avg	TD	Fum	Suc
M.Gordon	-68	-17.4%	184	641	3.5	0	5	43%
D.Woodhead	13	-5.5%	96	330	3.4	3	0	45%
D.Brown*	21	0.3%	59	229	3.9	1	0	36%
B.Oliver	27	10.1%	31	108	3.5	0	0	48%

Receiving

Player	DYAR	DVOA	Plays	Ctch	Yds	Y/C	YAC	TD	C%
K.Allen	173	11.9%	89	67	725	10.8	3.5	4	75%
M.Floyd*	16	-9.6%	69	30	561	18.7	2.9	3	43%
S.Johnson	76	2.1%	65	45	497	11.0	5.9	3	69%
D.Inman	32	-6.2%	63	35	486	13.9	5.1	3	56%
J.Herndon	-15	-19.1%	33	24	195	8.1	4.4	0	73%
T.Williams	15	21.9%	6	2	90	45.0	25.5	1	33%
T.Benjamin	38	-8.7%	125	68	973	14.3	4.8	5	54%
A.Gates	113	13.1%	85	56	630	11.3	4.3	5	66%
L.Green*	78	11.8%	63	37	429	11.6	6.0	4	59%
J.Phillips*	39	37.9%	11	10	69	6.9	2.4	1	91%
J.Cumberland	-35	-45.1%	14	5	77	15.4	10.0	0	36%
D.Woodhead	235	25.8%	108	82	761	9.3	8.9	6	76%
M.Gordon	-5	-16.1%	37	33	192	5.8	7.8	0	89%
B.Oliver	39	37.4%	15	13	112	8.6	10.4	0	87%
D.Brown*	-7	-24.8%	13	8	88	11.0	13.8	0	62%

Offensive Line

Player	Pos	Age	GS	Snaps	Pen	Sk	Pass	Run	Player	Pos	Age	GS	Snaps	Pen	Sk	Pass	Run
Joseph Barksdale	RT	27	16/16	1115	8	3.5	7.0	5.0	Orlando Franklin	LG	29	10/10	618	5	1.0	2.5	1.0
Trevor Robinson	C	26	16/13	978	5	2.5	2.5	1.0	King Dunlap	LT	31	7/7	313	1	2.0	2.0	0.0
D.J. Fluker	RG	25	12/12	861	12	1.0	2.0	6.0	Chris Watt	C	26	5/3	180	4	0.5	3.5	0.0
Kenny Wiggins	G/T	28	15/8	790	5	3.0	7.0	1.0	Matt Slauson	LG/C	30	16/16	1083	5	0.5	5.5	6.0
Chris Hairston	LT	27	16/11	785	8	6.0	7.0	6.0									

Year	Yards	ALY	Rank	Power	Rank	Stuff	Rank	2nd Lev	Rank	Open Field	Rank	Sacks	ASR	Rank	Press	Rank	F-Start	Cont.
2013	4.20	4.26	3	74%	5	12%	1	1.10	17	0.50	27	30	5.9%	8	22.0%	8	21	28
2014	3.51	3.29	31	78%	3	21%	28	0.95	28	0.52	27	37	6.1%	17	21.8%	9	14	27
2015	3.53	3.18	31	73%	6	20%	15	0.85	32	0.53	27	40	5.4%	11	24.3%	14	20	22

2015 ALY by direction:	Left End 3.65 (16)	Left Tackle 3.38 (24)	Mid/Guard 3.35 (31)	Right Tackle 2.1 (32)	Right End 2.13 (29)

King Dunlap has always struggled to stay on the field. When Dunlap played all 16 games in 2014, the only time he has ever done that in his career, he ranked third among left tackles in snaps per blown block. Dunlap doesn't need to perform like a star to have a heightened impact on the Chargers passing game. Philip Rivers can make an adequate left tackle an above-average player. ☞ Dunlap's main role is keeping Chris Hairston off the field. Hairston handcuffs the Chargers offense both as a run-blocker and pass-blocker. He ranked 26th among left tackles in snaps per blown block last season. ☞ Five players have started at center for the Chargers over the past two seasons. In response to those issues, the Chargers signed free-agent Matt Slauson (ex-Bears) and used a third-round selection on rookie Max Tuerk (USC) while retaining former third-round pick Chris Watt, the team's first-choice center from last season. Slauson is the favorite in any competition. *San Diego Union-Tribune* beat writer Kevin Acee called it "obvious" that Slauson will be the starting center after just one OTA. Slauson is transitioning to center having previously played guard, but Rivers said "You'd think he was playing center for all of his career" while also comparing him to former starter Nick Hardwick.

Defensive Front Seven

Defensive Line	Age	Pos	G	Snaps	Plays	TmPct	Rk	Stop	Dfts	BTkl	Runs	St%	Rk	RuYd	Rk	Sack	Hit	Hur	Dsrpt
						Overall						**vs. Run**				**Pass Rush**			
Kendall Reyes*	27	DE	16	656	36	4.7%	46	28	7	5	25	80%	26	2.0	39	2.0	5	14.5	2
Ricardo Mathews*	29	DE	16	511	22	2.9%	78	15	3	3	20	65%	74	3.7	82	1.0	0	3.5	0
Corey Liuget	26	DE	11	444	34	6.5%	26	26	9	1	28	75%	45	2.8	63	3.0	1	3.0	0
Sean Lissemore	29	DT	11	233	16	3.1%	--	10	1	1	15	60%	--	3.7	--	0.0	1	2.0	0
Darius Philon	22	DE	8	143	6	1.6%	--	5	3	1	4	75%	--	2.5	--	0.0	2	4.5	0
Brandon Mebane	31	DT	15	489	24	3.3%	69	18	5	3	19	84%	15	1.5	15	1.5	3	6.0	0

Edge Rushers	Age	Pos	G	Snaps	Plays	TmPct	Rk	Stop	Dfts	BTkl	Runs	St%	Rk	RuYd	Rk	Sack	Hit	Hur	Dsrpt
						Overall						**vs. Run**				**Pass Rush**			
Melvin Ingram	27	OLB	16	961	69	9.1%	1	48	26	5	31	65%	76	3.3	83	10.5	9	29.5	3
Jeremiah Attaochu	23	OLB	15	667	51	7.1%	8	38	19	5	37	73%	52	3.8	90	6.0	11	21.5	1
Kyle Emanuel	25	OLB	15	300	18	2.5%	--	14	4	6	14	79%	--	2.2	--	1.0	2	6.5	0

Linebackers	Age	Pos	G	Snaps	Plays	TmPct	Rk	Stop	Dfts	BTkl	Runs	St%	Rk	RuYd	Rk	Sack	Hit	Hur	Tgts	Suc%	Rk	AdjYd	Rk	PD	Int
						Overall						**vs. Run**				**Pass Rush**				**vs. Pass**					
Manti Te'o	25	ILB	12	710	84	14.7%	23	47	13	11	51	63%	48	3.4	37	0.5	3	5	24	33%	69	6.4	41	3	1
Donald Butler*	28	ILB	16	500	40	5.2%	87	25	5	6	25	68%	27	2.8	16	0.5	0	2.5	10	32%	--	11.7	--	0	0
Denzel Perryman	23	ILB	14	386	67	10.0%	62	41	12	3	44	73%	12	3.3	33	2.0	1	3	8	61%	--	6.4	--	0	0
Kavell Conner*	29	ILB	10	184	16	3.4%	--	7	2	2	9	44%	--	4.0	--	0.0	0	0	5	79%	--	6.9	--	1	0

Year	Yards	ALY	Rank	Power	Rank	Stuff	Rank	2nd Level	Rank	Open Field	Rank	Sacks	ASR	Rank	Press	Rank
2013	4.46	4.45	31	73%	26	16%	27	1.39	30	0.55	11	35	6.9%	15	22.0%	26
2014	4.03	4.02	20	58%	9	20%	14	1.20	22	0.56	7	26	5.5%	27	25.8%	11
2015	4.95	4.22	28	73%	27	18%	25	1.38	31	1.21	32	32	5.8%	26	25.2%	16

2015 ALY by direction:	Left End 3.41 (16)	Left Tackle 5.52 (32)	Mid/Guard 4.15 (24)	Right Tackle 4.14 (23)	Right End 4.29 (27)

The main reason for San Diego's low adjusted sack rate was a lack of talent on their three-man defensive line. Joey Bosa brings to the interior of the defense the kind of pass-rushing skill set that simply wasn't there last year. ☞ When the Chargers drafted Jeremiah Attaochu two years ago, they understood that he needed significant development. As an edge defender, Attaochu needs to add strength. Attaochu shows off the body control, explosiveness, and length to beat offensive tackles in different ways, but he struggles to disengage once caught. Attaochu has yet to play full-time but he has gradually improved over his first two seasons. His tape reflected his issues disengaging from blocks to finish plays, as he had only six sacks but 21.5 total hurries to rank 32nd in the league. Bosa, Attaochu, and Melvin Ingram have the potential to be one of the best pass-rushing trios in the league. Ingram is closer to his peak than the other two after his first 10-sack season in 2015. If Attaochu continues to improve on the other side and Bosa (with Brandon Mebane) offers a greater presence from the inside, Ingram's job should only get easier. ☞ The Chargers used two third-day picks to build depth at inside linebacker. Fourth-rounder Joshua Perry (Ohio State) is all-around solid and dependable but never really flashes with big plays. Fifth-rounder Jatavis Brown (Akron) is speedy but undersized and could play a Mark Barron-like "dollar linebacker" role in sub packages.

Defensive Secondary

Secondary	Age	Pos	G	Snaps	Plays	Overall TmPct	Rk	Stop	Dfts	BTkl	vs. Run Runs	St%	Rk	RuYd	Rk	vs. Pass Tgts	Tgt%	Rk	Dist	Suc%	Rk	AdjYd	Rk	PD	Int
Eric Weddle*	31	FS	13	751	81	13.1%	10	36	15	9	45	40%	36	6.8	35	19	6.9%	29	9.5	64%	19	6.5	29	5	0
Jason Verrett	25	CB	14	719	59	8.8%	32	28	15	2	9	33%	50	12.0	68	58	22.4%	55	15.2	61%	8	7.2	23	10	3
Jahleel Addae	26	SS	13	712	68	11.0%	23	20	7	13	34	32%	49	8.5	52	20	7.9%	39	17.7	56%	40	9.3	55	4	0
Patrick Robinson*	29	CB	16	692	57	7.5%	57	20	8	6	18	28%	59	6.6	33	47	18.8%	37	9.2	58%	13	4.9	3	5	1
Brandon Flowers	30	CB	11	603	37	7.1%	63	12	6	6	2	100%	1	3.0	3	47	21.6%	52	14.5	40%	72	10.6	74	3	0
Jimmy Wilson*	30	SS/FS	13	483	44	7.1%	64	19	7	9	16	38%	42	8.0	48	21	11.9%	61	11.2	51%	52	7.3	40	3	1
Steve Williams	25	CB	13	286	24	3.9%	--	11	6	8	2	50%	--	3.5	--	35	33.8%	--	13.7	43%	--	9.9	--	4	2
Craig Mager	24	CB	10	226	11	2.3%	--	5	3	1	2	100%	--	5.5	--	15	18.6%	--	13.4	53%	--	8.4	--	2	0
Adrian Phillips	24	FS	9	206	17	4.0%	--	6	5	3	6	33%	--	9.0	--	5	6.1%	--	9.6	9%	--	17.0	--	1	1
Dwight Lowery	30	FS	16	1088	84	10.0%	33	36	15	10	30	40%	36	8.1	50	39	8.6%	50	12.1	59%	31	7.9	46	9	4
Casey Hayward	27	CB	16	914	70	8.6%	36	39	15	9	19	68%	7	5.4	18	46	13.6%	3	9.4	57%	19	6.8	15	5	0

Year	Pass D Rank	vs. #1 WR	Rk	vs. #2 WR	Rk	vs. Other WR	Rk	vs. TE	Rk	vs. RB	Rk
2013	31	24.7%	31	24.5%	32	3.4%	18	-5.1%	11	7.9%	22
2014	25	-3.6%	13	11.2%	26	12.9%	26	-4.0%	16	17.3%	27
2015	21	4.9%	20	7.6%	19	-10.5%	9	34.8%	31	14.1%	26

From our viewpoint, Jason Verrett was the best cornerback in his class when he entered the NFL two years ago. There were only two knocks on Verrett: health and height. The first has proven to be an issue. Verrett entered the NFL with a shoulder issue and was considered an injury risk because of his 5-foot-10, 189-pound frame and past health problems. Verrett has missed time in both of his first two seasons, but managed to start 13 games in 2015. In those 13 starts, Verrett disproved the validity of the other knock. Had Verrett been one or two inches taller, he would have been a top-10 pick. Instead, Justin Gilbert went in the top 10 and Verrett fell to the Chargers in the 20s. Gilbert is now fighting for his roster spot in Cleveland whereas Verrett is a burgeoning star. What makes Verrett special is his footwork. He can mirror any receiver and track him through breaks, offsetting his lack of size with controlled aggression and awareness. ☞ The signing of Casey Hayward was a smart one. Hayward had a rough couple of years after playing phenomenally well during his rookie season, but his charting metrics were impressive in 2015. The Chargers recognized the risk in relying on someone who has proven to be inconsistent, but the value and skill set made him one of the smarter signings of the offseason. What makes Hayward even more fascinating in San Diego is the versatility he creates. The Chargers have two players who can thrive in the slot at a time when slot cornerbacks have never been more valuable. ☞ Brandon Flowers could move to safety to mitigate the impact of his declining athleticism. Otherwise, Jahleel Addae and Dwight Lowery are expected to start at the safety spots. Addae is a carryover piece whereas Lowery is a proven, consistent veteran who has been brought in to replace Eric Weddle. Lowery isn't as good as Weddle but the gap isn't as wide as their reputations would suggest.

Special Teams

Year	DVOA	Rank	FG/XP	Rank	Net Kick	Rank	Kick Ret	Rank	Net Punt	Rank	Punt Ret	Rank	Hidden	Rank
2013	0.8%	15	3.4	11	-0.8	17	-2.2	19	7.4	7	-3.8	21	-0.1	15
2014	-2.7%	23	0.6	13	-8.3	29	-1.4	20	-3.0	20	-1.6	13	-0.4	19
2015	-5.3%	31	-1.2	19	-2.7	22	-4.3	26	-12.3	29	-6.1	28	-7.8	25

The Chargers special teams have been in steady decline over the past three seasons, and punts have been a big issue. The "most prolific punter in franchise history," Mike Scifres was released during the offseason. At 35 years of age, Scifres is no longer the weapon he once was as a directional kicker, landing just 15 of 73 punts inside the opposition's 20-yard line. Drew Kaser from Texas A&M was drafted in the sixth round to replace Scifres. Scifres was a precision punter but Kaser's main selling point is his strength. His 47.5 yards per punt in 2015 ranked fourth in the nation and led the SEC. ☞ Rookie kicker Josh Lambo was unimpressive on field goals but ranked fourth with 3.5 points of estimated gross kickoff value. Unfortunately, poor coverage gave that back so kickoffs were a net negative for San Diego. ☞ Travis Benjamin ranked third in punt return value for Cleveland and should take the job from Javontee Herndon; kick returns should remain a mix of Herndon and Branden Oliver.

San Francisco 49ers

2015 record: 5-11	Total DVOA: -27.5% (32nd)	2016 Mean Projection: 5.4 wins	On the Clock (0-4): 37%
Pythagorean Wins: 3.8 (32nd)	Offense: -14.0% (28th)	Postseason Odds: 6.7%	Mediocrity (5-7): 45%
Snap-Weighted Age: 26.2 (27th)	Defense: 9.9% (27th)	Super Bowl Odds: 0.3%	Playoff Contender (8-10): 16%
Average Opponent: 8.6% (2nd)	Special Teams: -3.6% (27th)	Proj. Avg. Opponent: 5.3% (1st)	Super Bowl Contender (11+): 2%

2015: No team scored fewer points than the 49ers.

2016: The offense may still stink, but watch how fast they hike the ball.

If you were expecting Chip Kelly to revolutionize coaching in the NFL, then surely you are disappointed. While some great coaches only went on to find success after early failure and a second chance, there is little to suggest that Kelly, who saw his Eagles regress each year, is going to live up to the hype that followed him from Oregon to the pros in 2013.

Still, isn't a 26-21 record without stellar quarterbacks a pretty good start for a first-time head coach? Notable college coaches Steve Spurrier (12-20) and Nick Saban (15-17) combined to go just 27-37 in the NFL. The Eagles were only 22-26 in Andy Reid's last three years before Kelly took over. Kelly is the 26th coach since 1992 to be relieved of his duties after a three-season tenure. The other 25 coaches won 36.9 percent of their games, and only Wade Phillips (1998-2000 Bills) and Pete Carroll (1997-1999 Patriots), two coaches on their second tries in the NFL, had better records than Kelly. Carroll went on to incredible runs with USC and Seattle, while Phillips just won Super Bowl 50 as the mastermind of Denver's epic defense. The Eagles just may rue the day they pulled the plug on the Kelly experiment after 47 games.

But make no mistake about it. Chip Kelly the football coach did not get Kelly fired. Chip Kelly the lousy general manager created the rift with owner Jeffrey Lurie, ultimately leading to his demise in Philadelphia. Kelly wanted full control of player personnel decisions in 2015, and a hesitant Lurie granted him that. "There [are] dangers in that, in terms of having two 10-6 seasons in a row, and … making significant changes, you can easily achieve mediocrity. I think it would be [a] shame not to try, but the end result was mediocrity," Lurie said a day after firing Kelly.

After an offseason filled with several bizarre player acquisitions, it wasn't hard to predict the unhappy denouement of Kelly's tenure with the Eagles. He gave No. 1 cornerback money to a No. 2 cornerback (Byron Maxwell) from a great Seattle scheme. He jettisoned running back LeSean McCoy and replaced him with DeMarco Murray, who was coming off a 392-carry season. Kelly's love of sending players on a Reverse Oregon Trail to Philadelphia brought in Kiko Alonso, who may or may not have missed five games due to dysentery last year. To top it off, Kelly traded Nick Foles (plus significant draft compensation) for the often injured, always underwhelming Sam Bradford, who never had a season anywhere near as good as what Foles did in Kelly's system in 2013.

On March 9, the Eagles went all Katherine Hepburn in *Philadelphia Story* and started throwing away Kelly's possessions. Maxwell, Murray, and Alonso were all traded after one season with the team, while Bradford's days are numbered since the Eagles moved up to draft Carson Wentz. Rarely has a team tried to expunge the seeds of a bad offseason as quickly as the Eagles have distanced themselves from Kelly's mess.

Perhaps the most damning criticism of Kelly came from Lurie's December press conference. Lurie hoped his next coach would value "emotional intelligence" and open his heart to players. This is not just a knee-jerk reaction by a disappointed owner either. An unidentified player provided this quote to Bleacher Report's Mike Freeman in 2015: "The thing with Chip is he just doesn't see you as a person. He sees you as a commodity. The more players get that, the better off they'll be."

Lurie is far from the first person to question Kelly's personal skills. Cornerback Brandon Boykin, who was traded to Pittsburgh last summer, said that Kelly is "uncomfortable around grown men of our culture. [Kelly] can't relate and that makes him uncomfortable. He likes total control of everything, and he don't like to be uncomfortable." Former assistant coach Tra Thomas told FOX in 2015 that players "feel like there is a hint of racism." After being traded to Buffalo last year, McCoy told *ESPN The Magazine* that Kelly got rid of "especially all the good black players," likely referring to himself, DeSean Jackson, and Jeremy Maclin over the years. A former Eagles player, speaking anonymously to NJ Advance Media, talked about the reports that Kelly lost the locker room last season. "I can tell you, he never had the support of the team this year," the ex-Eagles player said. "It was a toxic situation from the moment I arrived. Those guys in that locker room almost universally despised him."

While he was not unemployed for long, these are questions Kelly is going to have to answer in San Francisco now. In fact, at his introductory press conference, a reporter asked Kelly what kind of guy he is. "I'm a football guy" was his generic response, because what else would a head coach say in that situation?

For this to work, the 49ers need Kelly to just leave the player personnel decisions to the general manager. Fortunately, the 49ers have a strong established personality in that role in Trent Baalke. Unfortunately, Baalke's relationship deteriorated with Jim Harbaugh, the last great coach the team had. This could

2016 49ers Schedule

Week	Opp.	Week	Opp.	Week	Opp.
1	LARM (Mon.)	7	TB	13	at CHI
2	at CAR	8	BYE	14	NYJ
3	at SEA	9	NO	15	at ATL
4	DAL	10	at ARI	16	at LARM (Sat.)
5	ARI (Thu.)	11	NE	17	SEA
6	at BUF	12	at MIA		

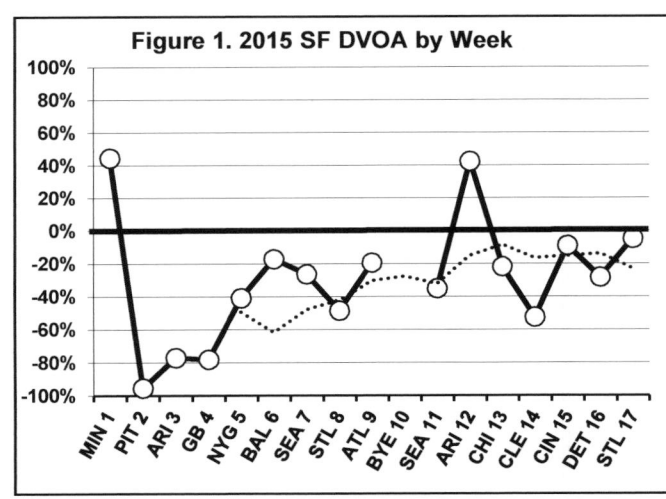

Figure 1. 2015 SF DVOA by Week

seed some drama down the road, but for 2016, we will just assume everyone plays nice as the 49ers attempt to rebuild.

Oh, it is certainly a rebuild. Even if Kelly wanted to retain his role of quasi-GM, fans would have no need to worry about him shipping away the team's best players. Most already left a year ago, leaving a small portion of the talent core from the teams that went to three straight NFC Championship Games. The departure of Harbaugh and the uninspiring promotion of Jim Tomsula to head coach probably influenced a few of those stunning retirements the team was hit with last offseason. That mass exodus of talent made the 49ers an easy choice to fall out of contention, and things never got better for Tomsula than they did in a surprising 20-3 Week 1 win on Monday night against the Vikings. Hopefully he cherished ESPN's graphic from that night showing him with the highest winning percentage (1.000) in 49ers' history, because it was all downhill from there.

There is a good argument that San Francisco was the worst team in football in 2015. The 49ers finished last in DVOA (-27.5%) and estimated wins (4.1). They played in a league-low six close games that were within one score in the fourth quarter, because most of their losses were not competitive. The main reason this team finished 5-11 instead of holding the No. 1 pick at 2-14 really came down to the outcome of three field goals. The Bears (Week 13) and Rams (Week 17) both missed game-winning field goals against the 49ers, while the Falcons (Week 9) kicked a field goal from the 1-yard line when they needed a late touchdown in a 17-16 upset. If anything, San Francisco actually overachieved by winning five games.

You could also make the argument that Kelly has moved to a team in a tougher division with more roster holes, more quarterback uncertainty and fewer offensive weapons. So how does he turn this around?

First, to understand what Kelly brings to a team, you have to understand what he is not about. While some of us hoped for Kelly to be a maverick amongst his peers, bucking conventional wisdom in favor of data-driven decision making, the truth is that Kelly became another member of the NFL's old boys club. There was once the thought that Kelly would take advantage of two-point conversions with the swinging gate formation on extra points that was successful for him at Oregon. After an embarrassing attempt in his third game in 2013, Kelly kept that gate closed. We use a stat called Aggressiveness Index (AI) to measure coaches' fourth-down decisions, and Kelly's AI ranks 29th out of 144 coaches since 1989. That

is not bad, but it does nothing to paint Kelly as a bad mamma jamma on fourth down. His AI is lower than that of the connected coaching trio of Bill Parcells (12th), Bill Belichick (14th), and Sean Payton (10th). The fourth-down revolution will have to wait for another leader to emerge.

This is not to say that Kelly has failed to create something unique in the NFL. He put his stamp on the Eagles, but it was more about style and the offensive system than it was advantageous decision making. And Kelly should have no problem in bringing his style to San Francisco.

The first obvious change Kelly brings is the high-tempo offense. Kelly's Eagles led the league in fewest seconds per play in each of his three seasons. In 2015, the Eagles averaged 22.2 seconds between plays, more than 5 seconds ahead of the league average. This may seem like a drastic change for a San Francisco offense that was always 30th or 31st in pace under Harbaugh. However, last year was good practice, as the 49ers ranked fifth in pace at 25.8 seconds. This could actually be a great change to an offense that used to routinely fight the play clock under Harbaugh and offensive coordinator Greg Roman. In fact, the 49ers led the league (or tied for the lead) in delay of game penalties for four years in a row (2011-2014), totaling 44 flags. Last season, the 49ers had just two such penalties, and that should be about the number in 2016 given Kelly's pace of getting in the play.

Of course, there is skepticism over the value of Kelly's hyper-speed offense, including concern over what it does to the bodies of players on both sides of the ball. Eagles offensive tackle Lane Johnson told CSNPhilly.com that Kelly's practices were too grueling. "We practice pretty much the same from OTAs until the end of the season. There's not a lot of the guys in the league that do that, continuous. It takes a toll on you, especially me, I expect a lot from myself so I've hit it hard since January, go out with [Jason Peters], bust some ass, and by the end of the year I feel like I'm gonna fall apart."

Kelly has never been a proponent for time of possession (TOP), and it is hard to blame him for that. Kelly won 73.3 percent of his games when his offense had at least 25 minutes of TOP, compared to a league average winning rate of 54.7 percent. He was 12-4 (75 percent) when his offense had the ball between 25 and 30 minutes (NFL average: 38.9 percent). The Eagles were last in TOP in 2015, but it should be noted that the 49ers weren't much better at 31st.

Kelly's focus has always been on the number of plays. The Eagles are tied with New England for the most games (32) with at least 60 plays on both sides of the ball since 2013. The Eagles are also tied with Denver for the most games (nine) with at least 70 plays on both sides of the ball. No one questions the success or pace of Denver and New England, but it's not like Kelly had Peyton Manning or Tom Brady to run his offense. The Eagles have ranked first, second, and first in plays run against their defense since 2013. That sounds less than ideal, but any complaint about TOP usually falls on deaf ears. If a defense wants to be on the field less, then find a way to get turnovers and third-down stops. If an offense wants to be on the field more, make plays and extend drives.

Playing better football usually cures any ails of TOP, but rest is a tricky concept in the NFL. There may be long-term health implications from running this up-tempo style for an extended number of years, but for three seasons in Philadelphia, the numbers do not support Kelly tiring out his players, especially the defense. In 2015, Philadelphia's defense was at its worst in the *first* quarter, ranked 27th in DVOA at a point in the game where fatigue should not have set in yet. In each of his three seasons with the Eagles, Kelly's defense ranked better in DVOA after halftime than it did before halftime. In his first two seasons, Kelly's defense ranked better in DVOA in the second half of the season than in the first half, when players should have been fresher. When the Eagles had a late lead, they usually held on, allowing six fourth-quarter comebacks—an average amount for the past three years. The noteworthy part is that none of the blown leads were larger than four points. Kelly was 26-1 when leading by at least five points in the second half. Carolina is the only other team with only one loss in that time span, and Kelly's lone loss happened in San Francisco in 2014. The offense actually struggled more in those comeback situations, as Kelly's 3-11 record at fourth-quarter comeback opportunities is the second-worst among active head coaches.

Then there are the smoothies and daily urine tests to track hydration, or parts of Kelly's famous sports science program. Some players may find this too invasive, which does not help Kelly's reputation as a dictator, but the results in Philadelphia were very encouraging. Adjusted Games Lost (AGL) is Football Outsiders' metric for quantifying injuries, and the Eagles ranked first, fifth, and sixth in AGL under Kelly. The 2004-2006 Texans and 2007-2011 Titans are the only other teams since 2002 to rank in the top six in AGL in at least three consecutive seasons. So despite the increased number of plays and opportunities for injuries, Kelly's teams were very healthy, avoiding many of the soft-tissue injuries that plague teams each season. Expect Kelly to bring this system to Silicon Valley, though he has already said that the 49ers have done similar things, but did not receive the credit Kelly did in Philadelphia. That is probably because the results have not been nearly as favorable for the 49ers. San Francisco finished first in AGL in 2012, but since then, the 49ers have been among the NFL's most injured teams, finishing 23rd, 28th, and 27th in AGL since 2013. A health boost in 2016 would really help the 49ers get back on track.

Another element of Kelly teams is the use of shotgun at never-before seen levels. San Francisco is the home of the shotgun, as the 1960 49ers were the first team to use it thanks to Red Hickey's innovation. Shotgun usage has only continued to increase since then, and three of the top four offenses that have used the shotgun the most in our database were coached by Kelly. The 2015 Eagles used shotgun (or pistol) on 93.6 percent of their plays, the highest rate in NFL history. This can be another big change for the 49ers, who used shotgun about 41 percent of the time under Harbaugh, and on 62.3 percent of plays in 2015. Running back Carlos Hyde should love the potential of playing in Kelly's offense. Last year, Hyde averaged 5.3 yards per carry and had the league's second-highest success rate (59 percent) on shotgun runs. Hyde was sensational against Minnesota in Week 1, but unfavorable scoring margins and injury limited him to just 470 rushing yards in seven games. Remember how San Francisco finished near the bottom in AGL? No backfield was hit with more injuries than the 49ers last year. San Francisco was down to the No. 5, 6, and 7 running backs on the depth chart to rush for over 100 yards against Detroit in Week 16. A healthy Hyde should be Kelly's new workhorse this season.

As for the starting quarterback, Kelly walked into a messy situation and may have made it even messier. In February, Colin Kaepernick's agents requested a trade, and for the next two months leading into the draft, there was a real possibility that Denver would be his new home this season. While that fell through, Kaepernick's offseason surgeries for his shoulder, thumb, and knee prohibited him from taking any reps in offseason activities, giving Blaine Gabbert all the first-team work. Kelly has been quick to praise Gabbert as a similar player, and expectations are that Gabbert will start in Week 1.

It is easy to sympathize with someone wanting a trade after getting benched repeatedly for Gabbert, who has the worst career passing DYAR (-1,769) of any quarterback since 1989. The so-called "improvement" Gabbert showed last season was like when a player goes from being the worst in the league to *one of* the worst. Technically, that is an improvement, but it's still lousy quarterback play. In Gabbert's eight starts, the 49ers scored 20 points once: the 26-20 overtime win in Chicago. That game was a perfect example of how close to the old Gabbert he still is. Through 10 drives, the 49ers were sitting on six points, and Gabbert's success rate was 29.4 percent (10-for-34). He was 0-for-5 on any pass thrown beyond 10 yards. Then Gabbert made a few scrambles, including a 44-yard touchdown run after Chicago safety Adrian Amos took a horrible angle on the tackle. Chicago missed a short game-winning field goal, and in overtime, blown coverage by Amos led to a 71-yard touchdown pass to Torrey Smith. For most of the day, Gabbert was still an ineffective mess against the 31st-ranked defense.

Kelly owes Kaepernick nothing, but it is bad business to bench a quarterback with a cap hit just south of $16 million this season. In playing devil's advocate, let's try to make some statistical sense of starting Gabbert over Kaepernick in 2016. Kaepernick is usually slow in his decision-making, and his rate of pressure (32.7 percent) was higher than Gabbert's (27.9 percent) despite similar personnel and system. Kelly certainly likes to have a quarterback who can make plays outside the pocket. Sam Bradford only threw 10.2 percent of his passes outside the pocket last year, but he ranked third in DVOA (53.2%) when doing so. In a similar pattern in 2014, Mark Sanchez had 3.9% DVOA in the pocket and 66.9% DVOA when out of the pocket. In 2013, Nick Foles was about equal in efficiency, but was also throwing 19.7 percent of his passes outside the pocket in Kelly's best offense. Kaepernick usually throws around 27 percent of his passes outside the pocket, but his DVOA sunk to -11.7% (ranked 30th) in 2015. Gabbert threw 20.7 percent of his passes outside the pocket, but finished fifth in DVOA (49.2%). Kelly likes to use play-action passing, but Kaepernick struggled there last season with -11.7% DVOA. Meanwhile, Gabbert had 34.2% DVOA with play-action, a significant improvement over his DVOA (3.3%) without play-action.

If only 2015 mattered, then Gabbert has a decent argument over Kaepernick. But it is hard to ignore their first four seasons and how much better Kaepernick was, and how much more physical talent he still has right now. Kelly has almost made it a point to prove a mobile quarterback is not necessary for his system, and what Nick Foles did in 2013 supports that. However, defenses soon caught on, and Kaepernick's mobility would definitely open up the read-option. While Kaepernick has been criticized as a "one-read quarterback" in the past, Kelly's system provides a lot of easy throws, and it has helped his troubled passers before. Away from Kelly, the aforementioned Foles was arguably the worst quarterback in the NFL in St. Louis last season. Mark Sanchez was a 55-percent passer who averaged 6.5 yards per attempt with the Jets. Under Kelly, Sanchez completed 64.3 percent of his passes and averaged 7.6 yards per attempt. Last year, Bradford cracked 7.0 yards per attempt for the first time and hit a career-high 65 percent of his passes despite the Eagles tying for the second-most dropped passes in the league.

Kelly's scheme has done a good job of providing a boost to his quarterbacks and receivers. Kaepernick's past success with throwing deep, avoiding turnovers, and being one of the best rushing threats ever from his position make him such an intriguing fit with Kelly that it would be a shame if the two never seize the opportunity to make this work. Gabbert is what he is: a bum.

Regardless of quarterback, the 49ers have quite arguably the least intimidating group of skill players in the NFL, which presents a major problem in Kelly getting this offense to be productive again. Anquan Boldin, who turns 36 in October, was not retained after leading the team with 111 targets last year. Eric Rogers, a CFL star, was signed in January as the only free-agent addition to the receivers. Michigan State wideout Aaron Burbridge was drafted in the sixth round as Baalke's only pass-catching draft pick in 2016. Torrey Smith is a great deep threat and should be in line for a career year in this offense, but there is not much help on the way. The 49ers will have to hope past underwhelming Baalke draft picks, including Quinton Patton, Bruce Ellington and tight end Vance McDonald, will finally have breakout years in 2016. That trio has combined for just 95 career catches.

More than ever, Kelly is going to have to scheme ways to get receivers open behind a fairly young offensive line with quarterbacks who need a lot of help to succeed. Needless to say, the offense has a lot of growing pains ahead of it, and NaVorro Bowman and the defense will have to lead the team again. New defensive coordinator Jim O'Neil is a Rex Ryan disciple who fits with San Francisco's 3-4 personnel, but his success in Cleveland over the last two seasons was limited. O'Neil has some reasonable talent on this defense, especially if veterans Glenn Dorsey and Antoine Bethea remain healthy this year. The lack of a dominant edge rusher could be a problem as Aaron Lynch and Ahmad Brooks were the only 49ers to surpass 2.5 sacks last season, finishing with 6.5 each. But O'Neil promises an attacking defense and Lynch will be just 23 this season.

Baalke's recent drafts have been among the worst in the NFL, but the 49ers may start to see some better returns this year. To Kelly's delight, the future of the defensive line is in the hands of two Oregon Ducks after back-to-back first-round picks were used on Arik Armstead (2015) and DeForest Buckner (2016), two good fits as 5-technique defensive ends in the 3-4 defense. In keeping with the theme of building up the trenches, Baalke traded back into the first round to grab Stanford guard Joshua Garnett. Garnett's noted lack of athleticism may raise a red flag for the up-tempo offense, but he could be a forceful road-grader for an offense expected to run often.

Despite the Kelly hiring, San Francisco did not go for a sexy offseason, because getting back to the basics is key for setting a new foundation. Only two teams since 1989 were able to make the playoffs after finishing last in DVOA the previous season. Not only did the 2000 Saints and 2013 Chiefs get a new head coach and quarterback, but they also each had an elite pass-rushing talent (La'Roi Glover and Justin Houston) and faced easy schedules. The only part of that equation the 2016 49ers nail is the new coach. The structure of the tough NFC West and the state of San Francisco's roster makes it likely this team resides in the basement for another year. The final record may only be a game or two better than what Tomsula managed a year ago, but patience must be shown with Kelly. As fast as he may want to go down the road to redemption, this is going to be a slow ride. Take it easy.

Scott Kacsmar

2015 49ers Stats by Week

Wk	vs.	W-L	PF	PA	YDF	YDA	TO	Total	Off	Def	ST
1	MIN	W	20	3	395	248	0	45%	37%	-20%	-13%
2	at PIT	L	18	43	409	453	-1	-95%	-22%	69%	-4%
3	at ARI	L	7	47	156	446	-3	-77%	-68%	12%	3%
4	GB	L	3	17	196	362	-1	-78%	-50%	15%	-13%
5	at NYG	L	27	30	380	525	1	-41%	0%	41%	0%
6	BAL	W	25	20	391	420	2	-17%	1%	12%	-6%
7	SEA	L	3	20	142	388	2	-26%	-41%	-7%	7%
8	at STL	L	6	27	189	388	1	-48%	-37%	13%	2%
9	ATL	W	17	16	318	302	-2	-19%	-9%	-2%	-13%
10	BYE										
11	at SEA	L	13	29	306	508	0	-35%	6%	43%	2%
12	ARI	L	13	19	368	337	-2	43%	23%	-21%	-1%
13	at CHI	W	26	20	291	364	1	-22%	-17%	-17%	-21%
14	at CLE	L	10	24	221	481	2	-52%	-39%	25%	12%
15	CIN	L	14	24	318	242	-3	-9%	-36%	-34%	-6%
16	at DET	L	17	32	322	371	-1	-28%	10%	29%	-9%
17	STL	W	19	16	458	364	-1	-5%	-4%	4%	3%

Trends and Splits

	Offense	Rank	Defense	Rank
Total DVOA	-13.9%	28	9.9%	27
Unadjusted VOA	-14.4%	27	14.3%	31
Weighted Trend	-12.1%	26	5.3%	21
Variance	8.1%	23	7.4%	27
Average Opponent	-3.5%	3	3.7%	2
Passing	-9.3%	30	25.0%	30
Rushing	-10.4%	21	-5.3%	23
First Down	-15.1%	31	11.3%	26
Second Down	-6.1%	22	17.7%	31
Third Down	-23.4%	29	-5.4%	12
First Half	-20.5%	31	7.6%	24
Second Half	-7.0%	23	12.4%	26
Red Zone	-13.6%	25	0.0%	16
Late and Close	-1.4%	16	14.0%	29

Five-Year Performance

Year	W-L	Pyth W	Est W	PF	PA	TO	Total	Rk	Off	Rk	Def	Rk	ST	Rk	Off AGL	Rk	Def AGL	Rk	Off Age	Rk	Def Age	Rk	ST Age	Rk
2011	13-3	12.3	10.8	380	229	+2	18.6%	6	-3.9%	18	-14.6%	3	7.8%	2	29.6	16	8.8	2	26.5	23	26.7	21	26.6	7
2012	11-4-1	11.4	12.5	397	273	+9	29.5%	4	16.5%	5	-14.4%	3	-1.5%	20	11.7	5	4.5	1	27.1	14	27.3	10	26.9	5
2013	12-4	11.5	10.6	406	272	+12	17.4%	7	9.1%	8	-4.6%	13	3.7%	7	34.7	17	46.8	27	27.8	5	27.4	9	26.9	4
2014	8-8	7.0	9.0	306	340	+7	6.6%	11	-0.4%	16	-10.1%	5	-3.0%	24	30.0	15	71.8	31	27.6	6	26.8	16	26.4	8
2015	5-11	3.8	4.1	238	387	-5	-27.5%	32	-14.0%	28	9.9%	27	-3.6%	27	58.2	28	25.8	11	27.7	6	25.4	32	25.1	31

2015 Performance Based on Most Common Personnel Groups

	SF Offense					SF Offense vs. Opponents					SF Defense				SF Defense vs. Opponents			
Pers	Freq	Yds	DVOA	Run%		Pers	Freq	Yds	DVOA	Run%	Pers	Freq	Yds	DVOA	Pers	Freq	Yds	DVOA
11	41%	5.1	-24.8%	17%		Base	42%	5.5	2.9%	51%	Base	30%	5.0	-5.5%	11	62%	6.5	19.2%
12	24%	5.0	0.3%	35%		Nickel	41%	4.7	-21.4%	23%	Nickel	56%	6.5	19.2%	12	15%	5.9	13.5%
21	15%	5.8	0.3%	46%		Dime+	15%	5.3	-19.8%	17%	Dime+	12%	6.5	9.8%	21	7%	4.4	-18.6%
13	9%	4.8	6.8%	60%		Goal Line	1%	0.4	-18.4%	45%	Goal Line	2%	0.4	5.3%	22	3%	2.9	-38.2%
22	9%	5.1	-12.8%	58%		Big	1%	9.6	-7.4%	60%					13	3%	5.5	-4.3%

Strategic Tendencies

Run/Pass		Rk	Formation		Rk	Pass Rush		Rk	Secondary		Rk	Strategy		Rk
Runs, first half	38%	13	Form: Single Back	71%	24	Rush 3	9.6%	6	4 DB	30%	22	Play action	25%	3
Runs, first down	45%	22	Form: Empty Back	2%	32	Rush 4	62.6%	19	5 DB	56%	14	Avg Box (Off)	6.42	3
Runs, second-long	34%	11	Pers: 3+ WR	41%	31	Rush 5	22.4%	15	6+ DB	12%	14	Avg Box (Def)	6.23	19
Runs, power sit.	44%	29	Pers: 2+ TE/6+ OL	44%	5	Rush 6+	5.5%	17	CB by Sides	96%	3	Offensive Pace	28.57	5
Runs, behind 2H	26%	14	Pers: 6+ OL	1%	25	Sacks by LB	55.4%	10	S/CB Cover Ratio	23%	15	Defensive Pace	30.73	25
Pass, ahead 2H	46%	19	Shotgun/Pistol	62%	18	Sacks by DB	17.9%	2	DB Blitz	11%	12	Go for it on 4th	1.00	13

Say goodbye to the 49ers offense that used extra blockers and old-school personnel packages more than any other in the NFL. The transition already began last year—San Francisco only used six linemen on a handful of plays—but Chip Kelly likes his offense very strictly structured. The Eagles used the same two personnel packages (11 and 12) on 95 percent of plays last year, and did not use more than five offensive linemen on a single play over the last two seasons. ☞ Although stats with and without play-action tend to fluctuate each season, the Chip Kelly offense clearly made play-action valuable. In each of his three seasons in Philadelphia, the Eagles were significantly better passing the ball with a play-action fake first. Last year, that difference was 3.9 yards per pass and 19.1% DVOA. The year before, the yardage gap was smaller but the DVOA gap wider. ☞ San Francisco ran the ball on just 17 percent of plays when it had three or more receivers on the field, the lowest rate in the league. The Eagles have been well above average in this category under Kelly. ☞ As bad as things were for the San Francisco offense last year, it could have been worse: the 49ers recovered 12 of their 15 fumbles on offense, the best rate in the league. ☞ The 49ers allowed 8.0 yards per pass with a standard pass rush but only 5.6 yards per pass when blitzing. Defensive back blitzes were even better, allowing just 4.1 yards per pass. ☞ The Niners were 14th in defensive DVOA at home but dead last on the road, the largest split of any defense in the league.

Passing

Player	DYAR	DVOA	Plays	NtYds	Avg	YAC	C%	TD	Int
B.Gabbert	-85	-15.6%	308	1866	6.1	6.1	63.1%	10	7
C.Kaepernick	-182	-21.5%	273	1446	5.3	5.8	59.0%	6	5

Rushing

Player	DYAR	DVOA	Plays	Yds	Avg	TD	Fum	Suc
C.Hyde	60	3.9%	115	470	4.1	4	1	49%
S.Draughn	-28	-18.4%	76	263	3.5	1	1	38%
C.Kaepernick	63	22.7%	40	260	6.5	1	3	-
M.Davis	-13	-17.3%	35	58	1.7	1	0	31%
D.Harris	23	12.1%	27	140	5.2	0	0	37%
B.Gabbert	34	16.2%	24	179	7.5	1	1	-
J.Hayne*	2	-5.8%	17	52	3.1	0	0	41%
K.Gaskins*	-23	-38.3%	16	38	2.4	0	0	31%
R.Bush*	-4	-26.0%	8	28	3.5	0	0	13%
T.Cadet*	-10	-53.7%	7	16	2.3	0	0	0%
B.Miller	19	37.0%	6	14	2.3	1	0	83%
P.Thomas*	-4	-37.7%	4	12	3.0	0	0	25%
D.Harris	-30	-45.0%	21	51	2.4	0	1	38%

Receiving

Player	DYAR	DVOA	Plays	Ctch	Yds	Y/C	YAC	TD	C%
A.Boldin*	41	-7.9%	111	69	789	11.4	4.1	4	62%
T.Smith	134	14.3%	62	33	663	20.1	6.6	4	53%
Q.Patton	-9	-14.7%	57	30	394	13.1	7.1	1	53%
B.Ellington	-27	-32.7%	19	13	153	11.8	8.5	0	68%
J.Simpson	-43	-42.2%	19	5	54	10.8	3.2	1	26%
V.McDonald	-34	-19.2%	46	30	326	10.9	6.1	3	65%
V.Davis*	-25	-20.7%	30	18	194	10.8	4.1	0	60%
G.Celek	25	5.4%	28	19	186	9.8	5.2	3	68%
B.Bell	-45	-35.1%	25	15	186	12.4	6.1	0	60%
S.Draughn	-9	-19.4%	32	25	175	7.0	7.0	0	78%
C.Hyde	-18	-33.9%	15	11	53	4.8	5.5	0	73%
B.Miller	38	25.6%	14	10	135	13.5	9.9	0	71%
D.Harris	21	12.1%	14	9	97	10.8	10.9	0	64%
M.Davis	-41	-62.7%	13	7	38	5.4	5.0	0	54%
K.Gaskins*	21	24.1%	10	8	69	8.6	6.9	0	80%
T.Cadet*	9	7.2%	10	7	66	9.4	9.0	0	70%
R.Bush*	-30	-64.2%	10	4	19	4.8	5.8	0	40%
J.Hayne*	-1	-15.0%	7	6	27	4.5	3.7	0	86%

Offensive Line

Player	Pos	Age	GS	Snaps	Pen	Sk	Pass	Run	Player	Pos	Age	GS	Snaps	Pen	Sk	Pass	Run
Erik Pears	RT	34	16/16	1015	11	3.5	8.5	3.0	Jordan Devey*	RG	28	15/9	390	2	3.5	6.5	2.0
Joe Staley	LT	32	16/16	1015	3	3.0	11.5	3.0	Daniel Kilgore	C	29	5/3	268	0	0.0	0.0	0.0
Marcus Martin	C	23	14/14	822	7	3.5	10.0	1.5	Trenton Brown	G	23	6/2	187	0	0.0	1.0	1.0
Alex Boone*	LG	29	13/13	768	4	1.0	3.0	3.0	Zane Beadles	LG	30	16/16	1058	4	3.0	8.0	6.0
Andrew Tiller	G	27	12/7	615	5	3.0	4.0	2.0									

Year	Yards	ALY	Rank	Power	Rank	Stuff	Rank	2nd Lev	Rank	Open Field	Rank	Sacks	ASR	Rank	Press	Rank	F-Start	Cont.
2013	4.05	3.57	29	55%	28	24%	29	1.12	15	0.98	5	39	7.8%	22	26.0%	19	19	39
2014	4.15	4.05	10	48%	32	21%	19	1.26	6	0.59	24	52	9.8%	30	30.5%	29	14	22
2015	3.51	3.16	32	67%	14	26%	31	1.05	22	0.57	26	53	9.1%	31	30.2%	28	16	35

2015 ALY by direction:	Left End 5.65 (1)	Left Tackle 3.07 (27)	Mid/Guard 3.02 (32)	Right Tackle 2.75 (28)	Right End 1.68 (31)

Joe Staley has made five consecutive Pro Bowls, but the last two look to be reputation-based selections. Still, left tackle is the right spot to have your best and most experienced lineman. ☞ At left guard, free-agent signing Zane Beadles is a slight downgrade from Alex Boone. Beadles disappointed in Jacksonville after being propped up in Denver by Peyton Manning's quick release. ☞ Marcus Martin has not impressed through 22 starts, and he had the third-worst average of snaps per blown block among centers in 2015. Daniel Kilgore only has 10 starts in five seasons, but should be the favorite to win this job if he's actually healthy. ☞ When a team trades up for a first-round guard, he is probably going to start in Week 1. Josh Garnett is a good fit for what Kelly will want to do in the ground game. ☙ This line could get instantly better depending on the reinstatement of right tackle Anthony Davis after his one-year sabbatical. We still don't know what kind of shape he's in or if he's willing to come back to the 49ers, so they may have to put up with another year of Erik Pears' mediocrity. ☙ Trenton Brown, a seventh-round pick last year, could also challenge Pears for that job, but past reports of his poor conditioning are troublesome when he'll be expected to keep up with the fastest offense in the league.

Defensive Front Seven

Defensive Line	Age	Pos	G	Snaps	Plays	Overall TmPct	Rk	Stop	Dfts	BTkl	vs. Run Runs	St%	Rk	RuYd	Rk	Pass Rush Sack	Hit	Hur	Dsrpt
Ian Williams	27	DT	16	659	66	7.5%	12	51	7	1	64	77%	41	3.0	71	1.0	1	5.0	1
Quinton Dial	26	DT	15	642	60	7.2%	14	41	7	3	45	71%	55	2.5	55	2.5	5	3.5	1
Arik Armstead	23	DE	16	375	19	2.2%	--	13	5	3	15	67%	--	2.7	--	2.0	7	14.0	0
Glenn Dorsey	31	DE	10	353	18	3.3%	71	11	0	1	17	59%	83	2.9	65	0.0	3	3.0	0
Tony Jerod-Eddie	26	DE	16	291	18	2.0%	--	14	7	1	12	83%	--	2.8	--	0.0	2	2.0	4
Mike Purcell	25	DT	8	288	15	3.4%	68	11	2	3	14	71%	54	2.1	42	1.0	0	1.0	0

Edge Rushers	Age	Pos	G	Snaps	Plays	Overall TmPct	Rk	Stop	Dfts	BTkl	vs. Run Runs	St%	Rk	RuYd	Rk	Pass Rush Sack	Hit	Hur	Dsrpt
Aaron Lynch	23	OLB	14	796	41	5.3%	40	29	17	3	22	64%	80	2.1	43	6.5	16	34.0	0
Ahmad Brooks	32	OLB	14	744	43	5.6%	35	33	12	7	28	68%	70	2.5	59	6.5	4	15.5	0
Eli Harold	22	OLB	16	337	13	1.5%	--	10	9	1	11	91%	--	0.5	--	0.0	3	4.0	0
Corey Lemonier	25	OLB	10	272	12	2.2%	--	6	0	1	8	38%	--	7.1	--	0.0	4	3.0	0

Linebackers	Age	Pos	G	Snaps	Plays	Overall TmPct	Rk	Stop	Dfts	BTkl	vs. Run Runs	St%	Rk	RuYd	Rk	Pass Rush Sack	Hit	Hur	vs. Pass Tgts	Suc%	Rk	AdjYd	Rk	PD	Int
NaVorro Bowman	28	ILB	16	1101	156	17.7%	7	82	15	19	103	57%	63	3.8	58	2.5	5	15	23	50%	52	7.2	55	1	0
Michael Wilhoite	30	ILB	12	617	86	13.0%	36	34	5	11	52	56%	70	3.8	60	0.0	0	1	13	46%	57	10.0	69	1	1
Gerald Hodges	24	ILB	14	518	70	9.1%	65	33	8	10	44	57%	67	3.0	22	0.0	2	4.5	11	42%	--	4.3	--	1	0

Year	Yards	ALY	Rank	Power	Rank	Stuff	Rank	2nd Level	Rank	Open Field	Rank	Sacks	ASR	Rank	Press	Rank
2013	3.88	4.12	22	66%	18	14%	31	0.99	6	0.42	2	38	6.0%	29	25.6%	13
2014	4.04	4.16	25	71%	25	16%	26	1.00	6	0.59	9	36	6.6%	16	26.0%	9
2015	4.19	4.16	27	64%	15	17%	29	1.01	5	0.81	18	28	5.4%	29	25.7%	14
2015 ALY by direction:		Left End 2.53 (4)			Left Tackle 4.11 (21)			Mid/Guard 4.32 (29)			Right Tackle 4.21 (24)			Right End 3.87 (23)		

Ian Williams had just as many stops (51) as Ndamukong Suh last season, and only six fewer than Aaron Donald. No, he's not on that level, but as a run-stopping nose tackle, Williams has come a long way since arriving as an undrafted free agent in 2011. He is playing on a cheap one-year deal after ankle surgeries, but a big 2016 could secure his financial future. ☙ Glenn Dorsey and Quinton Dial are there for depth, but it must be tempting for Kelly to start the two Oregon ends, Arik Armstead and rookie DeForest Buckner, after consecutive first-round picks were used on them. Buckner will be the better player, but both fit the mold for a 5-technique end. ☙ It was great to see a healthy NaVorro Bowman back, finishing third in the league with 82 stops. As with other top linebackers such as Lavonte David and Derrick Johnson, his high broken-tackle total is partly just a product of how often he gets to the ballcarrier. ☙ While the 49ers would like to see more out of Eli Harold and Corey "Earl of" Lemonier, the pass rush really comes down to Ahmad Brooks and Aaron Lynch. ☙ The good news for Lynch: he's only 23, and he had 34.5 hurries last season. Since 2012, we have charted 34 players with at least 30 hurries in a season. Twenty-five of those players had double-digit sacks, and only three had fewer than Lynch. If he keeps getting that much pressure, he is bound to see his sack production improve. The bad news for Lynch: he will serve a four-game suspension for violating the league's substance abuse policy, and could lose his starting job if Harold starts the season hot.

Defensive Secondary

Secondary	Age	Pos	G	Snaps	Plays	TmPct	Rk	Stop	Dfts	BTkl	Runs	St%	Rk	RuYd	Rk	Tgts	Tgt%	Rk	Dist	Suc%	Rk	AdjYd	Rk	PD	Int
						Overall						vs. Run					vs. Pass								
Eric Reid	25	FS	16	1116	71	8.0%	58	20	9	9	19	21%	61	9.9	59	24	6.6%	25	12.7	54%	45	6.7	32	7	0
Tramaine Brock	28	CB	15	1066	64	7.7%	52	23	13	4	14	29%	57	6.1	25	56	16.3%	14	19.2	60%	10	8.8	59	11	3
Kenneth Acker	24	CB	15	809	71	8.6%	38	23	9	9	22	36%	47	8.7	53	48	18.6%	30	16.1	47%	61	9.4	68	7	3
Jimmie Ward	25	CB	16	732	60	6.8%	66	30	14	4	17	59%	11	6.2	26	34	14.3%	5	7.8	50%	49	7.2	20	5	1
Jaquiski Tartt	24	SS	15	721	67	8.1%	56	26	9	13	27	48%	19	7.9	46	23	9.8%	55	8.8	56%	38	6.4	24	3	1
Antoine Bethea	32	SS	7	443	46	11.9%	--	15	5	4	19	37%	--	6.7	--	7	5.0%	--	17.0	47%	--	9.6	--	2	0
Dontae Johnson	25	CB	16	367	31	3.5%	--	9	2	3	1	100%	--	1.0	--	27	23.1%	--	12.8	44%	--	8.4	--	5	0

Year	Pass D Rank	vs. #1 WR	Rk	vs. #2 WR	Rk	vs. Other WR	Rk	vs. TE	Rk	vs. RB	Rk
2013	10	-9.5%	11	-1.2%	14	-0.6%	14	-15.0%	8	-13.6%	7
2014	4	-6.0%	11	-22.4%	4	-11.8%	8	-9.7%	9	-16.5%	8
2015	30	2.9%	18	22.0%	28	10.2%	23	9.1%	22	11.7%	25

Antoine Bethea had been the most reliable member of the secondary, but he missed a career-high nine games due to injury. When he did play, he was beaten deep on the vertical assaults the 49ers suffered against the Cardinals, Steelers, and Giants. ☞ Bethea returns as a starter, but second-round rookie Jaquiski Tartt gained invaluable experience and should be the future at the position. ☞ Eric Reid, the other starting safety, had his fifth-year option picked up in May. His best season was his rookie year of 2013, but he is not a liability. ☞ Defenses loved throwing deep against this secondary. Tramaine Brock, the default No. 1 cornerback, covered passes at an average of 19.2 yards per target, league-high among corners with at least 50 targets. That's a big reason why Brock's ranking in success rate is so much better than his ranking in adjusted yards per pass. Kenneth Acker, the No. 2 corner, ranked fourth at 16.1 yards per target. ☞ On the other end of the spectrum, nickelback Jimmie Ward faced the shortest targets (7.8) in the league and led the 49ers' secondary in stops. While Ward can be used in a variety of ways, he primarily played corner instead of safety last season. ☞ Third-round pick Will Redmond (Mississippi State) showed a lot of athleticism in college, but only played in 19 games and is recovering from a torn ACL. ☞ Fourth-round pick Rashard Robinson (LSU) shares similar traits: impressive physical tools, but low on production and experience.

Special Teams

Year	DVOA	Rank	FG/XP	Rank	Net Kick	Rank	Kick Ret	Rank	Net Punt	Rank	Punt Ret	Rank	Hidden	Rank
2013	3.7%	7	5.9	6	10.0	3	-4.6	26	10.7	3	-3.6	20	2.0	12
2014	-3.0%	24	-2.0	22	0.7	14	-0.8	17	-8.3	28	-4.8	25	-6.4	25
2015	-3.6%	27	0.7	15	-4.3	27	-5.3	28	-4.6	22	-4.4	22	11.3	4

At 41 years old, Phil Dawson was the lone bright spot for an otherwise poor special teams unit, and he seems to be on that Adam Vinatieri career arc. Since turning 36, Dawson has made 27 of his 33 field goals (81.8 percent) from 50-plus yards compared to 10-of-19 (52.6 percent) to start his career. Dawson also followed the Vinatieri career arc by giving up kickoff duties this last season. ☞ 21-year-old Bradley Pinion took over for a "legend" in punter Andy Lee, and the results were not favorable. Pinion's kickoffs were average, but his punts were worth an estimated minus-10.2 points of field position; only Jeff Locke of the Vikings had worse gross punt value. ☞ Bruce Ellington held both return jobs and did a little better with kickoffs than punts, but had negative value on both. Ellington's value was similar in 2014. ☞ Australian rugby star Jarryd Hayne made some buzz with his brief NFL career, returning eight punts for the 49ers last year. However, he announced his retirement after just one season of American football. ☞ San Francisco has not returned any type of kick for a touchdown since Ted Ginn Jr. had a pair in the 2011 season opener against Seattle.

Seattle Seahawks

2015 record: 10-6	**Total DVOA:** 38.1% (1st)	**2016 Mean Projection:** 10.5 wins	**On the Clock (0-4):** 1%
Pythagorean Wins: 11.8 (3rd)	**Offense:** 18.7% (1st)	**Postseason Odds:** 72.2%	**Mediocrity (5-7):** 9%
Snap-Weighted Age: 26.4 (22nd)	**Defense:** -15.2% (4th)	**Super Bowl Odds:** 23.1%	**Playoff Contender (8-10):** 36%
Average Opponent: 2.4% (15th)	**Special Teams:** 4.2% (3rd)	**Proj. Avg. Opponent:** 1.0% (10th)	**Super Bowl Contender (11+):** 54%

2015: The DVOA dynasty continued after a late-season surge.

2016: The window for a real dynasty may be starting to close.

Asking an NFL head coach about statistics and expecting a detailed answer is often a pipe dream, but Pete Carroll is not your typical coach. Carroll had plenty to say via Seahawks.com after his team finished another regular season on top in a particular stat. "We do know it. We've been aware of it. It's an interesting stat because it's so comprehensive, and it does take into account all three phases in great detail. I don't know how the structure of it, how accurate it is to tell you what kind of team you are, but it's pretty cool because it does involve everything you're doing. And they measure it against I think the average of what's going on in the league. That's a good sign of consistency is what it is."

The stat Carroll was referencing was in fact DVOA. While things looked bleak when the Seahawks were just 4-5, a strong finish kept alive an unprecedented run. Seattle finished No. 1 in DVOA for the fourth year in a row, breaking the tie with the 1992-94 Cowboys for the longest reign on record. Even if we were fortunate enough to calculate DVOA back to the beginning of the modern NFL, it is unlikely that any other team has pulled off this dynastic feat.[1] Readers may just think we are trying to toot our own horn and promote DVOA, but this Seahawks run can stand the test of time when measured by a variety of metrics. We often downplay the significance of something historic while it is currently happening, but Seattle deserves more credit for building arguably the most competitive team in NFL history.

Consistency was a great word choice by Carroll, because no team is more consistent than Seattle. The key to Seattle's dominance in DVOA is the lack of bad games. Seattle has just nine games with negative DVOA since 2012, compared to an average of 32.7 negative games for the rest of the NFL. Since 2012, Seattle and Denver are the only teams to not have a regular-season game with -40.0% DVOA or worse while the rest of the league has combined to do so 316 times. We emphasize the phrase "regular season" because Denver had -57.0% DVOA in Super Bowl XLVIII after Seattle delivered the only Super Bowl blowout in the last 13 seasons. That game was the pinnacle for Seattle's defense, the main reason the Seahawks are the first team in the Super Bowl era to allow the fewest points in the league for four straight seasons.

Seattle has bad halves here and there, but no one has been able to beat this team thoroughly for 60 minutes since Pittsburgh's 24-0 shutout in Week 2 of the 2011 season. Seattle has led or been within one score in the fourth quarter of 88 consecutive games (including playoffs), the longest streak in NFL history. The second-longest streak belongs to the 2008-2012 Packers at 69 games. Seattle also held a lead at some point in the first 70 games of Russell Wilson's career, another NFL record. This is not by accident either. When Carroll was the coach at USC (2001-2009), his 97-19 record included just three losses by more than 7 points. The Trojans led or were within one score in the fourth quarter in his first 110 games, only getting blown out twice in his final six games by Chip Kelly's Oregon Ducks and Jim Harbaugh's Stanford Cardinal.

Incredible stuff, but are we starting to see more cracks? Only three times in their 88-game streak have the Seahawks been unable to take possession of the ball when they had a one-score deficit in the fourth quarter. However, two of those games came in the last month of the 2015 season. In Week 16, the Rams stunned Seattle with a wire-to-wire 23-17 win on the road, completing the season sweep and ending that 70-game streak of Seattle having a lead. In the NFC divisional round, Seattle fell behind Carolina 31-0 at halftime before rallying to score the game's next 24 points. In each game the Seahawks were unable to recover an onside kick in the final 75 seconds after a late touchdown kept the "always within one score" streak alive by the slimmest of margins.

Before the elephant in the room gets any louder, or calls another ill-advised pass at the goal line, we know why there has not been more mainstream appreciation of these Seahawks. Longtime Football Outsiders readers know that 16 binary win/loss results won't always directly reflect the quality of over 1,000 different plays on the field, and postseason results won't always mirror regular-season results. Thus, Seattle's historic level of play since 2012 has only resulted in two NFC West titles. More importantly, the trophy case is occupied by just one Super Bowl win. Without another parade down Fourth Avenue, this DVOA dynasty may best be remembered as the team that left us wanting more—like a real dynasty.

Our sample size may be a miniscule six, but modern NFL

---

1 When Andreas Shepard estimated DVOA back to 1950 in a 2014 article on our website, the 1961-63 Packers and 1953-55 Browns were the only other teams to lead the NFL for three straight seasons.

2016 Seahawks Schedule

Week	Opp.	Week	Opp.	Week	Opp.
1	MIA	7	at ARI	13	CAR
2	at LARM	8	at NO	14	at GB
3	SF	9	BUF (Mon.)	15	LA (Thu.)
4	at NYJ	10	at NE	16	ARI (Sat.)
5	BYE	11	PHI	17	at SF
6	ATL	12	at TB		

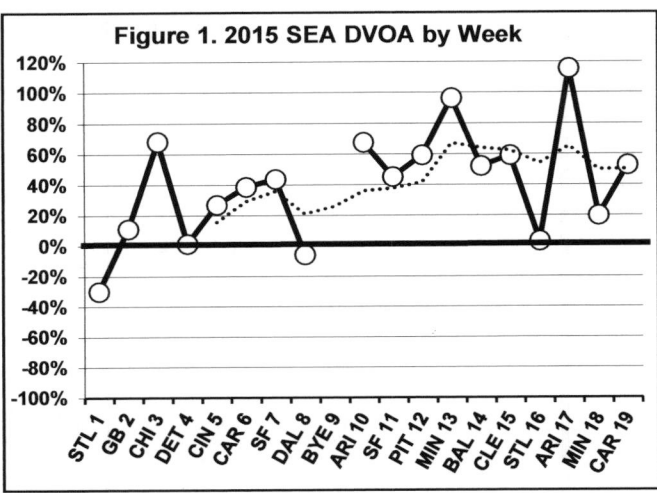

Figure 1. 2015 SEA DVOA by Week

history has taught us that a team of the decade always emerges. The Browns (1950s), Packers (1960s), Steelers (1970s), 49ers (1980s), Cowboys (1990s), and Patriots (2000s) are all known as dynasties for their consistent success in the regular season and having won at least three championships. Sometimes, these team-of-the-decade races are not decided until the decade is nearly over. For instance, the Steelers did not claim the '70s until defeating Dallas in Super Bowl XIII on January 21, 1979.

We still have four seasons to go in the 2010's race, but the trifecta to bet on right now is Seattle, New England, and Denver. Each has a Super Bowl win and a Super Bowl loss, often as the result of games against each other. But going back a few years, Seattle would have been the obvious choice for the NFL's next great dynasty. Thanks to a few great drafts that found maximum value in the later rounds, this team was loaded with young talent on both sides of the ball. But you can't keep all that talent when it comes time to sign those second contracts in the salary-cap era. Seattle has prioritized well in extending Wilson, Richard Sherman, Bobby Wagner, Kam Chancellor, and Earl Thomas, while saying goodbye to Russell Okung, Golden Tate, Byron Maxwell and Bruce Irvin.

Our time spent reminiscing about past Seattle feats does not make this a eulogy for an *almost* dynasty, nor are we closing the window on any *future* dynasty to come. Seattle is still a major contender in 2016, but what made this team so great in the first place is starting to lose its shine. Strong drafts? They have not been there for general manger John Schneider since 2013. The Seahawks did not have a first-round pick between 2013 and 2015, due to trades that brought in Percy Harvin (big disappointment), Paul Richardson (injury problems), and Jimmy Graham (underwhelming debut season). Throw in a surprise retirement from Marshawn Lynch, the heart and soul of this offense, and some free-agent moves that did not pan out (really, Cary Williams?), and we may be looking at a team that will rely more than ever on its star players to succeed. If faced with the challenge of a holdout or injury situation, the depth just may not be there anymore.

In other words, Seattle may be transitioning from the most balanced team in the NFL to one that relies heavily on its quarterback. Not that Wilson is a bad option for added responsibilities, but it makes Seattle more ordinary after such a special four years where running the ball and playing physical defense were always emphasized. We started to see the transition last season with more cracks in the defense and running game, and the late-season surge to No. 1 in DVOA was really

fueled by Wilson having one of the best seven-game stretches any quarterback has ever had.

As last year showed, this is Wilson's offense now. If you told someone before the 2015 season that Seattle's offense would finish No. 1 in DVOA, it would come as no surprise. An underrated receiving corps along with Lynch and the addition of Jimmy Graham seemed to give Wilson all the weapons he needed for a career year. Yet through nine games, the Seahawks were 4-5, Wilson was limited to one touchdown pass eight times, and the offense only managed to surpass 20 points (excluding return scores) twice. Lynch was barely a factor before missing nine games with a sports hernia. Graham struggled to fit in with his new team and tore his patellar tendon in Week 12. The prospects that Seattle would suddenly transform into an offensive juggernaut were poor. But it happened after Wilson threw 24 touchdowns and one interception over the final seven games. His passing DVOA for that stretch was 60.8%, which would be the highest season in our database (Peyton Manning finished 2004 at 58.9%). Wilson's DVOA was just -3.4% for the first nine games.

It really was a tale of two seasons for Wilson, and the stunning part is just how successful he was with Lynch and Graham sidelined. As always, when looking forward we are conflicted by whether to trust the second half or the whole season. Doug Baldwin caught 11 touchdowns from Wilson in a five-game span. It is unlikely these two turned into Joe Montana and Jerry Rice overnight. You can start by questioning the competition. The 49ers, Ravens, and Browns had poor defenses last season. The Rams were better, but that game was Wilson's low point during the run. Pittsburgh's defense struggled in Week 12, although so did Seattle's defense, and it was really important for Wilson to lead Seattle to a 39-30 shootout win—the Seahawks had been 0-12 in games under Wilson when the opponent scored at least 25 points. Minnesota was missing a few defensive starters in Week 13's bloodbath, and the Cardinals, minus Tyrann Mathieu, may not have been going all out to win in Week 17 when just about the only thing on the line was the DVOA trophy. Still, Wilson did not face a lineup of scrubs week after week, and it takes quite the passer to put up those types of numbers over seven games.

Wilson was not alone in his triumphs. Some efficient receivers can't maintain their performance with more volume, but Baldwin was excellent. Third-round pick Tyler Lockett shined as a rookie, both as a receiver and return specialist. Undrafted rookie running back Thomas Rawls exploded onto the scene to lead the NFL in rushing DYAR and success rate. He may have been Offensive Rookie of the Year if not for injury, and is a big reason why Seattle should be in decent shape to overcome Lynch's retirement. Rawls will be back, they are still trying to make Christine Michael happen, and the Seahawks drafted three running backs, including agile former Notre Dame wideout C.J. Prosise in the third round.

Of course, the Wilson-reliant offense did not fare well in the postseason. We can partly chalk up the 10-9 finish in Minnesota to the third-coldest game in NFL history. In Carolina, pressure led to two Wilson interceptions and a very quick 24-0 deficit. Wilson ended up dropping back 56 times and only handing the ball off eight times for a measly 29 yards in the comeback attempt.

Seattle's main weakness is the offensive line, which has probably been the case for three years now. When you have to pay some players handsomely, you cut corners elsewhere. Offensive line is a pretty wise place to do that when your quarterback is uniquely skilled to extend plays with his mobility and overcome pressure. It's just a dangerous game to play when one bad hit can end that quarterback's season, and then what do you do? A criminal arrest shut the door on veteran Tarvaris Jackson this offseason, leaving undrafted rookie Trevone Boykin as Wilson's backup. The TCU product may have a similar skill set, but he's not ready for prime time.

Wilson's 74 consecutive starts to begin his career is the fourth-longest streak in NFL history for a quarterback. Two of the players ahead of him, Andy Dalton and Joe Flacco, saw their streaks end in 2015, while the all-time leader, Peyton Manning, also dealt with injury costing him games for the second time in his career. Wilson's durability will be more important than ever this season. While Wilson can mask many of the pass protection issues, the same may not be true for Seattle's running game without Lynch's physical style. While Rawls may be a similar back, willing to "run through a mother****er's face," is he willing to do it over and over and over... and over and over and over for a full season? The only major change to Seattle's offensive line during last season was at center with Patrick Lewis taking over for Drew Nowak for the second half of the year. That move in itself did not stir such a change in Seattle's production.

The bad news for Seattle's offensive line is that it may have gotten worse this offseason with the free-agent departures of left tackle Russell Okung and right guard J.R. Sweezy, the latter being Seattle's only main starter to rank higher than 25th at his position in snaps per blown block in 2015. You can expect offensive line coach Tom Cable to go through many games of musical chairs this summer to field a starting five from this depth chart. Garry Gilliam was one of the worst right tackles last season, so it is hard to see him working out too well at left tackle this year. J'Marcus Webb was an ineffective guard in Oakland last year, and he could be the favorite to start at right

tackle in Seattle. Justin Britt, a second-round pick in 2014, struggled as a rookie right tackle and then struggled as a left guard last season. Britt was the player swallowed whole by Kawaan Short on Wilson's first dropback against Carolina in the playoffs. He is now moving to center to compete with Lewis, with 2015 fourth-round pick Mark Glowinski getting a good shot at the left guard spot. About the only certainty is that rookie first-round pick Germain Ifedi (Texas A&M) will start his career at right guard. A common knock on him is his lack of consistency and patience in pass protection, meaning he should fit right in with this bunch.

This line sounds like a major problem, but Seattle did allow the NFL's highest rate of pass pressure in 2013 when the Seahawks won the Super Bowl. As long as the run blocking is even close to adequate, you just have to count on Wilson keeping the offense in check.

Lest we forget, Wilson is the asterisk. Despite an ad-lib playing style, he is statistically the most consistent quarterback in the league when running coordinator Darrell Bevell's offense. In four NFL seasons, Wilson's completion percentage has never dipped below 63.1 percent and his passing yards per attempt has always been 7.7 or higher. He had 10 interceptions as a rookie and single digits each year since. Wilson has led the league in scrambles four years in a row, including 56 times last year. Wilson has ranked first or second in percentage of passes thrown out of the pocket for four years in a row, doing so about 30 percent of the time. Wilson has had one of the four highest pressure rates among quarterbacks in each of his seasons. So while things may look chaotic at times, Wilson has a pretty good idea of what he's doing out there. Maybe he never again reaches the high of his seven-game hot streak from last year, but Wilson's track record is good enough that we can trust he'll have his offense ready to compete this season. Getting Rawls, Lockett, and Graham more integrated in their second season with the Seahawks keeps the potential alive for a great offense.

Defensively, Seattle is as solid as it gets in this era... until the game is on the line. Remember that 4-5 start we've mentioned a few times in this chapter? The Seattle defense blew a fourth-quarter lead in all five losses. This has been the Achilles' heel of an otherwise epic defense throughout this run. Since 2012, Seattle's 15 blown fourth-quarter leads are second only to Tampa Bay (16). For reference, the Patriots have allowed 15 fourth-quarter comebacks in 15 years (2001-2015). Using a total is a little unfair to Seattle, which as we've seen has had more fourth-quarter leads to hold than any team in this era. But even when looking at records for preventing fourth-quarter comebacks, Seattle's defense leaves a lot to be desired at 23-15 (Table 1).

The ease with which opponents have driven down the field on Seattle in crunch time has been mystifying. It sure is good that Wilson holds the NFL record for the most game-winning drives (18) through a quarterback's first four seasons. Without some of those, that number of 15 blown leads would be even worse. The defense deserves more blame than it gets for these failures. Matt Ryan only needed 12 seconds to complete two passes and set up a game-winning field goal in the 2012 NFC divisional playoff loss in Atlanta. Tom Brady led the Patriots to a 10-point comeback in the final quarter of Super Bowl XLIX. Last season in Cincinnati, Seattle became the first team since the 2010 Giants to blow a 17-point lead in the fourth quarter. Seattle had always beaten Carolina in tight games, but last season, Cam Newton led a nine-point comeback in the fourth quarter in Week 6. Prior to that, the Panthers were 0-27 when trailing by more than three points in the fourth quarter under Ron Rivera.

Now think of some of the games where the Seattle defense was bailed out from allowing a game-winning drive. How about two Monday night controversies? The "Fail Mary" followed a go-ahead drive for Green Bay in 2012. Last year, the Seahawks stymied Detroit for most of the game. Then with six minutes left, Matthew Stafford suddenly started shredding the secondary, only to see Calvin Johnson fumble at the 1-yard line with a missed illegal bat penalty in the end zone. Or take the games where Seattle's defense never had to take the field in overtime. In Chicago in 2012, Jay Cutler only had 20 seconds to set up a game-tying field goal, and found Brandon Marshall for a 56-yard play. In Denver two years ago, Peyton Manning led the first ever one-minute drill with a two-point conversion for a team to force overtime after trailing by 8 points. Seattle's offense finished the game in overtime, sparing the defense again. Even in the playoffs this past year, Teddy Bridgewater and Kyle Rudolph beat Kam Chancellor twice to quickly get Minnesota into field-goal range. Blair Walsh just happened to miss the shortest do-or-die field goal (27 yards) in playoff history, allowing Seattle to escape with a 10-9 win instead of suffering another blown lead in the playoffs.

This is why Sherman tipping a pass intended for Michael Crabtree in the end zone in the 2013 NFC Championship Game is the biggest play in Seahawks history. Without that Malcolm Smith interception locking up a spot in Super Bowl

Table 1. Holding a One-Score Lead (1-8 Points) in Q4/OT, 2012-2015

Rk	Team	Record	Pct.	Rk	Team	Record	Pct.
1	ARI	28-3	90.3%	17	MIA	17-8	68.0%
2	IND	28-4	87.5%	18	CHI	18-9	66.7%
3	DEN	29-5	85.3%	19	MIN	16-8	66.7%
4	HOU	15-3	83.3%	20	PHI	18-10	64.3%
5	NE	23-5	82.1%	21	BAL	21-13	61.8%
6	NYJ	17-4	81.0%	22	SEA	23-15	60.5%
7	CAR	26-8	76.5%	23	OAK	9-6	60.0%
8	BUF	17-6	73.9%	24	JAC	13-9	59.1%
9	SF	19-7	73.1%	25	WAS	16-12	57.1%
10	GB	18-7	72.0%	26	NYG	14-11	56.0%
11	KC	17-7	70.8%	27	DET	17-14	54.8%
12	ATL	21-9	70.0%	28	NO	12-10	54.5%
13	CIN	20-9	69.0%	29	CLE	13-12	52.0%
14	DAL	22-10	68.8%	30	TEN	12-12	50.0%
15	PIT	22-10	68.8%	31	SD	13-14	48.1%
16	STL	11-5	68.8%	32	TB	12-16	42.9%

Includes regular season and playoffs.

XLVIII, who knows where this team's legacy sits right now?

Carroll says his team has not found a common link among the blown leads, because there really isn't one. You either make the big stops or you don't, and your legacy is greatly affected by success or failure in these moments. A defense with the likes of Sherman, Thomas, Chancellor, Wagner, K.J. Wright, Cliff Avril, and Michael Bennett should be faring better than it has in these moments, but that has not been the case. So you do get worried when this defense has to close a game. The talent core is still obviously strong, but it was not just newcomers such as Cary Williams that hurt the team last season when those five blown leads happened. Like the Vikings in the playoffs, the Bengals and Panthers took advantage of Chancellor with passes up the seam in their comeback victories. This season, the culprit might be the returning Brandon Browner, another odd free-agent signing by Schneider. While Browner used to be a solid corner for the original Legion of Boom, his grabby nature led to a dismal performance in New Orleans last season. Browner was penalized 24 times, the most ever since the league began keeping track of individual penalties in 1999. Browner projects to start opposite of Sherman, but it looks like another downgrade for this defense.

If you downgrade the running game and defense, then the quarterback just gets that much more important to your success. If the Seahawks can keep Wilson upright all year and hold onto enough leads, then there is no reason this team cannot challenge for another No. 1 seed in the NFC. Both Super Bowl appearances came in the seasons where Seattle had home-field advantage, because it is a significant one. Since 2012, the Seahawks are an NFC-best 31-5 (.861) at home.

The hidden advantage to playing at home is getting a favorable start time instead of one of those dreaded 10 a.m. "body clock games" that Pacific teams have to deal with. Since 2012, Seattle is just 9-10 in road games starting at 10 a.m., compared to 12-5 in road games that started later. This is magnified in the postseason against better competition. In three body clock playoff games, Seattle fell behind 20-0 in Atlanta (2012), 9-0 in Minnesota (2015) and 31-0 in Carolina (2015). In none of those games did Seattle score in the first half, something that has happened only twice in the other 71 games of the Wilson era. You may question the importance of the start time when you see Seattle smash Minnesota 38-7 in an early Week 13 game, and you may wonder how starting the game three hours later can help the offensive line block Kawann Short. Nonetheless, years of research show a significant disadvantage to West Coast teams playing in the early Sunday time slot.

Fortunately, Seattle's 2016 schedule only has two early starts: Week 4 at the Jets and Week 8 at the Saints. Unfortunately, other aspects of the schedule favor Arizona. In particular, the Seahawks have to travel to New England in Week 10, while the Cardinals get the Patriots at home to open the season—likely with Jimmy Garoppolo instead of Tom Brady at quarterback. Another strong finish may be necessary with the Seahawks hosting Carolina and Arizona in December with a trip to Green Bay in between. Those big games should go a long way in determining home-field advantage for the playoffs.

Is it greedy for fans and analysts to want more than one championship in an era where there has been no repeat champion for a dozen seasons? Seattle sure came the closest since then, if not for the costliest interception in NFL history at the 1-yard line. Maybe that moment was the breaking point between dynasty and just another great team. Maybe this decade is different and no team emerges as the undisputed team of the decade. But it sure would be disappointing if Seattle did not achieve a bigger payoff from this historically high level of play.

Scott Kacsmar

2015 Seahawks Stats by Week

Wk	vs.	W-L	PF	PA	YDF	YDA	TO	Total	Off	Def	ST
1	at STL	L	31	34	343	352	2	-30%	-7%	23%	0%
2	at GB	L	17	27	324	361	-1	11%	24%	19%	7%
3	CHI	W	26	0	371	146	0	68%	-15%	-43%	40%
4	DET	W	13	10	345	256	-2	1%	-18%	-10%	9%
5	at CIN	L	24	27	397	419	1	27%	21%	-14%	-7%
6	CAR	L	23	27	334	383	2	39%	36%	-1%	2%
7	at SF	W	20	3	388	142	-2	44%	4%	-42%	-2%
8	at DAL	W	13	12	323	220	-1	-6%	-15%	-11%	-2%
9	BYE										
10	ARI	L	32	39	343	451	2	68%	45%	-24%	-1%
11	SF	W	29	13	508	306	0	45%	54%	9%	0%
12	PIT	W	39	30	436	538	4	59%	56%	-2%	2%
13	at MIN	W	38	7	433	125	0	96%	40%	-71%	-15%
14	at BAL	W	35	6	424	302	1	52%	39%	-16%	-3%
15	CLE	W	30	13	423	230	1	59%	42%	-14%	4%
16	STL	L	17	23	312	205	-3	3%	-22%	-15%	10%
17	at ARI	W	36	6	354	232	3	116%	26%	-66%	24%
18	at MIN	W	10	9	226	183	0	20%	-12%	-37%	-5%
19	at CAR	L	24	31	403	295	-2	53%	47%	-3%	4%

Trends and Splits

	Offense	Rank	Defense	Rank
Total DVOA	18.5%	2	-15.2%	4
Unadjusted VOA	15.9%	4	-11.9%	6
Weighted Trend	28.0%	1	-21.0%	3
Variance	7.4%	20	7.2%	26
Average Opponent	-2.4%	9	-0.2%	18
Passing	44.2%	2	-9.8%	3
Rushing	7.4%	4	-22.9%	3
First Down	23.2%	1	-6.2%	9
Second Down	0.8%	18	-9.3%	5
Third Down	39.5%	1	-44.6%	1
First Half	16.2%	7	-13.3%	6
Second Half	20.9%	1	-17.3%	4
Red Zone	11.1%	12	-8.8%	11
Late and Close	16.5%	3	-1.5%	18

Five-Year Performance

Year	W-L	Pyth W	Est W	PF	PA	TO	Total	Rk	Off	Rk	Def	Rk	ST	Rk	Off AGL	Rk	Def AGL	Rk	Off Age	Rk	Def Age	Rk	ST Age	Rk
2011	7-9	8.2	8.1	321	315	+8	-1.5%	19	-8.7%	22	-7.1%	10	0.2%	16	53.4	30	25.2	14	25.8	31	26.2	26	26.0	26
2012	11-5	12.5	13.0	412	245	+13	38.7%	1	18.5%	4	-14.5%	2	5.7%	3	14.8	6	15.0	6	25.9	27	25.6	31	26.0	18
2013	13-3	12.8	13.0	417	231	+20	40.0%	1	9.4%	7	-25.9%	1	4.7%	5	43.8	22	16.2	7	25.7	32	26.0	27	26.1	14
2014	12-4	11.9	12.7	394	254	+10	31.9%	1	16.8%	5	-16.8%	1	-1.7%	19	39.5	24	35.3	13	25.3	31	26.3	23	25.8	24
2015	10-6	11.8	12.5	423	277	+7	38.1%	1	18.7%	1	-15.2%	4	4.2%	3	23.7	9	16.4	4	25.9	25	27.0	12	26.3	12

2015 Performance Based on Most Common Personnel Groups

SEA Offense					SEA Offense vs. Opponents					SEA Defense				SEA Defense vs. Opponents			
Pers	Freq	Yds	DVOA	Run%	Pers	Freq	Yds	DVOA	Run%	Pers	Freq	Yds	DVOA	Pers	Freq	Yds	DVOA
11	54%	6.7	39.8%	27%	Base	34%	5.2	6.8%	64%	Base	40%	4.3	-25.3%	11	52%	5.6	-10.6%
12	16%	5.1	-1.9%	45%	Nickel	50%	6.4	34.3%	31%	Nickel	58%	5.7	-6.6%	12	22%	4.7	-14.1%
21	13%	4.1	-11.7%	74%	Dime+	14%	7.0	64.4%	20%	Dime+	1%	6.1	-136.9%	21	6%	3.6	-50.8%
22	6%	3.3	-1.5%	75%	Goal Line	1%	0.8	1.5%	83%	Goal Line	0%	1.0	92.4%	22	5%	3.9	-28.4%
20	3%	11.2	114.4%	60%										10	5%	8.0	6.2%
01	2%	10.4	139.9%	0%										13	4%	3.8	-24.1%

Strategic Tendencies

Run/Pass		Rk	Formation		Rk	Pass Rush		Rk	Secondary		Rk	Strategy		Rk
Runs, first half	41%	9	Form: Single Back	70%	25	Rush 3	9.6%	7	4 DB	40%	7	Play action	24%	6
Runs, first down	48%	13	Form: Empty Back	11%	5	Rush 4	68.2%	12	5 DB	58%	9	Avg Box (Off)	6.20	19
Runs, second-long	38%	3	Pers: 3+ WR	61%	16	Rush 5	17.7%	26	6+ DB	1%	30	Avg Box (Def)	5.96	31
Runs, power sit.	67%	5	Pers: 2+ TE/6+ OL	26%	25	Rush 6+	4.5%	25	CB by Sides	72%	21	Offensive Pace	31.70	26
Runs, behind 2H	28%	12	Pers: 6+ OL	2%	16	Sacks by LB	21.6%	22	S/CB Cover Ratio	22%	19	Defensive Pace	31.85	31
Pass, ahead 2H	50%	9	Shotgun/Pistol	63%	15	Sacks by DB	8.1%	15	DB Blitz	5%	30	Go for it on 4th	0.89	17

Despite their strength in the running game, the Seahawks were shockingly mediocre using play-action in 2015. Seattle was the best team in the NFL without play-action, gaining 7.6 yards per play with 56.0% DVOA. But with play-action, that dropped to 5.7 yards per play and 25.4% DVOA. However, this may be a one-year fluke, as the Seahawks were about the same with and without play-action in 2014 and actually much better when using play-action in 2013. ☜ When we remove consideration of sacks, deliberate throwaways, and passes batted down at the line, the Seahawks had the highest passing DVOA in the league on both short passes (up to 15 yards through the air, 70.9% DVOA) and deep passes (over 16 yards through the air, 196.1% DVOA). ☜ If you want to pass on this defense, do it early in the down-and-distance sequence. Seattle was just 17th against passes on first down, but ranked No. 1 against passes on third down. ☜ This was the fourth straight year the Seahawks were 31st or 32nd in situation-neutral pace on defense, as opponents try to keep the ball out of their hands. ☜ The gap wasn't quite as bad as the year before, but once again the Seahawks committed far more penalties than their opponents, tied for ninth with 138 penalties but tied for 30th with 108 opponent penalties. Arizona's gap was just as big in the opposite direction, one of the reasons the Cardinals took the division title.

Passing

Player	DYAR	DVOA	Plays	NtYds	Avg	YAC	C%	TD	Int
R.Wilson	1190	24.3%	526	3744	7.1	5.6	68.7%	34	8
T.Jackson*	7	2.5%	7	31	4.4	5.8	66.7%	0	0

Rushing

Player	DYAR	DVOA	Plays	Yds	Avg	TD	Fum	Suc
T.Rawls	216	26.4%	147	830	5.6	4	1	62%
M.Lynch*	47	1.2%	111	417	3.8	3	0	50%
R.Wilson	123	17.4%	85	566	6.7	1	4	-
C.Michael	45	18.6%	39	192	4.9	0	0	51%
F.Jackson*	25	17.9%	26	100	3.8	0	0	46%
B.Brown*	15	5.0%	26	72	2.8	1	0	35%
D.Harris*	-30	-45.0%	21	51	2.4	0	1	38%
D.Coleman*	0	-7.4%	8	32	4.0	0	0	63%
T.Lockett	11	-5.7%	5	20	4.0	0	0	-
W.Tukuafu*	-3	-18.9%	4	6	1.5	1	1	75%

Receiving

Player	DYAR	DVOA	Plays	Ctch	Yds	Y/C	YAC	TD	C%
D.Baldwin	414	39.6%	103	78	1069	13.7	5.6	14	76%
T.Lockett	249	35.1%	69	51	664	13.0	5.0	6	74%
J.Kearse	227	29.8%	68	49	690	14.1	4.8	5	72%
C.Matthews*	-12	-28.8%	9	4	54	13.5	3.5	0	44%
R.Lockette*	15	15.5%	7	4	71	17.8	3.8	1	57%
J.Graham	110	14.8%	74	48	605	12.6	4.6	2	65%
L.Willson	30	10.5%	26	17	213	12.5	5.5	1	65%
C.Helfet	-31	-28.5%	22	13	130	10.0	6.1	0	59%
F.Jackson*	76	20.3%	41	32	257	8.0	8.0	2	78%
M.Lynch*	-24	-34.6%	21	13	80	6.2	6.7	0	62%
T.Rawls	13	5.8%	11	9	76	8.4	8.4	1	82%

Offensive Line

Player	Pos	Age	GS	Snaps	Pen	Sk	Pass	Run	Player	Pos	Age	GS	Snaps	Pen	Sk	Pass	Run
Justin Britt	LG	25	16/16	1079	8	1.0	5.5	7.0	Patrick Lewis	C	25	10/9	599	1	0.0	1.0	5.0
Garry Gilliam	RT	26	16/16	1059	6	4.5	14.0	4.0	Drew Nowak*	C	26	8/7	464	3	0.0	0.0	2.0
J.R. Sweezy*	RG	27	15/15	1006	10	2.5	3.5	2.0	Alvin Bailey*	OT	25	14/3	271	3	1.0	4.5	1.0
Russell Okung*	LT	29	13/13	851	6	3.0	7.0	7.0	J'Marcus Webb	RG	28	16/16	1056	6	2.0	10.0	5.0

Year	Yards	ALY	Rank	Power	Rank	Stuff	Rank	2nd Lev	Rank	Open Field	Rank	Sacks	ASR	Rank	Press	Rank	F-Start	Cont.
2013	4.03	4.05	9	49%	32	19%	15	1.17	13	0.59	23	44	9.6%	32	35.9%	32	21	29
2014	4.62	4.23	4	78%	2	17%	6	1.34	4	0.80	11	42	8.7%	24	39.3%	32	29	25
2015	4.44	4.18	4	71%	8	18%	5	1.20	15	0.81	12	46	9.0%	30	31.8%	30	21	30

2015 ALY by direction:	Left End 4.06 (10)	Left Tackle 4.53 (3)	Mid/Guard 4.1 (9)	Right Tackle 4.19 (6)	Right End 4.04 (8)

There was strong consideration to just write this comment as two words: "It blows," as in blown blocks. ✎ Look where Seattle's starting five ranked at their positions in snaps per blown block in 2015: left tackle Russell Okung (25th), left guard Justin Britt (28th), center Patrick Lewis (29th), right guard J.R. Sweezy (12th) and right tackle Garry Gilliam (32nd). ✎ Sweezy and Okung are gone now, but if there is a bright side, it's that Mark Glowinski and rookie Germain Ifedi have not yet proven they are poor players. Seattle could get better here, but as we know, this offense has worked at a high level in the past in spite of the offensive line.

Defensive Front Seven

Defensive Line	Age	Pos	G	Snaps	Plays	TmPct	Rk	Stop	Dfts	BTkl	Runs	St%	Rk	RuYd	Rk	Sack	Hit	Hur	Dsrpt
Brandon Mebane*	31	DT	15	489	24	3.3%	69	18	5	3	19	84%	15	1.5	15	1.5	3	6.0	0
Ahtyba Rubin	30	DT	16	476	37	4.8%	44	30	6	4	33	79%	38	2.5	53	2.0	3	8.5	0
Jordan Hill	25	DT	10	311	25	5.2%	39	16	6	0	19	68%	63	2.5	54	0.0	3	7.5	1
Sealver Siliga	26	DT	13	254	28	4.2%	--	21	2	1	27	74%	--	2.5	--	0.0	0	1.0	0

Edge Rushers	Age	Pos	G	Snaps	Plays	TmPct	Rk	Stop	Dfts	BTkl	Runs	St%	Rk	RuYd	Rk	Sack	Hit	Hur	Dsrpt
Michael Bennett	31	DE	16	808	50	6.5%	19	45	27	7	36	89%	6	0.8	4	10.0	21	27.0	0
Cliff Avril	30	DE	16	778	54	7.1%	10	44	24	10	28	86%	10	1.3	15	9.0	17	28.0	5
Frank Clark	23	DE	15	333	18	2.5%	--	14	7	0	9	89%	--	1.3	--	3.0	4	10.5	2
Chris Clemons	35	DE	16	662	14	1.6%	97	13	7	6	8	100%	1	0.5	3	3.0	7	18.5	1

Linebackers	Age	Pos	G	Snaps	Plays	TmPct	Rk	Stop	Dfts	BTkl	Runs	St%	Rk	RuYd	Rk	Sack	Hit	Hur	Tgts	Suc%	Rk	AdjYd	Rk	PD	Int
K.J. Wright	27	OLB	16	966	117	15.3%	14	65	19	3	63	59%	58	3.8	59	1.0	1	6.5	34	75%	5	3.6	7	3	0
Bobby Wagner	26	MLB	15	904	120	16.7%	10	63	18	13	56	66%	36	3.4	39	0.5	4	6	27	69%	11	5.1	18	7	0
Bruce Irvin*	29	OLB	15	710	40	5.6%	85	32	14	3	22	77%	5	2.6	8	5.5	11	16.5	6	100%	--	0.3	--	1	0

Year	Yards	ALY	Rank	Power	Rank	Stuff	Rank	2nd Level	Rank	Open Field	Rank	Sacks	ASR	Rank	Press	Rank
2013	3.75	3.73	13	70%	24	21%	11	1.06	11	0.55	12	44	7.6%	7	34.4%	1
2014	3.54	3.41	5	59%	10	23%	6	0.92	4	0.59	8	37	7.0%	13	25.4%	13
2015	3.54	3.60	12	72%	26	21%	15	0.94	3	0.42	3	37	6.7%	14	29.3%	2

2015 ALY by direction:	Left End 4.96 (29)	Left Tackle 4.04 (20)	Mid/Guard 3.02 (2)	Right Tackle 4.05 (22)	Right End 3.08 (14)

Michael Bennett and Cliff Avril are arguably the best duo of defensive ends in the NFL right now, combining for 55 hurries last season. ✎ Seattle's defensive line depth has been impressive over the years, and looks to be in good shape again with the young Frank Clark and return of veteran Chris Clemons, who played for Seattle from 2010 to 2013 and posted 23 hurries in 2013. ✎ Defensive tackles have been harder to retain for Seattle, and the departure of Brandon Mebane should open the door for Jordan Hill to finally be a starter in his fourth season. If not, Seattle also used a second-round pick on Jarran Reed (Alabama), an elite run defender who could play on early downs. ✎ K.J. Wright and Bobby Wagner are very good linebackers, though Wagner's 2015 was down from his 2014 level when Tony Dungy thought he was the NFL's MVP. ✎ Bruce Irvin was never a dominant pass-rusher, so look for Seattle to replace him with Michael Morgan (a veteran backup who played for Pete Carroll at USC) or 2014 fourth-round pick Kevin Pierre-Louis.

Defensive Secondary

Secondary	Age	Pos	G	Snaps	Plays	Overall TmPct	Rk	Stop	Dfts	BTkl	vs. Run Runs	St%	Rk	RuYd	Rk	vs. Pass Tgts	Tgt%	Rk	Dist	Suc%	Rk	AdjYd	Rk	PD	Int
Earl Thomas	27	FS	16	978	69	9.0%	45	20	12	12	24	17%	67	9.3	56	14	3.9%	7	20.1	73%	6	4.9	7	7	5
Richard Sherman	28	CB	16	975	64	8.4%	44	28	11	4	14	50%	20	4.9	13	58	16.0%	13	18.2	57%	21	7.5	36	14	2
Kam Chancellor	28	SS	11	635	76	14.5%	6	32	11	11	38	50%	16	4.9	9	24	10.2%	57	9.2	67%	12	5.4	11	4	2
Cary Williams*	32	CB	10	619	50	10.5%	12	15	9	3	18	22%	64	7.2	39	36	15.5%	9	13.9	44%	68	9.4	69	3	0
DeShawn Shead	27	CB	16	616	56	7.3%	--	16	8	6	10	30%	--	5.5	--	45	19.5%	--	16.3	44%	--	8.1	--	7	1
Kelcie McCray	28	FS	16	218	26	3.4%	--	11	0	0	14	50%	--	5.1	--	7	8.7%	--	5.1	36%	--	3.6	--	2	0
Marcus Burley	26	CB	13	203	19	3.1%	--	10	5	0	5	60%	--	3.8	--	14	18.6%	--	11.2	60%	--	5.5	--	2	1
Brandon Browner	32	CB	16	1024	86	10.6%	9	30	6	9	24	54%	17	8.4	51	69	17.9%	21	13.6	44%	67	11.0	75	11	1

Year	Pass D Rank	vs. #1 WR	Rk	vs. #2 WR	Rk	vs. Other WR	Rk	vs. TE	Rk	vs. RB	Rk
2013	1	-18.0%	4	-13.4%	7	-27.1%	3	-34.2%	3	-32.7%	1
2014	3	-22.0%	4	-18.3%	6	-19.2%	4	-0.8%	18	-2.0%	16
2015	3	-33.3%	1	-21.5%	5	-9.5%	10	20.0%	26	-17.8%	5

This famed secondary is getting very top-heavy with little trustworthy depth behind the three big stars. ☞ Earl Thomas is the best all-around safety in the game, but Kam Chancellor is the enforcer. Despite a few hiccups in big moments, Chancellor's overall coverage numbers still look good. Nonetheless, teams may want to target him more to get him out of his comfort level in the box. ☞ Our charting numbers for Richard Sherman will rarely blow you away, but so much of his value is intimidating opponents to not even throw in his direction. Sherman routinely faces about 60 targets per season. Seattle opponents threw 20.6 percent of passes to No. 1 receivers; only Arizona opponents threw to their top receiver less often. ☞ Finding a boundary corner to play opposite of Sherman has been difficult since Byron Maxwell left. Cary Williams was a poor replacement before Seattle cut him in December. Jeremy Lane is a talented nickelback, but really needs to stay in the slot, and his career has been limited by various injuries. DeShawn Shead was not much better than Williams, and now the Seahawks look serious about resurrecting Brandon Browner's career opposite of Sherman. It worked when the grabby corner was younger, but Browner embarrassed himself in New Orleans' system last season. If the end of the Legion of Doom was when Road Warrior Hawk fell off the Titantron, then Browner starting for Seattle in 2016 could mark the end of the Legion of Boom's dominance.

Special Teams

Year	DVOA	Rank	FG/XP	Rank	Net Kick	Rank	Kick Ret	Rank	Net Punt	Rank	Punt Ret	Rank	Hidden	Rank
2013	4.7%	5	4.3	8	5.6	7	-3.8	22	10.4	4	7.2	6	-2.6	19
2014	-1.7%	19	0.8	12	4.5	11	-7.5	31	-4.0	21	-2.4	15	5.3	8
2015	4.2%	3	6.6	4	0.8	13	7.6	4	-5.4	23	11.3	1	-8.9	29

Tyler Lockett's excellent rookie season earned him All-Pro honors as a return specialist. Lockett ranked third in kick return value and fourth in punt return value, scoring a touchdown on each type of return. ☞ Though he missed four extra points, Steven Hauschka had one of his best kicking seasons yet, including a perfect 6-for-6 on field goals of 50-plus yards. ☞ Punting was the weak link for an otherwise strong special teams unit. Jon Ryan had one of his better punting seasons, but the punt coverage—long a Seahawks strength—was among the weakest in the league. Tavon Austin burned the Seahawks again with a 75-yard punt return touchdown in Week 1.

Tampa Bay Buccaneers

2015 record: 6-10	**Total DVOA:** -9.1% (21st)		**2016 Mean Projection:** 7.2 wins	**On the Clock (0-4):** 15%	
Pythagorean Wins: 6.0 (24th)	**Offense:** -1.1% (17th)		**Postseason Odds:** 26.4%	**Mediocrity (5-7):** 41%	
Snap-Weighted Age: 25.9 (30th)	**Defense:** 3.3% (18th)		**Super Bowl Odds:** 2.3%	**Playoff Contender (8-10):** 34%	
Average Opponent: -7.7% (31st)	**Special Teams:** -4.7% (30th)		**Proj. Avg. Opponent:** 2.1% (6th)	**Super Bowl Contender (11+):** 10%	

2015: They've rebuilt well enough to can the head coach and make the offensive coordinator the new head coach. Trust us —it makes sense.

2016: With all these Smiths, the only appropriate question is: How Soon Is Now?

Lately the Buccaneers have been memorable, but for all the wrong reasons. Their new franchise quarterback threw a pick-six on his first career pass, losing to a team that finished the year 2-14. Star receiver Mike Evans created a snuff film of dropped passes against the Giants. They canned Lovie Smith for the audacity of improving the team four games last season, something unheard of in NFL circles. They drafted a kicker in the second round. For some reason they wanted their uniform numbers to look like alarm clocks. It's all very confusing.

But I want to draw your attention to one of those oft-popular "Player A versus Player B" comparisons. Player A is Crystal Pepsi, and … oops, I'm getting ahead of myself. Clearly, *one* of these players is Jameis Winston.

Table 1. Jameis Winston versus New Coke

	Comp %	TD-INT	Yards	DVOA	DYAR
Player A	58.9%	22-15	3,828	2.1%	467
Player B	55.0%	23-17	4,089	-5.1%	257

Player A is Winston. Player B is Andrew Luck's rookie season.

Now, we're aware that these statistics weren't compiled in a vacuum. Andrew Luck ran a Bruce Arians offense as a rookie, and his completion percentage clearly suffered for it. We get it. But outside of Tampa having better running backs, the context in which these two operated was actually quite similar.

Winston was asked to run a pro-style offense under coordinator (now head coach) Dirk Koetter from Day 1, and he made a ton of rookie mistakes because of it. This wasn't an offense that had jitterbugs ready to take quick screens for extra yardage. It had two big receivers, and asked Winston to throw to their routes with anticipation. Nothing came easy.

Just like Luck, Winston had nobody of note to throw to outside of those top two receivers. UDFAs such as Donteea Dyer and Adam Humphries were a major part of this offense. Just like Luck, Winston dealt with offensive linemen who continually tried to get him killed. Donovan Smith's rookie season at left tackle was rough, and stalwart veteran tackle Demar Dotson only played six games. Fill-in Gosder Cherilus only added to the party in his own backfield. Partly because of these fac-

tors, the Bucs ran more plays with six offensive linemen than any team besides Washington.

Just like Luck, Winston wasn't immediately sure what throws his arm could cash in the NFL. This led to a high interception total and helped drag down his completion percentage. And, just like Luck, Winston created some passes with his reads, mobility, and arm that only a handful of quarterbacks in the league today could recreate.

NFL media types spent a lot of time slagging Winston pre-draft because his 2014 season was objectively worse than his 2013 one. Football Outsiders won't claim to be an exception, either; Winston had a mediocre QBASE projection, and we criticized the decision to choose him over Marcus Mariota. Of course, even more digital ink was spilled on the subject of Winston's off-field behavior, which was at best eccentric and at worst a Johnny Manziel B-reel. (Of course, Peyton Manning also had some interesting off-field drama in college, let's not forget.) Nonetheless, Winston was clearly a special talent, one that merited the No. 1 overall pick in spite of the poor 2014 season. The idea of Winston having a full offseason to work with an NFL team, clean up his mechanics, and leave college baseball in the rearview mirror should scare the rest of the league.

The decision to retain Koetter as head coach so that he could continue Winston's development was interesting. Koetter has some head coach experience with Boise State and Arizona State. He also coordinated some NFL offenses that didn't look great on paper, but became much worse after he left. Koetter was one of the sacrificial lambs for the Jaguars after Blaine Gabbert and Luke McCown did exactly what you would expect them to do in 2011. The Jaguars offense didn't recover until last year. When Mike Smith was deposed in Atlanta, Koetter left as well after three years of running the Falcons' offense. Despite a better offensive line performance, the Falcons' passing game suddenly fell apart last year. Meanwhile, Tampa went from 32nd in offensive DVOA in 2014 to 17th last year—granted, they did fall into Winston, but Tennessee fell into Mariota and took over last place from the Bucs anyway. For what it's worth, there was also a sense that the Bucs had to promote Koetter or risk losing him: he was also chased by the 49ers, and was reportedly considered by the Eagles as well.

Lovie Smith's firing, in and of itself, wasn't a bad thing. Smith's in-game management was ridiculously conserva-

2016 Buccaneers Schedule

Week	Opp.	Week	Opp.	Week	Opp.
1	at ATL	7	at SF	13	at SD
2	at ARI	8	OAK	14	NO
3	LARM	9	ATL (Thu.)	15	at DAL
4	DEN	10	CHI	16	at NO (Sat.)
5	at CAR (Mon.)	11	at KC	17	CAR
6	BYE	12	SEA		

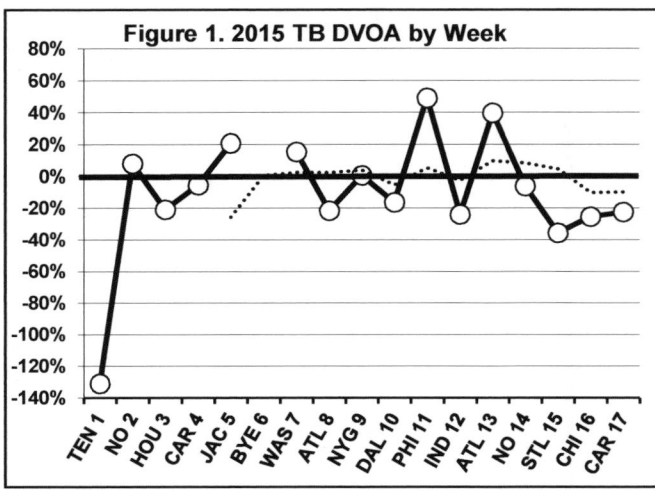

tive, and cost the Bucs points in games they could have used to mount a real playoff charge in a down NFC last year. No, Tampa didn't just play Tampa-2 all the time, but his defensive schemes either asked too much of his players or left underneath receivers free to pick up big chunks of yardage. It's easy to give a coach with as much of a track record as Smith the benefit of the doubt. But the fact that firing Smith was an aggressive move does not mean that Bucs management didn't also properly recognize that Smith's habits would haunt a contending team.

Tossing Smith overboard meant committing to Koetter's vision, which meant another Smith —Mike—is now running the defense. Koetter's former head coach with the Falcons told reporters in his opening presser that he wanted to run a more flexible defense than (Lovie) Smith did. Mike Smith's teams have always been built on stopping the run without much in the way of pass rush, which is ... pretty much exactly how Lovie Smith's teams have been built.

As Table 2 shows, Lovie was a very extreme coach in some ways. He refused to use six defensive backs, he finished last in percentage of three-man rushes in each of the last two years, and had the highest average defensive box in the league each of the last two seasons as well. All Mike has to do to be more flexible than Lovie is understand that other strategies exist.

Table 2. Major Strategic Differences Between Mike Smith and Lovie Smith (2013-2015)

Averages	Lovie Smith	Mike Smith
6+ DB	0.0%	21.0%
3-Man Rush	1.1%	6.2%
Average Box	6.50	6.33
Blitz Rate	28.4%	33.9%

How will things actually change? We suspect there won't be a huge difference between Lovie and Mike besides the fact that Mike will disguise things a little more. The base fronts will mostly be the same. You'll see slightly more blitzing. That means the Bucs will need to improve on their personnel.

Tampa's offseason was about addressing immediate areas of need, but most of their signings fall into the category of "he was a free agent for a reason." With guard Logan Mankins retiring, the team signed Seahawks guard J.R. Sweezy to a five-year deal with $14.5 million in guarantees. Sweezy is a scout's dream in that when he plays well, he looks incredible. He's strong

enough to bulldoze anyone in the run game. He was also a big part of the reason the Seattle offensive line was much-maligned under Russell Wilson. The contract is in no way an albatross— it's just that Sweezy is not an improvement on Mankins.

Edge-rusher Robert Ayers is an attempt at papering over another quick-fix signing that didn't work out: Michael Bennett. Once left for dead as a draft bust in Denver, Ayers finally became a source of rotational pressure for the Giants last year, notching nine sacks with 11 starts. But at age 31, with no previous track record as a full-time starter, it's fair to wonder just how consistently effective he can be in a full-time role.

Corner Brent Grimes and linebacker Daryl Smith were the kind of great, underrated players who could have turned this unit around—in 2012. Grimes has been more relevant for his wife's Twitter rants than his play over the past two seasons. Smith looked a step slow in Baltimore last year and was singled out as part of the problem as the Ravens tried to rebuild this offseason.

Rebuilding the Bucs from 2-14 has never been about the star power; as soon as Winston was on board, Tampa has had enough of that to compensate. But for the Bucs to succeed sooner rather than later, they need to win more of their tiny gambles. They need 2015 fifth-round Nebraska receiver Kenny Bell, a draftnik favorite, healthy and ready to produce as their third receiver. They need their second-round offensive linemen, Smith and Ali Marpet, to play like worthy starters. They need their free agents to be contributors rather than just players who keep them treading water. The big thing standing in the way of Tampa and success as of today is that they just don't have the depth of talent that some of the teams in front of them have.

The building blocks of a strong offense are in place. Tampa ranked fifth in both yards and plays per drive, and had the second-fewest punts and three-and-outs per drive. But between Winston's constant turnovers and red zone failures, most of the good production didn't actually lead to points. The flags the offensive line helped provide as part of a league-high in offensive penalties (for the second straight season) didn't help either.

Like all of the NFC South teams this year, the Bucs have a tough schedule with games against both West divisions.

We've got their defense shaking up a little bit higher than it did in the past couple of years. The biggest swing factor, though, will be just how high Winston can soar. That's a very difficult thing to project, because projection systems don't often encounter quarterbacks with the combination of high-pedigree quarterback skills and lack of refinement that Winston has. We can put a number on it, but our guess it that

the ceiling is much, much higher than we're going to get out of a computer forecast.

And if Winston can hit that in a hurry, there's no reason he can't take another page from Luck's book and lead an undeserving team to the playoffs.

Rivers McCown

2015 Buccaneers Stats by Week

Wk	vs.	W-L	PF	PA	YDF	YDA	TO	Total	Off	Def	ST
1	TEN	L	14	42	273	309	-1	-131%	-93%	45%	7%
2	at NO	W	26	19	333	323	1	8%	-25%	-26%	7%
3	at HOU	L	9	19	318	413	0	-21%	-6%	-5%	-19%
4	CAR	L	23	37	411	244	-4	-5%	-6%	-17%	-16%
5	JAC	W	38	31	369	325	2	21%	23%	14%	12%
6	BYE										
7	at WAS	L	30	31	479	355	0	16%	36%	23%	2%
8	at ATL	W	23	20	290	496	4	-22%	-1%	18%	-2%
9	NYG	L	18	32	383	327	-1	1%	-2%	-17%	-14%
10	DAL	W	10	6	327	216	-1	-16%	-19%	-17%	-14%
11	at PHI	W	45	17	521	383	3	49%	28%	-16%	5%
12	at IND	L	12	25	344	336	-1	-24%	-8%	8%	-9%
13	ATL	W	23	19	388	319	-1	40%	22%	-13%	5%
14	NO	L	17	24	291	388	0	-6%	-1%	2%	-3%
15	at STL	L	23	31	509	319	-2	-36%	18%	37%	-16%
16	CHI	L	21	26	389	327	-3	-25%	1%	10%	-16%
17	at CAR	L	10	38	386	366	-1	-22%	5%	23%	-4%

Trends and Splits

	Offense	Rank	Defense	Rank
Total DVOA	-1.4%	18	3.3%	18
Unadjusted VOA	-1.6%	19	4.0%	25
Weighted Trend	7.3%	13	4.5%	19
Variance	8.8%	25	4.5%	17
Average Opponent	3.6%	29	-3.3%	30
Passing	13.0%	17	20.6%	26
Rushing	-6.1%	11	-16.5%	9
First Down	9.5%	9	-0.4%	15
Second Down	-9.2%	23	3.7%	20
Third Down	-12.5%	24	9.9%	22
First Half	2.2%	14	1.8%	18
Second Half	-4.6%	19	4.9%	21
Red Zone	4.5%	15	26.7%	29
Late and Close	-4.7%	20	-2.2%	17

Five-Year Performance

Year	W-L	Pyth W	Est W	PF	PA	TO	Total	Rk	Off	Rk	Def	Rk	ST	Rk	Off AGL	Rk	Def AGL	Rk	Off Age	Rk	Def Age	Rk	ST Age	Rk
2011	4-12	3.2	5.5	287	494	-16	-25.1%	30	-11.5%	26	14.2%	31	0.6%	14	17.1	5	34.3	20	26.0	30	25.6	31	25.3	31
2012	7-9	7.9	7.8	389	394	+3	-6.6%	20	0.6%	14	2.9%	20	-4.3%	27	26.7	14	30.1	18	26.4	22	25.6	30	25.7	24
2013	4-12	5.3	6.3	288	389	+10	-5.1%	19	-10.4%	24	-6.8%	8	-1.5%	22	75.6	31	9.6	2	27.0	16	25.0	32	26.2	11
2014	2-14	4.4	4.1	277	410	-8	-28.3%	30	-26.3%	32	1.1%	18	-0.8%	17	31.1	17	56.1	25	27.5	7	25.7	30	26.0	18
2015	6-10	6.0	6.7	342	417	-5	-9.1%	21	-1.1%	17	3.3%	18	-4.7%	30	42.2	21	32.8	20	25.9	27	25.9	28	26.2	16

2015 Performance Based on Most Common Personnel Groups

TB Offense					TB Offense vs. Opponents					TB Defense				TB Defense vs. Opponents			
Pers	Freq	Yds	DVOA	Run%	Pers	Freq	Yds	DVOA	Run%	Pers	Freq	Yds	DVOA	Pers	Freq	Yds	DVOA
11	52%	5.8	-1.2%	24%	Base	41%	6.3	4.7%	60%	Base	39%	4.5	-11.3%	11	55%	5.8	13.6%
12	17%	6.8	7.3%	45%	Nickel	46%	6.0	0.3%	30%	Nickel	60%	5.9	14.3%	12	20%	5.4	-3.6%
21	12%	5.6	-28.4%	65%	Dime+	13%	5.9	10.9%	12%	Dime+	0%	3.0	-89.8%	21	10%	5.0	-7.1%
611	4%	8.1	61.9%	61%	Goal Line	1%	0.6	39.9%	88%					22	5%	4.5	-3.4%
612	4%	4.4	10.6%	69%										13	3%	2.4	-42.1%
13	3%	7.5	37.2%	58%										01	2%	4.8	-35.8%

Strategic Tendencies

Run/Pass		Rk	Formation		Rk	Pass Rush		Rk	Secondary		Rk	Strategy		Rk
Runs, first half	45%	4	Form: Single Back	72%	22	Rush 3	1.1%	32	4 DB	39%	9	Play action	19%	16
Runs, first down	54%	6	Form: Empty Back	5%	24	Rush 4	70.3%	6	5 DB	60%	6	Avg Box (Off)	6.29	12
Runs, second-long	27%	24	Pers: 3+ WR	53%	23	Rush 5	19.1%	22	6+ DB	0%	32	Avg Box (Def)	6.43	3
Runs, power sit.	57%	14	Pers: 2+ TE/6+ OL	34%	16	Rush 6+	9.5%	9	CB by Sides	79%	13	Offensive Pace	29.90	14
Runs, behind 2H	29%	7	Pers: 6+ OL	13%	2	Sacks by LB	23.7%	19	S/CB Cover Ratio	23%	16	Defensive Pace	29.31	6
Pass, ahead 2H	48%	11	Shotgun/Pistol	44%	30	Sacks by DB	3.9%	27	DB Blitz	9%	18	Go for it on 4th	0.63	29

We've seen since we began charting games that play-action performance is surprisingly inconsistent from season to season, but we've never seen anything like the Bucs in 2014 and 2015. Tampa Bay increased its play-action DVOA by over 100 percentage points from the year before, by far the largest year-to-year jump we've ever seen. The Bucs were by far the worst team with play-action in 2014 (-55.9% DVOA, 4.1 yards per pass) but last season ranked fourth in DVOA (49.2%) and fifth in yards per play (9.2). By comparison, the Bucs' DVOA in passes without play-action only increased from -9.1% in 2014 to 8.5% in 2015. ☜ Tampa ranked eighth in offensive DVOA on the road, but just 25th in home games. That was the largest "reverse split" in the league last year for offensive DVOA. ☜ The Bucs used extra offensive linemen more effectively than any offense in the league. Tampa had six or more O-linemen on 12.9 percent of its plays—second behind Washington—and compiled a 36.1% DVOA on these plays (third among teams with at least 20 such plays). ☜ Tampa had the league's best DVOA on wide receiver and tight end screens at 65.0%, but they only called 17 such plays all season, fourth-fewest in the league. ☜ If you watched a Tampa Bay game, you saw a lot of bad tackling. On offense, the Bucs finished fifth in the league in broken tackles and fourth in the rate of plays with broken tackles. But on defense, Tampa Bay had the most broken tackles in the league, 125, though Chicago had a slightly higher rate of plays with broken tackles.

Passing

Player	DYAR	DVOA	Plays	NtYds	Avg	YAC	C%	TD	Int
J.Winston	467	2.1%	560	3828	6.8	4.8	58.9%	22	15

Rushing

Player	DYAR	DVOA	Plays	Yds	Avg	TD	Fum	Suc
D.Martin	81	-1.6%	288	1402	4.9	6	4	48%
C.Sims	50	2.6%	107	529	4.9	0	1	57%
J.Winston	42	7.6%	41	223	5.4	6	3	-
B.Rainey*	-16	-118.2%	5	18	3.6	0	1	40%

Receiving

Player	DYAR	DVOA	Plays	Ctch	Yds	Y/C	YAC	TD	C%
M.Evans	187	2.8%	148	74	1211	16.4	3.3	3	50%
V.Jackson	111	11.2%	62	33	543	16.5	3.1	3	53%
A.Humphries	26	-4.1%	40	27	260	9.6	4.6	1	68%
D.Dye	-75	-45.4%	30	11	132	12.0	3.1	1	37%
L.Murphy	45	18.0%	18	10	198	19.8	3.7	0	56%
R.Shepard	-12	-29.2%	9	3	28	9.3	0.3	1	33%
A.Seferian-Jenkins	33	5.0%	39	21	338	16.1	4.6	4	54%
C.Brate	81	33.6%	30	23	288	12.5	2.2	3	77%
B.Myers	18	11.2%	17	12	127	10.6	1.8	0	71%
L.Stocker	-2	-9.2%	13	9	61	6.8	4.3	1	69%
C.Sims	150	29.2%	70	51	571	11.2	9.5	4	73%
D.Martin	11	-8.9%	44	33	271	8.2	7.0	1	75%

Offensive Line

Player	Pos	Age	GS	Snaps	Pen	Sk	Pass	Run	Player	Pos	Age	GS	Snaps	Pen	Sk	Pass	Run
Donovan Smith	LT	23	16/16	1093	13	4.0	18.0	7.0	Evan Smith	C	30	9/5	377	2	0.0	2.0	2.0
Logan Mankins*	LG	34	15/15	1023	7	0.0	4.0	6.0	Kevin Pamphile	OT	26	16/2	203	2	0.0	1.0	1.5
Joe Hawley	C	28	15/14	981	4	1.0	3.5	5.0	Demar Dotson	RT	31	6/3	201	2	0.0	1.5	0.0
Gosder Cherilus	RT	32	13/13	892	15	3.0	7.0	3.0	J.R. Sweezy	RG	27	15/15	1006	10	2.5	3.5	2.0
Ali Marpet	RG	23	13/13	824	6	2.0	6.0	3.0									

Year	Yards	ALY	Rank	Power	Rank	Stuff	Rank	2nd Lev	Rank	Open Field	Rank	Sacks	ASR	Rank	Press	Rank	F-Start	Cont.
2013	4.00	3.63	27	59%	22	21%	22	1.12	16	0.77	13	47	7.7%	21	30.4%	30	18	33
2014	3.73	3.21	32	69%	7	23%	32	0.99	25	0.79	13	52	9.4%	29	32.3%	31	17	33
2015	4.86	4.00	9	71%	8	20%	13	1.20	13	1.40	1	27	5.8%	14	29.3%	26	19	25
2015 ALY by direction:		Left End 4.94 (3)			Left Tackle 3.4 (22)			Mid/Guard 4.12 (8)				Right Tackle 3.77 (18)				Right End 3.61 (15)		

Donovan Smith's rookie year went about how you would expect from a toolsy left tackle who didn't play up to them in college. No full-time lineman allowed as many blown blocks per snap as Smith, and only fellow rookie Ereck Flowers really came close. ☞ The Bucs were much better down the stretch when a healthy Demar Dotson could take over for the obsolete Gosder Cherilus on the right side. It might be even better to put him back at left tackle and let Smith play a less demanding position. ☞ Tampa's other second-round rookie, Ali Marpet, had a more up-and-down season than Smith, and was impressive as a run-blocker. Unfortunately for the Bucs, Logan Mankins was the best this line had to offer last year and now he's gone.

Defensive Front Seven

Defensive Line	Age	Pos	G	Snaps	Plays	Overall TmPct	Rk	Stop	Dfts	BTkl	Runs	St%	vs. Run Rk	RuYd	Rk	Sack	Hit	Pass Rush Hur	Dsrpt
Gerald McCoy	28	DT	15	802	35	4.3%	56	27	16	1	22	68%	64	2.6	56	8.5	7	14.0	0
Henry Melton*	30	DT	16	512	32	3.7%	65	16	6	2	23	48%	84	3.4	80	2.0	11	12.0	2
Tony McDaniel*	31	DT	14	295	26	3.4%	--	18	4	3	24	67%	--	2.7	--	1.0	2	4.0	1
Akeem Spence	25	DT	8	289	11	2.5%	82	7	1	1	10	60%	81	3.0	67	1.0	4	3.0	0
Clinton McDonald	29	DT	6	246	31	9.5%	2	20	5	1	29	66%	73	2.8	62	0.0	0	1.0	0

Edge Rushers	Age	Pos	G	Snaps	Plays	Overall TmPct	Rk	Stop	Dfts	BTkl	Runs	St%	vs. Run Rk	RuYd	Rk	Sack	Hit	Pass Rush Hur	Dsrpt
William Gholston	25	DE	16	674	68	7.8%	4	50	13	3	61	74%	49	2.0	33	3.0	7	14.0	2
Jacquies Smith	26	DE	12	546	23	3.5%	77	19	12	2	12	75%	40	2.8	66	7.0	6	10.5	0
George Johnson	29	DE	11	433	23	3.8%	72	17	3	2	21	81%	21	1.2	13	0.0	4	4.5	0
Howard Jones	26	DE	12	386	14	2.1%	94	12	8	3	8	75%	40	2.4	48	5.0	3	13.0	0
Robert Ayers	*31*	*DE*	*12*	*569*	*45*	*6.7%*	*15*	*38*	*19*	*4*	*28*	*82%*	*15*	*2.0*	*38*	*9.5*	*13*	*23.0*	*3*
Quinton Coples	*26*	*OLB*	*15*	*291*	*8*	*1.1%*	*--*	*6*	*1*	*0*	*7*	*86%*	*--*	*1.3*	*--*	*0.0*	*4*	*9.5*	*0*

Linebackers	Age	Pos	G	Snaps	Plays	Overall TmPct	Rk	Stop	Dfts	BTkl	Runs	St%	vs. Run Rk	RuYd	Rk	Sack	Hit	Pass Rush Hur	Tgts	vs. Pass Suc%	Rk	AdjYd	Rk	PD	Int
Lavonte David	26	OLB	16	1090	158	18.1%	6	88	35	19	72	64%	45	2.5	5	3.0	2	8	31	55%	40	5.2	19	8	3
Kwon Alexander	22	OLB	12	816	100	15.3%	15	59	22	16	50	68%	27	3.1	28	3.0	1	5	19	57%	35	4.4	12	7	2
Danny Lansanah*	31	MLB	16	374	51	5.8%	--	34	11	4	33	76%	--	2.9	--	1.0	0	1	9	57%	--	3.9	--	2	0
Bruce Carter*	28	MLB	14	307	41	5.4%	--	23	6	2	28	61%	--	3.3	--	2.0	2	4	7	88%	--	1.5	--	2	0
Daryl Smith	*34*	*MLB*	*16*	*981*	*124*	*15.5%*	*11*	*68*	*18*	*14*	*83*	*58%*	*61*	*3.7*	*54*	*3.0*	*1*	*2*	*23*	*44%*	*61*	*6.8*	*46*	*3*	*1*

Year	Yards	ALY	Rank	Power	Rank	Stuff	Rank	2nd Level	Rank	Open Field	Rank	Sacks	ASR	Rank	Press	Rank
2013	3.95	3.62	7	66%	17	24%	5	1.07	13	0.80	21	35	6.2%	25	26.6%	8
2014	3.94	3.57	8	67%	20	25%	4	1.14	18	0.81	21	36	6.5%	19	21.9%	28
2015	3.55	3.73	15	69%	23	21%	16	1.07	13	0.29	1	38	7.6%	5	24.4%	23

2015 ALY by direction: Left End 2.88 (9) Left Tackle 3.75 (15) Mid/Guard 3.97 (18) Right Tackle 3.80 (20) Right End 3.26 (16)

The Bucs decided they had an answer in Kwon Alexander and promoted him to the starting lineup immediately as a fourth-round rookie. They key word in that sentence was "decided," because Alexander's rookie season was definitely a mixed bag. He tends to look very overmatched on film, and despite being suspended for the last month of the season, he managed an insane amount of missed tackles. His broken tackle rate was the highest of any qualifying linebacker with more than 40 tackles not named Paul Worrilow. Alexander was routinely suckered in on play-action, and while he made enough splashy plays to accumulate some Rookie Player of the Week honors, he was generally a dud. On most depth charts, a player like this wouldn't get to start as a rookie. But Alexander gets put on the spot and made to act as a "win" for the general manager because he was a rookie starter. ☞ Lavonte David was as dominant as usual, once again racking up more defeats than any defender except J.J. Watt. We're not sure what's going on with that broken tackles total; we charted David with more broken tackles in 2015 than in the three previous seasons combined. ☞ Gerald McCoy had a down year, but Tampa got some solid rotational play from Jacquies Smith and found enough linebacker sacks to generate a high adjusted sack rate. Their much lower rank in pressure rate suggests this was a bit of a fluke, as does the fact the Bucs had only 14 sacks marked as "blown block" compared to the NFL average of 16. These were good reasons to select Eastern Kentucky's Noah Spence in the second round of the draft. Spence had a really nice week at the Senior Bowl, but at 251 pounds, is going to have to bulk up to anchor against the run. SackSEER saw him as about an average second-round prospect, projecting 20.8 sacks by Year 5.

Defensive Secondary

Secondary	Age	Pos	G	Snaps	Plays	Overall TmPct	Rk	Stop	Dfts	BTkl	vs. Run Runs	St%	Rk	RuYd	Rk	vs. Pass Tgts	Tgt%	Rk	Dist	Suc%	Rk	AdjYd	Rk	PD	Int
Bradley McDougald	26	FS	16	893	90	10.3%	29	19	8	12	43	26%	56	6.3	28	25	7.9%	40	14.7	54%	48	6.8	34	5	2
Chris Conte	27	SS	14	731	82	10.7%	26	23	10	9	39	31%	52	7.3	40	18	6.8%	27	16.0	66%	14	5.8	18	6	2
Sterling Moore*	26	CB	16	706	51	5.8%	71	22	13	8	7	86%	2	2.6	1	47	18.8%	35	10.1	46%	66	8.0	42	6	1
Alterraun Verner	28	CB	16	578	57	6.5%	--	19	9	6	18	39%	--	6.0	--	37	18.1%	--	11.7	42%	--	7.5	--	5	1
Jude Adjei-Barimah	24	CB	13	468	41	5.8%	--	15	5	4	5	80%	--	1.6	--	35	21.1%	--	9.6	44%	--	8.5	--	1	0
Johnthan Banks	27	CB	14	435	26	3.4%	--	6	2	5	6	50%	--	3.7	--	20	12.6%	--	11.6	20%	--	11.6	--	1	0
Mike Jenkins*	31	CB	14	330	18	2.4%	--	6	2	4	2	50%	--	3.0	--	26	21.8%	--	13.9	48%	--	7.8	--	4	0
Keith Tandy	27	SS	14	285	38	5.0%	--	13	4	3	21	33%	--	5.4	--	2	1.5%	--	13.0	66%	--	13.7	--	0	0
Major Wright	28	SS	9	219	29	5.9%	--	7	2	4	11	27%	--	5.6	--	8	10.3%	--	9.3	48%	--	4.6	--	1	0
Brent Grimes	33	CB	15	960	62	7.5%	56	23	11	10	14	29%	57	10.4	61	75	22.6%	57	14.5	42%	71	9.8	72	13	4

Year	Pass D Rank	vs. #1 WR	Rk	vs. #2 WR	Rk	vs. Other WR	Rk	vs. TE	Rk	vs. RB	Rk
2013	11	-6.6%	13	-10.7%	8	20.6%	29	-7.4%	10	-19.5%	4
2014	23	27.1%	31	5.6%	21	-0.9%	16	4.0%	20	-17.9%	7
2015	26	-1.4%	16	41.6%	32	34.0%	32	2.9%	18	-8.0%	10

Cornerback was a major area of need for the Bucs heading into this offseason. In selecting Vernon Hargreaves of Florida 10th overall, they're trying to duplicate the Jameis Winston plan of using their first-round pick on a player who had a better season the year before he came out. Hargreaves coasted on talent in 2015, often eyeing the quarterback and trying to make the big play. Florida's opponents were able to use his aggression against him often. He also was able to play for a major SEC school as a true freshman, so it's not all bad. ☞ Alterraun Verner since signing his huge contract in Tampa: a 41 percent adjusted success rate in 2014 (74th of 77 qualifying corners) followed by a 42 percent success rate in 2015, when he didn't have enough targets to be ranked because he was benched for a washed-up Tim Jennings. This is the guy running with the first team in OTAs, but unless Lovie Smith's scheme implicitly wanted corners to surrender yards, it's hard to say it was earned. On the plus side, if you stack it up next to Johnthan Banks' 49 percent (2014, 49th of 77 qualifiers) and 20 percent (no, really, 20 percent in 2015), it doesn't look so bad. ☞ On any other depth chart, you know we'd be making Chris Conte tackling jokes. Here, what's the point? He didn't even chart out with as many broken tackles as Bradley McDougald.

Special Teams

Year	DVOA	Rank	FG/XP	Rank	Net Kick	Rank	Kick Ret	Rank	Net Punt	Rank	Punt Ret	Rank	Hidden	Rank
2013	-1.5%	22	-6.6	27	8.1	4	-7.2	31	-3.5	25	1.8	11	-7.9	26
2014	-0.8%	17	1.7	11	-1.4	18	-3.5	24	-0.6	18	-0.3	12	4.6	9
2015	-4.7%	30	-17.5	32	-3.1	23	0.2	12	1.1	17	-4.3	21	2.8	11

Kickers drafted in the first three rounds of the draft in the DVOA era: Sebastian Janikowski (17th overall, 2000), Jason Hanson (56th overall, 1992), Mike Nugent (47th overall, 2005), and now Roberto Aguayo (59th, 2016). Absent the sort of kicker who could effortlessly hit from 55 yards 90 percent of the time, it's hard to see using a premium draft pick on one as a worthwhile move. Of the six teams with the highest finish in our FG/XP points added last year, the highest pick spent on their kicker was a fourth-rounder—and a few of those teams (Seattle, the Giants, the Lions) signed their kicker as a free agent. In looking at last season's brutal finish, it's easy to conclude that kicker was an area of need for the Bucs. Spending a second-round pick on one is like going to the ER for a common cold. ☞ With Bobby Rainey gone to the Giants, the return jobs will probably go to one or two of the depth receivers. Adam Humphries returned punts at Clemson and Kenny Bell returned kickoffs at Nebraska, so that's a job share that makes sense.

Tennessee Titans

2015 record: 3-13	**Total DVOA:** -26.6% (31st)	**2016 Mean Projection:** 7.2 wins	**On the Clock (0-4):** 15%
Pythagorean Wins: 4.8 (30th)	**Offense:** -15.7% (32nd)	**Postseason Odds:** 28.9%	**Mediocrity (5-7):** 41%
Snap-Weighted Age: 26.0 (28th)	**Defense:** 7.1% (23rd)	**Super Bowl Odds:** 2.1%	**Playoff Contender (8-10):** 34%
Average Opponent: -5.6% (27th)	**Special Teams:** -3.8% (28th)	**Proj. Avg. Opponent:** -3.8% (32nd)	**Super Bowl Contender (11+):** 11%

2015: A team led by "Super Mario" is not supposed to be this dreadfully boring.

2016: The glorious potential of Marcus Mariota vs. a head coach who doesn't understand his skill set.

Amy Adams Strunk was a beacon of light for 72 days. For 72 days, the new Titans owner had an opportunity to take the franchise in a brand new direction. The Titans have been one of the most futile franchises in the NFL since their last playoff appearance seven seasons ago. A 41-71 record over that span ranks as the fifth-worst in the league, and no team has come close to losing as many games as they have over the past two seasons.

Those 72 days of promise began on November 4, 2015. That was the day when Strunk fired then-head coach Ken Whisenhunt. When the Titans hired Whisenhunt in 2014, he continued the franchise's commitment to languishing in the doldrums of the worst division in football. In fact, he surpassed the depths that his predecessors reached by watching the team go 3-20 with him in charge. After a 1-6 start in 2015, Strunk swiftly pulled the plug.

The timing of the move offered up reasons for hope. While Whisenhunt deserved to be fired, conventional wisdom suggested that he should have been given more time to work with Marcus Mariota. Mariota only played five games for Whisenhunt before the coach was dismissed, and Whisenhunt never got a chance to develop the quarterback he drafted. Strunk could justifiably disrupt the development of the franchise's cornerstone quarterback if the move was about accountability and creating a new franchise culture of high expectations. For 72 days it was reasonable to speculate that it was.

Then on January 16, the Titans announced the permanent hire of Mike Mularkey as Whisenhunt's replacement. Cue end of new franchise culture, and extinguish the beacon of light.

Mularkey is Whisenhunt 2.0. His career largely mimics that of the man he is replacing. Whisenhunt and Mularkey worked together in Pittsburgh, where Mularkey was initially the tight ends coach. When Mularkey was promoted to offensive coordinator, Whisenhunt became the tight ends coach. After Mularkey left to take his first head coaching position with the Bills, Whisenhunt replaced him as offensive coordinator. They reunited in Tennessee two years ago, when Whisenhunt became the head coach and Mularkey became the tight ends coach, and Mularkey served as interim head coach after Whisenhunt was let go. Most observers expected Mularkey to simply coach through the end of the year and then depart. And yet, despite having so much time to set up their coaching search and explore every possible option from the outside, the Titans and Strunk never appeared interested in the top available candidates.

CEO Steve Underwood was asked about the poor hiring process at the introductory press conference for Mularkey and new general manager Jon Robinson. Despite efforts to allay fears, Underwood unintentionally underlined exactly why everyone was so concerned: "There was already a pretty good working knowledge of Mike. We interviewed Mike once before to be a head coach, he had been our interim head coach... and we interviewed three other highly qualified candidates. So I'm not really sure what discomfort level you're talking about." The Titans spoke and acted like a team that had decided Mularkey was going to be their next head coach as soon as they fired Whisenhunt. Underwood all but admitted that by saying "Amy largely knew that she wanted to keep Mularkey."

Doug Marrone, Ray Horton, and Teryl Austin were the three other candidates who reportedly interviewed with the Titans. Horton was the team's defensive coordinator before being effectively supplanted by Dick LeBeau, while Marrone remains the offensive line coach in Jacksonville. Teryl Austin interviewed for four different head coaching positions but got no final offers, and went back to Detroit as defensive coordinator. He later told reporters that "half of his interviews weren't legitimate." He didn't name names, but two of his four interviews came with teams that eventually promoted from within: the Giants and the Titans.

It's hard to imagine the Titans doing less in their search for a head coach. They opened the blinds, looked through the keyhole, and picked up their Rooney Rule compliance letter through the mail slot before hiring the coach they were always going to hire. This might have made sense if the coach they were hiring had a track record to fall back on, but Mularkey's head coaching career has been less impressive than Whisenhunt's. Whisenhunt at least went to a Super Bowl in Arizona before going 3-20 as the Titans head coach. Mularkey has a career record of 18-39, has never made the playoffs, and has gone 4-21 over his past 25 games as a head coach.

Robinson and Mularkey didn't mask their intentions when they took over. To reverse the losing trend in Tennessee, they plan to build a "tough" team that looks to bully its opponents. Speaking after the draft, Robinson said "Teams are starting to build to play in sub defense now ... to counteract that, we can play a bigger game, and maybe move some of those smaller

2016 Titans Schedule

Week	Opp.	Week	Opp.	Week	Opp.
1	MIN	7	IND	13	BYE
2	at DET	8	JAC (Thu.)	14	DEN
3	OAK	9	at SD	15	at KC
4	at HOU	10	GB	16	at JAC (Sat.)
5	at MIA	11	at IND	17	HOU
6	CLE	12	at CHI		

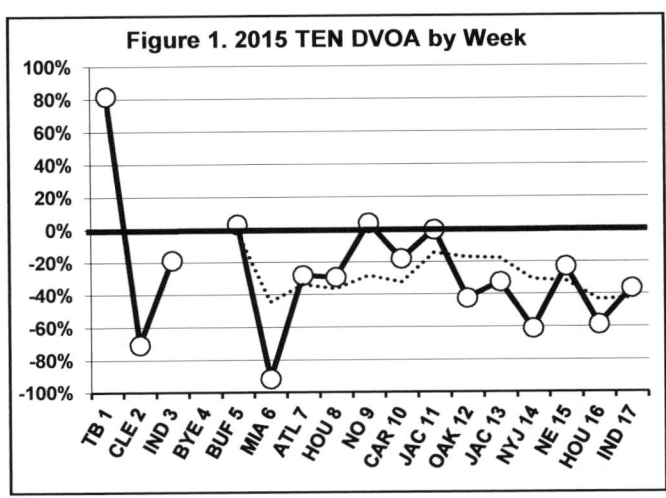

Figure 1. 2015 TEN DVOA by Week

guys off the ball." In theory, this is a smart approach. Robinson formerly worked for the New England Patriots and the Patriots have moved in this direction lately also, complementing Tom Brady's passing game with a power-run option and players who could physically overwhelm their opponents. The concern for the Titans is that while the Patriots create balance with these options in their offense, the Titans appear to be moving more towards a Rex Ryan-type of philosophy. Robinson further elaborated, "It shortens the game. If you can control the ball on offense and be able to run the ball, the clock is shortened. So you get a couple stops on defense, you can score, and it really limits the other team's offensive opportunities." This is an old-school line of thinking that doesn't recognize how that approach will limit the output of both offenses if it works. The Patriots invest in their offense so they can run the ball 45 times if they need to or pass the ball 45 times if they need to. That's not the direction the Titans are going in.

Mularkey is very much on the same page as Robinson. As the interim coach for the Titans, he went to a much more conservative offense than the one Whisenhunt had run, then described his philosophy after taking over the full-time role as "Exotic Smashmouth." This should be very concerning for Titans fans, and not just because you are imagining a version of "All Star" played on Peruvian pan flutes. Mularkey evoked the name Kordell Stewart as an example to follow. Stewart had success as the Steelers quarterback in 2001 with Mularkey as the offensive coordinator. The team went 13-3 and ranked seventh in points scored and third in yards gained. DVOA ranked the offense fourth (sixth passing and fourth rushing). But that success was short lived, as Stewart was benched and ultimately released the following year. Mularkey's offenses gradually declined by all measures until he departed after the 2003 season.

Stewart was a running quarterback who had physical throwing ability. He wasn't a nuanced passer or technician the way Mariota is. Putting Mariota in the type of offense that Mularkey is envisioning will limit his impact on the game. Mariota is the type of quarterback who can elevate his teammates by manipulating coverages with his eyes, mitigating pressure in the pocket, and throwing receivers open with anticipation against tight coverage. In a simplified offense that prioritizes the run, simplifies passing concepts, and uses eligible receivers as blockers instead of pass catchers, the quarterback is more reliant on the initial play design and how it matches up to the specific play call of the opposing defense.

This offseason, the Titans invested in not one but two bell-cow, between-the-tackles running backs who have limited receiving skills. DeMarco Murray came at a reduced cost. He is now 28 and coming off the worst season of his career. Rookie Derrick Henry was more expensive as a top-50 pick in the 2016 draft. After drafting Henry, the Titans publicly reassured Murray that he was still the primary ballcarrier. Both are expected to be featured heavily as the focal points of the offense, and this will force the Titans to keep their quarterback under center more. Mularkey acknowledged this in the same breath as he acknowledged Mariota is more effective from shotgun. The cognitive dissonance highlights how this coaching staff is trying to minimize the impact of its most talented player. Yes, Mariota should comfortably adapt to playing from under center more, but he can do more to elevate his offense from the shotgun.

Mularkey clearly doesn't recognize the talent that he has in front of him. When he became the interim coach, one of the things he constantly talked about was running Mariota more, though that went against his other stated goal of doing more to protect the quarterback. After he was hired full-time in February, he returned to this notion. Apparently, the *smashmouth* element of Mularkey's offense consists of Murray, Henry, and the most expensive right tackle in the history of the league, Jack Conklin. (The Michigan State product not only went in the top 10 of the 2016 draft but also cost the Titans first-, second-, and third-round picks to go and get him.) Does that mean that Mariota running around on read-options and bootlegs is supposed to be the *exotic* element? While Mariota is very athletic and showed off his ability to create big gains with his feet against the Jacksonville Jaguars last year, he isn't a creative runner. He's much more creative as a passer. Alas, that level of evaluation is likely too deep for Mularkey. He sees Mariota's athleticism and immediately stereotypes him as a running quarterback like any other quarterback who can run.

Despite his failings in Tennessee, of which there were many, it's relatively easy to argue that Whisenhunt was the better option to develop Mariota than Mularkey. At the very least, Whisenhunt has had success running the type of quick-passing, shotgun-heavy scheme that would suit Mariota's skill set. Even though it's debatable how much credit he deserved for the success of Kurt Warner and Philip Rivers, it's better to have a coach who recognizes the talents of his quarterback instead of one who seemingly sees all running quarterbacks as the same. It's not a good sign that Mularkey seems to look at Mariota and see Colin Kaepernick.

As the offense focuses on becoming run-reliant, Dick Le-Beau is building a defense that hopes to be run-repellant. The Titans defense ranked 23rd in DVOA last season and got worse as the year went on, finishing 30th in weighted DVOA. Our projections suggest that they will once again have one of the worst defenses in the league in 2016, but there are still reasons to feel confident about the direction they are going in. LeBeau hasn't managed a good defense in years, but, unlike Mularkey, he does have an obvious track record of sustained success to fall back on. LeBeau was the Steelers defensive coordinator from 2004 to 2014. Six of his defenses over those 11 seasons ranked first in either points or yards allowed. Five of his defenses ranked first or second in both categories in the same season. From 2004 through 2011, the Steelers were a constant force in the DVOA top 10, with the top-ranked defense twice and a top-three defense in five separate seasons (Table 1).

Table 1. Dick LeBeau's Steelers Defenses

Team	DVOA	DVOA Rank	Pass DVOA	Pass Rank	Rush DVOA	Rush Rank
2004	-18.9%	3	-20.0%	3	-17.6%	3
2005	-13.5%	3	-9.4%	5	-18.7%	1
2006	-7.2%	9	1.1%	14	-17.4%	4
2007	-12.5%	3	-8.6%	6	-18.0%	3
2008	-29.0%	1	-32.8%	1	-24.2%	2
2009	-4.6%	9	1.8%	14	-13.9%	8
2010	-20.7%	1	-15.7%	3	-29.0%	1
2011	-9.4%	7	-11.7%	3	-6.6%	15
2012	-2.9%	13	-2.4%	11	-3.6%	20
2013	4.0%	19	8.1%	1	-1.0%	21
2014	11.3%	30	24.9%	30	-7.3%	17

It must be noted that from 2004 to 2011, LeBeau's defenses ranked higher against the run than against the pass five times. In two of the other three years, they still ranked in the top three against the run. LeBeau's philosophy has always focused on creating a dominant run defense to force the offense to become one-dimensional. He invests in the spine of his defense, alleviating the pressure on his cornerbacks by relying on zone coverages from off alignments.

Cornerbacks in LeBeau's preferred scheme don't need to be versatile in coverage. They do need to be versatile in terms of playing both the run and the pass equally. LeBeau's cornerbacks are expected to offer intense, effective run support coming off the edge while being reliable tacklers in space. They can rely on their positioning and awareness in coverage, but have to bring physicality to the tackle point. It was no surprise that LeBeau brought in two cornerbacks who have previously played for him, free agents Antwon Blake and Brice McCain.

McCain will likely be second or third on the depth chart, though Blake will just be competing for a roster spot; he is a liability in coverage and led the league with 21 broken tackles last year. The most interesting cornerback for LeBeau is veteran Jason McCourty, who was on the roster last year but barely played because of a groin injury. When healthy, he is one of the best cornerbacks in the league. He offers length and versatility that LeBeau has rarely had. There is precedent for LeBeau asking more of one specific corner though; during his best years, LeBeau used Ike Taylor as a shadow corner and asked him to play more aggressive coverages than his teammates.

Athleticism and versatility in coverage matters more for the safeties in LeBeau's scheme. He doesn't need an Earl Thomas-like free safety, but whoever fills the role will need to have the range to act as a lone deep defender in single-high coverages. Playing that role in Pittsburgh, Ryan Clark was an ideal complement to Troy Polamalu not because he was a great athlete, but because he managed to play intelligent, disciplined coverage while still being very aggressive when opportunities arose. Rashad Johnson, signed away from Arizona, perfectly fits that description and should be the Titans starter at free safety. Third-round rookie Kevin Byard was described by Jon Robinson as someone who could play either free or strong safety, but Johnson's presence should push the rookie to strong safety, where he will compete for playing time with the incumbent Da'Norris Searcy. Byard consistently found the football at Middle Tennessee State, notching a total of 19 interceptions with at least four each season. He could be an ideal fit as the frenetic but intimidating and disruptive strong safety in LeBeau's defense.

Because of how LeBeau wants to prioritize stopping the run, the nose tackle position matters more to him than it does to most coaches. It matters so much that the Titans invested a top-50 pick in Penn State's Austin Johnson. Johnson isn't a penetrator; he is a space-eating, two-gapping defensive lineman who offers limited upside on passing downs. His place in the starting lineup over Al Woods will need to be earned on first and second downs, when Woods could spend some time at defensive end like he did early in his career.

Johnson was one of three second-round picks for the Titans in 2016. He was selected before Henry but after Clemson edge-rusher Kevin Dodd. Dodd was a polarizing prospect throughout the draft process because of his age and athletic testing. In particular, a disappointing performance at the combine helped contribute to a poor SackSEER projection, just 11.9 sacks over his first five years in the league. However, an outside linebacker in LeBeau's defense does more than just rush the passer. Dodd should provide help against the run and could also prove to be valuable in coverage. LeBeau's blitz packages on third down will afford him opportunities to drop into underneath zones. Dodd may not have tested well, but he did show off impressive balance, fluidity, and footwork in college, three elements that aren't accurately measured by combine drills. Another reason why SackSEER frowns on Dodd is that he didn't establish himself in a full-time role until his final season, but he also became more productive as the season went on. That suggests he takes well to coaching, and there isn't a coach with a better outside linebacker lineage than LeBeau.

Dodd won't need to start as a rookie. His depth could still prove to be valuable as the Titans defense suffered dramatically without Derrick Morgan last year. With Morgan in the lineup, they had -2.3% defensive DVOA and were first in adjusted sack rate. In the games he missed, they had a 20.8% DVOA, ahead of only New Orleans, and had an adjusted sack rate of just 3.8 percent.

Our spreadsheets are forecasting a nice step forward from the Titans in 2016. Some of that is the residue of the unrequited love affair between our QBASE projection system and Mariota, and it also helps that the Titans have the easiest projected schedule in the league. Nevertheless, with the oldest coaching staff in the league and such an antiquated focus on running

the ball, it's hard to feel optimistic about the Titans overall direction. Mularkey should at least last longer than Whisenhunt did, but that may only be because Amy Adams Strunk handpicked him for the role. Strunk will show patience with Mularkey so long as she is in position to do so—which may not be for the long term. She has only been the controlling owner since March 2015, when she replaced brother-in-law Tommy Smith. Another change of heart within the family could see her out just as quickly as she took power. Furthermore, Roger Goodell has continued to express dissatisfaction with the state of Tennessee's ownership structure. A sale, either voluntary or not, may be the only way to resolve that concern.

So much for those 72 days.

Cian Fahey

2015 Titans Stats by Week

Wk	vs.	W-L	PF	PA	YDF	YDA	TO	Total	Off	Def	ST
1	at TB	W	42	14	309	273	1	82%	34%	-49%	-1%
2	at CLE	L	14	28	385	274	-3	-71%	-34%	4%	-33%
3	IND	L	33	35	433	378	0	-19%	3%	24%	3%
4	BYE										
5	BUF	L	13	14	276	209	0	3%	-19%	-22%	0%
6	MIA	L	10	38	299	434	-2	-92%	-61%	37%	6%
7	ATL	L	7	10	256	378	0	-28%	-37%	-6%	3%
8	at HOU	L	6	20	211	270	-3	-29%	-35%	-6%	1%
9	at NO	W	34	28	483	416	1	4%	8%	5%	0%
10	CAR	L	10	27	242	303	-2	-18%	-1%	9%	-8%
11	at JAC	L	13	19	316	308	1	0%	-2%	-20%	-18%
12	OAK	L	21	24	249	407	0	-42%	-15%	24%	-3%
13	JAC	W	42	39	467	383	-1	-32%	16%	45%	-4%
14	at NYJ	L	8	30	292	439	-1	-61%	-31%	26%	-4%
15	at NE	L	16	33	282	346	-2	-23%	-14%	5%	-3%
16	HOU	L	6	34	257	330	-3	-59%	-39%	19%	-1%
17	at IND	L	24	30	231	327	0	-36%	-33%	5%	2%

Trends and Splits

	Offense	Rank	Defense	Rank
Total DVOA	-15.7%	32	7.0%	23
Unadjusted VOA	-16.8%	31	6.1%	23
Weighted Trend	-18.6%	31	12.1%	30
Variance	6.1%	12	5.6%	22
Average Opponent	1.5%	21	-2.7%	25
Passing	-9.0%	29	17.7%	24
Rushing	-18.2%	29	-4.5%	24
First Down	4.4%	10	12.0%	28
Second Down	-26.4%	31	3.2%	18
Third Down	-40.4%	32	3.3%	18
First Half	-15.4%	27	9.9%	27
Second Half	-16.0%	32	3.9%	18
Red Zone	8.3%	14	22.3%	28
Late and Close	-23.5%	31	-0.9%	21

Five-Year Performance

Year	W-L	Pyth W	Est W	PF	PA	TO	Total	Rk	Off	Rk	Def	Rk	ST	Rk	Off AGL	Rk	Def AGL	Rk	Off Age	Rk	Def Age	Rk	ST Age	Rk
2011	9-7	8.2	8.3	325	317	+1	6.6%	13	0.6%	15	0.3%	15	6.3%	3	20.0	7	17.7	9	28.1	3	25.7	30	26.4	14
2012	6-10	4.6	3.3	330	471	-4	-29.4%	30	-20.5%	29	7.5%	25	-1.4%	19	49.9	26	14.6	5	27.7	9	25.3	32	26.0	15
2013	7-9	7.5	6.6	362	381	0	-6.1%	21	1.4%	16	4.2%	22	-3.2%	26	28.3	12	15.6	6	27.3	13	26.2	20	26.4	8
2014	2-14	3.3	4.0	254	438	-10	-29.3%	31	-16.4%	29	11.2%	29	-1.8%	20	38.8	22	40.9	19	27.0	14	27.0	10	26.7	2
2015	3-13	4.8	4.4	299	423	-14	-26.6%	31	-15.7%	32	7.1%	23	-3.8%	28	38.7	20	26.5	13	25.6	29	26.5	18	25.7	24

2015 Performance Based on Most Common Personnel Groups

TEN Offense					TEN Offense vs. Opponents					TEN Defense				TEN Defense vs. Opponents			
Pers	Freq	Yds	DVOA	Run%	Pers	Freq	Yds	DVOA	Run%	Pers	Freq	Yds	DVOA	Pers	Freq	Yds	DVOA
12	42%	5.6	-6.0%	33%	Base	44%	5.1	-6.8%	59%	Base	50%	5.0	5.5%	11	46%	6.1	8.0%
11	29%	5.1	-25.0%	20%	Nickel	42%	5.6	-11.3%	18%	Nickel	33%	5.9	9.3%	12	24%	5.0	3.4%
21	11%	5.8	-18.3%	50%	Dime+	12%	4.8	-62.8%	3%	Dime+	16%	7.0	18.6%	13	7%	5.5	10.6%
13	9%	4.9	8.9%	58%	Goal Line	2%	0.9	16.5%	69%	Goal Line	1%	0.3	-54.0%	21	6%	5.1	9.0%
22	4%	4.2	-18.0%	74%										22	6%	3.5	-26.0%
														10	4%	6.9	42.2%

Strategic Tendencies

Run/Pass		Rk	Formation		Rk	Pass Rush		Rk	Secondary		Rk	Strategy		Rk
Runs, first half	39%	12	Form: Single Back	74%	19	Rush 3	3.5%	26	4 DB	50%	3	Play action	21%	10
Runs, first down	45%	21	Form: Empty Back	4%	28	Rush 4	52.4%	29	5 DB	33%	29	Avg Box (Off)	6.34	8
Runs, second-long	33%	12	Pers: 3+ WR	31%	32	Rush 5	33.3%	1	6+ DB	16%	11	Avg Box (Def)	6.45	2
Runs, power sit.	43%	30	Pers: 2+ TE/6+ OL	60%	1	Rush 6+	10.8%	6	CB by Sides	78%	16	Offensive Pace	31.70	25
Runs, behind 2H	25%	15	Pers: 6+ OL	1%	27	Sacks by LB	59.0%	7	S/CB Cover Ratio	23%	14	Defensive Pace	30.40	18
Pass, ahead 2H	44%	25	Shotgun/Pistol	59%	21	Sacks by DB	6.4%	17	DB Blitz	11%	11	Go for it on 4th	0.80	21

Tennessee recovered only eight of 22 fumbles on offense and only four of 12 fumbles on defense. The Titans even fumbled the ball away twice on special teams... but also recovered all four opponent fumbles on special teams. ☜ The Titans can hope that opponents drop a few more passes than they did a year ago. Tennessee opponents dropped just 11 passes, or 2.3 percent. Only Cleveland benefited less from opponent drops. ☜ The Titans were the only team in the league to use 11 personnel on less than 30 percent of plays; every other team except the Jets used this personnel at least 40 percent of the time. ☜ When the offense had three or more receivers on the field, the Titans ran the ball just 58 times, the lowest raw total of any offense. That's a good thing, because Tennessee's -49.2% DVOA and 3.24 yards per carry on those runs was the worst in the league. ☜ The defense didn't fare so well in those situations either, as their 11.6% DVOA against runs with three or more receivers on the field ranked 31st (4.80 yards per carry, 23rd). ☜ The Titans ranked 10th in defensive DVOA on the road but 30th in the same category at home, the largest "reverse" home-road split any defense exhibited last season. ☜ Tennessee's pass pressure was brought with its blitzes. We only recorded pass pressure 18 percent of the time when the Titans rushed four, the lowest rate in the league. That went to 31 percent with five pass rushers and 50 percent with six or more. The Titans allowed 7.7 yards per pass with four pass rushers, 6.8 yards with five, and 5.2 yards with six or more. ☜ Tennessee was the NFL's best defense at defending running back screens, compiling a -148.6% DVOA on 23 such plays. ☜ The Tennessee defense had a league-low 72 broken tackles, though this may be partly because the other three AFC South teams were the bottom three offenses in percentage of plays with a broken tackle.

Passing

Player	DYAR	DVOA	Plays	NtYds	Avg	YAC	C%	TD	Int
M.Mariota	-53	-13.2%	407	2551	6.3	5.1	62.5%	19	10
Z.Mettenberger*	-408	-46.4%	179	812	4.5	4.1	61.6%	4	7
A.Tanney	3	-8.5%	17	65	3.8	2.3	71.4%	1	0
M.Cassel	-172	-23.7%	216	1190	5.5	4.8	58.9%	5	6

Rushing

Player	DYAR	DVOA	Plays	Yds	Avg	TD	Fum	Suc
A.Andrews	-6	-9.5%	143	520	3.6	3	1	42%
D.McCluster	-12	-14.9%	55	247	4.5	1	1	31%
D.Cobb	-16	-16.4%	52	146	2.8	1	0	33%
B.Sankey	12	-1.5%	47	193	4.1	1	1	45%
M.Mariota	20	-0.6%	32	253	7.9	2	1	-
T.West*	-31	-51.8%	16	51	3.2	0	2	50%
J.Fowler	11	13.0%	7	13	1.9	1	0	71%
K.Wright	2	-31.1%	5	17	3.4	0	0	-
M.Cassel	-10	-29.3%	14	85	6.1	0	2	-
D.Murray	-29	-12.1%	193	704	3.6	6	2	45%

Receiving

Player	DYAR	DVOA	Plays	Ctch	Yds	Y/C	YAC	TD	C%
H.Douglas	-28	-17.4%	72	36	411	11.4	3.6	2	50%
D.Green-Beckham	77	1.8%	67	32	549	17.2	4.5	4	48%
K.Wright	21	-8.1%	60	36	408	11.3	4.0	3	60%
J.Hunter	70	17.0%	31	22	264	12.0	1.5	1	71%
R.Matthews	235	36.4%	61	43	662	15.4	5.5	4	70%
D.Walker	174	13.0%	133	94	1088	11.6	4.1	6	71%
A.Fasano	32	4.0%	42	26	289	11.1	5.8	2	62%
C.Stevens	3	-4.7%	16	12	121	10.1	3.4	2	75%
C.Coffman*	4	3.7%	6	4	42	10.5	2.0	0	67%
D.McCluster	5	-11.5%	41	31	261	8.4	6.3	1	76%
A.Andrews	10	-7.5%	29	21	174	8.3	8.3	0	72%
B.Sankey	26	6.4%	23	14	139	9.9	9.8	1	61%
J.Fowler	26	45.3%	6	5	44	8.8	8.4	1	83%
D.Murray	13	-9.3%	55	44	322	7.3	8.7	1	80%

Offensive Line

Player	Pos	Age	GS	Snaps	Pen	Sk	Pass	Run	Player	Pos	Age	GS	Snaps	Pen	Sk	Pass	Run
Byron Bell	RT	27	16/16	1029	5	5.5	8.5	3.5	Jeremiah Poutasi	RT	22	11/7	399	2	6.0	9.0	4.0
Taylor Lewan	LT	25	15/15	911	10	4.5	5.5	3.0	Jamon Meredith*	OT	30	13/3	394	3	3.0	6.0	0.5
Chance Warmack	RG	25	14/14	833	7	0.0	1.5	1.0	Quinton Spain	LG	25	7/6	383	2	0.0	1.0	1.0
Andy Gallik	C	25	12/8	505	1	3.0	5.0	1.0	Brian Schwenke	C	25	5/5	308	1	0.0	0.0	2.0
Joe Looney*	C/LG	26	8/6	425	2	3.0	3.5	2.0	Ben Jones	C	27	16/16	1186	6	2.0	5.0	1.0

Year	Yards	ALY	Rank	Power	Rank	Stuff	Rank	2nd Lev	Rank	Open Field	Rank	Sacks	ASR	Rank	Press	Rank	F-Start	Cont.
2013	3.83	3.82	19	55%	29	20%	19	1.05	21	0.60	22	37	6.7%	12	24.5%	14	9	29
2014	3.82	3.91	17	63%	17	17%	4	1.06	23	0.39	31	50	8.9%	26	26.0%	20	16	29
2015	3.66	3.65	20	37%	32	22%	20	0.95	31	0.58	25	54	9.6%	32	28.1%	24	10	24
2015 ALY by direction:		Left End 3.01 (25)			Left Tackle 3.87 (16)			Mid/Guard 3.63 (24)			Right Tackle 3.88 (13)			Right End 3.88 (11)				

Whenever you have a god-awful offensive line and you get not one, but *two* opportunities to pass on a generational talent in the draft, you have to take them. The Titans could have taken Laremy Tunsil to be their starter at left tackle in 2015 and for the foreseeable future. Instead they traded three picks away and moved up to select a run-blocking right tackle, Jack Conklin of Michigan State, with the eighth overall pick. Adding Conklin fits Mike Mularkey's philosophy but it's unlikely to improve the Titans pass protection issues. In 2015, the Titans had 27 sacks directly attributable to blown blocks. No other offense had more than 23. ☞ Last year's third-round pick, Jeremiah Poutasi, was near the top of the league in sacks allowed despite starting for only half the season. He finished one snap short of our minimum for the "snaps per blown block" rankings, but if you add a snap he would have finished dead last in the NFL with a blown block every 30.8 snaps. Poutasi was drafted to play right tackle but will compete for the starting left guard spot now that Conklin is in place on the right side. ☞ Right guard Chance Warmack and left tackle Taylor Lewan are former first-round picks who need to prove themselves. Warmack in particular really needs to help his career with an improved season, as the Titans declined to pick up his fifth-year option this offseason. ☞ Center Ben Jones was signed away from rival Houston; he's a limited talent but he fits Mularkey's philosophy as a run blocker.

Defensive Front Seven

Defensive Line	Age	Pos	G	Snaps	Plays	TmPct	Rk	Stop	Dfts	BTkl	Runs	St%	Rk	RuYd	Rk	Sack	Hit	Hur	Dsrpt
						Overall						**vs. Run**					**Pass Rush**		
Jurrell Casey	27	DE	16	826	56	7.2%	15	41	16	3	44	68%	64	2.6	56	7.0	7	12.5	2
DaQuan Jones	25	DE	16	672	45	5.8%	36	34	4	0	43	79%	36	1.9	30	0.0	5	9.5	0
Al Woods	29	DT	14	356	22	3.2%	--	13	3	1	22	59%	--	2.9	--	0.0	1	1.0	0
Karl Klug	28	DE	16	331	19	2.4%	--	11	8	2	11	45%	--	2.8	--	4.0	7	11.5	0
Sammie Lee Hill*	30	DT	10	188	12	2.5%	--	9	2	0	12	75%	--	1.8	--	0.0	0	0.0	0

Edge Rushers	Age	Pos	G	Snaps	Plays	TmPct	Rk	Stop	Dfts	BTkl	Runs	St%	Rk	RuYd	Rk	Sack	Hit	Hur	Dsrpt
						Overall						**vs. Run**					**Pass Rush**		
Brian Orakpo	30	OLB	16	959	56	7.2%	6	37	22	1	34	56%	90	3.1	77	7.0	3	18.5	3
David Bass	26	OLB	16	529	35	4.5%	55	22	6	3	23	61%	85	3.5	87	1.5	2	10.0	3
Derrick Morgan	27	OLB	10	528	25	5.1%	46	19	9	2	16	75%	40	2.8	66	4.5	5	14.5	1

Linebackers	Age	Pos	G	Snaps	Plays	TmPct	Rk	Stop	Dfts	BTkl	Runs	St%	Rk	RuYd	Rk	Sack	Hit	Hur	Tgts	Suc%	Rk	AdjYd	Rk	PD	Int
						Overall						**vs. Run**					**Pass Rush**				**vs. Pass**				
Avery Williamson	24	ILB	15	925	102	13.9%	31	56	12	7	77	61%	53	3.7	53	3.5	2	7	13	28%	71	8.3	62	1	1
Wesley Woodyard	30	ILB	16	499	84	10.8%	54	57	14	1	62	69%	21	2.7	13	5.0	2	3	11	90%	1	3.4	6	0	0
Zach Brown*	27	ILB	16	493	80	10.2%	59	42	16	6	47	55%	71	5.6	88	0.5	1	2	17	66%	16	7.5	57	3	2
Nate Palmer	26	ILB	16	539	66	8.1%	72	33	3	9	42	55%	72	3.5	44	1.0	1	1	17	55%	42	4.9	16	0	0
Sean Spence	26	ILB	15	270	34	4.3%	--	18	6	2	19	58%	--	3.4	--	1.0	0	0	7	45%	--	6.4	--	0	0

Year	Yards	ALY	Rank	Power	Rank	Stuff	Rank	2nd Level	Rank	Open Field	Rank	Sacks	ASR	Rank	Press	Rank
2013	4.03	4.15	23	61%	12	17%	23	1.17	22	0.52	10	36	6.6%	20	24.4%	19
2014	4.41	4.08	23	73%	27	19%	17	1.25	26	0.84	26	39	7.0%	11	20.8%	29
2015	3.91	4.10	26	56%	6	18%	26	1.10	14	0.44	4	39	7.8%	3	25.2%	16
2015 ALY by direction:		Left End 5.41 (31)			Left Tackle 4.31 (26)			Mid/Guard 3.98 (20)			Right Tackle 3.60 (14)				Right End 4.24 (26)	

Jurrell Casey should be a star in the NFL. Actually, he *is* a star in the NFL, he's just an unknown one. Playing defensive end in a 3-4 scheme typically means you are overlooked; playing in a 3-4 scheme on a boring Tennessee team with a bad defense means you're not even in the picture. As a 26-year-old with five seasons under his belt and 77 starts, Casey is entering the prime of his career. He has 28 career sacks, six pass deflections and four forced fumbles. More importantly, Casey consistently beats his blockers to penetrate the pocket and disrupt the design of running plays while also being stout against double-teams. Casey doesn't need to be surrounded by stars, but he needs the Titans to put more competent defenders around their unknown star. ☜ In Derrick Morgan and Brian Orakpo, the Titans have two established outside linebackers. They'll be backed up by second-round pick Kevin Dodd out of Clemson. Dodd has a horrific 9.0 percent SackSEER rating. Dodd had 12.5 sacks as a redshirt junior but zero in his freshman and sophomore seasons, and never batted down a pass in three seasons. He also disappointed in the combine drills mesasured by SackSEER. ☜ The defensive line is where the Titans need to see growth. DaQuan Jones showed some promise at defensive end in 2015, while rookie Austin Johnson (chosen 43rd overall out of Penn State) will play a huge role as the anchor in the spine of the defense at nose tackle. How impactful and consistent Johnson and Jones can be will have a major impact on Casey and the rest of the front seven.

Defensive Secondary

Secondary	Age	Pos	G	Snaps	Plays	TmPct	Rk	Stop	Dfts	BTkl	Runs	St%	Rk	RuYd	Rk	Tgts	Tgt%	Rk	Dist	Suc%	Rk	AdjYd	Rk	PD	Int
Coty Sensabaugh*	28	CB	16	1005	66	8.5%	42	26	11	9	17	47%	31	6.5	32	70	20.0%	41	13.9	47%	59	8.5	53	8	2
Michael Griffin*	31	FS	15	940	101	13.8%	8	44	10	10	50	64%	1	5.0	11	25	7.5%	36	12.3	38%	69	12.2	69	4	1
Da'Norris Searcy	28	SS	15	886	59	8.1%	57	20	7	4	24	42%	32	7.1	38	18	5.7%	17	11.5	58%	34	5.0	8	4	1
Perrish Cox	29	CB	13	701	37	5.8%	72	14	6	6	8	50%	20	4.5	10	50	20.5%	45	14.4	43%	69	8.1	45	6	1
Daimion Stafford	25	SS	16	331	25	3.2%	--	12	6	6	10	30%	--	7.0	--	15	12.6%	--	8.6	66%	--	5.1	--	2	0
Blidi Wreh-Wilson	27	CB	10	296	20	4.1%	--	6	2	3	3	67%	--	3.0	--	30	29.1%	--	14.7	37%	--	13.9	--	3	0
B.W. Webb	26	CB	9	256	24	5.5%	--	6	6	2	3	0%	--	13.3	--	26	29.2%	--	11.5	36%	--	9.8	--	2	1
Antwon Blake	26	CB	16	921	86	10.2%	14	33	14	21	17	53%	18	6.2	26	90	24.0%	64	12.3	40%	73	8.9	63	13	2
Brice McCain	30	CB	14	790	49	6.4%	68	22	9	6	15	47%	32	4.5	9	49	17.7%	19	14.9	49%	54	8.5	54	10	1

Year	Pass D Rank	vs. #1 WR	Rk	vs. #2 WR	Rk	vs. Other WR	Rk	vs. TE	Rk	vs. RB	Rk
2013	16	-13.2%	6	10.0%	23	-14.9%	7	8.6%	22	12.1%	26
2014	26	-6.3%	10	53.9%	32	-8.1%	10	9.0%	24	0.5%	18
2015	24	12.2%	27	33.3%	31	14.3%	25	15.8%	24	-39.0%	1

Michael Griffin and Jason McCourty have been staples of the Titans secondary over recent years, but that secondary has been a major problem for a defense that has ranked 24th and 26th against the pass by DVOA over the past two seasons. McCourty's inability to stay healthy further exposed a cornerback group that was always going to be overmatched, while Griffin's declining athleticism made him a liability both against the run and against the pass. The Titans cut Griffin in February after nine seasons with the team. ☞ To solve their cornerback problems, Dick LeBeau will hope that McCourty stays healthy and for either Perrish Cox or Brice McCain to establish himself on the other side of the field. Before spending last year in Miami, McCain had some success playing under LeBeau in Pittsburgh, ranking 37th in adjusted success rate in coverage in 2014.

Special Teams

Year	DVOA	Rank	FG/XP	Rank	Net Kick	Rank	Kick Ret	Rank	Net Punt	Rank	Punt Ret	Rank	Hidden	Rank
2013	-3.2%	26	-1.8	22	-4.5	27	-1.3	16	0.6	18	-9.1	29	5.3	8
2014	-1.8%	20	-0.1	17	-9.4	30	1.1	11	2.7	11	-3.3	20	-9.5	28
2015	-3.8%	28	1.5	12	-1.2	19	-10.0	32	-6.7	26	-2.4	19	-5.9	23

The Titans special teams were decidedly subpar in 2015; other than the usual random fluctuations in special teams performance, there is little reason to expect that to change in 2016. Kicker Ryan Succop is decidedly average. Punter Brett Kern was actually fantastic in our gross punting metric in 2015—only Johnny Hekker of the Rams was worth more—but the Titans gave up all that value and then some with poor coverage. ☞ There is some hope that the return game can improve, but it will hinge on Rishard Matthews getting opportunities or Tre McBride developing ahead of his second season. McBride is one of four players who remain on the Titans roster who returned a kick or punt in 2015, along with Dexter McCluster, Bishop Sankey, and Harry Douglas. Out of that group, McCluster is the most likely to assume both roles because he's the most likely to be on the roster: the coaching staff has repeatedly voiced their trust in him as part of the offense. ☞ One place Tennessee special teams will be better this season is out of their control: opposing punters averaged 48.2 gross yards per punt last season. The NFL average was 45.4 yards and no other team faced an average higher than 47.0 yards.

Washington Redskins

2015 record: 9-7	**Total DVOA:** -0.3% (15th)	**2016 Mean Projection:** 6.8 wins	**On the Clock (0-4):** 19%
Pythagorean Wins: 8.2 (14th)	**Offense:** 1.9% (12th)	**Postseason Odds:** 21.5%	**Mediocrity (5-7):** 44%
Snap-Weighted Age: 26.4 (21st)	**Defense:** 5.4% (21st)	**Super Bowl Odds:** 1.4%	**Playoff Contender (8-10):** 29%
Average Opponent: -5.0% (25th)	**Special Teams:** 3.2% (6th)	**Proj. Avg. Opponent:** 1.5% (9th)	**Super Bowl Contender (11+):** 8%

2015: We like that, especially the last two months.

2016: We like that... a lot less.

If you were frozen Han Solo-style back on New Year's Eve 2012 and woke up today, you might not think much has changed. Taylor Swift and Adele still blare incessantly through your car radio, everyone still watches *The Walking Dead* and *Game of Thrones*, and the Washington Redskins are still NFC East champs, led by a homegrown quarterback and offensive-minded head coach praised for his schematic ingenuity.

You would then realize that, no, that's not a different Donald Trump on the verge of the presidency, and yes, that is Kirk Cousins instead of Robert Griffin III emerging as the anointed savior for the long-suffering Washington franchise. The last four years of Redskins football have essentially amounted to three-and-a-half years of routine dysfunction balanced by two blissful second-half surges. Currently riding the upswing of one of those surges, the question now is whether Cousins and Jay Gruden can avoid the same devastating backslide that Griffin and Mike Shanahan suffered immediately after a similarly unexpected postseason berth four years earlier.

The answer to that question will largely reside in Cousins himself. Seemingly a lost cause after multiple failed stints as a turnover-prone starter, Cousins suddenly corrected his biggest weakness and spawned a catchphrase that enraptured the Mid-Atlantic, a scenario which would have seemed inconceivable in September. Over his first three seasons, Cousins' interception rate was an astounding 35 percent above the league average. That's worse than virtually every quarterback in NFL history who's ever earned even passing consideration as a starter. Among signal-callers with at least eight starts through his first three seasons, only one player threw more picks than Cousins when compared to the league average: Zeke Bratkowski, who was either a quarterback for the Bears in the mid-1950s or some sort of *Madden*-generated Nickelodeon character.

So naturally, in his fourth season, Cousins' turned in an interception rate right on par with league MVP Cam Newton. In fact, Cousins was above the league average in all nine standard passing categories recorded by Pro Football Reference.[1] This alone isn't particularly unique, as 10 other quarterbacks earned the same distinction last year. Of course, Cousins isn't a worshipped institution (yet) like Tom Brady or Drew Brees. Dating back to the start of the DVOA era in 1989, only 14

fourth-year quarterbacks have pulled off the same feat (Table 1). And when factoring in passing DVOA and DYAR, Cousins still posted a season which belonged alongside a largely impressive group of names.

Table 1. The Best of the Year 4 QBs, 1989-2015

Player	Year	Team	Pass DVOA	Pass DYAR
Jim Everett	1989	LARM	28.1%	1360
Chris Miller	1990	ATL	-0.1%	304
Mark Rypien	1991	WAS	41.9%	1,489
Troy Aikman	1992	DAL	28.1%	1,249
Mark Brunell	1997	JAC	26.9%	1,137
Brad Johnson	1997	MIN	20.2%	971
Tom Brady	2003	NE	8.7%	692
Drew Brees	2004	SD	31.4%	1,136
Ben Roethlisberger	2007	PIT	12.7%	668
Matt Cassel	2008	NE	1.1%	458
Aaron Rodgers	2008	GB	8.5%	708
Matt Ryan	2011	ATL	18.8%	1,120
Kirk Cousins	**2015**	**WAS**	**16.9%**	**1,023**
Russell Wilson	2015	SEA	24.3%	1,190

The majority of the players in Table 1 developed into serviceable starters at the minimum. Moreover, pre-1989 players who fit these criteria include Dan Marino during his legendary 1986 season and others such as Neil Lomax, Bert Jones, and Ken Anderson, all of whom emerged as Pro Bowl-level players beginning in their fourth seasons. Based on historic precedent alone, the odds of Cousins morphing back into the old pick-happy pumpkin appear rather low.

Then again, we don't need to look back further than November to understand why some might be optimistic about Cousins and the Redskins in general. From Weeks 1 to 9, Washington posted a mediocre -8.3% offensive DVOA, 22nd in the league over that span. But from Weeks 10 to 17, the Redskins were the fifth-best offense, surging to a 13.1% of-

---

1 The nine categories are completion percentage, yards per attempt, touchdown percentage, interception percentage, passer rating, sack percentage, adjusted yards per attempt, net yards per attempt, and adjusted net yards per attempt.

2016 Redskins Schedule

Week	Opp.	Week	Opp.	Week	Opp.
1	PIT (Mon.)	7	at DET	13	at ARI
2	DAL	8	at CIN (U.K.)	14	at PHI
3	at NYG	9	BYE	15	CAR (Mon.)
4	CLE	10	MIN	16	at CHI (Sat.)
5	at BAL	11	GB	17	NYG
6	PHI	12	at DAL (Thu.)		

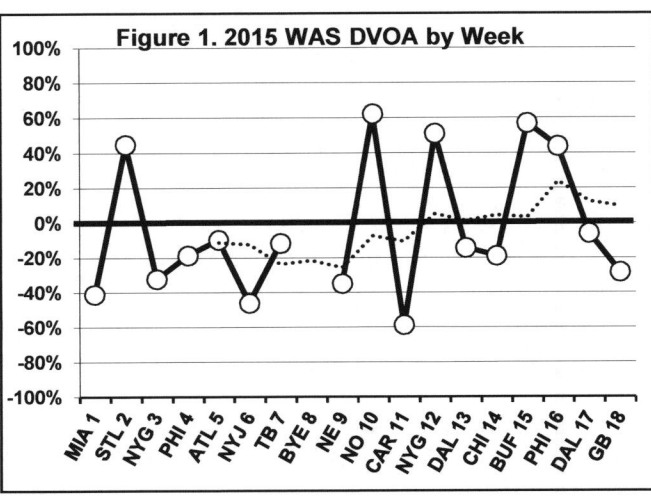

Figure 1. 2015 WAS DVOA by Week

fensive DVOA. Only the Seahawks and Lions improved more from the first half of the season to the second half, and in weighted offensive DVOA, the Redskins finished the regular season with an eye-popping 43.0% figure. Again, only Seattle bested Washington in that department. Perhaps most importantly, Cousins turned the ball over just four times in the final eight games, only two of which were interceptions.

That neat little division isn't a case of arbitrary endpoints. Week 9 marked the return of DeSean Jackson and Jordan Reed from injury, jumpstarting what had previously been an unimaginative offense filled with checkdowns and 2-yard runs up the gut. Jackson played a grand total of two series over the first seven games, and while Reed played an important role in Washington's franchise-record 24-point comeback against Tampa Bay (now immortalized as the "YOU LIKE THAT?!" game), he had scored just once while averaging under 70 yards per game in four other contests. From November on, though, both added sorely needed vertical elements to the passing game, with Jackson demanding safety help over the top and Reed subsequently punishing helpless linebackers and slot corners down the vacated seams. In the aforementioned second-half stretch, Cousins compiled 420 DYAR and posted a 116.2% DVOA on deep passes over 15 yards past the line of scrimmage, both of which were top-five marks over that span (minimum 50 deep attempts).

Assuming Cousins didn't secretly purchase Elwayian arm strength while Christmas shopping, we can attribute a lot of Washington's second-half offensive surge to not only healthy returns for Jackson and Reed, but also the growth of Jay Gruden in his second season. We tend to forget that coaches aren't just static cardboard figures with visors and pre-programmed press conference answers, especially young first-timers like Gruden. In that sense, Gruden's development on the sidelines was nearly as important as Cousins' development under center, as his play calling maximized his quarterback's strengths. Watch any Washington game from last year and you'll see lots of play-action rollouts, which keep the pass rush honest and simplify the processing for Cousins by only requiring a half-field read. Not surprisingly, Cousins fared extremely well on such plays; his 56.8% passing and rushing DVOA on play-action attempts was one of the five best in the league (min. 50 attempts). You would also see lots of well-designed "drive starters" like screens and shallow crossers and clever man coverage beaters to provide Cousins with bigger throwing windows.

This all sounds rosy in retrospect, but as is often the case with the Redskins, there's cold water to pour over the situation. So

far, we have spent this chapter explaining how Cousins turned into a top-five quarterback over the season's final two months, by far the most important factor in Washington's unexpected 6-2 finish to steal its much-maligned division. What's abundantly less clear is if Cousins can put up a full 16-game season that's even within shouting distance of his second-half breakthrough. Lurking underneath his shiny numbers are some clear weaknesses which give reasons for pause. Cousins remained a fairly conservative quarterback throughout 2015, finishing in the bottom third in both third-down Air Less EXpected (ALEX) and failed completion percentage. Even if you filter the sample size to Weeks 10-17, his ALEX was -0.8 yards on third downs, below the league average (-0.2) and trailing luminaries such as Blaine Gabbert and Brian Hoyer. The biggest concern is how poorly he fared while pressured, one of the most crippling limitations a quarterback can have. Cousins had the second-largest split in the league between DVOA with no pass pressure and DVOA under pressure, trailing only Hoyer. While every quarterback is better when J.J. Watt or Aaron Donald isn't about to consume them, Cousins' DVOA was an astonishing 179.1% worse when pressured. Teams like Dallas and Carolina effectively treated Cousins like a rookie, sending blitzes that would doom defenses against the best quarterbacks but instead resulted in a flurry of negative plays for Washington. Looking solely at passes where he was pressured, Cousins posted a -110.1% DVOA, worse than every qualifying passer besides Hoyer and Ryan Mallett.

Cousins isn't doomed to the mediocrity of those former New England backups, nor is he destined for stardom like many of the other quarterbacks from Table 1. The point is that there is very little historical precedent for a player like Cousins, one who appears hopelessly lost through three seasons before the light just suddenly flips on. That adds a huge layer of mystery to Washington's projection. The Redskins themselves are clearly not sure about Cousins, having franchised him this offseason without coming close to a long-term extension. Even if you believe in Cousins as the long-term quarterback, it's likelier than not that he'll regress a bit from his torrid finish. Thus, if Washington is going to earn consecutive postseason berths for the first time since 1991-92, we need to look at what other parts of this roster can pick up the slack.

A good place to start is in the trenches, where Washington was quietly excellent on passing downs. The Redskins were a top-10 team in adjusted sack rate (ASR) on both sides of the ball. Before last season, neither side had finished in the top 10 of ASR since the defensive line finished ninth in 2011. In fact, by ASR, Washington's pass protection was arguably the league's most improved, jumping from 31st in the category in 2014 to 10th last season. There's young cost-controlled talent on both lines here, a startling development for a franchise which has become the archetype for reckless spending. General manager Scott McCloughan's first two draft picks brought in one starter on each side, as both Brandon Scherff and Preston Smith became integral contributors by season's end. Few guards go fifth overall, but Scherff's pro-ready skill set coupled with Morgan Moses' development at right tackle accounted for much of Washington's improvement on the line. The Redskins averaged nearly a half-yard more per rush when running to the right side of the line than when going left, a positive reflection for the McCloughan draftees.

And on defense, Smith's emergence was particularly impressive: the second-rounder from Mississippi State played a marginal role to begin the season before turning into Washington's best edge-rusher down the stretch, ultimately finishing with 8 sacks and 12 hurries, both second on the team. Washington now has a viable edge-rushing rotation for the first time in forever, with minicamp buzz suggesting that Smith could even play snaps inside to allow the Redskins to deploy Smith, Ryan Kerrigan, and Junior Galette simultaneously on passing downs. Galette is the wild card here; though he accrued 22 sacks over his final two years in New Orleans, there are far safer bets than someone who just missed an entire season after tearing his Achilles. Nevertheless, Smith gives the Redskins' pass rush feasible depth alongside the eminently productive Ryan Kerrigan (who has 30 or more combined sacks and hurries each of the past three years).

After that, things begin to break down. Washington is as bad as any team in the league in terms of the run game, and did very little to fix it. The plodding Alfred Morris won't be missed in the backfield, but new starter Matt Jones appears largely cut from the same cloth. Washington ranked dead last in rushing DVOA as a team, and Jones finished last among 44 qualifying running backs in both rushing DVOA and DYAR. A lack of big plays doomed the Redskins to the basement, as Washington finished 27th in open field yards per carry (gained over 10 yards past the line of scrimmage) and 31st in percentage of rushing attempts which gained more than 10 yards (7.7 percent). Perhaps those numbers would have turned out better had Washington been allowed to run against its own front, which finished 30th in both open-field and second-level yards (gained 5 to 10 yards beyond the line of scrimmage).

As most of our readers surely understand, running the football well is far from a prerequisite for a winning team in today's NFL. That also does not mean it should go totally ignored. Fans complaining about McCloughan's tenure as GM are akin to fans of the archrival Cowboys who whine about Tony Romo while forgetting the days of Quincy Carter and Chad Hutchinson. And yet, it's curious that McCloughan

decided to overlook Washington's cap-strapped situation to fork over the league's priciest cornerback contract to Josh Norman. Norman undeniably produced in Carolina, finishing fourth in adjusted yards allowed per target last season, and adds much-needed talent to a secondary which was starting a pair of unheralded rookies (sixth-rounder Kyshoen Jarrett and undrafted Quinton Dunbar) by the end of 2015. But remember, Washington's pass defense was already an above-average unit because of its pressure, which has a fairly high ceiling this season for reasons already mentioned. It's inefficient to mortgage the cap on a player who reinforces a strength but does nothing for the team's biggest weaknesses. Norman should thrive in a defense which uses many of the zone principles he encountered in Carolina, but he won't carry the ball, stop the run, or regularly cover tight ends.

Thus, you don't even have to believe that Kirk Cousins is the second coming of Nick Foles to raise the caution flag in D.C. Washington's biggest offseason moves were largely spent on areas which already appeared steady, doing almost nothing to patch its biggest roster holes. There's a decent chance the Redskins' best-case scenario is probably exactly what we saw unfold last season. We can hope that first-round wide receiver Josh Doctson opens up the offense and helps Cousins sustain his second-half form. However, we know the all-too-familiar sight of Jones running into Kory Lichtensteiger's back will probably return to the offense. Similarly, we can hope that Norman elevates the pass defense and shuts down the likes of Dez Bryant and Odell Beckham Jr. (As an aside, the new bi-annual Norman-ODB matchups are the strongest proof yet of the NFL being the WWE's slightly more clandestine cousin.) But again, we know that Perry Riley, Mason Foster, and Will Compton are challenged at shedding blockers and dropping into coverage, and that DeAngelo Hall masquerading as a safety is somehow the best safety on the roster.

There's nothing wrong with trying to replicate a formula that resulted in a division title a year ago, except for the fact that Washington isn't starting from a particularly enviable position of strength. Despite the final two months, the Redskins' overall DVOA suggested they were almost exactly a league-average team. Only the Texans had a worse DVOA among playoff teams, the result of playing in the one division more execrable than the NFC East. Thus, Washington is a prime candidate to fall prey to the Plexiglass Principle. This is a simple statistical pattern in sports first stated clearly by Bill James: teams that dramatically improve from one season to the next tend to decline the following year, and vice versa.

Washington's overall DVOA jumped 26.7% from 2014, the fifth-largest improvement of any team in the league. We know this was driven largely by its offense, which saw its DVOA improve by 13.7%. The defense improved slightly, but remained below average for the fourth consecutive season. However, the Redskins offense jumping from bad to above-average isn't the same as, say, the Panthers and Bengals jumping from average to very good or great. Historically, offenses that make the Redskins' type of jump are much more likely to backslide than those which make the Panthers' or Bengals' type of jump. Since the last expansion in 2002, there have been 20 offenses which have improved their DVOA by 10% to 20% in their "breakout" season, yet still only ended up right around league average (an offensive DVOA between -5.0% and 5.0%). In other words, like the 2015 Redskins, these offenses have seemed rather vulnerable to the aforementioned Plexiglass Principle. If the 2016 Washington offense ends up being like its predecessors, history suggests that regression is likely coming in the upcoming season (Table 2).

Table 2. Plexiglass Principle for "Average" Offenses, 2002-2015

Year	Team	Off Y-1	Off	Off Y+1
2002	ATL	-11.5%	1.6%	-9.3%
2004	BAL	-12.7%	-2.1%	-11.7%
2004	HOU	-14.7%	-1.8%	-15.4%
2005	ATL	-10.5%	3.3%	-0.6%
2006	BAL	-11.7%	0.9%	-13.3%
2006	CHI	-17.1%	-5.0%	-22.1%
2006	STL	-7.9%	2.5%	-22.7%
2007	MIN	-17.9%	-0.8%	-9.9%
2008	BAL	-13.3%	-0.3%	12.8%
2009	CIN	-18.3%	-0.9%	1.7%
2010	NYJ	-12.5%	2.1%	-8.3%
2011	BUF	-14.5%	0.3%	-4.2%
2011	OAK	-8.3%	2.6%	-9.5%
2012	IND	-17.2%	-2.9%	4.3%
2012	MIN	-10.2%	0.3%	-4.7%
2012	TB	-11.5%	0.6%	-10.4%
2014	NYG	-22.0%	-0.3%	-1.8%
2015	NYJ	-11.2%	1.6%	--
2015	OAK	-19.4%	-1.3%	--
2015	**WAS**	**-11.8%**	**1.9%**	**--**
Average		*-13.6%*	*0.0%*	*-7.4%*

Average offenses are defined here as DVOA between -5.0% and 5.0%

This has to be at least a little concerning for Washington fans. Only three of the offenses in Table 2 improved again the following year. Many of the other teams regressed to below-average levels which were only marginally better than their former "pre-breakout" selves.

The Redskins also saw their overall DVOA jump 20 percentage points from 2014. For the 96 teams since 1989 to make that type of leap, the average win total the next season fell from 9.7 to 8.3, while the average overall DVOA fell from 11.6% to 2.2%. So while Washington has room to grow, history suggests it also has plenty of room to regress.

For a Washington fan seeking a reason for optimism, a hopeful recent comparison might be the 2008 Ravens. That Baltimore team posted an offensive DVOA slightly worse than Washington 2015, but had a similar improvement over the previous year. The following season, the 2009 Ravens offense posted a 12.8% DVOA and the Ravens were the No. 1 team in overall DVOA. Like Washington, that Baltimore team improved in part because of a massive upgrade at the quarterback position during Joe Flacco's rookie season. The comparison isn't perfect because Flacco enjoyed a lot more surrounding help from the running game and defense in Baltimore. Then again, apart from 2014, he's also never posted a season as strong as the one Cousins just had. Flacco leveraged a series of above-average seasons and one fortuitously timed Super Bowl run into a record-breaking contract; Cousins could similarly put Washington in a tough spot next offseason if his performance this year helps the Redskins stave off offensive regression.

Of course, Redskins fans would likely kill for the type of run the Ravens have enjoyed since 2008, as Baltimore did not suffer a losing season in the first seven years of the Flacco era. That type of consistency was once routine in D.C., but it's now been 24 years since the Redskins enjoyed such a streak.

To do it again, Washington will have to build a better machine with largely the same tools and parts. The Redskins played the eighth easiest schedule last season by average opponent DVOA, and Washington did not beat a single team all season which finished .500 or better. Now, facing a first-place schedule which projects as the ninth-toughest in the league, that option will be off the table if Washington hopes to return to the postseason. Complicating matters are the significantly easier paths for the rest of the division. There's a big difference between playing Carolina and Arizona compared to playing the other NFC South and West teams (although Philadelphia has to play Seattle). Meanwhile, the Cowboys get the No. 31 projected schedule just in time for the healthy return of the Tony Romo-to-Dez Bryant connection.

Washington is not without promise, an important bottom line for a starving franchise. Cousins gives the Redskins a second chance to recapture the future they lost with RG3's demise, and if he progresses this season, the win-loss total may ultimately be secondary. Washington would then encounter a brand new set of problems, namely building its roster on a budget after paying through the nose to keep Cousins off the open market. Considering the frustration and ridicule the organization has endured, though, anything different would surely be welcome. For the moment, Washington has an acceptable status quo it can cling to heading into a new season. Now, they can only hope they fare better than they did four years ago, the last time this team had any real expectations.

Sterling Xie

2015 Redskins Stats by Week

Wk	vs.	W-L	PF	PA	YDF	YDA	TO	Total	Off	Def	ST
1	MIA	L	10	17	349	256	-1	-41%	-21%	-1%	-21%
2	STL	W	24	10	373	213	-1	45%	33%	-12%	0%
3	at NYG	L	21	32	393	363	-3	-32%	-27%	24%	19%
4	PHI	W	23	20	417	320	1	-18%	4%	18%	-4%
5	at ATL	L	19	25	270	418	1	-10%	-22%	-12%	0%
6	at NYJ	L	20	34	225	474	1	-46%	-25%	24%	3%
7	TB	W	31	30	355	479	0	-12%	22%	37%	4%
8	BYE										
9	at NE	L	10	27	250	460	0	-35%	-35%	3%	4%
10	NO	W	47	14	510	350	2	62%	37%	-26%	-1%
11	at CAR	L	16	44	186	368	-5	-59%	-74%	16%	32%
12	NYG	W	20	14	407	332	3	51%	10%	-36%	5%
13	DAL	L	16	19	266	318	2	-14%	-15%	-10%	-9%
14	at CHI	W	24	21	374	377	0	-19%	5%	25%	1%
15	BUF	W	35	25	431	452	-1	57%	56%	5%	6%
16	at PHI	W	38	24	418	398	2	44%	43%	5%	6%
17	at DAL	W	34	23	437	512	4	-6%	16%	27%	5%
18	GB	L	18	35	354	346	0	-28%	-8%	25%	4%

Trends and Splits

	Offense	Rank	Defense	Rank
Total DVOA	1.9%	12	5.4%	21
Unadjusted VOA	6.9%	10	5.8%	17
Weighted Trend	7.5%	12	5.0%	20
Variance	11.6%	31	4.3%	13
Average Opponent	3.4%	28	-1.9%	24
Passing	31.5%	6	13.6%	19
Rushing	-23.6%	32	-5.5%	22
First Down	3.7%	12	8.3%	23
Second Down	-4.7%	20	6.9%	26
Third Down	8.2%	11	-2.9%	14
First Half	11.1%	9	-3.6%	13
Second Half	-7.7%	25	13.2%	28
Red Zone	10.5%	13	-12.4%	8
Late and Close	-2.7%	17	15.5%	30

Five-Year Performance

Year	W-L	Pyth W	Est W	PF	PA	TO	Total	Rk	Off	Rk	Def	Rk	ST	Rk	Off AGL	Rk	Def AGL	Rk	Off Age	Rk	Def Age	Rk	ST Age	Rk
2011	5-11	5.7	6.3	288	367	-14	-7.0%	21	-7.0%	19	-1.2%	14	-1.2%	21	54.3	31	13.2	7	27.3	14	27.3	15	26.9	3
2012	10-6	9.2	9.8	436	388	+17	9.3%	9	15.3%	6	1.7%	17	-4.3%	28	34.8	20	48.8	26	26.1	26	27.8	5	27.1	3
2013	3-13	4.8	4.2	334	478	-8	-26.2%	29	-10.0%	23	4.2%	21	-12.0%	32	14.6	4	26.8	13	27.0	15	28.0	3	27.1	2
2014	4-12	4.5	4.4	301	438	-12	-27.0%	28	-11.8%	28	9.9%	27	-5.4%	29	21.9	7	67.6	29	27.1	13	26.9	14	25.9	21
2015	9-7	8.2	7.8	388	379	+5	-0.3%	15	1.9%	12	5.4%	21	3.2%	6	44.0	24	75.1	32	25.9	26	27.1	7	26.0	17

2015 Performance Based on Most Common Personnel Groups

WAS Offense					WAS Offense vs. Opponents					WAS Defense				WAS Defense vs. Opponents			
Pers	Freq	Yds	DVOA	Run%	Pers	Freq	Yds	DVOA	Run%	Pers	Freq	Yds	DVOA	Pers	Freq	Yds	DVOA
11	64%	5.9	7.1%	27%	Base	32%	5.5	2.4%	64%	Base	26%	5.9	-0.8%	11	63%	6.1	9.0%
12	12%	5.7	5.6%	54%	Nickel	57%	5.5	-2.9%	34%	Nickel	60%	6.1	11.1%	12	16%	6.5	13.2%
611	4%	6.8	-5.9%	59%	Dime+	10%	8.3	70.0%	6%	Dime+	13%	7.3	0.7%	21	9%	6.9	2.5%
612	4%	5.7	21.7%	84%	Goal Line	1%	5.2	169.5%	67%	Goal Line	1%	0.5	-49.2%	13	3%	4.3	-28.1%
21	4%	5.6	3.8%	51%	Big	0%	1.0	-130.5%	100%					10	2%	7.3	7.5%
610	3%	4.7	2.3%	89%										22	1%	4.8	-4.4%

Strategic Tendencies

Run/Pass		Rk	Formation		Rk	Pass Rush		Rk	Secondary		Rk	Strategy		Rk
Runs, first half	42%	6	Form: Single Back	83%	5	Rush 3	6.5%	17	4 DB	26%	27	Play action	19%	15
Runs, first down	52%	8	Form: Empty Back	7%	18	Rush 4	71.8%	3	5 DB	60%	7	Avg Box (Off)	6.21	18
Runs, second-long	31%	16	Pers: 3+ WR	68%	8	Rush 5	16.8%	30	6+ DB	13%	13	Avg Box (Def)	6.07	28
Runs, power sit.	53%	22	Pers: 2+ TE/6+ OL	31%	19	Rush 6+	4.9%	23	CB by Sides	87%	7	Offensive Pace	32.49	29
Runs, behind 2H	18%	32	Pers: 6+ OL	15%	1	Sacks by LB	59.5%	6	S/CB Cover Ratio	22%	17	Defensive Pace	29.54	9
Pass, ahead 2H	43%	27	Shotgun/Pistol	50%	26	Sacks by DB	2.7%	28	DB Blitz	6%	25	Go for it on 4th	0.80	22

In 2014, Washington averaged 7.0 yards after the catch, the highest figure since we started charting YAC in 2005. Last year, that sunk to just 5.1 yards after the catch, below the NFL average. ☜ Washington had one of the league's biggest gaps between play-action passes and other pass plays, with 10.3 yards per play and 58.6% DVOA using play-action but 6.4 yards per play and 25.0% DVOA without play-action. It was the second straight year Washington had a very large advantage when using play-action. ☜ Washington's offense had the league's best first-down passing DVOA (51.3%) but the worst first-down rushing DVOA (-31.6%). ☜ Washington used six or more offensive linemen on a league-high 15.2 percent of plays, with 7.4% DVOA and 5.7 yards per play. ☜ The offense led the league with a 73.6% DVOA on plays with an empty backfield. ☜ The offense had the league's best DVOA on passes behind the line of scrimmage at 47.4%, but ranked 24th in percentage of passes thrown behind the line of scrimmage. ☜ Along those lines, Washington averaged 13.9 yards per pass with 125.0% DVOA on running back screens but used only 15 of these plays (compared to an NFL average of 25). ☜ When it came to passes thrown behind the line of scrimmage, the defense was almost as bad as the offense was good, ranking 26th in DVOA and conceding an average of 10.5 yards after the catch on such plays. Only the Saints allowed more YAC on these throws. ☜ The Washington defense benefited from a league-high 6.3 percent drop rate by opposing receivers. ☜ Washington's rate of blitzing plummeted from 2014, when they had sent five or more pass-rushers on 36.8 percent of passes compared to just 21.7 percent in 2015.

Passing

Player	DYAR	DVOA	Plays	NtYds	Avg	YAC	C%	TD	Int
K.Cousins	1023	16.9%	570	3979	7.0	5.0	69.8%	29	11
C.McCoy	22	20.9%	12	114	9.5	11.6	63.6%	1	0

Rushing

Player	DYAR	DVOA	Plays	Yds	Avg	TD	Fum	Suc
A.Morris*	-52	-15.0%	202	751	3.7	2	0	39%
M.Jones	-92	-23.4%	144	490	3.4	3	4	46%
C.Thompson	22	8.0%	35	216	6.2	0	1	43%
K.Cousins	8	-3.1%	14	52	3.7	5	3	-
P.Thomas*	1	-4.4%	11	52	4.7	0	0	36%
D.Young*	-29	-107.0%	6	10	1.7	0	1	33%

Receiving

Player	DYAR	DVOA	Plays	Ctch	Yds	Y/C	YAC	TD	C%
P.Garcon	128	2.4%	111	72	777	10.8	2.3	6	65%
J.Crowder	52	-4.4%	78	59	604	10.2	5.7	2	76%
D.Jackson	97	12.7%	49	30	528	17.6	5.3	4	61%
R.Grant	40	-1.1%	42	23	268	11.7	4.3	2	55%
A.Roberts*	-26	-28.6%	21	11	135	12.3	3.5	0	52%
R.Ross	63	45.4%	13	8	184	23.0	8.0	1	62%
J.Reed	206	20.1%	114	87	952	10.9	5.4	11	76%
D.Carrier	17	4.9%	22	17	141	8.3	4.5	1	77%
V.Davis	-6	-8.8%	58	38	395	10.4	3.8	0	66%
C.Thompson	-5	-15.6%	48	35	240	6.9	4.8	2	73%
M.Jones	75	38.9%	25	19	304	16.0	14.0	1	76%
A.Morris*	-10	-27.6%	13	10	55	5.5	3.8	0	77%
P.Thomas*	18	26.6%	11	9	84	9.3	7.0	0	82%
D.Young*	-11	-42.8%	6	6	22	3.7	3.3	0	100%

Offensive Line

Player	Pos	Age	GS	Snaps	Pen	Sk	Pass	Run	Player	Pos	Age	GS	Snaps	Pen	Sk	Pass	Run
Brandon Scherff	RG	25	16/16	1069	3	1.0	5.0	3.0	Josh LeRibeus	C	27	16/11	711	2	0.5	2.5	3.0
Morgan Moses	RT	25	16/16	1031	13	4.5	6.5	3.0	Kory Lichtensteiger	C	31	5/5	372	2	1.0	1.0	5.0
Trent Williams	LT	28	14/14	927	7	1.5	2.5	5.5	Tom Compton*	RT	27	13/1	210	1	0.0	1.0	0.0
Spencer Long	LG	26	13/13	843	0	0.5	2.5	3.5	Ty Nsekhe	OT	31	13/2	194	1	0.0	0.0	1.0

Year	Yards	ALY	Rank	Power	Rank	Stuff	Rank	2nd Lev	Rank	Open Field	Rank	Sacks	ASR	Rank	Press	Rank	F-Start	Cont.
2013	4.51	3.75	23	76%	4	22%	28	1.29	5	0.95	7	43	7.6%	19	26.5%	21	16	48
2014	4.22	3.87	19	58%	27	20%	16	1.26	7	0.75	14	58	9.8%	31	23.9%	16	20	29
2015	3.82	3.64	21	65%	18	22%	19	1.02	27	0.68	17	27	5.4%	10	20.4%	2	13	34

2015 ALY by direction:	Left End 3.56 (17)	Left Tackle 3.37 (25)	Mid/Guard 3.58 (28)	Right Tackle 3.87 (15)	Right End 3.89 (10)

Washington took two offensive linemen in the third round of the 2014 draft, Morgan Moses and Spencer Long, but they didn't play a significant role until last season. Considered a raw project coming out of Virginia, Moses largely held up in his first full season as a starter, finishing a respectable 24th among all tackles in snaps per bown block (108.5). However, the technique issues showed up in the number of flags Moses drew, as his 13 penalties were the third-most among all offensive linemen. Nine of those were holding calls, a figure only Greg Robinson exceeded. ☜ Long fared well at left guard after Shawn Lauvao went down at the end of September, and early buzz suggests he could supplant Kory Lichtensteiger as the starting center. Long actually played right guard at Nebraska, but could give Washington an opportunity to start its best five if Lauvao can fully recover after undergoing five foot surgeries.

Defensive Front Seven

Defensive Line	Age	Pos	G	Snaps	Plays	TmPct	Rk	Stop	Dfts	BTkl	Runs	St%	Rk	RuYd	Rk	Sack	Hit	Hur	Dsrpt
						Overall						**vs. Run**					**Pass Rush**		
Chris Baker	29	DT	16	617	53	6.7%	24	44	20	0	42	83%	19	1.4	6	6.0	11	9.0	1
Jason Hatcher*	34	DE	15	540	20	2.7%	81	14	7	7	16	69%	60	3.3	76	2.0	11	14.5	1
Ricky Jean-Francois	30	DE	16	385	26	3.3%	--	24	8	4	21	90%	--	0.7	--	2.0	2	7.0	1
Terrance Knighton*	30	DT	15	369	29	3.9%	--	27	8	4	25	92%	--	1.0	--	1.5	2	2.0	0
Stephen Paea	28	DE	11	215	16	2.9%	--	15	7	1	12	92%	--	1.3	--	1.5	4	5.0	0
Kendall Reyes	27	DE	16	656	36	4.7%	46	28	7	5	25	80%	26	2.0	39	2.0	5	14.5	2

Edge Rushers	Age	Pos	G	Snaps	Plays	TmPct	Rk	Stop	Dfts	BTkl	Runs	St%	Rk	RuYd	Rk	Sack	Hit	Hur	Dsrpt
						Overall						**vs. Run**					**Pass Rush**		
Ryan Kerrigan	28	OLB	16	886	44	5.5%	37	40	18	5	28	89%	5	1.2	14	9.5	4	29.0	3
Trent Murphy	26	OLB	16	671	32	4.0%	69	23	12	4	20	65%	73	1.9	31	3.5	8	8.0	0
Preston Smith	24	OLB	16	508	34	4.3%	62	20	10	1	18	44%	97	4.4	93	8.0	2	12.0	2

Linebackers	Age	Pos	G	Snaps	Plays	TmPct	Rk	Stop	Dfts	BTkl	Runs	St%	Rk	RuYd	Rk	Sack	Hit	Hur	Tgts	Suc%	Rk	AdjYd	Rk	PD	Int
						Overall						**vs. Run**				**Pass Rush**				**vs. Pass**					
Will Compton	27	ILB	16	715	95	12.0%	44	49	14	11	51	65%	41	2.7	9	1.0	1	3	20	46%	55	5.3	21	4	1
Keenan Robinson*	27	ILB	12	546	65	10.9%	53	33	10	11	31	58%	60	5.4	86	0.0	0	0	14	57%	34	7.1	52	3	1
Perry Riley	28	ILB	9	463	46	10.3%	57	21	6	4	26	54%	75	3.6	46	0.0	1	3	13	56%	39	8.0	60	3	2
Mason Foster	27	ILB	13	259	34	5.3%	--	15	3	1	19	58%	--	2.5	--	0.0	0	2	8	62%	--	8.7	--	1	0

Year	Yards	ALY	Rank	Power	Rank	Stuff	Rank	2nd Level	Rank	Open Field	Rank	Sacks	ASR	Rank	Press	Rank
2013	4.02	3.58	6	68%	22	23%	6	1.18	25	0.82	22	36	7.0%	13	26.4%	9
2014	3.97	3.77	12	60%	11	20%	13	1.04	8	0.69	16	36	6.6%	17	25.8%	12
2015	4.68	4.01	24	49%	1	19%	20	1.35	30	1.07	30	38	7.3%	9	22.6%	28
2015 ALY by direction:		Left End 4.10 (24)			Left Tackle 3.09 (7)			Mid/Guard 4.15 (24)			Right Tackle 3.64 (11)			Right End 3.07 (6)		

Watch any Redskins game from 2015 and you'll likely notice Chris Baker being the first to penetrate the backfield and reach the quarterback or ballcarrier. Baker had more sacks than he did during his first five years in the league combined, while also compiling the same number of defeats as Fletcher Cox. The 29-year-old won't receive the same mammoth contract as Cox, but he has an opportunity to earn a big raise if he can follow up 2015 with a similar season in the final year of his contract. ☞ Terrance Knighton may not have played a ton of snaps, but he was clearly the best run-stuffer on an otherwise subpar run defense. The Redskins opted not to replace Knighton with a true nose tackle, making for one of the smaller 3-4 fronts in the league. ☞ This wouldn't be a problem if Washington's inside linebackers were better at shedding blocks. Or do anything at an average or better level, for that matter. The Redskins started with a Perry Riley-Keenan Robinson duo and ended with Will Compton and Mason Foster in the middle, but saw largely uniform results throughout. Rookie Su'a Cravens figures to play a hybrid linebacker role to improve Washington's pass coverage at the position, but again, that makes a small Redskins front even smaller.

Defensive Secondary

Secondary	Age	Pos	G	Snaps	Plays	TmPct	Rk	Stop	Dfts	BTkl	Runs	St%	Rk	RuYd	Rk	Tgts	Tgt%	Rk	Dist	Suc%	Rk	AdjYd	Rk	PD	Int
						Overall						**vs. Run**							**vs. Pass**					
Dashon Goldson*	32	FS	15	968	110	14.8%	5	44	15	13	53	43%	29	5.7	19	15	3.9%	8	11.6	60%	28	6.8	36	3	1
Bashaud Breeland	24	CB	15	912	96	12.9%	1	44	15	7	36	53%	19	7.5	41	83	23.0%	60	13.7	52%	43	8.3	47	16	2
Will Blackmon	32	CB	15	786	54	7.3%	60	18	7	7	20	20%	66	11.5	66	48	15.4%	8	15.9	57%	18	9.2	66	7	2
Kyshoen Jarrett	23	SS	16	601	59	7.4%	62	27	10	9	24	50%	16	5.1	14	34	14.4%	66	8.9	51%	51	5.5	15	4	0
Trenton Robinson*	26	SS	9	439	53	11.9%	--	17	5	7	33	39%	--	7.1	--	6	3.5%	--	13.3	61%	--	6.6	--	1	1
DeAngelo Hall	33	CB/SS	11	427	50	9.2%	--	12	3	9	17	18%	--	9.5	--	24	14.0%	--	11.9	50%	--	8.9	--	2	0
Quinton Dunbar	24	CB	11	257	17	3.1%	--	7	2	2	4	25%	--	10.8	--	17	16.3%	--	10.8	52%	--	5.7	--	5	1
Jeron Johnson*	28	SS	14	196	20	2.9%	--	7	3	3	14	36%	--	5.2	--	4	4.5%	--	8.0	0%	--	9.6	--	0	0
Josh Norman	29	CB	16	1061	75	9.1%	30	39	15	9	12	50%	20	5.6	21	80	18.7%	32	14.2	63%	3	4.9	4	18	4
Greg Toler	31	CB	10	684	60	11.5%	4	19	9	3	7	14%	71	15.3	74	76	27.2%	73	14.3	52%	37	9.5	70	9	0
David Bruton	29	SS	13	481	50	7.5%	60	25	12	3	13	62%	3	6.4	29	25	14.2%	65	9.3	60%	27	5.5	14	4	2

Year	Pass D Rank	vs. #1 WR	Rk	vs. #2 WR	Rk	vs. Other WR	Rk	vs. TE	Rk	vs. RB	Rk
2013	22	13.6%	27	-14.1%	6	12.9%	25	7.5%	21	5.1%	20
2014	32	19.9%	29	32.5%	30	22.8%	29	21.7%	29	-18.0%	6
2015	20	13.2%	28	23.7%	30	-5.3%	13	8.0%	21	-17.8%	6

Josh Norman may have exaggerated when he dubbed himself one of the top five cornerbacks in league history, but he certainly achieved that lofty ranking last season. Norman saw fewer targets and posted a higher success rate than he did in 2014, a telltale sign of his growth into a premier No. 1 corner. ☞ With Norman now on the other side, Bashaud Breeland's workload figures to continue growing. By adjusted target percentage, only 15 out of 75 qualifying cornerbacks were targeted more than Breeland in his sophomore campaign. The long-armed Breeland shows good ball skills at times, but can be feast-or-famine. His Week 6 performance against the Jets embodied this trend, as he forced a fumble and picked off a pass in the first half, only to concede a back-breaking 35-yard touchdown in the second half. ☞ Let us know if you can figure out who Washington will start at safety this year. Kyshoen Jarrett likely would have been one starter after a pleasantly surprising rookie season, but Jarrett's career may have ended prematurely after an arm injury suffered in the regular season finale left him with severe nerve damage. DeAngelo Hall made the conversion from cornerback late last season, and Will Blackmon will do the same this summer. Maybe career special-teamer David Bruton will help the run as a thumping box safety, a role in which he showed some promise in Denver last season. Or maybe Dashon Goldson returns to reprise that role, an outcome neither Goldson nor the Redskins ruled out upon the 31-year-old's release in March. So yeah, let us know. ☞ Washington may have played more two-high safety coverages than any defense in the league. The average distance between tackles made by Redskins safeties was just 0.2 yards, the lowest figure in the league. (A table can be found in the Detroit chapter, page 79.)

Special Teams

Year	DVOA	Rank	FG/XP	Rank	Net Kick	Rank	Kick Ret	Rank	Net Punt	Rank	Punt Ret	Rank	Hidden	Rank
2013	-12.0%	32	-2.5	23	-8.3	28	-6.4	29	-33.3	32	-9.4	30	-0.4	16
2014	-5.4%	29	-0.5	19	-10.1	31	-4.0	25	-8.0	27	-4.1	21	-8.4	27
2015	3.2%	6	3.0	10	5.1	4	8.9	3	4.8	8	-5.8	27	2.5	13

Washington's long-beleaguered special teams suddenly transformed into a top-10 unit last season, an underrated factor in the Redskins' unexpected division title. The ranking was the team's highest since 1995. ☞ The biggest boost came from kickoff returns, where Washington got two return touchdowns after having just one kick return score the past eight seasons combined. Andre Roberts is no longer on the roster, but Rashad Ross was steady in his first extended run as the primary returner. ☞ Tress Way and the punting unit really turned things around after a rocky start. Despite conceding a return touchdown and blocked punt for a safety in the first three games, the punting unit still provided 4.8 points in net value, a huge leap from the minus-8.0 net points the unit supplied in 2014 and the horrific minus-33.3 points from 2013. ☞ A former Buffalo sixth-round pick, Dustin Hopkins finally got on the field in his third season and was above-average on both placekicking and gross kickoff value.

Quarterbacks

On the following pages, we provide the last three years of statistics for the top two quarterbacks on each team's depth chart, as well as a number of other quarterbacks who played significant time in 2015.

Each quarterback currently on a roster gets a projection from our KUBIAK fantasy football projection system, based on a complicated regression analysis that takes into account numerous variables including projected role, performance over the past two years, performance on third down vs. all downs, experience of the projected offensive line, historical comparables, collegiate stats, height, age, and strength of schedule.

It is difficult to accurately project statistics for a 162-game baseball season, but it is exponentially more difficult to accurately project statistics for a 16-game football season because of the small size of the data samples involved. With that in mind, we ask that you consider the listed projections not as a prediction of exact numbers, but the mean of a range of possible performances. What's important is not so much the exact number of yards and touchdowns we project, but whether or not we're projecting a given player to improve or decline. Along those same lines, rookie projections will not be as accurate as veteran projections due to lack of data.

Our quarterback projections look a bit different than our projections for the other skill positions. At running back and wide receiver, second-stringers see plenty of action, but, at quarterback, either a player starts or he does not start. We recognize that, when a starting quarterback gets injured in Week 8, you don't want to grab your *Football Outsiders Almanac* to find out if his backup is any good only to find that we've projected that the guy will throw 12 passes this year. Therefore, each year we project all quarterbacks to start all 16 games. If Aaron Rodgers goes down in November, you can look up Brett Hundley, divide the stats by 16, and get an idea of what we think he will do in an average week (and then, if you are a Green Bay fan, pass out). There are full-season projections for the top two quarterbacks on all 32 depth charts.

The first line of each quarterback table contains biographical data—the player's name, height, weight, college, draft position, birth date, and age. Height and weight are the best data we could find; weight, of course, can fluctuate during the offseason. **Age** is very simple: the number of years between the player's birth year and 2016, but birthdate is provided if you want to figure out exact age.

Draft position gives draft year and round, with the overall pick number with which the player was taken in parentheses. In the sample table, it says that Blake Bortles was chosen in the first round of the 2014 NFL draft, with the third overall pick. Undrafted free agents are listed as "FA" with the year they came into the league, even if they were only in training camp or on a practice squad.

To the far right of the first line is the player's **Risk** variable for fantasy football in 2016, which measures the likelihood of the player hitting his projection. The default rating for each player is Green. As the risk of a player failing to hit his projection rises, he's given a rating of Yellow or, in the worst cases, Red. The Risk variable is not only based on injury probability, but how a player's projection compares to his recent performance as well as our confidence (or lack thereof) in his offensive teammates. A few players with the strongest chances of surpassing their projections are given a Blue rating. Most players marked Blue will be backups with low projections, but a handful are starters or situational players who can be considered slightly better breakout candidates.

Next, we give the last three years of player stats. The majority of these statistics are passing numbers, although the final five columns on the right are the quarterback's rushing statistics.

The first few columns after the year and team the player played for are standard numbers: games and games started (**G/GS**), offensive **Snaps**, pass attempts (**Att**), pass completions (**Cmp**), completion percentage (**C%**), passing yards (**Yds**), passing touchdowns (**TD**). These numbers are official NFL totals and therefore include plays we leave out of our own metrics, such as clock-stopping spikes, and omit plays we include in our metrics, such as sacks and aborted snaps. (Other differences between official stats and Football Outsiders stats are described in the "Statistical Toolbox" introduction at the front of the book.)

The column for interceptions contains two numbers, representing the official NFL total for interceptions (**Int**) as well as our own metric for adjusted interceptions (**Adj**). For example, if you look at our sample table, Blake Bortles had 18 interceptions and 26 adjusted interceptions in 2015. Adjusted interceptions use game charting data to add dropped interceptions, plays where a defender most likely would have had an interception but couldn't hold onto the ball. Then we remove Hail Mary passes and interceptions thrown on fourth down when losing in the final two minutes of the game. We also remove "tipped interceptions," when a perfectly catchable ball deflected off the receiver's hands or chest and into the arms of a defender.

Blake Bortles Height: 6-4 Weight: 232 College: Central Florida Draft: 2014/1 (3) Born: 28-Apr-1992 Age: 24 Risk: Yellow

Year	Team	G/GS	Snaps	Att	Comp	C%	Yds	TD	INT/Adj	FUM	ASR	NY/P	Rk	DVOA	Rk	DYAR	Rk	YAR	Runs	Yds	TD	DVOA	DYAR	QBR
2014	JAC	14/13	896	475	280	58.9%	2908	11	17/20	7	10.5%	4.8	37	-40.7%	36	-955	37	-935	56	419	0	24.7%	100	21.9
2015	JAC	16/16	1058	606	355	58.6%	4428	35	18/26	14	8.0%	6.3	18	-9.9%	25	54	25	100	52	310	2	24.5%	86	46.4
2016	JAC		587	358	60.9%	4215	29	17	12		5.9		-12.6%						60	302	3	14.7%		

| 2014: | 57% Short | 30% Mid | 7% Deep | 5% Bomb | YAC: 5.8 (7) | ALEX: -0.8 | 2015: | 45% Short | 29% Mid | 19% Deep | 7% Bomb | YAC: 5.2 (21) | ALEX: 2.6 |

Overall, adjusted interception rate is higher than standard interception rate, so most quarterbacks will have more adjusted interceptions than standard interceptions. On average, a quarterback will have one additional adjusted interception for every 120 pass attempts. Once this difference is accounted for, adjusted interceptions are a better predictor of next year's interception total than standard interceptions.

The next column is fumbles (FUM), which adds together all fumbles by this player, whether turned over to the defense or recovered by the offense (explained in the essay "Pregame Show"). Even though this fumble total is listed among the passing numbers, it includes all fumbles, including those on sacks, aborted snaps, and rushing attempts. By listing fumbles and interceptions next to one another, we're giving readers a general idea of how many total turnovers the player was responsible for.

Next comes Adjusted Sack Rate (ASR). This is the same statistic you'll find in the team chapters, only here it is specific to the individual quarterback. It represents sacks per pass play (total pass plays = pass attempts + sacks) adjusted based on down, distance, and strength of schedule. For reference, the NFL average was 7.0 percent in 2013, 6.6 percent in 2014, and 6.4 percent in 2015.

The next two columns are Net Yards per Pass (NY/P), a standard stat but a particularly good one, and the player's rank (Rk) in Net Yards per Pass for that season. Net Yards per Pass consists of passing yards minus yards lost on sacks, divided by total pass plays.

The five columns remaining in passing stats give our advanced metrics: DVOA (Defense-Adjusted Value Over Average), DYAR (Defense-Adjusted Yards Above Replacement), and YAR (Yards Above Replacement), along with the player's rank in both DVOA and DYAR. These metrics compare each quarterback's passing performance to league-average or replacement-level baselines based on the game situations that quarterback faced. DVOA and DYAR are also adjusted based on the opposing defense. The methods used to compute these numbers are described in detail in the "Statistical Toolbox" introduction at the front of the book. The important distinctions between them are:

• DVOA is a rate statistic, while DYAR is a cumulative statistic. Thus, a higher DVOA means more value per pass play, while a higher DYAR means more aggregate value over the entire season.
• Because DYAR is defense-adjusted and YAR is not, a player whose DYAR is higher than his YAR faced a harder-than-average schedule. A player whose DYAR is lower than his YAR faced an easier-than-average schedule.

To qualify for a ranking in Net Yards per Pass, passing DVOA, and passing DYAR in a given season, a quarterback must have had 200 pass plays in that season. 40 quarterbacks are ranked for 2013, 37 quarterbacks for 2014, and 37 quarterbacks for 2015.

The final five columns contain rushing statistics, starting with Runs, rushing yards (Yds), and rushing touchdowns (TD). Once again, these are official NFL totals and include

kneeldowns, which means you get to enjoy statistics such as Drew Stanton rushing 13 times for minus-13 yards. The final two columns give DYAR and DVOA for quarterback rushing, which are calculated separately from passing. Rankings for these statistics, as well as numbers that are not adjusted for defense (YAR and VOA) can be found on our website, FootballOutsiders.com.

The last number listed is the Total QBR metric from ESPN Stats & Information. Total QBR is based on the expected points added by the quarterback on each play, then adjusts the numbers to a scale of 0-100. There are five main differences between Total QBR and DVOA:

• Total QBR incorporates information from game charting, such as passes dropped or thrown away on purpose.
• Total QBR splits responsibility on plays between the quarterback, his receivers, and his blockers. Drops, for example, are more on the receiver, as are yards after the catch, and some sacks are more on the offensive line than others.
• Total QBR has a clutch factor which adds (or subtracts) value for quarterbacks who perform best (or worst) in high-leverage situations.
• Total QBR combines passing and rushing value into one number and differentiates between scrambles and planned runs.
• Total QBR is not adjusted for strength of opponent.

The italicized row of statistics for the 2016 season is our 2016 KUBIAK projection, as detailed above. Again, in the interest of producing meaningful statistics, all quarterbacks are projected to start a full 16-game season, regardless of the likelihood of them actually doing so. (This year, as an exception, there are multiple totals listed for Tom Brady and Jimmy Garoppolo.)

The final line below the KUBIAK projection represents data from the Football Outsiders game charting project for the last two seasons. First, we break down charted passes based on distance: Short (5 yards or less), Mid (6-15 yards), Deep (16-25 yards), and Bomb (26 or more yards). These numbers are based on distance in the air only and include both complete and incomplete passes. Passes thrown away or tipped at the line are not included, nor are passes on which the quarterback's arm was hit by a defender while in motion.

We also list average yards after catch (YAC) with the rank in parentheses for the 37 quarterbacks who qualify. The final number listed is ALEX, or Air Less EXpected. This represents the distance between the quarterback's intended throwing distance and the first-down marker, measured on third downs only.

One other stat you'll see referenced a few times is failed completion rate. Failed completions are passes that are complete but fall short of our baselines for success: 45 percent of needed yards on first down, 60 percent of needed yards on second down, and 100 percent of needed yards on third or fourth down. This is a good way to measure quarterbacks who pad their completion percentage with short passes that aren't necessarily helpful.

A number of third- and fourth-string quarterbacks are briefly discussed at the end of the chapter in a section we call "Going Deep."

Top 20 QB by Passing DYAR (Total Value), 2015

Rank	Player	Team	DYAR
1	Carson Palmer	ARI	1,698
2	Tom Brady	NE	1,312
3	Russell Wilson	SEA	1,190
4	Andy Dalton	CIN	1,136
5	Ben Roethlisberger	PIT	1,114
6	Drew Brees	NO	1,111
7	Kirk Cousins	WAS	1,023
8	Philip Rivers	SD	847
9	Matthew Stafford	DET	804
10	Jay Cutler	CHI	642
11	Cam Newton	CAR	630
12	Derek Carr	OAK	582
13	Ryan Fitzpatrick	NYJ	542
14	Tyrod Taylor	BUF	536
15	Alex Smith	KC	468
16	Jameis Winston	TB	467
17	Aaron Rodgers	GB	406
18	Eli Manning	NYG	404
19	Matt Ryan	ATL	389
20	Brian Hoyer	HOU	201

Minimum 200 passes.

Top 20 QB by Passing DVOA (Value per Pass), 2015

Rank	Player	Team	DVOA
1	Carson Palmer	ARI	34.4%
2	Andy Dalton	CIN	31.7%
3	Russell Wilson	SEA	24.3%
4	Ben Roethlisberger	PIT	22.1%
5	Tom Brady	NE	19.5%
6	Kirk Cousins	WAS	16.9%
7	Drew Brees	NO	15.8%
8	Tyrod Taylor	BUF	9.8%
9	Jay Cutler	CHI	8.6%
10	Matthew Stafford	DET	8.0%
11	Philip Rivers	SD	7.8%
12	Cam Newton	CAR	7.6%
13	Derek Carr	OAK	4.1%
14	Ryan Fitzpatrick	NYJ	3.5%
15	Alex Smith	KC	3.0%
16	Jameis Winston	TB	2.1%
17	Aaron Rodgers	GB	-1.0%
18	Matt Ryan	ATL	-1.9%
19	Eli Manning	NYG	-1.9%
20	Brian Hoyer	HOU	-3.0%

Minimum 200 passes.

Derek Anderson

Height: 6-6 Weight: 229 College: Oregon State Draft: 2005/6 (213) Born: 15-Jun-1983 Age: 33 Risk: Red

Year	Team	G/GS	Snaps	Att	Comp	C%	Yds	TD	INT/Adj	FUM	ASR	NY/P	Rk	DVOA	Rk	DYAR	Rk	YAR	Runs	Yds	TD	DVOA	DYAR	QBR
2013	CAR	4/0	15	0	0	0.0%	0	0	0/0	0	0.0%	0.0	--	0.0%	--	0	--	0	5	0	0	27.7%	3	4.3
2014	CAR	6/2	177	97	65	67.0%	701	5	0/2	2	5.2%	6.7	--	27.8%	--	254	--	282	8	24	0	34.3%	14	82.8
2015	CAR	3/0	25	6	4	66.7%	36	0	0/0	1	1.8%	6.0	--	-11.9%	--	0	--	1	7	-2	0	-137.8%	-19	9.7
2016	CAR			481	286	59.5%	3514	21	15	8		6.4		-2.4%					23	70	1	2.4%		

2014: 40% Short 39% Mid 15% Deep 7% Bomb YAC: 2.8 (–) ALEX: 2.0 2015: 50% Short 0% Mid 33% Deep 17% Bomb YAC: 5.3 (–) ALEX: 0.7

Derek Anderson spent the previous three seasons becoming the master of small-sample size deep-ball success, but in 2015, he only found six total pass attempts playing behind an MVP. He's a good fit for the offense Carolina runs, and got a two-year extension out of it this offseason.

Blake Bortles

Height: 6-4 Weight: 232 College: Central Florida Draft: 2014/1 (3) Born: 28-Apr-1992 Age: 24 Risk: Yellow

Year	Team	G/GS	Snaps	Att	Comp	C%	Yds	TD	INT/Adj	FUM	ASR	NY/P	Rk	DVOA	Rk	DYAR	Rk	YAR	Runs	Yds	TD	DVOA	DYAR	QBR
2014	JAC	14/13	896	475	280	58.9%	2908	11	17/20	7	10.5%	4.8	37	-40.7%	36	-955	37	-935	56	419	0	24.7%	100	21.9
2015	JAC	16/16	1058	606	355	58.6%	4428	35	18/26	14	8.0%	6.3	18	-9.9%	25	54	25	100	52	310	2	24.5%	86	46.4
2016	JAC			587	358	60.9%	4215	29	17	12		5.9		-12.6%					60	302	3	14.7%		

2014: 57% Short 30% Mid 7% Deep 5% Bomb YAC: 5.8 (7) ALEX: -0.8 2015: 45% Short 29% Mid 19% Deep 7% Bomb YAC: 5.2 (21) ALEX: 2.6

At this point of his career, Bortles is an unrefined physical talent who needs to develop consistency and discipline. Bortles threw an impressive 35 touchdown passes, heavily relying on Allen Robinson and Allen Hurns, but he also led the league in interceptions with 18 and sacks with 51. Furthermore, Bortles' accuracy remained a major concern in his second season, as he once again couldn't cross 59 percent. Bortles needs to do one of two things to further his development in 2016: make better decisions to avoid so many interceptions, or show off tighter mechanics so that his short and intermediate accuracy can be as consistent as it needs to be. Look for his touchdown total to drop because the presence of Chris Ivory will change the way the Jags call plays in the red zone.

Trevone Boykin   Height: 6-0   Weight: 213   College: TCU   Draft: 2016/FA   Born: 22-Aug-1993   Age: 23   Risk: Yellow

Year	Team	G/GS	Snaps	Att	Comp	C%	Yds	TD	INT/Adj	FUM	ASR	NY/P	Rk	DVOA	Rk	DYAR	Rk	YAR	Runs	Yds	TD	DVOA	DYAR	QBR
2016	SEA		477	297	62.3%	3448	22	18		13		6.0		-16.6%					100	573	6	26.7%		

For a team with Super Bowl aspirations, it is best to have a veteran backup quarterback capable of keeping the ship afloat for a short stretch. Yet Seattle may be going with an undrafted rookie to back up Russell Wilson. The good news is that Boykin has a very similar skill set, so the offense would not have to change much to start him. A likely reason for Boykin going undrafted was the incident where he punched a patrol officer just days before the Alamo Bowl. Boykin improved as a passer each year at TCU and should have enough athleticism to run out of trouble at the pro level. If everything goes according to plan, Boykin won't have to play in the regular season and could make the second half of Seattle's preseason games less of a hate-watching chore. But it doesn't always go according to plan, does it?

Sam Bradford   Height: 6-4   Weight: 236   College: Oklahoma   Draft: 2010/1 (1)   Born: 8-Nov-1987   Age: 29   Risk: Yellow

Year	Team	G/GS	Snaps	Att	Comp	C%	Yds	TD	INT/Adj	FUM	ASR	NY/P	Rk	DVOA	Rk	DYAR	Rk	YAR	Runs	Yds	TD	DVOA	DYAR	QBR
2013	STL	7/7	450	262	159	60.7%	1687	14	4/5	3	6.0%	5.8	28	5.2%	14	304	19	387	15	31	0	-70.1%	-25	48.0
2015	PHI	14/14	987	532	346	65.0%	3725	19	14/15	9	6.2%	6.3	16	-8.2%	24	107	24	221	26	39	0	-76.7%	-43	41.8
2016	PHI		574	371	64.7%	3897	25	14		6		5.9		-1.3%					24	53	1	-4.2%		
													2015: 56%		Short 28%		Mid 12%		Deep 4%		Bomb		YAC: 5.6 (12)	

Long, long ago in a galaxy far, far away, Bradford was once an anointed franchise savior. Now, the former first overall pick is the one keeping the seat warm for the next big thing. Though Bradford made a bit of a fuss after Carson Wentz's selection, the reality is that he never showed enough during his first season in Philly to stop the Eagles' front office from scratching their itch for a quarterback. Bradford flashed periodically throughout the season, typically for 30 minutes at a time, but would also go long stretches completing nothing but screens, drags, and button hooks. Mustering up the willingness to stretch defenses has always been a struggle for Bradford, who might be hopelessly indoctrinated in the School of Shallow Crossers at this point. Last year, his persistent tendency to throw short of the sticks led Bradford to finish 31st in failed completion percentage and 34th in ALEX among a group of 37 qualified quarterbacks. That trend seems unlikely to change with Doug Pederson importing his West Coast offense from Kansas City, where he coached the grand poobah of checkdowns in Alex Smith. Bradford could really use some stability at this point in his career, as Pederson's offense will be the fifth he has learned in seven NFL seasons. Of course, with Wentz warming up in the bullpen, 2016 is far likelier to bring about more change and transition for the quarterback who keeps landing dates but can't find anyone to give him a ring (or a long-term contract).

Tom Brady   Height: 6-4   Weight: 225   College: Michigan   Draft: 2000/6 (199)   Born: 3-Aug-1977   Age: 39   Risk: Yellow

Year	Team	G/GS	Snaps	Att	Comp	C%	Yds	TD	INT/Adj	FUM	ASR	NY/P	Rk	DVOA	Rk	DYAR	Rk	YAR	Runs	Yds	TD	DVOA	DYAR	QBR
2013	NE	16/16	1197	628	380	60.5%	4343	25	11/8	9	6.1%	6.2	18	10.9%	11	979	6	859	32	18	0	-19.4%	-5	61.1
2014	NE	16/16	1062	582	373	64.1%	4109	33	9/11	6	3.9%	6.6	16	18.1%	5	1176	6	1096	36	57	0	-25.1%	-19	74.3
2015	NE	16/16	1105	624	402	64.4%	4770	36	7/9	6	6.5%	6.9	7	19.5%	5	1312	2	1269	34	53	3	6.5%	25	64.4
2016	NE (16 G)		626	414	66.1%	4754	35	11		6		6.8		13.3%					39	54	1	-6.5%		
2016	NE (12 G)		469	310	66.1%	3566	26	9		4		6.8		13.3%					30	40	1	-6.5%		
2014:	51% Short	32% Mid	11% Deep	5% Bomb	YAC: 5.0 (28)	ALEX: 1.8	2015:	50% Short	33% Mid	11% Deep	7% Bomb	YAC: 6.0 (6)	ALEX: 1.1											

The amount of pass pressure Brady faces has been creeping up every year since 2012. Brady was pressured on just 15.5 percent of pass plays that year (105 pass plays). The percentage increased to 20.3 percent (138 pass plays) the next year, 22.5 percent (140 pass plays) in 2014, and 25.7 percent (174 pass plays) last year. There are complex factors at work: shuffling and injuries on the offensive line; injuries at the skill positions (fewer dangerous receivers = more blitz opportunities and coverage-based pressure); a running game that can be safely ignored when it's not functioning well; and a general "Get Brady" philosophy among the other AFC contenders. Brady remains one of the NFL's best quarterbacks when pressured, but no quarterback is as good under pressure as he is with a clean pocket, and it's a bad idea to let Brady face more pressure as he ages, for obvious reasons. It's just another reminder to Patriots fans that not everything the team does is part of Belichick's grand and infallible design, and that while Brady remains outstanding, he won't be able to play until he's 55, or whatever age that caller on WEEI just suggested.

Drew Brees — Height: 6-0 — Weight: 209 — College: Purdue — Draft: 2001/2 (32) — Born: 15-Jan-1979 — Age: 37 — Risk: Yellow

Year	Team	G/GS	Snaps	Att	Comp	C%	Yds	TD	INT/Adj	FUM	ASR	NY/P	Rk	DVOA	Rk	DYAR	Rk	YAR	Runs	Yds	TD	DVOA	DYAR	QBR
2013	NO	16/16	1110	650	446	68.6%	5162	39	12/14	5	5.3%	7.2	6	26.9%	5	1701	3	1550	35	52	3	33.6%	36	70.5
2014	NO	16/16	1140	659	456	69.2%	4952	33	17/19	7	5.2%	7.0	8	15.7%	6	1225	4	1224	27	68	1	17.7%	27	71.6
2015	NO	15/15	1089	627	428	68.3%	4870	32	11/13	5	5.3%	7.0	5	15.8%	7	1111	6	1184	24	14	1	32.1%	21	75.5
2016	NO			642	430	67.1%	4974	32	11	5		6.8		12.6%					19	56	0	8.3%		

| 2014: | 56% Short | 27% Mid | 11% Deep | 7% Bomb | YAC: 4.8 (33) | ALEX: 3.1 | 2015: | 54% Short | 26% Mid | 13% Deep | 7% Bomb | YAC: 5.6 (15) | ALEX: 1.1 |

Analyzing last season for Brees is something that's hard to do from the outside, without greater knowledge of his injuries. From the injury report, we've got a torn plantar fascia in Weeks 16 and 17, and a shoulder sprain suffered in Week 2 that was listed until Week 4. In Weeks 2-5, Brees had a -11.4% DVOA. To put that in context, Brandon Weeden had a -10.7% DVOA in those weeks. But in Weeks 11-17, Brees ranked fourth in the league in passing DYAR. Brees no longer has the deep-ball touch he had in his prime, but compensates with anticipation throws well enough to keep his DVOA from plummeting. He's still a good enough quarterback to win with. If only there was a team around him that could help...

Teddy Bridgewater — Height: 6-2 — Weight: 214 — College: Louisville — Draft: 2014/1 (32) — Born: 10-Nov-1992 — Age: 24 — Risk: Green

Year	Team	G/GS	Snaps	Att	Comp	C%	Yds	TD	INT/Adj	FUM	ASR	NY/P	Rk	DVOA	Rk	DYAR	Rk	YAR	Runs	Yds	TD	DVOA	DYAR	QBR
2014	MIN	13/12	794	402	259	64.4%	2919	14	12/11	3	9.1%	6.1	23	-16.9%	34	-159	34	-82	47	209	1	-8.5%	8	50.2
2015	MIN	16/16	994	447	292	65.3%	3231	14	9/11	8	8.8%	6.0	29	-5.1%	22	187	21	93	44	192	3	5.3%	32	62.7
2016	MIN			494	325	65.8%	3592	20	11	5		6.2		-2.6%					47	195	2	18.3%		

| 2014: | 61% Short | 23% Mid | 9% Deep | 7% Bomb | YAC: 5.6 (12) | ALEX: -0.8 | 2015: | 56% Short | 25% Mid | 14% Deep | 6% Bomb | YAC: 6.2 (2) | ALEX: -0.7 |

As mentioned in the Vikings' chapter, Bridgewater got little help from an injury-ravaged offensive line—his pressure rate of 36.0 percent wasn't just the highest in the league last year, it was among the highest of the last six years. Does Bridgewater himself bear any blame for that though? In his rookie season, his pressure rate of 28.3 percent was still in the top 10. The Vikings' line had its share of injuries that season as well, with starters missing 14 games between them, but better pocket presence would go a long way in keeping Bridgewater productive and healthy.

Vikings general manager Rick Spielman has said that Minnesota's new domed stadium will be beneficial to Bridgewater, citing the quarterback's success indoors. It's a small sample size, but in his five indoor games, Bridgewater has completed 70.6 percent of his passes for 8.1 yards per attempt, with a much lower sack rate (7.5 percent) than in outdoor games (9.2 percent). Weirdly, he has fumbled more indoors (three in five games, compared to eight in 24 outdoor games), but that likely just shows how random fumble stats can be.

Jacoby Brissett — Height: 6-4 — Weight: 231 — College: North Carolina State — Draft: 2016/3 (91) — Born: 11-Dec-1992 — Age: 24 — Risk: Yellow

Year	Team	G/GS	Snaps	Att	Comp	C%	Yds	TD	INT/Adj	FUM	ASR	NY/P	Rk	DVOA	Rk	DYAR	Rk	YAR	Runs	Yds	TD	DVOA	DYAR	QBR
2016	NE			576	328	56.9%	3960	27	18	10		6.1		-9.1%					77	163	3	-1.4%		

Brissett is not a serious threat to Jimmy Garoppolo for Deflategate starts. The Patriots just don't like their quarterback prospects to rot in the back of the fridge, and by adding to the developmental pipeline every few years they make sure they won't be in a Brock Osweiler situation when Tom Brady's time comes. Frankly, Brissett looks more like a Gary Kubiak quarterback than a Bill Belichick/Josh McDaniels quarterback. He's big, strong-armed, and steady, but with a plodding delivery that can disrupt the timing of quick-trigger plays. Brissett only completed 60 percent of his passes last season, a big reason why he has a lousy QBASE projection of minus-381 (coincidentally, the same projection as a past Patriots third-round pick, Kevin O'Connell).

Derek Carr — Height: 6-3 — Weight: 220 — College: Fresno State — Draft: 2014/2 (36) — Born: 3/28/1991 — Age: 25 — Risk: Green

Year	Team	G/GS	Snaps	Att	Comp	C%	Yds	TD	INT/Adj	FUM	ASR	NY/P	Rk	DVOA	Rk	DYAR	Rk	YAR	Runs	Yds	TD	DVOA	DYAR	QBR
2014	OAK	16/16	986	599	348	58.1%	3270	21	12/16	10	4.0%	5.0	36	-14.9%	33	-150	33	-355	29	92	0	28.4%	40	38.4
2015	OAK	16/16	1014	573	350	61.1%	3987	32	13/15	10	4.6%	6.2	22	4.1%	13	582	12	428	33	138	0	-25.3%	-13	49.2
2016	OAK			619	390	63.0%	4283	28	14	11		6.1		-1.9%					44	143	1	-2.7%		

| 2014: | 54% Short | 29% Mid | 10% Deep | 7% Bomb | YAC: 4.2 (35) | ALEX: 1.2 | 2015: | 48% Short | 32% Mid | 12% Deep | 7% Bomb | YAC: 5.1 (23) | ALEX: 0.7 |

It's interesting to look back at the zeitgeist on Carr as of last season, which really showed a split between the numbers and the scouts. Numbers guys saw the high red zone touchdown rate and called fluke, then looked at the low yards per attempt numbers and cried "weak arm!" Carr's arm was never the problem, though. In fact, it was likely the strong arm that gave him the high red zone DVOA in the first place. (Carr's red zone DVOA regressed from 57.1% in 2014 to a still-strong 23.7% in 2015.) For all the hype about Oakland's improved receiving corps, Amari Cooper dropped a lot of passes and Michael Crabtree has no second gear. If Cooper breaks out, or if the Raiders can find a third receiver worth throwing to, there's no reason why Carr can't continue to climb. It's not like the offensive line is going to let him down, right?

Matt Cassel

Height: 6-5 Weight: 230 College: USC Draft: 2005/7 (230) Born: 17-May-1982 Age: 34 Risk: Yellow

Year	Team	G/GS	Snaps	Att	Comp	C%	Yds	TD	INT/Adj	FUM	ASR	NY/P	Rk	DVOA	Rk	DYAR	Rk	YAR	Runs	Yds	TD	DVOA	DYAR	QBR
2013	MIN	9/6	459	254	153	60.2%	1807	11	9/10	3	6.1%	6.4	16	-5.9%	23	92	23	-7	18	57	1	5.2%	10	48.7
2014	MIN	3/3	140	71	41	57.7%	425	3	4/3	3	7.7%	4.9	--	-40.4%	--	-147	--	-150	9	18	0	-10.5%	0	28.9
2015	2TM	9/8	415	204	119	58.3%	1276	5	7/7	4	6.6%	5.5	35	-23.7%	35	-172	34	-210	15	78	0	-29.3%	-10	33.7
2016	TEN			509	289	56.7%	3077	16	14	9		5.0		-24.3%					37	126	1	0.6%		

2014:	61% Short	25% Mid	9% Deep	5% Bomb	YAC: 7.2 (–)	ALEX: -1.9	2015:	48% Short	31% Mid	13% Deep	8% Bomb	YAC: 4.8 (30)	ALEX: 0.2

Cassel was supposed to be the steady veteran stopgap who could staunch the Cowboys' bleeding until Tony Romo returned. Alas, Cassel struggled after arriving via an October trade from Buffalo, demonstrating an unwillingness to push the ball downfield while also making dangerous throws into traffic all too frequently. As a result, he ended up being a bottom-four quarterback by DVOA, DYAR, and QBR. Granted, his first four starts came with Dez Bryant out of the lineup, leaving him with a motley crew of targets who had trouble separating. Nevertheless, Cassel's reputation as a reliable backup essentially rests on a single 382-yard day against Philadelphia from three years ago. At least in Tennessee, he likely won't have the burden of trying to keep a team in playoff contention if pressed into action.

Jimmy Clausen

Height: 6-3 Weight: 222 College: Notre Dame Draft: 2010/2 (48) Born: 21-Sep-1987 Age: 29 Risk: N/A

Year	Team	G/GS	Snaps	Att	Comp	C%	Yds	TD	INT/Adj	FUM	ASR	NY/P	Rk	DVOA	Rk	DYAR	Rk	YAR	Runs	Yds	TD	DVOA	DYAR	QBR
2014	CHI	4/1	89	48	26	54.2%	223	2	1/1	0	5.7%	4.0	--	-12.7%	--	-5	--	-37	3	9	0	15.2%	5	40.6
2015	2TM	4/3	217	125	72	57.6%	739	2	4/4	1	4.7%	5.3	--	-10.3%	--	6	--	-148	11	36	0	-50.8%	-17	28.6

2014:	57% Short	27% Mid	6% Deep	10% Bomb	YAC: 4.7 (–)	ALEX: 0.2	2015:	49% Short	26% Mid	17% Deep	9% Bomb	YAC: 4.1 (–)	ALEX: -2.3

How bad has he been? In this pass-happy era of the NFL, it took Clausen 21 appearances (13 starts) to have a 200-yard passing game. He actually did it against Seattle, a defense he got two cracks at last year—he was shut out 26-0 against the Seahawks while with the Bears, then threw for 274 yards in a 35-6 Baltimore loss. Clausen also threw for 281 yards against Kansas City, albeit with a Hail Mary included. He rightfully remains a free agent into July.

Kellen Clemens

Height: 6-2 Weight: 224 College: Oregon Draft: 2006/2 (49) Born: 6-Jun-1983 Age: 33 Risk: Red

Year	Team	G/GS	Snaps	Att	Comp	C%	Yds	TD	INT/Adj	FUM	ASR	NY/P	Rk	DVOA	Rk	DYAR	Rk	YAR	Runs	Yds	TD	DVOA	DYAR	QBR
2013	STL	10/9	554	242	142	58.7%	1673	8	7/9	7	7.7%	5.8	24	-7.5%	24	60	25	-133	23	64	0	-52.9%	-35	38.2
2014	SD	2/0	15	3	1	33.3%	10	0	0/0	0	23.6%	0.3	--	-92.7%	--	-20	--	-20	0	0	0	--	--	1.3
2015	SD	2/0	15	6	5	83.3%	63	1	0/0	0	-0.9%	10.5	--	157.4%	--	67	--	62	1	-1	0	--	--	99.9
2016	SD			591	372	62.9%	3937	19	18	11		5.6		-13.1%					41	85	1	-8.3%		

2014:	50% Short	50% Mid	0% Deep	0% Bomb	YAC: 2.0 (–)	ALEX: 2.0	2015:	17% Short	50% Mid	33% Deep	0% Bomb	YAC: 0.8 (–)	ALEX: 4.0

Clemens is one of those quarterbacks who has solidified his status as a trusted backup. The only way he loses his job is if he is forced to play for an extended period.

Kirk Cousins

| | | Height: 6-3 | | Weight: 214 | | College: Michigan State | | Draft: 2012/4 (102) | | Born: 19-Aug-1988 | | Age: 28 | | | Risk: Green |

Year	Team	G/GS	Snaps	Att	Comp	C%	Yds	TD	INT/Adj	FUM	ASR	NY/P	Rk	DVOA	Rk	DYAR	Rk	YAR	Runs	Yds	TD	DVOA	DYAR	QBR
2013	WAS	5/3	238	155	81	52.3%	854	4	7/7	3	4.1%	5.1	--	-42.6%	--	-314	--	-300	4	14	0	-6.6%	1	26.5
2014	WAS	6/5	357	204	126	61.8%	1710	10	9/9	2	3.8%	7.7	1	4.6%	14	223	22	213	7	20	0	9.0%	7	46.9
2015	WAS	16/16	1026	543	379	69.8%	4166	29	11/13	8	5.4%	7.0	6	16.9%	6	1023	7	1125	26	48	5	-3.1%	8	70.1
2016	WAS			560	356	63.5%	4226	26	18	7		6.7		3.3%					29	61	2	-0.2%		

| 2014: | 51% Short | 30% Mid | 12% Deep | 8% Bomb | YAC: 7.1 (2) | ALEX: 0.6 | 2015: | 58% Short | 23% Mid | 13% Deep | 6% Bomb | YAC: 5.0 (28) | ALEX: 0.9 |

It's no surprise that a quarterback from the class of 2012 is Washington's best hope for a long-awaited period of contention and stability. That it's Kirk Cousins instead of Robert Griffin III would have seemed unfathomable as recently as September, given Cousins' prior failures to exhibit starter potential during RG3's downfall. Beginning with the "YOU LIKE THAT?!" comeback win over Tampa Bay in Week 7, Cousins stunningly turned into a top-five quarterback the rest of the way. Only Carson Palmer, Russell Wilson, and Drew Brees accrued more DYAR in that span, and only Palmer and Wilson posted better passing DVOA figures. Most crucially, Cousins tossed only three interceptions the rest of the way, overcoming his historically woeful tendency to turn the ball over. Now, the question is whether Cousins can deliver an encore worthy of the rare optimism surrounding D.C. this summer. After protecting Cousins with lots of movement and quick reads in 2015, Jay Gruden seems likely to open up the offense to discover how far the fifth-year pro can really stretch himself. The tell-tale sign will be on third downs, where Cousins posted an overachieving 26.7% DVOA despite frequently throwing short of the sticks with a fairly conservative ALEX (23rd out of 37 qualifying quarterbacks). With the trio of DeSean Jackson, Jordan Reed, and rookie first-rounder Josh Doctson, Cousins certainly has an enviable array of field-stretchers at his disposal. Still, we've seen how high the ceiling rises and how low the floor sinks. KUBIAK lists his Risk as "Green" because a lot of regression is already built into the forecast—and because his performance in five 2014 starts was a lot better than most people realize.

Jay Cutler

| | | Height: 6-3 | | Weight: 220 | | College: Vanderbilt | | Draft: 2006/1 (11) | | Born: 29-Apr-1983 | | Age: 33 | | | Risk: Yellow |

Year	Team	G/GS	Snaps	Att	Comp	C%	Yds	TD	INT/Adj	FUM	ASR	NY/P	Rk	DVOA	Rk	DYAR	Rk	YAR	Runs	Yds	TD	DVOA	DYAR	QBR
2013	CHI	11/11	636	355	224	63.1%	2621	19	12/13	4	6.0%	6.7	10	5.5%	13	392	18	423	23	118	0	58.4%	48	66.4
2014	CHI	15/15	969	561	370	66.0%	3812	28	18/22	12	6.3%	6.0	26	-0.7%	21	398	16	351	39	191	2	38.3%	65	54.0
2015	CHI	15/15	992	483	311	64.4%	3659	21	11/14	8	5.2%	6.9	8	8.6%	9	659	10	556	38	201	1	43.7%	84	60.7
2016	CHI			547	346	63.2%	4080	28	13	10		6.5		4.1%					42	183	1	11.1%		

| 2014: | 60% Short | 26% Mid | 8% Deep | 7% Bomb | YAC: 5.5 (16) | ALEX: 0.1 | 2015: | 50% Short | 30% Mid | 11% Deep | 9% Bomb | YAC: 5.6 (13) | ALEX: 3.1 |

By both DYAR and DVOA, Cutler had his best season since 2008, his last year in Denver. And when you consider that he put those numbers together with Marquess Wilson and Marc Mariani as his leading wide receivers in snaps played, it was almost certainly the best campaign of his career. The key to Cutler's success was a remarkably good performance under pressure, where his DVOA was an NFL-best -4.3%. The second-best quarterback under pressure, Carson Palmer, was closer to sixth place than he was to Cutler. Cutler averaged 6.3 yards per play under pressure, which is more than one part-time starter (Ryan Mallett) averaged from a clean pocket. This has long been a strength of Cutler's—he was second in that category in 2013, and has been better than average in each of the past six seasons. Assuming the Bears have more health at receiver this year—and it can't get much worse—Cutler should have better fantasy stats in 2016.

Andy Dalton

| | | Height: 6-2 | | Weight: 215 | | College: TCU | | Draft: 2011/2 (35) | | Born: 29-Oct-1987 | | Age: 29 | | | Risk: Green |

Year	Team	G/GS	Snaps	Att	Comp	C%	Yds	TD	INT/Adj	FUM	ASR	NY/P	Rk	DVOA	Rk	DYAR	Rk	YAR	Runs	Yds	TD	DVOA	DYAR	QBR
2013	CIN	16/16	1117	586	363	61.9%	4293	33	20/21	4	5.2%	6.7	11	2.3%	18	541	16	612	61	183	2	13.0%	52	55.8
2014	CIN	16/16	1031	481	309	64.2%	3398	19	17/21	3	4.3%	6.5	19	-3.7%	24	237	21	238	60	169	4	-2.9%	26	55.2
2015	CIN	13/13	798	386	255	66.1%	3250	25	7/9	5	5.1%	7.7	3	31.7%	2	1135	4	1059	57	142	3	-8.1%	9	73.1
2016	CIN			511	333	65.2%	3908	30	14	5		7.0		10.0%					54	181	2	7.0%		

| 2014: | 54% Short | 29% Mid | 11% Deep | 6% Bomb | YAC: 5.6 (10) | ALEX: -0.4 | 2015: | 49% Short | 28% Mid | 14% Deep | 9% Bomb | YAC: 5.9 (8) | ALEX: 1.9 |

Dalton hadn't missed a single start in his career (81 straight, including playoffs) until he went down with the broken thumb that cost him the team's final five games (including the wild-card game). The heartbreak was worsened by the fact that no quarterback was pressured less in 2015. When he did come under duress, the Red Rifle was significantly better than he had been in recent years. His -51.4% DVOA when pressured ranked 12th among qualifying passers, putting to bed a previously held truism that Ginger would fold when his pocket collapsed. Naturally, his injury came not as a result of a sack but a tackle on an unhurried interception. Irony can be pretty ironic sometimes.

After what was easily Dalton's best season as a pro, KUBIAK projects some fall off. Part of that is natural regression, and part is the fact that he won't have the same panoply of weapons available to him in 2016, including offensive coordinator Hue Jackson. If Dalton can hold his numbers and/or efficiency despite the losses, it will be an indicator that he has taken an important step forward as a quarterback.

Chase Daniel

Height: 6-0   Weight: 225   College: Missouri   Draft: 2009/FA   Born: 7-Oct-1986   Age: 30   Risk: Red

Year	Team	G/GS	Snaps	Att	Comp	C%	Yds	TD	INT/Adj	FUM	ASR	NY/P	Rk	DVOA	Rk	DYAR	Rk	YAR	Runs	Yds	TD	DVOA	DYAR	QBR
2013	KC	5/1	100	38	25	65.8%	248	1	1/1	0	4.7%	5.9	–	-13.6%	–	-6	–	22	14	52	0	47.0%	18	78.7
2014	KC	3/1	67	28	16	57.1%	157	0	0/0	0	13.2%	4.4	–	-24.4%	–	-28	–	-18	4	15	0	84.8%	9	46.4
2015	KC	2/0	13	2	2	100.0%	4	0	0/0	0	-1.7%	2.0	–	-32.7%	–	-3	–	-1	2	-2	0	–	–	98.5
2016	PHI			561	348	62.1%	3978	25	16	11		5.8		-10.5%					35	109	1	-2.0%		
2014:	63% Short		25% Mid		6% Deep		6% Bomb		YAC: 4.1 (–)		ALEX: 1.5		2015:	100% Short		0% Mid		0% Deep		0% Bomb		YAC: 2.0 (–)		ALEX: -1.0

Daniel has now been in the NFL for six seasons and he has only five more completions in his career (50) than Drew Bledsoe did in a single game in 1994. Despite an almost entirely empty resume save for some stellar preseason work, Daniel still cashed in to the tune of $21 million for three years; he is likely to see at least two-thirds of both. Before the Eagles drafted Carson Wentz, Daniel also had a more plausible path to starting and adding $15 million in incentive pay to his haul. That scenario might still be feasible. If the Eagles find a taker for Sam Bradford—admittedly a fairly sizable if—Daniel could either start until Wentz is ready or take over for him should he struggle early.

Austin Davis

Height: 6-2   Weight: 221   College: Southern Mississippi   Draft: 2012/FA   Born: 2-Jun-1989   Age: 27   Risk: Red

Year	Team	G/GS	Snaps	Att	Comp	C%	Yds	TD	INT/Adj	FUM	ASR	NY/P	Rk	DVOA	Rk	DYAR	Rk	YAR	Runs	Yds	TD	DVOA	DYAR	QBR
2014	STL	10/8	548	284	180	63.4%	2001	12	9/12	5	9.5%	5.9	32	-8.8%	29	47	29	-2	16	36	0	4.6%	5	37.6
2015	CLE	3/2	159	94	56	59.6%	547	1	3/5	2	11.5%	4.0	–	-52.9%	–	-269	–	-287	7	33	0	-24.5%	-5	22.1
2016	CLE			530	305	57.5%	3477	15	16	12		5.2		-26.6%					42	126	1	-9.4%		
2014:	59% Short		22% Mid		9% Deep		10% Bomb		YAC: 5.0 (26)		ALEX: 2.1		2015:	47% Short		39% Mid		8% Deep		6% Bomb		YAC: 3.8 (–)		ALEX: 0.9

All the way back in 2014, Davis came off the bench and led the Rams to an upset of Seattle. Brett Favre, a fellow Southern Miss alum, likened Davis to other quarterbacks whose careers were rocky at first, actually invoking the names Brady and Warner to describe Davis. Yeah, no. While it's certainly unfair to judge Davis on his 105 attempts with the hapless Browns a year ago, imagining him as even an average starter (much less an all-time great) is *Game of Thrones*-level fantasy. We suppose that makes the Gunslinger a good ol' boy George R.R. Martin.

Ryan Fitzpatrick

Height: 6-2   Weight: 221   College: Harvard   Draft: 2005/7 (250)   Born: 24-Nov-1982   Age: 34   Risk: Green

Year	Team	G/GS	Snaps	Att	Comp	C%	Yds	TD	INT/Adj	FUM	ASR	NY/P	Rk	DVOA	Rk	DYAR	Rk	YAR	Runs	Yds	TD	DVOA	DYAR	QBR
2013	TEN	11/9	680	350	217	62.0%	2454	14	12/13	9	5.8%	6.4	14	-3.6%	20	179	21	112	43	225	3	34.8%	85	55.4
2014	HOU	12/12	727	312	197	63.1%	2483	17	8/13	5	5.8%	7.2	6	6.7%	12	383	17	485	50	184	2	2.8%	32	55.3
2015	NYJ	16/16	1046	562	335	59.6%	3905	31	15/23	5	3.9%	6.6	14	3.5%	14	542	13	670	60	270	2	18.0%	73	63.6
2016	NYJ			575	351	61.1%	4023	28	17	7		6.3		-2.4%					60	248	2	5.0%		
2014:	51% Short		31% Mid		14% Deep		5% Bomb		YAC: 5.5 (17)		ALEX: -0.1		2015:	42% Short		33% Mid		17% Deep		9% Bomb		YAC: 5.4 (19)		ALEX: 3.1

Fitzpatrick's magical season was the result of:
- A soft schedule. Fitzpatrick faced pass defenses that ranked 24th (Titans), 27th (Browns), 28th (Giants), 29th (Dolphins twice), and 31st (Jaguars) in DVOA. The only top-ten pass defense the Jets faced was the Texans. Fitzpatrick threw 16 touchdown passes and three interceptions against defenses ranked in the bottom quarter of the league.
- Great receivers. Watch the highlight film of any big Fitzpatrick pass play and you are likely to see Brandon Marshall leaping, diving, dragging a defender across the goal line, coming back for the ball, scooping it off the ground, or performing some other heroic feat to catch a pass 95 percent of NFL receivers would fail to make a play on. If Marshall is not involved, Eric Decker is probably exploiting a No. 2 cornerback.
- Smart game plans. Chan Gailey knew the strengths of the Jets offense were Marshall, Decker, and pass protection led by D'Brickashaw Ferguson and Nick Mangold. Not one to overcomplicate a simple situation, Gailey built the offense around spread-

ing the field and force-feeding Marshall and Decker 305 pass attempts. Fitzpatrick targeted Marshall and Decker 107 times between the opposing 40 and the end zone last year with passes that averaged 10.8 yards in air length. If the Jets were anywhere near the end zone, Gailey ordered Fitzpatrick to heave the ball in the general vicinity of his best receivers. Do you have a better idea?

• Fitzpatrick's own ability. It got cool among analytic circles to overcorrect for Fitzpatrick's big numbers last year (and for those annoying Harvard Hipster Hero press clippings) and claim that he was incapable of chewing gum on an escalator without falling to his death. Fitzpatrick has been among the league's best caretaker backup/spot starters for years. He has started at least eight games per season since 2008 and threw 121 touchdown passes before last season. The narrative-to-quality ratio has always been sky-high, but Fitzpatrick has been somewhere between the 25th and 35th best quarterback in the NFL for almost a decade, and still is.

Joe Flacco

Height: 6-6 Weight: 236 College: Delaware Draft: 2008/1 (18) Born: 16-Jan-1985 Age: 31 Risk: Red

Year	Team	G/GS	Snaps	Att	Comp	C%	Yds	TD	INT/Adj	FUM	ASR	NY/P	Rk	DVOA	Rk	DYAR	Rk	YAR	Runs	Yds	TD	DVOA	DYAR	QBR
2013	BAL	16/16	1129	614	362	59.0%	3912	19	22/29	8	7.4%	5.4	37	-18.1%	33	-296	36	-242	27	131	1	37.4%	53	46.7
2014	BAL	16/16	1070	554	344	62.1%	3986	27	12/16	5	4.5%	6.7	13	15.5%	7	987	8	962	39	70	2	-12.9%	-1	67.3
2015	BAL	10/10	717	413	266	64.4%	2791	14	12/14	5	4.2%	6.3	21	-10.5%	26	17	27	55	13	23	3	6.8%	15	40.9
2016	BAL			600	374	62.2%	4139	28	12	6		6.2		5.7%					28	54	1	-0.3%		

2014:	45% Short	38% Mid	8% Deep	8% Bomb	YAC: 5.1 (24)	ALEX: 2.2	2015:	59% Short	23% Mid	12% Deep	7% Bomb	YAC: 5.6 (14)	ALEX: 1.9

The Baltimore chapter details why Flacco needs to play much better this season, but one thing we've never had to talk about with Flacco is his durability. He never missed a start until last season, and he only appeared on the NFL's injury report six times between 2008 and 2014—the last appearance for a little cold that cost him a practice in 2014. Now that he tore his left ACL and MCL, it is worth thinking about going into the season.

Daunte Culpepper really never recovered from his major knee injury in 2005. Recovery science is better now, but conventional wisdom still says that it's not until that second season after the torn knee ligament that the player gets back to normal. Donovan McNabb was better in 2008 than he was in 2007. Tom Brady was better in 2010 than he was in 2009. Sam Bradford had the misfortune of tearing his ACL again in the 2014 preseason after ending his 2013 with a torn ACL. Carson Palmer has kind of refuted this, because his 2006 and 2015 seasons are the best of his career outside of the great 2005 season he had before he first tore his ACL in the playoffs. Flacco's a pocket passer, so there may not be much running involved in his game, but that ability to plant the leg and take a hit is something to watch for, especially if he continues to be sloppy with his mechanics and rely too much on arm strength.

Nick Foles

Height: 6-5 Weight: 243 College: Arizona Draft: 2012/3 (88) Born: 20-Jan-1989 Age: 27 Risk: Red

Year	Team	G/GS	Snaps	Att	Comp	C%	Yds	TD	INT/Adj	FUM	ASR	NY/P	Rk	DVOA	Rk	DYAR	Rk	YAR	Runs	Yds	TD	DVOA	DYAR	QBR
2013	PHI	13/10	703	317	203	64.0%	2891	27	2/4	4	9.2%	7.9	2	35.6%	2	1011	5	1111	57	221	3	23.1%	72	69.0
2014	PHI	8/8	545	311	186	59.8%	2163	13	10/12	4	2.7%	6.5	18	1.8%	19	264	19	280	16	68	0	9.5%	15	62.2
2015	STL	11/11	656	337	190	56.4%	2052	7	10/12	4	3.8%	5.6	34	-27.9%	37	-353	37	-428	17	20	1	32.0%	21	30.0
2016	LARM			497	287	57.7%	3205	20	16	9		5.4		-23.1%					28	98	0	-2.7%		

2014:	50% Short	24% Mid	16% Deep	10% Bomb	YAC: 5.3 (20)	ALEX: 3.7	2015:	51% Short	30% Mid	12% Deep	8% Bomb	YAC: 6.1 (3)	ALEX: 0.6

Whether right or wrong, Foles believes that he should be a starting quarterback in the NFL. It's easy to see why he thinks that; just two seasons ago he was the Philadelphia Eagles' future because of his outrageous success in Chip Kelly's system. Those thoughts could hurt Foles, though, because he's at the point of his career where his best-case scenario is holding down a backup position for the next decade or more. He has already done enough on the field to guarantee that he can hold onto one of those well-paid, relaxed roles so long as his ego allows him to accept it. If losing his job to Case Keenum, watching his coaching staff trade the farm for a prospect, and being put in position to compete with Sean Mannion won't push him in that direction, nothing will.

Josh Freeman

Height: 6-6 Weight: 248 College: Kansas State Draft: 2009/1 (17) Born: 13-Jan-1988 Age: 28 Risk: N/A

Year	Team	G/GS	Snaps	Att	Comp	C%	Yds	TD	INT/Adj	FUM	ASR	NY/P	Rk	DVOA	Rk	DYAR	Rk	YAR	Runs	Yds	TD	DVOA	DYAR	QBR
2013	2TM	4/4	260	147	63	42.9%	761	2	1/5	2	4.6%	4.5	--	-29.7%	--	-176	--	-208	5	20	0	-8.9%	0	18.9
2015	IND	1/1	60	28	15	53.6%	149	1	1/1	0	2.2%	4.9	--	-48.0%	--	-70	--	-58	8	24	0	24.4%	12	53.9

												2015: 63%	Short 22%	Mid 7%	Deep 7%	Bomb	YAC: 4.5 (–)

Freeman went from unemployed at the end of Week 16 to starting in Week 17 and leading the Colts to a win. It was his first game action since his 2013 appearance in the Rick Spielman-Leslie Frazier divorce case. For a while it looked like the Colts might keep him to back up Andrew Luck, but he was released in March and has not yet found a new team. Still just 28, his name could continue to pop up for the next five seasons, or we may never hear from him again.

Blaine Gabbert

Height: 6-4   Weight: 234   College: Missouri   Draft: 2011/1 (10)   Born: 15-Oct-1989   Age: 27   Risk: Yellow

Year	Team	G/GS	Snaps	Att	Comp	C%	Yds	TD	INT/Adj	FUM	ASR	NY/P	Rk	DVOA	Rk	DYAR	Rk	YAR	Runs	Yds	TD	DVOA	DYAR	QBR
2013	JAC	3/3	159	86	42	48.8%	481	1	7/5	2	11.0%	4.2	--	-84.1%	--	-429	--	-480	9	32	0	-29.2%	-8	1.8
2014	SF	1/0	9	7	3	42.9%	38	1	0/0	0	0.3%	5.4	--	37.7%	--	22	--	18	1	5	0	-34.2%	-1	91.4
2015	SF	8/8	511	282	178	63.1%	2031	10	7/6	4	8.0%	6.1	27	-15.6%	31	-85	31	-118	32	185	1	16.2%	34	42.6
2016	SF			566	349	61.8%	3991	20	15	8		5.9		-13.9%					50	177	2	2.1%		

2014:	38% Short	25% Mid	25% Deep	13% Bomb	YAC: 1.7 (–)	ALEX: 24.0	2015:	56% Short	28% Mid	12% Deep	4% Bomb	YAC: 6.1 (4)	ALEX: -2.4

Gabbert used short, ineffective passes to bolster his 2015 stats, but advanced stats are hip to that jive. Gabbert was next to last in failed completion rate. On third down, he threw short of the sticks 65 percent of the time, the highest rate by anyone since 2006. Although we named ALEX after Alex Smith, Gabbert has the lowest ALEX (-2.1) on third down of any quarterback in the last decade. Colin Kaepernick's accuracy may leave something to be desired, but his career passing plus-minus (minus-0.9) is still well ahead of Gabbert (minus-77.1), who has the third-worst mark since 2006. Chip Kelly's system should help Gabbert to the best season of his career, but you can bet it will still be an ineffective one. Kaepernick clearly has more talent than Gabbert, but it's easier for Kelly to reign in Gabbert under his control to run the offense the way he likes.

Jimmy Garoppolo

Height: 6-2   Weight: 226   College: Eastern Illinois   Draft: 2014/2 (62)   Born: 11-Feb-1991   Age: 25   Risk: Yellow

Year	Team	G/GS	Snaps	Att	Comp	C%	Yds	TD	INT/Adj	FUM	ASR	NY/P	Rk	DVOA	Rk	DYAR	Rk	YAR	Runs	Yds	TD	DVOA	DYAR	QBR
2014	NE	6/0	69	27	19	70.4%	182	1	0/0	0	14.0%	4.6	--	-13.8%	--	-5	--	-28	10	9	0	-14.3%	-1	19.2
2015	NE	5/0	13	4	1	25.0%	6	0	0/0	0	1.2%	1.5	--	-98.6%	--	-25	--	-21	5	-5	0	--	--	2.4
2016	NE (16 G)			596	360	60.4%	4201	29	17	9		6.2		-2.3%					57	113	2	2.1%		
2016	NE (4 G)			149	90	60.4%	1050	7	4	2		6.2		-2.3%					14	28	0	2.1%		

2014:	67% Short	18% Mid	12% Deep	3% Bomb	YAC: 6.3 (–)	ALEX: -6.2	2015:	75% Short	25% Mid	0% Deep	0% Bomb	YAC: 1.0 (–)	ALEX: 0.0

The Patriots released Matt Flynn on August 10 of 2015, three weeks before the first Deflategate suspension was repealed. They have not bothered acquiring a journeyman spot starter since, unless you consider Ryan Lindley a journeyman spot starter. (He's a camp arm.) Bryan Hoyer was on the free-agent market when the Deflategate suspension was reinstated, but the Patriots didn't pursue an inexpensive quarterback who knows their system and has proven he can provide a few games of minimum competency.

The Patriots' disinterest in veteran placeholders is the clearest endorsement of Garoppolo we have. Everything else is three-year-old scouting reports, preseason observations, and puffy speculation in the form of two summers' worth of "What Can We Expect from Jimmy Garoppolo?" think-pieces. No one knows how good Garoppolo could be. But the Patriots have been certain for two years that he can be better than Flynn or Hoyer over a four-game stretch. That's good enough to win two or three of those first four games (especially if J.J. Watt isn't playing in Week 3) and maintain Rob Gronkowski's fantasy value. What else are you looking for in 2016?

Mike Glennon

Height: 6-6   Weight: 218   College: North Carolina State   Draft: 2013/3 (73)   Born: 12-Dec-1989   Age: 27   Risk: Yellow

Year	Team	G/GS	Snaps	Att	Comp	C%	Yds	TD	INT/Adj	FUM	ASR	NY/P	Rk	DVOA	Rk	DYAR	Rk	YAR	Runs	Yds	TD	DVOA	DYAR	QBR
2013	TB	13/13	842	416	247	59.4%	2608	19	9/11	7	8.3%	5.1	40	-7.7%	25	99	22	-73	27	37	0	-45.6%	-22	45.6
2014	TB	6/5	363	203	117	57.6%	1417	10	6/8	2	7.7%	6.1	24	-3.1%	23	107	26	161	10	49	0	2.2%	6	56.0
2016	TB			524	302	57.7%	3368	22	16	8		5.3		-18.3%					36	70	1	-15.8%		

2014:	39% Short	35% Mid	18% Deep	8% Bomb	YAC: 3.6 (37)	ALEX: 0.6

Glennon wasn't half-bad when given a chance in 2013 and 2014. There's nothing he has shown to really recommend him as a star, but he's no different than Brock Osweiler or (to throw it back to yesteryear) Matt Cassel on the spectrum of Young Quarterbacks With Starting Potential. It's a bit surprising the Bucs haven't dealt him yet, given their lack of depth in other areas. Glennon is two years from free agency, so check back in 2018 when every football analysis blog on the Interwebs has to write a story on why he's not really worth $40 million in guarantees, but the (Cleveland Browns/San Francisco 49ers/etc.) were desperate to have a quarterback with a chance.

Jared Goff — Height: 6-4 — Weight: 215 — College: California — Draft: 2016/1 (1) — Born: 14-Oct-1994 — Age: 22 — Risk: Yellow

Year	Team	G/GS	Snaps	Att	Comp	C%	Yds	TD	INT/Adj	FUM	ASR	NY/P	Rk	DVOA	Rk	DYAR	Rk	YAR	Runs	Yds	TD	DVOA	DYAR	QBR
2016	LARM		502	304	60.7%	3345	18	14	8		5.9		-10.8%					48	73	1	-15.7%		

Goff should be the decisive player in Jeff Fisher's stint as the St. Louis/Los Angeles Rams head coach. Goff proved to be a well-rounded but unspectacular quarterback in college. He doesn't have a massive arm or great athleticism and didn't show off consistent decision-making or precision to every level of the field. Goff isn't your typical first overall pick and he wasn't the type of prospect who warranted a king's ransom to acquire. He just happened to be the best available quarterback at a time when the Rams were desperate for a quarterback. Goff's QBASE projection was clearly the best among this year's quarterback prospects, and is among the ten highest on record dating back to 1996.

Bruce Gradkowski — Height: 6-1 — Weight: 220 — College: Toledo — Draft: 2006/6 (194) — Born: 27-Jan-1983 — Age: 33 — Risk: Green

Year	Team	G/GS	Snaps	Att	Comp	C%	Yds	TD	INT/Adj	FUM	ASR	NY/P	Rk	DVOA	Rk	DYAR	Rk	YAR	Runs	Yds	TD	DVOA	DYAR	QBR
2014	PIT	1/0	7	0	0	0.0%	0	0	0/0	0	--	--	--	--	--	--	--	--	2	-2	0	--	--	--
2016	PIT		558	339	60.7%	4017	22	14	8		6.2		3.0%					31	77	0	0.7%		

Gradkowski has not thrown a pass in a regular-season game since the 2012 finale, but he did see some time in the 2014 wild-card playoff loss to Baltimore. Last summer, Gradkowski dislocated his finger, which led to Michael Vick joining the team. Gradkowski re-signed with his local team for one more year and should be the primary backup to Ben Roethlisberger this season.

Robert Griffin — Height: 6-2 — Weight: 223 — College: Baylor — Draft: 2012/1 (2) — Born: 12-Feb-1990 — Age: 26 — Risk: Yellow

Year	Team	G/GS	Snaps	Att	Comp	C%	Yds	TD	INT/Adj	FUM	ASR	NY/P	Rk	DVOA	Rk	DYAR	Rk	YAR	Runs	Yds	TD	DVOA	DYAR	QBR
2013	WAS	13/13	906	456	274	60.1%	3203	16	12/15	10	8.8%	6.0	21	-13.1%	29	-60	30	98	86	489	0	-0.9%	42	40.1
2014	WAS	9/7	457	214	147	68.7%	1694	4	6/6	9	13.7%	5.9	29	-34.2%	35	-374	35	-372	38	176	1	-25.5%	-23	30.8
2016	CLE		530	334	63.0%	4048	21	14	15		6.5		-9.0%					75	314	2	-6.0%		
2014:	73% Short		17% Mid		4% Deep		6% Bomb		YAC: 7.5 (1)		ALEX: -0.1													

Griffin's career trajectory seems like the type of tragic demise which would befall the Browns, so perhaps it's fitting that the two parties have joined forces this offseason. When we last saw RG3 toiling away at the end of the 2014 season, he had deteriorated into one of the three or four worst passers in the league. (That high completion rate was packed with failed completions on third down.) Worse, even an approaching-middle-age Tom Brady (!) accrued more rushing value than the once explosive Griffin that season. Thus, Cleveland is perhaps the only team this year that would have given Griffin a realistic chance at starting, assuming he still has enough juice to beat out Josh McCown. Hue Jackson provides at least some hope for those still hanging around the RG3 bandwagon, having elevated Andy Dalton's career and resuscitated Jason Campbell in recent years. A Griffin revival wouldn't be that much stranger than what he's already gone through over his first four seasons. Most likely, though, Griffin is just keeping the seat warm for Deshaun Watson or Brad Kaaya as Cleveland begins the most thorough rebuild this side of the 76ers.

Christian Hackenberg — Height: 6-4 — Weight: 223 — College: Penn State — Draft: 2016/2 (51) — Born: 14-Feb-1995 — Age: 21 — Risk: Yellow

Year	Team	G/GS	Snaps	Att	Comp	C%	Yds	TD	INT/Adj	FUM	ASR	NY/P	Rk	DVOA	Rk	DYAR	Rk	YAR	Runs	Yds	TD	DVOA	DYAR	QBR
2016	NYJ		539	304	56.3%	3616	21	19	9		5.6		-17.5%					24	36	1	-8.6%		

The *Optimum Scouting Draft Guide* for 2016 performed tape breakdowns of six games by each of the top quarterbacks in the draft class. The games they analyzed were randomized and included some games from before 2015, which should have worked in Hackenberg's favor. Among the results of their study:
• Hackenberg finished second-to-last among top prospects with a "true accuracy" of 61.1 percent, ahead of only Jacoby Brissett. True accuracy is an Optimum Scouting metric that factors the length of the dropback and the complexity/distance of the throw into each prospect's completion rate.
• Hackenberg finished last among top prospects in "explosive play percentage," which is basically the rate of 25-plus-yard completions or touchdown passes, at 6.13 percent.

- Hackenberg had the lowest third- or fourth-down completion rate among the top prospects at 36.6 percent.
- Hackenberg was just 32-of-72 (44.4 percent) on passes longer than 10 yards downfield. By contrast, Jared Goff was 67-of-121 (55.4 percent), Carson Wentz 56-of-94 (59.6 percent), and Paxton Lynch 73-of-133 (54.9 percent) on similar passes. The sheer paucity of attempts and completions is as informative as the rate itself: Hackenberg didn't throw even midrange passes often, and he did not throw them very well.

There was some good news in the study, most of it coming from Hackenberg's low interception rate. Overall, however, Hackenberg had the game tape of a Jacoby Brissett or Dak Prescott *at best*: someone to tinker with behind a Pro Bowl veteran, not a potential immediate starter. Jets scouts clearly saw something else. Who knows what they were looking at.

Matt Hasselbeck Height: 6-4 Weight: 223 College: Boston College Draft: 1998/6 (187) Born: 25-Sep-1975 Age: 41 Risk: N/A

Year	Team	G/GS	Snaps	Att	Comp	C%	Yds	TD	INT/Adj	FUM	ASR	NY/P	Rk	DVOA	Rk	DYAR	Rk	YAR	Runs	Yds	TD	DVOA	DYAR	QBR
2013	IND	3/0	23	12	7	58.3%	130	0	1/1	0	0.6%	10.8	--	-28.6%	--	-15	--	-9	2	-2	0	--	--	38.1
2014	IND	4/0	82	44	30	68.2%	301	2	0/1	1	5.3%	6.2	--	10.8%	--	71	--	96	8	-11	0	-216.5%	-9	71.6
2015	IND	8/8	460	256	156	60.9%	1690	9	5/6	3	6.6%	5.8	31	-13.4%	30	-41	29	57	16	15	0	-24.4%	-5	55.1

| 2014: | 50% Short | 31% Mid | 15% Deep | 4% Bomb | YAC: 6.1 (--) | ALEX: 4.5 | 2015: | 50% Short | 32% Mid | 13% Deep | 5% Bomb | YAC: 5.0 (26) | ALEX: 1.1 |

Hasselbeck won his first four starts in 2015, earning plaudits from those who value quarterback wins and leading them to suggest he should play even if Andrew Luck were healthy. The Colts lost their next two games by 35 points. Each. We rarely see 40-year-old quarterbacks because those who never had a strong arm tend to see their arm get even weaker, and their bodies cannot take the physical pounding. Hasselbeck will still be on your TV screens on Sundays, but it will now be as a talking head for ESPN.

Chad Henne Height: 6-2 Weight: 230 College: Michigan Draft: 2008/2 (57) Born: 2-Jul-1985 Age: 31 Risk: Red

Year	Team	G/GS	Snaps	Att	Comp	C%	Yds	TD	INT/Adj	FUM	ASR	NY/P	Rk	DVOA	Rk	DYAR	Rk	YAR	Runs	Yds	TD	DVOA	DYAR	QBR
2013	JAC	15/13	897	503	305	60.6%	3241	13	14/21	2	7.4%	5.6	34	-13.9%	31	-94	31	-149	27	77	0	-39.9%	-37	31.9
2014	JAC	3/3	141	78	42	53.8%	492	3	1/2	1	16.2%	4.2	--	-54.3%	--	-249	--	-210	4	25	0	38.3%	10	16.1
2016	JAC			569	323	56.8%	3575	20	15	6		4.8		-24.0%					34	110	0	-4.3%		

| 2014: | 55% Short | 28% Mid | 8% Deep | 9% Bomb | YAC: 5.1 (--) | ALEX: 1.8 |

So long as he never has to play another snap, Henne could carve out a long career for himself in Jacksonville. Henne has been commended for how he has carried himself as a backup, something that carries weight when evaluating that role.

Shaun Hill Height: 6-5 Weight: 210 College: Maryland Draft: 2002/FA Born: 9-Jan-1980 Age: 37 Risk: Green

Year	Team	G/GS	Snaps	Att	Comp	C%	Yds	TD	INT/Adj	FUM	ASR	NY/P	Rk	DVOA	Rk	DYAR	Rk	YAR	Runs	Yds	TD	DVOA	DYAR	QBR
2013	DET	1/0	2	0	0	0.0%	0	0	0/0	0	--	--	--	--	--	--	--	--	2	-2	0	--	--	--
2014	STL	9/8	452	229	145	63.3%	1657	8	7/5	7	7.5%	6.2	21	-14.1%	31	-46	31	-35	10	10	1	-41.0%	-8	38.1
2015	MIN	3/0	28	7	2	28.6%	15	0	0/0	0	11.5%	0.5	--	-77.4%	--	-35	--	-40	4	-5	0	--	--	1.4
2016	MIN			471	292	62.0%	3286	19	14	9		5.9		-9.9%					18	32	0	-9.4%		

| 2014: | 58% Short | 22% Mid | 11% Deep | 9% Bomb | YAC: 5.6 (13) | ALEX: 1.0 | 2015: | 33% Short | 50% Mid | 17% Deep | 0% Bomb | YAC: 4.5 (--) | ALEX: 2.0 |

Shaun Hill vs. Sam Bradford, Career Stats

	G/GS	W-L	C%	Yd/At	TD%	INT%	Sk%	NetY/P	DVOA	Avg. NFL Salary*
Shaun Hill	46/34	16-18	62%	6.77	4.1%	2.5%	6.5%	5.91	-6.1%	$1.7 million
Sam Bradford	63/63	25-37-1	60%	6.45	3.4%	2.3%	6.1%	5.64	-9.3%	$13.0 million

* Includes money and time on practice squads, but not Hill's lucrative stint with the Amsterdam Admirals. Source: Spotrac.com

Life can be so unfair. Hill has earned more than $20 million in his career, so there's no need to set up a GoFundMe in his name or anything. But that just ain't right.

Hill is a lock for the Vikings' backup job this season. His only competition is Joel Stave, an undrafted rookie who threw more interceptions than touchdowns in his last two seasons at Wisconsin.

Brian Hoyer

Height: 6-2 Weight: 215 College: Michigan State Draft: 2009/FA Born: 13-Oct-1985 Age: 31 Risk: Red

Year	Team	G/GS	Snaps	Att	Comp	C%	Yds	TD	INT/Adj	FUM	ASR	NY/P	Rk	DVOA	Rk	DYAR	Rk	YAR	Runs	Yds	TD	DVOA	DYAR	QBR
2013	CLE	3/3	151	96	57	59.4%	615	5	3/4	0	7.1%	5.5	--	-10.4%	--	5	--	27	6	16	0	20.4%	4	47.5
2014	CLE	14/13	911	438	242	55.3%	3326	12	13/20	4	5.4%	6.8	10	-5.3%	25	166	24	255	24	39	0	-64.8%	-59	43.1
2015	HOU	11/9	674	369	224	60.7%	2606	19	7/6	6	7.5%	6.1	26	-3.0%	20	201	20	372	15	44	0	57.9%	26	59.6
2016	CHI			549	322	58.7%	3624	25	18	8		5.6		-14.6%					28	58	0	-11.2%		

2014:	44% Short	35% Mid	13% Deep	9% Bomb	YAC: 5.6 (11)	ALEX: 1.1	2015:	44% Short	37% Mid	11% Deep	7% Bomb	YAC: 4.2 (36)	ALEX: 2.5

The longtime backup became the Texans' primary quarterback in 2015, and ended up playing like a longtime backup. He could succeed, to a degree, in carefully controlled situations, but lacks the talent and consistency to be beyond that. He functioned best under center (19.1% DVOA, compared to -13.4% in shotgun) and knew enough to throw the ball up to DeAndre Hopkins in the red zone (19 of 52 red zone targets) but struggled on third-and-long (-24.8% DVOA on third down with 7 or more yards to go). The postseason disaster against the Chiefs exposed his deep limitations, and the signing of Brock Osweiler meant his time in Houston was at an end. If managed properly, he could be effective as a Jay Cutler fill-in for a few games, but no more than that.

Brett Hundley

Height: 6-3 Weight: 226 College: UCLA Draft: 2015/5 (147) Born: 15-Jun-1993 Age: 23 Risk: Yellow

Year	Team	G/GS	Snaps	Att	Comp	C%	Yds	TD	INT/Adj	FUM	ASR	NY/P	Rk	DVOA	Rk	DYAR	Rk	YAR	Runs	Yds	TD	DVOA	DYAR	QBR
2016	GB			517	315	61.0%	3747	25	18	9		6.5		-1.3%					87	332	1	5.5%		

Some draftniks projected Hundley to go as high as the first round of the 2015 draft, but concerns about his pocket presence and ability to read defenses overshadowed his prodigious athletic ability, and he fell to Green Bay in Round 5, the sixth quarterback off the boards. Then in the preseason, he played like, well, a first-rounder, completing 69 percent of his passes for 9.7 yards per pass with seven touchdowns and one pick. Scott Tolzien's departure makes Hundley the top backup in 2016. He's not likely to start in Green Bay any time soon, but this franchise has a long track record of drafting quarterbacks and giving them time to develop into quality starters, from Mark Brunell to Matt Hasselbeck to Aaron Brooks to (of course) Aaron Rodgers. There's a good chance Hundley will join that list in a few years, whether in Green Bay or elsewhere.

Landry Jones

Height: 6-4 Weight: 218 College: Oklahoma Draft: 2013/4 (115) Born: 4-Apr-1989 Age: 27 Risk: Yellow

Year	Team	G/GS	Snaps	Att	Comp	C%	Yds	TD	INT/Adj	FUM	ASR	NY/P	Rk	DVOA	Rk	DYAR	Rk	YAR	Runs	Yds	TD	DVOA	DYAR	QBR
2015	PIT	7/2	109	55	32	58.2%	513	3	4/4	1	3.1%	8.7	--	-1.5%	--	37	--	-12	5	-5	0	--	--	35.9
2016	PIT			558	336	60.2%	4237	26	21	8		6.7		-1.1%					27	30	1	-13.0%		

						2015: 45%	Short 25%	Mid 19%	Deep 11%	Bomb	YAC: 8.8 (--)

Jones finally threw the first 55 passes of his regular-season career in 2015, but there was not much to like unless you enjoy watching Martavis Bryant's speed and size make the plays. Jones should revert to third-string quarterback now that Bruce Gradkowski is healthy, and it is hard to see him earning a second contract in Pittsburgh.

Colin Kaepernick

Height: 6-5 Weight: 233 College: Nevada Draft: 2011/2 (36) Born: 3-Nov-1987 Age: 29 Risk: Red

Year	Team	G/GS	Snaps	Att	Comp	C%	Yds	TD	INT/Adj	FUM	ASR	NY/P	Rk	DVOA	Rk	DYAR	Rk	YAR	Runs	Yds	TD	DVOA	DYAR	QBR
2013	SF	16/16	968	416	243	58.4%	3197	21	8/10	6	7.8%	6.5	12	16.6%	7	791	8	650	92	524	4	11.8%	91	68.6
2014	SF	16/16	1049	478	289	60.5%	3369	19	10/12	8	9.9%	5.7	34	-8.4%	28	91	27	176	104	639	1	7.5%	88	55.9
2015	SF	9/8	504	244	144	59.0%	1615	6	5/8	5	10.3%	5.3	36	-21.5%	34	-182	35	-249	45	256	1	22.7%	63	47.1
2016	SF			510	311	60.9%	3538	20	13	11		5.9		-16.1%					95	546	3	7.6%		

2014:	53% Short	29% Mid	10% Deep	7% Bomb	YAC: 4.8 (30)	ALEX: 2.3	2015:	59% Short	23% Mid	8% Deep	10% Bomb	YAC: 5.8 (9)	ALEX: 0.6

Yes, Kaepernick has seen his performance decline. Yes, his DVOA, QBR and yards per attempt have fallen each season. But between Kaepernick and Blaine Gabbert, who is the career bust and who once looked like a stud in leading the 49ers to within a 5-yard pass of a Super Bowl victory? Perhaps a trade still happens, or the preseason dictates a change, but it is difficult to believe that Gabbert gives the 49ers the best chance to win the few games the team will win this season. At least we know the potential for greatness is there with Kaepernick.

Case Keenum Height: 6-2 Weight: 209 College: Houston Draft: 2012/FA Born: 17-Feb-1988 Age: 28 Risk: Red

Year	Team	G/GS	Snaps	Att	Comp	C%	Yds	TD	INT/Adj	FUM	ASR	NY/P	Rk	DVOA	Rk	DYAR	Rk	YAR	Runs	Yds	TD	DVOA	DYAR	QBR
2013	HOU	8/8	461	253	137	54.2%	1760	9	6/8	6	7.4%	5.8	25	-22.4%	36	-191	34	-201	14	72	1	23.8%	27	34.5
2014	2TM	2/2	165	77	45	58.4%	435	2	2/2	1	2.8%	5.3	--	-20.8%	--	-50	--	-43	10	35	0	4.3%	9	43.7
2015	STL	6/5	297	125	76	60.8%	828	4	1/4	3	3.1%	6.2	--	-1.1%	--	83	--	144	12	5	0	-70.7%	-17	47.7
2016	LARM			485	276	56.9%	3176	16	13	9		5.7		-14.8%					34	111	1	-2.7%		

2014: 60% Short   26% Mid   7% Deep   6% Bomb   YAC: 5.8 (–)   ALEX: -2.4   2015: 50% Short   31% Mid   7% Deep   11% Bomb   YAC: 5.3 (–)   ALEX: 0.2

Hopefully Keenum didn't buy Jeff Fisher's declaration that he was the team's starting quarterback after the 2015 season. If he did, he was the only one. Keenum got a good deal from the Rams, including a first-round tender as a restricted free agent, and should be in position to be Jared Goff's backup for the foreseeable future. Keenum has bounced between the Rams and Texans rosters since he arrived in the NFL, so finding a full-time home will be a huge achievement.

Cody Kessler Height: 6-1 Weight: 220 College: USC Draft: 2016/3 (93) Born: 11-Apr-1993 Age: 23 Risk: Yellow

Year	Team	G/GS	Snaps	Att	Comp	C%	Yds	TD	INT/Adj	FUM	ASR	NY/P	Rk	DVOA	Rk	DYAR	Rk	YAR	Runs	Yds	TD	DVOA	DYAR	QBR
2016	CLE			496	310	62.6%	3308	15	16	10		5.3		-20.2%					22	66	1	4.2%		

The former USC Trojan was seemingly chosen thanks to Browns coach Hue Jackson's California Crush, which leaves him sweet on Left Coasters. Statistically, the likes of Dak Prescott and Kevin Hogan were superior, though Kessler was selected ahead of both. Profiles to be a less accomplished Colt McCoy as a pro, albeit with better coaching.

Andrew Luck Height: 6-4 Weight: 234 College: Stanford Draft: 2012/1 (1) Born: 12-Mar-1989 Age: 27 Risk: Yellow

Year	Team	G/GS	Snaps	Att	Comp	C%	Yds	TD	INT/Adj	FUM	ASR	NY/P	Rk	DVOA	Rk	DYAR	Rk	YAR	Runs	Yds	TD	DVOA	DYAR	QBR
2013	IND	16/16	1046	570	343	60.2%	3822	23	9/14	6	5.7%	6.0	22	4.6%	16	650	14	623	63	377	4	47.6%	151	62.0
2014	IND	16/16	1072	616	380	61.7%	4761	40	16/21	13	4.8%	7.1	7	9.2%	10	879	10	829	64	273	3	4.4%	40	63.8
2015	IND	7/7	508	293	162	55.3%	1881	15	12/16	3	5.4%	5.8	30	-17.5%	32	-126	33	-189	33	196	0	31.2%	59	47.6
2016	IND			608	366	60.3%	4670	34	17	6		6.8		4.4%					58	251	2	15.8%		

2014: 51% Short   30% Mid   12% Deep   7% Bomb   YAC: 5.8 (8)   ALEX: 3.5   2015: 41% Short   34% Mid   16% Deep   9% Bomb   YAC: 4.3 (35)   ALEX: 2.5

Amid all the downer numbers and film that said Luck was not the same quarterback in 2015 he had been his first three seasons in the NFL, he actually posted the best red zone DVOA of his career. After coming out right around average his first three seasons, his 39.9% DVOA in 2015 was seventh among the 37 passers with at least 25 red zone attempts. But as we chronicled in the team chapter, almost all his other numbers, especially on deeper throws, were down significantly. We are optimistic that 2015 was largely a fluke and the result of injury, that he will return to the form he showed in 2013 and 2014, and that his fantasy numbers will rebound accordingly.

Paxton Lynch Height: 6-7 Weight: 244 College: Memphis Draft: 2016/1 (26) Born: 12-Feb-1994 Age: 22 Risk: Red

Year	Team	G/GS	Snaps	Att	Comp	C%	Yds	TD	INT/Adj	FUM	ASR	NY/P	Rk	DVOA	Rk	DYAR	Rk	YAR	Runs	Yds	TD	DVOA	DYAR	QBR
2016	DEN			522	311	59.5%	3439	23	17	10		5.5		-16.8%					59	227	2	7.3%		

On NFL.com's draft page for Lynch, the first five sentences of weaknesses read as follows: "Needs to improve ball placement for catch-and-run throws. Inability to throw with desired accuracy on the move forced him to leave yards and plays on the field. Must learn to better anticipate routes and stay ahead in the rep. Doesn't quite have the quickness through progressions that he will need in the pros. Has to learn to move defenders around with his eyes to open throwing lanes." That scouting report reads a lot like those for recent flops such as Jake Locker. Given how noisy scouting and projection are (including our QBASE projection system for college quarterbacks), all this means is that we think Lynch's chances of succeeding are a little lower than you would want in a first-round pick. One day, we're going to get around to running a regression of NFL success on a variable for whether a prospect was lauded for having "elite arm talent." We expect the correlation not to be positive.

Ryan Mallett

| | Height: 6-7 | Weight: 253 | College: Arkansas | | Draft: 2011/3 (74) | Born: 5-Jun-1988 | Age: 28 | Risk: Red |

Year	Team	G/GS	Snaps	Att	Comp	C%	Yds	TD	INT/Adj	FUM	ASR	NY/P	Rk	DVOA	Rk	DYAR	Rk	YAR	Runs	Yds	TD	DVOA	DYAR	QBR
2014	HOU	3/2	157	75	41	54.7%	400	2	2/5	0	3.6%	5.3	--	14.5%	--	120	--	37	6	-2	0	31.6%	6	48.2
2015	2TM	8/6	421	244	136	55.7%	1336	5	6/10	0	3.0%	5.2	37	-12.3%	28	-19	28	-113	5	15	1	17.2%	8	55.1
2016	BAL		586	321		54.7%	3703	19	19	7		5.5		-18.5%					27	47	0	-16.9%		

| 2014: | 45% Short | 36% Mid | 11% Deep | 8% Bomb | YAC: 3.9 (--) | ALEX: 2.0 | 2015: | 41% Short | 42% Mid | 12% Deep | 5% Bomb | YAC: 3.5 (37) | ALEX: -0.1 |

After oversleeping and missing some team meetings, it was pretty obvious Mallett's time was not long in Houston. He signed with Baltimore in December and became the team's fourth starter of the season. Mallett probably had the best game of his NFL career in the Week 16 win over Pittsburgh. That should be enough to give him the job of being Joe Flacco's backup, though Mallett does struggle with his accuracy. Then again, so does Flacco after all of these years, so it's a good fit.

Eli Manning

| | Height: 6-4 | Weight: 218 | College: Mississippi | | Draft: 2004/1 (1) | Born: 3-Jan-1981 | Age: 35 | Risk: Yellow |

Year	Team	G/GS	Snaps	Att	Comp	C%	Yds	TD	INT/Adj	FUM	ASR	NY/P	Rk	DVOA	Rk	DYAR	Rk	YAR	Runs	Yds	TD	DVOA	DYAR	QBR
2013	NYG	16/16	986	551	317	57.5%	3818	18	27/31	7	7.7%	6.0	20	-20.2%	35	-335	37	-202	18	36	0	-76.6%	-27	36.5
2014	NYG	16/16	1109	601	379	63.1%	4410	30	14/20	7	4.7%	6.7	14	4.6%	15	642	11	735	12	31	1	41.3%	18	70.9
2015	NYG	16/16	1106	618	387	62.6%	4432	35	14/15	11	5.2%	6.6	13	-1.9%	19	404	18	535	20	61	0	-0.4%	5	60.5
2016	NYG		618	386		62.4%	4386	32	12	7		6.4		5.0%					27	60	0	-4.8%		

| 2014: | 47% Short | 35% Mid | 12% Deep | 7% Bomb | YAC: 5.1 (23) | ALEX: 1.1 | 2015: | 50% Short | 34% Mid | 9% Deep | 7% Bomb | YAC: 5.4 (18) | ALEX: 1.1 |

Now that he's Last Manning Standing, the good news is that Eli finally has an acceptably high floor to his game. Playing in Ben McAdoo's West Coast-derived system has all but eradicated Manning's old habit of squeezing throws into impossibly small windows. The player who thrice led the league in picks has been better than average in interception rate in each of the past two years. In fact, last season's 2.5-to-1 touchdown-to-interception ratio was the best of Manning's 12-year career.

However, as Manning approaches his age-35 season, the Giants are asking their aging quarterback to carry an increasingly greater burden, surrounding him with a mediocre running game and a mix of raw youngsters and longtime veteran backups on the offensive line. Fantasy owners will surely like the volume, and Manning's raw touchdown totals could approach a career high if he fares better in the red zone. Manning led the league with five red zone picks in 2015, and his -45.2% red zone DVOA was the worst of any quarterback with at least 50 attempts inside the opposing 20. Moreover, the addition of Sterling Shepard and reintroduction of Victor Cruz should (in theory) fit well with McAdoo's scheme, giving Manning more options to control the middle of the field and feed the ball to players capable of racking up yards after the catch. None of this guarantees that Manning will see his efficiency numbers return to their lofty 2008-12 peaks, especially if he continues to become conservative as his physical tools erode. Still, entering his third season in McAdoo's system, it appears the Giants no longer need to fret about which version of Eli will show up for the fall.

Peyton Manning

| | Height: 6-5 | Weight: 230 | College: Tennessee | | Draft: 1998/1 (1) | Born: 24-Mar-1976 | Age: 40 | Risk: N/A |

Year	Team	G/GS	Snaps	Att	Comp	C%	Yds	TD	INT/Adj	FUM	ASR	NY/P	Rk	DVOA	Rk	DYAR	Rk	YAR	Runs	Yds	TD	DVOA	DYAR	QBR
2013	DEN	16/16	1156	659	450	68.3%	5477	55	10/12	10	3.4%	7.9	1	43.2%	1	2475	1	2674	32	-31	1	-110.6%	-30	82.9
2014	DEN	16/16	1092	597	395	66.2%	4727	39	15/19	6	3.5%	7.5	4	23.9%	4	1412	3	1358	24	-24	0	-236.4%	-30	77.3
2015	DEN	10/9	593	331	198	59.8%	2249	9	17/21	1	4.5%	6.2	24	-25.8%	36	-326	36	-317	6	-6	0	--	--	45.0

| 2014: | 54% Short | 26% Mid | 12% Deep | 8% Bomb | YAC: 4.8 (31) | ALEX: 2.5 | 2015: | 45% Short | 31% Mid | 14% Deep | 9% Bomb | YAC: 4.9 (29) | ALEX: 1.6 |

Manning had the worst regular-season statistics, postseason numbers, and Super Bowl performance of any championship-winning quarterback in our database back to 1989. Between the regular season and playoffs, he threw a league-high 18 interceptions despite starting only 12 total games. Supporters will say that his appearance off the bench against San Diego in Week 17 saved home-field advantage for the Broncos, but critics can point out the top seed might have already been clinched by then were it not for Manning's 5-of-20, four-interception game against Kansas City that caused him to get benched for Brock Osweiler in the first place. It is more than fair to say that the 2016 version of Peyton Manning was the worst quarterback to win a Super Bowl in at least a quarter-century.

Which is ironic, because Manning was widely considered the best quarterback without a Super Bowl ring until his MVP performance against the Bears in Super Bowl XLI. It's very difficult to summarize Manning's career in a few hundred words. There are the raw numbers, of course: Manning retires with five MVP awards and seven first-team All-Pro appearances. He is the all-time leader in passing yards (71,940) and touchdowns (539), and second in attempts and completions. But he is only ninth in interceptions, and according to Pro-Football-Reference.com (which claims to have sack data back to 1969), he is 44th in sacks. Manning's brother Eli has already been sacked more than Peyton ever was, in 82 fewer starts.

His advanced numbers, if anything, are even more impressive. In his rookie season, he was already a good quarterback, finishing 12th in DYAR and 14th in DVOA. In the next *16 years*, save for the 2011 season he missed with a neck injury, he never finished lower than seventh in either category. Meanwhile, he was first in DYAR and DVOA six times each. His 58.9% DVOA in 2004 is still the highest we've ever measured in a season (minimum 200 passes), and he appears five other times in the top 25. The single-season DYAR record belongs to Tom Brady in 2007, but Manning is in second (2013), third (2004), and fourth (2006) place. Manning's career total of 26,290 DYAR is far more than anyone else. Brady is in second place with 19,759, which means he could add two seasons like his record 2007 campaign and he would still be in second place. Among quarterbacks with at least 1,000 passes, Manning's career passing DVOA of 29.9% trails only the 30.4% of Steve Young, but remember that this does not include Young's whole career. Manning will probably "pass" Young once we've computed DVOA for Young's formative seasons in Tampa Bay.

And somehow, not even that seems to do Manning justice. He is probably the best quarterback in the history of the Colts franchise, which would mean he is better than Johnny Unitas. His first three seasons in Denver were light years ahead of anything the Broncos have ever seen, and it would not be totally absurd to put Manning ahead of John Elway on that franchise's all-time list either. Mike Tanier covered each franchise's top-five quarterback list in 2011, and then updated it in 2014 for *A Good Walkthrough Spoiled: The Best of Mike Tanier at Football Outsiders*. (Available now on our website!) Here is what he wrote about Manning then:

> "There is nothing, absolutely nothing, in any of the records that looks like Manning's body of work. There is no run of 12-4 seasons and statistical dominance that lasts anywhere near as long, period. Terry Bradshaw and Tom Brady cannot touch it. John Elway does not come close. Neither does Dan Marino, who had a lot of great statistical years for 8-8 teams. Joe Montana has something more checkered, although it is brilliant enough to be arguably greater. Unitas has 1957-60 and several punctuation marks, so he has a case. Brett Favre has his four-year run and lots of (very good) stuffing. Otto Graham has something that looks better if you can stomach AAFC statistics. But really, Manning's statistical record is completely on its own, and to write it all off is to write this whole decade off."

Since Tanier wrote that, Manning had a 12-4, 4,727-yard, 39-touchdown season in 2015, and then won another Super Bowl ring last year, numbers be damned. In some ways, that last Lombardi Trophy was like a lifetime achievement award from the football gods. It was like he deserved to go out on top, not because he was particularly good in 2016, but because he had been so perpetually excellent for the better part of two decades before that.

EJ Manuel

Height: 6-5   Weight: 240   College: Florida State   Draft: 2013/1 (16)   Born: 19-Mar-1990   Age: 26   Risk: Red

Year	Team	G/GS	Snaps	Att	Comp	C%	Yds	TD	INT/Adj	FUM	ASR	NY/P	Rk	DVOA	Rk	DYAR	Rk	YAR	Runs	Yds	TD	DVOA	DYAR	QBR
2013	BUF	10/10	694	306	180	58.8%	1972	11	9/10	6	8.9%	5.5	35	-19.9%	34	-190	33	-87	53	186	2	11.0%	49	42.3
2014	BUF	5/4	259	131	76	58.0%	838	5	3/3	1	5.5%	5.8	--	-17.1%	--	-53	--	-36	16	52	1	-26.3%	-10	19.8
2015	BUF	7/2	155	84	52	61.9%	561	3	3/5	2	8.1%	5.7	--	-16.0%	--	-26	--	-12	17	64	1	20.8%	34	37.0
2016	BUF			481	287	59.6%	3206	18	13	7		5.8		-16.4%					66	214	1	-9.3%		

2014:	61% Short	20% Mid	14% Deep	5% Bomb	YAC: 7.0 (–)	ALEX: 2.7	2015:	38% Short	38% Mid	14% Deep	9% Bomb	YAC: 3.2 (–)	ALEX: 0.2

Manuel played fairly well in a pair of losses to the Bengals and Jaguars. He also made brief cameo appearances in a Wildcat; only the Bills would try to cross up opponents by inserting a *slower* quarterback to run the option. The Bills didn't bother with Manuel's fifth-year option, as he is no longer remotely in the team's quarterback-of-the-future plans. Manuel has a backup's skill set, however, so the Bills should keep him around as a Cardale Jones ego suppressant. Manuel will still be on some NFL bench eight years from now, and the giddy time that he rose into the first round of an almost homeopathically weak quarterback class will be a distant memory.

Johnny Manziel

Height: 6-0   Weight: 207   College: Texas A&M   Draft: 2014/1 (22)   Born: 6-Dec-1992   Age: 24   Risk: N/A

Year	Team	G/GS	Snaps	Att	Comp	C%	Yds	TD	INT/Adj	FUM	ASR	NY/P	Rk	DVOA	Rk	DYAR	Rk	YAR	Runs	Yds	TD	DVOA	DYAR	QBR
2014	CLE	5/2	75	35	18	51.4%	175	0	2/2	1	9.0%	3.9	--	-73.2%	--	-144	--	-180	9	29	1	-36.7%	-9	5.1
2015	CLE	9/6	438	223	129	57.8%	1500	7	5/8	6	7.8%	5.6	33	-18.4%	33	-105	32	-179	37	230	0	32.6%	68	54.7

2014:	60% Short	28% Mid	13% Deep	0% Bomb	YAC: 4.7 (–)	ALEX: 1.1	2015:	46% Short	37% Mid	12% Deep	4% Bomb	YAC: 5.7 (10)	ALEX: 1.8

It's hard now to recall through the blizzard of drunken Instagram snaps, TMZ ambush photos, and mug shots, but there was a moment or two in 2015 when it appeared Manziel might actually become at least a serviceable quarterback, if not a good one. Unfortunately, his personal demons deep-sixed his career in Cleveland. His poor mechanics, limited physical attributes, dicey decision-making, and inability to read defenses quickly will almost certainly have the same effect on whatever NFL opportunity may magically arise for him, if one ever does.

Marcus Mariota

Height: 6-4 Weight: 222 College: Oregon Draft: 2015/1 (2) Born: 30-Oct-1993 Age: 23 Risk: Red

Year	Team	G/GS	Snaps	Att	Comp	C%	Yds	TD	INT/Adj	FUM	ASR	NY/P	Rk	DVOA	Rk	DYAR	Rk	YAR	Runs	Yds	TD	DVOA	DYAR	QBR
2015	TEN	12/12	736	370	230	62.2%	2818	19	10/14	10	10.1%	6.3	17	-13.2%	29	-53	30	123	34	252	2	-0.6%	20	61.0
2016	TEN		528	325		61.6%	3936	26	13	11		6.6		1.5%					88	412	3	10.0%		
													2015: 38%		Short 40%		Mid 17%		Deep 5%		Bomb		YAC: 5.1 (25)	

Mariota's rookie season was embarrassing—embarrassing, that is, for those who labeled him a system quarterback during the draft process. Mariota transitioned to the NFL with ease. The perfect passer rating from his debut against the Tampa Bay Buccaneers obviously wasn't sustainable, but over 12 games he showed off all the traits of a franchise quarterback. Mariota threw the ball with precision while reading through progressions and making adjustments in the pocket. He wasn't reliant on running the ball, nor did he show a lack of poise working under pressure. Mariota only really has two concerns at this point: His health and his deep ball.

Mariota only played in 12 games because of multiple MCL tears. He suffered his first against the Miami Dolphins when Olivier Vernon hit him low and late. His second MCL injury occurred against the New England Patriots when Jamie Collins caused his body to crumble awkwardly, pushing his knees out at an uncomfortable angle. Whether Mariota was unlucky or has chronic issues is to be determined, but either way it's largely out of his control. His deep ball is under his control, though, and the quarterback got bigger and stronger during the offseason in the hopes of showing off more control and velocity on passes that travel further than 20 yards.

AJ McCarron

Height: 6-3 Weight: 220 College: Alabama Draft: 2014/5 (164) Born: 13-Sep-1990 Age: 26 Risk: Yellow

Year	Team	G/GS	Snaps	Att	Comp	C%	Yds	TD	INT/Adj	FUM	ASR	NY/P	Rk	DVOA	Rk	DYAR	Rk	YAR	Runs	Yds	TD	DVOA	DYAR	QBR
2015	CIN	7/3	257	119	79	66.4%	854	6	2/2	1	8.5%	6.0	--	6.9%	--	151	--	138	14	31	0	-8.2%	2	64.4
2016	CIN		506	332		65.7%	3453	23	15	8		5.9		-5.8%					44	128	1	-5.1%		
													2015: 50%		Short 25%		Mid 17%		Deep 8%		Bomb		YAC: 4.0 (−)	

In another dimension, the Bengals don't implode at the end of the playoff game/steel cage match with Pittsburgh, and McCarron is the toast of Cincinnati, the anti-Dalton who ended the franchise's numbing postseason futility. The rally he led in that furious fourth quarter would be part of Cincinnati lore, and Hot Take Nation might even have drummed up a quarterback controversy. (Imagine if the Bengals won the following round as well!) McCarron was hardly ready to supplant Dalton as starter, though he showed enough competence to remain a quality backup and potential trade chip. To his credit, McCarron largely avoided the mistakes that cripple young quarterbacks, though his fumbled snap in overtime of the regular-season game against Denver was crucial in costing the Bengals a bye week. AJ proved his scouting report correct—he is smart, tough, and poised. But for all his positive intangibles, his arm is mediocre, and he couldn't regularly take advantage of the mismatches the Bengals offense often provided.

Josh McCown

Height: 6-4 Weight: 215 College: Sam Houston State Draft: 2002/3 (81) Born: 4-Jul-1979 Age: 37 Risk: Red

Year	Team	G/GS	Snaps	Att	Comp	C%	Yds	TD	INT/Adj	FUM	ASR	NY/P	Rk	DVOA	Rk	DYAR	Rk	YAR	Runs	Yds	TD	DVOA	DYAR	QBR
2013	CHI	8/5	421	224	149	66.5%	1829	13	1/3	3	4.8%	7.6	5	32.1%	4	659	13	773	13	69	1	10.9%	10	85.1
2014	TB	11/11	630	327	184	56.3%	2206	11	14/13	10	10.4%	5.5	35	-41.9%	37	-665	36	-576	25	127	3	35.9%	47	35.7
2015	CLE	8/8	509	292	186	63.7%	2109	12	4/5	9	7.1%	6.2	23	-5.8%	23	110	23	81	20	98	1	0.7%	12	53.9
2016	CLE		542	335		61.8%	3966	21	16	16		6.2		-14.6%					43	124	1	-11.7%		
2014:	47% Short		33% Mid		11% Deep		9% Bomb		YAC: 4.0 (36)		ALEX: 2.5		2015:	51% Short		33% Mid		11% Deep		5% Bomb		YAC: 5.5 (17)	ALEX: 2.7

Though seemingly a poster boy for gawky old white quarterbacks, McCown has always possessed an athletic element to his game. However, to paraphrase Shaquille O'Neal, 36 ain't 26, bro. So McCown's bonzai charge toward the goal line in the season opener against the Jets wasn't surprising, and neither was the result—a concussion that led to the initial appearance of Johnny Football behind center in 2015. Injuries to McCown's shoulder and ribs followed in the weeks to come, followed by a season-ending broken collarbone. McCown was hardly even mentioned in the offseason despite the copious ink spilled about the Browns' search for a quarterback. That's a touch surprising—the elder McCown wasn't very good when he did play last year, but he might get Cleveland through a few games should Robert Griffin prove resistant to Hue Jackson's anti-suck serum injections. Somebody, if not the Browns, will employ McCown in 2016. Let's hope he acts his age.

Luke McCown

Height: 6-3   Weight: 208   College: Louisiana Tech   Draft: 2004/4 (106)   Born: 12-Jul-1981   Age: 35   Risk: Red

Year	Team	G/GS	Snaps	Att	Comp	C%	Yds	TD	INT/Adj	FUM	ASR	NY/P	Rk	DVOA	Rk	DYAR	Rk	YAR	Runs	Yds	TD	DVOA	DYAR	QBR
2013	NO	16/0	16	1	0	0.0%	0	0	0/0	0	-5.4%	0.0	--	-89.2%	--	-3	--	-4	3	-4	0	--	--	85.1
2015	NO	8/1	70	39	32	82.1%	335	0	1/1	0	2.3%	8.4	--	77.1%	--	220	--	154	0	0	0	--	--	84.9
2016	NO			609	385	62.6%	4051	26	18	9		6.0		-8.0%					23	73	0	0.8%		

2015: 57%	Short 27%	Mid 14%	Deep 3%	Bomb	YAC: 4.8 (–)

It was a big year for McCown, who dink-and-dunked his way into a shockingly strong statistical performance against a Panthers team missing the injured Luke Kuechly, then starred in a Verizon commercial before getting sent to IR with a back injury. He'll turn 35 before the season, and won't be taken seriously as a starting candidate anywhere, but he seems beloved enough behind the scenes to keep this up for another couple years.

Colt McCoy

Height: 6-1   Weight: 216   College: Texas   Draft: 2010/3 (85)   Born: 5-Sep-1986   Age: 30   Risk: Red

Year	Team	G/GS	Snaps	Att	Comp	C%	Yds	TD	INT/Adj	FUM	ASR	NY/P	Rk	DVOA	Rk	DYAR	Rk	YAR	Runs	Yds	TD	DVOA	DYAR	QBR
2013	SF	4/0	22	1	1	100.0%	13	0	0/0	0	-1.8%	13.0	--	256.6%	--	14	--	13	6	-6	0	--	--	95.0
2014	WAS	5/4	240	128	91	71.1%	1057	4	3/4	6	11.8%	6.5	--	-15.9%	--	-43	--	-9	16	66	1	-33.0%	-13	46.1
2015	WAS	2/0	44	11	7	63.6%	128	1	0/0	1	7.9%	9.5	--	20.9%	--	22	--	14	3	-3	0	--	--	36.8
2016	WAS			544	361	66.5%	3850	23	16	13		6.0		-10.0%					49	131	2	-5.7%		

2014:	61% Short	25% Mid	7% Deep	6% Bomb	YAC: 6.0 (–)	ALEX: -1.3	2015:	55% Short	27% Mid	0% Deep	18% Bomb	YAC: 11.6 (–)	ALEX: 1.8

McCoy probably saved his career with a respectable stint as Washington's part-time starter in 2014, and now appears ready to settle into life as an unofficial Savvy Veteran Backup. McCoy played only 44 snaps all year after Kirk Cousins broke through in 2015 and seized the starting job, but the once-erratic Cousins still feels as though he's a single five-picks-in-two-games stretch from falling back into the doghouse. Washington's leash for Cousins is longer than it has ever been after last season, but McCoy will stick around as the shaky insurance policy the Redskins hope they never need to bank on.

Matt McGloin

Height: 6-1   Weight: 210   College: Penn State   Draft: 2013/FA   Born: 2-Dec-1989   Age: 27   Risk: Yellow

Year	Team	G/GS	Snaps	Att	Comp	C%	Yds	TD	INT/Adj	FUM	ASR	NY/P	Rk	DVOA	Rk	DYAR	Rk	YAR	Runs	Yds	TD	DVOA	DYAR	QBR
2013	OAK	7/6	378	211	118	55.9%	1547	8	8/10	4	3.1%	6.9	8	-11.9%	27	-11	27	62	11	27	0	21.1%	7	49.5
2014	OAK	1/0	24	19	12	63.2%	129	1	2/1	0	4.7%	6.1	--	-54.4%	--	-58	--	-63	2	3	0	8.1%	2	10.3
2015	OAK	2/0	42	32	23	71.9%	142	2	1/1	1	6.1%	3.6	--	-21.5%	--	-26	--	-46	0	0	0	--	--	18.8
2016	OAK			611	363	59.4%	4042	21	15	11		5.5		-15.0%					33	80	0	-13.0%		

2014:	40% Short	45% Mid	5% Deep	10% Bomb	YAC: 4.8 (–)	ALEX: 1.0	2015:	66% Short	25% Mid	6% Deep	3% Bomb	YAC: 2.8 (–)	ALEX: -0.5

Garbage time called in Week 1 against Cincinnati, and McGloin answered the phone. Down 17-0 to the Bengals with about two quarters to play, McGloin continued to show cromulent backup quarterback attributes. He has held off Matt Schaub and Christian Ponder in consecutive seasons, and now finds Connor Cook in his path for 2016. If you compare McGloin's college statistics to his NFL statistics, you ... are slightly more optimistic about Christian Hackenberg?

Zach Mettenberger

Height: 6-4   Weight: 224   College: Louisiana State   Draft: 2014/6 (178)   Born: 16-Jul-1991   Age: 25   Risk: Red

Year	Team	G/GS	Snaps	Att	Comp	C%	Yds	TD	INT/Adj	FUM	ASR	NY/P	Rk	DVOA	Rk	DYAR	Rk	YAR	Runs	Yds	TD	DVOA	DYAR	QBR
2014	TEN	7/6	305	179	107	59.8%	1412	8	7/9	4	8.7%	6.5	--	-28.7%	--	-211	--	-235	5	4	0	64.8%	5	30.1
2015	TEN	7/4	271	166	101	60.8%	935	4	7/9	4	7.8%	4.6	--	-46.4%	--	-408	--	-486	9	8	1	7.9%	4	13.6
2016	SD			596	368	61.7%	3772	15	20	7		5.1		-21.4%					21	35	1	-5.7%		

2014:	50% Short	29% Mid	16% Deep	5% Bomb	YAC: 6.2 (–)	ALEX: -1.5	2015:	57% Short	27% Mid	9% Deep	7% Bomb	YAC: 4.1 (–)	ALEX: -1.8

In two years, Mettenberger showed less than Alex "Trick Shot" Tanney showed in one half. Mettenberger is your prototypical tall, big-armed quarterback who isn't good but will keep getting NFL opportunities because of his physical tools. Ken Whisenhunt drafted him in Tennessee, which is why he landed in San Diego where Whisenhunt is now offensive coordinator.

Kellen Moore

Height: 6-0 | Weight: 197 | College: Boise State | Draft: 2012/FA | Born: 12-Jul-1989 | Age: 27 | Risk: Yellow

Year	Team	G/GS	Snaps	Att	Comp	C%	Yds	TD	INT/Adj	FUM	ASR	NY/P	Rk	DVOA	Rk	DYAR	Rk	YAR	Runs	Yds	TD	DVOA	DYAR	QBR
2015	DAL	3/2	167	104	61	58.7%	779	4	6/4	1	5.4%	6.9	--	-9.7%	--	10	--	16	2	-1	0	--	--	19.0
2016	DAL			505	302	59.7%	3708	24	22	7		6.4		-8.1%					26	32	1	-13.9%		

2015: 40% | Short 39% | Mid 18% | Deep 3% | Bomb | YAC: 5.8 (-)

Following three years as a preseason fixture in Detroit, a change of scenery allowed Moore to finally see his first regular-season action. Playing the final two-and-a-half games in Dallas' lost season, the former Boise State star showed what you might expect from a physically limited player without much experience at processing NFL defenses. Like Matt Cassel and Brandon Weeden before him, Moore made plenty of mistakes, tossing six interceptions in his limited time (although one was a downfield almost-Hail Mary with 24 seconds left in a loss, and another was tipped to the defender by Brice Butler). The southpaw appeared especially uncomfortable under center—although he actually posted a positive passing DVOA out of shotgun formations, his -110.2% DVOA in non-shotgun passes was the second-worst among quarterbacks with at least 15 such plays, ahead of only Michael Vick. Considering the Cowboys figure to use more standard power formations with their current offensive personnel, Moore would seem ill-suited to serve as Tony Romo's No. 2. Thus, his tenure as the top backup might only last as long as it takes Dak Prescott to get up to speed.

Matt Moore

Height: 6-3 | Weight: 202 | College: Oregon State | Draft: 2007/FA | Born: 9-Aug-1984 | Age: 32 | Risk: Red

Year	Team	G/GS	Snaps	Att	Comp	C%	Yds	TD	INT/Adj	FUM	ASR	NY/P	Rk	DVOA	Rk	DYAR	Rk	YAR	Runs	Yds	TD	DVOA	DYAR	QBR
2013	MIA	1/0	6	6	2	33.3%	53	0	2/2	1	-2.7%	8.8	--	-120.6%	--	-36	--	-45	0	0	0	--	--	1.3
2014	MIA	2/0	30	4	2	50.0%	21	0	0/0	0	0.0%	5.3	--	28.4%	--	8	--	13	2	-2	0	--	--	72.4
2015	MIA	1/0	7	1	1	100.0%	14	0	0/0	0	-1.2%	14.0	--	340.2%	--	12	--	11	3	-2	0	--	--	98.1
2016	MIA			564	325	57.5%	3441	18	14	15		5.0		-23.8%					31	87	1	-3.6%		

2014: 25% Short | 25% Mid | 0% Deep | 50% Bomb | YAC: 5.0 (-) | ALEX: 8.0 | 2015: 100% Short | 0% Mid | 0% Deep | 0% Bomb | YAC: 9.0 (-) | ALEX: -

The Dolphins re-signed Moore to a two-year contract late in the free-agency period. The Dolphins were seeking a backup who might give Tannehill a little more of a nudge, and Moore was seeking a chance to throw more than 11 passes in three years so he could pursue a sweet, lucrative, Josh McCown-style late career, but a good compromise is one that leaves both parties dissatisfied.

Aaron Murray

Height: 6-1 | Weight: 207 | College: Georgia | Draft: 2014/5 (163) | Born: 10-Nov-1990 | Age: 26 | Risk: Yellow

Year	Team	G/GS	Snaps	Att	Comp	C%	Yds	TD	INT/Adj	FUM	ASR	NY/P	Rk	DVOA	Rk	DYAR	Rk	YAR	Runs	Yds	TD	DVOA	DYAR	QBR
2016	KC			463	283	61.2%	3076	23	16	9		5.9		-11.8%					58	86	1	-12.9%		

Murray posted very good college numbers as a four-year starter at Georgia. His total of 13,166 passing yards was over 2,000 more than anyone else in SEC history. With Chase Daniel now in Philadelphia, Murray currently rates as the most likely option to be Alex Smith's backup. Many scouts that Murray is too small to succeed in the NFL, but otherwise his scouting report reads like Alex Smith Jr. except he's less afraid to throw downfield (though not necessarily better at it). We like him over Tyler Bray, which is why he gets Kansas City's "every team needs a backup quarterback projection" spot. At least he's not the most unlikely quarterback to get a full table and projection; that would be Trevone Boykin.

Ryan Nassib

Height: 6-2 | Weight: 229 | College: Syracuse | Draft: 2013/4 (110) | Born: 10-Mar-1990 | Age: 26 | Risk: Green

Year	Team	G/GS	Snaps	Att	Comp	C%	Yds	TD	INT/Adj	FUM	ASR	NY/P	Rk	DVOA	Rk	DYAR	Rk	YAR	Runs	Yds	TD	DVOA	DYAR	QBR
2014	NYG	4/0	19	5	4	80.0%	60	0	0/0	1	28.0%	6.9	--	-48.7%	--	-18	--	-18	2	-3	0	--	--	29.4
2015	NYG	1/0	6	5	5	100.0%	68	1	0/0	0	0.6%	13.6	--	144.0%	--	65	--	64	0	0	0	--	--	99.3
2016	NYG			560	348	62.0%	3641	22	19	8		5.6		-8.1%					42	129	1	9.5%		

2014: 71% Short | 29% Mid | 0% Deep | 0% Bomb | YAC: 10.8 (-) | ALEX: -2.0 | 2015: 60% Short | 20% Mid | 20% Deep | 0% Bomb | YAC: 5.4 (-) | ALEX: -

We're officially past the point of no return with Nassib's hopes of becoming a useful NFL starter. Since the 1970 merger, 22 quarterbacks drafted in the first four rounds have only attempted 10 or fewer passes in their first three seasons. Literally none of them have developed into pro-level passers, and Brad Smith, the longtime Swiss Army knife for the Jets and Bills, was the only one whose career resulted in noteworthy production. Unless Nassib possesses a hidden penchant for running the Wildcat, he'll remain the questionable insurance policy the Giants hope they never need to actually use.

Cam Newton

						Height: 6-5		Weight: 248		College: Auburn			Draft: 2011/1 (1)		Born: 11-May-1989			Age: 27			Risk: Green
Year	Team	G/GS	Snaps	Att	Comp	C%	Yds	TD	INT/Adj	FUM	ASR	NY/P	Rk	DVOA	Rk	DYAR	Rk	YAR	Runs	Yds	TD	DVOA	DYAR	QBR
2013	CAR	16/16	1015	473	292	61.7%	3379	24	13/18	3	8.2%	5.9	23	1.7%	19	421	17	321	111	585	6	5.7%	102	56.2
2014	CAR	14/14	927	448	262	58.5%	3127	18	12/14	9	8.4%	5.9	30	-14.5%	32	-105	32	-46	103	539	5	16.3%	146	56.9
2015	CAR	16/16	1077	495	296	59.8%	3837	35	10/14	5	6.9%	6.8	11	7.6%	12	630	11	855	132	636	10	8.1%	142	66.0
2016	CAR			493	304	61.6%	3715	29	10	9		6.8		3.7%					117	557	8	19.5%		

2014:	47% Short	35% Mid	10% Deep	7% Bomb	YAC: 4.8 (34)	ALEX: 2.6	2015:	34% Short	42% Mid	12% Deep	11% Bomb	YAC: 5.0 (27)	ALEX: 3.0

One statistic that properly contextualizes how much Newton improved last year are his splits in the shotgun. The Panthers ran about 400 of Newton's 500 passes out of the gun each of the last two seasons. In 2014, Newton had a -17.8% DVOA on those passes. In 2015? 10.2% DVOA.

Regression will hit Newton to some extent next year. It would be quite improbable to see him get a combined 45 touchdowns again. However, his supporting cast should be better this year, with Kelvin Benjamin back and Devin Funchess given an extra year in the program. It's hard to see Newton as anything but one of the best two or three fantasy quarterbacks for next season, and that's even if you project him for 35 touchdowns instead of 45.

Dan Orlovsky

						Height: 6-5		Weight: 230		College: Connecticut			Draft: 2005/5 (145)		Born: 18-Aug-1983			Age: 33			Risk: Green
Year	Team	G/GS	Snaps	Att	Comp	C%	Yds	TD	INT/Adj	FUM	ASR	NY/P	Rk	DVOA	Rk	DYAR	Rk	YAR	Runs	Yds	TD	DVOA	DYAR	QBR
2013	TB	2/0	4	0	0	0.0%	0	0	0/0	0	--	--	--	--	--	--	--	--	0	0	0	--	--	--
2015	DET	2/0	46	40	22	55.0%	201	1	1/1	0	0.8%	5.0	--	0.4%	--	31	--	-1	0	0	0	--	--	50.8
2016	DET			595	328	55.2%	3914	23	18	8		5.3		-14.7%					26	51	0	-9.9%		

							2015: 50%	Short 33%	Mid 14%	Deep 3%	Bomb	YAC: 3.7 (–)

The Lions re-signed Orlovsky in March, then did little to address the quarterback position in the draft. Sixth-rounder Jake Rudock drew heavy criticism in OTAs from coach Jim Caldwell, so Orlovsky's position as Matthew Stafford's unneeded understudy (Stafford hasn't missed a start since 2010) looks safe.

Brock Osweiler

						Height: 6-7		Weight: 242		College: Arizona State			Draft: 2012/2 (57)		Born: 22-Nov-1990			Age: 26			Risk: Green
Year	Team	G/GS	Snaps	Att	Comp	C%	Yds	TD	INT/Adj	FUM	ASR	NY/P	Rk	DVOA	Rk	DYAR	Rk	YAR	Runs	Yds	TD	DVOA	DYAR	QBR
2013	DEN	4/0	51	16	11	68.8%	95	0	0/0	0	11.3%	4.8	--	-8.5%	--	3	--	18	3	2	0	29.9%	3	43.3
2014	DEN	4/0	37	10	4	40.0%	52	1	0/0	0	11.3%	4.2	--	-19.7%	--	-5	--	1	8	0	0	-85.5%	-6	10.2
2015	DEN	8/7	515	275	170	61.8%	1967	10	6/10	4	7.2%	6.1	25	-3.2%	21	153	22	140	21	61	1	-6.1%	6	48.8
2016	HOU			556	330	59.4%	4026	22	16	9		6.1		-10.0%					46	111	2	-3.9%		

2014:	70% Short	10% Mid	20% Deep	0% Bomb	YAC: 7.5 (–)	ALEX: 1.0	2015:	43% Short	38% Mid	11% Deep	8% Bomb	YAC: 5.2 (20)	ALEX: 1.7

Osweiler's QBASE projection is the most pessimistic for any top-100 draft pick in our database, going back to 1996. That comes with several large grains of salt attached since projecting on basic college stats is a noisy endeavor, but there is little in Osweiler's college production to suggest he will live up to his four-year, $72 million contract. That lack of college production should also carry greater weight in Osweiler's case given his small NFL sample. Perhaps reflecting its uncertainty about Osweiler really being the answer, Houston structured his deal so it can easily be changed to two years and $31 million without taking on a lot of dead money.

Carson Palmer

Height: 6-5 Weight: 230 College: USC Draft: 2003/1 (1) Born: 27-Dec-1979 Age: 37 Risk: Green

Year	Team	G/GS	Snaps	Att	Comp	C%	Yds	TD	INT/Adj	FUM	ASR	NY/P	Rk	DVOA	Rk	DYAR	Rk	YAR	Runs	Yds	TD	DVOA	DYAR	QBR
2013	ARI	16/16	1081	572	362	63.3%	4274	24	22/26	6	6.8%	6.5	13	2.7%	17	547	15	361	27	3	0	-30.4%	-3	51.9
2014	ARI	6/6	410	224	141	62.9%	1626	11	3/5	3	4.1%	6.7	15	8.5%	11	285	18	400	8	25	0	-94.8%	-20	64.8
2015	ARI	16/16	1039	537	342	63.7%	4671	35	11/18	6	4.9%	8.1	1	34.4%	1	1698	1	1755	25	24	1	-31.7%	-10	82.2
2016	ARI			547	353	64.5%	4471	31	12	5		7.5		21.3%					31	41	0	-10.8%		

2014:	54% Short	26% Mid	12% Deep	9% Bomb	YAC: 5.3 (21)	ALEX: 2.0	2015:	36% Short	37% Mid	16% Deep	11% Bomb	YAC: 5.1 (22)	ALEX: 4.3

The skepticism over Palmer joining forces with Bruce Arians in 2013 was that Palmer lacked the ability to break tackles or scramble away from pressure à la Ben Roethlisberger or Andrew Luck. When you play in an Arians offense, you are going to face pressure. The early results were poor, as in 2013 Palmer ranked 40th in DVOA while pressured, but ninth when not pressured. Apparently Palmer adapted to this offense, as he was 10th in DVOA under pressure in 2014, and climbed all the way to No. 2 in 2015. Palmer also faced his highest rate of pressure (28.1 percent) since 2010 last season, but still found ways to make plays. He will have to keep doing that because Arians loves vertical routes, which take more time to develop. No offense attacks the first-down marker more than Arizona. Palmer's air need percentage (average pass length divided by average yards to go) was a league-high 142.6 percent in 2015.

Bryce Petty

Height: 6-3 Weight: 230 College: Baylor Draft: 2015/4 (103) Born: 31-May-1991 Age: 25 Risk: Green

Year	Team	G/GS	Snaps	Att	Comp	C%	Yds	TD	INT/Adj	FUM	ASR	NY/P	Rk	DVOA	Rk	DYAR	Rk	YAR	Runs	Yds	TD	DVOA	DYAR	QBR
2016	NYJ			519	293	56.4%	3373	17	18	9		5.3		-20.9%					73	395	4	20.4%		

Petty was so unready last year that he was never even active after Week 4. Maybe Todd Bowles was afraid Petty would walk into the huddle and shout "Ask Madden! Ask Madden!" The Big 12 is the most offense-friendly environment in major 11-on-11 football; its baseball equivalent would be a AAA league where all the teams were in the Alps and had 375-foot power alleys. Baylor typically has the most pass-happy offense in the nation's most pass-friendly conference. Recent drafts suggest that scouts may still be coming to grips with the fact that they are watching some of the biggest, most prestigious programs in America play glorified sandlot football. Petty, like other Big 12 quarterbacks of the last few years, excelled at "run a post pattern past the blue Camry" style of football. There's a chance that skill will never translate to the NFL.

Philip Rivers

Height: 6-5 Weight: 228 College: North Carolina State Draft: 2004/1 (4) Born: 8-Dec-1981 Age: 35 Risk: Yellow

Year	Team	G/GS	Snaps	Att	Comp	C%	Yds	TD	INT/Adj	FUM	ASR	NY/P	Rk	DVOA	Rk	DYAR	Rk	YAR	Runs	Yds	TD	DVOA	DYAR	QBR
2013	SD	16/16	1100	544	378	69.5%	4478	32	11/13	3	5.9%	7.6	4	34.8%	3	1799	2	1884	28	72	0	-17.6%	-5	71.7
2014	SD	16/16	1052	570	379	66.5%	4286	31	18/18	8	6.0%	6.8	12	12.6%	9	918	9	803	37	102	0	-10.0%	3	66.8
2015	SD	16/16	1153	661	437	66.1%	4792	29	13/16	4	5.5%	6.4	15	7.8%	11	847	8	780	17	28	0	-9.8%	1	59.4
2016	SD			614	406	66.1%	4628	29	11	5		6.6		11.9%					30	42	0	-9.4%		

2014:	55% Short	27% Mid	10% Deep	8% Bomb	YAC: 5.1 (25)	ALEX: 1.9	2015:	56% Short	29% Mid	9% Deep	6% Bomb	YAC: 6 (7)	ALEX: 0.6

Only 15 percent of Rivers' passes travelled further than 16 yards downfield in 2015. That's a number the Chargers need to correct in 2016. For as good as Rivers is as a short and intermediate passer, the passing game as a whole needs to be opened up for the San Diego offense to reach its full potential. Rivers' arm showed signs of decline towards the end of last season, but his intelligence and precision should allow him to remain effective into the latter stages of his career. Developing a relationship with Travis Benjamin quickly will be crucial for Rivers' ability to create big plays downfield.

Aaron Rodgers

Height: 6-2 Weight: 223 College: California Draft: 2005/1 (24) Born: 2-Dec-1983 Age: 33 Risk: Yellow

Year	Team	G/GS	Snaps	Att	Comp	C%	Yds	TD	INT/Adj	FUM	ASR	NY/P	Rk	DVOA	Rk	DYAR	Rk	YAR	Runs	Yds	TD	DVOA	DYAR	QBR
2013	GB	9/9	582	290	193	66.6%	2536	17	6/5	4	7.6%	7.8	3	25.4%	6	740	10	762	30	120	0	6.8%	23	68.7
2014	GB	16/16	983	520	341	65.6%	4381	38	5/7	10	5.3%	7.6	2	32.2%	1	1564	2	1581	43	269	2	54.4%	104	82.6
2015	GB	16/16	1138	572	347	60.7%	3821	31	8/11	8	7.3%	5.7	32	-1.0%	17	406	17	258	58	344	1	37.1%	107	64.9
2016	GB			546	359	65.8%	4269	35	9	9		7.1		19.8%					66	272	1	9.4%		

2014:	54% Short	29% Mid	13% Deep	5% Bomb	YAC: 6.0 (6)	ALEX: 4.2	2015:	50% Short	30% Mid	11% Deep	8% Bomb	YAC: 5.6 (11)	ALEX: 3.5

Well, that sucked. In his first seven seasons as a starter, Rodgers' passing DVOA never dipped below 8.5%, and it had not gone lower than 23.4% since 2009. And he looked better than ever at the start of 2015, until eventually defenses realized that the Green Bay offense was very different without Jordy Nelson, and they had little to fear from the Randall Cobbs and Davante Adams of the world. Rodgers and the Packers seemed to get worse by the game, and by the end of the year he was statistically one of the worst quarterbacks in the league.

Aaron Rodgers' DVOA Throughout 2015

Games	DVOA	Rank
1-4	51.2%	2
5-8	-0.1%	16
9-12	-11.8%	24
13-17	-30.0%	27

There is ample evidence, though, that the problems had more to do with Rodgers' teammates than with the quarterback himself. We mentioned in the Green Bay chapter that Cobb and Adams often failed to make plays with the ball in their hands. They also had trouble getting the ball in their hands in the first place—both were among the top 10 wide receivers in drops, and Adams in particular had trouble even getting open. On top of all that (or maybe because of that), Rodgers was under more pressure than ever before. From 2010 to 2014, Rodgers was never pressured on more than 22 percent of his dropbacks, and never ranked higher than 20th in this category. In 2015, he was seventh with a pressure rate of 30 percent.

Viewers of *The Bachelorette* learned this summer that Jordan Rodgers, a former NFL quarterback himself and now a contestant on the show, is no longer speaking with his brother Aaron. Fans in Green Bay couldn't care less—they're far more interested in seeing Rodgers reunite with Jordy than with Jordan.

Ben Roethlisberger

Height: 6-5   Weight: 240   College: Miami (Ohio)   Draft: 2004/1 (11)   Born: 2-Mar-1982   Age: 34   Risk: Yellow

Year	Team	G/GS	Snaps	Att	Comp	C%	Yds	TD	INT/Adj	FUM	ASR	NY/P	Rk	DVOA	Rk	DYAR	Rk	YAR	Runs	Yds	TD	DVOA	DYAR	QBR
2013	PIT	16/16	1051	584	375	64.2%	4261	28	14/15	9	7.2%	6.4	15	6.6%	12	724	11	764	27	99	1	-41.5%	-26	54.3
2014	PIT	16/16	1104	608	408	67.1%	4952	32	9/14	8	5.8%	7.6	3	26.8%	3	1572	1	1505	33	27	0	-50.8%	-34	72.5
2015	PIT	12/11	794	469	319	68.0%	3938	21	16/18	1	4.3%	7.8	2	22.1%	4	1114	5	1056	15	29	0	-0.2%	4	76.9
2016	PIT			574	378	65.9%	4668	31	11	4		7.4		24.6%					28	45	0	-4.4%		

2014:	50% Short	31% Mid	11% Deep	8% Bomb	YAC: 5.6 (14)	ALEX: 2.3	2015:	44% Short	31% Mid	12% Deep	13% Bomb	YAC: 4.6 (33)	ALEX: 7.1

Since 2004, 13 different quarterbacks have received at least one vote for the NFL's MVP award. Ben Roethlisberger has not been one of them. He looks as poised as ever to be in that discussion this year, until you see people already picking Antonio Brown for the quarterback-heavy award.

Part of Roethlisberger's problem is health, as he has only started all 16 games in three of his 12 seasons. He somehow survived three trips to the injury cart last year without a season-ending injury, but did miss four full games and the start of a fifth. However, the games he has missed over the years have allowed Roethlisberger to show his value as much as any quarterback in the league. When he's out of the lineup, Pittsburgh's passing game becomes an afterthought. Ignoring the Cleveland game last year when Roethlisberger replaced an injured Landry Jones in the first seven minutes, the Steelers have started 22 games without Roethlisberger since 2004. They have won 12 of those 22 games, and Pittsburgh's replacement starters have passed for 3,507 yards, 16 touchdowns, 23 interceptions and a 68.6 passer rating. Only Charlie Batch, against the 2012 Ravens, was able to pass for at least 240 yards in a game. Roethlisberger averages 251.4 passing yards per game in his career, and that number has gone up to 283.0 since 2009. Roethlisberger's 2015 average of 328.2 passing yards per game was the third-highest season in NFL history.

It may not help that Roethlisberger still has the reputation for being "Backyard Ben," improvising and taking a punishment instead of beating defenses with his mind and precision passing. Yet in 2015, only Andy Dalton was pressured less often than Roethlisberger, who led the NFL with the highest rate of passes (94.7 percent) thrown from inside the pocket. Roethlisberger has had many better seasons than 2015 in terms of throwing touchdowns and interceptions, but he may have been at his most accurate and physical best throwing the ball last year with a career-high passing plus-minus of plus-26.2. With Peyton Manning retired and Tom Brady suspended for September, 2016 is a prime opportunity for Roethlisberger to shine in the spotlight as one of the best quarterbacks in the NFL.

Tony Romo Height: 6-2 Weight: 219 College: Eastern Illinois Draft: 2003/FA Born: 21-Apr-1980 Age: 36 Risk: Red

Year	Team	G/GS	Snaps	Att	Comp	C%	Yds	TD	INT/Adj	FUM	ASR	NY/P	Rk	DVOA	Rk	DYAR	Rk	YAR	Runs	Yds	TD	DVOA	DYAR	QBR
2013	DAL	15/15	919	535	342	63.9%	3828	31	10/10	4	6.7%	6.3	17	11.5%	10	839	7	898	20	38	0	44.3%	17	59.5
2014	DAL	15/15	971	435	304	69.9%	3705	34	9/12	7	6.3%	7.5	5	27.6%	2	1187	5	1266	26	61	0	50.9%	23	82.8
2015	DAL	4/4	233	121	83	68.6%	884	5	7/7	1	6.2%	6.7	--	-22.4%	--	-93	--	-65	4	13	0	-21.7%	-2	55.8
2016	DAL			502	332	66.1%	3897	29	12	4		6.9		16.1%					25	50	0	-3.3%		

2014:	48% Short	33% Mid	11% Deep	8% Bomb	YAC: 5.4 (19)	ALEX: 2.8	2015:	53% Short	34% Mid	8% Deep	6% Bomb	YAC: 5.1 (–)	ALEX: 1.5

If there's an upside to Romo's lost 2015 season, it's that Cowboys fans have seen him rebound from this exact same injury before. When a broken collarbone limited Romo to just six games in 2010, he came back and finished among the five best quarterbacks in the league in DVOA, DYAR, and QBR in 2011. At the very least, Romo should strive to recapture the ball security he showed during his 2011 comeback campaign, when he posted a career-low 1.9 percent interception rate. That figure soared over the four games he played in 2015, as his 5.8 percent interception rate was more than double his career rate to date. Still, the optimist can preach about small sample sizes, while also pointing out Romo's 34-to-9 touchdown-to-interception ratio from 2014, second-best in the league that year. If Dallas has its way, Romo will return to that comfort zone from 2014 when he attempted his fewest passes in any season as a healthy full-time starter, yet also put up the second-best DVOA of his career. Then again, the best laid plans of Jerry Jones often go awry. Ezekiel Elliott and the Cowboys' estimable offensive line might make plenty of sweet music, but the burden of making the highest leverage plays will remain squarely on Romo's surgically repaired shoulder. As Peyton Manning can attest, aging quarterbacks with metal plates in their bodies don't always age so gracefully. Entering his age-36 season, Romo not only faces the familiar challenge of battling his playoff demons, but also his own body.

Matt Ryan Height: 6-4 Weight: 228 College: Boston College Draft: 2008/1 (3) Born: 17-May-1985 Age: 31 Risk: Yellow

Year	Team	G/GS	Snaps	Att	Comp	C%	Yds	TD	INT/Adj	FUM	ASR	NY/P	Rk	DVOA	Rk	DYAR	Rk	YAR	Runs	Yds	TD	DVOA	DYAR	QBR
2013	ATL	16/16	1065	651	439	67.4%	4515	26	17/16	5	5.9%	6.1	19	13.3%	9	1124	4	825	17	55	0	54.5%	23	61.1
2014	ATL	16/16	1064	628	415	66.1%	4694	28	14/18	5	5.1%	6.9	9	14.9%	8	1101	7	1072	29	145	0	4.8%	23	67.0
2015	ATL	16/16	1116	614	407	66.3%	4591	21	16/20	13	5.2%	6.8	10	-1.9%	18	389	19	669	36	63	0	-9.6%	3	61.8
2016	ATL			612	389	63.6%	4486	25	13	6		6.4		4.4%					37	106	0	0.9%		

2014:	57% Short	25% Mid	14% Deep	4% Bomb	YAC: 5.0 (27)	ALEX: 2.1	2015:	47% Short	39% Mid	10% Deep	4% Bomb	YAC: 4.5 (34)	ALEX: 0.6

How big of an outlier was Ryan's 2015 season? The quarterback had never had a DVOA lower than 12.4% in a season before, and only once had he put up less than 1,000 DYAR (he had 702 in 2009). The standard stats don't really look much different from previous years, except for the touchdown and fumble totals, but DVOA sees just how easy Ryan's schedule was. Half his games came against teams ranked 24th or lower in pass defense DVOA. Ryan was uncharacteristically sloppy last season, and also suffered from a lack of targets not named Julio Jones. Mohammed Sanu is Atlanta's attempt to solve one of those issues—he should help, even if he doesn't play like prime Roddy White—and the turnovers could be mitigated by a second year in Kyle Shanahan's offense.

Of course, the real cause for concern for Ryan is that non-elite quarterbacks do tend to crash and burn pretty quickly when they lose a step. At 31, Matt Schaub was a mostly-efficient quarterback you could win with. At 32, he was a pick-six slot machine. Jake Delhomme went from a Pro Bowl quarterback to a playoff arsonist before he even turned 34. Ryan has more pedigree and is a better quarterback than those two ever were. He's also not even to his mid-thirties yet. But the end can sneak up on you, and there's a non-zero chance that last year's Ryan is the new normal.

Mark Sanchez Height: 6-2 Weight: 227 College: USC Draft: 2009/1 (5) Born: 11-Nov-1986 Age: 30 Risk: Red

Year	Team	G/GS	Snaps	Att	Comp	C%	Yds	TD	INT/Adj	FUM	ASR	NY/P	Rk	DVOA	Rk	DYAR	Rk	YAR	Runs	Yds	TD	DVOA	DYAR	QBR
2014	PHI	9/8	625	309	198	64.1%	2418	14	11/11	7	7.2%	6.8	11	-1.4%	22	210	23	255	34	87	1	-25.9%	-15	58.2
2015	PHI	4/2	169	91	59	64.8%	616	4	4/4	1	8.5%	5.6	--	-46.9%	--	-227	--	-154	6	22	0	20.9%	7	38.9
2016	DEN			562	341	60.6%	3845	21	17	11		5.8		-12.1%					32	64	1	-16.3%		

2014:	52% Short	33% Mid	12% Deep	4% Bomb	YAC: 5.7 (9)	ALEX: 0.8	2015:	54% Short	33% Mid	12% Deep	1% Bomb	YAC: 5.4 (–)	ALEX: -2.0

Despite the Eagles' collapse down the homestretch of the 2014 season, Chip Kelly had evidently seen enough in Sanchez to entrust him with the backup quarterback job for 2015. Though not as brazen as his other personnel decisions, sticking with Sanchez ended up being another turn on the roulette wheel that went against Kelly. Sanchez commandeered the Eagles' most disastrous stretch, a three-game fiasco in which they blew a 13-point lead at home to Miami, then lost by a combined score of 90-31 over four days against Tampa Bay and Detroit. In the process, Sanchez accrued an abysmal minus-227 DYAR over just 100 passes. So logically, he now holds the inside track to become the Week 1 starter for the defending Super Bowl champions. The partnership between Sanchez and the Broncos feels a bit like two people who need a date to senior prom and accidentally make eye contact from adjacent lunch tables. Denver will eventually ditch Sanchez to dance with Paxton Lynch, but the eighth-year pro will at least get to ride in the limo with his date. Sanchez's turnover-prone game is really the last thing the Broncos need. For all of their faults, Brock Osweiler and post-injury Peyton Manning managed to avoid giving the ball away down the stretch. History suggests that Sanchez, who has yet to post a positive passing DVOA in any season, won't be nearly as successful in staying out of the defense's way.

Matt Schaub

Height: 6-5 Weight: 235 College: Virginia Draft: 2004/3 (90) Born: 25-Jun-1981 Age: 35 Risk: Red

Year	Team	G/GS	Snaps	Att	Comp	C%	Yds	TD	INT/Adj	FUM	ASR	NY/P	Rk	DVOA	Rk	DYAR	Rk	YAR	Runs	Yds	TD	DVOA	DYAR	QBR
2013	HOU	10/8	610	358	219	61.2%	2310	10	14/19	2	6.1%	5.7	31	-16.2%	32	-123	32	-115	5	24	0	52.6%	9	37.3
2014	OAK	11/0	19	10	5	50.0%	57	0	2/3	2	22.9%	2.2	--	-220.7%	--	-158	--	-158	0	0	0	--	--	0.1
2015	BAL	2/2	137	80	52	65.0%	540	3	4/4	0	4.8%	6.2	--	-38.4%	--	-146	--	-71	4	10	0	-76.1%	-17	34.3
2016	ATL			609	395	64.9%	4260	22	15	7		6.1		-2.7%					29	46	0	-16.2%		

2014: 64% Short   27% Mid   9% Deep   0% Bomb   YAC: 4.8 (–)   ALEX: -10.0   2015:   46% Short   33% Mid   14% Deep   7% Bomb   YAC: 4.1 (–)   ALEX: -0.1

Remember the Bill Murray suicide montage in *Groundhog Day*? Ever since 2013, Matt Schaub has been experiencing that in quarterback form. He wakes up, goes to the stadium, and promptly throws a pick-six. Schaub managed to throw a pick-six in both of his starts for the Ravens last year. The one in Miami was worth minus-79 DYAR, the single least valuable pass in 2015. Schaub has returned to where his NFL career began in Atlanta, but should he see the field there, chances are we'll see another pick-six.

Trevor Siemian

Height: 6-3 Weight: 220 College: Northwestern Draft: 2015/7 (250) Born: 26-Dec-1991 Age: 25 Risk: Red

Year	Team	G/GS	Snaps	Att	Comp	C%	Yds	TD	INT/Adj	FUM	ASR	NY/P	Rk	DVOA	Rk	DYAR	Rk	YAR	Runs	Yds	TD	DVOA	DYAR	QBR
2015	DEN	1/0	1	0	0	0.0%	0	0	0/0	0	--	--	--	--	--	--	--	--	1	-1	0	--	--	--
2016	DEN			548	324	59.2%	3516	18	19	10		5.3		-19.4%					24	36	1	-12.5%		

Siemian's last college season was his worst statistically. He has impressed with his oodles of arm talent, but that strong arm couldn't stop him from averaging 5.6 yards per attempt with seven touchdowns and 11 interceptions in a difficult situation at Northwestern. Some have suggested that Siemian could challenge for the starting job in Denver, which would shatter any logical concept of what college production means for quarterbacks.

Alex Smith

Height: 6-4 Weight: 212 College: Utah Draft: 2005/1 (1) Born: 7-May-1984 Age: 32 Risk: Green

Year	Team	G/GS	Snaps	Att	Comp	C%	Yds	TD	INT/Adj	FUM	ASR	NY/P	Rk	DVOA	Rk	DYAR	Rk	YAR	Runs	Yds	TD	DVOA	DYAR	QBR
2013	KC	15/15	978	508	308	60.6%	3313	23	7/11	7	7.9%	5.7	29	-3.7%	21	262	20	416	76	431	1	18.7%	96	49.4
2014	KC	15/15	940	464	303	65.3%	3265	18	6/6	4	9.1%	5.9	28	4.1%	18	493	14	527	49	254	1	8.5%	38	49.4
2015	KC	16/16	989	470	307	65.3%	3486	20	7/11	4	8.6%	6.3	19	3.0%	15	468	15	359	84	498	2	11.5%	86	66.5
2016	KC			493	322	65.4%	3510	21	9	6		6.2		1.4%					65	317	2	21.2%		

2014: 62% Short   27% Mid   8% Deep   3% Bomb   YAC: 6.1 (5)   ALEX: -2.4   2015:   49% Short   36% Mid   9% Deep   6% Bomb   YAC: 6.3 (1)   ALEX: -3.4

In 2015, Smith was remarkably more successful throwing in the middle of the field than to the sidelines. Consider these directional splits for Smith:

Alex Smith By Throwing Direction, 2015

	Left	Middle	Right
Deep	41.7%	172.7%	-3.9%
Short	20.5%	68.5%	-1.5%
Overall	23.6%	87.0%	-1.8%

The rest of the league is also better down the middle than to the sidelines, but not nearly so starkly as Smith and the Chiefs. The rest of the league is not too far off to the left (17.9% DVOA) or the right (10.3%), but is much less efficient on throws to the middle of the field (39.8%). Smith's propensity for taking sacks accounts for the Chiefs only having average passing efficiency despite Smith's efficiency both in the short middle and his 19 throws to the deep middle.

Geno Smith Height: 6-3 Weight: 208 College: West Virginia Draft: 2013/2 (39) Born: 10-Oct-1990 Age: 26 Risk: Yellow

Year	Team	G/GS	Snaps	Att	Comp	C%	Yds	TD	INT/Adj	FUM	ASR	NY/P	Rk	DVOA	Rk	DYAR	Rk	YAR	Runs	Yds	TD	DVOA	DYAR	QBR
2013	NYJ	16/16	985	443	247	55.8%	3046	12	21/26	8	8.3%	5.6	32	-23.6%	37	-371	38	-434	72	366	6	9.5%	65	35.9
2014	NYJ	14/13	816	367	219	59.7%	2525	13	13/15	8	7.5%	6.0	27	-12.5%	30	-33	30	-21	59	238	1	-34.3%	-65	35.4
2015	NYJ	1/0	65	42	27	64.3%	265	2	1/1	0	7.5%	5.5	--	11.0%	--	72	--	83	2	34	0	168.6%	14	66.2
2016	NYJ			580	352	60.7%	3907	26	20	10		5.9		-11.9%					62	259	2	6.7%		

2014:	55% Short	29% Mid	11% Deep	6% Bomb	YAC: 5.5 (15)	ALEX: 3.2	2015:	37% Short	47% Mid	7% Deep	9% Bomb	YAC: 3.3 (–)	ALEX: 3.7

Smith replaced Ryan Fitzpatrick after a hand injury against the Raiders in Week 8, and on his first few series he looked like he hadn't thrown a football since middle school. Smith threw an interception and a variety of off-speed, off-kilter passes, finally getting some rhythm when the Raiders held a 28-6 lead and were getting generous on short underneath completions. Smith left the game late in the fourth quarter after a big hit by Marcus Smith, forcing Fitzpatrick to re-enter the lineup. If Smith plans to prove all the doubters and rabble-rousers wrong, he'd better get busy soon.

Matthew Stafford Height: 6-2 Weight: 225 College: Georgia Draft: 2009/1 (1) Born: 7-Feb-1988 Age: 28 Risk: Yellow

Year	Team	G/GS	Snaps	Att	Comp	C%	Yds	TD	INT/Adj	FUM	ASR	NY/P	Rk	DVOA	Rk	DYAR	Rk	YAR	Runs	Yds	TD	DVOA	DYAR	QBR
2013	DET	16/16	1125	634	371	58.5%	4650	29	19/27	12	4.5%	6.9	9	4.9%	15	690	12	838	37	69	2	-40.3%	-41	52.5
2014	DET	16/16	1093	602	363	60.3%	4257	22	12/15	8	7.0%	6.2	22	-0.7%	20	423	15	544	43	93	2	-15.4%	-4	55.1
2015	DET	16/16	1033	592	398	67.2%	4262	32	13/14	4	7.3%	6.3	20	8.0%	10	804	9	637	44	159	1	11.4%	35	62.6
2016	DET			605	402	66.5%	4342	29	14	5		6.1		3.4%					46	111	2	0.7%		

2014:	56% Short	28% Mid	10% Deep	6% Bomb	YAC: 6.1 (4)	ALEX: 2.3	2015:	56% Short	30% Mid	10% Deep	5% Bomb	YAC: 6.1 (5)	ALEX: -0.4

Stafford has been around the league so long that it's easy to forget how young he is. The first pick of the 2009 draft was born in 1988—the same year as 2012 draftees Russell Wilson, Kirk Cousins, and Ryan Tannehill. So even with seven NFL seasons under his belt, it's doubtful that Stafford has reached his peak yet. Stafford's completion percentage last year was a career high—he became the first quarterback in NFL history to complete at least 60 percent of his passes in each game of a 16-game season—and he finished in the top ten of DVOA for just the second time. Stafford's red zone DVOA of 61.2% was the best of any full-time starter last year, but that speaks more to the yo-yo nature of that stat than any particular talent the quarterback has near the goal line. Stafford's red zone DVOA in 2014 was -31.5%, and in 2013, it was 33.4%. So anything is on the table concerning his performance in 2016.

Drew Stanton Height: 6-3 Weight: 230 College: Michigan State Draft: 2007/2 (43) Born: 7-May-1984 Age: 32 Risk: Green

Year	Team	G/GS	Snaps	Att	Comp	C%	Yds	TD	INT/Adj	FUM	ASR	NY/P	Rk	DVOA	Rk	DYAR	Rk	YAR	Runs	Yds	TD	DVOA	DYAR	QBR
2014	ARI	9/8	469	240	132	55.0%	1711	7	5/13	1	4.3%	6.5	20	4.2%	16	238	20	185	25	63	0	36.2%	27	58.0
2015	ARI	7/0	65	25	11	44.0%	104	0	2/2	0	7.2%	3.6	--	-57.4%	--	-82	--	-99	13	-13	0	--	--	12.3
2016	ARI			543	312	57.5%	3788	25	14	5		6.1		-2.3%					49	100	0	-13.3%		

2014:	42% Short	35% Mid	14% Deep	10% Bomb	YAC: 4.9 (29)	ALEX: 4.1	2015:	32% Short	48% Mid	4% Deep	16% Bomb	YAC: 2.4 (–)	ALEX: 6.2

Stanton's claim to fame in 2015 was celebrating on the sideline with the joy of a little kid when the Cardinals scored a touchdown in Seattle in prime time. The 32-year-old backup fits Bruce Arians' offense well, meaning he'll hold the ball until the last possible second before throwing downfield. Since 2012, Stanton has taken 40 hits and 12 sacks, a 3.33-to-1 ratio that ranks second in the NFL and fits in with other recent Arians quarterbacks such as Andrew Luck (2.90) and Carson Palmer (2.24). There have been some rumblings that Stanton could be the future starter after Palmer eventually retires, but at this point, the best thing to say about Stanton is that he's not Ryan Lindley.

Ryan Tannehill

Height: 6-4   Weight: 221   College: Texas A&M   Draft: 2012/1 (8)   Born: 27-Jul-1988   Age: 28   Risk: Red

Year	Team	G/GS	Snaps	Att	Comp	C%	Yds	TD	INT/Adj	FUM	ASR	NY/P	Rk	DVOA	Rk	DYAR	Rk	YAR	Runs	Yds	TD	DVOA	DYAR	QBR
2013	MIA	16/16	1020	588	355	60.4%	3913	24	17/26	9	8.7%	5.5	36	-9.8%	26	54	26	22	40	238	1	19.0%	46	45.8
2014	MIA	16/16	1065	590	392	66.4%	4045	27	12/15	8	7.0%	5.8	33	4.1%	17	630	12	566	56	311	1	11.4%	51	59.1
2015	MIA	16/16	1026	586	363	61.9%	4208	24	12/15	10	7.6%	6.1	28	-10.6%	27	20	26	67	32	141	1	36.5%	49	43.2
2016	MIA			588	369	62.8%	4162	27	13	5		5.9		-4.8%					42	173	1	7.1%		

2014:	55% Short	30% Mid	10% Deep	4% Bomb	YAC: 4.8 (32)	ALEX: 1.2	2015:	45% Short	34% Mid	12% Deep	9% Bomb	YAC: 5.1 (24)	ALEX: 1.6

Tannehill's stat lines from last year verge on statistical gibberish. Coaching staffs changed monthly, philosophies almost weekly. Tannehill threw 58 passes in Week 11 and 19 passes in Week 12. He followed exceptional games (18-of-19, 282 yards, four touchdowns in a blowout over the Texans in Week 7) with miserable ones (two interceptions in a 36-7 loss to the Patriots in Week 8). Every stat line comes with a bushel of asterisks. Who was the head coach at that point? The offensive coordinator? Were the decision makers pro-Tannehill or anti-Tannehill? Was the team motivated or not that particular week?

It has been that way for four years, really. The 2013 data is polluted by 58 sacks and the Bullygate fiasco. The 2014 data is quieter—it's also Tannehill's best statistical season—though you have to wonder what it would look like without 115 passes launched into the vicinity of a not-totally-engaged Mike Wallace.

There's at least one Tannehill fiction that the 2015 numbers can lay to rest: Tannehill was a respectable 28-of-84 for 951 yards, five touchdowns, and one interception last season on passes of 20-plus yards. Tannehill can, in fact, throw deep when given permission and a set of motivated and reliable wide receivers. Data snapshots of the past show Tannehill able to complete short passes efficiently, run well, and do other things that franchise quarterbacks do. Maybe Adam Gase is the coach who can put all the pieces of Tannehill together into a complete quarterback. There's also a chance that Gase will be the one coping with the consequences when everything falls apart.

Tyrod Taylor

Height: 6-1   Weight: 216   College: Virginia Tech   Draft: 2011/6 (180)   Born: 3-Aug-1989   Age: 27   Risk: Yellow

Year	Team	G/GS	Snaps	Att	Comp	C%	Yds	TD	INT/Adj	FUM	ASR	NY/P	Rk	DVOA	Rk	DYAR	Rk	YAR	Runs	Yds	TD	DVOA	DYAR	QBR
2013	BAL	3/0	21	5	1	20.0%	2	0	1/2	0	0.4%	0.4	--	-236.3%	--	-75	--	-75	8	64	0	26.2%	15	44.8
2014	BAL	1/0	6	0	0	0.0%	0	0	0/0	0	--	--	--	--	--	--	--	--	4	-3	0	--	--	--
2015	BUF	14/14	923	380	242	63.7%	3035	20	6/11	8	8.5%	6.8	12	9.8%	8	536	14	486	104	568	4	19.8%	133	67.8
2016	BUF			459	287	62.6%	3575	23	11	6		7.0		-0.3%					100	516	5	12.3%		

												2015: 45%	Short 29%	Mid 10%	Deep 15%	Bomb	YAC: 4.7 (32)

Taylor's greatest weakness right now is his tendency to run at the first whisper of pass pressure. He scrambled 50 times last year, meaning that scrambles and sacks accounted for 18 percent of his dropbacks, and that's before throws on the run are factored in. Taylor's DVOA under pressure was a respectable -43.6%, which ranked eighth in the NFL—keep in mind that DVOA under pressure is always dreadful—but his inability/unwillingness to stand in the pocket and scan the field hurts his efficiency as a passer when teams know he must pass. Taylor's completion rate dropped to 55.0 percent when the Bills trailed by 9 to 16 points, and 56.6 percent (with four interceptions and five sacks in 53 pass attempts) in the last two minutes of halves. Taylor needed the running threat (both his own and his team's) to be effective as a passer last season.

Bills general manager Doug Whaley said in January that Taylor did enough in 2015 to "continue down the road to see if he can be the franchise guy of the future." If you ever see that written on one of your performance evaluations, dear reader, update your résumé immediately. The Bills were whispered to be in the quarterback market throughout free agency and declined to reopen Taylor's super-affordable little contract, which runs through 2017. The team eventually drafted Cardale Jones in the fourth round. None of these were terrible decisions, mind you, but it's the kind of lukewarm appreciation a player remembers after another Pro Bowl season or two.

Scott Tolzien

Height: 6-3   Weight: 205   College: Wisconsin   Draft: 2011/FA   Born: 9-Jan-1987   Age: 29   Risk: Green

Year	Team	G/GS	Snaps	Att	Comp	C%	Yds	TD	INT/Adj	FUM	ASR	NY/P	Rk	DVOA	Rk	DYAR	Rk	YAR	Runs	Yds	TD	DVOA	DYAR	QBR
2013	GB	3/2	158	90	55	61.1%	717	1	5/8	0	4.2%	7.6	--	-9.1%	--	13	--	19	5	55	1	117.5%	33	24.3
2015	GB	3/0	10	1	1	100.0%	4	0	0/0	1	48.3%	-2.0	--	-321.5%	--	-14	--	-17	3	-3	0	-224.2%	-16	0.2
2016	IND			607	363	59.8%	4065	17	27	11		5.3		-29.1%					30	85	1	-2.8%		

												2015: 100%	Short 0%	Mid 0%	Deep 0%	Bomb	YAC: 0.0 (–)

Tolzien was clearly outplayed by Brett Hundley in the 2015 preseason, and the Packers didn't much mind when the Colts offered him a two-year deal in free agency. Indianapolis released Josh Freeman and Ryan Lindley, so Tolzien will have little competition for the backup role behind Andrew Luck. It's not clear why the Colts preferred Tolzien to Freeman, who threw as many touchdowns in his Week 17 start last season as Tolzien has in his five-year NFL career, but it's their team, not ours.

Michael Vick

Height: 6-0   Weight: 215   College: Virginia Tech   Draft: 2001/1 (1)   Born: 26-Jun-1980   Age: 36   Risk: N/A

Year	Team	G/GS	Snaps	Att	Comp	C%	Yds	TD	INT/Adj	FUM	ASR	NY/P	Rk	DVOA	Rk	DYAR	Rk	YAR	Runs	Yds	TD	DVOA	DYAR	QBR
2013	PHI	7/6	325	141	77	54.6%	1215	5	3/3	4	10.5%	7.2	--	-6.9%	--	40	--	49	36	306	2	70.0%	128	58.8
2014	NYJ	10/3	272	121	64	52.9%	604	3	2/5	5	13.5%	3.6	--	-36.8%	--	-228	--	-273	26	153	0	-8.9%	3	22.2
2015	PIT	5/3	172	66	40	60.6%	371	2	1/1	2	13.2%	4.3	--	-57.4%	--	-207	--	-184	20	99	0	12.1%	15	31.8

2014:	63% Short	24% Mid	3% Deep	10% Bomb	YAC: 3.9 (--)	ALEX: 0.2	2015:	52% Short	23% Mid	16% Deep	10% Bomb	YAC: 4.8 (--)	ALEX: 0.5

Vick showed he could still run in three unexpected starts for the Steelers, but he also reminded us of the long overthrows, the missed reads, and the inability to stay healthy. If Vick's final game in the NFL ends up being the win he started against Arizona, the stat line is pretty fitting: 3-of-8 passing for 6 yards, with five runs for 47 yards.

Brandon Weeden

Height: 6-4   Weight: 221   College: Oklahoma State   Draft: 2012/1 (22)   Born: 14-Oct-1983   Age: 33   Risk: Red

Year	Team	G/GS	Snaps	Att	Comp	C%	Yds	TD	INT/Adj	FUM	ASR	NY/P	Rk	DVOA	Rk	DYAR	Rk	YAR	Runs	Yds	TD	DVOA	DYAR	QBR
2013	CLE	8/5	452	267	141	52.8%	1731	9	9/11	6	9.7%	5.3	39	-36.1%	40	-443	40	-429	12	44	0	12.4%	11	24.7
2014	DAL	5/1	89	41	24	58.5%	303	3	2/2	1	3.2%	7.0	--	-3.5%	--	21	--	25	6	-1	0	-158.1%	-26	15.4
2015	2TM	6/4	313	140	97	69.3%	1043	5	2/4	2	7.0%	6.5	--	3.8%	--	139	--	209	16	47	1	49.8%	27	66.2
2016	HOU		532	339		63.7%	3243	16	15	9		4.8		-25.3%					27	95	1	5.9%		

2014:	42% Short	44% Mid	5% Deep	9% Bomb	YAC: 6.7 (--)	ALEX: 2.3	2015:	50% Short	34% Mid	13% Deep	3% Bomb	YAC: 5.0 (--)	ALEX: -1.1

Weeden helping a team win its division may have been 2015's most surprising storyline, especially after the Cowboys released him in October. His main problem in Dallas was too many short passes—he completed 26 against the Patriots for just 188 yards. In December, he came off the bench at halftime to lead the Texans to a comeback and their first ever win in Indianapolis. He was much more efficient in Houston, posting a DVOA of 32.2% compared to -10.1% in Dallas, and his average pass traveled 9.4 yards in the air instead of 6.7. That was enough to earn him a shot at the backup gig behind Brock Osweiler, though Tom Savage may yet challenge him in his return from the shoulder injury that cost him all of 2015.

Carson Wentz

Height: 6-5   Weight: 237   College: North Dakota State   Draft: 2016/1 (2)   Born: 30-Dec-1992   Age: 24   Risk: Red

Year	Team	G/GS	Snaps	Att	Comp	C%	Yds	TD	INT/Adj	FUM	ASR	NY/P	Rk	DVOA	Rk	DYAR	Rk	YAR	Runs	Yds	TD	DVOA	DYAR	QBR
2016	PHI		534	342		64.2%	3614	21	17	9		5.9		-7.5%					64	281	2	14.2%		

What's the most you've ever lost on a coin toss? For Howie Roseman, the answer will be his career as a general manager if Wentz doesn't pan out. Even the highest drafted quarterbacks tend to be 50-50 propositions to develop into above-average long-term starters. And given that the Eagles traded five draft picks, the Liberty Bell, and a lifetime's supply of cheesesteaks to select Wentz, the North Dakota State product needs to become even more than above-average for the deal to pan out. Evaluating any quarterback prospect requires lots of extrapolation, but Wentz's level of competition adds an additional layer of guessing. Over the course of his collegiate career, he posted superior numbers to Joe Flacco, the current NFL comparison most often made given their similar builds and FCS backgrounds. Flacco averaged 7.2 yards per attempt and had a 41-to-15 touchdown-to-interception ratio at Delaware; Wentz averaged 8.4 yards per pass and had a 45-to-14 ratio. QBASE still isn't particularly optimistic on Wentz, giving him more than a 60 percent chance to be a bust, in large part because of the system's adjustments for opponent strength. The real source of hope lies in the fact that Wentz might possess the best foundation of physical and cerebral tools since Andrew Luck, and that those tools will continue to function when it's Panthers and Packers chasing him instead of Sycamores and Spiders. So long as Wentz can make that jump and placate a notoriously anxious fanbase that has waited 56 years and counting for a football championship, he should be just fine.

Charlie Whitehurst   Height: 6-4   Weight: 220   College: Clemson   Draft: 2006/3 (81)   Born: 6-Aug-1982   Age: 34   Risk: N/A

Year	Team	G/GS	Snaps	Att	Comp	C%	Yds	TD	INT/Adj	FUM	ASR	NY/P	Rk	DVOA	Rk	DYAR	Rk	YAR	Runs	Yds	TD	DVOA	DYAR	QBR
2013	SD	2/0	12	0	0	0.0%	0	0	0/0	0	--	--	--	--	--	--	--	--	6	-5	0	--	--	--
2014	TEN	7/5	357	185	105	56.8%	1326	7	2/4	3	8.8%	6.0	25	-7.2%	27	49	28	80	20	90	0	-5.9%	5	39.6
2015	2TM	5/0	65	32	16	50.0%	150	0	1/1	0	13.1%	3.3	--	-58.4%	--	-99	--	-86	2	1	0	21.2%	3	20.5

| 2014: | 53% Short | | 24% Mid | | 17% Deep | | 7% Bomb | | YAC: 5.2 (22) | | ALEX: 0.2 | | 2015: | 52% Short | | 21% Mid | | 21% Deep | | 7% Bomb | | YAC: 5.8 (–) | | ALEX: -1.0 |

It was announced in January that Whitehurst was dating Jewel, but unless the singer is running an NFL team, Whitehurst's career could be over after attempting all of 372 passes in 10 seasons. Not bad work, if you can get it.

Russell Wilson   Height: 5-11   Weight: 204   College: Wisconsin   Draft: 2012/3 (75)   Born: 29-Nov-1988   Age: 28   Risk: Yellow

Year	Team	G/GS	Snaps	Att	Comp	C%	Yds	TD	INT/Adj	FUM	ASR	NY/P	Rk	DVOA	Rk	DYAR	Rk	YAR	Runs	Yds	TD	DVOA	DYAR	QBR
2013	SEA	16/16	973	407	257	63.1%	3357	26	9/9	10	9.8%	6.9	7	15.6%	8	770	9	699	96	539	1	23.3%	134	58.9
2014	SEA	16/16	1054	452	285	63.1%	3475	20	7/12	11	8.8%	6.6	17	5.5%	13	503	13	488	118	849	6	43.7%	269	62.5
2015	SEA	16/16	1050	483	329	68.1%	4024	34	8/11	7	9.0%	7.1	4	24.3%	3	1190	3	1159	103	553	1	17.4%	123	74.9
2016	SEA			492	318	64.6%	3915	33	11	7		7.1		11.0%					100	496	4	11.9%		

| 2014: | 58% Short | | 26% Mid | | 11% Deep | | 6% Bomb | | YAC: 6.6 (3) | | ALEX: 0.3 | | 2015: | 48% Short | | 33% Mid | | 11% Deep | | 8% Bomb | | YAC: 5.6 (16) | | ALEX: 2.2 |

When you lead the league in scrambles in each of your first four seasons, you will gain the reputation for being a sandlot quarterback. But while there may be images of chaotic randomness in scrambling, Wilson's usage of mobility is a frighteningly consistent part of Seattle's offense. Scott Kacsmar studied it for our website prior to Super Bowl XLIX, and we have updated these metrics for the past season, including playoffs (terms explained below).

Russell Wilson: Play Breakdown (Includes Playoffs, Excludes Kneeldowns, Spikes and Lateral Passes)

Season	Plays	Throws	Sacks	Scramble Runs	Other Runs	Broken	Pressure	PRES%	Scrambles	SCRAM%	OFP	OFP%	MTP	MTP%
2012	593	455	40	58	36	4	186	33.6%	184	33.3%	398	67.6%	50	10.1%
2013	613	473	51	57	29	3	237	40.8%	204	35.1%	399	65.4%	59	11.3%
2014	687	523	52	57	48	7	227	35.9%	215	34.0%	459	67.5%	62	10.8%
2015	700	553	52	61	30	4	249	37.4%	228	34.2%	466	67.0%	41	6.8%
Total	2593	2004	195	233	143	18	899	37.0%	831	34.2%	1722	66.9%	212	9.6%

Pressure Rate (PRES%): Rate of Pressure on Throws + Sacks + Scramble Runs
Scramble Rate (SCRAM%): Rate of Scrambles on Throws + Sacks + Scramble Runs
Offensive Flow Play Rate (OFP%): Rate of Offensive Flow Plays on Plays (Broken Plays Excluded)
Move the Pocket Passes (MTP%): Rate of Move the Pocket Passes on Throws + Sacks

Wilson is one of the most-pressured quarterbacks in the league, facing pressure on at least a third of his plays each season. His scramble rate has remained remarkably close to 34 percent each season, which is to say he uses his feet to extend plays just over a third of the time. Plays that are run on time without Wilson having to move around are what we call plays happening in the offensive flow. Wilson's offensive flow play rate has been just over 67 percent in three of his seasons, with just a slight decline in the 2013 Super Bowl year. During Wilson's incredible seven-game stretch to close the 2015 regular season, his offensive flow play rate was 74.6 percent, so that run was sparked by more traditional play from the pocket and less improvising. During that stretch, Wilson's pressure rate fell to 29.5 percent, so there was better blocking as well. About the only thing that noticeably changed last year was the decrease in passes that moved the pocket by design.

Jameis Winston   Height: 6-4   Weight: 230   College: Florida State   Draft: 2015/1 (1)   Born: 6-Jan-1994   Age: 23   Risk: Yellow

Year	Team	G/GS	Snaps	Att	Comp	C%	Yds	TD	INT/Adj	FUM	ASR	NY/P	Rk	DVOA	Rk	DYAR	Rk	YAR	Runs	Yds	TD	DVOA	DYAR	QBR
2015	TB	16/16	1093	535	312	58.3%	4042	22	15/22	6	5.8%	6.8	9	2.1%	16	467	16	495	54	213	6	7.6%	42	58.6
2016	TB			540	330	61.0%	3957	27	14	9		6.6		0.4%					64	283	4	15.4%		

| | | | | | | | | | | | | | 2015: 36% | | Short 39% | | Mid 17% | | Deep 8% | | Bomb | | YAC: 4.8 (31) |

Winston had one of the lowest DVOA swings for any quarterback when facing pressure, diving from 44.0% DVOA without pressure to just -47.0% DVOA on the (many) plays when he was pressured. Only five other quarterbacks had a smaller difference in those situations. He was also one of seven quarterbacks to throw the ball outside of the pocket more than 100 times. Only three quarterbacks on that list maintained a DVOA higher than 20.0% outside the pocket, including scrambles: Russell Wilson, Aaron Rodgers, and Winston (37.6%). He's got a high football IQ and, more importantly, shows some good instincts when things are going wrong around him. Year 2's game plan should be simple: cut the unforced errors.

T.J. Yates　　Height: 6-3　　Weight: 195　　College: North Carolina　　Draft: 2011/5 (152)　　Born: 28-May-1987　　Age: 29　　Risk: N/A

Year	Team	G/GS	Snaps	Att	Comp	C%	Yds	TD	INT/Adj	FUM	ASR	NY/P	Rk	DVOA	Rk	DYAR	Rk	YAR	Runs	Yds	TD	DVOA	DYAR	QBR
2013	HOU	3/0	50	22	15	68.2%	113	0	2/2	1	6.6%	4.4	--	-78.0%	--	-109	--	-112	1	0	0	--	--	12.2
2014	ATL	1/0	17	4	3	75.0%	64	0	1/1	0	0.0%	16.0	--	-44.3%	--	-8	--	-4	0	0	0	--	--	21.1
2015	HOU	4/2	132	57	28	49.1%	370	3	1/1	1	7.9%	5.4	--	-7.0%	--	17	--	-18	6	0	0	81.8%	3	55.7

| 2014: | 50% Short | 25% Mid | 25% Deep | 0% Bomb | YAC: 8.7 (--) | ALEX: 4.5 | 2015: | 36% Short | 38% Mid | 16% Deep | 11% Bomb | YAC: 4.2 (--) | ALEX: 0.7 |

Yates failed to make the Falcons out of training camp. Houston picked him up, and when he was forced to start two games, he was surprisingly just mediocre instead of almost completely ineffective. A torn ACL in Week 15 had him on the mend the entire offseason, but he could return to speed dial in case of a quarterback injury in Atlanta, Houston, or elsewhere if he recovers quickly.

Going Deep

Tyler Bray, KC: Aaron Murray's main competition to be the Kansas City backup is essentially Murray's polar opposite: he's tall (6-foot-6) and has a rocket arm but no mobility and poor accuracy. He had a completion rate below 60 percent in each of his three years at Tennessee, part of why he went undrafted in 2013. He's been floating around the Chiefs' roster since then but keeps going on injured reserve instead of getting practice-squad time. He missed all of last season after he tore an ACL playing pickup basketball. Bray was the No. 2 quarterback at Kansas City OTAs but we expect Murray to pass him on the depth chart.

McLeod Bethel-Thompson, PHI: What is dead may never die.

Connor Cook, OAK: Character season's big loser. Cook's dad helped his draft slide by doing an impersonation of PFT Commenter, but without the irony. Cook also wasn't team captain, and has appeared at times to be stand-offish by renowned body language experts in sports studios everywhere. He's got a cannon arm, he's tough in the pocket, and acting like a douche isn't a terminal disease. The accuracy will need to improve, and he'll need to get smarter about testing the middle of the field. In a talented Michigan State offense that didn't face a particularly tough slate of defenses, Cook's 56.1 completion percentage in 2015 is a bad omen. QBASE projects him to be well below replacement level.

Brandon Doughty, MIA: Doughty made quite an impression during a motor-mouthed table interview at the NFL combine, referring to himself as a "Football Muffin" and rattling off wisdom along the lines of: "When you think about Brandon Doughty, you think about Christ and you think about football. Some guys play this game because they love it. Other guys play it because they are it. I AM football." When not sounding like the over-caffeinated roadie for a Christian metal band, this seventh-round pick was a heady, accurate short passer who threw for 9,885 yards and 97 touchdowns (!) in his final two seasons at Western Kentucky under Jeff Brohm. Doughty's deep touch is poor and his foot speed is nonexistent, but he's the kind of gamer who coaches fall in love with in the meeting rooms.

Jeff Driskel, SF: The buzz about Driskel making a run at the Niners' starting quarterback gig speaks both to the overzealousness of the spring NFL rumor mill and the sadness of San Francisco's QB depth chart. In fairness, Driskel did improve after transferring from Florida to Louisiana Tech, where he flashed the type of mobility and quick decision-making skills that project well into Chip Kelly's system. It wouldn't be unprecedented for a sixth-round rookie to see significant playing time: Marc Bulger usurped Kurt Warner in 2002, and Mark Rypien did the same to Doug Williams in 1988. Like Bulger and Rypien, Driskel will need injuries to open up playing time for him in the immediate future. Then again, who's exactly aching to see more from Blaine Gabbert or Colin Kaepernick?

Garrett Grayson, NO: Grayson was a third-round pick out of Colorado State a year ago. He projected poorly in QBASE, picking up an 80.6 percent chance of being a bust, with a mean projection of minus-274 DYAR. Of course, to put up a DYAR that low, he would have to actually see the field first. The Saints didn't even trust him enough to let Luke McCown walk. It's early, but it's getting late awfully fast here.

Jake Heaps, SEA: Heaps played at three different universities, transferring from BYU to Kansas when he lost a starting job and then from Kansas to Miami when he lost a starting job *again*. Between those three schools, his college completion rate was a horrendous 54.7 percent, with just 5.8 yards per attempt. He spent last year on the Jets' practice squad, but has now come home to Washington where he was a highly-regarded prospect at Skyline High School in Sammamish. Homecoming stories are fun, but seriously, this guy is Russell Wilson's backup if something happens to Trevone Boykin? Please, Seahawks, just sign a real backup quarterback already.

Kevin Hogan, KC: The seventh-round pick out of Stanford has a shot to challenge for the backup quarterback position. Hogan's stats (9.4 yards per attempt, 27 TD, 8 INT) in his senior season would project reasonably well if he had been drafted higher. But there's a reason guys like this aren't drafted higher, starting with poor mechanics, bad footwork, lack of pocket presence, and below-average arm strength.

Cardale Jones, BUF: Jones looked like a future NFL franchise quarterback for about five weeks between December of 2014 and January of 2015. Beating Wisconsin, Alabama, and Oregon in a row is great, but losing your starting job to sophomore J.T. Barrett the next season is not so great. Jones did not look dialed in for most of last season. Against Indiana, his passing mechanics were so mixed up that he couldn't throw a spiral, and he sometimes kept the ball on a read-option even with two defenders keying on him at the edge. Against Penn State, he sometimes faked handoffs to the wrong side and was overthrowing screen passes when he was finally pulled. You get the idea. Jones then ran a 4.83-second 40 at the combine before suffering a minor injury. Jones is not the kind of quarterback who bubbles up from the third string unless he matures and develops exponentially, or the coaching staff falls in love with something it saw in a bowl game two years ago and cannot let go. Rex Ryan is the coach who gave us Geno Smith and the Tim Tebow fake punt package, so … Jones may not have to mature and develop exponentially.

Sean Mannion, LARM: Mannion threw just seven passes during his rookie season. Those seven passes are likely to be the only ones he ever throws for the Rams. Mannion was a big-bodied, big-armed quarterback prospect whom the Rams drafted to develop in 2015. He was never given a real chance to prove himself as a rookie, and now the Rams have put their future on the shoulders of Jared Goff.

Dak Prescott, DAL: Prescott rose up draft boards as a trendy mid-round sleeper, a sentiment QBASE reflected in its pre-draft projection for the Mississippi State product. While QBASE still sees Prescott's bust potential as rather high, it also gives him a better chance to turn into a starter than either Carson Wentz or Paxton Lynch. (Sort of: technically, Prescott does not qualify for QBASE because he was taken late in the fourth round instead of in the top 100 picks.) Prescott should have some time to develop as the No. 3 option on the Cowboys' depth chart, but given Tony Romo's age, it's not unfeasible to think that he could become Romo's successor by the end of his rookie deal.

Jake Rudock, DET: Rudock wasn't an NFL-caliber prospect for most of his collegiate career, but steady growth under Jim Harbaugh convinced the Lions to take a sixth-round flier on him. After transferring from Iowa to Michigan, Rudock posted the best numbers of his career at Ann Arbor, peaking at the end of the season with 12 touchdowns in his final four games. Rudock profiles as a below-average prospect in most aspects of the position, but someone has to unseat Dan Orlovsky at some point, right?

Tom Savage, HOU: Though the Texans started four quarterbacks in 2015, a preseason shoulder injury meant that second-year man Savage was not one of them. Any hopes of earning the starting job were dashed by the signing of Brock Osweiler, leaving Savage competing for the backup job with Brandon Weeden. Savage has a big arm but a slow mental clock and his rookie deal is up in two seasons, at the end of the Osweiler tryout period.

Nate Sudfeld, WAS: Sudfeld posted some shiny numbers in Indiana's vertically inclined passing offense, averaging 8.7 yards per attempt as a senior and completing more than 60 percent of his passes in each of his three seasons as a starter. The sixth-rounder has the size (6-foot-6, 234 pounds) and maturity you'd want from your quarterback, having twice led missions to Uganda. Concerns about his shoddy mechanics and ability to read defenses dropped him down draft boards, but Washington, which has kept three quarterbacks each of the past four seasons, will likely afford him some time to develop.

Running Backs

In the following section we provide the last three years of statistics, as well as a 2016 KUBIAK projection, for every running back who either played a significant role in 2015 or is expected to do so in 2016.

The first line contains biographical data—each player's name, height, weight, college, draft position, birth date, and age. Height and weight are the best data we could find; weight, of course, can fluctuate during the offseason. **Age** is very simple, the number of years between the player's birth year and 2016, but birthdate is provided if you want to figure out exact age.

Draft position gives draft year and round, with the overall pick number with which the player was taken in parentheses. In the sample table, it says that Lamar Miller was chosen in the 2012 NFL draft in the fourth round with the 97th overall pick. Undrafted free agents are listed as "FA" with the year they came into the league, even if they were only in training camp or on a practice squad.

To the far right of the first line is the player's Risk for fantasy football in 2016. As explained in the quarterback section, the standard is for players to be marked Green. Players with higher than normal risk are marked Yellow, and players with the highest risk are marked Red. Players who are most likely to match or surpass our forecast—primarily second-stringers with low projections—are marked Blue. Risk is not only based on injury probability, but how a player's projection compares to his recent performance as well as our confidence (or lack thereof) in his offensive teammates.

Next we give the last three years of player stats. First come games played and games started (**G/GS**). Games played is the official NFL total and may include games in which a player appeared on special teams, but did not carry the ball or catch a pass. We also have a total of offensive **Snaps** for each season. The next four columns are familiar: **Runs**, rushing yards (**Yds**), yards per rush (**Yd/R**) and rushing touchdowns (**TD**).

The entry for fumbles (**FUM**) includes all fumbles by this running back, no matter whether they were recovered by the offense or defense. Holding onto the ball is an identifiable skill; fumbling it so that your own offense can recover it is not. (For more on this issue, see the essay "Pregame Show" in the front of the book.) This entry combines fumbles on both carries and receptions.

The next five columns give our advanced metrics for rushing: **DVOA** (Defense-Adjusted Value Over Average), **DYAR** (Defense-Adjusted Yards Above Replacement), and **YAR** (Yards Above Replacement), along with the player's rank (**Rk**) in both **DVOA** and **DYAR**. These metrics compare every carry by the running back to a league-average baseline based on the game situations in which that running back carried the ball. DVOA and DYAR are also adjusted based on the opposing defense. The methods used to compute these numbers are described in detail in the "Statistical Toolbox" introduction in the front of the book. The important distinctions between them are:

• DVOA is a rate statistic, while DYAR is a cumulative statistic. Thus, a higher DVOA means more value per play, while a higher DYAR means more aggregate value over the entire season.
• Because DYAR is defense-adjusted and YAR is not, a player whose DYAR is higher than his YAR faced a harder-than-average schedule. A player whose DYAR is lower than his YAR faced an easier-than-average schedule.

To qualify for ranking in rushing DVOA and DYAR, a running back must have had 100 carries in that season. Last year, 44 running backs qualified to be ranked in these stats, compared to 43 backs in 2014 and 47 backs in 2013.

Success rate (**Suc%**), listed along with rank, represents running back consistency as measured by successful running plays divided by total running plays. (The definition for success is explained in the "Statistical Toolbox" introduction in the front of the book.) A player with high DVOA and a low success rate mixes long runs with plays on which he was stuffed at or behind the line of scrimmage. A player with low DVOA and a high success rate generally gets the yards needed, but rarely gets more. The league-average success rate in 2015 was 47 percent. Success rate is not adjusted for the defenses a player faced.

We also give a total of broken tackles (**BTkl**) according to charting from Sports Info Solutions. This total includes broken tackles on both runs and receptions, but not special teams. Please note that SIS used a looser definition of broken tackles and therefore marked about 25 percent more broken tackles than last year, when our broken tackle numbers came from the Football Outsiders game charting project. Most running backs with consistent playing time will be listed with more broken tackles in 2015; it doesn't necessarily mean they suddenly became more powerful or elusive.

The shaded columns to the right of broken tackles give data

Lamar Miller   Height: 5-11   Weight: 212   College: Miami   Draft: 2012/4 (97)   Born: 25-Apr-1991   Age: 25   Risk: Red

Year	Team	G/GS	Snaps	Runs	Yds	Yd/R	TD	FUM	DVOA	Rk	DYAR	Rk	YAR	Suc%	Rk	BTkl	Rec	Pass	Yds	C%	Yd/C	TD	YAC	DVOA	Rk	DYAR	Rk
2013	MIA	16/15	622	177	709	4.0	2	1	-7.7%	31	6	31	5	46%	29	16	26	35	170	74%	6.5	0	6.8	-7.9%	31	11	32
2014	MIA	16/16	642	216	1099	5.1	8	2	17.8%	3	246	4	239	57%	1	24	38	52	275	73%	7.2	1	6.1	-10.7%	37	9	37
2015	MIA	16/16	631	194	872	4.5	8	1	1.7%	18	81	19	105	43%	34	26	47	57	397	82%	8.4	2	9.0	-3.6%	31	32	25
2016	HOU			283	1275	4.5	10	3	10.1%								36	46	279	78%	7.7	2		15.6%			

for each running back as a pass receiver. Receptions (**Rec**) counts passes caught, while Passes (**Pass**) counts total passes thrown to this player, complete or incomplete. The next four columns list receiving yards (**Yds**), catch rate (**C%**), yards per catch (**Yd/C**), receiving touchdowns (**TD**), and average yards after the catch (**YAC**).

Our research has shown that receivers bear some responsibility for incomplete passes, even though only their catches are tracked in official statistics. Catch rate represents receptions divided by all intended passes for this running back. The average NFL running back caught 74 percent of passes in 2015. Unfortunately, we don't have room to post the best and worst running backs in receiving plus-minus, but you'll find the top 10 and bottom 10 running backs in this metric listed in the statistical appendix.

Finally we have receiving DVOA and DYAR, which are entirely separate from rushing DVOA and DYAR. To qualify for ranking in receiving DVOA and DYAR, a running back must have 25 passes thrown to him in that season. There are 58 running backs ranked for 2015, 57 backs for 2014, and 49 backs for 2013. Numbers without opponent adjustment (YAR and VOA) can be found on our website, FootballOutsiders.com.

The italicized row of statistics for the 2016 season is our 2016 KUBIAK projection based on a complicated regression analysis that takes into account numerous variables including projected role, performance over the past two years, projected team offense and defense, historical comparables, height, age, experience of the offensive line, and strength of schedule.

It is difficult to accurately project statistics for a 162-game baseball season, but it is exponentially more difficult to ac-

Top 20 RB by Rushing DYAR (Total Value), 2015

Rank	Player	Team	DYAR
1	T.Rawls	SEA	216
2	M.Forte	CHI	192
3	De.Williams	PIT	184
4	T.Gurley	STL	170
5	L.Bell	PIT	162
6	A.Peterson	MIN	143
7	L.McCoy	BUF	139
8	Da.Johnson	ARI	133
9	R.Mathews	PHI	133
10	G.Bernard	CIN	131
11	J.Langford	CHI	123
12	R.Jennings	NYG	117
13	J.Forsett	BAL	117
14	M.Ingram	NO	108
15	D.Freeman	ATL	90
16	J.Hill	CIN	85
17	D.McFadden	DAL	83
18	D.Martin	TB	81
19	L.Miller	MIA	81
20	C.West	KC	77

Top 20 RB by Rushing DVOA (Value per Rush), 2015

Rank	Player	Team	DVOA
1	L.Bell	PIT	28.1%
2	T.Rawls	SEA	26.4%
3	R.Mathews	PHI	20.4%
4	Da.Johnson	ARI	15.7%
5	J.Langford	CHI	12.7%
6	De.Williams	PIT	12.1%
7	M.Forte	CHI	12.0%
8	G.Bernard	CIN	11.8%
9	T.Gurley	STL	10.0%
10	J.Forsett	BAL	9.1%
11	L.McCoy	BUF	8.8%
12	M.Ingram	NO	6.6%
13	R.Jennings	NYG	5.6%
14	C.Hyde	SF	3.9%
15	C.West	KC	2.8%
16	C.Sims	TB	2.6%
17	A.Peterson	MIN	2.2%
18	L.Miller	MIA	1.7%
19	M.Lynch	SEA	1.2%
20	L.Blount	NE	0.2%

Minimum 100 carries.

Top 10 RB by Receiving DYAR (Total Value), 2015

Rank	Player	Team	DYAR
1	D.Woodhead	SD	235
2	T.Riddick	DET	201
3	C.Sims	TB	150
4	J.White	NE	140
5	M.Reece	OAK	127
6	Da.Johnson	ARI	120
7	M.Forte	CHI	112
8	De.Williams	PIT	109
9	S.Vereen	NYG	103
10	J.Starks	GB	97

Top 10 RB by Receiving DVOA (Value per Pass), 2015

Rank	Player	Team	DVOA
1	J.Bell	DET	49.3%
2	M.Reece	OAK	42.3%
3	M.Jones	WAS	38.9%
4	A.Foster	HOU	35.0%
5	J.White	NE	33.3%
6	De.Williams	PIT	30.5%
7	C.Sims	TB	29.2%
8	B.Cunningham	STL	28.3%
9	D.Woodhead	SD	25.8%
10	T.Riddick	DET	24.6%

Minimum 25 passes.

curately project statistics for a 16-game football season. Consider the listed projections not as a prediction of exact numbers, but the mean of a range of possible performances. What's important is less the exact number of yards we project, and more which players are projected to improve or decline. Actual performance will vary from our projection less for veteran starters and more for rookies and third-stringers, for whom we must base our projections on much smaller career statistical samples. Touchdown numbers will vary more than yardage numbers.

Finally, in a section we call "Going Deep," we briefly discuss lower-round rookies, free-agent veterans, and practice-squad players who may play a role during the 2016 season or beyond.

Ameer Abdullah

Height: 5-9 **Weight:** 205 **College:** Nebraska **Draft:** 2015/2 (54) **Born:** 13-Jun-1993 **Age:** 23 **Risk:** Red

Year	Team	G/GS	Snaps	Runs	Yds	Yd/R	TD	FUM	DVOA	Rk	DYAR	Rk	YAR	Suc%	Rk	BTkl	Rec	Pass	Yds	C%	Yd/C	TD	YAC	DVOA	Rk	DYAR	Rk
2015	DET	16/9	355	143	597	4.2	2	4	-8.9%	37	-2	37	21	51%	7	16	25	38	183	66%	7.3	1	7.7	-11.3%	40	6	40
2016	DET			200	903	4.5	3	4	4.4%								40	56	282	71%	7.1	2		-6.3%			

The biggest story concerning Abdullah this offseason was shown on Amazon's show about the Arizona Cardinals, *All or Nothing*, which revealed that the Cardinals planned to select the running back in the second round until the Lions beat them to the punch. Abdullah's playing time dipped in the second half of the year as Jim Bob Cooter turned to a committee approach, and that's the plan again for this season. Abdullah played through a shoulder injury the last few games of 2015 and underwent surgery in January, but general manager Bob Quinn has said that Abdullah will be ready for training camp.

Jay Ajayi

Height: 6-0 **Weight:** 221 **College:** Boise State **Draft:** 2015/5 (149) **Born:** 15-Jun-1993 **Age:** 23 **Risk:** Green

Year	Team	G/GS	Snaps	Runs	Yds	Yd/R	TD	FUM	DVOA	Rk	DYAR	Rk	YAR	Suc%	Rk	BTkl	Rec	Pass	Yds	C%	Yd/C	TD	YAC	DVOA	Rk	DYAR	Rk
2015	MIA	9/0	158	49	187	3.8	1	0	-17.7%	--	-17	--	-3	39%	--	17	7	11	90	64%	12.9	0	11.1	38.1%	--	28	--
2016	MIA			170	779	4.6	4	2	2.9%								25	34	168	74%	6.7	0		-7.5%			

Ajayi gained 89 yards on his first 11 carries after coming off short-term injured reserve in the second half of the season. He tailed off quickly after that, though he got plenty of opportunities; Dan Campbell felt Ajayi was better than Lamar Miller but kept smashing his head into the reality that Miller was far more productive. There were conflicting reports that the Dolphins organization considered Ajayi a potential starter while the team simultaneously made offers to C.J. Anderson and courted Chris Johnson; the Dolphins are perfectly capable of thinking two contradictory thoughts and acting upon them simultaneously. Ajayi will battle the newly-signed Arian Foster for the starting job, with rookie Kenyon Drake assuming a third-down role. It meets the minimum standards of a "running back committee" in that both players are running backs and there is more than one of them.

Javorius Allen

Height: 6-0 **Weight:** 221 **College:** USC **Draft:** 2015/4 (125) **Born:** 27-Aug-1991 **Age:** 25 **Risk:** Green

Year	Team	G/GS	Snaps	Runs	Yds	Yd/R	TD	FUM	DVOA	Rk	DYAR	Rk	YAR	Suc%	Rk	BTkl	Rec	Pass	Yds	C%	Yd/C	TD	YAC	DVOA	Rk	DYAR	Rk
2015	BAL	16/6	393	137	514	3.8	1	2	-3.2%	29	31	30	0	47%	19	23	45	62	353	73%	7.8	2	6.7	-6.2%	33	27	29
2016	BAL			133	556	4.2	2	4	-7.0%								48	60	389	80%	8.1	1		8.9%			

Buck Allen did well enough as a rookie for the Ravens to basically draft a deluxe version of him in Kenneth Dixon. Justin Forsett does not become a free agent until 2018, but perhaps Allen and Dixon could be the future at running back for the Ravens. It is just hard to see where Allen's skill set fits between Forsett and Dixon in getting him touches this year. The days of Matt Schaub dumping 13 passes to Allen as the closest target to him while all the wide receivers and tight ends were hurt are thankfully over.

C.J. Anderson

Height: 5-8 **Weight:** 224 **College:** California **Draft:** 2013/FA **Born:** 2-Feb-1991 **Age:** 25 **Risk:** Yellow

Year	Team	G/GS	Snaps	Runs	Yds	Yd/R	TD	FUM	DVOA	Rk	DYAR	Rk	YAR	Suc%	Rk	BTkl	Rec	Pass	Yds	C%	Yd/C	TD	YAC	DVOA	Rk	DYAR	Rk
2013	DEN	5/0	21	7	38	5.4	0	0	53.0%	--	19	--	20	86%	--	1	0	1	0	0%	0.0	0	--	-91.1%	--	-5	--
2014	DEN	15/7	495	179	849	4.7	8	1	17.5%	4	196	7	215	51%	10	46	34	44	324	77%	9.5	2	8.3	13.0%	14	65	13
2015	DEN	15/6	500	152	720	4.7	5	2	-3.2%	27	34	28	70	41%	41	31	25	36	183	69%	7.3	0	6.0	-27.8%	53	-23	51
2016	DEN			232	1004	4.3	7	2	6.8%								44	58	329	76%	7.5	1		5.9%			

In 2014, Anderson succeeded in every direction, posting a DVOA of 4.3% on 59 runs charted to the left, 23.7% on 70 runs up the middle, and 23.2% on 50 runs to the right. In 2015, Anderson did well on runs to the left (23.7% DVOA on 61 carries), but poorly up the middle (-12.2% DVOA on 43 carries) and to the right (-28.0% DVOA on 48 carries). Those numbers suggest that Anderson's overall drop-off last season largely speaks to the problems on the offensive line. In snaps per blown block, both right guard Louis Vasquez (37th out of 39) and right tackle Michael Schofield (35th out of 38) ranked in the bottom five at their positions.

Antonio Andrews   Height: 5-10   Weight: 225   College: Western Kentucky   Draft: 2014/FA   Born: 17-Aug-1992   Age: 24   Risk: Red

Year	Team	G/GS	Snaps	Runs	Yds	Yd/R	TD	FUM	DVOA	Rk	DYAR	Rk	YAR	Suc%	Rk	BTkl	Rec	Pass	Yds	C%	Yd/C	TD	YAC	DVOA	Rk	DYAR	Rk
2014	TEN	4/0	13	0	0	0.0	0	0	0	--	0	--	0	--	--	0	2	2	11	100%	5.5	0	4.5	10.4%	--	2	--
2015	TEN	14/10	422	143	520	3.6	3	1	-9.5%	38	-6	38	-17	42%	39	31	21	29	174	72%	8.3	0	8.3	-7.5%	36	10	38
2016	TEN			24	109	4.6	1	1	6.7%								9	11	70	82%	7.8	0		10.2%			

Andrews can feel somewhat aggrieved by the way he was treated by the Titans coaching staff last year. He was playing relatively well behind an awful offensive line before being benched because of a fumble. Being an undrafted free agent who had worked his way up, Andrews' playing time was always going to be under threat to the higher draft picks on the roster. The arrivals of DeMarco Murray and Derrick Henry all but destroy Andrews' hopes of starring in the Titans offense in 2016, but he will compete for a roster spot with David Cobb and Bishop Sankey. He outperformed both in 2015.

Cameron Artis-Payne   Height: 5-10   Weight: 212   College: Auburn   Draft: 2015/5 (174)   Born: 23-Jun-1992   Age: 24   Risk: Green

Year	Team	G/GS	Snaps	Runs	Yds	Yd/R	TD	FUM	DVOA	Rk	DYAR	Rk	YAR	Suc%	Rk	BTkl	Rec	Pass	Yds	C%	Yd/C	TD	YAC	DVOA	Rk	DYAR	Rk
2015	CAR	7/0	113	45	183	4.1	1	0	-9.2%	--	-1	--	-10	38%	--	7	5	5	58	100%	11.6	0	12.2	90.1%	--	31	--
2016	CAR			64	245	3.8	1	2	-9.5%								11	13	66	85%	6.0	0		-0.3%			

It was Artis-Payne that took over the majority of the workload once the Panthers had clinched the playoffs and started resting Jonathan Stewart. The back didn't show much in his limited sample size to either recommend or denigrate him, then was inactive for the rest of the playoffs after losing a fumble against the Seahawks in the divisional round. Because older running backs are so much less likely to cough up the ball in the Super Bowl, right? Artis-Payne enters the offseason as the clear No. 2 back, but has limited value as a receiver. In a backfield with Mike Tolbert and Cam Newton, there are even fewer touchdowns to go around, so he's low-upside for fantasy purposes.

Matt Asiata   Height: 5-11   Weight: 220   College: Utah   Draft: 2011/FA   Born: 24-Jul-1987   Age: 29   Risk: Red

Year	Team	G/GS	Snaps	Runs	Yds	Yd/R	TD	FUM	DVOA	Rk	DYAR	Rk	YAR	Suc%	Rk	BTkl	Rec	Pass	Yds	C%	Yd/C	TD	YAC	DVOA	Rk	DYAR	Rk
2013	MIN	11/1	117	44	166	3.8	3	1	12.9%	--	41	--	24	55%	--	3	5	8	13	63%	2.6	0	4.4	-67.7%	--	-26	--
2014	MIN	15/9	524	164	570	3.5	9	1	1.0%	17	69	20	75	52%	6	10	44	63	312	70%	7.1	1	7.7	-23.9%	48	-33	48
2015	MIN	16/0	199	29	112	3.9	0	0	-11.8%	--	-3	--	-1	38%	--	7	19	22	132	86%	6.9	0	10.5	-19.5%	--	-6	--
2016	MIN			21	93	4.5	1	1	10.7%								23	29	180	79%	7.8	1		10.3%			

You'll often see Asiata described as a short-yardage specialist, but in fact he had only two carries in 2015 with 1 or 2 yards to go. Meanwhile, Adrian Peterson had 30, Teddy Bridgewater had seven, and Jerick McKinnon and Zach Line had four each. Really, Asiata is the "Adrian needs a breather" specialist—he had one carry in the first quarter and one in the third, but nine in the second and 18 in the fourth quarter or overtime. He's also a key special-teamer, on the field for 47 percent of Minnesota's kicking plays. The Vikings re-signed him to a one-year, $840,000 contract after the season.

Kenjon Barner   Height: 5-9   Weight: 196   College: Oregon   Draft: 2013/6 (182)   Born: 28-Apr-1989   Age: 27   Risk: Green

Year	Team	G/GS	Snaps	Runs	Yds	Yd/R	TD	FUM	DVOA	Rk	DYAR	Rk	YAR	Suc%	Rk	BTkl	Rec	Pass	Yds	C%	Yd/C	TD	YAC	DVOA	Rk	DYAR	Rk
2013	CAR	8/0	24	6	7	1.2	0	0	-67.2%	--	-14	--	-18	0%	--	0	2	3	7	67%	3.5	0	6.0	-51.2%	--	-5	--
2015	PHI	10/0	79	28	124	4.4	0	1	18.3%	--	30	--	22	54%	--	7	9	12	22	75%	2.4	0	4.8	-65.6%	--	-36	--
2016	PHI			28	112	4.0	3	1	17.1%								12	17	100	71%	8.3	1		1.1%			

Don't assume Barner stuck around in Philly last season simply because he saved his hall pass from Eugene. Chip Kelly's former Oregon protégé was a surprise inclusion on the 2015 roster, but eventually flashed enough to justify that decision. Barner even usurped big-ticket signee DeMarco Murray on the depth chart at one point, though a disastrous fumble in the final two minutes of the New England game sent him back to the bench until Week 17. Still, his efficiency in limited time was promising enough to earn him some first-team OTA snaps this spring. He likely won't keep that role entering the season, but considering Ryan Mathews' injury history and Darren Sproles' usage limitations, it would hardly be surprising to see Barner get his big break in 2016. Either way, Barner profiles as a Swiss Army knife who could eventually inherit Sproles' offensive and special teams roles down the line.

Joique Bell   Height: 5-11   Weight: 220   College: Wayne State   Draft: 2010/FA   Born: 4-Aug-1986   Age: 30   Risk: N/A

Year	Team	G/GS	Snaps	Runs	Yds	Yd/R	TD	FUM	DVOA	Rk	DYAR	Rk	YAR	Suc%	Rk	BTkl	Rec	Pass	Yds	C%	Yd/C	TD	YAC	DVOA	Rk	DYAR	Rk
2013	DET	16/4	547	166	650	3.9	8	4	2.0%	20	78	24	75	51%	10	24	53	69	547	77%	10.3	0	10.3	40.3%	3	196	2
2014	DET	15/6	615	223	860	3.9	7	5	-14.9%	38	-59	42	-19	45%	23	24	34	52	322	65%	9.5	1	9.9	6.2%	17	54	18
2015	DET	13/5	242	90	311	3.5	4	1	-12.5%	–	-15	–	-2	46%	–	18	22	27	286	81%	13.0	0	13.9	49.3%	1	97	11

As noted in the Detroit chapter, Bell was terrible in Joe Lombardi's zone-based blocking schemes, but played much better in the man-to-man concepts favored by Jim Bob Cooter. The Lions released him after the season, a move that saved them $2.5 million, and Bell remained unsigned as of mid-July. In all likelihood, he'll get a veteran minimum deal to be a backup somewhere this fall.

Le'Veon Bell   Height: 6-1   Weight: 230   College: Michigan State   Draft: 2013/2 (48)   Born: 18-Feb-1992   Age: 24   Risk: Yellow

Year	Team	G/GS	Snaps	Runs	Yds	Yd/R	TD	FUM	DVOA	Rk	DYAR	Rk	YAR	Suc%	Rk	BTkl	Rec	Pass	Yds	C%	Yd/C	TD	YAC	DVOA	Rk	DYAR	Rk
2013	PIT	13/13	677	244	860	3.5	8	1	-7.0%	28	17	28	15	47%	23	21	45	65	399	68%	8.9	0	10.0	-5.9%	30	28	28
2014	PIT	16/16	927	290	1361	4.7	8	0	8.6%	9	205	5	283	51%	9	59	83	105	854	79%	10.3	3	9.8	38.4%	3	316	1
2015	PIT	6/6	301	113	556	4.9	3	0	28.1%	1	162	5	127	50%	10	19	24	26	136	92%	5.7	0	5.8	-21.3%	49	-10	48
2016	PIT			201	905	4.5	7	1	13.9%								50	65	414	78%	8.2	2		22.6%			

Pittsburgh was poised for a big rushing performance last season from its lead back. If you add the numbers together for Le'Veon Bell and DeAngelo Williams, you get 313 carries for 1,463 yards and 346 rushing DYAR. Add his receiving capabilities and Bell could be looking at another season with more than 2,000 yards from scrimmage. Bell should be the favorite to lead the league in that category this year, unless his teammate Antonio Brown beats him to it. In 2014, Bell (2,215) and Brown (1,711) became the first teammates in NFL history to both go over 1,700 yards from scrimmage in the same season. Their 3,926 combined yards are the most by a pair in NFL history. The talent and circumstances are there to get them both over 2,000 yards this season, which would be a remarkable feat. Of course, health is going to be a huge factor here, and like Ben Roethlisberger, Bell has been far from perfect attendance throughout his career.

Sure enough, that last part proved to be prescient as just before we went to print, Bell was hit with a four-game suspension for multiple missed drug tests. While he can try blaming this on a changed phone number, it's not looking good for Bell to lead the league in any statistics or be worthy of the top pick in your fantasy draft. If the Steelers can take away any positives here, it would be that Bell's price just went down, and that's four fewer games he has to get hit in, so maybe he can be fresher for the stretch run. But Bell's unreliability is becoming a serious problem for Pittsburgh. The chances it becomes someone else's problem next season have also gone up.

Giovani Bernard   Height: 5-8   Weight: 202   College: North Carolina   Draft: 2013/2 (37)   Born: 22-Nov-1991   Age: 25   Risk: Green

Year	Team	G/GS	Snaps	Runs	Yds	Yd/R	TD	FUM	DVOA	Rk	DYAR	Rk	YAR	Suc%	Rk	BTkl	Rec	Pass	Yds	C%	Yd/C	TD	YAC	DVOA	Rk	DYAR	Rk
2013	CIN	16/0	614	170	695	4.1	5	1	-4.5%	27	28	27	69	48%	21	28	56	71	514	79%	9.2	3	9.4	29.4%	5	167	5
2014	CIN	13/9	509	168	680	4.0	5	0	-8.1%	32	3	32	8	39%	38	19	43	59	349	73%	8.1	2	8.4	0.8%	22	48	21
2015	CIN	16/1	580	154	730	4.7	2	1	11.8%	8	131	10	130	49%	13	37	49	66	472	74%	9.6	0	9.3	14.6%	16	97	12
2016	CIN			156	679	4.3	6	2	6.0%								53	70	464	76%	8.8	1		19.3%			

Nat Gio's high quality season was an afterthought amid all the other Bengals offensive success stories, but he set career highs in rushing yards and DVOA, as well as yards per carry and per reception. As a result, the team felt comfortable in handing out an extension during the summer, justified not only by Bernard's production but his age (just 25) and receiving skill. Recently paid Bengals have a checkered injury history (see Carson Palmer, Vontaze Burfict, Geno Atkins, etc.), but assuming Bernard stays healthy his impact on the offense should be more notable in 2016.

LeGarrette Blount   Height: 6-0   Weight: 247   College: Oregon   Draft: 2010/FA   Born: 5-Dec-1986   Age: 30   Risk: Red

Year	Team	G/GS	Snaps	Runs	Yds	Yd/R	TD	FUM	DVOA	Rk	DYAR	Rk	YAR	Suc%	Rk	BTkl	Rec	Pass	Yds	C%	Yd/C	TD	YAC	DVOA	Rk	DYAR	Rk
2013	NE	16/7	286	153	772	5.0	7	3	9.4%	10	117	16	131	54%	3	17	2	5	38	40%	19.0	0	20.5	-5.0%	--	3	--
2014	2TM	16/1	231	125	547	4.4	5	1	1.6%	15	56	22	54	46%	19	14	10	12	54	83%	5.4	0	6.1	-15.3%	--	-1	--
2015	NE	12/6	308	165	703	4.3	6	1	0.2%	20	64	21	91	52%	6	23	6	7	43	86%	7.2	1	5.2	39.5%	--	21	--
2016	NE			186	783	4.2	7	3	2.9%								12	17	86	71%	7.1	1		-2.6%			

Blount rushed 87 times for 406 yards (4.7 yards per carry) when the score margin was greater than 15 points and 78 times for 297 yards (3.9 yards per carry) when the score was closer. In other words, he's a moderately-priced clock muncher with some goal-line serviceability (four touchdowns in 14 goal-to-go carries) who the Patriots like to rent one year at a time. This year's rental cost $1 million for a player who was suspended for the season opener and missed December and the postseason with a hip injury. The Patriots could have found a running back in the draft capable of doing more than grinding out between-the-tackles yards, but they know precisely what they are getting. Blount, meanwhile, realized that annual chance to win a Super Bowl and associate himself with one of the greatest organizations in professional sports is as good as it's gonna get for a one-dimensional player prone to brain cramps.

Alfred Blue   Height: 6-2   Weight: 223   College: Louisiana State   Draft: 2014/6 (181)   Born: 27-Apr-1991   Age: 25   Risk: Yellow

Year	Team	G/GS	Snaps	Runs	Yds	Yd/R	TD	FUM	DVOA	Rk	DYAR	Rk	YAR	Suc%	Rk	BTkl	Rec	Pass	Yds	C%	Yd/C	TD	YAC	DVOA	Rk	DYAR	Rk
2014	HOU	16/3	336	169	528	3.1	2	0	-21.3%	43	-88	43	-60	39%	36	6	15	18	113	83%	7.5	1	5.0	25.4%	--	41	--
2015	HOU	16/9	368	183	698	3.8	2	2	-0.2%	22	61	22	10	45%	29	20	15	16	109	94%	7.3	1	4.5	26.1%	--	31	--
2016	HOU			96	309	3.2	1	1	-16.0%								11	14	73	79%	6.7	0		5.5%			

Blue will always be a between-the-tackles grinder—among the 44 backs with at least 100 carries, he ranked 42nd in open-field yards per carry—but he was much more effective at that task in 2015 than he had been as a rookie. That included going over 100 yards in two of the last three games, and adding 99 more in the playoff game against the Chiefs. Lamar Miller's arrival relegates him to no more than a secondary spot. The Texans did not add another grinder back to the roster, however, so Blue could still have a situational role.

Brandon Bolden   Height: 5-11   Weight: 220   College: Mississippi   Draft: 2012/FA   Born: 26-Jan-1990   Age: 26   Risk: Green

Year	Team	G/GS	Snaps	Runs	Yds	Yd/R	TD	FUM	DVOA	Rk	DYAR	Rk	YAR	Suc%	Rk	BTkl	Rec	Pass	Yds	C%	Yd/C	TD	YAC	DVOA	Rk	DYAR	Rk
2013	NE	12/2	266	55	271	4.9	3	0	13.1%	--	54	--	54	49%	--	5	21	29	152	72%	7.2	0	7.6	-14.6%	37	-1	37
2014	NE	16/2	72	28	89	3.2	1	0	-11.2%	--	-3	--	-6	43%	--	3	2	6	8	33%	4.0	0	5.5	-81.7%	--	-26	--
2015	NE	15/2	191	63	207	3.3	0	0	-24.3%	--	-40	--	-52	33%	--	23	19	30	180	63%	9.5	2	6.8	2.2%	24	26	30
2016	NE			49	161	3.3	1	1	-14.5%								19	24	173	79%	9.1	1		14.7%			

The Patriots have held so many commanding leads for so many years that a career special-teamer like Bolden, who typically only soaks up meaningless fourth-quarter carries, can rack up 1,192 career scrimmage yards. Bolden inherited an increased role late in the year when Dion Lewis and LeGarrette Blount were injured. He was awful, hammering out just 3.3 yards per carry in December (when the Patriots could use a little juice from the ground game) and five carries for 12 yards against the Broncos in the playoffs. Bolden's special teams value keeps him on the roster. He's a little too close to earning meaningful carries again for comfort.

Devontae Booker   Height: 5-11   Weight: 219   College: Utah   Draft: 2016/4 (136)   Born: 27-May-1992   Age: 24   Risk: Green

Year	Team	G/GS	Snaps	Runs	Yds	Yd/R	TD	FUM	DVOA	Rk	DYAR	Rk	YAR	Suc%	Rk	BTkl	Rec	Pass	Yds	C%	Yd/C	TD	YAC	DVOA	Rk	DYAR	Rk
2016	DEN			55	232	4.2	1	2	-3.2%								13	17	96	76%	7.4	1		-6.0%			

The Broncos' fourth-round pick ran for 2,773 yards (5.0 per carry) and 21 touchdowns in his last two years at Utah, adding 80 catches for 622 yards for good measure. He was second and fourth in yards from scrimmage in the Pac-12 the last two seasons. Booker was third behind Derrick Henry and Ezekiel Elliott in our new BackCAST projections for this year's draft class, and Denver running backs coach Eric Studesville praised his pass blocking and quick learning in OTAs. C.J. Anderson will start the season as Denver's clear No. 1 running back, but Booker will likely get more and more carries later in the year.

Donald Brown   Height: 5-11   Weight: 210   College: Connecticut   Draft: 2009/1 (27)   Born: 11-Apr-1987   Age: 29   Risk: Blue

Year	Team	G/GS	Snaps	Runs	Yds	Yd/R	TD	FUM	DVOA	Rk	DYAR	Rk	YAR	Suc%	Rk	BTkl	Rec	Pass	Yds	C%	Yd/C	TD	YAC	DVOA	Rk	DYAR	Rk
2013	IND	16/5	373	102	537	5.3	6	0	19.2%	2	117	14	122	54%	2	17	27	36	214	78%	7.9	2	8.8	6.2%	19	44	22
2014	SD	13/3	358	85	223	2.6	0	1	-23.9%	–	-51	–	-74	30%	–	9	29	42	211	71%	7.3	0	9.8	-23.7%	47	-22	47
2015	SD	10/2	120	59	229	3.9	1	1	0.3%	–	21	–	-3	36%	–	11	8	13	88	62%	11.0	0	13.8	-24.8%	–	-7	–
2016	NE			22	94	4.2	1	0	1.4%								9	12	79	75%	8.7	0		8.7%			

Whether it was an issue of age or scheme fit, Brown never looked as good in San Diego as he had in Indianapolis. Brown can be a valuable player in New England because of his skill set, but he needs to show off better consistency than he has throughout his career. Of course, that assumes he even makes the roster over one of the four returning backs from last year's team.

Travaris Cadet   Height: 6-1   Weight: 210   College: Appalachian State   Draft: 2012/FA   Born: 1-Feb-1989   Age: 27   Risk: Yellow

Year	Team	G/GS	Snaps	Runs	Yds	Yd/R	TD	FUM	DVOA	Rk	DYAR	Rk	YAR	Suc%	Rk	BTkl	Rec	Pass	Yds	C%	Yd/C	TD	YAC	DVOA	Rk	DYAR	Rk
2013	NO	13/0	11	0	0	0.0	0	0	0	–	0	–	0	–	–	0	2	2	5	100%	2.5	1	3.0	76.1%	–	11	–
2014	NO	15/1	205	10	32	3.2	0	2	-55.8%	–	-18	–	-16	50%	–	0	38	51	296	75%	7.8	1	6.4	5.4%	18	57	15
2015	3TM	7/1	117	11	28	2.5	0	1	-69.0%	–	-26	–	-19	27%	–	2	17	22	214	77%	12.6	1	9.0	51.6%	–	78	–
2016	NO			13	46	3.5	0	1	-8.5%								18	23	165	78%	9.1	1		14.7%			

It's a thin line between becoming the new Shane Vereen in New England and becoming a veteran passing-down back for hire. After losing out to Dion Lewis in a preseason competition, Cadet bounced around a few teams last season. Cadet can be a good receiving back, but he's more of a change-of-pace guy than the leader of a committee. All you have to do to understand that is look at his rush/reception splits.

Ka'Deem Carey   Height: 5-9   Weight: 207   College: Arizona   Draft: 2014/4 (117)   Born: 30-Oct-1992   Age: 24   Risk: Green

Year	Team	G/GS	Snaps	Runs	Yds	Yd/R	TD	FUM	DVOA	Rk	DYAR	Rk	YAR	Suc%	Rk	BTkl	Rec	Pass	Yds	C%	Yd/C	TD	YAC	DVOA	Rk	DYAR	Rk
2014	CHI	14/0	98	36	158	4.4	0	0	21.2%	–	47	–	48	53%	–	8	5	6	57	83%	11.4	0	8.6	43.5%	–	17	–
2015	CHI	11/1	77	43	159	3.7	2	1	21.2%	–	56	–	34	58%	–	4	3	3	19	100%	6.3	1	2.7	53.6%	–	18	–
2016	CHI			60	251	4.2	1	2	-2.3%								9	11	59	82%	6.5	0		1.2%			

Only three teams had more shotgun handoffs than Chicago last season, which is good news for Carey, who excels in space. Each of his 17 runs out of the shotgun last season gained at least 2 yards, 13 were successful plays, and only two were worth negative DYAR. That's not a one-year fluke either: his DVOA on 25 shotgun runs in 2014 (43.0%) was almost as good as what he did in 2015 (53.6%). Carey put up a pair of 1,800-yard seasons in Rich Rodriguez's spread offense with the Arizona Wildcats, so it shouldn't be surprising that he's at his best out of the shotgun in the NFL.

Jamaal Charles   Height: 5-11   Weight: 200   College: Texas   Draft: 2008/3 (73)   Born: 27-Dec-1986   Age: 30   Risk: Yellow

Year	Team	G/GS	Snaps	Runs	Yds	Yd/R	TD	FUM	DVOA	Rk	DYAR	Rk	YAR	Suc%	Rk	BTkl	Rec	Pass	Yds	C%	Yd/C	TD	YAC	DVOA	Rk	DYAR	Rk
2013	KC	15/15	845	259	1287	5.0	12	4	13.7%	7	247	3	258	51%	11	39	70	104	693	67%	9.9	7	9.4	8.5%	17	135	8
2014	KC	15/15	650	206	1033	5.0	9	5	19.9%	2	249	3	212	54%	2	30	40	60	291	68%	7.3	5	7.7	-13.5%	39	1	39
2015	KC	5/5	264	71	364	5.1	4	3	24.8%	–	96	–	90	48%	–	16	21	30	177	70%	8.4	1	9.8	-12.1%	42	3	42
2016	KC			213	1014	4.8	9	2	15.0%								48	63	385	76%	8.0	1		10.4%			

Is Charles a Hall of Famer? Three times he has finished first or second in rushing DVOA, and he was threatening to do it again before he was injured last season. He has averaged at least 5.0 yards in each of his eight seasons (although three of them featured fewer than 75 carries). Right now, the club with at least 7,000 rushing yards and a career average over 5.0 yards per carry has three members: Jim Brown (12,312 yards, 5.22 yd/car), Joe Perry (9,723 yards, 5.04 yd/car), and Charles (7,220 yards, 5.47 yd/car). If he can get through three healthy seasons, Charles would have a good chance to join Brown as the only running backs to hit 10,000 yards and at least 5.0 yards per carry. Charles has benefited from a limited workload and other current backs are posting impressive numbers as defenses scheme to stop the pass, but think of the quarterbacks that Charles has played with. If all of that adds up to a Hall of a Famer, it's hard to get past just how easy it was for the Chiefs to replace that Hall of Famer with two unknown players last year.

David Cobb Height: 5-11   Weight: 229   College: Minnesota   Draft: 2015/5 (138)   Born: 3-Jun-1993   Age: 23   Risk: Red

Year	Team	G/GS	Snaps	Runs	Yds	Yd/R	TD	FUM	DVOA	Rk	DYAR	Rk	YAR	Suc%	Rk	BTkl	Rec	Pass	Yds	C%	Yd/C	TD	YAC	DVOA	Rk	DYAR	Rk
2015	TEN	7/1	115	52	146	2.8	1	0	-16.4%	–	-16	–	-27	33%	–	4	1	2	-2	50%	-2.0	0	3.0	-158.4%	–	-14	–
2016	TEN			21	73	3.5	0	1	-10.2%								5	6	37	83%	7.5	0		8.4%			

Cobb has been dealt a cruel hand. Injuries early on during his rookie season prevented him from establishing himself. By the time he was fully healthy, the head coach who drafted him had already been fired. Cobb now faces an uphill battle for playing time with Derrick Henry and DeMarco Murray slotted in as the primary ballcarriers.

Tevin Coleman Height: 5-11   Weight: 206   College: Indiana   Draft: 2015/3 (73)   Born: 16-Apr-1993   Age: 23   Risk: Green

Year	Team	G/GS	Snaps	Runs	Yds	Yd/R	TD	FUM	DVOA	Rk	DYAR	Rk	YAR	Suc%	Rk	BTkl	Rec	Pass	Yds	C%	Yd/C	TD	YAC	DVOA	Rk	DYAR	Rk
2015	ATL	12/3	226	87	392	4.5	1	3	-11.9%	–	-12	–	13	49%	–	3	2	11	14	18%	7.0	0	5.5	-99.5%	–	-46	–
2016	ATL			134	622	4.6	5	4	6.6%								25	36	227	69%	9.1	1		3.9%			

Known for his track speed at Indiana, Coleman's first year in the NFL saw him falling far behind starter Devonta Freeman. Offensive coordinator Kyle Shanahan does tend to funnel his carries to one back naturally anyway, but Coleman's ability as a blocker, a receiver, and as a zone runner were all open questions. Three fumbles in 89 touches didn't help either. Atlanta's coaching staff and front office have gone on the warpath this offseason about how they want Coleman more involved in this offense. It's nice to want things, but it's all empty praise until all this supposed improvement shows up on the field. This time next year, we'll either be talking about Coleman as a bust or a potential star—there's not much space for an in-between.

Isaiah Crowell Height: 5-11   Weight: 225   College: Alabama State   Draft: 2014/FA   Born: 8-Jan-1993   Age: 23   Risk: Red

Year	Team	G/GS	Snaps	Runs	Yds	Yd/R	TD	FUM	DVOA	Rk	DYAR	Rk	YAR	Suc%	Rk	BTkl	Rec	Pass	Yds	C%	Yd/C	TD	YAC	DVOA	Rk	DYAR	Rk
2014	CLE	16/4	382	148	607	4.1	8	3	-3.6%	25	30	25	43	44%	28	6	9	14	87	64%	9.7	0	7.6	-3.6%	–	8	–
2015	CLE	16/9	476	185	706	3.8	4	0	-4.0%	30	36	27	-21	41%	40	25	19	22	182	86%	9.6	1	11.9	17.9%	–	37	–
2016	CLE			180	711	4.0	4	3	-5.2%								21	28	174	75%	8.3	1		10.1%			

Crowell is a tough plugger when carrying the ball, but has surprisingly good receiving skills. Like his backfield mate Duke Johnson, he was better catching the ball in space than attempting to run behind the Browns' oft-overwhelmed line. Surprisingly, the most similar running back since 1978 over his first two seasons is Mark Ingram (2012-2013), followed by T.J. Duckett (2002-2003), Fred Lane (1997-1998), Ron Dayne (2000-2001), and Herman Heard (1984-1985).

Benny Cunningham Height: 5-10   Weight: 217   College: Middle Tennessee State   Draft: 2013/FA   Born: 7-Jul-1990   Age: 26   Risk: Green

Year	Team	G/GS	Snaps	Runs	Yds	Yd/R	TD	FUM	DVOA	Rk	DYAR	Rk	YAR	Suc%	Rk	BTkl	Rec	Pass	Yds	C%	Yd/C	TD	YAC	DVOA	Rk	DYAR	Rk
2013	STL	14/0	138	47	261	5.6	1	2	-5.7%	–	5	–	20	45%	–	6	6	10	59	60%	9.8	0	10.2	3.6%	–	8	–
2014	STL	16/2	396	66	246	3.7	3	1	1.7%	–	26	–	7	38%	–	12	45	53	352	85%	7.8	1	7.0	25.7%	8	109	6
2015	STL	16/1	282	37	140	3.8	0	1	-14.9%	–	-10	–	-29	38%	–	21	26	36	250	72%	9.6	0	9.2	28.3%	8	67	20
2016	LARM			61	275	4.5	1	2	0.6%								34	50	239	68%	7.0	1		-7.0%			

A fully healthy and available Todd Gurley should have reduced Cunningham's role in the Rams offense. However, Tre Mason's off-field problems have pushed him even further away from relevance, leaving Cunningham with very little competition for touches behind Gurley. Cunningham should carry the ball more than last year but theoretically, he should be targeted less in the passing game, since Jeff Fisher is talking about getting Tavon Austin to 100 receptions. (We're a bit skeptical.) Regardless of Fisher's goals for Austin, Cunningham's greatest value to the Rams offense should be in pass protection, where his reliable skills will carry huge value for a team starting a rookie quarterback.

Knile Davis   Height: 5-11   Weight: 227   College: Arkansas   Draft: 2013/3 (95)   Born: 5-Oct-1991   Age: 25   Risk: Blue

Year	Team	G/GS	Snaps	Runs	Yds	Yd/R	TD	FUM	DVOA	Rk	DYAR	Rk	YAR	Suc%	Rk	BTkl	Rec	Pass	Yds	C%	Yd/C	TD	YAC	DVOA	Rk	DYAR	Rk
2013	KC	16/1	170	70	242	3.5	4	2	-19.4%	--	-29	--	-15	34%	--	7	11	15	75	73%	6.8	0	8.3	-27.0%	--	-11	--
2014	KC	16/1	304	134	463	3.5	6	4	-17.7%	42	-50	40	-70	37%	41	13	16	25	147	64%	9.2	1	9.8	-17.2%	42	-4	42
2015	KC	14/0	79	28	72	2.6	1	0	-25.7%	--	-19	--	-19	39%	--	2	2	3	24	67%	12.0	0	12.5	46.0%	--	7	--
2016	KC			26	97	3.7	2	1	0.1%								6	9	35	67%	5.8	0		-15.1%			

Davis appears unlikely to make the Chiefs' roster. The depth chart at running back leaves him exclusively as a kick return option, and rookie Tyreek Hill may take over that speedster returner role. Davis still has the third-highest Speed Score in our database (back to 1999). With all the success other running backs have had recently in Kansas City, Davis may be the poster child for speed and size not being enough.

Mike Davis   Height: 5-9   Weight: 217   College: South Carolina   Draft: 2015/4 (126)   Born: 19-Feb-1993   Age: 23   Risk: Green

Year	Team	G/GS	Snaps	Runs	Yds	Yd/R	TD	FUM	DVOA	Rk	DYAR	Rk	YAR	Suc%	Rk	BTkl	Rec	Pass	Yds	C%	Yd/C	TD	YAC	DVOA	Rk	DYAR	Rk
2015	SF	6/0	125	35	58	1.7	0	0	-17.3%	--	-13	--	-42	31%	--	6	7	13	38	54%	5.4	0	5.0	-62.7%	--	-41	--
2016	SF			28	93	3.3	1	1	-16.2%								6	8	41	75%	6.9	0		-1.6%			

Injuries to Carlos Hyde and Reggie Bush set up Mike Davis to take over, but the fourth-round rookie was also bit by the injury bug (a fractured hand). When he did play, Davis made Glen Coffee proud with his 1.66 yards per carry. You have to go back to Willie Spencer in 1978 for the last time a running back had at least 30 carries and averaged under 1.70 yards per carry. Never heard of Spencer? Yeah, that is kind of the problem here. Davis was especially stymied on second downs, gaining at least 50 percent of needed yardage on only 2 of 14 carries. The 49ers do not have much of a presence behind Hyde, so the No. 2 job is there for the taking, but Davis' rookie season rests in a graveyard of bad seasons by forgettable backs from the last 40 years. The prospects are not very good.

Kenneth Dixon   Height: 5-10   Weight: 215   College: Louisiana Tech   Draft: 2016/4 (134)   Born: 21-Jan-1994   Age: 22   Risk: Green

Year	Team	G/GS	Snaps	Runs	Yds	Yd/R	TD	FUM	DVOA	Rk	DYAR	Rk	YAR	Suc%	Rk	BTkl	Rec	Pass	Yds	C%	Yd/C	TD	YAC	DVOA	Rk	DYAR	Rk
2016	BAL			69	312	4.5	1	1	2.2%								19	27	140	70%	7.4	1		-10.6%			

Dixon scored 87 career touchdowns at Louisiana Tech, the second most in FBS history. Who's No. 1? Navy quarterback Keenan Reynolds, who was also drafted by the Ravens this year. Dixon had 13 touchdown catches in his last two years at Louisiana Tech and was regarded as the best receiving back in the draft. That could help him see the field this year, though some concerns with his pass protection and fumbles (13 in the last three years) could keep him on the bench.

Kenyan Drake   Height: 6-1   Weight: 210   College: Alabama   Draft: 2016/3 (73)   Born: 26-Jan-1994   Age: 22   Risk: Blue

Year	Team	G/GS	Snaps	Runs	Yds	Yd/R	TD	FUM	DVOA	Rk	DYAR	Rk	YAR	Suc%	Rk	BTkl	Rec	Pass	Yds	C%	Yd/C	TD	YAC	DVOA	Rk	DYAR	Rk
2016	MIA			44	180	4.1	1	2	-6.0%								31	36	221	86%	7.1	1		0.6%			

Drake caught 29 passes for 276 yards and one touchdown for Alabama last year as Derrick Henry's change-up back, adding a dramatic kickoff return touchdown in the BCS Championship Game. It's hard to squeeze out playing time on college depth charts that feature Eddie Lacy, T.J. Yeldon, and Henry, so Drake showed up at the Senior Bowl and demonstrated just how good a third-down back and return man he could be, if not a full-fledged featured back. Drake doesn't look like much as a between-the-tackles runner but is incredibly quick with great hands and big-play capability in the open field.

Shaun Draughn   Height: 6-0   Weight: 205   College: North Carolina   Draft: 2011/FA   Born: 7-Dec-1987   Age: 29   Risk: Green

Year	Team	G/GS	Snaps	Runs	Yds	Yd/R	TD	FUM	DVOA	Rk	DYAR	Rk	YAR	Suc%	Rk	BTkl	Rec	Pass	Yds	C%	Yd/C	TD	YAC	DVOA	Rk	DYAR	Rk
2013	BAL	3/0	9	4	2	0.5	0	0	-58.5%	--	-10	--	-11	25%	--	0	0	--	0	--	0.0	0	--	--	--	--	--
2014	3TM	10/0	20	10	19	1.9	0	0	-62.7%	--	-20	--	-22	40%	--	0	0	--	0	--	0.0	0	--	--	--	--	--
2015	2TM	11/6	263	78	273	3.5	1	1	-16.8%	--	-24	--	-27	40%	--	13	27	35	176	77%	6.5	0	6.5	-27.3%	52	-25	52
2016	SF			71	240	3.4	1	2	-17.5%								24	31	168	77%	7.0	0		-8.1%			

In answering questions about San Diego's running back situation last year, we said the Chargers were paying Donald Brown $4 million to get a few touches you should pay someone like Shaun Draughn the league minimum to carry out. Draughn's name really just came up as one of those random journeymen backs that hang on for a few years without making much of an impact. San Francisco has another one on the roster in DuJuan Harris, and the two could be battling each other for a roster spot. Draughn ended up starting six games for the injury-ravaged 49ers, but was not very effective. Still, the fact that he was healthy and getting 18-plus touches for a month straight actually had people wanting to use him on their fantasy teams. Draughn earned those paychecks, while Brown touched the ball 67 times in San Diego for 317 yards. There is no point overspending on deep-bench running backs.

Andre Ellington

Height: 5-9 **Weight:** 199 **College:** Clemson **Draft:** 2013/6 (187) **Born:** 3-Feb-1989 **Age:** 27 **Risk:** Green

Year	Team	G/GS	Snaps	Runs	Yds	Yd/R	TD	FUM	DVOA	Rk	DYAR	Rk	YAR	Suc%	Rk	BTkl	Rec	Pass	Yds	C%	Yd/C	TD	YAC	DVOA	Rk	DYAR	Rk
2013	ARI	15/1	405	118	652	5.5	3	1	17.5%	4	117	15	107	46%	30	28	39	57	371	68%	9.5	1	6.7	22.3%	10	117	10
2014	ARI	12/12	528	201	660	3.3	3	2	-12.3%	35	-29	36	-87	39%	37	13	46	65	395	72%	8.6	2	7.7	-2.6%	27	44	23
2015	ARI	10/2	213	45	289	6.4	3	1	24.4%	–	64	–	63	58%	–	7	15	24	148	63%	9.9	0	5.3	3.7%	–	27	–
2016	ARI			45	188	4.2	1	1	1.2%								19	25	205	76%	10.8	1		24.2%			

Ellington was very effective in 2013 and 2015, and poor in 2014 when he had more work on his plate (also, more injuries). Health has definitely been an issue, but the good thing is the Cardinals have David Johnson and Chris Johnson to use as well. There is still a role for Ellington as a change-of-pace back and occasional receiver.

Ezekiel Elliott

Height: 6-0 **Weight:** 225 **College:** Ohio State **Draft:** 2016/1 (4) **Born:** 22-Jul-1995 **Age:** 21 **Risk:** Yellow

Year	Team	G/GS	Snaps	Runs	Yds	Yd/R	TD	FUM	DVOA	Rk	DYAR	Rk	YAR	Suc%	Rk	BTkl	Rec	Pass	Yds	C%	Yd/C	TD	YAC	DVOA	Rk	DYAR	Rk
2016	DAL			285	1267	4.4	10	4	8.4%								36	43	251	84%	7.0	1		-3.2%			

It's hard to recall a rookie who faced more pressure to immediately contribute than Elliott. This is what happens when you pair the consensus best rookie running back with the consensus best offensive line on the league's most visible franchise (which also has a decorated history of great running backs, no less). On the plus side, Elliott probably has one of the higher floors of any running back this season, even as a rookie. He has a clean bill of health and had a fumble rate of a measly 0.7 percent in 2015. And Dallas' offensive line just dragged a Darren McFadden-led backfield to a top-10 rushing DVOA mark, while also finishing sixth in adjusted line yards. Now, as the logic goes, imagine how the run game will look when they get to block for a player who just averaged 6.6 yards per carry and rushed for 41 touchdowns the past two seasons!

At the same time, it's a little presumptuous to start carving Elliott's name in the Cowboys' Ring of Honor. Ohio State's running game was highly prolific even when Elliott didn't carry the ball, a reflection of superior surrounding talent. This is why Elliott actually wasn't the best running back in this class according to BackCAST projections, which favored Derrick Henry. Elliott also finished behind Henry in Speed Score, though his 112.7 is also historically impressive. To be clear, Elliott still possesses terrific height-weight-speed measurables and strong game film from college, and should likely finish as an RB1 in fantasy this season. But a lot of projections seem to reflect his ceiling rather than his median outcome, so even a productive rookie season might not satisfy everyone.

Tyler Ervin

Height: 5-10 **Weight:** 192 **College:** San Jose State **Draft:** 2016/4 (119) **Born:** 7-Oct-1993 **Age:** 23 **Risk:** Blue

Year	Team	G/GS	Snaps	Runs	Yds	Yd/R	TD	FUM	DVOA	Rk	DYAR	Rk	YAR	Suc%	Rk	BTkl	Rec	Pass	Yds	C%	Yd/C	TD	YAC	DVOA	Rk	DYAR	Rk
2016	HOU			24	98	4.1	0	1	-3.4%								8	10	46	80%	5.7	0		-15.4%			

Ervin rushed for more than 1,600 yards with San Jose State in 2015, but the Texans took him in the fourth round as more of a space player. His 6.0 highlight yards per opportunity in college and physical talent (including a 4.41 40-yard dash, 39-inch vertical jump, and 130-inch broad jump) suggest he could succeed there. How exactly that squares with Lamar Miller, a quality space player in his own right, is a question that remains to be answered, especially after a quad injury cost Ervin part of the offseason.

Justin Forsett

Height: 5-8 | Weight: 194 | College: California | Draft: 2008/7 (233) | Born: 14-Oct-1985 | Age: 31 | Risk: Green

Year	Team	G/GS	Snaps	Runs	Yds	Yd/R	TD	FUM	DVOA	Rk	DYAR	Rk	YAR	Suc%	Rk	BTkl	Rec	Pass	Yds	C%	Yd/C	TD	YAC	DVOA	Rk	DYAR	Rk
2013	JAC	9/0	99	6	31	5.2	0	1	20.8%	--	7	--	9	33%	--	3	15	16	82	94%	5.5	0	7.2	-28.0%	--	-11	--
2014	BAL	16/14	707	235	1266	5.4	8	1	6.7%	12	149	11	207	44%	29	25	44	60	263	75%	6.0	0	7.4	-33.5%	51	-64	55
2015	BAL	10/10	477	151	641	4.2	2	0	9.1%	10	117	13	101	46%	22	12	31	41	153	76%	4.9	0	4.5	-42.6%	57	-64	57
2016	BAL			164	699	4.3	4	3	1.4%								30	39	192	77%	6.4	0		-7.2%			

Before breaking his arm, Forsett's rushing production was about on pace with his 2014 season, adjusting for the loss of Gary Kubiak, fewer leads, and some injuries on the offensive line. What could keep Forsett on the bench more this season is Baltimore's plethora of backs, including Buck Allen and rookie Kenneth Dixon. One area of Forsett's game that has not been good is receiving, which is a big part of Marc Trestman's offense. Forsett's receiving DVOA has been lower than -25.0% in four of the last five seasons, and Forsett ranked dead last in YAC+ last year after a bottom-six finish in 2014.

Matt Forte

Height: 6-2 | Weight: 218 | College: Tulane | Draft: 2008/2 (44) | Born: 10-Dec-1985 | Age: 31 | Risk: Yellow

Year	Team	G/GS	Snaps	Runs	Yds	Yd/R	TD	FUM	DVOA	Rk	DYAR	Rk	YAR	Suc%	Rk	BTkl	Rec	Pass	Yds	C%	Yd/C	TD	YAC	DVOA	Rk	DYAR	Rk
2013	CHI	16/16	928	289	1339	4.6	9	3	7.4%	15	193	4	191	47%	26	24	74	96	594	79%	8.0	3	6.8	8.5%	16	113	11
2014	CHI	16/16	975	266	1038	3.9	6	2	0.9%	18	113	12	112	50%	12	30	102	131	808	79%	7.9	4	7.7	5.0%	19	127	3
2015	CHI	13/13	600	218	898	4.1	4	2	12.0%	7	192	2	147	48%	17	37	44	58	389	76%	8.8	3	8.0	23.5%	11	112	7
2016	NYJ			253	1116	4.4	3	3	3.4%								49	69	412	71%	8.4	2		9.4%			

You could find backs that are bigger or faster, but what sets Forte apart is the way he makes everything look so smooth. He reads his blockers and defenders well, and almost never leaves you thinking that he left yards on the field. That's a big reason the Bears' offensive line had the NFL's second-lowest stuff rate last year. And of course he has perennially been one of the top receiving backs in the league, with at least 300 receiving yards in each of his eight NFL seasons. The Jets have also talked about using him as a slot receiver; he had nine catches for 61 yards out of the slot in 2015. On the other hand, with Bilal Powell around (and with Forte turning 31 this year), he might not get as many catches as he has with the Bears. And with only four 20-yard runs in 218 carries last year, his home-run burst is pretty much gone. All in all, though, he should be a huge upgrade over anyone the Jets had last season.

Arian Foster

Height: 6-1 | Weight: 225 | College: Tennessee | Draft: 2009/FA | Born: 24-Aug-1986 | Age: 30 | Risk: Red

Year	Team	G/GS	Snaps	Runs	Yds	Yd/R	TD	FUM	DVOA	Rk	DYAR	Rk	YAR	Suc%	Rk	BTkl	Rec	Pass	Yds	C%	Yd/C	TD	YAC	DVOA	Rk	DYAR	Rk
2013	HOU	8/8	327	121	542	4.5	1	0	11.4%	8	99	19	85	50%	16	9	22	35	183	63%	8.3	1	9.5	-9.2%	33	9	33
2014	HOU	13/13	621	260	1246	4.8	8	2	7.5%	10	167	9	159	46%	21	43	38	59	327	64%	8.6	5	6.8	0.7%	23	46	22
2015	HOU	4/4	190	63	163	2.6	1	2	-29.7%	--	-51	--	-55	40%	--	8	22	28	227	79%	10.3	2	7.3	35.0%	4	80	13
2016	MIA			112	475	4.3	4	2	2.1%								30	41	229	73%	7.6	1		-1.3%			

We wrote in *Football Outsiders Almanac 2015* about the thin line for Foster between remaining an effective and smart runner who may miss a couple games, or morphing into an injury-riddled back who cannot be what he once was. The 2015 season clearly argued the latter case—he struggled to find any running room at all on a lousy offense early, then tore his Achilles in the fourth quarter of a Week 7 blowout. (If ever put in charge of an NFL team, we at Football Outsiders like to think we would do a better job of managing important injury-prone players in blowouts than NFL teams do, even with the constraints of a 46-man active roster.) Signed with Miami in July.

Devonta Freeman

Height: 5-8 | Weight: 206 | College: Florida State | Draft: 2014/4 (103) | Born: 15-Mar-1992 | Age: 24 | Risk: Yellow

Year	Team	G/GS	Snaps	Runs	Yds	Yd/R	TD	FUM	DVOA	Rk	DYAR	Rk	YAR	Suc%	Rk	BTkl	Rec	Pass	Yds	C%	Yd/C	TD	YAC	DVOA	Rk	DYAR	Rk
2014	ATL	16/0	234	65	248	3.8	1	1	-22.9%	--	-38	--	-47	31%	--	15	30	37	225	81%	7.5	1	5.7	4.1%	20	33	26
2015	ATL	15/13	768	265	1056	4.0	11	3	-0.5%	24	90	15	122	46%	23	54	73	97	578	75%	7.9	3	6.0	-1.2%	28	68	19
2016	ATL			222	932	4.2	8	3	3.1%								59	84	481	70%	8.2	1		-1.3%			

The final rankings belie a back that didn't rush for more than 76 yards in a game in the second half of the season, but Freeman was a success in his sophomore season and was able to show enough burst to be a lead back. Freeman was also productive in the passing game despite being wildly over-targeted by a team with no one else to turn to after Julio Jones. In an ideal world, Freeman would do more with less touches. That ideal world relies more on a breakout seasons from Tevin Coleman and Justin Hardy than anything Freeman does.

Toby Gerhart   Height: 6-0   Weight: 231   College: Stanford   Draft: 2010/2 (51)   Born: 18-Mar-1987 Age: 29   Risk: N/A

Year	Team	G/GS	Snaps	Runs	Yds	Yd/R	TD	FUM	DVOA	Rk	DYAR	Rk	YAR	Suc%	Rk	BTkl	Rec	Pass	Yds	C%	Yd/C	TD	YAC	DVOA	Rk	DYAR	Rk
2013	MIN	14/0	196	36	283	7.9	2	1	73.6%	--	105	--	102	50%	--	8	13	19	88	68%	6.8	0	6.4	10.7%	--	22	--
2014	JAC	14/7	302	101	326	3.2	2	1	-16.1%	39	-35	38	-27	43%	33	15	20	24	186	83%	9.3	0	11.5	27.5%	--	53	--
2015	JAC	7/1	87	20	44	2.2	0	0	-50.8%	--	-47	--	-38	35%	--	0	3	5	23	60%	7.7	0	7.7	-0.8%	--	3	--

The arrival of Chris Ivory in Jacksonville ended any hopes that Gerhart had of returning. Gerhart's own struggles as a short-yardage back forced the Jaguars to look elsewhere. He had five goal-line carries in 2015, gaining 1 total yard while being stopped for no gain on four of the five plays.

Mike Gillislee   Height: 5-11   Weight: 208   College: Florida   Draft: 2013/5 (164)   Born: 1-Nov-1990 Age: 26   Risk: Green

Year	Team	G/GS	Snaps	Runs	Yds	Yd/R	TD	FUM	DVOA	Rk	DYAR	Rk	YAR	Suc%	Rk	BTkl	Rec	Pass	Yds	C%	Yd/C	TD	YAC	DVOA	Rk	DYAR	Rk
2013	MIA	3/0	8	6	21	3.5	0	0	29.1%	--	8	--	4	50%	--	0	0	--	0	--	0.0	0	--	--	--	--	--
2015	BUF	5/1	112	47	267	5.7	3	1	20.9%	--	54	--	20	36%	--	4	6	7	29	86%	4.8	0	5.2	-4.0%	--	4	--
2016	BUF			53	226	4.3	2	2	0.6%								5	7	35	71%	6.9	0		-3.8%			

Runs of 30, 50 and 60 yards accounted for 52 percent of Gillislee's rushing total last year. Remove them and his yards per carry average drops from 5.7 to 2.9. His Strat-o-Matic card will probably have a Long Gain on a Wrong defensive guess for a dice roll of 8 or 9, with lots of minus-2- to 2-yard results everywhere else.

Gillislee produced one of the most mind-boggling stat lines of the year in Week 17 against the Jets: 24 carries, 28 yards, one fumble. LeSean McCoy was unavailable and Karlos Williams was hurt early in the game, so the Bills force-fed Gillislee (who had some productive early runs) over and over again while clinging to a narrow lead. The strategy "worked" in that the Bills won, thanks to some clutch plays by Tyrod Taylor and Ryan Fitzpatrick showing his true colors with three interceptions. Gillislee is a replacement-level third running back who should never get 24 carries in a month, let alone one game.

Melvin Gordon   Height: 6-1   Weight: 215   College: Wisconsin   Draft: 2015/1 (15)   Born: 13-Apr-1993 Age: 23   Risk: Green

Year	Team	G/GS	Snaps	Runs	Yds	Yd/R	TD	FUM	DVOA	Rk	DYAR	Rk	YAR	Suc%	Rk	BTkl	Rec	Pass	Yds	C%	Yd/C	TD	YAC	DVOA	Rk	DYAR	Rk
2015	SD	14/12	395	184	641	3.5	0	6	-17.4%	43	-68	43	-94	43%	32	38	33	37	192	89%	5.8	0	7.8	-16.1%	46	-5	45
2016	SD			256	913	3.6	5	6	-14.9%								38	54	284	70%	7.5	1		-10.8%			

The odds are stacked against Gordon. First, he will have to prove his health. Gordon had offseason microfracture surgery, so it's unclear what kind of shape he is going to be in once training camp starts. If he's fully healthy, he will then need to prove his quality. Gordon didn't show off enough flashes last year to pass off his overall disappointment as unfortunate or just a result of the need to adapt to a new level of football. Finally, Gordon has to find a way to fit into Philip Rivers' offense. Gordon would be better off in a power-run offense, but the Chargers are locked into their shotgun-heavy scheme because Rivers thrives in it. Last year they ranked second in the league, using shotgun or pistol formations on 88 percent of their snaps.

Frank Gore   Height: 5-9   Weight: 215   College: Miami   Draft: 2005/3 (65)   Born: 14-May-1983 Age: 33   Risk: Yellow

Year	Team	G/GS	Snaps	Runs	Yds	Yd/R	TD	FUM	DVOA	Rk	DYAR	Rk	YAR	Suc%	Rk	BTkl	Rec	Pass	Yds	C%	Yd/C	TD	YAC	DVOA	Rk	DYAR	Rk
2013	SF	16/16	745	276	1128	4.1	9	3	-0.8%	24	91	20	40	42%	38	15	16	26	141	62%	8.8	0	6.3	-16.3%	39	-3	39
2014	SF	16/16	647	255	1106	4.3	4	2	6.3%	13	154	10	118	50%	11	19	11	19	111	58%	10.1	1	9.3	-14.4%	--	-1	--
2015	IND	16/16	690	260	967	3.7	6	4	-8.6%	36	0	36	-65	40%	42	41	34	58	267	59%	7.9	1	8.0	-32.1%	56	-60	56
2016	IND			256	923	3.6	7	2	-4.3%								31	46	184	67%	5.9	0		-24.0%			

Gore called 2015 the "toughest 967 [yards] I ever got," which sounds like an accurate statement after he posted the worst success rate of his career and dipped below 4.0 yards per carry for the first time ever. Most teams would look to move on from a back who turned 33 in May and has over 2,800 career carries, but Gore faces no significant competition for his job. As fans of football, we would like to see Gore do well, but Gore is in a battle with age and time he will eventually lose. The Colts are hoping that is not in 2016.

Jonas Gray Height: 5-10 Weight: 225 College: Notre Dame Draft: 2012/FA Born: 27-Jun-1990 Age: 26 Risk: Green

Year	Team	G/GS	Snaps	Runs	Yds	Yd/R	TD	FUM	DVOA	Rk	DYAR	Rk	YAR	Suc%	Rk	BTkl	Rec	Pass	Yds	C%	Yd/C	TD	YAC	DVOA	Rk	DYAR	Rk
2014	NE	8/3	158	89	412	4.6	5	0	29.1%	--	152	--	152	65%	--	3	1	3	7	33%	7.0	0	3.0	-38.7%	--	-4	--
2015	2TM	8/0	137	45	176	3.9	0	0	-5.8%	--	5	--	14	42%	--	2	7	8	76	88%	10.9	0	8.4	81.6%	--	29	--
2016	JAC			23	78	3.4	0	1	-13.0%								7	8	40	88%	5.7	0		2.0%			

Gray shot to fame during his brief stint with the New England Patriots (remember his 201-yard game on Sunday night against the Colts?) because of his discipline as a runner. He's a smart back who lacks the explosiveness to thrive as a starter in the NFL. The Patriots got the most out of him by providing clean running lanes for him to attack. When he was in Miami, the Dolphins tried to use him as a receiving back—a move that was akin to making Peyton Manning a scrambler. The Jaguars signed him off the Dolphins' practice squad in December. He'll compete with Denard Robinson for carries behind Chris Ivory and T.J. Yeldon this fall.

Jonathan Grimes Height: 5-10 Weight: 209 College: William & Mary Draft: 2012/FA Born: 21-Dec-1989 Age: 27 Risk: Green

Year	Team	G/GS	Snaps	Runs	Yds	Yd/R	TD	FUM	DVOA	Rk	DYAR	Rk	YAR	Suc%	Rk	BTkl	Rec	Pass	Yds	C%	Yd/C	TD	YAC	DVOA	Rk	DYAR	Rk
2013	HOU	2/1	58	21	73	3.5	1	1	21.7%	--	27	--	26	48%	--	0	6	6	76	100%	12.7	0	9.7	22.0%	--	10	--
2014	HOU	16/0	164	39	153	3.9	0	0	-24.0%	--	-22	--	-3	49%	--	2	6	8	86	75%	14.3	0	12.5	72.4%	--	33	--
2015	HOU	14/0	282	56	282	5.0	1	0	20.0%	--	54	--	42	38%	--	6	26	31	173	84%	6.7	1	5.0	-13.3%	44	1	44
2016	HOU			28	98	3.5	0	1	-10.3%								21	28	176	75%	8.4	1		9.8%			

What happens to a space back on a team that a) signs a big free-agent deal with a back who excels in space and caught 47 passes in 2015, and b) drafts another space back in the fourth round? Grimes is about to find out, as Lamar Miller and Tyler Ervin threaten to cut into his snap total. The Texans decided the RFA tender amount of $1.67 million was too much for Grimes and re-signed him for less, even *before* they added Miller or Ervin. That seems like a hint. Special teams work like he did in 2014 could save his job, but don't expect more touches than 2015 barring injury.

Todd Gurley Height: 6-1 Weight: 222 College: Georgia Draft: 2015/1 (10) Born: 3-Aug-1994 Age: 22 Risk: Green

Year	Team	G/GS	Snaps	Runs	Yds	Yd/R	TD	FUM	DVOA	Rk	DYAR	Rk	YAR	Suc%	Rk	BTkl	Rec	Pass	Yds	C%	Yd/C	TD	YAC	DVOA	Rk	DYAR	Rk
2015	STL	13/12	456	229	1106	4.8	10	3	10.0%	9	170	4	124	43%	36	46	21	26	188	81%	9.0	0	9.6	2.1%	25	25	31
2016	LARM			320	1495	4.7	10	5	5.6%								41	55	300	75%	7.3	0		-5.1%			

Todd Gurley is the Los Angeles Rams offense. Expectations can't be too high for the second-year back out of Georgia. His rookie season showed that he is on the fast track to success and only two things can hold him back: his situation and his health. Sometimes it's that simple. Gurley has every trait to not just be a great back, but a truly special one on par with Adrian Peterson during his prime.

DuJuan Harris Height: 5-7 Weight: 197 College: Troy Draft: 2011/FA Born: 3-Sep-1988 Age: 28 Risk: Green

Year	Team	G/GS	Snaps	Runs	Yds	Yd/R	TD	FUM	DVOA	Rk	DYAR	Rk	YAR	Suc%	Rk	BTkl	Rec	Pass	Yds	C%	Yd/C	TD	YAC	DVOA	Rk	DYAR	Rk
2014	GB	15/0	51	16	64	4.0	0	0	11.0%	--	14	--	13	56%	--	3	1	2	11	50%	11.0	0	10.0	23.1%	--	4	--
2015	2TM	4/1	98	48	189	3.9	0	1	-12.4%	--	-7	--	-31	38%	--	10	9	14	97	64%	10.8	0	10.9	12.1%	--	21	--
2016	SF			40	161	4.0	1	2	-1.3%								11	14	77	79%	7.0	0		1.0%			

Harris has been signed by eight franchises in his five-year career, including three last December alone. San Francisco was so banged up at running back that Harris was signed on December 23 and led the team in rushing in a game played four days later. He even chipped in eight catches for 86 yards against the Rams in Week 17 after entering the game with five career catches. Teams keep taking an interest in Harris, but with a healthier group this year, San Francisco's interest may be for the third-string at best.

Roy Helu Height: 5-11 Weight: 216 College: Nebraska Draft: 2011/4 (105) Born: 7-Dec-1988 Age: 28 Risk: Red

Year	Team	G/GS	Snaps	Runs	Yds	Yd/R	TD	FUM	DVOA	Rk	DYAR	Rk	YAR	Rk	Suc%	Rk	BTkl	Rec	Pass	Yds	C%	Yd/C	TD	YAC	DVOA	Rk	DYAR	Rk
2013	WAS	16/0	526	62	274	4.4	4	2	8.5%	–	48	–	51		45%	–	9	31	42	251	74%	8.1	0	6.1	-15.0%	38	-3	38
2014	WAS	14/0	364	40	216	5.4	1	2	15.7%	–	42	–	43		55%	–	21	42	47	477	89%	11.4	2	11.6	31.2%	5	108	7
2015	OAK	9/0	91	17	39	2.3	0	0	-30.1%	–	-16	–	-10		41%	–	4	9	16	75	56%	8.3	1	9.7	18.2%	–	30	–
2016	OAK			13	59	4.5	0	1	8.7%									24	33	196	73%	8.2	1		4.4%			

Signed to be a third-down option on a team that could desperately use one, Helu suffered through hip injuries in 2015 and had surgery to fix impingements on both sides of his body. Fifth-rounder DeAndre Washington is in town to push him. Successful rehab and holding off the youngster will give Helu a great chance to establish some value behind this offensive line heading into free agency next season. Anything less than that? You're looking at someone whose career could be done soon.

Derrick Henry Height: 6-3 Weight: 247 College: Alabama Draft: 2016/2 (45) Born: 17-Jul-1994 Age: 22 Risk: Green

Year	Team	G/GS	Snaps	Runs	Yds	Yd/R	TD	FUM	DVOA	Rk	DYAR	Rk	YAR	Rk	Suc%	Rk	BTkl	Rec	Pass	Yds	C%	Yd/C	TD	YAC	DVOA	Rk	DYAR	Rk
2016	TEN			126	514	4.1	7	2	4.7%									12	17	103	71%	8.6	0		-7.0%			

During his final season in college, Henry was a foundational piece of a National Championship-winning offense. He won the Heisman and proved his durability as a feature back. Yet, despite his positives, Henry was one of the most divisive prospects amongst draft analysts in 2016. Comparisons to Trent Richardson were made inevitable by the running lanes that Henry was given. Henry played behind a dominant offensive line, which meant he never had to be creative or show off subtle movements in tight spaces. Furthermore, he didn't break as many tackles as teams typically want from their bigger backs, and he showed off no skill set as a receiver.

On the other hand, our new BackCAST projection system actually gave Henry the top score among all this year's prospects, even higher than Ezekiel Elliott. Henry played a larger role in the offense than Elliott (or Richardson back in his day), and Henry averaged 5.97 yards per carry during his college career compared to 4.98 yards per carry on all other Alabama runs. That's similar to the gap with Elliott (6.69 vs. 5.61 for the rest of Ohio State) and slightly higher than what Richardson had (5.80 vs. 5.05). No, that doesn't mean the scouts are wrong and Henry is actually a better prospect than Elliott. But Richardson was really a black swan event of universal scouting failure, and it's unlikely Henry is going to follow in his footsteps.

Tim Hightower Height: 6-0 Weight: 226 College: Richmond Draft: 2008/5 (149) Born: 23-May-1986 Age: 30 Risk: Green

Year	Team	G/GS	Snaps	Runs	Yds	Yd/R	TD	FUM	DVOA	Rk	DYAR	Rk	YAR	Rk	Suc%	Rk	BTkl	Rec	Pass	Yds	C%	Yd/C	TD	YAC	DVOA	Rk	DYAR	Rk
2015	NO	8/3	192	96	375	3.9	4	0	16.5%	–	110	–	95		56%	–	10	12	13	129	92%	10.8	0	11.2	56.5%	–	51	–
2016	NO			79	311	3.9	3	3	-3.4%									16	20	141	80%	8.8	1		14.1%			

It's an incredible story that Hightower fought his way back into the league in 2015, four years removed from his last job. The way things are stacked against older backs in NFL circles, even making a roster was miraculous. And to have an actual role, swing fantasy football leagues across the nation, and get re-signed for next season to boot? It says a lot about Hightower's passion for the game, work ethic, and willingness to do the gritty special teams stuff. He's a completely fungible talent at this point, but you should be pulling for him anyway.

Jeremy Hill Height: 6-1 Weight: 233 College: Louisiana State Draft: 2014/2 (55) Born: 10/20/1992 Age: 24 Risk: Yellow

Year	Team	G/GS	Snaps	Runs	Yds	Yd/R	TD	FUM	DVOA	Rk	DYAR	Rk	YAR	Rk	Suc%	Rk	BTkl	Rec	Pass	Yds	C%	Yd/C	TD	YAC	DVOA	Rk	DYAR	Rk
2014	CIN	16/8	501	222	1124	5.1	9	5	12.6%	6	204	6	231		54%	4	26	27	32	215	84%	8.0	0	8.3	-3.7%	30	17	31
2015	CIN	16/15	458	223	794	3.6	11	3	0.1%	21	85	16	64		49%	12	23	15	19	79	79%	5.3	1	5.8	-13.4%	–	0	–
2016	CIN			238	979	4.1	9	5	-2.6%									21	29	152	72%	7.3	0		-5.9%			

Hill was a candidate to win the rushing title after his stellar 2014, but he had a poor sophomore season, despite his high touchdown total. Hill was reportedly asked by Hue Jackson to gain leg strength before the season, and it appeared to render him plodding rather than powerful. Though less elusive, Hill doubled down by trying to turn too many singles into home runs by dancing outside, to deleterious effect. Hill did reduce his fumbling in the regular season, only to cough one up at the worst possible time in the playoffs. Mainly, Hill was sacrificed to the Bengals' success in three-wide sets. With the wideout corps at reduced strength, the team could go back to more 2014-vintage powerball, which would benefit Hill—assuming he's all the way back mentally.

Ronnie Hillman Height: 5-9 Weight: 200 College: San Diego State Draft: 2012/3 (67) Born: 14-Sep-1991 Age: 25 Risk: Green

Year	Team	G/GS	Snaps	Runs	Yds	Yd/R	TD	FUM	DVOA	Rk	DYAR	Rk	YAR	Suc%	Rk	BTkl	Rec	Pass	Yds	C%	Yd/C	TD	YAC	DVOA	Rk	DYAR	Rk
2013	DEN	10/0	157	55	218	4.0	1	2	-6.9%	--	4	--	3	55%	--	2	12	14	119	86%	9.9	0	6.3	41.1%	--	45	--
2014	DEN	8/4	311	106	434	4.1	3	1	-1.4%	22	31	24	10	43%	31	6	21	34	139	62%	6.6	1	5.1	-18.3%	44	-8	43
2015	DEN	16/10	524	207	863	4.2	7	3	-6.2%	33	21	34	75	45%	28	29	24	35	111	69%	4.6	0	5.1	-59.0%	58	-89	58
2016	DEN			101	431	4.3	2	1	1.7%								28	36	224	78%	8.0	1		8.1%			

With C.J. Anderson getting lead back money and the Broncos spending a fourth-round pick on Utah's Devontae Booker, Hillman would seem to be the odd man out in Denver's backfield. But just two weeks before the draft, the Broncos signed Hillman to a one-year deal for $2 million that included $500,000 guaranteed. That potential dead money hit, and the sunk cost fallacy, may help Hillman keep his roster spot.

Jordan Howard Height: 6-0 Weight: 230 College: Indiana Draft: 2016/5 (150) Born: 2-Nov-1994 Age: 22 Risk: Green

Year	Team	G/GS	Snaps	Runs	Yds	Yd/R	TD	FUM	DVOA	Rk	DYAR	Rk	YAR	Suc%	Rk	BTkl	Rec	Pass	Yds	C%	Yd/C	TD	YAC	DVOA	Rk	DYAR	Rk
2016	CHI			92	401	4.4	5	2	9.0%								20	26	180	77%	9.0	1		1.9%			

At 230 pounds, the fifth-round rookie figures to be the power back in Chicago's rotation this year. He is a workhorse—he was first in Conference USA and fourth in the nation in carries when he played for Alabama-Birmingham, then fourth in the Big Ten in carries after transferring to Indiana in 2015.

Carlos Hyde Height: 6-0 Weight: 230 College: Ohio State Draft: 2014/2 (57) Born: 9/20/1991 Age: 25 Risk: Yellow

Year	Team	G/GS	Snaps	Runs	Yds	Yd/R	TD	FUM	DVOA	Rk	DYAR	Rk	YAR	Suc%	Rk	BTkl	Rec	Pass	Yds	C%	Yd/C	TD	YAC	DVOA	Rk	DYAR	Rk
2014	SF	14/0	292	83	333	4.0	4	1	3.0%	--	38	--	25	46%	--	21	12	16	68	75%	5.7	0	5.4	-38.5%	--	-21	--
2015	SF	7/7	295	115	470	4.1	3	1	3.9%	14	60	23	27	49%	14	24	11	15	53	73%	4.8	0	5.5	-33.9%	--	-18	--
2016	SF			299	1149	3.8	6	5	-11.4%								36	54	279	67%	7.7	1		-9.7%			

Either Hyde will be the centerpiece to Kelly's improved offense, or his 2-yard runs on first down will lead off the fastest three-and-out drives in the league. Hyde's 2015 started in grand fashion with a 168-yard rushing performance against Minnesota, but that honestly looks like the outlier so far. Though he can blame a stress fracture for ending his 2015 season, Hyde still has plenty to prove as the new lead back in San Francisco after Frank Gore was so productive for so long. Hyde's lack of receiving ability also hurts him. Through two seasons, he has 23 catches for just 121 yards. That average of 5.3 yards per catch ranks among the bottom 20 in NFL history for anyone with at least 20 catches. Still, the 49ers have talked a lot about using him more in the passing game this year.

Mark Ingram Height: 5-11 Weight: 215 College: Alabama Draft: 2011/1 (28) Born: 21-Dec-1989 Age: 27 Risk: Green

Year	Team	G/GS	Snaps	Runs	Yds	Yd/R	TD	FUM	DVOA	Rk	DYAR	Rk	YAR	Suc%	Rk	BTkl	Rec	Pass	Yds	C%	Yd/C	TD	YAC	DVOA	Rk	DYAR	Rk
2013	NO	11/3	168	78	386	4.9	1	0	4.6%	--	45	--	41	49%	--	15	7	11	68	64%	9.7	0	10.9	-5.4%	--	5	--
2014	NO	13/9	470	226	964	4.3	9	3	2.7%	14	108	14	129	50%	13	30	29	36	145	81%	5.0	0	5.0	-40.9%	56	-54	54
2015	NO	12/10	534	166	769	4.6	6	2	6.6%	12	108	14	120	45%	30	34	50	60	405	83%	8.1	0	9.2	4.0%	21	59	21
2016	NO			226	964	4.3	8	4	1.6%								55	87	402	63%	7.3	1		-25.6%			

It really feels like the lead back in New Orleans should be a consistent fantasy football star, right? But instead, Ingram has mostly teased Saints fans and fantasy football players alike. After 2014's breakout, 2015 saw him take a step back by heading to injured reserve for the final month of the season. Ingram has played all 16 games just once in five seasons—that's a feature, not a bug. As long as he's as involved in the passing game as he was last year, he'll have a ton of value in fantasy. But don't be afraid to cash him out as soon as you can get a more reliable asset.

Chris Ivory Height: 6-0   Weight: 222   College: Tiffin   Draft: 2010/FA   Born: 22-Mar-1988   Age: 28   Risk: Red

Year	Team	G/GS	Snaps	Runs	Yds	Yd/R	TD	FUM	DVOA	Rk	DYAR	Rk	YAR	Suc%	Rk	BTkl	Rec	Pass	Yds	C%	Yd/C	TD	YAC	DVOA	Rk	DYAR	Rk
2013	NYJ	15/6	331	182	833	4.6	3	2	-8.3%	33	2	33	38	44%	33	20	2	7	10	29%	5.0	0	4.0	-58.2%	--	-19	--
2014	NYJ	16/10	446	198	821	4.1	6	2	-0.6%	20	69	21	60	44%	25	33	18	27	123	67%	6.8	1	6.7	-15.4%	41	-2	41
2015	NYJ	15/14	537	247	1070	4.3	7	4	-11.5%	39	-31	40	23	43%	35	45	30	37	217	81%	7.2	1	9.2	-4.3%	32	21	32
2016	JAC			155	621	4.0	5	2	0.7%								22	29	169	76%	7.7	0		3.5%			

The latest Jaguars attempt to acquire a Marshawn Lynch-type for their Junior Achievement Seahawks (see Toby Gerhart), Ivory started last season with some big games against bad defenses (20-91-2 against the Browns, 29-166-1 against the Dolphins, 20-146-1 against Washington). He then dealt with minor hamstring and quad injuries that caused a 38-carry, 43-yard stretch over two games and sapped his effectiveness for most of the second half of the season. Ivory was among last year's top tackle-breakers, which will happen when you face the Browns, Titans, and Dolphins in power-saver mode, but it's also an indication of his value as a power/speed threat. That value is not worth anywhere near $32 million (over five years), but the Jaguars had cap space to burn, and Ivory will have room to run in their wide-open offense.

Fred Jackson Height: 6-1   Weight: 215   College: Coe College   Draft: 2007/FA   Born: 20-Feb-1981   Age: 35   Risk: N/A

Year	Team	G/GS	Snaps	Runs	Yds	Yd/R	TD	FUM	DVOA	Rk	DYAR	Rk	YAR	Suc%	Rk	BTkl	Rec	Pass	Yds	C%	Yd/C	TD	YAC	DVOA	Rk	DYAR	Rk
2013	BUF	16/6	663	206	890	4.3	9	3	9.1%	11	163	8	170	51%	9	27	47	66	387	71%	8.2	1	8.8	0.8%	23	52	20
2014	BUF	14/9	548	141	525	3.7	2	4	-4.7%	27	23	27	26	46%	20	25	66	90	501	73%	7.6	1	8.8	-21.5%	46	-38	51
2015	SEA	16/0	256	26	100	3.8	0	1	17.9%	--	25	--	16	46%	--	11	32	41	257	78%	8.0	2	8.0	20.3%	13	76	15

The undrafted veteran has had a fine career, but at age 34, he was not much help to Seattle, losing a costly fumble in Green Bay in Week 2. A team would have to be pretty desperate to sign a now 35-year-old back, but hey, the 49ers were using their seventh running back late in the season last year. It could happen.

Rashad Jennings Height: 6-1   Weight: 231   College: Liberty   Draft: 2009/7 (250)   Born: 26-Mar-1985   Age: 31   Risk: Red

Year	Team	G/GS	Snaps	Runs	Yds	Yd/R	TD	FUM	DVOA	Rk	DYAR	Rk	YAR	Suc%	Rk	BTkl	Rec	Pass	Yds	C%	Yd/C	TD	YAC	DVOA	Rk	DYAR	Rk
2013	OAK	15/8	548	163	733	4.5	6	0	15.8%	5	164	7	158	47%	25	9	36	46	292	76%	8.1	0	8.7	3.3%	22	44	21
2014	NYG	11/9	418	167	639	3.8	4	1	7.0%	11	112	13	75	47%	16	26	30	41	226	73%	7.5	0	10.4	-29.3%	50	-35	49
2015	NYG	16/16	425	195	863	4.4	3	2	5.6%	13	117	12	161	56%	4	25	29	40	296	73%	10.2	1	10.7	-0.9%	27	29	27
2016	NYG			208	891	4.3	5	3	4.4%								28	38	231	74%	8.3	1		7.5%			

Although he remains slightly underqualified as a lead back, Jennings did set a career-high in yards from scrimmage while remaining one of the league's more quietly efficient runners. The 31-year-old remains the best candidate to assume the early-down rushing duties for New York. First down was both Jennings' most productive and prolific down in 2015, as he posted a 13.5% rushing DVOA while receiving nearly 60 percent of his carries on that down. Jennings' total rushing attempts have increased every single season he's been in the league (excluding 2011, when he missed the whole year with a knee injury). So while no one thinks of Jennings as a workhorse, he could conceivably eclipse 200 carries for the first time in his career in 2016, given the stagnation of Andre Williams and the fact that rookie Paul Perkins seems more suited to contribute on passing downs right now. The Giants don't give Jennings nearly enough goal-line scoring opportunities to make him an exciting fantasy proposition, but the touches should be there, which is more than you can depend on for most backs nowadays.

Chris Johnson Height: 5-11   Weight: 197   College: East Carolina   Draft: 2008/1 (24)   Born: 23-Sep-1985   Age: 31   Risk: Green

Year	Team	G/GS	Snaps	Runs	Yds	Yd/R	TD	FUM	DVOA	Rk	DYAR	Rk	YAR	Suc%	Rk	BTkl	Rec	Pass	Yds	C%	Yd/C	TD	YAC	DVOA	Rk	DYAR	Rk
2013	TEN	16/16	798	279	1077	3.9	6	3	1.5%	22	110	17	75	46%	31	18	42	52	345	81%	8.2	4	9.4	10.8%	14	66	16
2014	NYJ	16/6	398	155	663	4.3	1	1	-6.0%	30	16	30	31	45%	24	10	24	34	151	71%	6.3	1	6.1	-13.8%	40	0	40
2015	ARI	11/9	366	196	814	4.2	3	2	-5.4%	31	26	32	24	47%	18	25	6	13	58	46%	9.7	0	10.5	-47.0%	--	-23	--
2016	ARI			105	416	4.0	4	1	3.3%								11	14	116	79%	10.5	0		19.6%			

The elder Johnson did a respectable job for Arizona last season, but he's no longer a star. This is the "Earnest Byner in Washington" stage of his career. Even just on success rate, ignoring all of David Johnson's long gains, the running game worked better with David Johnson carrying the ball (56 percent) than it did Chris (47 percent). While Bruce Arians has hinted at Chris still starting games this season, his offenses have traditionally featured one workhorse back. If that's not David Johnson this year, then something is wrong in Arizona. Don't forget that a decline in receptions from a veteran back is usually the sign that rushing efficiency will drop off in a year or two.

David Johnson
Height: 6-1 **Weight:** 224 **College:** Northern Iowa **Draft:** 2015/3 (86) **Born:** 16-Dec-1991 **Age:** 25 **Risk:** Green

Year	Team	G/GS	Snaps	Runs	Yds	Yd/R	TD	FUM	DVOA	Rk	DYAR	Rk	YAR	Suc%	Rk	BTkl	Rec	Pass	Yds	C%	Yd/C	TD	YAC	DVOA	Rk	DYAR	Rk
2015	ARI	16/5	412	125	581	4.6	8	3	15.7%	4	133	8	149	56%	3	27	36	57	457	63%	12.7	4	9.6	22.1%	12	120	6
2016	ARI			253	1160	4.6	10	4	9.6%								48	73	443	66%	9.2	1		2.0%			

Boy, general manager Steve Keim sure found a third-round steal in David Johnson. Of course, we know now that Arizona was determined to draft Ameer Abdullah in the second round before Detroit snatched him. We also know the Cardinals planned to start Andre Ellington and brought in post-gunshot wound Chris Johnson in August. Even after scoring two long touchdowns in his first two games, the rookie Johnson was still mostly confined to the bench, never earning double-digit carries until Week 13 after the other backs were injured. Johnson rushed for more than 90 yards in each of his next three starts, but was quiet to end the season. Still, he scored 13 touchdowns on limited touches (including one on a kick return) and should be a major factor in balancing the offense this season.

Duke Johnson
Height: 5-9 **Weight:** 207 **College:** Miami **Draft:** 2015/3 (77) **Born:** 23-Sep-1993 **Age:** 23 **Risk:** Green

Year	Team	G/GS	Snaps	Runs	Yds	Yd/R	TD	FUM	DVOA	Rk	DYAR	Rk	YAR	Suc%	Rk	BTkl	Rec	Pass	Yds	C%	Yd/C	TD	YAC	DVOA	Rk	DYAR	Rk
2015	CLE	16/7	561	104	379	3.6	0	1	-1.4%	25	30	31	9	45%	26	47	61	74	534	82%	8.8	2	8.0	2.3%	23	68	18
2016	CLE			154	657	4.3	3	2	0.1%								68	85	616	80%	9.1	2		18.9%			

Injuries during the preseason meant that the Browns previous coaching staff was reluctant to fully embrace Johnson during his rookie season. Johnson fell to the third round of the 2015 draft because of durability questions. Despite his limited role, he still thrived as a receiver showing off a skill set that is special. Johnson isn't just elusive and reliable, he's also versatile and precise in everything he does as a receiver. The question with Sir Duke isn't if he can thrive in Hue Jackson's offense, but rather how much Jackson will trust his ability to stay healthy. Johnson isn't just your typical receiving back; he is an aggressive, nuanced runner with the explosiveness and balance to create and exploit space. If he were 10 or 15 pounds heavier, he'd be an every-down back.

Matt Jones
Height: 6-2 **Weight:** 231 **College:** Florida **Draft:** 2015/3 (95) **Born:** 7-Mar-1993 **Age:** 23 **Risk:** Yellow

Year	Team	G/GS	Snaps	Runs	Yds	Yd/R	TD	FUM	DVOA	Rk	DYAR	Rk	YAR	Suc%	Rk	BTkl	Rec	Pass	Yds	C%	Yd/C	TD	YAC	DVOA	Rk	DYAR	Rk
2015	WAS	13/0	340	144	490	3.4	3	5	-23.4%	44	-92	44	-54	46%	23	19	19	25	304	76%	16.0	1	14.0	38.9%	3	75	16
2016	WAS			257	1027	4.0	4	5	-6.0%								27	39	218	69%	8.1	1		-2.7%			

Meet 2015's least productive NFL running back. After an auspicious two-score, 123-yard game in Week 2, Jones struggled with fumbles and stuffs at the line for the rest of his rookie season. Jones wasn't historically inefficient—remember, Trent Richardson was a starter not so long ago—and he was surprisingly productive on receiver screens after rarely catching the ball in college. However, following that promising Week 2 glimpse, Jones posted a positive rushing DVOA or DYAR in just two games the rest of the season. Somehow, this all convinced Washington to hand him the keys to the backfield. While it wasn't a hard decision to jettison Alfred Morris, the Redskins did nothing else to shake up their league-worst rushing game, signing no free agents and waiting until Round 7 to draft a back.

Jones may never be an explosive home run threat, but Washington would likely settle for better production near the goal line. Jones has the physical profile of a powerful goal-line back and ran for 11 touchdowns during his final year at Florida, yet ended up with a -23.5% rushing DVOA in the red zone, scoring just twice in 27 attempts. He will apparently receive ample opportunity to correct that and thus holds fantasy relevance, but don't be surprised if Washington adds more competition at some point before the regular season.

Eddie Lacy   Height: 5-11   Weight: 240   College: Alabama   Draft: 2013/2 (61)   Born: 1-Jan-1990   Age: 27   Risk: Yellow

Year	Team	G/GS	Snaps	Runs	Yds	Yd/R	TD	FUM	DVOA	Rk	DYAR	Rk	YAR	Suc%	Rk	BTkl	Rec	Pass	Yds	C%	Yd/C	TD	YAC	DVOA	Rk	DYAR	Rk
2013	GB	15/15	680	284	1178	4.1	11	1	5.3%	18	160	9	171	46%	27	29	35	44	257	80%	7.3	0	8.9	-3.5%	27	26	29
2014	GB	16/16	687	246	1139	4.6	9	3	9.8%	8	189	8	159	48%	15	51	42	55	427	76%	10.2	4	10.3	23.0%	9	112	4
2015	GB	15/12	471	187	758	4.1	3	4	-8.3%	35	3	35	42	49%	15	29	20	28	188	71%	9.4	2	10.7	-0.6%	26	20	33
2016	GB			228	1030	4.5	7	4	9.9%								32	42	253	76%	7.9	1		9.3%			

Lacy has always been a big back, and he ballooned in 2015, with some reports that he was playing at 260 pounds or more as he lost his starting job to James Starks. Somebody then went through Lacy's Twitter history, and lo and behold, the man loves to talk about food, including such delicacies as McGriddles, Gummi Bears, and Sonic burgers. Mike McCarthy called him out on his weight gain after the season, and Lacy took heed, showing up at OTAs in the 240-pound range after intense sessions of P90X. Lacy is a prime candidate to bounce back in his contract year, but buyer beware: a hefty payday may just encourage Lacy to super-size his meal at the drive-thru.

Jeremy Langford   Height: 6-0   Weight: 208   College: Michigan State   Draft: 2015/4 (106)   Born: 6-Dec-1991   Age: 25   Risk: Green

Year	Team	G/GS	Snaps	Runs	Yds	Yd/R	TD	FUM	DVOA	Rk	DYAR	Rk	YAR	Suc%	Rk	BTkl	Rec	Pass	Yds	C%	Yd/C	TD	YAC	DVOA	Rk	DYAR	Rk
2015	CHI	16/2	391	148	537	3.6	6	0	12.7%	5	123	11	111	47%	20	13	22	42	279	52%	12.7	1	10.4	-6.6%	34	16	34
2016	CHI			195	787	4.0	4	2	0.5%								35	56	261	63%	7.5	1		-15.2%			

Since 1989, there have been 233 running back seasons with at least 100 carries and a DVOA of at least 10.0%. Only one of those runners had a lower average gain than Langford last year: Edgar Bennett, who had an 11.5% DVOA and averaged 3.5 yards on 159 carries for the Packers in 1993. And Langford wasn't especially consistent either, with a success rate of 47 percent that was almost exactly average. Langford's DVOA was so high not because of anything special he did right, but of how little he did wrong: his stuff rate was among the five lowest in football, and he didn't fumble all season. That's obviously not sustainable, but Langford does have a track record of sure hands—he fumbled only five times in 609 touches in his last two years at Michigan State. Langford should be Chicago's lead rusher more often than not this fall, but John Fox has always favored a committee approach. Ka'Deem Carey, Jacquizz Rodgers, and Jordan Howard will all get their carries too.

Dion Lewis   Height: 5-7   Weight: 195   College: Pittsburgh   Draft: 2011/5 (149)   Born: 27-Sep-1990   Age: 26   Risk: Yellow

Year	Team	G/GS	Snaps	Runs	Yds	Yd/R	TD	FUM	DVOA	Rk	DYAR	Rk	YAR	Suc%	Rk	BTkl	Rec	Pass	Yds	C%	Yd/C	TD	YAC	DVOA	Rk	DYAR	Rk
2015	NE	7/6	298	49	234	4.8	2	2	28.1%	–	77	–	83	55%	–	25	36	50	388	72%	10.8	2	9.6	14.7%	15	78	14
2016	NE			96	438	4.6	2	1	5.8%								60	77	654	78%	10.9	3		32.1%			

Lewis suffered an ACL injury in November. He was back on the field during the Patriots minicamp in June. Like LeGarrette Blount, he's a one-skill back rescued from rock bottom by the Patriots, whose system allows otherwise replacement-level rushers to excel at the one thing they are good at. While Blount's skill is breaking tackles up the middle, Lewis' is open-field jukes; he started his career in Philadelphia as a Brian Westbrook surrogate but was too injury-/fumble-/mistake-prone to stay on the roster. The Patriots handed him the Danny Woodhead role, and 6-98-0 and 6-93-1 receiving lines ensued. Lewis has fantasy PPR value until he gets hurt again or the Patriots discover an even more obscure alternative. But he may be overdrafted in non-PPR leagues by people who don't realize he had only one game with more than 8 carries on the ground.

Marshawn Lynch   Height: 5-11   Weight: 215   College: California   Draft: 2007/1 (12)   Born: 22-Apr-1986   Age: 30   Risk: N/A

Year	Team	G/GS	Snaps	Runs	Yds	Yd/R	TD	FUM	DVOA	Rk	DYAR	Rk	YAR	Suc%	Rk	BTkl	Rec	Pass	Yds	C%	Yd/C	TD	YAC	DVOA	Rk	DYAR	Rk
2013	SEA	16/16	710	301	1257	4.2	12	4	5.9%	17	185	5	146	48%	19	59	36	44	316	82%	8.8	2	7.9	9.1%	15	55	19
2014	SEA	16/14	704	280	1306	4.7	13	3	23.1%	1	359	2	307	53%	5	88	37	48	367	77%	9.9	4	10.9	21.8%	11	93	9
2015	SEA	7/6	310	111	417	3.8	3	0	1.2%	19	47	25	54	50%	11	24	13	21	80	62%	6.2	0	6.7	-34.6%	–	-24	–

No more action, boss.

Early retirement does not come as much of a surprise from Lynch, who reportedly told teammates during the 2013 season that he might retire if the Seahawks won the Super Bowl. They won, he returned, and then he was denied a chance at the game-winning touchdown run in Super Bowl XLIX. Had Lynch been able to bask in that glory and follow it up with a typically productive 2015, then he would have two rings and more than 10,000 rushing yards. His Hall of Fame case would be in good shape, and what a crazy speech that might be.

The reality is 2015 was an injury-plagued disappointment, and now there may not be much of a push to induct the NFL's 35th all-time leading rusher, who had a tumultuous relationship with the media. Still, from the moment of the Beast Quake against the 2010 Saints through the point he should have carried the Seahawks to back-to-back titles, he really was the best back not named Adrian Peterson in his time. In an era that has tried to limit the workhorse back, Lynch's impact was undeniable, and the team built its offense around him. Seattle can continue a great run of success, but Lynch will still be remembered as one of the central figures from this era.

We just had to state his Hall of Fame case so we don't get fined.

Doug Martin

Height: 5-9 Weight: 210 College: Boise State Draft: 2012/1 (31) Born: 13-Jan-1989 Age: 27 Risk: Yellow

Year	Team	G/GS	Snaps	Runs	Yds	Yd/R	TD	FUM	DVOA	Rk	DYAR	Rk	YAR	Suc%	Rk	BTkl	Rec	Pass	Yds	C%	Yd/C	TD	YAC	DVOA	Rk	DYAR	Rk
2013	TB	6/6	303	127	456	3.6	1	1	-14.9%	40	-31	38	-53	39%	41	6	12	24	66	50%	5.5	0	4.8	-54.2%	--	45	--
2014	TB	11/11	345	134	494	3.7	2	0	-12.9%	36	-21	34	5	36%	43	7	13	20	64	65%	4.9	0	4.8	-47.2%	--	35	--
2015	TB	16/16	622	288	1402	4.9	6	5	-1.6%	26	81	18	150	48%	16	63	33	44	271	75%	8.2	1	7.0	-8.9%	38	11	36
2016	TB			289	1270	4.4	7	3	0.8%								35	49	285	71%	8.1	1		3.7%			

Doug Martin was unquestionably great last year. Tampa Bay finished first in open-field yards in 2015, as well as 13th in second-level yards; Martin was the key factor behind that, as you may have gleaned from the league-leading broken tackle total listed in his table. However, the decision to give Martin a big contract is somewhat more questionable. The Bucs have a ready back behind Martin in Charles Sims, and two of Martin's four NFL seasons have been dreadful. The Bucs were so worried about him as of last offseason that they turned down his fifth-year option. While the contract price wasn't incredibly prohibitive, it does tie Martin to the roster through 2017 in any logical scenario, and he has to repeat 2015 to be worth his cap number again. It's a fair deal, but not one without risk.

Tre Mason

Height: 5-8 Weight: 207 College: Auburn Draft: 2014/3 (75) Born: 8-Jun-1993 Age: 23 Risk: Red

Year	Team	G/GS	Snaps	Runs	Yds	Yd/R	TD	FUM	DVOA	Rk	DYAR	Rk	YAR	Suc%	Rk	BTkl	Rec	Pass	Yds	C%	Yd/C	TD	YAC	DVOA	Rk	DYAR	Rk
2014	STL	12/9	368	179	765	4.3	4	2	-0.9%	21	55	23	10	44%	30	14	16	26	148	62%	9.3	1	10.3	28.3%	6	55	17
2015	STL	13/3	184	75	207	2.8	1	3	-41.7%	--	-99	--	-90	39%	--	18	18	21	88	86%	4.9	0	6.6	-31.5%	--	-18	--
2016	LARM			28	114	4.1	0	1	-5.7%								8	12	51	67%	6.4	0		-10.1%			

Tre Mason's career appears to be a secondary issue at this point. Mason had an arrest warrant issued then withdrawn soon after the 2015 season came to a close. After that point, it emerged that police were called to his home on at least five separate occasions and family members became concerned with his well-being. When the Rams had a mandatory team meeting at the start of training camp, Mason was an unexplained absence. While we don't know what is happening to the former Auburn running back, we shouldn't expect him to be a factor for the Rams this year.

Ryan Mathews

Height: 6-0 Weight: 218 College: Fresno State Draft: 2010/1 (12) Born: 1-May-1987 Age: 29 Risk: Green

Year	Team	G/GS	Snaps	Runs	Yds	Yd/R	TD	FUM	DVOA	Rk	DYAR	Rk	YAR	Suc%	Rk	BTkl	Rec	Pass	Yds	C%	Yd/C	TD	YAC	DVOA	Rk	DYAR	Rk
2013	SD	16/14	472	285	1255	4.4	6	2	3.6%	19	141	10	120	49%	17	13	26	33	189	79%	7.3	1	7.3	19.9%	11	61	17
2014	SD	6/6	165	74	330	4.5	3	1	11.3%	--	62	--	37	47%	--	8	9	10	69	90%	7.7	0	7.0	37.6%	--	32	--
2015	PHI	13/6	245	106	539	5.1	6	3	20.4%	3	133	9	106	53%	5	16	20	28	146	71%	7.3	1	7.6	-22.2%	50	-11	49
2016	PHI			190	828	4.4	5	3	3.1%								31	40	234	78%	7.6	1		7.7%			

During Philly's running back overhaul following the 2014 season, Mathews' arrival got lost in the shuffle of the LeSean McCoy-DeMarco Murray swap and the Frank Gore renege. As it turns out, Mathews had a better year than any of the former All-Pros, thriving as an ancillary piece in the Eagles' running back rotation and posting the best rushing DVOA and success rate figures of his six-year career. With Murray banished to Tennessee and Philly making no significant additions to the backfield, Mathews may return to the alpha dog role he once held in San Diego. It's unclear if this would actually be a boost to his real-life or fantasy value, however. Mathews has played all 16 games just once in his career, and even then, he played through a high-ankle sprain during the last month of the season. He didn't make it through 2015 totally unscathed either, undergoing minor offseason groin surgery. The Eagles struck the right balance with Mathews' workload last year. Now the question is whether Philly can maintain that equilibrium, which would likely require Kenjon Barner or rookie Wendall Smallwood to prove ready for carries. If not, Mathews will have to risk his health and efficiency by carrying a larger burden.

Dexter McCluster   Height: 5-9   Weight: 172   College: Mississippi   Draft: 2010/2 (36)   Born: 26-Aug-1988   Age: 28   Risk: Green

Year	Team	G/GS	Snaps	Runs	Yds	Yd/R	TD	FUM	DVOA	Rk	DYAR	Rk	YAR	Suc%	Rk	BTkl	Rec	Pass	Yds	C%	Yd/C	TD	YAC	DVOA	Rk	DYAR	Rk
2013	KC	15/6	581	8	5	0.6	0	0	-89.6%	8	-25	8	-27	0%	0	6	53	83	511	64%	9.6	2	4.9	-16.0%	78	-22	76
2014	TEN	14/2	233	40	131	3.3	0	0	-20.2%	--	-19	--	-7	41%	--	8	26	37	197	73%	7.6	1	7.2	-0.8%	26	26	28
2015	TEN	11/2	305	55	247	4.5	1	2	-14.9%	--	-12	--	-1	31%	--	9	31	41	260	76%	8.4	1	6.3	-11.5%	41	5	41
2016	TEN			29	137	4.7	1	0	9.8%								35	48	279	73%	8.0	0		-0.3%			

Although his career has largely been a disappointment, McCluster has proven to be a reliable receiving back in Tennessee. He won't see many carries in 2016 because of the new additions in the backfield, but he should have the receiving role locked up. The Titans ideally won't feature McCluster heavily, but his versatility working underneath will be valuable situationally.

LeSean McCoy   Height: 5-11   Weight: 198   College: Pittsburgh   Draft: 2009/2 (53)   Born: 12-Jul-1988   Age: 28   Risk: Green

Year	Team	G/GS	Snaps	Runs	Yds	Yd/R	TD	FUM	DVOA	Rk	DYAR	Rk	YAR	Suc%	Rk	BTkl	Rec	Pass	Yds	C%	Yd/C	TD	YAC	DVOA	Rk	DYAR	Rk
2013	PHI	16/16	873	314	1607	5.1	9	1	18.1%	3	341	1	321	52%	8	51	52	64	539	81%	10.4	2	11.3	23.8%	9	137	7
2014	PHI	16/16	775	312	1319	4.2	5	4	-1.6%	24	87	15	93	45%	22	40	28	39	155	77%	5.5	0	6.6	-18.2%	43	-9	44
2015	BUF	12/12	598	203	895	4.4	3	2	8.8%	11	139	7	110	47%	21	39	32	50	292	64%	9.1	2	9.0	-2.0%	29	30	26
2016	BUF			223	947	4.2	7	1	5.2%								38	61	328	62%	8.6	1		-9.6%			

McCoy didn't fit Chip Kelly's *Big Bang Theory*-meets-SXSW-sidestage team culture in Philly. Rex Ryan's barely-controlled anarchy? *That's* more like it.

Shady got into a little barroom brawl and hosted an "All the Single Ladies" social. He wore his Kelly grudge on his sleeve in the Eagles rematch. (McCoy rushed for 74 yards and caught four passes for another 35; the Bills lost because of 15 penalties, many by McCoy's blockers.) He bounced every run he didn't like to the outside, but he was so effective in the open field that his low success rate didn't hurt the bottom line.

McCoy averaged 3.4 yards per rush on 93 carries between the guards and 5.3 yards per rush off tackle and to the outside (111 carries). Inability/unwillingness to poke through the middle of the line of scrimmage will be McCoy's undoing as soon as he loses a half-step of elusiveness. It also exacerbates the boom-or-bust nature of the Bills offense, though McCoy's success rates are no lower than Frank Gore's rates were in Greg Roman's system. Karlos Williams and/or Mike Gillislee will cut into Shady's carries, but there are plenty of carries to go around in Buffalo. McCoy should enjoy at least one more 1,000-yard season before 11 different issues/habits/injuries/defenders catch up to him all at once.

Darren McFadden   Height: 6-1   Weight: 211   College: Arkansas   Draft: 2008/1 (4)   Born: 27-Aug-1987   Age: 29   Risk: Green

Year	Team	G/GS	Snaps	Runs	Yds	Yd/R	TD	FUM	DVOA	Rk	DYAR	Rk	YAR	Suc%	Rk	BTkl	Rec	Pass	Yds	C%	Yd/C	TD	YAC	DVOA	Rk	DYAR	Rk
2013	OAK	10/7	336	114	379	3.3	5	1	-17.0%	42	-38	40	-31	34%	46	6	17	25	108	68%	6.4	0	7.4	-8.8%	32	7	34
2014	OAK	16/12	513	155	534	3.4	2	1	-13.9%	37	-33	37	-40	40%	35	14	36	56	212	64%	5.9	0	7.3	-37.5%	53	-75	56
2015	DAL	16/10	614	239	1089	4.6	3	3	-0.4%	23	83	17	103	50%	8	22	40	53	328	75%	8.2	0	7.9	6.9%	19	56	22
2016	DAL			54	255	4.7	2	1	14.4%								15	19	149	79%	9.9	1		19.3%			

While it wasn't quite as prolific as his breakout 2010 season, McFadden's 2015 campaign was the most important in the star-crossed career of the former fourth overall pick. Running on fumes after seven years in Oakland, McFadden found new life in Dallas after unexpectedly inheriting the bell-cow role from the troubled Joseph Randle in Week 7. From that point forward, McFadden finished 14th in rushing DYAR, and only Adrian Peterson carried the ball more often (202 carries). The brittle back set a career-high in total touches (279) during his age-28 season, helping him to post his first positive DYAR in four years.

Of course, one only needs to look at his Raiders days to understand the fallibility of banking on a second consecutive healthy and productive season from McFadden. Indeed, McFadden couldn't even make it through OTAs, breaking his elbow in a home accident. With Ezekiel Elliott as the undisputed alpha dog and Alfred Morris also around to provide relief, it's doubtful McFadden ever tastes as large a slice of the backfield pie as he did last season. Nevertheless, if he recovers from the broken elbow and stays healthy with a limited workload, perhaps McFadden can extend his career as a useful source of relief off the bench.

Jerick McKinnon Height: 5-9 Weight: 209 College: Georgia Southern Draft: 2014/3 (96) Born: 5-Mar-1992 Age: 24 Risk: Green

Year	Team	G/GS	Snaps	Runs	Yds	Yd/R	TD	FUM	DVOA	Rk	DYAR	Rk	YAR	Suc%	Rk	BTkl	Rec	Pass	Yds	C%	Yd/C	TD	YAC	DVOA	Rk	DYAR	Rk
2014	MIN	11/6	331	113	538	4.8	0	0	11.5%	7	82	16	72	42%	34	12	27	41	135	66%	5.0	0	6.4	-53.1%	57	-83	57
2015	MIN	16/0	160	52	271	5.2	2	0	15.3%	–	50	–	61	50%	–	17	21	29	173	72%	8.2	1	8.4	2.4%	22	27	28
2016	MIN			64	342	5.3	2	3	18.2%								27	35	228	77%	8.4	1		11.8%			

Adrian Peterson's return obviously meant a smaller role, but if anything McKinnon was even more spectacular in 2015. Seventeen broken tackles in only 73 touches? That's one broken tackle every 4.3 touches, a better rate than the 1-in-5.1 mark produced by Tampa Bay's Doug Martin, who led the league with 63 total broken tackles. McKinnon's usage was somewhat random last year, with four games with zero carries and four games with six or more. And his high yards per carry average is fluky—take away his 68-yard touchdown against the Giants and it drops just below 4.0. Still, he was more reliable, consistent, and explosive than Adrian Peterson last year on a per-carry basis, and should get more playing time in 2016. Mike Zimmer has specifically mentioned that he wants McKinnon to catch more passes this year.

Christine Michael Height: 5-10 Weight: 220 College: Texas A&M Draft: 2013/2 (62) Born: 9-Nov-1990 Age: 26 Risk: Blue

Year	Team	G/GS	Snaps	Runs	Yds	Yd/R	TD	FUM	DVOA	Rk	DYAR	Rk	YAR	Suc%	Rk	BTkl	Rec	Pass	Yds	C%	Yd/C	TD	YAC	DVOA	Rk	DYAR	Rk
2013	SEA	4/0	26	18	79	4.4	0	0	10.6%	–	14	–	17	78%	–	0	0	–	0	–	0.0	0	–	–	–	–	–
2014	SEA	10/0	73	34	175	5.1	0	1	10.0%	–	25	–	19	50%	–	8	1	2	12	50%	12.0	0	18.0	23.8%	–	3	–
2015	2TM	8/2	100	54	243	4.5	0	0	13.2%	–	51	–	29	48%	–	11	3	6	16	50%	5.3	0	6.0	-70.0%	–	-14	–
2016	SEA			51	209	4.1	1	1	0.2%								7	8	62	88%	8.9	0		19.7%			

The Cowboys took a flier on the former second-round pick when the Seahawks essentially traded Michael for some packing peanuts after the preseason. However, Michael was a healthy scratch the first three games of the season, and despite whispers that he could assume the starting job, no role ever materialized for him in Dallas. And yet, just as Michael's prospect status fizzled out, injuries to Marshawn Lynch and Thomas Rawls afforded him the most extended work of his career back in Seattle. Over the final three weeks of the regular season, Michael finished 10th in rushing DYAR and posted an impressive 18.6% rushing DVOA. Michael's roster status is still no lock with Rawls returning and three rookie running backs in tow, but he likely flashed enough glimpses of his long-rumored talent to earn a chance somewhere.

Lamar Miller Height: 5-11 Weight: 212 College: Miami Draft: 2012/4 (97) Born: 25-Apr-1991 Age: 25 Risk: Red

Year	Team	G/GS	Snaps	Runs	Yds	Yd/R	TD	FUM	DVOA	Rk	DYAR	Rk	YAR	Suc%	Rk	BTkl	Rec	Pass	Yds	C%	Yd/C	TD	YAC	DVOA	Rk	DYAR	Rk
2013	MIA	16/15	622	177	709	4.0	2	1	-7.7%	31	6	31	5	46%	29	16	26	35	170	74%	6.5	0	6.8	-7.9%	31	11	32
2014	MIA	16/16	642	216	1099	5.1	8	2	17.8%	3	246	4	239	57%	1	24	38	52	275	73%	7.2	1	6.1	-10.7%	37	9	37
2015	MIA	16/16	631	194	872	4.5	8	1	1.7%	18	81	19	105	43%	34	26	47	57	397	82%	8.4	2	9.0	-3.6%	31	32	25
2016	HOU			283	1275	4.5	10	3	10.1%								36	46	279	78%	7.7	2		15.6%			

Miller only received more than 20 carries in a game once in four years with the Dolphins. Limiting a running back's carries has its merits, of course, but by last season the Dolphins were so hesitant to unleash Tannehill and so stubborn about limiting Miller that they sometimes looked ready to punt on second down.

When Zac Taylor replaced Bill Lazor as offensive coordinator, Miller disappeared from the passing game, with just nine catches on 12 targets for 56 yards in his final five games. Lazor, for his part, would abandon the run roughly every other week, but at least Miller could count on five to seven catches per week when the passing game was in a manic phase.

Miller chose the Texans specifically because he would be used as more of a featured back, with Alfred Blue and Jonathan Grimes competing for more of a power back/short-yardage complementary role. Look for Miller to get a steady 20 touches per week. He won't be a high success-rate back, but Miller will be able to provide more big plays for a team less likely to forget that he's on the roster.

Alfred Morris   Height: 5-10   Weight: 219   College: Florida Atlantic   Draft: 2012/6 (173)   Born: 12-Dec-1988   Age: 28   Risk: Green

Year	Team	G/GS	Snaps	Runs	Yds	Yd/R	TD	FUM	DVOA	Rk	DYAR	Rk	YAR	Suc%	Rk	BTkl	Rec	Pass	Yds	C%	Yd/C	TD	YAC	DVOA	Rk	DYAR	Rk
2013	WAS	16/16	605	276	1275	4.6	7	6	2.0%	21	121	13	133	48%	20	24	9	12	78	75%	8.7	0	8.8	-12.0%	--	1	--
2014	WAS	16/16	595	265	1074	4.1	8	2	-1.4%	23	77	17	77	46%	18	28	17	26	155	65%	9.1	0	9.1	-8.7%	36	7	38
2015	WAS	16/16	385	202	751	3.7	1	0	-15.0%	41	-52	42	9	39%	44	12	10	13	55	77%	5.5	0	3.8	-27.6%	--	-10	--
2016	DAL			82	331	4.1	2	1	1.8%								10	14	76	71%	7.6	1		1.5%			

Robert Griffin III isn't the only one who misses the 2012 Redskins. Like his former backfield partner in crime, Morris saw his role deteriorate over the course of his time in Washington, ultimately getting squeezed out and sent away into the cold of free agency. Signing in Dallas to run behind the league's best offensive line seemed like a logical route to rejuvenate his career, but that was before the Cowboys said their vows with Ezekiel Elliott. Now, Morris will compete with Darren McFadden for the rest of the scraps in the running game. Ultimately, despite what the Cowboys O-line squeezed out of McFadden last season, that's probably the best for all parties involved. After 55 of his rookie-year carries went for 10 or more yards, Morris has had just 69 such rush attempts the past three seasons combined. Given his lack of contributions in the passing game, Morris will require an injury to Elliott or McFadden to reemerge on anyone's radar.

DeMarco Murray   Height: 6-0   Weight: 213   College: Oklahoma   Draft: 2011/3 (71)   Born: 12-Feb-1988   Age: 28   Risk: Yellow

Year	Team	G/GS	Snaps	Runs	Yds	Yd/R	TD	FUM	DVOA	Rk	DYAR	Rk	YAR	Suc%	Rk	BTkl	Rec	Pass	Yds	C%	Yd/C	TD	YAC	DVOA	Rk	DYAR	Rk
2013	DAL	14/14	672	217	1121	5.2	9	3	24.0%	1	295	2	288	53%	6	35	53	66	350	80%	6.6	1	7.2	-3.5%	26	40	24
2014	DAL	16/16	782	392	1845	4.7	13	5	14.8%	5	382	1	369	54%	3	51	57	64	416	89%	7.3	0	8.8	3.0%	21	58	14
2015	PHI	15/8	482	193	702	3.6	6	2	-12.1%	40	-29	39	19	45%	31	33	44	55	322	80%	7.3	1	8.7	-9.3%	39	13	35
2016	TEN			203	807	4.0	7	3	-0.1%								26	35	201	74%	7.7	1		0.9%			

Like Spider-Man donning the black suit, Murray's foray into new colors didn't turn out so well. A season removed from winning Offensive Player of the Year and sprinting away with the rushing title, Murray left for Philadelphia's (midnight) green pastures, only to realize he belonged in Dallas all along. Murray lurching sideways on ill-fated outside sweeps is a strangely indelible image from Chip Kelly's unceremonious final season, as things never meaningfully improved after he began the year with an impossibly disastrous 21-carry, 11-yard stat line through two weeks. After posting career-worsts in virtually every traditional or advanced metric, Murray is surely happy to be anywhere besides Philadelphia, even if Tennessee is far from the spotlight of the big NFC East markets. Bizarrely, the Titans have decided to construct an under-center, power-based offense, which accentuates Murray's strengths but not those of franchise quarterback Marcus Mariota. This is a fortunate break for Murray, as the ideal Mariota offense would bear a strong resemblance to what Murray just suffered through in 2015. On carries from the shotgun last year, Murray posted a -12.9% DVOA, by far the worst figure of the Philly running backs. Murray may not shine as brightly or burn out as spectacularly as he has the past two seasons, but a quietly effective campaign in a downhill running scheme could be just what he needs.

Latavius Murray   Height: 6-2   Weight: 223   College: UCF   Draft: 2013/6 (181)   Born: 18-Jan-1990   Age: 26   Risk: Yellow

Year	Team	G/GS	Snaps	Runs	Yds	Yd/R	TD	FUM	DVOA	Rk	DYAR	Rk	YAR	Suc%	Rk	BTkl	Rec	Pass	Yds	C%	Yd/C	TD	YAC	DVOA	Rk	DYAR	Rk
2014	OAK	15/3	275	82	424	5.2	2	1	1.7%	--	35	--	26	44%	--	3	17	23	143	74%	8.4	0	9.0	-6.6%	--	8	--
2015	OAK	16/16	680	266	1066	4.0	6	4	-5.6%	32	32	29	27	39%	43	39	41	53	232	77%	5.7	0	6.0	-30.6%	55	-47	54
2016	OAK			239	911	3.8	5	4	-7.2%								41	62	343	66%	8.4	1		-7.5%			

Oakland spent all offseason openly wondering about whether they should bring in a top-level back, but the chips didn't fall that way. Instead, we've got Murray, who had one of the least impressive 300-touch seasons in recent memory, at the head of the backfield again. The strength of the Oakland offensive line was able to pull the run game up, but Murray has no special qualities as a back to exploit them. He's a JAG masquerading as a No. 1 back, and the bubble is going to burst sooner rather than later for fantasy football owners. The question is: Can he sneak in one more nice year? Only Ezekiel Elliott has more help in front of him.

Branden Oliver

Height: 5-8 — Weight: 203 — College: Buffalo — Draft: 2014/FA — Born: 7-May-1991 — Age: 25 — Risk: Red

Year	Team	G/GS	Snaps	Runs	Yds	Yd/R	TD	FUM	DVOA	Rk	DYAR	Rk	YAR	Suc%	Rk	BTkl	Rec	Pass	Yds	C%	Yd/C	TD	YAC	DVOA	Rk	DYAR	Rk
2014	SD	14/7	373	160	582	3.6	3	0	-5.5%	28	20	29	24	44%	26	29	36	45	271	80%	7.5	1	9.4	15.3%	12	68	12
2015	SD	8/1	90	31	108	3.5	0	0	10.1%	--	27	--	23	48%	--	5	13	15	112	87%	8.6	0	10.4	37.4%	--	39	--
2016	SD			40	133	3.3	3	2	-4.1%								16	19	131	84%	8.2	1		12.5%			

Oliver got everyone talking during the preseason last year. An impressive display against the Dallas Cowboys and one big reception against the Seattle Seahawks saw him outperform Melvin Gordon. Ultimately that proved to be more of an indictment of Gordon than a sign of Oliver's quality. Oliver struggled once the regular season began before landing on injured reserve with turf toe after Week 8. Oliver is a fine back to have rostered but his limited skill set suggests he's better suited to remaining a backup.

Paul Perkins

Height: 5-10 — Weight: 208 — College: UCLA — Draft: 2016/5 (149) — Born: 16-Nov-1994 — Age: 22 — Risk: Green

Year	Team	G/GS	Snaps	Runs	Yds	Yd/R	TD	FUM	DVOA	Rk	DYAR	Rk	YAR	Suc%	Rk	BTkl	Rec	Pass	Yds	C%	Yd/C	TD	YAC	DVOA	Rk	DYAR	Rk
2016	NYG			49	223	4.6	0	2	3.2%								10	13	61	77%	6.1	0		-14.3%			

Perkins enters his rookie year as the clear future of the Giants backfield, but someone who might be blocked for the present. He was a universal sleeper among draftniks this spring thanks to his impressive all-around game at UCLA. Perkins averaged 6.0 yards per touch in college, catching or carrying the ball 701 times over three seasons. Moreover, he displayed an advanced aptitude for pass-blocking and fumbled on just 0.4 percent of his carries last season, qualities which could endear him to the Giants coaching staff. However, New York has the duo of Rashad Jennings and Shane Vereen under contract for the next two seasons, and both have skill sets which overlap with Perkins and make the rookie redundant. At some point, Perkins' youth and superior upside will allow him to surpass Jennings and Vereen on the depth chart. It's just not clear if that opportunity will arrive in 2016.

Adrian Peterson

Height: 6-2 — Weight: 217 — College: Oklahoma — Draft: 2007/1 (7) — Born: 21-Mar-1985 — Age: 31 — Risk: Yellow

Year	Team	G/GS	Snaps	Runs	Yds	Yd/R	TD	FUM	DVOA	Rk	DYAR	Rk	YAR	Suc%	Rk	BTkl	Rec	Pass	Yds	C%	Yd/C	TD	YAC	DVOA	Rk	DYAR	Rk
2013	MIN	14/14	674	279	1266	4.5	10	5	-3.1%	26	60	25	135	44%	32	42	29	41	171	73%	5.9	1	5.5	-22.8%	45	-20	43
2014	MIN	1/1	43	21	75	3.6	0	0	-1.8%	--	5	--	-4	43%	--	1	2	3	18	67%	9.0	0	10.0	53.4%	--	10	--
2015	MIN	16/16	665	327	1485	4.5	11	7	2.2%	17	143	6	133	45%	25	51	30	36	222	83%	7.4	0	8.6	-16.3%	47	-5	47
2016	MIN			324	1493	4.6	10	6	9.2%								25	32	184	78%	7.4	1		2.6%			

Peterson returned from his year in exile to produce perhaps his finest season, leading the league in carries, rushing yards and touchdowns, with ten more runs of double-digit yardage than any other player, despite an offensive line that was missing two starters all year and a passing game that scared no defense. His advanced stats weren't great because he was stuffed too much, his success rate was mediocre, and he still fumbled a lot, but given his workload and the mess around him, it's hard to argue that any runner did more to carry his team on his shoulders last year. There were signs he was slowing down at the end of the year, though—in the last six games of the season, including the playoffs, he averaged only 61.0 yards per game and 3.2 yards per carry. Peterson admitted after the season that retirement had crossed his mind, and that the mental grind of year-round training and the repetitive nature of OTAs and practice were starting to get to him. Will Peterson last long enough to put his name in the record books? He is currently 17th in NFL history with 11,675 rushing yards. A thousand yards in 2016 would put him in the top ten. Emmitt Smith's record of 18,355 seems safe, but if Peterson has just a couple of good years left, he should get the 2,009 yards he needs to pass LaDainian Tomlinson and move into the top five.

Chris Polk

Height: 5-11 — Weight: 222 — College: Washington — Draft: 2012/FA — Born: 16-Dec-1989 — Age: 27 — Risk: N/A

Year	Team	G/GS	Snaps	Runs	Yds	Yd/R	TD	FUM	DVOA	Rk	DYAR	Rk	YAR	Suc%	Rk	BTkl	Rec	Pass	Yds	C%	Yd/C	TD	YAC	DVOA	Rk	DYAR	Rk
2013	PHI	15/0	46	11	98	8.9	3	0	120.4%	--	64	--	59	64%	--	4	4	5	61	80%	15.3	0	12.3	81.6%	--	22	--
2014	PHI	14/0	97	46	172	3.7	4	0	12.9%	--	43	--	42	54%	--	3	2	3	16	67%	8.0	0	10.5	-19.9%	--	-1	--
2015	HOU	15/2	267	99	334	3.4	1	0	-17.0%	--	-31	--	-21	33%	--	12	16	28	109	57%	6.8	1	3.6	-30.1%	54	-26	53

Polk missed the cutoff for our running back rankings by a single carry, so Alfred Morris's 39 percent, not Polk's 33 percent, was the worst success rate by any back in 2015. It's not like Polk was ripping off big runs, either, as he had even fewer open-field yards per carry than Alfred Blue. Unsigned as of July.

Bilal Powell

Height: 5-10   Weight: 205   College: Louisville   Draft: 2011/4 (126)   Born: 27-Oct-1988   Age: 28   Risk: Green

Year	Team	G/GS	Snaps	Runs	Yds	Yd/R	TD	FUM	DVOA	Rk	DYAR	Rk	YAR	Suc%	Rk	BTkl	Rec	Pass	Yds	C%	Yd/C	TD	YAC	DVOA	Rk	DYAR	Rk
2013	NYJ	16/11	618	176	697	4.0	1	1	-8.7%	34	-1	34	37	43%	35	13	36	57	272	63%	7.6	0	8.7	-20.2%	44	-20	44
2014	NYJ	15/1	237	33	141	4.3	1	0	7.6%	–	22	–	24	45%	–	3	11	15	92	73%	8.4	0	8.7	2.2%	–	14	–
2015	NYJ	11/2	367	70	313	4.5	1	2	1.0%	–	25	–	48	46%	–	20	47	63	388	75%	8.3	2	8.9	-3.3%	30	36	24
2016	NYJ			103	369	3.6	1	2	-12.7%								48	64	385	75%	8.0	1		6.6%			

Powell is the dictionary definition of the "other" back in a committee. He's like James Starks with a little less sizzle. Powell boasted a career-high 47 catches last year as he took over third-down duties from Chris Ivory in the second half of last season and the Jets stopped pretending they would ever throw a pass to a tight end. Matt Forte can take care of himself and his quarterback on third downs than the players Powell backed up in the past. But the Jets coaching staff has made it clear that they don't want to overuse the 30-year-old Forte, so Powell will get a healthy dose of rotation touches. Also, the Jets still aren't exactly stacked at tight end, so both backs will catch their share of passes. Powell's greatest asset for five years has been his reliability and the fact that he never causes drama or a financial crunch. Those assets are always in short supply at Jets headquarters.

C.J. Prosise

Height: 6-0   Weight: 220   College: Notre Dame   Draft: 2016/3 (90)   Born: 20-May-1994   Age: 22   Risk: Green

Year	Team	G/GS	Snaps	Runs	Yds	Yd/R	TD	FUM	DVOA	Rk	DYAR	Rk	YAR	Suc%	Rk	BTkl	Rec	Pass	Yds	C%	Yd/C	TD	YAC	DVOA	Rk	DYAR	Rk
2016	SEA			65	296	4.6	3	2	9.0%								24	31	224	77%	9.4	1		6.6%			

Seattle selected three running backs in this year's draft, and Prosise has the best shot at making an immediate impact. Is that because he was the highest draft pick, or was he just the first one the Seahawks drafted because they knew he was the top back on their list? We would like to trust Seattle here, but recent picks such as Christine Michael and Robert Turbin did not exactly pan out, which is why Marshawn Lynch is largely going to be replaced by an undrafted player (Thomas Rawls) and Prosise, a converted wide receiver. Between Prosise and Jimmy Graham, Seattle could run 11 personnel while fielding five players who are basically wide receivers, even if some of them are versatile enough to be labeled something else.

Joseph Randle

Height: 6-0   Weight: 204   College: Oklahoma State   Draft: 2013/5 (151)   Born: 29-Dec-1991   Age: 25   Risk: N/A

Year	Team	G/GS	Snaps	Runs	Yds	Yd/R	TD	FUM	DVOA	Rk	DYAR	Rk	YAR	Suc%	Rk	BTkl	Rec	Pass	Yds	C%	Yd/C	TD	YAC	DVOA	Rk	DYAR	Rk
2013	DAL	13/2	119	54	164	3.0	2	0	-8.1%	–	1	–	-9	44%	–	2	8	10	61	80%	7.6	0	7.6	-10.6%	–	2	–
2014	DAL	16/0	93	51	343	6.7	3	2	26.3%	–	68	–	63	51%	–	13	4	5	23	80%	5.8	0	6.8	-19.8%	–	-2	–
2015	DAL	6/6	144	76	315	4.1	4	1	-3.5%	–	16	–	43	45%	–	14	10	10	86	100%	8.6	0	7.8	41.0%	–	36	–

The man who called out DeMarco Murray for leaving "meat on the bone" in 2014 has ironically wasted as much talent as almost any player in recent memory. Randle's first season as Murray's successor began innocently enough, peaking with a three-touchdown performance in Week 3 against Atlanta. But then Randle began to spiral out of control, complaining about losing his starting job to Darren McFadden following an oblique injury and subsequently refusing to show up for treatment. The previously promising prospect still doesn't turn 25 until the end of December, but with four arrests since his release and six overall since January 2015, Randle's NFL career is good as gone. Jerry Jones expressed some ominous concerns about Randle's mental health upon the running back's release. Clearly, football needs to remain on the backburner as Randle struggles to hold his life together.

Thomas Rawls

Height: 5-9   Weight: 215   College: Central Michigan   Draft: 2015/FA   Born: 8-Aug-1993   Age: 23   Risk: Yellow

Year	Team	G/GS	Snaps	Runs	Yds	Yd/R	TD	FUM	DVOA	Rk	DYAR	Rk	YAR	Suc%	Rk	BTkl	Rec	Pass	Yds	C%	Yd/C	TD	YAC	DVOA	Rk	DYAR	Rk
2015	SEA	13/7	289	147	830	5.6	4	1	26.4%	2	216	1	224	62%	1	27	9	11	76	82%	8.4	1	8.4	5.8%	–	13	–
2016	SEA			255	1200	4.7	8	3	11.0%								18	25	126	72%	7.0	0		-5.2%			

If not for a fractured ankle in December, Rawls could have pulled off the incredible feat of winning Offensive Rookie of the Year as an undrafted player. He really was that good in an offense that did not start out well even with Marshawn Lynch getting the bulk of the carries. Rawls' success rate (62 percent) was the fifth-highest season by a running back since 1989 (minimum 100 carries). Rawls averaged 6.0 yards per carry on first down, and only Le'Veon Bell had a higher rushing DVOA. The small sample size, the ankle, and the state of Seattle's offensive line provide risk for Rawls, but there is potential for a stud fantasy season here with an offense that you know will commit to the run.

Theo Riddick Height: 5-10 Weight: 201 College: Notre Dame Draft: 2013/6 (199) Born: 4-May-1991 Age: 25 Risk: Yellow

Year	Team	G/GS	Snaps	Runs	Yds	Yd/R	TD	FUM	DVOA	Rk	DYAR	Rk	YAR	Suc%	Rk	BTkl	Rec	Pass	Yds	C%	Yd/C	TD	YAC	DVOA	Rk	DYAR	Rk
2013	DET	14/0	43	9	25	2.8	1	0	16.2%	--	9	--	5	44%	--	3	4	8	26	50%	6.5	0	4.3	-22.0%	--	-4	--
2014	DET	14/2	172	20	51	2.6	0	0	-34.4%	--	-22	--	-17	40%	--	4	34	50	316	68%	9.3	4	9.0	14.7%	13	76	11
2015	DET	16/1	470	43	133	3.1	0	1	-24.5%	--	-29	--	-19	42%	--	40	80	99	697	81%	8.7	3	8.2	24.6%	10	201	2
2016	DET			93	389	4.2	1	2	-0.5%								75	94	717	80%	9.6	3		22.1%			

Obscure records department: in 2015, Riddick became the first player in NFL history to gain at least 25 yards receiving in 16 games without ever gaining 75 yards or more in any one contest. Riddick is on his way to becoming one of the premier receiving backs of his era. In the last two years, only Matt Forte has more receptions or more receiving yards among running backs, and only Le'Veon Bell has more receiving DYAR. On the other hand, Riddick has hardly ever run the ball, and when he has, he has been terrible at it. You've got to go back an awful long way to find a player with similar numbers in his first three seasons. The best match might be a former Lion, Cloyce Box, who spent a good chunk of his rookie year in 1949 as a running back before Detroit moved him to receiver (or "left end," in the parlance of those times) permanently. You've got to think a similar move could be in Riddick's future.

Stevan Ridley Height: 6-0 Weight: 223 College: Louisiana State Draft: 2011/3 (73) Born: 27-Jan-1989 Age: 27 Risk: Red

Year	Team	G/GS	Snaps	Runs	Yds	Yd/R	TD	FUM	DVOA	Rk	DYAR	Rk	YAR	Suc%	Rk	BTkl	Rec	Pass	Yds	C%	Yd/C	TD	YAC	DVOA	Rk	DYAR	Rk
2013	NE	14/6	333	178	773	4.3	7	4	10.2%	9	135	11	133	52%	7	14	10	12	62	83%	6.2	0	5.7	-27.6%	--	-9	--
2014	NE	6/5	187	94	340	3.6	2	0	-9.9%	--	-6	--	17	53%	--	3	4	5	20	80%	5.0	0	7.8	-20.2%	--	-2	--
2015	NYJ	8/1	86	36	90	2.5	0	0	-45.5%	--	-51	--	-36	28%	--	7	4	5	-2	80%	-0.5	0	2.8	-127.8%	--	-35	--
2016	DET			53	209	3.9	1	2	-1.9%								12	15	101	80%	8.4	1		11.8%			

The Jets paid Ridley to spend a season slowly rehabbing his ACL injury, then let him leave for the Lions as a free agent. They replaced Ridley with Khiry Robinson, who is on the mend from a broken leg. It's not hard to draft a powerful committee back at the end of the draft who works cheap and is actually healthy enough to contribute to the team. The Jets just prefer not to do so. Meanwhile, Ridley will battle Zach Zenner for the power-back role in the Detroit offense formerly filled by Joique Bell.

Denard Robinson Height: 5-11 Weight: 210 College: Michigan Draft: 2013/5 (135) Born: 22-Sep-1990 Age: 26 Risk: Blue

Year	Team	G/GS	Snaps	Runs	Yds	Yd/R	TD	FUM	DVOA	Rk	DYAR	Rk	YAR	Suc%	Rk	BTkl	Rec	Pass	Yds	C%	Yd/C	TD	YAC	DVOA	Rk	DYAR	Rk
2013	JAC	16/0	52	20	66	3.3	0	3	-86.1%	--	-61	--	-60	35%	--	0	0	1	0	0%	0.0	0	--	-102.0%	--	-2	--
2014	JAC	13/9	391	135	582	4.3	4	2	-8.1%	33	3	33	31	38%	40	9	23	31	124	74%	5.4	0	8.7	-39.2%	55	-43	52
2015	JAC	13/3	254	67	266	4.0	1	3	-24.4%	--	-43	--	-38	36%	--	7	21	30	164	70%	7.8	0	7.5	-8.6%	37	9	39
2016	JAC			35	155	4.4	0	1	0.4%								15	18	104	83%	6.9	0		4.9%			

Over the course of his career, Robinson has proven to be a more natural runner than expected. Robinson has dealt with nerve issues in his hand but had enough opportunities to show off his elusiveness and decisiveness as a runner. His path to playing time is blocked by T.J. Yeldon and Chris Ivory now, so Robinson's best hopes of making an impact will be with his explosiveness on misdirection plays.

Khiry Robinson Height: 6-0 Weight: 220 College: West Texas A&M Draft: 2013/FA Born: 28-Dec-1989 Age: 27 Risk: Green

Year	Team	G/GS	Snaps	Runs	Yds	Yd/R	TD	FUM	DVOA	Rk	DYAR	Rk	YAR	Suc%	Rk	BTkl	Rec	Pass	Yds	C%	Yd/C	TD	YAC	DVOA	Rk	DYAR	Rk
2013	NO	10/0	73	54	224	4.1	1	0	-11.9%	--	-7	--	4	41%	--	5	0	0	0	--	0.0	0	--	--	--	--	--
2014	NO	10/3	156	76	362	4.8	3	1	8.9%	--	57	--	67	58%	--	16	8	11	63	73%	7.9	0	10.8	-8.8%	--	3	--
2015	NO	8/0	133	56	180	3.2	4	0	3.0%	--	29	--	24	43%	--	12	17	20	115	85%	6.8	0	9.1	-14.7%	--	-1	--
2016	NYJ			17	49	3.0	0	1	-19.1%								8	10	44	80%	5.5	0		-7.3%			

A non-factor in the passing game, Robinson is the latest Jets retread back you probably won't need to remember. (See: Stacy, Zac.) Clearly behind Matt Forte and Bilal Powell in the pecking order for carries, Robinson had a nice little career for a UDFA find, but nothing we've seen in the last two years leads us to believe he's going to bust out this season.

Bishop Sankey Height: 5-9   Weight: 209   College: Washington   Draft: 2014/2 (54)   Born: 9/15/1992   Age: 24   Risk: Red

Year	Team	G/GS	Snaps	Runs	Yds	Yd/R	TD	FUM	DVOA	Rk	DYAR	Rk	YAR	Suc%	Rk	BTkl	Rec	Pass	Yds	C%	Yd/C	TD	YAC	DVOA	Rk	DYAR	Rk
2014	TEN	16/9	354	152	569	3.7	2	2	-4.5%	26	24	26	34	44%	27	18	18	23	133	78%	7.4	0	8.2	7.0%	--	26	--
2015	TEN	13/3	179	47	193	4.1	1	1	-1.5%	--	12	--	18	45%	--	9	14	23	139	61%	9.9	1	9.8	6.4%	--	26	--
2016	TEN			13	58	4.4	1	1	10.0%								11	14	91	79%	8.3	0		9.0%			

During his rookie season, Sankey struggled to get on the field because of poor footwork. It was an issue Ken Whisenhunt repeatedly talked about. During his second season, Sankey saw the field but was phased out of the offense as the season wore on. He lacks the physicality to make any impact at the tackle point and he is neither agile or fast enough to create or take advantage of space. He'll be lucky to make the Titans roster in 2016.

Charles Sims Height: 6-0   Weight: 214   College: West Virginia   Draft: 2014/3 (69)   Born: 9/19/1990   Age: 26   Risk: Green

Year	Team	G/GS	Snaps	Runs	Yds	Yd/R	TD	FUM	DVOA	Rk	DYAR	Rk	YAR	Suc%	Rk	BTkl	Rec	Pass	Yds	C%	Yd/C	TD	YAC	DVOA	Rk	DYAR	Rk
2014	TB	8/0	231	66	185	2.8	1	2	-42.1%	--	-84	--	-77	35%	--	9	19	27	190	70%	10.0	0	10.4	-4.4%	31	12	33
2015	TB	16/0	457	107	529	4.9	0	2	2.6%	16	50	24	71	57%	2	36	51	70	561	73%	11.0	4	9.5	29.2%	7	150	3
2016	TB			95	448	4.7	1	1	6.3%								57	77	538	74%	9.4	1		12.5%			

Incredibly productive with his touches, Sims is a natural pass-catcher who grew up in Air Raid offenses at Houston and West Virginia. Last year was a breakout year on the ground as well, where he sent would-be tacklers sprawling around him with an array of dazzling moves. With Doug Martin back in Tampa, Sims is still just a third-down back. But he may be the best in the business at this point.

Wendell Smallwood Height: 5-10   Weight: 208   College: West Virginia   Draft: 2016/5 (153)   Born: 29-Jan-1994   Age: 22   Risk: Yellow

Year	Team	G/GS	Snaps	Runs	Yds	Yd/R	TD	FUM	DVOA	Rk	DYAR	Rk	YAR	Suc%	Rk	BTkl	Rec	Pass	Yds	C%	Yd/C	TD	YAC	DVOA	Rk	DYAR	Rk
2016	PHI			68	319	4.7	1	3	1.6%								20	22	176	91%	8.8	1		14.8%			

The compact West Virginia product relied on consistency over flash, stringing together streaks of quality runs en route to 1,679 yards from scrimmage and 6.4 yards per carry during his junior season in Morgantown. Smallwood also has an element of explosiveness and ranked seventh in his class with a Speed Score of 104.2, ahead of more highly-touted backs such as Kenneth Dixon and Paul Perkins. Smallwood's three-down skill set makes him an intriguing arrival to the Eagles backfield, which subtracted DeMarco Murray without adding a significant replacement.

C.J. Spiller Height: 5-11   Weight: 195   College: Clemson   Draft: 2010/1 (9)   Born: 15-Aug-1987   Age: 29   Risk: Yellow

Year	Team	G/GS	Snaps	Runs	Yds	Yd/R	TD	FUM	DVOA	Rk	DYAR	Rk	YAR	Suc%	Rk	BTkl	Rec	Pass	Yds	C%	Yd/C	TD	YAC	DVOA	Rk	DYAR	Rk
2013	BUF	15/10	389	202	933	4.6	2	4	-17.8%	43	-70	43	-49	36%	44	18	33	40	185	83%	5.6	0	6.9	-17.8%	40	-8	41
2014	BUF	9/5	188	78	300	3.8	0	3	-33.2%	--	-76	--	-80	40%	--	10	19	22	125	86%	6.6	1	9.7	7.8%	--	28	--
2015	NO	13/2	200	36	112	3.1	0	1	-28.5%	--	-29	--	-24	36%	--	3	34	44	239	77%	7.0	2	7.5	-12.9%	43	2	43
2016	NO			38	156	4.1	1	2	-1.4%								52	63	446	83%	8.6	2		18.1%			

Spiller blamed his poor 2015 on preseason arthroscopic surgery from which he never recovered. For his sake, we hope that's true. He was noticeably slower last year, and it's possible that all the injuries he has sustained over the years simply caught up to him all at once. He was running behind Tim Hightower at OTAs, and if that holds true, he could very well be cut before the season.

Darren Sproles Height: 5-6   Weight: 181   College: Kansas State   Draft: 2005/4 (130)   Born: 20-Jun-1983   Age: 33   Risk: Green

Year	Team	G/GS	Snaps	Runs	Yds	Yd/R	TD	FUM	DVOA	Rk	DYAR	Rk	YAR	Suc%	Rk	BTkl	Rec	Pass	Yds	C%	Yd/C	TD	YAC	DVOA	Rk	DYAR	Rk
2013	NO	15/4	357	53	220	4.2	2	1	1.4%	--	21	--	25	49%	--	14	71	89	604	80%	8.5	2	7.3	23.9%	8	174	4
2014	PHI	15/0	337	57	329	5.8	6	2	30.4%	--	86	--	87	41%	--	18	40	63	387	65%	9.7	0	10.1	-3.1%	28	37	24
2015	PHI	16/4	393	83	317	3.8	3	1	14.8%	--	80	--	64	49%	--	14	55	83	388	66%	7.1	1	6.5	-24.9%	51	-50	55
2016	PHI			117	465	4.0	1	2	-3.5%								63	90	480	70%	7.6	2		-2.8%			

As bigger, faster, and stronger running backs come and go, one of the NFL's smallest jitterbugs continues to roll on. Sproles' multifaceted skill set has allowed him to age well while continuing to chip in as a runner, receiver, and punt returner. The latter is his best skill at this point, as Sproles led the league in points added on punt returns for the second consecutive season. Moreover, his two return touchdowns ended up being the winning scores in upset road victories over the Jets and Patriots. It wasn't all perfect for Sproles, who posted his worst receiving efficiency numbers since becoming a full-time rotation player eight seasons ago. However, he also maintained strong rushing numbers despite logging his most carries since 2011, and the departure of DeMarco Murray could require the Eagles to use Sproles as a runner a little more than usual. There has been some trade smoke surrounding Sproles this offseason, but no matter where he plays in 2016, he'll continue to command snaps on passing downs while also serving as one of the game's better returners.

Zac Stacy   Height: 5-8   Weight: 216   College: Vanderbilt   Draft: 2013/5 (160)   Born: 9-Apr-1991   Age: 25   Risk: Green

Year	Team	G/GS	Snaps	Runs	Yds	Yd/R	TD	FUM	DVOA	Rk	DYAR	Rk	YAR	Suc%	Rk	BTkl	Rec	Pass	Yds	C%	Yd/C	TD	YAC	DVOA	Rk	DYAR	Rk
2013	STL	14/12	566	250	973	3.9	7	1	-0.7%	23	80	23	55	42%	39	15	26	35	141	74%	5.4	1	5.7	-19.7%	43	-11	42
2014	STL	13/5	201	76	293	3.9	1	2	-8.8%	–	-1	–	3	50%	–	7	18	23	152	78%	8.4	0	8.7	23.2%	–	48	–
2015	NYJ	8/0	140	31	89	2.9	1	0	-24.0%	–	-17	–	-16	35%	–	1	9	12	65	75%	7.2	0	8.9	-18.6%	–	-3	–
2016	NYJ			13	43	3.3	0	1	-13.1%								9	11	63	82%	7.0	0		4.9%			

Stacy was a non-factor for the Jets after arriving from the Rams in the wake of his "Uh-Oh" Tweet when Todd Gurley was drafted. He saw most of his action in mop-up duty or when Bilal Powell was unavailable. Stacy is still on the Jets roster but did not comment on any social networks when the team signed Matt Forte or Khiry Robinson. He didn't really have to.

James Starks   Height: 6-2   Weight: 218   College: Buffalo   Draft: 2010/6 (193)   Born: 25-Feb-1986   Age: 30   Risk: Green

Year	Team	G/GS	Snaps	Runs	Yds	Yd/R	TD	FUM	DVOA	Rk	DYAR	Rk	YAR	Suc%	Rk	BTkl	Rec	Pass	Yds	C%	Yd/C	TD	YAC	DVOA	Rk	DYAR	Rk
2013	GB	13/1	220	89	493	5.5	3	1	19.2%	–	110	–	130	54%	–	13	10	13	89	77%	8.9	1	10.9	38.0%	–	36	–
2014	GB	16/0	260	85	333	3.9	2	1	-8.6%	–	0	–	-8	40%	–	14	18	29	140	62%	7.8	0	6.7	-27.1%	49	-20	46
2015	GB	16/4	528	148	601	4.1	2	5	-15.8%	42	-46	41	-49	43%	37	18	43	53	392	81%	9.1	3	11.4	17.3%	14	97	10
2016	GB			116	492	4.3	3	2	6.1%								30	38	213	79%	7.1	1		4.3%			

If Eddie Lacy was sharing junk food with his teammates, then Starks called dibs on all the butterfingers. Starks fumbled five times in 191 touches in 2015; that's as many fumbles as he had in 470 touches in his first five seasons. Four of those fumbles came in December, meaning 40 percent of the fumbles in his career hit the ground in that one month. Starks talked with the Patriots and Dolphins in free agency, but ended up re-signing with Green Bay for two years and $6 million. Starks' reception total soared last year, but if the Packers' offense returns to form, they likely won't be dumping off to the running backs so often.

Jonathan Stewart   Height: 5-10   Weight: 235   College: Oregon   Draft: 2008/1 (13)   Born: 21-Mar-1987   Age: 29   Risk: Yellow

Year	Team	G/GS	Snaps	Runs	Yds	Yd/R	TD	FUM	DVOA	Rk	DYAR	Rk	YAR	Suc%	Rk	BTkl	Rec	Pass	Yds	C%	Yd/C	TD	YAC	DVOA	Rk	DYAR	Rk
2013	CAR	6/1	110	48	180	3.8	0	1	-7.4%	–	2	–	1	48%	–	4	7	7	44	100%	6.3	0	6.0	30.1%	–	18	–
2014	CAR	13/8	546	175	809	4.6	3	2	1.3%	16	72	18	71	51%	7	32	25	31	181	81%	7.2	1	8.6	7.8%	16	35	25
2015	CAR	13/13	607	242	989	4.1	6	3	-6.2%	34	23	33	78	43%	33	49	16	21	99	76%	6.2	1	7.3	-5.4%	–	10	–
2016	CAR			240	1097	4.6	6	4	6.5%								23	28	183	82%	8.0	0		17.8%			

You know what you're getting with Jonathan Stewart at this point. He's a productive back with burst and power, he's going to bust tackles, and he's going to sit out at least a few games every season. A sprained left foot that sidelined Stewart once the Panthers clinched was re-aggravated in the Super Bowl, and he still had soreness in the foot as of June. Stewart has three years left on a contract that makes him one of the highest-paid running backs in football. With only $3.5 million in guarantees left after this season, it wouldn't be surprising if this is his last hurrah in Carolina.

Chris Thompson

			Height: 5-8			Weight: 187			College: Florida State				Draft: 2013/5 (154)		Born: 20-Oct-1990		Age: 26			Risk: Green	

Year	Team	G/GS	Snaps	Runs	Yds	Yd/R	TD	FUM	DVOA	Rk	DYAR	Rk	YAR	Suc%	Rk	BTkl	Rec	Pass	Yds	C%	Yd/C	TD	YAC	DVOA	Rk	DYAR	Rk
2013	WAS	4/0	0	0	0	0.0	0	--	--	--	--	--	--	--	--	--	0	--	0	--	0.0	0	--	--	--	--	--
2014	WAS	2/0	30	3	12	4.0	0	0	18.5%	--	3	--	3	67%	--	0	6	7	27	86%	4.5	1	6.0	-12.4%	--	1	--
2015	WAS	13/0	274	35	216	6.2	0	2	8.0%	--	22	--	25	43%	--	8	35	48	240	73%	6.9	2	4.7	-15.6%	45	-5	46
2016	WAS			47	201	4.3	1	2	-0.9%								39	50	393	78%	10.1	1		21.2%			

A former fifth-round pick whose career was teetering on the verge of extinction, Thompson not only made Washington's roster in 2015, but emerged as the Redskins' best running back. The diminutive third-year pro was the only Washington back to post a positive rushing DVOA or DYAR, and never relinquished the third-down role after earning it out of training camp. Thompson probably doesn't have the size to absorb much more than the 70 touches he had last season—his pro career almost never happened after he broke two vertebrae while at Florida State—but it's not inconceivable that he could demand a larger role given the mediocrity in the rest of the Redskins' backfield. At the very least, he'll have some marginal value in PPR leagues. Thompson's role is likely the safest of any running back on the Washington roster, a stark turnaround from his prospects at this time last year.

Mike Tolbert

			Height: 5-9			Weight: 243			College: Coastal Carolina				Draft: 2008/FA		Born: 23-Nov-1985		Age: 31			Risk: Blue	

Year	Team	G/GS	Snaps	Runs	Yds	Yd/R	TD	FUM	DVOA	Rk	DYAR	Rk	YAR	Suc%	Rk	BTkl	Rec	Pass	Yds	C%	Yd/C	TD	YAC	DVOA	Rk	DYAR	Rk
2013	CAR	16/13	599	101	361	3.6	5	0	9.0%	12	86	22	69	50%	13	11	27	32	184	84%	6.8	2	7.1	29.0%	6	77	14
2014	CAR	8/6	220	37	78	2.1	0	0	-53.2%	--	-72	--	-68	27%	--	2	12	17	93	71%	7.8	0	8.3	-39.4%	--	-21	--
2015	CAR	16/3	422	62	256	4.1	1	0	9.8%	--	54	--	53	56%	--	12	18	23	154	78%	8.6	3	7.6	25.3%	--	56	--
2016	CAR			59	213	3.6	1	2	-4.6%								17	21	123	81%	7.2	0		7.2%			

After recovering from last season's hairline leg fracture, Tolbert resumed his career objectives of a) being a bowling ball and b) recreating Mike Alstott's career in a more low-usage environment for goal-line backs. On a new two-year deal, the Panthers will continue to get heady play from the veteran until he loses a step.

Robert Turbin

			Height: 5-10			Weight: 222			College: Utah State				Draft: 2012/4 (106)		Born: 2-Dec-1989		Age: 27			Risk: Red	

Year	Team	G/GS	Snaps	Runs	Yds	Yd/R	TD	FUM	DVOA	Rk	DYAR	Rk	YAR	Suc%	Rk	BTkl	Rec	Pass	Yds	C%	Yd/C	TD	YAC	DVOA	Rk	DYAR	Rk
2013	SEA	16/0	231	77	264	3.4	0	0	-17.0%	--	-25	--	-28	44%	--	4	8	12	60	67%	7.5	0	8.0	-24.2%	--	-6	--
2014	SEA	16/3	260	74	310	4.2	0	1	9.5%	--	57	--	41	61%	--	5	16	20	186	80%	11.6	2	10.5	83.3%	--	104	--
2015	2TM	10/0	150	50	199	4.0	1	0	13.5%	--	45	--	32	48%	--	9	7	10	23	70%	3.3	0	3.7	-89.2%	--	-31	--
2016	IND			54	212	4.0	0	2	-7.8%								9	11	96	82%	10.6	1		28.0%			

After the Christine Michael experiment failed, the Cowboys tried their luck with another Seahawks reclamation project and signed Turbin in mid-November. The stout fourth-year back saw a high ankle sprain end his time in Seattle, and never really caught up when Cleveland claimed him off waivers shortly before the season began. Once Turbin was healthy, though, he actually performed well in limited carries spelling Darren McFadden, compiling 28 rushing DYAR and a 13.4% rushing DVOA during his time in Dallas. However, Turbin got squeezed out when the Cowboys upgraded their backfield this offseason. Now competing for the No. 2 role in Indianapolis, Turbin remains the quintessential fantasy handcuff you draft in the final round and immediately dump for whichever unknown receiver has three catches for 80 yards in Week 1.

Shane Vereen

			Height: 5-10			Weight: 205			College: California				Draft: 2011/2 (56)		Born: 2-Mar-1989		Age: 27			Risk: Green	

Year	Team	G/GS	Snaps	Runs	Yds	Yd/R	TD	FUM	DVOA	Rk	DYAR	Rk	YAR	Suc%	Rk	BTkl	Rec	Pass	Yds	C%	Yd/C	TD	YAC	DVOA	Rk	DYAR	Rk
2013	NE	8/1	295	44	208	4.7	1	1	-5.0%	--	6	--	6	39%	--	11	47	69	427	68%	9.1	3	5.9	25.1%	7	151	6
2014	NE	16/6	595	96	391	4.1	2	0	-7.4%	--	4	--	-2	41%	--	15	52	77	447	68%	8.6	3	7.3	-3.1%	29	49	20
2015	NYG	16/0	431	61	260	4.3	0	1	-4.8%	--	9	--	20	41%	--	15	59	81	494	73%	8.4	4	7.2	8.4%	17	103	9
2016	NYG			78	356	4.6	1	2	5.6%								59	78	527	76%	8.9	1		10.8%			

Vereen's receiving efficiency experienced a nice rebound after moving from Foxborough to East Rutherford. Though Vereen received the fewest carries per game since his abbreviated rookie season, the Giants did feed him a career-high in targets. And while he did fare slightly worse as a third-down receiver (12.7% DVOA after eclipsing 20.0% each of the past two years in New England), he compensated with obscene red zone efficiency. Vereen's 12 red zone targets were the second-highest total on the team, and he converted four of his nine receptions into touchdowns, good for a 54.5% DVOA. He might not maintain that kind of small-sample size efficiency in 2016, but Vereen will remain a slippery mismatch in space against opposing linebackers, capable of doing damage in any part of the field. Vereen probably has a higher floor and clearer role than any Giants running back at the moment, so even with the selection of intriguing rookie Paul Perkins, the sixth-year vet should remain one of Eli Manning's preferred targets.

Spencer Ware   Height: 5-10   Weight: 228   College: Louisiana State   Draft: 2013/6 (194)   Born: 23-Nov-1991   Age: 25   Risk: Green

Year	Team	G/GS	Snaps	Runs	Yds	Yd/R	TD	FUM	DVOA	Rk	DYAR	Rk	YAR	Suc%	Rk	BTkl	Rec	Pass	Yds	C%	Yd/C	TD	YAC	DVOA	Rk	DYAR	Rk
2013	SEA	2/0	7	3	10	3.3	0	0	-26.7%	--	-2	--	2	33%	--	0	0	0	0	--	0.0	0	--	--	--	--	--
2015	KC	11/2	159	72	403	5.6	6	0	25.8%	--	106	--	144	58%	--	12	6	6	5	100%	0.8	0	2.0	-167.8%	--	-42	--
2016	KC			87	386	4.4	5	1	9.4%								24	32	180	75%	7.5	1		3.6%			

Ware's efficiency and usage almost exactly matched Jamaal Charles' injury-shortened 2015 numbers. An ankle injury prevented Ware from seeing action in the divisional round loss to the Patriots, which was an underappreciated obstacle to the Chiefs' maintaining their No. 1 ranked ground attack in the 27-20 loss. In the offseason, Ware signed a three-year, $4.2 million extension and appears likely to be the first option to get carries behind Charles, particularly near the goal line. Reporters also noticed Ware spending a lot more time on passing drills in OTAs.

Charcandrick West   Height: 5-10   Weight: 205   College: Abilene Christian   Draft: 2014/FA   Born: 2-Jun-1991   Age: 25   Risk: Green

Year	Team	G/GS	Snaps	Runs	Yds	Yd/R	TD	FUM	DVOA	Rk	DYAR	Rk	YAR	Suc%	Rk	BTkl	Rec	Pass	Yds	C%	Yd/C	TD	YAC	DVOA	Rk	DYAR	Rk
2015	KC	15/9	497	160	634	4.0	4	1	2.8%	15	77	20	74	45%	27	29	20	34	214	59%	10.7	1	11.9	-20.4%	48	-13	50
2016	KC			64	260	4.0	2	1	-0.5%								14	20	101	70%	7.2	0		-5.0%			

"Tidget" (yes, that's really his nickname) signed a three-year, $4.2 million extension on March 30, the same day that fellow back Spencer Ware signed a contract that appears to be identical in all dimensions. In 2015, West saw more action but was the less efficient back. By the time the playoffs arrived, West had fallen behind Ware on the depth chart, and that's where he appears to be going into the 2016 season.

Terrance West   Height: 5-9   Weight: 225   College: Towson   Draft: 2014/3 (94)   Born: 1/28/1991   Age: 25   Risk: Green

Year	Team	G/GS	Snaps	Runs	Yds	Yd/R	TD	FUM	DVOA	Rk	DYAR	Rk	YAR	Suc%	Rk	BTkl	Rec	Pass	Yds	C%	Yd/C	TD	YAC	DVOA	Rk	DYAR	Rk
2014	CLE	14/6	401	171	673	3.9	4	1	-5.7%	29	21	28	39	47%	17	21	11	13	64	85%	5.8	1	4.8	17.5%	--	20	--
2015	2TM	8/0	125	62	231	3.7	0	2	-17.2%	--	-22	--	-35	42%	--	8	4	5	21	80%	5.3	0	4.5	-40.7%	--	-7	--
2016	BAL			13	59	4.5	0	1	6.9%								5	6	34	83%	6.8	0		6.7%			

Three teams in two years is bad news for a third-round pick. West put himself in the doghouse in Cleveland and has not cracked the 4.0 barrier in yards per carry for any team yet. The Ravens should have four backs ahead of him on the depth chart going into the preseason. Baltimore can only carry so many skill players, so look for West to come up short in the race to make the roster unless someone gets injured.

James White   Height: 5-9   Weight: 204   College: Wisconsin   Draft: 2014/4 (130)   Born: 3-Feb-1992   Age: 24   Risk: Green

Year	Team	G/GS	Snaps	Runs	Yds	Yd/R	TD	FUM	DVOA	Rk	DYAR	Rk	YAR	Suc%	Rk	BTkl	Rec	Pass	Yds	C%	Yd/C	TD	YAC	DVOA	Rk	DYAR	Rk
2014	NE	3/0	31	9	38	4.2	0	0	-7.1%	--	0	--	4	56%	--	0	5	5	23	100%	4.6	0	4.8	4.0%	--	5	--
2015	NE	14/1	290	22	56	2.5	2	0	-22.1%	--	-12	--	-13	32%	--	9	40	54	410	74%	10.3	4	8.7	33.3%	5	140	4
2016	NE			33	122	3.7	1	1	-9.0%								18	23	169	78%	9.4	1		15.5%			

White replaced the injured Dion Lewis in the second half of last season and began producing Lewis-like stat lines. In other words, he produced fifth generation Kevin Faulk-Danny Woodhead-Shane Vereen-Lewis stat lines, with five to seven catches per game, some big plays, and a carry now and then. The Patriots haven't shown much interest in using White as even their version of a traditional running back in two years, and he's now behind the recovering Lewis on the depth chart. White is one Lewis injury or mistake away from a regular role, but he's also a lackluster camp away from falling off the back of the roster.

Fozzy Whittaker   Height: 5-10   Weight: 202   College: Texas   Draft: 2012/FA   Born: 2-Feb-1989   Age: 27   Risk: Green

Year	Team	G/GS	Snaps	Runs	Yds	Yd/R	TD	FUM	DVOA	Rk	DYAR	Rk	YAR	Suc%	Rk	BTkl	Rec	Pass	Yds	C%	Yd/C	TD	YAC	DVOA	Rk	DYAR	Rk
2013	2TM	14/2	167	28	79	2.8	0	0	-25.2%	–	-17	–	-11	43%	–	1	21	35	155	60%	7.4	2	7.4	-5.5%	29	18	30
2014	CAR	10/1	84	32	145	4.5	1	0	22.7%	–	33	–	37	41%	–	2	5	6	60	83%	12.0	1	15.6	53.6%	–	24	–
2015	CAR	15/1	155	25	108	4.3	1	0	2.0%	–	11	–	20	44%	–	6	12	15	64	80%	5.3	0	9.3	-42.5%	–	-21	–
2016	CAR			24	93	3.8	0	1	-6.1%								16	20	124	80%	7.8	0		7.1%			

Returns kicks, plays a little running back when everyone gets hurt, and gives a damn on special teams. It's the perfect blueprint for a consistent NFL paycheck. Whittaker isn't fantasy-relevant unless he's on the Giants or someone brings the Giants curse onto his team, but he's functional depth with an established floor.

Andre Williams   Height: 5-11   Weight: 230   College: Boston College   Draft: 2014/4 (113)   Born: 28-Aug-1992   Age: 24   Risk: Red

Year	Team	G/GS	Snaps	Runs	Yds	Yd/R	TD	FUM	DVOA	Rk	DYAR	Rk	YAR	Suc%	Rk	BTkl	Rec	Pass	Yds	C%	Yd/C	TD	YAC	DVOA	Rk	DYAR	Rk
2014	NYG	16/7	520	217	721	3.3	7	1	-11.4%	34	-24	35	-54	38%	39	23	18	37	130	49%	7.2	0	8.2	-37.6%	54	-48	53
2015	NYG	16/0	157	88	257	2.9	1	0	-30.9%	–	-83	–	-64	34%	–	7	1	3	7	33%	7.0	0	3.0	-53.6%	–	-6	–
2016	NYG			50	197	3.9	3	2	5.5%								7	9	44	78%	6.3	0		-3.4%			

Once a fearsome bruiser at Boston College, the NFL version of Williams has turned into a bowling ball incapable of knocking over any pins. His physical profile makes him a logical goal-line choice for the Giants, but after a stellar rookie year in this role, Williams scored just once on seven carries inside the 5-yard line. That is 2.6 scores worse than what the average back would have been expected to convert; only Chris Johnson was a more inefficient goal-line back in 2015. If Williams isn't producing near the goal line, it's hard to imagine what role he'll have in New York. The pre-draft concerns about his lack of burst have clearly come to fruition. Among running backs with at least 300 carries over their first two seasons, Williams' 3.2 yards per carry average is the worst since the 1970 merger, right behind Lawrence Phillips and Trent Richardson. That's terrifying company to be around, and bodes quite ominously for the rest of Williams' pro career.

Damien Williams   Height: 5-11   Weight: 221   College: Oklahoma   Draft: 2014/FA   Born: 3-Apr-1992   Age: 24   Risk: Green

Year	Team	G/GS	Snaps	Runs	Yds	Yd/R	TD	FUM	DVOA	Rk	DYAR	Rk	YAR	Suc%	Rk	BTkl	Rec	Pass	Yds	C%	Yd/C	TD	YAC	DVOA	Rk	DYAR	Rk
2014	MIA	16/0	158	36	122	3.4	0	0	-9.7%	–	-2	–	-6	47%	–	12	21	27	187	78%	8.9	1	7.2	40.1%	2	90	10
2015	MIA	16/0	159	16	59	3.7	0	1	-49.1%	–	-28	–	-27	31%	–	7	21	28	142	75%	6.8	1	4.2	-7.4%	35	10	37
2016	MIA			27	112	4.2	0	1	-0.3%								10	13	72	77%	7.2	0		1.1%			

The ultimate Dolphins role-playing running back: a fumble-prone quasi-all purpose back with no big-play capability. Williams inexplicably started getting regular playing time as a third-down back late last year because Dan Campbell's staff had some strange aversion to Lamar Miller. He could remain in the picture this year as the third running back in the Dolphins' dreary committee, or the arrival of Arian Foster might leave him without a roster spot.

DeAngelo Williams   Height: 5-8   Weight: 210   College: Memphis   Draft: 2006/1 (27)   Born: 25-Apr-1983   Age: 33   Risk: Green

Year	Team	G/GS	Snaps	Runs	Yds	Yd/R	TD	FUM	DVOA	Rk	DYAR	Rk	YAR	Suc%	Rk	BTkl	Rec	Pass	Yds	C%	Yd/C	TD	YAC	DVOA	Rk	DYAR	Rk
2013	CAR	15/15	470	201	843	4.2	3	3	7.2%	16	126	12	76	43%	34	17	26	36	333	72%	12.8	1	14.3	16.0%	12	57	18
2014	CAR	6/6	135	62	219	3.5	0	1	-15.2%	–	-17	–	-22	45%	–	7	5	6	44	83%	8.8	0	11.4	-3.3%	–	4	–
2015	PIT	16/10	701	200	907	4.5	11	3	12.1%	6	184	3	162	50%	9	31	40	47	367	85%	9.2	0	9.2	30.5%	6	109	8
2016	PIT			153	715	4.7	4	1	12.7%								31	40	236	78%	7.6	1		9.3%			

Williams can make an easy claim to being the best backup running back in the NFL right now. He did a fantastic job in filling in for Le'Veon Bell last season. To keep their backs healthier, Pittsburgh must find a way to use Williams more. Bell has dominated the snap count when he has played the last two seasons. When Bell returned from his two-game suspension last year, Williams played just 32 offensive snaps in the next five games before Bell tore his MCL. Why not use both backs together? Todd Haley should consider splitting Bell, a good receiver, out wide in a favorable matchup with linebackers while putting Williams in the backfield. Williams' KUBIAK projection gets an extra boost from four games as the starter while Bell serves his likely early-season suspension.

Karlos Williams Height: 6-1 Weight: 230 College: Florida State Draft: 2015/5 (155) Born: 4-May-1993 Age: 23 Risk: Red

Year	Team	G/GS	Snaps	Runs	Yds	Yd/R	TD	FUM	DVOA	Rk	DYAR	Rk	YAR	Suc%	Rk	BTkl	Rec	Pass	Yds	C%	Yd/C	TD	YAC	DVOA	Rk	DYAR	Rk
2015	BUF	11/3	243	93	517	5.6	7	2	30.4%	--	159	--	150	56%	--	14	11	14	96	79%	8.7	2	4.0	-2.0%	--	11	--
2016	BUF			107	516	4.8	5	3	7.4%								11	14	74	74%	7.0	0		-0.8%			

Williams recorded five rushes of 20-plus yards to beautify his yards-per-carry rate, but it dips to a still-respectable 4.01 without his longest runs, three of which came late in lopsided wins over the Dolphins. Williams looks like a bruiser suited to do the dirty work LeSean McCoy won't touch (runs between the tackles, mainly), but a concussion and a shoulder injury slowed him for much of the season. Whenever he got a start in place of the injured McCoy, Williams would suffer his own injury. Williams then showed up overweight to OTAs, explaining that his wife's pregnancy forced him to gain sympathy weight. (That excuse *totally* wouldn't work for Russell Wilson.) Oh, and he got hit with a four-game PED suspension right before we went to press. Mike Gillislee is still around, and the Bills added Jonathan Williams in the draft, so don't make too many assumptions about the change-up role behind Shady.

Danny Woodhead Height: 5-9 Weight: 200 College: Chadron State Draft: 2008/FA Born: 25-Jan-1985 Age: 31 Risk: Yellow

Year	Team	G/GS	Snaps	Runs	Yds	Yd/R	TD	FUM	DVOA	Rk	DYAR	Rk	YAR	Suc%	Rk	BTkl	Rec	Pass	Yds	C%	Yd/C	TD	YAC	DVOA	Rk	DYAR	Rk
2013	SD	16/2	491	106	429	4.0	2	1	13.7%	6	104	18	105	60%	1	12	76	87	605	87%	8.0	6	6.1	41.2%	2	282	1
2014	SD	3/0	68	15	38	2.5	0	0	-30.3%	--	-14	--	-21	33%	--	2	5	6	34	83%	6.8	0	6.6	46.4%	--	24	--
2015	SD	16/2	594	98	336	3.4	3	0	-5.5%	--	13	--	14	45%	--	21	80	108	755	76%	9.4	6	8.9	25.8%	9	235	1
2016	SD			94	421	4.5	4	2	9.7%								78	101	741	77%	9.5	2		17.2%			

As a 31-year-old running back with a small frame, Woodhead isn't the guy you're supposed to rely on to carry your running game. And yet, that is where the Chargers could find themselves in 2016. Woodhead was the best back on the roster last year. He offers the Chargers versatility and consistency that they haven't seen from their other backs. His importance was highlighted by the reaction to an injury scare during OTAs when Woodhead rolled his ankle. Woodhead previously missed the majority of the 2014 season with a broken fibula, so any lower-leg issue is met with fear.

T.J. Yeldon Height: 6-1 Weight: 226 College: Alabama Draft: 2015/2 (36) Born: 2-Oct-1993 Age: 23 Risk: Green

Year	Team	G/GS	Snaps	Runs	Yds	Yd/R	TD	FUM	DVOA	Rk	DYAR	Rk	YAR	Suc%	Rk	BTkl	Rec	Pass	Yds	C%	Yd/C	TD	YAC	DVOA	Rk	DYAR	Rk
2015	JAC	12/12	620	182	740	4.1	2	0	-3.2%	28	39	26	31	42%	38	38	36	46	279	78%	7.8	1	8.3	5.7%	20	52	23
2016	JAC			159	678	4.3	3	2	0.9%								31	42	235	74%	7.6	1		0.6%			

The concern with Yeldon coming out of Alabama was that he lacked one truly great trait to rely on. That concern proved true during his rookie season, as Yeldon struggled to make a consistent impact behind an inconsistent offensive line. The Jaguars were expecting to see more of the kind of dynamism he showed off against the Buffalo Bills in London during his best game of the season, when he had 20 carries for 115 yards and a touchdown. But overall, the coaching staff appeared wary of asking too much of the youngster, making his usage inconsistent. They were completely allergic to using Yeldon at the goal line, a big reason why Blake Bortles had so many passing touchdowns. Toby Gerhart (5) and even Denard Robinson (5) had almost as many carries inside the 5-yard line as Yeldon (6).

Yeldon is the type of back who could put up huge numbers behind a good offensive line, but the Jaguars don't have a good run-blocking line and the arrival of Chris Ivory suggests that Yeldon's workload is about to go down rather than up.

Going Deep

Mack Brown, WAS: A twice-waived second-year running back wouldn't generate much interest in most backfields. But in a backfield as perilously thin as Washington's, even a longshot like Brown will get a real look this summer. Brown shuttled on and off of the Redskins practice squad last year before receiving a futures contact in January, and doesn't possess particularly intriguing measurables or collegiate production. The Florida product ran a 4.6 40 at his pro day, and his only noteworthy season at Gainesville came when he rushed for 543 yards on 148 carries as the lead back for a miserable 4-8 Gators team in 2013.

Alex Collins, SEA: Not that it matters, but *Madden 17* gave Collins, Seattle's fifth-round choice, a higher rookie rating (77) than third-round pick C.J. Prosise (75). Collins is a downhill runner who could see red zone touches, but he's not going to break tackles like a Marshawn Lynch or Thomas Rawls, nor will he catch the ball as well as Prosise. Still, there is definitely a spot for this Arkansas product on a team that needed youth and depth at the position.

John Crockett, GB: The undrafted rookie out of North Dakota State spent most of the year on the practice squad, then played in the final two games. He packed a lot of excitement into his nine carries, with gains of 10 and 12 yards, but also losses of 4 and 8. His average gain was 2.3 yards, but the standard deviation on those carries was 6.3 yards. With his only competition a trio of undrafted rookies, Crockett is the favorite to win the third running back job behind Eddie Lacy and James Starks this year.

Lance Dunbar, DAL: Dunbar was all set to break out in his first extended stretch of playing time last season before a debilitating hit in New Orleans left him with a torn ACL and MCL in his left knee. As the Cowboys' primary passing back, Dunbar fared well in the three-and-a-half games he did play, emerging as a capable receiving threat either out of the backfield or split out wide. Unfortunately, Dunbar was exclusively limited to rehab work during OTAs, and will almost certainly start the year on the PUP list. In Dallas' crowded backfield, Dunbar has a lot to prove if he hopes to reclaim the role he enjoyed all too briefly in 2015. (Full 2015 stats: 5 carries for 67 yards, 107.9% DVOA, plus 21 catches on 23 passes for 215 yards, 23.1% DVOA.)

Josh Ferguson, IND: Chuck Pagano described this undrafted rookie out of Illinois as a "mismatch out in space" in June. The departure of Ahmad Bradshaw creates an obvious opening for a third-down back, and Ferguson is as good a candidate as any to fill the position.

Taiwan Jones, OAK: For sale: Al Davis speed, never properly used on a football field. The Raiders made Jones a cornerback for a while, then switched him back to offense last year. As an occasional switch-up, he had 16 carries for 74 yards. He also managed 106 yards receiving on just 7 catches, mostly because of a 59-yard touchdown reception against the Jets in Week 8. Jones could play a role this year, but it's more likely the fullbacks scoop up any carries that don't go to Latavius Murray or DeAndre Washington.

Keith Marshall, WAS: Meet your all-time Speed Score champion. Once a top recruit, knee injuries at Georgia forced Marshall to take a backseat to Todd Gurley and Nick Chubb over his last three collegiate seasons. But Marshall proved there was still plenty of juice left in his knees at the combine, running a 4.31 40 while weighing in at 219 pounds. Having a great Speed Score alone won't make a career, as Mario Fannin and Knile Davis can attest. Still, Marshall is entering a barren backfield in Washington, and did average 6.5 yards per carry when given the chance to start as a freshman. If his health cooperates, Marshall is far more intriguing than your average seventh-round back.

Jacquizz Rodgers, CHI: The long-time Falcon missed most of his first season in Chicago with a broken arm. When healthy, he had only 14 carries for 41 yards in five games, and just a single pass reception. Still only 26, Rodgers figures to play a small role in Chicago's running back rotation this fall, primarily on passing downs.

Lorenzo Taliaferro, BAL: Taliaferro had a chance to replace Justin Forsett when he was injured last year, but a foot injury limited Taliaferro to three appearances. (He did have 13 carries for 47 yards, with a touchdown and 31.4% DVOA.) He's not really on the roster bubble yet, but he may only be the fourth-best back in town after the emergence of Buck Allen and drafting of Kenneth Dixon.

Juwan Thompson, DEN: ESPN.com's current projections have Thompson making Denver's roster as the fourth running back. But Thompson's versatility to play fullback could be undermined by the Broncos' choice of Andy Janovich in the sixth round to play that position.

Fitzgerald Toussaint, PIT: As Pittsburgh's third running back last year, Toussaint only saw 18 regular-season carries, and did very little with them (42 yards and a horrifying -52.3% DVOA). He did an admirable job in Cincinnati in the playoffs as the lead back, then had that big fumble in Denver a week later. Now he sits behind a window marked "in case of marijuana test-skipping emergency, break glass."

Terron Ward, ATL: This 2015 UDFA out of Oregon State is in the Jacquizz Rodgers mode of short, stout backs. He can help on kick returns, though he didn't get much of an opportunity to do so last year. As a pure runner, he doesn't have much to recommend him over any of the league's other journeymen. In fact, his decision-making between the tackles is questionable. But hey, he did get some garbage time runs against the Texans. He'll always have that. (Full 2015 stats: 29 carries for 95 yards and a touchdown, -12.3% DVOA, plus 9 catches for 73 yards, -33.4% DVOA.)

DeAndre Washington, OAK: Future Sproles Squad member, current fifth-round rookie. Washington (5-foot-8, 204 pounds) profiles as an NFL passing-down back and was also surprisingly successful as a runner in Texas Tech's Air Raid offense. The Oakland backfield isn't packed to the gills with talent, and one Latavius Murray could make Washington the next Devonta Freeman. He's a good name to pack in the back of your mind for Dynasty Leagues.

Terrell Watson, CLE: As an undrafted rookie, Watson led the Bengals in rushing in the preseason. This caught the eye of Hue Jackson, who snagged Watson almost immediately after he drove across Ohio to take over the Browns. Freed from the Cincy logjam, Watson has a decidedly non-zero chance to see decent playing time, especially if Isaiah Crowell loses time to his bad online judgment. You should pull hard for Watson (especially over a knucklehead like Crowell)—incredibly, as an infant Watson was left in a basket on the porch of a couple who took him in and raised him as their own. He overcame severe learning and social disabilities to dominate at tiny Azusa Pacific. That indefatigable nature speaks well for Watson's potential to contribute to the Browns offense going forward.

Jonathan Williams, BUF: Williams missed his senior season at Arkansas with a foot injury, was limited to light duties during Senior Bowl week, and could not run for scouts until his March pro day, when he produced solid-but-unspectacular results. Flashy 40 times aren't what Williams is about, anyway. He's a between-the-tackles runner with an excellent mixture of burst, short-area quickness and vision. He makes quick, economical cuts, finishes his runs with authority, and can catch and block well enough to stay on the field in any situation. His weaknesses include ball security and a tendency to get choosy about his holes, plus the injury concerns and a July drunk-driving arrest. It sounds like the Bills drafted a new running back who encapsulates all the strengths and weaknesses of all of their established running backs. Williams should push Karlos Williams in one of the most confusing all-Williams depth chart battles of Bills training camp.

Zach Zenner, DET: As Joe Redemann of NumberFire.com pointed out, Zenner's combine numbers are remarkably similar to those of Joique Bell, Detroit's power back last year. Bell's release was inspired in part by Zenner, who was a very pleasant surprise as an undrafted rookie out of South Dakota State before his season ended due to a rib injury. (Full 2015 stats: 17 carries for 60 yards, -0.3% DVOA, and a 53 percent success rate.)

Wide Receivers

In the following two sections we provide the last three years of statistics, as well as a 2016 KUBIAK projection, for every wide receiver and tight end who either played a significant role in 2015 or is expected to do so in 2016.

The first line contains biographical data—each player's name, height, weight, college, draft position, birth date, and age. Height and weight are the best data we could find; weight, of course, can fluctuate during the off-season. **Age** is very simple, the number of years between the player's birth year and 2016, but birth date is provided if you want to figure out exact age.

Draft position gives draft year and round, with the overall pick number with which the player was taken in parentheses. In the sample table, it says that Odell Beckham was chosen in the 2014 NFL draft with the 12th overall pick in the first round. Undrafted free agents are listed as "FA" with the year they came into the league, even if they were only in training camp or on a practice squad.

To the far right of the first line is the player's **Risk** for fantasy football in 2016. As explained in the quarterback section, the standard is for players to be marked Green. Players with higher than normal risk are marked Yellow, and players with the highest risk are marked Red. Players who are most likely to match or surpass our forecast—primarily second- stringers with low projections—are marked Blue. Risk is not only based on injury probability, but how a player's projection compares to his recent performance as well as our confidence (or lack thereof) in his offensive teammates.

Next we give the last three years of player stats. Note that rushing stats are not included for receivers, but that any receiver with at least five carries last year will have his 2015 rushing stats appear in his team's chapter.

Next we give the last three years of player stats. First come games played and games started (**G/GS**). Games played represents the official NFL total and may include games in which a player appeared on special teams, but did not play wide receiver or tight end. We also have a total of offensive **Snaps** for each season. Receptions (**Rec**) counts passes caught, while Passes (**Pass**) counts passes thrown to this player, complete or incomplete. Receiving yards (**Yds**) is the official NFL total for each player.

Catch rate (**C%**) includes all passes listed in the official play-by-play with the given player as the intended receiver, even if those passes were listed by our game charters as "Thrown Away," "Tipped at Line," or "Quarterback Hit in Motion." The average NFL wide receiver has caught between 58 and 60 percent of passes over the last three seasons; tight ends caught between 64 and 65 percent of passes over the last three seasons.

Plus/minus (+/-) is a metric that we introduced in *Football Outsiders Almanac 2010*. It estimates how many passes a receiver caught compared to what an average receiver would have caught, given the location of those passes. Unlike simple catch rate, plus/minus does not consider passes listed as "Thrown Away," "Tipped at Line," or "Quarterback Hit in Motion." Player performance is compared to a historical baseline of how often a pass is caught based on the pass distance, the distance required for a first down, and whether it is on the left, middle, or right side of the field. Note that plus/minus is not scaled to a player's target total.

Yards per catch (**Yd/C**) and receiving touchdowns (**TD**) are standard stats. Drops (**Drop**) list the number of dropped passes according to our game charting data. Our totals may differ from the drop totals kept by other organizations, and 2015 data is a combination of data from ESPN Stats & Info and Sports Info Solutions.

Next we list yards after catch (**YAC**), rank (**Rk**) in yards after catch, and **YAC+**. YAC+ is similar to plus-minus; it estimates how much YAC a receiver gained compared to what we would have expected from an average receiver catching passes of similar length in similar down-and-distance situations. This is imperfect—we don't specifically mark what route a player runs, and obviously a go route will have more YAC than a comeback—but it does a fairly good job of telling you if this receiver gets more or less YAC than other receivers with similar usage patterns. We also give a total of broken tackles (**BTkl**) according to Sports Info Solutions game charting.

The next five columns include our main advanced metrics for receiving: **DVOA** (Defense-Adjusted Value Over Average), **DYAR** (Defense-Adjusted Yards Above Replacement), and **YAR** (Yards Above Replacement), along with the player's rank in both DVOA and DYAR. These metrics compare every pass intended for a receiver and the results of that pass to a league-average baseline based on the game situations in which passes were thrown to that receiver. DVOA and DYAR are also adjusted based on the opposing defense and include defensive pass interference yards on passes intended for that receiver. The methods used to compute these numbers are described in detail in the "Statistical Toolbox" introduction in the front of the book. The important distinctions between them are:

Odell Beckham			Height: 5-11		Weight: 198		College: Louisiana State			Draft: 2014/1 (12)		Born: 5-Nov-1992		Age: 24		Risk: Green		
Year	Team	G/GS	Snaps	Rec	Pass	Yds	C%	+/-	Yd/C	TD	Drop	YAC	Rk	YAC+	BTkl	DVOA	Rk	DYAR	Rk	YAR	Short	Mid	Deep	Bomb
2014	NYG	12/11	771	91	130	1305	70%	+11.1	14.3	12	2	5.3	20	+0.2	14	25.8%	9	396	6	429	33%	40%	14%	12%
2015	NYG	15/15	998	96	158	1450	61%	+4.6	15.1	13	4	6.2	8	+2.0	12	10.3%	27	304	10	345	25%	50%	9%	16%
2016	NYG			98	161	1426	61%	--	14.5	12							12.8%							

• DVOA is a rate statistic, while DYAR is a cumulative statistic. Thus, a higher DVOA means more value per pass play, while a higher DYAR means more aggregate value over the entire season.

• Because DYAR is defense-adjusted and YAR is not, a player whose DYAR is higher than his YAR faced a harder-than-average schedule. A player whose DYAR is lower than his YAR faced an easier-than-average schedule.

To qualify for ranking in YAC, receiving DVOA, or receiving DYAR, a wide receiver must have had 50 passes thrown to him in that season. We ranked 87 wideouts in 2015, 87 wideouts in 2012, and 90 in 2013. Tight ends qualify with 25 targets in a given season; we ranked 51 tight ends in 2015, 50 tight ends in 2014, and 51 in 2013.

The final four columns break down passes based on distance through the air, including both complete and incomplete passes. The categories are **Short** (5 yards or less), **Mid** (6-15 yards), **Deep** (16-25 yards), and **Bomb** (26 or more yards).

The italicized row of statistics for the 2016 season is our 2016 KUBIAK projection based on a complicated regression analysis that takes into account numerous variables including projected role, performance over the past two years, projected team offense and defense, projected quarterback statistics, historical comparables, height, age, and strength of schedule.

It is difficult to accurately project statistics for a 162-game baseball season, but it is exponentially more difficult to accurately project statistics for a 16-game football season. Consider the listed projections not as a prediction of exact numbers, but as the mean of a range of possible performances. What's important is less the exact number of yards we project, and more which players are projected to improve or decline. Actual performance will vary from our projection less for veteran starters and more for rookies and third-stringers, for whom we must base our projections on much smaller career statistical samples. Touchdown numbers will vary more than yardage numbers. Players facing suspension or recovering from injury have those missed games taken into account.

Note that the receiving totals for each team will add up to higher numbers than the projection for that team's starting quarterback, because we have done KUBIAK projections for more receivers than will actually make the final roster.

A few low-round rookies, guys listed at seventh on the depth chart, and players who are listed as wide receivers but really only play special teams are briefly discussed at the end of the chapter in a section we call "Going Deep."

Two notes regarding our advanced metrics: We cannot yet fully separate the performance of a receiver from the performance of his quarterback. Be aware that one will affect the other. In addition, these statistics measure only passes thrown to a receiver, not performance on plays when he is not thrown the ball, such as blocking and drawing double-teams.

Top 20 WR by Receiving DYAR (Total Value), 2015

Rank	Player	Team	DYAR
1	A.Brown	PIT	517
2	D.Baldwin	SEA	414
3	A.J.Green	CIN	414
4	L.Fitzgerald	ARI	363
5	Jo.Brown	ARI	352
6	J.Jones	ATL	343
7	C.Johnson	DET	319
8	A.Robinson	JAC	318
9	S.Watkins	BUF	312
10	O.Beckham	NYG	304
11	B.Marshall	NYJ	303
12	E.Decker	NYJ	278
13	D.Hopkins	HOU	268
14	M.Floyd	ARI	256
15	T.Lockett	SEA	249
16	A.Hurns	JAC	236
17	R.Matthews	MIA	235
18	J.Maclin	KC	234
19	J.Kearse	SEA	227
20	J.Jones	GB	206

Top 20 WR by Receiving DVOA (Value per Pass), 2015

Rank	Player	Team	DVOA
1	D.Baldwin	SEA	39.6%
2	R.Matthews	MIA	36.4%
3	T.Lockett	SEA	35.1%
4	Jo.Brown	ARI	29.9%
5	J.Kearse	SEA	29.8%
6	S.Watkins	BUF	28.9%
7	A.J.Green	CIN	26.5%
8	M.Floyd	ARI	24.0%
9	A.Brown	PIT	19.7%
10	L.Fitzgerald	ARI	18.9%
11	M.Wilson	CHI	17.0%
12	A.Hurns	JAC	16.1%
13	J.Cotchery	CAR	14.8%
14	T.Smith	SF	14.3%
15	C.Johnson	DET	14.0%
16	A.Robinson	JAC	14.0%
17	E.Decker	NYJ	13.6%
18	J.Jones	GB	13.6%
19	S.Roberts	OAK	13.3%
20	D.Jackson	WAS	12.7%

Minimum 50 targets

Davante Adams

Height: 6-1 | Weight: 212 | College: Fresno State | Draft: 2014/2 (53) | Born: 12/24/1992 | Age: 24 | Risk: Yellow

Year	Team	G/GS	Snaps	Rec	Pass	Yds	C%	+/-	Yd/C	TD	Drop	YAC	Rk	YAC+	BTkl	DVOA	Rk	DYAR	Rk	YAR	Short	Mid	Deep	Bomb
2014	GB	16/11	738	38	66	446	58%	+1.0	11.7	3	4	4.6	44	+0.2	2	-9.0%	59	19	63	28	32%	50%	11%	6%
2015	GB	13/12	763	50	94	483	53%	-7.1	9.7	1	6	3.0	78	-1.7	6	-27.8%	84	-109	86	-131	39%	38%	16%	8%
2016	GB			43	75	483	57%	--	11.2	3						-6.7%								

There were six games by wide receivers last year that scored minus-50 DYAR or worse. Adams had two of them, in Week 10 against Detroit and Week 12 against Chicago, with a combined 12 catches for 93 yards on 32 targets. Adams and Oakland's Michael Crabtree were the only wide receivers to finish in the bottom ten in both plus-minus and YAC+. And Adams wasn't just in the bottom ten in overall DVOA; he was in the bottom ten in short routes, on deep balls, and passes over the middle, and he was dead last on passes to the outside. He was absolutely terrible in almost any situation, and when you consider the caliber of his quarterback, he was on the short list last year of the worst starters at any position. This wasn't a fluke: by DVOA, the two worst qualifying seasons of any Green Bay wideout in the Aaron Rodgers era belong to Adams in 2014 and again in 2015. Jordy Nelson's return pushes Randall Cobb to the No. 2 slot and Adams back to third receiver, assuming he beats out Ty Montgomery and playoff sensation Jeff Janis.

Nelson Agholor

Height: 6-0 | Weight: 198 | College: USC | Draft: 2015/1 (20) | Born: 24-May-1993 | Age: 23 | Risk: Yellow

Year	Team	G/GS	Snaps	Rec	Pass	Yds	C%	+/-	Yd/C	TD	Drop	YAC	Rk	YAC+	BTkl	DVOA	Rk	DYAR	Rk	YAR	Short	Mid	Deep	Bomb
2015	PHI	13/12	670	23	44	283	52%	-3.0	12.3	1	2	4.0	--	-0.9	4	-21.3%	--	-31	--	-16	44%	31%	13%	11%
2016	PHI			43	73	543	59%	--	12.6	4						-3.6%								

Playmaker Score was extremely high on Agholor coming out of college but as the Eagles offense sputtered, the USC product never distinguished himself as a player worthy of that optimism or his first-round draft status. Agholor became the 14th first-round wide receiver since 1992 to garner at least 40 targets and reach the end zone one or fewer times. The last to do so was one of the most spectacular busts in recent memory, Jonathan Baldwin in 2011. Of course, Agholor is not doomed to failure just yet. Part of the issue was his usage, as he spent much of the season as an isolated split-end decoy on the right side of the field. Moreover, a midseason high-ankle sprain caused him to miss three weeks and valuable game reps, leading to a slide down the depth chart. The Eagles inked Reuben Randle and Chris Givens in the offseason, but Agholor still appears entrenched as Philly's No. 2 receiver. Perhaps more snaps from the slot, where he thrived in college, could help begin to unlock Agholor's potential.

Kamar Aiken

Height: 6-2 | Weight: 219 | College: UCF | Draft: 2011/FA | Born: 30-May-1989 | Age: 27 | Risk: Green

Year	Team	G/GS	Snaps	Rec	Pass	Yds	C%	+/-	Yd/C	TD	Drop	YAC	Rk	YAC+	BTkl	DVOA	Rk	DYAR	Rk	YAR	Short	Mid	Deep	Bomb
2014	BAL	16/0	273	24	32	267	75%	+3.5	11.1	3	1	2.5	--	-1.4	0	29.7%	--	106	--	100	22%	56%	13%	9%
2015	BAL	16/14	937	75	127	944	59%	-0.1	12.6	5	2	2.8	80	-1.4	10	-2.7%	57	101	46	118	28%	42%	17%	13%
2016	BAL			57	94	664	61%	--	11.6	3						-5.7%								

Aiken has a few legs up on the bloated Baltimore receiving corps: he is healthy and coming off his best season. He had at least 73 receiving yards in eight games last season, making the most of his opportunity after being an undrafted player in 2011. Aiken is not a speed demon or a YAC machine, but he runs solid routes and can reliably catch the ball, much like Derrick Mason used to in his days. There is definitely a place for Aiken in this offense, but Baltimore has to figure out where.

Keenan Allen

Height: 6-2 | Weight: 206 | College: California | Draft: 2013/3 (76) | Born: 27-Apr-1992 | Age: 24 | Risk: Yellow

Year	Team	G/GS	Snaps	Rec	Pass	Yds	C%	+/-	Yd/C	TD	Drop	YAC	Rk	YAC+	BTkl	DVOA	Rk	DYAR	Rk	YAR	Short	Mid	Deep	Bomb
2013	SD	15/14	946	71	104	1046	68%	+8.6	14.7	8	2	5.9	13	+1.5	10	28.2%	5	343	8	351	37%	43%	17%	3%
2014	SD	14/14	837	77	122	783	63%	+1.4	10.2	4	1	3.9	57	-0.8	6	-8.0%	57	43	55	29	46%	38%	11%	4%
2015	SD	8/8	540	67	89	725	75%	+8.0	10.8	4	2	3.5	67	-0.8	6	11.9%	22	173	24	181	47%	41%	8%	5%
2016	SD			101	147	1222	69%	--	12.1	7						8.7%								

Allen had nine or more receptions on four occasions last year despite only playing in eight games. It was Allen's breakout season, or at least it was supposed to be. Allen is going to be the focal point of this passing game moving forward, assuming more of Antonio Gates' role the further into his career he goes. Even though Allen only averaged 10.8 yards per reception, that shouldn't be considered a slight against his ability. It was simply a product of the offense in which he was playing. He can create separation downfield against different types of coverage; it's just a question of how the Chargers want (or are able) to use him.

Danny Amendola | Height: 5-11 | Weight: 186 | College: Texas Tech | Draft: 2008/FA | Born: 2-Nov-1985 | Age: 31 | Risk: Green

Year	Team	G/GS	Snaps	Rec	Pass	Yds	C%	+/-	Yd/C	TD	Drop	YAC	Rk	YAC+	BTkl	DVOA	Rk	DYAR	Rk	YAR	Short	Mid	Deep	Bomb
2013	NE	12/6	571	54	83	633	65%	+0.9	11.7	2	4	4.7	43	-0.2	2	12.3%	21	163	27	116	45%	40%	9%	6%
2014	NE	16/4	456	27	42	200	64%	-1.3	7.4	1	2	2.7	--	-2.6	0	-17.7%	--	-16	--	-14	49%	30%	12%	9%
2015	NE	14/7	576	65	87	648	75%	+8.2	10.0	3	2	4.1	54	-0.8	12	8.6%	33	139	30	132	53%	36%	9%	2%
2016	NE			56	83	568	67%	--	10.1	3						-4.8%								

Amendola took a pay cut after his best season in five years to remain with the Patriots. This is a great example of "Championomics"—the ability of a perennial contender to retain the services of quality role players at discounted rates in exchange for the likelihood of a championship. Amendola and Julian Edelman produced spookily similar stat lines in totally different ways. Edelman began the season as a starter in a familiar Wes Welker-like role. Amendola was nominally a starter but only played 30 or 40 offensive snaps per game and caught just 10 passes for 91 yards in his first four games. Amendola's role increased as Aaron Dobson, Dion Lewis, and eventually Edelman got injured. Amendola had his own injury issues but enjoyed roughly a dozen targets per game for several weeks (most of them short and slotty) before Edelman returned for the playoffs.

Both Edelman and Amendola had injury issues in the offseason. The Patriots are wise to keep a spare, considering how much these slot types mean to their offense. Remember, however, that a healthy Edelman outranks Amendola in the Patriots slot hierarchy.

Tavon Austin | Height: 5-8 | Weight: 174 | College: West Virginia | Draft: 2013/1 (8) | Born: 15-Mar-1991 | Age: 25 | Risk: Green

Year	Team	G/GS	Snaps	Rec	Pass	Yds	C%	+/-	Yd/C	TD	Drop	YAC	Rk	YAC+	BTkl	DVOA	Rk	DYAR	Rk	YAR	Short	Mid	Deep	Bomb
2013	STL	13/3	422	40	69	418	58%	-4.3	10.5	4	6	5.8	17	+0.2	7	-19.4%	81	-36	80	-38	54%	30%	7%	9%
2014	STL	15/8	534	31	44	242	70%	-1.8	7.8	0	2	5.5	--	-0.9	8	-5.8%	--	24	--	13	67%	20%	7%	7%
2015	STL	16/15	742	52	88	473	60%	-6.1	9.1	5	2	6.8	3	-0.6	34	-30.6%	86	-122	87	-122	57%	24%	8%	11%
2016	LARM			67	103	685	65%	--	10.2	3						-9.1%								

Tavon Austin is a unique player in today's NFL. Our wide receiver tables don't have room for rushing totals, and what's the point, since most wide receivers will have just a carry or two per year. Austin, however, carried the ball 51 times last year for 427 yards and 4 touchdowns. That worked out to 253 rushing DYAR, making Austin the first player who nominally was a wide receiver to ever top 200 rushing DYAR.

Averaging 8.4 yards per carry is remarkable, but the Rams have Todd Gurley to tote the rock 300 times. Austin is supposed to be catching the ball and getting yards after the catch. Jeff Fisher has told reporters this summer that he wants to get Austin to 100 receptions in 2016. That's not as significant a milestone as it used to be, but for Austin it would be a major leap. Regardless of how many passes Austin catches in 2015, he has to average more yards per reception. Ten yards per reception is a paltry number, and Austin hasn't even scratched that in either of the past two seasons. Part of that is due to the quarterback situation in St. Louis and how he was used, but Austin himself hasn't shown enough proficiency as a route-runner or pass-catcher downfield either.

All those long runs are valuable, but you don't take a player in the top-ten picks of the draft so you can use on gadget plays. At this point of his career, despite all that running value, Austin sure looks like a bust. At least the big plays give us *some* hope that he can be a real threat moving forward. His KUBIAK projection includes 44 carries for 291 yards and 3 touchdowns.

Jason Avant | Height: 6-0 | Weight: 210 | College: Michigan | Draft: 2006/4 (109) | Born: 20-Apr-1983 | Age: 33 | Risk: N/A

Year	Team	G/GS	Snaps	Rec	Pass	Yds	C%	+/-	Yd/C	TD	Drop	YAC	Rk	YAC+	BTkl	DVOA	Rk	DYAR	Rk	YAR	Short	Mid	Deep	Bomb
2013	PHI	16/13	789	38	76	447	50%	-3.4	11.8	2	0	2.1	88	-2.2	1	-24.5%	85	-68	85	-55	26%	41%	24%	9%
2014	2TM	16/0	554	34	62	353	55%	-4.9	10.4	1	2	4.3	48	-1.2	1	-16.5%	79	-18	78	-29	37%	46%	10%	7%
2015	KC	16/1	345	15	24	119	63%	-1.4	7.9	0	0	3.3	--	-1.5	2	-15.7%	--	-6	--	-9	38%	50%	8%	4%

The 69 yards receiving that Avant had in the divisional-round game against the Patriots was his highest total in the last 47 games. After the Chiefs did not resign him this offseason, Avant has been searching for a new team, and there are no takers so far. If Andy Reid isn't interested, Avant may be in for a long wait.

Stedman Bailey Height: 5-10 Weight: 193 College: West Virginia Draft: 2013/3 (92) Born: 11-Nov-1990 Age: 26 Risk: N/A

Year	Team	G/GS	Snaps	Rec	Pass	Yds	C%	+/-	Yd/C	TD	Drop	YAC	Rk	YAC+	BTkl	DVOA	Rk	DYAR	Rk	YAR	Short	Mid	Deep	Bomb
2013	STL	16/2	188	17	25	226	68%	+3.3	13.3	0	0	2.7	--	-1.1	1	7.5%	--	36	--	33	33%	43%	24%	0%
2014	STL	14/3	404	30	46	435	65%	+3.7	14.5	1	2	6.1	--	+1.5	8	16.8%	--	103	--	98	29%	44%	12%	15%
2015	STL	8/3	254	12	25	182	48%	-1.8	15.2	1	1	5.9	--	+0.3	0	-19.4%	--	-12	--	-15	36%	23%	41%	0%

Bailey was serving a four-game PED suspension last season when his family was attacked while sitting in a car in Miami. He survived two gunshots to the head and worked out with the Rams during OTAs but was waived with a non-football injury designation in June. Bailey is hoping to return to the field but it's unlikely to happen in 2016. In the meantime, he's returned to West Virginia to serve as an assistant coach and try to finish his degree.

Doug Baldwin Height: 5-11 Weight: 189 College: Stanford Draft: 2011/FA Born: 21-Sep-1988 Age: 28 Risk: Green

Year	Team	G/GS	Snaps	Rec	Pass	Yds	C%	+/-	Yd/C	TD	Drop	YAC	Rk	YAC+	BTkl	DVOA	Rk	DYAR	Rk	YAR	Short	Mid	Deep	Bomb
2013	SEA	16/9	749	50	73	778	68%	+7.3	15.6	5	3	4.6	47	-0.2	2	33.3%	2	274	13	269	27%	45%	18%	11%
2014	SEA	16/16	879	66	99	825	68%	+6.1	12.5	3	3	5.2	24	-0.2	8	5.5%	34	137	32	140	38%	38%	18%	6%
2015	SEA	16/16	798	78	103	1069	76%	+13.3	13.7	14	1	5.6	14	+1.0	15	39.6%	1	414	2	391	40%	38%	14%	7%
2016	SEA			80	111	1069	72%	--	13.4	9							21.7%								

Baldwin has one of the NFL's better success stories. He broke out in 2010 as Andrew Luck's leading receiver at Stanford, but went undrafted in 2011. He still led the Seahawks with 788 receiving yards as a rookie with Tarvaris Jackson at quarterback. Now Russell Wilson's most-targeted receiver, Baldwin has twice finished first or second DVOA, something no other wideout has done since Vincent Jackson in 2008-09. Baldwin's 80-yard touchdown to put away the Steelers was worth 50 DYAR, the single most valuable reception in 2015. Baldwin was the only wide receiver to finish in the top 10 in both plus-minus and YAC+ in 2015, yet was not one of the 12 players invited to the Pro Bowl at his position. He can take comfort in his new four-year deal worth $46 million. Baldwin had 15 touchdown catches in his first four seasons before leading the league with 14 last year, including 11 scores in a five-game stretch. While this makes him one of the easiest picks ever for touchdown regression, Baldwin should still be Wilson's favorite target in an offense that may actually start passing more.

Cole Beasley Height: 5-8 Weight: 177 College: Southern Methodist Draft: 2012/FA Born: 26-Apr-1989 Age: 27 Risk: Green

Year	Team	G/GS	Snaps	Rec	Pass	Yds	C%	+/-	Yd/C	TD	Drop	YAC	Rk	YAC+	BTkl	DVOA	Rk	DYAR	Rk	YAR	Short	Mid	Deep	Bomb
2013	DAL	14/3	242	39	54	368	72%	+3.4	9.4	2	1	4.7	40	-0.3	3	1.5%	42	59	58	74	61%	37%	2%	0%
2014	DAL	16/2	434	37	49	420	76%	+4.0	11.4	4	0	6.6	6	+2.1	4	16.7%	13	117	36	134	47%	45%	4%	4%
2015	DAL	16/3	563	52	75	536	69%	+1.2	10.3	5	4	6.2	7	+1.4	7	-1.9%	53	64	58	73	68%	30%	1%	1%
2016	DAL			44	62	486	71%	--	11.0	3							7.6%								

The diminutive slot receiver set career-highs in counting stats across the board, but like Dallas' other receivers, Beasley saw his overall receiving efficiency dip with Tony Romo out of the lineup. Entering his fifth season, Beasley is a known commodity: he'll come in when the Cowboys utilize their 11 personnel on passing downs and run a slippery route that picks up 6 yards on third-and-5. Even with no Romo, Beasley still reliably moved the chains in 2015, posting a 42.2% receiving DVOA on third and fourth downs. At the same time, it's clear Dallas does not envision a bigger role for him, given that the likes of Devin Street and Brice Butler received starting snaps ahead of Beasley last season. There's nothing wrong with Beasley's current role, and in certain game plans, he'll play an integral role in keeping the offense humming along.

Odell Beckham Height: 5-11 Weight: 198 College: Louisiana State Draft: 2014/1 (12) Born: 5-Nov-1992 Age: 24 Risk: Green

Year	Team	G/GS	Snaps	Rec	Pass	Yds	C%	+/-	Yd/C	TD	Drop	YAC	Rk	YAC+	BTkl	DVOA	Rk	DYAR	Rk	YAR	Short	Mid	Deep	Bomb
2014	NYG	12/11	771	91	130	1305	70%	+11.1	14.3	12	2	5.3	20	+0.2	14	25.8%	9	396	6	429	33%	40%	14%	12%
2015	NYG	15/15	998	96	158	1450	61%	+4.6	15.1	13	4	6.2	8	+2.0	12	10.3%	27	304	10	345	25%	50%	9%	16%
2016	NYG			98	161	1426	61%	--	14.5	12							12.8%								

As far as sequels go, Beckham's encore to his record-breaking rookie year was closer to *The Godfather Part II* than *Jaws 2*. Although Beckham saw his efficiency dip somewhat, he remained one of the league's most electrifying threats, particularly in the open field. Beckham led all wide receivers in YAC+ (even though the statistic naturally favors more traditional deep threats such as Martavis Bryant and Ted Ginn), terrorizing defenders in the open field on slants, curls, and other routes that provided him room to operate. At this point, the only things likely to derail Beckham are his persistent hamstring issues, which popped up and played a role in limiting him to 64 yards per game from Weeks 4-7, and his ongoing feud with Josh Norman, with whom he'll now spar twice a year. Apart from that caveat, Beckham might be the safest wide receiver fantasy option this side of Antonio Brown, given the steady number of targets he'll see every week. New York's top receiver has seen at least seven targets in 25 consecutive contests, and has eclipsed 100 receiving yards in 15 of his 27 career games. And over the past two years, no one, not even Brown or Rob Gronkowski, has more receiving touchdowns than Beckham's 25. With Ben McAdoo succeeding Tom Coughlin, the same offensive system that propelled Beckham to stardom will remain in place, likely leading to more of the same in Year 3.

Kelvin Benjamin

Height: 6-5 — Weight: 240 — College: Florida State — Draft: 2014/1 (28) — Born: 5-Feb-1991 — Age: 25 — Risk: Green

Year	Team	G/GS	Snaps	Rec	Pass	Yds	C%	+/-	Yd/C	TD	Drop	YAC	Rk	YAC+	BTkl	DVOA	Rk	DYAR	Rk	YAR	Short	Mid	Deep	Bomb
2014	CAR	16/15	925	73	145	1008	50%	-7.8	13.8	9	7	2.3	86	-2.0	3	-11.8%	67	9	67	33	18%	49%	15%	18%
2016	CAR			70	120	1023	58%	--	14.6	9						6.9%								

Torn ACL in the rearview mirror, all signs point to Benjamin being ready for training camp. Not much has changed in his situation. Carolina still has no other established receivers besides Greg Olsen. Benjamin still needs to work on his 2014 efficiency numbers. ACL tears are a pretty clean comeback at this point, so Benjamin shouldn't be limited in any way. If Carolina plays as well as they did last year, he probably won't draw 150 targets again. But maybe that's for the best.

Travis Benjamin

Height: 5-10 — Weight: 172 — College: Miami — Draft: 2012/4 (100) — Born: 29-Dec-1989 — Age: 27 — Risk: Red

Year	Team	G/GS	Snaps	Rec	Pass	Yds	C%	+/-	Yd/C	TD	Drop	YAC	Rk	YAC+	BTkl	DVOA	Rk	DYAR	Rk	YAR	Short	Mid	Deep	Bomb
2013	CLE	8/3	143	5	13	105	38%	-1.8	21.0	0	1	12.0	--	+7.7	1	-8.3%	--	4	--	-2	23%	31%	23%	23%
2014	CLE	16/0	383	18	46	314	39%	-6.5	17.4	3	3	2.4	--	-2.6	2	-10.2%	--	9	--	5	20%	35%	15%	30%
2015	CLE	16/15	851	68	125	966	54%	-4.1	14.2	5	4	4.8	34	-0.4	8	-8.7%	69	38	65	37	37%	31%	18%	13%
2016	SD			50	88	777	57%	--	15.5	5						3.7%								

The speedy Benjamin got off to a fast start in 2015, with 10 grabs for 249 yards and four touchdowns in the first three games. He was the lone receiver whose game was enhanced when Johnny Manziel was quarterback—when Manziel improvised and got outside the pocket, Benjamin went deep, and was rewarded with bombs. When the air went out of Johnny Football, Benjamin was deflated as well, though his deep-threat (and kick-return) capabilities are such that San Diego signed him away without much fight from the rebuilding Browns. It remains to be seen whether Philip Rivers can extend plays long enough to truly benefit his new target.

Anquan Boldin

Height: 6-1 — Weight: 218 — College: Florida State — Draft: 2003/2 (54) — Born: 3-Oct-1980 — Age: 36 — Risk: Yellow

Year	Team	G/GS	Snaps	Rec	Pass	Yds	C%	+/-	Yd/C	TD	Drop	YAC	Rk	YAC+	BTkl	DVOA	Rk	DYAR	Rk	YAR	Short	Mid	Deep	Bomb
2013	SF	16/16	803	85	129	1179	66%	+9.9	13.9	7	4	5.0	30	+0.6	9	25.8%	9	386	3	409	30%	48%	20%	2%
2014	SF	16/16	952	83	131	1062	63%	+3.6	12.8	5	7	4.8	34	+0.6	12	9.3%	28	222	19	240	33%	48%	14%	5%
2015	SF	14/13	762	69	111	789	62%	-4.0	11.4	4	3	4.1	53	-0.9	11	-7.9%	65	41	64	13	52%	34%	9%	5%
2016	DET			49	80	532	61%	--	10.9	3						-6.4%								

There wasn't much of a market for a wideout going on 36 who is probably better served to come off the bench these days. It was surprising to not see San Francisco bring Boldin back simply due to the lack of skill players there, but it would have been a one-year solution for a team that needs to rebuild for the future and focus on youth anyway. Signed with Detroit right before we went to press.

Tyler Boyd

Height: 6-1 — Weight: 197 — College: Pittsburgh — Draft: 2016/2 (55) — Born: 15-Nov-1994 — Age: 22 — Risk: Yellow

Year	Team	G/GS	Snaps	Rec	Pass	Yds	C%	+/-	Yd/C	TD	Drop	YAC	Rk	YAC+	BTkl	DVOA	Rk	DYAR	Rk	YAR	Short	Mid	Deep	Bomb
2016	CIN			43	72	553	60%	--	12.9	3						-3.6%								

Boyd's collegiate production at Pitt profiles him as a chain-moving slot possession guy. His catch rate was higher than any top wideout prospect save Josh Doctson and Sterling Shepard, but his yards per catch average (10.2) is miles behind those two and the other highly drafted receivers. In that sense, he seems closer to the departed Mo Sanu than the departed Marvin Jones. Boyd is already the only option at slot receiver for the Bengals, and he'll be counted on to be effective, if not superb, early. Given the shot putters he had as quarterbacks in college, there is some extra upside to his pro potential.

Kenny Britt

Height: 6-3   Weight: 218   College: Rutgers   Draft: 2009/1 (30)   Born: 19-Sep-1988   Age: 28   Risk: Green

Year	Team	G/GS	Snaps	Rec	Pass	Yds	C%	+/-	Yd/C	TD	Drop	YAC	Rk	YAC+	BTkl	DVOA	Rk	DYAR	Rk	YAR	Short	Mid	Deep	Bomb
2013	TEN	12/3	299	11	35	96	31%	-9.2	8.7	0	5	1.2	--	-2.1	3	-48.5%	--	-101	--	-108	20%	46%	17%	17%
2014	STL	16/13	783	48	84	748	57%	+2.9	15.6	3	2	3.5	67	-1.2	2	12.4%	18	163	28	161	35%	22%	13%	30%
2015	STL	16/14	650	36	72	681	50%	-1.4	18.9	3	3	3.3	73	-1.4	5	11.0%	26	139	31	141	16%	47%	15%	22%
2016	LARM			50	97	790	52%	--	15.8	5						-0.1%								

Britt should be the biggest benefactor from an improvement at the quarterback position in Los Angeles. Britt isn't the player he was when he entered the league—an ACL tear sapped some of his immense athleticism and he has struggled with his consistency catching the ball—but he is capable of making impressive adjustments downfield against tight coverage. Britt needs a quarterback who can put the ball in the right spot for him to attack it. Nobody he's played with in the NFL has done that consistently.

Antonio Brown

Height: 5-10   Weight: 186   College: Central Mighican   Draft: 2010/6 (195)   Born: 10-Jul-1988   Age: 28   Risk: Green

Year	Team	G/GS	Snaps	Rec	Pass	Yds	C%	+/-	Yd/C	TD	Drop	YAC	Rk	YAC+	BTkl	DVOA	Rk	DYAR	Rk	YAR	Short	Mid	Deep	Bomb
2013	PIT	16/14	954	110	167	1499	66%	+10.1	13.6	8	6	5.2	27	-0.2	15	15.0%	15	361	5	346	40%	35%	12%	13%
2014	PIT	16/16	1061	129	181	1698	71%	+16.5	13.2	13	5	4.6	39	-0.2	18	25.7%	10	554	1	525	36%	39%	15%	10%
2015	PIT	16/16	1029	136	193	1834	70%	+18.2	13.5	10	4	4.4	45	-0.5	18	19.7%	9	517	1	490	38%	29%	21%	12%
2016	PIT			124	175	1636	71%	--	13.2	11						20.4%								

Normally, you would never predict with any real confidence that an NFL player would break significant records, but do not sleep on the 150-catch, 2,000-yard season for Brown this year. He has the right quarterback, who just needs to stay healthy. Brown has caught at least five passes in each of the last 46 games Ben Roethlisberger started. Brown certainly has the skill to do it, beating any type of coverage and rarely ever finding a cornerback who has his number. Brown's plus-18.2 last year is the highest single-season plus-minus since 2006. He also may have the right situation to break records thanks to the suspension of Martavis Bryant and retirement of Heath Miller. The perfect storm is forming, and about the only thing that can mess it up is injury, or NFL defenses growing a brain and actually double-teaming Brown for most of the game. But the double-team is not a commonly used tactic, which is why Brown should continue to be the league's most productive receiver and one of the most fun to watch.

Corey Brown

Height: 5-11   Weight: 180   College: Ohio State   Draft: 2014/FA   Born: 16-Dec-1991   Age: 25   Risk: Blue

Year	Team	G/GS	Snaps	Rec	Pass	Yds	C%	+/-	Yd/C	TD	Drop	YAC	Rk	YAC+	BTkl	DVOA	Rk	DYAR	Rk	YAR	Short	Mid	Deep	Bomb
2014	CAR	13/3	307	21	36	296	58%	-0.2	14.1	2	1	2.5	--	-2.4	2	7.7%	--	59	--	67	24%	42%	16%	18%
2015	CAR	14/11	753	31	54	447	57%	+3.8	14.4	4	2	2.6	83	-1.1	3	8.8%	32	89	50	101	14%	41%	27%	18%
2016	CAR			17	29	222	59%	--	13.0	1						-2.6%								

Brown showed up big when it counted, leading the Panthers with 80 receiving yards in the Super Bowl before being forced to leave with a concussion. His basic archetype is still "speedy, inefficient slot receiver," but he doesn't have the size to be as much of a matchup problem as most of Carolina's collection of similar types. He heads into 2016 looking to beat out Ted Ginn for third receiver duties.

John Brown

Height: 5-10   Weight: 179   College: Pittsburg St. (KS)   Draft: 2014/3 (91)   Born: 4-Mar-1990   Age: 26   Risk: Green

Year	Team	G/GS	Snaps	Rec	Pass	Yds	C%	+/-	Yd/C	TD	Drop	YAC	Rk	YAC+	BTkl	DVOA	Rk	DYAR	Rk	YAR	Short	Mid	Deep	Bomb
2014	ARI	16/5	633	48	103	696	47%	-7.3	14.5	5	2	3.8	62	-1.7	0	-12.5%	69	1	69	-5	21%	43%	22%	15%
2015	ARI	15/11	826	65	101	1003	64%	+6.6	15.4	7	5	4.8	32	+0.0	7	29.9%	4	352	5	345	27%	37%	14%	22%
2016	ARI			67	110	994	61%	--	14.8	7						7.8%								

A year ago, there were rumblings that Brown was ready to take over for Larry Fitzgerald as the No. 1 wide receiver in Arizona. Of course, Fitzgerald was incredible again in 2015, but Brown was only 11 DYAR behind his teammate, and finished fourth in the NFL in DVOA. With roughly the same number of targets as his rookie season, Brown increased his receptions by 17, his yards by 307, and his touchdowns by two. Brown does not yet draw the attention of an Odell Beckham, Sammy Watkins, or Mike Evans, but he is holding his own through two seasons in what could go down as the greatest wide receiver draft class in NFL history.

Marlon Brown

Height: 6-4   Weight: 205   College: Georgia   Draft: 2013/FA   Born: 22-Apr-1991   Age: 25   Risk: N/A

Year	Team	G/GS	Snaps	Rec	Pass	Yds	C%	+/-	Yd/C	TD	Drop	YAC	Rk	YAC+	BTkl	DVOA	Rk	DYAR	Rk	YAR	Short	Mid	Deep	Bomb
2013	BAL	14/12	791	49	83	524	59%	-2.4	10.7	7	2	4.8	35	+0.4	6	4.9%	31	117	41	106	44%	32%	16%	8%
2014	BAL	14/1	375	24	31	255	77%	+5.0	10.6	0	0	4.1	--	+0.0	1	13.9%	--	61	--	59	38%	52%	0%	10%
2015	BAL	10/2	404	14	30	112	47%	-4.3	8.0	0	2	3.3	--	-1.9	0	-52.1%	--	-91	--	-99	63%	19%	11%	7%

Brown's unexpected seven touchdown catches as an undrafted rookie in 2013 look to be simply the result of Baltimore not having other red zone options that year. He has not caught a touchdown since, and only averages 10.2 yards per catch in his career. Brown ended 2015 on injured reserve with a back injury and was last seen working out for the Redskins, where he was forced to catch passes from Jimmy Clausen again.

Dez Bryant

Height: 6-2   Weight: 225   College: Oklahoma State   Draft: 2010/1 (24)   Born: 4-Nov-1988   Age: 28   Risk: Yellow

Year	Team	G/GS	Snaps	Rec	Pass	Yds	C%	+/-	Yd/C	TD	Drop	YAC	Rk	YAC+	BTkl	DVOA	Rk	DYAR	Rk	YAR	Short	Mid	Deep	Bomb
2013	DAL	16/16	933	93	160	1233	58%	-1.7	13.3	13	6	5.7	18	+1.4	7	3.7%	33	215	18	242	32%	42%	17%	9%
2014	DAL	16/16	896	88	137	1320	64%	+6.7	15.0	16	4	4.6	41	+0.1	18	27.0%	5	430	5	456	31%	39%	17%	13%
2015	DAL	9/9	444	31	72	401	43%	-8.5	12.9	3	6	4.2	49	+0.1	6	-26.8%	83	-86	85	-88	24%	44%	17%	15%
2016	DAL			90	144	1327	63%	--	14.7	12						17.1%								

His career game log will read that he played nine games, but in reality, Bryant's 2015 season was effectively over after three quarters. The All-Pro receiver, who underwent foot and ankle surgeries this offseason, admitted that he was never close to 100 percent after rushing back from a broken foot suffered in the season opener. Of course, one look at his putrid metrics would tell the same story, as last year was the first time in Bryant's six-year career that he posted negative DVOA or DYAR figures. While the Cowboys certainly would have preferred to avoid the season from hell in the first year of Bryant's lucrative five-year deal, there's really no reason to believe this contract will turn into another albatross on Dallas' perpetually messy cap sheet. One of the game's most physically imposing specimens, Bryant had played at least 15 games in each of the four seasons prior to 2015, and will not turn 28 until November. Having caught a league-leading 41 touchdowns from 2012-14, Bryant should once again feast in an offense with a dearth of reliable secondary targets for Tony Romo. So long as Bryant is healthy enough to participate in training camp as expected, his place as one of the game's premier receivers should remain secure.

Martavis Bryant

Height: 6-4   Weight: 211   College: Clemson   Draft: 2014/4 (118)   Born: 20-Dec-1991   Age: 25   Risk: N/A

Year	Team	G/GS	Snaps	Rec	Pass	Yds	C%	+/-	Yd/C	TD	Drop	YAC	Rk	YAC+	BTkl	DVOA	Rk	DYAR	Rk	YAR	Short	Mid	Deep	Bomb
2014	PIT	10/3	295	26	49	549	53%	-0.8	21.1	8	3	7.3	--	+1.7	2	22.9%	--	137	--	129	31%	22%	14%	33%
2015	PIT	11/5	511	50	92	765	54%	-3.7	15.3	6	6	7.0	2	+1.7	14	-2.4%	54	75	56	47	30%	34%	10%	26%

While Bryant could make breathtaking plays, he was far from an efficient receiver. In fact, the lowest passing plus-minus Ben Roethlisberger has to any target since 2006 is Bryant at minus-4.3. Some of this is the added difficulty in going deep, but Bryant also struggled at the catch point too often. In a game against Seattle where Roethlisberger passed for 456 yards, Bryant actually left about 100 more yards on the field with a few bad plays. The physical traits are up there with the best in the league, but clearly Bryant needs help and guidance in his personal life, or else the Steelers are looking at their own Josh Gordon situation.

Brice Butler

| | | | | | Height: 6-3 | | | | Weight: 205 | | | College: San Diego State | | | Draft: 2013/7 (209) | | Born: 29-Jan-1990 | | Age: 26 | | Risk: Blue |

Year	Team	G/GS	Snaps	Rec	Pass	Yds	C%	+/-	Yd/C	TD	Drop	YAC	Rk	YAC+	BTkl	DVOA	Rk	DYAR	Rk	YAR	Short	Mid	Deep	Bomb
2013	OAK	10/2	210	9	17	103	53%	-1.5	11.4	0	2	3.4	--	-2.2	0	-28.1%	--	-19	--	-20	35%	24%	41%	0%
2014	OAK	15/0	271	21	36	280	58%	-0.1	13.3	2	1	4.0	--	-0.4	2	1.9%	--	42	--	24	26%	57%	9%	9%
2015	DAL	7/2	261	12	26	258	46%	-0.9	21.5	0	2	8.0	--	+3.5	2	0.3%	--	28	--	30	17%	50%	25%	8%
2016	DAL			4	8	53	50%	--	13.3	1						-11.6%								

Traded from Oakland to Dallas in September, Butler never really got a chance to play with Tony Romo, receiving just a single target from the Dallas starter in 2015. Moreover, a hamstring injury on Butler's first signature play as a Cowboy—a 67-yard catch against New Orleans—set him back until the end of the season. Butler did get a longer look once the Cowboys' season was lost, starting each of the final three games. Receivers who stand 6-foot-3 and run 4.37 40-yard dashes don't come around very often, a fact which has kept Butler's career alive to date. However, he'll need to erase some of the mental mistakes that precipitated his exit from Oakland if he hopes to avoid the same fate in Dallas—and the likely move back to a run-heavy offense with the arrival of Ezekiel Elliott makes it unlikely we'll see much production past the Cowboys' top three receivers.

Jeremy Butler

| | | | | | Height: 6-2 | | | | Weight: 219 | | | College: Tennessee Martin | | | Draft: 2014/FA | | Born: 21-Apr-1991 | | Age: 25 | | Risk: Blue |

Year	Team	G/GS	Snaps	Rec	Pass	Yds	C%	+/-	Yd/C	TD	Drop	YAC	Rk	YAC+	BTkl	DVOA	Rk	DYAR	Rk	YAR	Short	Mid	Deep	Bomb
2015	BAL	8/0	385	31	44	363	70%	+2.3	11.7	0	2	4.8	--	-0.3	6	-1.4%	--	38	--	33	45%	33%	19%	2%
2016	BAL			4	6	43	67%	--	10.7	0						-0.4%								

When you consider Butler came off the practice squad to catch most of his passes from the ungodly trio of Jimmy Clausen, Matt Schaub, and Ryan Mallett, his high catch rate actually impresses. The problem is Baltimore just has way too many bodies at wide receiver right now, and Butler lacks some of the skills that would help him lock up a roster spot by playing special teams. But he should be able to find work somewhere in the NFL this season.

Leonte Carroo

| | | | | | Height: 6-0 | | | | Weight: 211 | | | College: Rutgers | | | Draft: 2016/3 (86) | | Born: 24-Jan-1994 | | Age: 22 | | Risk: Green |

Year	Team	G/GS	Snaps	Rec	Pass	Yds	C%	+/-	Yd/C	TD	Drop	YAC	Rk	YAC+	BTkl	DVOA	Rk	DYAR	Rk	YAR	Short	Mid	Deep	Bomb
2016	MIA			13	21	198	62%	--	15.3	1						8.9%								

Carroo came on strong late in the draft cycle. He caught six total touchdowns against Indiana and Michigan State in his senior season, plus seven catches and a touchdown in the final game of his career. Then he put in a solid showing at Senior Bowl practices before suffering a minor injury. Carroo is a route technician by NCAA standards, but the measurables don't blow anyone away, and despite 19.5 yards per reception in 2015, Playmaker Score is not too impressed by a senior with one collegiate 1,000-yard season. Carroo enters the season in the old Rishard Matthews role as the No. 4 receiver the Dolphins forget they have until he ends up catching 40 passes.

Sammie Coates

| | | | | | Height: 6-1 | | | | Weight: 212 | | | College: Auburn | | | Draft: 2015/3 (87) | | Born: 31-Mar-1993 | | Age: 23 | | Risk: Red |

Year	Team	G/GS	Snaps	Rec	Pass	Yds	C%	+/-	Yd/C	TD	Drop	YAC	Rk	YAC+	BTkl	DVOA	Rk	DYAR	Rk	YAR	Short	Mid	Deep	Bomb
2015	PIT	6/0	34	1	2	11	50%	-0.3	11.0	0	0	4.0	--	+0.3	0	-26.8%	--	-2	--	-2	0%	100%	0%	0%
2016	PIT			33	62	604	53%	--	18.3	4						10.8%								

Coates wasn't exactly an immediate fit in Pittsburgh, disappointing coaches with poor conditioning and difficulty picking up the playbook. He produced a single 11-yard catch in the regular season. But he had a chance to step up in the postseason in Denver and looked good on two catches for 61 yards. Apparently, the coaches are much happier with him after his first full offseason in the program, and now Coates will get every opportunity to beat out Darrius Heyward-Bey for the No. 3 receiver role. That sounds like a piece of cake, but DHB seems to have borrowed those Will Blackwell photos to keep earning playing time from Mike Tomlin. There is good reason to trust the Steelers on these mid-round wide receiver picks, and Coates averaged 21.4 yards per catch at Auburn. He is not on the same freakish scale as Martavis Bryant, but he could be a deep threat in this offense this season.

Randall Cobb

Height: 5-11 Weight: 190 College: Kentucky Draft: 2011/2 (64) Born: 22-Aug-1990 Age: 26 Risk: Green

Year	Team	G/GS	Snaps	Rec	Pass	Yds	C%	+/-	Yd/C	TD	Drop	YAC	Rk	YAC+	BTkl	DVOA	Rk	DYAR	Rk	YAR	Short	Mid	Deep	Bomb
2013	GB	6/4	333	31	47	433	66%	+4.8	14.0	4	1	5.6	--	+0.0	5	21.1%	--	121	--	105	43%	35%	15%	8%
2014	GB	16/16	922	91	127	1287	72%	+8.4	14.1	12	2	6.4	7	+1.9	10	35.7%	1	479	4	501	46%	32%	21%	2%
2015	GB	16/15	1050	79	129	829	61%	-2.3	10.5	6	6	5.5	18	+0.2	16	-5.1%	60	77	53	54	46%	37%	14%	2%
2016	GB			80	120	1009	67%	--	12.6	8							9.8%								

Someday we'll build the Second Banana Hall of Fame to celebrate receivers who looked great as sidekicks to elite wideouts, but crashed and burned when put into place as the top guy. And when we do, you'll find Cobb's bust there next to the likes of Alvin Harper and Peerless Price. For now, Cobb will step back into the comfort of Jordy Nelson's shadow. The punctured lung that left Cobb coughing up blood on the sidelines against Arizona in the playoffs has thankfully healed, and there's no reason not to expect him to bounce back to his prior level of production.

Brandon Coleman

Height: 6-6 Weight: 220 College: Rutgers Draft: 2014/FA Born: 22-Jun-1992 Age: 24 Risk: Green

Year	Team	G/GS	Snaps	Rec	Pass	Yds	C%	+/-	Yd/C	TD	Drop	YAC	Rk	YAC+	BTkl	DVOA	Rk	DYAR	Rk	YAR	Short	Mid	Deep	Bomb
2015	NO	16/4	430	30	49	454	61%	+2.3	15.1	2	1	4.0	--	-0.5	2	17.9%	--	113	--	104	25%	33%	29%	13%
2016	NO			25	44	327	57%	--	13.1	3							-5.9%								

Seen by general manager Mickey Loomis as the "heir apparent" to Marques Colston, Coleman produced plenty of value in the offense when various other Saints receivers were dealing with injuries. Of course, now with Michael Thomas in the fold, Coleman has no easy path to a starting job again. A third-year UDFA out of Rutgers, he has been a nice find for the Saints. But as of now, he may just be functional depth.

Corey Coleman

Height: 5-11 Weight: 194 College: Baylor Draft: 2016/1 (15) Born: 6-Jul-1994 Age: 22 Risk: Yellow

Year	Team	G/GS	Snaps	Rec	Pass	Yds	C%	+/-	Yd/C	TD	Drop	YAC	Rk	YAC+	BTkl	DVOA	Rk	DYAR	Rk	YAR	Short	Mid	Deep	Bomb
2016	CLE			57	104	825	55%	--	14.5	4							-5.8%								

Hey, it's Playmaker Score's favorite wide receiver of 2016! Coleman was extremely productive in college, but as with all Baylor products, take that with a grain of salt. His route tree doesn't have many branches on it—the overwhelming majority of his patterns were hitches, slants, and gos, with the odd screen thrown in. And his new coach Hue Jackson called him out during rookie camp, saying Coleman "needed to get in better shape." Assuming he hits the gym, Coleman has the explosion and sudden direction change to be extremely dangerous, especially with the ball in his hands. He sinks his hips and changes speed and angles very well. He's not very physical, but like a slightly bigger DeSean Jackson he'll be capable of hitting homers from all manner of plays, not just bombs. Defensive coordinators will have to account for him at all times.

As the first receiver drafted, and the top pick of the new Cleveland regime, Coleman will be under intense scrutiny, which is unfair—he isn't quite the prospect previous top receivers have been, and the 2014 class set an impossibly high bar. The current status of the Cleveland quarterback room doesn't exactly help things.

Marques Colston

Height: 6-4 Weight: 225 College: Hofstra Draft: 2006/7 (252) Born: 5-Jun-1983 Age: 33 Risk: N/A

Year	Team	G/GS	Snaps	Rec	Pass	Yds	C%	+/-	Yd/C	TD	Drop	YAC	Rk	YAC+	BTkl	DVOA	Rk	DYAR	Rk	YAR	Short	Mid	Deep	Bomb
2013	NO	15/11	750	75	110	943	68%	+9.3	12.6	5	2	3.4	78	-0.6	4	19.5%	14	276	12	283	32%	47%	17%	4%
2014	NO	16/13	876	59	99	902	60%	-1.8	15.3	5	6	5.0	30	+1.0	3	13.0%	16	201	23	211	32%	39%	22%	7%
2015	NO	13/5	569	45	67	520	67%	+0.8	11.6	4	4	4.4	46	+0.0	4	7.1%	39	103	45	106	40%	48%	10%	1%

Now retired, Colston will finish with 2,611 receiving DYAR in just ten seasons. It was in an ideal role in an ideal passing offense, yes, but that puts him in some really nice company.

Top WRs by DYAR, 1989-2015

Name	DYAR	Seasons	Name	DYAR	Seasons
Jerry Rice	4,261	16*	Michael Irvin	3,106	9*
Randy Moss	3,980	14	Isaac Bruce	3,084	16
Marvin Harrison	3,653	13	Tim Brown	2,976	16*
Terrell Owens	3,481	15	Hines Ward	2,703	14
Reggie Wayne	3,240	14	**Marques Colston**	**2,612**	**10**
Not including seasons played earlier than 1989					

Is that enough to make him a Hall of Famer? We kind of doubt it, even despite the statistical company. Nobody from this era is going to put Colston over players like Steve Smith or Andre Johnson who finished with less DYAR in less ideal situations. But what a beautiful, unappreciated ride it was. From the moment he was an instant 1,000-yard rookie tight end in your Yahoo! league until last season, Colston did nothing but deliver value for the Saints.

Chris Conley Height: 6-2 Weight: 213 College: Georgia Draft: 2015/3 (76) Born: 25-Oct-1992 Age: 24 Risk: Red

Year	Team	G/GS	Snaps	Rec	Pass	Yds	C%	+/-	Yd/C	TD	Drop	YAC	Rk	YAC+	BTkl	DVOA	Rk	DYAR	Rk	YAR	Short	Mid	Deep	Bomb
2015	KC	16/5	369	17	31	199	55%	-1.1	11.7	1	3	4.1	--	-0.1	3	2.7%	--	39	--	39	23%	45%	16%	16%
2016	KC			39	63	485	62%	--	12.4	4						3.1%								

Conley is the 13th wide receiver that the Chiefs have drafted in the first three rounds since 1981. Of the previous 12, just two (Dwayne Bowe and Dexter McCluster) topped 200 career receptions. The Chiefs' depth chart certainly leaves an opening for Conley to make a mark. From the pessimist's perspective, Conley is a deep threat on a team that throws deep less often than any other. The optimist would say that Conley's provides the Chiefs with an important weapon to add the downfield passing they need so badly.

Brandin Cooks Height: 5-10 Weight: 189 College: Oregon State Draft: 2014/1 (20) Born: 25-Sep-1993 Age: 23 Risk: Green

Year	Team	G/GS	Snaps	Rec	Pass	Yds	C%	+/-	Yd/C	TD	Drop	YAC	Rk	YAC+	BTkl	DVOA	Rk	DYAR	Rk	YAR	Short	Mid	Deep	Bomb
2014	NO	10/7	534	53	69	550	77%	+9.7	10.4	3	1	3.2	75	-2.3	1	9.7%	26	124	34	125	51%	29%	9%	11%
2015	NO	16/12	959	84	130	1138	65%	+5.8	13.5	9	3	4.6	41	-0.8	4	7.1%	40	192	21	186	44%	20%	19%	17%
2016	NO			83	132	1106	63%	--	13.3	8						4.5%								

Not a complete receiver, but someone who can thrive in the New Orleans offense. Cooks is a headache in the slot, where his size doesn't matter quite as much as his speed. He wins routes early with startling acceleration. Cooks can still get pressed on the outside, but with Kenny Stills gone he got a much wider share of the deep targets. If he can keep hauling them in like he did last year, he should be able to have a productive career as a lower-tier No. 1 receiver.

Amari Cooper Height: 6-1 Weight: 211 College: Alabama Draft: 2015/1 (4) Born: 18-Jun-1994 Age: 22 Risk: Yellow

Year	Team	G/GS	Snaps	Rec	Pass	Yds	C%	+/-	Yd/C	TD	Drop	YAC	Rk	YAC+	BTkl	DVOA	Rk	DYAR	Rk	YAR	Short	Mid	Deep	Bomb
2015	OAK	16/15	900	72	130	1070	55%	-6.6	14.9	6	10	5.2	23	+0.0	11	-1.0%	50	122	37	130	33%	43%	13%	10%
2016	OAK			87	145	1251	60%	--	14.4	8						3.8%								

For someone who was supposed to come into the league so polished, it was a little odd to see Cooper drop so many balls as a rookie. Our projection for his output this season is adjusted for the fact that he played through a foot injury in the last month of the season, reeling in more than 20 yards in just one of those games. Drop-prone receivers aren't necessarily shaky investments in the long-term as long as they deliver everything else you need, and Cooper certainly projects to do that.

Pharoh Cooper Height: 5-11 Weight: 203 College: South Carolina Draft: 2016/4 (117) Born: 7-Mar-1995 Age: 21 Risk: Blue

Year	Team	G/GS	Snaps	Rec	Pass	Yds	C%	+/-	Yd/C	TD	Drop	YAC	Rk	YAC+	BTkl	DVOA	Rk	DYAR	Rk	YAR	Short	Mid	Deep	Bomb
2016	LARM			18	30	222	60%	--	12.3	1						-5.8%								

When speaking about his new receivers after the draft, Rams general manager Les Snead said that each had a "specific role or skill set. Pharoh in the slot, kind of a weapon role. Michael [Thomas] as an outside guy." For Thomas that doesn't mean much but for Cooper it's a problem. The Rams already have a version of Cooper entrenched in their starting lineup—they drafted him with the eighth overall pick a few years ago. Even if Cooper continues to run precise routes and thrive on underneath patterns in space in the NFL, it's hard to see how he ever takes over Tavon Austin's role in the offense. For Cooper to be relevant in 2016, he will need to prove his quality in training camp and hope that the Rams use more four-receiver sets than they ever have in the Jeff Fisher era.

Riley Cooper — Height: 6-4 — Weight: 222 — College: Florida — Draft: 2010/5 (159) — Born: 9-Sep-1987 — Age: 29 — Risk: N/A

Year	Team	G/GS	Snaps	Rec	Pass	Yds	C%	+/-	Yd/C	TD	Drop	YAC	Rk	YAC+	BTkl	DVOA	Rk	DYAR	Rk	YAR	Short	Mid	Deep	Bomb
2013	PHI	16/15	981	47	84	835	56%	+0.5	17.8	8	4	4.9	32	+0.1	4	20.6%	13	212	19	214	26%	37%	20%	18%
2014	PHI	16/16	956	55	95	577	58%	-1.7	10.5	3	2	2.8	81	-2.2	2	-17.8%	80	-38	80	-20	33%	36%	19%	12%
2015	PHI	16/13	571	21	41	327	51%	-1.7	15.6	2	1	3.0	—	-1.4	0	-6.2%	—	20	—	27	23%	43%	18%	18%

Cooper's reputation as a Chip Kelly favorite didn't really help his approval rating in Philadelphia, which had already scapegoated him following a miserable 2014 season. Last season wasn't nearly as disastrous, but mostly because Cooper was phased out of the offense altogether. Apart from a couple touchdowns off of deep post routes early in the season, Cooper spent 2015 tethered to the sideline, even as the rest of Philly's young receiving corps underwhelmed. Excising Cooper and his $5.3 million cap hit was one of the easier decisions for the Eagles' new regime. There was some smoke afterwards that Kelly might bring him as a carry-on to San Francisco, but nothing has materialized on that front thus far. And if Kelly doesn't want him, it's hard to envision where exactly Cooper might latch on to continue his career.

Jerricho Cotchery — Height: 6-1 — Weight: 200 — College: North Carolina State — Draft: 2004/4 (108) — Born: 16-Jun-1982 — Age: 34 — Risk: N/A

Year	Team	G/GS	Snaps	Rec	Pass	Yds	C%	+/-	Yd/C	TD	Drop	YAC	Rk	YAC+	BTkl	DVOA	Rk	DYAR	Rk	YAR	Short	Mid	Deep	Bomb
2013	PIT	16/6	635	46	76	602	61%	-0.8	13.1	10	3	4.7	41	+0.4	7	26.2%	8	235	16	214	32%	49%	14%	5%
2014	CAR	15/13	783	48	78	580	62%	+0.7	12.1	1	2	4.0	54	-0.6	4	-3.7%	50	55	53	49	34%	41%	20%	5%
2015	CAR	14/3	419	39	54	485	72%	+2.8	12.4	3	1	5.0	27	+0.3	7	14.8%	13	112	40	122	45%	36%	11%	8%

A veteran with reliable hands and no speed, Cotchery could probably still deliver as an underneath option for some team lacking proven targets in 2016. That team won't be Carolina, as they told him they have no plans to re-sign him. And as a 34-year-old receiver, getting the attention of an organization won't be simple. The odds of Cotchery continuing his career look long at this point.

Michael Crabtree — Height: 6-2 — Weight: 215 — College: Texas Tech — Draft: 2009/1 (10) — Born: 14-Sep-1987 — Age: 29 — Risk: Green

Year	Team	G/GS	Snaps	Rec	Pass	Yds	C%	+/-	Yd/C	TD	Drop	YAC	Rk	YAC+	BTkl	DVOA	Rk	DYAR	Rk	YAR	Short	Mid	Deep	Bomb
2013	SF	5/5	237	19	33	284	58%	+1.8	14.9	1	1	7.2	—	+3.0	1	3.7%	—	42	—	42	38%	41%	14%	7%
2014	SF	16/16	722	68	108	698	64%	-0.8	10.3	4	5	3.9	58	-1.2	9	-9.9%	63	24	59	50	47%	30%	17%	6%
2015	OAK	16/15	809	85	146	922	58%	-6.7	10.8	9	6	3.1	75	-1.4	14	-13.0%	76	-4	77	3	41%	37%	13%	8%
2016	OAK			81	128	890	63%	—	11.0	6						-3.8%								

Now That's What I Call A Reclamation Project! Crabtree was left for dead after his torn Achilles, signing a one-year prove-it deal with Oakland. He bounced back in a big way, delivering a consistent underneath target and absorbing a lot of volume in an Oakland passing game with little depth. The big reward? A four-year extension with nearly $17 million in guarantees. Crabtree could be more efficient if Oakland had better talent around him, but sometimes the usage tells you a lot about how good a player is.

Jamison Crowder — Height: 5-8 — Weight: 185 — College: Duke — Draft: 2015/4 (105) — Born: 17-Jun-1993 — Age: 23 — Risk: Green

Year	Team	G/GS	Snaps	Rec	Pass	Yds	C%	+/-	Yd/C	TD	Drop	YAC	Rk	YAC+	BTkl	DVOA	Rk	DYAR	Rk	YAR	Short	Mid	Deep	Bomb
2015	WAS	16/6	734	59	78	604	76%	+5.1	10.2	2	2	5.7	12	+0.1	4	-4.4%	59	52	62	49	69%	17%	12%	3%
2016	WAS			43	67	476	64%	—	11.1	2						-5.5%								

Crowder pulled off the type of progression you might hope for from a rookie, beginning the year on the sidelines before gradually carving out a larger and steadier role in Washington's offense. This is the part where you might normally start discussing his sophomore breakout promise, but that's hard to envision given the Redskins' crowded wide receiver depth chart. Moreover, Crowder had a mediocre Playmaker Score which ranked in the bottom third of his receiver draft class, and was hardly the chain-mover you expect your slot receiver to be (-9.0% DVOA in third and fourth downs). Not all is lost for him, however, as both DeSean Jackson and Pierre Garcon are on the wrong side of 30 and entering the final year of their contracts. If Crowder can flash well in in his opportunities this season, it could keep him in an important role even after Josh Doctson passes him on the depth chart.

Victor Cruz Height: 6-1   Weight: 200   College: Massachusetts   Draft: 2010/FA   Born: 11-Nov-1986   Age: 30   Risk: Red

Year	Team	G/GS	Snaps	Rec	Pass	Yds	C%	+/-	Yd/C	TD	Drop	YAC	Rk	YAC+	BTkl	DVOA	Rk	DYAR	Rk	YAR	Short	Mid	Deep	Bomb
2013	NYG	14/12	785	73	121	998	60%	+2.4	13.7	4	3	3.4	76	-0.8	7	1.0%	44	133	35	172	25%	52%	12%	11%
2014	NYG	6/6	372	23	41	337	56%	-1.4	14.7	1	6	7.7	–	+2.5	7	-9.0%	–	13	--	21	29%	37%	22%	12%
2016	NYG			47	80	582	59%	--	12.4	5						-1.6%								

Starting from scratch is nothing new for someone who was once an undrafted free agent. However, if Cruz successfully makes it back after nearly two years since his last official game, he'll be coming back to an entirely new world. Once the centerpiece of a Super Bowl-winning offense, Cruz will no longer have a significant role preordained for him as he approaches his 30th birthday. Cruz was already in the midst of a four-year decline in receiving yardage and receiving DVOA at the time of his debilitating knee injury, so it's unclear how much juice he had even then. With New York drafting Sterling Shepard to eventually take Cruz's slot receiver role from him, Cruz is back to where he started: an underdog striving to exceed expectations and gain the trust of the coaching staff.

Eric Decker Height: 6-3   Weight: 217   College: Minnesota   Draft: 2010/3 (87)   Born: 15-Mar-1987   Age: 29   Risk: Green

Year	Team	G/GS	Snaps	Rec	Pass	Yds	C%	+/-	Yd/C	TD	Drop	YAC	Rk	YAC+	BTkl	DVOA	Rk	DYAR	Rk	YAR	Short	Mid	Deep	Bomb
2013	DEN	16/16	1050	87	136	1288	64%	+4.3	14.8	11	7	4.3	58	-0.4	5	21.3%	12	381	4	382	35%	39%	17%	9%
2014	NYJ	15/15	812	74	115	962	64%	+5.4	13.0	5	5	4.4	47	-0.2	1	9.4%	27	199	24	176	33%	44%	15%	9%
2015	NYJ	15/13	906	80	132	1027	61%	+4.2	12.8	12	5	2.7	82	-1.1	1	13.6%	17	278	12	290	23%	48%	22%	7%
2016	NYJ			75	123	938	61%	--	12.5	7						2.1%								

Decker caught 35 of 55 passes (63.6 percent) of 10 to 20 yards in air length last season for 582 yards: pretty darn good for medium-length passes sprayed by a journeyman with wobbly downfield accuracy. Decker slipped naturally back to the No. 2 possession receiver role behind Brandon Marshall after a miscast year as the Jets' go-to guy. He also showed solidarity with Marshall when the pair skipped a portion of OTAs to let the organization know how they felt about the team's quarterback situation. Decker dealt with both the Geno Smith and Tim Tebow experiences and knows he can be productive enough on screens and other easy throws to survive a bad quarterback. But he prefers the 80-1,000-10 stat lines that he can produce with even a baseline competent quarterback, and so should the Jets.

Stefon Diggs Height: 6-0   Weight: 195   College: Maryland   Draft: 2015/5 (146)   Born: 29-Nov-1993   Age: 23   Risk: Yellow

Year	Team	G/GS	Snaps	Rec	Pass	Yds	C%	+/-	Yd/C	TD	Drop	YAC	Rk	YAC+	BTkl	DVOA	Rk	DYAR	Rk	YAR	Short	Mid	Deep	Bomb
2015	MIN	13/9	654	52	84	720	62%	+4.0	13.8	4	2	5.6	15	+0.8	14	3.8%	43	108	44	85	35%	39%	15%	10%
2016	MIN			69	114	908	61%	--	13.2	6						-0.4%								

Diggs was the hottest waiver-wire pickup in every fantasy league after he busted out with 419 yards in his first four games, but it was a mirage—he totaled only 301 yards in nine games after that, never gaining more than 66 yards in a game. It's not clear precisely how the Vikings' wide receiver situation will shake out this season, but given Laquon Treadwell's lack of straight-line speed, perhaps the rookie will handle the majority of shorter and midrange routes while Diggs finds himself going deep more often.

Aaron Dobson

| | | Height: 6-3 | | Weight: 210 | | College: Marshall | | | Draft: 2013/2 (59) | | Born: 23-Jul-1991 | | Age: 25 | | Risk: Red |

Year	Team	G/GS	Snaps	Rec	Pass	Yds	C%	+/-	Yd/C	TD	Drop	YAC	Rk	YAC+	BTkl	DVOA	Rk	DYAR	Rk	YAR	Short	Mid	Deep	Bomb
2013	NE	12/9	546	37	72	519	51%	-2.8	14.0	4	7	5.0	30	+0.9	2	-5.4%	63	46	62	41	22%	45%	18%	14%
2014	NE	4/1	56	3	5	38	60%	-0.3	12.7	0	0	7.0	--	+1.9	1	13.3%	--	13	--	11	50%	33%	0%	17%
2015	NE	8/3	212	13	21	141	62%	+0.6	10.8	0	1	2.2	--	-1.9	0	15.1%	--	49	--	46	40%	45%	5%	10%
2016	NE			10	17	116	59%	--	11.6	1						-9.5%								

The ultimate Patriots second-round draft pick: a wide receiver with reliability and injury issues who slowly slides down the depth chart behind low-priced free agents and late-round role players. Dobson caught seven passes for 87 yards in Week 2 last year, as Bill Belichick emptied his bench to embarrass Rex Ryan with players he had never even heard of, then ping-ponged between healthy scratches and blowout duties before suffering a high ankle sprain. Dobson is poised over Chad Jackson's little corner of oblivion.

Josh Doctson

| | | Height: 6-2 | | Weight: 202 | | College: TCU | | | Draft: 2016/1 (22) | | Born: 3-Dec-1992 | | Age: 24 | | Risk: Blue |

Year	Team	G/GS	Snaps	Rec	Pass	Yds	C%	+/-	Yd/C	TD	Drop	YAC	Rk	YAC+	BTkl	DVOA	Rk	DYAR	Rk	YAR	Short	Mid	Deep	Bomb
2016	WAS			13	24	207	54%	--	15.9	2						0.7%								

Doctson's numbers improved in each of his four seasons at TCU, and the Redskins' first-round pick topped out in 2015 at 1,326 receiving yards on 17.0 yards per reception and 14 touchdowns. In a wide receiver class without a lot of size among the top prospects, Doctson's sinewy 6-foot-3, 195-pound frame certainly stood out. That size projects him to a prototypical split end role, where he'll put his superior acceleration and ability to snare jump balls to good use. Because he came out as a senior, Playmaker Score didn't have a particularly high projection on Doctson, ranking him behind less heralded prospects like Tyler Boyd and Pharoh Cooper. Even for those who don't believe in Playmaker, it's a good idea to tap the brakes on the 2016 hype given the depth at receiver in Washington. However, with DeSean Jackson and Pierre Garcon over 30 and hitting free agency next year, 2017 looks like the season where Doctson should become Kirk Cousins' primary target. Expect Washington to periodically showcase their first-round pick before truly loosening the reins in Doctson's second year. A much better pick in dynasty fantasy leagues than redraft leagues.

Phillip Dorsett

| | | Height: 5-10 | | Weight: 185 | | College: Miami | | | Draft: 2015/1 (29) | | Born: 5-Jan-1993 | | Age: 24 | | Risk: Yellow |

Year	Team	G/GS	Snaps	Rec	Pass	Yds	C%	+/-	Yd/C	TD	Drop	YAC	Rk	YAC+	BTkl	DVOA	Rk	DYAR	Rk	YAR	Short	Mid	Deep	Bomb
2015	IND	11/0	212	18	39	225	46%	-2.8	12.5	1	0	3.3	--	-1.5	0	-32.4%	--	-59	--	-49	32%	27%	19%	22%
2016	IND			54	103	779	52%	--	14.4	6						-5.6%								

Barring injury, Dorsett is locked in as the Colts' third receiver in 2016. What that means for his numbers is a more open question. The Colts flashed signs of manufacturing touches for him late in the year; whether that was more about his skills and 4.33 40-level speed or trying to find something with an inept Luck-less offense is more of an open question. Perhaps more than any other player, Luck's arm injury and concurrent deep-ball struggles prevented Dorsett from doing more in 2015. This year should bring more of the Dorsett-Luck deep ball combination we expected, and give us a more fair evaluation of whether Dorsett is good enough at that to justify that first-round pick. Plus, there is basically nothing on the depth chart underneath him.

Harry Douglas

| | | Height: 5-11 | | Weight: 176 | | College: Louisville | | | Draft: 2008/3 (84) | | Born: 16-Sep-1984 | | Age: 32 | | Risk: Red |

Year	Team	G/GS	Snaps	Rec	Pass	Yds	C%	+/-	Yd/C	TD	Drop	YAC	Rk	YAC+	BTkl	DVOA	Rk	DYAR	Rk	YAR	Short	Mid	Deep	Bomb
2013	ATL	16/11	926	85	132	1067	64%	+1.0	12.6	2	7	6.0	9	+1.2	8	3.6%	34	171	26	147	48%	38%	8%	6%
2014	ATL	12/6	557	51	74	556	69%	+1.7	10.9	2	1	4.7	38	+0.1	3	5.9%	32	108	38	102	49%	31%	15%	5%
2015	TEN	14/12	719	36	72	411	50%	-6.7	11.4	2	2	3.6	64	-0.4	1	-17.4%	81	-28	81	-24	26%	46%	18%	11%
2016	TEN			15	27	169	56%	--	11.2	1						-15.6%								

When Douglas was with the Atlanta Falcons, he was usually the fourth option in the offense. Playing behind Julio Jones, Roddy White, and Tony Gonzalez obviously helped put him in more favorable situations. He isn't afforded that luxury in Tennessee, but that's not Douglas' biggest issue. His legs have gone. Douglas is a smaller receiver who doesn't run precise routes or dominate at the catch point. Now that his athleticism is spiraling, he can't create separation. As the season wore on last year, his greatest contributions to his offense came via defensive pass interference penalties (4 for 69 yards). Ironically, he drew so many because he couldn't separate against tight coverage.

Donteea Dye   Height: 6-0   Weight: 185   College: Heidelburg   Draft: 2015/FA   Born: 20-Aug-1993   Age: 23   Risk: Blue

Year	Team	G/GS	Snaps	Rec	Pass	Yds	C%	+/-	Yd/C	TD	Drop	YAC	Rk	YAC+	BTkl	DVOA	Rk	DYAR	Rk	YAR	Short	Mid	Deep	Bomb
2015	TB	10/5	384	11	30	132	37%	-5.2	12.0	1	2	3.1	–	-1.2	4	-45.4%	–	-75	–	-79	36%	36%	14%	14%
2016	TB			4	9	58	44%	–	14.5	1						-19.7%								

The less successful of Tampa Bay's two UDFA receivers, Dye got some run after Louis Murphy went on injured reserve. This is the kind of stat line that makes you wonder about the general manager. There was no one better situated on the free-agent line? Not a single person the Bucs could have called on? Dye's future in this league is on special teams. If you see him with a full table in a future edition of this book, something went wrong.

Julian Edelman   Height: 6-0   Weight: 198   College: Kent State   Draft: 2009/7 (232)   Born: 22-May-1986   Age: 30   Risk: Red

Year	Team	G/GS	Snaps	Rec	Pass	Yds	C%	+/-	Yd/C	TD	Drop	YAC	Rk	YAC+	BTkl	DVOA	Rk	DYAR	Rk	YAR	Short	Mid	Deep	Bomb
2013	NE	16/11	1021	105	151	1056	70%	+5.7	10.1	6	6	4.7	42	-0.8	11	4.3%	32	204	22	164	52%	29%	13%	6%
2014	NE	14/13	805	92	133	972	69%	+7.1	10.6	4	10	4.6	40	-0.1	8	0.2%	42	137	31	102	53%	34%	9%	4%
2015	NE	9/9	525	61	88	692	69%	+2.6	11.3	7	6	5.1	25	+0.5	15	8.1%	35	144	28	159	51%	36%	6%	7%
2016	NE			99	141	1104	70%	–	11.1	8						8.1%								

Edelman is coming off a November foot injury. Health information being as forthcoming as it is out of Foxborough, Edelman could either be full-go by the time you read this or an amputee. Assuming he is healthy, Edelman's weekly 6-to-10 catch allotment should remain secure and reliable. Though Danny Amendola was often better in the same role last year. And Martellus Bennett will earn some catches as the second tight end. And newcomers like Chris Hogan, Nate Washington and/or Malcolm Mitchell are likely to push for touches. Phew! It's a good thing the Patriots never run the ball until anymore.

Bruce Ellington   Height: 5-9   Weight: 197   College: South Carolina   Draft: 2014/4 (106)   Born: 22-Aug-1991   Age: 25   Risk: Red

Year	Team	G/GS	Snaps	Rec	Pass	Yds	C%	+/-	Yd/C	TD	Drop	YAC	Rk	YAC+	BTkl	DVOA	Rk	DYAR	Rk	YAR	Short	Mid	Deep	Bomb
2014	SF	13/0	95	6	12	62	50%	-1.1	10.3	2	0	5.5	–	+0.0	1	-1.5%	–	11	–	4	45%	27%	9%	18%
2015	SF	13/0	143	13	19	153	68%	+0.1	11.8	0	1	8.5	–	-0.1	2	-32.7%	–	-27	–	-34	58%	16%	5%	21%
2016	SF			52	76	559	68%	–	10.7	2						-4.1%								

With Torrey Smith running the deep routes and Quinton Patton trying to find his way, Ellington's role as slot receiver should lead him to a career-best season in Chip Kelly's offense. (That's not a tough forecast since a career-best season wouldn't even require 200 yards.) It is hard to project much for a fourth-round pick with just 19 catches in two seasons, but someone has to fake the jet sweep and catch short, ineffective passes from Blaine Gabbert in San Francisco, right?

Quincy Enunwa   Height: 6-2   Weight: 225   College: Nebraska   Draft: 2014/6 (209)   Born: 31-May-1992   Age: 24   Risk: Green

Year	Team	G/GS	Snaps	Rec	Pass	Yds	C%	+/-	Yd/C	TD	Drop	YAC	Rk	YAC+	BTkl	DVOA	Rk	DYAR	Rk	YAR	Short	Mid	Deep	Bomb
2015	NYJ	12/6	522	22	46	315	48%	-6.9	14.3	0	5	6.7	–	+1.9	7	-27.0%	–	-48	–	-40	42%	28%	23%	7%
2016	NYJ			24	38	302	63%	–	12.6	3						-2.6%								

Enunwa was the third option in a two-option passing game for most of the year. When healthy, he played 40 to 55 snaps per game in Chad Gailey's wide-open offense, but he sandwiched lots of two-catch, 20-something-yard stat lines around a four-game domestic violence suspension and a neck injury. Like an off-brand Brandon Marshall, Enunwa combined big plays like his 48-yard flat-and-run reception against the Patriots with half-a-dozen dropped passes, some of them ugly. Enunwa is in line for the No. 3 receiver role again this year. He's not that great a prospect, and it's not that great of a role.

Mike Evans   Height: 6-5   Weight: 231   College: Texas A&M   Draft: 2014/1 (7)   Born: 21-Aug-1993   Age: 23   Risk: Green

Year	Team	G/GS	Snaps	Rec	Pass	Yds	C%	+/-	Yd/C	TD	Drop	YAC	Rk	YAC+	BTkl	DVOA	Rk	DYAR	Rk	YAR	Short	Mid	Deep	Bomb
2014	TB	15/15	768	68	123	1051	55%	+3.8	15.5	12	4	2.5	82	-2.3	4	11.4%	21	222	17	234	21%	38%	22%	19%
2015	TB	15/14	857	74	148	1206	50%	-6.2	16.3	3	10	3.3	74	-0.9	4	2.8%	44	187	22	153	14%	46%	23%	16%
2016	TB			84	150	1309	56%	–	15.6	8						2.5%								

Fun with randomness: Mike Evans red zone DVOA 2015: -58.1%. Mike Evans red zone DVOA 2014: 40.1%. Evans slogged through a tough year, at various times this offseason calling himself out for a lack of fundamentals and focus on the field. Being force-fed targets as the only semi-healthy receiver on the squad didn't help either, as his catch rate plummeted into the Chris Chambers Zone. Jameis Winston's sophomore season should see a rise in Evans' efficiency, if not his fantasy value.

Larry Fitzgerald

Height: 6-3 | Weight: 225 | College: Pittsburgh | Draft: 2004/1 (3) | Born: 31-Aug-1983 | Age: 33 | Risk: Yellow

Year	Team	G/GS	Snaps	Rec	Pass	Yds	C%	+/-	Yd/C	TD	Drop	YAC	Rk	YAC+	BTkl	DVOA	Rk	DYAR	Rk	YAR	Short	Mid	Deep	Bomb
2013	ARI	16/16	998	82	136	954	62%	+0.3	11.6	10	1	4.2	61	-0.9	6	-0.6%	49	132	36	152	37%	37%	20%	6%
2014	ARI	14/13	857	63	104	784	61%	-1.2	12.4	2	1	5.3	22	+0.4	8	-5.8%	55	54	54	58	37%	37%	20%	6%
2015	ARI	16/16	984	109	146	1215	75%	+14.7	11.1	9	2	4.2	48	-0.6	8	18.9%	10	363	4	356	42%	40%	14%	3%
2016	ARI			88	125	1034	70%	--	11.8	9						15.5%								

There was some concern that Fitzgerald was no longer a top threat after three straight years without a 1,000-yard season. However, the problems were more with the delivery system. Fitzgerald's career offers a great argument for the importance of competent quarterback play. When Arizona has had that, Fitzgerald has been at his best, especially in the postseason where he is off the charts with 942 yards and 10 touchdowns in nine games. Last season was the first time since 2008 that Fitzgerald finished in the top 10 in DVOA, largely thanks to Palmer's efficient season. Fitzgerald also finished second in receiving plus-minus, a stat where he is plus-20.6 with Palmer, plus-28.0 with Kurt Warner, and minus-36.8 with Arizona's lousy cast of other passers since 2006. Fitzgerald is 33 this season, but even if he takes a step or two back, the Cardinals will still boast arguably the best wide receiving corps in the NFL.

Malcom Floyd

Height: 6-5 | Weight: 201 | College: Wyoming | Draft: 2004/FA | Born: 8-Sep-1981 | Age: 35 | Risk: N/A

Year	Team	G/GS	Snaps	Rec	Pass	Yds	C%	+/-	Yd/C	TD	Drop	YAC	Rk	YAC+	BTkl	DVOA	Rk	DYAR	Rk	YAR	Short	Mid	Deep	Bomb
2013	SD	2/2	88	6	11	149	55%	-0.5	24.8	0	0	2.0	--	-3.8	0	40.9%	--	47	--	45	25%	17%	50%	8%
2014	SD	16/16	942	52	91	856	57%	+7.2	16.5	6	1	2.4	84	-2.0	2	23.1%	12	252	14	245	13%	46%	16%	25%
2015	SD	15/13	833	30	69	561	43%	-4.1	18.7	3	2	2.9	79	-1.9	1	-9.6%	72	16	72	18	10%	37%	20%	33%

There haven't been many deep threats like Malcom Floyd. Floyd averaged 17.3 yards per reception for his career but rarely ran away from defensive backs. Floyd ran a 4.44 40 at the combine, but it took so long for him to get on the field that this speed was never really felt in the NFL. Floyd worked with Philip Rivers because of his ability to run good routes and tower over defensive backs to pluck the ball out of the air consistently. Since he entered the league in 2004, Floyd is one of 71 wide receivers to see at least 500 targets. Among that group, only Jordy Nelson (27.7%) has a better career DVOA than Floyd's 22.5%. That does not mean that Floyd has been the second-best receiver in the league over the past decade, but it does show how effective he was playing a specific role with a very good quarterback, usually as the third or fourth option in the San Diego offense.

Michael Floyd

Height: 6-3 | Weight: 220 | College: Notre Dame | Draft: 2012/1 (13) | Born: 27-Nov-1989 | Age: 27 | Risk: Yellow

Year	Team	G/GS	Snaps	Rec	Pass	Yds	C%	+/-	Yd/C	TD	Drop	YAC	Rk	YAC+	BTkl	DVOA	Rk	DYAR	Rk	YAR	Short	Mid	Deep	Bomb
2013	ARI	16/16	930	65	112	1041	58%	+3.5	16.0	5	4	4.3	57	-0.2	5	12.9%	20	220	17	229	18%	49%	20%	13%
2014	ARI	16/14	944	47	100	841	48%	-5.2	17.9	6	3	2.5	83	-2.4	2	-1.9%	47	81	44	81	15%	41%	16%	29%
2015	ARI	15/6	652	52	89	849	58%	+2.8	16.3	6	3	4.1	52	+0.0	4	24.0%	8	256	14	227	12%	46%	26%	17%
2016	ARI			59	101	933	58%	--	15.8	6						7.8%								

Places where Floyd could be a No. 1 wide receiver in 2016: Cleveland, Baltimore, Tennessee, San Francisco, Los Angeles... and we could probably debate a couple of other teams. Alas, he is just the Third Man in Arizona, but what a way to round out the trio with size and big-play ability. This could be the last season Arizona has its trio intact, with Floyd set to hit free agency next March. There should be a few suitors waiting, but he is a good fit in Arizona.

Bennie Fowler

Height: 6-1 | Weight: 212 | College: Michigan State | Draft: 2014/FA | Born: 10-Jun-1991 | Age: 25 | Risk: Green

Year	Team	G/GS	Snaps	Rec	Pass	Yds	C%	+/-	Yd/C	TD	Drop	YAC	Rk	YAC+	BTkl	DVOA	Rk	DYAR	Rk	YAR	Short	Mid	Deep	Bomb
2015	DEN	16/1	264	16	25	203	64%	-0.5	12.7	0	0	6.1	--	+1.4	8	-3.4%	--	20	--	24	42%	54%	4%	0%
2016	DEN			13	22	154	59%	--	11.8	0						-8.2%								

Fowler was a training-camp star over the past two years, but that hasn't yet translated to breaking through in the regular season. This year, he'll fight with Cody Latimer and Jordan Norwood for Denver's No. 3 receiver position. Last year, Fowler received credit from special teams coach Joe DeCamillis for being the unsung hero of the playoffs thanks to his work as a gunner in punt coverage.

Will Fuller

Height: 6-0   Weight: 186   College: Notre Dame   Draft: 2016/1 (21)   Born: 16-Apr-1994   Age: 22   Risk: Red

Year	Team	G/GS	Snaps	Rec	Pass	Yds	C%	+/-	Yd/C	TD	Drop	YAC	Rk	YAC+	BTkl	DVOA	Rk	DYAR	Rk	YAR	Short	Mid	Deep	Bomb
2016	HOU			48	87	794	55%	--	16.5	4						2.4%								

Fuller has college production backed up by measurables, as he ran a 4.32 40-yard dash to show the 20.3 yards per catch average in his final season in South Bend was not a fluke. Playmaker Score liked him second-best in this year's draft class, behind only Corey Coleman, and the dimension he adds to a Houston offense desperately lacking in speed last season is obvious. Fuller's NFL success will depend on how quickly he can get on the same page with Brock Osweiler on those deep throws, and whether he ever finds a second dimension to move beyond the Ashley Lelies of the world.

Devin Funchess

Height: 6-4   Weight: 232   College: Michigan   Draft: 2015/2 (41)   Born: 21-May-1994   Age: 22   Risk: Red

Year	Team	G/GS	Snaps	Rec	Pass	Yds	C%	+/-	Yd/C	TD	Drop	YAC	Rk	YAC+	BTkl	DVOA	Rk	DYAR	Rk	YAR	Short	Mid	Deep	Bomb
2015	CAR	16/5	493	31	63	473	49%	-5.1	15.3	5	3	3.6	63	-0.4	3	-10.7%	73	9	73	32	15%	63%	12%	10%
2016	CAR			49	89	718	55%	--	14.7	7						1.7%								

This is about the rookie year you expect from a player this raw coming out of Michigan. Funchess had trouble getting off the line of scrimmage, and has no real release moves. He was used mostly on rudimentary route concepts last season. The Panthers should not be surprised by this development—he simply was forced to play because the depth chart was barren. With another offseason of work—he was the *Charlotte Observer*'s "star of OTAs"— there is still reason to be optimistic that he will develop into a quality NFL receiver. Just remember that there's still plenty of growing to do.

Taylor Gabriel

Height: 5-8   Weight: 167   College: Abilene Christian   Draft: 2014/FA   Born: 17-Feb-1991   Age: 25   Risk: Green

Year	Team	G/GS	Snaps	Rec	Pass	Yds	C%	+/-	Yd/C	TD	Drop	YAC	Rk	YAC+	BTkl	DVOA	Rk	DYAR	Rk	YAR	Short	Mid	Deep	Bomb
2014	CLE	16/2	610	36	74	621	51%	-5.4	17.3	1	2	7.3	3	+1.2	4	-9.0%	60	21	61	19	32%	33%	17%	18%
2015	CLE	13/4	401	28	48	241	58%	-4.4	8.6	0	4	3.9	--	-2.3	2	-31.8%	--	-74	--	-95	51%	30%	13%	6%
2016	CLE			11	21	118	52%	--	10.7	0						-24.3%								

The Browns drafted approximately 2,647 wide receivers this spring, including *Air Bud: Golden Receiver*. Gabriel is extra-wee (he barely weighs more than the cinematic dog) and has been hampered this spring with leg injuries. His battle for a roster spot is uphill, and Josh Gordon's reinstatement makes it even steeper.

Pierre Garcon

Height: 6-0   Weight: 210   College: Mount Union   Draft: 2008/6 (205)   Born: 8-Aug-1986   Age: 30   Risk: Yellow

Year	Team	G/GS	Snaps	Rec	Pass	Yds	C%	+/-	Yd/C	TD	Drop	YAC	Rk	YAC+	BTkl	DVOA	Rk	DYAR	Rk	YAR	Short	Mid	Deep	Bomb
2013	WAS	16/16	978	113	181	1346	62%	+0.2	11.9	5	6	5.8	15	+0.5	7	-5.2%	62	104	45	132	44%	36%	14%	6%
2014	WAS	16/14	872	68	105	752	65%	+0.1	11.1	3	0	5.0	29	-0.1	6	-14.6%	75	-15	76	0	49%	33%	9%	9%
2015	WAS	16/16	811	72	111	777	65%	+3.9	10.8	6	2	2.3	86	-2.1	3	2.4%	45	128	33	129	39%	33%	20%	8%
2016	WAS			56	92	640	61%	--	11.4	4						-6.6%								

His high-volume 2013 season was clearly an aberration, but Garcon remains one of the league's steadier possession receivers as he enters his thirties. Though Jordan Reed and DeSean Jackson received most of the attention among Redskins receivers, especially during their season-ending surge, it was Garcon who served as Kirk Cousins' favorite third-down target. While every other wide receiver on the roster had a negative DVOA on third and fourth downs, Garcon accrued a 31.3% DVOA on such plays, converting 22 of his 43 targets into first downs. The league isn't overflowing with split ends who can make contested catches against big perimeter cornerbacks, so Garcon's route-running diversity might prolong his career a few more seasons. But he's absolutely no threat after the catch, as his minus-2.1 YAC+ figure came in dead last among 81 qualified receivers.

Garcon is entering the final year of his deal, and Washington's receiver room now houses first-rounder Josh Doctson and promising second-year slot receiver Jamison Crowder. Garcon seems quite likely to leave in free agency next year, and if the youngsters can pick up the playbook, his numbers may take an uncharacteristic dive in 2016.

Ted Ginn — Height: 5-11 — Weight: 178 — College: Ohio State — Draft: 2007/1 (9) — Born: 12-Apr-1985 — Age: 31 — Risk: Green

Year	Team	G/GS	Snaps	Rec	Pass	Yds	C%	+/-	Yd/C	TD	Drop	YAC	Rk	YAC+	BTkl	DVOA	Rk	DYAR	Rk	YAR	Short	Mid	Deep	Bomb
2013	CAR	16/2	502	36	68	556	53%	-0.1	15.4	5	3	5.9	14	+0.8	2	0.3%	47	65	56	68	31%	42%	3%	24%
2014	ARI	16/0	151	14	26	190	54%	-0.7	13.6	0	2	3.3	--	-1.9	1	-15.5%	--	-6	--	-4	35%	27%	19%	19%
2015	CAR	15/13	670	44	96	739	46%	-6.4	16.8	10	7	5.5	19	+1.4	2	-2.5%	55	77	52	106	14%	50%	12%	24%
2016	CAR			34	65	522	52%	--	15.4	4						-1.1%								

In overtime against the Colts, Cam Newton placed a perfect throw over Ted Ginn's shoulder that should have won the game. Ginn dropped it. It was the perfect single image of what it was like to be Newton last season—and also the perfect image for Ginn's career. Ginn will always hang around a roster as long as his track-star speed and punt return ability are still evident. Don't expect 10 touchdowns ever again. Carolina would probably be happiest if he went back to a 40- or 50-target role. That would mean the youth around him has developed properly. If it doesn't? Well, time to roll the dice on every deep ball.

Chris Givens — Height: 5-11 — Weight: 198 — College: Wake Forest — Draft: 2012/4 (96) — Born: 6-Dec-1989 — Age: 27 — Risk: Blue

Year	Team	G/GS	Snaps	Rec	Pass	Yds	C%	+/-	Yd/C	TD	Drop	YAC	Rk	YAC+	BTkl	DVOA	Rk	DYAR	Rk	YAR	Short	Mid	Deep	Bomb
2013	STL	16/13	779	34	83	569	41%	-9.2	16.7	0	3	7.6	3	+2.9	1	-22.8%	82	-68	84	-66	31%	33%	24%	12%
2014	STL	14/0	197	11	20	159	55%	+1.1	14.5	1	0	4.0	--	-2.5	0	-12.9%	--	0	--	-4	41%	12%	24%	24%
2015	2TM	15/6	488	20	54	353	37%	-7.5	17.7	1	3	2.6	84	-2.9	1	-29.8%	85	-70	83	-70	29%	31%	16%	24%
2016	PHI			8	16	108	50%	--	14.6	1							-9.2%								

Givens signed a one-year deal worth $840,000 in March with the Eagles, likely meaning a short-lived reunion with Sam Bradford trying to find him deep down the field. The real question is, why did Baltimore let a cheap deep threat go after trading a seventh-round pick during the season for him? Givens caught 6-of-15 passes thrown at least 20 yards beyond the line of scrimmage last season. Mike Wallace has caught 7-of-30 such passes since 2014, and will cost more than five times what Givens is making for the Eagles while possibly stunting the development of Breshad Perriman. Again, Ozzie Newsome's plan for the skill players this season has us dazed and confused.

Josh Gordon — Height: 6-4 — Weight: 220 — College: Baylor — Draft: 2012/2 (SUP) — Born: 12-Apr-1991 — Age: 25 — Risk: Red

Year	Team	G/GS	Snaps	Rec	Pass	Yds	C%	+/-	Yd/C	TD	Drop	YAC	Rk	YAC+	BTkl	DVOA	Rk	DYAR	Rk	YAR	Short	Mid	Deep	Bomb
2013	CLE	14/14	900	87	159	1646	55%	+1.8	18.9	9	10	7.3	4	+2.8	6	14.4%	17	336	9	321	25%	38%	23%	14%
2014	CLE	5/5	233	24	47	303	51%	-3.9	12.6	0	1	6.7	--	+1.5	1	-22.7%	--	-35	--	-38	33%	40%	16%	11%
2016	CLE			47	89	730	53%	--	15.4	5							-1.1%								

Will the fourth time around be the charm? Assuming he doesn't petition the league for all Browns kickoffs to be moved to 4:20 PM, a Gordon on the straight and narrow can only help Cleveland and its legion of dubious quarterbacks and raw wide receivers. But he has played in just 35 of the 64 potential games since his career began. Even if he makes it through all 12 games after he serves his season-opening four-game suspension, assuming he will recapture his 2013 form is highly optimistic, even for the newly pumped Believeland. Needless to say his projection risk is the bright red of candy apples and fire engines, not the dusky red of merlots and sangrias.

Ryan Grant — Height: 6-0 — Weight: 199 — College: Tulane — Draft: 2014/5 (142) — Born: 19-Dec-1990 — Age: 26 — Risk: Yellow

Year	Team	G/GS	Snaps	Rec	Pass	Yds	C%	+/-	Yd/C	TD	Drop	YAC	Rk	YAC+	BTkl	DVOA	Rk	DYAR	Rk	YAR	Short	Mid	Deep	Bomb
2014	WAS	16/2	178	7	15	68	47%	-1.3	9.7	0	0	3.3	--	-0.6	0	-37.3%	--	-27	--	-18	29%	36%	29%	7%
2015	WAS	16/5	456	23	42	268	55%	-0.4	11.7	2	2	4.3	--	-0.1	2	-1.1%	--	40	--	31	49%	30%	16%	5%
2016	WAS			17	35	187	49%	--	11.0	1							-28.9%								

When DeSean Jackson went down with a hamstring injury in Week 1, Grant earned the first prolonged stretch of playing time in his career. The results were unspectacular. Grant certainly did not embarrass himself, but it is difficult to remember a particularly impactful moment from his time as a starter in Washington's three-receiver sets. Thus, it was hardly surprising to see Jackson's return spell the end of Grant's playing time, as he caught just six passes the rest of the year. Entering his third season, Grant smells like a player who will live annually on the roster bubble. Redskins beat writers have praised his route-running ability, and that certainly shows up in the diversity of his route tree. However, Grant is also quite thin-framed and lacks elite quickness or speed, making it difficult to consistently feature him in any offense. Maybe he'll pop up somewhere on a less crowded depth chart, but don't count on a breakthrough in D.C.

A.J. Green

Height: 6-4   Weight: 207   College: Georgia   Draft: 2011/1 (4)   Born: 31-Jul-1988   Age: 28   Risk: Green

Year	Team	G/GS	Snaps	Rec	Pass	Yds	C%	+/-	Yd/C	TD	Drop	YAC	Rk	YAC+	BTkl	DVOA	Rk	DYAR	Rk	YAR	Short	Mid	Deep	Bomb
2013	CIN	16/16	1055	98	178	1426	55%	-1.6	14.6	11	5	4.1	65	-0.6	7	1.9%	41	207	20	185	27%	44%	14%	15%
2014	CIN	13/13	648	69	116	1041	59%	+4.2	15.1	6	2	4.5	46	+0.3	9	4.1%	38	158	29	161	23%	45%	20%	12%
2015	CIN	16/16	932	86	132	1297	65%	+13.2	15.1	10	3	3.9	57	-0.3	6	26.5%	7	414	3	403	26%	38%	22%	13%
2016	CIN			92	151	1341	61%	--	14.6	9				7.7%										

Five years in the league, five seasons with 1,000-plus yards receiving. The only receiver besides Green to accomplish that? Randy Moss. Blessed with a plethora of weapons alongside him, Green found his sweet spot in 2015. Capable of blowing open any game on any play, he also cleared out space for the rest of a wondrously talented offense. Now that unit has been depleted, and Green again figures to shoulder a heavier load than preferred. He has proven, however, that he can handle the weight.

Dorial Green-Beckham

Heigh t:65   Weight: 237   College: Oklahoma   Draft: 2015/2 (40)   Born: 12-Apr-1993   Age: 23   Risk: Red

Year	Team	G/GS	Snaps	Rec	Pass	Yds	C%	+/-	Yd/C	TD	Drop	YAC	Rk	YAC+	BTkl	DVOA	Rk	DYAR	Rk	YAR	Short	Mid	Deep	Bomb
2015	TEN	16/5	580	32	67	549	48%	-2.5	17.2	4	3	4.5	42	+0.8	4	1.8%	47	77	54	90	23%	35%	36%	6%
2016	TEN			35	67	586	52%	--	16.8	6				3.6%										

Green-Beckham has all the physical talent to be a great receiver. He showed flashes of that talent on occasions last year, most notably his touchdown reception against the Cleveland Browns. Green-Beckham worked through his in route on the backside of a fourth-and-6 play. Mariota worked through his progression and found him with a high pass in the end zone that Green-Beckham pulled in by fully extending away from the defensive back trying to cover him. It was a great play, but physical talent isn't valuable if you don't know where to be or if you can't get there at the right time. Green-Beckham has a long way to go to be successful in the NFL. His routes were a constant issue during his rookie season and his stamina limited his ability to create separation.

Rashad Greene

Height: 5-11   Weight: 182   College: Florida State   Draft: 2015/5 (139)   Born: 23-Sep-1992   Age: 24   Risk: Green

Year	Team	G/GS	Snaps	Rec	Pass	Yds	C%	+/-	Yd/C	TD	Drop	YAC	Rk	YAC+	BTkl	DVOA	Rk	DYAR	Rk	YAR	Short	Mid	Deep	Bomb
2015	JAC	9/0	168	19	35	93	54%	-4.6	4.9	2	3	2.8	--	-3.2	2	-33.8%	--	-61	--	-66	51%	34%	11%	3%
2016	JAC			41	63	402	65%	--	9.8	2				-11.3%										

Greene proved himself to be an outstanding football player while catching passes from Jameis Winston at Florida State, but the undersized receiver fell in the draft because of his size and because of his hands. Greene can get open and he can make big plays. His size doesn't matter as he primarily acts as a slot receiver, but his hands need to improve if he is going to reach his potential.

Leonard Hankerson

Height: 6-2   Weight: 209   College: Miami   Draft: 2011/3 (79)   Born: 7-May-1988   Age: 28   Risk: Blue

Year	Team	G/GS	Snaps	Rec	Pass	Yds	C%	+/-	Yd/C	TD	Drop	YAC	Rk	YAC+	BTkl	DVOA	Rk	DYAR	Rk	YAR	Short	Mid	Deep	Bomb
2013	WAS	10/7	390	30	50	375	60%	+1.8	12.5	3	2	4.4	55	-0.0	1	-0.6%	50	46	61	72	40%	40%	20%	0%
2014	WAS	1/0	21	0	1	0	0%	+0.0	0.0	0	0	0.0	--	+0.0	0	-118.9%	--	-9	--	-7	--	--	--	--
2015	3TM	10/0	350	26	46	327	57%	-3.0	12.6	3	6	4.6	--	+1.0	1	1.1%	--	51	--	57	36%	50%	11%	2%
2016	BUF			4	11	47	36%	--	11.9	0				-42.6%										

Hankerson played eight games for Atlanta last season, went on injured reserve with a hamstring issue, then was released following an injury settlement. He spent ten days on New England's roster and then was picked up for Week 17 by Buffalo, playing one game each with no targets for the Pats and Bills. Buffalo has no depth at wide receiver behind Sammy Watkins, and Hankerson has a good chance at making the roster. He could even end up winning the slot receiver job.

Justin Hardy — Height: 5-10 — Weight: 192 — College: East Carolina — Draft: 2015/4 (107) — Born: 18-Dec-1991 — Age: 25 — Risk: Red

Year	Team	G/GS	Snaps	Rec	Pass	Yds	C%	+/-	Yd/C	TD	Drop	YAC	Rk	YAC+	BTkl	DVOA	Rk	DYAR	Rk	YAR	Short	Mid	Deep	Bomb
2015	ATL	9/1	337	21	36	194	58%	-1.6	9.2	0	2	3.1	--	-1.0	0	-24.8%	--	-32	--	-20	42%	48%	3%	6%
2016	ATL			48	78	596	62%	--	12.4	4						-0.3%								

The big bugaboo with Hardy coming out of East Carolina was that he got jammed really easily. Falcons head coach Dan Quinn parroted Hardy's need to work on the issue again this offseason, which tells you all you need to know about how successful he was against press coverage in 2015. He's a clean projection to the slot receiver role as long as he can actually get off the line of scrimmage, but we haven't seen any sign of that coming to fruition yet.

Dwayne Harris — Height: 5-10 — Weight: 200 — College: East Carolina — Draft: 2011/6 (176) — Born: 16-Sep-1987 — Age: 29 — Risk: Blue

Year	Team	G/GS	Snaps	Rec	Pass	Yds	C%	+/-	Yd/C	TD	Drop	YAC	Rk	YAC+	BTkl	DVOA	Rk	DYAR	Rk	YAR	Short	Mid	Deep	Bomb
2013	DAL	13/3	147	9	14	80	64%	-0.5	8.9	2	4	4.0	--	-2.0	2	7.3%	--	20	--	16	64%	21%	14%	0%
2014	DAL	16/0	155	7	12	116	58%	-0.2	16.6	0	0	5.1	--	-2.0	1	-2.3%	--	8	--	8	27%	55%	9%	9%
2015	NYG	15/6	623	36	57	396	63%	+0.0	11.0	4	4	3.8	58	-0.5	2	-2.7%	56	45	63	60	39%	43%	16%	2%
2016	NYG			14	22	139	64%	--	9.9	0						-9.5%								

Harris claimed that playing the largest offensive role of his career detracted from his ability as a returner, but the numbers hardly back up that claim. In fact, after a down year returning kicks during his last season in Dallas, Harris re-emerged as one of the league's best special teams weapons during his first season in New York. As a punt and kick returner, Harris was one of four players to deliver more than 10 points of combined return value. As a receiver, the results were a little more spotty, though he wasn't a disaster playing both the slot and split end roles. With Sterling Shepard on board and Victor Cruz hopefully healthy again, the Giants figure to scale back Harris' offensive role in 2016. On the other hand, given that both Shepard and Cruz are most comfortable in the slot, it's not out of the question that Harris plays a significant role in three-receiver packages once again. Either way, anything beyond stellar special teams contributions will be a bonus for the Giants.

Brian Hartline — Height: 6-2 — Weight: 195 — College: Ohio State — Draft: 2009/4 (108) — Born: 22-Nov-1986 — Age: 30 — Risk: N/A

Year	Team	G/GS	Snaps	Rec	Pass	Yds	C%	+/-	Yd/C	TD	Drop	YAC	Rk	YAC+	BTkl	DVOA	Rk	DYAR	Rk	YAR	Short	Mid	Deep	Bomb
2013	MIA	16/15	907	76	133	1016	57%	-2.9	13.4	4	7	3.7	71	-0.3	6	-0.7%	51	123	38	135	26%	54%	14%	6%
2014	MIA	16/16	813	39	63	474	62%	-0.1	12.2	2	4	3.5	66	-0.5	1	2.6%	40	77	47	73	37%	43%	14%	6%
2015	CLE	12/4	515	46	77	523	60%	-1.6	11.4	2	5	3.6	65	-0.8	2	-9.2%	71	21	71	9	38%	47%	11%	4%

Hartline had his moments in the NFL, but few came in his lone year in Cleveland. Pushed out in favor of an extreme youth movement, Hartline remains unemployed at press time, not having supplied much quality tape last season. His best hope to regain employment would seem to be a rash of injuries along some team's wideout corps, which isn't the sort of thing one feels good about hoping for in the wee small hours of the evening.

Percy Harvin — Height: 5-11 — Weight: 192 — College: Florida — Draft: 2009/1 (22) — Born: 28-May-1988 — Age: 28 — Risk: N/A

Year	Team	G/GS	Snaps	Rec	Pass	Yds	C%	+/-	Yd/C	TD	Drop	YAC	Rk	YAC+	BTkl	DVOA	Rk	DYAR	Rk	YAR	Short	Mid	Deep	Bomb
2013	SEA	1/0	19	1	1	17	100%	+0.4	17.0	0	0	5.0	--	+1.7	0	102.4%	--	8	--	9	0%	100%	0%	0%
2014	2TM	13/12	541	51	78	483	65%	-1.7	9.5	1	2	5.1	28	-1.0	10	-21.4%	84	-55	83	-65	62%	22%	7%	9%
2015	BUF	5/5	240	19	30	218	63%	+1.1	11.5	1	1	4.4	--	-0.8	2	-6.5%	--	14	--	24	42%	32%	0%	26%

After eight seasons in search of the perfect equilibrium of being unable to take the field, unwilling to take the field, impossible to catch in the open field, unable to avoid sizzling locker-room rumors, and uninterested in giving straight answers about his health or future which might impact his earning potential, Harvin reportedly retired in April. He was outstanding in brief spurts. If he returns in September, he'll be gone again in October.

Andrew Hawkins
Height: 5-7   **Weight:** 175   **College:** Toledo   **Draft:** 2008/FA   **Born:** 10-Mar-1986   **Age:** 30   **Risk:** Green

Year	Team	G/GS	Snaps	Rec	Pass	Yds	C%	+/-	Yd/C	TD	Drop	YAC	Rk	YAC+	BTkl	DVOA	Rk	DYAR	Rk	YAR	Short	Mid	Deep	Bomb
2013	CIN	8/0	118	12	18	199	67%	-0.1	16.6	0	2	11.3	--	+4.1	0	8.7%	--	31	--	30	53%	24%	18%	6%
2014	CLE	15/15	647	63	113	824	57%	-5.2	13.1	2	3	6.4	9	+1.1	9	-11.4%	66	11	65	29	40%	41%	15%	4%
2015	CLE	8/8	415	27	43	276	63%	-1.4	10.2	0	0	4.7	--	-0.5	1	-26.0%	--	-42	--	-44	54%	37%	7%	2%
2016	CLE			46	74	557	62%	--	12.1	2						-7.4%								

Baby Hawk had his season ruined by a pair of concussions that landed him on injured reserve after Week 10. He spent much of the offseason commuting from Florida to New York to take sports management classes at Columbia, so it seems he wisely is already thinking about his post-football life. The elite slot quickness that carved his NFL career is dwindling, but he still might have a productive season or two in his legs. Then Hawkins can don an elegant three-piece suit and haggle with the front office full time.

Javontee Herndon
Height: 6-1   **Weight:** 194   **College:** Arkansas   **Draft:** 2014/FA   **Born:** 21-Jun-1991   **Age:** 25   **Risk:** Blue

Year	Team	G/GS	Snaps	Rec	Pass	Yds	C%	+/-	Yd/C	TD	Drop	YAC	Rk	YAC+	BTkl	DVOA	Rk	DYAR	Rk	YAR	Short	Mid	Deep	Bomb
2015	SD	8/2	288	24	33	195	73%	-0.5	8.1	0	2	4.4	--	-1.8	2	-19.1%	--	-15	--	-15	64%	30%	3%	3%
2016	SD			9	14	101	64%	--	11.3	0						-2.7%								

Herndon's first regular-season play in the NFL didn't go very well: not only did he drop his first target, but he committed pass interference to get open in the first place. He had only found his way onto the field for the Chargers because of Keenan Allen's injury. After his initial faux pas, things got a lot better for Herndon. He has good size and speed, showing off consistent catching ability even if his ball skills on the whole aren't spectacular. Herndon has the versatility to move around the field on offense and contributed as a returner on special teams, though two fumbles on punt returns won't help his case. He will compete with Dontrelle Inman for the fourth receiver spot in 2016. Fun fact: Herndon inexplicably has two Wikipedia pages.

Darrius Heyward-Bey
Height: 6-2   **Weight:** 210   **College:** Maryland   **Draft:** 2009/1 (7)   **Born:** 26-Feb-1987   **Age:** 29   **Risk:** Green

Year	Team	G/GS	Snaps	Rec	Pass	Yds	C%	+/-	Yd/C	TD	Drop	YAC	Rk	YAC+	BTkl	DVOA	Rk	DYAR	Rk	YAR	Short	Mid	Deep	Bomb
2013	IND	16/11	603	29	64	309	45%	-7.4	10.7	1	6	4.5	50	-0.4	0	-24.5%	84	-63	83	-77	34%	43%	14%	9%
2014	PIT	16/1	123	3	5	33	60%	+0.3	11.0	0	1	1.3	--	-4.2	0	-26.0%	--	-7	--	-7	17%	33%	17%	33%
2015	PIT	16/4	401	21	39	314	54%	-0.1	15.0	2	0	3.5	--	-2.0	1	-4.6%	--	25	--	23	32%	24%	13%	32%
2016	PIT			16	27	210	59%	--	13.2	1						0.8%								

Heyward-Bey has become Limas Sweed with a better work ethic. He saw 26 of his 39 targets early last season when Martavis Bryant was out. His workload could be going back up should he beat Sammie Coates for the No. 3 wide receiver job. Heyward-Bey has the speed to get deep, and Ben Roethlisberger can certainly find him, but the Steelers are better off playing Coates, assuming he grasps the playbook. Heyward-Bey is considered a good tutor for Pittsburgh's younger receivers, but he is also still a mistake-prone player. In Week 1 at New England, he cost the Steelers a touchdown before halftime by not knowing where he was on the field and stepping out of bounds in the end zone. Later, he intentionally gave himself up a yard short of the first-down marker on a second-and-10, which is something you would never see on the other side from Julian Edelman or Danny Amendola.

T.Y. Hilton
Height: 5-10   **Weight:** 183   **College:** Florida International   **Draft:** 2012/3 (92)   **Born:** 14-Nov-1989   **Age:** 27   **Risk:** Yellow

Year	Team	G/GS	Snaps	Rec	Pass	Yds	C%	+/-	Yd/C	TD	Drop	YAC	Rk	YAC+	BTkl	DVOA	Rk	DYAR	Rk	YAR	Short	Mid	Deep	Bomb
2013	IND	16/10	759	82	140	1083	60%	+0.1	13.2	5	5	4.8	39	-0.7	7	1.1%	43	155	29	152	36%	34%	17%	13%
2014	IND	15/15	831	82	131	1345	63%	+11.9	16.4	7	5	4.5	45	-0.1	5	16.5%	14	303	11	283	22%	45%	14%	19%
2015	IND	16/15	925	69	134	1124	51%	-7.8	16.3	5	1	5.5	17	+0.9	8	-7.7%	64	52	61	77	24%	44%	17%	15%
2016	IND			87	152	1412	57%	--	16.2	9						7.4%								

Hilton's average target from Andrew Luck came 13.7 yards downfield. That was right in line with the 13.9 figure from 2014 and better than the 12.0 average target depth with the other Colts quarterbacks. Of course, Luck's struggles throwing deep meant that this difference was not reflected in DVOA: Hilton was at -7.4% with Luck and a surprisingly similar -7.9% with all the other Colts quarterbacks. If Luck is the Luck we saw in 2014, then Hilton should look a lot more like the Hilton we saw in 2014.

Chris Hogan

				Height: 6-1			Weight: 220			College: Monmouth				Draft: 2012/FA		Born: 24-Oct-1988		Age: 28		Risk: Green

Year	Team	G/GS	Snaps	Rec	Pass	Yds	C%	+/-	Yd/C	TD	Drop	YAC	Rk	YAC+	BTkl	DVOA	Rk	DYAR	Rk	YAR	Short	Mid	Deep	Bomb
2013	BUF	16/0	187	10	17	83	59%	-0.5	8.3	0	1	2.7	--	-1.5	2	-25.3%	--	-17	--	-23	44%	44%	13%	0%
2014	BUF	16/2	461	41	61	426	67%	+1.0	10.4	4	2	4.6	43	-0.6	5	-8.1%	58	21	60	10	51%	32%	14%	3%
2015	BUF	16/4	612	36	59	450	61%	+1.3	12.5	2	5	2.8	81	-1.8	5	-12.4%	75	1	75	15	38%	28%	12%	22%
2016	NE			33	55	419	60%	--	12.7	2						-3.7%								

Hogan had some "rising star" buzz for a few weeks in 2014 but tailed off to become a possession receiver on a team with no idea what to do with a possession receiver. Hogan's playing time and target rates rose and fell based on injuries to Sammy Watkins, Robert Woods, and others; he never had a clearly defined role and would sometimes play 30 or 50 snaps in a game with zero or one reception. Now in New England, Hogan will replace Brandon LaFell as the designated veteran boundary receiver. He's the fourth or fifth option in the passing game, but at least he's an option, and Hogan has some deep-threat capability. Hogan was a respectable 6-of-17 on deep passes (16-plus yards) and would have been better if not for some wild throws when he was open. Wild throws will no longer be a problem, at least not after Week 5.

Andre Holmes

				Height: 6-5			Weight: 206			College: Hillsdale				Draft: 2011/FA		Born: 16-Jun-1988		Age: 28		Risk: Green

Year	Team	G/GS	Snaps	Rec	Pass	Yds	C%	+/-	Yd/C	TD	Drop	YAC	Rk	YAC+	BTkl	DVOA	Rk	DYAR	Rk	YAR	Short	Mid	Deep	Bomb
2013	OAK	10/4	380	25	52	431	48%	-3.6	17.2	1	4	4.4	51	+0.1	0	-2.1%	54	42	64	46	21%	42%	23%	15%
2014	OAK	16/13	714	47	98	693	48%	-4.6	14.7	4	4	4.1	52	-0.4	1	-7.2%	56	42	56	22	25%	36%	22%	18%
2015	OAK	16/1	346	14	33	201	42%	-2.7	14.4	4	2	3.1	--	-0.3	1	-15.9%	--	-8	--	-7	30%	30%	17%	23%
2016	OAK			22	42	299	52%	--	13.6	3						-9.1%								

Holmes has always looked the part of a deep sleeper, with his huge frame and decent combine results (6.69-second 3-cone, 130-inch broad jump). But he's got Donald Trump hands, and the catch rates back up how that limits him. He's an excellent special teams player who should float around the bottom of a good receiving depth chart. Just don't get fooled by the size and speed into thinking he just needs a chance. It's not happening.

DeAndre Hopkins

				Height: 6-1			Weight: 214			College: Clemson				Draft: 2013/1 (27)		Born: 6-Jun-1992		Age: 24		Risk: Green

Year	Team	G/GS	Snaps	Rec	Pass	Yds	C%	+/-	Yd/C	TD	Drop	YAC	Rk	YAC+	BTkl	DVOA	Rk	DYAR	Rk	YAR	Short	Mid	Deep	Bomb
2013	HOU	16/16	995	52	91	802	57%	+2.6	15.4	2	1	3.5	75	-1.1	1	6.9%	28	139	34	132	28%	38%	19%	15%
2014	HOU	16/16	1053	76	127	1210	60%	+4.4	15.9	6	2	4.9	32	+0.3	7	10.3%	23	237	15	223	22%	43%	23%	13%
2015	HOU	16/16	1150	111	192	1521	58%	+4.5	13.7	11	3	2.0	87	-1.7	5	4.8%	41	268	13	307	15%	54%	20%	11%
2016	HOU			94	164	1336	57%	--	14.2	9						-0.5%								

Hopkins' greatness is a bit of a puzzle. He's not the fastest, not the quickest, not the most precise, not the biggest, but still extraordinarily successful. He has enough of each of those skills, plus incredible physical awareness and the ability to catch the ball easily in a variety of body positions. All those skills help him to overcome some trying circumstances, including poor quarterback play and a lack of other options to draw defensive coverage. He has vowed to improve his lousy yards after catch totals, but that will depend on more routes that give him a better opportunity to run and better ball placement from his quarterback—not a certainty with Brock Osweiler. Either way, he will still be the one that makes the passing game go in Houston.

Josh Huff

				Height: 5-11			Weight: 206			College: Oregon				Draft: 2014/3 (86)		Born: 10/14/1991		Age: 25		Risk: Yellow

Year	Team	G/GS	Snaps	Rec	Pass	Yds	C%	+/-	Yd/C	TD	Drop	YAC	Rk	YAC+	BTkl	DVOA	Rk	DYAR	Rk	YAR	Short	Mid	Deep	Bomb
2014	PHI	12/0	210	8	18	98	44%	-3.7	12.3	0	3	9.6	--	+3.8	6	-48.9%	--	-49	--	-51	41%	29%	24%	6%
2015	PHI	15/4	537	27	40	312	68%	+1.8	11.6	3	2	6.7	--	+1.5	4	13.5%	--	89	--	102	48%	40%	10%	3%
2016	PHI			22	36	232	61%	--	10.6	0						-11.8%								

One of several Ducks to flock over to the Chip Kelly pond, Huff is in a precarious position following Kelly's ouster in Philadelphia. The former third-rounder has yet to carve out a consistent offensive role, making the occasional long run-after-the-catch play but mostly sitting behind decaying vets such as Riley Cooper and Miles Austin. And after bursting on the scene as one of the league's five best kick returners in his rookie season, Huff regressed to a roughly league-average returner in his sophomore year, adding just 0.2 points of value. Given the potential marginalization of the kickoff with the new touchback rule, it's time for Huff to sink or swim on offense and climb his way up a very manageable depth chart.

Adam Humphries   Height: 5-11   Weight: 195   College: Clemson   Draft: 2015/FA   Born: 24-Jun-1993   Age: 23   Risk: Blue

Year	Team	G/GS	Snaps	Rec	Pass	Yds	C%	+/-	Yd/C	TD	Drop	YAC	Rk	YAC+	BTkl	DVOA	Rk	DYAR	Rk	YAR	Short	Mid	Deep	Bomb
2015	TB	13/0	437	27	40	260	68%	-0.8	9.6	1	2	4.6	--	-0.7	4	-4.1%	--	26	--	24	53%	33%	15%	0%
2016	TB			11	19	117	58%	--	10.6	0						-17.3%								

How far off the radar was Humphries in last year's draft class? He was a tryout camp receiver for Tampa Bay, one who caught just 127 passes in his entire career at Clemson. He looked adept at running the bottom of the route tree for the Bucs, and obviously was more consistent than the rest of their UDFAs, somehow. But at 195 pounds, there's not much reason to believe he'll continue to stick in the NFL. Now, Jason Licht's NFL, where we can continually ignore receiver problems? Maybe.

Justin Hunter   Height: 6-4   Weight: 196   College: Tennessee   Draft: 2013/2 (34)   Born: 20-Apr-1991   Age: 25   Risk: Red

Year	Team	G/GS	Snaps	Rec	Pass	Yds	C%	+/-	Yd/C	TD	Drop	YAC	Rk	YAC+	BTkl	DVOA	Rk	DYAR	Rk	YAR	Short	Mid	Deep	Bomb
2013	TEN	14/0	334	18	42	354	43%	-3.2	19.7	4	1	5.1	--	-0.1	2	-3.6%	--	30	--	45	12%	44%	17%	27%
2014	TEN	12/8	593	28	67	498	42%	-8.7	17.8	3	2	6.4	10	+1.7	5	-13.4%	72	-4	72	-22	21%	34%	30%	15%
2015	TEN	9/5	378	22	31	264	71%	+2.9	12.0	1	1	1.5	--	-2.6	0	17.0%	--	70	--	72	25%	50%	19%	6%
2016	TEN			14	26	199	54%	--	14.2	2						-5.3%								

It's hard to call Hunter anything but disappointing at this point of his career. His physical talent hasn't resulted in consistent deep separation like the Titans hoped it would. As such, he has been put in more contested catch situations where he has struggled. Hunter broke his ankle during the 2015 season, then hurt it again when leaping in the locker room for a bet during the offseason. That injury didn't linger for more than a few days, but it didn't help his case as he entered training camp behind Rishard Matthews, Kendall Wright and Tajae Sharpe, instead competing with Harry Douglas and Andre Johnson for a roster spot. The odds are stacked against Hunter even if he comes back at 100 percent from injury.

Allen Hurns   Height: 6-3   Weight: 195   College: Miami   Draft: 2014/FA   Born: 12-Nov-1991   Age: 25   Risk: Green

Year	Team	G/GS	Snaps	Rec	Pass	Yds	C%	+/-	Yd/C	TD	Drop	YAC	Rk	YAC+	BTkl	DVOA	Rk	DYAR	Rk	YAR	Short	Mid	Deep	Bomb
2014	JAC	16/8	788	51	97	677	53%	-6.8	13.3	6	5	4.2	51	-0.7	5	-14.4%	74	-13	75	-16	38%	37%	13%	11%
2015	JAC	15/15	865	64	105	1031	61%	+5.2	16.1	10	1	5.4	20	+1.2	5	16.1%	12	236	16	243	29%	36%	30%	6%
2016	JAC			63	107	919	59%	--	14.6	7						4.0%								

Some eyes were raised when Hurns signed a four-year, $40 million contract extension this offseason. They shouldn't have been. Hurns has proven to be a well-rounded receiver who can mask some of Blake Bortles' ball placement issues. Hurns is a big-play threat and possession receiver who played through injuries last year to catch 10 touchdowns. The 24-year-old should be a fixture in the Jaguars passing game for years to come.

Dontrelle Inman   Height: 6-3   Weight: 205   College: Virginia   Draft: 2011/FA   Born: 31-Jan-1989   Age: 27   Risk: Green

Year	Team	G/GS	Snaps	Rec	Pass	Yds	C%	+/-	Yd/C	TD	Drop	YAC	Rk	YAC+	BTkl	DVOA	Rk	DYAR	Rk	YAR	Short	Mid	Deep	Bomb
2014	SD	7/0	120	12	17	158	71%	+2.5	13.2	0	1	1.2	--	-2.7	1	24.0%	--	49	--	42	12%	47%	35%	6%
2015	SD	14/7	691	35	63	486	56%	-0.5	13.9	3	3	5.1	26	+1.0	4	-6.2%	61	32	67	35	32%	38%	24%	6%
2016	SD			16	28	203	57%	--	12.7	2						-6.0%								

Inman is 27 years old and entering his third year in the league after two seasons in Canada. If he was a few years younger, he'd be a more intriguing development prospect for the Chargers. In his second season, he proved to be a fluid mover who could run a variety of routes. He also proved to be an aggressive hands catcher who could make difficult adjustments to pull the ball in. However, Inman was way too inconsistent completing catches and working against tight coverage. His 56 percent catch rate highlighted that. Inman is clearly an inferior talent to Travis Benjamin and will now compete for the fourth receiver spot on the roster.

DeSean Jackson

Height: 5-9 | Weight: 169 | College: California | Draft: 2008/2 (49) | Born: 1-Dec-1986 | Age: 30 | Risk: Yellow

Year	Team	G/GS	Snaps	Rec	Pass	Yds	C%	+/-	Yd/C	TD	Drop	YAC	Rk	YAC+	BTkl	DVOA	Rk	DYAR	Rk	YAR	Short	Mid	Deep	Bomb
2013	PHI	16/16	987	82	125	1332	66%	+12.2	16.2	9	4	5.9	12	+0.4	5	23.7%	10	358	6	374	36%	26%	22%	17%
2014	WAS	15/13	755	56	95	1169	60%	+0.8	20.9	6	1	8.5	1	+2.5	3	27.0%	6	306	10	300	36%	33%	6%	24%
2015	WAS	9/9	359	30	49	528	61%	+5.3	17.6	4	0	5.3	22	-0.6	4	12.7%	20	97	47	99	27%	29%	18%	27%
2016	WAS			57	101	991	56%	--	17.4	6						8.9%								

It's probably presumptuous to call Jackson's return from a hamstring injury the straw that stirred the drink of the Washington offense, but it did add an undeniably critical element to a previously stagnant passing game. Despite the lack of route-running variety and week-to-week inconsistency in production, Jackson's status as one of the game's premier deep threats has long preserved his role in any offense (well, at least ones not run by Chip Kelly). Among players with at least 20 charted deep targets, Jackson's 70.5% DVOA on such plays ranked eighth in the league. There's not much mystery as to how the Redskins will utilize Jackson entering his ninth season, and his boom-or-bust stat lines will continue to toy with the heartstrings of fantasy owners everywhere. However, Jackson's future in D.C. is considerably less secure, as the speed-reliant receiver will turn 30 in December and enter free agency next spring. First-rounder Josh Doctson should theoretically develop into a larger version of Jackson and provide more value in the confinement of the red zone, where Jackson has posted woeful DVOA figures each of his two Washington seasons. Jackson can continue marching to his own drumbeat so long as he keeps beating safeties over the top, but if he slips up or gets hurt again, his status as the No. 1 receiver is no longer preordained.

Vincent Jackson

Height: 6-5 | Weight: 241 | College: Northern Colorado | Draft: 2005/2 (61) | Born: 14-Jan-1983 | Age: 33 | Risk: Green

Year	Team	G/GS	Snaps	Rec	Pass	Yds	C%	+/-	Yd/C	TD	Drop	YAC	Rk	YAC+	BTkl	DVOA	Rk	DYAR	Rk	YAR	Short	Mid	Deep	Bomb
2013	TB	16/16	968	78	161	1224	49%	-13.2	15.7	7	11	4.2	63	-0.2	5	-3.3%	57	122	39	138	21%	52%	13%	13%
2014	TB	16/16	903	70	142	1002	49%	-7.8	14.3	2	1	2.1	87	-1.8	5	-12.3%	68	4	68	30	11%	56%	19%	15%
2015	TB	10/9	533	33	62	543	53%	-1.2	16.5	3	1	3.1	76	-0.9	2	11.2%	25	111	42	104	11%	56%	31%	2%
2016	TB			51	90	673	57%	--	13.2	5						-4.9%								

Tampa Bay had to rely on the bottom of their roster last year because Jackson was hurt, and boy did those players ever show how much the team needed Jackson healthy. Jackson has made it to the last year of a five-year, $55 million contract in Tampa despite some real falloffs in his game. Jackson's 53 percent catch rate last year was the best he's posted in the last five seasons. It's not often we truly get to test "replacement level" against a receiver in decline, but that's exactly the reason Jackson isn't being pushed this year.

Alshon Jeffery

Height: 6-3 | Weight: 216 | College: South Carolina | Draft: 2012/2 (45) | Born: 14-Feb-1990 | Age: 26 | Risk: Yellow

Year	Team	G/GS	Snaps	Rec	Pass	Yds	C%	+/-	Yd/C	TD	Drop	YAC	Rk	YAC+	BTkl	DVOA	Rk	DYAR	Rk	YAR	Short	Mid	Deep	Bomb
2013	CHI	16/14	962	89	150	1421	59%	+7.1	16.0	7	6	4.7	44	-0.3	8	8.3%	26	248	14	255	26%	43%	17%	13%
2014	CHI	16/16	956	85	145	1133	59%	+0.1	13.3	10	5	5.5	19	+0.1	7	11.1%	22	278	13	266	38%	31%	12%	18%
2015	CHI	9/8	506	54	94	807	57%	+1.8	14.9	4	1	3.3	71	-1.1	3	4.1%	42	126	35	134	20%	44%	17%	18%
2016	CHI			85	152	1184	56%	--	13.9	9						0.2%								

Jeffery is taking a gamble this season. He failed to come to a long-term deal with Chicago, and will play 2016 under the franchise tag on a one-year contract for $14.6 million. The gamble is that he will stay healthy and have a big year, then sign a long-term deal with somebody for an average payout in the $15 million range. The Bears, though, have refused to invest in Jeffery's long-term future. It's one thing to move on from players in their thirties such as Brandon Marshall or Matt Forte, but No. 1 receivers like Jeffery don't often hit the market in the prime of their careers. A bidding war for Jeffery's services could be the highlight of the 2017 free-agent period.

Greg Jennings

Height: 5-11 | Weight: 195 | College: Western Michigan | Draft: 2006/2 (52) | Born: 21-Sep-1983 | Age: 33 | Risk: N/A

Year	Team	G/GS	Snaps	Rec	Pass	Yds	C%	+/-	Yd/C	TD	Drop	YAC	Rk	YAC+	BTkl	DVOA	Rk	DYAR	Rk	YAR	Short	Mid	Deep	Bomb
2013	MIN	15/15	742	68	105	804	65%	+4.7	11.8	4	3	5.0	29	+0.1	4	2.6%	38	127	37	112	39%	34%	18%	9%
2014	MIN	16/13	870	59	92	742	64%	+3.6	12.6	6	4	3.4	70	-1.1	4	5.0%	36	125	33	148	32%	40%	18%	10%
2015	MIA	16/5	307	19	36	208	53%	-0.7	10.9	1	2	3.5	--	-1.1	1	-31.1%	--	-51	--	-55	42%	42%	10%	6%

Jennings had the official "it's over" season last year, falling behind Kenny Stills to fourth on the Miami depth chart and being reduced to running mostly shallow underneath routes. As of April, he was leaving voicemails with Vikings general manager Rick Speilman asking for an opportunity. The Vikings opted for Laquon Treadwell and a kid from Germany instead.

Andre Johnson Height: 6-3 Weight: 219 College: Miami Draft: 2003/1 (3) Born: 11-Jul-1981 Age: 35 Risk: N/A

Year	Team	G/GS	Snaps	Rec	Pass	Yds	C%	+/-	Yd/C	TD	Drop	YAC	Rk	YAC+	BTkl	DVOA	Rk	DYAR	Rk	YAR	Short	Mid	Deep	Bomb
2013	HOU	16/16	994	109	181	1407	60%	+2.6	12.9	5	5	3.7	70	-0.7	8	-2.3%	55	150	31	178	31%	45%	17%	8%
2014	HOU	15/15	926	85	147	936	58%	-6.9	11.0	3	6	4.6	42	-0.7	6	-19.8%	81	-86	86	-81	34%	43%	16%	6%
2015	IND	16/14	710	41	77	503	53%	-6.2	12.3	4	2	3.5	68	-0.7	3	-8.2%	67	27	68	20	40%	29%	28%	3%

Johnson found a rapport with Matt Hasselbeck, catching plenty of short throws from the veteran after failing to link up with Andrew Luck on deeper throws (his average Luck target came 11.3 yards downfield, compared to just 8.5 with Hasselbeck). On the whole, though, 2015 mostly confirmed the impression we all got in 2014 that Johnson has likely reached the end of his career. If so, it was a pretty good one, including four top-eight finishes in DYAR with Matt Schaub throwing him the ball. Signed with Tennessee right before we went to press, but probably won't make the team.

Calvin Johnson Height: 6-5 Weight: 239 College: Georgia Tech Draft: 2007/1 (2) Born: 25-Sep-1985 Age: 31 Risk: N/A

Year	Team	G/GS	Snaps	Rec	Pass	Yds	C%	+/-	Yd/C	TD	Drop	YAC	Rk	YAC+	BTkl	DVOA	Rk	DYAR	Rk	YAR	Short	Mid	Deep	Bomb
2013	DET	14/14	877	84	156	1492	54%	+0.3	17.8	12	10	5.5	22	+1.2	6	14.9%	16	347	7	343	15%	46%	30%	9%
2014	DET	13/13	695	71	128	1077	55%	-0.1	15.2	8	3	3.3	72	-0.7	1	10.2%	24	231	16	253	16%	53%	19%	12%
2015	DET	16/16	1001	88	149	1214	59%	+4.0	13.8	9	5	3.4	70	-0.5	2	14.0%	15	319	7	274	25%	43%	18%	14%

Since Johnson was drafted in 2007, he ranks seventh among wide receivers with 731 catches, but first in yardage (11,619), receiving touchdowns (83), and 100-yard games (46). Johnson led the league in receiving touchdowns in 2008, in receiving yardage in 2011, and in receptions and yardage (the latter an all-time record of 1,964) in 2012. He finished in the top ten in receptions just twice, but in the top ten for yardage six times and for touchdowns four times. He was especially effective as a deep threat. In 455 career targets that came more than 15 yards past the line of scrimmage, he had 185 catches for 5,338 yards and 36 touchdowns. That's 87 more targets, 31 more catches, 864 more yards, and eight more touchdowns than any other player had on deep balls in the same timeframe.

Johnson always got a ton of targets in Detroit's high-volume passing game (and a lot of those targets came on plays called "Throw The Ball To Megatron Whether He's Open Or Not"), and so his advanced stats aren't quite as dominant—he was seventh in DVOA in 2011, his only season in the top ten in that category. But he finished in the top ten in DYAR six times, leading the league in both 2011 and 2012, and finishing eighth last season. Still, he leads all wide receivers with 2,551 DYAR in the last nine years, and of the 54 wideouts with at least 500 targets in that timeframe, only seven had a higher average DVOA than Johnson's 11.6%.

There is a dark side to Johnson's success and longevity. In an interview with ESPN, Johnson said he had been taking addictive opioid-based painkillers "like candy," and ingesting powerful drugs like Vicodin and Toradol "every day." He also claimed that NFL players suffered concussions every third play. There's undoubtedly some exaggeration in these claims, but given that Johnson has earned tens of millions of dollars in his career, you can't blame him for abandoning the football field to fill his Instagram feed with things like pictures of monkeys in Bali.

Charles Johnson Height: 6-2 Weight: 215 College: Grand Valley State Draft: 2013/7 (216) Born: 27-Feb-1989 Age: 27 Risk: Yellow

Year	Team	G/GS	Snaps	Rec	Pass	Yds	C%	+/-	Yd/C	TD	Drop	YAC	Rk	YAC+	BTkl	DVOA	Rk	DYAR	Rk	YAR	Short	Mid	Deep	Bomb
2014	MIN	12/6	440	31	59	475	53%	-3.1	15.3	2	2	5.6	18	+1.2	1	-16.2%	78	-16	77	2	26%	41%	16%	17%
2015	MIN	11/4	218	9	13	127	69%	+1.1	14.1	0	0	3.1	--	-1.4	1	19.5%	--	37	--	40	43%	7%	36%	14%
2016	MIN			22	37	296	59%	--	13.4	2							0.9%								

Johnson didn't see a single target after Week 9 and was a healthy inactive for the wild-card game. He was considered a long shot to make Minnesota's roster for 2016, but might have clinched a job with a strong performance in OTAs. Minnesota's depth chart at receiver is barren after Laquon Treadwell and Stefon Diggs, and Johnson could conceivably be the team's third wideout this fall. He could also fail to make the team. Neither would be a surprise.

Steve Johnson   Height: 6-2   Weight: 202   College: Kentucky   Draft: 2008/7 (224)   Born: 22-Jul-1986   Age: 30   Risk: Green

Year	Team	G/GS	Snaps	Rec	Pass	Yds	C%	+/-	Yd/C	TD	Drop	YAC	Rk	YAC+	BTkl	DVOA	Rk	DYAR	Rk	YAR	Short	Mid	Deep	Bomb
2013	BUF	12/12	701	52	102	597	52%	-9.1	11.5	3	8	4.2	60	-0.3	7	-15.6%	77	-25	78	-29	46%	39%	12%	4%
2014	SF	13/1	292	35	50	435	70%	+4.1	12.4	3	1	5.3	22	+1.1	4	23.4%	11	139	30	140	41%	43%	12%	4%
2015	SD	10/8	590	45	65	497	69%	+1.5	11.0	3	2	5.9	11	+1.1	5	2.1%	46	76	55	94	56%	38%	7%	0%
2016	SD			43	69	474	62%	--	11.0	2						-6.2%								

The Chargers ran the perfect offense for Johnson in 2015. Johnson has never been a deep threat, so getting open quickly on short and intermediate routes suited his skill set more than playing in a vertical offense. With Travis Benjamin and Keenan Allen as the primary starters, Johnson should remain in a possession role for the 2016 season. Johnson will turn 30 before the start of next season, but because his game has never been based on speed he should take longer to reach his physical decline.

James Jones   Height: 6-1   Weight: 208   College: San Jose State   Draft: 2007/3 (78)   Born: 31-Mar-1984   Age: 32   Risk: N/A

Year	Team	G/GS	Snaps	Rec	Pass	Yds	C%	+/-	Yd/C	TD	Drop	YAC	Rk	YAC+	BTkl	DVOA	Rk	DYAR	Rk	YAR	Short	Mid	Deep	Bomb
2013	GB	14/14	846	59	93	817	63%	+3.3	13.8	3	3	6.2	6	+1.1	8	2.1%	40	110	42	114	38%	37%	12%	13%
2014	OAK	16/10	717	73	112	666	65%	+4.3	9.1	6	2	3.0	79	-2.2	7	-14.7%	76	-18	79	-45	47%	36%	10%	7%
2015	GB	16/15	1045	50	99	890	51%	+0.0	17.8	8	3	4.4	44	+0.1	4	13.6%	18	206	20	193	20%	39%	17%	24%

Following one year in Oakland, Jones signed with the Giants, but then asked for his release when he realized he would be a fourth receiver at best in New York. The Packers were eager to re-acquire him after Jordy Nelson was injured, and they should be grateful they did—Jones was the only man in Green Bay last year capable of any kind of big-play consistency. Ten of his catches gained 30 yards or more; the rest of the team combined for 11 such catches, and nobody else had more than two. Still, Jones' age and low catch rate scared Green Bay away after the season, and they made it very clear they were not interested in re-signing him. Unless he finds a job somewhere, his lasting legacy may be the sweatshirt he wore under his uniform in 2015, the hood flapping back over the name on his jersey. The league tightened its already draconian uniform rules afterwards to ban hoodies, while most fans just wondered why you'd want to wear a sweatshirt under your uniform in places like Arizona.

Julio Jones   Height: 6-3   Weight: 220   College: Alabama   Draft: 2011/1 (6)   Born: 3-Feb-1989   Age: 27   Risk: Green

Year	Team	G/GS	Snaps	Rec	Pass	Yds	C%	+/-	Yd/C	TD	Drop	YAC	Rk	YAC+	BTkl	DVOA	Rk	DYAR	Rk	YAR	Short	Mid	Deep	Bomb
2013	ATL	5/5	296	41	60	580	68%	+5.3	14.1	2	2	6.0	10	+0.3	4	0.4%	45	60	57	71	50%	21%	20%	9%
2014	ATL	15/15	868	104	163	1593	64%	+7.2	15.3	6	4	5.2	25	+0.4	14	16.2%	15	356	7	353	34%	26%	30%	10%
2015	ATL	16/16	970	136	203	1871	67%	+10.6	13.8	8	7	4.7	38	-0.1	21	8.5%	34	343	6	409	37%	41%	15%	7%
2016	ATL			117	181	1633	65%	--	14.0	10						8.8%								

Just your casual "hampered by a hurt hamstring for the first nine weeks" 1,800-yard season. The efficiency suffered because the Falcons had no one else to throw to and often had to force Jones to create underneath. If Mohamed Sanu can keep defenses honest in 2016, Jones could have stupid good numbers by adding more deep balls to the volume of targets he received in 2015. "Usually, explosive plays have never been an issue," offensive coordinator Kyle Shanahan told ESPN during the offseason. "Julio got a bunch at the beginning of the year, but it's a little harder when there's always a second guy over the top." 2,000 yards may be in play here if everything goes right.

Marvin Jones   Height: 6-2   Weight: 199   College: California   Draft: 2012/5 (166)   Born: 12-Mar-1990   Age: 26   Risk: Yellow

Year	Team	G/GS	Snaps	Rec	Pass	Yds	C%	+/-	Yd/C	TD	Drop	YAC	Rk	YAC+	BTkl	DVOA	Rk	DYAR	Rk	YAR	Short	Mid	Deep	Bomb
2013	CIN	16/3	542	51	80	712	64%	+4.2	14.0	10	2	4.4	53	-0.3	11	32.4%	3	279	11	269	24%	54%	14%	8%
2015	CIN	16/13	901	65	104	816	63%	+5.3	12.6	4	3	4.6	40	-0.6	11	7.6%	37	171	25	149	42%	23%	13%	23%
2016	DET			64	106	826	60%	--	12.9	5						0.5%								

Cincinnati wanted to re-sign Jones, but pay him like a No. 2 wideout. Detroit came through with No. 1 receiver dollars, and thus Jones swapped franchises named for big predatory cats. By the numbers, the Bengals were correct not to pony up the big dough, though of course, with A.J. Green around, Jones would never really get to know if he could step up in class. In Detroit, Jones will be unfairly saddled with some drunken "He's no Megatron" barbs, but Jones tracks the ball well, is tough with it in his hands, and is a willing blocker. He may not be exceptional enough to "earn" the contract he received, but Lions fans should be happy to have him.

T.J. Jones

Height: 5-11   Weight: 188   College: Notre Dame   Draft: 2014/6 (189)   Born: 19-Jul-1992   Age: 24   Risk: Yellow

Year	Team	G/GS	Snaps	Rec	Pass	Yds	C%	+/-	Yd/C	TD	Drop	YAC	Rk	YAC+	BTkl	DVOA	Rk	DYAR	Rk	YAR	Short	Mid	Deep	Bomb
2015	DET	10/0	159	10	18	132	56%	-1.8	13.2	1	1	4.1	--	-0.9	1	-7.8%	--	7	--	-5	39%	33%	22%	6%
2016	DET			34	54	396	63%	--	11.6	3						0.6%								

Jones' first two NFL seasons were extremely limited due to nerve damage in his shoulder that left him without feeling in his hands, which naturally sounds troublesome for a wide receiver. Now fully recovered from surgery to correct the problem, Jones was everyone's favorite surprise at OTAs this spring, drawing praise from coach Jim Caldwell and quarterback Matthew Stafford. Jones will battle Jeremy Kerley and other assorted journeymen for the Lions' third receiver spot this fall.

Jermaine Kearse

Height: 6-1   Weight: 209   College: Washington   Draft: 2012/FA   Born: 6-Feb-1990   Age: 26   Risk: Green

Year	Team	G/GS	Snaps	Rec	Pass	Yds	C%	+/-	Yd/C	TD	Drop	YAC	Rk	YAC+	BTkl	DVOA	Rk	DYAR	Rk	YAR	Short	Mid	Deep	Bomb
2013	SEA	15/5	469	22	38	346	58%	+1.5	15.7	4	3	1.7	--	-3.0	0	26.2%	--	116	--	108	16%	42%	24%	18%
2014	SEA	15/14	792	38	69	537	55%	-1.0	14.1	1	3	5.9	11	+0.4	4	-9.1%	61	19	62	22	31%	33%	23%	13%
2015	SEA	16/16	771	49	68	685	72%	+7.5	14.0	5	3	4.8	37	+0.4	6	29.8%	5	227	19	217	28%	43%	21%	9%
2016	SEA			41	71	595	58%	--	14.5	4						0.0%								

Maybe if a certain pass from the 1-yard line had gone to Kearse, he would be the Robert Horry of the NFL. Not much to see in the regular season as the third or fourth target on a low-volume passing team, but Kearse's highlight reel is built on the postseason, where he has 28 catches for 471 yards in his last eight games. Kearse's 6 touchdown catches in the playoffs are already more than Terrell Owens (5), Tim Brown (3), and Marvin Harrison (2) had in their longer, far more prestigious careers. Kearse will make a great answer to a trivia question some day. He was quietly the third Seattle wideout to rank in the top five in DVOA last year.

Jeremy Kerley

Height: 5-9   Weight: 188   College: TCU   Draft: 2011/5 (153)   Born: 8-Nov-1988   Age: 28   Risk: Red

Year	Team	G/GS	Snaps	Rec	Pass	Yds	C%	+/-	Yd/C	TD	Drop	YAC	Rk	YAC+	BTkl	DVOA	Rk	DYAR	Rk	YAR	Short	Mid	Deep	Bomb
2013	NYJ	12/8	567	43	72	523	60%	+1.3	12.2	3	0	4.1	64	-1.0	1	6.0%	29	97	46	95	37%	38%	20%	5%
2014	NYJ	16/7	734	38	75	409	51%	-4.3	10.8	1	3	3.9	55	-0.7	2	-21.2%	83	-51	82	-67	29%	52%	15%	3%
2015	NYJ	16/1	223	16	26	152	62%	-2.2	9.5	2	1	5.9	--	+1.0	3	-5.3%	--	14	--	10	50%	46%	4%	0%
2016	DET			10	15	100	67%	--	10.0	1						-15.4%								

Kerley led the Jets in receiving twice, in 2012 and 2013. You can look it up. A 5-foot-9 slots-and-returns type led a 21st-century NFL team with 56-827-2 and 43-523-3 receiving stat lines. The arrivals of Eric Decker and Brandon Marshall moved Kerley down the depth chart to where he belongs. He led the league with 48 punt returns last year, only playing a significant role on offense when Quincy Enunwa was suspended. The Lions are getting a useful spare part who can take Golden Tate off punt return duty, play the screens-and-reverses game, and provide a little Wildcat chicanery. The Jets may miss a role player who did everything they asked of him for five years, and then some.

Brandon LaFell

Height: 6-3   Weight: 211   College: Louisiana State   Draft: 2010/3 (78)   Born: 4-Nov-1986   Age: 30   Risk: Red

Year	Team	G/GS	Snaps	Rec	Pass	Yds	C%	+/-	Yd/C	TD	Drop	YAC	Rk	YAC+	BTkl	DVOA	Rk	DYAR	Rk	YAR	Short	Mid	Deep	Bomb
2013	CAR	16/16	907	49	85	627	58%	-2.2	12.8	5	6	5.2	25	+0.5	2	-6.2%	64	44	63	50	26%	44%	23%	7%
2014	NE	16/13	913	74	119	953	62%	-0.2	12.9	7	3	5.0	31	+0.3	8	5.7%	33	174	27	158	34%	43%	16%	7%
2015	NE	11/7	659	37	74	515	50%	-8.9	13.9	0	6	6.1	9	-0.2	1	-20.1%	82	-43	82	-52	39%	32%	11%	18%
2016	CIN			45	75	575	60%	--	12.8	4						-2.2%								

The Patriots can turn mediocre players into stars, but the effect is often short-lived. LaFell's 74-catch 2014 season was mostly Patriots pixie dust, with Tom Brady's brilliance and a scheme that forces opponents to worry about Rob Gronkowski and the slot receivers combining to make LaFell look like more than just a drop-prone boundary receiver. Last year, the drops returned and Brady lost confidence in LaFell, who became a glorified decoy in the second half of the season. The Bengals are looking for a receiver to soak up catches that Marvin Jones and Mohammed Sanu used to make, but LaFell is a No. 4 receiver trying to do a No. 2 receiver's work.

Jarvis Landry

Height: 5-11   Weight: 205   College: Louisiana State   Draft: 2014/2 (63)   Born: 11/28/1992   Age: 24   Risk: Green

Year	Team	G/GS	Snaps	Rec	Pass	Yds	C%	+/-	Yd/C	TD	Drop	YAC	Rk	YAC+	BTkl	DVOA	Rk	DYAR	Rk	YAR	Short	Mid	Deep	Bomb
2014	MIA	16/11	683	84	112	758	75%	+8.7	9.0	5	3	5.1	26	-0.3	10	-0.8%	45	102	39	86	58%	36%	4%	2%
2015	MIA	16/14	868	110	167	1157	66%	+2.3	10.5	4	6	4.8	33	-1.1	33	-7.1%	63	72	57	55	48%	36%	9%	6%
2016	MIA			102	147	1066	69%	--	10.5	6						-1.0%								

Landry led the NFL in failed completions with 35 after finishing second in the NFL in 2014 with 31. Landry's failed completion rate has almost nothing to do with Landry and everything to do with a) Ryan Tannehill's reluctance to throw deep; and b) the Dolphins' various offensive playcallers' reluctance to do anything remotely sensible. Landry's failed completion lowlights were 7- and 9-yard gains on third-and-22 and third-and-25 against the Cowboys. It's not Landry's fault that he didn't swerve through the defense for first-down yardage, or even Tannehill's fault for completing passes to his best receiver. It was the coaches' fault for calling plays that left their top receiver 15 yards short of the sticks.

Landry will never be a true deep threat, mind you, but better playcalling should turn many of his failed completions into successes. Better game planning may also decrease his target total, but fantasy owners (outside of PPR leagues, anyway) should take heart that Landry's 10-67-0 stat lines could turn into 6-80-1 type stat lines, much to the benefit of everyone.

Marqise Lee

Height: 6-0   Weight: 192   College: USC   Draft: 2014/2 (39)   Born: 11/25/1991   Age: 25   Risk: Yellow

Year	Team	G/GS	Snaps	Rec	Pass	Yds	C%	+/-	Yd/C	TD	Drop	YAC	Rk	YAC+	BTkl	DVOA	Rk	DYAR	Rk	YAR	Short	Mid	Deep	Bomb
2014	JAC	13/8	492	37	68	422	54%	-5.7	11.4	1	4	4.8	36	-0.4	7	-20.3%	82	-41	81	-37	48%	38%	6%	8%
2015	JAC	10/1	240	15	32	191	47%	-3.4	12.7	1	2	6.1	--	+0.9	5	-13.4%	--	-2	--	9	43%	27%	10%	20%
2016	JAC			34	62	413	55%	--	12.2	2						-13.6%								

The Jaguars took Lee before Allen Robinson and Allen Hurns in the 2014 draft, yet Lee is the one on the outside looking in after two seasons. The receiver has dealt with health issues, but more significantly he has consistently struggled to catch the ball, showing off poor technique all too often. Lee and Rashad Greene will be competing for the third receiver spot in the offense, both receivers hoping to lessen their consistency issues by creating big plays with their elusiveness.

Dezmin Lewis

Height: 6-4   Weight: 214   College: Central Arkansas   Draft: 2015/7 (234)   Born: 5-Dec-1992   Age: 24   Risk: Red

Year	Team	G/GS	Snaps	Rec	Pass	Yds	C%	+/-	Yd/C	TD	Drop	YAC	Rk	YAC+	BTkl	DVOA	Rk	DYAR	Rk	YAR	Short	Mid	Deep	Bomb
2015	BUF	1/0	9	0	0	0	--	--	--	0	0	--	--	--	--	--	--	--	--	--	--	--	--	--
2016	BUF			35	61	527	57%	--	15.0	3						1.5%								

Lewis was a star of the 2015 Senior Bowl. He made a bunch of Odell Beckham-like catches along the sidelines during practices. He then dropped a bunch of passes in Bills training camp, prompting the team to banish him to the practice squad. However, Lewis was singled out by several coaches during OTAs as being one of the most improved young players on the Bills roster. With slots two through five on the receiver depth chart up for grabs, Lewis could emerge as the big-play complement to Sammy Watkins or just get lost in a sea of Kolby Linstenbee types for a team that doesn't like to pass much. Lewis has Marvin Jones upside, but if Tyrod Taylor saw Marvin Jones isolated in single coverage along the sideline, he would scramble.

Tyler Lockett

Height: 5-10   Weight: 182   College: Kansas State   Draft: 2015/3 (69)   Born: 28-Sep-1992   Age: 24   Risk: Green

Year	Team	G/GS	Snaps	Rec	Pass	Yds	C%	+/-	Yd/C	TD	Drop	YAC	Rk	YAC+	BTkl	DVOA	Rk	DYAR	Rk	YAR	Short	Mid	Deep	Bomb
2015	SEA	16/8	664	51	69	664	74%	+8.1	13.0	6	2	5.0	28	-0.4	7	35.1%	3	249	15	242	38%	29%	10%	22%
2016	SEA			59	93	821	63%	--	13.9	7						9.1%								

Golden Tate was an underrated receiver during in his time in Seattle, but Tyler Lockett is going to do a great job of filling that void in the offense. He was already named a first-team All-Pro as a return specialist last year, with both punt and kickoff touchdowns. He also improved as a receiver as the season wore on, and he should be second to Doug Baldwin on the depth chart now. Lockett's big-play ability makes him one of the most exciting young players to keep an eye on this season.

Jeremy Maclin Height: 6-0   Weight: 198   College: Missouri   Draft: 2009/1 (19)   Born: 11-May-1988   Age: 28   Risk: Green

Year	Team	G/GS	Snaps	Rec	Pass	Yds	C%	+/-	Yd/C	TD	Drop	YAC	Rk	YAC+	BTkl	DVOA	Rk	DYAR	Rk	YAR	Short	Mid	Deep	Bomb
2014	PHI	16/16	1022	85	143	1318	59%	-1.5	15.5	10	2	5.8	12	+0.8	4	7.4%	30	222	18	245	31%	39%	16%	14%
2015	KC	15/15	828	87	124	1088	70%	+9.6	12.5	8	3	3.8	59	-0.7	3	11.3%	24	234	18	217	28%	50%	11%	11%
2016	KC			80	123	1058	65%	--	13.2	8						12.0%								

After just one year in Kansas City, Maclin already holds the Chiefs' all-time record for receptions in a season. That stellar performance made it all the more devastating when Maclin sustained a high ankle sprain in the wild-card win over the Texans, seemingly depriving the Chiefs of their lone game-breaking threat in the divisional round matchup against the Patriots. Maclin surprised everyone by playing through the injury, but on a one-receiver team, the Chiefs' offense was not the same without him anywhere near full strength. This offseason, Maclin stayed in Kansas City to train with the two young receivers just behind him on the depth chart, Albert Wilson and Chris Conley. If Maclin's leadership and toughness transfer to those players, the Chiefs might finally add some zip.

Bradley Marquez Height: 5-11   Weight: 200   College: Texas Tech   Draft: 2015/FA   Born: 14-Dec-1992   Age: 24   Risk: Yellow

Year	Team	G/GS	Snaps	Rec	Pass	Yds	C%	+/-	Yd/C	TD	Drop	YAC	Rk	YAC+	BTkl	DVOA	Rk	DYAR	Rk	YAR	Short	Mid	Deep	Bomb
2015	STL	16/1	170	13	22	88	59%	-2.0	6.8	0	0	1.8	--	-3.6	0	-51.4%	--	-61	--	-60	43%	48%	10%	0%
2016	LARM			15	28	166	54%	--	11.0	0						-22.5%								

As the incumbent, Marquez will have an advantage over the incoming rookies when the Rams enter training camp. Marquez played sparingly last year but flashed enough on a few plays to suggest that he could have a place in the Rams offense. However, Pharoh Cooper, Mike Thomas, and Duke Williams all have the talent to surpass him on the depth chart if they earn the trust of the coaching staff in August.

Brandon Marshall Height: 6-4   Weight: 229   College: UCF   Draft: 2006/4 (119)   Born: 23-Mar-1984   Age: 32   Risk: Yellow

Year	Team	G/GS	Snaps	Rec	Pass	Yds	C%	+/-	Yd/C	TD	Drop	YAC	Rk	YAC+	BTkl	DVOA	Rk	DYAR	Rk	YAR	Short	Mid	Deep	Bomb
2013	CHI	16/16	987	100	163	1295	61%	+4.7	13.0	12	12	2.8	83	-2.0	9	9.5%	22	284	10	291	26%	47%	14%	13%
2014	CHI	13/13	753	61	106	721	58%	-2.1	11.8	8	4	3.8	60	-0.8	7	-3.3%	48	78	46	82	31%	49%	8%	13%
2015	NYJ	16/16	1059	109	173	1502	63%	+7.0	13.8	14	8	4.0	56	+0.0	15	9.3%	31	303	11	343	26%	46%	17%	11%
2016	NYJ			95	161	1225	59%	--	12.9	10						1.6%								

Marshall had the best season of his career last year, but it was very much a Brandon Marshall season. He consistently made breathtaking catches on bad throws, but he also dropped 11 passes, fumbled three times (including a brain-cramp lateral attempt), and became the team's unofficial spokesman/mood ring by the offseason. Marshall openly pined for Ryan Fitzpatrick's return throughout the spring and joined Eric Decker in a mini-protest holdout for a portion of the OTAs. The dual wide receiver/general manager role is one reason teams tire of Marshall after two or three seasons. Marshall is the key to the Jets' offensive success this year and the development of their young quarterbacks, and he knows it.

Keshawn Martin Height: 5-11   Weight: 194   College: Michigan State   Draft: 2012/4 (121)   Born: 15-Mar-1990   Age: 26   Risk: Blue

Year	Team	G/GS	Snaps	Rec	Pass	Yds	C%	+/-	Yd/C	TD	Drop	YAC	Rk	YAC+	BTkl	DVOA	Rk	DYAR	Rk	YAR	Short	Mid	Deep	Bomb
2013	HOU	16/1	373	22	40	253	55%	-1.4	11.5	2	1	4.0	--	+0.0	3	-13.0%	--	-1	--	0	37%	54%	6%	3%
2014	HOU	16/0	233	6	12	78	50%	-1.0	13.0	0	0	9.5	--	+4.4	3	-30.4%	--	-16	--	-13	50%	42%	0%	8%
2015	NE	9/8	0	24	37	269	65%	-0.5	11.2	2	3	3.2	--	-1.5	2	14.9%	--	84	--	75	35%	35%	20%	10%
2016	NE			9	16	107	56%	--	11.9	0						-12.8%								

The Patriots found yet another Wes Welker type ... and this one's African-American! Progress! Martin signed a two-year contract extension in January after a bunch of three-catch, 20-something-yard games when Julian Edelman was hurt, plus 7 catches for 68 yards against the Jets in Week 16 and some punt returns. And so the Patriots stockpile of itty-bitty slot receivers grows and their shortage of normal receivers who can get open more than 8 yards downfield continues. The heart wants what it wants, and often wins the Super Bowl with it, so don't criticize.

Chris Matthews

Height: 6-5 Weight: 218 College: Kentucky Draft: 2011/FA Born: 6-Oct-1989 Age: 27 Risk: Blue

Year	Team	G/GS	Snaps	Rec	Pass	Yds	C%	+/-	Yd/C	TD	Drop	YAC	Rk	YAC+	BTkl	DVOA	Rk	DYAR	Rk	YAR	Short	Mid	Deep	Bomb
2014	SEA	3/0	19	0	0	0	--	--	--	0	0	--	--	--	--	--	--	--	--	--	--	--	--	--
2015	2TM	13/0	243	13	25	151	52%	-1.1	11.6	1	1	3.2	--	-1.1	2	-17.1%	--	-9	--	-8	25%	46%	13%	17%
2016	BAL			4	7	46	57%	--	11.6	0						-10.1%								

The Super Bowl XLIX hero saw just nine targets in nine games before Seattle released him last November. Baltimore gave him a shot and he did catch his first regular-season touchdown in the upset win over Pittsburgh in Week 16. However, Matthews faces a huge battle just for a roster spot this year, let alone any significant playing time.

Jordan Matthews

Height: 6-3 Weight: 212 College: Vanderbilt Draft: 2014/2 (42) Born: 7/16/1992 Age: 24 Risk: Yellow

Year	Team	G/GS	Snaps	Rec	Pass	Yds	C%	+/-	Yd/C	TD	Drop	YAC	Rk	YAC+	BTkl	DVOA	Rk	DYAR	Rk	YAR	Short	Mid	Deep	Bomb
2014	PHI	16/10	764	67	103	872	65%	+0.1	13.0	8	3	5.8	15	+0.8	6	11.6%	20	194	25	214	47%	37%	13%	4%
2015	PHI	16/12	919	85	128	997	66%	+2.2	11.7	8	5	4.9	31	+0.4	10	-1.8%	52	112	41	120	48%	34%	14%	4%
2016	PHI			86	135	1027	64%	--	11.9	7						2.1%								

If there were an award for Junktime Fantasy MVP, Matthews would have won last season in a Steph Curry-style landslide. Though the Eagles' top receiver saw his counting stats increase across the board from his rookie season, much of that production was fool's gold. Five of Matthews' eight touchdowns came in the fourth quarter of games where the score differential was at least two possessions. In reality, Matthews was a far less efficient receiver when the outcome was still in doubt than he was in 2014. A broken hand in early October coincided with an ugly case of the drops from Weeks 4-7, a stretch in which Matthews averaged just under 42 yards per game, failed to reach the end zone, and compiled a ghastly minus-77 receiving DYAR, the worst figure of any wide receiver or tight end in that period. Times should be better for Matthews in 2016, who rebounded slightly at the end of last season and fits well as a run-after-the-catch threat in Doug Pederson's West Coast offense. The Eagles didn't make a big splash at receiver this offseason, so clearly the new coaching staff still holds some degree of faith in the Chip Kelly draft pick. With Pederson using fewer three-receiver sets than Kelly did, Matthews might even get his first shot to start on the perimeter after almost exclusively sticking to the slot his first two seasons.

Rishard Matthews

Height: 6-0 Weight: 217 College: Nevada Draft: 2012/7 (227) Born: 12-Oct-1989 Age: 27 Risk: Green

Year	Team	G/GS	Snaps	Rec	Pass	Yds	C%	+/-	Yd/C	TD	Drop	YAC	Rk	YAC+	BTkl	DVOA	Rk	DYAR	Rk	YAR	Short	Mid	Deep	Bomb
2013	MIA	16/5	519	41	67	448	61%	+0.7	10.9	2	2	3.9	68	-0.6	0	-7.7%	68	27	67	43	38%	46%	14%	2%
2014	MIA	14/0	210	12	23	135	57%	-0.3	11.3	2	1	3.5	--	-1.0	2	-14.5%	--	-3	--	-15	35%	35%	26%	4%
2015	MIA	11/11	520	43	61	662	70%	+6.3	15.4	4	4	5.7	13	+1.4	2	36.4%	2	235	17	237	28%	47%	17%	8%
2016	TEN			45	73	634	62%	--	14.1	5						6.6%								

Mathews slowly worked his way up from the seventh round of the draft in 2012 to become the Dolphins' best big-play receiver at the start of last season, with ten receptions of 20-plus yards in his first 11 games before a rib injury. Matthews then became an afterthought in the Dolphins' annual roster churn. The Titans signed him to $15 million over three years while the Dolphins were busy seeking big-name free agents to overpay. Matthews should slip naturally into Nate Washington's old role as the Titans receiver you assume retired three years ago who is still somehow catching 47 passes per year.

Donte Moncrief

Height: 6-2 Weight: 221 College: Mississippi Draft: 2014/3 (90) Born: 8-Jun-1993 Age: 23 Risk: Green

Year	Team	G/GS	Snaps	Rec	Pass	Yds	C%	+/-	Yd/C	TD	Drop	YAC	Rk	YAC+	BTkl	DVOA	Rk	DYAR	Rk	YAR	Short	Mid	Deep	Bomb
2014	IND	16/2	411	32	49	444	65%	+3.1	13.9	3	2	6.5	--	+1.2	9	-0.2%	--	47	--	61	48%	20%	11%	22%
2015	IND	16/10	836	64	105	733	61%	-0.3	11.5	6	2	4.2	51	-0.3	7	1.1%	49	110	43	121	35%	43%	17%	6%
2016	IND			80	128	1015	63%	--	12.7	7						2.4%								

Reasons to expect Donte Moncrief not to explode in 2016: offseason injury for a turf toe problem that bothered him in December and had him in a walking boot into June.

Reasons to expect Donte Moncrief to explode in 2016: just about everything else.

Leading the Colts' qualifying receivers in DYAR and DVOA might not be a great accomplishment, considering Andrew Luck's injury and, well, backup quarterbacks being backup quarterbacks. But it was a good sign of the continued development in Moncrief's game. He has improved greatly as a route runner and technician, excels on contested catches, and was the Colts' most effective red zone weapon. Plus, this year Ryan Grigson did not add a possibly washed-up veteran receiver to take a spot ahead of him on the depth chart.

Ty Montgomery

Height: 6-0 Weight: 221 College: Stanford Draft: 2015/3 (94) Born: 22-Jan-1993 Age: 23 Risk: Blue

Year	Team	G/GS	Snaps	Rec	Pass	Yds	C%	+/-	Yd/C	TD	Drop	YAC	Rk	YAC+	BTkl	DVOA	Rk	DYAR	Rk	YAR	Short	Mid	Deep	Bomb
2015	GB	6/3	242	15	19	136	79%	+2.1	9.1	2	0	6.1	--	+0.9	4	32.3%	--	74	--	67	60%	20%	5%	15%
2016	GB			23	35	278	66%	--	12.1	2						7.1%								

A multipurpose tool in search of a purpose. Montgomery saw just one offensive snap in Week 1 and 25 in Week 2, but then was on the field for 199 of 209 snaps in the next three weeks. For all those snaps, though, he was primarily a decoy, with only 13 targets and two runs in those three games. His season ended the next week with an ankle injury that would eventually require surgery to fix. Though most of that time was spent out wide, Montgomery also occasionally lined up in the slot, and was at running back for four snaps (carrying the ball twice). He also saw 20 snaps on special teams, and though he only had seven kickoff returns, he managed gains of 41 and 46 yards against the Bears in the opener. The Packers have plenty of options at receiver, running back, and returner, and it's still not clear how Montgomery fits into their plans in 2016.

Lance Moore

Height: 5-9 Weight: 177 College: Toledo Draft: 2005/FA Born: 31-Aug-1983 Age: 33 Risk: N/A

Year	Team	G/GS	Snaps	Rec	Pass	Yds	C%	+/-	Yd/C	TD	Drop	YAC	Rk	YAC+	BTkl	DVOA	Rk	DYAR	Rk	YAR	Short	Mid	Deep	Bomb
2013	NO	13/5	441	37	54	457	69%	+6.4	12.4	2	3	1.8	90	-2.2	0	22.1%	11	150	30	153	28%	50%	15%	7%
2014	PIT	14/2	262	14	26	198	54%	-1.2	14.1	2	2	2.9	--	-1.2	1	-2.8%	--	20	--	16	35%	27%	31%	8%
2015	DET	14/8	577	29	43	337	67%	+3.3	11.6	4	0	2.1	--	-1.8	0	10.1%	--	79	--	69	34%	41%	22%	2%

Moore had eight productive years as a small cog in a great New Orleans offensive machine, but it looks like the Saints were right to cut him in a cap-related move after the 2013 season. Moore hasn't accomplished much in two years since leaving Bourbon Street, and the Lions opted to bring in oodles of other veteran wide receivers rather than re-sign Moore this offseason. Moore remained un-signed in mid-July with no likely suitors. He was reportedly considering an acting career after a brief appearance in a Key & Peele sketch, an opportunity that came about after the comedians saw Moore do the Hingle McCringleberry touchdown celebration in a game in 2013.

Keith Mumphery

Height: 6-0 Weight: 215 College: Michigan State Draft: 2015/5 (175) Born: 5-Jun-1992 Age: 24 Risk: Blue

Year	Team	G/GS	Snaps	Rec	Pass	Yds	C%	+/-	Yd/C	TD	Drop	YAC	Rk	YAC+	BTkl	DVOA	Rk	DYAR	Rk	YAR	Short	Mid	Deep	Bomb
2015	HOU	16/3	318	14	32	129	44%	-5.0	9.2	0	4	1.4	--	-3.2	0	-50.0%	--	-93	--	-89	29%	42%	26%	3%
2016	HOU			6	10	72	60%	--	12.0	1						-6.3%								

Mumphery paired a terrible catch rate with a dismal average gain in his rookie season. He was also next to last in punt return value and below average on kickoff returns. The fifth-rounder out of Michigan State has done three jobs poorly and no jobs well and seems a long shot to stick in Houston.

Louis Murphy

Height: 6-3 Weight: 203 College: Florida Draft: 2009/4 (124) Born: 11-May-1987 Age: 29 Risk: Green

Year	Team	G/GS	Snaps	Rec	Pass	Yds	C%	+/-	Yd/C	TD	Drop	YAC	Rk	YAC+	BTkl	DVOA	Rk	DYAR	Rk	YAR	Short	Mid	Deep	Bomb
2013	NYG	14/0	99	6	13	37	46%	-1.6	6.2	1	1	1.0	--	-2.9	0	-61.2%	--	-50	--	-48	38%	54%	0%	8%
2014	TB	11/3	456	31	56	380	55%	-3.1	12.3	2	5	4.1	53	-0.2	4	-15.3%	77	-11	74	-3	24%	48%	20%	7%
2015	TB	6/1	211	10	18	198	56%	+0.0	19.8	0	1	3.7	--	-1.2	0	18.0%	--	45	--	45	17%	50%	11%	22%
2016	TB			17	31	239	55%	--	14.1	2						-4.3%								

The highlight of Murphy's offseason was when he got drunk at the wedding of ex-Florida teammate Deonte Thompson, fell asleep, and woke up trapped in a museum in the middle of the night. We are going to assume that like Ben Stiller, he had adventures with dinosaurs and Neanderthals and a mummy, and you can't tell us any different. Murphy tore his ACL last October but should be ready for Tampa Bay's training camp, where he will battle Kenny Bell for the Bucs' third receiver spot.

J.J. Nelson Height: 5-10 Weight: 156 College: Alabama-Birmingham Draft: 2015/5 (159) Born: 24-Apr-1992 Age: 24 Risk: Yellow

Year	Team	G/GS	Snaps	Rec	Pass	Yds	C%	+/-	Yd/C	TD	Drop	YAC	Rk	YAC+	BTkl	DVOA	Rk	DYAR	Rk	YAR	Short	Mid	Deep	Bomb
2015	ARI	11/2	148	11	27	299	41%	+0.0	27.2	2	0	5.1	--	+0.4	2	25.7%	--	84	--	82	7%	24%	34%	34%
2016	ARI			18	32	380	56%	--	21.1	1						20.8%								

"When this boy runs quick, he is FAST" might sound like Michael Irvin describing Nelson, but there is not much else to say beyond his speed. It's amazing, and it helped him average 27.2 yards per catch last season. The only problem is he plays in Arizona, so there are at least three wide receivers ahead of him on the depth chart. But if you watch the 64-yard touchdown he caught against Cincinnati last season, you'll see that Nelson is a talent that Bruce Arians needs to find a way to get more balls to this year.

Jordy Nelson Height: 6-2 Weight: 217 College: Kansas State Draft: 2008/2 (36) Born: 31-May-1985 Age: 31 Risk: Green

Year	Team	G/GS	Snaps	Rec	Pass	Yds	C%	+/-	Yd/C	TD	Drop	YAC	Rk	YAC+	BTkl	DVOA	Rk	DYAR	Rk	YAR	Short	Mid	Deep	Bomb
2013	GB	16/16	1083	85	127	1314	67%	+14.2	15.5	8	4	4.8	37	-0.1	11	26.7%	6	402	2	408	37%	33%	20%	10%
2014	GB	16/16	959	98	151	1519	65%	+11.6	15.5	13	3	5.1	27	+0.6	11	26.8%	8	482	2	487	27%	45%	16%	12%
2016	GB			84	133	1229	63%	--	14.6	11							18.5%	x	x	x	x	x	x	x	x

What kind of weapon did Green Bay lose when Nelson tore his ACL in a preseason game against the Steelers? Nelson has 1,950 DYAR since he was drafted in 2008; only Calvin Johnson (2,465) and Marques Colston (an even 2,000) have more. Nelson's DVOA of 27.7% is best among the 208 wideouts with at least 100 targets over that span. Now, context is important—Nelson has benefited from playing with a Hall of Fame-caliber quarterback, and for most of those years he was not the No. 1 receiver in Green Bay—but the fact is that no regular receiver has been as productive as Nelson on a per-target basis for the better part of a decade now. The Packers were being understandably cautious with Nelson's rehab, but he told reporters in June that if there had been a game that weekend, he could have played. It's hard to overstate the impact a healthy and productive Nelson could have on Green Bay's offense.

Jordan Norwood Height: 5-11 Weight: 179 College: Penn State Draft: 2009/FA Born: 29-Sep-1986 Age: 30 Risk: Yellow

Year	Team	G/GS	Snaps	Rec	Pass	Yds	C%	+/-	Yd/C	TD	Drop	YAC	Rk	YAC+	BTkl	DVOA	Rk	DYAR	Rk	YAR	Short	Mid	Deep	Bomb
2015	DEN	11/5	378	22	32	207	69%	+0.2	9.4	0	1	3.1	--	-2.0	3	-14.9%	--	-6	--	-3	53%	31%	6%	9%
2016	DEN			26	42	277	62%	--	10.6	1							-9.9%								

Norwood's 61-yard punt return in the second quarter against the Panthers was the longest in Super Bowl history. That broke Norwood's previous career mark by 47 yards. Yes, Norwood only had 13 previous career punt returns, but that lack of previous work speaks to just how unexpected a game-changing play from Norwood was in that spot. He can also catch some balls out of the slot and has the inside track on the third spot on the Denver depth chart this season.

DeVante Parker Height: 6-3 Weight: 209 College: Louisville Draft: 2015/1 (14) Born: 20-Jan-1993 Age: 23 Risk: Red

Year	Team	G/GS	Snaps	Rec	Pass	Yds	C%	+/-	Yd/C	TD	Drop	YAC	Rk	YAC+	BTkl	DVOA	Rk	DYAR	Rk	YAR	Short	Mid	Deep	Bomb
2015	MIA	14/4	468	26	50	494	52%	+1.3	19.0	3	3	3.8	61	-0.7	6	11.4%	23	93	48	90	13%	57%	13%	17%
2016	MIA			66	115	1029	57%	--	15.6	8							5.4%								

Nine of Parker's 26 receptions last year netted 20 or more yards. That's a remarkable figure for the Dolphins, a team that never met a 7-yard pass to Jarvis Landry on third-and-22 it didn't like.

Parker also battled a foot injury last season. Weekly statements from Dan Campbell indicated that the foot was "fine" and that Parker wasn't playing because of a lack of "fundamentals" but the Dolphins eventually admitted there was soft-tissue damage in Parker's foot, which underwent surgery in the summer of 2015. In April, the *Miami Herald* reported that Parker actually tore scar tissue from the surgery. Under the circumstances, Parker's late-season surge was both encouraging and extraordinary. Most coaching staffs would have shut down a first-round pick with a troubling injury late in a meaningless season. But most coaching staffs don't believe that torn scar tissue in a surgically repaired foot represents a shortcoming of manliness the way the Campbell Crew did.

Quinton Patton Height: 6-0   Weight: 204   College: Louisiana Tech   Draft: 2013/4 (128)   Born: 9-Aug-1990   Age: 26   Risk: Green

Year	Team	G/GS	Snaps	Rec	Pass	Yds	C%	+/-	Yd/C	TD	Drop	YAC	Rk	YAC+	BTkl	DVOA	Rk	DYAR	Rk	YAR	Short	Mid	Deep	Bomb
2013	SF	6/0	60	3	5	34	60%	-0.2	11.3	0	0	2.7	--	-3.6	0	-36.5%	--	-9	--	-11	40%	40%	20%	0%
2014	SF	4/0	86	3	8	44	38%	-1.4	14.7	0	0	0.0	--	-5.4	0	-37.2%	--	-18	--	-18	38%	50%	0%	13%
2015	SF	16/4	424	30	57	394	53%	-5.6	13.1	1	3	7.1	1	+1.6	6	-14.7%	79	-9	78	-23	48%	33%	12%	8%
2016	SF			41	70	541	59%	--	13.2	3							-4.9%								

The good: Patton finished fourth in YAC+ in 2015. The bad: Patton's catch rate was 10.5 points lower than we would expect given the location of his targets, third worst among 2015 wideouts. The ugly: Patton has only 36 catches in three seasons. The scary: Patton could be the second or third-most targeted receiver in this offense in 2016.

Breshad Perriman Height: 6-2   Weight: 212   College: UCF   Draft: 2015/1 (26)   Born: 10-Sep-1993   Age: 23   Risk: Red

Year	Team	G/GS	Snaps	Rec	Pass	Yds	C%	+/-	Yd/C	TD	Drop	YAC	Rk	YAC+	BTkl	DVOA	Rk	DYAR	Rk	YAR	Short	Mid	Deep	Bomb
2016	BAL			44	77	716	57%	--	16.3	4							7.8%								

When he was a rookie, the thought was for Perriman to replace Torrey Smith as Baltimore's deep threat. This year, Perriman could replace an aging Steve Smith, or he could be replaced himself by a declining Mike Wallace. His role and placement on the depth chart are mysteries going into the season, but we know his roster spot is secure as a first-round pick. That does not mean he is going to be a success, and losing his entire rookie season to what coach John Harbaugh called "probably one of the all-time slowest healing sprained PCLs ever" was not a good start. Perriman saved us some extensive research on injured starts to careers by not losing his entire second season to a knee injury after an erroneous report said he had a partially torn ACL. For what it's worth, Perriman joins Chicago's Kevin White and 1997 pick Yatil Green (Dolphins) as the only first-round wide receivers since 1988 to spend their rookie seasons on injured reserve. Hopefully Perriman and White can contribute this year and not end up like Green, who caught 18 passes in an injury-plagued career.

Brian Quick Height: 6-4   Weight: 220   College: Appalachian State   Draft: 2012/2 (33)   Born: 5-Jun-1989   Age: 27   Risk: Red

Year	Team	G/GS	Snaps	Rec	Pass	Yds	C%	+/-	Yd/C	TD	Drop	YAC	Rk	YAC+	BTkl	DVOA	Rk	DYAR	Rk	YAR	Short	Mid	Deep	Bomb
2013	STL	16/5	353	18	34	302	53%	-1.4	16.8	2	2	5.8	--	+1.3	3	12.6%	--	72	--	67	44%	29%	15%	12%
2014	STL	7/7	339	25	39	375	64%	+4.1	15.0	3	1	2.9	--	-1.0	1	24.5%	--	115	--	119	16%	42%	21%	21%
2015	STL	13/2	351	10	32	102	31%	-7.6	10.2	0	1	3.9	--	-0.7	0	-56.7%	--	-110	--	-118	22%	41%	19%	19%
2016	LARM			33	63	492	52%	--	14.9	4							-6.3%								

Ball-winning receivers can be very valuable crutches for rookie quarterbacks. As they adjust to the pace of the professional league, a receiver who can erase the need for precision gives them one less thing to worry about. Quick has the talent to be a ball-winning receiver for Jared Goff, but he needs to prove his health. Quick's career was nearly ended two years ago by a shoulder injury that obviously limited him during the 2015 season. Quick has a chance to be the Rams' leading receiver, but he could find himself fighting for his roster spot if he can't get back to his previous level of athleticism and comfort.

Rueben Randle Height: 6-3   Weight: 210   College: Louisiana State   Draft: 2012/2 (63)   Born: 7-May-1991   Age: 25   Risk: Yellow

Year	Team	G/GS	Snaps	Rec	Pass	Yds	C%	+/-	Yd/C	TD	Drop	YAC	Rk	YAC+	BTkl	DVOA	Rk	DYAR	Rk	YAR	Short	Mid	Deep	Bomb
2013	NYG	16/3	578	41	79	611	52%	-2.1	14.9	6	4	4.8	36	+0.1	6	-1.5%	53	71	53	87	22%	39%	24%	15%
2014	NYG	16/13	961	71	127	938	56%	-4.8	13.2	3	4	3.3	72	-0.9	9	-9.3%	62	34	58	54	26%	51%	13%	10%
2015	NYG	16/16	995	57	90	797	63%	+0.9	14.0	8	2	3.7	62	-0.9	4	10.0%	29	167	26	193	32%	48%	5%	14%
2016	PHI			36	65	478	55%	--	13.3	4							-5.5%								

Randle took a sizable step forward in Year 2 within Ben McAdoo's system, blowing away his previous career-high in DYAR and posting his first positive DVOA since his rookie year in 2012. And yet, whether due to the decline in his traditional receiving numbers or the inability to shake his reputation as an inconsistent and mistake-prone player, Randle was an afterthought in free agency for the Giants. After jumping ship to New York's NFC East rival, Randle has a shot to stick on a receiver-hungry Eagles squad. Early reports out of Philly suggest that Randle holds the inside track for the No. 3 receiver job, which makes sense given Jordan Matthews' ability to play the slot. That would likely lead to a downturn in playing time for Randle, though Doug Pederson still used three-receiver sets on 50 percent of his plays in Kansas City last season. The former second-round pick never developed into the featured weapon the Giants hoped he would, but Randle is still just 25, and perhaps a reduced role in Philadelphia will help improve his efficiency.

Paul Richardson   Height: 6-0   Weight: 175   College: Colorado   Draft: 2014/2 (45)   Born: 4/13/1992   Age: 24   Risk: Blue

Year	Team	G/GS	Snaps	Rec	Pass	Yds	C%	+/-	Yd/C	TD	Drop	YAC	Rk	YAC+	BTkl	DVOA	Rk	DYAR	Rk	YAR	Short	Mid	Deep	Bomb
2014	SEA	15/6	497	29	44	271	66%	+4.1	9.3	1	1	2.2	--	-2.6	2	-15.2%	--	-8	--	-1	35%	43%	8%	15%
2015	SEA	1/0	6	1	1	40	100%	+0.7	40.0	0	0	12.0	--	+3.4	0	253.5%	--	21	--	21	0%	0%	0%	100%
2016	SEA			13	21	159	62%	--	12.3	2						0.6%								

Injuries to his ACL and hamstring have ended Richardson's first two seasons. He can hope to be the fourth wide receiver on the depth chart this year, used mostly for shorter passes in the way Percy Harvin was in 2014, but as a much cheaper alternative.

Andre Roberts   Height: 5-11   Weight: 195   College: The Citadel   Draft: 2010/3 (88)   Born: 9-Jan-1988   Age: 28   Risk: Blue

Year	Team	G/GS	Snaps	Rec	Pass	Yds	C%	+/-	Yd/C	TD	Drop	YAC	Rk	YAC+	BTkl	DVOA	Rk	DYAR	Rk	YAR	Short	Mid	Deep	Bomb
2013	ARI	16/2	605	43	76	471	57%	-3.2	11.0	2	1	2.6	86	-2.3	2	-15.3%	76	-15	75	-5	31%	40%	17%	12%
2014	WAS	16/4	693	36	73	453	49%	-7.0	12.6	2	5	5.7	17	+0.8	3	-14.2%	73	-9	73	-27	36%	41%	17%	6%
2015	WAS	9/0	260	11	21	135	52%	-2.2	12.3	0	2	3.5	--	-1.7	0	-28.6%	--	-26	--	-20	38%	33%	19%	10%
2016	DET			7	12	86	58%	--	12.3	0						-4.8%								

Roberts won't go down as one of the most memorable or damaging of Washington's myriad free-agent busts during the Dan Snyder era. Still, Roberts was just about the only receiver who didn't surge at the same time as the rest of Washington's offense, disappearing after an unproductive September and never reappearing beyond a kick return touchdown at Carolina. In six seasons, Roberts has never posted a positive DVOA, and his only positive DYAR season came four years ago. He'll have to battle a number of other veterans including Jeremy Kerley, Anquan Boldin, and Andre Caldwell for a place on a receiver-hungry Lions roster, and after what unfolded during two unhappy Redskins seasons, it's hard to envision Roberts finally becoming a productive regular in his late twenties.

Seth Roberts   Height: 6-2   Weight: 195   College: West Alabama   Draft: 2014/FA   Born: 22-Feb-1991   Age: 25   Risk: Green

Year	Team	G/GS	Snaps	Rec	Pass	Yds	C%	+/-	Yd/C	TD	Drop	YAC	Rk	YAC+	BTkl	DVOA	Rk	DYAR	Rk	YAR	Short	Mid	Deep	Bomb
2015	OAK	16/5	565	32	55	480	58%	-0.8	15.0	5	4	4.2	50	-0.2	2	13.3%	19	114	38	127	39%	43%	11%	7%
2016	OAK			32	57	432	56%	--	13.5	3						-5.3%								

Roberts rode a big preseason (15 catches, 243 yards and a score) into eventually overtaking Andre Holmes for the third receiver job. Coming out of Maclay High School in Tallahassee, he had no scholarship offers from four-year programs, and spent two seasons at a community college before ending up at West Alabama. He had a perfectly cromulent year in the slot, but is a bit limited by his size.

Allen Robinson   Height: 6-2   Weight: 220   College: Penn State   Draft: 2014/2 (61)   Born: 8/24/1993   Age: 23   Risk: Green

Year	Team	G/GS	Snaps	Rec	Pass	Yds	C%	+/-	Yd/C	TD	Drop	YAC	Rk	YAC+	BTkl	DVOA	Rk	DYAR	Rk	YAR	Short	Mid	Deep	Bomb
2014	JAC	10/8	516	48	81	548	59%	-0.2	11.4	2	1	3.3	71	-1.0	3	-11.1%	64	10	66	9	27%	53%	9%	11%
2015	JAC	16/16	983	80	151	1400	53%	+1.4	17.5	14	5	4.5	43	+0.2	8	14.0%	16	318	8	343	22%	30%	30%	17%
2016	JAC			89	157	1368	57%	--	15.4	10						4.1%								

The scheme change in Jacksonville was huge for Robinson. Before his rookie season was cut short by injury, previous offensive coordinator Jedd Fisch showed off a complete misunderstanding of Robinson's skill set. Fisch asked Robinson to run short routes where he would need to create yards with the ball in his hands to attain significant gains. When Greg Olson took over, he immediately unleashed Robinson downfield, allowing him to compete with defensive backs at the catch point for the ball in the air. Robinson won most of those battles because of his natural ball skills and impressive athleticism.

Eddie Royal Height: 5-9   Weight: 184   College: Virginia Tech   Draft: 2008/2 (42)   Born: 21-May-1986   Age: 30   Risk: Yellow

Year	Team	G/GS	Snaps	Rec	Pass	Yds	C%	+/-	Yd/C	TD	Drop	YAC	Rk	YAC+	BTkl	DVOA	Rk	DYAR	Rk	YAR	Short	Mid	Deep	Bomb
2013	SD	15/3	705	47	67	631	70%	+4.3	13.4	8	2	7.1	5	+1.6	4	31.6%	4	238	15	255	43%	28%	19%	10%
2014	SD	16/11	760	62	91	778	68%	+7.0	12.5	7	3	5.8	13	-0.1	6	12.8%	17	183	26	159	51%	22%	16%	11%
2015	CHI	9/9	477	37	50	238	74%	-1.0	6.4	1	3	4.8	35	-1.8	8	-34.0%	87	-81	84	-83	71%	24%	2%	4%
2016	CHI			48	76	527	63%	--	11.0	2						-6.0%								

Let's not gloss over that tenth column in that table, the one that reads "6.4" in 2015. That is, 6.4 yards per catch. 6.4 yards. *SIX. POINT. FOUR..* That's not even 20 *feet*. No other wide receiver in league history has come close to such a paltry average gain with at least 32 catches in a season. The prior record belonged to Danny Amendola, whose average reception with the Rams in 2013 gained 7.6 yards. Royal fell short of that by more than a yard. If anyone ever breaks Royal's record, they might actually be running backwards. And the most amazing thing is, this wasn't even Royal's worst year—he was last in the NFL with a DVOA of -45.2% with Denver in 2011 (the Tim Tebow season). Royal is now the only wide receiver in our database to qualify for our leaderboards with a DVOA of -30.0% or worse three different times. Early Doucet is the only other player to do it twice.

To be fair, Royal was struggling through knee and ankle injuries and illnesses all season. The Bears are hopeful he can rebound to at least be a viable third receiver behind Alshon Jeffery and Kevin White. It's not like he can get much worse.

Emmanuel Sanders Height: 5-11   Weight: 186   College: Southern Methodist   Draft: 2010/3 (82)   Born: 17-Mar-1987   Age: 29   Risk: Green

Year	Team	G/GS	Snaps	Rec	Pass	Yds	C%	+/-	Yd/C	TD	Drop	YAC	Rk	YAC+	BTkl	DVOA	Rk	DYAR	Rk	YAR	Short	Mid	Deep	Bomb
2013	PIT	16/10	796	67	113	740	60%	-0.5	11.0	6	2	4.4	54	-0.9	7	-10.2%	71	22	69	-1	37%	35%	14%	15%
2014	DEN	16/16	1000	101	141	1404	72%	+16.3	13.9	9	0	3.5	65	-1.4	6	29.6%	4	481	3	457	40%	27%	15%	19%
2015	DEN	15/15	859	76	137	1135	55%	-0.7	14.9	6	6	4.8	36	+0.0	5	-4.1%	58	90	49	110	24%	38%	19%	20%
2016	DEN			75	126	1010	60%	--	13.5	6						0.6%								

Sanders is reportedly seeking a contract extension in the neighborhood of four years, $48 million, with $24 million guaranteed. If he gets close to what he's looking for, Sanders will be getting paid in large part for his huge 2014, making him the last in a line of receivers who can trace a chunk of their net worth to the good fortune of playing with The Sheriff.

Mohamed Sanu Height: 6-2   Weight: 211   College: Rutgers   Draft: 2012/3 (83)   Born: 22-Aug-1989   Age: 27   Risk: Yellow

Year	Team	G/GS	Snaps	Rec	Pass	Yds	C%	+/-	Yd/C	TD	Drop	YAC	Rk	YAC+	BTkl	DVOA	Rk	DYAR	Rk	YAR	Short	Mid	Deep	Bomb
2013	CIN	16/14	749	47	78	455	60%	+1.2	9.7	2	6	5.4	23	+0.1	2	-10.0%	69	17	71	2	45%	33%	11%	11%
2014	CIN	16/13	986	56	98	790	57%	-6.7	14.1	5	6	5.8	16	+0.7	6	0.1%	43	99	40	91	35%	40%	12%	12%
2015	CIN	16/4	643	33	49	394	67%	-0.2	11.9	0	0	6.2	--	+1.0	7	-8.3%	--	16	--	14	57%	23%	15%	4%
2016	ATL			62	99	815	63%	--	13.1	5						3.0%								

Like his former teammate in Cincinnati, Marvin Jones, Sanu was bowled over by a huge offer to depart via free agency. Unlike Jones, who may not be a true No. 1 but should do just fine in Detroit, Sanu may well disappoint if expected to be a true "deuce," as Atlanta general manager Thomas Dimitroff called him. Less is more with Mo, who had his targets cut in half after being Cincy's top receiver by default for much of the injury-plagued 2014 season. His catch rate improved as a result, though his efficiency didn't because of the shorter routes. As the Bengals' fourth or fifth option, Sanu could make plays against bottom-level defensive backs. He doesn't separate or attack the ball well enough to threaten defenses as a No. 2 option, even with Julio Jones playing the A.J. Green role on the other side. However, Sanu does bring other gifts to the table, including strong blocking and an unblemished mark as a passer out of gadget formations.

Tajae Sharpe Height: 6-2   Weight: 194   College: Massachusetts   Draft: 2016/5 (140)   Born: 23-Dec-1994   Age: 22   Risk: Yellow

Year	Team	G/GS	Snaps	Rec	Pass	Yds	C%	+/-	Yd/C	TD	Drop	YAC	Rk	YAC+	BTkl	DVOA	Rk	DYAR	Rk	YAR	Short	Mid	Deep	Bomb
2016	TEN			25	45	328	56%	--	13.1	3						-7.4%								

Sharpe is a receiver the Titans coaching staff is high on. The rookie was given a starting role during the offseason alongside Rishard Matthews. It may have only been a ploy to motivate Dorial Green-Beckham, but if the Titans wanted to do that they didn't need to include Sharpe, they could have just started Kendall Wright. Sharpe is long with impressive body control, but he needs to add strength and he doesn't offer much speed on deep routes. The idea that a team might start a fifth-round rookie with a Playmaker Score of 14.3 percent just seems weird.

Sterling Shepard Height: 5-10   Weight: 194   College: Oklahoma   Draft: 2016/2 (40)   Born: 10-Feb-1994   Age: 22   Risk: Red

Year	Team	G/GS	Snaps	Rec	Pass	Yds	C%	+/-	Yd/C	TD	Drop	YAC	Rk	YAC+	BTkl	DVOA	Rk	DYAR	Rk	YAR	Short	Mid	Deep	Bomb
2016	NYG			64	105	841	61%	--	13.1	6						3.6%								

Shepard rose up draft boards this spring because of his polished skill set and strong testing numbers, and should get a chance to immediately contribute for a Giants offense starving for targets behind Odell Beckham Jr. Though he's probably limited to the slot given his size and usage at Oklahoma, Shepard was highly prolific as the Sooners' top target last season, generating 1,288 yards and 11 touchdowns with an impressive 74 percent catch rate. From a personnel perspective, Shepard's redundancy with Victor Cruz isn't ideal, given New York's lack of viable receiver depth and the fact that both are true slot receivers. That could create some playing time challenges, especially if Cruz is finally healthy after nearly two years away. Still, it's hard to imagine the Giants won't give their second-round pick plenty of opportunities. Given the attention Beckham commands from opposing defenses, Shepard should have plenty of room to roam and make an immediate impression.

Cecil Shorts Height: 6-0   Weight: 200   College: Mount Union   Draft: 2011/4 (114)   Born: 22-Dec-1987   Age: 29   Risk: Green

Year	Team	G/GS	Snaps	Rec	Pass	Yds	C%	+/-	Yd/C	TD	Drop	YAC	Rk	YAC+	BTkl	DVOA	Rk	DYAR	Rk	YAR	Short	Mid	Deep	Bomb
2013	JAC	13/13	759	66	125	777	53%	-5.5	11.8	3	7	4.2	62	-0.7	3	-16.3%	79	-36	79	-32	36%	36%	18%	10%
2014	JAC	13/12	741	53	110	557	48%	-13.2	10.5	1	4	4.9	33	+0.0	5	-33.7%	87	-183	87	-187	39%	44%	13%	4%
2015	HOU	11/4	567	42	75	484	56%	-5.8	11.5	2	5	5.0	28	-0.1	4	-11.9%	74	4	74	-4	44%	41%	9%	6%
2016	HOU			39	68	436	57%	--	11.2	2						-14.1%								

No, really, Shorts once averaged more than 17 yards per catch with Blaine Gabbert throwing him the ball. That the Texans drafted a pair of wideouts in the first three rounds said a lot about the state of their non-DeAndre Hopkins receivers. He could continue to see work in the slot as Braxton Miller transitions to the NFL, but the offseason moves and a blah 2015 suggest his future is not that bright.

Devin Smith Height: 6-0   Weight: 196   College: Ohio State   Draft: 2015/2 (37)   Born: 3-Mar-1992   Age: 24   Risk: Red

Year	Team	G/GS	Snaps	Rec	Pass	Yds	C%	+/-	Yd/C	TD	Drop	YAC	Rk	YAC+	BTkl	DVOA	Rk	DYAR	Rk	YAR	Short	Mid	Deep	Bomb
2015	NYJ	10/3	312	9	28	115	32%	-4.9	12.8	1	2	2.0	--	-1.8	0	-46.1%	--	-71	--	-62	11%	25%	32%	32%
2016	NYJ			12	24	189	50%	--	15.8	2						-7.0%								

Smith tore an ACL in December and is unlikely to be available for the season opener. His 2015 season was a mess before the injury: he dropped an easy touchdown pass against the Texans, fumbled a kickoff return, battled minor injuries, and was relegated to a "go deep and we'll fake it to ya" role in an offense full of four-receiver formations because he did not pick the system up quickly. He's another young player who increases the Jets' reliance on old players.

Steve Smith Height: 5-9   Weight: 185   College: Utah   Draft: 2001/3 (74)   Born: 12-May-1979   Age: 37   Risk: Yellow

Year	Team	G/GS	Snaps	Rec	Pass	Yds	C%	+/-	Yd/C	TD	Drop	YAC	Rk	YAC+	BTkl	DVOA	Rk	DYAR	Rk	YAR	Short	Mid	Deep	Bomb
2013	CAR	15/15	770	64	110	745	58%	-0.3	11.6	4	5	2.8	84	-1.7	12	-3.7%	58	74	51	80	27%	52%	13%	8%
2014	BAL	16/16	822	79	134	1065	59%	-3.7	13.5	6	5	4.7	37	+0.3	13	-5.4%	53	79	45	57	33%	44%	12%	11%
2015	BAL	7/7	348	46	73	670	63%	+2.3	14.6	3	1	5.6	16	+0.3	6	9.4%	30	125	36	113	36%	38%	20%	6%
2016	BAL			67	115	836	58%	--	12.5	8						1.3%								

Back in *Football Outsiders Almanac 2014*, we ran a table that showed the most receiving yards any receiver had in his debut season with a new team at age 35-plus. Smith beat expectations with 1,065 yards for the Ravens in 2014—only Jerry Rice (1,139 yards for the 2001 Raiders at age 39) had topped 1,000 yards in that circumstance. Smith was off to another great start in 2015 before tearing his Achilles in what was supposed to be his final season. Perhaps the allure of 1,000 career receptions being 39 catches away motivated Smith for one more try, but coming off a serious injury at age 37, it is hard to see him doing much more than putting a stamp on a career that should ignite many Hall of Fame debates. Smith also needs just 169 receiving yards to move ahead of Andre Johnson (14,100 yards) for ninth all-time.

Only five players have caught 50 passes in a season at age 37-plus: Jerry Rice (five times), Charlie Joiner (twice), Tim Brown (2003), Terrell Owens (2010), and Tony Gonzalez (2013). We wouldn't dare tell Smith to his face that he cannot join that group, but every big play and memorable quote Smith gives us at this point is something to be grateful for.

Torrey Smith — Height: 6-1 — Weight: 204 — College: Maryland — Draft: 2011/2 (58) — Born: 26-Jan-1989 — Age: 27 — Risk: Red

Year	Team	G/GS	Snaps	Rec	Pass	Yds	C%	+/-	Yd/C	TD	Drop	YAC	Rk	YAC+	BTkl	DVOA	Rk	DYAR	Rk	YAR	Short	Mid	Deep	Bomb
2013	BAL	16/16	1099	65	137	1128	47%	-4.3	17.4	4	3	5.5	21	+0.7	2	0.0%	48	139	33	98	25%	32%	22%	21%
2014	BAL	16/16	788	49	92	767	53%	-3.0	15.7	11	5	3.4	69	-1.0	6	26.8%	7	310	9	304	16%	46%	17%	22%
2015	SF	16/12	775	33	62	663	53%	+0.3	20.1	4	4	6.6	5	+1.1	1	14.3%	14	134	32	112	20%	42%	20%	17%
2016	SF			65	115	1074	57%	--	16.5	8						6.4%								

Smith's San Francisco debut on a five-year deal worth $40 million was an odd one. Sure, Anquan Boldin was getting more targets, much like when they were teammates in Baltimore in 2011 and 2012, but back then it was nearly a 50-50 split. Last season, a 35-year-old Boldin had 49 more targets than Smith, and he even missed two games. It's not like Smith was ineffective. He led the NFL with 20.2 yards per reception, finishing 14th among wide receivers in DVOA and ninth in YAC+. But 62 targets on a limited offense that desperately needed big plays to make up all those huge score deficits is crazy.

Smith's lone 1,000-yard season came in 2013 when the Ravens lost Boldin and could only field a cast of Jacoby Jones, Marlon Brown, and the corpses of Dallas Clark and Brandon Stokley around him. He should have a similar experience this year with Boldin gone and the 49ers behind him barely having any professional experience. Add in the fact that Chip Kelly's No. 1 wide receiver, played by three different guys in Philadelphia, has always caught at least 82 passes, and it could be a career year for Smith. But this is really just a classic example of being the best receiver on a lousy offense. The accuracy issues of the quarterbacks combined with the vertical routes Smith runs best at won't boost his receptions to the usual Kelly level, but there will be ample opportunities for some hollow yardage.

Willie Snead — Height: 5-11 — Weight: 195 — College: Ball State — Draft: 2014/FA — Born: 17-Oct-1992 — Age: 24 — Risk: Green

Year	Team	G/GS	Snaps	Rec	Pass	Yds	C%	+/-	Yd/C	TD	Drop	YAC	Rk	YAC+	BTkl	DVOA	Rk	DYAR	Rk	YAR	Short	Mid	Deep	Bomb
2015	NO	15/8	780	69	101	984	68%	+8.8	14.3	3	2	5.0	28	+0.5	9	10.1%	28	175	23	198	35%	42%	14%	9%
2016	NO			62	104	951	60%	--	15.3	5						3.7%								

New Orleans was able to get quite a bit of production from the third-year UDFA last year. He's not going to win on 9-routes over the top or anything, but Snead showed some remarkable route-running prowess in his first season in the NFL. He is able to find and work to holes in zones, and he's the kind of pest who can annoy a team underneath if he gets off press. Physically, Snead isn't much. His arm and hand size are nice, but he was in the 20th percentile or lower versus other wideouts at the combine in the 40-yard dash, bench press, and all jumps and shuttles. Luckily for Snead, football isn't a drill.

Kenny Stills — Height: 6-0 — Weight: 194 — College: Oklahoma — Draft: 2013/5 (144) — Born: 22-Apr-1992 — Age: 24 — Risk: Yellow

Year	Team	G/GS	Snaps	Rec	Pass	Yds	C%	+/-	Yd/C	TD	Drop	YAC	Rk	YAC+	BTkl	DVOA	Rk	DYAR	Rk	YAR	Short	Mid	Deep	Bomb
2013	NO	16/10	689	32	51	641	65%	+6.4	20.0	5	1	6.2	7	+1.5	1	40.1%	1	206	21	218	31%	24%	22%	22%
2014	NO	15/7	617	63	84	931	75%	+15.5	14.8	3	3	3.0	80	-1.6	2	30.3%	3	285	12	301	32%	35%	19%	15%
2015	MIA	16/8	594	27	63	440	43%	-5.9	16.3	3	4	3.8	60	-1.3	0	-17.2%	80	-22	80	-26	16%	34%	26%	23%
2016	MIA			48	90	741	53%	--	15.4	4						-3.8%								

Stills seamlessly replaced Mike Wallace as the receiver who jogs halfheartedly downfield and watches Ryan Tannehill passes sail over his head out of bounds. Stills, who became expendable in New Orleans because of his lackluster practice habits, never met a sideline pass he couldn't bobble or catch with only one foot in bounds, nor a difficult over-the-shoulder bomb he couldn't try to flag down with one hand. His timing with Tannehill was dreadful, and of course Tannehill isn't exactly a sniper on the deep out to begin with. So Stills and Tannehill combined for some amazing 1-of-6, 0-of-4, and 2-of-10 catch-to-target lines, often looking like a quarterback and wide receiver who just met in the parking lot.

Stills has the ability to be a go-to receiver, as evidenced by a handful of highlight receptions last year and the amazing catches he made for Drew Brees in New Orleans. But DeVante Parker could take over his role as the big-play threat, and the new coaches will have limited patience with the habits that turned off Sean Payton two years ago. Meanwhile, the Dolphins proved they learned their lessons about trading for another team's frustrating talent by acquiring Byron Maxwell.

Rod Streater | Height: 6-3 | Weight: 200 | College: Temple | Draft: 2012/FA | Born: 9-Feb-1988 | Age: 28 | Risk: Blue

Year	Team	G/GS	Snaps	Rec	Pass	Yds	C%	+/-	Yd/C	TD	Drop	YAC	Rk	YAC+	BTkl	DVOA	Rk	DYAR	Rk	YAR	Short	Mid	Deep	Bomb
2013	OAK	16/14	748	60	100	888	61%	+4.4	14.8	4	4	5.1	28	+0.3	3	13.6%	18	204	23	203	31%	42%	17%	10%
2014	OAK	3/3	86	9	13	84	69%	+0.4	9.3	1	0	3.3	--	-1.2	0	2.0%	--	15	--	18	31%	54%	0%	15%
2015	OAK	1/0	10	1	1	8	100%	+0.3	8.0	0	0	1.0	--	-0.8	0	46.9%	--	7	--	6	0%	100%	0%	0%
2016	KC			5	9	66	56%	--	13.2	0						-6.5%								

An odd year for Streater, who missed time in the preseason with what was dubbed cryptically as an "illness" and fell behind Andre Holmes and Seth Roberts on the depth chart despite having more of a pedigree. Streater received a second-round tender from the Raiders last offseason, and was the one player they chose to use the IR-designated to return spot on in 2014. Then they suddenly decided to cut bait on him. The Chiefs could benefit, getting him on a low-risk one-year deal. Streater's lanky, but he can fly. If he's healthy, he could very well end up as the third receiver for KC.

Jaelen Strong | Height: 6-2 | Weight: 197 | College: Arizona State | Draft: 2015/3 (70) | Born: 25-Jan-1994 | Age: 22 | Risk: Yellow

Year	Team	G/GS	Snaps	Rec	Pass	Yds	C%	+/-	Yd/C	TD	Drop	YAC	Rk	YAC+	BTkl	DVOA	Rk	DYAR	Rk	YAR	Short	Mid	Deep	Bomb
2015	HOU	10/1	282	14	24	161	58%	-0.8	11.5	3	1	4.5	--	+0.3	1	7.1%	--	35	--	45	50%	27%	14%	9%
2016	HOU			45	80	580	56%	--	12.9	3						-10.0%								

It seemed reasonable to wonder how long Strong's NFL career might be after a February marijuana possession arrest followed an unproductive rookie season where he struggled to find the field despite a thin depth chart. Fortunately, the arrest seems to have taught him the need to work—he dropped his weight from 230 pounds to 197 and paid serious attention to his craft, earning praise from Bill O'Brien as one of the Texans' most improved players. The key will be whether he can still be as successful on contested catches as he was when he was bigger, or if the weight loss gives him a better ability to separate. Oh, and whether the Texans will feel the need to put rookie Will Fuller opposite DeAndre Hopkins to give them the speed they crave.

Golden Tate | Height: 5-10 | Weight: 199 | College: Notre Dame | Draft: 2010/2 (60) | Born: 2-Aug-1988 | Age: 28 | Risk: Yellow

Year	Team	G/GS	Snaps	Rec	Pass	Yds	C%	+/-	Yd/C	TD	Drop	YAC	Rk	YAC+	BTkl	DVOA	Rk	DYAR	Rk	YAR	Short	Mid	Deep	Bomb
2013	SEA	16/13	762	64	100	898	66%	+5.4	14.0	5	4	7.6	1	+2.0	23	12.9%	19	196	24	206	44%	30%	11%	14%
2014	DET	16/16	924	99	144	1331	69%	+4.9	13.4	4	2	7.0	4	+1.5	18	6.7%	31	214	22	244	49%	33%	13%	4%
2015	DET	16/16	926	90	128	813	70%	+1.7	9.0	6	5	5.9	10	+0.1	27	-1.7%	51	113	39	74	58%	32%	7%	3%
2016	DET			91	131	1067	69%	--	11.7	7						11.7%								

In a sense, Tate has always been the Lions' No. 1 receiver—he led the team in catches and catches per game in each of the last two seasons. This just goes to show you how overrated receptions can be as a measuring stick. Now that he enters the 2016 season as Detroit's No. 1 wideout in reality, it will be interesting to see if they use him as a downfield weapon more often. In each of four seasons in Seattle, at least 22 percent of Tate's targets came more than 15 yards past the line of scrimmage. That rate dipped to 17 percent in his first year in Detroit and then just 10 percent last year. It's hard to be an effective top receiver if you don't try to take the top off the defense once in a while. Either way, we know Tate won't go down easy—he was third among wide receivers in broken tackles last year after finishing first in both 2013 and 2014.

Adam Thielen | Height: 6-2 | Weight: 195 | College: Minnesota State | Draft: 2013/FA | Born: 22-Aug-1990 | Age: 26 | Risk: Blue

Year	Team	G/GS	Snaps	Rec	Pass	Yds	C%	+/-	Yd/C	TD	Drop	YAC	Rk	YAC+	BTkl	DVOA	Rk	DYAR	Rk	YAR	Short	Mid	Deep	Bomb
2014	MIN	16/2	152	8	13	137	62%	+0.3	17.1	1	0	4.3	--	+0.2	0	31.3%	--	43	--	44	8%	62%	15%	15%
2015	MIN	16/2	218	12	18	144	67%	+1.4	12.0	0	0	3.9	--	+0.0	3	-8.4%	--	6	--	-5	29%	53%	12%	6%
2016	MIN			4	7	50	57%	--	12.6	0						-6.6%								

The second-leading receiver in the prestigious history of Minnesota State (whose nickname, shockingly, is the Mavericks and not the Screaming Eagles), Thielen earned a spot on the Vikings' practice squad in 2013, then made a name for himself in the kicking game. He blocked a punt and recovered it for a touchdown in 2014, and finished second on the club in special teams snaps last year while successfully fielding two onside kicks and converting a fourth-and-3 with a 41-yard gain on a fake punt against Green Bay. In addition to that play, Thielen ran three end-arounds last year, each picking up a first down and gaining 48 total yards. Thielen may not see much time at receiver in 2016, but he'll remain a key special teamer and occasional secret weapon.

De'Anthony Thomas Height: 5-9   Weight: 174   College: Oregon   Draft: 2014/4 (124)   Born: 5-Jan-1993   Age: 24   Risk: Green

Year	Team	G/GS	Snaps	Rec	Pass	Yds	C%	+/-	Yd/C	TD	Drop	YAC	Rk	YAC+	BTkl	DVOA	Rk	DYAR	Rk	YAR	Short	Mid	Deep	Bomb
2014	KC	12/3	188	23	32	156	75%	-0.3	6.8	0	2	8.0	--	-0.4	4	-34.9%	--	-55	--	-44	93%	0%	3%	3%
2015	KC	10/1	172	17	25	140	72%	-1.3	8.2	1	1	8.3	--	+0.6	2	-26.4%	--	-26	--	-41	79%	21%	0%	0%
2016	KC			20	31	178	65%	--	8.9	0						-27.6%								

Thomas missed the last six regular season games after sustaining a concussion in late November. The last two games in Thomas' absence were for off-field reasons that are unclear, except that all involved agree it was not related to the concussion. With the arrival of fifth-round pick Tyreek Hill to handle return duties, Thomas may not have a place on the roster.

Demaryius Thomas Height: 6-3   Weight: 224   College: Georgia Tech   Draft: 2010/1 (22)   Born: 25-Dec-1987   Age: 29   Risk: Green

Year	Team	G/GS	Snaps	Rec	Pass	Yds	C%	+/-	Yd/C	TD	Drop	YAC	Rk	YAC+	BTkl	DVOA	Rk	DYAR	Rk	YAR	Short	Mid	Deep	Bomb
2013	DEN	16/16	1106	92	142	1430	65%	+6.2	15.5	14	4	7.6	2	+2.5	8	26.5%	7	430	1	465	48%	24%	17%	11%
2014	DEN	16/16	1021	111	184	1619	60%	-3.8	14.6	11	8	5.8	14	+1.2	7	9.2%	29	317	8	282	43%	32%	19%	6%
2015	DEN	16/16	937	105	177	1304	59%	-3.3	12.4	6	9	4.7	39	+0.0	15	-8.7%	70	56	60	80	38%	38%	16%	9%
2016	DEN			90	151	1170	60%	--	13.0	8						-0.6%								

Thomas put up poor efficiency numbers no matter who was under center for the Broncos in 2015. With Peyton Manning, Thomas posted a -5.5% DVOA in 101 targets. With Brock Osweiler, Thomas posted a -12.8% DVOA in 80 targets. Thomas' 181 targets ranked fourth in the league. Usually all that attention means the connection is succeeding. Not so with Thomas. Only Michael Crabtree had a lower DVOA than Thomas among the 43 wide receivers with at least 100 targets. The quarterbacking doesn't exactly get better this season.

Michael Thomas Height: 6-3   Weight: 212   College: Ohio State   Draft: 2016/2 (47)   Born: 3-Mar-1994   Age: 22   Risk: Red

Year	Team	G/GS	Snaps	Rec	Pass	Yds	C%	+/-	Yd/C	TD	Drop	YAC	Rk	YAC+	BTkl	DVOA	Rk	DYAR	Rk	YAR	Short	Mid	Deep	Bomb
2016	NO			45	66	600	68%	--	13.3	4						11.1%								

Thomas was part of an offensive collapse at Ohio State in 2015, but it wasn't his fault. With offensive coordinator Tom Hermann leaving for Houston, the passing game disintegrated. Thomas isn't a burner, but he's the sort of receiver who comes in NFL-ready because of his efficiency releasing at the line of scrimmage and his use of good footwork. The Saints are throwing Thomas right into the Marques Colston role. It'd be foolhardy to project a rookie to do what Colston did at his peak, but he can definitely do more than Colston did last year. Michael Crabtree is one logical comparison for an optimistic outcome for Thomas.

Kenbrell Thompkins Height: 6-1   Weight: 196   College: Cincinnati   Draft: 2013/FA   Born: 29-Jul-1988   Age: 28   Risk: Green

Year	Team	G/GS	Snaps	Rec	Pass	Yds	C%	+/-	Yd/C	TD	Drop	YAC	Rk	YAC+	BTkl	DVOA	Rk	DYAR	Rk	YAR	Short	Mid	Deep	Bomb
2013	NE	12/8	574	32	70	466	46%	-10.5	14.6	4	5	4.3	56	-0.1	4	-11.9%	73	4	74	8	32%	43%	17%	7%
2014	2TM	12/6	394	21	47	262	45%	-6.8	12.5	0	2	4.5	--	-0.2	3	-28.4%	--	-56	--	-66	30%	46%	9%	15%
2015	NYJ	7/2	281	17	33	165	52%	-1.6	9.7	0	0	4.0	--	-1.6	0	-38.8%	--	-68	--	-69	36%	30%	15%	18%
2016	NYJ			11	19	138	58%	--	12.5	1						-7.8%								

The Jets re-signed Tompkins to a one-year, $1.67 million contract after the former Patriots receiver showed brief flashes of usefulness in the second half of last season. Tompkins is still dining out on his 15-catch preseason for the Patriots in 2013; both the Raiders and Jets have searched in vain for the "next Deion Branch" they saw in August three years ago. Tellingly, the Patriots gave up looking as soon as Danny Amendola and Rob Gronkowski got healthy that year. Tompkins is not particularly big, fast, or reliable, but no AFC East team ever gives up on a former Patriots player without making absolutely sure he won't return to Foxborough and haunt their nightmares.

Laquon Treadwell Height: 6-2   Weight: 221   College: Mississippi   Draft: 2016/1 (23)   Born: 14-Jun-1995   Age: 21   Risk: Red

Year	Team	G/GS	Snaps	Rec	Pass	Yds	C%	+/-	Yd/C	TD	Drop	YAC	Rk	YAC+	BTkl	DVOA	Rk	DYAR	Rk	YAR	Short	Mid	Deep	Bomb
2016	MIN			65	103	846	63%	--	13.0	5						2.3%								

Playmaker Score was not impressed with Treadwell's college production, and nobody was impressed with the 4.63 40-yard dash he ran at Mississippi's pro day. Vikings offense coordinator Norv Turner, though, looks at Treadwell and sees hints of another over-sized wide receiver with iffy straight-line speed. The best receiver Norv Turner ever coached in the NFL was Michael Irvin, the Dallas Cowboys' Hall of Famer whose 591 DYAR in 1995 is still the most for any wideout we've ever measured in a single season. At 6-foot-2 and 207 pounds, Irvin was a big receiver for his day, and though he wasn't a Randy Moss-style home run threat, he was a doubles hitter, specializing in the skinny post route that Turner liked to call the Bang 8. "You want to widen the cornerback with your release," Turner explained to Matt Vensel of *Minneapolis Star-Tribune*. "When you get [about 12 yards downfield], you make a high-angle cut to the post. It's usually caught 20, 22 yards deep on the inside edge of the numbers." Enter Laquon Treadwell, a big receiver himself (and the heaviest of this year's first-round rookie wideouts by 19 pounds). Treadwell was used mainly on shorter routes at Mississippi, but the Vikings believe he has the physical skills to develop into a modern-day version of Irvin. If they're right, he'll fill a hole in their offense—the Vikings were tied for last in the league with only three receptions in that 20- to 22-yard range last year. The Jaguars led the league with 17. Julio Jones had eight by himself.

Mike Wallace Height: 6-0 Weight: 199 College: Mississippi Draft: 2009/3 (84) Born: 1-Aug-1986 Age: 30 Risk: Green

Year	Team	G/GS	Snaps	Rec	Pass	Yds	C%	+/-	Yd/C	TD	Drop	YAC	Rk	YAC+	BTkl	DVOA	Rk	DYAR	Rk	YAR	Short	Mid	Deep	Bomb
2013	MIA	16/16	951	73	141	930	52%	-4.2	12.7	5	7	3.9	67	-0.9	5	-14.8%	75	-24	77	-37	26%	44%	9%	22%
2014	MIA	16/16	819	67	115	862	58%	+3.2	12.9	10	4	3.5	63	-1.0	10	11.8%	19	221	20	216	27%	39%	19%	15%
2015	MIN	16/12	751	39	72	473	54%	-2.7	12.1	2	4	4.3	47	-0.5	4	-6.4%	62	36	66	16	35%	37%	20%	8%
2016	BAL			25	46	305	54%	--	12.2	2						-10.4%								

The year was 2010. Spain won a World Cup event that is remembered for vuvuzelas as much as anything that happened on the pitch. Bode Miller, Lindsey Vonn, and Shaun White were some of the stars of the Winter Olympics. And in his second season, Pittsburgh's Mike Wallace led all NFL receivers in DVOA and DYAR. It didn't last—Wallace was top-ten in both categories again the next season, but then horrible in his last season with the Steelers in 2012, and mediocre at best since then. Wallace was sure to throw Teddy Bridgewater under the bus on his way out of Minnesota, telling reporters there that there was no way he was going to re-sign with the Vikings, adding "I need a good quarterback. I need a quarterback who I know is proven and can get things done." It's fair to question, then, why he chose to sign with Baltimore. In fairness, though, Wallace has always been a deep-ball specialist, and Joe Flacco's cannon arm may give him an opportunity to make plays downfield that Bridgewater was simply unable to provide.

Bryan Walters Height: 6-0 Weight: 190 College: Cornell Draft: 2010/FA Born: 4-Nov-1987 Age: 29 Risk: Blue

Year	Team	G/GS	Snaps	Rec	Pass	Yds	C%	+/-	Yd/C	TD	Drop	YAC	Rk	YAC+	BTkl	DVOA	Rk	DYAR	Rk	YAR	Short	Mid	Deep	Bomb
2013	SEA	4/1	50	0	0	0	--	--	--	0	0	--	--	--	--	--	--	--	--	--	--	--	--	--
2014	SEA	13/0	106	6	11	57	55%	-0.8	9.5	0	0	6.5	--	-0.6	0	-27.2%	--	-12	--	-19	60%	20%	20%	0%
2015	JAC	11/1	313	32	45	368	71%	+4.1	11.5	1	1	3.8	--	-1.1	0	11.4%	--	87	--	86	45%	36%	19%	0%
2016	JAC			4	7	43	57%	--	10.7	0						-16.6%								

Walters caught 32 passes last season. That's… surprising. Walters played more than he would have been expected to because of injuries. But with Allen Robinson, Allen Hurns, Julius Thomas, Marqise Lee, Rashad Greene, and Marcedes Lewis all ahead of him as pass-catching options, he'll likely need even more injuries to even reach double-digit receptions in 2016.

Nate Washington Height: 6-1 Weight: 185 College: Tiffin Draft: 2005/FA Born: 28-Aug-1983 Age: 33 Risk: Red

Year	Team	G/GS	Snaps	Rec	Pass	Yds	C%	+/-	Yd/C	TD	Drop	YAC	Rk	YAC+	BTkl	DVOA	Rk	DYAR	Rk	YAR	Short	Mid	Deep	Bomb
2013	TEN	16/15	886	58	104	919	56%	+3.7	15.8	3	3	4.0	66	-0.4	3	7.4%	27	162	28	165	13%	58%	14%	15%
2014	TEN	16/11	765	40	72	647	56%	-0.5	16.2	2	4	3.5	64	-0.7	2	5.3%	35	97	41	94	18%	46%	24%	11%
2015	HOU	14/14	795	47	94	658	50%	-7.4	14.0	4	7	3.4	69	-0.5	1	-13.2%	77	-4	76	23	30%	48%	14%	8%
2016	NE			10	16	126	63%	--	12.6	0						0.7%								

Washington is best suited as a No. 3 with the ability to play outside and in the slot, and to work against an opposing team's third corner or find the soft spot in zone coverage on intermediate routes. With Houston, quarterback play hurt him a lot. He had a -4.1% DVOA with Brian Hoyer, but only -27.0% with the other passers. New England's lack of depth at outside receiver gives him a shot at a roster spot, but June reports had him struggling to get on the same page as Tom Brady. That's a veteran tradition in New England. Just ask Chad Johnson. Or Reggie Wayne. Or Joey Galloway.

Sammy Watkins

Height: 6-1   **Weight:** 211   **College:** Clemson   **Draft:** 2014/1 (4)   **Born:** 14-Jun-1993   **Age:** 23   **Risk:** Red

Year	Team	G/GS	Snaps	Rec	Pass	Yds	C%	+/-	Yd/C	TD	Drop	YAC	Rk	YAC+	BTkl	DVOA	Rk	DYAR	Rk	YAR	Short	Mid	Deep	Bomb
2014	BUF	16/16	1027	65	128	982	51%	-8.5	15.1	6	2	5.3	21	+0.9	9	-5.7%	54	71	48	48	30%	33%	23%	14%
2015	BUF	13/13	714	60	96	1047	63%	+9.6	17.5	9	2	3.0	77	-1.2	2	28.9%	6	312	9	312	28%	29%	13%	30%
2016	BUF			77	129	1258	60%	--	16.3	11							13.8%							

Watkins missed much of this past offseason with a broken bone in his foot. Watkins missed most of the 2015 offseason with hip surgery, was limited in training camp with a glute injury, then missed time with calf and ankle injuries. Maybe the problem is just working its way down and out of his system and Watkins is just a pinkie-toe strain away from 100 percent health.

Watkins averaged just 2.9 yards after the catch on passes labeled as "short" (less than 15 yards) on the official play-by-play. He was one of the best receivers in the nation with the ball in his hands in college, but Watkins was rarely targeted for screens or other ball-in-space plays last year. Many of his short catches were quick hitters in the flat from bunch formations; Watkins would catch a 3- or 4-yard pass between a defender and the sideline, leaving him little choice but to run out of bounds. The Bills were generally peculiar about getting Watkins the ball on non-bombs, which may have reflected Watkins' rustiness after a missed offseason, Tyrod Taylor's limitations, or just the generally inscrutability of the Bills offense.

When healthy, Watkins is one of the league's most talented receivers, but his statistics will remain disappointing as long as OTAs are convalescent periods and game plans remain arch-conservative.

Markus Wheaton

Height: 5-11   **Weight:** 189   **College:** Oregon   **Draft:** 2013/3 (79)   **Born:** 7-Feb-1991   **Age:** 25   **Risk:** Green

Year	Team	G/GS	Snaps	Rec	Pass	Yds	C%	+/-	Yd/C	TD	Drop	YAC	Rk	YAC+	BTkl	DVOA	Rk	DYAR	Rk	YAR	Short	Mid	Deep	Bomb
2013	PIT	12/1	159	6	13	64	46%	-1.4	10.7	0	0	6.0	--	+0.6	0	-30.5%	--	-18	--	-14	33%	42%	8%	17%
2014	PIT	16/11	745	53	86	644	62%	+4.7	12.2	2	1	3.2	76	-1.2	8	-0.2%	44	84	43	69	20%	52%	17%	11%
2015	PIT	16/8	699	44	79	749	56%	+0.0	17.0	5	3	3.6	66	-0.7	4	12.4%	21	159	27	140	22%	47%	15%	16%
2016	PIT			55	93	835	59%	--	15.2	5							7.5%							

For much of Wheaton's early career in Pittsburgh, he never looked to be on the same page with Ben Roethlisberger. In Weeks 6-10 last season, Wheaton was barely a participant in the offense, catching 7-of-14 targets for 45 yards. Then, in Seattle of all places, the explosion came: Wheaton caught 9 passes for 201 yards and a 69-yard touchdown. Wheaton's production picked up from there and he should be eyeing a career season in a contract year as the new No. 2 wideout thanks to Martavis Bryant's suspension. The skill set is not nearly as dynamic as Bryant's, but Wheaton can earn his spot in Pittsburgh, or sign big somewhere else, with a good 2016.

Kevin White

Height: 6-3   **Weight:** 215   **College:** West Virginia   **Draft:** 2015/1 (7)   **Born:** 25-Jun-1992   **Age:** 24   **Risk:** Red

Year	Team	G/GS	Snaps	Rec	Pass	Yds	C%	+/-	Yd/C	TD	Drop	YAC	Rk	YAC+	BTkl	DVOA	Rk	DYAR	Rk	YAR	Short	Mid	Deep	Bomb
2016	CHI			62	112	915	55%	--	14.8	6							-0.7%							

Injuries can happen to anyone, and you wouldn't think one lost season would torpedo a player's entire career, but the track record for first-round wide receivers who missed all or most of their rookie seasons is shockingly bad. Through 2014, there were 23 first-round wideouts who played in fewer than 10 games in their rookie seasons. Only four—Santana Moss (2001), Haywood Jeffires (1987), Mike Quick (1982), and Frank Lewis (1971)—ever had a 1,000-yard season. A handful of others, including Robert Meachem and Ike Hilliard, enjoyed long careers as role players in successful offenses. Still, this history paints a dim picture for White (and for Baltimore's Breshad Perriman).

White's entire rookie season was wiped out by stress fractures in his shin, but he claimed at OTAs that he had been 100 percent for months. Some reports had him looking "strong and fast" in June, while others called him a "work in progress," noting that he was dropping passes left and right. White's Playmaker Score coming out of college was underwhelming, but the Bears are hopeful he can develop the hands and routes to go with the 4.35-second 40 speed he flashed at the 2015 combine.

Roddy White

Height: 6-1 **Weight:** 201 **College:** Alabama-Birmingham **Draft:** 2005/1 (27) **Born:** 2-Nov-1981 **Age:** 35 **Risk:** N/A

Year	Team	G/GS	Snaps	Rec	Pass	Yds	C%	+/-	Yd/C	TD	Drop	YAC	Rk	YAC+	BTkl	DVOA	Rk	DYAR	Rk	YAR	Short	Mid	Deep	Bomb
2013	ATL	13/13	782	63	97	711	65%	+2.6	11.3	3	4	1.8	89	-2.3	0	2.7%	37	118	40	117	34%	45%	14%	6%
2014	ATL	14/14	870	80	125	921	64%	+3.0	11.5	7	5	2.3	85	-1.7	1	-1.3%	46	113	37	115	34%	46%	16%	4%
2015	ATL	16/16	936	43	70	506	61%	+1.6	11.8	1	2	2.4	85	-1.7	1	-8.5%	68	23	69	37	31%	48%	16%	4%

"At this point of my career, I don't want to be dragging my feet in Week 13 just to have an opportunity to be 4-10 next week," White told the *Atlanta Journal-Constitution*. He was linked to Tampa Bay right after he was cut by the Falcons, but the harsh truth is that White doesn't have a lot to offer at this point. He was a big part of the problem in Atlanta last season, no matter how much he wants to blame Kyle Shanahan for putting him in bad positions. White insists he wants to play, so we'll hold off on the career retrospective, but there's realistically not much more to be added to it.

Nick Williams

Height: 5-10 **Weight:** 184 **College:** Connecticut **Draft:** 2013/FA **Born:** 23-Nov-1990 **Age:** 26 **Risk:** Blue

Year	Team	G/GS	Snaps	Rec	Pass	Yds	C%	+/-	Yd/C	TD	Drop	YAC	Rk	YAC+	BTkl	DVOA	Rk	DYAR	Rk	YAR	Short	Mid	Deep	Bomb
2013	WAS	5/0	54	3	11	15	27%	-2.0	5.0	0	0	0.3	–	-3.3	0	-63.7%	–	-47	–	-53	38%	50%	13%	0%
2015	ATL	14/0	200	17	25	159	68%	-0.8	9.4	2	2	5.7	–	+0.5	1	0.8%	–	27	–	25	54%	38%	8%	0%
2016	ATL			12	21	127	57%	–	10.6	0						-18.8%								

Dear sports teams: There are too many Nick Williams(es). Please eliminate three. P.S.: I am NOT a crackpot. The non-Phillies prospect, non-defensive tackle Williams was an all-Big East kick returner. As a live body with working knowledge of how to catch balls, he was also targeted by Atlanta a few times last season.

Terrance Williams

Height: 6-2 **Weight:** 208 **College:** Baylor **Draft:** 2013/3 (74) **Born:** 18-Sep-1989 **Age:** 27 **Risk:** Yellow

Year	Team	G/GS	Snaps	Rec	Pass	Yds	C%	+/-	Yd/C	TD	Drop	YAC	Rk	YAC+	BTkl	DVOA	Rk	DYAR	Rk	YAR	Short	Mid	Deep	Bomb
2013	DAL	16/8	677	44	75	736	60%	+1.9	16.7	5	2	4.6	46	-0.1	3	3.0%	36	92	48	128	28%	41%	16%	15%
2014	DAL	16/16	811	37	65	621	57%	+3.4	16.8	8	2	3.0	78	-1.4	2	30.6%	2	220	21	239	17%	39%	19%	25%
2015	DAL	16/13	789	52	93	840	56%	-0.7	16.2	3	4	5.3	21	+0.8	5	7.4%	38	140	29	147	17%	45%	27%	11%
2016	DAL			57	96	896	59%	–	15.7	6						9.4%								

Williams ran headlong into the Peter Principle during his third season, turning from an excellent No. 2 option into an underwhelming No. 1 receiver when the Cowboys asked him to carry a heavier burden with Dez Bryant hobbled. Perhaps it's unfair to criticize Williams too harshly, as he still posted per-game and per-catch numbers which were largely in line with his career rates. But his sparkling 2014 DVOA suggested bigger things, and when given the opportunity to shine, Williams' alpha dog potential ended up being a mirage. Perhaps not coincidentally, Williams' receiving DVOA was an excellent 31.6% in the four games where Tony Romo suited up and a less impressive -2.1% in the 12 other games. Dallas did not add a single free agent or draft pick to its wide receiver corps this offseason, so for now, Williams' role is likely safe.

Albert Wilson

Height: 5-9 **Weight:** 200 **College:** Georgia State **Draft:** 2014/FA **Born:** 12-Jul-1992 **Age:** 24 **Risk:** Yellow

Year	Team	G/GS	Snaps	Rec	Pass	Yds	C%	+/-	Yd/C	TD	Drop	YAC	Rk	YAC+	BTkl	DVOA	Rk	DYAR	Rk	YAR	Short	Mid	Deep	Bomb
2014	KC	12/2	215	16	28	260	57%	-0.9	16.3	0	1	7.4	–	+2.7	6	14.8%	–	57	–	56	38%	38%	12%	12%
2015	KC	14/12	654	35	57	451	61%	-1.0	12.9	2	2	6.3	6	+1.0	10	1.5%	48	61	59	59	38%	36%	16%	11%
2016	KC			38	60	428	63%	–	11.3	2						-5.6%								

Last season, Wilson only ran 10.8 percent of his routes from the slot, perhaps surprising for a receiver of his height. In offseason workouts, the Chiefs were putting Wilson in the slot more often, perhaps foreshadowing more targets from his short-route-loving quarterback. Last season, Wilson was already the unusual receiver who had a higher DVOA on short routes (5.0%, 43 targets) than on long ones (-9.1%, 15 targets).

Marquess Wilson Height: 6-3   Weight: 194   College: Washington State   Draft: 2013/7 (236)   Born: 14-Sep-1992   Age: 24   Risk: Yellow

Year	Team	G/GS	Snaps	Rec	Pass	Yds	C%	+/-	Yd/C	TD	Drop	YAC	Rk	YAC+	BTkl	DVOA	Rk	DYAR	Rk	YAR	Short	Mid	Deep	Bomb
2013	CHI	10/1	75	2	3	13	67%	+0.5	6.5	0	0	4.5	--	-2.7	3	-38.5%	--	-7	--	-5	33%	67%	0%	0%
2014	CHI	7/6	373	17	32	140	53%	-2.8	8.2	1	3	3.0	--	-1.0	1	-25.0%	--	-31	--	-34	45%	36%	9%	9%
2015	CHI	11/6	641	28	51	464	55%	+0.6	16.6	1	3	6.6	4	+2.0	4	17.0%	11	127	34	112	28%	32%	22%	18%
2016	CHI			13	24	179	54%	--	13.7	2						-6.3%								

Like most Chicago wide receivers, Wilson was hurt last year, his season ending due to a broken foot in Week 12. Wilson was considered to be on the bubble to make the roster in 2016; if that was the case, his job might have been saved when he broke the same foot in June, making him a candidate to start the season on the reserve/PUP list. Wilson's injury opens the door for Josh Bellamy to step into Chicago's fourth receiver position.

Robert Woods Height: 6-0   Weight: 201   College: USC   Draft: 2013/2 (41)   Born: 10-Apr-1992   Age: 24   Risk: Green

Year	Team	G/GS	Snaps	Rec	Pass	Yds	C%	+/-	Yd/C	TD	Drop	YAC	Rk	YAC+	BTkl	DVOA	Rk	DYAR	Rk	YAR	Short	Mid	Deep	Bomb
2013	BUF	14/14	910	40	85	587	47%	-6.0	14.7	3	1	2.8	85	-1.4	2	-11.7%	72	6	72	-6	19%	46%	23%	12%
2014	BUF	16/15	899	65	104	699	63%	-0.3	10.8	5	5	3.1	77	-1.9	2	-11.4%	65	11	64	12	43%	32%	19%	7%
2015	BUF	14/9	774	47	80	552	59%	-2.8	11.7	3	2	3.3	72	-0.7	3	-14.6%	78	-12	79	-3	26%	55%	12%	8%
2016	BUF			58	94	689	62%	--	11.9	4						-4.9%								

A very ordinary short-route possession receiver with a tendency to draw flags when he tries to block (six penalties last year, most for holding or peelbacks), Woods somehow walked away from the offseason with the Bills' No. 2 role all sewn up. Chris Hogan left for New England, Percy Harvin either retired or disappeared like the Cheshire Cat, and Marquise Goodwin focused on the Olympics, leaving Greg Salas and Kolby Listenbee as the top competitors with Woods for playing time. Woods is effective enough on underneath routes to catch 80 passes (for 801 yards and four touchdowns) in the right system. He's in just the opposite of a right system.

Jarius Wright Height: 5-10   Weight: 182   College: Arkansas   Draft: 2012/4 (118)   Born: 25-Nov-1989   Age: 27   Risk: Green

Year	Team	G/GS	Snaps	Rec	Pass	Yds	C%	+/-	Yd/C	TD	Drop	YAC	Rk	YAC+	BTkl	DVOA	Rk	DYAR	Rk	YAR	Short	Mid	Deep	Bomb
2013	MIN	16/3	417	26	43	434	60%	+3.4	16.7	3	1	4.5	--	-0.4	4	22.7%	--	117	--	109	30%	28%	30%	13%
2014	MIN	16/7	512	42	62	588	68%	+3.3	14.0	2	3	7.8	2	+2.2	3	0.7%	41	64	51	86	44%	31%	12%	14%
2015	MIN	16/3	431	34	50	442	68%	+5.2	13.0	0	2	5.1	24	+0.2	3	7.6%	36	78	51	68	40%	31%	24%	4%
2016	MIN			42	67	505	63%	--	12.0	1						-4.7%								

Wright signed a contract extension just before the 2015 season started that will make him Minnesota's highest-paid receiver this fall. That's one deal that Rick Spielman would probably like to have back—we're four seasons into Wright's career now, and he has rarely looked like anything more than a marginal possession receiver. Wright has said that he wants to be a starter, but playing behind Stefon Diggs and Laquon Treadwell, that seems unlikely.

Kendall Wright Height: 5-10   Weight: 196   College: Baylor   Draft: 2012/1 (20)   Born: 12-Nov-1989   Age: 27   Risk: Green

Year	Team	G/GS	Snaps	Rec	Pass	Yds	C%	+/-	Yd/C	TD	Drop	YAC	Rk	YAC+	BTkl	DVOA	Rk	DYAR	Rk	YAR	Short	Mid	Deep	Bomb
2013	TEN	16/12	808	94	140	1079	67%	+2.3	11.5	2	8	5.9	11	+0.6	14	-3.7%	59	95	47	96	49%	33%	13%	5%
2014	TEN	14/11	662	57	93	715	61%	-1.2	12.5	6	1	6.4	8	+0.8	14	-3.3%	49	67	50	48	46%	26%	18%	9%
2015	TEN	10/9	412	36	60	408	60%	+0.3	11.3	3	3	4.0	55	-0.9	8	-8.1%	66	21	70	17	29%	46%	12%	14%
2016	TEN			59	100	726	59%	--	12.3	6						-3.8%								

Wright caught 13 passes for 213 yards and two touchdowns over the first three weeks of the 2015 season, and it appeared that he was going to be the biggest benefactor of Marcus Mariota's presence in the Titans offense. His season was ultimately derailed by injuries to both Mariota and himself, limiting his output to just 23 catches for 195 yards and one score over the rest of the year. Wright excels on short and intermediate routes and can be a constant threat in space with the ball in his hands. He needs a quarterback who can throw with timing and accuracy to get the most out of his skill set. Mariota thrives in those areas, so he should allow Wright to prosper. The Titans offense as a whole needs to be more stable for the duo to highlight each other's quality, though.

Going Deep

Jared Abbrederis, GB: Abbrederis had 16 targets in the regular season, then 16 more in the playoffs as Green Bay receivers started filling up the trainer's room. In all those postseason targets, though, he had only six catches for 69 yards. In the regular season, he had nine catches for 111 yards with -36.2% DVOA. Unlikely to make the team this year.

Demarcus Ayers, PIT: Ayers is a slot receiver, but the seventh-round pick from the University of Houston can best help himself make the team by putting in work on special teams. Kick returner is where Pittsburgh can really use some help, and he may factor into that battle. Pittsburgh has four locks at wide receiver, but there is definitely a spot or two available for Ayers to make the team.

Josh Bellamy, CHI: After bouncing from one special teams roster to another for several years, Bellamy finally saw extended time at wide receiver for Chicago last season and was surprisingly effective. Marquess Wilson's injury means Bellamy will start the year as the Bears' fourth receiver; the Bears would be happy to see him pass Eddie Royal for the third spot as well. (2015 stats: 19-of-34, 224 yards, 2 TD, -16.8% DVOA.)

Kenny Bell, TB: A 2015 fifth-round pick out of Nebraska who was stashed on injured reserve after a hamstring injury. Bell comes with risk, but he is also extremely polished and more physical than you would expect a 197-pounder to be. He has some tweener fit to him because of the size, but he has the skill set to play a huge role in the Tampa Bay offense. And on this depth chart, talent will play. He's a deep sleeper, but keep an eye on him near the end of your fantasy drafts if he gets training camp and preseason buzz.

Moritz Boehringer, MIN: Boehringer ist der erste europäische Spieler in der NFL Draft ausgewählt zu werden, ohne College-Football zu spielen. Zuletzt für die Unicorns Schwäbisch Hall gesehen spielt der Deutschen Fußball-Liga, er ist groß (6- Fuß -4) und schnell (4,43 Sekunden 40) und dem Vernehmen nach in Wikinger Lager ohne Idee kam , was er tat und wenig Geschick fangen ein Fußball. Ein langer Schuss das Team zu machen .

Quan Bray, IND: An undrafted rookie out of Auburn, Bray moved from the practice squad to the active roster at midseason, and from the active roster to the field as the punt and kickoff returner. He was a bit better than average at both tasks, and a significant upgrade on what else the Colts had trotted out there. If there is an offensive breakout coming after he played just four snaps there in 2015, no signs of it have been spotted yet. But the Colts' depth chart at receiver is a wasteland after the top three guys.

Jaron Brown, ARI: When you have the best wide receiver corps in the league, you can say silly things like "Arizona has the best WR5 in the NFL!" Yes, Brown might be able to make that claim, but we rarely talk about WR5s since they don't see the field much. In Arizona, Brown has caught at least 11 passes in all three of his years, and he could step up in case an injury occurs to one of the top guys. He just lacks the speed of J.J. Nelson, the physical threat of Michael Floyd, and the consistency of Larry Fitzgerald and John Brown. (2015 stats: 11-for-23, 144 yards, 1 TD, -16.1% DVOA.)

Andre Caldwell, DET: Caldwell is on the fringes of the Lions' potential 53-man roster, competing with a number of other veterans including Jeremy Kerley, Andre Roberts, and Corey Fuller. Caldwell's potential usefulness for depth on kickoff returns could see him onto the roster. (2015 stats: 10-of-22, 72 yards, 2 TD, -39.8% DVOA.)

Michael Campanaro, BAL: A series of injuries have limited Campanaro to just eight games in two years. Facing so much competition at wide receiver, Campanaro's argument to make the team is that he can be a productive slot receiver if given the chance. Baltimore is lacking in that area, so a diverse skill set might help Campanaro hang on if he can stay out of the trainer's room.

Marquise Goodwin, BUF: Goodwin focused on Olympic track this offseason; he won a silver medal in the long jump in last year's Pan Am games and remains one of the most athletic individuals in the NFL. Assuming he remains in the NFL, of course. Goodwin missed most of last season with broken ribs and certainly seems more enthusiastic about Olympic glory than getting tackled. Bills general manager Greg Whaley has a thing for extreme athleticism at wide receiver, which is why he has shown extra patience with both Goodwin and Percy Harvin. But rookie Kolby Listenbee is pretty darn fast and wants to play football, which will probably give him the leg up on the Bills' screen-and-bomb role that no one appears to want.

Rashard Higgins, CLE: "Hollywood" Higgins put up big numbers at Colorado State—238 catches, 3,648 yards and 31 touchdowns in three seasons at Fort Collins. Unfortunately, he ran a pedestrian 4.64 40-yard dash at the combine, dropping his value to the fifth round, where the Browns scooped him up. Rangy, athletic, and very good at plucking the ball at its apogee, Higgins has a chance to be a playmaker, though adding strength will be crucial. Outfighting corners in the Mountain West is one thing, but it'll take more than mad ups to snag passes on the perimeter in the NFL. One thing for sure—his outgoing personality and throwback high-top fade should make Higgins one of the more popular players of this new era in Browns Town.

Tyreek Hill, KC: A controversial fifth-round pick by Kansas City. Hill played at West Alabama last season after being forced to leave Oklahoma State for assaulting his pregnant girlfriend. He had 465 yards on kick returns last season, and only 444 yards on receptions. Likely useful for special teams only.

Jeff Janis, GB: Last seen catching seven passes for 145 yards and two scores in the playoff loss to Arizona (including the game-tying Hail Mary, and 101 total yards on the final drive). Janis will fight for the third receiver spot (and kickoff return job) this fall. Before we raise our expectations too high, let's remember that last year at this time, we were wondering how Chris Matthews would follow up on his 109-yard, nigh-MVP performance in the Super Bowl against New England. Well, he followed it up by getting cut in November. (2015 stats: 2-of-12, 79 yards, -17.0% DVOA.)

Darius Jennings, CLE: First Jennings coughed up his No. 10 jersey number to incoming reclamation project Robert Griffin III. Then he was slapped across the other cheek when the Browns drafted numerous receivers, clearly hoping that they wouldn't have to issue Jennings any other numbers. Jennings has some special teams value, which be his saving grace come preseason. (2015 stats: 14-of-21, 118 yards, -36.8% DVOA.)

Cody Latimer, DEN: It's make-it-or-break-it time for Latimer, who went ahead of both Allen Robinson and Jarvis Landry in the 2014 draft. Latimer has personified the concept of draft bust so far. Yes, he has Demaryius Thomas and Emmanuel Sanders ahead of him on the depth chart, but that doesn't explain why he also fell behind Bennie Fowler, Jordan Norwood, and Andre Caldwell. Latimer is in the race for this year's No. 3 wide receiver role, but he is certainly not the favorite. (2015 stats: 6-of-11, 59 yards, 1 TD, 7.5% DVOA.)

Kenny Lawler, SEA: Lawler was Jared Goff's touchdown target at Cal, but he slipped to the seventh round of the draft while his quarterback went first overall. He has a good shot to be Seattle's fifth wideout because his size, catch radius, and red zone ability give him a different skill set than the other four.

Kolby Listenbee, BUF: This sixth-round pick is a blessedly fast deep threat from Texas Christian. He caught 30 passes for 19.9 yards per reception last year, usually hauling in a bomb or two per game from Trevone Boykin when all of the coverage was rolled to Josh Doctson's side of the field. Listenbee became a #DraftTwitter binky, because #DraftTwitter doesn't realize that the Big 12 is practically a high-profile sandlot league in terms of offensive production and doesn't notice when a receiver makes all his plays against a No. 2 cornerback with no safety help. The Bills have been searching for a speedster to run fly routes and draw safeties away from Sammy Watkins, and all of their other choices try out for the Olympics or spend months contemplating retirement instead.

Ricardo Louis, CLE: This Cleveland fourth-round selection is best remembered as the Auburn wide receiver who hauled in the miracle deflection of 2014 against Georgia. Louis is a boom-or-bust type, with good speed but a 55 percent catch rate. He admitted that he didn't get much development in Gus Malzahn's offense, so the learning curve to Hue Jackson's scheme will be steep as the Himalayas.

Marc Mariani, CHI: With all of Chicago's wideouts broken, the veteran kick returner spent more time on offense than ever before, and he was shockingly effective, with an 18.8% DVOA on 33 targets. Everyone else is healthy now, though, which means Mariani will have to earn his new one-year, $840,000 contract exclusively as a returner again. (2015 stats: 22-of-33, 300 yards, 18.8% DVOA.)

Cameron Meredith, CHI: You know your wideouts are damaged when you're throwing passes to undrafted rookies from Illinois State. It was a good local-kid-makes-good story (Meredith went to high school at St. Joseph's in the Chicago suburb of Westchester), but Meredith enters camp this year as the seventh wideout at best and is a longshot to make the team. (2015 stats: 11-of-16, 120 yards, -6.3% DVOA.)

Braxton Miller, HOU: The former quarterback converted to wide receiver his final season at Ohio State. He had just 341 receiving yards on a loaded Buckeyes team that threw the ball around, but has the athleticism to do a lot more, including taking carries out of the backfield and even serving as a Wildcat quarterback. He described his likely 2016 role as a "playmaker," which customarily means he won't get many touches as a rookie and too many of them will be at or behind the line of scrimmage.

Malcolm Mitchell, NE: Author of the children's book The Magic Hat, Mitchell was not allowed to appear in any promotional materials for the book wearing Georgia Bulldogs gear or even mentioning his college football semi-stardom, lest the NCAA renounce his eligibility and accuse him of war crimes. Now he's in the emotionally open and forthcoming Land o' Belichick, where his next children's book will just be 32 blank pages. Mitchell is a tall, sure-handed receiver who ran pretty good routes in college and has a no-nonsense attitude and outstanding character. For some reason, the Patriots have a miserable track record with receivers like him.

Chris Moore, BAL: Oh look, another Baltimore wideout. To be fair, this team needs a young, healthy receiver with a chance to be part of the long-term plan. Moore can be brought along slowly, but there's not much more to his game than running go routes, which shouldn't bother Joe Flacco. A fourth-round rookie, Moore averaged 22.1 yards per catch for the Cincinnati Bearcats in 2015.

Cordarrelle Patterson, MIN: A victim of bad timing, Patterson is undoubtedly one of the all-time great kickoff returners (his 30.1-yard career average is second only to Gale Sayers' 30.6) who happens to play in an era when the NFL is doing nearly all it can to limit kickoff returns. That's unfortunate, because as electrifying as Patterson is on special teams, he is a dirt-terrible wide receiver, and his team knows it. Despite a limited passing game, Minnesota stopped trying to make Patterson the wide receiver happen, throwing him two passes in 16 games after 144 targets in his first two seasons. Yes, he is also a dangerous runner, with a 12.1-yard average and four touchdowns on 24 career carries, but Patterson's self-admitted laziness has left him far short of his potential.

Jordan Payton, CLE: One of the horde of rookie wideouts in Cleveland, Payton profiles as an inside, move-the-chains type. Since he's African-American, let's go out of our way to compare him to Julian Edelman for kicks, though Payton's preferred pro comp would be former Bengal T.J. Houshmandzadeh. (Payton's older brother Michael was a teammate and close friend of Houshmandzadeh at Oregon State.) Well more than half of Payton's targets last season at UCLA were within ten yards of the line of scrimmage, while he struggles to separate on deeper routes. He also showed very good blocking skills, which will always endear a receiver to a coach—in this case, Houshmandzadeh's former position coach, Hue Jackson, who is now head coach of Payton's new team.

Terrelle Pryor, CLE: Pryor has finally embraced the fact that he won't be playing pro quarterback. That doesn't mean he will make it at his new position, of course, but at least he's sitting in the wide receivers meeting room without craning his neck and trying to catch a glimpse of what is going on over with the passers. His extreme athleticism and big frame tantalize coaches, in particular Hue Jackson, who tried Pryor in Cincinnati and is giving him another crack with the Browns. But with the deep aggregation of actual wideouts in camp, Pryor will have to do more than just commit to the position in order to stick.

Keenan Reynolds, BAL: Reynolds was very prolific in Navy's triple-option offense, and he was instantly willing to make the conversion from quarterback to wide receiver after Baltimore chose him in the sixth round of this April's draft. There may be some interesting ways to work him into the offense right away, but chances are special teams will be his key to fighting through the receiver logjam to make this roster.

Demarcus Robinson, KC: Robinson was drafted in the fourth round, about two rounds higher than most draft projections (NFL.com projected Round 6 or 7). But our Playmaker Rating for Robinson ranked him 14th amongst this year's wide receivers, and so it's fitting that he was the 14th receiver selected.

Eli Rogers, PIT: This 2015 UDFA played three years with Teddy Bridgewater at Louisville. He had one of the most consistent college careers you'll ever see, catching 41 to 46 passes for roughly 500 yards in each of his four seasons. The only problem is that Rogers never improved his marginal production, and it is hard to see him cracking Pittsburgh's talented lineup at the position this year. But the Martavis Bryant suspension does open up a roster spot, and Pittsburgh has carried six wideouts in the past.

Eric Rogers, SF: We probably have grown tired of these all-stars from up north trying to join the NFL (see: Duron Carter), but Rogers has a shot to make the 49ers just because of how little there is at the wide receiver position. He reportedly visited 16 different NFL teams before signing with San Francisco, which was probably the wisest choice in maximizing his probability of making a 53-man roster this September. Rogers has good size, he's only 25, and he both led the CFL in receiving yards (1,448) and tied for the lead in touchdowns (10) last year.

Jerome Simpson, SF: Simpson was a second-round pick in 2008, and all we have really gotten to know him for in that time is his front-flip touchdown in 2011, and several drug-related incidents that have led to suspensions and a police investigation. Simpson only caught 5-of-19 targets in San Francisco last year, with 54 yards and a touchdown, but 10 of the incompletions were defensed or underthrown. He had one drop.

DeAndre Smelter, SF: The latest in a long line of oversized freak athlete wideouts from Georgia Tech who are difficult to evaluate because they played in the Yellow Jackets' run-heavy option offense. Smelter was a fourth-round pick a year ago but took a redshirt year because of a late 2014 ACL tear.

Griff Whalen, MIA: The Stanford connection in action: on 14 targets from Andrew Luck, Whalen had 12 receptions for 151 yards and a 69.3% DVOA. On 12 targets from non-Luck Colts passers, Whalen had seven catches for 54 yards and a -48.6% DVOA before heading to injured reserve. (Not included in those stats: snapping the ball on the worst fake punt we've ever seen.) Now in Miami, where he does not have Luck but does have coach Clyde Christensen and another shot at a fifth receiver job.

DeAndrew White, SF: White made the 53-man roster in San Francisco after a strong finish to his preseason, but he only caught two passes in 30 offensive snaps in the regular season. Even with a lean receiving corps, White will have to show more this year to make the team again.

Lucky Whitehead, DAL: An undrafted rookie, Whitehead got his break as a result of the Cowboys' offensive injuries and incompetence. Beginning in Week 7, the Florida Atlantic product carved out a niche as a speedy threat on screens, end arounds, and returns. Whitehead struggled as a punt returner, at one point fielding a punt on the 1-yard line, but was a borderline top-10 kick returner, adding 1.9 points in value on just 16 return attempts. He also caught 6-of-8 passes for only 16 yards and had 10 runs for 107 yards. Given the uniqueness of his skill set, expect Whitehead to stick around for some specialty plays in 2016.

Tyrell Williams, SD: A 2015 UDFA from Division II Western Oregon, Williams caught an 80-yard touchdown from Philip Rivers in Week 17. He's 6-foot-4 and runs a 4.43 40, but of course has very little experience with the complexity of the pro game and the quality of competition that he faces in the NFL.

Tight Ends

Top 20 TE by DYAR (Total Value), 2015

Rank	Player	Team	DYAR
1	T.Eifert	CIN	247
2	R.Gronkowski	NE	235
3	G.Barnidge	CLE	218
4	J.Reed	WAS	206
5	D.Walker	TEN	174
6	G.Olsen	CAR	132
7	A.Gates	SD	113
8	J.Graham	SEA	110
9	T.Kelce	KC	110
10	B.Celek	PHI	107
11	Z.Miller	CHI	104
12	C.Gillmore	BAL	95
13	B.Watson	NO	87
14	Dar.Fells	ARI	86
15	C.Brate	TB	81
16	L.Green	SD	78
17	J.Tamme	ATL	68
18	E.Ebron	DET	64
19	Z.Ertz	PHI	56
20	W.Tye	NYG	51

Top 20 TE by DVOA (Value per Play), 2015

Rank	Player	Team	DVOA
1	T.Eifert	CIN	42.0%
2	B.Celek	PHI	36.8%
3	Dar.Fells	ARI	35.8%
4	C.Brate	TB	33.6%
5	Z.Miller	CHI	25.6%
6	C.Gillmore	BAL	22.7%
7	R.Gronkowski	NE	21.0%
8	J.Reed	WAS	20.1%
9	G.Barnidge	CLE	19.7%
10	J.Graham	SEA	14.8%
11	A.Gates	SD	13.1%
12	D.Walker	TEN	13.0%
13	L.Green	SD	11.8%
14	R.Griffin	HOU	11.5%
15	L.Willson	SEA	10.5%
16	T.Kelce	KC	9.3%
17	G.Olsen	CAR	8.9%
18	E.Ebron	DET	6.5%
19	S.Chandler	NE	5.8%
20	J.Tamme	ATL	5.7%

Minimum 25 targets

Dwayne Allen

Height: 6-3 Weight: 255 College: Clemson Draft: 2012/3 (64) Born: 24-Feb-1990 Age: 26 Risk: Yellow

Year	Team	G/GS	Snaps	Rec	Pass	Yds	C%	+/-	Yd/C	TD	Drop	YAC	Rk	YAC+	BTkl	DVOA	Rk	DYAR	Rk	YAR	Short	Mid	Deep	Bomb
2013	IND	1/1	30	1	2	20	50%	-0.1	20.0	1	0	5.0	--	+1.0	1	84.3%	--	12	--	14	0%	50%	50%	0%
2014	IND	13/13	619	29	50	395	58%	-2.7	13.6	8	4	5.6	13	+1.2	3	22.7%	6	104	12	91	34%	46%	16%	4%
2015	IND	13/12	509	16	29	109	55%	-1.7	6.8	1	0	3.1	46	-1.5	0	-31.4%	49	-48	45	-59	56%	37%	7%	0%
2016	IND			48	76	572	63%	--	11.9	7						8.1%								

The 2016 Colts will be running Rob Chudzinski's offense. That was news to Allen's ears after he was targeted just 29 times in 2015, and enough to convince him to accept Indianapolis' offer of $29 million over four seasons to not go anywhere. He is a quality blocker at the point of attack, and a solid receiver even if not as explosive as the league's top receiving tight ends. If he can stay on the field for all 16 games for the first time since his rookie season, his numbers should take a big jump.

Jace Amaro

Height: 6-5 Weight: 265 College: Texas Tech Draft: 2014/2 (49) Born: 6/26/1992 Age: 24 Risk: Green

Year	Team	G/GS	Snaps	Rec	Pass	Yds	C%	+/-	Yd/C	TD	Drop	YAC	Rk	YAC+	BTkl	DVOA	Rk	DYAR	Rk	YAR	Short	Mid	Deep	Bomb
2014	NYJ	14/4	374	38	53	345	72%	+2.3	9.1	2	6	4.4	23	-0.7	2	-7.0%	32	1	32	-1	58%	33%	8%	2%
2016	NYJ			39	60	401	65%	--	10.3	2						-6.1%								

Amaro tore a labrum at the end of the preseason and missed the entire 2015 season. He was a pass-dropping disaster with no big-play capability as a rookie. Todd Bowles made some rather dismissive remarks about Amaro during OTAs: "He's competing for a spot like everybody else … He missed a year. I haven't seen him play yet." Bowles hinted that Amaro will have to make the team as an H-back, a far cry from the playmaker the previous Jets regime thought they drafted. Chan Gailey has coached everyone from Jay Novacek to Tony Gonzalez and would happily feature the tight end in his offense, but he won't bother if there is no tight end worth featuring.

Gary Barnidge   Height: 6-6   Weight: 243   College: Louisville   Draft: 2008/5 (141)   Born: 22-Sep-1985   Age: 31   Risk: Red

Year	Team	G/GS	Snaps	Rec	Pass	Yds	C%	+/-	Yd/C	TD	Drop	YAC	Rk	YAC+	BTkl	DVOA	Rk	DYAR	Rk	YAR	Short	Mid	Deep	Bomb
2013	CLE	16/12	529	13	18	127	72%	+0.7	9.8	2	0	7.0	--	+2.1	0	-10.7%	--	-4	--	3	71%	18%	6%	6%
2014	CLE	13/2	358	13	25	156	52%	-2.8	12.0	0	0	3.2	43	-1.4	2	-0.3%	27	10	29	-5	46%	29%	21%	4%
2015	CLE	16/13	942	79	125	1043	63%	+1.5	13.2	9	4	4.6	24	+0.3	8	19.7%	9	218	3	188	35%	51%	13%	1%
2016	CLE			70	111	842	63%	--	12.0	6						6.4%								

If Barnidge played for any other team, his improbable late-career explosion would have been a much bigger story. During his first seven seasons, Barnidge amassed a total of 43 catches and three touchdowns. In 2015, with the tragicomic Browns quarterback corps tossing him passes, he nearly doubled his career catch total, and tripled his touchdown total. Players over the age of 30 hardly ever post career years that far outside of their proven capabilities. The bust-out earned Barnidge, who underwent sports hernia surgery in the offseason, a new three-year, $12 million deal—a tip of the hat for his unlikely breakout, while not so much dough that the team will agonize should his 2015 be a one-off, which is highly possible.

Martellus Bennett   Height: 6-6   Weight: 259   College: Texas A&M   Draft: 2008/2 (61)   Born: 10-Mar-1987   Age: 29   Risk: Red

Year	Team	G/GS	Snaps	Rec	Pass	Yds	C%	+/-	Yd/C	TD	Drop	YAC	Rk	YAC+	BTkl	DVOA	Rk	DYAR	Rk	YAR	Short	Mid	Deep	Bomb
2013	CHI	16/15	951	65	94	759	69%	+5.9	11.7	5	5	5.7	11	+0.4	14	3.4%	23	65	16	59	51%	38%	7%	5%
2014	CHI	16/15	954	90	128	916	70%	+1.6	10.2	6	8	5.0	17	-0.1	19	3.0%	20	88	14	51	57%	31%	12%	1%
2015	CHI	11/11	728	53	80	439	66%	-0.9	8.3	3	3	4.3	31	-1.0	9	-10.7%	35	-18	38	-30	55%	29%	13%	4%
2016	NE			46	74	500	62%	--	10.9	4						-2.3%								

With Chicago's top wide receivers spending more time in the training room than on the field, Bennett was often the top priority for opposing defenses, and his totals and rate stats plummeted as a result. Then he missed the final four games of the season with allegedly injured ribs, but Dan Wiederer of the *Chicago Tribune* later reported that Bennett had been healthy, and the Bears had reported a phony injury to begin a divorce process that was completed in an offseason trade to New England. Bennett had already worn out his welcome with the Cowboys and Giants, and his vocal and emotional nature made him a bad fit in the buttoned-down culture John Fox is trying to build in Chicago. The Patriots, though, have a long history of success with players who burned bridges elsewhere, from Corey Dillon to Randy Moss to LeGarrette Blount. And on the field, Bennett seems a perfect fit as the second piece in what figures to be a heavy dose of two-tight end sets with Rob Gronkowski. All that and a sixth-round draft pick for the low cost of a fourth-rounder? This might have been the best deal of the offseason.

Cameron Brate   Height: 6-5   Weight: 235   College: Harvard   Draft: 2014/FA   Born: 13-Jul-1991   Age: 25   Risk: Green

Year	Team	G/GS	Snaps	Rec	Pass	Yds	C%	+/-	Yd/C	TD	Drop	YAC	Rk	YAC+	BTkl	DVOA	Rk	DYAR	Rk	YAR	Short	Mid	Deep	Bomb
2014	TB	5/1	44	1	1	17	100%	+0.3	17.0	0	0	4.0	--	-0.3	0	114.4%	--	9	--	8	0%	100%	0%	0%
2015	TB	14/4	341	23	30	288	77%	+3.8	12.5	3	0	2.2	51	-2.0	1	33.6%	4	81	15	85	23%	50%	20%	7%
2016	TB			28	43	277	65%	--	9.9	2						-6.5%								

You mean there's another Harvard kid besides Ryan Fitzpatrick? Yes, and he had a big year in relief of Austin Sefarian-Jenkins. He's more of a fourth- or fifth-wheel in a functioning offense than some sort of burgeoning star. Then again, with Sefarian-Jenkins on the hot seat at OTAs and Dirk Koetter talking Brate up, maybe he's this year's Gary Barnidge. Either way, he made a nice find as the organization struggled to find Jameis Winston targets last year.

Jordan Cameron   Height: 6-5   Weight: 220   College: USC   Draft: 2011/4 (102)   Born: 7-Aug-1988   Age: 28   Risk: Green

Year	Team	G/GS	Snaps	Rec	Pass	Yds	C%	+/-	Yd/C	TD	Drop	YAC	Rk	YAC+	BTkl	DVOA	Rk	DYAR	Rk	YAR	Short	Mid	Deep	Bomb
2013	CLE	15/14	969	80	118	917	68%	+11.6	11.5	7	1	3.0	45	-1.6	0	5.6%	21	99	9	79	39%	40%	15%	6%
2014	CLE	10/9	475	24	48	424	50%	-5.0	17.7	2	1	7.0	5	+1.9	0	-17.5%	38	-34	40	-30	45%	28%	19%	9%
2015	MIA	16/16	744	35	70	386	50%	-5.2	11.0	3	1	2.3	50	-1.9	2	-17.9%	42	-50	47	-65	34%	43%	10%	13%
2016	MIA			43	75	446	57%	--	10.4	4						-6.2%								

The Dolphins spent $15 million over two years on a player, then forgot about him? Shocking! As soon as the Dan Campbell Clan took over the coaching staff, Cameron went from two or three catches per game (often on eight or nine targets) to a long series of one-catch, 5-yard type stat lines. No explanation was given, because real men like Campbell don't explain themselves.

Cameron accepted a pay cut to stay in Miami, and the Adam Gase staff believes Cameron was misused last year, which is something that can be said about 70 percent of the Dolphins' offensive contributors.

Brent Celek Height: 6-4   Weight: 261   College: Cincinnati   Draft: 2007/5 (162)   Born: 25-Jan-1985   Age: 31   Risk: Green

Year	Team	G/GS	Snaps	Rec	Pass	Yds	C%	+/-	Yd/C	TD	Drop	YAC	Rk	YAC+	BTkl	DVOA	Rk	DYAR	Rk	YAR	Short	Mid	Deep	Bomb
2013	PHI	16/15	845	32	51	502	63%	+0.7	15.7	6	3	8.8	5	+3.2	2	18.3%	10	89	12	100	52%	23%	21%	4%
2014	PHI	16/15	815	32	51	340	63%	-0.0	10.6	1	2	4.1	27	-1.1	2	-20.8%	42	-49	43	-58	53%	26%	15%	6%
2015	PHI	16/13	601	27	35	398	77%	+6.5	14.7	3	0	6.3	7	+2.1	1	36.8%	2	107	10	116	34%	47%	19%	0%
2016	PHI			26	40	272	65%	--	10.5	2						-0.8%								

Though he has taken a back seat to Zach Ertz the past two seasons, the 31-year-old Celek has arguably become a better player by maximizing his more limited opportunities. Celek posted the best receiving DVOA of his nine-year career in 2016, as well as his highest DYAR figure since 2009. Though he only received five targets inside the 20 all season, he caught all of them and turned three of those catches into touchdowns. The Eagles rewarded that efficiency with a three-year extension this offseason, paying Celek like a borderline No. 1 tight end in the process. Multi-tight end sets were vital to Doug Pederson's offense in Kansas City, so if anything, the veteran figures to see an increase in his workload this season. There are a few too many targets and not enough consistency at the quarterback position to make Celek a viable standard-league fantasy option, but he should continue providing plenty of run-blocking and receiving value to the Eagles.

Garrett Celek Height: 6-5   Weight: 252   College: Michigan State   Draft: 2012/FA   Born: 29-May-1988   Age: 28   Risk: Green

Year	Team	G/GS	Snaps	Rec	Pass	Yds	C%	+/-	Yd/C	TD	Drop	YAC	Rk	YAC+	BTkl	DVOA	Rk	DYAR	Rk	YAR	Short	Mid	Deep	Bomb
2013	SF	12/1	123	2	4	38	50%	-0.5	19.0	0	1	11.0	--	+5.7	0	-91.9%	--	-19	--	-20	25%	50%	25%	0%
2014	SF	3/1	35	2	2	53	100%	+1.2	26.5	0	0	3.5	--	-2.8	0	169.2%	--	24	--	23	0%	0%	50%	50%
2015	SF	11/8	399	19	28	186	68%	+1.1	9.8	3	0	5.2	17	+0.5	1	5.4%	21	25	29	29	62%	27%	12%	0%
2016	SF			27	42	230	64%	--	8.5	1						-16.7%								

Chip Kelly is used to having a second tight end named Celek, but Garrett is no Brent in the receiving department. Kelly may convert the weekly Bruce Miller catch into a Celek dumpoff, but do not expect much production from the backup tight end.

Scott Chandler Height: 6-7   Weight: 270   College: Iowa   Draft: 2007/4 (129)   Born: 23-Jul-1985   Age: 31   Risk: N/A

Year	Team	G/GS	Snaps	Rec	Pass	Yds	C%	+/-	Yd/C	TD	Drop	YAC	Rk	YAC+	BTkl	DVOA	Rk	DYAR	Rk	YAR	Short	Mid	Deep	Bomb
2013	BUF	16/7	918	53	81	655	65%	+3.6	12.4	2	4	5.2	15	+0.7	3	-1.3%	33	32	28	26	39%	44%	16%	1%
2014	BUF	16/5	749	47	70	497	67%	+2.6	10.6	3	5	4.1	28	-0.7	1	-3.6%	28	17	26	36	52%	34%	12%	1%
2015	NE	15/4	381	23	42	259	55%	-3.1	11.3	4	1	3.1	45	-0.9	2	5.8%	19	39	23	32	36%	38%	19%	7%

Chandler underwent knee surgery in April and is expected to at least miss the 2016 season. His career is probably over. He only got to enjoy one year of life as the No. 2 tight end for the Patriots, where you often get covered by a linebacker or quality control coach in the red zone.

Charles Clay Height: 6-3   Weight: 239   College: Tulsa   Draft: 2011/6 (174)   Born: 13-Feb-1989   Age: 27   Risk: Green

Year	Team	G/GS	Snaps	Rec	Pass	Yds	C%	+/-	Yd/C	TD	Drop	YAC	Rk	YAC+	BTkl	DVOA	Rk	DYAR	Rk	YAR	Short	Mid	Deep	Bomb
2013	MIA	16/15	855	69	102	759	68%	+3.5	11.0	6	5	5.2	16	+0.5	13	6.0%	20	88	13	92	49%	40%	9%	2%
2014	MIA	14/14	745	58	84	605	69%	+3.6	10.4	3	1	4.4	22	-1.0	6	-6.9%	31	2	31	8	52%	34%	14%	0%
2015	BUF	13/13	764	51	77	528	66%	-1.5	10.4	3	5	4.6	22	-0.9	11	-6.0%	32	6	32	-2	54%	25%	18%	3%
2016	BUF			50	77	553	65%	--	11.1	4						-0.6%								

Clay is a great fit in the Greg Roman offense, which has a more distinct role for an H-back type than it has for second or third wide receivers. Clay was an effective run blocker on Roman's many flavors of outside rushing plays, caught lots of short dump-offs in the middle of the field, and snuck up the seam on play-action surprises now and then. All the hard work resulted in a late-season injury and three-year lows in receptions and yards for a player trying to justify a five-year, $38 million contract. The Clay signing weakened the Dolphins more than it strengthened the Bills. That's the kind of zero-sum AFC East thinking that helps Bill Belichick sleep like a baby.

Jared Cook   Height: 6-6   Weight: 246   College: South Carolina   Draft: 2009/3 (89)   Born: 7-Apr-1987   Age: 29   Risk: Red

Year	Team	G/GS	Snaps	Rec	Pass	Yds	C%	+/-	Yd/C	TD	Drop	YAC	Rk	YAC+	BTkl	DVOA	Rk	DYAR	Rk	YAR	Short	Mid	Deep	Bomb
2013	STL	16/13	718	51	86	671	59%	+0.5	13.2	5	6	5.1	19	+0.7	1	2.8%	24	58	21	65	39%	41%	16%	5%
2014	STL	16/6	682	52	99	634	53%	-8.1	12.2	3	3	5.1	16	+0.6	6	-13.4%	37	-39	41	-47	40%	43%	13%	3%
2015	STL	16/12	673	39	75	481	52%	-6.6	12.3	0	3	5.1	18	-0.1	3	-23.5%	44	-76	51	-71	41%	39%	13%	7%
2016	GB			41	68	495	60%	--	12.1	4						1.8%								

The Green Bay Packers had limited, unreliable receiving options last season. Their only addition of note to that group, discounting the return of Jordy Nelson, was Cook, a proud advocate of being a limited and unreliable receiver. Cook will have a chance to succeed like any player who plays with Aaron Rodgers, but only he can reverse the trend of a career that has featured his unreliable hands over and over and over again.

Owen Daniels   Height: 6-3   Weight: 245   College: Wisconsin   Draft: 2006/4 (98)   Born: 9-Nov-1982   Age: 34   Risk: N/A

Year	Team	G/GS	Snaps	Rec	Pass	Yds	C%	+/-	Yd/C	TD	Drop	YAC	Rk	YAC+	BTkl	DVOA	Rk	DYAR	Rk	YAR	Short	Mid	Deep	Bomb
2013	HOU	5/5	352	24	41	252	59%	-1.4	10.5	3	0	3.5	40	-1.1	2	-2.4%	34	14	35	4	42%	50%	8%	0%
2014	BAL	15/13	818	48	79	527	61%	-2.4	11.0	4	3	3.7	35	-0.9	0	2.2%	22	49	16	42	32%	59%	7%	3%
2015	DEN	16/16	827	46	77	517	60%	-3.4	11.2	3	2	5.8	13	+0.5	7	-2.1%	29	26	28	19	42%	44%	11%	3%

As of late June, Daniels was unsigned and reportedly contemplating retirement. Despite being submerged in the dumpster fire of the 2015 Broncos' passing game during the regular season, Daniels had one last moment in the sun in the playoffs. His two touchdown passes gave Denver 14 of their 20 points in the win over the Patriots. On the second of those, Daniels toasted Pro Bowl linebacker Jamie Collins on a double-move.

Vernon Davis   Height: 6-3   Weight: 250   College: Maryland   Draft: 2006/1 (6)   Born: 31-Jan-1984   Age: 32   Risk: Green

Year	Team	G/GS	Snaps	Rec	Pass	Yds	C%	+/-	Yd/C	TD	Drop	YAC	Rk	YAC+	BTkl	DVOA	Rk	DYAR	Rk	YAR	Short	Mid	Deep	Bomb
2013	SF	15/15	810	52	84	850	62%	+5.6	16.3	13	3	5.1	20	+0.2	3	29.3%	3	199	3	189	30%	34%	21%	15%
2014	SF	14/14	830	26	51	245	51%	-3.5	9.4	2	4	1.9	49	-2.2	3	-28.4%	46	-66	45	-71	29%	44%	17%	10%
2015	2TM	15/9	621	38	58	395	66%	+2.5	10.4	0	3	3.8	39	-0.9	4	-8.8%	34	-6	34	1	41%	37%	15%	7%
2016	WAS			16	25	176	64%	--	11.0	2						0.0%								

It's almost unfathomable that Davis is just three years removed from a 13-touchdown season as one of the league's elite tight ends. Now playing on his third team in three seasons, the 32-year-old hasn't reached the end zone since Week 1 of the 2014 season and was invisible in Denver after a midseason trade to the Broncos. The Redskins took a low-risk flier by signing Davis to a one-year, $2.4 million deal, potentially to serve as insurance given the injury histories of Jordan Reed and Niles Paul. However, if Washington's top two tight ends are healthy, Davis isn't even a sure bet to make the final roster, let alone contribute in a meaningful capacity.

Larry Donnell   Height: 6-6   Weight: 269   College: Grambling State   Draft: 2011/FA   Born: 1-Nov-1988   Age: 28   Risk: Yellow

Year	Team	G/GS	Snaps	Rec	Pass	Yds	C%	+/-	Yd/C	TD	Drop	YAC	Rk	YAC+	BTkl	DVOA	Rk	DYAR	Rk	YAR	Short	Mid	Deep	Bomb
2013	NYG	16/1	105	3	6	31	50%	-0.5	10.3	0	0	3.3	--	-0.0	0	-19.2%	--	-5	--	-6	0%	67%	17%	17%
2014	NYG	16/12	866	63	92	623	68%	+4.2	9.9	6	2	3.5	39	-1.2	0	-10.2%	34	-18	36	-16	44%	40%	13%	3%
2015	NYG	8/8	386	29	41	223	71%	+0.1	7.7	2	1	3.0	49	-1.8	3	-12.6%	36	-15	35	-26	61%	29%	7%	2%
2016	NYG			37	54	380	69%	--	10.3	4						4.1%								

To this point, Donnell's career has produced one sublime three-touchdown performance on national TV and not much else. Still, it's a small win for Donnell that he's even still going after a broken bone in his neck ended his 2015 season and threatened to do the same to his career. Thankfully, Donnell appears fine to return, enough so that the Giants signed him at his affordable restricted free-agent tender this offseason. However, he's no longer the unquestioned No. 1 tight end, with Will Tye putting together a surprisingly strong eight-game audition during Donnell's absence. Though Donnell is a bigger player, his receiving-based skill set overlaps quite a bit with that of Tye's, likely forcing the Giants to choose between the two. It would help Donnell if he actually lived up to his reputation as a red zone threat, as he's posted red zone DVOA figures of -32.4% and -28.8% the past two seasons. In a Giants offense that leans on three-receiver sets, there is probably only room for one tight end to see significant snaps.

Eric Ebron | Height: 6-4 | Weight: 250 | College: North Carolina | Draft: 2014/1 (10) | Born: 10-Apr-1993 | Age: 23 | Risk: Green

Year	Team	G/GS	Snaps	Rec	Pass	Yds	C%	+/-	Yd/C	TD	Drop	YAC	Rk	YAC+	BTkl	DVOA	Rk	DYAR	Rk	YAR	Short	Mid	Deep	Bomb
2014	DET	13/7	445	25	47	248	53%	-4.0	9.9	1	4	5.0	18	+0.3	1	-28.6%	47	-65	44	-49	50%	26%	11%	13%
2015	DET	14/8	613	47	70	537	67%	-2.4	11.4	5	7	6.2	8	+1.3	3	6.5%	18	64	18	81	57%	35%	7%	0%
2016	DET			49	80	587	61%	--	12.0	6						3.7%								

Perhaps the only player in Detroit who didn't benefit from Jim Bob Cooter's promotion to offensive coordinator. Ebron gained 268 yards in five games under Joe Lombardi, then 269 yards in nine games under Cooter. There was the usual positive chatter over the offseason about Ebron losing weight and feeling good and taking a bigger role in the offense to fill Calvin Johnson's shoes, and he did take a big step forward after a terrible rookie season, but Ebron still has a long way to go to live up to his top-ten draft status.

Tyler Eifert | Height: 6-6 | Weight: 251 | College: Notre Dame | Draft: 2013/1 (21) | Born: 8-Sep-1990 | Age: 26 | Risk: Red

Year	Team	G/GS	Snaps	Rec	Pass	Yds	C%	+/-	Yd/C	TD	Drop	YAC	Rk	YAC+	BTkl	DVOA	Rk	DYAR	Rk	YAR	Short	Mid	Deep	Bomb
2013	CIN	15/15	673	39	59	445	66%	+1.3	11.4	2	2	5.8	9	+1.2	6	-14.0%	45	-27	47	-6	54%	29%	13%	5%
2014	CIN	1/1	8	3	3	37	100%	+1.1	12.3	0	0	2.7	--	-1.6	0	47.1%	--	11	--	13	33%	33%	33%	0%
2015	CIN	13/12	751	52	74	615	70%	+7.2	11.8	13	5	4.5	28	+0.4	5	42.0%	1	247	1	230	40%	44%	16%	0%
2016	CIN			53	76	606	70%	--	11.5	6						13.1%								

2015 was the breakout season long awaited from the Bengals' top 2013 draft pick. He was arguably the best tight end in the non-Gronk universe (Ty actually doubled the the big 'Ski in DVOA), and particularly dangerous in the red zone, where he routinely devoured single coverage. But his old bugaboo, injuries, popped up in the most unlikely place. In late spring Eifert announced he was undergoing ankle surgery after hurting the crucial joint in the—wait for it—Pro Bowl. Like an Aussie discovering a venomous spider in the bathroom, it came as a shock, yet hardly a surprise. Needless to say, a fully healthy Eifert is critical to Cincy's success, but hard to rely upon. Our projection assumes he won't go on PUP but will still miss the first couple weeks of the season.

Zach Ertz | Height: 6-5 | Weight: 249 | College: Stanford | Draft: 2013/2 (35) | Born: 10-Nov-1990 | Age: 26 | Risk: Green

Year	Team	G/GS	Snaps	Rec	Pass	Yds	C%	+/-	Yd/C	TD	Drop	YAC	Rk	YAC+	BTkl	DVOA	Rk	DYAR	Rk	YAR	Short	Mid	Deep	Bomb
2013	PHI	16/3	450	36	56	469	64%	+3.3	13.0	4	2	4.4	30	-0.5	0	9.8%	17	60	20	71	34%	42%	17%	8%
2014	PHI	16/5	587	58	89	702	65%	+3.5	12.1	3	2	3.9	31	-0.5	3	13.3%	12	127	8	130	34%	37%	23%	6%
2015	PHI	15/7	788	75	112	853	67%	+4.9	11.4	2	4	4.0	36	-0.5	4	0.2%	27	56	19	55	45%	36%	19%	0%
2016	PHI			70	104	824	67%	--	11.8	5						4.3%								

Ertz's target and reception totals would suggest that he was one of the focal points in Philadelphia's passing attack, but that didn't really manifest itself until the end of the season. Like many of the Eagles' "skill players," Ertz's flashes of excellence in 2015 were interspersed among all-too-frequent stretches of invisibility. The physically imposing tight end didn't reach the end zone until Week 12; in fact, over the first half of the season, Ertz's -20 DYAR made him one of the least efficient tight ends in the league. The Eagles eventually woke up and featured him prominently down the stretch, as more than half of Ertz's receiving yards for the season came in the final four weeks. Still, it's stunning that a player of Ertz's physical stature has caught just nine touchdowns through three seasons. To really tap into his potential, Ertz must fare better in the red zone, where he compiled a hideous -55.2% receiving DVOA in 2015. Given the success Travis Kelce enjoyed under Doug Pederson in Kansas City, Ertz looms as one of the position's prime breakout candidates for 2016.

Anthony Fasano | Height: 6-4 | Weight: 255 | College: Notre Dame | Draft: 2006/2 (53) | Born: 20-Apr-1984 | Age: 32 | Risk: Green

Year	Team	G/GS	Snaps	Rec	Pass	Yds	C%	+/-	Yd/C	TD	Drop	YAC	Rk	YAC+	BTkl	DVOA	Rk	DYAR	Rk	YAR	Short	Mid	Deep	Bomb
2013	KC	9/9	503	23	33	200	70%	+1.3	8.7	3	2	3.2	44	-1.4	2	-12.7%	43	-12	42	5	45%	48%	0%	6%
2014	KC	15/13	671	25	36	226	69%	+0.6	9.0	4	2	3.2	42	-1.8	0	2.0%	23	23	23	21	50%	31%	17%	3%
2015	TEN	16/11	549	26	42	289	62%	+0.0	11.1	2	1	5.8	12	+1.3	1	4.0%	25	32	26	18	58%	26%	16%	0%
2016	TEN			19	32	217	59%	--	11.4	2						-2.1%								

As the second tight end in what is expected to be a run-heavy offense, Fasano's 2016 season is likely going to show off his skills as a pass protector more than his skills as a receiver.

Darren Fells   Height: 6-7   Weight: 281   College: Cal-Irvine   Draft: 2013/FA   Born: 22-Apr-1986   Age: 30   Risk: Green

Year	Team	G/GS	Snaps	Rec	Pass	Yds	C%	+/-	Yd/C	TD	Drop	YAC	Rk	YAC+	BTkl	DVOA	Rk	DYAR	Rk	YAR	Short	Mid	Deep	Bomb
2014	ARI	10/5	225	5	11	71	45%	-0.9	14.2	0	1	4.2	--	-0.2	1	-10.7%	--	-2	--	-10	22%	67%	11%	0%
2015	ARI	14/12	672	21	28	311	75%	+2.5	14.8	3	1	6.7	5	+2.9	3	35.8%	3	86	14	106	39%	43%	18%	0%
2016	ARI			27	37	295	73%	--	10.9	4						8.9%								

Tight end is really the only area on offense where Arizona is not strong, but Fells was good when targeted last season. He deserves more opportunities over the slower Jermaine Gresham.

C.J. Fiedorowicz   Height: 6-5   Weight: 265   College: Iowa   Draft: 2014/3 (65)   Born: 10/22/1991   Age: 25   Risk: Yellow

Year	Team	G/GS	Snaps	Rec	Pass	Yds	C%	+/-	Yd/C	TD	Drop	YAC	Rk	YAC+	BTkl	DVOA	Rk	DYAR	Rk	YAR	Short	Mid	Deep	Bomb
2014	HOU	15/8	471	4	7	28	57%	-0.9	7.0	1	0	2.5	--	-1.5	0	-19.1%	--	-5	--	-4	71%	14%	14%	0%
2015	HOU	16/14	650	17	24	167	71%	+0.0	9.8	1	1	4.5	--	-0.1	0	-19.6%	--	-19	--	-9	78%	22%	0%	0%
2016	HOU			26	42	287	62%	--	11.0	2						-4.4%								

Head coach Bill O'Brien declared in June that the former third-round pick heading into his third season "knows the plays better" and is a "really, really hard worker." That's better than the alternative for a team that needs more than the mediocre blocking and lousy receiving they got in Fiedorowicz's first two seasons. Unless he has improved even more dramatically than O'Brien suggested, his near- and long-term outlook remains dim.

Coby Fleener   Height: 6-6   Weight: 247   College: Stanford   Draft: 2012/2 (34)   Born: 20-Sep-1988   Age: 28   Risk: Yellow

Year	Team	G/GS	Snaps	Rec	Pass	Yds	C%	+/-	Yd/C	TD	Drop	YAC	Rk	YAC+	BTkl	DVOA	Rk	DYAR	Rk	YAR	Short	Mid	Deep	Bomb
2013	IND	16/12	815	52	87	608	60%	-2.3	11.7	4	1	4.9	23	+0.4	0	-11.3%	42	-24	45	-21	44%	40%	15%	1%
2014	IND	16/12	787	51	92	774	55%	-3.6	15.2	8	5	5.8	11	+1.3	3	10.1%	15	112	10	115	35%	38%	19%	8%
2015	IND	16/11	732	54	84	491	64%	-0.3	9.1	3	3	3.3	42	-1.4	2	-15.9%	40	-49	46	-38	49%	31%	17%	4%
2016	NO			69	101	782	68%	--	11.3	6						4.2%								

If you're a one-dimensional receiving tight end with good speed and the ability to play out wide, and you can find your way to New Orleans, and you can get a lucrative contract notwithstanding the Saints' seemingly perennial cap issues, then you should do it in a heartbeat. That is just what Fleener did this offseason, leaving his collegiate teammate in Central Indiana for the Crescent City and $36 million over five years. Drew Brees was suitably effusive in June, declaring that Fleener had an "uncanny ability to separate." Sure, if you don't necessarily expect him to always haul the ball in after he's separated. Fleener isn't Jimmy Graham, especially in his ability to make contested catches, but athletically he is much closer than Benjamin Watson was in 2015.

Antonio Gates   Height: 6-4   Weight: 260   College: Kent State   Draft: 2003/FA   Born: 18-Jun-1980   Age: 36   Risk: Red

Year	Team	G/GS	Snaps	Rec	Pass	Yds	C%	+/-	Yd/C	TD	Drop	YAC	Rk	YAC+	BTkl	DVOA	Rk	DYAR	Rk	YAR	Short	Mid	Deep	Bomb
2013	SD	16/15	970	77	113	872	68%	+4.0	11.3	4	5	4.8	24	+0.3	8	0.7%	29	63	18	62	54%	36%	7%	3%
2014	SD	16/14	770	69	98	821	70%	+7.8	11.9	12	1	3.7	34	-0.5	1	24.1%	4	204	2	224	45%	39%	8%	8%
2015	SD	11/4	496	56	85	630	66%	+3.2	11.3	5	3	4.3	32	+0.0	4	13.1%	11	113	7	91	46%	43%	10%	1%
2016	SD			64	98	745	65%	--	11.6	7						9.3%								

36-year-old Antonio Gates has new competition in San Diego with the arrival of second-round pick Hunter Henry. Gates fended off Ladarius Green for four years with ease despite the way Green flashed whenever he was used; he should do the same with Henry even though this challenger was selected two rounds higher than Green and Gates is past the twilight of his career. Gates' athleticism is obviously declining but he is still a very impressive route runner who can dominate at the catch point to be productive.

Crockett Gillmore

| | | | Height: 6-6 | | | Weight: 260 | | | College: Colorado State | | | | Draft: 2014/3 (99) | | Born: 11/16/1991 | | Age: 25 | | Risk: Yellow |

Year	Team	G/GS	Snaps	Rec	Pass	Yds	C%	+/-	Yd/C	TD	Drop	YAC	Rk	YAC+	BTkl	DVOA	Rk	DYAR	Rk	YAR	Short	Mid	Deep	Bomb
2014	BAL	15/1	372	10	15	121	67%	+0.5	12.1	1	1	5.9	--	+1.0	0	11.2%	--	20	--	21	54%	46%	0%	0%
2015	BAL	10/10	520	33	47	412	70%	+1.5	12.5	4	0	7.4	3	+2.3	5	22.7%	6	95	12	99	57%	26%	17%	0%
2016	BAL			20	31	238	65%	--	11.9	2						4.0%								

If any player in the league is going to hang his touchdown balls up with his raccoon pelts, it would be someone with the name of Crockett Gillmore. He was a solid contributor in his second season, finishing fourth among tight ends in YAC+. A couple of injuries shortened his season to just 10 games, and Baltimore's logjam at tight end is likely to limit his progression in his third season.

Jimmy Graham

| | | | Height: 6-6 | | | Weight: 260 | | | College: Miami | | | | Draft: 2010/3 (95) | | Born: 24-Nov-1986 | | Age: 30 | | Risk: Red |

Year	Team	G/GS	Snaps	Rec	Pass	Yds	C%	+/-	Yd/C	TD	Drop	YAC	Rk	YAC+	BTkl	DVOA	Rk	DYAR	Rk	YAR	Short	Mid	Deep	Bomb
2013	NO	16/12	755	86	143	1215	60%	+5.1	14.1	16	4	4.7	26	+0.3	9	15.7%	12	223	1	212	36%	44%	11%	9%
2014	NO	16/13	775	85	124	889	69%	+3.7	10.5	10	5	3.5	40	-0.7	7	6.8%	17	124	9	113	41%	46%	10%	2%
2015	SEA	11/11	571	48	74	605	65%	+2.3	12.6	2	2	4.6	27	-0.3	4	14.8%	10	110	8	72	37%	49%	11%	3%
2016	SEA			70	106	788	66%	--	11.3	6						4.8%								

Graham was viewed as a transformative piece for the Seattle offense, especially in the red zone. You want to throw from the 1-yard line again? You get a Jimmy Graham, even if it costs a first-round pick and center Max Unger. The price always felt too high for a run-based offense that would prefer a legitimate blocking tight end to one who argued with the NFL that he was a wideout. Little did we expect that Graham's two touchdowns in 2015 would both come in September when the offense struggled. It was even stranger when the Seattle offense went on a seven-game tear that happened largely without Graham, who tore his patellar tendon in Week 12 against the Steelers. It is a difficult injury to return from, but if he can make it back, Graham should see similar numbers to last year with a likely improved touchdown count. However, those days of the fantasy numbers he shared with Drew Brees in New Orleans are over. To be honest, they never should have been expected in Seattle even before the injury.

Ladarius Green

| | | | Height: 6-6 | | | Weight: 237 | | | College: Louisiana-Lafayette | | | | Draft: 2012/4 (110) | | Born: 27-Jan-1991 | | Age: 25 | | Risk: Red |

Year	Team	G/GS	Snaps	Rec	Pass	Yds	C%	+/-	Yd/C	TD	Drop	YAC	Rk	YAC+	BTkl	DVOA	Rk	DYAR	Rk	YAR	Short	Mid	Deep	Bomb
2013	SD	16/10	365	17	30	376	57%	-0.1	22.1	3	1	9.8	1	+5.0	0	45.3%	1	113	7	109	23%	45%	26%	6%
2014	SD	14/4	289	19	25	226	76%	+2.8	11.9	0	1	6.0	8	+0.5	1	15.9%	9	41	18	32	60%	20%	20%	0%
2015	SD	13/11	662	37	63	429	59%	+0.7	11.6	4	4	6.0	11	+1.3	3	11.8%	13	78	16	42	50%	32%	14%	4%
2016	PIT			60	87	733	69%	--	12.2	5						10.6%								

Green's skill set isn't that of a tight end, but rather of an over-sized receiver. Green is lean and athletic, and he can move in space, accelerate away from linebackers, and make difficult adjustments when the ball is in the air. The Steelers may have signed him as a tight end, but he's more likely to play the Martavis Bryant role as a field-stretching ball-winner than the Heath Miller role as a key run blocker and possession receiver.

Green never established himself in San Diego but it's not like he was showered with repeated opportunities. The Steelers should offer him that kind of chance, though it is concerning that he missed OTAs because of ankle surgery.

Virgil Green

| | | | Height: 6-5 | | | Weight: 240 | | | College: Nevada | | | | Draft: 2011/7 (204) | | Born: 3-Aug-1988 | | Age: 28 | | Risk: Yellow |

Year	Team	G/GS	Snaps	Rec	Pass	Yds	C%	+/-	Yd/C	TD	Drop	YAC	Rk	YAC+	BTkl	DVOA	Rk	DYAR	Rk	YAR	Short	Mid	Deep	Bomb
2013	DEN	16/3	319	9	12	45	75%	+0.0	5.0	0	0	1.9	--	-2.7	0	-61.0%	--	-44	--	-44	92%	8%	0%	0%
2014	DEN	13/9	394	6	6	74	100%	+1.7	12.3	1	0	7.7	--	+2.8	0	71.5%	--	35	--	41	83%	0%	17%	0%
2015	DEN	16/5	383	12	15	173	80%	+1.8	14.4	1	0	10.1	--	+5.9	3	51.3%	--	66	--	62	79%	21%	0%	0%
2016	DEN			34	57	341	60%	--	10.0	2						-10.6%								

The rest of Denver's tight end depth chart (2015 third-round pick Jeff Heuerman, who missed all of his rookie season, and free-agent signee Garrett Graham) leaves the door wide-open for Green to finally break through. That was also true last season, however, and the Broncos decided to make a midseason trade for Vernon Davis. Green missed most of OTAs after having finger surgery.

Ryan Griffin

		Height: 6-6		Weight: 247			College: Connecticut			Draft: 2013/6 (201)		Born: 11-Jan-1990		Age: 26		Risk: Red	

Year	Team	G/GS	Snaps	Rec	Pass	Yds	C%	+/-	Yd/C	TD	Drop	YAC	Rk	YAC+	BTkl	DVOA	Rk	DYAR	Rk	YAR	Short	Mid	Deep	Bomb
2013	HOU	15/8	362	19	28	244	68%	+2.1	12.8	1	0	5.2	17	+0.2	0	13.9%	13	38	26	43	50%	23%	15%	12%
2014	HOU	16/2	334	10	16	91	63%	-1.1	9.1	1	2	3.6	--	-1.0	0	-2.7%	--	5	--	7	56%	19%	19%	6%
2015	HOU	9/4	351	20	34	251	59%	-2.2	12.6	2	2	5.0	19	+0.1	2	11.5%	14	42	22	39	44%	41%	9%	6%
2016	HOU			21	32	233	66%	--	11.1	2						-0.8%								

Given the depth chart competition and desperate need for a quality option other than DeAndre Hopkins, 2015 could have been Griffin's breakout season. But inconsistent quarterback play, a missed half-season due to an MCL injury, and then a late-season Achilles injury meant it was not to be. His most notable play was failing to hold on to a touchdown pass in the playoff loss to Kansas City. The Achilles injury kept him out of the entire offseason, so consider him questionable for 2016 production as well.

Rob Gronkowski

		Height: 6-6		Weight: 264			College: Arizona			Draft: 2010/2 (42)		Born: 14-May-1989		Age: 27		Risk: Yellow	

Year	Team	G/GS	Snaps	Rec	Pass	Yds	C%	+/-	Yd/C	TD	Drop	YAC	Rk	YAC+	BTkl	DVOA	Rk	DYAR	Rk	YAR	Short	Mid	Deep	Bomb
2013	NE	7/6	383	39	66	592	59%	-0.2	15.2	4	1	5.0	21	+1.0	4	12.9%	14	91	11	115	25%	45%	22%	7%
2014	NE	15/10	825	82	131	1124	63%	+2.3	13.7	12	5	5.6	14	+1.3	24	19.7%	7	237	1	253	34%	45%	17%	4%
2015	NE	15/15	939	72	120	1176	60%	-0.1	16.3	11	1	7.7	2	+3.3	14	21.0%	7	235	2	211	35%	40%	19%	6%
2016	NE			74	119	1059	62%	--	14.3	11						15.8%								

Patriots Receivers, 20-Plus-Yard Passes, 2015

Player	Rec	Tgt	Yards	TD	Player	Rec	Tgt	Yards	TD
Gronk	8	20	300	1	Julian Edelman	1	8	27	0
Brandon LaFell	4	16	167	0	Danny Amendola	3	6	87	0
Scott Chandler	3	8	78	0	Others	5	12	191	1

As you can see, Gronk is responsible for a huge percentage of Tom Brady's deep production, which is why Patriots fans are perpetually jittery about his health status.

Gronk was not on the field for the first half of mandatory minicamp in June, though he practiced with the team at least once before minicamp ended. Gronk's absence was a national story during the pre-summer doldrums; keep in mind that this was not a holdout but just some missed open-to-the-media practice sessions, which were almost certainly spent doing some sports science stuff to keep him healthy through the season. The Patriots were typically vague and creepy about Gronk's status, because saying "Gronk was working with trainers to strengthen his knee and back" would make Bill Belichick's spleen explode and give the Jets some sort of inexplicable competitive advantage. The Patriots' obsession with secrecy only made everyone suspicious and turned a minor non-issue into a major conspiracy. Those who do not learn from the past, and all of that.

Hunter Henry

		Height: 6-5		Weight: 250			College: Arkansas			Draft: 2016/2 (35)		Born: 7-Dec-1994		Age: 22		Risk: Red	

Year	Team	G/GS	Snaps	Rec	Pass	Yds	C%	+/-	Yd/C	TD	Drop	YAC	Rk	YAC+	BTkl	DVOA	Rk	DYAR	Rk	YAR	Short	Mid	Deep	Bomb
2016	SD			29	46	348	63%	--	12.0	3							2.0%							

Despite being the consensus top tight end prospect in 2016, Henry couldn't crack the first round of the draft. That is because he lacks the vertical athleticism that teams have prioritized at the position in recent years. He isn't the deep threat that the Lions hoped Eric Ebron could be, but he can become a better player in San Diego by relying on his versatility. Henry is a strong blocker with the fluidity and quickness to get open on short and intermediate routes. He is a consistent catcher of the ball with the ability to make difficult adjustments over the middle of the field or against tight coverage. Henry should be an ideal complement to Antonio Gates in the immediate future before fitting seamlessly into his starting role for the next decade or so.

Jeff Heuerman

		Height: 6-5		Weight: 254			College: Ohio State			Draft: 2015/3 (92)		Born: 24-Nov-1992		Age: 24		Risk: Yellow	

Year	Team	G/GS	Snaps	Rec	Pass	Yds	C%	+/-	Yd/C	TD	Drop	YAC	Rk	YAC+	BTkl	DVOA	Rk	DYAR	Rk	YAR	Short	Mid	Deep	Bomb
2016	DEN			42	65	473	65%	--	11.3	3							-0.1%							

Just a week after the 2015 draft, Heuerman tore his ACL at post-draft rookie minicamp. Now recovered, the Broncos are hoping that Heuerman will be the top tight end this season. At Ohio State, Heuerman topped out with 26 receptions (17.9 yards per catch) as a junior. His production fell as a senior (17 receptions, 12.2 YPC) as he battled a foot injury and inconsistent quarterback play. His most impressive catch did not come in a football uniform. According to NFL.com, Heuerman once caught a 200-pound tarpon, which Wikipedia defines as a large fish of the genus *Megalops*.

Josh Hill

Height: 6-5　　Weight: 229　　College: Idaho State　　Draft: 2013/FA　　Born: 21-May-1990　　Age: 26　　Risk: Green

Year	Team	G/GS	Snaps	Rec	Pass	Yds	C%	+/-	Yd/C	TD	Drop	YAC	Rk	YAC+	BTkl	DVOA	Rk	DYAR	Rk	YAR	Short	Mid	Deep	Bomb
2013	NO	14/3	176	6	10	44	60%	-0.8	7.3	1	1	5.5	--	+0.5	0	-14.7%	--	-6	--	-6	60%	30%	10%	0%
2014	NO	16/3	288	14	20	176	70%	+0.9	12.6	5	1	7.1	--	+2.2	0	32.0%	--	57	--	58	68%	11%	16%	5%
2015	NO	16/7	424	16	30	120	53%	-6.0	7.5	2	0	4.8	21	-0.3	2	-27.9%	48	-44	43	-42	73%	17%	10%	0%
2016	NO			22	31	208	71%	--	9.4	2						-3.1%								

The Saints matched Chicago's restricted free-agent offer for the Idaho State product, but he's now comfortably buried behind Coby Fleener on the depth chart. We live in a world of ever-increasing information, which can make it hard to find the 20 percent of information that matters in life. The other 80 percent, one assumes, is made up of glowing Josh Hill fantasy football reports circa May 2015.

Travis Kelce

Height: 6-5　　Weight: 255　　College: Cincinnati　　Draft: 2013/3 (63)　　Born: 5-Oct-1989　　Age: 27　　Risk: Green

Year	Team	G/GS	Snaps	Rec	Pass	Yds	C%	+/-	Yd/C	TD	Drop	YAC	Rk	YAC+	BTkl	DVOA	Rk	DYAR	Rk	YAR	Short	Mid	Deep	Bomb
2013	KC	1/0	0	0	0	0	--	--	--	0	0	--	--	--	--	--	--	--	--	--	--	--	--	--
2014	KC	16/11	668	67	87	862	77%	+9.9	12.9	5	4	7.2	4	+2.2	12	23.0%	5	174	4	196	53%	35%	12%	0%
2015	KC	16/16	923	72	103	875	70%	+0.2	12.2	5	5	7.3	4	+1.8	14	9.3%	16	110	9	108	57%	35%	8%	0%
2016	KC			71	101	853	70%	--	12.0	5						8.8%								

Before last season, Kelce was tabbed as the breakout tight end of 2015 by approximately 8,000 football forecasters and fantasy fanatics. And while Kelce's targets did go up, they were the only one of his counting stats to take a leap. Kelce finished the season seventh in total fantasy points among tight ends and ninth in fantasy points per game. If he breaks out this season, it wouldn't be the first time a potential breakout waited a year before launching.

Lance Kendricks

Height: 6-3　　Weight: 243　　College: Wisconsin　　Draft: 2011/2 (47)　　Born: 30-Jan-1988　　Age: 28　　Risk: Green

Year	Team	G/GS	Snaps	Rec	Pass	Yds	C%	+/-	Yd/C	TD	Drop	YAC	Rk	YAC+	BTkl	DVOA	Rk	DYAR	Rk	YAR	Short	Mid	Deep	Bomb
2013	STL	15/13	575	32	46	258	70%	+0.7	8.1	4	3	3.4	42	-1.4	1	-6.4%	38	3	38	0	72%	23%	5%	0%
2014	STL	16/14	594	27	38	259	71%	+1.4	9.6	5	2	3.9	32	-1.0	0	11.8%	13	51	15	52	64%	25%	11%	0%
2015	STL	15/12	570	25	40	245	63%	-1.5	9.8	2	1	5.2	16	-0.3	2	-13.6%	37	-17	37	-7	62%	27%	3%	8%
2016	LARM			40	56	400	71%	--	10.0	4						2.1%								

Jared Cook's departure suggests that Kendricks' role can grow in the Rams offense. Kendricks is a capable receiving option, but not a good one. He doesn't run precise routes, he doesn't have great ball skills, and he won't show off much creativity after the catch. The Rams know what they have in Kendricks, a tight end who can contribute as a blocker and receiver but not a difference-making talent.

Vance McDonald

Height: 6-4　　Weight: 267　　College: Rice　　Draft: 2013/2 (55)　　Born: 13-Jun-1990　　Age: 26　　Risk: Green

Year	Team	G/GS	Snaps	Rec	Pass	Yds	C%	+/-	Yd/C	TD	Drop	YAC	Rk	YAC+	BTkl	DVOA	Rk	DYAR	Rk	YAR	Short	Mid	Deep	Bomb
2013	SF	15/4	480	8	19	119	42%	-2.4	14.9	0	2	5.9	--	+1.2	1	-23.8%	--	-20	--	-27	41%	29%	18%	12%
2014	SF	8/4	214	2	7	30	29%	-1.3	15.0	0	0	13.0	--	+8.0	0	-99.1%	--	-46	--	-46	60%	20%	0%	20%
2015	SF	14/11	473	30	46	326	65%	-0.5	10.9	3	5	6.1	9	+1.2	4	-19.2%	43	-34	40	-29	52%	28%	13%	7%
2016	SF			45	69	466	65%	--	10.4	2						-8.9%								

This is really the now-or-never season for McDonald, a second-round pick in 2013. He only has 40 career receptions and never formed a competitive duo with Vernon Davis. Now with a chance to shine as the No. 1 tight end in a more pass-friendly system, McDonald could secure himself financially with a big year, or add his name to the long list of second-round busts in NFL history. Chances are he'll at least surpass his career receiving totals in 2016 alone.

Heath Miller

Height: 6-5   Weight: 256   College: Virginia   Draft: 2005/1 (30)   Born: 22-Oct-1982   Age: 34   Risk: N/A

Year	Team	G/GS	Snaps	Rec	Pass	Yds	C%	+/-	Yd/C	TD	Drop	YAC	Rk	YAC+	BTkl	DVOA	Rk	DYAR	Rk	YAR	Short	Mid	Deep	Bomb
2013	PIT	14/14	901	58	78	593	74%	+8.1	10.2	1	3	3.9	38	-0.9	3	-2.8%	35	23	29	22	53%	33%	11%	3%
2014	PIT	16/16	1081	66	91	761	73%	+5.9	11.5	3	4	4.9	19	+0.2	2	13.5%	11	127	7	110	43%	45%	11%	0%
2015	PIT	15/15	924	60	82	535	74%	+3.9	8.9	2	0	3.6	40	-1.3	1	1.2%	26	48	21	34	57%	35%	8%	0%

Miller retired in February with 592 receptions, sixth-most in NFL history by a tight end. If there was ever a Hall of Very Good, he would be a lock for it. Pittsburgh always featured a wide receiver rather than Miller, which made it hard for him to compare statistically to his lofty AFC peers such as Tony Gonzalez, Antonio Gates, and Rob Gronkowski. Miller also had a lot of blocking responsibilities given the poor quality of Pittsburgh's offensive line for much of his 11-season career. Miller finished first among tight ends in fewest snaps per blown block in 2015, but clearly his receiving impact was starting to diminish. Still, he was an excellent security blanket for Ben Roethlisberger, and DVOA loved him, with eight top-15 finishes.

Zach Miller

Height: 6-4   Weight: 233   College: Nebraska-Omaha   Draft: 2009/6 (180)   Born: 4-Oct-1984   Age: 32   Risk: Yellow

Year	Team	G/GS	Snaps	Rec	Pass	Yds	C%	+/-	Yd/C	TD	Drop	YAC	Rk	YAC+	BTkl	DVOA	Rk	DYAR	Rk	YAR	Short	Mid	Deep	Bomb
2015	CHI	15/14	579	34	46	439	74%	+5.0	12.9	5	0	6.5	6	+2.4	12	25.6%	5	104	11	105	57%	26%	14%	2%
2016	CHI			52	75	582	69%	--	11.2	4							5.2%								

Once upon a time, Miller was a promising young player with the Jacksonville Jaguars, among the top 25 tight ends in both DVOA and DYAR in 2009 and 2010. Then injuries wiped out most of his third season, and Miller spent nearly four years bouncing on and off the rosters of Jacksonville, Tampa Bay, and Chicago. Finally healthy in 2015, he found playing time on a desperate Bears team that was running out of quality receiving options. Thirty-one of Miller's 34 catches last year came in Week 9 or later; from that point forward, only two tight ends had more DYAR, and only six gained more yardage. The Bears liked Miller enough to sign him to a two-year, $5.5 million deal and trade away Martellus Bennett, but you have to question the decision to rely so heavily on a 32-year-old who has played only 19 games in the past five years.

Greg Olsen

Height: 6-6   Weight: 254   College: Miami   Draft: 2007/1 (31)   Born: 11-Mar-1985   Age: 31   Risk: Green

Year	Team	G/GS	Snaps	Rec	Pass	Yds	C%	+/-	Yd/C	TD	Drop	YAC	Rk	YAC+	BTkl	DVOA	Rk	DYAR	Rk	YAR	Short	Mid	Deep	Bomb
2013	CAR	16/16	1001	73	111	816	66%	+7.7	11.2	6	5	4.5	29	-0.1	4	3.8%	22	83	14	65	39%	44%	13%	5%
2014	CAR	16/16	1067	84	123	1008	68%	+5.1	12.0	6	1	4.0	29	-0.3	1	14.7%	10	178	3	183	37%	49%	12%	3%
2015	CAR	16/16	1057	77	124	1104	62%	+3.3	14.3	7	2	4.5	29	+0.3	1	8.9%	17	132	6	184	28%	48%	15%	9%
2016	CAR			71	109	922	65%	--	13.0	7							12.1%								

It's been an interesting career path for Olsen, who came into the league as a 7th Floor Crew member and now, at 31, finds himself as one of the more highly regarded and thoughtful players in the league. In 2015, Olsen had his best year yet, becoming the de facto No. 1 receiver for an offense with no actual wide receivers of note. Catch rates and DVOA will tell you he would be better off in a less-volume intensive role, but the fact that Olsen could handle it almost got the Panthers all the way to the Super Bowl trophy. Olsen is getting to the age where tight ends begin to hit the wall, but he has shown no signs of slowing up yet.

Niles Paul

Height: 6-1   Weight: 225   College: Nebraska   Draft: 2011/5 (155)   Born: 9-Aug-1989   Age: 27   Risk: Yellow

Year	Team	G/GS	Snaps	Rec	Pass	Yds	C%	+/-	Yd/C	TD	Drop	YAC	Rk	YAC+	BTkl	DVOA	Rk	DYAR	Rk	YAR	Short	Mid	Deep	Bomb
2013	WAS	15/4	150	4	8	51	50%	-0.7	12.8	0	0	5.5	--	+0.6	0	-26.8%	--	-11	--	-14	57%	29%	14%	0%
2014	WAS	16/7	562	39	52	507	75%	+3.5	13.0	1	3	6.6	7	+1.6	4	24.4%	3	110	11	87	62%	20%	14%	4%
2016	WAS			30	44	292	68%	--	9.7	2							-4.0%								

Fresh off a breakout year, Paul appeared primed to become a focal point of the Washington passing game. That vision never made it to the field, as Paul's season ended in the first quarter of the preseason opener with a gruesome ankle injury that his surgeon called "the worst he's ever seen." The silver lining to the injury is that it occurred early enough for Paul to return fully for the offseason program. Of course, the complexion of Wasington's tight end picture has changed dramatically since Paul last suited up, with Jordan Reed finally delivering on his potential as a game-changing mismatch. But while Paul will no longer sit atop the depth chart, he should still occupy a clear niche on a team that used an extra tight end or offensive lineman on 27 percent of its offensive snaps last season. Paul has reportedly bulked up this offseason to potentially take on more of a blocking role, but given Reed's injury history, he may yet get a chance to have a part in the passing game.

Jordan Reed Height: 6-2 Weight: 236 College: Florida Draft: 2013/3 (85) Born: 3-Jul-1990 Age: 26 Risk: Yellow

Year	Team	G/GS	Snaps	Rec	Pass	Yds	C%	+/-	Yd/C	TD	Drop	YAC	Rk	YAC+	BTkl	DVOA	Rk	DYAR	Rk	YAR	Short	Mid	Deep	Bomb
2013	WAS	9/4	379	45	60	499	75%	+3.5	11.1	3	3	5.5	12	+0.5	2	19.5%	9	98	10	124	48%	45%	5%	2%
2014	WAS	11/2	364	50	65	465	77%	+1.9	9.3	0	0	5.7	12	+0.5	10	-10.8%	35	-15	35	-8	66%	28%	6%	0%
2015	WAS	14/8	704	87	114	952	76%	+9.6	10.9	11	2	5.4	15	+0.9	19	20.1%	8	206	4	213	64%	25%	11%	1%
2016	WAS			78	105	870	74%	--	11.1	6						9.6%								

After spending his first two seasons teasing with glimpses of excellence, everything finally came together for Reed down the stretch. The oft-injured tight end looked as though he was falling into a familiar pattern when he suffered a concussion in Week 4, causing him to miss two games. Beginning with his Week 7 return, though, Reed out-produced every other tight end in the league, leading the position with 170 DYAR from that point forward. Also starting from that point, Doug Baldwin was the only player at any position to score more touchdowns than Reed's 10. As you might expect, Reed was a terror in the red zone, finishing with 97 DYAR in that part of the field alone, sixth-most in the league and more than any tight end besides Tyler Eifert. Though he'll never be an asset as a blocker, Reed clearly has enough ability to become the best receiving tight end in the league. Now the question is whether he can stay healthy enough to stake a legitimate claim to that title. The 14 games he played last season represented a career-high, and he has dealt with a cocktail of lower-body problems throughout his three seasons (including a sprained MCL he played through in 2015). Reed's body may very well be the toughest competition he faces, because if last season is any indication, there aren't many defenses capable of containing him themselves.

Mychal Rivera Height: 6-3 Weight: 242 College: Tennessee Draft: 2013/6 (184) Born: 8-Sep-1990 Age: 26 Risk: Green

Year	Team	G/GS	Snaps	Rec	Pass	Yds	C%	+/-	Yd/C	TD	Drop	YAC	Rk	YAC+	BTkl	DVOA	Rk	DYAR	Rk	YAR	Short	Mid	Deep	Bomb
2013	OAK	16/3	592	38	60	407	63%	+2.5	10.7	4	4	2.4	51	-2.1	3	8.1%	19	60	19	57	42%	44%	11%	4%
2014	OAK	16/10	818	58	99	534	59%	-2.7	9.2	4	7	3.0	44	-1.8	1	-22.6%	45	-97	49	-112	51%	31%	14%	4%
2015	OAK	16/0	401	32	46	280	70%	+1.4	8.8	1	1	3.9	38	-1.6	2	-25.7%	45	-51	48	-56	55%	20%	18%	7%
2016	OAK			22	35	213	63%	--	9.7	2						-7.7%								

Usurped in the pecking order by Clive Walford late last year, Rivera is a reliable lower-rung receiver who hasn't really learned how to be the low man as a blocker. He doesn't do much with the ball once he catches it, but you could do a lot worse than that package out of your second tight end.

Richard Rodgers Height: 6-4 Weight: 257 College: California Draft: 2014/3 (98) Born: 1/22/1992 Age: 24 Risk: Yellow

Year	Team	G/GS	Snaps	Rec	Pass	Yds	C%	+/-	Yd/C	TD	Drop	YAC	Rk	YAC+	BTkl	DVOA	Rk	DYAR	Rk	YAR	Short	Mid	Deep	Bomb
2014	GB	16/5	478	20	30	225	67%	-0.1	11.3	2	1	2.4	47	-2.5	1	-10.9%	36	-8	34	-7	59%	24%	10%	7%
2015	GB	16/12	799	58	85	510	68%	+2.4	8.8	8	2	4.0	35	-0.9	4	-3.7%	30	21	30	30	55%	36%	5%	4%
2016	GB			40	59	445	68%	--	11.1	3						2.6%								

Rodgers' 61-yard Hail Mary touchdown to beat Detroit was the longest game-winning score in the last ten seconds of a game since at least 1994. (Only two other such touchdowns have been longer than 50 yards; both were Hail Marys thrown by Tim Couch, of all people.) Rodgers finished that game 8-of-8 for 146 yards, and it got him a lot of attention from opposing defensive coordinators—in his next three games, he totaled three catches for 12 yards. With Jared Cook in town and Mike McCarthy's preference for three-receiver sets, Rodgers' playing time figures to drop sharply in 2016.

Kyle Rudolph Height: 6-6 Weight: 265 College: Notre Dame Draft: 2011/2 (43) Born: 9-Nov-1989 Age: 27 Risk: Yellow

Year	Team	G/GS	Snaps	Rec	Pass	Yds	C%	+/-	Yd/C	TD	Drop	YAC	Rk	YAC+	BTkl	DVOA	Rk	DYAR	Rk	YAR	Short	Mid	Deep	Bomb
2013	MIN	8/8	424	30	46	313	65%	+0.3	10.4	3	1	4.0	37	-0.7	6	-13.9%	44	-21	43	-13	44%	36%	20%	0%
2014	MIN	9/8	434	24	34	231	71%	+1.8	9.6	2	3	4.8	20	+0.3	1	0.0%	25	17	25	11	65%	26%	6%	3%
2015	MIN	16/16	847	49	73	495	67%	+6.0	10.1	5	3	3.9	37	-0.4	7	-6.3%	33	5	33	12	63%	20%	14%	3%
2016	MIN			58	85	586	68%	--	10.1	4						0.6%								

Two years ago, in an interview with the *St. Paul Pioneer Press*, Rudolph declared himself the best tight end in football. This June, the paper asked Rudolph if he still felt this way. With two more years of experience in the league and two more years of wisdom gained on the earth, Rudolph replied "absolutely." He went on to complain about fantasy football and how fans only cared about receiving stats, and while he may not have the numbers of someone like Rob Gronkowski, "if I did my job in the run game and pass protection, [Mike Zimmer] is going to be happy."

First of all, in the modern day of the NFL, catching passes is probably more than half the job for most tight ends, and it's not as if the Vikings have a Jimmy Graham-type receiving specialist to take targets away from Rudolph. Second, Rudolph might have been impressed with himself on film, but the charters at Sports Info Solutions weren't—they ranked him 36th among tight ends in snaps per blown block. Gronkowski, meanwhile, was second. This is some very crude statistical analysis, and it goes without saying that tight ends like Gronk who catch lots of passes will have fewer opportunities to miss blocks. But there's little in Rudolph's receiving or blocking metrics to suggest that he's the best at anything.

Austin Seferian-Jenkins Height: 6-5 Weight: 262   College: Washington   Draft: 2014/2 (38)   Born: 9/29/1992   Age: 24   Risk: Red

Year	Team	G/GS	Snaps	Rec	Pass	Yds	C%	+/-	Yd/C	TD	Drop	YAC	Rk	YAC+	BTkl	DVOA	Rk	DYAR	Rk	YAR	Short	Mid	Deep	Bomb
2014	TB	9/9	447	21	38	221	55%	-0.0	10.5	2	2	2.0	48	-1.8	1	-18.7%	40	-29	38	-30	30%	55%	15%	0%
2015	TB	7/3	218	21	39	338	54%	-2.9	16.1	4	1	4.6	26	+1.2	3	5.0%	23	33	25	62	26%	50%	21%	3%
2016	TB			50	82	615	61%	--	12.3	6							4.5%							

Highly drafted due to his size (6-foot-5, 262 pounds) and speed (4.56 40-yard dash), Seferian-Jenkins was an inconsistent player at Washington and has carried that into the pros by missing 16 games in his first two years. The talent is evident, both as a blocker and as a receiver. But the straight-line speed doesn't show up on tape, and he has yet to show much in the way of absorbing contact or attacking the ball. When it all comes together on a guy like this, you get Rob Gronkowski. After kicking him out of a spring practice for mouthing off to coaches, Tampa may be ready to move on.

Jacob Tamme Height: 6-3   Weight: 236   College: Kentucky   Draft: 2008/4 (127)   Born: 15-Mar-1985   Age: 31   Risk: Green

Year	Team	G/GS	Snaps	Rec	Pass	Yds	C%	+/-	Yd/C	TD	Drop	YAC	Rk	YAC+	BTkl	DVOA	Rk	DYAR	Rk	YAR	Short	Mid	Deep	Bomb
2013	DEN	16/1	264	20	25	184	80%	+3.9	9.2	1	0	3.3	43	-0.7	1	23.7%	7	56	22	53	44%	48%	4%	4%
2014	DEN	15/0	275	14	28	109	50%	-3.9	7.8	2	1	1.6	50	-3.2	1	-42.8%	50	-67	47	-70	34%	41%	17%	7%
2015	ATL	15/8	772	59	81	657	73%	+5.6	11.1	1	1	3.3	41	-1.0	4	5.7%	20	68	17	100	38%	53%	8%	1%
2016	ATL			51	76	553	67%	--	10.8	2							-2.0%							

Freed from his duties as a wandering Peyton Manning disciple, Tamme stumbled into an optimal situation for himself in Atlanta. The team needed him to catch balls, because nobody else besides Julio Jones was doing it. The vast majority of the time he was more of a fourth option, but he came up with 24 catches in three games against Washington, San Francisco, and Tampa Bay. Tamme can definitely continue to produce in this role: decent blocker, decent receiver. Just don't ask him to do anything with the ball after he catches it.

Julius Thomas Height: 6-5   Weight: 251   College: Portland State   Draft: 2011/4 (129)   Born: 27-Jun-1988   Age: 28   Risk: Yellow

Year	Team	G/GS	Snaps	Rec	Pass	Yds	C%	+/-	Yd/C	TD	Drop	YAC	Rk	YAC+	BTkl	DVOA	Rk	DYAR	Rk	YAR	Short	Mid	Deep	Bomb
2013	DEN	14/14	901	65	90	788	72%	+6.0	12.1	12	3	6.2	6	+1.5	6	27.0%	4	214	2	214	58%	24%	18%	0%
2014	DEN	13/10	691	43	62	489	69%	+4.3	11.4	12	1	3.8	33	-0.5	3	24.7%	2	140	6	142	58%	31%	8%	3%
2015	JAC	12/10	541	46	80	455	58%	-4.3	9.9	5	5	3.2	44	-0.8	3	-17.7%	41	-57	49	-42	50%	34%	14%	1%

Thomas blamed his rough first season in Jacksonville on the broken hand he suffered during training camp. Thomas said he couldn't get his timing down or find his spot in the offense because of the time he missed. While the injury likely didn't help, the real issue appeared to be that Thomas was out of shape. His frame looked decidedly rotund compared to the lean figure he had cut while destroying defenses for the Denver Broncos. Thomas could still be hugely valuable for the Jaguars, but he has to prove that he didn't get lazy after getting paid.

Will Tye Height: 6-2 Weight: 262 College: Stony Brook Draft: 2015/FA Born: 4-Nov-1991 Age: 25 Risk: Green

Year	Team	G/GS	Snaps	Rec	Pass	Yds	C%	+/-	Yd/C	TD	Drop	YAC	Rk	YAC+	BTkl	DVOA	Rk	DYAR	Rk	YAR	Short	Mid	Deep	Bomb
2015	NYG	13/7	543	42	62	464	68%	-0.5	11.0	3	4	4.6	23	+0.2	11	5.1%	22	51	20	44	64%	25%	10%	0%
2016	NYG			37	60	412	62%	--	11.1	4						-1.0%								

Compared to all the former basketball players and imposing physical specimens lining up to play tight end these days, the stodgy 6-foot-2 Tye hardly looks the part of a starter. And yet, when Larry Donnell went down with a neck injury last season, the undrafted rookie out of football powerhouse Stony Brook delivered a pleasantly surprising stretch for the Giants. Tye started each of New York's final seven games, effectively becoming Eli Manning's No. 2 option behind Odell Beckham Jr. and ranking second on the offense in targets, receptions, and receiving yards. And most impressively, Tye ranked fourth among tight ends in receiving DYAR over that stretch, ahead of the likes of Rob Gronkowski and Greg Olsen. He's not a future All-Pro, but all those contested catches down the seam didn't smell like a fluke either. While Donnell will be back to challenge for the starting job, Tye likely holds the inside track based on his strong finish to 2015.

Clive Walford Height: 6-4 Weight: 251 College: Miami Draft: 2015/3 (68) Born: 21-Oct-1991 Age: 25 Risk: Yellow

Year	Team	G/GS	Snaps	Rec	Pass	Yds	C%	+/-	Yd/C	TD	Drop	YAC	Rk	YAC+	BTkl	DVOA	Rk	DYAR	Rk	YAR	Short	Mid	Deep	Bomb
2015	OAK	16/2	439	28	50	329	56%	-2.1	11.8	3	1	4.4	30	-0.8	5	-4.1%	31	10	31	-6	38%	32%	26%	4%
2016	OAK			50	79	603	63%	--	12.1	6						5.9%								

Walford's rookie season was about what you'd expect. A decent technical blocker without much strength, he contributed in goal-line packages and had the speed to stretch the seam. There wasn't much in the way of consistency here, but Walford came out of Miami a bit raw. This is a big year for Walford. If he can establish himself as a Dwayne Allen-esque player in Oakland, there will be plenty of targets for him to work with.

Delanie Walker Height: 6-1 Weight: 241 College: Central Missouri Draft: 2006/6 (175) Born: 12-Aug-1984 Age: 32 Risk: Green

Year	Team	G/GS	Snaps	Rec	Pass	Yds	C%	+/-	Yd/C	TD	Drop	YAC	Rk	YAC+	BTkl	DVOA	Rk	DYAR	Rk	YAR	Short	Mid	Deep	Bomb
2013	TEN	15/11	762	60	86	571	70%	+6.8	9.5	6	4	2.9	47	-1.5	4	-0.7%	31	38	25	37	45%	36%	14%	5%
2014	TEN	15/14	769	63	106	890	59%	-1.2	14.1	4	3	6.0	10	+1.4	14	-5.6%	30	12	28	9	40%	40%	14%	6%
2015	TEN	15/10	688	94	133	1088	71%	+9.9	11.6	6	5	4.1	34	-0.3	11	13.0%	12	174	5	164	42%	42%	12%	4%
2016	TEN			72	109	879	66%	--	12.2	5						4.2%								

Despite being a tight end, and a tight end who built his career on being a blocker with the San Francisco 49ers, Walker has somehow become the Tennessee Titans' No. 1 receiver. Walker is one of the most underrated players in the league because of the quarterbacks with whom he has played since signing with the Titans. Though both suffered with injuries last year, Walker and Marcus Mariota established a strong rapport quickly. Mariota was able to throw Walker open down the seams, something his previous quarterbacks couldn't do, while also helping Walker create YAC more easily with his ball placement. The ceiling for Walker's production with Mariota as his quarterback should be very high.

Benjamin Watson Height: 6-3 Weight: 255 College: Duke Draft: 2004/1 (32) Born: 18-Dec-1980 Age: 36 Risk: Red

Year	Team	G/GS	Snaps	Rec	Pass	Yds	C%	+/-	Yd/C	TD	Drop	YAC	Rk	YAC+	BTkl	DVOA	Rk	DYAR	Rk	YAR	Short	Mid	Deep	Bomb
2013	NO	15/7	494	19	30	226	63%	+2.2	11.9	2	0	4.9	22	-0.0	0	2.5%	25	22	31	21	46%	25%	14%	14%
2014	NO	16/8	571	20	31	136	65%	+0.5	6.8	2	2	3.9	30	-1.5	1	-21.3%	43	-29	39	-29	68%	21%	11%	0%
2015	NO	16/16	984	74	110	825	67%	+5.1	11.1	6	5	3.3	43	-1.0	3	4.9%	24	87	13	102	48%	33%	14%	6%
2016	BAL			44	64	506	69%	--	11.5	4						8.5%								

Twenty-two active players last year were drafted in 2004, and many of them were active only in sub roles or as last-chance options. The only non-kickers who look like they're coming into 2016 with a guaranteed role are Eli Manning, Philip Rivers, Ben Roethlisberger, Larry Fitzgerald, DeAngelo Hall, Vince Wilfork, Karlos Dansby, and Watson. Not a bad little career for the final first-rounder of that draft. Watson was rejuvenated in New Orleans last year, dusted off after years of being a block-first tight end, and helped absorb targets after the loss of Jimmy Graham. In Baltimore, he'll give the Ravens what they couldn't count on from their youth and the perpetually hurt Dennis Pitta: reliable play as both a blocker and a receiver.

Maxx Williams Height: 6-4   Weight: 249   College: Minnesota   Draft: 2015/2 (55)   Born: 12-Apr-1994   Age: 22   Risk: Yellow

Year	Team	G/GS	Snaps	Rec	Pass	Yds	C%	+/-	Yd/C	TD	Drop	YAC	Rk	YAC+	BTkl	DVOA	Rk	DYAR	Rk	YAR	Short	Mid	Deep	Bomb
2015	BAL	14/7	477	32	48	268	67%	+0.0	8.4	1	2	4.6	25	-1.0	1	-14.6%	39	-23	39	-40	57%	30%	11%	2%
2016	BAL			33	48	371	69%	--	11.2	2						2.9%								

Baltimore thought it was getting the best receiving tight end in the 2015 draft with Williams in the second round. His rookie year was a struggle and he did not generate many big plays, but this is not uncommon for rookies at the position. The signing of free agent Ben Watson makes it seem pretty unlikely that Williams will be a big contributor in 2016. For such a high draft pick, that would be a disappointment.

Luke Willson Height: 6-5   Weight: 250   College: Rice   Draft: 2013/5 (158)   Born: 15-Jan-1990   Age: 26   Risk: Green

Year	Team	G/GS	Snaps	Rec	Pass	Yds	C%	+/-	Yd/C	TD	Drop	YAC	Rk	YAC+	BTkl	DVOA	Rk	DYAR	Rk	YAR	Short	Mid	Deep	Bomb
2013	SEA	16/7	404	20	28	272	71%	+2.5	13.6	1	1	8.9	4	+4.2	3	18.2%	11	48	24	43	64%	24%	8%	4%
2014	SEA	15/10	556	22	40	362	55%	-2.2	16.5	3	4	9.7	1	+4.0	5	0.6%	24	20	24	21	42%	26%	18%	13%
2015	SEA	14/7	451	17	26	213	65%	+0.4	12.5	1	1	5.5	14	+0.6	4	10.5%	15	30	27	32	44%	44%	8%	4%
2016	SEA			21	32	267	66%	--	12.7	3						7.5%								

He only has 59 catches in three seasons, but Willson has been a reliable target for Russell Wilson, and is capable of making big plays. Should Jimmy Graham be slow to recover this season, Willson is more than capable of holding the fort as the No. 1 tight end in Seattle. It still boggles the mind that Willson (or any Seattle tight end) was never targeted in Super Bowl XLIX.

Jason Witten Height: 6-6   Weight: 265   College: Tennessee   Draft: 2003/3 (69)   Born: 6-May-1982   Age: 34   Risk: Yellow

Year	Team	G/GS	Snaps	Rec	Pass	Yds	C%	+/-	Yd/C	TD	Drop	YAC	Rk	YAC+	BTkl	DVOA	Rk	DYAR	Rk	YAR	Short	Mid	Deep	Bomb
2013	DAL	16/16	984	73	111	851	66%	-0.2	11.7	8	4	4.3	31	-0.2	7	11.2%	15	134	5	120	39%	44%	15%	2%
2014	DAL	16/16	1047	64	90	703	71%	+6.0	11.0	5	2	3.6	37	-0.7	3	17.9%	8	146	5	171	31%	53%	12%	3%
2015	DAL	16/16	1019	77	104	713	74%	+7.9	9.3	3	0	3.0	48	-1.3	3	-1.9%	28	36	24	37	45%	46%	7%	2%
2016	DAL			65	95	687	68%	--	10.6	5						5.8%								

Et tu, Jason? Witten had been one of the steadiest tight ends in the Football Outsiders era, finishing fifth or better in receiving DYAR in 10 of 11 seasons from 2004-14. However, even the 10-time Pro Bowler was not immune to Dallas' self-destruction in 2015, finishing with the worst DVOA and DYAR rankings of his entire career. Ideally, Witten would see his workload scaled back as he commences his 14th season, but appointed heir apparent Gavin Escobar has never developed. Beyond Escobar, the Cowboys have a humdrum cavalcade of blockers and recent seventh-round picks at tight end, leaving Witten to shoulder the load once again. Assuming Tony Romo stays healthier, it's reasonable to expect Witten's numbers to rebound towards more respectable levels. The future Hall of Famer could probably run his short-to-intermediate routes between the seams for another 20 years, but Witten's days as a game-altering weapon may have reached expiration.

Going Deep

Jerell Adams, NYG: Adams was projected as high as the third round by NFL Draft Scout, but fell into the Giants' lap in the sixth round instead. Adams' receiving numbers at South Carolina won't wow you, in part because of the Gamecocks' woeful quarterback play. But his polished blocking should allow Adams to see the field early on, and his 6-foot-5 frame and 4.64 speed have the potential to open eyes. Adams isn't particularly refined as a receiver yet, but his measurables give him a chance to catch on for a New York offense lacking much upside at tight end.

Stephen Anderson, HOU: A hybrid wideout/tight end at Cal, Anderson went undrafted, but good athletic testing results got him noticed. Houston is a team lacking in tight end options and an interest in getting faster, which should give Anderson a shot at making the team and carving out a modest role.

Blake Bell, SF: Bell was kind of like old-school Tim Tebow at Oklahoma: a quarterback brought in to take advantage of his size in the power-running game. Unlike Tebow, Bell was willing to move to tight end. He might actually be the best receiving tight end in San Francisco, but the 49ers also have Vance McDonald and Garrett Celek, and have converted fullback Bruce Miller to tight end. That's a lot of competition in a passing game that still looks like it will struggle this year.

Jeff Cumberland, SD: The Jets spent three years trying to talk themselves into Cumberland as a pass-catching weapon at tight end, getting 23 to 29 receptions per year for their troubles. Chan Gailey saw a big, slow receiver masquerading as a tight end and buried Cumberland in a situational role. Cumberland signed with the Chargers, who drafted Hunter Henry as their second tight end and heir apparent to Antonio Gates. That 29-catch season was probably the high-water mark.

Kellen Davis, NYJ: They don't make tight end stat lines like Davis' anymore. He played 58 snaps in the Jets' first meeting with the Dolphins without getting targeted for a pass. He played 40 snaps against Washington the following week but was targeted just once. Davis' high-water mark for targets last season was three against the Giants; he caught one 8-yard pass in 35 offensive snaps. Davis has never had the receiving chops of Kellen Winslow, but he veered into sixth-lineman territory in 2015. Davis is still on the Jets roster but will see his playing time dwindle if Jace Amaro gets healthy and his act together. It's hard to imagine Davis' productivity dwindling without a position switch to right guard.

Seth DeValve, CLE: Not since the days of Knowlton "Snake" Ames (who was named to the first All-America team in 1889), or perhaps Dick Kazmeier (Heisman Trophy winner, 1951), has the Princeton gridiron known such glory. DeValve was plucked from the New Jersey Ivy by the Browns with the 138th pick in the draft, the highest spot a Tiger has ever been tabbed. DeValve was a wideout/wingback/tight end/all-around chess piece at Princeton, using his imposing frame to outfight opposing brainiacs. The Browns front office, many of whom went to rival Harvard, envision DeValve as a potential mismatch in twin-tight end sets. To meet that expectation, DeValve will have to avoid the multiple foot surgeries that cost him double-digit games over his last two seasons at Princeton.

Glenn Gronkowski, BUF: Gronkowski should be every bit as successful as his more famous older brothers Chris and Dan, who were fullback/H-back types for several teams at the start of the decade. Like those two particular older siblings, Gronk is a solid lead blocker with some rudimentary receiving chops. He played mostly short-yardage fullback at Kansas State, but he had a somewhat impressive Senior Bowl as a pass-catching tight end. Look for Glenn to continue in the proud tradition of the majority of his older brothers by becoming a serviceable NFL role player.

Tyler Higbee, LARM: A fourth-round pick with Higbee's receiving talent and only Lance Kendricks to beat out should feel confident of earning a starting role. Higbee may still do that, but he had a knee injury during his final year at Western Kentucky and pled not guilty to assault charges in the offseason.

Austin Hooper, ATL: Atlanta has the void to fill, and Hooper has the skills to play right away. Hooper was a solid in-line blocker for the Stanford Cardinal, and while that skill hasn't always translated to "Great NFL blocker straight off the shelf" in recent years, he shows the aptitude to be good at it. Hooper has the skill to take contact, and he can run the seam rather well. The question of his ultimate upside is how well he can deal with more pass-oriented NFL concepts. But on talent, nobody on this Atlanta tight end depth chart is Hangin' with Mr. Hooper.

Jesse James, PIT: James not only has a name made for headlines and TV highlight packages, but also a good story as a local boy made good. He grew up in the Pittsburgh suburb of Glassport before playing at Penn State and now for the Steelers. Ladarius Green is still the tight end you want for fantasy purposes, but there's no question that James will have a role in an offense that uses plenty of two-tight end sets. Steelers fans just have to remember that when the large white guy catches the ball, they no longer should chant "Heath!"

Tyler Kroft, CIN: The Bengals have one excellent tight end named Tyler—why not two? OK, no one puts Kroft in Eifert's class, but as a rookie from Rutgers this Ty played well when the "other Ty" was inevitably injured. Now Kroft will be the No. 1 tight end through the summer, and possibly into the fall. He won't cause mismatches like Eifert, or overpower anyone on the line of scrimmage, but he provides a decent enough mix of the two skills required from the position. When Eifert returns, he, Kroft, and rookie wideout Tyler Boyd can form the Tyler Trio and confuse teams by putting their first names on the back of their jerseys.

Troy Niklas, ARI: Niklas has caught 100 percent of his NFL targets. Unfortunately, the 52nd overall pick in the 2014 draft has only seen seven targets in two years. That may not change with Darren Fells and Jermaine Gresham still in town and the Cardinals employing a passing game focused almost entirely on wide receivers. Niklas only had one year of production at Notre Dame, so maybe this shouldn't be too surprising.

Dion Sims, MIA: Start with an offense that forces its best receiver to run mostly 5- to 10-yard drag, slant, and flat routes. Now, imagine how short the routes must be for the H-back/fullback/second tight end. Sims' stat lines include one catch for minus-1 yards in the second meeting with the Jets, one catch for minus-3 against the Texans, plus the usual one-catch, 6-yard lines you expect from the fifth option in the passing game. Sims is athletic and versatile enough to do more; "H-back" was just too subtle a concept for the late-season Dolphins offensive coaches to grasp.

Cole Wick, DET: The local media came away from Detroit OTAs raving about this undrafted rookie from Incarnate Word University, an FCS school that didn't even have football until 2009. Wick's wide catch radius should make him an excellent red zone target, although his actual height seems to be up for debate; different Internet sites list him as everything from 6-foot-5 to 6-foot-7. He's also a strong blocker, which was more of his focus in college. Reports that Wick might actually beat out Eric Ebron as the starting tight end seem a bit far-fetched, but he'll clearly make the roster and is an interesting player to watch in dynasty leagues.

2016 Kicker Projections

listed below are the 2016 KUBIAK projections for kickers. Due to the inconsistency of field-goal percentage from year to year, kickers are projected almost entirely based on team forecasts, although a handful of individual factors do come into play:

- More experience leads to a slightly higher field-goal percentage in general, with the biggest jump between a kicker's rookie and sophomore seasons.
- Kickers with a better career field-goal percentage tend to get more attempts, although they are not necessarily more accurate.
- Field-goal percentage on kicks over 40 yards tends to regress to the mean.

Kickers are listed with their total fantasy points based on two different scoring systems. For **Pts1**, all field goals are worth three points. For **Pts2**, all field goals up to 39 yards are worth three points, field goals of 40-49 yards are worth four points, and field goals over 50 yards are worth five points. Kickers are also listed with a Risk of Green, Yellow, or Red, as explained in the introduction to the section on quarterbacks.

Note that field-goal totals below are rounded, but "fantasy points" are based on the actual projections, so the total may not exactly equal (FG * 3 + XP).

Fantasy Kicker Projections, 2016

Kicker	Team	FG	Pct	XP	Pts1	Pts2	Risk	Kicker	Team	FG	Pct	XP	Pts1	Pts2	Risk
Stephen Gostkowski	NE	32-35	91%	45	140	154	Green	Steven Hauschka	SEA	25-29	86%	45	119	131	Green
Graham Gano	CAR	30-35	86%	48	137	150	Yellow	Robbie Gould	CHI	27-33	82%	37	118	133	Green
Chandler Catanzaro	ARI	30-35	86%	43	133	147	Green	Dan Carpenter	BUF	25-30	83%	41	115	127	Green
Mason Crosby	GB	29-34	85%	44	132	146	Green	Kai Forbath	NO	23-28	82%	44	114	126	Red
Brandon McManus	DEN	33-39	85%	32	130	147	Green	Greg Zuerlein	LARM	26-31	84%	33	111	126	Red
Blair Walsh	MIN	30-36	83%	40	130	145	Yellow	Nick Novak	HOU	25-29	86%	35	109	121	Green
Mike Nugent	CIN	28-33	85%	43	127	139	Yellow	Caleb Sturgis	PHI	24-28	86%	36	108	120	Red
Chris Boswell	PIT	29-37	78%	39	126	140	Green	Roberto Aguayo	TB	23-31	74%	38	108	118	Red
Josh Brown	NYG	30-34	88%	37	126	140	Yellow	Jason Myers	JAC	23-29	79%	36	105	117	Yellow
Justin Tucker	BAL	30-37	81%	36	126	143	Green	Travis Coons	CLE	25-31	81%	27	103	115	Yellow
Cairo Santos	KC	29-34	85%	38	125	138	Red	Phil Dawson	SF	22-28	79%	29	96	108	Green
Dan Bailey	DAL	27-32	84%	42	124	137	Green	Ryan Succop	TEN	20-22	91%	37	96	105	Green
Adam Vinatieri	IND	28-32	88%	41	124	137	Green	Andrew Franks	MIA	20-25	80%	35	95	104	Red
Sebastian Janikowski	OAK	30-36	83%	34	124	141	Green								
Dustin Hopkins	WAS	31-36	86%	31	124	137	Red								
Josh Lambo	SD	28-32	88%	39	123	135	Red								
Nick Folk	NYJ	29-34	85%	34	122	135	Yellow								
Matt Prater	DET	28-34	82%	37	121	134	Yellow								
Matt Bryant	ATL	27-31	87%	38	120	132	Yellow								

Other kickers who may win jobs:							
Kicker	Team	FG	Pct	XP	Pts1	Pts2	Risk
Zach Hocker	NO	24-29	82%	44	113	124	Red
Carey Spear	CLE	25-33	76%	26	104	118	Red

2016 Fantasy Defense Projections

Listed below are the 2016 KUBIAK projections for fantasy team defense. The projection method is discussed in an essay in *Pro Football Prospectus 2006*, the key conclusions of which were:

• Schedule strength is very important for projecting fantasy defense.
• Categories used for scoring in fantasy defense have no consistency from year-to-year whatsoever, with the exception of sacks and interceptions.

Fumble recoveries and defensive touchdowns are forecast solely based on the projected sacks and interceptions, rather than the team's totals in these categories from a year ago. This is why the 2016 projections may look very different from the fantasy defense values from the 2015 season. Safeties and shutouts are not common enough to have a significant effect on the projections. Team defenses are also projected with Risk factor of Green, Yellow, or Red; this is based on the team's projection compared to performance in recent seasons.

In addition to projection of separate categories, we also give an overall total based on our generic fantasy scoring formula: one point for a sack, two points for a fumble recovery or interception, and six points for a touchdown. Remember that certain teams (in particular, the Seahawks) will score better if your league also gives points for limiting opponents' scoring or yardage. Special-teams touchdowns are listed separately and are not included in the fantasy scoring total listed.

Fantasy Team Defense Projections, 2016

Team	Fant Pts	Sack	Int	Fum Rec	Def TD	Risk	ST TD	Team	Fant Pts	Sack	Int	Fum Rec	Def TD	Risk	ST TD
DEN	122	47.3	15.5	10.5	3.8	Yellow	0.9	PIT	102	37.6	15.9	8.0	2.7	Green	0.7
NE	115	44.0	15.9	11.6	2.6	Yellow	0.7	NYJ	101	35.8	14.0	9.5	3.0	Yellow	0.7
SEA	112	40.9	14.4	11.0	3.5	Yellow	0.9	JAC	100	36.8	12.6	10.8	2.8	Yellow	0.9
ARI	112	42.6	16.7	10.1	2.6	Green	0.8	PHI	100	36.1	13.1	10.1	2.9	Green	1.7
CIN	111	41.1	15.7	11.8	2.4	Yellow	0.9	MIA	99	35.8	10.6	11.5	3.1	Yellow	0.9
KC	109	41.4	15.9	10.5	2.4	Yellow	0.7	BAL	98	41.7	12.1	10.5	1.8	Yellow	1.0
MIN	108	35.2	14.6	12.0	3.2	Yellow	1.8	SD	98	37.3	13.2	9.5	2.5	Red	1.0
DAL	107	32.3	14.7	12.5	3.4	Red	0.9	WAS	97	34.6	13.0	8.2	3.4	Yellow	1.0
CAR	107	38.9	14.7	10.5	2.9	Green	0.8	TEN	97	38.0	12.7	10.0	2.3	Yellow	0.9
NYG	105	37.1	13.4	11.7	3.0	Yellow	1.0	TB	97	35.3	12.7	9.7	2.8	Green	0.9
LARM	105	39.1	14.3	10.1	2.8	Yellow	0.6	CHI	97	34.9	13.3	10.0	2.5	Red	1.1
BUF	104	37.9	14.8	11.1	2.5	Yellow	0.8	OAK	95	35.5	12.2	9.9	2.5	Yellow	0.8
HOU	104	37.3	13.3	10.0	3.3	Yellow	0.8	NO	93	33.7	12.3	9.1	2.8	Red	1.1
DET	104	38.5	13.4	11.7	2.5	Yellow	0.9	ATL	87	28.9	12.2	10.1	2.3	Yellow	1.3
GB	103	39.2	14.9	10.2	2.3	Yellow	0.7	SF	86	33.0	9.7	9.6	2.4	Yellow	0.7
IND	103	37.5	12.7	11.8	2.8	Green	0.8	CLE	85	31.5	11.5	7.8	2.4	Green	1.0

Projected Defensive Leaders, 2016

Solo Tackles			Total Tackles			Sacks			Interceptions		
Player	Team	Tkl	Player	Team	Tkl	Player	Team	Sacks	Player	Team	Int
N.Bowman	SF	106	L.David	TB	146	J.J.Watt	HOU	14.3	M.Peters	KC	3.4
L.David	TB	93	N.Bowman	SF	142	K.Mack	OAK	12.9	R.Darby	BUF	3.3
L.Kuechly	CAR	93	L.Kuechly	CAR	142	E.Ansah	DET	12.4	T.Johnson	LARM	3.2
D.Levy	DET	91	D.Jackson	IND	136	C.Jones	ARI	12.2	R.Johnson	TEN	3.2
T.Smith	JAC	88	C.J.Mosley	BAL	129	V.Miller	DEN	11.4	R.Jones	MIA	3.1
M.Smith	OAK	86	B.Wagner	SEA	122	R.Quinn	LARM	11.0	T.Mathieu	ARI	3.0
R.Jones	MIA	86	T.Smith	JAC	121	E.Dumervil	BAL	10.7	M.Adams	IND	3.0
J.Hicks	PHI	85	A.Ogletree	LARM	120	J.Pierre-Paul	NYG	10.7	B.Grimes	TB	3.0
A.Ogletree	LARM	85	S.Lee	DAL	118	R.Kerrigan	WAS	10.6	R.Nelson	OAK	3.0
P.Posluszny	JAC	84	P.Brown	BUF	117	C.Barwin	PHI	10.5	D.House	JAC	3.0
C.J.Mosley	BAL	84	L.Timmons	PIT	116	M.Williams	MIA	10.3	L.David	TB	3.0
D.Bucannon	ARI	83	M.Barron	LARM	114	E.Griffen	MIN	10.2	G.Quin	DET	3.0

College Football Introduction and Statistical Toolbox

Welcome to the Football Outsiders College Football Almanac and our deep dive into the numbers that will shape the 2016 season. Since 2003, Brian Fremeau has been developing and enhancing the drive-based Fremeau Efficiency Index (FEI) and its companion statistics; for the last nine years, Bill Connelly has explored play-by-play and drive data to refine his system, the S&P+ ratings. Both systems are opponent-adjusted and effective in evaluating team strengths and weaknesses.

Consensus isn't our objective. By taking two distinct statistical approaches, we often find that our respective ratings systems disagree about some teams in significant ways. A team that finds success at the play level but isn't as efficient on drives is one that might be worth drilling into for more detail. The FEI and S&P+ distinctions sometimes highlight essential information about a team and its capacity to win the rivalry game, the division crown, or the national championship.

The combination of FEI and S&P+ is our F/+ ratings, designed to balance out the distinctions and best summarize the overall quality of each team. For the first time in our collaborative history, our projection models for the upcoming season are in lock step at the top. The four best teams in 2016 according to both FEI and S&P+ projections will be the Alabama Crimson Tide, LSU Tigers, Clemson Tigers, and Oklahoma Sooners. Consensus is disconcerting.

Alabama and LSU could play out the year as the two best teams in college football, but there may only be room for one of them on the College Football Playoff dance card in the end. As SEC West division rivals, they'll face off in Baton Rouge in early November, potentially with a division championship on the line. Five years ago, these two programs slugged it out in the regular season only to be rewarded with a rematch in the BCS championship game. The playoff format is still in its infancy, and the selection committee hasn't yet been forced to consider the merits of a pair of teams from the same conference for inclusion in the playoff.

The ACC Atlantic division may present the same dilemma. Clemson returns nearly all of the explosive and dynamic offensive weapons they used to take Alabama down to the wire in January, but their division rival Florida State Seminoles have one of the most loaded rosters in the game and will play host to the Tigers in late October. How will the selection committee handle their process if the only undefeated and one-loss teams at season's end are concentrated in two conferences?

Our projections pose interesting questions for the other conferences as well. The off-season turmoil that rocked the football program at Baylor doesn't register in our numbers. Will the Bears be a Big 12 conference contender as their recent program data points indicate, or will the coaching staff shakeup and institutional issues ultimately render them weaker than the sum of their parts?

The highest ranked team out of the Big Ten according to our F/+ projections is Ohio State, but no team needs to replace more key contributors than the Buckeyes. In November they'll face the Michigan Wolverines, a team getting loads of attention and preseason accolades from media and fans as a potential national championship contender, but one that doesn't have the recent performance history to be ranked quite that highly in our projections.

We're confident in the overall accuracy of our F/+ projection model, but we're also absolutely certain that our data will miss the mark on several teams as well. Consensus isn't nearly as fun as chaos, and we can't wait to find out how the college football season will surprise us again this year.

The College Statistical Toolbox section that follows this introduction explains the methodology of FEI, S&P+, F/+, and other stats you will encounter in the college section of this book. There are similarities to Football Outsiders' NFL-based DVOA ratings in the combined approach, but college football presents a unique set of challenges different from the NFL. All football stats must be adjusted according to context, but how? If Team A and Team B do not play one another and don't share any common opponents, how can their stats be effectively compared? Should a team from the SEC or Big 12 be measured against that of an average team in its own conference, or an average team across all conferences?

Our mission is to continue to drill deeper into the statistical measures that fuel success on the field for each and every FBS team, though this book is particularly focused on the playoff and conference contenders for the year ahead. Each of the 50 team capsules provides a snapshot of the team's projection for 2016 and the statistical factors that went into the projection. The capsules also include a game-by-game graphic highlighting our projected win likelihoods for the year ahead. Supplementing the stat work, college football staff writers Chad Peltier and Ian Boyd explore player and coaching personnel changes, offensive and defensive advantages and deficiencies, and schedule highlights and pitfalls in a thorough summary of each team's keys to the upcoming season.

For each of the 128 FBS teams, we project the likelihood of every possible regular-season record, conference and nonconference alike. We've included division, overall conference, and College Football Playoff projections for every team as well.

By taking two different statistical approaches to reach one exciting series of answers to college football's most important questions, we feel we are at the forefront of the ongoing debates. Enjoy the college football section of *Football Outsiders Almanac 2016*, and join us at www.FootballOutsiders.com/college throughout the season.

College Statistics Toolbox

Regular readers of FootballOutsiders.com may be familiar with the FEI and S&P+ stats published throughout the year. Others may be learning about our advanced approach to college football stats analysis for the first time by reading this book. In either case, this College Statistics Toolbox section is highly recommended reading before getting into the team capsules. The stats that form the building blocks for F/+, FEI, and S&P+ are constantly being updated and refined.

Each team profile begins with a statistical snapshot. The projected overall and conference records—rounded from the team's projected Mean Wins—are listed alongside the team name in the header. Other stats and rankings provided in the team snapshot and highlighted in the team capsules are explained below.

DRIVE-BY-DRIVE DATA

Fremeau Efficiency Index: The Fremeau Efficiency Index (FEI) is based on opponent-adjusted drive efficiency. Approximately 20,000 possessions are contested annually in FBS vs. FBS games. First-half clock-kills and end-of-game garbage drives are filtered out. Unadjusted game efficiency is a measure of net success on non-garbage possessions, the success of the offensive, defensive, and special teams units in terms of maximizing the team's own scoring opportunities and minimizing those of its opponent. FEI opponent adjustments are calculated with an emphasis placed on quality performances against good teams, win or lose.

Offensive and Defensive FEI: Maximizing success on offensive possessions and minimizing success on opponent possessions begins with an understanding of the value of field position. An average offense facing an average defense may expect to score 2.1 points on average at the conclusion of the drive. If that drive begins at the offense's own 15-yard line, the average scoring value is only 1.5 points. If it begins at the opponent's 15-yard line, the average scoring value is 4.9

points. Offensive and defensive efficiency is in part a function of the variable value of starting field position.

Likewise, drive-ending field position is an important component as well. Touchdowns represent the ultimate goal of an offensive possession, but drives that fall short of the end zone can add scoring value as well. National field goal success rates correlate strongly with proximity to the end zone, and an offense that drives deep into opponent territory to set up a chip shot field goal generates more scoring value than one that ends a drive at the edge of or outside field goal range.

The basic value generated by an offense on a given possession is the difference between the drive-ending value and the value of field position at the start of the drive. Offensive efficiency is the average per-possession value generated or lost by the offense. Defensive efficiency is the average per-possession value generated or lost by the defense. Offensive FEI and Defensive FEI are the opponent-adjusted per-possession values generated or lost by these units.

PLAY-BY-PLAY DATA

Success Rates: More than one million plays over the last ten years in college football have been collected and evaluated to determine baselines for success for every situational down in a game. Similarly to DVOA, basic success rates are determined by national standards. The distinction for college football is in defining the standards of success. We use the following determination of a "successful" play:

- First down success = 50 percent of necessary yardage
- Second down success = 70 percent of necessary yardage
- Third/Fourth down success = 100 percent of necessary yardage

On a per-play basis, these form the standards of efficiency for every offense in college football. Defensive success rates are based on preventing the same standards of achievement.

Equivalent Points and Points per Play: All yards are not created equal. A 10-yard gain from a team's own 15-yard

No. 1 Alabama Crimson Tide (11-1, 7-1)

2016 Projections		Projection Factors		Projected Win Likelihood by Game				
F/+	71.3 (1)	2015 F/+	71.3 (1)	Date	Opponent (Proj Rank)	PWL	Projected Loss	Projected Win
FEI	.290 (1)	2015 FEI	.333 (1)	Sep 3	vs USC (12)	87%		
S&P+	26.8 (1)	2015 S&P+	30.0 (1)	Sep 10	vs W. Kentucky (46)	99%		
Total Wins	10.8	5-Year F/+	65.7 (1)	Sep 17	at Ole Miss (5)	77%		
Conf Wins	6.9	5-Year FEI	.317 (1)	Sep 24	vs Kent St. (101)	99%		
SOS	.016 (6)	5-Year S&P+	27.3 (1)	Oct 1	vs Kentucky (89)	99%		
Conf SOS	.027 (6)	2-Year Recruiting	97.3 (1)	Oct 8	at Arkansas (18)	87%		
Div Champ	.577	5-Year Recruiting	98.2 (1)	Oct 15	at Tennessee (10)	82%		
Conf Champ	.346	Ret. Offense	.448	Oct 22	vs Texas A&M (23)	96%		
CFP Berth	.374	Ret. Defense	.660	Nov 5	at LSU (2)	59%		
				Nov 12	vs Mississippi St. (21)	96%		
				Nov 19	vs Chattanooga (FCS)	100%		
				Nov 26	vs Auburn (24)	97%		

line does not have the same value as a 10-yard gain that goes from the opponent's 10-yard line into the end zone. Based on expected scoring rates by field position, we calculate a point value for each play in a drive. Equivalent Points (EqPts) are calculated by subtracting the value of the resulting yard line from the initial yard line of a given play. This assigns credit to the yards that are most associated with scoring points, the end goal in any possession.

With EqPts, the game can be broken down and built back up again in a number of ways. With the addition of penalties, turnovers, and special teams play, EqPts provides an accurate assessment of how a game was played on a play-by-play basis. Average EqPts per play (PPP) measures consistency and IsoPPP measures EqPts per play on successful plays only as a way to isolate of explosiveness.

S&P: Like OPS (on-base percentage plus slugging average) in baseball, we created a measure that combines consistency with power. S&P represents a combination of efficiency (Success Rates) and explosiveness (Points per Play) to most accurately represent the effectiveness of a team or individual player.

A boom-or-bust running back may have an excellent per carry average and PPP, but his low Success Rate will lower his S&P. A consistent running back who gains between 4 and 6 yards every play, on the other hand, will have a strong Success Rate but possibly low PPP. The best offenses in the country can maximize both efficiency and explosiveness on a down-by-down basis. Reciprocally, the best defenses can limit both.

S&P+: As with the FEI stats discussed above, context matters in college football. Adjustments are made to the S&P unadjusted data with a formula that takes into account a team's production, the quality of the opponent, and the quality of the opponent's opponent. To eliminate the noise of less-informative blowout stats, we filtered the play-by-play data to include only those that took place when the game was "close." This excludes plays where the score margin is larger than 28 points in the first quarter, 24 points in the second quarter, 21 points in the third quarter, or 16 points in the fourth quarter.

Beginning in 2013, we also factored in a drive efficiency measure that is calculated in a similar fashion to PPP, by comparing the expected value of a given drive (based on starting field position) to the actual value a team produces and adjusting it for the opponent at hand. The ability to finish drives is a singular skill that isn't perfectly encapsulated in a measure that only looks at play-by-play data.

The combination of the play-by-play and drive data gives us S&P+, a comprehensive measure that represents a team's efficiency and explosiveness as compared to all other teams in college football. S&P+ values are calibrated around an average rating of 100. An above-average team, offensively or defensively, will have an S&P+ rating greater than 100. A below-average team will have an S&P+ rating lower than 100. The "+" adjustment can be used for other components, as well, such as Success Rate+ and PPP+.

Five Factors: In January 2014, Bill Connelly introduced a new set of concepts for analysis and debate within the realm of college football stats. At Football Study Hall, a college football stats site within the SB Nation network, he wrote the following: "Over time, I've come to realize that the sport comes down to five basic things, four of which you can mostly control. You make more big plays than your opponent, you stay on schedule, you tilt the field, you finish drives, and you fall on the ball. Explosiveness, efficiency, field position, finishing drives, and turnovers are the five factors to winning football games."

Unlike the Four Factors used by ESPN's Dean Oliver for discussion of basketball, these factors are heavily related to each other, and at press time, work to unpack each one is still ongoing. But for team tables in this section, we are including the following measures, which represent each of the five factors as currently constituted: Success Rate+ (the opponent-adjusted version of Success Rate), IsoPPP+ (an opponent-adjusted look at the average PPP gained only in successful plays), FPA (Brian Fremeau's Field Position Advantage measure), Red Zone S&P+, and Adjusted Turnover Margin (a comparison of a team's actual turnover margin to what would have been expected with neutral luck).

Highlight Yards: Highlight yards represent the yards gained by a runner outside of those credited to the offensive line through Adjusted Line Yards. The ALY formula, much like the same stat in the NFL, gives 100 percent credit to all yards gained between 0 and 4 yards and 50 percent strength to yards between 5 and 10 to the offensive line. If a runner gains 12 yards in a given carry, and we attribute 7.0 of those yards to the line, and the player's highlight yardage on the play is 5.0 yards. Beginning in 2013, we began calculating highlight yardage averages in a slightly different manner: Instead of dividing total highlight yardage by a player's overall number of carries, we divide it only by the number of carries that gain more than 4 yards; if a line is given all credit for gains smaller than that, then it makes sense to look at highlight averages only for the carries on which a runner got a chance to create a highlight.

Opportunity Rate: Opportunity Rate represents the percentage of a runner's carries that gained at least 5 yards. This gives us a look at a runner's (and his line's) consistency and efficiency to go along with the explosiveness measured by Highlight Yards.

Adjusted Score/Adjusted Points: Taking a team's single-game S&P+ for both offense and defense, and applying it to a normal distribution of points scored in a given season, can give us an interesting, descriptive look at a team's performance in a given game and season. Adjusting for pace and opponent, Adjusted Score asks the same question of every team in every game: if Team A had played a perfectly average opponent in a given game, how would they have fared? Adjusted Score allows us to look at in-season trends as well, since the week-to-week baseline is opponent-independent.

COMBINATION DATA

F/+: Introduced in *Football Outsiders Almanac 2009*, the F/+ measure combines FEI and S&P+. There is a clear distinction between the two individual approaches, and merging the two diminishes certain outliers caused by the quirks of each method. The resulting metric is both powerfully predictive and sensibly evaluative.

Projected F/+: Relative to the pros, college football teams are much more consistent in year-to-year performance. Breakout seasons and catastrophic collapses certainly occur, but generally speaking, teams can be expected to play within a reasonable range of their baseline program expectations. The idea of a Football Outsiders program rating began with the introduction of Program FEI in *Pro Football Prospectus 2008* as a way to represent those individual baseline expectations.

As the strength of the F/+ system has been fortified with more seasons of full drive-by-drive and play-by-play data, the Program F/+ measure has emerged. Program F/+ is calculated from five years of FEI and S&P+ data. The result not only represents the status of each team's program power, but provides the first step in projecting future success. For each team statistical profile, we provide each team's five-year ratings profile and other projection factors that are included in the formula for the Projected FEI, Projected S&P+, and Projected F/+ ratings.

Recruiting success rates are based on a blend of Rivals. com and 247Sports.com recruiting ratings. The percentile rating for each team's two-year recruiting success and five-year recruiting success reflect the potential impact for both recent star-studded classes and the depth of talent for each team. For the first time this year, our returning experience data represents the percentage of production that returns to the roster this fall rather than a simple count of players labeled as starters. Program F/+ ratings are a function of program ratings and these recruiting and returning production transition factors.

Strength of Schedule: Unlike other rating systems, our Strength of Schedule (SOS) calculation is not a simple average of the Projected F/+ data of each team's opponents. Instead, it represents the likelihood that an elite team (typical top-five team) would win every game on the given schedule. The distinction is valid. For any elite team, playing No. 1 Alabama and No. 128 Massachusetts in a two-game stretch is certainly more difficult than playing No. 64 Arizona and No. 65 Cincinnati. An average rating might judge these schedules to be equal.

The likelihood of an undefeated season is calculated as the product of individual game projected win likelihoods. Generally speaking, an elite team may have a 75 percent chance of defeating a team ranked No. 10, an 85 percent chance of defeating a team ranked No. 20, and a 95 percent chance of defeating a team ranked No. 40. Combined, the elite team has a 61 percent likelihood of defeating all three (0.75 x 0.85 x 0.95 = 0.606).

A lower SOS rating represents a lower likelihood of an elite team running the table, and thus a stronger schedule. For our calculations of FBS versus FCS games, with all due apologies to North Dakota State et al., the likelihood of victory is 100 percent in the formula.

Mean Wins and Win Probabilities: To project records for each team, we use Projected F/+ and win likelihood formulas to estimate the likelihood of victory for a given team in its individual games. The probabilities for winning each game are added together to represent the average number of wins the team is expected to tally over the course of its scheduled games. Potential conference championship games and bowl games are not included.

The projected records listed next to each team name in the conference chapters are rounded from the mean wins data listed in the team capsule. Mean Wins are not intended to represent projected outcomes of specific matchups; rather they are our most accurate forecast for the team's season as a whole. The correlation of mean projected wins to actual wins is 0.69 for all games, 0.61 for conference games.

Win likelihoods are also used to produce the likelihood of each team winning a division or championship. Our College Football Playoff appearance likelihoods are a function of each team's likelihood to go undefeated or finish the season with one loss as well as the strength of the team's conference and overall schedule, factors that the CFP selection committee considers in their process.

The Win Probability tables that appear in each conference chapter are also based on the game-by-game win likelihood data for each team. The likelihood for each record is rounded to the nearest whole percent.

Brian Fremeau and Bill Connelly

NCAA Top 50 Teams

No. 1 Alabama Crimson Tide (11-1, 7-1)

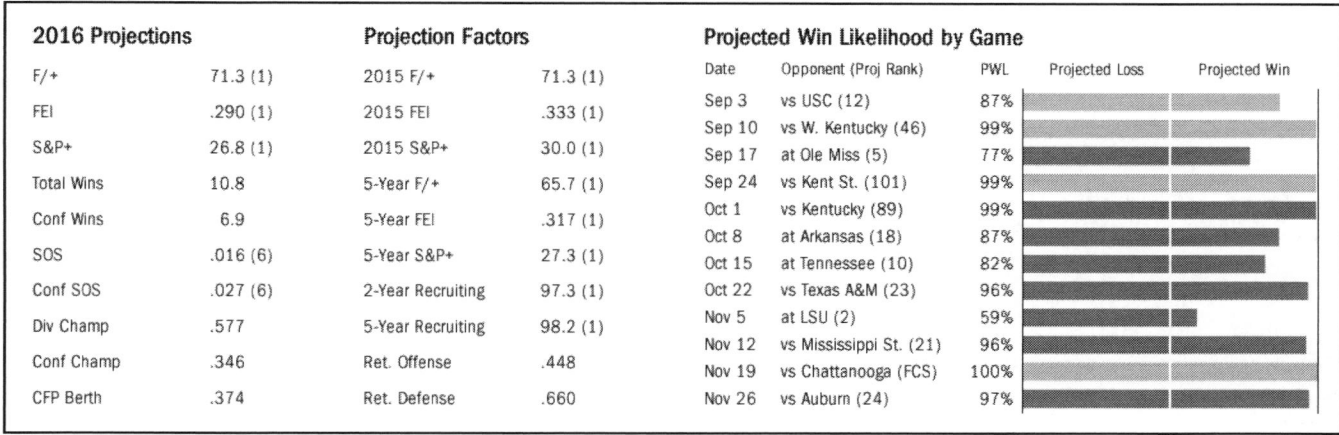

2016 Projections			Projection Factors		
F/+	71.3 (1)		2015 F/+	71.3 (1)	
FEI	.290 (1)		2015 FEI	.333 (1)	
S&P+	26.8 (1)		2015 S&P+	30.0 (1)	
Total Wins	10.8		5-Year F/+	65.7 (1)	
Conf Wins	6.9		5-Year FEI	.317 (1)	
SOS	.016 (6)		5-Year S&P+	27.3 (1)	
Conf SOS	.027 (6)		2-Year Recruiting	97.3 (1)	
Div Champ	.577		5-Year Recruiting	98.2 (1)	
Conf Champ	.346		Ret. Offense	.448	
CFP Berth	.374		Ret. Defense	.660	

Projected Win Likelihood by Game

Date	Opponent (Proj Rank)	PWL
Sep 3	vs USC (12)	87%
Sep 10	vs W. Kentucky (46)	99%
Sep 17	at Ole Miss (5)	77%
Sep 24	vs Kent St. (101)	99%
Oct 1	vs Kentucky (89)	99%
Oct 8	at Arkansas (18)	87%
Oct 15	at Tennessee (10)	82%
Oct 22	vs Texas A&M (23)	96%
Nov 5	at LSU (2)	59%
Nov 12	vs Mississippi St. (21)	96%
Nov 19	vs Chattanooga (FCS)	100%
Nov 26	vs Auburn (24)	97%

The reigning national champions have a program that doesn't rebuild, it reloads. Alabama is in the same position it has been for the better part of the last decade: the team most likely to contend for the SEC championship and the College Football Playoff.

The Crimson Tide defense returns the top three pass-rushers from the most dominant pass-rushing unit that Nick Saban has ever fielded in Tuscaloosa. With defensive end Jonathan Allen back (12 sacks in 2015) along with outside linebackers Tim Williams (9.5 sacks) and Ryan Anderson (6.5 sacks), the Tide can once again combine tight coverage in the secondary with intense pressure up front, the formula that produced the third-ranked passing down defense in 2015.

Alabama's top-ranked rushing S&P and standard down defensive rankings may be more difficult to replicate with inside linebacker Reggie Ragland and nose tackle Jarron Reed now playing on Sundays. The Tide's interior defense was insanely dominant in 2015, yielding 100 rushing yards only three times all season. Georgia was bottled up in a 38-10 thrashing except for one 83-yard touchdown sprint from Nick Chubb. Tennessee averaged only 3.4 yards per carry against the Tide. Clemson only averaged 3.8 yards per carry in the championship game and found most of its rushing success on Deshaun Watson scrambles. If five-star sophomore tackle Da'Ron Payne and five-star senior linebacker Reuben Foster play to their elite potential, Alabama's interior defense will be fine.

The secondary will feature a pair of 6-foot-1 sophomores at cornerback in Minkah Fitzpatrick and Marlon Humphrey, key positions to press and lock down receivers to buy time for the Tide pass rush. Senior Eddie Jackson (six interceptions in 2015) moves from cornerback to strong safety alongside sophomore free safety Ronnie Harrison. The young defensive backs will be in good hands with Jeremy Pruitt back on Saban's staff to coordinate the defense and help oversee the secondary. Pruitt was the secondary coach for Alabama's legendary 2011 secondary before taking a job as the defensive coordinator at Florida State where he coached another legendary secondary in 2013, winning national championships on each occasion.

The offense will have to overcome losses such as quarterback Jake Coker, center Ryan Kelly, and star running back Derrick Henry, but it does return potential first-round left tackle Cam Robinson (pending legal issues), most of the offensive line, superstar tight end O.J. Howard, and a collection of young wide receivers that shined in the playoffs a year ago while eviscerating the Michigan State and Clemson pass defenses.

Alabama's typical "pound the ball between the tackles with inside zone" approach has been bolstered by more spread sets and run/pass option plays since offensive coordinator Lane Kiffin arrived in 2014. This combination has had the effect of forcing defenses to handle star wide receivers like Amari Cooper while also keeping a lid on backs like T.J. Yeldon and Derrick Henry. The results have been remarkably gaudy stats for their offensive bellcows achieved through relatively simple and turnover-averse tactics.

Running backs Bo Scarborough and Damien Harris are now competing for the carries while wideout Calvin Ridley figures to be the primary target on the perimeter. There's excitement in Tuscaloosa about true freshman and early enrollee quarterback Jalen Hurts, but traditionally Saban has plugged in veterans who specialize in distributing the ball to the athletes while avoiding mistakes. Alabama ranked 45th nationally a year ago in sacks allowed and took five against both Clemson and Tennessee. This is due to Saban hard-wiring his quarterbacks to take sacks before taking risks with the football. Alabama wants their quarterbacks to have to do as little as possible in the Tide formula for victory. With that history in mind, redshirt junior Cooper Bateman seems most likely to take the baton as the eldest signal-caller on campus.

A bet on Alabama is a bet on Nick Saban and his staff successfully leveraging all the returning talent while plugging in pieces from each of the top-ranked recruiting classes the Tide have secured in the last five years.

No. 2 LSU Tigers (10-2, 6-2)

2016 Projections		Projection Factors	
F/+	61.2 (2)	2015 F/+	39.1 (10)
FEI	.236 (2)	2015 FEI	.167 (15)
S&P+	24.4 (2)	2015 S&P+	18.6 (9)
Total Wins	10.3	5-Year F/+	43.4 (5)
Conf Wins	6.4	5-Year FEI	.168 (12)
SOS	.030 (9)	5-Year S&P+	19.0 (2)
Conf SOS	.035 (8)	2-Year Recruiting	92.5 (8)
Div Champ	.344	5-Year Recruiting	93.9 (7)
Conf Champ	.206	Ret. Offense	.962
CFP Berth	.201	Ret. Defense	.883

Projected Win Likelihood by Game

Date	Opponent (Proj Rank)	PWL	Projected Loss / Projected Win
Sep 3	vs Wisconsin (36)	95%	
Sep 10	vs Jacksonville St. (FCS)	100%	
Sep 17	vs Mississippi St. (21)	91%	
Sep 24	at Auburn (24)	85%	
Oct 1	vs Missouri (40)	97%	
Oct 8	at Florida (26)	86%	
Oct 15	vs Southern Miss (77)	99%	
Oct 22	vs Ole Miss (5)	78%	
Nov 5	vs Alabama (1)	41%	
Nov 12	at Arkansas (18)	78%	
Nov 19	vs S. Alabama (111)	99%	
Nov 24	at Texas A&M (23)	84%	

Any hesitation in proclaiming Alabama the kings of the SEC West again comes from the stiff competition in the rest of the division, starting with their rivals down in Baton Rouge.

The 2015 LSU Tigers looked a lot like most of the other squads in the Les Miles era. They pounded the ball on the ground with a massive offensive line filled with NFL prospects and a freakishly talented feature running back to land just enough kill shots with their play-action passing game to overcome suspect quarterback play. On defense, they enjoyed lockdown coverage from a stable of exceptional defensive backs while bringing the heat on passing downs with their line. All of this is likely to ring true for 2016 as well.

The offense is young yet experienced, with the trio of quarterback Brandon Harris, running back Leonard Fournette, and wide receiver Malachi Dupre certain to be the focal point of the Tiger attack. Fournette ranked as one of the most explosive backs in the country in 2015, finishing with 6.83 highlight yards per carry despite heavy usage (just over 300 carries on the year). At 6-foot-1 and 230 pounds, he has an extraordinary blend of speed and size that allows him to be effective at running through arm tackles at the first level and then either stiff-arming or simply out-running defensive backs at the second level. Malachi Dupre was effective in 2015, leading all wide receivers with 698 yards and six touchdowns, but figures to be the primary beneficiary from any growth by quarterback Brandon Harris as he enters his third year in the system and second as the full-time starter.

Whether LSU breaks through into the top 10 in offensive S&P (12th in 2015) and manages to successfully challenge Alabama will likely depend on how well Harris provides an explosive constraint to teams that try to load the box to stop Fournette. The Tigers were 9-1 in 2015 when Harris threw the ball less than 30 times (the single loss was to Alabama) and 0-2 in games where Harris threw 30 or more passes. It was difficult to force the Tigers to throw the ball in 2015, but if teams could do it then that was pretty much all she wrote. That will need to change in 2016 for LSU to compete for the division crown.

The offensive line will have a part to play in this as well, of

course, and returns Maea Teuhema (moving from guard to left tackle), William Clapp (left guard), and Ethan Pocic (center). As is typically the case, there's a lot of size and talent in this group. If Teuhema, who started as a true freshman a year ago, is ready to make another leap and lock down the left tackle position, then the prognosis is good.

On defense the Tigers have always enjoyed the advantage of having one of the most athletic squads in the country, but now they add defensive coordinator Dave Aranda, who for the last several years has been molding top defenses at Wisconsin with much slower players across the board than he's found at LSU.

Aranda's "smart aggression" philosophy is all about crafting blitzes that can attack soft spots in protection with only four or five pass-rushers while still dropping back into their base coverages. This LSU secondary doesn't necessarily need that same kind of protection but there's little doubt that they could thrive if allowed to play at advantage behind a good pass rush.

The Tigers are returning three proven cornerbacks in Tre'Davious White, Kevin Tolliver II, and Ed Paris along with both starting safeties in Ricky Jefferson and Jamal Adams. This could be one of the better secondaries in the country in 2016 with White and Adams as the key pieces. Adams had four interceptions and six pass break-ups a year ago while also serving as LSU's box safety/rover. He's an exceptional and versatile athlete that will be featured in a defensive scheme that regularly asks players to handle multiple positions as part of the blitz package.

Up front the new Tigers defensive coordinator also has a fair amount of experience and talent returning, highlighted by junior defensive lineman Davon Godchaux and senior middle linebacker Kendal Beckwith, both of whom will enjoy having blitz packages designed to set them up with favorable matchups. Those two combined to rack up 9.5 sacks a year ago but will be positioned to really run wild in 2016.

The big question mark is the run defense, which ranked 50th in 2015 according to S&P and has struggled to field defensive tackles that could hold up to mauling double-teams of the sort that rivals like Alabama bring on Saturdays. Against SEC West opponents the Tigers gave up 993 yards on 222 carries at 4.5 yards per carry—not terrible, but not up to their usual standards either.

Another year under legendary defensive line coach Ed Orgeron should help here, but if LSU isn't strong on standard downs, there will be fewer opportunities for Aranda's brilliant pass-rushing tactics to come to bear on passing downs.

No. 3 Clemson Tigers (11-1, 7-1)

2016 Projections			Projection Factors		
F/+	60.9 (3)		2015 F/+	61.2 (2)	
FEI	.235 (3)		2015 FEI	.270 (2)	
S&P+	24.2 (3)		2015 S&P+	27.4 (2)	
Total Wins	11.2		5-Year F/+	33.3 (12)	
Conf Wins	7.4		5-Year FEI	.226 (4)	
SOS	.196 (57)		5-Year S&P+	14.5 (13)	
Conf SOS	.275 (50)		2-Year Recruiting	92.9 (6)	
Div Champ	.739		5-Year Recruiting	91.6 (14)	
Conf Champ	.502		Ret. Offense	.897	
CFP Berth	.531		Ret. Defense	.498	

Projected Win Likelihood by Game

Date	Opponent (Proj Rank)	PWL	Projected Loss / Projected Win
Sep 3	at Auburn (24)	85%	
Sep 10	vs Troy (105)	99%	
Sep 17	vs S. Carolina St. (FCS)	100%	
Sep 22	at Georgia Tech (41)	95%	
Oct 1	vs Louisville (19)	89%	
Oct 7	at Boston College (53)	98%	
Oct 15	vs NC State (55)	98%	
Oct 29	at Florida St. (6)	67%	
Nov 5	vs Syracuse (58)	99%	
Nov 12	vs Pittsburgh (34)	96%	
Nov 19	at Wake Forest (78)	99%	
Nov 26	vs South Carolina (59)	99%	

Alabama and LSU are both leaning on returning multiple NFL talents at various skill positions across their lineup to help young or inexperienced quarterbacks find success. Meanwhile Clemson is losing some NFL talents, yet returning arguably the best quarterback in the college ranks.

Deshaun Watson single-handedly helped Clemson evolve their offense from being a simple "spread to run" attack to including a lethal quick passing game. That attack reached an elite level down the stretch when walk-on slot receiver Hunter Renfrow joined tight end Jordan Leggett to give the Tigers a dominant pair of inside receivers. They'll be rejoined by potential star wideout Mike Williams (who missed 2015) as well as returning receivers Artavis Scott (an explosive hybrid) and Deon Cain. Star running back Wayne Gallman is back as well, giving Clemson perhaps the most experienced and proven offensive skill talent in the nation. The Clemson offensive line also returns three starters, including left tackle Mitch Hyatt, who played last year as a true freshman.

This team has shown it has the personnel and skill to line up and knock people over with the running game before throwing deep off play-action or, alternatively, to spread people out and pick them apart with quick passes and quarterback runs. Their skill in each facet is only likely to improve with so much chemistry returning. It's hard to see a scenario where Deshaun Watson plays a healthy season in Clemson and the Tiger offense isn't one of the nation's elite units.

Defensively the Tigers are facing a much different scenario in which defensive end Shaq Lawson, middle linebacker B.J. Goodson, cornerback Mackensie Alexander, and strong safety Jayron Kearse have all departed for the NFL. However, there was a similar story to be told in 2015 when Clemson was facing the monumental task of replacing defensive end Vic

Beasley and six of their top seven defensive linemen, linebacker Stephon Anthony, and defensive backs Garry Peters and Robert Smith. The general consensus was that Clemson would struggle to field another top-10 defense in S&P without all of that NFL talent. Instead the Tigers' defensive S&P only dropped from second place to fourth overall. Clemson fielded a unit that was dominant in every regard save for passing downs, where they slipped from first to 59th without star pass-rusher Vic Beasley.

Clearly defensive coordinator Brent Venables knows what he's doing and will be able to craft another good unit out of the emerging players on the roster for 2016. Those players will include cornerback Cordrea Tankersley, who had five interceptions and nine pass break-ups while being targeted opposite Alexander; disruptive defensive tackle Carlos Watkins; and steady linebacker Ben Boulware. Young talents to keep an eye on include young defensive end Clelin Ferrell and safety Van Smith. There's always a new star waiting in the wings for Venables, who's now working with a defensive roster comprising entirely of players he recruited himself.

Concerns for the Tigers include rebuilding the passing down defense while replacing two defensive ends who both topped 10 sacks on the year in Kevin Dodd and Shaw. The Tigers also have a difficult schedule to navigate. Besides the obvious, looming showdown in Tallahassee against our projected No. 6 Florida State, Clemson also has road trips to No. 24 Auburn and No. 41 Georgia Tech while drawing No. 19 Louisville and No. 34 Pitt at home.

There's plenty of room for a slip-up on that schedule, and if Florida State proves an even match, then that road trip could be easily be a defeat. It's hard to repeat an undefeated stretch in regular season play, even when you return your quarterback and most of your offense.

No. 4 Oklahoma Sooners (11-1, 8-1)

2016 Projections		Projection Factors	
F/+	53.1 (4)	2015 F/+	49.9 (4)
FEI	.200 (4)	2015 FEI	.220 (6)
S&P+	22.0 (4)	2015 S&P+	22.6 (4)
Total Wins	10.7	5-Year F/+	41.1 (6)
Conf Wins	8.1	5-Year FEI	.192 (6)
SOS	.185 (54)	5-Year S&P+	18.0 (5)
Conf SOS	.286 (52)	2-Year Recruiting	88.8 (16)
Div Champ	-	5-Year Recruiting	88.7 (16)
Conf Champ	.666	Ret. Offense	.723
CFP Berth	.540	Ret. Defense	.657

Projected Win Likelihood by Game

Date	Opponent (Proj Rank)	PWL
Sep 3	vs Houston (38)	91%
Sep 10	vs UL-Monroe (123)	99%
Sep 17	vs Ohio St. (13)	77%
Oct 1	at TCU (25)	78%
Oct 8	vs Texas (37)	91%
Oct 15	vs Kansas St. (54)	97%
Oct 22	at Texas Tech (45)	92%
Oct 29	vs Kansas (114)	99%
Nov 3	at Iowa St. (79)	99%
Nov 12	vs Baylor (7)	73%
Nov 19	at West Virginia (35)	87%
Dec 3	vs Oklahoma St. (27)	89%

The 2015 Oklahoma Sooners are a bit of a statistical enigma. On the one hand, they had a mostly impressive run through non-conference and Big 12 play with only a single hiccup against a fired-up young Texas team playing for their coach's job. On the other hand, the Sooners defeated top Big 12 opponents TCU, Oklahoma State, and Baylor when those teams were without their starting quarterbacks. The resulting stat and perception boost those wins provided for the Sooners makes it more difficult to quantify exactly how strong their returning core will be in 2016.

The Sooners defense is one of the trickier units to figure out in college football, as they benefitted much more than the offense from facing so many second-string quarterbacks. They finished 16th in S&P defense with strong numbers across the board against run or pass, passing down or standard down, and in limiting big plays.

They face some tough losses this year with defensive end Charles Tapper (seven sacks), linebackers Eric Striker (seven sacks) and Dominique Sanders (104 tackles), and cornerback Zach Sanchez (13 interceptions in two years) all departing. Bob Stoops and his brother Mike will be hoping to get playmaking from another pass-rusher at Striker's outside linebacker position while finding another cornerback who can attack routes with the same aggression and sticky fingers as Sanchez.

The Sooners do return a strong foundation for their defense with four prominent defensive backs returning, including rising cover corner Jordan Thomas and strong safety Steven Parker. Oklahoma will also feature defensive lineman Charles Walker, who was nearly impossible to block in limited snaps in 2015, totaling six sacks and ten tackles for loss. If OU can find another pass-rusher like Striker then everything should be set.

On offense the picture is much clearer with the loaded backfield cast of quarterback Baker Mayfield and running backs Samaje Perine and Joe Mixon all returning. Their skill sets perfectly complement each other, as Mayfield is more than capable in the option game, Perine is a powerful downhill back, and Mixon is equally adept running between the tackles or being a pitch man or wide receiver on the perimeter. The Sooners have been developing plays in which opponents have to be ready to simultaneously defend a quick pass to Mixon, inside run to Perine, or perimeter dash by Mayfield.

The Sooners also return a pair of athletic young tackles in Orland Brown and Dru Samia who experienced a baptism by fire as starters in their freshman seasons facing the likes of Clemson in the Orange Bowl. Top guard Jonathan Alvarez also returns and will move inside to center to help anchor an offensive line with a lot of promise.

The main hang-up is replacing Giants second-round pick Sterling Shepard, who had 1,288 yards and 11 touchdowns last season. The Sooners do return second leading wide receiver Dede Westbrook and promising young tight end Mark Andrews, and will look to find another weapon from their ranks of young receivers or perhaps from Penn State transfer Geno Lewis.

Should any of their wide receivers emerge as the kind of option that needs to be double-teamed, then Oklahoma is primed to have an absolute juggernaut offense in 2016. The biggest place this would show up would be on passing downs, where OU ranked a lowly 61st last year due to inexperience at the tackle spots.

No. 5 Ole Miss Rebels (8-4, 5-3)

2016 Projections		Projection Factors	
F/+	46.7 (5)	2015 F/+	48.4 (5)
FEI	.182 (8)	2015 FEI	.221 (5)
S&P+	18.9 (7)	2015 S&P+	21.2 (5)
Total Wins	8.4	5-Year F/+	24.3 (22)
Conf Wins	5.0	5-Year FEI	.187 (8)
SOS	.009 (4)	5-Year S&P+	12.4 (20)
Conf SOS	.016 (4)	2-Year Recruiting	89.0 (15)
Div Champ	.052	5-Year Recruiting	85.9 (20)
Conf Champ	.031	Ret. Offense	.736
CFP Berth	.022	Ret. Defense	.540

Projected Win Likelihood by Game

Date	Opponent (Proj Rank)	PWL	Projected Loss / Projected Win
Sep 5	vs Florida St. (6)	54%	
Sep 10	vs Wofford (FCS)	100%	
Sep 17	vs Alabama (1)	23%	
Sep 24	vs Georgia (8)	64%	
Oct 1	vs Memphis (66)	97%	
Oct 15	at Arkansas (18)	60%	
Oct 22	at LSU (2)	22%	
Oct 29	vs Auburn (24)	83%	
Nov 5	vs Ga. Southern (51)	95%	
Nov 12	at Texas A&M (23)	69%	
Nov 19	at Vanderbilt (75)	97%	
Nov 26	vs Mississippi St. (21)	79%	

The breakthrough 2013 recruiting class that helped position Ole Miss as a legitimate national contender over the last few years is already nearly depleted, leaving head coach Hugh Freeze to prove that subsequent solid classes are ready to take the helm. That 2013 class included NFL draft picks like defensive tackle Robert Nkemdiche, left tackle Laremy Tunsil, and wide receiver Laquon Treadwell.

Now the Rebels will have to plug in a new generation of talent such as left tackle Greg Little, who may start in 2016 as a true freshman. What should help this transition is the return of starting quarterback Chad Kelly, who had more than 4,500 yards of total offense and 41 touchdowns a year ago. Kelly's size and speed made the Ole Miss run game come alive and caused serious dilemmas for defenses looking to get numbers in the box while still holding up outside against Treadwell, fellow wideout Cody Core, and the rest of the passing game. The Rebels ranked ninth in offensive S&P, 23rd in rushing, and first on standard downs thanks to the dilemmas they were able to pose to defenses.

Ole Miss basically baited Alabama into loading up to stuff the run, only to then throw for 341 yards and three touchdowns in a shocking upset (also, admittedly, aided by an uncharacteristic five-turnover day from the Tide).

Treadwell, Core, and virtually the entire offensive line now departs, but the run game should still be sturdy simply thanks to the arithmetic problems caused by Kelly's wheels. Meanwhile the skill positions can just reload around tight end Evan Engram (464 receiving yards last year) and wide receivers Damore'ea Stringfellow (503 yards), Quincy Adeboyejo (604 yards), and Markell Pack (380 yards) who all saw significant action in 2015.

On defense the Rebels bring back leading pass-rusher Marquis Haynes and fellow defensive end Fadol Brown, who will now be looking to find advantages against protection schemes without the aid of Nkemdiche drawing attention inside. They also have some experienced talent back on the perimeter with cornerback Tony Bridges and nickelback Tony Conner. The problem is up the middle of the defense, as the Rebels are losing both starting defensive tackles, both starting inside linebackers, and both starting safeties.

The Rebels ranked 21st in defensive S&P a year ago thanks largely to their sturdy standard down and rushing defense (24th and 18th nationally respectively) so there could be a real drop-off here given the serious losses up the middle of the defense. Besides the grievous loss of losing the ultra-disruptive Nkemdiche, safeties Mike Hilton and Trae Elston were a big part of the Rebels' defensive identity. Ole Miss was aggressive in playing their safeties close to the action, and those two combined for 140 tackles, 17.5 tackles for loss, six interceptions, and 25 passes defended in 2015.

The positives for the Rebels are that seven of their vacant starting positions on either side of the ball will be filled by seniors, and Hugh Freeze is now replenishing the roster with players chosen and developed for his system. The negatives include trying to get a team with so little experience going against a schedule that features Florida State, Alabama, and Georgia in the first four games and later takes them on the road to play Arkansas, LSU, and Texas A&M. This could be one of the best teams in the country and still lose more than a few times.

There's nearly zero margin for growing pains in that schedule. Any failures to reform the offensive identity with new athletes on the outside or the defense with new faces in their normally swarming defensive backfield will see the Rebels punished. If Freeze is able to plug in developed talent around Kelly then there's enough firepower for another strong season, even if the Rebels drop a couple of games.

No. 6 Florida State Seminoles (9-3, 6-2)

2016 Projections

F/+	44.5 (6)
FEI	.160 (11)
S&P+	19.6 (5)
Total Wins	9.4
Conf Wins	6.3
SOS	.070 (19)
Conf SOS	.164 (32)
Div Champ	.182
Conf Champ	.124
CFP Berth	.089

Projection Factors

2015 F/+	36.4 (12)
2015 FEI	.137 (25)
2015 S&P+	20.0 (7)
5-Year F/+	39.8 (7)
5-Year FEI	.168 (13)
5-Year S&P+	16.8 (7)
2-Year Recruiting	96.3 (3)
5-Year Recruiting	96.3 (3)
Ret. Offense	.765
Ret. Defense	.493

Projected Win Likelihood by Game

Date	Opponent (Proj Rank)	PWL
Sep 5	vs Ole Miss (5)	46%
Sep 10	vs Charleston So. (FCS)	100%
Sep 17	at Louisville (19)	58%
Sep 24	at South Florida (44)	85%
Oct 1	vs North Carolina (28)	85%
Oct 8	at Miami-FL (39)	81%
Oct 15	vs Wake Forest (78)	98%
Oct 29	vs Clemson (3)	33%
Nov 5	at NC State (55)	88%
Nov 11	vs Boston College (53)	95%
Nov 19	at Syracuse (58)	89%
Nov 26	vs Florida (26)	82%

Florida State's talent level is on par with Alabama and Ohio State as one of the best in the country. Given the overall talent foundation, it's no surprise that the only people standing in the Seminoles' way are last year's playoff runner-up, Deshaun Watson and the Clemson Tigers. Last season may have ended on a sour note for FSU with a two-touchdown loss to Houston, but expectations heading in to 2016 are rightfully high for a team that returns nearly everyone but a quarterback on offense and has a host of talent on defense.

It's no secret that this team will rise and fall with quarterback play. The primary options are the veteran Sean Maguire, who may have a low ceiling but is an experienced option who ended up mostly out-performing Everett Golson by season's end last fall. The other option is Deondre Francois, a mobile redshirt freshman who hasn't played a down at Florida State yet. Maguire had a higher interception rate than anyone would like (3.2 percent), but he averaged a decent, if unspectacular 7.4 yards per attempt last year. Francois has been noted for his early leadership capabilities and mobility, with a few third-down scrambles in Florida State's spring game.

If one of the two can be more effective than the Golson/Maguire combination was last season, then this immediately sets Florida State on a championship-level trajectory. That's because almost the entire offense returns around the quarterback. Dalvin Cook and his backup, sophomore Jacques Patrick (a five-star recruit in his own right), return at running back. The entire receiving corps returns, with Travis Rudolph, Jesus Wilson, and Kermit Whitfield forming the core, and the entire offensive line returns as well. If there's any area that could be better, it's the offensive line that was 31st in adjusted

line yards and 39th in adjusted sack rate. There are plenty of former blue-chip players in the room, so depth is incredible, but the overall consistency of the line could improve—making Cook and Patrick more efficient than just the 54th overall opportunity rate. But Cook has been incredible even when his line has just been average at efficient run blocking. Cook sets himself apart from other top running backs in his extreme explosiveness. Though he had just a 41 percent opportunity rate (a function of the line, mostly), he made the most of his opportunity averaging 10.1 highlight yards per opportunity.

The defense is forced to reload at linebacker and in the secondary, and needs viable rotational players along the defensive line. The good news is that Florida State certainly has the talent on the depth chart to fill those roles. Derwin James, a sophomore who should contend for All-American status, should erase any fears of losing versatile Jalen Ramsey to the NFL. He'll be surrounded by former five-stars Tavarus McFadden and true freshman Lavonta Taylor (among other blue chip candidates) to fill in the three holes in the starting secondary lineup. While the secondary just needs to reload with top-flight talent, the linebackers can reload but have extremely limited depth after losing five contributors. Injuries could sink the position group even though the overall talent level is high. What's more, four of the eight linebackers are freshmen—all blue chips to be sure, but still completely inexperienced freshmen. It will be imperative that the secondary provides leadership while linemen like DeMarcus Walker and Josh Sweat put heavy pressure on opposing quarterbacks to make things easier for the young linebackers.

No. 7 Baylor Bears (10-2, 7-2)

2016 Projections		Projection Factors	
F/+	43.0 (7)	2015 F/+	36.0 (14)
FEI	.181 (9)	2015 FEI	.171 (13)
S&P+	16.4 (13)	2015 S&P+	15.6 (14)
Total Wins	10.2	5-Year F/+	35.3 (10)
Conf Wins	7.2	5-Year FEI	.174 (11)
SOS	.171 (47)	5-Year S&P+	15.1 (10)
Conf SOS	.174 (36)	2-Year Recruiting	79.9 (27)
Div Champ	-	5-Year Recruiting	74.9 (30)
Conf Champ	.248	Ret. Offense	.710
CFP Berth	.199	Ret. Defense	.663

Projected Win Likelihood by Game

Date	Opponent (Proj Rank)	PWL
Sep 3	vs Northwestern St. (FCS)	100%
Sep 10	vs SMU (102)	99%
Sep 17	at Rice (118)	99%
Sep 24	vs Oklahoma St. (27)	81%
Oct 1	at Iowa St. (79)	96%
Oct 15	vs Kansas (114)	99%
Oct 29	at Texas (37)	79%
Nov 5	vs TCU (25)	80%
Nov 12	at Oklahoma (4)	27%
Nov 19	vs Kansas St. (54)	94%
Nov 25	vs Texas Tech (45)	88%
Dec 3	at West Virginia (35)	79%

It's hard to know where to begin with Baylor. Before the sexual assault scandal rocked Waco this offseason, leading to Art Briles getting fired and the exit of a large portion of this year's freshman recruiting class, the on-field talk about Baylor was all positive. Baylor returns two elite quarterbacks in Seth Russell and Jarrett Stidham, and had proved they were the most adaptable explosive offense in the nation by running up gaudy stats in a neo-wishbone offense in a bowl game romp over North Carolina.

Now it's hard to say what kind of Baylor we'll see in 2016. Jim Grobe, all-around good guy and former Wake Forest head coach, will be the acting head coach for the short term. It's hard to imagine that Grobe will change the Baylor system, especially considering all assistant coaches are set to return. So at least on offense, the most glaring personnel losses were at receiver. Corey Coleman and Jay Lee accounted for almost half of the team's targets, and each averaged more than 18 yards per reception. KD Cannon is the clear No. 1 receiver, and a close approximation to Coleman statistically, with just a slightly lower catch rate (55 percent to 61 percent) and fewer targets. Sophomores Chris Platt and Ishmael Zamora, as well as redshirt freshman Blake Lynch, will take on bigger roles, but Baylor could have benefitted from Devin Duvernay, a top receiver recruit who opted to go to Texas following the scandal.

It's unclear who will be throwing to these receivers. After Seth Russell was injured, true freshman Jarrett Stidham stepped in and played just as well, if not better, than the senior. Both averaged 10.3 yards per attempt, and Stidham completed about nine percent more of his passes, but took six percent more sacks as well. Either way, the offense should hum at its typical absurdly efficient pace. It certainly helps that rushers Shock Linwood and Johnny Jefferson both return, fresh after dueling 1,000-yard seasons and nearly identical efficiency and explosiveness numbers (5.6 highlight yards per opportunity and low-50s percent opportunity rate).

The defense is a little different. Last season the run defense allowed opposing running backs to be a little too efficient (57th in rushing success rate) and quarterbacks to be too explosive (97th in passing IsoPPP), and they've lost leading tackler Grant Campbell, plus sack leaders Jamal Palmer, Shawn Oakman, and Andrew Billings. It's hard to see the defensive line replacements replicating that group's 20th-ranking in defensive line havoc rate.

We don't have a way to calculate the impact of the coaching shake-up and our projection factors clearly indicate that the pieces are in place for another strong year on the field for Baylor. It's hard to imagine the off-field issues won't have some impact, but with a back-loaded schedule, we may not know much about Baylor's candidacy as a contender until deep into the year.

No. 8 Georgia Bulldogs (10-2, 6-2)

2016 Projections		Projection Factors	
F/+	42.9 (8)	2015 F/+	21.4 (30)
FEI	.185 (6)	2015 FEI	.099 (31)
S&P+	16.2 (15)	2015 S&P+	10.0 (32)
Total Wins	9.8	5-Year F/+	38.8 (8)
Conf Wins	6.1	5-Year FEI	.159 (14)
SOS	.143 (43)	5-Year S&P+	16.5 (8)
Conf SOS	.183 (38)	2-Year Recruiting	92.8 (7)
Div Champ	.571	5-Year Recruiting	94.0 (6)
Conf Champ	.228	Ret. Offense	.755
CFP Berth	.164	Ret. Defense	.765

Projected Win Likelihood by Game

Date	Opponent (Proj Rank)	PWL	Projected Loss	Projected Win
Sep 3	vs North Carolina (28)	77%		
Sep 10	vs Nicholls St. (FCS)	100%		
Sep 17	at Missouri (40)	80%		
Sep 24	at Ole Miss (5)	36%		
Oct 1	vs Tennessee (10)	61%		
Oct 8	at South Carolina (59)	88%		
Oct 15	vs Vanderbilt (75)	98%		
Oct 29	vs Florida (26)	73%		
Nov 5	at Kentucky (89)	99%		
Nov 12	vs Auburn (24)	79%		
Nov 19	vs UL-Lafayette (104)	99%		
Nov 26	vs Georgia Tech (41)	91%		

Georgia's offense has a lot of uncertainty heading into 2016, and it starts with the quarterback position. Greyson Lambert, the incumbent starting quarterback and Virginia transfer, was not terrible last season, no matter what popular perception suggests. He was at times too safe and the offense as a whole had a limited ceiling as a result. The passing game ranked 27th in passing S&P+ but lacked any kind of explosive capability (104th in passing IsoPPP). Lambert minimized mistakes with just two interceptions all year, and maintained a respectable 7 yards per passing attempt.

The hope is that freshman Jacob Eason can fill the explosive play void thanks to his NFL-caliber arm. He enrolled early and took part in Georgia's record-setting spring game, which only fueled the hype after a 19-for-29, 244-yard performance. That said, if new head coach Kirby Smart follows the example of his former employer Alabama, then it's unlikely he and new offensive coordinator Jim Chaney will trust the offense to a true freshman, regardless of how talented he is. Pro-style quarterbacks are generally brought on more slowly in offenses that feature fewer pre-snap reads and rely more on natural athletic ability than system knowledge. Would Eason be given the full playbook or a limited, digestible version of it if he does win the job?

Regardless of whether Eason, Lambert, or dark horse third option Brice Ramsey gets the nod, the starter will need his retooled offensive line to perform at a high level immediately. FCS graduate transfer Tyler Catalina could be the answer. Coming from Rhode Island, the late bloomer looks like a textbook left tackle, and slotting him in there would allow new offensive line coach Sam Pittman incredible flexibility to create a potentially dominating offensive line. The line will likely include some combination of Catalina, Isaiah Wynn, Greg Pyke, center Brandon Kublanow, Dyshon Sims, and potentially true freshman Ben Cleveland. All of these guys have NFL potential, but their order and cohesion aren't there yet.

A truly elite player elevates the rest of the team around him, and that's exactly what Nick Chubb was able to do, turning small holes in to big gains thanks to excellent balance and

vision with cutback lanes and the strength to run through tackles. When Chubb went down against Tennessee, the Bulldogs were fortunate enough to replace him with five-star back Sony Michel. Michel has excellent balance and top-end speed of his own (15th-ranked rushing IsoPPP) but he was less efficient than Chubb (92nd in rushing success rate and 81st in opportunity rate). A healthy Chubb-Michel combination is hard to beat as the best running back tandem in the country and takes the pressure off of not just the incoming quarterback, but also the receivers.

Terry Godwin has the athletic ability to be the No. 1 receiver while Jayson Stanley and Reggie Davis are other potential options. Georgia certainly has enough elite tight ends on the roster at least, with entrenched starter and viable receiving option Jeb Blazevich, Jackson Harris, and incoming five-star Issac Nauta, who joined Eason for a touchdown in the spring game. As one of the most talented position groups on the team, look for Georgia's tight ends to be an active part of the passing offense.

On the other side of the ball, a certain level of stability from last year's 11th-ranked S&P+ defense is expected due to Smart's bona fides at Alabama. That's a tough ask, though, considering the loss of pass-rushers Leonard Floyd and Jordan Jenkins, along with team MVP Jake Ganus. Georgia's pass defense led the way at 28th in passing S&P+ and now has a stream of talent, including incoming five-star Mecole Hardman and fellow-five star sophomore Rico McGraw, but the Bulldogs need Lorenzo Carter and Davin Bellamy to step up at outside linebacker for the trend to continue. The two outside linebackers, along with defensive lineman Trenton Thompson, will be critical for the Bulldogs to contend for the SEC East.

The SEC East itself is fairly wide open, with Florida, Georgia, and Tennessee all in roughly the same ballpark. We'll know Georgia's ceiling by the second week of October, as the Bulldogs face North Carolina, Missouri, Ole Miss, and Tennessee all in the first month and a half. While all of those games are winnable on their own, starting the season 4-1 would be a huge win for the Bulldogs.

No. 9 Stanford Cardinal (9-3, 7-2)

2016 Projections		Projection Factors	
F/+	41.4 (9)	2015 F/+	48.1 (6)
FEI	.183 (7)	2015 FEI	.265 (3)
S&P+	15.3 (16)	2015 S&P+	18.4 (10)
Total Wins	9.1	5-Year F/+	44.2 (4)
Conf Wins	6.7	5-Year FEI	.232 (3)
SOS	.075 (20)	5-Year S&P+	18.0 (6)
Conf SOS	.131 (25)	2-Year Recruiting	82.3 (24)
Div Champ	.261	5-Year Recruiting	88.3 (18)
Conf Champ	.131	Ret. Offense	.331
CFP Berth	.080	Ret. Defense	.608

Projected Win Likelihood by Game

Date	Opponent (Proj Rank)	PWL
Sep 2	vs Kansas St. (54)	93%
Sep 17	vs USC (12)	59%
Sep 24	at UCLA (17)	50%
Sep 30	at Washington (14)	46%
Oct 8	vs Washington St. (43)	91%
Oct 15	at Notre Dame (15)	46%
Oct 22	vs Colorado (86)	98%
Oct 29	at Arizona (64)	89%
Nov 5	vs Oregon St. (90)	99%
Nov 12	at Oregon (11)	43%
Nov 19	at California (72)	92%
Nov 26	vs Rice (118)	99%

The Cardinal may need a new quarterback after Kevin Hogan's departure, but who better to pair with a green quarterback than Christian McCaffrey? After rushing for more than 2,000 yards and being the leading receiver for Stanford, McCaffrey will surely be centerpiece again. But besides the quarterback question, can the Cardinal solve their run defense and leaky pass defense issues?

Defense has always been a strength for the Cardinal since Jim Harbaugh put Stanford on their current course, but the 2015 defense ranked just 42nd in S&P+ and had notable problems containing explosive runs (120th in rushing IsoPPP and 88th in adjusted line yards), limiting opponent pass efficiency, and pressuring the quarterback. Pac-12 North teams like Oregon and Washington may be able to exploit that weakness if it continues in to 2016. Stanford had to bend, not break with their pass defense (92nd in passing success rate, eighth in passing IsoPPP), forcing the red zone defense to hold up under pressure. Adding to that pressure, Stanford returns just 63 percent of their defensive experience for next season. There is certainly talent in the form of players like junior defensive end Solomon Thomas, but they will need young players like de-

fensive tackle Wesley Annan and defensive end Dylan Jackson to step up.

The offense will be led by either Ryan Burns or Keller Chryst. Though Chryst was the higher-rated recruit, Burns might be slightly ahead coming into fall camp. Either way, Stanford doesn't necessarily need a superstar running the offense—they simply need someone to make sound decisions to distribute the ball to McCaffrey, fellow do-everything back Bryce love, rising receiver Trent Irwin, and tight end Dalton Schultz. There's good reason to think the offense won't dip very much as long as the new quarterback is merely competent. Of course, the offensive line could stand to improve as well, considering it was 62nd in adjusted sack rate last season.

The first half of the season is rough for Stanford. Opening with Kansas State, the Cardinal see USC and UCLA early, then face Pac-12 media darling Washington to end September. Tough games against Washington State and Notre Dame are the first two games in October. There are many potential losses on the schedule, but Stanford has consistently met and often exceeded expectations in the recent past.

No. 10 Tennessee Volunteers (9-3, 6-2)

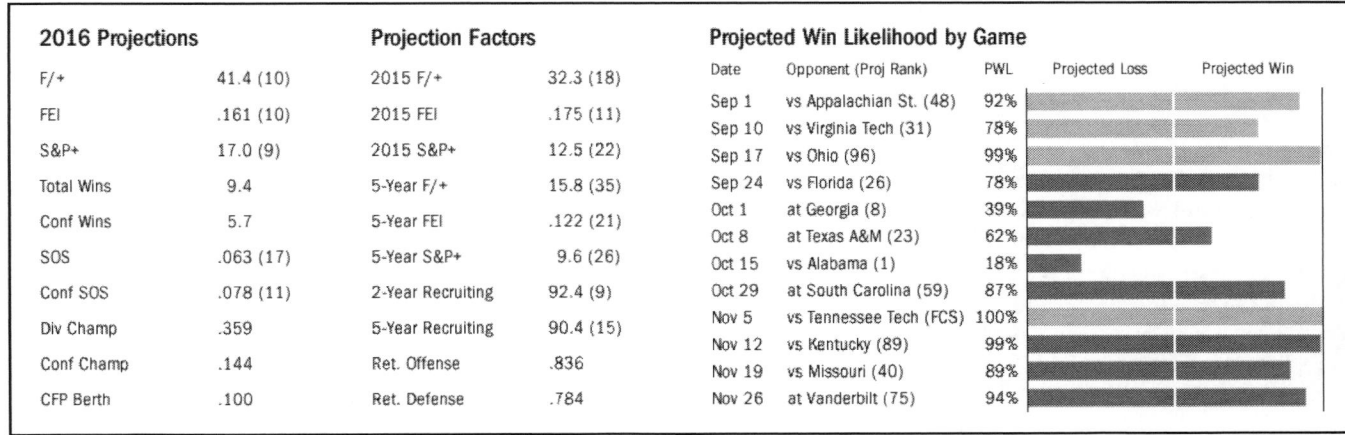

2016 Projections		Projection Factors	
F/+	41.4 (10)	2015 F/+	32.3 (18)
FEI	.161 (10)	2015 FEI	.175 (11)
S&P+	17.0 (9)	2015 S&P+	12.5 (22)
Total Wins	9.4	5-Year F/+	15.8 (35)
Conf Wins	5.7	5-Year FEI	.122 (21)
SOS	.063 (17)	5-Year S&P+	9.6 (26)
Conf SOS	.078 (11)	2-Year Recruiting	92.4 (9)
Div Champ	.359	5-Year Recruiting	90.4 (15)
Conf Champ	.144	Ret. Offense	.836
CFP Berth	.100	Ret. Defense	.784

Projected Win Likelihood by Game

Date	Opponent (Proj Rank)	PWL
Sep 1	vs Appalachian St. (48)	92%
Sep 10	vs Virginia Tech (31)	78%
Sep 17	vs Ohio (96)	99%
Sep 24	vs Florida (26)	78%
Oct 1	at Georgia (8)	39%
Oct 8	at Texas A&M (23)	62%
Oct 15	vs Alabama (1)	18%
Oct 29	at South Carolina (59)	87%
Nov 5	vs Tennessee Tech (FCS)	100%
Nov 12	vs Kentucky (89)	99%
Nov 19	vs Missouri (40)	89%
Nov 26	at Vanderbilt (75)	94%

If this isn't the year that Butch Jones' Volunteers make a run at the SEC East division title, then it's hard to imagine when it will be. The stage is perfectly set. First, Florida and Georgia both need new quarterbacks, so the East competition is wide open. Second, new defensive coordinator Bob Shoop, who has had excellent, hard-hitting defenses at Penn State, begins his tenure at Tennessee. Third, the Volunteers have a ton of talent returning on both sides of the ball. Finally, the Volunteers have recruited extremely well throughout Jones' tenure in Knoxville. Now Tennessee just has to put it all together.

Big plays were a problem for Tennessee last year on offense and defense. The most explosive runner for the Vols ended up being quarterback Josh Dobbs, who averaged 6.4 highlight yards per opportunity. But starting running back Jalen Hurd received more than twice as many carries as Dobbs and Alvin Kamara combined, yet had inferior numbers—4.6 highlight yards per opportunity and just a 35.5 percent opportunity rate. It wasn't because of the offensive line, which was 19th in adjusted line yards, either. In the receiving corps, juniors Josh Malone and Josh Smith were the best options last year, but they both averaged less than 13.5 yards per catch and less than

a 60 percent catch rate. Neither one has proven to be a go-to guy yet, and Dobbs is especially desperate for a big-play threat (5.8 yards per pass) in particular. Tight end Ethan Wolf and Alvin Kamara are the most reliable receiving targets, averaging north of 71 percent catch rates.

The defense was talented, but very young in 2014 and 2015, which means Bob Shoop inherits an experienced group that should be more exciting than the offense. There are a few stars, including former blue-chip linemen Kahlil McKenzie and pass-rushing specialist Derek Barnett. Incoming freshman and Tennessee's highest-rated recruit this class, Nigel Warrior, could make an impact at safety this season. That talent, plus Stoops' coaching, should be a scary prospect for the young offenses around the SEC East. If the defense can generate more of a pass rush (64th in adjusted sack rate) and clamp down on explosive plays (70th in IsoPPP), then the defense might be a top-ten level defense.

We're likely to know all we need to about Tennessee by the mid-point of October, since they have dangerous out-of-conference games against Appalachian State and Virginia Tech to open, followed by games against Florida, Georgia, Texas A&M, and Alabama.

No. 11 Oregon Ducks (10-2, 7-2)

2016 Projections		Projection Factors		Projected Win Likelihood by Game				
				Date	Opponent (Proj Rank)	PWL	Projected Loss	Projected Win
F/+	41.2 (11)	2015 F/+	28.1 (23)	Sep 3	vs UC Davis (FCS)	100%		
FEI	.187 (5)	2015 FEI	.144 (23)	Sep 10	vs Virginia (71)	96%		
S&P+	15.0 (18)	2015 S&P+	11.6 (25)	Sep 17	at Nebraska (22)	60%		
Total Wins	9.6	5-Year F/+	46.6 (2)	Sep 24	vs Colorado (86)	98%		
Conf Wins	7.0	5-Year FEI	.191 (7)	Oct 1	at Washington St. (43)	81%		
				Oct 8	vs Washington (14)	62%		
SOS	.142 (42)	5-Year S&P+	18.2 (4)	Oct 21	at California (72)	92%		
Conf SOS	.203 (44)	2-Year Recruiting	86.5 (19)	Oct 29	vs Arizona St. (60)	94%		
Div Champ	.417	5-Year Recruiting	87.3 (19)	Nov 5	at USC (12)	43%		
				Nov 12	vs Stanford (9)	58%		
Conf Champ	.209	Ret. Offense	.494	Nov 19	at Utah (32)	74%		
CFP Berth	.138	Ret. Defense	.791	Nov 26	at Oregon St. (90)	99%		

It's a little early to write the eulogy for Oregon as an elite program. A four-loss season in 2015 was out of character for the Ducks, but everyone expected some drop-off in the immediate post-Marcus Mariota years. But has it really been so terrible? Three of the four losses came by seven points or fewer, and Oregon looked fine for the portion of the season when Vernon Adams was healthy. Another graduate transfer, Montana State's Dakota Prukop, looks to take over the quarterback position this fall. A successful year from Prukop and a resurrection of the defense by new defensive coordinator Brady Hoke could push the Ducks back to the top of the Pac-12 in a heartbeat.

The offense will be absolutely loaded assuming Prukop plays to his potential. At Montana State, Prukop averaged 9.7 and 8.8 yards per attempt in two years along with rushing for 1,956 yards. He excels both in his vision running the football and in connecting on play-action passes. While he didn't

run exactly the same system at Montana State, his skill set should align well with Oregon's run/pass options and the explosiveness that the Ducks are accustomed to (13th in passing IsoPPP). He'll have plenty of skill talent around him, from electric Darren Carrington (19 yards per catch) and Charles Nelson (who should have even more rushing, passing and RPO bubble opportunities next year), to running backs Royce Freeman and Taj Griffin.

Freeman, a legitimate Heisman contender and the steadier option (44.4 percent opportunity rate), still has explosiveness, but Griffin averaged an insane 12.3 highlight yards per opportunity on about a quarter of Freeman's opportunities last year. That pair, combined with Prukop, should ensure the second-overall rushing S&P+ offense doesn't fall far. If there were any areas that the Ducks could improve on offense last season, it would be finishing drives, where they averaged only five points per trip inside the 40 (40th), and in pass protection along the line, where they were a dismal 109th.

The biggest individual personnel loss on defense was DeForest Buckner, who racked up 17 tackles for loss and 10.5 sacks last season. Former blue chip sophomore Canton Kaumatule looks to be his replacement, but he'll need help from a new set of linebackers. Hoke will install his 4-3 under defense, and it's likely that at least schematically that the Ducks should be more prepared for the power attacks of USC and Stanford.

The problem in projecting a return to the nation's elite for Oregon is that the Pac-12 is extremely competitive this year and schedule doesn't exactly set the Ducks up for success. November begins with a rough three-game stretch of USC, Stanford, and Utah, each capable of bruising efficiency. Before that, the Ducks face Washington State, who scored an upset in Eugene last year, and the Washington Huskies in back-to-back weeks.

No. 12 USC Trojans (8-4, 6-3)

2016 Projections		Projection Factors	
F/+	40.6 (12)	2015 F/+	33.6 (17)
FEI	.153 (13)	2015 FEI	.156 (17)
S&P+	17.3 (8)	2015 S&P+	14.9 (17)
Total Wins	8.1	5-Year F/+	33.0 (14)
Conf Wins	6.4	5-Year FEI	.154 (15)
SOS	.017 (7)	5-Year S&P+	14.3 (14)
Conf SOS	.111 (19)	2-Year Recruiting	96.4 (2)
Div Champ	.311	5-Year Recruiting	97.5 (2)
Conf Champ	.156	Ret. Offense	.538
CFP Berth	.082	Ret. Defense	.774

Projected Win Likelihood by Game

Date	Opponent (Proj Rank)	PWL	Projected Loss	Projected Win
Sep 3	vs Alabama (1)	13%		
Sep 10	vs Utah St. (73)	96%		
Sep 17	at Stanford (9)	41%		
Sep 23	at Utah (32)	73%		
Oct 1	vs Arizona St. (60)	94%		
Oct 8	vs Colorado (86)	98%		
Oct 15	at Arizona (64)	88%		
Oct 27	vs California (72)	96%		
Nov 5	vs Oregon (11)	57%		
Nov 12	at Washington (14)	45%		
Nov 19	at UCLA (17)	49%		
Nov 26	vs Notre Dame (15	61%		

The Trojans main priorities this off-season are finding quarterback Cody Kessler's replacement and rebuilding the defensive front seven. The current race between former five-star redshirt junior Max Browne and redshirt freshman Sam Darnold has the potential to make or break the Trojans season in Clay Helton's first full season as USC's permanent head coach. The schedule leaves no room for error either.

Browne has been in the program a long time now, but he's almost as much of an uncertainty as Darnold. Completing eight of 12 passes last season at 9.4 yards per attempt, Browne hasn't been able to put much separation between himself and Darnold, who appears to be a more mobile option. The offense was fairly efficient last fall but could have used more explosiveness. Browne has the better deep ball, and he has plenty of weapons around him, from potential top overall wide receiver Juju Smith-Schuster, to both running backs, Justin Davis and Ronald Jones II. Davis was slightly more efficient than Jones, but Jones, now just a sophomore, averaged 2.3 more highlight yards per opportunity than Davis. Each has the potential to break the 1,000-yard mark this season.

Smith-Schuster is reliable and explosive (16.3 yards per catch), but if there's any problem with the receiving corps it's that Kessler was over-reliant on him, targeting him on nearly a third of his throws. The second-leading receiver had less than a quarter of Smith-Schuster's total receiving yards. That means there are plenty of opportunities for four blue chip freshmen receivers that they signed this season to step up and contribute. Two receivers, Michael Pittman and Josh Imatorbhebhe, enrolled early, while Tyler Vaughns is the third-ranked receiver overall in the 2016 class. If just one of the freshmen emerges as a reliable option—and particularly as a deep threat option—then the offense has the potential to be a top-ten group in the country. Whoever starts at quarterback will also benefit from a stocked offensive line that returns every starter. Of course, the line should have performed much better than it did last season given the recruiting pedigree of its members. At just 55th in adjusted line yards and 89th in adjusted sack rate, the line should benefit from experience and continuity.

Experience and continuity won't be a strong point for the defensive front seven, however, with six starters moving on from last season. Su'a Cravens and Delvon Simmons are the big losses, but there is nonetheless a lot of talent waiting for their shot. There is a ton of potential, with now-sophomores Cameron Smith, Porter Gustin, and Osa Masina all returning. Cameron Smith had three interceptions and was second on the team in tackles, while Gustin tied for the team lead in sacks as a true freshman. There's likely space in the rotation for top overall freshman weakside defensive end Oluwole Betiku, who enrolled in January and should help the Trojans maintain a pass rush that ranked 23rd in adjusted sack rate. The bigger concern might be the run defense and the interior of the line, though former five-star Rasheem Green is reportedly coming in to his own. Finally, the secondary is set to be one of the best in the country thanks to all-world cornerback Adoree' Jackson and now-sophomore Iman Marshall. If they can improve on their 47th-ranked passing S&P+ defense, then the team overall looks to be as talented as anyone in the country.

No. 13 Ohio State Buckeyes (9-3, 7-2)

2016 Projections		Projection Factors	
F/+	39.6 (13)	2015 F/+	54.7 (3)
FEI	.154 (12)	2015 FEI	.248 (4)
S&P+	16.4 (14)	2015 S&P+	24.0 (3)
Total Wins	9.3	5-Year F/+	44.3 (3)
Conf Wins	7.1	5-Year FEI	.248 (2)
SOS	.101 (27)	5-Year S&P+	18.3 (3)
Conf SOS	.282 (51)	2-Year Recruiting	93.5 (5)
Div Champ	.302	5-Year Recruiting	95.5 (4)
Conf Champ	.196	Ret. Offense	.225
CFP Berth	.128	Ret. Defense	.365

Projected Win Likelihood by Game

Date	Opponent (Proj Rank)	PWL
Sep 3	vs Bowling Green (69)	95%
Sep 10	vs Tulsa (91)	99%
Sep 17	at Oklahoma (4)	23%
Oct 1	vs Rutgers (84)	98%
Oct 8	vs Indiana (68)	95%
Oct 15	at Wisconsin (36)	76%
Oct 22	at Penn St. (42)	79%
Oct 29	vs Northwestern (47)	91%
Nov 5	vs Nebraska (22)	72%
Nov 12	at Maryland (74)	92%
Nov 19	at Michigan St. (20)	52%
Nov 26	vs Michigan (16)	60%

Few teams are as interesting as the Buckeyes going in to 2016. Just a field goal away from an undefeated regular season and returning to the Big Ten Championship and a potential playoff berth, a Fiesta Bowl win over Notre Dame couldn't shake the feeling of a little disappointment in Ohio State's 2015 campaign.

Now a couple of things are clear for the Buckeyes. First, after a historic NFL Draft that saw twelve Buckeyes selected, including ten in the first hundred picks, many are calling this Ohio State's rebuilding year. By returning experience, Ohio State is second-to-last behind the University of Massachusetts, with just 22 percent of offense and 36 percent of defensive experience returning. What's more, the percentage of returning passes broken up seems to correlate most with next season's defensive S&P+, and the Buckeyes lost all but one cornerback (Gareon Conley) to the NFL. The losses also include three starting offensive linemen, leading receiver Michael Thomas, and star running back Ezekiel Elliott. Those losses would be a deathblow to most teams.

But Ohio State isn't "most teams." The Buckeyes have recruited better than everyone but Alabama over the last four years, with about a 68 percent blue chip percentage (the percentage of a recruiting class that are four- or five-star recruits). Four-star sophomore Marcus Lattimore is projected to slide in for Eli Apple at cornerback. Sam Hubbard, a four-star defensive end is set to replace Joey Bosa, and he racked up 6.5 sacks last season (Bonus: Bosa's five-star true freshman brother Nick just arrived on campus, too). Blue chips Dante Booker and Jerome Baker are fighting for linebacker spots. The list goes on. The Buckeyes lost a lot of star talent, but they're also replacing those NFL players with future stars.

J.T. Barrett returns at quarterback, the role finally all his after swapping back and forth with Cardale Jones to open 2015. His numbers were down significantly last season from his stellar redshirt freshman debut—he averaged 2.7 fewer yards per attempt—but the passing offense was still 26th in S&P+. Barrett offers a different dimension in the run game as well, as he averaged a 53.2 percent opportunity rate. The major question will be whether Barrett can be as effective after losing his top three receivers from last season. Their potential replacements are all extremely talented, especially Noah Brown, who missed all of last season to injury, and Torrance Gibson, who is still new to receiver and not assured a starting spot, but has incredible potential as one of the tallest receivers on the roster. Senior Corey Smith, electric H-back/running back Curtis Samuel, and Parris Campbell might get the first crack at starting roles. The passing offense missed Devin Smith and the deep threat component of Urban's offense last season. If Ohio State finds one, the rest of the Big Ten should watch out.

The schedule is fairly unforgiving. Ohio State opens with three-straight Air Raid teams in Bowling Green, Tulsa, and Oklahoma, all of whom will test the Buckeyes' green secondary. Then, beginning in mid-October, they hit a four-game stretch of pesky games against Wisconsin, Penn State, Northwestern, and Nebraska. No individual game in that stretch is impossible, but all four teams rank between 27th and 48th in the F/+ projections. Finally, they close with Michigan State and Michigan. The Buckeyes will be more talented than every team on their schedule, but it will take time to put those pieces together and figure out who will be the go-to guys. Are two games enough of a warm up before the Buckeyes travel to a loaded Oklahoma team coming off a playoff appearance?

It's hard to bet against both Urban Meyer and the amount of accumulated talent he's been able to recruit to Columbus. But there are definite question marks—secondary, defensive line, receiver—and not much time in the schedule to get answers before they're thrown into the fire. Nevertheless, anything less than ten wins would be a major disappointment, and this team's ceiling is another playoff berth.

No. 14 Washington Huskies (10-2, 7-2)

2016 Projections		Projection Factors	
F/+	39.1 (14)	2015 F/+	36.0 (13)
FEI	.144 (15)	2015 FEI	.154 (19)
S&P+	17.0 (10)	2015 S&P+	17.1 (12)
Total Wins	9.6	5-Year F/+	15.0 (39)
Conf Wins	6.7	5-Year FEI	.119 (22)
SOS	.182 (51)	5-Year S&P+	7.2 (39)
Conf SOS	.185 (39)	2-Year Recruiting	78.2 (30)
Div Champ	.311	5-Year Recruiting	77.5 (29)
Conf Champ	.156	Ret. Offense	.722
CFP Berth	.109	Ret. Defense	.795

Projected Win Likelihood by Game

Date	Opponent (Proj Rank)	PWL
Sep 3	vs Rutgers (84)	98%
Sep 10	vs Idaho (110)	99%
Sep 17	vs Portland St. (FCS)	100%
Sep 24	at Arizona (64)	87%
Sep 30	vs Stanford (9)	54%
Oct 8	at Oregon (11)	39%
Oct 22	vs Oregon St. (90)	99%
Oct 29	at Utah (32)	71%
Nov 5	at California (72)	90%
Nov 12	vs USC (12)	55%
Nov 19	vs Arizona St. (60)	93%
Nov 25	at Washington St. (43)	79%

With the Pac-12 North wide open, given Oregon, Cal, and Stanford's new quarterbacks, Washington has been the early beneficiary of preseason love and expectations given that they have their answer at quarterback in Jake Browning. Browning was an elite recruit with a stellar freshman debut, averaging eight yards per attempt and completing 63 percent of his passes. The Huskies were far from perfect last season and it's understandable that there would be skepticism about slotting a 7-6 team right behind Ohio State, but the Huskies ended the season on a tear and seemed poised for bigger things in 2016. The optimism comes from identifying Browning as the answer at quarterback, discovering Myles Gaskin at running back, and the defense not missing a beat despite heavy personnel losses.

The Huskies have a lot of experience returning on defense this season—79 percent of last year's production is back. The two leading tacklers were both sophomores, while young defensive backs like Budda Baker and Sidney Jones suggest the pass defense might even improve on last year's 27th ranking in the S&P+. The only concern is replacing two prolific pass-rushers who fueled a 17th ranking in adjusted sack rate—Brian Lay and Cory Littleton. The pair combined for 28.5 tackles for loss and 14 sacks, responsible for the sixth-best overall havoc rate in the country. No one else on the team had more than 4.5 sacks. Their dynamism will be missed, but they return Kieshawn Bierria and Zeem Victor and have with reinforcements coming in the form of blue chip freshmen Camilo Eifler and Brandon Wellington. You would like to see a little more pass-rushing ability from the defensive line, however—especially with Littleton and Lay gone. Junior Elijah Qualis looks like the best option from here, picking up 4.5 sacks for a line that was just 108th in defensive line havoc rate.

While Browning seemed to grow throughout his freshman season, he unfortunately loses his top two receiving weapons, forcing juniors Brayden Lenius and Dante Pettis to step in to starting roles. Lenius is an interesting option at 6-foot-5 and with a 74 percent catch rate. But the real excitement is in the return of John Ross III, who missed last season due to injury. Pettis leads returning receivers with 13.8 average yards per catch, but the group as a whole could certainly be more explosive at just 94th in passing IsoPPP last season. Better line play—the Huskies were 83rd in adjusted sack rate—would give Browning more time in the pocket and for receivers to get open downfield. Browning is complimented by freshman Myles Gaskin, who appeared out of nowhere to rush for more than 1,000 yards and 6.8 highlight yards per opportunity. That indicates good explosiveness, but Gaskin wasn't as efficient as you'd like, with only 39 percent of his rushes gaining 5 yards or more. With his offensive line ranking just 50th in adjusted line yards, better line play would improve those efficiency numbers and keep the Huskies offense moving consistently—they ranked just 97th in creating value drives last season.

The schedule sets up well for the Huskies. With easy games early, Browning, Gaskin, and the defense have time to get in sync before a tough two-game stretch against Stanford and Oregon, followed by a physical game against Utah in late October. Though November features tough games in the Apple Cup and against USC, the one to watch for is against Cal on November 5—if the Cal offense begins to click with Davis Webb, then a bruising game against Utah the week before could create a body blow situation where the Bears slice and dice the 61st-ranked passing success rate Washington defense.

No. 15 Notre Dame Fighting Irish (10-2)

2016 Projections		Projection Factors	
F/+	38.9 (15)	2015 F/+	43.3 (7)
FEI	.145 (14)	2015 FEI	.202 (7)
S&P+	16.7 (11)	2015 S&P+	18.8 (8)
Total Wins	9.5	5-Year F/+	34.9 (11)
Conf Wins	-	5-Year FEI	.177 (9)
SOS	.183 (53)	5-Year S&P+	15.7 (9)
Conf SOS	-	2-Year Recruiting	92.0 (10)
Div Champ	-	5-Year Recruiting	93.8 (8)
Conf Champ	-	Ret. Offense	.605
CFP Berth	.068	Ret. Defense	.467

Projected Win Likelihood by Game

Date	Opponent (Proj Rank)	PWL
Sep 4	at Texas (37)	75%
Sep 10	vs Nevada (82)	98%
Sep 17	vs Michigan St. (20)	66%
Sep 24	vs Duke (52)	92%
Oct 1	vs Syracuse (58)	89%
Oct 8	at NC State (55)	84%
Oct 15	vs Stanford (9)	54%
Oct 29	vs Miami-FL (39)	86%
Nov 5	vs Navy (57)	89%
Nov 12	vs Army (107)	99%
Nov 19	vs Virginia Tech (31)	82%
Nov 26	at USC (12)	39%

The biggest obstacles to a playoff appearance for the Irish include a reloading defense, a need for wide receivers to step up, and a sneaky-tough schedule. And head coach Brian Kelly still needs to settle the quarterback battle between DeShone Kizer and Malik Zaire.

The Irish were consistently strong on offense behind Kizer's admirable relief for Zaire after his broken ankle early in 2015. The passing offense was top 10 in passing S&P+ and benefitted from an explosive, veteran receiving corps as well as the running back duo of C.J. Prosise and Josh Adams. First, the running backs: even though Prosise is off to the NFL this year, surprise sophomore Adams leads a group of young, explosive talent. And that's before you count the return of Tarean Folston from injury. Get ready for a tandem of backs carrying the ball, as Adams provides a level of explosiveness that Folston hadn't shown (averaging 7.8 highlight yards per carry to 3.5 for Folston, with similar opportunity rates). But the key to their success was a powerful offensive line that saw the departure of three starters, including star left tackle Ronnie Stanley. The cupboard is far from bare, however, with former blue chips Hunter Bivin, Colin McGovern, Sam Mustipher, and others ready for starting roles—assuming they can hold off a trio of highly-regarded true freshmen.

The run game shouldn't miss a beat—the bigger concern is certainly with the passing game. Despite returning two quarterbacks that could start for nearly anyone in the country, the combination of replacing wide receivers and offensive linemen could create a setback until new go-to options emerge. It's entirely possible that the line's mediocre No. 52 ranking in adjusted sack rate had more to do with having a mobile quarterback than anything else, but replacing three starters is difficult nonetheless. But the bigger issue is that the three-most targeted wide receivers all departed, including explosive play specialist Will Fuller. The receivers room is stocked with young talent, but they'll need at least two young options to emerge—especially someone who offers a deep threat. As for the quarterbacks, Notre Dame fans should have faith in either one starting. The question will be more about how the coaches handle their quarterbacks, not whether one of them is up to the challenge.

The defense was the team's weak spot last season, ranking 33rd in success rate but 57th in IsoPPP+. They were particularly vulnerable to explosive rushing opponents, ranking 67th in rushing PPP+. Now the front seven has to replace four starters, including stars Sheldon Day and Jaylon Smith, as well as leading pass rusher Romeo Okwara. The Irish don't have a returning player with more than 7.5 tackles for loss or three sacks, so the pass rush, which was already just 77th in adjusted sack rate, is a concern. The good news is that there is young talent across the board that is ready to step in. There are a lot of young defensive backs on the roster, so it's very likely that true freshmen will litter the two-deep.

Notre Dame's overall talent base is high enough that it's unreasonable to expect anything but a top-15 or maybe top-20 team from the Irish. But losses on the line, at wide receiver, and throughout the defense are the most critical areas to reload. While 2015 Ohio State showed that it is possible to mismanage a glut of talent at quarterback, that shouldn't be too much of a concern. Instead, the biggest challenge might be a difficult schedule that offers few true lightweight opponents. The Irish have at least three peer opponents (Michigan State, Stanford, and USC) and six other games where our projections favor the Irish by fewer than two scores. If the Irish end the season with an 11-1 record then they will certainly have earned it.

No. 16 Michigan Wolverines (10-2, 7-2)

2016 Projections		Projection Factors	
F/+	38.3 (16)	2015 F/+	41.6 (8)
FEI	.123 (22)	2015 FEI	.167 (14)
S&P+	19.3 (6)	2015 S&P+	21.1 (6)
Total Wins	10.1	5-Year F/+	26.7 (19)
Conf Wins	7.2	5-Year FEI	.131 (19)
SOS	.261 (69)	5-Year S&P+	13.0 (17)
Conf SOS	.269 (49)	2-Year Recruiting	89.1 (14)
Div Champ	.336	5-Year Recruiting	92.9 (9)
Conf Champ	.219	Ret. Offense	.534
CFP Berth	.161	Ret. Defense	.727

Projected Win Likelihood by Game

Date	Opponent (Proj Rank)	PWL
Sep 3	vs Hawaii (121)	99%
Sep 10	vs Central Florida (93)	99%
Sep 17	vs Colorado (86)	98%
Sep 24	vs Penn St. (42)	88%
Oct 1	vs Wisconsin (36)	86%
Oct 8	at Rutgers (84)	96%
Oct 22	vs Illinois (83)	98%
Oct 29	at Michigan St. (20)	50%
Nov 5	vs Maryland (74)	96%
Nov 12	at Iowa (33)	70%
Nov 19	vs Indiana (68)	94%
Nov 26	at Ohio St. (13)	40%

It would be easy to overhype Jim Harbaugh's Wolverines after he took a 5-7 team to a 10-3 season. However, this team still has some questions to answer and some payback to administer after a nightmarish defeat at home against Michigan State and a crushing defeat in round one of the Jim vs. Urban era of football's fiercest rivalry.

The Wolverines underachieved for several years BH (Before Harbaugh, the date by which Ann Arbor residents now set their calendar) which hurts them in projection models that use the past to project the future. That said, there are a lot of reasons to believe Michigan might make the leap and be a national contender in 2016.

The strongest point in their favor might be the roster losses suffered by Big 10 East division rivals Michigan State and Ohio State. After that, you have to mention a defense that ranked second in S&P a year ago and returns many of the best players that made that success possible.

The defensive line is an absolute embarrassment of riches, highlighted by Chris Wormley (14.5 tackles for loss and 6.5 sacks) and Ryan Glasgow, who missed much of 2015 with injury. The Wolverines also bring back defensive linemen Willie Henry (6.5 sacks) and Taco Charlton (5.5 sacks) and can easily rotate bodies along one of the biggest and most intimidating defensive fronts in college football.

Behind that, the Wolverines are losing a couple of experienced linebackers but return even more riches in the secondary. Cornerback Jourdan Lewis is the key piece after a season in which he defended 20 passes and moved around between the nickelback and both cornerback positions to shadow his assignments with press-man coverage. The other featured star is SAM linebacker Jabrill Peppers, a 6-foot-1, 205-pound explosive dynamo who new defensive coordinator Don Brown intends to use as a rover around the box.

Michigan was at their best in 2015 playing a 3-2-6 dime package that allowed them to lock down spread offenses with man coverage while shooting their two linebackers into the backfield on the blitz from every conceivable angle. The Wolverines ranked 13th on passing downs and could see those numbers go up in Brown's aggressive blitz package. The Wolverines should again be formidable in both nickel and dime sub-packages next year.

The offense is set up for success as well for whichever quarterback wins the starting job (likely Houston transfer John O'Korn). The top three receivers are back, including tight end Jake Butt who plays a major role in Harbaugh's West Coast passing game in attacking the middle of the field. The offensive line ranked 13th in adjusted sack rate a year ago and returns four starters. They're moving junior Mason Cole from left tackle to center in order to make room for sophomore Grant Newsome. Given the success the Wolverines had in protection last year, such a move can only signify a talent upgrade.

The problem on offense was a struggle to impose their will in the Harbaugh power run game—their Power success rate in 2015 only ranked 50th nationally. Running back De'Veon Smith leads a stable of runners that could mimic the success Toby Gerhart enjoyed under Harbaugh back at Stanford if Michigan can match that program's brilliance along the offensive line. Senior fullback Khalid Hill (6-foot-2, 270) and redshirt freshman tight end Tyrone Wheatley (6-foot-6, 280) may also play significant roles in helping this vision of power football be realized. If John O'Korn wins the quarterback job then Michigan will also be able to add a scrambling element to their offense, which would help them match 2015's impressive tenth-place finish on passing downs.

Michigan's schedule doesn't present a major challenge until late October, when the likely undefeated Wolverines roll into East Lansing. This team figures to be in the playoff hunt throughout the regular season.

No. 17 UCLA Bruins (9-3, 7-2)

2016 Projections		Projection Factors	
F/+	36.9 (17)	2015 F/+	23.8 (28)
FEI	.133 (20)	2015 FEI	.095 (32)
S&P+	16.5 (12)	2015 S&P+	12.4 (23)
Total Wins	9.4	5-Year F/+	22.8 (24)
Conf Wins	7.2	5-Year FEI	.111 (26)
SOS	.206 (60)	5-Year S&P+	11.6 (22)
Conf SOS	.357 (58)	2-Year Recruiting	91.7 (11)
Div Champ	.637	5-Year Recruiting	92.2 (13)
Conf Champ	.318	Ret. Offense	.615
CFP Berth	.184	Ret. Defense	.879

Projected Win Likelihood by Game

Date	Opponent (Proj Rank)	PWL
Sep 3	at Texas A&M (23)	56%
Sep 10	vs UNLV (115)	99%
Sep 17	at BYU (30)	65%
Sep 24	vs Stanford (9)	50%
Oct 1	vs Arizona (64)	93%
Oct 8	at Arizona St. (60)	84%
Oct 15	at Washington St. (43)	77%
Oct 22	vs Utah (32)	81%
Nov 3	at Colorado (86)	96%
Nov 12	vs Oregon St. (90)	99%
Nov 19	vs USC (12)	52%
Nov 26	at California (72)	89%

The Bruins went all in on freshman quarterback Josh Rosen in 2015 and were rewarded with 3,669 yards, 23 touchdowns, and 11 interceptions. In 2016 they are doubling down with a new, pro-style offense that will focus a lot of control in the sophomore's hands while putting greater emphasis on the run game and vertical passing attack. If Rosen can wield the audibles and varying tempos he's being armed with this offseason, it should make the entire offense more dangerous. As Peyton Manning spent his career proving in the NFL, a player who can adjust to minimize threats and maximize opportunities with decisions at the line is very difficult to counter.

The Bruins are bringing back both offensive tackles to help keep Rosen upright while moving stud athlete and cornerback Ishmael Adams over to play wide receiver so he can use his speed to run past defensive backs. Thomas Duarte, a 6-foot-3 senior, will also be a featured target for Rosen on deep throws down the sideline. The Bruins ranked 23rd in offensive S&P in 2015 despite finishing only 73rd on standard downs thanks to ranking 20th on passing downs. Much of that is attributable to Rosen's ability to hit difficult throws on third-and-long, which should only improve.

The Bruins also have the personnel in place to build a fearsome running game to open up the play-action opportunities thanks to the return of both starting guards, fullback Nate Iese, and explosive running back Soso Jamabo, who ran for 404 yards at 6.1 yards per carry in 2015 as a back-up.

The defense had to grow up fast in 2015 after losing defensive tackle Eddie Vanderdoes, cornerback Fabian Moreau, and linebacker Myles Jack to injury. As a result of those losses they slipped from 25th in defensive S&P to 51st in 2015. Moreau and Vanderdoes return in 2016, though Jack is moving on to the NFL. The Bruins should be loaded in the secondary thanks to the return of all four starters.

Hard-hitting safety Jaleel Wadood is a standout and finished third in tackles a year ago and middle linebacker Jayon Brown is back after leading the team in tackles as a junior. If Vanderdoes can keep the linebackers clean, then the overall speed and aggressiveness of the Bruins defensive backfield should allow a return to the top 30 or better on defense.

No. 18 Arkansas Razorbacks (7-5, 4-4)

2016 Projections		Projection Factors	
F/+	35.5 (18)	2015 F/+	36.7 (11)
FEI	.134 (18)	2015 FEI	.181 (9)
S&P+	15.2 (17)	2015 S&P+	15.3 (15)
Total Wins	7.4	5-Year F/+	21.5 (27)
Conf Wins	3.8	5-Year FEI	.142 (16)
SOS	.015 (5)	5-Year S&P+	11.7 (21)
Conf SOS	.021 (5)	2-Year Recruiting	81.0 (25)
Div Champ	.015	5-Year Recruiting	73.8 (31)
Conf Champ	.009	Ret. Offense	.367
CFP Berth	.006	Ret. Defense	.889

Projected Win Likelihood by Game

Date	Opponent (Proj Rank)	PWL
Sep 3	vs Louisiana Tech (85)	98%
Sep 10	at TCU (25)	57%
Sep 17	vs Texas St. (124)	99%
Sep 24	vs Texas A&M (23)	61%
Oct 1	vs Alcorn St. (FCS)	100%
Oct 8	vs Alabama (1)	13%
Oct 15	vs Ole Miss (5)	40%
Oct 22	at Auburn (24)	55%
Nov 5	vs Florida (26)	71%
Nov 12	vs LSU (2)	22%
Nov 19	at Mississippi St. (21)	50%
Nov 26	at Missouri (40)	72%

The Hogs have a clear identity as a program, which is basically to field the biggest, strongest team on the field every Saturday and bash skulls until they impose their will. That's a tough vision to realize in the rough-and-tumble SEC West, but head hog Brett Bielema will have a squad in 2016 that might be his best yet.

The offensive line has been retooled after losing several starters over the last two years but some of the key pieces are still around. Big 6-foot-10 right tackle Dan Skipper and 6-foot-5 guard Frank Ragnow are back, and Arkansas is looking to plug in a 6-foot-4 Dane named Hjalte Froholdt and redshirt freshman Colton Jackson on the left side as the foundation of the next generation of Arkansas offensive line. Texas grad transfer Jake Raulerson could factor in at center and allow Ragnow to stay at guard where he has excelled.

The skill positions are reasonably well stocked despite losing tight end Hunter Henry and running back Alex Collins to the NFL. The No. 1 and 3 receivers (Drew Morgan and Dominique Reed) return, while 2014's leading receiver Keon Hatcher is back after a foot injury that sidelined him for all last season. Even at quarterback things should look familiar with Brandon Allen's younger brother Austin stepping in.

The defense is facing a tougher challenge after leapfrogging from 82nd to sixth in defensive S&P from 2013 to 2014 but then dropping back down to 71st in 2015. Arkansas plays fairly conservative defense and relies on sturdy play up front and playmaking at linebacker to allow the safeties to drop back and bracket troublesome wide receivers. When this is working well it allows them to shut down even elite talents like Amari Cooper, who was held to 22 yards on two catches in 2014.

In 2015 this was ineffective and the Hogs finished 102nd in defending standard downs. In 2016 they return some key pieces along the defensive line that may improve the situation. A key to their strategy will be usage of under-shifted fronts that pair defensive tackle Jeremiah Ledbetter (7.5 tackles for loss in 2015) with defensive end Deatrich Wise (eight sacks) on the weak side while moving nose tackle Taiwan Johnson back to his natural position and aligning 280-pound defensive end Tevin Beanum with him on the strong side.

Behind them the Hogs return both inside linebackers Brooks Ellis and Dre Greenlaw to clean things up, and they hired former Iowa State head coach Paul Rhoads to coach up their secondary to better balance run support with a conservative coverage approach. If the Hogs can win the battles in the trenches more often than not, the rest of their roster could be good enough to take advantage.

No. 19 Louisville Cardinals (9-3, 6-2)

2016 Projections		Projection Factors	
F/+	34.8 (19)	2015 F/+	17.2 (39)
FEI	.137 (17)	2015 FEI	.054 (51)
S&P+	14.4 (20)	2015 S&P+	10.9 (28)
Total Wins	9.3	5-Year F/+	19.7 (31)
Conf Wins	5.8	5-Year FEI	.083 (36)
SOS	.103 (29)	5-Year S&P+	8.1 (36)
Conf SOS	.131 (26)	2-Year Recruiting	69.1 (39)
Div Champ	.079	5-Year Recruiting	69.7 (39)
Conf Champ	.054	Ret. Offense	.976
CFP Berth	.046	Ret. Defense	.765

Projected Win Likelihood by Game

Date	Opponent (Proj Rank)	PWL
Sep 1	vs Charlotte (122)	99%
Sep 9	at Syracuse (58)	81%
Sep 17	vs Florida St. (6)	42%
Sep 24	at Marshall (62)	82%
Oct 1	at Clemson (3)	12%
Oct 14	vs Duke (52)	89%
Oct 22	vs NC State (55)	90%
Oct 29	at Virginia (71)	87%
Nov 5	at Boston College (53)	79%
Nov 12	vs Wake Forest (78)	96%
Nov 17	at Houston (38)	70%
Nov 26	vs Kentucky (89)	98%

The story of 2016 Lousiville will begin and end with true sophomore quarterback Lamar Jackson, an athletic terror who rushed for more than 1,000 yards in 2016 and whose development will now be the focus of head coach Bobby Petrino's offseason.

Petrino and offensive line coach/run game coordinator Chris Klenakis have installed elements of the Nevada Pistol offense to marry Petrino's pro-style personnel preferences to the shotgun zone-read system. The result is an imposing run game. Opponents that want to try and focus defenders in the box to control running back Brandon Radcliff will be faced with the prospect of stopping Jackson on the perimeter running behind multiple lead blockers. If that sounds remotely appealing to any defensive coordinators, they can ask Texas A&M how that approach went for them in the Music City Bowl, when Jackson ran for 226 yards and two scores.

If Petrino can get Jackson further along in his passing game, there are weapons here as well with three of the four leading receivers back and athletic, converted quarterback Reggie Bonnafon focusing his time running routes this offseason. The offensive line has to find three starters, but the option run game should offer enough advantages to allow an easy transition for the replacements.

On defense the Cardinals must say goodbye to star defensive lineman Sheldon Rankins, but they do welcome back nose tackle DeAngelo Brown and star pass-rusher Devonte Fields (10 sacks in 2015). The secondary also returns four starters and is at its best when playing a nickel package that features 6-foot-5 hybrid Josh Harvey-Clemons over the slot where he can impact the run or the pass.

The Cardinals finished 23rd in defensive S&P a year ago thanks largely to a stout run defense that finished seventh in rushing S&P. With leading tackler and weakside linebacker Keith Kelsey returning along with Brown and Harvey-Clemons, there's a good chance that the Cardinals will continue to be strong up front.

No. 20 Michigan State Spartans (9-3, 7-2)

2016 Projections		Projection Factors	
F/+	34.0 (20)	2015 F/+	39.1 (9)
FEI	.141 (16)	2015 FEI	.198 (8)
S&P+	13.5 (22)	2015 S&P+	15.9 (13)
Total Wins	9.1	5-Year F/+	36.5 (9)
Conf Wins	7.0	5-Year FEI	.194 (5)
SOS	.210 (64)	5-Year S&P+	14.7 (12)
Conf SOS	.390 (60)	2-Year Recruiting	88.0 (18)
Div Champ	.344	5-Year Recruiting	83.9 (21)
Conf Champ	.224	Ret. Offense	.265
CFP Berth	.129	Ret. Defense	.637

Projected Win Likelihood by Game

Date	Opponent (Proj Rank)	PWL
Sep 2	vs Furman (FCS)	100%
Sep 17	at Notre Dame (15)	34%
Sep 24	vs Wisconsin (36)	82%
Oct 1	at Indiana (68)	84%
Oct 8	vs BYU (30)	75%
Oct 15	vs Northwestern (47)	87%
Oct 22	at Maryland (74)	88%
Oct 29	vs Michigan (16)	50%
Nov 5	at Illinois (83)	93%
Nov 12	vs Rutgers (84)	97%
Nov 19	vs Ohio St. (13)	48%
Nov 26	at Penn St. (42)	73%

The Spartans run of dominance over the last three years that featured two conference championships may be coming to an end thanks to a tough Big Ten East division and the departure of quarterback Connor Cook.

In three years as the starter, Cook was 36-5 with a sterling 22-2 record in conference play and 5-1 record against the Buckeyes and Wolverines. He's now gone, along with left tackle Jack Conklin, from an offense that ranked 12th on passing downs in 2015. They'll be bringing in senior quarterback Tyler O'Connor to replace Cook while redshirt junior Dennis Finley is next man up at the crucial left tackle spot. The Spartans will enjoy the return of two very good tight ends in Josiah Price (six touchdowns in 2015) and Jamal Lyles as well as second leading wide receiver R.J. Shelton.

Undoubtedly the Spartans will lean chiefly on their running game, which returns three different 500-yard backs from 2015. With several returning faces along the interior offensive line, the drop-off shouldn't be too severe so long as the passing game doesn't collapse without Cook.

On defense the Spartans look really imposing on paper. The front returns star defensive tackle Malik McDowell along with three good inside linebackers in Jon Reschke, Ed Davis, and Riley Bullough to fill two spots. On the back end they return both safeties with Demetrious Cox and Montae Nicholson both back, and they hope to bolster their weak pass coverage with cornerback Vayante Copeland's return from injury after a promising start to 2015.

On the field the Spartans have taken some hits over the last few years from teams that used spread alignments to attack their aggressive safeties in coverage. Their insistence on playing big tacklers over the slot and in both safety positions to swarm opposing running games makes it more difficult to hold up against the pass, but if teams can't threaten them in the middle of the field then they'll continue to swarm Big Ten foes with a deeper and more experienced group than took the field in 2015.

No. 21 Mississippi State Bulldogs (7-5, 4-4)

2016 Projections		Projection Factors	
F/+	31.0 (21)	2015 F/+	33.9 (16)
FEI	.117 (23)	2015 FEI	.157 (16)
S&P+	13.6 (21)	2015 S&P+	15.0 (16)
Total Wins	7.5	5-Year F/+	22.9 (23)
Conf Wins	3.9	5-Year FEI	.142 (17)
SOS	.008 (3)	5-Year S&P+	11.0 (24)
Conf SOS	.010 (3)	2-Year Recruiting	82.8 (23)
Div Champ	.010	5-Year Recruiting	77.9 (27)
Conf Champ	.006	Ret. Offense	.436
CFP Berth	.004	Ret. Defense	.685

Projected Win Likelihood by Game

Date	Opponent (Proj Rank)	PWL
Sep 3	vs South Alabama (111)	99%
Sep 10	vs South Carolina (59)	83%
Sep 17	at LSU (2)	9%
Sep 24	at Massachusetts (128)	99%
Oct 8	vs Auburn (24)	63%
Oct 14	at BYU (30)	57%
Oct 22	at Kentucky (89)	94%
Oct 29	vs Samford (FCS)	100%
Nov 5	vs Texas A&M (23)	62%
Nov 12	at Alabama (1)	4%
Nov 19	vs Arkansas (18)	50%
Nov 26	at Ole Miss (5)	21%

On top of the annual challenge of competing in the SEC West, Dan Mullen's squad must also deal this year with the departure of three-year starting quarterback Dak Prescott and defensive coordinator Manny Diaz. The Bulldogs are also losing several other talents due to graduation or early departure to the NFL, including wide receivers De'Runnya Wilson and Fred Brown, defensive tackle Chris Jones, and linebacker Beniquez Brown.

The loss of Dak Prescott and the unclear succession to the next quarterback is probably the scariest issue for MSU, as his unique talents were key in driving the Bulldogs' run-pass balance that saw them finish in the S&P top 30 for rushing and top 15 in passing last year. With good size and deceptive speed, Prescott was able to allow the Bulldogs to stress multiple parts of the field from spread sets in the passing game while also serving as an inside running threat.

Prescott served as the go-to ball carrier in short-yardage situations, and that ability allowed the Bulldogs to run the ball from four- and five-wide sets. The Bulldogs could even afford to go small in the backfield with scatback Brandon Holloway at running back since the position's physical demands were made lighter by Prescott's role as an inside runner. The offensive line returns three starters and should provide some stability for Holloway and others, but replacing Dak's production will be very difficult.

On defense the Bulldogs are adjusting to the departure of Diaz and defensive lineman Chris Jones by moving to more of a 3-4 defensive look and leaning on a veteran secondary that returns three starters and looks to plug in redshirt senior Cedric Jiles into the vacant cornerback spot.

The Bulldogs were 19th nationally on passing downs last year, largely due to the 10.5 sacks that starting inside linebackers Richie Brown and Beniquez Brown (departed) had in Diaz's blitz schemes. The Bulldogs return a good deal of experience in the secondary as well as Richie Brown, so there shouldn't be too much of a drop-off here so long as new defensive coordinator Peter Sirmon can scheme pressures with their young pass-rushers.

No. 22 Nebraska Cornhuskers (9-3, 7-2)

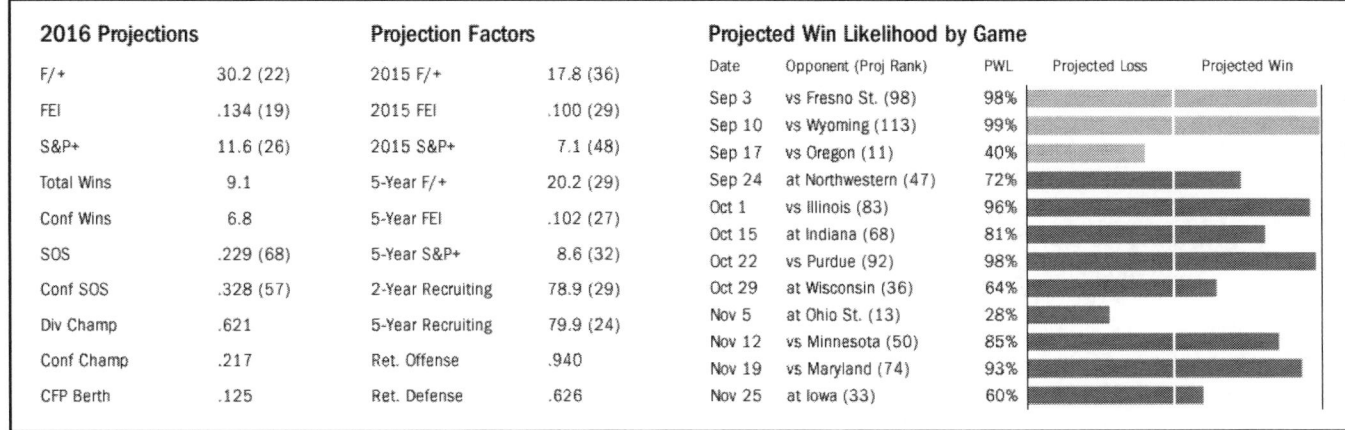

2016 Projections		Projection Factors	
F/+	30.2 (22)	2015 F/+	17.8 (36)
FEI	.134 (19)	2015 FEI	.100 (29)
S&P+	11.6 (26)	2015 S&P+	7.1 (48)
Total Wins	9.1	5-Year F/+	20.2 (29)
Conf Wins	6.8	5-Year FEI	.102 (27)
SOS	.229 (68)	5-Year S&P+	8.6 (32)
Conf SOS	.328 (57)	2-Year Recruiting	78.9 (29)
Div Champ	.621	5-Year Recruiting	79.9 (24)
Conf Champ	.217	Ret. Offense	.940
CFP Berth	.125	Ret. Defense	.626

Projected Win Likelihood by Game

Date	Opponent (Proj Rank)	PWL
Sep 3	vs Fresno St. (98)	98%
Sep 10	vs Wyoming (113)	99%
Sep 17	vs Oregon (11)	40%
Sep 24	at Northwestern (47)	72%
Oct 1	vs Illinois (83)	96%
Oct 15	at Indiana (68)	81%
Oct 22	vs Purdue (92)	98%
Oct 29	at Wisconsin (36)	64%
Nov 5	at Ohio St. (13)	28%
Nov 12	vs Minnesota (50)	85%
Nov 19	vs Maryland (74)	93%
Nov 25	at Iowa (33)	60%

The Cornhuskers should have been well-positioned for success ever since they made the move from the Big 12 to the Big 10 West, where their main competition comes from non-blueblood programs such as Wisconsin and Iowa. In 2015 they finished 6-7 with a record of 1-6 in games determined by five points or less. This poor luck in close games can perhaps be partly explained by the fact that Nebraska recovered the third lowest percentage of their own fumbles in FBS football.

In 2016 Nebraska hopes to be luckier in that regard but will need more than just good fortune to handle a schedule that includes Pac-12 contender Oregon and sends them on the road against Big 10 West contenders Wisconsin and Iowa, plus Big 10 East powerhouse Ohio State.

The Huskers figure to field a reasonably strong offense thanks to the returns of starting quarterback Tommy Armstrong from the nation's 25th passing S&P offense and leading wide receiver Jordan Westerkramp. Nebraska also brings back speedy wideout Demornay Pierson-El, who missed most of 2015 with injury and whose skill set should fit like a glove into head coach Mike Riley's offense.

The bigger issue in terms of losing experience is across the offensive line, where the Huskers return only two starters, both of whom are moving to fill out the crucial left tackle (Nick Gates) and center (Dylan Utter) positions. The advantage here is that the unit had previously been molded to feature lighter, quicker players along the offensive line to execute an Oregon-style outside zone/spread approach, whereas Riley prefers tall and wide players that can roadgrade in his downhill, inside zone running schemes. As a result of the graduation of three starters, the average size of the starting 'Husker offensive line is going from 6-foot-4, 293 pounds in 2015 to 6-foot-5, 299 as they began to reflect the new vision for the Nebraska run game.

On defense the Huskers are losing much of their defensive line, especially at tackle, where both starters and most of the likely replacements are gone. They're hoping that the development of a young defensive backfield will allow them to improve from a 57th place finish in defensive S&P. Between cornerback Joshua Kalu and strong safety Nate Gerry, the Huskers bring back their two leading tacklers, plus seven interceptions. The defensive line is hoping that the move of defensive ends Freedom Akinmoladun and Ross Dzuris into full-time starting roles will result in a better base pass rush. Nebraska also returns a wealth of experience at linebacker to help mitigate the youth movement underway at defensive tackle.

No. 23 Texas A&M Aggies (6-6, 3-5)

2016 Projections		Projection Factors		Projected Win Likelihood by Game					
				Date	Opponent (Proj Rank)	PWL		Projected Loss	Projected Win
F/+	28.7 (23)	2015 F/+	19.7 (34)	Sep 3	vs UCLA (17)	44%			
FEI	.111 (24)	2015 FEI	.110 (26)	Sep 10	vs Prairie View A&M (FCS)	100%			
S&P+	12.5 (25)	2015 S&P+	7.7 (42)	Sep 17	at Auburn (24)	44%			
Total Wins	6.3	5-Year F/+	33.2 (13)	Sep 24	vs Arkansas (18)	39%			
Conf Wins	2.8	5-Year FEI	.112 (24)	Oct 1	at South Carolina (59)	76%			
SOS	.007 (2)	5-Year S&P+	14.8 (11)	Oct 8	vs Tennessee (10)	38%			
Conf SOS	.009 (2)	2-Year Recruiting	90.2 (13)	Oct 22	at Alabama (1)	4%			
Div Champ	.001	5-Year Recruiting	92.5 (10)	Oct 29	vs N. Mexico St. (120)	99%			
Conf Champ	.001	Ret. Offense	.586	Nov 5	at Mississippi St. (21)	38%			
CFP Berth	.000	Ret. Defense	.722	Nov 12	vs Ole Miss (5)	31%			
				Nov 19	vs UTSA (112)	99%			
				Nov 24	vs LSU (2)	16%			

The Aggies could have been in really strong position to make a move in 2016. Newly installed defensive coordinator John Chavis of LSU was able to translate A&M's strong defensive recruiting into a jump in S&P defense from 58th place in 2014 to 29th in 2015. The offense is loaded with talent, including wide receivers Speedy Noil, Ricky Seals-Jones, Christian Kirk, and Josh Reynolds. All they needed this offseason was to rally around one of the two young blue-chip quarterbacks on the roster and continue to make strides on defense and the offensive line, and A&M would have had the makings of an elite squad.

But quarterbacks Kyler Murray and Kyle Allen both transferred this off-season, the offensive coordinator was let go and replaced with UCLA's Noel Mazzone and a new system, and the timeline was reset. Still, the Aggies are only passable quarterback play and improvements at linebacker away from still fielding one of the more talented teams in a loaded SEC West.

The defensive leap under Chavis was largely the result of a year's growth from ultra-talented defensive end tandem Myles Garrett and Daeshon Hall, who combined for 18.5 sacks. They'll be rejoined by up-and-coming defensive tackles Zaycoven Henderson and Daylon Mack, who combined for 16 tackles behind the line. Chavis also got great play out of the back end, leaning heavily on then-sophomore, now-junior free safety Armani Watts (126 tackles a year ago). The Aggies also return strong safety Justin Evans and all of their linebackers from a year ago, suggesting the possibility of major improvements in run defense.

The run defense has been the Achilles heel of the Aggie defense for the last several years, and still only ranked 82nd according to S&P a year ago, but with everyone back up front and so much talent in the defensive line, it should be possible for the linebacker unit to make big strides.

Hopes on offense rest largely on OU transfer quarterback Trevor Knight mastering the system this offseason and finally making good on the promise he showed while shredding Nick Saban's Crimson Tide defense back in 2013. Knight will have an embarrassment of riches at wide receiver, but the offensive line protecting him will be rebuilt after losing four starters. Mazzone's concept-based spread passing attack should be relatively familiar and simple for Knight—his problem has been a tendency to lock in on targets and a lack of accuracy when going to his second or third progression. If those issues can be cured, A&M could surprise in a major way.

No. 24 Auburn Tigers (6-6, 3-5)

2016 Projections		Projection Factors	
F/+	27.7 (24)	2015 F/+	20.6 (33)
FEI	.103 (28)	2015 FEI	.095 (33)
S&P+	12.5 (24)	2015 S&P+	9.7 (35)
Total Wins	6.0	5-Year F/+	19.8 (30)
Conf Wins	2.9	5-Year FEI	.112 (25)
SOS	.003 (1)	5-Year S&P+	11.1 (23)
Conf SOS	.007 (1)	2-Year Recruiting	94.2 (4)
Div Champ	.001	5-Year Recruiting	94.9 (5)
Conf Champ	.001	Ret. Offense	.641
CFP Berth	.000	Ret. Defense	.607

Projected Win Likelihood by Game

Date	Opponent (Proj Rank)	PWL
Sep 3	vs Clemson (3)	16%
Sep 10	vs Arkansas St. (87)	96%
Sep 17	vs Texas A&M (23)	56%
Sep 24	vs LSU (2)	15%
Oct 1	vs UL-Monroe (123)	99%
Oct 8	at Mississippi St. (21)	37%
Oct 22	vs Arkansas (18)	45%
Oct 29	at Ole Miss (5)	17%
Nov 5	vs Vanderbilt (75)	93%
Nov 12	at Georgia (8)	21%
Nov 19	vs Alabama A&M (FCS)	100%
Nov 26	at Alabama (1)	3%

Back in 2010 when Malzahn was the offensive coordinator for Auburn and looking to replace a senior quarterback and take the offense to another level, they plugged in a juco transfer named Cam Newton. The rest was history. When Malzahn returned to Auburn in 2013 he recruited another juco signal caller to step in and help. That player was Nick Marshall, and with him at the helm Auburn again won the SEC title and returned to the national championship game before falling short against Florida State.

In 2015 the Tigers took a step back without Marshall. His successors Sean White and Jeremy Johnson couldn't execute the quarterback-option offense, and the unit struggled without this core piece of their identity. The effect was felt in the run game where the offense slipped from 15th in both rushing S&P and standard downs to 40th and 66th respectively. They slipped even further in their passing game, which was built off the run game, going from first in passing S&P to 41st and from second on passing downs to 24th.

The Auburn skill talent is largely turned over, but the offensive line returns three starters, including standouts Alex Kozan and Braden Smith, and has a young stable of fullbacks that could be ready to provide the kind of lead blocking Malzahn's offense enjoyed back when wrecking ball Jay Prosch was on campus.

The hope is that incoming juco quarterback John Franklin III can reignite the run game with his blazing speed while new defensive coordinator Kevin Steele continues Will Muschamp's attempt to transform the Tigers defense with Nick Saban's schemes.

On defense the Tigers return their young defensive tackles and hope to have pass-rushing specialist Carl Lawson back at full strength. The linebacker corps takes a hit with Cassanova McKinzy and Kris Frost leaving, but safeties Johnathan Ford and Tray Matthews return to try and anchor the interior defense.

No. 25 TCU Horned Frogs (8-4, 6-3)

2016 Projections		Projection Factors	
F/+	26.8 (25)	2015 F/+	30.5 (19)
FEI	.130 (21)	2015 FEI	.173 (12)
S&P+	9.7 (31)	2015 S&P+	11.4 (26)
Total Wins	8.2	5-Year F/+	27.5 (18)
Conf Wins	5.7	5-Year FEI	.175 (10)
SOS	.123 (36)	5-Year S&P+	10.9 (25)
Conf SOS	.159 (31)	2-Year Recruiting	77.1 (31)
Div Champ	-	5-Year Recruiting	72.0 (35)
Conf Champ	.039	Ret. Offense	.286
CFP Berth	.023	Ret. Defense	.679

Projected Win Likelihood by Game

Date	Opponent (Proj Rank)	PWL
Sep 3	vs S. Dakota St. (FCS)	100%
Sep 10	vs Arkansas (18)	43%
Sep 17	vs Iowa St. (79)	93%
Sep 23	at SMU (102)	98%
Oct 1	vs Oklahoma (4)	22%
Oct 8	at Kansas (114)	99%
Oct 22	at West Virginia (35)	58%
Oct 29	vs Texas Tech (45)	80%
Nov 5	at Baylor (7)	20%
Nov 19	vs Oklahoma St. (27)	59%
Nov 25	at Texas (37)	60%
Dec 3	vs Kansas St. (54)	83%

The numbers were somewhat unfair to TCU last season. The Horned Frogs lost most of their great 2014 defense to graduation or the NFL and then lost many of the top replacements to injury during fall camp or early in the season. Now facing the departures of several offensive linemen, first-round wide receiver Josh Doctson, running back Aaron Green, and quarterback Trevone Boykin, the Frogs could actually hold steady if they simply have better luck with injuries.

Last fall marked the first time since joining the Big 12 that TCU didn't field a top-15 defense by S&P (58th!), and you can reasonably expect defensive-minded head coach Gary Patterson to fix that in 2016. The Frogs return middle linebacker and leading tackler Travin Howard, up-and-coming strong safety Denzel Johnson, versatile weak safety Nick Orr, and leading pass-rusher Josh Carraway (eight sacks) this year while also regaining injured stars from a year ago in cornerback Ranthony Texada and defensive end James McFarland.

While the offense was gutted by graduation, many contributors last year were never expected to be great in the first place. They came alive in the Air Raid system that co-offensive coordinators Doug Meacham and Sonny Cumbie installed in 2014. The Frogs still have several offensive linemen who played regularly thanks to injuries in 2015 and a large cast of potential weapons at wide receiver, including the ultra-explosive Kavontae Turpin who had 765 total yards and eight touchdowns as a true freshman.

The Frogs offense should be just fine and simply has to rally behind either Texas A&M transfer quarterback Kenny Hill or redshirt sophomore Foster Sawyer, who turned heads in spring camp.

No. 26 Florida Gators (7-5, 4-4)

2016 Projections		Projection Factors	
F/+	26.7 (26)	2015 F/+	24.0 (27)
FEI	.079 (36)	2015 FEI	.081 (38)
S&P+	14.5 (19)	2015 S&P+	14.3 (18)
Total Wins	7.5	5-Year F/+	26.1 (20)
Conf Wins	4.3	5-Year FEI	.092 (32)
SOS	.040 (10)	5-Year S&P+	12.9 (18)
Conf SOS	.079 (12)	2-Year Recruiting	86.3 (20)
Div Champ	.060	5-Year Recruiting	92.3 (12)
Conf Champ	.024	Ret. Offense	.629
CFP Berth	.012	Ret. Defense	.590

Projected Win Likelihood by Game

Date	Opponent (Proj Rank)	PWL
Sep 3	vs Massachusetts (128)	99%
Sep 10	vs Kentucky (89)	96%
Sep 17	vs North Texas (127)	99%
Sep 24	at Tennessee (10)	22%
Oct 1	at Vanderbilt (75)	83%
Oct 8	vs LSU (2)	14%
Oct 15	vs Missouri (40)	75%
Oct 29	vs Georgia (8)	27%
Nov 5	at Arkansas (18)	29%
Nov 12	vs South Carolina (59)	85%
Nov 19	vs Presbyterian (FCS)	100%
Nov 26	at Florida St. (6)	19%

Jim McElwain's Gators had a fairly successful inaugural season, but a 10-1 start was marred by three ugly losses down the stretch. Quarterback Will Grier looked good early on but was suspended for a positive PED test and has since transferred out of the program. Florida also needs to replace more than half their offensive line, starting running back Kelvin Taylor, and second leading receiver Demarcus Robinson. Leading wide receiver and true sophomore Antonio Callaway could also be missing for the Gators next season due to suspension.

For a group that finished 56th in S&P a year ago and 73rd in rushing S&P, a breakthrough season led by several unknown stars asserting themselves is desperately needed to spark the offense. McElwain earned the opportunity to coach at Florida due to a resume of turning unknown players into stars at Colorado State, and the Florida roster is always loaded with young talent.

On defense the picture is a little brighter, despite the departure of cornerback Vernon Hargreaves, safety Keanu Neal, defensive end Jonathan Bullard, nickelback Brian Poole, and linebacker Antonio Morrison. The Gators finished ranked in the top 10 in every category measured by S&P in 2015 save

for standard downs, where they were 29th, and they still bring back a lot of production from that unit.

Florida will be built around returning cornerback Jalen Tabor, safety Marcus Maye, and a defensive line featuring defensive ends CeCe Jefferson and Bryan Cox Jr., along with returning defensive tackle Caleb Brantley. There's young blue-chip talent stepping in at multiple positions and "minister of mayhem" defensive coordinator Geoff Collins (who's secretly all about sound defense branded with fun buzz words).

Florida's late-season slide may continue, but the quality of coaching combined with the quality of recruiting suggests that they're more likely to right the ship in short order.

No. 27 Oklahoma State Cowboys (8-4, 6-3)

2016 Projections		Projection Factors	
F/+	26.2 (27)	2015 F/+	16.9 (40)
FEI	.091 (29)	2015 FEI	.060 (47)
S&P+	12.6 (23)	2015 S&P+	9.9 (33)
Total Wins	8.2	5-Year F/+	30.3 (16)
Conf Wins	5.6	5-Year FEI	.071 (38)
SOS	.100 (26)	5-Year S&P+	13.5 (16)
Conf SOS	.111 (18)	2-Year Recruiting	68.7 (40)
Div Champ	-	5-Year Recruiting	71.7 (38)
Conf Champ	.031	Ret. Offense	.789
CFP Berth	.019	Ret. Defense	.685

Projected Win Likelihood by Game

Date	Opponent (Proj Rank)	PWL	Projected Loss	Projected Win
Sep 3	vs SE Louisiana (FCS)	100%		
Sep 10	vs C. Michigan (80)	93%		
Sep 17	vs Pittsburgh (34)	69%		
Sep 24	at Baylor (7)	20%		
Oct 1	vs Texas (37)	73%		
Oct 8	vs Iowa St. (79)	93%		
Oct 22	at Kansas (114)	99%		
Oct 29	vs West Virginia (35)	72%		
Nov 5	at Kansas St. (54)	70%		
Nov 12	vs Texas Tech (45)	80%		
Nov 19	at TCU (25)	41%		
Dec 3	at Oklahoma (4)	11%		

Like much of the Big 12, Oklahoma State was defined in 2015 by an explosive offense (22nd in offensive S&P) and an overmatched defense (64th in defensive S&P). They still managed to finish 10-3 and were undefeated before a final three-game stretch against Baylor, Oklahoma, and Ole Miss, the latter two of whom dispatched the Cowboys with relative ease.

In 2016 the Cowboys return a great deal of skill and experience, but lose key athletes on both sides of the ball that may prove difficult to replace. On offense, head coach Mike Gundy's squad returns what may be the most explosive offensive combination in the league in quarterback Mason Rudolph and wide receiver James Washington, who had a 1,000-yard season that included 20.5 yards per reception and 10 touchdowns.

However, the Cowboys lose back-up quarterback and red zone specialist J.W. Walsh, responsible for 13 touchdowns a year ago and a key asset for the Cowboys' power success rate that ranked 75th despite ranking 122nd in standard down line

yards. The 'Pokes return everyone across the offensive line, although given the quality of their blocking a year ago the value of that experience may be dubious. The OSU staff will need to either get considerably better run blocking from the offensive line or find more creative solutions for converting short-yardage opportunities in order to make the most of Rudolph and the passing game.

The Cowboys defense also returns a wealth of experience at positions that struggled a year ago, with both starting defensive tackles, inside linebackers, and safeties returning from a squad that ranked 48th in rushing S&P. The biggest challenge for the Cowboys defense will be in taking a step forward despite losing their top cornerback in Kevin Peterson and starting defensive ends Jimmy Bean and Emmanuel Ogbah, who combined for 18 sacks last season. If OSU can't reload successfully, then it will be too difficult to improve enough on defense and win a Big 12 championship while Rudolph is still on campus.

No. 28 North Carolina Tar Heels (8-4, 5-3)

2016 Projections		Projection Factors		Projected Win Likelihood by Game			
				Date	Opponent (Proj Rank)	PWL	
F/+	23.3 (28)	2015 F/+	27.2 (24)	Sep 3	vs Georgia (8)	23%	
FEI	.082 (34)	2015 FEI	.149 (21)	Sep 10	at Illinois (83)	85%	
S&P+	11.3 (27)	2015 S&P+	10.6 (29)	Sep 17	vs James Madison (FCS)	100%	
Total Wins	8.0	5-Year F/+	11.0 (45)	Sep 24	vs Pittsburgh (34)	64%	
Conf Wins	4.9	5-Year FEI	.087 (35)	Oct 1	at Florida St. (6)	15%	
SOS	.178 (50)	5-Year S&P+	6.3 (42)	Oct 8	vs Virginia Tech (31)	62%	
Conf SOS	.293 (54)	2-Year Recruiting	80.2 (26)	Oct 15	at Miami-FL (39)	55%	
Div Champ	.289	5-Year Recruiting	80.6 (23)	Oct 22	at Virginia (71)	76%	
Conf Champ	.093	Ret. Offense	.503	Nov 5	vs Georgia Tech (41)	73%	
CFP Berth	.048	Ret. Defense	.776	Nov 10	at Duke (52)	66%	
				Nov 19	vs Citadel (FCS)	100%	
				Nov 25	vs NC State (55)	80%	

Coming off a humiliating bowl game defeat to Baylor in which they gave up 645 rushing yards to a team playing without a quarterback, and facing the need to replace their own starting quarterback Marquise Williams (more than 4,000 total yards and 38 touchdowns in 2015), North Carolina doesn't have a great deal of hype around their program.

But the Tar Heels have a lot going for them heading into 2016, including the offensive infrastructure to make their transition to the Mitch Trubisky quarterback era an easy one, plus an older and more experienced defense.

Trubisky was very effective in spot duty over the last few years, and he'll be stepping in on an offense that has three seniors back at wide receiver, a young tight end in Brandon Fritts (who played with Trubisky in high school) who can block and run routes, and a potentially phenomenal offensive line. That Tar Heels offensive line ranked third in adjusted line yards a year ago and 27th in adjusted sack rate and now returns four starters while sliding backup left tackle John Ferranto into the guard position spot left vacant by departing All-

American Landon Turner.

All the pieces are in place for UNC to duplicate a successful attack that saw them finish 17th in offensive S&P a year ago. On defense though, where UNC was 67th overall and 106th in rushing S&P, there needs to be major improvement to allow the Tar Heels to have any hope of competing with the ACC elite.

The Gene Chizik game plan revolves around playing conservative, sound defenses that lean on consistent fundamentals up front and reliable tackling from the back end. In 2015 they lacked playmaking at defensive end and struggled to inflict enough negative plays on opponents to expect to bend without breaking.

The returning experience in the secondary and additional year in Chizik's schemes should allow the Tar Heels to be better at executing the fundamentals of his 4-3 defense, but they'll need senior defensive end Mikey Bart to make the most of increased opportunities and young linebackers Cayson Collins and Andre Smith to have an impact in the blitz package.

No. 29 Boise State Broncos (11-1, 8-0)

2016 Projections		Projection Factors		Projected Win Likelihood by Game			
				Date	Opponent (Proj Rank)	PWL	
F/+	22.4 (29)	2015 F/+	17.7 (37)	Sep 3	at UL-Lafayette (104)	97%	
FEI	.109 (25)	2015 FEI	.090 (37)	Sep 10	vs Washington St. (43)	74%	
S&P+	8.3 (36)	2015 S&P+	7.8 (41)	Sep 24	at Oregon St. (90)	90%	
Total Wins	10.7	5-Year F/+	28.3 (17)	Oct 1	vs Utah St. (73)	87%	
Conf Wins	7.5	5-Year FEI	.100 (28)	Oct 7	at New Mexico (100)	94%	
SOS	.766 (122)	5-Year S&P+	12.7 (19)	Oct 15	vs Colorado St. (95)	97%	
Conf SOS	.915 (122)	2-Year Recruiting	49.1 (65)	Oct 20	vs BYU (30)	59%	
Div Champ	.894	5-Year Recruiting	47.1 (69)	Oct 29	at Wyoming (113)	99%	
Conf Champ	.537	Ret. Offense	.866	Nov 4	vs San Jose St. (94)	97%	
CFP Berth	.027	Ret. Defense	.525	Nov 12	at Hawaii (121)	99%	
				Nov 18	vs UNLV (115)	99%	
				Nov 25	at Air Force (81)	82%	

Every year of the young College Football Playoff era carries the ultimate "what if" question for the scenario in which a program like Boise State runs the table. Would an undefeated non-Power 5 team receive an invitation to the playoffs? Perhaps this year's Broncos can make a run and answer the question with certainty.

The Broncos were middling on offense a year ago, finishing only 54th in S&P, but they at least found their man at quarterback in true freshman Brett Rypien, who will now look to avoid a sophomore slump. He'll be surrounded by a fair amount of talent, including star running back Jeremy McNichols and top wide receivers Thomas Sperbeck and Chaz Anderson. The Boise offensive line also returns several veterans and should find it easy to continue opening holes for McNichols, especially with defenses having to worry about a budding passing game

The defense is facing tough losses, with most of the defensive line departing along with third-round draft pick Darian Thompson, a safety who finished second on the team in tackles a year ago and picked off five passes. Boise is also losing defensive coordinator Marcell Yates to Arizona and will have to lean on a less proven staff to develop the defensive line and a new safety to enable the Broncos' very effective blitz package. If the Broncos can't disrupt offenses via the blitz, then a defensive tackle tandem consisting of players under 280 pounds could struggle.

Still, Boise State ranks as one of the most likely teams in the nation to run through the regular season unscathed. They'll face only two top-50 opponents, and none ranked among the top-25.

No. 30 BYU Cougars (8-4)

2016 Projections

F/+	22.0 (30)
FEI	.104 (27)
S&P+	8.4 (35)
Total Wins	7.6
Conf Wins	-
SOS	.208 (61)
Conf SOS	-
Div Champ	-
Conf Champ	-
CFP Berth	.000

Projection Factors

2015 F/+	19.2 (35)
2015 FEI	.091 (36)
2015 S&P+	8.9 (38)
5-Year F/+	19.4 (32)
5-Year FEI	.093 (30)
5-Year S&P+	8.1 (35)
2-Year Recruiting	47.0 (66)
5-Year Recruiting	46.8 (70)
Ret. Offense	.673
Ret. Defense	.730

Projected Win Likelihood by Game

Date	Opponent (Proj Rank)	PWL	Projected Loss	Projected Win
Sep 3	vs Arizona (64)	77%		
Sep 10	at Utah (32)	46%		
Sep 17	vs UCLA (17)	35%		
Sep 24	vs West Virginia (35)	58%		
Sep 30	vs Toledo (56)	79%		
Oct 8	at Michigan St. (20)	25%		
Oct 14	vs Mississippi St. (21)	43%		
Oct 20	at Boise St. (29)	41%		
Nov 5	at Cincinnati (65)	71%		
Nov 12	vs Southern Utah (FCS)	100%		
Nov 19	vs Massachusetts (128)	99%		
Nov 26	vs Utah St. (73)	87%		

When Bronco Mendenhall moved on from the difficult task of recruiting top units within BYU's unique institutional parameters to take over at Virginia, the Cougars tagged another defensive-minded coach in Kalani Sitake to take over. Sitake comes from the Kyle Whittingham/Gary Andersen coaching tree and he brought old BYU quarterback Ty Detmer to bring back the power-coast offense of BYU's past.

Back in those days it was assumed that BYU's success with the drop-back passing game and two-back run game was a result of having a roster full of married 24-year-olds who could handle the system's complexity. Detmer will have an interesting initial choice to make in choosing between prototypical pro-style signal-caller Tanner Mangum, who started most of last year as a 22-year-old true freshman, and ultra-athletic Taysom Hill, who's back from injury.

Either way, the Cougars will try to feature a more physical and fearsome rushing attack then they did a year ago, when they finished only 63rd in rushing S&P. Given that their roster isn't loaded with blocking tight ends as it was back in Detmer's day, they'll likely maintain some spread-option elements to their playbook and lean on Taysom Hill to boost this attack.

On defense, Sitake is inheriting a very stout defensive front but a secondary that regularly lacked athleticism and forced Mendenhall to mix in conservative coverages to go along with his blitz packages. In 2015 that resulted in the nation's 45th ranked defense by passing S&P and they were 24th on passing downs thanks to a "psycho" third-down package that replaced defensive linemen with linebackers who all stood up at the line of scrimmage and alternated who blitzed while the secondary sat back in Cover-2.

Sitake has traditionally relied on playing man coverage, but while the Cougars return cornerback Michael Davis and defensive back Micah Hanneman there may be growing pains transitioning to that style.

No. 31 Virginia Tech Hokies (7-5, 5-3)

2016 Projections		Projection Factors	
F/+	20.9 (31)	2015 F/+	7.0 (59)
FEI	.084 (33)	2015 FEI	.032 (56)
S&P+	9.3 (32)	2015 S&P+	4.2 (59)
Total Wins	7.3	5-Year F/+	18.2 (33)
Conf Wins	5.1	5-Year FEI	.063 (43)
SOS	.172 (48)	5-Year S&P+	8.6 (33)
Conf SOS	.458 (63)	2-Year Recruiting	75.0 (32)
Div Champ	.364	5-Year Recruiting	79.8 (25)
Conf Champ	.117	Ret. Offense	.663
CFP Berth	.054	Ret. Defense	.822

Projected Win Likelihood by Game

Date	Opponent (Proj Rank)	PWL
Sep 3	vs Liberty (FCS)	100%
Sep 10	vs Tennessee (10)	22%
Sep 17	vs Boston College (53)	77%
Sep 24	vs East Carolina (70)	84%
Oct 8	at North Carolina (28)	38%
Oct 15	at Syracuse (58)	66%
Oct 20	vs Miami-FL (39)	66%
Oct 27	at Pittsburgh (34)	45%
Nov 5	at Duke (52)	63%
Nov 12	vs Georgia Tech (41)	70%
Nov 19	at Notre Dame (15)	18%
Nov 26	vs Virginia (71)	85%

After years of combining aggressive and often dominant defense with middling offense, Virginia Tech's longtime head coach Frank Beamer retired and was replaced by spread offensive guru Justin Fuente from Memphis. Fuente then immediately secured the services of star juco quarterback Jerod Evans and recruited longtime defensive coordinator Bud Foster to stay and continue churning out top defenses.

If Evans can win the job he'll find a lot of weapons on the roster to help him, including the most spread-friendly tight end/fullback tandem you could hope to find in Bucky Hodges (530 receiving yards, six touchdowns) and Sam Rogers (193 receiving yards, two touchdowns). The top two wide receivers Isaiah Ford and Cam Phillips are also back, as are four starters from the offensive line. The potential is there for a major leap forward from a team that finished 72nd in offensive S&P a year ago if Evans can provide a big upgrade at quarterback and all of the returning contributors take well to Fuente's system.

On defense the Hokies struggled (relative to their norms), finishing 40th in S&P with poor numbers against the pass. They return their three main coverage defenders, cornerbacks Brandon Facyson and Greg Stroman along with free safety Chuck Clark, but the defensive front took some hits. Linebackers Deon Clarke and Andrew Motuapuaka are moving on, along with defensive tackle Luther Maddy and defensive end Dadi Nicholas. Foster will be relying on the secondary to help create margin for what will be a young defensive front.

No. 32 Utah Utes (7-5, 5-4)

2016 Projections		Projection Factors	
F/+	19.5 (32)	2015 F/+	29.0 (22)
FEI	.091 (30)	2015 FEI	.155 (18)
S&P+	7.8 (39)	2015 S&P+	11.4 (27)
Total Wins	7.4	5-Year F/+	13.8 (41)
Conf Wins	4.9	5-Year FEI	.134 (18)
SOS	.183 (52)	5-Year S&P+	6.0 (44)
Conf SOS	.205 (45)	2-Year Recruiting	64.6 (43)
Div Champ	.049	5-Year Recruiting	65.0 (46)
Conf Champ	.025	Ret. Offense	.219
CFP Berth	.012	Ret. Defense	.761

Projected Win Likelihood by Game

Date	Opponent (Proj Rank)	PWL
Sep 1	vs Southern Utah (FCS)	100%
Sep 10	vs BYU (30)	54%
Sep 17	at San Jose St. (94)	90%
Sep 23	vs USC (12)	27%
Oct 1	at California (72)	73%
Oct 8	vs Arizona (64)	81%
Oct 15	at Oregon St. (90)	88%
Oct 22	at UCLA (17)	19%
Oct 29	vs Washington (14)	29%
Nov 10	at Arizona St. (60)	65%
Nov 19	vs Oregon (11)	27%
Nov 26	at Colorado (86)	83%

At one point in 2015 Utah was 6-0 and looking like a potential Pac-12 champion after dismantling Oregon 62-20 and taking down both Cal and Arizona State. They had a 15th-ranked defense by S&P combined with an offense that ended up finishing only 53rd, but featured a potent rushing attack headlined by running back Devontae Booker.

Now the Utes have to replace quarterback Travis Wilson, Booker, and their top three wide receivers. Utah does return a fairly experienced offensive line and has some replacements lined up at the skill positions, but after their spring game the quarterback battle remained a three-way tie. It will likely prove difficult for the Utes to develop a strong offensive identity in time for the fall unless it's another simple rushing attack built around prospective starting running back Joe Williams.

On defense the picture is much brighter, with an absolutely loaded defensive line that includes defensive ends Hunter Dimick (10 sacks in 2014, injured after four games in 2015) and Kylie Fitts (seven sacks in 2015) along with defensive tackle Lowell Lotulelei (younger brother of the Carolina Panthers' Star Lotulelei) and sturdy nose tackle Filipo Mokofisi.

The defense has to replace both starting linebackers, but returns both cornerbacks and the safety/nickelback duo of Marcus Williams and Justin Thomas, who combined for eight interceptions a year ago. The Utes' penchant for bringing withering pressure with zone blitzes combined with a very solid and experienced secondary should allow them to stay in games while their offense figures things out.

Their biggest problem might be on special teams, which generated a ton of margin for both their offensive and defensive units, thanks largely to Aussie punter Tom Hackett who averaged 48 yards per kick. He must now be replaced as well.

No.33 Iowa Hawkeyes (9-3, 6-3)

2016 Projections

F/+	19.4 (33)		2015 F/+	17.5 (38)
FEI	.085 (32)		2015 FEI	.094 (34)
S&P+	8.1 (38)		2015 S&P+	7.3 (47)
Total Wins	8.6		5-Year F/+	8.6 (48)
Conf Wins	5.7		5-Year FEI	.070 (39)
SOS	.422 (81)		5-Year S&P+	3.9 (48)
Conf SOS	.430 (61)		2-Year Recruiting	60.9 (49)
Div Champ	.218		5-Year Recruiting	61.9 (51)
Conf Champ	.076		Ret. Offense	.724
CFP Berth	.043		Ret. Defense	.716

Projected Win Likelihood by Game

Date	Opponent (Proj Rank)	PWL
Sep 3	vs Miami-OH (108)	98%
Sep 10	vs Iowa St. (79)	89%
Sep 17	vs N. Dakota St. (FCS)	100%
Sep 24	at Rutgers (84)	83%
Oct 1	vs Northwestern (47)	73%
Oct 8	at Minnesota (50)	60%
Oct 15	at Purdue (92)	89%
Oct 22	vs Wisconsin (36)	63%
Nov 5	at Penn St. (42)	53%
Nov 12	vs Michigan (16)	30%
Nov 19	at Illinois (83)	82%
Nov 25	vs Nebraska (22)	40%

In 2015 the Hawkeyes were a solid team that capitalized on a favorable schedule to go 12-0 before meeting their match in the Big 10 Championship against Michigan State. They then were supremely overmatched in their bowl match-up against Christian McCaffrey and the Stanford Cardinal, losing by 29 points in a game that was over before halftime. Iowa was only the nation's 31st best defense by S&P and 57th best offense by the same metric, yet they are a team with interesting opportunities in 2016 to win a lot of games once again.

To begin with, the Hawkeyes return quarterback C.J. Beathard, who threw for 2,809 yards and 17 touchdowns to only five interceptions a year ago while adding six more touchdowns on the ground. Beathard also returns his top wide receiver Matt Vandeberg and up-and-coming tight end Henry Krieger-Coble. The Iowa offensive line, always the bulwark of the Kirk Ferentz's zone running-based offense, returns three starters for 2015's second leading rusher LeShun Daniels Jr. This may not be the most explosive rushing attack the Hawkeyes have seen in the Ferentz era, but their floor is never too low.

The defense was very sturdy on rushing downs if only pedestrian at getting pressure on third down. Star cornerback Desmond King is back to anchor the secondary after picking off eight passes in 2015, and the linebacker corps has a very strong foundation in returning starters Ben Niemann and Josey Jewell, both back after combining for 171 tackles, 14 tackles for loss, and six sacks last year.

The Hawkeyes will once again be very sound and difficult to beat, and they'll face one of the weakest schedules in the Power 5 yet again. A special season from Beathard and young defensive end Parker Hesse could bring the Hawkeyes back to the Big 10 title game.

No. 34 Pittsburgh Panthers (7-5, 4-4)

2016 Projections		Projection Factors	
F/+	19.3 (34)	2015 F/+	14.5 (46)
FEI	.062 (37)	2015 FEI	.056 (48)
S&P+	10.3 (29)	2015 S&P+	8.2 (40)
Total Wins	7.1	5-Year F/+	11.3 (43)
Conf Wins	4.3	5-Year FEI	.046 (47)
SOS	.094 (23)	5-Year S&P+	6.3 (43)
Conf SOS	.135 (27)	2-Year Recruiting	71.9 (35)
Div Champ	.150	5-Year Recruiting	71.9 (37)
Conf Champ	.048	Ret. Offense	.718
CFP Berth	.024	Ret. Defense	.723

Projected Win Likelihood by Game

Date	Opponent (Proj Rank)	PWL
Sep 3	vs Villanova (FCS)	100%
Sep 10	vs Penn St. (42)	68%
Sep 17	at Oklahoma St. (27)	31%
Sep 24	at North Carolina (28)	36%
Oct 1	vs Marshall (62)	78%
Oct 8	vs Georgia Tech (41)	67%
Oct 15	at Virginia (71)	72%
Oct 27	vs Virginia Tech (31)	55%
Nov 5	at Miami-FL (39)	48%
Nov 12	at Clemson (3)	4%
Nov 19	vs Duke (52)	75%
Nov 26	vs vs Syracuse (58)	78%

Pat Narduzzi's Pittsburgh project went quite well in Year 1, with the defense making modest gains while the offense continued to run over opponents despite the loss of star running back James Conner to a knee injury and cancer treatments.

In 2016 they return quarterback Nate Peterman after a solid year and now have two bruising lead backs, with Conner cancer-free and setting his sights on Qadree Wilson for a reclamation of the starting job. Whoever gets the bulk of the carries will benefit greatly from an offensive line that returns four starters and some talented options at both fullback and tight end. The challenge will be in replacing wide receiver Tyler Boyd, who caught 91 balls a year ago as the go-to target.

The defensive front brings back star pass-rusher Ejuan Price along with the rest of the defensive line and both inside linebackers. The Panthers will continue to unleash strong safety Jordan Whitehead near the action after his breakout 110-tackle season as a true freshman. Free safety Terrish Webb and cornerback Avonte Maddox will continue to develop tricks of the trade that come from playing in Narduzzi's extra-aggressive defense that defers stress back to the secondary.

With nine returning starters on defense and a solid outlook on offense, the pieces are in place for Pittsburgh to continue its ascension in the ACC. They may not be a conference championship threat this year, but they could be the top of the league's next tier.

No. 35 West Virginia Mountaineers (7-5, 5-4)

2016 Projections		Projection Factors	
F/+	17.2 (35)	2015 F/+	21.4 (31)
FEI	.056 (41)	2015 FEI	.079 (41)
S&P+	9.2 (33)	2015 S&P+	12.0 (24)
Total Wins	6.6	5-Year F/+	10.3 (46)
Conf Wins	4.5	5-Year FEI	.067 (40)
SOS	.136 (40)	5-Year S&P+	5.2 (47)
Conf SOS	.171 (34)	2-Year Recruiting	65.1 (42)
Div Champ	-	5-Year Recruiting	63.2 (50)
Conf Champ	.006	Ret. Offense	.861
CFP Berth	.003	Ret. Defense	.379

Projected Win Likelihood by Game

Date	Opponent (Proj Rank)	PWL
Sep 3	vs Missouri (40)	62%
Sep 10	vs Youngstown St. (FCS)	100%
Sep 24	vs BYU (30)	42%
Oct 1	vs Kansas St. (54)	73%
Oct 15	at Texas Tech (45)	54%
Oct 22	vs TCU (25)	42%
Oct 29	at Oklahoma St. (27)	29%
Nov 5	vs Kansas (114)	99%
Nov 12	at Texas (37)	45%
Nov 19	vs Oklahoma (4)	13%
Nov 26	at Iowa St. (79)	76%
Dec 3	vs Baylor (7)	22%

Dana Holgorsen's Mountaineers have struggled to enjoy a breakthrough season since joining the Big 12 and were victimized in 2015 by a brutal October scheduling stretch that sent them to Norman to face OU, back home to play OSU, to Waco to take on the Bears, and then north to Fort Worth to play TCU. West Virginia opened their conference slate 0-4

against the league's best teams. They went 8-1 against the rest of their schedule, with the nation's 35th ranked offense and 28th ranked defense according to S&P+.

Heading into 2016 the Mountaineers look very strong on one side of the ball and potentially awful on the other. The offense returns an interior offensive line of upperclassmen that new offensive line coach Joe Wickline should find easy to mold into one of the league's best units, third-year starter Skyler Howard at quarterback, and a cast of wide receivers that could quietly be the league's best. Four of the top five returning receivers are back, and redshirt juniors Shelton Gibson and Karaun White have star potential. Howard found his rhythm down the stretch last year, and another leap forward could have explosive results for the Mountaineer offense.

The story is exactly the reverse on defense, where defensive coordinator Tony Gibson has to replace all but one starter from the defensive backfield in his 3-3-5 unit. That returning starter, free safety Dravon Askew-Henry, will need to be ready to anchor a wildly inexperienced unit that is desperately looking for cornerbacks and safeties that can play man coverage and allow Gibson to continue to bring the heat on the blitz as they've done the last two years. Returning defensive ends Noble Nwachukwu and Christian Brown will also be relied on to help protect a green cast of linebackers. West Virginia has all the makings of a team destined for shootouts this fall.

No. 36 Wisconsin Badgers (6-6, 4-5)

2016 Projections		Projection Factors		Projected Win Likelihood by Game				
				Date	Opponent (Proj Rank)	PWL	Projected Loss	Projected Win
F/+	16.1 (36)	2015 F/+	20.9 (32)	Sep 3	vs LSU (2)	5%		
FEI	.058 (40)	2015 FEI	.091 (35)	Sep 10	vs Akron (99)	96%		
S&P+	8.3 (37)	2015 S&P+	10.3 (31)	Sep 17	vs Georgia St. (106)	98%		
Total Wins	6.3	5-Year F/+	32.6 (15)	Sep 24	at Michigan St. (20)	18%		
Conf Wins	4.3	5-Year FEI	.115 (23)	Oct 1	at Michigan (16)	15%		
SOS	.056 (15)	5-Year S&P+	13.6 (15)	Oct 15	vs Ohio St. (13)	25%		
Conf SOS	.174 (35)	2-Year Recruiting	73.9 (33)	Oct 22	at Iowa (33)	37%		
Div Champ	.048	5-Year Recruiting	72.9 (34)	Oct 29	vs Nebraska (22)	36%		
Conf Champ	.017	Ret. Offense	.337	Nov 5	at Northwestern (47)	53%		
CFP Berth	.008	Ret. Defense	.535	Nov 12	vs Illinois (83)	89%		
				Nov 19	at Purdue (92)	86%		
				Nov 26	vs Minnesota (50)	70%		

The Badgers had one of the quietest ten-win seasons in the country last year and ended the season with a close bowl game win over the USC Trojans. Wisconsin was solid on defense, ranking 11th in defensive FEI, but struggled on offense without key members of previously formidable Wisconsin rushing attacks. Besides reviving their offense (97th in rushing S&P+, 111th rushing success rate) they must replace more experience on both sides of the ball than nearly everyone. Wisconsin returns just 34 percent of their experience on offense and 54 percent on defense, which is seventh-worst in the country and second-worst in the Big Ten. This will be almost a totally new team in 2016—for better and for worse.

Heading into last season, Corey Clement was expected to take the mantle from Melvin Gordon as the next great Badgers running back, but injuries kept Clement off the field for much of the season, meaning a rotation of players like Dare Ogunbowale and Taiwan Deal had to compensate for a superstar at running back. Neither player managed very much in terms of either opportunity rate (34.5 percent and 37.6 percent, respectively), nor in highlight yards per opportunity (3.8 and 2.1), meaning that the Badgers were often inefficient and hardly ever explosive on the ground.

Now that quarterback Joel Stave is gone and Clement is rehabbing, the spring gave Badgers fans a first look at their new offensive talent. The quarterback race is between Stave's backup Bart Houston and redshirt freshman Alex Hornibrook. Besides Clement, Ogunbowale, and Deal, another name to join the running back rotation will likely be redshirt freshman Bradrick Shaw. Look for Jazz Peavy and George Rushing to step up to replace Alex Erickson's production (77 receptions) at receiver.

Defensively, an excellent pass defense must replace linebacker Joe Schoebert and safety Michael Caputo. Vince Biegel returns as the team's (and one of the conference's) most productive pass-rushers. With fewer losses than on offense, the defense must continue to lead the way for the Badgers in a top-heavy Big Ten. The Badgers' schedule doesn't do them any favors either, as they open with one of the SEC's best (LSU) before facing the Big Ten's best all before the end of October, including road games at Michigan State, Michigan, and Iowa, while getting Ohio State at home. Winning even two of those games would be very impressive for this rebuilding team.

No. 37 Texas Longhorns (6-6, 4-5)

2016 Projections		Projection Factors	
F/+	15.8 (37)	2015 F/+	-2.2 (68)
FEI	.046 (44)	2015 FEI	-.002 (69)
S&P+	9.2 (34)	2015 S&P+	-0.3 (72)
Total Wins	6.4	5-Year F/+	14.4 (40)
Conf Wins	4.5	5-Year FEI	.010 (67)
SOS	.106 (32)	5-Year S&P+	8.5 (34)
Conf SOS	.150 (30)	2-Year Recruiting	91.3 (12)
Div Champ	-	5-Year Recruiting	92.4 (11)
Conf Champ	.009	Ret. Offense	.794
CFP Berth	.004	Ret. Defense	.810

Projected Win Likelihood by Game

Date	Opponent (Proj Rank)	PWL
Sep 4	vs Notre Dame (15)	25%
Sep 10	vs UTEP (126)	99%
Sep 17	at California (72)	69%
Oct 1	at Oklahoma St. (27)	27%
Oct 8	vs Oklahoma (4)	9%
Oct 15	vs Iowa St. (79)	86%
Oct 22	at Kansas St. (54)	56%
Oct 29	vs Baylor (7)	21%
Nov 5	at Texas Tech (45)	52%
Nov 12	vs West Virginia (35)	56%
Nov 19	at Kansas (114)	99%
Nov 25	vs TCU (25)	40%

This appears to be a make-or-break year for Charlie Strong. With the program hoping to avoid another reset, Strong brought in Sterlin Gilbert to implement an up-tempo, Baylor-esque scheme in Austin. Some offensive change was needed, particularly for a passing game that ranked 114th in passing S&P+, though a consistent offensive identity is maybe the most critical development.

Gilbert isn't the only new face on offense. Texas spring game attendees got the first look at the Longhorns' fourth blue-chip quarterback currently on the roster, Shane Buechele. Senior Tyrone Swoopes barely managed a 50 percent pass completion rate last year, and former blue-chipper Jerrod Heard had a 15 percent sack rate, so improvement at the position is critical. Buechele's development (or Heard's, who was held out of spring practice due to injury) and understanding of Gilbert's system will likely determine not only the offense's trajectory, but the entire team's. But the running backs should provide some level of consistency this year as well. Former blue-chip running back Jonathan Gray is gone, though he averaged a 15 percent lower opportunity rate and more than 4 highlight yards per opportunity less than D'Onta Foreman and Chris Warren III. Outside of quarterback, the offensive line remains a concern, with two long-term starters leaving a line that ranked just 67th in adjusted line yards and second-to-last in adjusted sack rate. There are a few promising incoming freshmen, but the rest of the depth is largely inexperienced (only four linemen have starting experience on the roster) and unheralded (besides the three returning blue-chip starters and two incoming freshmen, all linemen were two- or three-star recruits). Whichever quarterback earns the start will likely be using mobile pockets and a quick-passing game to deflect leaky pass protection.

The most glaring defensive deficiency last season was the 78th-ranked S&P+ rushing defense. Opposing offenses could consistently move the ball on the ground against Texas, which is a large reason why the Longhorns were just 57th in success rate+ last season. Much like the offensive line, the Longhorns defensive line is largely undermanned—without the degree of top-end talent and quality, experienced depth that you'd expect for Texas. The top-three tacklers on the line return, along with a stellar group of linebackers, who might have to account for the line's run-stopping shortcomings. Malik Jefferson is the all-world leader of the linebacker corps now that Peter Jinkens is gone, though Jefferson will have help from a very deep group of linebackers, including incoming five-star Erick Fowler and sophomore Anthony Wheeler. The secondary was young last season, but still ranked 20th in passing S&P+—with limited personnel losses, the pass defense should be just fine.

Texas' major points of concern are obvious: breaking in a new offensive coordinator/yet another scheme change, settling on and developing a likely young quarterback, and creating some kind of depth on both lines. Based on the numbers (127th in offensive adjusted sack rate and 74th in defensive adjusted line yards) the lines will determine how far this team goes in 2016—and whether Charlie Strong will get the chance to continue the rebuilding effort in 2017.

No. 38 Houston Cougars (9-3, 6-2)

2016 Projections		Projection Factors	
F/+	15.8 (38)	2015 F/+	24.9 (26)
FEI	.104 (26)	2015 FEI	.175 (10)
S&P+	4.4 (53)	2015 S&P+	7.6 (44)
Total Wins	8.9	5-Year F/+	9.4 (47)
Conf Wins	6.5	5-Year FEI	.124 (20)
SOS	.276 (70)	5-Year S&P+	2.8 (50)
Conf SOS	.791 (81)	2-Year Recruiting	51.3 (61)
Div Champ	.644	5-Year Recruiting	47.3 (68)
Conf Champ	.354	Ret. Offense	.724
CFP Berth	.015	Ret. Defense	.444

Projected Win Likelihood by Game

Date	Opponent (Proj Rank)	PWL
Sep 3	vs Oklahoma (4)	9%
Sep 10	vs Lamar (FCS)	100%
Sep 15	at Cincinnati (65)	63%
Sep 24	at Texas St. (124)	99%
Sep 29	vs Connecticut (76)	85%
Oct 8	at Navy (57)	59%
Oct 15	vs Tulsa (91)	94%
Oct 22	at SMU (102)	92%
Oct 29	vs Central Florida (93)	94%
Nov 12	vs Tulane (119)	99%
Nov 17	vs Louisville (19)	30%
Nov 25	at Memphis (66)	64%

Expectations might be a little too high for Houston in 2016. After defeating Florida State in the Peach Bowl last season, our collective reference points for Houston immediately jumped through the roof, establishing last year's 12-1 record for Tom Herman's rookie season as a head coach as the baseline. And with star quarterback Greg Ward Jr. returning, it's easy to get lost in the hype. That is, until you look at the numbers.

One of the best ways to measure luck is by looking at expected turnovers and recoveries. Houston was second in the country in recovering its own fumbles, falling on 65 percent of lost balls. Including the percentage of interceptions from passes defended, Houston ranked 23rd in this metric in 2015.

There is also a huge difference between the projected FEI and projected S&P+ for Houston in 2016—26th and 53rd, respectively—indicating a mismatch of per-play and per-drive success. The problem with Houston isn't that they were a fraud last year, that their success was <i>all</i< luck, or that the bowl win over the Seminoles shouldn't matter. Instead, it's important to just recognize that national expectations were likely adjusted to Houston's ceiling rather than their mean level of play.

So what does this actually mean for 2016? First, while Ward was the leading rusher last season, Houston has lost their top four running backs (if you include cornerback Brandon Wil-son in that group). Texas transfer and former blue-chipper Duke Catalon should help, and fairly explosive sophomore Kaliq Kokuma will as well. An arguably bigger issue is that four starting offensive linemen have also departed, leaving a group of experienced linemen (only three of the 12 linemen are freshmen) waiting to take over. This leaves a lot of uncertainty, not only for a new starting running back, but also for a quarterback who already had to deal with the 80th-ranked line in adjusted sack rate last season.

Houston ranked 80th in defensive passing S&P+ last season and then lost four of its top five members of the secondary. Opposing offenses are likely to pass early and often, much like they did last season. However, incoming five-star defensive end Ed Oliver, who some argue could have the most immediate impact of any incoming freshman in the country, joins an experienced front seven that suffered few losses. The pass rush, which was just 83rd in the country last season, should see an immediate upgrade.

Overall, there's a lot of personnel turnover on offense, and a lot to improve on defense when it comes to the passing game. There's no doubt that Tom Herman has the program heading in the right direction, and with a schedule that features just two teams ranked higher than 66th in projected F/+, the Cougars may have little trouble making another run at ten or more wins.

No. 39 Miami Hurricanes (7-5, 4-4)

2016 Projections		Projection Factors	
F/+	15.6 (39)	2015 F/+	5.6 (62)
FEI	.038 (48)	2015 FEI	.001 (65)
S&P+	10.0 (30)	2015 S&P+	6.0 (51)
Total Wins	6.5	5-Year F/+	12.7 (42)
Conf Wins	3.9	5-Year FEI	.028 (56)
SOS	.176 (49)	5-Year S&P+	7.7 (37)
Conf SOS	.327 (56)	2-Year Recruiting	86.0 (21)
Div Champ	.094	5-Year Recruiting	88.6 (17)
Conf Champ	.030	Ret. Offense	.777
CFP Berth	.014	Ret. Defense	.617

Projected Win Likelihood by Game

Date	Opponent (Proj Rank)	PWL
Sep 3	vs Florida A&M (FCS)	100%
Sep 10	vs Florida Atlantic (103)	97%
Sep 17	at Appalachian St. (48)	53%
Oct 1	at Georgia Tech (41)	46%
Oct 8	vs Florida St. (6)	19%
Oct 15	vs North Carolina (28)	45%
Oct 20	at Virginia Tech (31)	34%
Oct 29	at Notre Dame (15)	14%
Nov 5	vs Pittsburgh (34)	52%
Nov 12	at Virginia (71)	68%
Nov 19	at NC State (55)	57%
Nov 26	vs Duke (52)	70%

Though we're sure getting fired at Georgia didn't exactly feel great for Mark Richt, there couldn't have been a better landing place than his alma mater, Miami. The Hurricanes have recruited well—third-best in the ACC over the last five years and 17th overall—and he inherits Brad Kaaya, who should be one of the best quarterbacks in the country next season. And Richt has a history developing quarterbacks (see: Aaron Murray, Matt Stafford).

But he also inherits a poor rushing offense, which ranked 117th in rushing S&P+ despite two blue-chippers in Joseph Yearby and Mark Walton. Yearby cleared the 1,000-yard mark, but was neither explosive (4.4 highlight yards per opportunity) nor consistent (39 percent opportunity rate), and Walton was worse. This was mostly due to an offensive line that was 113th in adjusted line yards and 91st in stuff rate. The good news is that nearly everyone returns on the offensive line, save for a single backup guard. If experience on the line counts for anything, then it's hard to see anything but the rushing offense getting better.

Kaaya loses his top two receiving threats, but has a number of talented replacements waiting in the wings, including slot receiver Sam Bruce and two other four-star freshmen. If the offense provides some run game balance, expect Kaaya and whichever receivers step up to the plate to have a great season.

As bad as the rushing offense was, the run defense may have been worse, ranking 102nd in adjusted line yards and 115th in rushing S&P+. New defensive coordinator Manny Diaz will certainly bring the pressure, but he has to get more production out of the fairly talented front seven. Many of the Hurricanes' highest-ranked linemen have yet to produce to the level of their recruiting rankings, and it is up to Diaz to get the most out of his defense's high athleticism. The good news is that Diaz is paired with former Missouri defensive line coach Craig Kuligowski, who helped produce players like Shane Ray and Michael Sam in his 15 seasons. If the run defense can come together and the offensive line can bring offensive balance, then Miami has the pieces for a successful debut season for Mark Richt—potentially only behind Florida State and Clemson in the ACC pecking order.

No. 40 Missouri Tigers (6-6, 3-5)

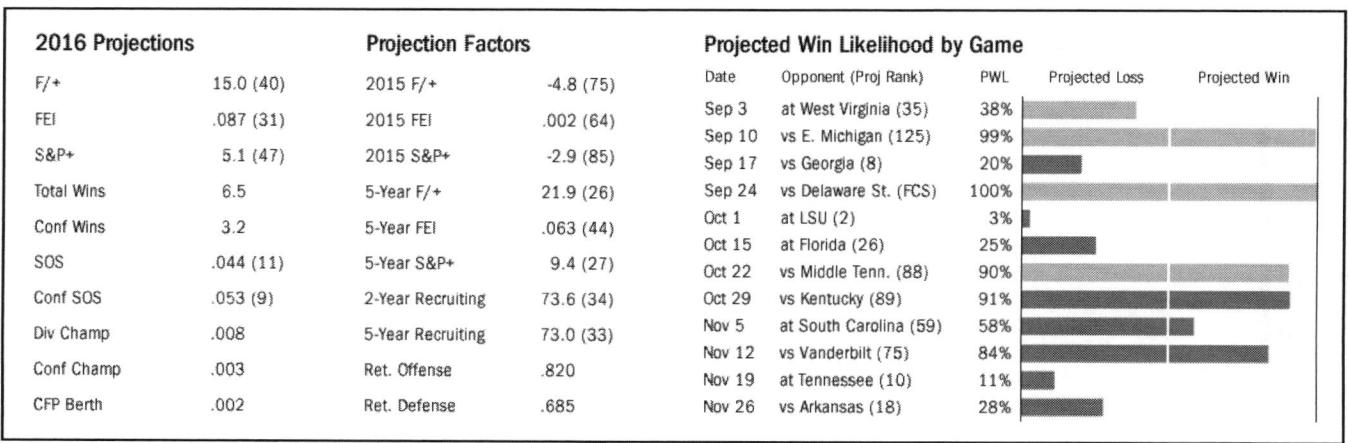

2016 Projections		Projection Factors	
F/+	15.0 (40)	2015 F/+	-4.8 (75)
FEI	.087 (31)	2015 FEI	.002 (64)
S&P+	5.1 (47)	2015 S&P+	-2.9 (85)
Total Wins	6.5	5-Year F/+	21.9 (26)
Conf Wins	3.2	5-Year FEI	.063 (44)
SOS	.044 (11)	5-Year S&P+	9.4 (27)
Conf SOS	.053 (9)	2-Year Recruiting	73.6 (34)
Div Champ	.008	5-Year Recruiting	73.0 (33)
Conf Champ	.003	Ret. Offense	.820
CFP Berth	.002	Ret. Defense	.685

Projected Win Likelihood by Game

Date	Opponent (Proj Rank)	PWL
Sep 3	at West Virginia (35)	38%
Sep 10	vs E. Michigan (125)	99%
Sep 17	vs Georgia (8)	20%
Sep 24	vs Delaware St. (FCS)	100%
Oct 1	at LSU (2)	3%
Oct 15	at Florida (26)	25%
Oct 22	vs Middle Tenn. (88)	90%
Oct 29	vs Kentucky (89)	91%
Nov 5	at South Carolina (59)	58%
Nov 12	vs Vanderbilt (75)	84%
Nov 19	at Tennessee (10)	11%
Nov 26	vs Arkansas (18)	28%

Last year went about as poorly as it could have gone for the Tigers. From the SEC Championship in 2014 to not making a bowl at all a year later, the Tigers regressed on offense from 47th in S&P+ to 120th. That drop made Missouri a half-team where even their typically stellar defense couldn't compensate.

Missouri started true freshman and former blue chip quarterback Drew Lock, though he wasn't yet the savior that Missouri fans expected. The Tigers were the second-worst in the FBS in points per game, averaging just 13.6 (behind winless UCF!) in large part because the inefficient offense (126th in success rate) couldn't take advantage of scoring opportunities. The Tigers were dead last in points per trip inside the 40 and in rushing success rate, and 121st in passing success rate. A large part of that undoubtedly falls on the offensive line, which was 102nd in adjusted line yards, and now-junior running back Ish Witter averaged just a 33.3 percent opportunity rate. Offensive line depth is still a concern for 2016, but there's hope that more experience, potential slight scheme changes from Josh Heupel, and simple regression to the mean will improve the line's play. If spring game play can be predictive in any way, then Lock at least appears to be more efficient after his first offseason of practices at Missouri.

The defense should be typically stellar. Last season the Tigers defense was extremely bend-don't-break-oriented, with the top overall IsoPPP rating and 29th-rating in success rate. They also were second in the country in points per opponent trip in the 40, meaning that while Missouri's offense hardly scored, the defense ensured plenty of close, low-scoring games too. The defense held five opponents to ten points or fewer in 2015, and that was even with a dropoff in the pass rush to 56th in adjusted sack rate. The defense ranked tenth in overall havoc rate, a critical factor in shortening opposing drives and preventing drives from turning in to points. Big-time defensive end Charles Harris returns, as do sophomore linemen Terry Beckner Jr. and Walter Brady, but all three faced some kind of offseason injury. Their health, and the offensive line's growth, will likely determine whether Missouri has any chance of challenging what now looks like a three-horse race in the SEC East. This team, and new head coach Barry Odom's tenure, are still young, which may mean that this year's benchmark for success is setting the stage for a 2017 SEC East title chase again.

No. 41 Georgia Tech Yellow Jackets (6-6, 4-4)

2016 Projections		Projection Factors		Projected Win Likelihood by Game				
				Date	Opponent (Proj Rank)	PWL	Projected Loss	Projected Win
F/+	13.3 (41)	2015 F/+	0.5 (64)	Sep 3	vs Boston College (53)	60%		
FEI	.081 (35)	2015 FEI	.008 (61)	Sep 10	vs Mercer (FCS)	100%		
S&P+	4.4 (54)	2015 S&P+	1.0 (68)	Sep 17	vs Vanderbilt (75)	82%		
Total Wins	6.1	5-Year F/+	16.8 (34)	Sep 22	vs Clemson (3)	6%		
Conf Wins	3.5	5-Year FEI	.072 (37)	Oct 1	vs Miami-FL (39)	54%		
SOS	.090 (22)	5-Year S&P+	7.6 (38)	Oct 8	at Pittsburgh (34)	33%		
Conf SOS	.175 (37)	2-Year Recruiting	62.2 (48)	Oct 15	vs Ga. Southern (51)	66%		
Div Champ	.060	5-Year Recruiting	65.1 (45)	Oct 29	vs Duke (52)	67%		
Conf Champ	.019	Ret. Offense	.973	Nov 5	at North Carolina (28)	27%		
CFP Berth	.009	Ret. Defense	.421	Nov 12	at Virginia Tech (31)	30%		
				Nov 19	vs Virginia (71)	78%		
				Nov 26	at Georgia (8)	9%		

The Yellow Jackets were one of the biggest surprises of last season, right alongside teams like Texas A&M and Auburn as terribly disappointing. Georgia Tech plummeted to a 3-9 record and a final F/+ rank of 64th after finishing eighth in the 2014 F/+ rankings. So what was responsible for the decline?

Returning quarterback Justin Thomas wasn't enough to offset the complete loss of the Tech offensive backfield. Freshmen Marcus Marshall and Clinton Lynch grew into their roles as explosive rushing options, but the offense as a whole couldn't produce enough explosive plays (from third to 73rd in IsoPPP). Thomas and Stanford graduate transfer Patrick Skov received the most carries, but neither had above a 36 percent opportunity rate and Skov averaged just 1.7 highlight yards per opportunity. Both Marshall and Lynch return as sophomores, while Tech faithful are excited for redshirt freshman Quaide Weimerskirch's development.

But the explosive play problems were also a function of an inefficient receiving corps. There are only two returning players with more than seven catches, and neither had above a 42 percent catch rate last year. Now the offensive line must replace three starters, including the entire left side, on a unit that was stuffed on a fifth of all runs last season (81st last season). The good news is that tackle Chris Griffin returns after missing last season due to injury, but the line is still a major uncertainty. If Tech opponents are able to spend so much time in the backfield (78th in adjusted sack rate), then it's hard to imagine the offense significantly improving for 2016—though Georgia Tech is known for unpredictable swings. The biggest bright spot is that Tech returns 97 percent of adjusted offensive experience for next year, and that experience, some big-play potential from the running backs, and Griffin's return on the offensive line could make a big difference.

The defense only returns 42 percent of last year's adjusted experience—and that 42 percent almost entirely comes from the defensive line. Unfortunately, that amounts to five players with significant game experience but only five total sacks (112th in adjusted sack rate). Four of the top five members of the secondary are gone, and one of the top linebackers as well. The Jackets will start a number of inexperienced guys on defense, which could be a challenge to improve a defense that struggled defending the red zone, allowing touchdowns far more often than forcing field goals (4.4 points per red zone trip, 93rd in red zone S&P+). Overall there's a lot of uncertainty for the Yellow Jackets in 2016—there's reason to expect improvement on offense but a defensive front seven that doesn't apply much pressure suggests the Jackets will not challenge Florida State, Clemson, Louisville, or any upstarts in the chase for the ACC crown.

No. 42 Penn State Nittany Lions (7-5, 5-4)

2016 Projections

F/+	13.1 (42)
FEI	.009 (66)
S&P+	11.3 (28)
Total Wins	6.7
Conf Wins	4.8
SOS	.227 (66)
Conf SOS	.287 (53)
Div Champ	.017
Conf Champ	.011
CFP Berth	.006

Projection Factors

2015 F/+	13.6 (47)
2015 FEI	.028 (57)
2015 S&P+	10.4 (30)
5-Year F/+	15.3 (37)
5-Year FEI	.030 (53)
5-Year S&P+	9.3 (29)
2-Year Recruiting	88.1 (17)
5-Year Recruiting	79.5 (26)
Ret. Offense	.528
Ret. Defense	.632

Projected Win Likelihood by Game

Date	Opponent (Proj Rank)	PWL
Sep 3	vs Kent St. (101)	95%
Sep 10	at Pittsburgh (34)	32%
Sep 17	vs Temple (61)	71%
Sep 24	at Michigan (16)	12%
Oct 1	vs Minnesota (50)	66%
Oct 8	vs Maryland (74)	80%
Oct 22	vs Ohio St. (13)	22%
Oct 29	at Purdue (92)	84%
Nov 5	vs Iowa (33)	47%
Nov 12	at Indiana (68)	61%
Nov 19	at Rutgers (84)	77%
Nov 26	vs Michigan St. (20)	28%

It's getting to be make-or-break time for James Franklin at Penn State. The Christian Hackenberg era is over, and this season also will see the introduction of several new coaching hires, including the promotion of defensive coordinator Brent Pry (who takes over for Bob Shoop after he left for Tennessee) and offensive coordinator Joe Moorhead (who came from his alma mater, Fordham). They have a lot of work to do. It's an easier job for Pry, who was already instrumental creating the previous seasons' fourth- and 15th-place finishes in the defensive S&P+ rankings. But Moorhead is implementing a new, wide-open spread, all while breaking in a new quarterback.

Moorhead's offense uses West Coast passing concepts; no-huddle, one-back formations; and plenty of tight end looks to move quickly and adjust to what the defense is doing. He'll have quality skill players in leading receivers Chris Godwin and DaeSean Hamilton, tight end Mike Gesicki, and one of the country's best freshman running backs from last season in Saquon Barkley, who averaged 7.3 highlight yards per opportunity. Penn State also has the top overall running back recruit in the 2016 class, Miles Sanders, who should immediately share snaps with Barkley.

The main problems are that no one knows who will take the reins at quarterback or whether the offensive line can improve regardless of who they're blocking for. Sophomore Trace McSorley seems like a likely candidate, and his spring game performance of 23-for-27 with four touchdowns seemed like a good omen for winning the starting job. But there are questions about whether he has the size or arm strength to make the long-distance throws to Godwin, Hamilton, or deep-threat specialist Saeed Blacknall. The offensive line ranked 111th in adjusted sack rate last season. Matchups with teams like Pittsburgh, Michigan, Temple (ten sacks against Penn State last season), and Ohio State could be rough if the line doesn't come together.

Only 63 percent of last year's defensive experience will return for 2016, which is a shame considering Bob Shoop orchestrated another top-15 S&P+ finish. They were especially good at limiting big passing plays and pressuring the quarterback thanks to pass-rushing phenom Carl Nassib, who had 19.5 tackles for loss and 15.5 sacks. But he and his partner on the line, Anthony Zettel, are both gone for 2016. Penn State's claim on the nickname Linebacker U looks strong, with the formidable trio of Brandon Bell, Jason Cabinda, and Nyeem Wartman-White. It's fair to expect the defense to take a slight step back with the change in defensive coordinators and the loss of two pass-rushers like Nassib and Zettel, but this will still be a solid group.

No. 43 Washington State Cougars (7-5, 4-5)

2016 Projections		Projection Factors	
F/+	11.6 (43)	2015 F/+	10.4 (54)
FEI	.059 (38)	2015 FEI	.080 (40)
S&P+	5.0 (48)	2015 S&P+	2.9 (63)
Total Wins	6.5	5-Year F/+	-9.7 (82)
Conf Wins	4.3	5-Year FEI	.025 (58)
SOS	.157 (45)	5-Year S&P+	-2.5 (81)
Conf SOS	.199 (41)	2-Year Recruiting	55.8 (56)
Div Champ	.011	5-Year Recruiting	55.0 (57)
Conf Champ	.005	Ret. Offense	.871
CFP Berth	.003	Ret. Defense	.712

Projected Win Likelihood by Game

Date	Opponent (Proj Rank)	PWL
Sep 3	vs E. Washington (FCS)	100%
Sep 10	at Boise St. (29)	26%
Sep 17	vs Idaho (110)	98%
Oct 1	vs Oregon (11)	19%
Oct 8	at Stanford (9)	9%
Oct 15	vs UCLA (17)	23%
Oct 22	at Arizona St. (60)	54%
Oct 29	at Oregon St. (90)	82%
Nov 5	vs Arizona (64)	72%
Nov 12	vs California (72)	77%
Nov 19	at Colorado (86)	76%
Nov 25	vs Washington (14)	21%

Their Apple Cup rivals in Seattle may be getting all of the attention in the Pac-12 North division this offseason, but Mike Leach's Cougars won nine games and look every bit as dangerous this season. Leach has finally managed to implement his system from Texas Tech up in Washington State. His Air Raid offense is efficient if not explosive, while his defense is just good enough to keep every game from becoming a shootout (though, most certainly were last season). After a shocking opening week loss to Portland State, the Cougars only lost three more games, and two of them were by a total of eight points—Cal out-Air Raided them, while Stanford bludgeoned the Cougars, and Washington hit their stride by the time the Apple Cup came around.

The best news for any Mike Leach team is that his steady, efficient quarterback is returning. Luke Falk was fifth in the country in total passing yards last season and completed almost 70 percent of his throws. Sure, his yards per attempt average (6.3) and passing IsoPPP rank (119th) demonstrate that these were mostly short, safe passes, but he was extremely successful with what he was asked to do last season. And all but one in his receiving corps returns this year, including leading receiver Gabe Marks. The receivers are nearly all reliable, with 70-plus percent catch rates, but they lack a real vertical threat right now, ranking just 54th in passes of 30-plus yards and 103rd in passes of 40-plus yards last season, despite the fact that they threw on 70 percent of standard downs. The offense should continue to hum along regardless—and that will likely be enough to keep Wazzu as a conference contender in this year's wide-open race.

The defense had bend-don't-break tendencies, and the secondary's ability to defend against explosive plays seems to have made all of the difference in the world in Wazzu's defensive growth. They ranked 14th in fewest passes of 20-plus yards given up (31), a huge leap forward from the prior year when they ranked 125th (58). The defensive front actually managed a strong pass rush, ranking 37th in adjusted sack rate, though they lose two top defensive ends. All-name teamer Hercules Mata'afa led the team in sacks and returns again, at least. And the secondary is mostly intact, losing just strong safety Taylor Taliulu, but returning four other starters. Front seven depth is likely to be a concern, but the return of most of the secondary along with Mata'afa should ensure that the Cougars can build on last year's great improvement in pass defense. The issue will likely be run defense again (92nd in rushing S&P+), and Stanford, Oregon, and Washington are each poised to exploit this weakness.

No. 44 South Florida Bulls (8-4, 6-2)

2016 Projections		Projection Factors		Projected Win Likelihood by Game				
				Date	Opponent (Proj Rank)	PWL	Projected Loss	Projected Win
F/+	10.3 (44)	2015 F/+	15.1 (44)	Sep 3	vs Towson (FCS)	100%		
FEI	.024 (61)	2015 FEI	.080 (39)	Sep 10	vs Northern Illinois (67)	71%		
S&P+	7.2 (41)	2015 S&P+	6.5 (50)	Sep 17	at Syracuse (58)	51%		
Total Wins	8.0	5-Year F/+	-9.2 (81)	Sep 24	vs Florida St. (6)	15%		
Conf Wins	5.6	5-Year FEI	-.011 (73)	Oct 1	at Cincinnati (65)	55%		
SOS	.466 (88)	5-Year S&P+	-2.3 (79)	Oct 8	vs East Carolina (70)	72%		
Conf SOS	.769 (78)	2-Year Recruiting	57.4 (54)	Oct 15	vs Connecticut (76)	80%		
Div Champ	.373	5-Year Recruiting	63.4 (49)	Oct 21	at Temple (61)	52%		
Conf Champ	.168	Ret. Offense	.889	Oct 28	vs Navy (57)	66%		
CFP Berth	.007	Ret. Defense	.700	Nov 12	at Memphis (66)	56%		
				Nov 19	at SMU (102)	88%		
				Nov 26	vs Central Florida (93)	91%		

It was a difficult first two years at South Florida for Willie Taggart, but the former Western Kentucky coach has new life after last season's 8-5 record. Though the season ended with a ten-point loss to his former employer, it was a success in both the win column and in the trend line. After an early-season loss to Maryland (76th in F/+), the Bulls beat everyone they were supposed to beat and dominated several teams down the stretch.

The turnaround was built on an explosive ground game with now-juniors Quinton Flowers and Marlon Mack. The former, the Bulls' quarterback, added more than a thousand yards on the ground and a consistent 45.7 percent opportunity rate, while the latter averaged nearly 7 highlight yards per opportunity while nearly matching Flowers' rushing efficiency. Together, the pair led the 18th-overall rushing S&P+ offense, which was 33rd in opponent-adjusted explosiveness. Yes, passing was inefficient (83rd in passing success rate) and was a large reason why the offense's overall success rate+ was just 71st, but Flowers at least only threw eight interceptions. His 6.1 percent sack rate, inflated somewhat by his rushing numbers, was an efficiency issue as well. This year, almost every skill player returns, including both Mack and Flowers and the top five receivers. Further, UCLA transfer Asiantii Woulard is the heir apparent behind Flowers, and should be more than a capable backup. However, three starting offensive linemen have gone, including All-AAC guard Thor Jozwiak. There is plenty of depth, but it's nevertheless mostly untested, which likely means similarly poor pass protection (73rd in adjusted sack rate).

The defense is good, but not great, in nearly every category, but a few bright spots stick out. First, despite ranking in the 50s n both IsoPPP+ and success rate+, the Bulls had a top-thirty opponent-adjusted red zone defense. Similarly, they greatly improved from standard to passing downs, going from 65th to 22nd in success rate. Taken together, the Bulls defense performed its best with its back against the wall. They will unfortunately be without disruptive defensive end Eric Lee, but leading tackler Auggie Sanchez is back at linebacker, and every defensive back save Jamie Byrd returns as well. Byrd and Lee combined for ten sacks on a defense that was 27th in adjusted sack rate. Someone will have to replace their production, but the answers on the line aren't obvious considering four of the Bulls' top five linemen are gone for next season.

No. 45 Texas Tech Red Raiders (6-6, 4-5)

2016 Projections		Projection Factors		Projected Win Likelihood by Game				
				Date	Opponent (Proj Rank)	PWL	Projected Loss	Projected Win
F/+	10.2 (45)	2015 F/+	6.7 (60)	Sep 3	vs SF Austin (FCS)	100%		
FEI	.030 (56)	2015 FEI	.037 (53)	Sep 10	at Arizona St. (60)	52%		
S&P+	6.5 (43)	2015 S&P+	3.5 (62)	Sep 17	vs Louisiana Tech (85)	86%		
Total Wins	6.0	5-Year F/+	'0.3 (58)	Sep 29	vs Kansas (114)	98%		
Conf Wins	3.7	5-Year FEI	.009 (68)	Oct 8	at Kansas St. (54)	47%		
SOS	.131 (39)	5-Year S&P+	2.3 (52)	Oct 15	vs West Virginia (35)	46%		
Conf SOS	.142 (28)	2-Year Recruiting	66.7 (41)	Oct 22	vs Oklahoma (4)	8%		
Div Champ	-	5-Year Recruiting	66.4 (42)	Oct 29	at TCU (25)	20%		
Conf Champ	.001	Ret. Offense	.759	Nov 5	vs Texas (37)	48%		
CFP Berth	.001	Ret. Defense	.723	Nov 12	at Oklahoma St. (27)	20%		
				Nov 19	at Iowa St. (79)	68%		
				Nov 25	vs Baylor (7)	12%		

Texas Tech ended 2015 with a 7-6 record, but it can by and large be considered a success—the Red Raiders won every game they were supposed to win plus one they weren't against Arkansas. They faced a difficult conference schedule and a bowl game against SEC stalwart LSU. Several losses were close, too—Tech lost to TCU and West Virginia by a combined eight points. The disparity between the offense (third in S&P+) and the defense (121st) once again put the Red Raiders in a number of shootouts. Three-quarters of both offensive and defensive experience return for 2016, so can we expect more of the same for next season?

The Red Raiders offense, led by quarterback Patrick Mahomes II, ranked in the top 15 in both adjusted efficiency and explosiveness. If there was any knock on last year's offense, it was a tendency to slow down in the red zone, ranking 42nd in red zone S&P+. And as good as Mahomes was, the rushing offense was actually more efficient than the passing offense, ranking fourth compared to 40th in adjusted success rate. The worst news is that the drivers of that rushing offense are no longer in Lubbock. Three starting offensive linemen, including two All-Big 12 selections, are gone, as is the dependable and explosive DeAndre Washington. Rushing for nearly 1,500 yards while averaging a 43 percent success rate and more than 6 highlight yards per opportunity, Washington was the total package. He ranked fifth in receiving yards and hauled in 72 percent of passes thrown his way. Luckily junior running back Justin Stockton had nearly identical efficiency and explosive-

ness numbers, averaging 6.3 highlight yards per opportunity and a 46 percent opportunity rate. Besides Stockton, redshirt freshman Corey Dauphine was a highly sought-after recruit, and sophomore Demarcus Felton was very explosive in limited action for his freshman year. But replacing the offensive line will be more difficult, considering there are only three returning linemen with starting experience and then a host of sophomores and redshirt freshmen waiting for their opportunity. Expectations are high for Mahomes this season, but the line will have to replicate its performance (ninth in adjusted line yards and 22nd in adjusted sack rate) for Texas Tech to repeat its level of shootout ability from a year ago.

It's tough to find reasons for optimism in the Texas Tech defense outside of the relative stability in the secondary. The defense can't perform much worse in 2016 than it did in 2015, however. It was one of the 20 worst defensive teams by almost every opponent-adjusted metric you can use—including explosive plays (113th), efficiency (112th), rushing (124th), and adjusted sack rate (114th). On top of those numbers, the defense has lost its top three defensive linemen and two of its top four linebackers (along with three backup linebackers as well). The relatively good news is that in terms of adjusted experience, Tech returns 72 percent of its defensive experience thanks to seven of its top eight defensive backs returning. Outside of departed linebacker Micah Awe, the majority of the leading tacklers were in the secondary, and most return as juniors or seniors.

No. 46 Western Kentucky Hilltoppers (10-2, 7-1)

2016 Projections		Projection Factors		Projected Win Likelihood by Game				
				Date	Opponent (Proj Rank)	PWL	Projected Loss	Projected Win
F/+	10.2 (46)	2015 F/+	35.8 (15)	Sep 1	vs Rice (118)	98%		
FEI	.040 (46)	2015 FEI	.149 (22)	Sep 10	at Alabama (1)	1%		
S&P+	5.6 (45)	2015 S&P+	17.5 (11)	Sep 17	at Miami-OH (108)	93%		
Total Wins	9.6	5-Year F/+	1.9 (56)	Sep 24	vs Vanderbilt (75)	79%		
Conf Wins	6.8	5-Year FEI	.090 (34)	Oct 1	vs Houston Baptist (FCS)	100%		
SOS	.129 (37)	5-Year S&P+	0.6 (64)	Oct 8	at Louisiana Tech (85)	74%		
Conf SOS	.870 (109)	2-Year Recruiting	25.4 (92)	Oct 15	at Middle Tenn. (88)	76%		
Div Champ	.503	5-Year Recruiting	25.1 (89)	Oct 22	vs Old Dominion (117)	98%		
Conf Champ	.312	Ret. Offense	.338	Oct 29	at Florida Atlantic (103)	89%		
CFP Berth	.013	Ret. Defense	.593	Nov 5	vs Florida Int'l (116)	98%		
				Nov 12	vs North Texas (127)	99%		
				Nov 26	at Marshall (62)	52%		

Western Kentucky has rolled since hiring Willie Taggart, but the most recent levels of success—including last season's 12-2 campaign—were largely due to the offensive marks set by quarterback Brandon Doughty. No offense was more explosive and only four were more efficient or better in the red zone last season than the Hilltoppers. So can they replace Doughty and continue on as the best of Conference USA?

The most experienced option is senior Nelson Fishback, an unrated recruit out of high school who has been efficient in extremely limited action as Doughty's reserve. The primary

challenger might be South Florida transfer Mike White, who started for the Bulls as a true freshman, though he had just a 50.4 percent completion rate that year. There are several other options too, including senior Tyler Ferguson, by way of Louisville and Penn State, and younger players Drew Eckels, Reese Ryan, and Steven Duncan. Ryan had the highest rating coming out of high school, though he hasn't had any game experience at the college level.

Regardless, given the skill position talent that returns, the new quarterback's job should be a little easier. The top three running backs all return, including last season's leading rusher Anthony Wales, who was incredibly efficient (55.5 percent opportunity rate) if not particularly explosive (just 5.1 highlight yards per opportunity), and potentially 2014's star back Leon Allen will as well. Allen ran for 1,542 yards in 2014 and was slightly more explosive than Wales, but his ability to return to form following a 2015 knee injury is still unclear. The top two leading receivers also return, including go-to senior Taywan Taylor and the relatively explosive Nicholas Morris. The other three of Doughty's top five receivers are gone, but the receivers room is honestly a little crowded at this point anyway, with seven other receivers who could make an impact in the Hilltoppers' system. Just as meaningful, the entire starting offensive line returns for 2016—including all-conference left tackle Forrest Lamp.

The defense was serviceable in 2015, but prone to late-game collapses and certainly not at the level of the elite offense. Ranking in the mid-60s in both explosiveness and efficiency, and 55th and 73rd in rushing and passing S&P+, the Hilltoppers defense was extremely average. But the defense

steadily declined throughout most games, falling from 20th in first-quarter defensive S&P+ to 118th in fourth-quarter defensive S&P+. Similarly, the defense was at its relative worst in the red zone, ranking 86th in red zone S&P+. So the defense seemed to be fine—even relatively good—at the beginning of games and drives, but seemed to run out of steam. One major issue is that the line couldn't seem to get much pressure, ranking 117th in adjusted sack rate. But the front seven will look much different in 2016, losing four of its top seven linemen and three of its top five linebackers. Both safeties return, but the corners are both gone. So a pass rush would certainly give new life to a mediocre defense and ease the pressure on two green corners.

Finally, despite personnel losses on offense, the Hilltoppers will benefit from an extremely favorable schedule that could see them favored in every game except for the sacrificial matchup with Alabama. Marshall, Vanderbilt, Lousiana Tech, Florida Atlantic, and Middle Tennessee should at least all be competitive, but the majority of Western Kentucky's opponents are ranked 100th or worse in the projected F/+ rankings.

No. 47 Northwestern Wildcats (6-6, 4-5)

2016 Projections		Projection Factors	
F/+	9.5 (47)	2015 F/+	11.0 (52)
FEI	.040 (47)	2015 FEI	.054 (49)
S&P+	5.1 (46)	2015 S&P+	5.5 (56)
Total Wins	6.3	5-Year F/+	4.1 (54)
Conf Wins	4.0	5-Year FEI	.047 (46)
SOS	.205 (59)	5-Year S&P+	1.0 (61)
Conf SOS	.219 (47)	2-Year Recruiting	64.2 (46)
Div Champ	.031	5-Year Recruiting	66.3 (43)
Conf Champ	.011	Ret. Offense	.679
CFP Berth	.005	Ret. Defense	.583

Projected Win Likelihood by Game

Date	Opponent (Proj Rank)	PWL	Projected Loss / Projected Win
Sep 3	vs W. Michigan (63)	66%	
Sep 10	vs Illinois St. (FCS)	100%	
Sep 17	vs Duke (52)	61%	
Sep 24	vs Nebraska (22)	28%	
Oct 1	at Iowa (33)	27%	
Oct 15	at Michigan St. (20)	13%	
Oct 22	vs Indiana (68)	70%	
Oct 29	at Ohio St. (13)	9%	
Nov 5	vs Wisconsin (36)	47%	
Nov 12	at Purdue (92)	80%	
Nov 19	at Minnesota (50)	44%	
Nov 26	vs Illinois (83)	84%	

Apart from maybe Georgia, Northwestern had one of the quietest ten-win seasons you're ever going to see in 2015. The season began with a huge upset win over Stanford, which was quickly followed by a victory over fellow elite academic school Duke, and had quality wins over Penn State and Nebraska. But when the Wildcats lost, they were pummeled: 38-0 against Michigan, 40-10 at the hands of the Hawkeyes, and then a bowl-game blowout of 45-6 from Tennessee. The bowl loss in particular is primarily responsible for why few media members are singling out the Wildcats for preseason praise.

Northwestern had been known for its effective spread offense under quarterbacks like Dan Persa and Mike Kafka, but the offense fell off the rails in 2015. At 113th in passing S&P+ and 99th in rushing S&P+, the defense had to carry the team—and it did, as the fifth overall defense according to the S&P+. That's generally what happens when you start a freshman quarterback in Clayton Thorson. Thorson

threw more interceptions than touchdowns, had nearly a 7 percent sack rate, and averaged just 4.3 yards per attempt, but the good news is that a) he was a freshman, and b) he was extremely effective on the ground, leading the team in yards per carry (6.9) and opportunity rate (44.3 percent) and far out-pacing leading running back Justin Jackson in explosiveness (7.6 highlight yards per opportunity). His ineffective passing numbers might have been due to extremely poor offensive line play, where the Wildcats were 102nd in adjusted sack rate. Simple stability and a consistent lineup should do wonders for his sophomore season.

Sophomore running back Justin Jackson had an interesting place in the offense. He was the clear focal point of the offense and ended the season with 1,418 rushing yards, but his advanced stats were less than stellar. Jackson averaged just 4.4 highlight yards per opportunity and a poor 33.2 percent opportunity rate. He was run as often as almost anyone in the country—only Derrick Henry and Christian McCaffrey got more touches—but wasn't very efficient or explosive behind that offensive line.

Outside of occasionally allowing explosive passing plays, the defense locked most opponents down. They dominated passing downs (tenth in passing downs S&P+) and slowed most run games down (26th in adjusted line yards), even hold-ing Christian McCaffrey to just 66 yards. But the losses of sack specialist Deonte Gibson and cornerback Nick VanHoose will certainly be tough to replace. Luckily, since recruiting has picked up (the Wildcats average the 51st overall class over the last four years according to 247 Sports Composite) depth has been solid on defense, and the Wildcats will likely have a very similar defensive efficiency profile for 2016.

No. 48 Appalachian State Mountaineers (10-2, 7-1)

2016 Projections		Projection Factors	
F/+	9.3 (48)	2015 F/+	15.9 (42)
FEI	.055 (42)	2015 FEI	.074 (44)
S&P+	3.7 (59)	2015 S&P+	7.7 (43)
Total Wins	9.5	5-Year F/+	-6.1 (73)
Conf Wins	7.1	5-Year FEI	.031 (52)
SOS	.439 (84)	5-Year S&P+	-2.4 (80)
Conf SOS	.849 (105)	2-Year Recruiting	18.4 (115)
Div Champ	-	5-Year Recruiting	16.8 (112)
Conf Champ	.445	Ret. Offense	.724
CFP Berth	.018	Ret. Defense	.781

Projected Win Likelihood by Game

Date	Opponent (Proj Rank)	PWL
Sep 1	at Tennessee (10)	8%
Sep 10	vs Old Dominion (117)	98%
Sep 17	vs Miami-FL (39)	47%
Sep 24	at Akron (99)	84%
Oct 1	vs Georgia St. (106)	96%
Oct 12	at UL-Lafayette (104)	89%
Oct 22	vs Idaho (110)	98%
Oct 27	at Ga. Southern (51)	44%
Nov 5	vs Texas St. (124)	99%
Nov 12	at Troy (105)	91%
Nov 19	vs UL-Monroe (123)	98%
Nov 26	at New Mexico St. (120)	97%

The Mountaineers are built on an explosive running game—and one that entirely returns in 2016. Appalachian State is coming off of an 11-2 season and has 72 percent of its total offensive experience and 78 percent of its total defensive experience returning for 2016—in short, expectations should be high once again in Boone. Outside of an expected Clemson loss last season, the Mountaineers split the two games where they played relatively poorly—against Troy and Arkansas State.

The 42nd-ranked offensive FEI team was built on running often (68.4 percent of standard downs compared to a 60.3 percent national average), doing so explosively (24th in IsoPPP+), and scoring despite poor field position (119th in defensive field position+). But despite the incredible raw numbers, where Appalachian State was sixth in overall rushing yards per game, there were some inefficiencies. First, the 31st-overall rushing S&P+ attack was only 61st in rushing success rate. That suggests the Mountaineers were effective by being explosive rather than efficient.

Second, passing downs were a big problem. The Mountaineers ranked just 95th in passing downs success rate even though they again ranked 25th in passing S&P+. Then-sophomore quarterback Taylor Lamb was reasonably effective, only throwing nine interceptions and averaging nearly 8 yards per attempt.

But the run game was where the Mountaineers were most effective. Senior running back Marcus Cox led a group of three players with more than 500 rushing yards last season, but like the total rushing efficiency stats suggest, he was much more explosive (6.7 highlight yards per opportunity) than efficient (40.7 percent opportunity rate). Backup running backs Jalin Moore and Terrence Upshaw were slightly more efficient per-carry, and Moore in particular appears to have a higher upside, averaging 7.4 highlight yards per opportunity along with an efficient 46.5 percent opportunity rate. Unfortunately, however, out of three All-Sun Belt performers on an offensive line that was excellent in both run- and pass-blocking, only senior guard Parker Collins returns. On top of those losses up front, three of Lamb's top four receiving targets from 2015 are also gone, and he'll need to develop a rapport with a number of young and inexperienced receivers.

The Mountaineers were pretty solid defensively in almost everything they were asked to do, but were obviously geared to be a bend-don't-break defense. Ranking 33rd in overall IsoPPP+ and 61st in success rate+, the problem is clear when you look at passing downs, where the Mountaineers were just 91st in passing downs success rate. If someone in their star front seven couldn't get to the quarterback (12th in adjusted sack rate), then it often resulted in a first down at most, thanks to strong safety play. However, replacing defensive end Ronald Blair's production will be a challenge, as he led the team in tackles for loss with 19 and in sacks with 7.5. The good news is that nearly everyone else returns, and most everyone was effective—so while no individual may match Blair's production, the unit as a whole should be solid.

No. 49 San Diego State Aztecs (10-2, 7-1)

2016 Projections		Projection Factors		Projected Win Likelihood by Game				
				Date	Opponent (Proj Rank)	PWL	Projected Loss	Projected Win
F/+	8.5 (49)	2015 F/+	15.6 (43)	Sep 3	vs New Hampshire (FCS)	100%		
FEI	.045 (45)	2015 FEI	.076 (42)	Sep 10	vs California (72)	73%		
S&P+	4.0 (55)	2015 S&P+	7.3 (45)	Sep 17	at Northern Illinois (67)	54%		
Total Wins	10.1	5-Year F/+	1.0 (57)	Oct 1	at South Alabama (111)	95%		
Conf Wins	6.8	5-Year FEI	.046 (48)	Oct 8	vs UNLV (115)	98%		
SOS	.835 (128)	5-Year S&P+	0.9 (62)	Oct 14	at Fresno St. (98)	83%		
Conf SOS	.904 (120)	2-Year Recruiting	32.8 (79)	Oct 21	vs San Jose St. (94)	91%		
Div Champ	.766	5-Year Recruiting	32.8 (74)	Oct 28	at Utah St. (73)	59%		
Conf Champ	.306	Ret. Offense	.518	Nov 5	vs Hawaii (121)	98%		
CFP Berth	.014	Ret. Defense	.793	Nov 12	at Nevada (82)	69%		
				Nov 19	at Wyoming (113)	95%		
				Nov 26	vs Colorado St. (95)	91%		

Outside of a rough three-game September stretch that saw losses to Cal, South Alabama, and Penn State, the Aztecs rolled through their schedule, with only a single game decided by less than two scores. San Diego State now has the chance to build on that foundation, but will have to replace nearly half of its offensive experience from last season. But like last season, the Aztecs will likely lead with their defense, anyway.

The offense was run-heavy (running the ball on 81 percent of standard downs compared to a 60 percent national average) and plodding (32.4 percent adjusted pace) and wasn't particularly explosive or efficient (80th and 84th in IsoPPP+ and success rate+). It wasn't splashy, but they did move the chains at least once on 74 percent of their drives (47th). They will need to replace quarterback Maxwell Smith, though like the run percentages above suggest, Smith was much more of a game manager, only attempting 200 passes on the year and averaging 6.5 yards per attempt. Sophomore Christian Chapman served as Smith's backup last season and appeared to improve on all of Smith's numbers, so that can be considered a potential bright spot for now. The run game featured two thousand-yard rushers, including returning starter Donnel Pumphrey and the departed Chase Price. Pumphrey was more explosive than efficient while Price was the steadier rusher. Junior Rashaad Penny (44.3 percent opportunity rate) or one of three freshmen backs will likely be a steady second option for the Aztecs this year.

But the strength of the team is in the defense, where the Aztecs absolutely dominated passing downs (fifth in passing downs S&P+), and still were effective against the run (fifth in rushing S&P+). They only got better as the game went on, ranking between 32nd and 28th in the first through third quarters, only to clamp down and jump to sixth overall in defensive S&P+ in the fourth. It started up front for the Aztecs, who were seventh in adjusted line yards thanks in large part to the efforts of linebacker Calvin Munson, who had 15 tackles for loss and 9.5 sacks. There are three open spots in the front six, but there's plenty of experience and talent in a crowded linebacker room. Finally, all but one member of the secondary returns as well, so it's fair to expect the same level of excellence from the defense again in 2016.

No. 50 Minnesota Golden Gophers (8-4, 5-4)

2016 Projections		Projection Factors		Projected Win Likelihood by Game				
				Date	Opponent (Proj Rank)	PWL	Projected Loss	Projected Win
F/+	8.4 (50)	2015 F/+	8.9 (55)	Sep 1	vs Oregon St. (90)	89%		
FEI	.011 (65)	2015 FEI	-.001 (67)	Sep 10	vs Indiana St. (FCS)	100%		
S&P+	7.0 (42)	2015 S&P+	9.1 (37)	Sep 24	vs Colorado St. (95)	91%		
Total Wins	7.6	5-Year F/+	-1.1 (63)	Oct 1	at Penn St. (42)	35%		
Conf Wins	4.8	5-Year FEI	.011 (66)	Oct 8	vs Iowa (33)	40%		
SOS	.433 (83)	5-Year S&P+	2.0 (55)	Oct 15	at Maryland (74)	61%		
Conf SOS	.441 (62)	2-Year Recruiting	57.5 (53)	Oct 22	vs Rutgers (84)	84%		
Div Champ	.081	5-Year Recruiting	52.6 (58)	Oct 29	at Illinois (83)	70%		
Conf Champ	.028	Ret. Offense	.836	Nov 5	vs Purdue (92)	89%		
CFP Berth	.015	Ret. Defense	.484	Nov 12	at Nebraska (22)	15%		
				Nov 19	vs Northwestern (47)	56%		
				Nov 26	at Wisconsin (36)	30%		

The Golden Gophers' fortunes hinged on the results of a half-dozen close games last year. After a six-point loss to TCU in the opener, Minnesota would play five more games decided by less than a touchdown, going 2-3 in those games. So was last season's disappointing 6-7 record a result of unfortunate bounces in close games or was it indicative of what's to come for 2016?

Quarterback Mitch Leidner is getting some attention as a potential top pick in the 2017 NFL Draft. His measurables (6-foot-4, 237 pounds) and rushing ability (4.1 yards per attempt) are certainly appealing to the NFL, but he completed just 59.5 percent of his passes for just 6.6 yards per attempt last fall. Entering this fall, Leidner loses his clear top receiver K.J. Maye, whom he targeted with nearly a third of his passes. Drew Wolitarsky now takes the mantle along with tight end Brandon Lingen, but there are a number of other options who caught at least 15 passes last season—it just remains to be seen whether Lediner will develop a rapport with them.

The strength of last year's team was the defense, which ranked 23rd in S&P+. They only ranked 69th in success rate, but third in IsoPPP. However, the Gophers' defense will be without leading tackler Antonio Johnson and third-leading tackler De'Vondre Campbell. In fact, the top three tacklers in the secondary are all gone, which will certainly stress the defense's bend-don't-break strategy.

The schedule isn't terribly challenging—the Gophers avoid Michigan, Michigan State, and Ohio State from the East division — but Penn State and Iowa in the first half of the season plus Nebraska, Northwestern and Wisconsin down the stretch all have the potential to be closely contested. Something like eight to ten wins could be possible if fortune favors the Gophers, but there's a chance they'll flirt with .500 again as well.

NCAA Win Projections

Projected Win Probabilities For ACC Teams

ACC Atlantic	Overall Wins													Conference Wins								
	12-0	11-1	10-2	9-3	8-4	7-5	6-6	5-7	4-8	3-9	2-10	1-11	0-12	8-0	7-1	6-2	5-3	4-4	3-5	2-6	1-7	0-8
Boston College	-	-	-	4	13	27	30	18	6	2	-	-	-	-	-	1	5	17	31	30	14	2
Clemson	42	41	14	3	-	-	-	-	-	-	-	-	-	50	40	9	1	-	-	-	-	-
Florida State	3	15	30	29	16	5	2	-	-	-	-	-	-	9	33	36	17	4	1	-	-	-
Louisville	2	12	30	31	17	6	2	-	-	-	-	-	-	2	21	40	27	9	1	-	-	-
NC State	-	-	-	1	4	13	26	30	19	6	1	-	-	-	-	1	5	17	32	30	13	2
Syracuse	-	-	-	-	1	7	17	27	26	16	5	1	-	-	-	-	4	13	28	32	18	5
Wake Forest	-	-	-	-	2	8	20	31	27	11	1	-	-	-	-	-	1	5	18	34	31	11
ACC Coastal	12-0	11-1	10-2	9-3	8-4	7-5	6-6	5-7	4-8	3-9	2-10	1-11	0-12	8-0	7-1	6-2	5-3	4-4	3-5	2-6	1-7	0-8
Duke	-	-	-	1	7	17	27	27	15	5	1	-	-	-	-	3	11	25	31	22	7	1
Georgia Tech	-	-	1	4	12	23	28	21	9	2	-	-	-	-	2	5	16	29	29	15	4	-
Miami-FL	-	-	1	7	17	25	25	16	7	2	-	-	-	-	3	9	21	29	24	11	3	-
North Carolina	-	2	11	23	28	21	10	3	2	-	-	-	-	1	9	24	31	23	10	2	-	-
Pittsburgh	-	1	3	13	23	27	20	10	2	1	-	-	-	-	3	14	28	30	17	6	2	-
Virginia	-	-	-	-	2	5	14	24	28	19	7	1	-	-	-	-	4	10	23	32	24	7
Virginia Tech	-	2	5	15	25	26	17	8	2	-	-	-	-	2	12	25	30	20	8	3	-	-

Projected Win Probabilities For American Teams

American East	Overall Wins													Conference Wins								
	12-0	11-1	10-2	9-3	8-4	7-5	6-6	5-7	4-8	3-9	2-10	1-11	0-12	8-0	7-1	6-2	5-3	4-4	3-5	2-6	1-7	0-8
Central Florida	-	-	-	-	1	6	17	29	29	15	3	-	-	-	-	-	3	14	31	34	15	3
Cincinnati	-	2	6	16	24	25	17	8	2	-	-	-	-	1	5	16	27	27	17	6	1	-
Connecticut	-	-	-	2	7	16	26	26	16	6	1	-	-	-	1	4	14	29	32	17	3	-
East Carolina	-	-	2	8	18	26	24	15	5	2	-	-	-	2	6	19	30	27	13	3	-	-
South Florida	-	3	11	22	27	21	11	4	1	-	-	-	-	4	19	31	27	14	4	1	-	-
Temple	1	6	19	29	26	14	4	1	-	-	-	-	-	3	16	29	29	16	5	2	-	-
American West	12-0	11-1	10-2	9-3	8-4	7-5	6-6	5-7	4-8	3-9	2-10	1-11	0-12	8-0	7-1	6-2	5-3	4-4	3-5	2-6	1-7	0-8
Houston	-	6	23	34	25	9	3	-	-	-	-	-	-	16	36	31	13	4	-	-	-	-
Memphis	-	1	4	14	25	28	19	8	1	-	-	-	-	2	6	19	30	27	13	3	-	-
Navy	-	2	10	23	29	22	10	3	1	-	-	-	-	2	13	29	31	18	6	1	-	-
SMU	-	-	-	-	-	1	4	14	31	34	15	1	-	-	-	-	1	4	16	34	35	10
Tulane	-	-	-	-	-	-	1	6	20	35	30	8	-	-	-	-	-	-	4	15	41	40
Tulsa	-	-	-	-	3	10	22	30	23	10	2	-	-	-	-	1	7	21	34	27	8	2

Projected Win Probabilities For Big 12 Teams

Big 12	Overall Wins													Conference Wins									
	12-0	11-1	10-2	9-3	8-4	7-5	6-6	5-7	4-8	3-9	2-10	1-11	0-12	9-0	8-1	7-2	6-3	5-4	4-5	3-6	2-7	1-8	0-9
Baylor	8	33	35	18	5	1	-	-	-	-	-	-	-	8	34	35	17	5	1	-	-	-	-
Iowa State	-	-	-	-	-	2	8	22	34	26	7	1	-	-	-	-	-	1	8	24	38	26	3
Kansas	-	-	-	-	-	-	-	-	1	8	38	53	-	-	-	-	-	-	-	-	2	21	77
Kansas State	-	-	-	1	4	14	28	31	18	4	-	-	-	-	-	-	4	13	28	32	18	5	-
Oklahoma	25	38	25	9	3	-	-	-	-	-	-	-	-	34	41	19	5	1	-	-	-	-	-
Oklahoma State	-	2	12	27	30	19	7	3	-	-	-	-	-	-	4	17	33	29	13	4	-	-	-
TCU	-	3	12	25	30	20	8	2	-	-	-	-	-	1	6	20	32	27	12	2	-	-	-
Texas	-	-	1	5	15	25	27	18	7	2	-	-	-	-	1	4	15	28	30	17	5	-	-
Texas Tech	-	-	-	3	11	22	29	22	10	3	-	-	-	-	-	1	6	18	30	29	14	2	-
West Virginia	-	-	2	7	17	26	25	16	6	1	-	-	-	-	1	4	16	28	29	16	5	1	-

Projected Win Probabilities For Big 10 Teams

Big Ten East	Overall Wins													Conference Wins									
	12-0	11-1	10-2	9-3	8-4	7-5	6-6	5-7	4-8	3-9	2-10	1-11	0-12	9-0	8-1	7-2	6-3	5-4	4-5	3-6	2-7	1-8	0-9
Indiana	-	-	-	1	8	20	29	25	13	3	1	-	-	-	-	-	3	12	27	32	20	5	1
Maryland	-	-	-	-	3	13	27	31	19	6	1	-	-	-	-	-	1	6	18	33	30	11	1
Michigan	8	30	36	20	5	1	-	-	-	-	-	-	-	9	30	36	19	5	1	-	-	-	-
Michigan State	2	12	26	30	20	8	2	-	-	-	-	-	-	8	27	34	21	8	2	-	-	-	-
Ohio State	2	14	29	30	17	6	2	-	-	-	-	-	-	11	29	33	19	6	2	-	-	-	-
Penn State	-	-	2	8	19	27	24	13	5	2	-	-	-	-	2	7	20	30	26	12	3	-	-
Rutgers	-	-	-	-	-	2	5	16	30	30	14	3	-	-	-	-	-	1	6	19	34	30	10
Big Ten West	12-0	11-1	10-2	9-3	8-4	7-5	6-6	5-7	4-8	3-9	2-10	1-11	0-12	9-0	8-1	7-2	6-3	5-4	4-5	3-6	2-7	1-8	0-9
Illinois	-	-	-	-	-	1	5	15	28	31	17	3	-	-	-	-	-	2	7	23	36	26	6
Iowa	1	7	18	28	25	14	6	1	-	-	-	-	-	1	7	20	29	25	13	4	1	-	-
Minnesota	-	1	7	18	28	26	15	4	1	-	-	-	-	-	2	8	20	30	25	12	3	-	-
Nebraska	2	11	27	31	20	8	1	-	-	-	-	-	-	5	22	35	26	10	2	-	-	-	-
Northwestern	-	-	1	5	14	24	27	19	8	2	-	-	-	-	-	2	9	23	31	23	9	3	-
Purdue	-	-	-	-	-	1	3	10	22	31	25	8	-	-	-	-	-	1	3	12	27	37	20
Wisconsin	-	-	1	4	13	25	30	20	6	1	-	-	-	-	-	3	12	26	31	20	6	2	-

Projected Win Probabilities For Conference USA Teams

Conf USA East	Overall Wins													Conference Wins								
	12-0	11-1	10-2	9-3	8-4	7-5	6-6	5-7	4-8	3-9	2-10	1-11	0-12	8-0	7-1	6-2	5-3	4-4	3-5	2-6	1-7	0-8
Charlotte	-	-	-	-	-	3	11	24	31	22	8	1	-	-	-	-	4	14	29	32	17	4
Florida Atlantic	-	-	-	1	6	18	31	27	13	4	-	-	-	-	1	8	27	35	21	6	2	-
Florida International	-	-	-	-	-	1	5	14	25	28	19	7	1	-	-	-	4	11	26	33	21	5
Marshall	1	7	25	35	23	8	1	-	-	-	-	-	-	18	42	30	9	1	-	-	-	-
Middle Tennessee	-	-	2	7	20	30	26	12	3	-	-	-	-	1	10	29	35	19	5	1	-	-
Old Dominion	-	-	-	-	-	4	14	28	30	18	5	1	-	-	-	-	4	16	31	31	15	3
Western Kentucky	-	18	38	30	11	3	-	-	-	-	-	-	-	24	43	25	6	2	-	-	-	-
Conf USA West	12-0	11-1	10-2	9-3	8-4	7-5	6-6	5-7	4-8	3-9	2-10	1-11	0-12	8-0	7-1	6-2	5-3	4-4	3-5	2-6	1-7	0-8
Louisiana Tech	-	-	5	17	33	30	12	3	-	-	-	-	-	2	15	35	33	12	3	-	-	-
North Texas	-	-	-	-	-	-	3	10	27	38	22	-	-	-	-	-	-	1	5	21	42	31
Rice	-	-	-	-	2	12	27	32	20	6	1	-	-	-	-	1	7	23	35	25	8	1
Southern Miss	-	9	27	34	21	7	2	-	-	-	-	-	-	16	40	31	11	2	-	-	-	-
UTEP	-	-	-	-	1	3	12	23	29	22	9	1	-	-	-	-	3	13	28	33	19	4
UTSA	-	-	-	-	1	7	19	30	27	13	3	-	-	-	-	4	15	30	31	16	4	-

Projected Win Probabilities For Independent Teams

Independents	Overall Wins												
	12-0	11-1	10-2	9-3	8-4	7-5	6-6	5-7	4-8	3-9	2-10	1-11	0-12
Army	-	-	-	-	2	11	29	35	19	4	-	-	-
BYU	-	2	7	18	26	25	15	6	1	-	-	-	-
Massachusetts	-	-	-	-	-	-	-	2	10	27	39	22	-
Notre Dame	4	18	30	27	14	5	2	-	-	-	-	-	-

Projected Win Probabilities For MAC Teams

MAC East	Overall Wins													Conference Wins								
	12-0	11-1	10-2	9-3	8-4	7-5	6-6	5-7	4-8	3-9	2-10	1-11	0-12	8-0	7-1	6-2	5-3	4-4	3-5	2-6	1-7	0-8
Akron	-	-	-	-	1	6	16	26	27	17	5	2	-	-	-	3	12	25	30	21	7	2
Bowling Green	-	2	13	28	31	19	6	1	-	-	-	-	-	6	26	38	22	6	2	-	-	-
Buffalo	-	-	-	-	-	2	6	17	29	28	15	3	-	-	-	-	1	8	23	34	26	8
Kent State	-	-	-	-	3	10	24	31	22	9	1	-	-	-	-	2	10	23	31	23	9	2
Miami-OH	-	-	-	-	-	2	10	20	29	25	12	2	-	-	-	1	7	19	30	27	13	3
Ohio	-	-	1	5	17	28	27	15	6	1	-	-	-	-	1	8	23	33	25	9	1	-
MAC West	12-0	11-1	10-2	9-3	8-4	7-5	6-6	5-7	4-8	3-9	2-10	1-11	0-12	8-0	7-1	6-2	5-3	4-4	3-5	2-6	1-7	0-8
Ball State	-	-	-	2	9	19	27	24	13	4	2	-	-	-	-	4	16	31	30	15	4	-
Central Michigan	-	-	3	13	27	30	19	7	1	-	-	-	-	1	8	24	34	23	8	2	-	-
Eastern Michigan	-	-	-	-	-	-	-	2	13	31	37	17	-	-	-	-	-	-	1	13	42	44
Northern Illinois	-	4	13	25	28	19	8	3	-	-	-	-	-	4	17	32	29	14	4	-	-	-
Toledo	2	9	24	30	22	10	3	-	-	-	-	-	-	9	29	34	20	6	2	-	-	-
Western Michigan	2	7	19	27	25	14	5	1	-	-	-	-	-	10	29	33	20	7	1	-	-	-

Projected Win Probabilities For MWC Teams

MWC Mountain	Overall Wins													Conference Wins								
	12-0	11-1	10-2	9-3	8-4	7-5	6-6	5-7	4-8	3-9	2-10	1-11	0-12	8-0	7-1	6-2	5-3	4-4	3-5	2-6	1-7	0-8
Air Force	-	2	11	24	28	21	10	3	1	-	-	-	-	1	9	26	33	22	8	1	-	-
Boise State	23	40	26	9	2	-	-	-	-	-	-	-	-	61	32	6	1	-	-	-	-	-
Colorado State	-	-	-	1	6	18	29	27	14	4	1	-	-	-	-	4	13	30	32	17	4	-
New Mexico	-	-	1	3	11	23	28	21	10	3	-	-	-	-	-	2	12	27	32	20	6	1
Utah State	-	-	3	9	23	30	22	10	3	-	-	-	-	1	9	26	33	21	8	2	-	-
Wyoming	-	-	-	-	-	-	2	7	20	34	28	9	-	-	-	-	-	2	8	26	41	23
MWC West	12-0	11-1	10-2	9-3	8-4	7-5	6-6	5-7	4-8	3-9	2-10	1-11	0-12	8-0	7-1	6-2	5-3	4-4	3-5	2-6	1-7	0-8
Fresno State	-	-	-	1	3	11	22	29	22	10	2	-	-	-	2	4	14	28	31	17	4	-
Hawaii*	-	-	-	-	-	-	-	2	9	26	37	22	4	-	-	-	-	2	9	29	41	19
Nevada	-	2	10	23	29	22	10	3	1	-	-	-	-	2	16	31	30	16	4	1	-	-
San Diego State	9	28	33	21	7	2	-	-	-	-	-	-	-	25	42	25	7	1	-	-	-	-
San Jose State	-	-	-	1	4	12	24	29	21	8	1	-	-	-	-	4	15	31	31	16	3	-
UNLV	-	-	-	-	-	1	5	16	29	30	16	3	-	-	-	-	1	7	21	35	28	8

*Hawaii will play 13 regular season games; for projected overall records, 12-0 means 13-0, 11-1 means 12-1, etc.

Projected Win Probabilities For Pac-12 Teams

Pac 12 North	12-0	11-1	10-2	9-3	8-4	7-5	6-6	5-7	4-8	3-9	2-10	1-11	0-12	9-0	8-1	7-2	6-3	5-4	4-5	3-6	2-7	1-8	0-9
						Overall Wins											Conference Wins						
California	-	-	-	-	-	1	5	14	26	30	19	5	-	-	-	-	-	2	6	20	35	29	8
Oregon	4	18	31	27	14	4	2	-	-	-	-	-	-	8	27	35	22	7	1	-	-	-	-
Oregon State	-	-	-	-	-	-	-	3	13	30	36	18	-	-	-	-	-	-	2	9	27	40	22
Stanford	2	10	25	31	22	9	1	-	-	-	-	-	-	4	19	34	29	12	2	-	-	-	-
Washington	5	20	33	27	12	3	-	-	-	-	-	-	-	5	20	33	27	12	3	-	-	-	-
Washington State	-	-	1	5	16	28	28	15	5	2	-	-	-	-	-	3	13	28	31	18	6	1	-

Pac 12 South	12-0	11-1	10-2	9-3	8-4	7-5	6-6	5-7	4-8	3-9	2-10	1-11	0-12	9-0	8-1	7-2	6-3	5-4	4-5	3-6	2-7	1-8	0-9
Arizona	-	-	-	-	3	10	24	32	22	7	2	-	-	-	-	-	1	7	22	34	26	9	1
Arizona State	-	-	-	1	6	14	26	28	18	6	1	-	-	-	-	-	2	8	22	32	25	9	2
Colorado	-	-	-	-	-	3	13	29	34	18	3	-		-	-	-	-	-	5	16	35	34	10
UCLA	4	16	29	28	16	6	1	-	-	-	-	-	-	11	31	34	18	5	1	-	-	-	-
USC	-	3	12	24	29	21	9	2	-	-	-	-	-	2	15	30	31	16	5	1	-	-	-
Utah	-	1	4	15	26	28	18	7	1	-	-	-	-	-	2	8	22	32	24	10	2	-	-

Projected Win Probabilities For SEC Teams

SEC East	12-0	11-1	10-2	9-3	8-4	7-5	6-6	5-7	4-8	3-9	2-10	1-11	0-12	8-0	7-1	6-2	5-3	4-4	3-5	2-6	1-7	0-8
						Overall Wins											Conference Wins					
Florida	-	-	4	14	30	33	16	3	-	-	-	-	-	-	2	11	29	36	18	4	-	-
Georgia	6	23	33	24	10	4	-	-	-	-	-	-	-	8	30	35	20	6	1	-	-	-
Kentucky	-	-	-	-	-	-	2	10	29	38	20	1	-	-	-	-	-	-	3	19	45	33
Missouri	-	-	1	4	15	29	31	16	4	-	-	-	-	-	-	2	9	27	37	21	4	-
South Carolina	-	-	-	-	3	10	24	31	22	8	2	-	-	-	-	1	3	14	30	33	17	2
Tennessee	2	14	31	31	16	5	1	-	-	-	-	-	-	2	18	37	30	11	2	-	-	-
Vanderbilt	-	-	-	-	-	1	5	16	30	30	15	3	-	-	-	-	-	3	12	33	38	14

SEC West	12-0	11-1	10-2	9-3	8-4	7-5	6-6	5-7	4-8	3-9	2-10	1-11	0-12	8-0	7-1	6-2	5-3	4-4	3-5	2-6	1-7	0-8
Alabama	24	40	26	8	2	-	-	-	-	-	-	-	-	27	43	23	6	1	-	-	-	-
Arkansas	-	1	5	15	26	27	18	7	1	-	-	-	-	-	2	8	21	30	25	11	3	-
Auburn	-	-	-	2	8	22	32	26	9	1	-	-	-	-	-	1	6	20	34	28	10	1
LSU	13	34	32	16	4	1	-	-	-	-	-	-	-	13	36	32	14	4	1	-	-	-
Mississippi State	-	-	3	15	30	30	16	4	2	-	-	-	-	-	-	6	23	36	26	8	1	-
Ole Miss	-	4	16	28	28	16	6	2	-	-	-	-	-	1	8	25	33	23	8	2	-	-
Texas A&M	-	-	1	4	13	25	29	20	7	1	-	-	-	-	-	1	7	20	31	27	12	2

Projected Win Probabilities For Sun Belt Teams

Sun Belt	12-0	11-1	10-2	9-3	8-4	7-5	6-6	5-7	4-8	3-9	2-10	1-11	0-12	8-0	7-1	6-2	5-3	4-4	3-5	2-6	1-7	0-8
						Overall Wins											Conference Wins					
Appalachian State	2	14	36	34	12	2	-	-	-	-	-	-	-	32	51	15	2	-	-	-	-	-
Arkansas State	-	1	4	17	30	28	15	4	1	-	-	-	-	6	26	36	23	8	1	-	-	-
Georgia Southern	-	6	23	35	25	9	2	-	-	-	-	-	-	30	44	21	5	-	-	-	-	-
Georgia State	-	-	-	-	2	10	22	29	23	12	2	-	-	-	-	3	15	29	31	18	4	-
Idaho	-	-	-	-	3	12	23	28	21	10	3	-	-	-	1	6	17	28	27	15	5	1
New Mexico State	-	-	-	-	-	1	3	10	22	29	23	10	2	-	-	-	2	9	25	35	24	5
South Alabama	-	-	-	-	2	9	22	30	24	10	3	-	-	-	-	2	8	21	31	25	11	2
Texas State	-	-	-	-	1	4	12	25	31	21	6	-	-	-	-	-	3	11	24	32	23	7
Troy	-	-	-	1	5	17	29	27	15	5	1	-	-	-	-	4	17	30	29	15	5	-
UL-Lafayette	-	-	-	1	5	17	29	27	15	5	1	-	-	-	1	7	23	33	24	10	2	-
UL-Monroe	-	-	-	-	-	1	3	14	29	32	18	3	-	-	-	-	2	11	28	34	20	5

NCAA F/+ Projections

NCAA Teams, No. 1 to No. 128

Rk	Team	Rec	Conf	F/+	MW	CW	SOS	Rk	CSOS	Rk	Div	Conf	CFP
1	Alabama	11-1	7-1	71.3%	10.8	6.9	0.016	6	0.027	6	0.577	0.346	0.374
2	LSU	10-2	6-2	61.2%	10.3	6.4	0.030	9	0.035	8	0.344	0.206	0.201
3	Clemson	11-1	7-1	60.9%	11.2	7.4	0.196	57	0.275	50	0.739	0.502	0.531
4	Oklahoma	11-1	8-1	53.1%	10.7	8.1	0.185	54	0.286	52	-	0.666	0.540
5	Ole Miss	8-4	5-3	46.7%	8.4	5.0	0.009	4	0.016	4	0.052	0.031	0.022
6	Florida State	9-3	6-2	44.5%	9.4	6.3	0.070	19	0.164	32	0.182	0.124	0.089
7	Baylor	10-2	7-2	43.0%	10.2	7.2	0.171	47	0.174	36	-	0.248	0.199
8	Georgia	10-2	6-2	42.9%	9.8	6.1	0.143	43	0.183	38	0.571	0.228	0.164
9	Stanford	9-3	7-2	41.4%	9.1	6.7	0.075	20	0.131	25	0.261	0.131	0.080
10	Tennessee	9-3	6-2	41.4%	9.4	5.7	0.063	17	0.078	11	0.359	0.144	0.100
11	Oregon	10-2	7-2	41.2%	9.6	7.0	0.142	42	0.203	44	0.417	0.209	0.138
12	USC	8-4	6-3	40.6%	8.1	6.4	0.017	7	0.111	19	0.311	0.156	0.082
13	Ohio State	9-3	7-2	39.6%	9.3	7.1	0.101	27	0.282	51	0.302	0.196	0.128
14	Washington	10-2	7-2	39.1%	9.6	6.7	0.182	51	0.185	39	0.311	0.156	0.109
15	Notre Dame	10-2	-	38.9%	9.5	-	0.183	53	-	-	-	-	0.068
16	Michigan	10-2	7-2	38.3%	10.1	7.2	0.261	69	0.269	49	0.336	0.219	0.161
17	UCLA	9-3	7-2	36.9%	9.4	7.2	0.206	60	0.357	58	0.637	0.318	0.184
18	Arkansas	7-5	4-4	35.5%	7.4	3.8	0.015	5	0.021	5	0.015	0.009	0.006
19	Louisville	9-3	6-2	34.8%	9.3	5.8	0.103	29	0.131	26	0.079	0.054	0.046
20	Michigan State	9-3	7-2	34.0%	9.1	7.0	0.210	64	0.390	60	0.344	0.224	0.129
21	Mississippi State	7-5	4-4	31.0%	7.5	3.9	0.008	3	0.010	3	0.010	0.006	0.004
22	Nebraska	9-3	7-2	30.2%	9.1	6.8	0.229	68	0.328	57	0.621	0.217	0.125
23	Texas A&M	6-6	3-5	28.7%	6.3	2.8	0.007	2	0.009	2	0.001	0.001	0.000
24	Auburn	6-6	3-5	27.7%	6.0	2.9	0.003	1	0.007	1	0.001	0.001	0.000
25	TCU	8-4	6-3	26.8%	8.2	5.7	0.123	36	0.159	31	-	0.039	0.023
26	Florida	7-5	4-4	26.7%	7.5	4.3	0.040	10	0.079	12	0.060	0.024	0.012
27	Oklahoma State	8-4	6-3	26.2%	8.2	5.6	0.100	26	0.111	18	-	0.031	0.019
28	North Carolina	8-4	5-3	23.3%	8.0	4.9	0.178	50	0.293	54	0.289	0.093	0.048
29	Boise State	11-1	8-0	22.4%	10.7	7.5	0.766	122	0.915	122	0.894	0.537	0.027
30	BYU	8-4	-	22.0%	7.6	-	0.208	61	-	-	-	-	0.000
31	Virginia Tech	7-5	5-3	20.9%	7.3	5.1	0.172	48	0.458	63	0.364	0.117	0.054
32	Utah	7-5	5-4	19.5%	7.4	4.9	0.183	52	0.205	45	0.049	0.025	0.012
33	Iowa	9-3	6-3	19.4%	8.6	5.7	0.422	81	0.430	61	0.218	0.076	0.043
34	Pittsburgh	7-5	4-4	19.3%	7.1	4.3	0.094	23	0.135	27	0.150	0.048	0.024
35	West Virginia	7-5	5-4	17.2%	6.6	4.5	0.136	40	0.171	34	-	0.006	0.003
36	Wisconsin	6-6	4-5	16.1%	6.3	4.3	0.056	15	0.174	35	0.048	0.017	0.008
37	Texas	6-6	4-5	15.8%	6.4	4.5	0.106	32	0.150	30	-	0.009	0.004
38	Houston	9-3	6-2	15.8%	8.9	6.5	0.276	70	0.791	81	0.644	0.354	0.015
39	Miami-FL	7-5	4-4	15.6%	6.5	3.9	0.176	49	0.327	56	0.094	0.030	0.014
40	Missouri	6-6	3-5	15.0%	6.5	3.2	0.044	11	0.053	9	0.008	0.003	0.002
41	Georgia Tech	6-6	4-4	13.3%	6.1	3.5	0.090	22	0.175	37	0.060	0.019	0.009
42	Penn State	7-5	5-4	13.1%	6.7	4.8	0.227	66	0.287	53	0.017	0.011	0.006
43	Washington State	7-5	4-5	11.6%	6.5	4.3	0.157	45	0.199	41	0.011	0.005	0.003
44	South Florida	8-4	6-2	10.3%	8.0	5.6	0.466	88	0.769	78	0.373	0.168	0.007
45	Texas Tech	6-6	4-5	10.2%	6.0	3.7	0.131	39	0.142	28	-	0.001	0.001
46	Western Kentucky	10-2	7-1	10.2%	9.6	6.8	0.129	37	0.870	109	0.503	0.312	0.013
47	Northwestern	6-6	4-5	9.5%	6.3	4.0	0.205	59	0.219	47	0.031	0.011	0.005
48	Appalachian State	10-2	7-1	9.3%	9.5	7.1	0.439	84	0.849	105	-	0.445	0.018
49	San Diego State	10-2	7-1	8.5%	10.1	6.8	0.835	128	0.904	120	0.766	0.306	0.014
50	Minnesota	8-4	5-4	8.4%	7.6	4.8	0.433	83	0.441	62	0.081	0.028	0.015

Rk	Team	Rec	Conf	F/+	MW	CW	SOS	Rk	CSOS	Rk	Div	Conf	CFP
51	Georgia Southern	9-3	7-1	8.0%	8.9	7.0	0.348	75	0.894	117	-	0.451	0.019
52	Duke	6-6	3-5	7.8%	5.6	3.2	0.169	46	0.315	55	0.032	0.010	0.004
53	Boston College	6-6	3-5	7.5%	6.3	2.6	0.103	30	0.106	17	0.001	0.001	0.000
54	Kansas State	5-7	3-6	7.3%	5.4	3.4	0.053	14	0.095	15	-	0.000	0.000
55	NC State	5-7	3-5	6.9%	5.3	2.7	0.052	13	0.075	10	0.000	0.000	0.000
56	Toledo	9-3	6-2	6.8%	9.0	6.1	0.657	109	0.838	99	0.364	0.200	0.008
57	Navy	8-4	5-3	5.3%	8.0	5.3	0.491	90	0.747	75	0.237	0.131	0.005
58	Syracuse	5-7	2-6	5.2%	4.6	2.4	0.057	16	0.090	13	0.000	0.000	0.000
59	South Carolina	5-7	2-6	5.2%	5.1	2.5	0.051	12	0.200	43	0.001	0.000	0.000
60	Arizona State	5-7	3-6	4.7%	5.4	3.0	0.113	33	0.119	21	0.002	0.001	0.000
61	Temple	9-3	5-3	4.6%	8.6	5.4	0.712	118	0.830	97	0.330	0.148	0.006
62	Marshall	9-3	7-1	4.5%	9.0	6.7	0.573	100	0.890	116	0.413	0.256	0.011
63	Western Michigan	9-3	6-2	4.3%	8.6	6.1	0.763	121	0.889	114	0.348	0.191	0.008
64	Arizona	5-7	3-6	2.5%	5.2	2.9	0.138	41	0.165	33	0.001	0.000	0.000
65	Cincinnati	7-5	4-4	2.5%	7.4	4.4	0.678	114	0.770	79	0.123	0.055	0.002
66	Memphis	7-5	5-3	1.8%	7.3	4.7	0.341	74	0.737	74	0.112	0.062	0.003
67	Northern Illinois	8-4	6-2	1.6%	8.2	5.6	0.698	117	0.819	91	0.185	0.102	0.004
68	Indiana	6-6	3-6	1.5%	5.8	3.3	0.190	55	0.196	40	0.001	0.001	0.000
69	Bowling Green	8-4	6-2	1.1%	8.3	6.0	0.456	87	0.822	93	0.704	0.317	0.013
70	East Carolina	7-5	5-3	0.9%	6.7	4.7	0.533	96	0.734	72	0.143	0.064	0.003
71	Virginia	4-8	2-6	-1.0%	4.4	2.1	0.212	65	0.382	59	0.010	0.003	0.001
72	California	3-9	2-7	-1.6%	3.4	1.9	0.103	31	0.123	22	0.000	0.000	0.000
73	Utah State	7-5	5-3	-1.9%	7.0	5.1	0.328	72	0.720	71	0.050	0.030	0.001
74	Maryland	5-7	3-6	-3.4%	5.3	2.7	0.195	56	0.199	42	0.000	0.000	0.000
75	Vanderbilt	4-8	2-6	-5.0%	3.6	1.5	0.099	25	0.128	24	0.001	0.000	0.000
76	Connecticut	6-6	3-5	-6.2%	5.6	3.5	0.547	97	0.629	65	0.026	0.012	0.000
77	Southern Miss	9-3	7-1	-6.4%	9.0	6.6	0.228	67	0.906	121	0.740	0.281	0.012
78	Wake Forest	5-7	2-6	-6.5%	4.9	1.8	0.098	24	0.105	16	0.000	0.000	0.000
79	Iowa State	4-8	2-7	-6.8%	4.0	2.1	0.121	35	0.148	29	-	0.000	0.000
80	Central Michigan	7-5	5-3	-7.7%	7.3	5.0	0.584	101	0.807	84	0.092	0.050	0.002
81	Air Force	8-4	5-3	-8.3%	8.0	5.0	0.777	126	0.817	86	0.052	0.031	0.001
82	Nevada	8-4	5-3	-9.0%	7.9	5.4	0.523	94	0.889	113	0.205	0.082	0.003
83	Illinois	4-8	2-7	-10.6%	3.5	2.0	0.198	58	0.229	48	0.002	0.001	0.000
84	Rutgers	4-8	2-7	-11.9%	3.6	1.9	0.130	38	0.219	46	0.000	0.000	0.000
85	Louisiana Tech	8-4	6-2	-12.2%	7.6	5.5	0.510	93	0.890	115	0.241	0.092	0.004
86	Colorado	3-9	2-7	-12.4%	3.4	1.7	0.067	18	0.111	20	0.000	0.000	0.000
87	Arkansas State	8-4	6-2	-13.2%	7.5	5.9	0.623	106	0.897	118	-	0.096	0.004
88	Middle Tennessee	7-5	5-3	-13.8%	6.8	5.2	0.678	113	0.840	100	0.073	0.045	0.002
89	Kentucky	3-9	1-7	-14.7%	3.3	0.9	0.019	8	0.030	7	0.000	0.000	0.000
90	Oregon State	2-10	1-8	-18.1%	2.5	1.3	0.101	28	0.124	23	0.000	0.000	0.000
91	Tulsa	5-7	3-5	-18.7%	5.0	2.9	0.403	78	0.697	70	0.006	0.003	0.000
92	Purdue	3-9	1-8	-18.8%	3.1	1.4	0.444	86	0.460	64	0.000	0.000	0.000
93	Central Florida	5-7	3-5	-19.0%	4.6	2.5	0.397	77	0.670	66	0.006	0.003	0.000
94	San Jose State	5-7	4-4	-21.1%	5.2	3.5	0.609	104	0.680	68	0.014	0.005	0.000
95	Colorado State	6-6	3-5	-21.9%	5.6	3.4	0.600	102	0.674	67	0.002	0.001	0.000
96	Ohio	7-5	4-4	-22.2%	6.5	3.9	0.468	89	0.846	104	0.110	0.050	0.002
97	Ball State	6-6	4-4	-22.4%	5.8	3.5	0.774	125	0.830	96	0.011	0.006	0.000
98	Fresno State	5-7	3-5	-22.5%	5.1	3.4	0.570	99	0.878	111	0.015	0.006	0.000
99	Akron	5-7	3-5	-23.5%	4.5	3.2	0.665	111	0.873	110	0.044	0.020	0.001
100	New Mexico	6-6	3-5	-23.8%	6.1	3.3	0.793	127	0.817	87	0.002	0.001	0.000
101	Kent State	5-7	3-5	-24.4%	5.1	3.0	0.115	34	0.861	106	0.084	0.038	0.002
102	SMU	4-8	2-6	-27.3%	3.5	1.7	0.339	73	0.737	73	0.000	0.000	0.000
103	Florida Atlantic	6-6	4-4	-28.7%	5.7	4.1	0.651	108	0.840	101	0.011	0.007	0.000
104	UL-Lafayette	6-6	4-4	-30.3%	5.6	3.9	0.393	76	0.822	95	-	0.002	0.000
105	Troy	6-6	4-4	-31.9%	5.6	3.5	0.210	63	0.822	94	-	0.001	0.000
106	Georgia State	5-7	3-5	-33.2%	5.0	3.4	0.683	116	0.818	88	-	0.003	0.000

Rk	Team	Rec	Conf	F/+	MW	CW	SOS	Rk	CSOS	Rk	Div	Conf	CFP
107	Army	5-7	-	-33.2%	5.3	-	0.510	92	-	-	-	-	0.000
108	Miami-OH	4-8	3-5	-35.1%	3.9	2.8	0.661	110	0.889	112	0.056	0.025	0.001
109	Buffalo	4-8	2-6	-36.7%	3.7	2.0	0.721	119	0.805	83	0.003	0.002	0.000
110	Idaho	5-7	4-4	-39.1%	5.1	3.6	0.441	85	0.841	102	-	0.002	0.000
111	South Alabama	4-8	3-5	-39.9%	4.0	2.9	0.156	44	0.897	119	-	0.000	0.000
112	UTSA	5-7	3-5	-40.2%	4.7	3.5	0.647	107	0.922	123	0.010	0.004	0.000
113	Wyoming	3-9	1-7	-40.2%	2.9	1.2	0.555	98	0.804	82	0.000	0.000	0.000
114	Kansas	2-10	0-9	-41.3%	1.6	0.2	0.089	21	0.095	14	-	0.000	0.000
115	UNLV	4-8	2-6	-41.8%	3.6	1.9	0.419	79	0.680	69	0.000	0.000	0.000
116	Florida International	3-9	2-6	-42.4%	3.4	2.3	0.772	124	0.820	92	0.000	0.000	0.000
117	Old Dominion	4-8	3-5	-42.8%	4.4	2.5	0.671	112	0.819	89	0.001	0.000	0.000
118	Rice	4-8	3-5	-42.9%	4.3	3.0	0.320	71	0.834	98	0.005	0.002	0.000
119	Tulane	3-9	1-7	-43.5%	2.9	0.8	0.731	120	0.754	76	0.000	0.000	0.000
120	New Mexico State	3-9	2-6	-43.5%	3.1	2.1	0.615	105	0.869	108	-	0.000	0.000
121	Hawaii	3-10	1-7	-44.2%	3.2	1.3	0.425	82	0.765	77	0.000	0.000	0.000
122	Charlotte	4-8	2-6	-44.6%	4.1	2.4	0.527	95	0.869	107	0.001	0.000	0.000
123	UL-Monroe	3-9	2-6	-45.4%	3.4	2.3	0.210	62	0.774	80	-	0.000	0.000
124	Texas State	3-9	2-6	-47.9%	3.3	2.2	0.503	91	0.841	103	-	0.000	0.000
125	Eastern Michigan	2-10	1-7	-49.8%	2.5	0.7	0.681	115	0.808	85	0.000	0.000	0.000
126	UTEP	4-8	2-6	-50.8%	4.2	2.4	0.771	123	0.922	124	0.003	0.001	0.000
127	North Texas	2-10	1-7	-56.0%	2.4	1.0	0.603	103	0.819	90	0.000	0.000	0.000
128	Massachusetts	2-10	-	-58.8%	2.3	-	0.419	80	-	-	-	-	0.000

FO Rookie Projections

Over the years, Football Outsiders has developed a number of methods for forecasting the NFL success of highly-drafted players at various positions. Here is a rundown of those methods and what they say about players drafted in 2016.

Quarterbacks: QBASE

The QBASE (Quarterback Adjusted Stats and Experience) system analyzes the last 20 years of rookie quarterbacks chosen among the top 100 picks of the NFL draft, and uses regression analysis to determine which factors helped predict their total passing DYAR in Years 3-5 of their careers. (We use these years to account for the fact that many highly-drafted quarterbacks may not play regularly until their second or even third seasons.)

The primary factor in QBASE is the quarterback's college performance, analyzed with three metrics: completion rate, yards per attempt adjusted based on touchdowns and interceptions, and team passing S&P+ from Football Outsiders' college stats. We then adjust based on strength of schedule and strength of teammates. The latter element gives credit based on the draft-pick value of offensive linemen and receivers drafted in the quarterback's draft year as well as the projected draft position of younger teammates in 2017.

The measurement of past performance is then combined with two other factors: college experience and draft position. The latter factor accounts for what scouts will see but a statistical projection system will not, including personality, leadership, and projection of physical attributes to the next level.

QBASE also looks at the past performance of quarterbacks compared to their projection and using 50,000 simulations, produces a range of potential outcomes for each prospect: Elite quarterback (over 2500 DYAR in Years 3-5), Upper Tier quarterback (1500-2500 DYAR), Adequate Starter (500-1500 DYAR), or Bust (less than 500 DYAR in Years 3-5).

Here are QBASE projections for quarterbacks chosen in the top 100 picks of the 2016 NFL draft:

Player	College	Team	Rd	Pick	QBASE	Elite	Upper Tier	Adequate	Bust
J.Goff	Cal	LARM	1	1	1179	14.2%	23.5%	34.1%	28.3%
C.Wentz	N.Dak. St.	PHI	1	2	209	3.8%	10.0%	24.3%	61.9%
P.Lynch	Memphis	DEN	1	26	75	2.9%	8.7%	21.3%	67.2%
C.Hackenberg	Penn St.	NYJ	2	51	-436	1.2%	5.1%	13.6%	80.1%
J.Brissett	N.C.St.	NE	3	91	-381	1.3%	5.4%	14.2%	79.1%
C.Kessler	USC	CLE	3	93	-201	1.9%	6.5%	16.7%	75.1%
C.Cook	Mich. St.	OAK	4	100	-380	1.3%	5.4%	14.2%	79.1%

QBASE was created by Andrew Healy.

Running Backs: Speed Score

Speed Score was introduced in *Pro Football Prospectus 2008*. The basic theory is simple: not all 40-yard dash times are created equal. A fast time means more from a bigger running back, and the range of 40 times for backs is so small that even a miniscule difference can be meaningful. The formula for Speed Score is:

$$\textbf{(Weight x 200) / 40 time \textasciicircum 4}$$

In general, you want a back chosen in the first couple rounds to be above 100. 2016 was one of the strongest years ever for Speed Score, with Keith Marshall setting an all-time record at 126.9 and five other backs scoring above 105.

Here are the Speed Scores for all backs chosen in the first three rounds, as well as the top five Speed Scores for backs chosen in the final four rounds and two UDFAs with Speed Scores above 100. Note that Jordan Howard and Devontae Booker did not run at the combine and therefore do not have an official Speed Score.

Player	College	Team	Round	Pick	Weight	40 Time	Speed Score
E.Elliott	Ohio St.	DAL	1	4	225	4.47	112.7
D.Henry	Alabama	TEN	2	45	247	4.54	116.3
K.Drake	Alabama	MIA	3	73	210	4.45	107.1
C.J.Prosise	Notre Dame	SEA	3	90	220	4.48	109.2
T.Ervin	San Jose St.	HOU	4	119	192	4.41	101.5
D.Washington	Texas Tech	OAK	5	143	204	4.49	100.4
W.Smallwood	W. Virginia	PHI	5	153	208	4.47	104.2
D.Lasco	California	NO	7	237	209	4.46	105.6
K.Marshall	Georgia	WAS	7	242	219	4.31	126.9
M.Coprich	Illinois St.	NYG	UDFA	--	207	4.47	103.7
B.Wilds	S. Carolina	ATL	UDFA	--	220	4.54	103.6

Speed Score was created by Bill Barnwell.

Running Backs: BackCAST

In April, Football Outsiders introduced a new system called BackCAST that attempts to expand projection of running backs past Speed Score to incorporate other combine drills as well as a running back's college performance and usage.[1] BackCAST incorporates the following elements:

- 40-yard dash time and weight, similar to Speed Score.
- "Yards Over Expected per game," which compares the back's college performance to the performance of his teammates.
- Peak percentage of team rushing attempts.
- Receiving yards per game.

BackCAST is expressed with two ratings. The first rating (BackCAST) represents the percentage that the player is expected to outperform (or underperform) the average running back prospect. The second rating (RecIndex) measures whether the back is more likely to become a third-down receiving back (positive) or a two-down ground-and-pound back (negative).

Here are the BackCAST results for all running backs who both attended the combine and were chosen in this year's draft:

Player	College	Team	Rd	Pick	Back-CAST	Rec-Index
Ezekiel Elliott	Ohio State	DAL	1	4	+46.2%	-0.04
Derrick Henry	Alabama	TEN	2	45	+63.1%	-0.41
Kenyan Drake	Alabama	MIA	3	73	-8.6%	+0.13
C.J. Prosise	Notre Dame	SEA	3	90	+18.2%	+0.64
Tyler Ervin	San Jose State	HOU	4	119	+8.6%	+0.52
Kenneth Dixon	Louisiana Tech	BAL	4	134	+16.6%	+0.40
Devontae Booker	Utah	DEN	4	136	+23.4%	+0.67
DeAndre Washington	Texas Tech	OAK	5	143	+14.2%	+0.58
Paul Perkins	UCLA	NYG	5	149	+8.1%	+0.34
Jordan Howard	Indiana	CHI	5	150	+18.1%	-0.23
Wendell Smallwood	West Virginia	PHI	5	153	-2.9%	+0.30
Jonathan Williams	Arkansas	BUF	5	156	-39.0%	-0.16
Alex Collins	Arkansas	SEA	5	171	-22.6%	-0.34
Kelvin Taylor	Florida	SF	6	211	-58.4%	-0.20
Daniel Lasco	California	NO	7	237	+15.2%	+0.02
Keith Marshall	Georgia	WAS	7	242	-29.8%	-0.10

BackCAST was created by Nathan Forster and should be considered a work in progress; we'll be working on improvements for 2017.

Edge Rushers: SackSEER

SackSEER is a method that projects sacks for edge rushers, including both 3-4 outside linebackers and 4-3 defensive ends, using the following criteria:

- An "explosion index" that measures the prospect's scores in the forty-yard dash, the vertical jump, and the broad jump in pre-draft workouts.
- Sacks per game, adjusted for factors such as early entry in the NFL Draft and position switches during college.
- Passes defensed per game.
- Missed games of NCAA eligibility due to academic problems, injuries, benchings, suspensions, or attendance at junior college.

SackSEER outputs two numbers. The first, SackSEER Rating, solely measures how high the prospect scores compared to players of the past. The second, SackSEER Projection, represents a forecast of sacks for the player's first five years in the NFL. It synthesizes metrics with conventional wisdom by adjusting based on the player's expected draft position (interestingly, not his actual draft position) based on pre-draft analysis at the site NFLDraftScout.com.

Here are the SackSEER numbers for edge rushers drafted in the first three rounds of the 2016 draft, along with later-round picks (and one UDFA) with a high SackSEER Rating.

Name	College	Team	Rnd	Pick	SackSEER Projection	SackSEER Rating
Joey Bosa	Ohio State	SD	1	3	26.8	87.8%
Leonard Floyd	Georgia	CHI	1	9	26.9	81.0%
Shaq Lawson	Clemson	BUF	1	19	22.9	72.6%
Emmanuel Ogbah	Oklahoma St.	CLE	2	32	25.6	97.3%
Kevin Dodd	Clemson	TEN	2	33	11.9	9.0%
Noah Spence	E. Kentucky	TB	2	39	20.8	64.1%
Kamalei Correa	Boise State	BAL	2	42	14.1	31.3%
Jihad Ward	Illinois	OAK	2	44	4.9	12.0%
Carl Nassib	Penn State	CLE	3	65	12.3	47.0%
Yannick Ngakoue	Maryland	JAC	3	69	7.0	55.7%
Bronson Kaufusi	BYU	BAL	3	70	14.9	90.8%
Jonathan Bullard	Florida	CHI	3	72	12.1	34.5%
Shilique Calhoun	Michigan St.	OAK	3	75	17.5	50.8%
Jordan Jenkins	Georgia	NYJ	3	83	10.0	25.8%
Charles Tapper	Oklahoma	DAL	4	101	14.3	69.6%
Dean Lowry	Northwestern	GB	4	137	6.6	90.8%
James Cowser	S. Utah	OAK	UDFA	–	12.8	84.2%

SackSEER was created by Nathan Forster.

---

1 You can read the full introduction to BackCAST at http://www.footballoutsiders.com/stat-analysis/2016/introducing-backcast

Wide Receivers: Playmaker Score

Playmaker Score projects success for NFL wide receivers using the following criteria:

• The wide receiver's peak season for receiving yards per team attempt and receiving touchdowns per team attempt.
• Differences between this prospect's peak season and most recent season, to adjust for players who declined in their final college year.
  • College career yards per reception.
  • Rushing attempts per game.
  • Vertical jump from pre-draft workouts.
• A binary variable that rewards players who enter the draft as underclassmen.

Like SackSEER, Playmaker Score outputs two numbers. The first, Playmaker Rating, solely measures how high the prospect scores compared to players of the past. The second, Playmaker Projection, represents a forecast of average receiving yards per year in the player's first five seasons, synthesizing metrics with conventional wisdom by adjusting based on the player's expected draft position.

Here are the Playmaker Score numbers for players drafted in the first three rounds of the 2016 draft, along with later-round picks (and two UDFAs) with a high Playmaker Rating.

Name	College	Team	Rnd	Pick	Playmaker Projection	Playmaker Rating
C.Coleman	Baylor	CLE	1	15	820	99.8%
W.Fuller	Notre Dame	HOU	1	21	514	94.7%
J.Doctson	TCU	WAS	1	22	409	70.8%
L.Treadwell	Mississippi	MIN	1	23	479	69.5%
S.Shepard	Oklahoma	NYG	2	40	328	71.0%
M.Thomas	Ohio State	NO	2	47	463	80.4%
T.Boyd	Pittsburgh	CIN	2	55	486	89.9%
L.Carroo	Rutgers	MIA	3	86	333	74.7%
P.Cooper	S. Carolina	LARM	4	117	493	89.5%
R.Higgins	Colorado St.	CLE	5	172	476	89.5%
R.Lewis	Bowling Green	NYG	UDFA	--	323	84.0%
D.Ayers	Houston	PIT	7	229	263	79.6%
B.Addison	Oregon	DEN	UDFA	--	315	78.2%
D.Robinson	Florida	KC	4	126	112	62.4%
M.Thomas	Southern Miss.	LARM	6	206	137	58.7%
R.Louis	Auburn	CLE	4	114	115	56.0%

Playmaker Score was originally created by Vincent Verhei and then further developed by Nathan Forster.

Top 25 Prospects

Every year, Football Outsiders takes it upon ourselves to put together a list of the NFL's best and brightest that have barely played. Eighty percent of the draft-day discussion is about first-round picks, and 10 percent is about the players that should have been first-round picks, but instead went in the second round.

This list is about the others. Everybody knows that Andrew Luck and Jameis Winston are good. There's a cottage industry around the idea of hyping every draft's No. 1 quarterback as a potential superstar. This is a list of players that have a strong chance to make an impact in the NFL despite their lack of draft stock and the fact that they weren't immediate NFL starters. Previous instances of the list have hyped players such as Geno Atkins, Elvis Dumervil, Malcolm Butler, and Jamaal Charles before they blew up. Rotoworld has referred to this list as "an all-star team of waiver pickups" after we hit on players such as Arian Foster and Miles Austin.

This is the tenth anniversary of the list. We're still relying on the same things we always do: scouting, statistics, measurables, context, expected role, and what we hear from other sources. The goal is still to bring your attention to players who are still developing in their second and third seasons, even after the draftniks have forgotten them. We have made one change to freshen up the list this year, and that's to determine eligibility based on snap counts rather than games started. It's something we couldn't have done when the list was first launched, but with the increased usage of nickel defenses over the last few seasons, it didn't make sense to keep counting slot cornerbacks as prospects just because they don't start many games.

Here's our full criteria:

- Drafted in the third round or later, or signed as an undrafted free agent
- Entered the NFL between 2013 and 2015
- Fewer than 500 career offensive or defensive snaps
- Have not signed a contract extension (players who have bounced around the league looking for the right spot, however, still qualify for the list)
- Age 26 or younger in 2016

The debate for spots on this year's list was intense, but, like Martavis Bryant last year, No. 1 wasn't much of a debate.

1 David Johnson, RB, Cardinals
412 offensive snaps, third-round pick (2015), age 25

You may remember Mr. Johnson as a major swing factor for your fantasy football league last winter. His advanced statistics certainly backed up the touchdowns: Johnson finished fourth in DVOA and eighth in DYAR in his rookie season. And while he's not a dumbfoundingly obvious talent like Todd Gurley is, that's the reason the Cardinals were able to get Johnson in the third round. At 6-foot-1, 224 pounds, Johnson is built to be a workhorse back. He also made outstanding plays as a receiver, finishing sixth in receiving DYAR among running backs and averaging 4.0 yards after the catch more than expected given where he caught those passes. The usual caveats about running backs—high attrition, increased role-splitting—apply, but Johnson sure looks like a franchise running back as we enter 2016.

2 Danielle Hunter, DE, Vikings
393 defensive snaps, third-round pick (2015), age 22

Hunter came out of LSU incredibly raw. He scored fairly low in our SackSEER projection system not because of his athleticism, but because of his lack of on-field production. Hunter managed just 4.5 sacks in three seasons at LSU. That dropped him to the third round, where the Vikings decided that a 252-pounder who ran a 4.57 40-yard dash at the combine might, in fact, be someone to groom. Hunter notched six sacks and a handful of hurries in his debut, and he's coming for Brian Robison's job sooner rather than later.

3 Henry Anderson, DE, Colts
450 defensive snaps, third-round pick (2015), age 25

Anderson only qualifies for this list because he tore his ACL in the middle of the season. A strong run-stopping 5-technique end, Anderson surprised the NFL with how much pass pressure he was able to get. He picked up ten quarterback pressures in our charting despite playing on the interior in the Indy 3-4. His rehab from injury aside, this is as nice a player as you can hope to find in the third round. The explosion off the line is rare for an interior player.

4 Thomas Rawls, RB, Seahawks
289 offensive snaps, undrafted (2015), age 23

In his rookie campaign, Rawls led all running backs in rushing DYAR and finished second in DVOA. He did this despite the poor Seattle offensive line, following in the footsteps of his predecessor Marshawn Lynch by leading ESPN Stats & Info charting with 2.68 average yards after contact. (No other back with at least 100 carries was over 2.3.) So why isn't he our No. 1 prospect instead of Johnson? Context has a lot to say here. The Seahawks spent three picks on running backs this year. Rawls wasn't allowed to be much of a receiver, and third-round pick C.J. Prosise would seem to fit that role better going forward. Rawls is also a UDFA, and despite playing for a team that regularly boasts about their UDFAs, he wasn't drafted for a reason. (Actually, a lot of reasons: three felony charges, a knee injury, and an academic suspension from Central Michigan's 2014 appearance in the Bahamas Bowl.) We still really like Rawls' talent. He just has a few more knocks against him.

5 Owamagbe Odihghizuwa, DE, Giants
127 defensive snaps, third-round pick (2015), age 24

Odihghizuwa was regarded as a steal by draftniks after he fell into New York's lap in the third round. His SackSEER score was rather pedestrian, but that's in large part because UCLA used him often as a 3-4 defensive end. Like Hunter, his production was obscured by factors outside the scope of his control. The Giants recognized this, but unlike the Vikings, didn't have much of a role for their third-round pick this year. Odihghizuwa's talent is obvious, and that's why he's still on this list. A 4.62 40-yard-dash and good jump numbers point to how explosive he is at the line of scrimmage. His short-term role is up for grabs after the Giants spent heavily to bring in Olivier Vernon and Damon Harrison this offseason.

6 Jordan Hicks, LB, Eagles
450 defensive snaps, third-round pick (2015), age 24

As with Anderson's knee, the torn pec that ended Hicks' season preserved his eligibility for this list. Hicks played an immediate role for the Eagles, with the highest run stop rate among all linebackers on the team last year. Going forward, he projects as a true three-down linebacker. The only question we have is: can he stay on the field? Hicks lost two seasons at Texas to hip problems and an Achilles injury. This is starting to become a trend, and it's the reason he's a bit lower on this list even though he has top-five talent.

7 Brett Hundley, QB, Packers
0 snaps, fifth-round pick (2015), age 23

Hundley fell to the Packers in the draft because he wasn't really asked to do much for UCLA. Jim Mora's scheme didn't let him audible at the line, and the offensive line made Hundley's job hell. Despite all that, Hundley fits the new mold of dual-threat quarterback that has taken hold in this league: the ones that can actually pass, too. Hundley tore up the preseason, completing 69.1 percent of his passes with seven touchdowns and only one pick. That doesn't mean he's ready to start tomorrow, but as with Tyrod Taylor last year, it's certainly proof that he's earned a real shot. Hundley won't get that shot for a bit—this Aaron Rodgers fella is alright—but he's our favorite quarterback prospect nobody is talking about.

8 Grady Jarrett, DT, Falcons
267 defensive snaps, fifth-round pick (2015), age 23

On paper, Jarrett fit the Geno Atkins role of "undersized SEC defensive tackle who blows everyone up" coming into the draft. Then, he was ignored just like Atkins was, and the comparisons got stronger. He didn't play much in Atlanta until the last month of the season, but he played well enough to draw a lot of praise from his coaching staff this offseason. The Falcons want to try him at nose tackle, which is an odd projection for someone who measures in at 304 pounds in today's NFL, but Jarrett may just be good enough in the trenches to pull it off.

9 Daryl Williams, OT, Panthers
58 offensive snaps, fourth-round pick (2015), age 24

Williams was a trade-up target for Panthers general manager Dave Gettleman, and played extremely well in the pre-season even though Carolina handed the starting right tackle job to Mike Remmers. Williams has done nothing in his limited sample size to show himself as unworthy of starting. The future may not be here tomorrow, but someday soon, he'll be anchoring one of Cam Newton's sides.

10 Chris Conley, WR, Chiefs
369 offensive snaps, third-round pick (2015), age 24

Conley was a true workout warrior, blowing up the combine with a 4.35 40-yard dash time and off-the-charts broad and vertical jump scores. Playing mostly behind Albert Wilson in his rookie year, Conley finished 16th in DVOA among all receivers with ten to 49 targets, and he's got the size to be an NFL outside receiver. The Kansas City depth chart at receiver looks wide open after Jeremy Maclin. Conley has come a long way in a few seasons: he didn't start until he was a junior at Georgia, and if he continues to improve his game, we might see him as an actual threat to stretch the field. Or whatever kind of threat a receiver like that can be with Alex Smith as his quarterback.

11 J.C. Tretter, OL, Packers
431 offensive snaps, fourth-round pick (2014), age 25

Another embarrassment of riches on the Green Bay depth chart. Tretter came in cold off the bench against Washington in the playoffs, shifted to left tackle to replace David Bahktiari, and helped hold the Skins to just one sack. He's an interior lineman by trade, but with the line as strong as it is today, it's hard to see an open spot for him—at least until the annual Bryan Bulaga injury, anyway.

12 Clive Walford, TE, Raiders
439 offensive snaps, third-round pick (2015), age 25

Walford came out of Miami as a pure power player. He's a good blocker who hits with force, and he's a good straight-line runner who can catch the ball in tight traffic. He started to eat more and more into Mychal Rivera's snaps as the season went along, and should be the starter in Oakland this season. We have our doubts that Walford is going to become an actual pass-catching tight end you want to target in fantasy football, but developing into the poor man's Dwayne Allen might be in the cards.

13 Sammie Coates, WR, Steelers
34 offensive snaps, third-round pick (2015), age 23

Coates, like Conley, is a pure physical projection. As a strong 6-foot-1, 212-pound receiver with decent wheels and awesome broad and vertical jump numbers, his athleticism is very apparent. He was also one of Playmaker Score's favorite receivers of the 2015 draft, with an asterisk: he was a high-volume receiver in a run-heavy Auburn offense, which has been one of Playmaker's blind spots. Coates wasn't exactly an immediate fit in Pittsburgh, disappointing coaches with poor conditioning and difficulty picking up the playbook. He's been talked up a lot more this preseason, and many in the Steelers press feel he's finally earned the confidence of the coaches. We're not entirely sure what side to believe in, but when you see Darrius Heyward-Bey and Markus Wheaton as the only obstacles in Coates' way of becoming the next Martavis Bryant, the upside is pretty tantalizing.

14 Quandre Diggs, CB, Lions
471 defensive snaps, sixth-round pick (2015), age 25

Diggs had a 56 percent success rate on 38 targets last season, and allowed just 8.5 yards per pass. While his size (5-foot-9, 197 pounds) and arm length (29 5/8 inches) are sure signs that most teams would never put him inside, the potential of having an ace slot cornerback is pretty valuable in today's NFL. We've been doing this list for a lot of years, though, and have seen our share of hyped slot corner prospects with one good year of statistics fail. Thus, Diggs is here instead of in the top 10.

15 Tevin Coleman, RB, Falcons
226 offensive snaps, third-round pick (2015), age 23

Coleman was mostly down in his rookie year. Devonta Freeman seized the starting job when Coleman missed two early games with a fractured rib, and all the college bugaboos about him came true. He wasn't great running zone plays, he ran high at times, and he didn't exactly seize his chance when Freeman was out with a concussion in the middle of the season. Coleman has the kind of speed you dream of, though, and the upside merits a slot on this list. He's a low-floor player, though, and one that has a good running back ahead of him on the depth chart.

16 Eli Harold, OLB, 49ers
337 defensive snaps, third-round pick (2015), age 22

Unlike Coleman, we would describe Harold as a high-floor player. He had the fourth-highest SackSEER projection for the 2015 class. There was nothing pointing to him being a bust-out star, but there was plenty of reason to expect him to become a steady, valuable edge rusher. However, he was stuck behind Ahmad Brooks last year and didn't play much. Will that change in 2016? It depends on how high the new coaching staff is on Brooks. In the meantime, Harold will get an opportunity to shine right away with Aaron Lynch's four-game suspension opening up a spot in the starting lineup.

17 Jay Ajayi, RB, Dolphins
158 offensive snaps, fifth-round pick (2015), age 23

Ajayi was a draftnik favorite in his class before everyone discovered the state of his knee. A lack of cartilage in his knee scared off teams, letting Ajayi freefall into the fifth round. The Dolphins siphoned some carries away from a productive Lamar Miller to Ajayi down the stretch. Even if you look at Ajayi's knee as something that could end his career at any moment, he's still a back with enough burst to be productive. With Arian Foster in town and Kenyan Drake a highly-drafted contender to play on passing downs, Ajayi's fantasy value for this year has taken a hit. But as long as he stays healthy, he's still the runner in this backfield we believe in most.

18 P.J. Williams, CB, Saints
0 defensive snaps, third-round pick (2015), age 23

Williams has a lot of strikes against him as a prospect. His timed speed at the combine wasn't that fast. His college career was very inconsistent, with Williams giving up a lot of space at times. He was a very poor tackler in college. On the other hand, he's the only guy on this list who has the skill set to be an outside NFL corner tomorrow. He reads the quarterback well, and his gambling mentality can also create a lot of turnovers. And he's definitely going to get an opportunity in New Orleans, where the depth chart after Delvin Breaux is a shrugging emoticon. This is a high-risk, high-reward pick.

19 Kevin Pierre-Louis, LB, Seahawks
184 defensive snaps, fourth-round pick (2014), age 25

Pierre-Louis has all the traits you want in a three-down linebacker. He ran a 4.51 40-yard dash at the combine, his 4.02 20-yard shuttle was one of the best scores in his class, and he shined in coverage at Boston College. The downside is that, at 6-foot-0, 232 pounds, he doesn't fit the size prototype of a linebacker. However, those standards have been changing for a long time now, since the days of Jimmy Johnson and Derrick Brooks, and we think Pierre-Louis can play. The Seahawks may not need him to, since they have Bobby Wagner and K.J. Wright, but it's nice to have a player this talented waiting in reserve.

20 Rashad Greene, WR, Jaguars
168 offensive snaps, fifth-round pick (2015), age 24

Greene was Jameis Winston's security blanket at Florida State, catching tight balls in coverage and getting vertical with ease against college corners. At 5-foot-11, 182 pounds, it's hard to project Greene as an outside receiver on pure size. But as a shifty slot receiver, he's definitely got a chance. The Jaguars haven't seen much from Marquise Lee yet, and Blake Bortles could use another reliable target over the middle. Greene will have to improve on last season's 53 percent catch rate to be that target.

21 Davis Tull, DE, Saints
0 defensive snaps, fifth-round pick (2015), age 25

Tull came into the league with a frightening combination of college production and agility. At the combine, he recorded vertical and broad jumps of 42.5 inches and 11 feet, respectively, and he added a 4.57-second 40-yard dash at his pro day. Late-round picks from small schools (in this case, Chattanooga) have a decent success rate as edge rushers, including players such as Robert Mathis and Jared Allen. We've seen dip-diddly to indicate that Tull is going to have a real role with the Saints this year, but with Hau'oli Kikaha out for the season with a torn ACL, they have a dire need for pass-rushing help next to Cameron Jordan on the outside. Tull could be that player.

22 Kenny Bell, WR, Bucs
0 offensive snaps, fifth-round pick (2015), age 24

The Bucs wasted a lot of wide receiver snaps on practice squad-quality players last year, and didn't do much to upgrade the position this offseason. Enter Bell, a tough Nebraska receiver who missed all last season with a hamstring issue. Bell has tweener size for an outside guy at 6-foot-1, 197 pounds, but he plays bigger, offers good explosion off the line, and won early in the down with his technique against press coverage in college. How that projects in Tampa is still up for interpretation, but with only an aging Vincent Jackson in front of him for the No. 2 job, Bell could rise quickly if he impresses.

23 AJ McCarron, QB, Bengals
257 offensive snaps, fifth-round pick (2014), age 26

Forced into work after Andy Dalton's season-ending injury, McCarron wasn't half bad in a limited sample, posting a 6.9% DVOA in 132 dropbacks. The caveats were a) this was a Bengals offense absolutely stacked with talent and b) all Cincy asked McCarron to do was be a caretaker for the offense. We don't think McCarron is going to be a star, but he could absolutely hang around the league for 12 more years as one of the 25 or 35 best quarterbacks in the league.

24 J.J. Nelson, WR, Cardinals
148 offensive snaps, fifth-round pick (2015), age 24

Last year, Nelson was a situational speedster, the guy who rocketed through the middle of the defense to catch Carson Palmer bombs. This is the sort of skill set that, in a good offense, leads to 27.2 yards per reception. Nelson's future in the league is harder to forecast. He's tiny enough (listed 5-foot-10, 160 pounds) that it's hard to buy him as an outside receiver. He came out of UAB with almost zero ability to make tacklers miss. Head coach Bruce Arians is big on the receiver's future, calling him "unique" at tracking the ball over his shoulder. It's possible that Arians sees a lot of a player he drafted with the Colts—T.Y. Hilton—in Nelson. For the near future, Nelson is behind three great receivers on the depth chart. To become

more, he'll need to show more ability to deal with the physical grind of the league. He'll also need to get better after the catch—he gained more than 3 yards after the catch on a grand total of two of his receptions.

25 Quinton Dunbar, CB, Washington
257 defensive snaps, undrafted (2015), age 24

Dunbar, an undrafted free agent out of Florida, converted from wideout to cornerback for Washington after they noticed how good he was jamming gunners on punt coverage. Dunbar combines modern corner size (6-foot-2, 201 pounds) with wideout speed, and impressed down the stretch for the Skins as they made their playoff push. Dunbar allowed just 5.7 adjusted yards per pass in limited time, and now he's had a full offseason to work on the fundamentals of a position he never played before last season. Washington just might have found something here.

Honorable Mention

DT Carl Davis, Ravens
C/G Max Garcia, Broncos
FS Clayton Geathers, Colts
WR Jeff Janis, Packers
RB Matt Jones, Washington
RB Jeremy Langford, Bears
OLB Shaq Riddick, Cardinals
WR Eric Rogers, 49ers
RB Karlos Williams, Bills

Rivers McCown

Fantasy Projections

H ere are the top 275 players according to the KUBIAK projection system, ranked by projected fantasy value (FANT) in 2016. We've used the following generic scoring system:

- 1 point for each 10 yards rushing, 10 yards receiving, or 20 yards passing
- 6 points for each rushing or receiving TD, 4 points for each passing TD
- -2 points for each interception or fumble lost
- 1 point for each extra point, 3 points for each field goal
- Team defense: 2 points for a fumble recovery, interception, or safety, 1 point for a sack, and 6 points for a touchdown.

These totals are then adjusted based on each player's listed Risk for 2016:

- **Green:** Standard risk, no change
- **Yellow:** Higher than normal risk, value dropped by five percent
- **Red:** Highest risk, value dropped by 10 percent
- **Blue:** Significantly lower than normal risk, value increased by five percent

Note that fantasy totals may not exactly equal these calculations, because each touchdown projection is not necessarily a round number. (For example, a quarterback listed with 2 rushing touchdowns may actually be projected with 2.4 rushing touchdowns, which will add 14 fantasy points to the player's total rather than 12.) Fantasy value does not include adjustments for week-to-week consistency,

Players are ranked in order based on marginal value of each player, the idea that you draft based on how many more points a player will score compared to the worst starting player at that position, not how many points a player scores overall. We've ranked players by value in a 12-team league working with three sets of rules:

- **Flex Rk:** starts 1 QB, 2 RB, 2 WR, 1 FLEX (RB/WR), 1 TE, 1 K, and 1 D.
- **3WR Rk:** starts 1 QB, 2 RB, 3 WR, 1 TE, 1 K, and 1 D.
- **PPR Rk:** starts 1 QB, 2 RB, 2 WR, 1 FLEX (RB/WR), 1 TE, 1 K, and 1 D. Also adds one point per reception to scoring.

The rankings also include half value for the first running back on the bench, and reduce the value of kickers and defenses to reflect the general drafting habits of fantasy football players. We urge you to draft using common sense, not a strict reading of these rankings.

A customizable spreadsheet featuring these projections is also available at FootballOutsiders.com for a $20 fee. This spreadsheet is updated based on injuries and changing forecasts of playing time during the preseason, and also has a version which includes individual defensive players.

The projections for Le'Veon Bell, Tom Brady, and Josh Gordon account for four-game suspensions. However, the fantasy value listed incorporates four weeks of "replacement-level" value for each player, accounting for the fact that a fantasy team that drafts one of these players will still get points from a bench player during those weeks. The same is true for Tyler Eifert, except his projection estimates that he will miss three games due to injury. These players are marked with an asterisk (*).

Player	Team	Bye	Pos	Age	PaYd	PaTD	INT	Ru	RuYd	RuTD	Rec	RcYd	RcTD	FL	XP	FG	Fant	Risk	Flex Rk	3WR Rk	PPR Rk
Todd Gurley	LARM	8	RB	22	0	0	0	320	1495	10	41	300	0	3	0	0	237	Green	1	2	8
Antonio Brown	PIT	8	WR	28	0	0	0	5	33	0	124	1636	11	0	0	0	233	Green	2	1	1
Julio Jones	ATL	11	WR	27	0	0	0	0	0	0	117	1633	10	0	0	0	224	Green	3	3	2
David Johnson	ARI	9	RB	25	0	0	0	253	1160	10	48	443	1	2	0	0	224	Green	4	4	10
Adrian Peterson	MIN	6	RB	31	0	0	0	324	1493	10	25	184	1	3	0	0	217	Yellow	5	6	23
Odell Beckham	NYG	8	WR	24	0	0	0	2	10	0	98	1426	12	0	0	0	216	Green	6	5	3
Le'Veon Bell	PIT	8	RB	24	0	0	0	201	905	7	50	414	2	1	0	0	207*	Yellow	7	7	13
Cam Newton	CAR	7	QB	27	3715	29	10	117	557	8	0	0	0	4	0	0	377	Green	8	9	17
Lamar Miller	HOU	9	RB	25	0	0	0	283	1275	10	36	279	2	2	0	0	200	Red	9	10	33
Ezekiel Elliott	DAL	7	RB	21	0	0	0	285	1267	10	36	251	1	2	0	0	199	Yellow	10	11	34
Allen Robinson	JAC	5	WR	23	0	0	0	2	15	0	89	1368	10	0	0	0	197	Green	11	8	4
Rob Gronkowski	NE	9	TE	27	0	0	0	0	0	0	74	1059	11	0	0	0	163	Green	12	17	16
Dez Bryant	DAL	7	WR	28	0	0	0	0	0	0	90	1327	12	0	0	0	193	Yellow	13	12	7
Jamaal Charles	KC	5	RB	30	0	0	0	213	1014	9	48	385	1	1	0	0	189	Yellow	14	18	32
A.J. Green	CIN	9	WR	28	0	0	0	0	0	0	92	1341	9	0	0	0	188	Green	15	13	5
Jordy Nelson	GB	4	WR	31	0	0	0	2	7	0	84	1229	11	0	0	0	188	Green	16	14	9
T.Y. Hilton	IND	10	WR	27	0	0	0	2	11	0	87	1412	9	0	0	0	187	Yellow	17	15	11
DeAndre Hopkins	HOU	9	WR	24	0	0	0	2	9	0	94	1336	9	0	0	0	186	Green	18	16	6
Doug Martin	TB	6	RB	27	0	0	0	289	1270	7	35	285	1	2	0	0	185	Yellow	19	19	44
Devonta Freeman	ATL	11	RB	24	0	0	0	222	932	8	59	481	1	2	0	0	184	Yellow	20	21	24
Mark Ingram	NO	5	RB	27	0	0	0	226	964	8	55	402	1	2	0	0	181	Green	21	22	28

Player	Team	Bye	Pos	Age	PaYd	PaTD	INT	Ru	RuYd	RuTD	Rec	RcYd	RcTD	FL	XP	FG	Fant	Risk	Flex Rk	3WR Rk	PPR Rk
Mike Evans	TB	6	WR	23	0	0	0	2	13	0	84	1309	8	0	0	0	180	Green	22	20	12
LeSean McCoy	BUF	10	RB	28	0	0	0	223	947	7	38	328	1	1	0	0	176	Green	23	23	47
Andrew Luck	IND	10	QB	27	4670	34	17	58	251	2	0	0	0	3	0	0	347	Yellow	24	27	38
Russell Wilson	SEA	5	QB	28	3915	33	11	100	496	4	0	0	0	4	0	0	347	Yellow	25	28	39
Brandon Marshall	NYJ	11	WR	32	0	0	0	0	0	0	95	1225	10	0	0	0	170	Yellow	26	24	14
Thomas Rawls	SEA	5	RB	23	0	0	0	255	1200	8	18	126	0	2	0	0	170	Yellow	27	29	76
Sammy Watkins	BUF	10	WR	23	0	0	0	2	9	0	77	1258	11	0	0	0	169	Red	28	25	25
Aaron Rodgers	GB	4	QB	33	4269	35	9	66	272	1	0	0	0	4	0	0	342	Yellow	29	35	42
Matt Forte	NYJ	11	RB	31	0	0	0	253	1116	3	49	412	2	1	0	0	168	Yellow	30	31	48
Alshon Jeffery	CHI	9	WR	26	0	0	0	2	12	0	85	1184	9	0	0	0	166	Yellow	31	26	20
Carlos Hyde	SF	8	RB	25	0	0	0	299	1149	6	36	279	1	3	0	0	166	Yellow	32	32	61
Amari Cooper	OAK	10	WR	22	0	0	0	3	15	0	87	1251	8	0	0	0	165	Yellow	33	30	21
C.J. Anderson	DEN	11	RB	25	0	0	0	232	1004	7	44	329	1	1	0	0	165	Yellow	34	36	54
Drew Brees	NO	5	QB	37	4974	32	11	19	56	0	0	0	0	3	0	0	338	Yellow	35	40	46
Eddie Lacy	GB	4	RB	26	0	0	0	228	1030	7	32	253	1	2	0	0	164	Yellow	36	37	68
Greg Olsen	CAR	7	TE	31	0	0	0	0	0	0	71	922	7	0	0	0	132	Green	37	42	37
Demaryius Thomas	DEN	11	WR	29	0	0	0	0	0	0	90	1170	8	0	0	0	161	Green	38	33	19
Brandin Cooks	NO	5	WR	23	0	0	0	5	31	0	83	1106	8	0	0	0	161	Green	39	34	22
Keenan Allen	SD	11	WR	24	0	0	0	2	16	0	101	1222	7	0	0	0	158	Yellow	40	38	18
Doug Baldwin	SEA	5	WR	28	0	0	0	2	9	0	80	1069	9	0	0	0	158	Green	41	39	26
Kelvin Benjamin	CAR	7	WR	25	0	0	0	2	10	0	70	1023	9	0	0	0	156	Green	42	41	36
Tom Brady	NE	9	QB	39	3566	26	9	30	40	1	0	0	0	2	0	0	329*	Yellow	43	50	55
Duke Johnson	CLE	13	RB	23	0	0	0	154	657	3	68	616	2	1	0	0	155	Green	44	47	41
Jarvis Landry	MIA	8	WR	24	0	0	0	14	81	1	102	1066	6	0	0	0	154	Green	45	43	15
Randall Cobb	GB	4	WR	26	0	0	0	12	57	0	80	1009	8	0	0	0	154	Green	46	44	29
Jeremy Hill	CIN	9	RB	24	0	0	0	238	979	9	21	152	0	3	0	0	154	Yellow	47	48	101
Jonathan Stewart	CAR	7	RB	29	0	0	0	240	1097	6	23	183	0	2	0	0	153	Yellow	48	49	99
Jeremy Maclin	KC	5	WR	28	0	0	0	0	0	0	80	1058	8	0	0	0	152	Green	49	45	35
Giovani Bernard	CIN	9	RB	25	0	0	0	156	679	6	53	464	1	1	0	0	152	Green	50	51	58
Larry Fitzgerald	ARI	9	WR	33	0	0	0	0	0	0	88	1034	9	0	0	0	151	Yellow	51	46	30
Carson Palmer	ARI	9	QB	37	4471	31	12	31	41	0	0	0	0	3	0	0	321	Green	52	58	62
Travis Kelce	KC	5	TE	27	0	0	0	0	0	0	71	853	5	0	0	0	116	Green	53	60	52
Jordan Reed	WAS	9	TE	26	0	0	0	0	0	0	78	870	6	0	0	0	116	Yellow	54	61	51
Golden Tate	DET	10	WR	28	0	0	0	6	31	0	96	1066	8	0	0	0	146	Yellow	55	52	27
Ben Roethlisberger	PIT	8	QB	34	4668	31	11	28	45	0	0	0	0	2	0	0	319	Yellow	56	63	63
Latavius Murray	OAK	10	RB	26	0	0	0	239	911	5	41	343	1	2	0	0	145	Yellow	57	56	83
Melvin Gordon	SD	11	RB	23	0	0	0	256	913	5	38	284	1	3	0	0	145	Green	58	57	86
Delanie Walker	TEN	13	TE	32	0	0	0	0	0	0	72	879	5	0	0	0	114	Green	59	65	53
Julian Edelman	NE	9	WR	30	0	0	0	5	38	0	99	1104	8	0	0	0	144	Red	60	53	31
Donte Moncrief	IND	10	WR	23	0	0	0	2	9	0	80	1015	7	0	0	0	143	Green	61	54	40
Emmanuel Sanders	DEN	11	WR	29	0	0	0	5	33	0	75	1010	6	0	0	0	141	Green	62	55	45
Zach Ertz	PHI	4	TE	26	0	0	0	0	0	0	70	824	5	0	0	0	110	Green	63	71	59
Ryan Mathews	PHI	4	RB	29	0	0	0	190	828	5	31	234	1	2	0	0	140	Green	64	67	108
Frank Gore	IND	10	RB	33	0	0	0	256	923	7	31	184	0	1	0	0	140	Yellow	65	68	115
Danny Woodhead	SD	11	RB	31	0	0	0	94	421	4	78	741	2	1	0	0	140	Yellow	66	75	49
Tyler Eifert	CIN	9	TE	26	0	0	0	0	0	0	53	606	6	0	0	0	109*	Yellow	67	73	71
Gary Barnidge	CLE	13	TE	31	0	0	0	0	0	0	70	842	6	0	0	0	109	Red	68	74	67
John Brown	ARI	9	WR	26	0	0	0	3	13	0	67	994	7	0	0	0	139	Green	69	59	56
Matt Jones	WAS	9	RB	23	0	0	0	257	1027	4	27	218	1	2	0	0	139	Yellow	70	77	133
Eric Decker	NYJ	11	WR	29	0	0	0	3	19	0	75	938	7	0	0	0	138	Green	71	62	50
Jordan Matthews	PHI	4	WR	24	0	0	0	0	0	0	86	1027	7	0	0	0	137	Yellow	72	64	43
Julius Thomas	JAC	5	TE	28	0	0	0	0	0	0	63	720	7	0	0	0	106	Yellow	73	78	73
Coby Fleener	NO	5	TE	28	0	0	0	0	0	0	69	782	6	0	0	0	106	Yellow	74	79	69
Andy Dalton	CIN	9	QB	29	3908	30	14	54	181	2	0	0	0	3	0	0	310	Green	75	80	75
Torrey Smith	SF	8	WR	27	0	0	0	0	0	0	65	1074	8	0	0	0	136	Red	76	66	64
Philip Rivers	SD	11	QB	35	4628	29	11	30	42	0	0	0	0	2	0	0	309	Yellow	77	84	77
Tavon Austin	LARM	8	WR	25	0	0	0	44	291	3	67	685	3	0	0	0	135	Green	78	69	60
Stephen Gostkowski	NE	9	K	32	0	0	0	0	0	0	0	0	0	0	45	32	137	Green	79	76	87
Antonio Gates	SD	11	TE	36	0	0	0	0	0	0	64	745	7	0	0	0	103	Red	80	89	84
Tyrod Taylor	BUF	10	QB	27	3575	23	11	100	516	5	0	0	0	3	0	0	307	Yellow	81	90	80
Blake Bortles	JAC	5	QB	24	4215	29	17	60	302	3	0	0	0	6	0	0	307	Yellow	82	91	81
DeVante Parker	MIA	8	WR	23	0	0	0	2	17	0	66	1029	8	0	0	0	133	Red	83	70	70
Jeremy Langford	CHI	9	RB	25	0	0	0	195	787	4	35	261	1	1	0	0	133	Green	84	81	120
Dion Lewis	NE	9	RB	26	0	0	0	96	438	2	60	654	3	1	0	0	133	Yellow	85	82	72
DeMarco Murray	TEN	13	RB	28	0	0	0	203	807	7	26	201	1	1	0	0	133	Yellow	86	83	147
Jimmy Graham	SEA	5	TE	30	0	0	0	0	0	0	70	788	6	0	0	0	102	Red	87	95	74

Player	Team	Bye	Pos	Age	PaYd	PaTD	INT	Ru	RuYd	RuTD	Rec	RcYd	RcTD	FL	XP	FG	Fant	Risk	Flex Rk	3WR Rk	PPR Rk
Allen Hurns	JAC	5	WR	25	0	0	0	2	9	0	63	919	7	0	0	0	132	Green	88	72	65
Broncos D	DEN	11	D	--	0	0	0	0	0	0	0	0	0	0	0	0	111	Yellow	89	87	92
Matthew Stafford	DET	10	QB	28	4342	29	14	46	111	2	0	0	0	2	0	0	304	Yellow	90	101	88
Eli Manning	NYG	8	QB	35	4386	32	12	27	60	0	0	0	0	3	0	0	304	Yellow	91	102	89
Chandler Catanzaro	ARI	9	K	25	0	0	0	0	0	0	0	0	0	0	43	30	133	Green	92	88	95
Rashad Jennings	NYG	8	RB	31	0	0	0	208	891	5	28	231	1	2	0	0	130	Red	93	85	151
Derek Carr	OAK	10	QB	25	4283	28	14	44	143	1	0	0	0	6	0	0	303	Green	94	104	90
Jameis Winston	TB	6	QB	22	3957	27	14	64	283	4	0	0	0	4	0	0	302	Yellow	95	107	93
Mason Crosby	GB	4	K	32	0	0	0	0	0	0	0	0	0	0	44	29	131	Green	96	98	98
Ameer Abdullah	DET	10	RB	23	0	0	0	200	903	3	40	282	2	2	0	0	128	Red	97	92	134
DeSean Jackson	WAS	9	WR	30	0	0	0	2	9	0	57	991	6	0	0	0	126	Yellow	98	86	91
Cardinals D	ARI	9	D	--	0	0	0	0	0	0	0	0	0	0	0	0	106	Green	99	106	100
Michael Crabtree	OAK	10	WR	29	0	0	0	0	0	0	81	890	6	0	0	0	125	Green	100	93	57
Tyler Lockett	SEA	5	WR	24	0	0	0	5	25	0	59	821	7	0	0	0	125	Green	101	94	82
Brandon McManus	DEN	11	K	25	0	0	0	0	0	0	0	0	0	0	32	33	127	Green	102	108	102
Graham Gano	CAR	7	K	29	0	0	0	0	0	0	0	0	0	0	48	30	127	Yellow	103	109	103
Willie Snead	NO	5	WR	24	0	0	0	2	10	0	62	951	5	0	0	0	124	Green	104	96	78
Theo Riddick	DET	10	RB	25	0	0	0	93	389	1	75	717	3	1	0	0	124	Yellow	105	97	66
Jason Witten	DAL	7	TE	34	0	0	0	0	0	0	65	687	5	0	0	0	93	Yellow	106	124	97
Ladarius Green	PIT	8	TE	25	0	0	0	0	0	0	60	733	5	0	0	0	93	Red	107	125	116
Michael Floyd	ARI	9	WR	27	0	0	0	0	0	0	59	933	6	0	0	0	123	Yellow	108	99	94
DeAngelo Williams	PIT	8	RB	33	0	0	0	153	715	4	31	236	1	1	0	0	123	Green	109	100	153
Seahawks D	SEA	5	D	--	0	0	0	0	0	0	0	0	0	0	0	0	103	Yellow	110	114	105
Eric Ebron	DET	10	TE	23	0	0	0	0	0	0	49	587	6	0	0	0	92	Green	111	130	135
Dwayne Allen	IND	10	TE	26	0	0	0	0	0	0	48	572	7	0	0	0	92	Yellow	112	132	144
Chris Boswell	PIT	8	K	25	0	0	0	0	0	0	0	0	0	0	39	29	125	Green	113	113	109
Steve Smith	BAL	8	WR	37	0	0	0	0	0	0	67	836	8	0	0	0	122	Yellow	114	103	79
Vikings D	MIN	6	D	--	0	0	0	0	0	0	0	0	0	0	0	0	102	Yellow	115	118	110
Patriots D	NE	9	D	--	0	0	0	0	0	0	0	0	0	0	0	0	102	Yellow	116	119	111
Justin Tucker	BAL	8	K	27	0	0	0	0	0	0	0	0	0	0	36	30	124	Green	117	117	117
Josh Gordon	CLE	13	WR	25	0	0	0	0	0	0	47	730	5	0	0	0	121*	Red	118	105	96
Panthers D	CAR	7	D	--	0	0	0	0	0	0	0	0	0	0	0	0	101	Green	119	123	118
Clive Walford	OAK	10	TE	25	0	0	0	0	0	0	50	603	6	0	0	0	90	Yellow	120	139	145
Bengals D	CIN	9	D	--	0	0	0	0	0	0	0	0	0	0	0	0	100	Yellow	121	127	119
Sebastian Janikowski	OAK	10	K	38	0	0	0	0	0	0	0	0	0	0	34	30	122	Green	122	128	121
Adam Vinatieri	IND	10	K	44	0	0	0	0	0	0	0	0	0	0	41	28	122	Green	123	129	122
Dan Bailey	DAL	7	K	28	0	0	0	0	0	0	0	0	0	0	42	27	122	Green	124	131	123
Eagles D	PHI	4	D	--	0	0	0	0	0	0	0	0	0	0	0	0	99	Green	125	135	124
Austin Seferian-Jenkins	TB	6	TE	24	0	0	0	0	0	0	50	615	6	0	0	0	87	Red	126	151	152
Blair Walsh	MIN	6	K	26	0	0	0	0	0	0	0	0	0	0	40	30	120	Yellow	127	138	130
Stefon Diggs	MIN	6	WR	23	0	0	0	3	15	0	69	908	6	0	0	0	117	Yellow	128	115	85
LeGarrette Blount	NE	9	RB	30	0	0	0	186	783	7	12	86	1	1	0	0	117	Red	129	110	205
Colts D	IND	10	D	--	0	0	0	0	0	0	0	0	0	0	0	0	97	Green	130	143	131
Chiefs D	KC	5	D	--	0	0	0	0	0	0	0	0	0	0	0	0	97	Yellow	131	144	132
Matt Ryan	ATL	11	QB	31	4486	25	13	37	106	0	0	0	0	3	0	0	290	Yellow	132	154	125
Marcus Mariota	TEN	13	QB	23	3936	26	13	88	412	3	0	0	0	6	0	0	290	Red	133	155	126
Markus Wheaton	PIT	8	WR	25	0	0	0	2	12	0	55	835	5	0	0	0	116	Green	134	120	106
Kirk Cousins	WAS	9	QB	28	4226	26	18	29	61	2	0	0	0	4	0	0	289	Green	135	156	128
Mike Nugent	CIN	9	K	34	0	0	0	0	0	0	0	0	0	0	43	28	118	Yellow	136	147	136
Josh Brown	NYG	8	K	37	0	0	0	0	0	0	0	0	0	0	37	30	118	Yellow	137	148	137
Terrance Williams	DAL	7	WR	27	0	0	0	0	0	0	57	896	6	0	0	0	115	Yellow	138	126	112
Tevin Coleman	ATL	11	RB	23	0	0	0	134	622	5	25	227	1	2	0	0	115	Green	139	111	176
Giants D	NYG	8	D	--	0	0	0	0	0	0	0	0	0	0	0	0	95	Yellow	140	149	138
Steelers D	PIT	8	D	--	0	0	0	0	0	0	0	0	0	0	0	0	95	Green	141	150	139
Kevin White	CHI	9	WR	24	0	0	0	0	0	0	62	915	6	0	0	0	114	Red	142	133	113
Jay Ajayi	MIA	8	RB	23	0	0	0	170	779	4	25	168	0	1	0	0	114	Green	143	112	181
Mohamed Sanu	ATL	11	WR	27	25	0	0	8	51	0	62	815	5	0	0	0	113	Yellow	144	136	107
Phillip Dorsett	IND	10	WR	23	0	0	0	6	31	0	54	779	6	0	0	0	112	Yellow	145	140	140
Sterling Shepard	NYG	8	WR	22	0	0	0	6	34	0	64	841	6	0	0	0	112	Red	146	141	114
Jay Cutler	CHI	9	QB	33	4080	28	13	42	183	1	0	0	0	5	0	0	285	Yellow	147	164	141
T.J. Yeldon	JAC	5	RB	23	0	0	0	159	678	3	31	235	1	1	0	0	110	Green	148	116	173
Kyle Rudolph	MIN	6	TE	27	0	0	0	0	0	0	58	586	4	0	0	0	79	Yellow	149	169	148
Darren Sproles	PHI	4	RB	33	0	0	0	117	465	1	63	480	2	1	0	0	109	Green	150	121	104
Justin Forsett	BAL	8	RB	31	0	0	0	154	657	4	34	274	1	2	0	0	108	Yellow	151	122	177
Charles Clay	BUF	10	TE	27	0	0	0	0	0	0	50	553	4	0	0	0	77	Green	152	170	158
Zach Miller	CHI	9	TE	32	0	0	0	0	0	0	52	582	4	0	0	0	77	Yellow	153	171	159

Player	Team	Bye	Pos	Age	PaYd	PaTD	INT	Ru	RuYd	RuTD	Rec	RcYd	RcTD	FL	XP	FG	Fant	Risk	Flex Rk	3WR Rk	PPR Rk
Alex Smith	KC	5	QB	32	3510	21	9	65	317	2	0	0	0	3	0	0	281	Green	154	174	146
Kendall Wright	TEN	13	WR	27	0	0	0	3	14	0	59	726	6	0	0	0	107	Green	155	157	129
Marvin Jones	DET	10	WR	26	0	0	0	3	14	0	64	826	5	0	0	0	106	Yellow	156	159	127
Kenny Britt	LARM	8	WR	28	0	0	0	0	0	0	50	790	5	0	0	0	106	Green	157	160	149
Charles Sims	TB	6	RB	26	0	0	0	95	448	1	57	538	1	1	0	0	105	Green	158	134	143
Laquon Treadwell	MIN	6	WR	21	0	0	0	6	33	0	65	846	5	0	0	0	104	Red	159	162	142
Buck Allen	BAL	8	RB	25	0	0	0	133	556	2	48	389	1	2	0	0	103	Green	160	137	156
Ryan Tannehill	MIA	8	QB	28	4162	27	13	42	173	1	0	0	0	3	0	0	276	Red	161	182	155
Corey Coleman	CLE	13	WR	22	0	0	0	4	24	0	57	825	4	0	0	0	102	Yellow	162	166	150
Devin Funchess	CAR	7	WR	22	0	0	0	2	11	0	49	718	7	0	0	0	102	Red	163	167	165
Jordan Cameron	MIA	8	TE	28	0	0	0	0	0	0	43	446	4	0	0	0	70	Green	164	188	187
Derrick Henry	TEN	13	RB	22	0	0	0	126	514	7	12	103	0	1	0	0	100	Green	165	142	235
Brock Osweiler	HOU	9	QB	26	4026	22	16	46	111	2	0	0	0	4	0	0	273	Green	166	192	157
Isaiah Crowell	CLE	13	RB	23	0	0	0	180	711	4	21	174	1	1	0	0	99	Red	167	145	223
Jacob Tamme	ATL	11	TE	31	0	0	0	0	0	0	51	553	2	0	0	0	68	Green	168	196	168
Chris Ivory	JAC	5	RB	28	0	0	0	155	621	5	22	169	0	1	0	0	98	Red	169	146	226
Martellus Bennett	NE	9	TE	29	0	0	0	0	0	0	46	500	4	0	0	0	67	Red	170	198	201
Geno Smith	NYJ	11	QB	26	3907	26	20	62	259	2	0	0	0	5	0	0	271	Yellow	171	199	161
Travis Benjamin	SD	11	WR	27	0	0	0	3	23	0	50	777	5	0	0	0	97	Red	172	177	167
Benjamin Watson	BAL	8	TE	36	0	0	0	0	0	0	44	506	4	0	0	0	66	Red	173	201	203
Robert Griffin	CLE	13	QB	26	4048	21	14	75	314	2	0	0	0	8	0	0	270	Yellow	174	203	162
Vincent Jackson	TB	6	WR	33	0	0	0	0	0	0	51	673	5	0	0	0	96	Green	175	179	163
Will Tye	NYG	8	TE	25	0	0	0	0	0	0	37	412	4	0	0	0	65	Green	176	205	208
Joe Flacco	BAL	8	QB	31	4139	28	12	28	54	1	0	0	0	3	0	0	269	Red	177	208	164
Steven Hauschka	SEA	5	K	31	0	0	0	0	0	0	0	0	0	0	45	25	117	Green	178	184	169
Kenny Stills	MIA	8	WR	24	0	0	0	2	17	0	48	741	4	0	0	0	95	Yellow	179	181	174
Shane Vereen	NYG	8	RB	27	0	0	0	78	356	1	59	527	1	1	0	0	95	Green	180	152	154
Bills D	BUF	10	D	--	0	0	0	0	0	0	0	0	0	0	0	0	94	Yellow	181	185	170
Lions D	DET	10	D	--	0	0	0	0	0	0	0	0	0	0	0	0	94	Yellow	182	186	171
Rams D	LARM	8	D	--	0	0	0	0	0	0	0	0	0	0	0	0	94	Yellow	183	187	172
Will Fuller	HOU	9	WR	22	0	0	0	2	14	0	48	794	4	0	0	0	94	Red	184	183	183
James Starks	GB	4	RB	30	0	0	0	116	492	3	30	213	1	1	0	0	94	Green	185	153	211
Jared Cook	GB	4	TE	29	0	0	0	0	0	0	41	495	4	0	0	0	63	Red	186	214	216
Teddy Bridgewater	MIN	6	QB	24	3592	20	11	47	195	2	0	0	0	2	0	0	267	Green	187	216	166
Robbie Gould	CHI	9	K	34	0	0	0	0	0	0	0	0	0	0	37	27	116	Green	188	191	178
Texans D	HOU	9	D	--	0	0	0	0	0	0	0	0	0	0	0	0	93	Yellow	189	193	179
Bucs D	TB	6	D	--	0	0	0	0	0	0	0	0	0	0	0	0	93	Green	190	194	180
Rishard Matthews	TEN	13	WR	27	0	0	0	2	8	0	45	634	5	0	0	0	92	Green	191	189	184
Jeff Heuerman	DEN	11	TE	24	0	0	0	0	0	0	42	473	3	0	0	0	61	Yellow	192	221	214
Richard Rodgers	GB	4	TE	24	0	0	0	0	0	0	33	445	4	0	0	0	61	Yellow	193	222	228
Packers D	GB	4	D	--	0	0	0	0	0	0	0	0	0	0	0	0	92	Yellow	194	200	182
Robert Woods	BUF	10	WR	24	0	0	0	2	12	0	58	689	4	0	0	0	91	Green	195	195	160
Jordan Howard	CHI	9	RB	22	0	0	0	92	401	5	20	180	1	1	0	0	91	Green	196	158	238
Lance Kendricks	LARM	8	TE	28	0	0	0	0	0	0	40	400	4	0	0	0	60	Green	197	234	217
Nick Folk	NYJ	11	K	32	0	0	0	0	0	0	0	0	0	0	34	29	114	Yellow	198	209	186
Ravens D	BAL	8	D	--	0	0	0	0	0	0	0	0	0	0	0	0	91	Yellow	199	210	188
Cowboys D	DAL	7	D	--	0	0	0	0	0	0	0	0	0	0	0	0	91	Red	200	211	189
Jaguars D	JAC	5	D	--	0	0	0	0	0	0	0	0	0	0	0	0	91	Yellow	201	212	190
Breshad Perriman	BAL	8	WR	23	0	0	0	2	14	0	44	716	4	0	0	0	88	Red	202	204	206
Spencer Ware	KC	5	RB	25	0	0	0	87	386	5	24	180	1	0	0	0	88	Green	203	161	236
Larry Donnell	NYG	8	TE	28	0	0	0	0	0	0	37	380	4	0	0	0	57	Yellow	204	244	229
Vance McDonald	SF	8	TE	26	0	0	0	0	0	0	45	466	2	0	0	0	57	Green	205	245	209
Matt Prater	DET	10	K	32	0	0	0	0	0	0	0	0	0	0	37	28	113	Yellow	206	217	194
Dan Carpenter	BUF	10	K	31	0	0	0	0	0	0	0	0	0	0	41	25	113	Green	207	218	195
Dolphins D	MIA	8	D	--	0	0	0	0	0	0	0	0	0	0	0	0	90	Yellow	208	219	196
Jets D	NYJ	11	D	--	0	0	0	0	0	0	0	0	0	0	0	0	90	Yellow	209	220	197
Tony Romo	DAL	7	QB	36	3897	29	12	25	50	0	0	0	0	2	0	0	259	Red	210	250	185
Matt Bryant	ATL	11	K	41	0	0	0	0	0	0	0	0	0	0	38	27	112	Yellow	211	231	198
Titans D	TEN	13	D	--	0	0	0	0	0	0	0	0	0	0	0	0	89	Yellow	212	229	199
Redskins D	WAS	9	D	--	0	0	0	0	0	0	0	0	0	0	0	0	89	Yellow	213	230	200
Arian Foster	MIA	8	RB	30	0	0	0	112	475	4	30	229	1	1	0	0	84	Red	214	163	239
Sam Bradford	PHI	4	QB	29	3897	25	14	24	53	1	0	0	0	3	0	0	257	Yellow	215	255	192
Blaine Gabbert	SF	8	QB	27	3991	20	15	50	177	2	0	0	0	4	0	0	257	Yellow	216	257	193
Kamar Aiken	BAL	8	WR	27	0	0	0	0	0	0	57	664	3	0	0	0	83	Green	217	232	175
Jermaine Kearse	SEA	5	WR	26	0	0	0	0	0	0	41	595	4	0	0	0	83	Green	218	233	210
Ted Ginn	CAR	7	WR	31	0	0	0	5	39	0	34	522	4	0	0	0	82	Green	219	236	227

Player	Team	Bye	Pos	Age	PaYd	PaTD	INT	Ru	RuYd	RuTD	Rec	RcYd	RcTD	FL	XP	FG	Fant	Risk	Flex Rk	3WR Rk	PPR Rk
Dorial Green-Beckham	TEN	13	WR	23	0	0	0	0	0	0	35	586	6	0	0	0	82	Red	220	237	230
Pierre Garcon	WAS	9	WR	30	0	0	0	0	0	0	56	640	4	0	0	0	82	Yellow	221	238	191
Bilal Powell	NYJ	11	RB	28	0	0	0	103	369	1	48	385	1	1	0	0	82	Green	222	165	202
Darren Fells	ARI	9	TE	30	0	0	0	0	0	0	27	295	4	0	0	0	51	Green	223	260	244
Ronnie Hillman	DEN	11	RB	25	0	0	0	101	431	2	28	224	1	1	0	0	81	Green	224	168	240
Jace Amaro	NYJ	11	TE	24	0	0	0	0	0	0	39	401	2	0	0	0	50	Green	225	265	237
Cairo Santos	KC	5	K	25	0	0	0	0	0	0	0	0	0	0	38	29	109	Red	226	251	207
Maxx Williams	BAL	8	TE	22	0	0	0	0	0	0	33	371	2	0	0	0	47	Yellow	227	270	245
Dustin Hopkins	WAS	9	K	26	0	0	0	0	0	0	0	0	0	0	31	31	108	Red	228	254	212
Josh Lambo	SD	11	K	26	0	0	0	0	0	0	0	0	0	0	39	28	108	Green	229	256	213
Raiders D	OAK	10	D	--	0	0	0	0	0	0	0	0	0	0	0	0	85	Yellow	230	258	215
Victor Cruz	NYG	8	WR	30	0	0	0	0	0	0	47	582	5	0	0	0	77	Red	231	252	222
Karlos Williams	BUF	10	RB	23	0	0	0	107	516	5	11	74	0	2	0	0	77	Red	232	172	252
Chris Johnson	ARI	9	RB	31	0	0	0	105	416	4	11	116	0	1	0	0	77	Green	233	173	251
Tyler Kroft	CIN	9	TE	24	0	0	0	0	0	0	27	285	3	0	0	0	46	Green	234	271	247
Michael Thomas	NO	5	WR	22	0	0	0	4	26	0	45	600	4	0	0	0	76	Red	235	253	224
Nick Novak	HOU	9	K	35	0	0	0	0	0	0	0	0	0	0	35	25	107	Green	236	272	218
Bears D	CHI	9	D	--	0	0	0	0	0	0	0	0	0	0	0	0	84	Red	237	261	219
Chargers D	SD	11	D	--	0	0	0	0	0	0	0	0	0	0	0	0	84	Red	238	262	220
Sammie Coates	PIT	8	WR	23	0	0	0	0	0	0	33	604	4	0	0	0	75	Red	239	259	242
Hunter Henry	SD	11	TE	22	0	0	0	0	0	0	29	348	3	0	0	0	44	Red	240	273	249
Jerick McKinnon	MIN	6	RB	24	0	0	0	64	342	2	27	228	1	1	0	0	74	Green	241	175	243
Justin Hardy	ATL	11	WR	25	0	0	0	0	0	0	48	596	4	0	0	0	73	Red	242	263	225
Tyler Boyd	CIN	9	WR	22	0	0	0	4	21	0	43	553	3	0	0	0	73	Yellow	243	264	231
Luke Willson	SEA	5	TE	26	0	0	0	0	0	0	21	267	3	0	0	0	42	Green	244	274	254
Brandon LaFell	CIN	9	WR	30	0	0	0	0	0	0	45	575	4	0	0	0	72	Red	245	266	234
Danny Amendola	NE	9	WR	31	0	0	0	0	0	0	56	568	3	0	0	0	72	Red	246	267	204
Nelson Agholor	PHI	4	WR	23	0	0	0	0	0	0	43	543	4	0	0	0	72	Yellow	247	268	232
Quinton Patton	SF	8	WR	26	0	0	0	0	0	0	41	541	3	0	0	0	72	Green	248	269	233
C.J. Spiller	NO	5	RB	29	0	0	0	38	156	1	52	446	2	1	0	0	72	Yellow	249	176	221
Brent Celek	PHI	4	TE	31	0	0	0	0	0	0	26	272	2	0	0	0	41	Green	250	275	250
C.J. Prosise	SEA	5	RB	22	0	0	0	65	296	3	24	224	1	1	0	0	71	Green	251	178	246
Chris Thompson	WAS	9	RB	26	0	0	0	47	201	1	39	393	1	1	0	0	69	Green	252	180	241
Tim Hightower	NO	5	RB	30	0	0	0	79	311	3	16	141	0	1	0	0	61	Green	253	190	256
Benny Cunningham	LARM	8	RB	26	0	0	0	61	275	1	34	239	1	1	0	0	59	Green	254	197	248
Alfred Morris	DAL	7	RB	28	0	0	0	82	331	2	10	76	1	1	0	0	54	Green	255	202	261
Kenyan Drake	MIA	8	RB	22	0	0	0	44	180	1	31	223	1	1	0	0	53	Blue	256	206	253
Darren McFadden	DAL	7	RB	29	0	0	0	54	255	2	15	149	1	1	0	0	52	Red	257	207	260
Wendell Smallwood	PHI	4	RB	22	0	0	0	68	319	1	20	176	1	1	0	0	51	Yellow	258	213	257
Andre Ellington	ARI	9	RB	27	0	0	0	45	188	1	19	205	1	0	0	0	49	Green	259	215	258
Charcandrick West	KC	5	RB	25	0	0	0	64	260	2	14	101	0	1	0	0	45	Green	260	223	264
Kenneth Dixon	BAL	8	RB	22	0	0	0	69	312	1	13	96	1	1	0	0	45	Green	261	224	265
Dexter McCluster	TEN	13	RB	28	0	0	0	29	137	1	35	279	0	0	0	0	45	Green	262	225	255
Zach Zenner	DET	10	RB	25	0	0	0	58	227	2	12	96	1	1	0	0	44	Green	263	226	267
Kenjon Barner	PHI	4	RB	27	0	0	0	28	112	3	12	100	1	1	0	0	44	Green	264	227	268
Shaun Draughn	SF	8	RB	29	0	0	0	71	240	1	24	168	0	1	0	0	44	Green	265	228	259
Brandon Bolden	NE	9	RB	26	0	0	0	49	161	1	19	173	1	1	0	0	43	Green	266	235	263
Jacquizz Rodgers	CHI	9	RB	26	0	0	0	43	162	0	23	181	1	1	0	0	41	Green	267	239	262
Mike Tolbert	CAR	7	RB	31	0	0	0	59	213	1	17	123	0	1	0	0	39	Blue	268	240	266
Branden Oliver	SD	11	RB	25	0	0	0	40	133	3	16	131	1	1	0	0	39	Red	269	241	269
Alfred Blue	HOU	9	RB	25	0	0	0	96	309	1	11	73	0	0	0	0	38	Yellow	270	242	272
Andre Williams	NYG	8	RB	24	0	0	0	50	197	3	7	44	0	1	0	0	38	Red	271	243	274
DeAndre Washington	OAK	10	RB	23	0	0	0	63	276	1	14	78	0	1	0	0	37	Green	272	246	271
Devontae Booker	DEN	11	RB	24	0	0	0	55	232	1	11	60	0	1	0	0	36	Green	273	247	273
James White	NE	9	RB	24	0	0	0	33	122	1	18	169	1	0	0	0	35	Green	274	248	270
Mike Gillislee	BUF	10	RB	26	0	0	0	53	226	2	5	34	0	1	0	0	35	Green	275	249	275

Statistical Appendix

Broken Tackles by Team, Offense

Rk	Team	Plays	Plays w/ BTkl	Pct	Total BTkl
1	STL	910	120	13.2%	136
2	MIN	965	121	12.5%	139
3	SEA	1013	124	12.2%	138
4	TB	1010	115	11.4%	132
5	NE	1038	115	11.1%	135
6	DEN	1052	107	10.2%	114
7	CAR	1042	105	10.1%	116
8	BUF	1000	99	9.9%	115
9	KC	944	93	9.9%	109
10	SF	962	94	9.8%	103
11	DET	1022	99	9.7%	113
12	OAK	1003	95	9.5%	107
13	MIA	972	91	9.4%	103
14	CHI	1025	95	9.3%	111
15	CLE	1037	95	9.2%	113
16	SD	1100	98	8.9%	102
17	NYJ	1067	94	8.8%	104
18	PIT	1004	86	8.6%	95
19	PHI	1102	92	8.3%	101
20	GB	1055	88	8.3%	97
21	CIN	995	81	8.1%	95
22	ATL	1065	86	8.1%	95
23	NO	1078	86	8.0%	91
24	TEN	978	78	8.0%	90
25	ARI	1024	81	7.9%	92
26	DAL	965	73	7.6%	76
27	BAL	1079	81	7.5%	91
28	WAS	1003	75	7.5%	81
29	NYG	1057	78	7.4%	89
30	IND	1037	75	7.2%	84
31	JAC	1011	72	7.1%	86
32	HOU	1112	65	5.8%	68

Play total includes Defensive Pass Interference.

Broken Tackles by Team, Defense

Rk	Team	Plays	Plays w/ BTkl	Pct	Total BTkl
1	TEN	982	61	6.2%	72
2	BAL	1002	68	6.8%	83
3	NE	1045	77	7.4%	81
4	CAR	1054	81	7.7%	90
5	BUF	1008	82	8.1%	94
6	SEA	942	77	8.2%	87
7	NYJ	1008	83	8.2%	94
8	IND	1065	89	8.4%	103
9	DEN	1027	86	8.4%	97
10	NYG	1094	93	8.5%	100
11	MIN	1010	87	8.6%	97
12	OAK	1090	95	8.7%	107
13	HOU	974	85	8.7%	107
14	CLE	990	88	8.9%	100
15	PHI	1133	101	8.9%	111
16	NO	994	90	9.1%	102
17	SF	1059	96	9.1%	112
18	ARI	977	89	9.1%	104
19	CIN	1026	94	9.2%	103
20	STL	1077	99	9.2%	113
21	MIA	1066	100	9.4%	110
22	KC	1037	98	9.5%	104
23	ATL	989	95	9.6%	107
24	DET	988	95	9.6%	105
25	DAL	984	96	9.8%	104
26	JAC	1085	111	10.2%	122
27	WAS	1009	104	10.3%	113
28	PIT	1047	108	10.3%	124
29	SD	950	98	10.3%	108
30	GB	1012	106	10.5%	119
31	TB	1031	115	11.2%	125
32	CHI	972	110	11.3%	123

Play total includes Defensive Pass Interference.

Most Broken Tackles, Defenders

Rk	Player	Team	BTkl	Rk	Player	Team	BTkl	Rk	Player	Team	BTkl
1	A.Blake	PIT	21	10	K.Alexander	TB	16	19	M.Jenkins	PHI	14
2	P.Worrilow	ATL	20	10	J.Cyprien	JAC	16	19	R.Jones	MIA	14
3	N.Bowman	SF	19	10	K.Fuller	CHI	16	19	E.Kendricks	MIN	14
3	L.David	TB	19	10	D.Johnson	KC	16	19	S.McClellin	CHI	14
5	B.Church	DAL	18	10	D.Kirkpatrick	CIN	16	19	V.Rey	CIN	14
5	M.Smith	OAK	18	15	E.Berry	KC	15	19	D.Smith	BAL	14
5	L.Timmons	PIT	18	15	D.Davis	NYJ	15	19	T.Smith	JAC	14
8	D.Jackson	IND	17	15	M.Kendricks	PHI	15				
8	T.Mathieu	ARI	17	15	R.Parker	KC	15				

Top 20 Defenders, Broken Tackle Rate

Rk	Player	Team	BTkl	Tkl	Rate
1	W.Woodyard	TEN	1	74	1.3%
2	K.Mack	OAK	1	65	1.5%
3	D.Harrison	NYJ	1	57	1.7%
4	I.Williams	SF	1	52	1.9%
5	B.Orakpo	TEN	1	44	2.2%
6	J.Taylor	MIA	1	43	2.3%
7	C.Graham	BUF	3	101	2.9%
8	K.Wright	SEA	3	85	3.4%
9	C.Dunlap	CIN	2	49	3.9%
10	J.Freeman	IND	4	90	4.3%
11	J.Verrett	SD	2	44	4.3%
12	C.Heyward	PIT	2	43	4.4%
12	L.Joseph	MIN	2	43	4.4%
12	D.Wolfe	DEN	2	43	4.4%
15	S.Smith	KC	2	41	4.7%
16	B.Maxwell	PHI	3	61	4.7%
17	G.Iloka	CIN	2	40	4.8%
17	N.Robey	BUF	2	40	4.8%
17	D.Perryman	SD	3	60	4.8%
20	P.Amukamara	NYG	3	59	4.8%

Broken Tackles divided by Broken Tackles + Solo Tackles.
Special teams not included; min. 40 Solo Tackles

Bottom 20 Defenders, Broken Tackle Rate

Rk	Player	Team	BTkl	Tkl	Rate
1	K.Fuller	CHI	16	47	25.4%
2	A.Blake	PIT	21	64	24.7%
3	J.Wilcox	DAL	13	40	24.5%
4	B.Meriweather	NYG	13	45	22.4%
5	T.J.Carrie	OAK	12	47	20.3%
6	E.Berry	KC	15	59	20.3%
7	J.Simon	HOU	10	40	20.0%
8	D.Kirkpatrick	CIN	16	65	19.8%
9	T.McDonald	STL	12	49	19.7%
9	E.Thomas	SEA	12	49	19.7%
11	P.Worrilow	ATL	20	84	19.2%
12	D.House	JAC	13	56	18.8%
13	K.Alexander	TB	16	70	18.6%
14	J.Addae	SD	13	57	18.6%
14	D.Amerson	2TM	13	57	18.6%
16	B.Grimes	MIA	10	44	18.5%
17	T.Whitehead	DET	9	40	18.4%
18	K.Robinson	WAS	11	49	18.3%
19	J.Tartt	SF	13	58	18.3%
20	D.Davis	NYJ	15	68	18.1%

Broken Tackles divided by Broken Tackles + Solo Tackles.
Special teams not included; min. 40 Solo Tackles

Most Broken Tackles, Running Backs

Rk	Player	Team	BTkl
1	D.Martin	TB	63
2	D.Freeman	ATL	54
3	A.Peterson	MIN	51
4	J.Stewart	CAR	49
5	D.Johnson	ARI	47
6	T.Gurley	STL	46
7	C.Ivory	NYJ	45
8	F.Gore	IND	41
9	T.Riddick	DET	40
10	L.McCoy	BUF	39
10	L.Murray	OAK	39
12	M.Gordon	SD	38
12	T.Yeldon	JAC	38
14	G.Bernard	CIN	37
14	M.Forte	CHI	37
16	C.Sims	TB	36
17	M.Ingram	NO	34
18	D.Murray	PHI	33
19	C.Anderson	DEN	31
19	A.Andrews	TEN	31
19	D.Williams	PIT	31

Most Broken Tackles, WR/TE

Rk	Player	Team	BTkl
1	T.Austin	STL	34
2	J.Landry	MIA	33
3	G.Tate	DET	27
4	J.Jones	ATL	21
5	J.Reed	WAS	19
6	A.Brown	PIT	18
7	R.Cobb	GB	16
8	D.Baldwin	SEA	15
8	J.Edelman	NE	15
8	B.Marshall	NYJ	15
8	D.Thomas	DEN	15
12	M.Bryant	PIT	14
12	M.Crabtree	OAK	14
12	S.Diggs	MIN	14
12	R.Gronkowski	NE	14
12	T.Kelce	KC	14
17	D.Amendola	NE	12
17	O.Beckham	NYG	12
17	Z.Miller	CHI	12
20	6 tied with		11

Most Broken Tackles, Quarterbacks

Rk	Player	Team	Behind LOS	Beyond LOS	BTkl	Rk	Player	Team	Behind LOS	Beyond LOS	BTkl
1	C.Newton	CAR	14	10	24	5	J.Cutler	CHI	9	3	12
1	T.Taylor	BUF	19	5	24	5	A.Smith	KC	10	2	12
3	T.Bridgewater	MIN	21	0	21	5	J.Winston	TB	10	2	12
3	R.Wilson	SEA	16	5	21	9	A.Luck	IND	11	0	11
5	B.Bortles	JAC	11	1	12	10	J.Manziel	CLE	10	0	10

Best Broken Tackle Rate, Offensive Players (min. 80 touches)

Rk	Player	Team	BTkl	Touch	Rate	Rk	Player	Team	BTkl	Touch	Rate
1	T.Austin	STL	34	104	32.7%	11	M.Lynch	SEA	24	124	19.4%
2	T.Riddick	DET	40	123	32.5%	12	T.Mason	STL	18	93	19.4%
3	D.Lewis	NE	25	85	29.4%	13	C.Hyde	SF	24	126	19.0%
4	D.Johnson	ARI	47	165	28.5%	14	J.Stewart	CAR	49	258	19.0%
5	G.Tate	DET	27	96	28.1%	15	A.Andrews	TEN	31	164	18.9%
6	B.Bolden	NE	23	82	28.0%	16	T.Gurley	STL	46	250	18.4%
7	J.Landry	MIA	33	128	25.8%	17	G.Bernard	CIN	37	203	18.2%
8	C.Sims	TB	36	158	22.8%	18	C.Anderson	DEN	31	177	17.5%
9	J.Reed	WAS	19	87	21.8%	19	M.Gordon	SD	38	217	17.5%
10	D.Martin	TB	63	321	19.6%	20	T.Yeldon	JAC	38	218	17.4%

Top 20 Defenders, Passes Defensed

Rk	Player	Team	PD
1	D.Amerson	2TM	25
2	M.Peters	KC	22
3	J.Joseph	CIN	21
3	D.House	JAC	21
5	R.Darby	BUF	18
5	D.Breaux	NO	18
5	S.Gilmore	BUF	18
5	J.Norman	CAR	18
9	M.Butler	NE	17
10	B.Breeland	WAS	16
11	V.Davis	IND	15
11	R.Nelson	CIN	15
13	R.Sherman	SEA	14
13	T.Newman	MIN	14
13	J.Jenkins	STL	14
13	D.Rodgers-Cromartie	NYG	14
13	L.Ryan	NE	14
13	T.Johnson	STL	14
19	7 tied with		13

Note: Based on the definition given in the Statistical Toolbox, not NFL totals.

Top 20 Defenders, Defeats

Rk	Player	Team	Dfts
1	J.J.Watt	HOU	42
2	M.Barron	STL	35
2	L.David	TB	35
4	K.Mack	OAK	32
5	A.Donald	STL	31
5	T.Mathieu	ARI	31
7	T.Smith	JAC	30
8	M.Jenkins	PHI	29
9	M.Bennett	SEA	27
9	C.J.Mosley	BAL	27
9	L.Timmons	PIT	27
12	M.Ingram	SD	26
13	G.Atkins	CIN	25
13	J.Collins	NE	25
13	M.Smith	OAK	25
13	O.Vernon	MIA	25
17	C.Avril	SEA	24
17	K.Dansby	CLE	24
17	L.Kuechly	CAR	24
17	P.Posluszny	JAC	24
17	K.Short	CAR	24

Top 20 Defenders, Run Tackles for Loss

Rk	Player	Team	TFL
1	J.J.Watt	HOU	18
2	M.Barron	STL	17
3	A.Donald	STL	15
4	N.Suh	MIA	13
5	M.Bennett	SEA	12
5	D.Lawrence	DAL	12
5	K.Sheppard	MIA	12
8	D.Harrison	NYJ	11
8	S.Lee	DAL	11
8	B.Logan	PHI	11
8	T.Smith	JAC	11
12	C.Baker	WAS	10
12	C.Campbell	ARI	10
12	W.Hayes	STL	10
12	D.Jackson	IND	10
12	P.Posluszny	JAC	10
12	O.Vernon	MIA	10
12	L.Williams	NYJ	10
19	8 tied with		9

Top 20 Defenders, Quarterback Hits

Rk	Player	Team	Hits
1	J.J.Watt	HOU	33
2	O.Vernon	MIA	30
3	A.Donald	STL	27
4	E.Ansah	DET	23
4	V.Miller	DEN	23
6	M.Bennett	SEA	21
7	C.Dunlap	CIN	20
7	E.Griffen	MIN	20
9	C.Avril	SEA	17
9	M.Wilkerson	NYJ	17
9	L.Williams	NYJ	17
12	C.Campbell	ARI	16
12	E.Dumervil	BAL	16
12	A.Lynch	SF	16
15	G.Hardy	DAL	15
15	T.Johnson	MIN	15
17	J.Allen	CAR	14
17	A.Clayborn	ATL	14
17	P.McPhee	CHI	14
17	O.Schofield	ATL	14

Top 20 Defenders, QB Knockdowns (Sacks + Hits)

Rk	Defender	Team	KD
1	J.J.Watt	HOU	52
2	O.Vernon	MIA	41
3	A.Donald	STL	39
4	E.Ansah	DET	37
4	C.Dunlap	CIN	37
6	V.Miller	DEN	35
7	M.Bennett	SEA	31
7	E.Griffen	MIN	31
9	C.Avril	SEA	28
9	M.Wilkerson	NYJ	28
11	K.Mack	OAK	27
12	E.Dumervil	BAL	24
12	A.Lynch	SF	24
14	R.Ayers	NYG	23
14	C.Campbell	ARI	23
14	C.Jordan	NO	23
17	G.Hardy	DAL	22
17	M.Ingram	SD	22
19	G.Atkins	CIN	21
19	F.Cox	PHI	21
19	T.Johnson	MIN	21
19	N.Suh	MIA	21
19	L.Williams	NYJ	21

Full credit for whole and half sacks; includes sacks cancelled by penalty.
Does not include strip sacks.

Top 20 Defenders, Hurries

Rk	Defender	Team	Hur
1	J.J.Watt	HOU	51.0
2	C.Dunlap	CIN	37.5
3	V.Miller	DEN	37.0
4	O.Vernon	MIA	35.5
5	F.Cox	PHI	34.0
5	A.Lynch	SF	34.0
7	J.Hughes	BUF	32.5
7	C.Jordan	NO	32.5
9	J.Pierre-Paul	NYG	32.0
10	A.Donald	STL	31.0
11	M.Wilkerson	NYJ	30.5
12	G.Atkins	CIN	29.5
12	M.Ingram	SD	29.5
12	K.Mack	OAK	29.5
15	E.Griffen	MIN	29.0
15	R.Kerrigan	WAS	29.0
17	E.Dumervil	BAL	28.5
18	C.Avril	SEA	28.0
19	E.Ansah	DET	27.0
19	M.Bennett	SEA	27.0

Top 20 Quarterbacks, QB Hits

Rk	Player	Team	Hits
1	J.Winston	TB	96
2	C.Palmer	ARI	79
3	P.Rivers	SD	74
4	R.Wilson	SEA	72
5	N.Foles	STL	71
6	R.Tannehill	MIA	69
7	A.Rodgers	GB	68
8	T.Brady	NE	65
9	M.Ryan	ATL	61
10	K.Cousins	WAS	58
11	S.Bradford	PHI	57
11	E.Manning	NYG	57
13	D.Brees	NO	56
14	M.Stafford	DET	55
15	T.Bridgewater	MIN	53
16	R.Fitzpatrick	NYJ	48
17	J.McCown	CLE	46
18	A.Luck	IND	44
19	J.Cutler	CHI	43
20	B.Bortles	JAC	41

Top 20 Quarterbacks, QB Knockdowns (Sacks + Hits)

Rk	Player	Team	KD
1	J.Winston	TB	123
2	A.Rodgers	GB	116
2	R.Wilson	SEA	116
4	R.Tannehill	MIA	114
5	P.Rivers	SD	113
6	C.Palmer	ARI	106
7	T.Brady	NE	103
7	M.Stafford	DET	103
9	T.Bridgewater	MIN	95
10	M.Ryan	ATL	93
11	B.Bortles	JAC	91
12	D.Brees	NO	90
13	S.Bradford	PHI	89
14	N.Foles	STL	85
15	K.Cousins	WAS	83
16	E.Manning	NYG	82
17	A.Smith	KC	79
18	J.McCown	CLE	72
19	J.Cutler	CHI	70
19	M.Mariota	TEN	70

Includes sacks cancelled by penalties
Does not include strip sacks or "self sacks" with no defender listed.

Top 10 Quarterbacks, Knockdowns per Pass

Rk	Player	Team	KD	Pct
1	N.Foles	STL	85	23.0%
2	J.McCown	CLE	72	21.2%
3	R.Wilson	SEA	116	21.2%
4	J.Winston	TB	123	20.2%
5	T.Bridgewater	MIN	95	18.3%
6	A.Luck	IND	58	18.1%
7	C.Palmer	ARI	106	17.6%
8	B.Osweiler	DEN	54	17.2%
9	M.Hasselbeck	IND	50	17.2%
10	C.Kaepernick	SF	48	17.1%

Min. 200 passes; includes passes cancelled by penalty

Bottom 10 Quarterbacks in Knockdowns per Pass

Rk	Player	Team	KD	Pct
1	A.Dalton	CIN	35	8.0%
2	B.Roethlisberger	PIT	45	8.5%
3	J.Flacco	BAL	41	9.1%
4	D.Carr	OAK	63	10.0%
5	R.Fitzpatrick	NYJ	67	11.1%
6	R.Mallett	2TM	29	11.2%
7	C.Newton	CAR	66	11.8%
8	E.Manning	NYG	82	11.8%
9	B.Hoyer	HOU	53	12.8%
10	D.Brees	NO	90	12.8%

Min. 200 passes; includes passes cancelled by penalty

Top 10 Most Passes Tipped at Line, Quarterbacks

Rk	Player	Team	Total
1	B.Bortles	JAC	21
2	R.Fitzpatrick	NYJ	20
3	M.Ryan	ATL	19
4	S.Bradford	PHI	15
5	R.Tannehill	MIA	14
6	T.Bridgewater	MIN	13
7	C.Newton	CAR	12
8	P.Rivers	SD	11
9	T.Brady	NE	10
9	D.Carr	OAK	10
9	M.Cassel	DAL	10
9	A.Dalton	CIN	10

Top 10 Tipped at the Line, Defenders

Rk	Player	Team	Total
1	J.J.Watt	HOU	8
2	J.Clowney	HOU	6
2	M.Jackson	DEN	6
2	J.Pierre-Paul	NYG	6
5	C.Avril	SEA	5
5	C.Barwin	PHI	5
5	C.Jordan	NO	5
5	R.Ninkovich	NE	5
5	N.Suh	MIA	5
10	7 tied with		4

2015 Quarterbacks with and without Pass Pressure

Rank	Player	Team	Plays	Pct Pressure	DVOA with Pressure	Yds with Pressure	DVOA w/o Pressure	Yds w/o Pressure	DVOA Dif	Rank
1	A.Dalton	CIN	439	18.5%	-51.4%	2.9	78.6%	8.7	-129.9%	30
2	B.Roethlisberger	PIT	507	18.9%	-41.0%	5.4	61.0%	8.8	-102.0%	13
3	R.Mallett	2TM	254	19.3%	-115.7%	1.7	31.9%	6.1	-147.6%	33
4	S.Bradford	PHI	580	19.8%	-81.5%	3.4	27.3%	7.2	-108.8%	17
5	K.Cousins	WAS	580	20.5%	-110.1%	2.2	69.0%	8.4	-179.1%	36
6	D.Carr	OAK	628	20.5%	-65.2%	3.4	47.7%	7.2	-112.8%	18
7	B.Hoyer	HOU	399	20.8%	-144.9%	0.4	45.0%	7.7	-190.0%	37
8	M.Hasselbeck	IND	284	21.1%	-105.0%	1.7	18.2%	7.0	-123.2%	27
9	D.Brees	NO	661	21.6%	-57.2%	2.7	51.1%	8.3	-108.2%	16
10	M.Stafford	DET	668	21.7%	-79.0%	2.1	48.1%	7.5	-127.1%	28
11	R.Fitzpatrick	NYJ	617	22.0%	-28.3%	4.3	39.9%	7.4	-68.3%	2
12	J.Flacco	BAL	429	22.8%	-66.0%	2.7	29.2%	7.4	-95.2%	7
13	E.Manning	NYG	665	23.5%	-77.5%	2.6	38.9%	8.0	-116.4%	22
14	M.Ryan	ATL	663	24.3%	-67.6%	3.5	32.8%	7.9	-100.4%	10
15	P.Manning	DEN	350	24.3%	-74.0%	3.9	5.5%	7.0	-79.4%	4
16	P.Rivers	SD	719	24.5%	-73.9%	3.1	54.7%	7.5	-128.6%	29
17	A.Smith	KC	574	25.1%	-90.8%	2.5	59.6%	7.9	-150.4%	34
18	M.Cassel	2TM	232	25.4%	-90.1%	3.3	11.3%	6.4	-101.4%	11
19	T.Brady	NE	678	25.7%	-38.5%	4.1	60.1%	8.1	-98.6%	8
20	M.Mariota	TEN	431	25.8%	-107.4%	3.5	49.2%	7.7	-156.6%	35
21	C.Newton	CAR	558	26.0%	-55.9%	2.8	59.4%	8.3	-115.3%	19
22	B.Bortles	JAC	689	27.4%	-45.6%	4.2	34.1%	7.4	-79.7%	5
23	B.Gabbert	SF	333	27.9%	-63.7%	3.3	40.7%	7.4	-104.4%	15
24	C.Palmer	ARI	580	28.1%	-22.5%	4.9	76.9%	9.6	-99.4%	9
25	R.Tannehill	MIA	643	28.1%	-80.1%	3.2	35.7%	7.4	-115.8%	20
26	N.Foles	STL	357	28.3%	-109.5%	1.4	11.5%	7.6	-121.0%	26
27	A.Luck	IND	332	28.6%	-95.7%	3.1	48.4%	7.2	-144.1%	32
28	T.Taylor	BUF	470	29.1%	-43.6%	4.6	58.0%	8.0	-101.6%	12
29	J.Winston	TB	601	29.3%	-47.0%	3.2	44.0%	8.6	-91.1%	6
30	J.Cutler	CHI	534	29.8%	-4.3%	6.3	40.8%	7.5	-45.0%	1
31	A.Rodgers	GB	673	30.2%	-64.1%	3.6	54.3%	7.4	-118.4%	24
32	B.Osweiler	DEN	313	31.0%	-69.8%	2.9	46.5%	7.6	-116.3%	21
33	J.McCown	CLE	328	31.1%	-37.0%	4.2	31.4%	7.2	-68.4%	3
34	R.Wilson	SEA	584	31.7%	-32.4%	4.3	86.4%	8.5	-118.9%	25
35	C.Kaepernick	SF	297	32.7%	-106.3%	0.8	35.9%	7.8	-142.2%	31
36	J.Manziel	CLE	268	35.4%	-66.2%	3.4	36.9%	7.0	-103.1%	14
37	T.Bridgewater	MIN	525	36.0%	-62.9%	3.2	53.8%	7.8	-116.7%	23

Includes scrambles and Defensive Pass Interference. Does not include aborted snaps. Minimum: 200 passes.

Top 20 Players, Passes Dropped

Rk	Player	Team	Total
1	A.Cooper	OAK	10
1	M.Evans	TB	10
3	D.Thomas	DEN	9
4	D.Freeman	ATL	8
4	B.Marshall	NYJ	8
6	E.Ebron	DET	7
6	T.Ginn	CAR	7
6	J.Jones	ATL	7
6	N.Washington	HOU	7
10	D.Adams	GB	6
10	D.Bryant	DAL	6
10	M.Bryant	PIT	6
10	R.Cobb	GB	6
10	M.Crabtree	OAK	6
10	J.Edelman	NE	6
10	L.Hankerson	ATL	6
10	B.LaFell	NE	6
10	J.Landry	MIA	6
10	E.Sanders	DEN	6
20	19 tied with		5

Top 20 Players, Pct. Passes Dropped

Rk	Player	Team	Drops	Passes	Pct
1	B.Sankey	TEN	5	23	21.7%
2	L.Hankerson	3TM	6	46	13.0%
3	K.Mumphery	HOU	4	32	12.5%
4	Q.Enunwa	NYJ	5	46	10.9%
4	V.McDonald	SF	5	46	10.9%
6	E.Ebron	DET	7	70	10.0%
7	J.Langford	CHI	4	42	9.5%
8	D.Murray	PHI	5	55	9.1%
9	C.Hogan	BUF	5	59	8.5%
10	D.Bryant	DAL	6	72	8.3%
10	T.Gabriel	CLE	4	48	8.3%
12	D.Freeman	ATL	8	97	8.2%
13	B.LaFell	NE	6	74	8.1%
14	A.Cooper	OAK	10	130	7.7%
15	N.Washington	TEN	7	94	7.4%
16	T.Ginn	CAR	7	96	7.3%
17	S.Roberts	OAK	4	55	7.3%
18	D.Harris	NYG	4	57	7.0%
19	M.Forte	CHI	4	58	6.9%
19	F.Gore	IND	4	58	6.9%

Min. four drops

Top 10 Teams, Pct Passes Dropped

Rk	Team	Passes	Drops	Pct
1	BAL	625	17	2.7%
2	PIT	567	16	2.8%
3	NO	643	19	3.0%
4	IND	575	17	3.0%
5	WAS	532	17	3.2%
6	ARI	525	17	3.2%
7	STL	441	16	3.6%
8	SEA	451	17	3.8%
9	KC	443	17	3.8%
10	SD	625	24	3.8%

Top 20 Intended Receivers on Interceptions

Rk	Player	Team	Total
1	B.Marshall	NYJ	9
2	A.Brown	PIT	8
2	D.Thomas	DEN	8
4	T.Y.Hilton	IND	6
4	A.Robinson	JAC	6
6	D.Bryant	DAL	5
6	R.Cooper	PHI	5
6	M.Evans	TB	5
6	M.Floyd	SD	5
6	P.Garcon	WAS	5
6	T.Ginn	CAR	5
6	J.Jones	GB	5
6	J.Witten	DAL	5
14	19 tied with		4

Bottom 10 Teams, Pct Passes Dropped

Rk	Team	Passes	Drops	Pct
23	CLE	571	27	4.7%
24	JAC	560	27	4.8%
25	NYG	594	29	4.9%
26	SF	501	25	5.0%
27	TEN	521	26	5.0%
28	NYJ	575	29	5.0%
29	HOU	589	30	5.1%
30	PHI	588	31	5.3%
31	OAK	575	31	5.4%
32	ATL	583	32	5.5%

Top 10 Plus/Minus for Running Backs

Rk	Player	Team	Pass	+/-
1	D.Johnson	CLE	70	+5.5
2	L.Bell	PIT	25	+3.4
3	T.Riddick	DET	95	+3.2
4	C.J.Spiller	NO	39	+3.0
5	L.Miller	MIA	53	+2.8
6	D.Freeman	ATL	91	+2.8
7	J.Allen	BAL	54	+2.3
8	A.Peterson	MIN	33	+2.1
9	M.Ingram	NO	58	+2.0
10	M.Gordon	SD	37	+1.9

Min. 25 passes; plus/minus adjusted for passes tipped/thrown away.

Bottom 10 Plus/Minus for Running Backs

Rk	Player	Team	Pass	+/-
1	J.Langford	CHI	41	-8.2
2	F.Gore	IND	48	-5.9
3	C.West	KC	31	-5.6
4	G.Bernard	CIN	65	-4.3
5	L.McCoy	BUF	45	-3.8
6	D.Johnson	ARI	53	-3.4
7	C.Polk	HOU	25	-3.1
8	E.Lacy	GB	27	-2.7
9	D.Sproles	PHI	72	-2.7
10	D.Lewis	NE	48	-2.3

Min. 25 passes; plus/minus adjusted for passes tipped/thrown away.

Top 10 Plus/Minus for Wide Receivers

Rk	Player	Team	Pass	+/-
1	A.Brown	PIT	186	+18.2
2	L.Fitzgerald	ARI	139	+14.7
3	D.Baldwin	SEA	97	+13.3
4	A.J.Green	CIN	123	+13.2
5	J.Jones	ATL	193	+10.6
6	J.Maclin	KC	121	+9.6
7	S.Watkins	BUF	91	+9.6
8	W.Snead	NO	94	+8.8
9	D.Amendola	NE	81	+8.2
10	T.Lockett	SEA	68	+8.1

Min. 50 passes; plus/minus adjusted for passes tipped/thrown away.

Bottom 10 Plus/Minus for Wide Receivers

Rk	Player	Team	Pass	+/-
1	B.LaFell	NE	71	-8.9
2	D.Bryant	DAL	65	-8.5
3	T.Y.Hilton	IND	129	-7.8
4	N.Washington	HOU	88	-7.4
5	D.Adams	GB	88	-7.1
6	H.Douglas	TEN	70	-6.7
7	M.Crabtree	OAK	143	-6.7
8	A.Cooper	OAK	121	-6.6
9	T.Ginn	CAR	90	-6.4
10	M.Evans	TB	143	-6.2

Min. 50 passes; plus/minus adjusted for passes tipped/thrown away.

Top 10 Plus/Minus for Tight Ends

Rk	Player	Team	Pass	+/-
1	D.Walker	TEN	127	+9.9
2	J.Reed	WAS	110	+9.6
3	J.Witten	DAL	99	+7.9
4	T.Eifert	CIN	66	+7.2
5	B.Celek	PHI	32	+6.5
6	K.Rudolph	MIN	64	+6.0
7	J.Tamme	ATL	78	+5.6
8	B.Watson	NO	104	+5.1
9	Z.Miller	CHI	42	+5.0
10	Z.Ertz	PHI	104	+4.9

Min. 25 passes; plus/minus adjusted for passes tipped/thrown away.

Bottom 10 Plus/Minus for Tight Ends

Rk	Player	Team	Pass	+/-
1	M.Lewis	JAC	33	-7.2
2	J.Cook	STL	68	-6.6
3	J.Hill	NO	30	-6.0
4	J.Cameron	MIA	63	-5.2
5	J.Thomas	JAC	75	-4.3
6	O.Daniels	DEN	71	-3.4
7	S.Chandler	NE	41	-3.1
8	Jenkins	TB	38	-2.9
9	E.Ebron	DET	68	-2.4
10	R.Griffin	HOU	33	-2.2

Min. 25 passes; plus/minus adjusted for passes tipped/thrown away.

Top 10 Quarterbacks, Yards Gained on Defensive Pass Interference

Rk	Player	Team	Pen	Yds
1	A.Rodgers	GB	14	364
2	B.Roethlisberger	PIT	14	297
3	C.Palmer	ARI	16	253
4	T.Brady	NE	10	233
5	E.Manning	NYG	13	192
6	J.Cutler	CHI	9	191
6	S.Bradford	PHI	11	176
8	D.Carr	OAK	8	165
9	J.Winston	TB	6	153
10	B.Bortles	JAC	8	145

Top 10 Receivers, Yards Gained on Defensive Pass Interference

Rk	Player	Team	Pen	Yds
1	A.Brown	PIT	7	196
2	J.Brown	ARI	5	136
3	M.Jones	CIN	5	122
4	M.Evans	TB	5	113
5	O.Beckham	NYG	6	109
6	M.Bennett	CHI	4	95
6	J.Jones	GB	3	93
8	A.Cooper	OAK	3	86
9	J.Cook	STL	2	81
10	D.Hopkins	HOU	5	77
10	K.Britt	STL	3	77

Top 10 Defenders, Yards Allowed on Defensive Pass Interference

Rk	Player	Team	Pen	Yds
1	J.Smith	BAL	4	112
2	T.Williams	CLE	3	107
3	M.Peters	KC	4	89
4	M.Butler	NE	5	88
5	K.Fuller	CHI	3	83
6	R.Alford	ATL	4	72
6	D.J.Hayden	OAK	4	72
6	X.Rhodes	MIN	4	72
9	J.Bademosi	CLE	3	71
10	R.Sherman	SEA	3	70

Top 20 First Downs/Touchdowns Allowed, Coverage

Rk	Player	Team	Grand Total
1	A.Blake	PIT	47
2	B.Grimes	MIA	38
3	D.House	JAC	36
3	B.Maxwell	PHI	36
3	M.Peters	KC	36
3	L.Ryan	NE	36
7	B.Breeland	WAS	35
8	M.Butler	NE	33
8	D.Kirkpatrick	CIN	33
10	T.Williams	CLE	31
11	S.Gilmore	BUF	30
11	G.Toler	IND	30
13	B.Browner	NO	29
13	C.Sensabaugh	TEN	29
13	B.Skrine	NYJ	29
16	B.Carr	DAL	28
16	R.Darby	BUF	28
18	D.Butler	IND	27
18	D.J.Hayden	OAK	27
18	J.Jenkins	STL	27
18	J.Powers	ARI	27
18	D.Randall	GB	27
18	X.Rhodes	MIN	27
18	J.Smith	BAL	27

Includes Defensive Pass Interference.

Top 20 Passing Yards Allowed, Coverage

Rk	Player	Team	Yards
1	A.Blake	PIT	814
2	M.Peters	KC	713
3	M.Butler	NE	710
4	B.Grimes	MIA	696
5	G.Toler	IND	666
6	L.Ryan	NE	655
7	B.Maxwell	PHI	640
8	B.Breeland	WAS	621
9	B.Browner	NO	614
9	T.Williams	CLE	614
11	D.House	JAC	575
12	D.Kirkpatrick	CIN	549
13	C.Sensabaugh	TEN	545
14	D.Randall	GB	543
15	A.Cromartie	NYJ	541
16	B.Carr	DAL	535
16	T.Newman	MIN	535
18	J.Powers	ARI	520
19	S.Gilmore	BUF	514
20	R.Cockrell	PIT	505

Includes Defensive Pass Interference.

Fewest Yards After Catch Allowed, Coverage by Cornerbacks

Rk	Player	Team	YAC
1	V.Davis	IND	1.5
2	D.Trufant	ATL	1.5
3	J.Norman	CAR	1.6
4	K.Jackson	HOU	1.7
5	J.Bethel	ARI	1.8
6	K.Johnson	HOU	1.8
7	S.Smith	KC	1.9
8	A.Jones	CIN	2.0
9	R.Darby	BUF	2.0
10	X.Rhodes	MIN	2.0
11	W.Gay	PIT	2.3
12	C.Sensabaugh	TEN	2.3
13	B.Roby	DEN	2.4
14	B.Grimes	MIA	2.5
15	D.Amerson	2TM	2.5
16	C.Tillman	CAR	2.6
17	P.Amukamara	NYG	2.6
18	D.Slay	DET	2.6
19	A.Talib	DEN	2.6
20	T.Porter	CHI	2.7

Min. 50 passes or 8 games started.

Most Yards After Catch Allowed, Coverage by Cornerbacks

Rk	Player	Team	YAC
1	R.Alford	ATL	6.4
2	B.Benwikere	CAR	6.1
3	A.Cromartie	NYJ	6.0
4	B.Browner	NO	5.9
5	M.Claiborne	DAL	5.8
6	D.Breaux	NO	5.7
7	B.Jones	DAL	5.6
8	N.Carroll	PHI	4.8
9	B.Flowers	SD	4.7
10	S.Moore	TB	4.7
11	D.Randall	GB	4.5
12	W.Blackmon	WAS	4.4
13	T.Johnson	STL	4.3
14	C.Munnerlyn	MIN	4.2
15	G.Toler	IND	4.2
16	D.Revis	NYJ	4.2
17	T.Brock	SF	4.2
18	B.Maxwell	PHI	4.2
19	J.Ward	SF	4.2
20	M.Butler	NE	4.1

Min. 50 passes or 8 games started.

Most Dropped Interceptions, 2015

Rk	Player	Team	Drops
1	D.Rodgers-Cromartie	NYG	4
2	K.Alexander	TB	3
2	M.Peters	KC	3
4	23 tied with		2

Most Dropped Interceptions, 2013-2015

Rk	Player	Team	Drops
1	M.Jenkins	NO/PHI	5
2	P.Cox	SF/TEN	5
3	D.House	GB/JAC	5
4	J.Haden	CLE	5
5	D.Smith	BAL	5
6	D.Rodgers-Cromartie	DEN/NYG	4
7	K.Wright	SEA	4
8	N.Bowman	SF	4
9	T.Williams	GB/CLE	4
10	K.Lewis	KC/HOU/BAL	4
11	A.Rolle	NYG/CHI	4
12	25 tied with		3

Fewest Avg Yards on Run Tackle, Defensive Line or Edge Rusher

Rk	Player	Team	Tkl	Avg
1	J.J.Watt	HOU	56	0.7
2	M.Bennett	SEA	36	0.8
3	T.Knighton	WAS	25	1.0
4	J.Sheard	NE	26	1.0
5	G.Atkins	CIN	29	1.1
6	B.Robison	MIN	27	1.1
7	T.Hali	KC	31	1.1
8	D.Shelby	MIA	31	1.1
9	R.Kerrigan	WAS	28	1.2
10	H.Anderson	IND	29	1.2
11	C.Avril	SEA	28	1.3
12	A.Donald	STL	54	1.3
13	C.Baker	WAS	42	1.4
14	W.Hayes	STL	37	1.4
15	O.Vernon	MIA	43	1.4
16	D.Harrison	NYJ	69	1.4
17	R.Miller	JAC	33	1.5
18	N.Suh	MIA	48	1.5
19	M.Neal	GB	27	1.5
20	M.Brockers	STL	37	1.5

Min. 25 run tackles

Fewest Avg Yards on Run Tackle, LB

Rk	Player	Team	Tkl	Avg
1	A.Klein	CAR	25	1.8
2	K.Minter	ARI	59	2.0
3	M.Smith	OAK	49	2.0
4	J.Mayo	NE	29	2.3
5	A.Ayers	STL	28	2.5
6	L.David	TB	72	2.5
7	S.Thompson	CAR	29	2.6
8	J.Jenkins	MIA	49	2.6
9	P.Posluszny	JAC	69	2.6
10	W.Compton	WAS	51	2.7
11	D.Skuta	JAC	30	2.7
12	B.Marshall	DEN	59	2.7
13	S.Tulloch	DET	64	2.7
14	W.Woodyard	TEN	62	2.7
15	J.Durant	ATL	31	2.7
16	C.Matthews	GB	36	2.8
17	D.Butler	SD	25	2.8
18	M.Lawson	BUF	30	2.8
19	J.Brinkley	NYG	44	2.8
20	V.Burfict	CIN	45	2.8

Min. 25 run tackles

Fewest Avg Yards on Run Tackle, DB

Rk	Player	Team	Tkl	Avg
1	P.Chung	NE	44	3.5
2	J.Ihedigbo	DET	33	3.9
3	A.Colvin	JAC	26	4.1
4	L.Ryan	NE	21	4.2
5	T.Newman	MIN	20	4.4
6	T.Jefferson	ARI	30	4.6
7	K.Vaccaro	NO	56	4.7
8	H.Smith	MIN	35	4.7
9	M.Jenkins	PHI	38	4.8
10	B.Church	DAL	63	4.9
11	K.Chancellor	SEA	38	4.9
12	R.Jones	MIA	79	5.0
13	M.Griffin	TEN	50	5.0
14	T.J.Ward	DEN	26	5.0
15	R.Harper	CAR	41	5.1
16	K.Jarrett	WAS	24	5.1
17	L.Collins	NYG	50	5.1
18	J.Taylor	MIA	21	5.2
19	K.Tandy	TB	21	5.4
20	C.Pryor	NYJ	32	5.5

Min. 20 run tackles

Top 20 Offensive Tackles, Blown Blocks

Rk	Player	Pos	Team	Sacks	All Pass	All Run	Total
1	D.Smith	LT	TB	4.0	18.0	7.0	25.0
2	E.Flowers	LT	NYG	3.0	21.0	1.0	22.0
3	M.Schofield	RT	DEN	7.0	15.0	4.0	19.0
4	G.Gilliam	RT	SEA	4.5	14.0	4.0	18.0
4	M.Kalil	LT	MIN	6.0	11.5	6.5	18.0
6	T.J.Clemmings	RT	MIN	4.5	12.0	5.0	17.0
7	D.Newton	RT	HOU	7.0	11.0	4.0	15.0
8	E.Fisher	LT	KC	3.0	11.5	3.0	14.5
8	J.Fox	RT	MIA	6.5	10.5	4.0	14.5
8	R.Harris	LT	DEN	2.0	10.5	4.0	14.5
8	J.Reid	RT	KC	2.0	11.5	3.0	14.5
8	J.Staley	LT	SF	3.0	11.5	3.0	14.5
13	C.Glenn	LT	BUF	4.0	9.0	5.0	14.0
13	R.Okung	LT	SEA	3.0	7.0	7.0	14.0
13	A.Villanueva	LT	PIT	6.0	11.0	3.0	14.0
16	K.Long	RT	CHI	6.5	11.5	2.0	13.5
16	D.Penn	LT	OAK	4.5	13.5	0.0	13.5
16	J.Peters	LT	PHI	4.5	9.5	4.0	13.5
19	D.Barclay	RT	GB	8.0	10.0	3.0	13.0
19	C.Hairston	LT	SD	6.0	7.0	6.0	13.0
19	L.Joeckel	LT	JAC	3.0	13.0	0.0	13.0
19	M.Oher	LT	CAR	6.0	10.0	3.0	13.0
19	J.Poutasi	RT	TEN	6.0	9.0	4.0	13.0

Top 20 Offensive Tackles in Snaps per Blown Block

Rk	Player	Pos	Team	Sacks	All Pass	All Run	Total	Snaps	Snaps per BB
1	J.Poutasi	RT	TEN	6.0	9.0	4.0	19.0	399	30.8
2	D.Barclay	RT	GB	8.0	10.0	3.0	21.0	423	32.5
3	J.Reid	RT	KC	2.0	11.5	3.0	16.5	608	41.9
4	D.Smith	LT	TB	4.0	18.0	7.0	29.0	1093	43.7
5	E.Flowers	LT	NYG	3.0	21.0	1.0	25.0	963	43.8
6	M.Schofield	RT	DEN	7.0	15.0	4.0	26.0	872	45.9
7	A.Villanueva	LT	PIT	6.0	11.0	3.0	20.0	753	53.8
8	M.Kalil	LT	MIN	6.0	11.5	6.5	24.0	1014	56.3
9	J.Peters	LT	PHI	4.5	9.5	4.0	18.0	761	56.4
10	E.Fisher	LT	KC	3.0	11.5	3.0	17.5	826	57.0
11	J.Fox	RT	MIA	6.5	10.5	4.0	21.0	829	57.2
12	D.Stephenson	LT	KC	1.0	8.5	1.0	10.5	555	58.4
12	L.Waddle	RT	2TM	2.0	7.0	0.0	9.0	409	58.4
14	G.Gilliam	RT	SEA	4.5	14.0	4.0	22.5	1059	58.8
15	T.J.Clemmings	RT	MIN	4.5	12.0	5.0	21.5	1016	59.8
16	C.Hairston	LT	SD	6.0	7.0	6.0	19.0	785	60.4
17	R.Okung	LT	SEA	3.0	7.0	7.0	17.0	851	60.8
18	J.Hurst	LT	BAL	1.5	9.0	0.0	10.5	572	63.6
19	S.Henderson	RT	BUF	1.0	7.0	2.0	10.0	593	65.9
20	L.Joeckel	LT	JAC	3.0	13.0	0.0	16.0	900	69.2

Minimum: 399 snaps

Top 20 Interior Linemen, Blown Blocks

Rk	Player	Pos	Team	Sacks	All Pass	All Run	Total
1	B.Fusco	LG	MIN	1.0	10.0	6.5	16.5
2	J.Miller	RG	BUF	3.0	14.0	2.0	16.0
3	M.Tobin	RG	PHI	4.5	12.5	3.0	15.5
4	D.Thomas	LG	MIA	5.0	14.0	1.0	15.0
4	S.Mason	LG	NE	2.0	12.0	3.0	15.0
4	J.Webb	RG	OAK	2.0	10.0	5.0	15.0
7	Z.Beadles	LG	JAC	3.0	8.0	6.0	14.0
7	J.Berger	C	MIN	4.0	8.0	6.0	14.0
9	L.Vasquez	RG	DEN	1.0	7.0	6.0	13.0
10	J.Britt	LG	SEA	1.0	5.5	7.0	12.5
10	C.Chester	RG	ATL	4.0	9.0	3.5	12.5
10	C.Wallace	C	PIT	3.0	8.0	4.5	12.5
13	R.Incognito	LG	BUF	2.0	7.0	5.0	12.0
13	L.Tomlinson	LG	DET	2.0	4.0	8.0	12.0
15	J.Kelce	C	PHI	0.0	2.0	9.5	11.5
15	M.Martin	C	SF	3.5	10.0	1.5	11.5
15	M.Slauson	LG/C	CHI	0.5	5.5	6.0	11.5
18	T.Barnes	C	STL	0.5	4.5	6.0	10.5
18	E.Mathis	LG	DEN	2.0	7.5	3.0	10.5
20	B.Brooks	RG	HOU	1.0	5.0	5.0	10.0
20	V.Ducasse	G	CHI	2.0	5.0	5.0	10.0
20	C.Erving	C	CLE	4.5	7.0	3.0	10.0
20	L.Mankins	LG	TB	0.0	4.0	6.0	10.0

Top 20 Interior Linemen in Snaps per Blown Block

Rk	Player	Pos	Team	Sacks	All Pass	All Run	Total	Snaps	Snaps per BB
1	J.Miller	RG	BUF	3.0	14.0	2.0	19.0	647	40.4
2	C.Erving	C	CLE	4.5	7.0	3.0	14.5	425	42.5
3	S.Mason	LG	NE	2.0	12.0	3.0	17.0	737	49.1
4	B.Stork	C	NE	3.0	7.0	1.0	11.0	491	61.4
5	B.Fusco	LG	MIN	1.0	10.0	6.5	17.5	1021	61.9
6	M.Tobin	RG	PHI	4.5	12.5	3.0	20.0	982	63.4
7	J.Brown	LG/RG	STL	2.0	3.0	5.0	10.0	533	66.6
8	L.Vasquez	RG	DEN	1.0	7.0	6.0	14.0	878	67.5
9	D.Thomas	LG	MIA	5.0	14.0	1.0	20.0	1032	68.8
10	J.Webb	RG	OAK	2.0	10.0	5.0	17.0	1056	70.4
11	M.Martin	C	SF	3.5	10.0	1.5	15.0	822	71.5
12	J.Berger	C	MIN	4.0	8.0	6.0	18.0	1022	73.0
13	V.Ducasse	LG/RG	CHI	2.0	5.0	5.0	12.0	752	75.2
14	Z.Beadles	LG	JAC	3.0	8.0	6.0	17.0	1058	75.6
15	E.Mathis	LG	DEN	2.0	7.5	3.0	12.5	809	77.0
16	J.Looney	C/LG	TEN	3.0	3.5	2.0	8.5	425	77.3
17	A.Peat	LG/LT	NO	3.0	4.0	1.5	8.5	426	77.5
18	M.Garcia	C	DEN	0.0	5.0	2.0	7.0	543	77.6
19	L.Tomlinson	LG	DET	2.0	4.0	8.0	14.0	986	82.2
20	A.Gallik	C	TEN	3.0	5.0	1.0	9.0	505	84.2

Minimum: 400 snaps

Top 20 Non-Offensive Linemen, Blown Blocks

Rk	Player	Pos	Team	Sacks	All Pass	All Run	Total
1	D.Fells	TE	ARI	0.0	1.0	7.5	8.5
2	G.Barnidge	TE	CLE	1.5	2.0	4.0	6.0
2	T.Kelce	TE	KC	0.0	2.0	4.0	6.0
2	K.Rudolph	TE	MIN	1.0	2.0	4.0	6.0
5	D.Johnson	RB	CLE	3.5	5.5	0.0	5.5
5	L.Smith	TE	OAK	1.5	4.5	1.0	5.5
5	J.Tamme	TE	ATL	0.0	3.0	2.5	5.5
5	J.Witten	TE	DAL	1.0	3.0	2.5	5.5
9	B.Celek	TE	PHI	0.0	2.0	3.0	5.0
9	P.DiMarco	FB	ATL	1.0	2.0	3.0	5.0
9	T.Eifert	TE	CIN	2.0	2.0	3.0	5.0
9	C.Fiedorowicz	TE	HOU	0.0	1.0	4.0	5.0
9	D.Freeman	RB	ATL	1.0	5.0	0.0	5.0
9	Z.Line	FB	MIN	0.0	0.0	5.0	5.0
9	J.Reed	TE	WAS	0.0	0.0	5.0	5.0
9	L.Stocker	TE	TB	0.0	0.0	5.0	5.0
9	W.Tye	TE	NYG	1.0	1.0	4.0	5.0
18	T.Bohanon	FB	NYJ	0.0	0.0	4.5	4.5
19	12 tied with						4.0

Most Penalties, Offense

Rk	Player	Team	Pen	Yds
1	G.Robinson	STL	16	114
2	G.Cherilus	TB	15	81
3	C.Wallace	PIT	13	110
3	D.Smith	TB	13	80
3	L.Johnson	PHI	13	75
3	M.Remmers	CAR	13	70
3	M.Moses	WAS	13	68
8	D.Fluker	SD	12	107
8	J.Reed	WAS	12	99
8	D.Bakhtiari	GB	12	79
11	M.Evans	TB	11	110
11	A.Levitre	ATL	11	95
11	E.Pears	SF	11	95
11	A.Smith	CIN	11	80
11	Z.Martin	DAL	11	60
11	J.Peters	PHI	11	33
17	J.Sweezy	SEA	10	100
17	R.Gronkowski	NE	10	69
17	Z.Strief	NO	10	65
17	E.Flowers	NYG	10	63
17	J.Fox	MIA	10	60
17	T.Lewan	TEN	10	59
17	T.Smith	DAL	10	56
17	M.Kalil	MIN	10	55

Includes declined and offsetting, but not special teams or penalties on turnover returns.

Most False Starts, Offense

Rk	Player	Team	Pen
1	D.Free	DAL	8
2	L.Johnson	PHI	7
2	M.Remmers	CAR	7
4	J.Barksdale	SD	6
5	D.Ferguson	NYJ	5
5	C.Hairston	SD	5
5	B.Jones	HOU	5
5	B.Marshall	NYJ	5
5	J.Peters	PHI	5
5	A.Smith	CIN	5
5	L.Smith	OAK	5
5	Z.Strief	NO	5
5	J.Thomas	CLE	5
5	J.Witten	DAL	5
15	15 tied with		4

Most Penalties, Defense

Rk	Player	Team	Pen	Yds	Rk	Player	Team	Pen	Yds
1	B.Browner	NO	22	192	12	V.Miller	DEN	9	81
2	N.Suh	MIA	15	61	12	M.Claiborne	DAL	9	78
3	D.Kirkpatrick	CIN	14	110	12	J.Howard	KC	9	75
4	X.Rhodes	MIN	12	96	12	D.House	JAC	9	42
4	J.Hughes	BUF	12	79	12	P.Peterson	ARI	9	35
6	O.Vernon	MIA	11	110	18	V.Davis	IND	8	83
6	D.Breaux	NO	11	73	18	J.J.Watt	HOU	8	79
8	D.J.Hayden	OAK	10	84	18	T.J.Carrie	OAK	8	78
8	A.Brooks	SF	10	73	18	N.Thorpe	OAK	8	72
8	B.Maxwell	PHI	10	60	18	D.Trufant	ATL	8	67
8	M.Bennett	SEA	10	46	18	E.Ansah	DET	8	61
12	M.Peters	KC	9	119	18	M.Ingram	SD	8	40

Includes declined and offsetting, but not special teams or penalties on turnover returns.

Top 10 Kickers, Gross Kickoff Value over Average

Rk	Player	Team	Kick Pts+	Net Pts+	Kicks
1	J.Tucker	BAL	+5.5	+4.5	72
2	P.McAfee	IND	+4.6	+4.8	73
3	S.Hauschka	SEA	+4.4	+1.2	87
4	J.Lambo	SD	+3.5	-2.5	70
5	J.Myers	JAC	+3.3	+2.4	78
6	S.Gostkowski	NE	+3.1	+8.2	94
7	G.Gano	CAR	+2.5	-4.7	101
8	S.Martin	DET	+2.3	-2.9	68
9	C.Santos	KC	+2.2	+0.6	85
10	D.Hopkins	WAS	+2.1	+4.4	74

Min. 20 kickoffs; squibs and onside not included

Bottom 10 Kickers, Gross Kickoff Value over Average

Rk	Player	Team	Kick Pts+	Net Pts+	Kicks
1	J.Brown	NYG	-5.7	-3.1	83
2	T.Coons	CLE	-4.5	+1.4	68
3	N.Novak	HOU	-3.6	+1.5	59
4	R.Gould	CHI	-3.2	-15.0	75
5	S.Janikowski	OAK	-2.6	-5.8	74
5	B.McManus	DEN	-2.6	+0.1	76
7	K.Forbath	2TM	-1.9	+0.7	52
8	D.Bailey	DAL	-1.5	-6.2	70
8	C.Catanzaro	ARI	-1.5	+0.4	96
10	N.Folk	NYJ	-1.1	+1.1	36

Min. 20 kickoffs; squibs and onside not included

Top 10 Punters, Gross Punt Value over Average

Rk	Player	Team	Punt Pts+	Net Pts+	Punts
1	J.Hekker	STL	+13.0	+10.4	96
2	B.Kern	TEN	+11.7	-6.7	88
3	P.McAfee	IND	+11.5	-0.1	85
4	D.Colquitt	KC	+9.1	+16.2	75
5	A.Lee	CLE	+6.4	-2.4	69
6	S.Koch	BAL	+5.2	+16.0	74
7	C.Jones	DAL	+5.0	+13.3	69
8	C.Schmidt	BUF	+4.8	+4.0	83
9	T.Way	WAS	+4.2	+4.8	71
10	M.King	OAK	+4.1	+14.0	84

Min. 20 punts

Bottom 10 Punters, Gross Punt Value over Average

Rk	Player	Team	Punt Pts+	Net Pts+	Punts
1	J.Locke	MIN	-12.5	+1.1	66
2	B.Pinion	SF	-10.2	-4.9	91
3	D.Butler	ARI	-9.4	-12.7	61
4	T.Masthay	GB	-8.4	+4.7	81
5	M.Scifres	SD	-8.0	-12.3	73
6	J.Schum	TB	-7.6	+1.1	56
7	B.Colquitt	DEN	-5.2	+5.5	84
8	D.Jones	PHI	-4.1	+1.0	88
9	R.Quigley	NYJ	-3.8	-15.7	76
10	S.Lechler	HOU	-3.5	-14.5	95

Min. 20 punts

Top 10 Kick Returners, Value over Average

Rk	Player	Team	Pts+	Returns
1	C.Patterson	MIN	+14.5	32
2	D.Harris	NYG	+7.8	22
3	T.Lockett	SEA	+6.9	32
4	B.Cunningham	STL	+4.5	25
5	J.Janis	GB	+4.0	14
6	D.Thompson	CHI	+3.7	14
6	R.Ross	WAS	+3.7	28
8	D.Johnson	ARI	+3.1	22
8	A.Abdullah	DET	+3.1	37
10	L.Whitehead	DAL	+1.9	16

Min. eight returns

Bottom 10 Kick Returners, Value over Average

Rk	Player	Team	Pts+	Returns
1	D.Williams	MIA	-7.1	21
2	J.Jones	2TM	-5.8	18
3	B.Sankey	TEN	-3.9	9
4	T.McBride	TEN	-3.7	10
5	K.Williams	ARI	-3.1	8
6	O.Bolden	DEN	-2.2	15
7	D.McCluster	TEN	-2.0	13
8	K.Mumphery	HOU	-1.9	14
9	G.Whalen	IND	-1.9	9
10	M.Thigpen	BUF	-1.2	16

Min. eight returns

Top 10 Punt Returners, Value over Average

Rk	Player	Team	Pts+	Returns
1	D.Sproles	PHI	+11.6	38
2	R.Greene	JAC	+11.1	18
3	T.Benjamin	CLE	+8.6	28
4	T.Lockett	SEA	+7.3	40
5	J.Landry	MIA	+6.1	35
6	K.Clay	BAL	+5.4	23
7	D.Amendola	NE	+4.7	23
8	M.Sherels	MIN	+4.0	34
9	E.Weems	ATL	+3.7	19
10	D.Harris	NYG	+3.5	34

Min. eight returns

Bottom 10 Punt Returners, Value over Average

Rk	Player	Team	Pts+	Returns
1	J.Jones	2TM	-4.7	11
2	K.Mumphery	HOU	-4.5	36
3	M.Thigpen	2TM	-4.4	19
4	B.Rainey	TB	-4.3	29
5	L.Whitehead	DAL	-4.0	19
6	E.Sanders	DEN	-3.9	17
7	P.Peterson	ARI	-3.4	32
7	M.Hyde	GB	-3.4	27
9	J.Crowder	WAS	-3.3	30
10	H.Douglas	TEN	-2.9	11

Min. eight returns

Top 20 Special Teams Plays

Rk	Player	Team	Plays	Rk	Player	Team	Plays
1	B.Peters	HOU	17	11	J.Bethel	ARI	13
2	J.Bademosi	CLE	16	11	N.Dzubnar	SD	13
2	C.Peerman	CIN	16	11	M.Herzlich	NYG	13
2	M.Slater	NE	16	14	T.Burton	PHI	12
5	N.Bellore	SF	15	14	N.Ebner	NE	12
5	D.Carey	DET	15	14	E.Henderson	NYJ	12
5	C.Dahl	NYG	15	14	J.Janis	GB	12
5	S.Paysinger	MIA	15	14	B.King	NE	12
9	M.Bullough	HOU	14	14	T.Reilly	NYJ	12
9	M.Thomas	MIA	14	20	7 tied with		11

lays = tackles + assists; does not include onside or end-half squib kicks.

Top 10 Offenses, 3-and-out per drive

Rk	Team	Pct
1	ARI	14.9%
2	TB	15.3%
3	MIN	15.7%
4	ATL	16.9%
5	PIT	17.1%
6	SEA	18.8%
7	SD	18.9%
8	NO	19.0%
9	NE	20.3%
10	BAL	20.5%

Top 10 Defenses, 3-and-out per drive

Rk	Team	Pct
1	NE	31.5%
2	NYJ	29.9%
3	HOU	27.5%
4	SEA	27.1%
5	DEN	26.2%
6	TEN	25.1%
7	CHI	24.7%
8	CIN	24.3%
9	SD	24.0%
10	PHI	23.7%

Top 10 Offenses, Yards per drive

Rk	Team	Yds/Dr
1	ARI	38.62
2	NO	37.09
3	PIT	35.75
4	ATL	35.36
5	TB	34.56
6	SEA	34.16
7	NYG	33.91
8	SD	33.21
9	NE	33.10
10	CIN	32.64

Top 10 Defenses, Yards per drive

Rk	Team	Yds/Dr
1	DEN	24.47
2	HOU	25.29
3	CAR	26.54
4	NYJ	26.91
5	ARI	27.62
6	SEA	28.45
7	NE	28.96
8	KC	29.71
9	CIN	29.94
10	TEN	30.27

Bottom 10 Offenses, 3-and-out per drive

Rk	Team	Pct
23	WAS	25.3%
24	IND	25.7%
25	OAK	25.9%
26	JAC	26.1%
27	HOU	26.2%
28	NYJ	26.4%
29	STL	27.0%
30	DEN	27.6%
31	TEN	27.9%
31	BUF	27.9%

Bottom 10 Defenses, 3-and-out per drive

Rk	Team	Pct
23	JAC	20.7%
24	NO	20.5%
25	ARI	20.3%
25	PIT	20.3%
27	CLE	19.7%
28	ATL	19.3%
29	NYG	19.1%
30	WAS	18.4%
31	SF	18.2%
32	TB	17.1%

Bottom 10 Offenses, Yards per drive

Rk	Team	Yds/Dr
23	PHI	29.86
24	DEN	29.84
25	JAC	29.43
26	OAK	28.86
27	HOU	28.53
28	MIA	28.47
29	IND	28.01
30	SF	27.12
31	TEN	26.37
32	STL	25.51

Bottom 10 Defenses, Yards per drive

Rk	Team	Yds/Dr
23	JAC	32.83
24	MIA	32.88
25	WAS	33.18
26	SD	33.19
27	TB	33.28
28	ATL	33.95
29	SF	34.51
30	CLE	35.72
31	NYG	36.30
32	NO	38.62

Top 10 Offenses, avg LOS to start drive

Rk	Team	LOS
1	KC	31.2
2	CAR	30.5
3	NE	30.4
4	CIN	30.0
5	MIN	29.9
6	CHI	29.5
7	OAK	29.4
8	NYJ	29.1
9	SEA	28.9
10	GB	28.1

Top 10 Defenses, avg LOS to start drive

Rk	Team	LOS
1	SEA	23.6
2	NE	23.7
3	KC	24.4
4	CIN	24.6
5	MIN	25.1
6	NYG	25.4
7	CHI	26.4
8	STL	26.5
9	GB	26.6
9	ATL	26.6

Top 10 Offenses, Points per drive

Rk	Team	Pts/Dr
1	CAR	2.57
2	ARI	2.52
3	NE	2.47
4	CIN	2.40
5	SEA	2.32
6	NO	2.24
7	PIT	2.20
8	NYG	2.07
9	KC	2.05
10	BUF	2.03

Top 10 Defenses, Points per drive

Rk	Team	Pts/Dr
1	DEN	1.43
2	CAR	1.46
3	CIN	1.47
4	SEA	1.50
4	NYJ	1.50
6	HOU	1.54
7	KC	1.55
8	STL	1.57
9	NE	1.59
10	GB	1.67

Bottom 10 Offenses, avg LOS to start drive

Rk	Team	LOS
23	TB	26.2
24	ATL	26.1
25	PHI	26.0
26	DEN	25.5
26	MIA	25.5
26	DET	25.5
29	HOU	25.3
30	DAL	24.4
31	SF	23.8
32	SD	22.9

Bottom 10 Defenses, avg LOS to start drive

Rk	Team	LOS
23	JAC	28.2
24	PIT	28.6
24	TEN	28.6
26	SF	28.8
27	CLE	28.9
28	HOU	29.3
29	DEN	29.5
30	DET	29.6
31	TB	29.9
32	SD	31.0

Bottom 10 Offenses, Points per drive

Rk	Team	Pts/Dr
23	HOU	1.65
24	DEN	1.64
25	BAL	1.63
26	IND	1.60
27	DAL	1.56
28	MIA	1.54
29	TEN	1.51
30	CLE	1.49
31	STL	1.33
32	SF	1.32

Bottom 10 Defenses, Points per drive

Rk	Team	Pts/Dr
23	PHI	2.08
24	SD	2.11
24	SF	2.11
26	JAC	2.16
27	TEN	2.19
28	DET	2.24
29	NYG	2.27
30	CLE	2.34
31	TB	2.36
32	NO	2.64

Top 10 Offenses, Better DVOA with Shotgun

Rk	Team	% Plays Shotgun	DVOA Shot	DVOA Not	Yd/Play Shot	Yd/Play Not	DVOA Dif
1	SD	88%	7.1%	-37.0%	5.8	3.3	44.1%
1	CAR	72%	24.3%	-19.8%	6.6	3.5	44.1%
3	BUF	78%	19.1%	-17.4%	6.1	4.9	36.5%
4	CIN	63%	30.4%	1.6%	6.4	4.9	28.7%
5	CHI	74%	14.9%	-12.1%	6.0	4.1	27.0%
6	NO	54%	24.3%	-2.7%	7.1	4.7	26.9%
7	SEA	63%	28.2%	4.5%	6.5	5.0	23.7%
8	JAC	61%	4.1%	-18.2%	6.0	5.1	22.3%
9	PIT	67%	25.5%	3.4%	7.1	5.7	22.0%
10	NE	58%	25.4%	4.6%	6.6	5.1	20.9%

Top 10 Offenses, Better DVOA with Play-Action

Rk	Team	% PA	DVOA PA	DVOA No PA	Yd/Play PA	Yd/Play No PA	DVOA Dif
1	STL	24%	33.8%	-28.4%	9.0	5.0	62.2%
2	BUF	17%	72.3%	13.6%	9.9	6.2	58.7%
3	TB	19%	49.2%	8.5%	9.2	6.5	40.6%
4	MIA	19%	35.1%	-5.0%	8.6	5.7	40.1%
5	IND	16%	27.1%	-9.1%	8.0	5.3	36.2%
6	ARI	17%	70.7%	35.8%	10.5	7.6	34.9%
7	WAS	19%	58.6%	25.0%	10.3	6.4	33.6%
8	DAL	15%	13.7%	-16.8%	7.4	6.1	30.5%
9	ATL	22%	30.3%	0.8%	8.8	6.2	29.5%
10	MIN	27%	29.0%	3.0%	7.4	5.6	25.9%

Bottom 10 Offenses, Better DVOA with Shotgun

Rk	Team	% Plays Shotgun	DVOA Shot	DVOA Not	Yd/Play Shot	Yd/Play Not	DVOA Dif
23	DAL	54%	-15.5%	-0.2%	6.1	5.1	-0.2%
24	MIA	77%	-7.1%	-0.3%	5.4	6.1	-0.3%
25	TB	44%	-0.7%	-0.9%	6.2	6.0	-0.9%
26	DEN	65%	-6.9%	-3.0%	5.8	4.9	-3.0%
27	TEN	59%	-12.6%	-5.8%	5.7	4.4	-5.8%
28	BAL	47%	-2.7%	-6.0%	5.5	5.1	-6.0%
29	ATL	49%	-2.6%	-10.5%	5.8	5.6	-10.5%
30	PHI	94%	0.3%	-11.1%	5.5	4.7	-11.1%
31	MIN	45%	4.8%	-11.8%	5.3	5.6	-11.8%
32	STL	42%	-3.0%	-32.7%	4.9	5.7	-32.7%

Bottom 10 Offenses, Better DVOA with Play-Action

Rk	Team	% PA	DVOA PA	DVOA No PA	Yd/Play PA	Yd/Play No PA	DVOA Dif
23	NYJ	16%	25.9%	26.6%	7.1	6.6	-0.7%
24	BAL	24%	5.0%	7.2%	6.7	6.0	-2.2%
25	CIN	20%	46.5%	51.4%	7.9	7.1	-4.9%
26	CHI	17%	18.5%	24.8%	7.7	6.7	-6.3%
27	KC	20%	15.6%	25.6%	6.1	6.6	-9.9%
28	NO	18%	15.4%	33.6%	6.2	7.3	-18.2%
29	CAR	27%	8.8%	37.1%	6.4	7.1	-28.3%
30	SEA	24%	25.4%	56.0%	5.7	7.6	-30.6%
31	PIT	14%	3.6%	39.0%	8.3	7.7	-35.4%
32	GB	16%	-10.8%	26.6%	5.2	6.4	-37.3%

Top 10 Defenses, Better DVOA vs. Shotgun

Rk	Team	% Plays Shotgun	DVOA Shot	DVOA Not	Yd/Play Shot	Yd/Play Not	DVOA Dif
1	HOU	64%	-15.7%	0.8%	5.0	5.5	-16.5%
2	STL	56%	-16.9%	-3.1%	5.6	5.5	-13.8%
3	ARI	63%	-18.7%	-11.2%	5.7	4.7	-7.5%
4	DET	72%	-0.6%	6.6%	5.7	6.1	-7.3%
5	PHI	60%	1.1%	5.6%	5.9	5.6	-4.5%
6	GB	69%	-8.4%	-5.1%	5.8	5.1	-3.3%
7	CHI	55%	11.7%	11.0%	5.8	5.9	0.7%
8	KC	74%	-9.8%	-15.7%	5.4	4.7	5.9%
9	CAR	68%	-15.9%	-22.8%	5.3	4.3	6.9%
10	NE	70%	-1.0%	-8.0%	5.6	4.9	7.1%

Top 10 Defenses, Better DVOA vs. Play-Action

Rk	Team	% PA	DVOA PA	DVOA No PA	Yd/Play PA	Yd/Play No PA	DVOA Dif
1	BUF	20%	-9.6%	20.4%	6.0	6.7	-30.0%
2	OAK	19%	-10.7%	12.2%	7.1	6.2	-22.9%
3	KC	16%	-23.2%	-3.7%	5.5	5.9	-19.5%
4	DEN	25%	-38.9%	-22.1%	5.2	5.5	-16.8%
5	NYG	20%	13.9%	26.6%	8.4	7.0	-12.6%
6	JAC	20%	18.8%	31.0%	7.2	7.0	-12.2%
7	STL	23%	-10.7%	-1.3%	6.5	6.5	-9.4%
8	CLE	19%	20.9%	25.4%	7.0	8.0	-4.5%
9	MIN	23%	2.6%	6.7%	7.4	6.1	-4.0%
10	BAL	23%	22.3%	20.5%	8.3	6.2	1.8%

Bottom 10 Defenses, Better DVOA vs. Shotgun

Rk	Team	% Plays Shotgun	DVOA Shot	DVOA Not	Yd/Play Shot	Yd/Play Not	DVOA Dif
23	WAS	71%	12.1%	-6.0%	6.3	5.7	18.1%
24	TEN	65%	15.9%	-2.5%	6.2	4.9	18.5%
25	CLE	72%	19.6%	0.1%	7.3	5.1	19.5%
25	MIN	69%	5.1%	-14.4%	5.9	4.8	19.5%
27	ATL	68%	16.1%	-4.1%	6.5	4.9	20.2%
28	BAL	71%	13.3%	-7.2%	5.9	5.1	20.4%
29	TB	78%	13.5%	-8.1%	6.0	4.6	21.6%
30	JAC	74%	21.0%	-3.7%	6.4	4.8	24.7%
31	OAK	78%	9.0%	-16.6%	6.0	4.7	25.7%
32	NO	71%	37.2%	11.4%	6.9	6.6	25.9%

Bottom 10 Defenses, Better DVOA vs. Play-Action

Rk	Team	% PA	DVOA PA	DVOA No PA	Yd/Play PA	Yd/Play No PA	DVOA Dif
23	ATL	20%	34.1%	13.5%	8.0	6.7	20.6%
24	PIT	17%	24.2%	3.0%	8.2	6.2	21.2%
25	WAS	22%	32.6%	10.3%	9.4	6.2	22.3%
26	ARI	20%	14.3%	-14.0%	7.1	6.0	28.4%
27	DAL	22%	32.1%	3.3%	7.3	6.8	28.9%
28	CHI	21%	45.3%	12.5%	9.6	6.2	32.8%
29	SF	24%	54.2%	14.3%	9.7	6.4	39.8%
30	GB	17%	27.5%	-12.6%	7.8	6.0	40.1%
31	TEN	22%	60.1%	7.2%	8.6	6.3	52.9%
32	HOU	17%	54.9%	-19.2%	9.0	5.0	74.2%

2015 Defenses with and without Pass Pressure

Rank	Team	Plays	Pct Pressure	DVOA with Pressure	Yds with Pressure	DVOA w/o Pressure	Yds w/o Pressure	DVOA Dif	Rank
1	DEN	655	32.7%	-104.1%	2.8	12.6%	6.8	-116.7%	7
2	SEA	614	29.3%	-68.8%	3.4	17.1%	7.0	-86.0%	24
3	ARI	638	29.3%	-79.7%	3.9	19.8%	7.2	-99.5%	19
4	STL	674	28.3%	-76.9%	2.6	25.9%	8.0	-102.8%	15
5	KC	694	28.1%	-82.6%	2.8	21.6%	7.0	-104.2%	14
6	NYJ	674	28.0%	-82.7%	2.7	29.5%	7.3	-112.2%	11
7	MIN	633	28.0%	-63.3%	3.4	32.3%	7.5	-95.6%	22
8	HOU	619	27.0%	-68.6%	2.7	18.0%	6.8	-86.6%	23
9	CIN	713	26.6%	-73.1%	2.8	25.0%	6.8	-98.1%	20
10	GB	630	26.5%	-93.4%	2.4	27.6%	7.7	-121.0%	5
11	IND	646	26.5%	-54.3%	3.7	29.0%	8.0	-83.3%	25
12	CAR	726	26.3%	-114.4%	1.8	20.6%	6.9	-135.0%	4
13	NYG	684	25.9%	-34.9%	4.2	43.5%	8.4	-78.4%	27
14	SF	607	25.7%	-29.4%	4.9	43.1%	8.0	-72.6%	29
15	MIA	594	25.3%	-78.7%	3.4	61.6%	8.4	-140.3%	2
16	SD	567	25.2%	-88.7%	2.9	52.8%	8.5	-141.4%	1
17	TEN	567	25.2%	-68.4%	3.0	47.6%	8.1	-116.0%	8
18	DET	602	24.9%	-65.5%	4.2	43.3%	7.8	-108.8%	13
19	PHI	696	24.9%	-99.0%	2.3	39.2%	7.9	-138.3%	3
20	CHI	587	24.7%	-56.5%	3.8	44.1%	7.9	-100.6%	17
21	NE	677	24.7%	-67.6%	3.1	31.9%	7.2	-99.5%	18
22	DAL	564	24.6%	-75.8%	2.7	37.9%	8.3	-113.6%	9
23	TB	591	24.4%	-64.3%	2.8	47.0%	8.0	-111.3%	12
24	PIT	694	24.2%	-69.8%	2.5	31.1%	7.9	-101.0%	16
25	OAK	715	24.1%	-41.4%	4.5	23.6%	6.9	-65.0%	32
26	BAL	623	23.9%	-53.7%	3.7	43.7%	7.5	-97.4%	21
27	CLE	567	23.6%	-35.0%	4.6	43.7%	8.7	-78.7%	26
28	WAS	628	22.6%	-76.4%	1.8	44.0%	8.4	-120.4%	6
29	BUF	650	21.8%	-36.4%	5.0	29.8%	7.0	-66.2%	31
30	JAC	664	21.7%	-27.4%	4.8	43.2%	7.6	-70.6%	30
31	ATL	610	21.5%	-42.7%	4.7	35.1%	7.6	-77.7%	28
32	NO	606	21.3%	-40.5%	2.9	72.8%	9.3	-113.2%	10
NFL AVERAGE			25.6%	-67.3%	3.3	35.5%	7.7	-102.7%	

Includes scrambles and Defensive Pass Interference. Does not include aborted snaps.

Author Bios

Editor-in-Chief and NFL Statistician

Aaron Schatz is the creator of FootballOutsiders.com and the proprietary NFL statistics within *Football Outsiders Almanac*, including DVOA, DYAR, adjusted line yards, and the KUBIAK fantasy football projections. He writes regularly for ESPN Insider and *ESPN The Magazine*, and he has done custom research for a number of NFL teams. *The New York Times Magazine* has referred to him as "the Bill James of football." He has a B.A. in Economics from Brown University and lives in Framingham, Massachusetts. He promises that someday Bill Belichick will retire, the Patriots will be awful, and he will write very mean and nasty things about them.

Layout and Design

Vincent Verhei has been a writer and editor for Football Outsiders since 2007. In addition to writing for *Football Outsiders Almanac 2016*, he did all layout and design on the book. During the season, he writes the "Quick Reads" column covering the best and worst players of each week according to Football Outsiders metrics. His writings have also appeared in *ESPN The Magazine* and in Maple Street Press publications, and he has done layout on a number of other books for Football Outsiders and Prospectus Entertainment Ventures. His other night job is as a writer and podcast host for pro wrestling/MMA website Figurefouronline.com. He is a graduate of Western Washington University.

College Football Statisticians

Bill Connelly has contributed college football play-by-play stats to Football Outsiders for nearly a decade. He's also the College Sports Editor and Analytics Director for SB Nation, where he runs the college football blog Football Study Hall. His first book, *Study Hall: College Football, Its Stats and Its Stories*, was published in July 2013. He grew up a numbers and sports nerd in western Oklahoma, but now lives in Missouri with his wife, pets, and young daughter.

Brian Fremeau joined Football Outsiders in 2006 and is a regular contributor to ESPN Insider and *Blue & Gold Illustrated*. He spends every home football Saturday cheering for his beloved Fighting Irish in the south end zone of Notre Dame Stadium. He lives in South Bend, Indiana with his wife and two daughters, each of whom prefers HGTV over college football.

Contributors

Ian Boyd is a history major graduate from the University of Texas, now based in southeast Michigan, who loves studying the trends and stories of college football. You can also find his work at SB Nation's Football Study Hall and Inside Texas websites.

It was a single moment that brought **Cian Fahey** to the NFL when he was 12 years old. Like many fans, it came at the behest of a family member. Unlike most fans, it came at 1 a.m. on Christmas Eve in Ireland. His uncle Dex had implored him to watch on as Brett Favre threw one of his many game-winning touchdown passes. The excitement of that moment began a journey that would stretch over the next decade and more. Cian owes his career to his grandfather, Eddie Brennan, who constantly inspires and pushes every member of his family towards their goals.

Tom Gower joined the FO writing staff in 2009 after serving three seasons as a game charter. He writes a weekly Sunday Night Football preview column for NBC Sports and his work has also appeared on ESPN.com and *ESPN The Magazine*. He has degrees from Georgetown University and the University of Chicago, whose football programs have combined for an Orange Bowl appearance and seven Big Ten Titles but are still trying to find success after Pearl Harbor. When not writing about football, he practices law in the Chicago area.

Scott Kacsmar has covered the NFL as a full-time analyst since 2011. He joined Football Outsiders as an Assistant Editor in 2013. Some of his unique contributions include the first standardized database of fourth-quarter comebacks and game-winning drives, quantifying catch radius, and ALEX. He will not stop writing about the value of drive stats and the dominance of the quarterback sneak, and he continues to help the NFL fix the most mundane of statistical errors, such as Tony Graziani's 1998 rushing totals. (*Yes, they were fixed just this summer*). His work has appeared on SI.com, Bleacher Report, ESPN Insider and NFL Network. Scott lives near Pittsburgh and has an Industrial Engineering degree from the University of Pittsburgh.

Rivers McCown is a freelance writer whose work has appeared at ESPN.com, Bleacher Report, *USA Today*, and Deadspin, among other places. He lives in Houston, Texas, and hopes to one day root for a team that has an actual quarterback.

Chad Peltier was raised to be an Ohio State fan, but four years of "Run the damn ball, Bobo!" at the University of Georgia and living in Athens have made him a Bulldawgs fan as well. In addition to writing two columns on college football at Football Outsiders, Chad also contributes to the SB Nation blogs Land Grant Holy Land and Football Study Hall. He currently lives in New Haven, Connecticut, working in aerospace and defense, but misses SEC country.

This is **Mike Tanier**'s 12th *Football Outsiders Almanac* or *Almanac*-like publication. He has been with FO since the days of individual kicker comments and publisher-mandated May deadlines, since before NFL Game Rewind made verifying plays or scouting an unknown player a breeze, since before social networking as we now know it, and since before any of us could ever get a press credential, let alone sometimes chew the ear of an actual player/coach/GM. Mike has gone from *The New York Times* to Sports on Earth to NFL lead writer at Bleacher Report, another thing that didn't exist when we starting writing annuals. He no longer teaches high school math in Joe Flacco's hometown, but still lives with his wife and two sons just one minute from the base of the Walt Whitman Bridge in South Jersey.

Robert Weintraub is the author of the *New York Times* bestseller *No Better Friend: One Man, One Dog, and their Extraordinary Story of Courage and Survival in WWII*, as well as *The Victory Season* and *The House That Ruth Built*. He is also a regular contributor to Sports on Earth, Grantland, Slate, *Columbia Journalism Review*, and *The New York Times*.

Sterling Xie grew up in the Division II football hotbed of West Virginia, where the Shepherd Rams' annual playoff letdowns have allowed him to sympathize with residents of Kansas City and Cincinnati. He recently graduated from Hamilton College and now works for ESPN's Stats & Info group when not writing for Football Outsiders. Sterling's work previously appeared at Advanced Football Analytics, Bleacher Report and ESPN.com. His last name is pronounced "Z" but he is no relation to Jay.

Acknowledgements

We want to thank all the Football Outsiders readers, all the people in the media who have helped to spread the word about our website and books, and all the people in the NFL who have shown interest in our work. This is our 12th annual book as part of the *Pro Football Prospectus* or *Football Outsiders Almanac* series. Bill James only wrote a dozen editions of the *Bill James Baseball Abstract*, so when we publish another book next year we will officially qualify as insane.

A few specific acknowledgements:

- FO techmaster Steven Steinman.
- Marc Helmick for additional help with proofreading and edits.
- Mike Harris for help with the season simulation.
- Premium programmer Sean McCall, Excel macro master John Argentiero, and drive stats guru Jim Armstrong.
- FO writers who did not write for the book, including Ben Muth and Andrew Healy.
- Nathan Forster, creator of SackSEER and current curator of Playmaker Score.
- Jason McKinley, creator of Offensive Line Continuity Score.
- Jeremy Snyder, our incredibly prolific transcriber of old play-by-play gamebooks. (Stay tuned to FootballOutsiders.com for the unveiling of DVOA from the 1986-1988 seasons very soon. Yes, we keep saying that. Yes, it really is coming.)
- Roland Beech of the Sacramento Kings, formerly of TwoMinuteWarning.com, who came up with the original ideas behind our individual defensive stats.
- Our editors at ESPN.com and *ESPN The Magazine*, including Daniel Kaufman, Scott Miller, and Chris Sprow.
- Everybody at ESPN Stats & Information, for all the charting data and for listening to us when we suggested endless revisions to all the charting data. Special props to our brothers in model-building: Ben Alamar, Brian Burke, and Jeff Bennett.
- Our friends at Sports Info Solutions who have really expanded what we can do with game charting, including Scott Spratt, Greg Thomas, and Ben Jedlovic.
- Bill Simmons, for constantly promoting us on his podcast, and Peter King, for lots of promotion on The MMQB.
- Michael Katzenoff at the NFL, for responding to our endless questions about specific items in the official play-by-play.
- All the friends we've made on coaching staffs and in front offices across the National Football League, who generally don't want to be mentioned by name. You know who you are.
- Our comrades in the revolution: Doug Drinen (creator of the indispensable Pro Football Reference), Bill Barnwell (our long lost brother), Neil Paine, Robert Mays, and K.C. Joyner, plus the kids at Numberfire, the football guys from footballguys.com, and our friends at Prospectus Entertainment Ventures.
- Also, our scouting buddies, including Greg Bedard, Andy Benoit, Chris Brown, Greg Cosell, Doug Farrar, and Russ Lande.
- Joe Alread and William Schautz, who handle the special Football Outsiders cards in Madden Ultimate Team, and the other folks at EA Sports who make FO a part of the Madden universe.

- Interns who helped prepare data over the past year or for this book specifically, including Zach Binney, Andrew Potter, Matthew Russo, Brent Schwartz, and Carl Yedor.
- All those who volunteered their time and effort for the Football Outsiders game charting project in past seasons. We would like to specifically thank charters who also pitched in this year to help us check our charting from multiple sources:

Mike Bonner, Jason Dooley, Michael Dunn, Dave DuPlantis, Willy Hu, Bo Hurley, Augie Salick, Matthew Weston, and Mark Wierichs.

And as always, thanks to our family and friends for putting up with this nonsense.

— Aaron Schatz

Follow Football Outsiders on Twitter

Follow the official account announcing new Football Outsiders articles at **@fboutsiders**. You can follow other FO and *FOA 2016* writers at these Twitter addresses:

Ian Boyd: **@Ian_A_Boyd**
Bill Connelly: **@SBN_BillC**
Cian Fahey: **@cianaf**
Brian Fremeau: **@bcfremeau**
Tom Gower: **@ThomasGower**
Scott Kacsmar: **@FO_ScottKacsmar**
Rivers McCown: **@RiversMcCown**
Ben Muth: **@FO_WordofMuth**
Chad Peltier: **@cgpeltier**
Aaron Schatz: **@FO_ASchatz**
Mike Tanier: **@MikeTanier**
Vince Verhei: **@FO_VVerhei**
Robert Weintraub: **@robwein**
Sterling Xie: **@SterlingXie**

Follow Football Outsiders on Facebook

https://www.facebook.com/footballoutsiders

Listen to Football Outsiders on Podcast

Check out the weekly Off The Charts podcast, featuring Aaron Schatz and Scott Spratt of Sports Info Solutions reviewing the world of the NFL through advanced stats and charting data. You can find episodes on iTunes or at http://www.footballoutsiders.com/podcasts/.

Made in the USA
San Bernardino, CA
13 August 2016